Value-based Management

Trademarks

Value-based Management: Context and Application

Edited by

GLEN ARNOLD AND MATT DAVIES

JOHN WILEY & SONS, LTD

Chichester · New York · Weinheim · Brisbane · Singapore · Toronto

Other Wiley Editorial Offices

John Wiley & Sons, Inc., 605 Third Avenue,
New York, NY 10158-0012, USA

Wiley-VCH GmbH, Pappelallee 3,
D-69469 Weinheim, Germany

Jacaranda Wiley Ltd, 33 Park Road, Miton,
Queensland 4064, Australia

John Wiley & Sons (Asia) Pte Ltd, 2 Clementi Loop #02-01,
Jin Xing Distripark, Singapore 129809

John Wiley & Sons (Canada) Ltd, 22 Worcester Road,
Rexdale, Ontario M9W 1L1, Canada

Library of Congress Cataloging-in-Publication Data

Value-based management : context and application / edited by Glen Arnold
and Matt Davis.
    p. cm.
  Includes bibliographical references and index.
  ISBN 0-471-89986-0 (cloth : alk. paper)
  1. Industrial management. 2. Managerial accounting. 3. Value analysis (Cost control)
  4. Value. I. Arnold, Glen. II. Davies, Matt, 1960–

  HD31.V3165 2000
  658.15'52—dc21   99-056803

British Library Cataloguing in Publication Data

A catalogue record for this book is available from the British Library

ISBN 0-471-89986-0

Typeset in 10/12 Palatino by Aarontype Ltd, Easton, Bristol
Printed and bound in Great Britain by Biddles Ltd, Guildford and King's Lynn
This book is printed on acid-free paper responsibly manufactured from sustainable forestry, in
which at least two trees are planted for each one used for paper production.

Contents

About the Editors

Glen Arnold is a lecturer in finance and value-based strategy at Aston Business School, Aston University, Birmingham. He is author of the best-selling UK-based corporate finance textbook *Corporate Financial Management* and has considerable experience teaching, researching and publishing in the areas of investment, corporate finance and strategy.

Matt Davies is a Director of ATC Limited, a company which specialises in the provision of financial training and consultancy. He previously spent six years as a member of the Finance and Accounting Group at Aston Business School, where he developed a specialism in shareholder value and value-based management. He co-authored *Shareholder Value*, published by the *Financial Times* in 1997. He is currently researching the use of value-based management within top UK companies.

Contributors

Glen Arnold *Aston University*

Ron Azair *Northwest Airlines*

John Byrd *Ft Lewis College*

Christopher Carter *Leicester University*

Steve Conway *Aston University*

Stuart Cooper *Aston University*

David Crowther *Aston University*

Matt Davies *ATC Ltd*

Jochen Drukarczyk *Universität Regensburg*

John Forker *Queen's University, Belfast*

Graham Francis *Open University Business School*

Kent Hickman *Gonzaga University*

Leon Kamhi *Deloitte Consulting/Braxton Associates*

Clare Minchington *Open University Business School*

Phil Molyneux *Institute of European Finance, University of Wales*

Gareth Owen *School of Finance and Management, London*

Ronan Powell *Queen's University, Belfast*

Janette Rutterford *Open University Business School*

Andreas Schueler *Universität Regensburg*

Mark Whittington *Warwick Business School*

1 Introduction

GLEN ARNOLD AND MATT DAVIES

Hundreds of leading companies have adopted, or at least say they have adopted, value-based management principles and one or more of the associated metrics. A few, such as Coca-Cola and Procter and Gamble in the US and Lloyds TSB in the UK, have been leading the way for 15 years or more. Many of these pioneers are regarded as highly successful and have stimulated potential emulators to discover 'the secret of their success'. Consultants, many of whom have worked with the leaders, are happy to oblige the new converts by providing guidance for the difficult task of understanding, accepting, inculcating and implementing the principles of value-based management.

As value-based management has become more widespread, business executives, journalists and academics increasingly use the phrase 'shareholder value'. Firms espouse the creation of value for shareholders as their central purpose. Consultancies have prospered by selling prescriptions for developing a value-orientated firm. Managers thought to be excellent in generating shareholder value are held in high esteem and command huge salaries. Now is the time to take stock of this accelerating bandwagon, and to try to explore the opposing views that this is merely another management fad thrust upon a workforce already punch-drunk, disillusioned and cynical about new management paradigms, or that at its core value-based management contains fundamental and radical truths which are able to lead to the kind of transformation which promotes shareholder and societal well-being.

Value-based management is an approach to corporate strategy, operations and organisation in which the primary purpose is always shareholder wealth maximisation. It draws on the theory of finance in requiring every activity to produce a return greater than the return finance providers could have obtained (for the same risk) elsewhere by, for example, investing in shares of another firm. This underlying principle is applied both on the microscale (e.g. looking for positive net present value projects, such as replacing machine tools) and on the macroscale in which decisions of great importance to the future of the firm are tested against the value-based management standard. So strategic decisions, such as whether to exit a particular product market or to merge with another firm, are examined in quantitative terms by applying value-based metrics as well as being considered in traditional qualitative terms.

Value principles have been applied across the globe to guide a variety of business decisions. For planning purposes, value-based management metrics assist with the allocation of scarce resources. Once the funds are committed, value metrics can help maintain control and monitor performance, leading to analysis of areas for improvement. They have been used extensively for managerial reward systems to encourage the congruence of goals of individual managers with those of the firm.

Value-based management has its roots in a number of disciplines from finance and strategy to accounting and human resource management. It draws on academic and practical traditions stretching back decades, but it is only in the last 15 years or so that it has developed into an approach which can be regarded as distinct from its progenitor traditions. But these are early days. There are many unanswered questions and many improvements to techniques still to be made. Each consulting firm has developed a unique approach and metrics and, naturally, sells them with fervour. We would not expect these organisations to highlight the weaknesses of their approach or to discuss some of the possible flaws in the underlying principles of value-based management. This book contributes to the growing maturity of value-based management by bringing into the open many of the hidden questions, doubts and difficulties, as well as pointing to its achievements. It questions the validity of some of the assumptions underlying value-based management and tackles some of the key technical issues. It also presents new empirical evidence of the difficulties of value-based management in practice.

THE STRUCTURE OF THE BOOK

The book is organised into four parts. Part I sets the scene by providing a critical review of the state of current knowledge on value-based management. In Chapter 2 Arnold focuses on the intellectual and theoretical heritage of VBM, showing how VBM has grown out of its roots in economics and finance. He outlines the extent to which VBM has developed and dealt with numerous theoretical and practical problems as well as discussing the major issues which remain unresolved. The success or otherwise of the VBM approach will depend upon how effectively it addresses these outstanding issues.

Davies then analyses the state of knowledge on VBM in business today. Chapter 3 establishes a framework for judging the relative merits of empirical evidence then applies it to evaluate existing research into VBM use. Davies demonstrates that whilst a number of surveys into VBM practice have been performed, much more research is still needed. The evidence, such as it is, suggests that VBM is not used in practice in the way advocated by its main protagonists. The reason for this is unclear.

The cornerstone of VBM is its assumption that the company should be run with one clear and unambiguous objective: to maximise the value of the owners' interest in the firm. Whilst this may be consistent with the modern theory of finance, it is far from uncontroversial. Part II challenges the appropriateness of this assumption.

In Chapter 4 Carter and Conway critically examine the assumptions underlying the use of VBM tools. In particular, they argue that because capital markets are 'short-termist', an emphasis on shareholder value is misplaced.

Cooper devotes Chapter 5 to questioning the assumption that the pursuit of shareholder wealth will lead to benefits to all stakeholders. He considers the question of whether shareholder wealth will lead to societal welfare, using a stakeholder analysis of the privatised electricity industry in England and Wales.

Crowther considers the same question in Chapter 6. He begins with a critical interpretation of the general nature and role of financial measurement and reporting, then specifically addresses the potential dichotomy between shareholder wealth and societal welfare. He argues that this dichotomy is more apparent than real – in the long run the interests of shareholders and other stakeholders, including society in general, will coincide.

In Part III the emphasis shifts to VBM practice. Rutterford addresses a pivotal issue relating to the use of VBM concepts – the cost of capital. Her Chapter 7 presents empirical evidence of how top UK firms calculate and use the cost of capital. Empirical evidence on the nature and use of VBM concepts is relatively limited. Chapter 8, a noteworthy contribution by Francis and Minchington, presents new information on the use of value-based metrics as divisional performance measures. They find relatively little take-up, though growing interest in VBM measures.

Byrd, Hickman and Azair use Chapter 9 to examine the rationality, of both managers and markets, which VBM takes for granted. Drawing on behavioural economics and psychology, they discuss a number of potential biases in judgements and their potential effects on corporate decisions, and ultimately on the value of a firm. They emphasise how decision making can be improved through a recognition of the types of systematic biases and errors that occur.

Then comes a detailed account of the experiences of VBM at Lloyds TSB, one of its best-known protagonists. The experience of Lloyds TSB, as described by Davies in Chapter 10, suggests that the way in which VBM is implemented may be more important than its technical specifications. Continuing with this theme, Kamhi draws on his experience of working with a number of top companies which have adopted VBM. In Chapter 11 he explains the key steps needed to embed VBM within a company.

Chapter 12 is the final chapter of Part III. Here Molyneux demonstrates the application of shareholder value thinking in the context of banking. He applies a shareholder value perspective to evaluate the performance of US and European banks; he then uses it to identify opportunities for improvements in shareholder value within the sector, and also to highlight some limitations of the shareholder value approach.

Part IV focuses on the measurement of value. Much has been written about the various value-based measures and their relative merits. The various shareholder value consultants devote much effort to selling their own favoured 'value metric'. The relative 'accuracy' of alternative measures in terms of their ability to explain share price behaviour is a source of much debate (Metric Wars, *CFO Magazine*, October 1996). However, much of this literature, including 'evidence' regarding the degree of association between performance as measured by a particular value metric and share price movements, has been provided by the very consultancy firms which promote their use. There is a lack of independent 'research-oriented' work in this field. Part IV contains four contributions which help to address this gap in the literature. Forker and Powell use Chapter 13 to consider the economic foundations of both VBM measures and accounting measures, and they provide an independent review of the empirical evidence with respect to the relative ability of such measures to explain share price behaviour.

In Chapter 14 Drukarczyk and Schueler consider the difficulties in establishing measures of performance which can be used not only to generate valuations compatible with discounted cash flow, but also to measure the periodic shareholder value performance of a business. Having developed criteria for evaluating alternative periodic measures of performance, they apply them to assess the relative merits of residual income measures, earned economic income and Rappaport's shareholder value added approach. They argue that residual income based on book values should be used at the divisional and business unit level, whilst residual income based on market values should be used at the firm level. They also outline a monitoring system that incorporates these measures.

Owen considers the relationship between accounting, economic and VBM approaches to performance measurement. His Chapter 15 focuses on the market value added and economic value added concepts, arguing that they should be considered as an economic modification of the traditional accounting model, which therefore suffers from the drawbacks of both. He also demonstrates how the market value added concept might provide new leads in the search for a solution to perhaps the most controversial issue in financial reporting – the treatment of goodwill.

Chapter 16 shifts the emphasis to more practical issues as Whittington considers the relative ease with which alternative VBM measures can be applied, and the difficulties encountered given that many value metrics are based on accounting data. He focuses on accounting measurement difficulties, including those which arise in an international context.

Part I

THE STATE OF
VBM KNOWLEDGE:
THEORY AND EVIDENCE

2 Tracing the Development of Value-based Management

GLEN ARNOLD

INTRODUCTION

Over the last 20 years the principles, concepts and techniques underlying value-based management (VBM) have become increasingly influential in the organisation and strategies of corporations around world. The US can be regarded as the heartland of this way of managing. Indeed, the effect of the arch-practitioners of value-based management in the US has been so significant that the conversion of their firms from a focus on traditional earnings figures to value metrics is frequently cited as their greatest contribution during their long careers. In 1997 in an obituary of Roberto Goizueta, the CEO of Coca-Cola, entitled 'A man of monomaniacal vision' the *Financial Times* drew attention to the three broad characteristics he displayed, the most important of which concern his credentials as a value-based management leader: 'the first, an unremitting concentration on shareholder value, was demonstrated as soon as he took over the leadership of the company. At that time, he calculated, Coca-Cola's cost of capital was about 16%, considerably higher than the returns being generated by what had been perceived as successful activities. The soda fountain operation for instance, was making only 12.5%' (*Financial Times*, 20 October 1997).

The UK also has a number of strong advocates for value-based management. Boots plc, the large retailer, have in Lord Blyth, the chairman, and David Thompson, the finance director, firm believers in VBM. 'The managers are clear,' Lord Blyth says, 'that they have a contract with me to maximise value' (*Financial Times*, 19 January 1998). Mr Thompson says, 'we've had a lot of difficulty with people within Boots who were brought up to believe in things like market share and sales per square foot'. 'Whether you're building a plant or investing in Christmas advertising,' Lord Blyth says, 'it's all cash, and requires a return'. Many other British firms, have now adopted VBM, including LucasVarity, Diageo, GEC, Blue Circle, and Lloyds TSB. In October 1997 Siemens, the German group, caused quite a stir in the home of 'stakeholder capitalism' when they announced a switch to economic value shareholders' money in ways that are contrary to the best interests of the owners of the organisation. This can manifest itself in many ways; for example, continuing to invest in a business regardless of industry attractiveness or competitive position, tolerance of underperforming business units, a refusal to divest, excessive overhead cost, a refusal to merge despite underlying logic, a focus on maximising returns to parties other than shareholders, a mindset that encourages incentive programmes which reward executives for mediocre performance, an obsession with company size.

The history of VBM is one in which consultants, managers and some academics interested in shareholder wealth maximisation try to overcome one or both of these two forces. At first this was piecemeal. Strategists and economists had their particular foci, on competitive strength, industry structure, and so on. Accountants and finance experts brought their insights to bear on the identification, quantification and realisation of value-creating activity. Some organisational behaviouralists examined issues such as culture, motivation, leadership and change management for the impact on shareholder value. For most of this century each discipline tended to remain within its own boundaries and rarely ventured outside. However, in recent years we have witnessed a coming together of these disparate powers with their vital insights, concepts and frameworks to fight the twin negative forces. The process of weaving the various threads together to make up the fabric of the modern discipline of value-based management has begun. Complementary developments in different fields, when combined, now provide useful competitive weapons in the armoury of value-based corporations. Conceptual hurdles have been cleared at various points in the eighteenth, nineteenth and twentieth centuries. However, despite this progress there are important issues which remain to be resolved as we enter the twenty-first century if we are to declare that VBM is a true, fully-fledged, rigorous and coherent new managerial discipline – or superdiscipline which overarches a number of already well-established fields of study and practice.

The value-based management family tree shown in Figure 2.1 provides a framework for considering the origins of VBM and helps to structure this chapter.

CORPORATE GOVERNANCE AND THE OBJECTIVE OF THE FIRM

Value-based management is firmly rooted in the tradition in which shareholder primacy is unquestioned. There are no apologies for this from the defenders of VBM, no room for doubt. We will look at some of the arguments supporting this position. The first argument has a long antecedence. It concerns the well-being of society and was best expressed over two hundred years ago by Adam Smith:

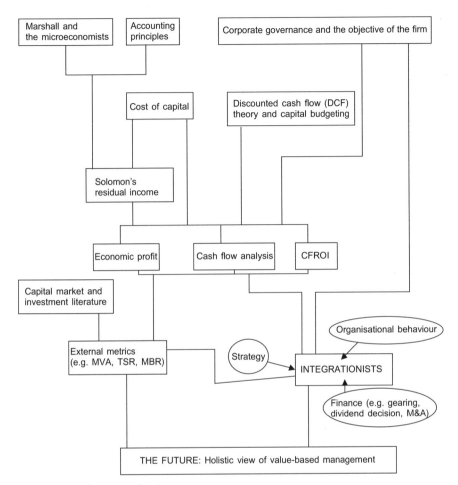

Figure 2.1. The VBM family tree

The businessman by directing ... industry in such a manner as its produce may be of the greatest value, intends only his own gain, and he is in this, as in many other cases, led by an invisible hand to promote an end which was no part of his intention. Nor is it always the worse for the society that it was no part of it. By pursuing his own interest he frequently promotes that of the society more effectually than when he really intends to promote it. I have never known much good done by those who affected to trade for the public good. It is an affectation, indeed, not very common among merchants. (*The Wealth of Nations*, 1776, p. 400)

Hayek (1960) believed that corporations should be confined to one specific goal if they are to be beneficial to society. By making the sole purpose the achievement of 'the highest long-term return on their capital' they will

(1) provide a safeguard against the acquisition by management of arbitrary and politically dangerous powers; (2) allocate resources to those firms which can make best use of them for society, and (3) substitute clear, specific and controllable goals for vagueness, drift and indefinable social responsibility. Milton Friedman (1958) also pointed out the dangers to the freedom of the individual if managers started to get a confused idea of their role and started to accept social responsibilities other than to make as much money as possible. These advocates of shareholder wealth primacy are not the rabid laissez-faire 'devil take the hindmost' pro-capitalist thinkers they are often caricatured to be. Monopolistic-exploitative capitalism, crony capitalism and gangster capitalism are condemned by these intellectuals as much as by others. They argue for *relatively* unfettered free markets, but also call for restraints set by legal and moral rules.

A second argument frequently advanced is that maximising shareholder wealth will lead to the maximisation of all stakeholder claims. This argument tends to be most forcefully expressed by the major consulting groups involved in selling value-based management change programmes. The next quotation is taken from page 22 of an influential book written by Copeland et al. (1995) of the McKinsey & Co. consultancy group:

> Empirical evidence indicates that increasing shareholder value does not conflict with the long-run interests of other stakeholders. Winning companies seem to create relatively greater value for all stakeholders: customers, labor, the government (via taxes paid) and suppliers of capital ... shareholders are the only stakeholders of a corporation who simultaneously maximise everyone's claim in seeking to maximise their own.

And on page 25:

> A labour union that is successful in winning abnormally high wages and benefits in the short run may actually decrease the value of labour's claim on the company if the company is forced out of business or loses market share in the long run. A company that pays below market wages in the short run will lose productive labourers and end up worse off in the long run. A company that milks the market with high product prices in the near term may destroy shareholder value in the long term if the high prices accelerate the entry of strong new competitors into the market.

Lloyds Bank, in a short report to shareholders dated 1991, put the issue in a nutshell: 'We can only create value for our shareholders if we create value for our customers'.

The next argument concerns national competitiveness and wealth. Here it is claimed that if companies do not focus on the interests of shareholders, those providers of risk capital, then there will be capital flight from the country, leading to economic decline. Copeland et al. (1995) expressed it thus:

If countries whose economic systems are not based on maximising shareholder value give investors lower returns on capital than those who do, they will slowly be starved of capital, as capital markets continue to globalise, falling farther and farther behind in global competition. (P. 4)

Nations who don't provide global investors with adequate returns on invested capital are doomed to fall further behind in the race for global competitiveness and suffer a stagnating or decreasing standard of living. (P. 27)

Then there is the issue of the strength of the corporation. It is claimed that without continual reference to a single fundamental objective, based around shareholder wealth, corporations will decline, and eventually will not be able to compete. 'We will argue that maximising shareholder value is superior to any other governing objective a company might adopt because it will lead managers to make the decisions most likely to increase the company's competitive, organisational, and financial strength over time' (McTaggart et al., 1994, p. 10)

Possibly the simplest argument of all is that shareholders own the firm and therefore could expect it to be run in their interests. Going back centuries, or even millennia, it has been argued that societies built on private property rights and freedom for enterprise have as an inalienable element the notion that the owners of businesses are entitled to expect their property to be employed so as to maximise their return.

If the above arguments do not persuade managers to act in shareholders' best interests then the VBM advocates suggest that the argument concerning managerial replacement will be more effective. This generally points out that if managers do not pursue shareholder wealth then the consequence may be that pain will be inflicted on these agents of shareholders. Management that is not acting in the best interests of owners 'will be replaced sooner or later' (Ezra Solomon, 1963, p. 24). Alfred Rappaport (1986) said:

the threat of takeover is an essential means of constraining corporate managers who might choose to pursue personal goals at the expense of shareholders. Any significant exploitation of shareholders should be reflected in a lower stock price. This lower price, relative to what it might be with more efficient management, offers an attractive takeover opportunity for another company which in many cases will replace incumbent management. (P. 8)

Treynor (1981, p. 69) expresses this more succinctly: 'any management — no matter how powerful and independent — that flouts the financial objective of maximising share value does so at its own peril'.

To round off this section we will consider the 'contractual theory'. The logic behind this is as follows: most of the parties with a claim on a commercial organisation operating in a competitive environment bargain for a restricted risk and a concomitant limited reward. For example, bankers when making a loan try to control risk but in return the company does not offer any income beyond the amount set in a loan agreement regardless of how well the firm performs. Likewise, suppliers contract with a firm to provide goods and services for a fixed return; they do not expect to benefit from any extraordinary surplus generated by the business. Ordinary share-holders, on the other hand, are not guaranteed any return at all. If the firm does badly they can lose their entire investment. These individuals are making a sacrifice by putting their money into a particular firm so that it can invest in real assets. This money is put at high risk and therefore, according to the contractual theory, shareholders should receive any surplus after all those claimants that bargained for a limited risk and a limited pay-off have been satisfied.

RESIDUAL INCOME

Shareholder wealth maximisation provides the driving purpose behind value-based management but it needs to be coupled with a mechanism for achieving this objective. The metrics used to guide modern VBM draw on the work of early microeconomists, accountants and finance experts. In 1890 Alfred Marshall promoted the idea that a return to shareholders is a basic requirement of business, and should be included as part of the overall cost of capital (Marshall, 1947). This required minimum return, or opportunity cost, is at the core of VBM. Marshall was presumably inspired by the work of earlier economists. Robert Hamilton, for example, wrote the following in 1777:

> in all commercial countries there is a fixed rate of interest, and the merchant's gain should only be estimated by the excess of its gross profits above the interest of his stock. The latter may be obtained with little risk or trouble; the former alone is the reward of his industry, and the compensation for his hazard. And, if the profit of his trade be less than his stock would have yielded at common interest, he may properly account it a losing one. (Vol. II, p. 246)

Adam Smith (1776), in characteristically folksy but profound style, pointed out the necessity of allowing for an adequate return to the providers of capital:

> the owner of this capital, though he is thus discharged of almost all labour, still expects that his profits should bear a regular proportion to his capital. In the price of commodities, therefore, the profits of stock constitute a component part. . . . In the price of corn, for example, one part pays the rent of the landlord, another pays the wages or maintenance of the labourers or labouring cattle employed in producing it, and a third pays the profit of the farmer. These three parts seem either immediately or ultimately to make up the whole price of corn. (Vol. 1, pp. 43–44)

The accounting profession and its academic contributors provided valuable planning, control and evaluatory techniques. However, by the mid 1960s it was becoming plain that accounting metrics did not solve all the practical business problems. David Solomons (1965) asked the question, What is the appropriate way to measure success for venture and a manager? An obvious answer, following the accounting literature, is profit. However, 'profit as measured in accordance with generally accepted accounting principles is a somewhat unsure gauge of success. Profits can be kept up for some years while the business is being "milked" by cutting down on research, maintenance, and certain kinds of advertising, or by realising assets which have been steadily appreciating in value for several years' (p. 60). Also if one manager makes a larger profit than another, we cannot assume that he performed better, because he may have had access to more capital. So Solomons identified two problems with profit as a gauge of success: (a) distortions in the accounting process and (b) non-allowance for the quantity of capital employed. The second obvious answer is to make use of an accounting rate of return, which takes account of the quantity of capital used to generate a profit. But as Solomons (1965, p. 61) said, 'Is a high rate of return on a small capital better or worse than a lower but still satisfactory return on a larger capital?' If a manager has been told to maximise the rate of return then, in the example below, venture A is preferable to venture B:

	Venture A	Venture B
Capital invested ($)	1000	5000
Net annual return ($)	200	750
Rate of return on capital (%)	20	15

If the highest absolute profit is set as the objective for managers then venture B is the more successful. This question can only be properly answered by taking account of the cost of capital. Supposing this to be 17.5%, then venture A alone is successful, while venture B is a misapplication of capital (value destructive). But if the cost of capital is 12% then venture B is the more successful:

	Venture A	Venture B
Net annual return ($)	200	750
12% on capital invested ($)	120	600
Excess earnings over 12% ($)	80	150

If the cost of capital is 14%, venture A generates more excess earnings over the required rate of return:

	Venture A	Venture B
Net annual return ($)	200	750
14% on capital invested ($)	140	700
Excess earnings over 14% (residual income) ($)	60	50

Solomons referred to the excess of net earnings over the cost of capital as 'residual income', a term originally coined by the General Electric Company which had been using the concept for some time prior to the publication of Solomons' seminal book. 'There is no simple answer to the question of which venture is more successful in terms of the excess of its earnings over the cost of capital it employs. While venture B is more successful at low rates of interest, A is more successful at high rates. A mere comparison of rates of return obscures this fact' (Solomons, 1965, p. 63).

The General Electric Company was not the only American firm using residual income. As early as 1965 over one-quarter of the largest US firms were using residual income for divisional performance measurement (Mauriel and Anthony,1966). Residual income has a number of endearing features. Its flexibility is useful: the required rate can be varied from period to period, division to division, and it is practicable to use different rates of return for different types of assets and investment risks (Dearden,1969). It is also easy for managers to understand because they are asked to maximise a number, not a ratio (Mauriel and Anthony, 1966). Tomkins (1973) shows that under certain assumptions (e.g. depreciation is calculated in a particular manner) residual income is consistent with maximisation of net present value. In addition residual income avoids one of the problems of accounting rates of return (ARR), namely, that managers incentivised on an ARR basis may be unwilling to expand investment if that will lower the ARR through an increase in the denominator. Managers incentivised on the basis of residual income can increase value by undertaking any investment that yields a return higher than the required percentage. Furthermore, as Mepham (1980) pointed out, residual income has the important quality that it is useful for both ex ante appraisal of investment opportunities and ex post analyses of investment performance.

The development of residual income analysis was an important advance but it did not prove to be the panacea to planning and evaluation problems. Solomons continued to use net earnings (profit) as an input to the residual income calculation with all the concomitant drawbacks. He asserted that 'most companies will, perhaps, be prepared to accept these shortcomings with no more than purely subjective corrections on the part of management whenever some recognition of them is thought to be necessary. It is a reflection of the art of accounting that these corrections have to be made in the form of mental reservations by managers rather than explicitly by accountants. However, for the present, this has to be accepted, and perhaps it will always be so' (Solomons, 1965, p. 66). Emmanuel and Otley (1976) drew attention to the potential for manipulation of accounting data designed to improve the appearance of current or near-term performance; for example, the acceptance of projects with relatively high initial cash inflows but with net present values less than zero. They called for research to discover accounting methods which will minimise this distortion. Much of the work which has taken place in the 1980s and 1990s has been aimed at addressing this problem. For example, Stern Stewart and Co., the value consultants, make dozens of adjustments to standard accounts, and incentive systems based upon them, in an attempt to achieve greater compliance with economic income principles.

Solomons also questioned the use of balance sheet assets figures for 'capital invested'. He was critical of the accounting approach in which research expenditure is written off in the year in which it occurs, implying that no intangible or tangible assets are deemed to result from it. There are similar problems with expenditure on 'developing harmonious relations with customers, suppliers and employees — the constituents of valuable goodwill' (Solomons, 1965, p. 124). At best the balance sheet shows only tangible investment, and in many cases it fails to represent even this. Solomons did suggest some modifications to the balance sheet data but many substantial problems remained.

A further problem with residual income is that it is technically impossible to evaluate an investment ex post until the end of the project's life. 'It is conceptually impossible to evaluate an investment decision on ex post figures until all returns have occurred. Residual income may do no more than compare actual cash flows with those expected for the single accounting period being considered' (Emmanuel and Otley, 1976, p. 46). Tomkins (1973, p. 121) says 'there are advantages in converting the cash flows of capital projects which are undertaken into a residual income stream in order to provide a standard against which to compare actual residual income earned'. But Tomkins goes on to say that a simpler approach is to compare budgeted and actual cash flows. Both methods, according to Tomkins, are better than conventional accounting methodology but cash flow comparison is easier than residual income comparison.

Finally, there is the crucial issue of calculating an appropriate cost of capital. The methods used by the early writers were extremely crude and there was a tendency to gloss over the difficulties, as indeed do many of the consultancies selling VBM programmes today. We now turn to this key aspect of modern value-based management.

THE COST OF CAPITAL

David Solomons gave thought to the fundamental requirements for estimating an appropriate cost of capital (required rate of return) for investment
appraisal and evaluation. 'The cost of capital ... is its opportunity cost.
By this is meant the sacrifice which has to be made when any scarce resource
is applied to one use and therefore shut out from another' (p. 156). He also
pointed out the necessity of taking into account the fact that most firms
obtain finance in a variety of forms: 'If debt finance is used to provide some
of the capital invested in divisions, then the cost of capital is not the cost
of raising money from one source. It is, rather, the weighted average of all of
them' (p. 158).

Prior to the development of more theoretically sound methods for calculating the cost of capital, businesses fell back on rules of thumb; for
example, limiting the size of the capital budget to the amount of internally
available funds, or insisting that all proposed projects exceed an arbitrarily
chosen cut-off rate of the order of 10%, 12% or 20% per annum (Solomon,
1955). These approaches did not, except by accident, lead to shareholder
wealth optimal decision making. Other methods were used, but they were
only marginally better. The return on investment method dictated that if a
company had been earning an accounting rate of return of $x\%$ per year on
book assets, an investment proposal would only be accepted if it offered at
least $x\%$ (Solomon, 1963). The popular dividend yield (the current dividend
divided by the share price) and the earnings yield (the current income per
share divided by the share price) methods both failed to recognise that a
share's dividends and earnings can be expected to grow (Solomon, 1963;
Gordon and Shapiro, 1956). The earnings yield method also failed to recognise that a company's earnings per share do not represent payments made to
the shareholder.

In 1955 Ezra Solomon tried to formulate a theoretically correct and non-
arbitrary system for calculating the cost of capital. He was faced with a
number of problems, including these two:

(a) Equity capital does not involve clear unambiguous fixed outpayments
    (e.g. dividends) so the equity cost is difficult to establish.
(b) Capital is derived from more than one source (debt, ordinary shares,
    preference shares, convertibles, etc.).

Solomon said that a refinement of the earnings divided by the share price
method is the 'only valid criterion for the cost of equity capital' (pp. 242–43).
In his model the numerator should not represent current earnings per share,
as managers tended to use at that time, but 'management's best estimate of
what average future earnings would be if the proposed capital expenditure
were not made'. Unfortunately, this approach is based on an inward-focused

opportunity cost of capital, not the more appropriate outward market-wide focused opportunity cost, and is therefore unacceptable. So Ezra Solomon did not solve either problem in his 1955 paper.

In 1961 Hirshleifer promoted the use of an equity cost of capital derived from the rate of return being offered on other investments in the same risk class in the markets. This was a significant advance on the work of Irving Fisher (1930), who had said that the required rate of return should be adjusted for risk but did not point to an objective external criterion for doing this. He said the discount rate should be adjusted on the basis of the decision maker's 'caution coefficient' which expressed the decision maker's preferences toward risk bearing. By the time he wrote his 1963 book, Ezra Solomon had accepted the need to use the market-derived opportunity cost of capital for equity, k_e:

> Stockholders are perfectly capable of investing their dividend receipts at a rate equivalent to k_e, either in the same company or elsewhere, and management should deprive them of this opportunity by withholding dividends for internal investment if, and only if, the promised return is at least equal to k_e. . . . The return available on such external investments [in other firms' shares] is appropriately measured by k_e and this represents a minimum rate of earnings required from internal investment or reinvestment proposals. (P. 53)

Perhaps Ezra Solomon's most important contribution is the weighted average cost of capital in 1963. He was helped by advances made by earlier researchers. Joel Dean (1951) hinted that there was a need to use a weighted average cost of capital, but did not go on to demonstrate how this might be achieved. Durand (1952) laid some of the groundwork by investigating alternative bases for measuring the cost of debt and equity funds, and Modigliani and Miller (1958) sought to simplify the cost of capital question and stimulate debate by discussing how the cost of capital behaves as the proportion of debt in the financial structure changes. It was Ezra Solomon who first formally developed the weighted average approach to the cost of capital. The WACC, or combined capitalisation rate, is the weighted average of the cost of equity capital, k_e, and the cost of debt funds, k_i, with the total market value of the share and debt components used as weights:

$$WACC = k_e W_1 + k_i W_2$$

where $W_1 =$ the proportion of total market value (debt plus equity) contributed by equity capital

$W_2 =$ the proportion of total market value (debt plus equity) contributed by debt capital

Knowing that the market-based opportunity cost of capital should be used to obtain the equity component of the WACC is a useful theoretical advance.

However, actually calculating the rates of return offered on shares has proved to be extremely difficult. The most influential model in the early 1960s (and one which is still in extensive use today) was created by Gordon and Shapiro (1956), and further developed by Gordon (1962). Suppose a company's shares priced at P produce earnings of E per share and pay a dividend of D per share. The company has a policy of retaining a fraction b of its earnings each year to use for internal investments. If the rate of return (discount or capitalisation rate) required on shares of this risk class is k_e, then under certain restrictive conditions it can be shown that earnings, dividends and reinvestment will all grow continuously at a rate of $g = br$, where r is the rate of return on the reinvestment of earnings, and we have

$$P = D/(k_e - g)$$

Solving for k_e we have

$$k_e = D/P + g$$

That is, the rate of return investors require on a share is equal to the dividend yield plus the rate at which the dividend stream is expected to grow. A major problem in the practical employment of this model is obtaining a trustworthy estimate of the future growth rate of dividends to an infinite horizon. Gordon and Shapiro (1956) told us to derive this figure from known data in an objective manner, using 'common sense' and with reference to the past rate of growth in a corporation's dividend. This advice, whilst eminently sensible, does not get us very far given that objective data from the past is less significant than 'common sense' in forecasting an unpredictable future.

In the mid 1960s an alternative approach was developed by Sharpe (1964), Lintner (1965) and Mossin (1966), called the capital asset pricing model. Here systematic risk, as measured by β, is the only factor affecting the level of return required on the share. A share's return is determined by the risk-free rate of return, r_f, the risk premium for the average share over the risk-free rate, $r_m - r_f$ (r_m = the expected return on market portfolio), and the share's β:

$$k_e = r_f + \beta(r_m - r_f)$$

CAPITAL BUDGETING AND DISCOUNTED CASH FLOW ANALYSIS

Capital budgeting is the discovery, screening, evaluation and selection of capital investments using established criteria which are consistent with the firm's objective and understandable to the component parts of the firm. In many respects VBM is merely net present value analysis or internal rate return analysis (discounted cash flow techniques used for capital budgeting) writ large and applied to strategies, business units, product lines, and so on. Therefore it is important to appreciate the origins of this field of analytical thought.

In the the 1930s and 1940s the allocation of corporate resources among projects was often determined by 'persistence of persuasion' by influential executives rather than by objective indices of company welfare (Dean, 1951). By the early 1960s most large firms were employing formal evaluatory techniques to assess the profitability of proposed investment opportunities. The four most important techniques were payback, accounting rate of return, internal rate return and net present value. Payback has the well-known defects of ignoring cash flows after the payback period and failing to take into account the time value of money. The accounting rate of return method also fails to allow for the time value of money as well as suffering from the absence of a theoretical base for selecting an appropriate cut-off rate. In addition, there is a confusing array of methods of calculating an accounting rate of return for a project, leading to potential for manipulation and misunderstanding.

Joel Dean's *Capital Budgeting*, published in 1951, was the first to demonstrate the significance of rigorous analysis in capital budgeting. Dean called for business acceptance of improved methods of capital budgeting evaluation, in particular the discounting of cash flows to derive an estimate of an investment's potential for value creation. Irving Fisher (1930) was the originator of the present value rule for estimating the total current value of future cash incomes, but it wasn't until 1958 that Jack Hirshleifer produced the classic article showing the theoretical justification for the use of net present value. By 1963 sufficient theoretical groundwork had been laid for Ezra Solomon to declare that net present worth (net present value) or internal rate return were to be used as *the* guiding metrics to maximise shareholder wealth in investment project appraisal:

> Any business proposal requiring the use of funds can be expected to increase net present worth and hence should be accepted:
>
> 1. If the present worth of the estimated stream of net incremental benefits it promises is larger than the present worth of the estimated stream of net capital outlays required for its implementation, when both streams are capitalised (or discounted) at rate k that measures the 'cost of capital'.
> 2. If the rate of return promised (correctly computed from expected outlays and benefits) exceeds the cost of capital k. (Solomon, 1963, p. 27)

NPV and IRR were significant advances on the techniques of payback and ARR. However, even today most firms confine the application of this knowledge to the appraisal of major capital expenditures within business units. The value-based approach is to extend these principles to a wide variety of business decisions, from strategic moves (such as mergers) to product lines and entire strategic business units.

INTERNAL VALUE METRICS

By the 1970s we had in place the theoretical foundations for modern value-based management. Value is created when investment produces a rate of return greater than that required for the risk class of the investment. Shareholder value is driven by the four factors shown in Figure 2.2 (Arnold, 1998). The difference between the second and third elements in Figure 2.2 creates the *performance spread.* Value is destroyed if element 3 is greater than element 2, and is created when element 2 is greater than element 3. The absolute amount of value generated in a year is determined by the quantity of capital invested multiplied by the performance spread. If a firm has an opportunity cost of capital of 10% and actually produces a return of 12% on an investment base of £2 million then it will create £40 000 of value per year. In value-based management there is usually an assumption that the difference between the required rate of return and the actual rate of return will eventually disappear, perhaps as a result of competition. The estimated time at which this will happen is called the planning horizon. The value action pentagon (Figure 2.3) shows the five possible actions available to a VBM firm (Arnold, 1998).

Building on the work of David Solomons, Ezra Solomon and others, theoreticians, consultants and practitioners have developed metrics which assist the process of managing a firm based on value principles. These so-called internal metrics allow managers to assess the performance of different areas and activities of the business. They assist the valuation of proposed and past resource allocations and are useful for target setting and managerial reward systems.

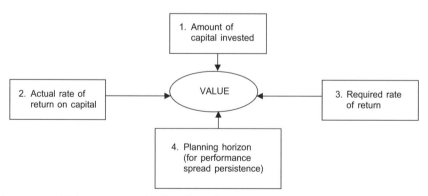

Figure 2.2. Value creation: the four key elements

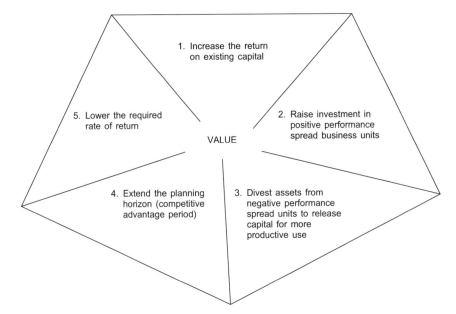

1. Increase the return
   on existing capital

5. Lower the required
   rate of return

VALUE

2. Raise investment in
   positive performance
   spread business units

4. Extend the planning
   horizon (competitive
   advantage period)

3. Divest assets from
   negative performance
   spread units to release
   capital for more
   productive use

Figure 2.3. The value action pentagon

In 1997 the *Economist* noted that one of the possible approaches under the VBM umbrella was already widely used: 'Altogether more than 300 firms worldwide have adopted EVA-based systems' (*Economist*, 2 August 1997). Economic value added (EVA was trademarked by Stern Stewart and Co.) is a variant of economic profit, which is the modern term for residual income. Economic profit for a period is the amount earned by business after deducting all operating expenses *and* a charge for the opportunity cost of capital employed. There are two ways to calculate economic profit:

● The performance spread approach

$$\text{Economic profit} = \text{performance spread} \times \text{invested capital}$$

$$\text{Economic profit} = (\text{return on capital} - \text{WACC}) \times \text{invested capital}$$

● The profit less capital charge approach

$$\text{Economic profit} = \left(\begin{array}{c}\text{operating profit before}\\\text{interest and after tax}\end{array}\right) - \text{capital change}$$

$$\text{Economic profit} = \left(\begin{array}{c}\text{operating profit before}\\\text{interest and after tax}\end{array}\right) - (\text{invested capital} \times \text{WACC})$$

A major advantage of this metric is its relative simplicity. Managers can quickly understand and use it for ex ante and ex post analysis. It uses accounting numbers and therefore requires little modification to the existing planning, performance and control systems. Because managers are familiar with being evaluated on the basis of accounting systems, they are more likely to respond favourably to a change in performance measurement and reward systems if profits continue to be used. There are three alternative approaches to target setting and performance measurement making use of economic profit. First, at the initiation of a strategy, performance targets for the business could be set on a year-by-year basis, progress could then be tracked through the established accounting system. An alternative use could be to set managers the target of improving economic profit year on year. Finally, managers could simply be told to generate as much economic profit as possible without being set explicit targets (Cornelius and Davies, 1997).

With economic profit it is possible to introduce an integrated financial planning and control system in which, using the same metric, investments can be selected, subsequent performance is evaluated and managers are rewarded. Economic profit has a direct link to value creation if 'profits' and 'invested capital' are properly defined and measured (using flow-through accounting): corporate value = all future economic profits discounted at the cost of capital + initial capital invested.

Economic profit per unit can be calculated; two examples are economic profit per square foot and economic profit per unit of output. It is arguable that managers receive a more powerful signal when told that the economic price per unit is £11 but the economic cost is £11.50, rather than being told that an operating profit margin of, say, 7% has been achieved. Measuring in absolute amounts of money rather than a percentage provides a sense of scale to value creation.

Although economic profit has many advantages, it also suffers from some drawbacks. For example, the book value of capital is frequently misleading. Balance sheets are not designed to provide information on the present economic value of assets being used in a business. Generally balance sheets significantly understate the capital employed, and this understatement can cause economic profit to appear high. Book value often results from a decision of past managers, so basing a capital charge on book value unfairly penalises some managers and unfairly assists others. There is also the problem of the large potential for manipulation of profit figures. This is compounded by firms which, in implementing economic profit-based systems, do not make appropriate adjustments to conventional accounts so that they comply with value principles.

Even if profit and balance sheet figures are kept pure, there are great difficulties in allocating assets and costs which are shared by a number of business units to the appropriate managers or business units. Consultants tend to be overoptimistic about the ability of accountants and managers to do this in a theory-compliant and precise manner. Managers resent having costs over which they have no control being imposed upon them. This can lead to a loss of respect for economic profit, and VBM generally. There are great difficulties with intra-company transfer prices and the allocation of the company's debt to each business unit, which in many cases becomes an arbitrary exercise. There is also the danger of managers being encouraged to give excessive emphasis to short-term economic profit and thereby losing the long-term perspective. Managers may refuse positive net present value investments if this will reduce near-term economic profit. They may be encouraged to milk a business by reducing capital spend, research and development, marketing, training, etc.

To deal with some of the problems associated with traditional economic profit, Stern Stewart and Co. developed economic value added in which up to 164 adjustments are made. Many of these adjustments are designed to encourage managers to take a long-term view when making decisions. These adjustments include putting a value on certain expenditures so they can be carried as part of capital invested, rather than being written off against profits in the year of payment. This would include expenditures such as research and development, training and goodwill on acquisitions. This allows the cost of these expenditures to be spread over the period the business is expected to benefit from these outlays. Stern Stewart and Co have made a number of important contributions to the development of value-based management, but attempts to deal with the inaccuracies of economic profit have tended to lead to greater complexity and away from economic profit's greatest virtue – simplicity. Also, it has been argued that many of the adjustments call for excessive reliance on 'judgment', or as some would put it more bluntly, arbitrary decisions.

As we have seen, the technique of projecting cash flows for proposed capital investment and then discounting them has been a firmly established method of valuation for some time. In addition, analysts have long valued shares using discounted cash flow projections. Alfred Rappaport (1986) has taken the basic concept of cash flow discounting and developed a simplified method of analysis which is particularly useful for the evaluation of strategies for business units or the entire corporation. In investment appraisal and share valuation the component elements of the annual cash flows do not change systematically and smoothly from year to year. Rappaport generally uses illustrations in which it is assumed that regular percentage changes in various cash flow elements from one year to the next will occur (they are all taken to be related to the sales level which grows at a constant rate). These elements are then discounted back to the present, using the WACC. These cash flows arise in two periods: within the forecast period (usually between 5 and 10 years), and outside of the forecast period. The values of those cash flows outside of the forecast period are reduced to a single number called the

residual value. Within the forecast period each year's cash flows are estimated as follows:

cash flow = cash inflow − cash outflow

$\qquad$ = (sales in prior year) (1 + sales growth rate)

$\qquad\qquad$ × (operating profit margin) (1 − cash income tax rate)

$\qquad\qquad$ − incremental fixed plus working capital investment

Shareholder value analysis is useful for valuing current and proposed
strategies as it helps to answer questions like these:

- Which business units in the current portfolio are creating most value?
- Which of the alternative strategies under consideration will lead to greatest
  value?
- How sensitive is a particular strategy's value potential to internal and
  external business factors not contemplated in the 'most likely' scenario?
- What is the optimal investment level for business?
- What is the maximum price the firm should pay for an acquisition?
- Should the financial gearing ratio be changed?

Rappaport also provides a link between the shareholder value (cash flow)
perspective and the use of profit as a performance metric. He introduces the
concept of threshold margin, which represents

> the minimum operating profit margin a business needs to attain in any period
> in order to maintain shareholder value in that period. Threshold margin is a
> *value-orientated* economic break-even analysis. Stated in yet another way,
> threshold margin represents the operating profit margin level at which the
> business will earn exactly its minimum acceptable rate of return, that is, it's
> cost of capital. ... Threshold margin can be used to evaluate the past
> performance of the business as well as establish performance targets for the
> future. (Rappaport, 1998, p. 52)

He goes on to compare the merits of shareholder value in evaluating
managerial performance with those of residual income and economic value
added. His conclusion is that shareholder value is best if three- to five-year
rolling measures are used. Many might agree that shareholder value, if we
overlook its simplifications, does indeed meet Rappaport's first condition for
a good performance measure, that is, it is economically sound. However, it
seems reasonable to doubt whether his proposed system meets his second
and third criteria, being easily understood and easily tracked. Other
objections to Rappaport's approach include the difficulties associated with

calculating the residual value, the fact that managers are more used to setting performance targets in terms of profit rather than cash flow, and the potential for short-termist value-destructive behaviour encouraged by a reward system which almost inevitably fails to link managerial incentives to the cash flows over the entire lifespan of an investment or strategy. Nevertheless, shareholder value analysis has proved its worth in a number of corporations, not least by forcing managers to identify the drivers of value.

Cash flow return on investment (CFROI) owes its roots to the internal rate of return literature and has been promoted by the Boston Consulting Group, Holt Value Associates and Braxton Associates. The multiperiod CFROI can be obtained by finding the discount rate which equates future discounted operating cash flows with the current cash value of net operating assets (similar to an IRR calculation). This can then be compared with the company's cost of capital. The single-period CFROI is a one-year measure that incorporates multi-year projection data. By focusing on cash flows rather than profit, these methods are said to overcome some of the deficiencies of economic profit. However, they suffer from a number of other problems; for example, the calculations are often based on subjective assumptions.

EXTERNAL METRICS

The external metrics used in VBM consider the company from the perspective of the investor community. Three principal techniques are used, and each attempts to assess the performance of the company as a whole over a period of time. Total shareholder return (TSR) shows the total return shareholders have earned on their shares over a stated period of time. Total returns include dividend returns and share price changes. *Management Today* (March 1997, p. 48) comments that 'performance against this type of measure is now used as the basis for calculating the major component of directors' bonuses in over half of FTSE 100 companies. ... TSR reflects the measures of success closest to the heart of a company's investors: what they have actually gained or lost from investing in one set of executives rather than in another'. Market value added (MVA) is a concept which has been developed by Stern Stewart and Co. It is the difference between the total amount of capital put into the business by finance providers (debt and equity) and the current market value of the company's shares and debt. Market to book ratio (MBR) is the current market value divided by capital invested.

These three metrics have important contributions to make in judging the performance of senior management and determining their rewards. They each suffer from drawbacks; for example, TSR is vulnerable to distortion by the selection of time period over which it is measured. MVA and MBR require an accurate figure for the capital invested, extremely difficult, if not impossible, to calculate for a firm which has been trading for a number of years, e.g. to what extent should R&D, goodwill or expenditure on brands be regarded as assets?

THE INTEGRATIONISTS

Creating a range of techniques and metrics for VBM was important for the development of the discipline. This work is continuing, but in recent times centre stage has been taken by the integrationists. Over the last 10 to 15 years there has been a push towards integrating the principles and techniques of VBM with knowledge gained from the spheres of strategic planning, economics, organisational behaviour, accounting and finance. For example, Rappaport (1992, pp. 84–85) has emphasised the connections between competitive advantage and value creation:

> Long-term productivity lies at the root of both sustainable competitive advantage and consistent results for the shareholder. ... A company creates competitive advantage when the long-term value of its output or sales is greater than its total costs, including the cost of capital. This advantage can be achieved by providing superior value or lower costs to customers. It is also productivity that the stock market reacts to when pricing a company's shares. Embedded in all share prices is a long-term forecast about a company's productivity – that is, its ability to create value in excess of the cost of producing it.

Tomkins (1991, pp. 176–77) calls for an incorporation of 'far more rigorous financial knowledge into the assessment of an SBU's position in respect of both market attractiveness and competitive position'. A few pages later he proposes:

> There is considerable scope for both academic research and practice-orientated analysis of the possible interrelationships between financial management and strategic portfolio analysis. ... The objective would be to demonstrate more clearly how to increase the value of the company. (Pp. 181–82)

Cornelius and Davies (1997) have pointed out that the VBM approach calls for accounting and other decision-making systems to be value focused:

> A key feature of the VBM company is that all key decision-making processes and planning and control systems are designed to be fully consistent with the shareholder value maximisation objective. ... The key planning and control systems and decision areas for business might be summarised as follows: strategic decision-making and strategic planning, resource allocation, target setting, performance

measurement and managerial compensation schemes. For a typical non-VBM company, different measures and criteria are often used for each of these areas. (P. 60)

McTaggart et al. (1994) require that the culture of the organisation and the processes be changed so that

> companies and their managers are truly 'value based' in their thinking and decision-making processes. ... Value based management has three main elements: beliefs, principles, and processes. The beliefs imbue the organisation with a sense of purpose and a basis for decision-making. The principles provide the knowledge and guidelines for making decisions consistent with the beliefs. And the processes provide the institutional capability to manage effectively within the framework of the beliefs and principles. (Pp. 47–48)

They go on: 'The impact of culture on wealth creation is clearly important. A company, undoubtedly has a set of cultural characteristics – such as being outward looking, imaginative, open, objective, demanding, energetic, focused – that are consistent with, but do not necessarily guarantee value creation' (p. 206). McTaggart et al. also described the ways in which taking on a VBM culture affects the role of the chief executive:

> The primary responsibility for making sure that the company performs well for its owners rests, of course, with the chief executive and, by extension, with his or her direct reports in the corporate centre. ... The three main tasks (for the CEO and the corporate centre of any firm) are as follows:
>
> - Making the rules, including the governing objective, by which the company will be managed;
> - Creating the organisation needed to achieve the company's governing objective;
> - Ensuring that all corporate and business unit strategies support the achievement of the governing objective. (Pp. 202–3)

They also comment on how senior managers should be rewarded: 'The goal of senior managers' incentive compensation plans should be to reward them for creating wealth' (p. 197).

Using VBM has led to a focus on the amount of capital used to generate returns in a merger. The viability of a merger is judged not on the potential for earnings per share dilution next year, or the year after, but on the returns above those required given the capital consumed in acquisition and integration. This may lead to greater hesitancy to raise the takeover premium. It may also reduce the tendency to empire build. This focus on the capital invested also leads to an examination of operations with a more critical eye.

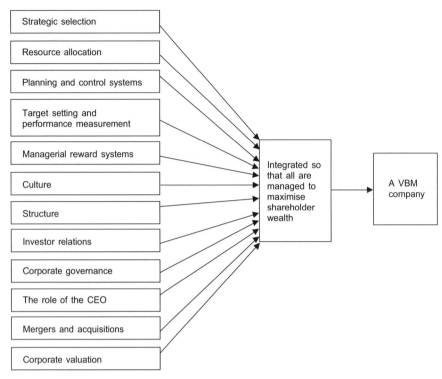

Figure 2.4. Some managerial tasks influenced by VBM

For example, firms which have switched to VBM often discover large amounts of value destroyed by holding excessive inventories. Another way in which VBM has benefited shareholders is by forcing managers to consider the cost of capital used, and whether it is possible to reduce its cost by, for instance, increasing the proportion of capital obtained through cheaper debt finance rather than equity. VBM is also used by security analysts who require tools which permit insights into the value potential of a company given the industry economics and competitive position.

For an integrationist the emphasis is less on the details of accounting, finance and economics and more on the inspirational impetus that the value-based management philosophy can provide in stimulating managers to look anew at operating units and corporate strategy (Figure 2.4). The focus is on providing a value-based environment and culture wherein decisions are made under the almost subliminal influence of value-based principles. This is achieved by widespread inculcation and acceptance of value-based ideas, precepts and norms, and requires leadership with a firm belief in the virtues of value-based principles, widespread education and training, and modified motivational systems. The quantitative analysis is used merely as a backdrop to the more important qualitative assessment of options for change.

OUTSTANDING ISSUES

VBM has grown remarkably, both in terms of widespread adoption by managers, and in terms of the development of techniques to assist a firm in becoming value focused. In their search for answers to difficult questions associated with directing and controlling a corporation and motivating people within, consultants, academics and practitioners have drawn on numerous disciplines. We have travelled far. However, this is a young discipline and there is a long way go. There are a number of unresolved issues which call for significant work over the next few decades.

There remains a need for a measure, or system of measures, which provide an accurate, meaningful and motivational periodic evaluation of performance which is consistent with the long-term valuation criteria. At present there is no short-term metric able to provide a reliable and accurate signal concerning the contribution to long-term shareholder wealth. Without this link to the objective of the firm, short-term performance measures may lead to action which is not value based. The wide variety in methods of value measurement causes confusion. The fundamental assumptions on which they are founded are often different, let alone the information systems, computational skills and conceptual understanding necessary to implement them. Is there a need for some consolidation to send a coherent message? Or are we content to encourage alternatives in the belief that there is no one best solution? Perhaps some metrics are suitable for particular circumstances while others are more suitable for firms in different situations. Perhaps there is a case for using multiple methods within the same firm, or business unit, because each gives insight from alternative perspectives. Or perhaps the explanation for the proliferation of metrics is less rational, being due to each consultancy group needing to sell its unique formula. Here lies an opportunity for objective academic work.

Progress needs to be made in producing techniques which are less vulnerable to managerial bias and manipulation. Existing techniques have the power if misused and misunderstood to turn a system which is nominally shareholder wealth enhancing into one which contributes to the destruction of value. In a poorly designed system, managers may be incentivised to promote the short-term pay-off option over the long-term shareholder wealth maximising option. They may distort the financial case presented to achieve their ends. Establishing executive reward systems which align the interests of managers with those of shareholders is difficult. For example, share option schemes often reward executives for mediocre performance.

The returns under these schemes are often greatly influenced by general market movements rather than company-specific performance. Another problem is the period of time over which performance is measured. Using long-term performance indicators may not have the required motivational impact that is sometimes exhibited by more immediate, and non-VBM metrics. In addition, tying managerial compensation too closely to firm performance may lead to excessive risk-averse behaviour.

There is also the perennial problem of managerial cynicism and scepticism of new techniques. This is likely to be heightened because of the practical problems of implementing VBM. For example, identifying and allocating assets to business units, estimation of the competitive advantage period and the valuing of real options. Adjusting for and analysing the uncertainty associated with estimating future financial outcomes is bound to be subjective and reliant on judgment. It is very important that the VBM advocates acknowledge the subjective and uncertain basis of their calculations and recommendations, and do not attempt to overstate their case. Perhaps they need to move away from giving undue weight to the quantifiable elements in their analysis to take proper account of non-financial and strategic factors. Operating managers can be put off by an excessive quantitative emphasis with the often impenetrable finance-based jargon and complex technical solutions. It does not have to be like this. There is a need to explain clearly the simple truths behind VBM and engender support and commitment rather than blind with science.

VBM metrics seem easier to apply in some industries than others. It is more difficult to establish reliable capital investment figures in industries where assets are generally intangible, e.g. software, brand names or patents. It is also problematic for very young companies with highly uncertain future cash flows and profits. Important business advances are often totally unquantifiable at the outset, e.g. Microsoft's innovations in the Internet market. An overreliance on VBM metrics may lead to a failure to pursue the right strategy and innovative thrust, simply because the high-risk nature of the investment does not lend itself to numerical analysis. Sometimes it is right to back a hunch and the entrepreneurial energy of an innovator. Perhaps it can be said that VBM is less all-encompassing than is claimed by the consultants. Perhaps the metrics are good at identifying the sources of sickness within the firm, allowing managers to remove the abnormality in the spirit of shareholder wealth maximisation, but they are less good at directing a strategic thrust; worse, they may even inhibit positive non-quantifiable action.

There is a mass of technical issues, ranging from the complications associated with valuing foreign operations to the unsuitability of external metrics for unquoted firms, but the primary outstanding technical difficulty has to be the difficulty of establishing a reliable cost of capital. There continues to be a lively debate over the extent to which β is useful for calculating the equity component. There is also a fierce debate about the level of the equity risk premium, with some saying 2–3% should be added to the risk-free return, and others saying the premium is between 7–8%. It is difficult enough to calculate the cost of capital for a company as a whole; however, VBM often evaluates sub-parts of the firm. Sectional cost of capital is incredibly difficult to establish with any certainty, given the problems in identifying systematic risk levels and debt/equity ratio levels.

A fundamental problem for VBM is that there is no universal acceptance among managers that the firm should be run entirely for the benefit of shareholders. If you add to this the fact that implementing a VBM programme properly is very expensive and time-consuming and requires enormous senior managerial commitment, then perhaps we should think it remarkable that so many of the world's largest firms have committed themselves to it.

'As is the case with other good ideas, shareholder value has moved from being ignored to being rejected to becoming self-evident' (Rappaport, 1998, pp. 2–3). The main contribution VBM makes to the field of management is not the valuation numbers it produces but the rich insights revealed in the process of investigating and analysing the value potential of strategies, businesses and investments. The qualitative, subjective and motivational aspects that impinge on business success are highlighted by the use of value principles, and this is what makes VBM a vitally important business approach despite its current limitations.

REFERENCES

Adedeji, A. (1997) A Test of CAPM and the three factor model on the London Stock Exchange. Paper presented at the British Accounting Association Northern Accounting Group 1997 Annual Conference, 10 September 1997, Loughborough University.

Arnold, G. (1998) *Corporate Financial Management*. Financial Times Pitman, London.

Buffett, W. (1989) Berkshire Hathaway 1989 annual report, p. 22.

Copeland, T., Koller, T. and Murrin, J. (1995) *Valuation: measuring and managing the value of companies*, 2nd edn. John Wiley, New York.

Cornelius, I. and Davies, M. (1997) *Shareholder Value*. Pearson Professional, London

Dean, J. (1951) *Capital Budgeting*. Columbia University Press, New York.

Dearden, J. (1969) The case against ROI control. *Harvard Business Review*, May/June, 124–35.

Durand, D. (1952) Growth stocks and the Petersburg paradox. *Journal of Finance*, **12**, 348–63.

Economist (1997) Valuing companies: a star to sail by? 2 August, pp. 61–63

Emmanuel, C.R. and Otley, D.T. (1976) The usefulness of residual income. *Journal of Business Finance and Accounting*, **3**(4), 43–51.

Financial Times (1997) A man of monomaniacal vision, an obituary of Roberto Goizueta. 20 October 1997.

Financial Times (1998) Registering the value of cash. Tony Jackson. 19 January 1998, p. 14.

Financial Times (1998) Japan's ray of hope. Paul Abrahams. 6 May 1998.

Fisher, I. (1930) *The Theory of Interest.* Reprinted 1977 by Porcupine Press.

Friedman, M. (1958) Three major factors in business management: leadership, decision-making, and social responsibility. Summary by Walter A. Diehm, Social Science Seminar, 19 March 1958.

Gordon, M.J. (1962) *The Investment, Financing and Valuation of the Corporation.* Richard D. Irwin, Homewood IL.

Gordon, M.J. and Shapiro, E. (1956) Capital equipment analysis: the required rate of profit. *Management Science,* **III**, 102–10.

Hamilton, R. (1777) *An Introduction to Merchandise.* Vol. II. Edinburgh.

Hayek, F.A. (1960) The corporation in a democratic society: in whose interest ought it and will it be run? Reproduced 1969 in *Business Strategy* (ed. H. Igor Ansoff). Penguin, London.

Hirshleifer, J. (1961) Risk, the discount rate and investment decisions. *American Economic Review,* May, 112–20.

Lintner, J. (1965) The valuation of risky assets and the selection of risky investments in stock portfolios and capital budgets. *Review of Economics and Statistics,* **47**, 13–37.

Lloyds Bank (1991) Short report to shareholders, p. 5

McTaggart, J.M., Kontes, P.W. and Mankins, M.C. (1994) *The Value Imperative.* Free Press, New York.

Management Today (1997) March, p. 48

Marshall, A. (1947) *Principles of Economics,* 8th edn. Macmillan, London. First edition 1890.

Mauriel, J.J. and Anthony, R.N. (1966) Misevaluation of investment center performance. *Harvard Business Review,* March/April, 98–105

Mepham, M.J. (1980) The residual income debate. *Journal of Business Finance and Accounting,* **7**(2), 183–99

Modigliani, F. and Miller, M.H. (1958) The cost of capital, corporation finance, and the theory of investment. *American Economic Review,* **XLVIII**, 261–97.

Mossin, J. (1966) Equilibrium in a capital asset market. *Econometrica,* **34**, 768–83.

Rappaport, A. (1986) *Creating Shareholder Value.* Free Press, New York.

Rappaport, A. (1992) CFOs and strategists: forging a common framework. *Harvard Business Review,* May/June, 84–91.

Rappaport, A. (1998) *Creating Shareholder Value,* 2nd edn. Free Press, New York.

Sharpe, W.F. (1964) Capital asset prices: a theory of market equilibrium under conditions of risk. *Journal of Finance,* **19**, 425–42.

Smith, A. (1776) *The Wealth of Nations.* Reproduced 1910 in two volumes by J.M. Dent, London.

Solomon, E. (1955) Measuring a company's cost of capital. *Journal of Business,* **XXVIII**, 240–52.

Solomon, E. (1963) *The Theory of Financial Management.* Columbia University Press, New York.

Solomons, D. (1965) *Divisional Performance: Measurement and Control.* Reproduced 1985, by M. Wiener Publishing.

Strong, N. and Xu, X.G. (1997) Explaining the cross-section of UK expected stock returns. *British Accounting Review,* **29**, 1–23.

Tomkins, C. (1973) *Financial Planning in Divisionalised Companies*. Accountancy Age Books, London.

Tomkins, C. (1991) *Corporate Resource Allocation*. Basil Blackwell, Oxford.

Treynor, J.L. (1981) The financial objective in the widely held corporation. *Financial Analysts Journal*, March/April.

3 Value-based Management in Practice: A Critical Review

MATT DAVIES

INTRODUCTION

Although a relatively recent innovation, value-based management (VBM) has rapidly achieved a high-profile status. In recent years the approach, its related measures and its advocates have been given much exposure in the business and professional press. An increasing number of large companies have publicly expressed their commitment to VBM, including Lloyds TSB, Cadbury Schweppes, and Boots. Growing interest in VBM among practitioners is evidenced by recent surveys and by the increase in VBM literature and conference activities.

The expanding literature on VBM has tended to originate from those consultants and consultant academics who advocate its use. The literature tends, therefore, to take a predominantly positive stance and can largely be characterised as comprising descriptions of the various alternative prescriptive 'VBM recipes' available. Whilst this literature is interspersed with examples of companies which are reported to have successfully applied such ideas, there remains a need for independent research into VBM in practice.

The purpose of this chapter is to review the state of VBM practice via a critical review of available evidence. The chapter is organised as follows. First, the need for research into VBM practice will be discussed, and a number of key research questions will be identified. Secondly, potential sources of empirical evidence on VBM practice will be evaluated and a set of criteria for appraising specific research findings will be established. Thirdly, the state of VBM practice will be reviewed, with a critique of the available evidence. The concluding comments will identify aspects of VBM practice requiring further investigation by future researchers.

THE NEED FOR EMPIRICAL EVIDENCE

There are several reasons why research into the application of VBM in practice is important. In management research generally, observations of practice are a critical feature, both for theory development and for theory testing.

In the context of VBM, however, there are more specific reasons why such empirical research is of particular relevance.

Since VBM emerged in the 1980s (Rappaport, 1986; Reimann, 1989), a number of alternative VBM recipes have been promoted, with much written by their respective advocates on why and how each should be applied and the likely benefits from doing so (Rappaport, 1986, 1998; Stewart, 1991; McTaggart et al., 1994; Copeland et al., 1996; Madden, 1999). Although there are important differences between these different approaches, the most important of which will be briefly considered below, it is nevertheless possible to discern a common theme.

At the heart of VBM is the assumption that the company should be managed explicitly for shareholder value creation. This means that managers are required to seek to maximise the net present value of the ownership equity of the company through both new investment in positive net present value opportunities, and through improvements in the economic returns achieved on existing assets employed. With VBM, shareholder value creation is the primary objective of the company, the primary decision-making criterion, and the primary measure of performance. In addition, VBM requires that a company's planning and control systems, including managerial reward schemes, be aligned so as to promote shareholder value creation at all levels of the business.

A further feature of VBM is its emphasis upon so-called value-based measures rather than traditional accounting measures of performance. VBM advocates argue that traditional accounting measures, such as earnings per share and net profit, provide a relatively poor guide to shareholder value creation (Rappaport, 1986; Stewart, 1991). Thus, a number of alternative measures have been proposed, each of which has the same objective: to provide a 'calculating machine consistent with the principles of economic income' (Bromwich, 1998).

Before considering the differences between the alternative VBM approaches, it is necessary to briefly consider VBM's theoretical foundations. It can be seen from the foregoing discussion that VBM relies on two important propositions: firstly, that shareholder value creation is the primary corporate objective and, secondly, that economic income is the primary measure of corporate performance. Whilst these propositions are not uncontroversial, there is a major stream within the finance and accounting literature in which these views are taken to be the ideal, thereby providing a justification for the VBM stance.

Whilst the alternative VBM approaches share these essential characteristics, there are differences between them, both in terms of the specific measures used but also in the way in which the approach is applied. Firstly, the different VBM recipes employ different measures of shareholder value creation. McTaggart et al. (1994) and Stewart (1991) favour a residual income approach (economic profit and economic value added, respectively),

Rappaport advocates shareholder value added, and Madden promotes cash flow return on investment (CFROI). The different measures and their main proponents are summarised in Table 3.1.

There has been much discussion of the theoretical and practical merits of these different measures, particularly in terms of their relative accuracy and complexity (Cornelius and Davies, 1997). It is beyond the scope of this chapter to review the relevant arguments here, but it is argued that the experience of practitioners who have attempted to apply these measures could offer much to this debate.

Secondly, in terms of differences in application, McTaggart et al. (1994) particularly emphasise both the process and content of strategic planning under their version of VBM. Stewart (1991), on the other hand, emphasises the technical adjustments required in order to improve the accuracy of the economic value added (EVA) calculation. Indeed, Stern Stewart have identified up to 164 such EVA adjustments.

Advocates of VBM have made strong claims on its behalf, in particular that its use will lead to the creation of shareholder value. McTaggart et al. (1994, p. 51) argue that VBM will 'greatly improve the quality of decision-making, by improving the quality of the alternatives that management has to consider as well as building a bias for choosing and implementing the best available alternatives'. Meanwhile Stern Stewart (1995, p. 5) claim: 'The major benefit $EVA^{®}$ firms can expect is a higher market value'. They also cite other significant benefits: 'a common language for planning and managing, more accountability for delivering value, a greater concern for managing assets, a greater willingness to rationalise and redirect resources, better bridges to link

Table 3.1. Alternative value measures and their main proponents

Consultancy firm	Preferred measures
Boston Consulting Group (1996)	Cash flow return on investment, total business returns
Braxton Associates (1991)	Various, including cash flow return on investment and total business returns
Holt (Madden, 1998)	Cash flow return on investment
LEK/Alcar (Rappaport, 1986, 1998)	Shareholder value added
Marakon (McTaggart et al., 1994)	Economic profit, warranted equity value
McKinsey (Copeland et al., 1996)	Various, including economic profit
Stern Stewart (Stewart, 1991; Ehrbar, 1998)	Economic value added, market value added

Source: Adapted from 'Keeping Score: Metric Wars', *CFO Magazine*, October 1996. Reprinted with permission.

operations and strategy with financial results, more collaborative long-term planning'. As a further example, Copeland et al. (1996, p. 98) argue: 'The management processes ... provide decision-makers at all levels of the organisation with the right information and incentives to make value creating decisions'.

The VBM literature is currently dominated by highly prescriptive contributions from those consultants and consultant academics who have a vested interest in promoting the virtues of their particular VBM approach. There is therefore a need for this literature to be counterbalanced by independent evidence on whether and how VBM is applied in practice. Moreover, there is a need for independent verification of whether the claims advanced on behalf of VBM generally, and individual VBM approaches specifically, are justified.

The foregoing discussion demonstrates the need for research into VBM practice and identifies broad areas of VBM practice which require investigation. Next the focus is narrowed through a more detailed consideration of specific areas where research into practice would be appropriate. Potential areas of research will be considered under two headings: descriptive research and explanatory research.

DESCRIPTIONS OF VBM PRACTICE

There is a need for research which provides a reliable picture of the state of VBM practice. It would address questions like these:

- How much VBM is being practised?
- Why is it being used?
- Where is it being practised?
- How is it being practised?
- How is it being implemented?
- What effect has its use had on adopting companies?

Such research is important for a number of reasons. Advocates of VBM imply that all companies should be run on this basis. If one accepts this, then descriptive research is useful to establish whether there is a gap between theory and practice. A gap might exist because companies are not doing it at all, or not doing it properly, and this leads to a consideration of what needs to be done to 'educate' apparently ignorant or misguided managers.

Such research might also help establish which of the various value metrics are most popular, what factors and issues have arisen in the adoption of VBM, and how any problems encountered have been overcome. Such research might prove particularly useful to practitioners, including existing VBM users and those contemplating its use.

However, the utility of such research is seriously limited, since descriptions of practice do not explain what has been observed. Take, for example, descriptions of the extent and nature of VBM use. To find that VBM (or a particular VBM recipe) is being widely used cannot in itself justify the assumption that VBM (or the particular approach) can therefore be regarded as best practice. On the other hand, to find that VBM is not widely used cannot justify the assumption that it should be.

Accounting research has given much attention to the apparent gap between textbook theory and observed practice. Explanations for this gap originally emphasised the potential ignorance of practitioners or that perhaps there was a time lag between the development of new theory and its implementation in practice (Drury, 1996). More recently, however, there has been an increasing recognition that a failure to adopt textbook techniques might be due to a logical trade-off between the benefits and costs from their introduction, or due to the failure of such normative theories to address the realities experienced by managers (Ryan et al., 1992). In other words, it is the theory not the practice which is in need of revision. It would not be enough therefore to simply compare VBM theory with VBM practice and to suggest changes in practice as a result of any apparent gap. It may be that the theory of VBM needs adapting to the realities experienced by companies attempting to use it.

In addition, descriptive research might find that companies doing VBM (or a particular recipe) are more successful than non-users (or users of other VBM approaches), or that they enjoy certain benefits or advantages. This raises two questions: What is meant by 'success'? And how do we measure the benefits and advantages accruing from the use of VBM? Benefits and advantages may be measured via managers' perceptions of the impact of VBM use, in which case the inherent subjectivity and the risk of bias are problematic. Even with more objective measures, descriptive research does not demonstrate that the success or benefits enjoyed by companies using VBM can be unequivocally attributed to its adoption. Similarly, a description of the implementation and use of VBM within what is deemed a successful VBM company does not in itself mean that this should be regarded as best practice in this field.

Nevertheless, despite these limitations, a description of the nature and form of existing VBM practice is a necessary first step to understanding VBM practice, and so has an important role to play.

EXPLANATIONS OF VBM PRACTICE

Explanatory research is widely regarded as being superior to descriptive research since it seeks to help us understand observed practice (Sekaran, 1992). In the context of VBM, the literature generally suggests that all companies should adopt one of the VBM recipes, that the same recipe is equally applicable to all companies and that the steps to be taken to implement the VBM recipe are the same for all companies. Explanatory research would address these assertions by looking at questions like these:

- Why is VBM used in the ways it is used by adopting companies? What are the effects of using VBM, and why do they occur?
- Do the different approaches to VBM have different effects, and if so what different aspects of VBM approaches have different outcomes, and why is this?
- Does VBM have different effects in different circumstances, and if so what circumstances affect what outcomes, and why?
- Do different implementation approaches have different effects, and if so what implementation approaches affect what outcomes, and why?

One potential output of explanatory research is a model of the relationships between variables relevant to a particular phenomenon. This could lead ultimately to what might be described as a contingency theory of VBM, which seeks to identify the key variables that are matched with features of VBM systems observed in practice.

The more powerful the explanatory model, the more useful it is likely to be for predictive purposes. Understanding the past is important, but even more useful is a model which can predict the future, given certain circumstances and factors. A strong predictive model would enable people to prescribe how to increase the likelihood of certain desirable outcomes. In other words, it could help to predict whether VBM would be useful to a particular company, and if so, it could prescribe how VBM should be applied and implemented.

ALTERNATIVE SOURCES OF EMPIRICAL EVIDENCE

The previous section highlighted specific areas of potentially useful descriptive and explanatory research. This section looks at sources of evidence and the next section examines the evidence itself; the next section also considers the extent to which these areas have indeed been addressed by researchers. Any consideration of the state of VBM practice must, it is argued, be accompanied by an appraisal of the significance which can be attached to the evidence upon which such a consideration is based. Without such an appraisal, undue significance may be placed upon potentially questionable evidence. This means that issues relating to research methods and methodology become important not only to academics, but to anyone interested in understanding VBM practice.

This section begins by establishing criteria for judging the quality of empirical research. These criteria will then be used to evaluate the alternative empirical methods of research available. Finally, the criteria established will be refined and extended in order for them to be used as a basis for evaluating individual pieces of research evidence.

CRITERIA FOR EVALUATING ALTERNATIVE METHODS

Four criteria are commonly used to evaluate alternative empirical methods (Yin, 1994, p. 33):

Construct validity

Construct validity refers to the need to establish operational measures which accurately capture the relevant concepts under investigation. For example, is a questionnaire instrument which is supposed to be measuring the extent and nature of VBM use in companies actually likely do this? Poorly worded or leading questions, among others, are examples of problems which might reduce the construct validity of such research.

Internal validity

Internal validity is concerned with the extent to which the identified causes or stimuli actually produce the reported effects or responses, and thus only applies in the context of explanatory research studies. For a study to have high internal validity this means that changes in the dependent variable have been brought about by changes in the independent variable, and not as a result of other confounding factors. Thus internal validity requires that control is exerted over extraneous variables. For example, a study of the effect of VBM adoption on companies' total shareholder returns (TSR) must ensure that appropriate and sufficient controls are used to provide confidence that the effects of other variables potentially impacting upon TSR performance have been ruled out.

External validity

External validity is concerned with the extent to which research findings can be generalised beyond the immediate research setting in which the study was conducted. For example, are the size and representativeness of a sample of companies surveyed to establish the extent and nature of VBM use such that one can extrapolate these findings to a larger population of companies? Note that both construct validity and internal validity are necessary but not sufficient conditions for external validity (Birnberg et al., 1990).

Reliability

Reliability is concerned with the consistency of the research results obtained. In other words, how likely is it that another researcher following the same procedures adopted by the original investigator would generate the same findings and conclusions? Reliability requires firstly that biases and errors are avoided, and secondly that the procedures employed in the research are disclosed in sufficient detail to enable another researcher to repeat the original investigation.

MERITS OF ALTERNATIVE METHODS

There are three main methods of empirical research: experiments (and quasi-experiments), surveys and case studies. The criteria established above will now be used to assess the potential contribution of each of these methods. The relevance of each method to VBM research will also be considered.

A number of authors provide a detailed assessment of the relative merits of each method in terms of their relative validity and reliability (Birnberg et al., 1990; and Gill and Johnson, 1997). For the purposes of this chapter, a summary of the key points is sufficient (Table 3.2).

Experiments and quasi-experiments

True experimental research in management is rare, for fairly obvious reasons, including the fact that that we are dealing with social phenomena, and this method may be considered to offer little to VBM research. Nevertheless, the logic of the true experiment underpins a number of what are described as quasi-experimental approaches, the main objective of which is to analyse causal relationships between variables.

The quasi-experimental approach is potentially highly relevant to VBM research. There are three main forms of quasi-experimental research and each could be applied to VBM practice: pre-test/post-test, interrupted time series and correlational designs. There are similarities between the first two forms in that both seek to measure the change in the dependent variable (which in the context of VBM could be total shareholder returns) resulting from a particular change (perhaps the adoption of VBM). Correlational designs, on

Table 3.2. A summary evaluation of alternative methods of empirical research

	Experiments and quasi-experiments	Surveys	Case studies
Construct validity	low to high	low to high	low to high
Internal validity	high	high	low
External validity	low to medium	medium	low to high
Reliability	high	high	low

Source: Adapted from Birnberg et al. (1990, pp. 36–37). Reprinted with permission.

the other hand, involve identifying the extent of association between certain variables, and they could be used to establish the degree of association between VBM use and TSR performance. Remember, however, that evidence of correlation does not itself prove causality.

Such approaches could potentially be used to provide the explanatory research identified earlier as fundamental to our understanding of VBM practice and in particular to investigate whether there is evidence that VBM actually works. In each of these forms of quasi-experimental research, the ability to control for alternative explanatory variables is of critical importance. In addition, the statistical significance of the results of such studies is dependent upon factors such as sample size, the representativeness of the sample and the number of measures taken for the relevant variables. These requirements may limit the scope for using such methods at the current time, since the relatively recent emergence of VBM might mean there are insufficient companies with a sufficiently long history of using it in practice.

Surveys

Although surveys tend to be used for descriptive purposes, that is to identify characteristics of a specific population of subjects, they may also be used for explanatory research. Explanatory research uses analytic surveys to seek evidence of a correlation between variables. The survey approach could usefully be applied in the context of VBM to provide insights into the extent and nature of the use of VBM in practice, the impact of its use on performance, and the benefits and problems associated with its use.

Case studies

Case study research has in recent years achieved growing acceptance as an appropriate method for researching management practice. Many authors have expressed concerns that questionnaire surveys offer little more than a partial and superficial representation of the state of practice (Ryan et al., 1992). Consequently, there have been many calls for the increasing use of field studies and case studies to provide a more detailed picture of company practices, with much greater sensitivity to the context in which such practices occur (Osborne, 1996).

As well as providing rich descriptions of practice, case studies may also be used in more explanatory research studies, in which the aim is to develop new theories or modify existing theories to provide good explanations of what has been observed in the specific cases examined. Such research involves an inductive approach, in which the emphasis is upon the development of theory grounded in empirical observations (Glaser and Strauss, 1967).

Compared with VBM questionnaire surveys, case studies provide scope for gaining a more complete understanding of how VBM is being used on the ground and the range of issues and factors that are relevant to its use. Whilst this itself enhances our knowledge of VBM practice, of even greater potential benefit would be case-based research which went further and attempted to develop a model that helped to explain VBM practice.

SUMMARY OF CRITERIA

It is important to recognise that the potential merits of a piece of research are to a certain extent constrained by the choice of empirical method. The key strengths and weaknesses have just been summarised for the three main empirical research methods in terms of their relative validity and reliability. The actual merits of any specific research findings, however, are also determined by the way in which the particular research study has been conducted. It is also necessary, therefore, to evaluate each individual piece of research evidence against the specific criteria by which the quality of research findings can be appraised.

To this end, although the four criteria – construct validity, internal validity, external validity, reliability – provide a useful general framework, some refinement is necessary. For descriptive research, internal validity does not apply, since descriptive research does not seek to establish relationships between variables. And except for case-based research, the size and representativeness of the sample is a critical feature of descriptive research. This is because sampling has a direct bearing on the external validity of descriptive research findings, whereas it affects not only the external validity but also the internal validity of explanatory research findings. The sample size and method of sample selection therefore warrant specific consideration.

There are also some additional criteria relevant to the appraisal of the merits of a specific research study. Firstly, more weight should be attached to the conclusions produced by research which involved multiple sources of data. Secondly, more faith should be placed in findings obtained via independent research. For example, in this context evidence presented by advocates of VBM (including consultants selling VBM advice) cannot be regarded as carrying the weight of an independent researcher, all other things being equal. Finally, more weight should be attached to research findings which have appeared in refereed academic journals since these will have been subjected to a process of academic peer review, which should provide a degree of quality control.

Following these refinements, a revised set of criteria can be established which can then be used to appraise the relative merits of contributions to VBM research:

- Construct validity
- Internal validity
- External validity

- Sample size and method of sample selection
- Replicability
- Sources of data
- Independence of the researcher
- Has the research been published in a refereed academic journal?

Internal validity is not relevant for descriptive research; for quasi-experimental designs it requires specific consideration of whether sufficient control has been exerted over extraneous variables.

THE STATE OF VBM PRACTICE: A CRITICAL REVIEW

Having established a set of criteria with which to evaluate the merits of particular research findings, it is time to consider the state of VBM practice, paying specific attention to the quality of the evidence upon which such knowledge is based. This review will be organised into two parts: (1) a review of descriptive research addressing the extent and nature of VBM use and the effects of VBM use, and (2) a review of the explanatory research into VBM practice.

DESCRIPTIVE RESEARCH INTO VBM PRACTICE

The extent and nature of use

There have been a number of surveys of VBM practice (Table 3.3). These surveys tend to indicate that whilst there is growing interest in VBM and shareholder value plus a recognition of its importance, they are neither widely used in practice nor well understood. A 1996 Deloitte & Touche survey of finance directors in UK companies revealed that among PLCs, 67% regard the concept of shareholder value as a key strategic driver, yet only 41% actually apply shareholder value techniques for decision making, and furthermore, only 29% claimed to have a good understanding of what 'shareholder value' means.

Such findings are supported by a 1996 KPMG survey of European companies which found that whilst 70% were aware of the concept of economic value, only 35% claimed to use it for managerial purposes, and only 8% were found to be 'true users of VBM' (defined as 'using VBM for key business decisions', including the management of product and market portfolios at the business unit level). Similarly, a 1997 PA Consulting survey of top UK and Irish companies found that whilst 96% of companies claimed to subscribe to the VBM philosophy in some form, only 5% applied 'full VBM' (determined according to whether positive responses were received

Table 3.3. Surveys into VBM practice

Survey	Sample size	Sampling method	Questionnaire	Responses (response rate)	Independent study?	Published in refereed academic journal?
Deloitte & Touche (1996)	not stated	A cross-section of FDs covering the top 500 UK companies and all CIMA FDs	postal	561 (?%)	?	no
KPMG (1996)	not stated	Large companies in 8 European countries	postal	468 (?%)	?	no
Mills et al. (1996)	250 companies	Largest UK companies by market value	telephone and postal	101 (40.4%)	yes	no
Coopers and Lybrand (1997)	not stated	Wide range of public and private companies in 12 European countries and Canada	postal	277 (?%)	?	no

PA Consulting (1997)	540 companies	FTSE 500 and top 40 in ISEQ	postal	132 (24.4%)	?	no
Wallace (1998)	76 US companies using residual income (RI)	US companies reported to be using RI	postal	14 out of 40 (35%) using RI for managerial incentives; 15 out of other 36 (41.7%)	yes	no
KPMG (1999)	not stated	Leading companies in 7 European countries	telephone	435 (?%)	?	no
Francis and Minchington (Chapter 8)	2331	Random sample of CIMA accountants in large UK companies	postal	258 (11.1%)	yes	no

for questions relating to principles, processes and actions considered consistent with VBM). Such evidence is confirmed by Francis and Minchington (Chapter 8), who also find evidence of very limited adoption of so-called value-based metrics.

A 1997 Coopers and Lybrand survey of shareholder value management issues carried out across 13 countries, found evidence that VBM ideas are perhaps more widely applied than the above studies suggest. It revealed that 80% of companies surveyed use VBM-related approaches for routine planning and investment decisions and 83% for 'major business decisions' (such as acquisitions and disposals and substantial capital expenditures). Note, however, the study also found that profit-based measures are used marginally more often than shareholder value measures for routine decisions, and profit-related, accounting rate of return (ARR) and payback measures are all used alongside shareholder value measures for 'major business decisions', with no single approach clearly preferred. This is contrary to VBM theory which contends that value-based measures are superior to such traditional accounting numbers (Rappaport, 1986; Stewart, 1991). Also, with respect to performance measurement, the study found that 50% of companies emphasised shareholder value measures, in contrast to 92% which emphasised profit-related measures and 76% ARR-related measures.

This picture is confirmed by a 1999 KPMG survey, in which although 64% of companies claim to use VBM, profit or earnings-based measures continue to be the most popular performance measures, being used by 90% of respondents. In addition, such measures are also the most commonly used as a basis for managerial reward schemes. Some 76% of respondents reported using profit or earnings-based measures for managerial incentives, whilst only 36% and 35% used shareholder value added and economic profit, respectively.

Whilst surveys provide a potentially useful indication of the extent of and 'broad nature' of usage, they are less helpful in examining practice in anything other than a relatively superficial manner (Ryan et al., 1992). Moreover, questionnaire surveys are notoriously open to misinterpretation, a problem likely to be exacerbated in the case of a relatively new phenomenon such as VBM. It is argued, therefore, that to gain a clearer picture of how VBM is used in practice, detailed independent field studies are essential (O'Hanlon and Peasnell, 1998). Few such case studies exist, however, and of the three most relevant UK sources, two are relatively long-standing (Table 3.4). The three main sources are Grundy (1992), Handler (1998) and Hennell and Warner (1998).

Grundy (1992) describes the experiences of BP in the period from the late 1980s to 1991, during which time a Rappaport-style VBM approach was adopted. Handler (1998), on the other hand, provides a similar account of the experiences of BP at around the same time as the Grundy study, and also reports the VBM experiences of Dixons and Lloyds Bank. Handler describes Dixons' 1990s plan for creating shareholder value through a strategy for

Table 3.4. Case studies of VBM practice

Study	Case companies	Sources of data	Independent study?	Published in refereed academic journal?
Grundy (1992)	BP	Multiple, including workshops and interviews	yes	no
Handler (1998)	BP, Dixons and Lloyds Bank	Not stated	?	yes
Hennell and Warner (1998)	Boots, Unilever and an anonymous US company	Multiple, including interviews and company documentation	?	no

building long-term customer satisfaction. The features of this strategy included new concepts in systems, service and merchandising. Whilst the objective of such changes is shareholder value creation, there is no mention of the use within the company of any specific VBM tools or measures. It is not clear from the case details that Dixons could (at the time of the study at least) be regarded as using VBM. The Lloyds Bank case is also interesting. The case reports how shareholder value ideas were applied within the company from 1983, when Sir Brian Pitman became CEO, to the early 1990s. During this period, key features of its shareholder value methodology included the objective (at the corporate and business unit levels) of achieving a net return on equity in excess of the company's cost of capital, and an emphasis on the creation of free cash flows.

More recently, Hennell and Warner (1998) describe the VBM experiences of Unilever, Boots and an anonymous US company. The Unilever case describes how in the mid 1990s the company shifted its emphasis away from traditional accounting-based measures, focusing instead on trading contribution (a form of residual income) for shorter-term performance measurement, and in 1997 it adopted total business returns (TBR) as the key measure of performance at the strategic level. Boots, on the other hand, is reported to use a discounted cash flow model for strategic planning from which key value drivers are identified and used for subsequent performance management. Finally, whilst Unilever and Boots are used as examples of successful VBM adoption, Warner and Hennell also briefly relate the experience of an anonymous US company which is reported to have failed to successfully implement an EVA-based system. Although the company adopted EVA, the authors argue that the measure was not well understood internally and had little impact on managers who continued to focus on EBIT (earnings before interest and tax) as the key financial measure.

The effects of VBM use

Considerable claims have been made on behalf of VBM by its advocates. Available evidence of whether such claims can be justified as a result of the experiences of adopting companies is limited in terms of both quantity and to some extent quality. The surveys cited above offer some insights into perceptions among managers of VBM companies, though this does not provide strong evidence that reported effects are necessarily those which have been experienced.

Although the 1996 Deloitte and Touche survey found that in companies implementing VBM the approach totally met or exceeded expectations in less than 40% of cases, survey evidence largely suggests that VBM is perceived to have a beneficial impact by adopting companies. The 1996 KPMG survey found that respondents were very positive about the financial effects of using VBM, particularly on cash flows, return on investment and profits, but less so on stock price and sales growth. The same study also revealed that 90% of 'real VBM users' and 79% of other users of VBM believed it had added moderate or much value to their organisation.

Further evidence in a US context, where the use of VBM is more established, is provided by Wallace (1998), who examines the management actions associated with a change to an EVA-based performance measurement system. This study involves a survey sent to 76 companies that have adopted EVA, with respondents indicating that such firms are more selective in choosing new projects, more willing to dispose of underperforming assets, more aware of the firm's cost of capital and better able to manage all three areas of working capital: accounts receivable, inventory and accounts payable. Wallace concludes that EVA performance measures appear to help align the interests of management with shareholders, with the emphasis shifting from bottom-line earnings to earning more than the cost of capital employed.

In terms of the more specific consequences of adopting VBM, the 1997 Coopers and Lybrand survey found that the two main benefits from the use of VBM were (1) the alignment of shareholder and company goals using a clear and consistent approach which reflects the cost of funding, and (2) that it allows the analysis of performance and strategic actions in terms of their effect on shareholder value.

The 1996 KPMG survey, on the other hand, reports that organisations stated how VBM had a positive impact on 'the company overall' (not defined), improving strategic decisions, the performance of management, enhancing market value, and understanding market forces. The survey also reports that the more broadly and deeply VBM is used, the greater the perceived benefits to the organisation.

Although some attention is given to implementation issues, problems with the use of VBM are largely neglected in the prescriptive VBM literature. Survey evidence suggests, however, that adopting VBM is far from easy. The 1999 KPMG survey found that over 80% of VBM users had experienced some difficulty in implementing VBM. It found that 'cultural change' and 'motivating management' were the two most common difficulties.

The 1997 Coopers and Lybrand survey, on the other hand, found the following potential barriers to the adoption of VBM: the need for specialist financial skills; the need for cultural change and the cost of implementation; the reliance on assumptions; the lack of applicability to R&D companies; difficulties relating to how the role of the HQ could be evaluated; and the lack of applicability to financial institutions. Unfortunately, however, this study does not clarify whether these are the views of those who have actual experience with VBM, or those who have merely contemplated its use.

The few case studies on VBM provide some additional insights into the potential benefits and problems of using the approach. Grundy (1992) reports that the benefits to BP from applying VBM were as follows: it provided a common framework for integrating strategy, capital investment, acquisition and divestment decisions and budgeting; through the link to managerial rewards, behaviour and motivation are aligned to decision and control processes; specific divestments and refocusing activities; and performance management became much more outwardly focused.

Grundy also reflects on some of the difficulties experienced by BP and offers the following advice to other companies implementing VBM: avoid excessive attention to number crunching; limit the scope for manipulation of terminal values; do not apply only to a discrete process; and avoid the temptation to accept compromises in order to maintain momentum. Handler's (1991) study of the BP experience at around the same time reports that the techniques were initially met with scepticism, for the following reasons: difficult arithmetic; no earth-shattering revelations; difficulties in dealing with major external uncertainties; and a culture which emphasised short-term performance.

The Hennell and Warner (1998) cases provide additional insights. Taking the Unilever case first, at the time of the study it is too early for reflections on the success or otherwise of the adoption of VBM. There are, however, reported to be high expectations for VBM: 'Unilever's top management is under no illusion that this change [to shareholder value-based measures] is going to provide competitive advantage' (p. 91). The Boots case, on the other hand, is described by the authors as 'the best example of success [in VBM adoption] we have seen'. The study does not, however, report the perceptions of Boots managers in terms of the benefits and problems that have arisen from the use of VBM. Finally, for the anonymous US company which introduced a 'lip-service EVA approach', it is reported that 'earnings per share growth, ROS and ROCE were still all better than competitors. ... None of the company's managers could understand why the share price was so low' (p. 112). No evidence is presented, however, to support these assertions.

EXPLANATORY RESEARCH INTO VBM PRACTICE

Although there is generally a dearth of explanatory research into VBM practice, two studies are worthy of mention (Table 3.5). First, Wallace (1997) uses an interrupted time series approach to study the internal management decisions associated with EVA-type compensation plans. He investigates the investing, financing and operating decisions made by managers in a sample of 40 firms that use an EVA-type measure in compensation plans, compared to a matched group of 40 firms that continue to use traditional accounting measures. Wallace finds statistically significant increases in EVA for the firms adopting EVA relative to the control firms, and statistically weak evidence of improved shareholder returns. He also finds that the firms that adopt EVA decrease their new investment and increase their disposition of assets, leading to a decrease in net investment; increase their payouts to shareholders through share repurchases; and increase their utilisation of assets in place.

Although Wallace argues that these actions are consistent with managers overcoming potential agency conflicts, and concludes therefore that EVA appears to cause managers to act more like owners, this interpretation is open to question. Decreases in investment, increases in asset disposals, and increases in share buy-backs cannot be unambiguously interpreted as congruent with shareholders' interests. For example, each may point to a short-termist orientation and a failure to maximise long-term value through profitable growth. This is potentially supported by the study's own findings; that is, there was a lack of strong evidence of improved shareholder returns for the treatment firms in the study.

In 1997 PA Consulting used an analytical survey approach to study the relationship between the 'extent of VBM adoption' and TSR performance. Companies are allocated to one of four categories reflecting progressively increasing use of VBM: (1) negative about VBM, (2) positive about principles but not processes, (3) positive about principles and processes but not actions, and (4) positive about principles, processes and actions. TSR is found to increase as the extent of VBM adoption increases, with average TSR ranging from 13% for category 1 to 21% for category 4. Although the study concludes that increasing use of VBM leads to a higher TSR performance, it does suffer from a number of limitations, the most important of which are discussed below.

For a study to establish a causal relationship between variables – in this case the impact of increasing VBM use upon a company's TSR performance – it must possess high internal validity. This means, among other

Table 3.5. Explanatory studies into VBM practice

Study	Sample size	Sampling method	Sources of data	Responses (response rate)	Control over extraneous variables	Independent study?	Published in refereed academic journal?
Wallace (1997)	40 US companies	US companies reported to be using RI measures for managerial incentives	Published financial data	NA	Matched-pair control group	yes	yes
PA Consulting (1997)	540 companies	FTSE 500 and top 40 ISEQ companies	Postal questionnaire and published financial data	132 (24.4%)	None	?	no

NA = not applicable

things, that the study should include appropriate and sufficient controls to provide confidence that differences in TSR performance are due to the extent of VBM use and are not the effect of other explanatory variables. No such controls, however, were used in this study.

The conclusions of the PA Consulting study regarding the existence of a causal relationship between VBM use and improved TSR performance, although they may be open to question, they do not preclude the possibility that the variables are correlated. In other words, there may be an association between increased VBM use and improved TSR performance. Details of the statistical significance or otherwise of the study's findings are not provided, however, and without them one is left to speculate on the likely strength of the association between the extent of VBM use and TSR performance revealed by this study. The study also suffers from further problems relating to construct validity, the size and representativeness of the respondent group of companies, among others. Further research is clearly needed.

CONCLUSION

It is clear that the research into VBM practice is lacking both in terms of the quantity and quality of work performed. Much of the evidence is provided by descriptive surveys, a method which provides only relatively superficial insights into the nature of VBM use. Specific problems with many of the individual VBM surveys, including a poor sampling method and a lack of independence, reduce the weight of this evidence further.

The case study approach offers scope for a more detailed understanding of the way in which VBM is actually used, but few such studies have been performed. Those that have tend to adopt a rather uncritical stance and merely report what might be described as the company line, particularly with regard to the benefits arising from its use.

If the descriptive evidence on VBM is weak, research seeking to explain the VBM phenomenon is almost non-existent. Admittedly there are some difficulties in applying quasi-experimental methods to a field in which potentially there are relatively few true VBM companies, and of these, fewer still have long experience of using the approach.

The available evidence points to a wide variation in the interpretation (among researchers and practitioners) in terms of what VBM actually means in practice. It would appear that even though companies claim to recognise the importance of shareholder value creation, VBM is still not widely used. VBM concepts are more likely to be applied in a decision-making context, but even then it appears that companies remain focused on traditional accounting numbers. Full VBM requires an integrated value-oriented planning and control system, and it is seldom practised.

This suggests perhaps that lip service is often paid to VBM, with companies failing to properly implement a VBM approach, and remaining focused upon traditional accounting numbers. Alternatively, perhaps VBM theory as prescribed by its advocates does not meet the needs of practitioners and that a more appropriate version is applied in practice. In that case it is the theory rather than the practice which is in need of modification.

Either way, much more research is needed to ascertain how companies implement VBM in practice, what technical features exist, what behavioural and other problems are encountered and how they are addressed. It is argued, therefore, that the case study approach is likely to be a very useful means of developing a better understanding of what doing VBM actually means, and an appreciation of the likely consequences arising from its use.

REFERENCES

Birnberg, J.G., Shields, M.D. and Young, S.M. (1990) The case for multiple methods in empirical management accounting research (with an illustration from budget setting). *Journal of Management Accounting Research*, Fall, 33–66.

Boston Consulting Group (1996) *Shareholder Value Metrics*. Shareholder Value Management Series, Booklet 2.

Braxton Associates (1991) *The Fundamentals of Value Creation*. Insights: Braxton on Strategy.

Bromwich, M. (1998) Value based financial management systems. *Management Accounting Research*, **9**, 387–89.

Coopers and Lybrand (1997) *International Survey of Shareholder Value Management Issues*.

Copeland, T., Koller, T. and Murrin, J. (1996) *Valuation*, 2nd edn. John Wiley, New York.

Cornelius, I.G. and Davies, M.L. (1997) *Shareholder Value*. Financial Times Publishing, London.

Deloitte & Touche (1996) *Financial Management Survey 1996*.

Drury, C. (1996) *Cost and Management Accounting*, 4th edn. International Thomson Business Press, London.

Ehrbar, A. (1998) *EVA: The Real Key to Creating Wealth*. John Wiley, New York.

Gill, J. and Johnson, P. (1997) *Research Methods for Managers*, 2nd edn. Paul Chapman, London.

Glaser, B.G. and Strauss, A.L. (1967) *The Discovery of Grounded Theory*. Aldine, Chicago IL.

Grundy, T. (1992) *Corporate Strategy and Financial Decisions*. Kogan Page, London.

Handler, S. (1998) The emphasis on value-based strategic management in UK companies. In *The Strategic Change Decision Challenge* (ed. D. Hussey). John Wiley, Chichester, pp. 75–100.

Hennell, A. and Warner, A. (1998) *Financial Performance Measurement and Shareholder Value Explained*. Financial Times Management, London.

KPMG (1996) *Value Based Management: A Survey of European Industry*.

KPMG (1999) *Value Based Management: The Growing Importance of Shareholder Value in Europe*.

McTaggart, J.M., Kontes, P.W. and Mankins, M.C. (1994) *The Value Imperative*. Free Press, New York.

Madden, B.J. (1999) *CFROI Valuation: A Total Systems Approach to Valuing the Firm*. Butterworth-Heinemann, Oxford.

Mills, R., De Bono, J., De Bono, V., Ewers, D., Parker, D. and Print, C. (1996) The use of shareholder value analysis in acquisition and divestment decisions by large UK companies. Working paper, Henley Management College.

O'Hanlon, J. and Peasnell, K. (1998) Wall Street's contribution to management accounting: the Stern Stewart EVA financial management system. *Management Accounting Research*, **9**, 421–44.

Osborne, P. (1996) The state of relevance in management accounting research. In *In Search of Relevance in Financial Management Research* (eds C. Tomkins, J. Grinyer, L. McAulay, P. Osborne and M. Walker). Research Monograph 1, British Accounting Association.

PA Consulting (1997) *Managing for Shareholder Value*.

Rappaport, A. (1986) *Creating Shareholder Value: The New Standard for Business Performance*. Free Press, New York.

Rappaport, A. (1998) *Creating Shareholder Value: A Guide for Managers and Investors*. Free Press, New York.

Reimann, B.C. (1989) *Managing for Value – A Guide to Value-Based Strategic Management*. Basil Blackwell, Oxford.

Ryan, B., Scapens, R.W. and Theobald, M. (1992) *Research Method and Methodology in Finance and Accounting*. Academic Press, New York.

Sekaran, U. (1992) *Research Methods for Business: A Skill Building Approach*, 2nd edn. John Wiley, New York.

Stern Stewart (1995) *The EVA Company*. Stern Stewart & Co., New York.

Stewart, B. (1991) *The Quest for Value: A Guide for Senior Managers*. Harper Collins, New York.

Wallace, J.S. (1997) Adopting residual income-based compensation plans: do you get what you pay for? *Journal of Accounting and Economics*, **24**(3), 275–300.

Wallace, J.S. (1998) EVA financial systems: managerial perspectives. *Advances in Management Accounting*, **6**, 1–15.

Yin, R.K. (1994) *Case Study Research: Design and Methods*, 2nd edn. Sage, London.

Part II

CHALLENGING SHAREHOLDER
WEALTH MAXIMISATION

4 A Manifesto for Corporate Myopia: A Cautionary Note on Shareholder Value Techniques

CHRISTOPHER CARTER AND STEVE CONWAY

THE RISE OF THE MANAGERIAL RECIPE

The ability of the American academic-consulting complex (Grey and Mitev, 1995) to generate seductive panaceas for organisational action is not in doubt. Recent years have seen the quality movement (Oakland, 1993), the excellence tradition (Peters and Waterman, 1982) and business process re-engineering (Hammer and Champy, 1993) become part of the corporate lexicon, a feature of the organisational world. Shareholder value is part of this tradition; it is a device, a set of techniques, a philosophy which lays claim to improving organisational performance, and therefore the returns to share-holders. All of these movements are characterised by an attention to promotion, in which grand claims are made, imploring individual managers and organisations to adopt and enrol within a given technique. In short, new managerial ideas are aggressively marketed, promising a great deal to adopting organisations (Egan, 1995; Wilson, 1992); they are at once rhetoric and image intensive (Alvesson, 1998).

Egan (1995) suggests that it is pertinent to question whether a new initiative amounts to a bauble or a breakthrough, while Grey and Mitev (1995) argue that any initiative which is making grand claims and is likely to have an impact within the corporate world, demands the closest scrutiny. This is all the more the case given the litany of movements that have failed to match their high expectations (Wilson, 1992). In his account of management consultants, Sturdy (1997) seeks to demonstrate how new ideas have such currency within the organisational world because of their ability to imbue managers with a sense of control, or of order, in an uncertain economic environment. Carter et al. (1998) are more up front in their treatment of such initiatives as amounting to postmodern consumerism: I consume therefore I am. This is a position whereby it is argued that both individual managers and organisations constitute their identities (Du Gay, 1996) through a variety of cultural signs (such as shareholder value), a process that seeks to legitimate their fitness to manage or to compete within a given market. Such a view demonstrates how such initiatives can produce 'positive effects' (Foucault, 1977); this is reflected in Huczynski's (1993) observation that the motivation to adopt a particular initiative can very often be accounted for by the career aspirations of an individual manager. Social theorists such as Bourdieu (1998) and Baudrillard (1988) place great emphasis on cultural signs in terms of their ability to construct identity and as such to create reality.

Such analyses do two things: first, they problematise the notion of a new managerial technique as being neutral (Alvesson and Wilmott, 1998); second, they suggest there may be many different reasons why an organisation adopts a particular initiative. As such we take the view that an organisational analyst would be wise to deconstruct any such initiative in order to scrutinise its efficacy. This is a vital endeavour given the far-reaching effects that decisions made by organisations can have upon stakeholders within their environment. Therefore, the unquestioning hyperbole that generally accompanies managerial initiatives should be placed in a dialectical relationship with a critical anti-managerialist perspective. To quote Knights and MacCabe (1995), we are arguing for a 'careful empirical examination when journeying through the paradise gardens of the gurus and the beastly jungles of their critics'.

It is beyond doubt that shareholder value (SHV) is an in-vogue technique for organisations and analysts alike. The high fashion status that is currently enjoyed by SHV is demonstrated by the case of Cadbury Schweppes (Crowther and Carter, 1998); the organisation saw its share price rise after the announcement that it was going to adopt SHV. Clearly, at the time of writing, SHV is rich in symbolic capital (Bourdieu, 1998). The aim of this chapter is therefore to reflexively examine the SHV approach within its broader societal context. It will review two analytically distinct issues which are nevertheless closely interconnected: the first is a critique of the underlying assumptions of the SHV approach; the second is the question of the impact of stock exchange expectations on organisations, the very nature of the City. The nature of the City is important in discussing the impact of SHV, since at the very heart of the approach is a reorientating of organisational focus and power in favour of the City and away from other stakeholders, such as employees, customers, suppliers, and local communities.

DECONSTRUCTING SHAREHOLDER VALUE

The emergence of the SHV approach represents the ascendancy of a new paradigm in the measurement of organisational performance. This notion of paradigmatic shift is based on the work of Kuhn (1962), whose work centred on the growth of scientific knowledge. He proposed that the growth and development of scientific knowledge in a particular field occurs as a result of the development of a paradigm or model of scientific achievement that sets guidelines for research. As a result, the attention of scientists is focused and scientific knowledge grows in a systematic and cumulative fashion. After a period of what Kuhn (1962) terms 'normal' science, phenomena that the paradigm cannot explain become inescapable and the field goes through a period of crisis during which a new paradigm is proposed and eventually accepted (Feyerabend, 1975; Foucault, 1972). In another version of this model, Kroeber (1957) argues that the period of growth leads to a kind of crescendo of activity ending in an exhaustion of the ideas that had stimulated the growth. The emergence of the SHV paradigm could be attributed, at least partially, to both of these hypotheses. Crane (1972, p. 34) attempts to link the growth of knowledge in a research area to the social organisation of the respective scientific community, arguing that:

> growth of a research area reflects a social interaction process in which contact between scientists contributes to the cumulative growth of knowledge. This suggests that there is an interaction between cognitive events and social events in the development of a research area.

The growth of the SHV community, comprising both academics and practitioners, can be seen to parallel the growth in the sophistication and usage of SHV techniques. The development of a powerful discourse in support of SHV highlights the attempt by the proponents of the SHV approach to create 'legitimacy' and to bring about the desired paradigmatic shift. Hajer (1995) provides two concepts that allow an insightful analysis of this discourse: storylines and discourse coalitions. A storyline is a

> subtle mechanism of creating and maintaining discursive order . . . it is a generative sort of narrative that allows actors to draw upon various discursive categories to give meaning to specific physical or social phenomena.

Discourse coalitions are

> narratives on social reality through which elements from many different domains are combined and that provide actors with a set of symbolic references that suggest a common understanding. Story-lines are essential political devices that allow the overcoming of fragmentation and the achievement of discourse closure.

A textual analysis of the canon of SHV literature reveals much about the assumptions and the world view of SHV apparatchiks. The textual analysis approach seeks to deconstruct a text in order to elicit the key storylines or narratives that underpin a particular discourse. This makes it possible to understand how the discourse functions: how it circulates, how it is reinforced, and for whom it speaks. The following sections outline a number of storylines that were elicited from a sample of texts on the SHV approach.

STORYLINE I: A CALL TO ACTION

The SHV literature provides a clear and uncompromising 'call to action' for the 'noble' goal of maximising shareholder wealth; 'it's a tough job, but someone has to do it':

> We believe that all companies, especially publicly owned companies, should be managed to create as much wealth as possible. ... This is an enormously demanding objective. ... Creating wealth is much more than a fiduciary responsibility, it is a hallmark of great management and great companies. (McTaggart et al., 1994, p. 7)

> Maximising shareholder value is not an abstract, shortsighted, impractical, or even, some might think, sinister objective. On the contrary, it is a concrete, future-oriented, pragmatic, and worthy objective, the pursuit of which motivates and enables managers to make substantially better strategic and organisational decisions than they would in pursuit of any other goal. (Ibid., p. 21)

STORYLINE II: THE MANTRA OF THE VIRTUOUS MARKET

The authors and proponents of SHV appear to have a total faith in the perfection of the market to deliver the spoils of shareholder wealth creation to society in general. For them the market is a virtuous device for ensuring the best possible use of a society's scarce resources. This economic Darwinism requires the existence of a market that is as free as possible, to ensure companies come under the discipline of the market, which as Bauman (1987) notes, acts as the 'meta-validating authority'.

There are three clear elements behind this argument. Firstly, shareholders are the only stakeholder who need and act upon 'complete information' in their decision-making process, and consequently are the only stakeholder likely to increase the claims of all stakeholders:

> Equity holders who are the residual claimants on the cash flows of a company ... need to consider all revenues and all payments to other stakeholders when they make decisions that affect their claim. They take the greatest risk, but even more important, they are the only claimants who need information concerning all other claims in order to make good decisions on their own behalf. ... All claimants benefit when shareholders (or their agents) use complete information and their decision-making authority to maximise their own value. (Copeland et al., 1995, pp. 26–27)

Secondly, proponents of SHV sidestep the ethical and moral responsibilities of organisations, by arguing that managers are poorly placed and insufficiently skilled at delivering benefits to a broad range of stakeholders:

In a market-based economy that recognises the rights of private property, the only social responsibility of business is to create shareholder value and to do so legally and with integrity ... corporate management has neither the political legitimacy nor the expertise to decide what is in the social interest. (Rappaport, 1998, p. 5)

Key to the above argument is the central element in the 'mantra of the virtuous market'; a total and unyielding faith in the perfection of the market for diffusing the benefits of shareholder wealth (once created) to a broad constituency of stakeholders:

Wealth creation is not a zero-sum game where an increment to shareholder value must somehow diminish the welfare of other stakeholders. Indeed, the reverse is true − increments to total welfare can come only from creating wealth. (McTaggart et al., 1994, p. 18)

Pursuing the objective of maximising value for shareholders also maximises the economic interests of all employees over time, even when, regrettably, management is forced to downsize the company. (Ibid., p. 20)

If one were to be charitable, it could be argued that this reflects a misguided belief in the perfection of the market. However, the more cynical might suggest that this is simply a crude attempt to shirk the social, ethical, moral, and environmental responsibilities of organisations.

Copeland et al. (1995) link the adoption of SHV by US firms with higher GDP per capita in the US compared to Germany, Japan and UK − who dilute shareholder power by taking account of a wider constituency of stakeholders:

Until 1980 the other countries [Japan, France, Germany and the UK] had been closing the [GDP per capita] gap [with the US]. However, since then only Japan has been catching up. The US, with shareholder value focus, remains the GDP leader. (Copeland et al. 1995, p. 10)

In this sense the importance of the shareholder as an agent in a successful economy is explicit. Furthermore, advocates of SHV draw a direct and positive relationship between the application of the approach and a nation's economic success. The extent to which this view privileges the role of the market and the shareholder as determinants of economic success is remarkable, with other competing explanations (e.g. knowledge, innovation capacity, role of the state) being silenced. However, even if we were to accept that the widespread adoption of SHV techniques would yield a growth in GDP, the evidence suggests that this growth in wealth would not be widely distributed. One only has to look at the UK to illustrate how a rise in GDP per capita conceals a growing concentration of wealth in the top 5% of the population and the growth in poverty and the underclass (Hutton,

1995; Lash and Urry, 1994). Indeed, there has been a great deal of coverage of the fracturing of British society which has, among other things, seen the emergence of an underclass largely excluded from the mainstream of British life. This process has not been confined to Britain alone, it has also been a striking feature of contemporary American society. As such the trickle-down thesis championed by the New Right in the 1980s has not happened; growth of GDP has not led to an increase in the common wealth.

STORYLINE III: SHV – SOCIETAL ALCHEMY

The SHV approach advocates the adoption of discounted cash flow analysis (DCF) to assess the value of cash flows resulting from a range of possible courses of action for an organisation. It is argued that the longer time frame focus of DCF over other forms of analysis, such as earnings per share ratios, provides organisations with a more sympathetic environment for longer-term decision making:

> Value is the best metric for performance that we know. . . . Value (discounted cash flows) is best because it is the only measure that requires complete information. To understand value creation one must use a long-term point of view, manage all cash flows on both the income statement and the balance sheet, and understand how to compare cash flows from different time periods on a risk adjusted basis. . . . Value cannot be short-term, but other measures can be. (Copeland et al., 1995, pp. 22–23)

However, the assumed link between the use of tools that focus on a longer time horizon, and the adoption of a long-term mentality in decision making is extremely tenuous (Myers, 1984). The key to encouraging long-term decision making is the acceptance of risk, since the further into the future cash flows are expected, the more doubt exists as to the certainty or value of these flows. Thus, the more risk averse an organisation, the more likely it is to seek cash flows in the near future regardless of the financial tools at its disposal. Once again, one can witness a blind faith in the approach, i.e. tools focusing on the longer term, automatically leading to a longer-term per-spective by an organisation. It is of interest that some advocates of SHV acknowledge, contra Marsh (1990), that there has been a tendency for the City to be short-termist, but they argue this is because of the tools used to evaluate investments (e.g. EPS, ROCE); tools such as EPS and ROCE are extremely demanding in terms of their expectation for short-term perform-ance, often with the requirement that a project will finance itself in two or three years (Hutton, 1995). SHV opens up an interesting proposition, namely that within a relationship the nature of the performance measures used is a filter through which reality about an organisation is produced. However, to what degree does SHV really constitute a significant reframing of the tem-poral reckoning systems of industry?

STORYLINE IV: A TECHNIQUE WHOSE TIME HAS COME

SHV is represented as a panacea for improving the performance of organisations; this is dawning on the corporate world as it moves to a stage of enlightenment:

> As is the case with other good ideas, shareholder value has moved from being ignored, to being rejected, to becoming self-evident. (Rappaport, 1998, p. 3)

The self-evident superiority of SHV is beginning to be recognised as the 'natural order' of things, the 'best way of organising'. In this sense it is reminiscent of movements such as scientific management whereby a 'one best way' is advocated (Thompson and McHugh, 1990; Wilson, 1992). However, undeterred by such self-congratulatory nonsense, the hyperbole and audacity of some proponents of SHV can be seen to rise to even greater heights; it is argued, for example, that in a highly competitive age, many managers are too short-sighted (and perhaps too cowardly) to deliver the necessary medicine to ensure the competitiveness of their organisations. In stark contrast, adopters of SHV are portrayed as enlightened and gutsy, and in the longer-term will be vindicated for taking 'difficult' decisions:

> It is important to distinguish between the causes of layoffs and the CEOs who as agents of change respond to ensure the competitiveness and survival of their companies. Spare the messenger. The tradeoff is a 10% reduction now or a possible loss of jobs for many more if not all employees in the near future. Experience teaches the bitter lesson that this type of kindness often turns into unintended cruelty. (Rappaport, 1998, p. 9)

STORYLINE V: THE POLICING OF MANAGEMENT DECISIONS

Two clear themes emerge from the SHV literature with regard to the need to police management: the first is indicative of a deep mistrust of the goals of managers as guardians of the interests of shareholders; the second is perhaps even more damning, in that it takes a swipe at the very heart of managerial competence – the ability to think and act strategically. The mistrust of senior managers by shareholders appears to be based on a mixture of self-righteousness and a deep paranoia of an emergence of new 'us and them', of beleaguered shareholders against an 'unholy' alliance of management and a motley assortment of stakeholders, from employees to suppliers. Rappaport argues:

> The stakeholder model that attempts to balance the interests of everyone with a stake in the company makes it easier for corporate managers to justify uneconomic diversification or over-investment in a declining core business, since these moves are likely to be endorsed by constituencies other than shareholders. (Rappaport, 1998, p. 7)

Furthermore, he legitimates and elevates the pursuit of shareholders interests, whilst dismissing managerial aspirations as inherently self-centred:

> The theory of a market economy is, after all, based on individuals promoting their *self-interests* via market transactions to bring about an efficient allocation of resources. In a world in which principals (e.g. stockholders) have imperfect control over their agents (e.g. managers), these agents may not always engage in transactions solely in the *best-interests* of the principals. (Ibid., p. 3, emphasis added)

Another reoccurring theme in the SHV literature is the belief that SHV techniques allow institutional investors to shine the spotlight on poor strategic decision making, hence on underperforming companies and senior managers:

> Many companies, particularly those in mature sectors such as oil, allocated their very substantial excess cash flow toward uneconomic reinvestment or ill-advised diversification. Other companies failed to seek the highest valued use for their assets. (Ibid., p. 1)

> Managers are generally not better than investors at estimating value, even though they typically have better information. In fact, it is only by understanding how investors determine values and set share prices that managers can begin to ensure that their strategic investment decisions will lead to consistent and significant wealth creation. (McTaggart et al., 1994, p. 13)

Such arguments ignore the benefits afforded by hindsight, and arrogantly elevate the strategic decision-making abilities of institutional investors above senior managers. Furthermore, they accredit a rationality to the City that is hard to support by the day-to-day activities of institutional investors. Furthermore, evidence suggests that the sector-specific knowledge of City analysts is sometimes poor (Moody, 1989; Innovation Advisory Board, 1990).

SHV AND THE ISSUE OF SHORT-TERMISM

Two key concerns emerge through the deconstruction of the discourse of SHV when placed in the British social, economic and political context: the first relates to the tightening of the hegemony of shareholder interests through the subjugation of the interests of all other stakeholders; the second, and related concern, is the likelihood of increased pressure for the continuation of short-termism within British industry to appease a dominant and short-termist City. Proponents of the SHV approach argue that the long-term nature of SHV techniques will bring about long-term decision making; yet the link made between 'tool' and 'behaviour' is extremely tenuous (Myers, 1984). The second half of this chapter explores the issue of short-termism. The essence of the concern expressed here is that in bolstering the influence of the City through the adoption of SHV techniques, businesses will become increasingly focused on creating shareholder value for the short term. The social, economic and environmental arguments supporting the desirability of maintaining a plurality of stakeholders is also of great import, but these are discussed in Chapter 5.

SHORT-TERMISM: AN ENDEMIC BRITISH DISEASE?

As many commentators have noted (Child, 1984; Clark and Staunton, 1989), there is a tendency for an organisation to exhibit properties that reveal an innovation emphasis or an efficiency emphasis. This perspective stresses that very often there exists a tension between the two orientations, which gives rise to the innovation/efficiency dilemma, i.e. how does an organisation go about managing the tension between these two dialectically opposed orientations? Child (1984) notes that innovation is increasingly viewed as a key source of competitive advantage. However, many British organisations possess an efficiency orientation. Perhaps this is not surprising; Demirag (1995, p. 247) argues that 'short-term performance pressures on the manufacturing sector in the UK have had a negative impact on R&D spending, patenting rates and on market shares'.

Given that research by eminent academics has highlighted a positive correlation between successful technological innovation and national economic performance (Schumpeter, 1939; Mensch, 1979), the issue of corporate short-termism can be seen to be extremely important to the economic welfare of a nation. However, it is also worth noting that the relationship between investment in R&D and successful technological innovation is not straightforward (Pavitt, 1980). That is, the innovation process cannot be usefully considered in terms of a simple input/output model; far from it, evidence suggests that the technical complexities and uncertainties inherent in many technological fields are further complicated by the deeply political and social nature of the innovation process (Burns and Stalker, 1961; Frost and Egri, 1990; Knights and Murray, 1994; Conway 1999). Nevertheless, investment in the R&D process and investment in the infrastructure that supports this process, such as the training and education of scientists and engineers, are important components of the complex mix that is required for successful and sustained innovation at the level of the organisation and nation alike. Such investments are also a key indicator of the commitment of institutional investors, managers, and policy-makers to the longer term. Yet it is clear from OECD statistics that the UK lags behind many of it's 'peer group' with regard to it's investment in R&D as a percentage of GDP (this is ignoring the fact that large chunks of the UK R&D spend are channelled into the defence sector). Rothwell and Zegveld (1985) have long highlighted the need to increase the availability of 'patient' money in the UK for long-term R&D investments.

The prevalance and consequences of short-termism within British industry do not seem to be in question; for example, in reviewing the literature, Demirag (1995, p. 248) notes that 'most authors agree that short-termism is one of the main reasons for the decline of the manufacturing industry in this country'. Indeed, the present debate on short-termism centres on revealing the causes of this endemic 'British disease' and to apportioning blame. The popular belief is that short-termism within the City is forcing short-termist decision making among senior managers of British companies. This view is supported by many different voices, including the DTI's Innovation Advisory Board (1990), those representing both the Labour Party and Conservative Party, the British press, and various 'captains of industry' (Marsh, 1990). In opposition are academics such as Marsh (1990), who dismisses this view as the 'popular verdict'. For Marsh (1990, p. 1–2), 'the direct perpetrators of short-termism are managers, and not financiers or shareholders', since 'ultimately the future of long-term investment lies in the hands of corporate management'. However, Demirag (1995, p. 247) hypothesises that 'whether these external pressures actually exist or not matters little: for if the managers perceive capital markets as short-termist, they will behave in a short-term manner'.

Marsh (1990, p. 1) observes that 'the succession of outpourings on short-termism and the associated "hype" have been accompanied by a paucity of hard evidence, and by some rather weak and partial analysis. Polarisation, prejudice, and position taking have been more in evidence than genuine debate'. Marsh has a point, though he too could easily be viewed as being guilty of position taking and employing anecdotal evidence and reasoning in presenting his counter-argument. Furthermore, Demirag (1995, p. 248) notes that most studies of short-termism 'have been of an *ad hoc* nature, dealing specifically with one aspect of the whole web of issues and fail to develop a consistent framework in which arguments can be evaluated'. The reality is that the findings of research on this issue are far from conclusive and sometimes contradictory; for example, a recent survey of 74 FTSE 100 finance directors found that 98% believed that investors were long-term orientated (Shares in the Action, *Financial Times*, 27 April 1998, p. 21). This is in complete contrast to an earlier survey that revealed 91% of finance directors thought that the City had been justifiably criticised for being too focused on short-term earnings (3i, 1990); this in itself can only 'fan the fire' of blame and counterblame. Nevertheless, we believe what emerges from a review of this debate is that even if there exists little hard evidence to lay the blame firmly and solely in the lap of the City, there is sufficient support to raise grave concerns, particularly in the light of the SHV debate which argues for an even greater focus on the shareholder and of value creation for shareholders. The support for these concerns is outlined in the following section.

TURNING THE SPOTLIGHT ON THE CITY

Marsh's (1990) influential diatribe on short-termism purports to expose as a myth the long-established notion that the British industrial context – UK plc to draw from his lexicon – is hampered by the short-termist demands of a rapacious City. However, his authority to speak (Foucault, 1972), or to legislate (Bauman, 1987), as a professor of an eminent UK business school, is undermined by the fact that his research for *Short-termism on Trial* was commissioned and bankrolled by the Institute of Fund Managers Association. Furthermore, as this report notes, he is also a non-executive director of M&G Investment Management, and a consultant to the Securities and Investment Board, and the International Stock Exchange, among others. In our view, this implodes the veracity of his message; not only is Marsh's position to speak potentially compromised, but his research methods are also open to question. Indeed, much of his evidence appears anecdotal. The inductivism inherent in his project allows him to find what he wants to find; we wonder what he would have found had he adopted a Popperian falsification approach.

Even though Marsh (1990, pp. 14 and 66) concedes in his polemic that 'this is not to imply that the City and Wall Street are necessarily blameless, or that financial institutions should receive a clean bill of health in the debate on short-termism', he nevertheless argues that 'no remedies are required for share-price short-termism – because the evidence indicates that the problem is imagined rather than real'. In coming to this conclusion, Marsh (1990) identifies the 'real culprits' as popular misconceptions and misunderstandings of the stock market's pricing mechanism; managerial short-termism; the performance measurement and management accounting techniques, as well as the capital budgeting and project appraisal systems employed by businesses; the internal structures of multidivisional companies; and the lack of profitable investment opportunities. Marsh's (1990, p. 68) closing words neatly sum up his position: 'The message is simple, if trite. The way ahead for both City and industry is for UK managers to get on with managing as if tomorrow mattered.' In short, Marsh blames all but the City in his woeful tale of 'rough justice'.

Yet this conclusion is odd, since Marsh (1990, p. 20) also raises, but plays down, a number of issues relating to a general lack of competence and short-termism among analysts within the City:

> Part of the problem may lie in the uneven quality of analysts (CBI, 1987) ... 'stars' are relatively few. Many analysts are ... not hugely impressive.

It would appear that finance directors, to a certain extent, have been responsible for the external short-term pressures upon them. However, institutional shareholders also bear some of the responsibility. They ultimately have responsibility and power, and it is hard to envisage significant improvement unless the institutions which are the major shareholders are willing to take a closer interest in the affairs of the companies they own. (Ibid., p. 277)

The two positions outlined above are clearly in dialectical opposition to one another, although they both argue for a continuation of capitalism, they envision very different roles for the City. The view of Marsh (1990) is one in which a resounding approval is given to the City; Hutton (1995) would like to see it replaced by a financial system whereby the long-term interests of organisations are served.

STRUCTURAL POSES AND DISCIPLINARY MECHANISMS

The discussion above clearly identifies conflicting conceptions of the role of the City; concomitantly, this also opens up questions of managerial behaviour. For instance, why do managers behave in a short-term manner? It is not sufficient just to say that managers act on their perceptions of City expectations. Instead, it is important to attempt to understand the mechanism through which City expectations translate into managerial behaviours, such as decision making and project management. In order to try make sense of this complex and inherently contested domain, it is important to draw upon insights provided by organisational theory.

Central to a consideration of whether an organisation is able to develop a particular capability (e.g. the ability to innovate, the ability to mass-produce a standardised product) is the notion of the 'corporate repertoire' (Clark, 1996, 1999; Clark and Carter, 1999). The premise is that an organisation possesses a firm-specific repertoire; that is, there are certain things that an organisation can do: it possesses particular structural poses (Clark and Staunton, 1989). For instance, a McDonald's restaurant is able to provide standardised meals with very little waiting time for customers. As Ritzer (1993) chronicles, there is predictability and calculability. In contrast is Gordon Ramsey's celebrated 'The Ivy' restaurant in London, which specialises in exclusive, haute cuisine for limited numbers of people during a sitting. The point is that both organisations can be considered to be a success, but both possess very different structural poses within their repertoire: would McDonald's be able to respond to a request for a lightly done burger and fries cooked in olive oil? Would 'The Ivy' restaurant be able to deal with an impromptu party of 30 wanting to have eaten their meal within half an hour? Both of these examples are illustrative of how an organisation possesses a repertoire which is firm-specific; it consists of standard operating procedures, the capacity to innovate and the ability to deal with unusual or crisis situations. This repertoire is shaped by the founding conditions of the organisation and the environment within which an organisation operates. An organisational repertoire is likely to be deeply embedded within the organisation and as such it can be considered to be recursive (Clark, 1996).

In his seminal study on carceral institutions, Foucault (1977) demonstrated how disciplinary mechanisms (such as interim profit figures) place individuals (such as chief executives) or organisations under powerful pressures to normalise (Goffman, 1968). Furthermore, disciplinary mechanisms have a panoptic quality (Foucault, 1986; Ball and Wilson, 1997) whereby the objects of the gaze (such as a board of directors) internalise the expectations espoused by the performance measures (i.e. high return on capital employed) and discipline themselves. A number of writers (Foucault, 1977; Townley, 1994; Du Gay, 1996; Carter, 1999) have highlighted how dominant discourses are enforced through disciplinary mechanisms which in turn constitute people as subjects: the corollary being that finance directors are constituted as finance subjects through the dominant discourses of finance, which are upheld, among other things, by the operation of disciplinary performance measures. This insight is important, as it gives an indication of how institutions operate, and more importantly how the apparently negative effects to industry are recursive (Clark, 1996) over time. Moreover, it tells us a good deal about the relative relations of power (Clegg, 1989), whereby within the British context, the discourse of the City, sustained through institutions, performance measures and people, is dominant over other discourses. Lash and Urry (1987) reflect this point by suggesting that Britain is best described as a 'makler' polity: that is to say a capitalist economy which is characterised by its 'short-term' trader properties, which are the corollary of Britain's long history as an epicentre for the flows in international trade and finance. The makler polity model stands in contrast to alternative, extant capitalist economies (i.e. the continental European modes of capitalism). There has been considerable recent discussion within the organisation sciences, whereby numerous writers (Lam, 1998; Lane, 1989; Sorge, 1991) have sought to explain the evident differences between capitalist economies. Clearly, differences between economies are variegated and inherently complex.

Thus, the performance measures that an organisation is subjected to can play a significant factor in orientating the repertoire of a particular organisation. This point is illustrated by Tinker (1985); it is also central to the quasi-Foucaultian turn to be found within organisational studies (McKinlay and Starkey, 1998). The argument is thus: the mechanism which provides the measure of performance on an organisation objectifies the organisation; this allows it to be ranked relative both to its own history as well as to other organisations within the same sector. This process of objectification plays a crucial role in the constitution of an identity for those within the organisation, i.e. is a manager within a successful organisation or a failing organisation?

As such the performance of an organisation must be regarded as a social construct rather than an ontological category (Hardy and Clegg, 1996). Thus, the social construction of an organisation's reality takes place through performance measures, which act to delineate 'normal' performance. This is something that enforces the prevailing power structures within the organisation and its environment: performance measures are important in terms of guiding the behaviour, the objectives and the perceptual mindset (Lam, 1998) of an organisation. Clearly this is a deterministic view, but it also recognises that organisations operate within particular contexts (Pettigrew, 1985; Child and Smith, 1987) which have a powerful normalising effect. As such the panoply of techniques immanent to the discourse of accounting exert a powerful influence on the shaping of an organisational agenda, and over the longer term can have a formative influence on the repertoire of an organisation.

The significance of these various insights is that constraints are placed on an organisation's ability to exercise strategic choice (Child, 1972). Child's seminal piece emphasises that while an organisation is subject to deterministic pressures from its environment it does possess a choice over its future corporate direction; this finding, whilst important, is ultimately a fantasy as it ignores the interdependencies, the antecedents and the performance measures that an organisation is objectified by and subjectified to. The 'zone of manoeuvre' (Clark, 1996) of an organisation is far more limited than is suggested by Child's theorising.

CONCLUSION

The analysis presented demonstrates that organisational analysts should be wary of the claims made on behalf of shareholder value. This is the case because shareholder value techniques are seriously reductionist in their conceptualisations of organisations: complexity is abandoned in favour of a world view that relies on simple truisms. The foundations of SHV techniques have been deconstructed, a process which clearly illustrated both the paucity of empirical evidence, and the theoretical inadequacies of the SHV approach. Perhaps the most astonishing feature of SHV techniques is the unblinkered faith that they place on the market, which is elevated to the status of a deity: the mantra of the market.

This chapter is highly sceptical of such claims; it urges academics, practitioners and students alike to consider the wider possibilities of SHV. To do this is to engage with the nature of organisations themselves; it is to transcend the banal binarism of SHV; it is to recognise that an organisation possesses a repertoire — the ability to do certain things — that is shaped, among other things, by its antecedents, its context and performance measures. This insight leads us ineluctably to the view that, pace Hutton, performance measures can have an injurious effect on the robustness of an organisation: to satisfy the caprice of the City is to orient the organisation to short-term performance. In support of this view, evidence presented in this chapter suggests that the ability of UK organisations to invest in R&D and training is chronically undermined by the need to be able to meet the short-term demands of the City. Moreover, given the well-documented problems that British industry has experienced in the successful management of the innovation process it seems perverse to embark upon an SHV adventure which may well exacerbate such problems. In summary, while SHV is currently the darling of the corporate fashion catwalk, it is vital to look, reflexively, beyond the rhetoric-intensive claims of SHV apparatchiks.

REFERENCES

3i (1990) *Corporate Attitudes to Stock Market Valuations: 3i Shareholder Value Survey*. 3i, London.

Alvesson, M. (1998) Knowledge ambiguity. Paper presented at the Knowledge Management Workshop, Warwick University, November.

Alvesson, M. and Wilmott, H. (1996) *Making Sense of Management: A Critical Introduction*. Sage, London.

Arnold, J. and Moizer, P. (1984) A survey of the methods used by UK investment analysts to appraise investments in ordinary shares. *Accounting and Business Research*, Summer, 195–207.

Ashton, D., Crossland, M. and Moizer, P. (1991) The performance evaluation of fund managers. Paper presented at the British Accounting Association Annual Conference, University of Salford, April.

Ball, K. and Wilson, D. (1997) Computer based monitoring in organizations. Paper presented at the European Group Organization Studies Colloquium, Budapest.

Barnett, C. (1986) *The audit of war: the illusion and reality of Britain as a great nation*, Macmillan, London.

Baudrillard, J. (1988) *Selected Writings*. Polity Press, Cambridge.

Bauman, Z. (1987) *Legislators and Interpreters*. Polity Press, Cambridge.

Bourdieu, P. (1998) *Distinction: a social critique of the judgement of taste*. Routledge, London. First published in English 1984.

Burns, T. and Stalker, G. (1961) *The Management of Innovation*. Pergamon, London.

Carter, C. (1999) Making lecturers: the discursive constitution of the professional subject. Paper presented at the Teaching and Learning in Higher Education Workshop, University of North London.

Carter, C. and Crowther, D. (1999) Unravelling a profession: the case of engineers in a British regional electricity company. *Critical Perspectives in Accounting*, in press.

Carter, C., Crowther, D. and Cooper, S. (1998) Organizational consumerism: the appropriation of packaged managerial knowledge. Paper presented at the British Academy of Management Conference, University of Nottingham.

CBI (1987) *Investing for Britain's Future: Report of the City/Industry Task Force*, Confederation of British Industry, London.

Child, J. (1972) Organizational structure, environment and performance: the role of strategic choice, *Sociology*, 6(1), 1–22.

Child, J. (1984) *Organization: A Guide to Problems and Practice*, 2nd edn. Harper & Row, London.

Child, J. and Smith, C. (1987) The firm in sector perspective. *Journal of Management Studies*, September.

Clark P.A. (1996) Structural activation, recursiveness, temporal duality and national specificities in a strategy for organizational change. Paper presented at the British Academy of Management Conference, Aston Business School, September.

Clark, P. (1999) *Organisations in Action*. Routledge, London.

Clark, P. and Carter, C. (1999) Academic capitalism, cool Britannia and explicit knowledge. Paper presented at the Organizational Knowledge Conference, University of Massachusetts.

Clark, P. and Staunton, N. (1989) *Innovation in Technology and Organisation*. Routledge, London.

Clegg, S. (1989) *Frameworks of Power*. Sage, London.

Conway, S. (1999) Social network mapping and the analysis of informal organisation. Research paper, Aston Business School Research Institute.

Copeland, T., Koller, T. and Murrin, J. (1995) *Valuation: Measuring and Managing the Value of Companies*, 2nd edn. John Wiley, New York.

Cosh, A., Hughes, A. and Singh, A. (1990) Take-overs, short-termism and finance-industry relations in the UK economy. Unpublished seminar discussion paper, Institute of Public Policy Research. Cited by Demirag, I. (1995) Assessing short-term perceptions of group finance directors of UK companies. *British Accounting Review*, **27**, 247–81.

Crane, D. (1972) *Invisible Colleges: Diffusion of Knowledge in Scientific Communities*. University of Chicago Press, Chicago IL.

Crowther, D. and Carter, C. (1998) Managing accounting and the Copernican metonymy. Paper presented at the MARG Conference, Aston University, September.

Day, J. (1986) The use of annual reports by UK investment analysts. *Accounting and Business Research*, Autumn, 295–307.

Demirag, I. (1995) Assessing short-term perceptions of group finance directors of UK companies. *British Accounting Review*, **27**, 247–81.

Demirag, I. and Goddard, S. (1994) *Financial Management for International Business*. McGraw-Hill, Maidenhead.

Doyle, P. (1987) Marketing and the British chief executive. *Journal of Marketing Management*, Winter, 121–32.

Du Gay, P. (1996) *Consumption and Identity at Work*. Sage, London

Egan, C. (1995) *Creating Organizational Advantage*. Butterworth-Heinemann, London.

Feyerabend, P. (1975) *Against Method: Outline of an Anarchistic Theory of Knowledge*. NLB, London.

Foucault, M. (1972) *The Archaeology of Knowledge*. Tavistock Publications, London. Translated by A. Sheridan.

Foucault, M. (1977) *Discipline and Punish: The Birth of the Prison*. Allen Lane, London. Translated by A. Sheridan.

Foucault M. (1986) *The Foucault Reader*. Penguin, Harmondsworth. Edited by Paul Rabinow.

Frost, P. and Egri, C. (1990) Influence of political action on innovation: part II. *Leadership and Organizational Development Journal*, **11**(2), 4–11.

Goffman, E. (1968) *Asylums: Essays on the Social Situation of Mental Patients and Other Inmates*. Penguin, Harmondsworth.

Grey, C. and Mitev, N. (1995) Re-engineering organizations: a critical appraisal. *Personnel Review*, **24**(1), 6–18.

Hajer, M. (1995) *The Politics of Environmental Discourse*. Oxford University Press, Oxford.

Hammer, M. and Champy, J. (1993) *Reengineering the Corporation: A Manifesto for Business Revolution*. Nicholas Brearley, London.

Hardy, C. and Clegg, S. (1996) Relativity without relativism: reflexivity in post-paradigm, organization studies. Paper presented at the British Academy of Management Annual Conference, Aston University, September 1996.

Hopkinson, D. (1990) Relations between the city and industry in the 1990s. In *Creative Tension?* National Association of Pension Funds, London.

Huczynski, A. (1993) *Management gurus: what makes them and how to become one*. Routledge, London.

Hutton, W. (1995) *The State We're In*. Cape, London.

Innovation Advisory Board (1990) *Innovation: City Attitudes and Practices*. DTI, London.

Keegan, W. (1984) *Mrs Thatcher's Economic Experiment*. Penguin, Harmondsworth.

Keegan, W. (1992) *The spectre of capitalism: the future of the world economy after the fall*. Radius, London.

Kennedy, P. (1989) *The rise and fall of the great powers: economic change and military conflict*. Fontana, London: Fontana.

Knights, D. and Macabe, D. (1998) When 'life is but a dream': obliterating politics through business process reengineering. *Human Relations*, **51**(6).

Knights, D. and Murray, F. (1994) *Managers Divided: Planning, Implementation and Control*, 8th edn. John Wiley, Chichester.

Kroeber, A. (1957) *Style and Civilizations*. Cornell University Press, New York.

Kuhn, T. (1962) *The Structure of Scientific Revolutions*. University of Chicago Press, Chicago IL.

Lam, A. (1998) Embedded firms, embedded knowledge: problems of collaboration and knowledge transfer in global cooperative ventures. *Organization Studies*, **18**(6), 973–96.

Lane, C. (1989) *Management and Labour in Europe*. Edward Elgar, Aldershot.

Lash, S. and Urry, J. (1987) *The End of Organized Capitalism*. Polity, Cambridge.

Lash, S. and Urry, J. (1994) *Economies of Signs and Space*. Sage, London.

Lyons, D. (1973) *In the interest of the governed: a study in Bentham's philosophy of utility*. Clarendon Press, Oxford.

McKinlay, A. and Starkey, K. (eds) (1998) *Foucault, Management and Organization Theory*. Sage, London.

McTaggart, J., Kontes, P. and Mankins, M. (1994) *The Value Imperative: Managing for Superior Shareholder Returns*. Free Press, New York.

Marsh, P. (1990) *Short-termism on Trial*. Institutional Fund Managers Association, London.

Mayhew, K. (1991) Training – the problem for employers. *Employment Institute Economic Report*, **5**(10).

Mensch, G. (1979) *Stalemate in Technology*. Ballinger, Cambridge.

Moody, J. (1989) *How the City Appraises Technology Investments*. Scientific Resources Ltd, Cambridge.

Myers, S. (1984) Finance theory and financial strategy. *Interfaces*, **14**, 126–37.

Oakland, J. (1993) *Total quality management: the route to improving performance*, 2nd edn. Butterworth-Heinemann, Oxford.

Pavitt, K. (1980) *Technical Innovation and British Economic Performance*. Macmillan, London.

Peters, T. and Waterman, R. (1982) *In Search of Excellence*. Harper and Row, New York.

Pettigrew, A. (1985) *The Awakening Giant: Continuity and Change in ICI*. Blackwell, Oxford.

Porter, M. (1990) *The Competitive Advantage of Nations*. Macmillan, London.

Ramsie, H. (1996) Managing sceptically: a critique of organizational fashion. In *The Politics of Management Knowledge*. (eds S. Clegg and G. Palmer). Sage, London.

Rappaport, A. (1998) *Creating Shareholder Value*. Free Press, New York.

Ritzer, G. (1993) *The McDonaldization of society: an investigation into the changing character*. Pine Forge Press, London.

Rothwell, R. and Zegveld, W. (1985) *Reindustrialisation and Technology*. Longman, Harlow.

Schumpeter, J. (1939) *Business cycles: a theoretical, historical and statistical analysis of the capitalist process*. McGraw-Hill, New York.

Sorge, A. (1991) *Technological Change, Employment, Qualifications and Training*. European Centre for the Development of Vocational Training, Berlin.

Sturdy, A (1997) The consultancy process – an insecure business. *Journal of Management Studies*, **34**(3).

Thompson, P. and McHugh, D. (1990) *Work Organizations*. Macmillan, Basingstoke.

Tinker, T. (1985) *Paper Prophets: A Social Critique of Accounting*. Holt, Rinehart and Winston, London.

Townley, B. (1994) *Reframing human resource management: power, ethics and the subject at work*. Sage, London.

Williams, R. (1986) British technology policy. In *Product Design and Technological Innovation* (eds R. Robin and D. Wield). Open University Press, Milton Keynes, pp. 219–24.

Wilson, D. (1992) *A Strategy of Change*. Routledge, London.

5 Shareholder Wealth or Societal Welfare: A Stakeholder Perspective

STUART COOPER

INTRODUCTION

It has long been argued that corporations should be run in order to maximise shareholder wealth. This is now a widely accepted premise according to Rappaport (1986). Similarly, Friedman (1970) posited that the sole aim of a firm should be to maximise profits; to do anything else would be against the primary objective of the firm. The requirement to maximise shareholder wealth has been operationalised recently in the increased interest and use of shareholder value techniques (and value-based management). However, over a similar period of time there has also been a greater academic consideration of corporate social responsibility and stakeholder theory.

This chapter considers the appropriateness of shareholder wealth maximisation not from the position of whether it constitutes an appropriate strategy for an individual firm, operating within the confines of a Western advanced capitalist economy, but instead from the perspective of the society within which the firm operates. The question of shareholder wealth or societal welfare will be explored through a stakeholder analysis of the electricity industry in England and Wales. This industry was sold to the private sector as part of the larger privatisation programme of successive Conservative governments from 1979 to 1997. As a consequence, the privatised electricity companies are owned by shareholders, as opposed to being a government-owned public service, and are therefore required to meet the expectations of these shareholders as would any other such organisation. The change in the performance of these companies provides a valuable insight into the effects of shareholder wealth maximising strategies.

THE ROOTS OF SHAREHOLDER WEALTH MAXIMISATION

The recent phenomenon of shareholder wealth as an all-encompassing objective for businesses is justified on the premise that this will result in optimal wealth creation for the business and subsequently for society. It has been likened to a win-win situation; when businesses correctly implement this strategy not only do the shareholders benefit but so does everybody else. This is not a new idea and utilitarian views have, for a long time, advocated the pursuance of individual self-interest as a way of best maximising the wealth of all (Bentham, 1789). John Stuart Mill (1863) was one of the earliest critics of this conception of self-interested behaviour when he attempted to refine the theory through a consideration of other effecting actions and the distinction between higher and lower interests. The first of these criticisms recognised the possibility of certain self-interested actions having a detrimental effect on others, which would therefore not necessarily result in an overall improvement of welfare. Secondly he argued that certain actions are more worthwhile, 'higher', and should therefore be given a certain degree of precedence.

The utilitarianist thoughts were very much based on the actions of individuals and it was the economic theory of Adam Smith (1776) which championed a similar strategy for businesses. He effectively suggested that businesses should operate in a self-interested way as the marketplace would regulate their behaviour. The 'invisible hand' of the free market would ensure that businesses' actions would benefit society. However, Smith was not blind to the potential problems that might arise from allowing businesses to pursue profits unchecked. In fact, he predicted that if this were the case, profits would be achieved not through gaining a competitive advantage but rather by eliminating competition (Monks and Minow, 1991). This was exemplified by the contention that when two 'businessmen' met they would spend their time colluding to the detriment of the operations of the market in order to improve profits.

The workings of modern Western economies have changed significantly since the time Smith was writing, not least through the increasing separation of ownership from control. Therefore when Smith discussed 'businessmen' he was referring to both the owner and the manager as these people were one and the same. The business was controlled and managed by the owner in such a way as to maximise his or her own wealth. The separation of ownership and control and the potential problems it causes are well known and the principal–agent relationship has resulted in a rich literature on agency theory. This theory is concerned with ensuring that managers are managing a business for the benefit of the owners. In fact, Friedman and others have suggested that the firm's sole purpose should be to operate for shareholders. The shareholders are the owners of the business and therefore on the basis of private property rights they should expect to see the returns from that property.

A contrary view is that the present capitalist societies differ from those envisaged by Smith and Mill in another fundamental respect. When promoting the self-interest theories it is posited that Smith and Mill both took for granted a supporting social principle (Hirsch, 1978). This implies that a following of self-interest is beneficial but would be within a society that shares certain moral and ethical standards. Hirsch argues that this construct within which self-interest is beneficial has been 'curiously neglected' (p. 128) and is no longer reflected in the Western capitalist societies where the model is most used. Hirsch also suggests that Keynes' view of the economic system was separated into two distinct parts: micromanagers responsible for managing business units, and macromanagers responsible for overseeing the system. An implicit assumption within this view was that the macromanagers would be 'cleverer' than the micromanagers and that they would be following a more moral and ethical code of conduct through which society would benefit. Again this requirement of the present economic system appears to have been awarded limited attention.

This section considers the often neglected theoretical roots of shareholder wealth maximisation. These utilitarian, self-interested theories have been criticised for several reasons but this is rarely acknowledged in the shareholder wealth literature that is still justified as being beneficial to all. This chapter will now consider the corporate social responsibility and stakeholder literature, as this appears to offer a significantly different view of the objectives of organisations.

CORPORATE SOCIAL RESPONSIBILITY AND STAKEHOLDER THEORY

Both shareholder wealth maximisation and corporate social responsibility have been of increasing academic interest in recent years. Woodward (1998) suggests that serious academic consideration of corporate social responsibility commenced in the early 1970s and has resulted in a relatively new field of research into the relationship between business and society. As the name suggests, corporate social responsibility is concerned with the effects of the actions of businesses (corporations) on the society within which they operate. Effectively it is suggested that these businesses should be managed in such a way as to recognise their impact on society and that they should be held responsible for their actions. An even more recent development is stakeholder theory that actually identifies numerous different factions within a society to whom an organisation may have some responsibility. Jones (1995) suggests that stakeholder theory is an integrative theme for the corporate social responsibility field; this would appear to be supported in the use of the stakeholder concept in considering the social performance and responsibilities of firms (Litz, 1996; Roberts, 1992).

Before we explore stakeholder theory further, we need a better definition of the term 'stakeholder' and its uses. Many trace the origins of stakeholder theory to Freeman (1984), although Freeman actually cites an internal memorandum at the Stanford Research Institute in 1963 as an earlier use of the term. But even the definition of what constitutes a stakeholder has not remained static. Sternberg (1997) demonstrates that Freeman himself has used multiple definitions of stakeholders and cites the following two:

> Those groups without whose support the organization would cease to exist. (P. 31)

> Any group or individual who can affect or is affected by the achievement of the organization's objectives. (P. 46)

Sternberg states that the second of these definitions, which is now the more commonly used, has increased the number of stakeholders to be considered by management adopting a stakeholder approach. Therefore a group can be affected by an organisation without necessarily being able to bring about its cessation by withdrawing its support. In fact, the difference in these two definitions has resulted in a distinction between primary and secondary stakeholders (Clarkson, 1995). Where a primary stakeholder is one whose continued support is necessary if the firm is not to be seriously damaged. Again this appears to be another modification of the definition where instead of an organisation ceasing to exist it is 'seriously damaged' by the with-drawal of support.

It is intended, for the purposes of this chapter, to amalgamate the corpor-ate social responsibility and stakeholder theory research. This is justified for two reasons: firstly, stakeholder theory is seen by many to be an integrative theme for the business and society field; and secondly both the social responsibility and the stakeholder literature propose that shareholders should not be the sole primary concern of businesses. Corporate social responsibility implies a primacy of society and stakeholder theory recognises the needs of other groups within society. This does not mean that these areas of research are synonymous or identical and it is acknowledged that a social issue is not necessarily a stakeholder issue and vice versa (Clarkson, 1995).

At first glance the two ideas of shareholder wealth maximisation and corporate social responsibility (or stakeholder management) would appear to be diametrically opposed; a firm cannot serve both its shareholders and society (or other stakeholders) at the same time. However, this has not been borne out by several field studies which have been completed in the area. These studies attempt to link socially responsible behaviour with improved economic performance and hence shareholder wealth maximisation (Aup-perle et al., 1985; Waddock and Graves, 1997; Greenley and Foxall, 1997). An underlying assumption which is not always explicitly recognised in these studies is that the firm should be operating for shareholders, i.e. they should be shareholder wealth maximising. The studies are searching for a correlation between social responsibility and economic performance. Therefore social responsibility is not an end in itself but is simply seen as a means for improv-ing economic performance. These studies appear to legitimate corporate social responsibility through its usefulness in achieving a firm's primary objective, namely maximising shareholder wealth. This assumption is often implicit, although it is clearly stated by A. A. Atkinson et al. (1997).

Another illustration of how stakeholders have been considered to be means to shareholder wealth maximisation is the 'balanced scorecard' performance measurement system (Kaplan and Norton, 1992, 1993, 1996a, 1996b). This system, it is claimed, actually balances the competing needs of an organisation. In its original form (1992) the balanced scorecard was credited with the ability to 'allow managers to look at the business from four important perspectives':

- Customer perspective
- Internal perspective
- Innovation and learning perspective
- Financial perspective

Shareholders and customers are two specific stakeholders that are mentioned within the balanced scorecard; however, continuous improvement and innovation would also indicate the need for employee development. In fact, each business is expected to design and adopt its own scorecard to meet its own needs. Therefore it is not unlikely that the perspective of each primary stakeholder would be incorporated at some point within the balanced scorecard and as such it could be considered to be a stakeholder-based performance measurement system. However, the overarching objective of the balanced scorecard is to achieve both short-term and long-term financial success and is actually competing with other more explicitly shareholder value based approaches as a method to enable businesses to achieve this.

This approach to corporate social responsibility (and stakeholder management) raises a critical issue with regard to what is ethical or moral behaviour. The work of Kant has been considered in the fields of corporate social responsibility (L'Etang, 1995) and stakeholder management (Evans and Freeman, 1988) and raises two relevant issues. Firstly, it is argued that it is 'wrong to use people as a means for one's own needs'. Therefore, consideration of stakeholders, and the use of individuals within a stakeholder group, merely to improve shareholder wealth would be considered wrong under this criterion. Secondly, it is the intention that is important in deciding the moral worth of an act. Therefore it is argued that acts which are motivated through self-interest are 'lacking in moral worth', whether or not the outcome is socially responsible. This is obviously a very different stance to that of utilitarianism and the proponents of shareholder wealth maximisation when considering the appropriateness of self-interested action.

Donaldson and Preston (1995) examine stakeholder theory and suggest that the theory has been justified on the basis of three aspects. These three aspects are its 'descriptive accuracy, instrumental power, and normative validity'. It has been argued, therefore, that stakeholder theory is of importance as it correctly reflects how businesses operate – not by simply considering shareholders but other stakeholders as well. Within this framework the studies which attempt to justify a corporate social responsibility, or stakeholder approach, as a means of improving economic performance would be classified as concerned with the instrumental power of the theories. This is to say that stakeholder theory is a tool that can be used to improve results. However, the normative validity justifications refer to the moral rights of individuals and therefore may require a complete reconsideration of the bases of modern Western capitalist societies. It is not sufficient to say that shareholder wealth should be maximised, or that stakeholder theory should be used to achieve this end, without first considering its ethical appropriateness.

At this point there is a need to distinguish between wealth creation and welfare distribution. Much of the value-based management literature concentrates on the idea of wealth creation for the shareholders. This is believed to maximise the wealth of a society and (as a result of the free market) will result in the whole of society benefiting. Firstly, it should be recognised that wealth, as measured by monetary units, is only a part of what makes up the welfare or utility of an individual or a society. The measures used within value-based management are very much in money or wealth terms and therefore fail to encapsulate the wider utility or welfare issues. This aspect of welfare rather than wealth will be revisited later as part of the case study specifically when considering the employee stakeholder.

The premise that shareholder wealth maximisation results in the whole of society benefiting has little supporting evidence to date. To provide some evidence of wealth creation, the two studies reported below analyse differences in GDP per capita for different countries. The dichotomy used is between the shareholder countries of the US and the UK and the more stakeholder-orientated countries of Germany, Japan and France. The analysis below is based on the assumption, in these studies, that it is the level of shareholder focus which is responsible for differences. However, it is acknowledged here that there are many other differences between these economies which may influence the performance reported, not least is the possible long-term effects of World War II.

Copeland et al. (1996) analyse GDP per capita in the US, UK, Germany, France and Japan over the period from 1950 to 1990. They show that the 'U.S., with shareholder value focus remains the GDP leader' (p. 10) despite acknowledging that the other, less shareholder value focused countries were actually closing the gap in the period 1950–1980. In fact, the country which has closed the gap least of all is the UK, arguably the second most shareholder value focused country. Similarly, the *Economist* (Anon, 1996) reported that annual growth in GDP per capita has, over the last 40 years, been at 5.5% in Japan, 3.0% in Germany, 2.0% in Britain, and 1.7% in America. Again this work suggests that the shareholder-focused countries,

Britain and America, are creating less wealth over this period than the more stakeholder orientated economies of Japan and Germany. Both studies place great emphasis on the fact that the improvements in Germany and Japan do not appear to have continued in the last 10 years. This does not change the fact that over the last 40 years Germany and Japan have outperformed, in terms of creating GDP per capita, the US and UK. If we then consider wealth distribution we see that the more shareholder value focused economies are shown to have a larger inequality of distribution.

One of the commonly used indices of distribution inequality is the Gini coefficient (A. B. Atkinson, 1996) where a coefficient of 0% is when each unit has the same income and 100% is when a single unit has all of the income and the rest none. Atkinson collates, from various studies, the Gini coefficients for different countries over the period from 1970 to 1992 and this indicates that firstly the inequality of distribution of income in the UK has increased from a low point of 23.4% in 1977 to 33.7% in 1991. Over the period from 1970 the US has also seen an increase from 39.4% to 43.3%, Japan an increase from 27.3% in 1980 to 29.6% in 1991 and in Germany it has been very consistent at 25–26%.

Of the economies discussed, the US shows the highest GDP per capita, although by a reducing margin, and the highest level of inequality; therefore it could be argued that the higher inequality can be justified by a higher overall level of wealth. However, the second shareholder-focused economy, the UK, shows the lowest GDP per capita and the second most unequal income distribution. Proving the superiority of shareholder focus through GDP per capita studies is problematic as there are many differences between the economies considered other than their shareholder focus. In addition this average figure does not accommodate the separate but no less important issue of wealth, or welfare, distribution. The rest of this chapter will further consider these issues, not from this economy-wide perspective but from a specific industry case.

Rawls (1973) developed a framework for considering ethical concepts specifically with regard to distribution and justice. He derived two principles from his 'original position' of a 'veil of ignorance' which were firstly that individuals have certain equal rights to basic liberties; and secondly that social and economic inequalities are 'just only if they result in compensating benefits for everyone, and in particular for the least advantaged'. Thus Rawls is not a utilitarian; although certain individual rights are protected, there is a need for some distributive justice (Moore, 1999). Following Rawls's argument, if society as a whole is to benefit then the distribution of welfare within that society must at least be considered. Wood (1994) suggests that a 'normative stakeholder theory is much more compatible with a Rawlsian view of just distribution than with an egocentric or firm-centric view of wants'.

The actual distribution of welfare within a society is dependent on an individual's or group's power within that society. Within modern Western capitalist society we see large corporations in a position of considerable power (L'Etang, 1995). As noted above it is widely regarded that the primary objective of these powerful corporations is the satisfaction of shareholder wants. Therefore this large amount of power is focused upon generating wealth for one part of society. Considering further the role of power within society, stakeholder management theory has suggested that a stakeholder group should be managed and managers' time allotted to a stakeholder group dependent upon their power (Carroll, 1993; Starik 1994). The implication of these approaches is that stakeholders should be ranked according to their power and receive appropriate management attention dependent upon this ranking.

If a stakeholder has limited or no power within a society or over a business, it will be ignored by an organisation. This will mean that the organisation can attempt to redistribute welfare away from the less powerful groups towards the more powerful groups. Similarly, if a stakeholder group's power is reduced, they will receive less management attention and also less of the wealth created by the organisation. Monks and Minow (1991) suggest that one way in which profits can be enhanced is by externalising costs. Specifically they suggest that reduced employee conditions and product quality actually reduce a business's costs at the expense of employees and consumers and could therefore potentially create wealth for shareholders. If this were the case then the wealth would be created not through maximisation of wealth but through a redistribution of wealth away from other stakeholders.

The source of power within society can be linked to the resources available to each stakeholder group. A stakeholder group is more likely to be considered or accommodated as their power increases. Therefore primary stakeholders are in a position of significant power as they can cause the decline of or seriously damage a powerful organisation. However, secondary stakeholders may not receive the same consideration. Furthermore, these secondary stakeholders may not have sufficient power in society to have their needs appropriately reflected. In fact, they may be powerless. As a powerless group they will not receive any attention and are unlikely to receive any of the wealth created by an organisation. Morris (1987) takes this further and suggests that if a member of society has no power within that society then this should represent a condemnation of the society itself.

One way in which a group can protect its welfare or ensure an equitable distribution of welfare within a society is through government legislation. Certainly this has been the case for both employment and environmental issues in recent years. These items have been recognised and addressed within the legislation of individual countries and as such would be classified as social issues by Clarkson (1995). However, the ability to get such legislation on the agenda will depend upon the power and the resources open to a stakeholder group. So again a powerless group in society may well fail to be protected through legislation, as they do not have sufficient influence.

Until now this chapter has argued that the efficacy of value-based man-agement techniques can be questioned from an ethical standpoint — the claim that all of society benefits is as yet unsubstantiated. A normative validity justification of stakeholder theory contends that distributive effects, in addition to those of wealth creation, should be accounted for when consider-ing its appropriateness. Therefore the next section looks at the effects on stakeholders of a shareholder-orientated strategy. It does this by considering the privatised electricity industry in England and Wales.

THE CASE OF THE ELECTRICITY INDUSTRY IN ENGLAND AND WALES

It is first necessary to explain why it is appropriate to use the electricity industry in England and Wales as a relevant case study. This industry was privatised in the early 1990s by the then Conservative government after it had been owned and operated within the public sector for decades. This was as part of one of the largest privatisation programmes in the world and witnessed the sale, to the private sector, of companies operating in both competitive industries and more controversially (Ogden and Anderson, 1995) the utility industries (telecommunications, gas, water, electricity and rail). The primary rhetoric of the time argues the case for privatisation on economic grounds, with the implicit assumption that private ownership would lead to more efficient service provision. Furthermore, it has been argued that the long-term success of the privatisation programme will be judged on the grounds of economic efficiency (Vickers and Yarrow, 1988). Dunsire et al. (1991) argue that the most commonly suggested mechanisms by which privatisation influences an organisation's performance, which has been taken to mean improved economic efficiency, are

(a) the policing role of the capital market (Kay and Thompson, 1986); and/or (b) an increase in competition (Millward and Parker, 1983); and/or (c) a change in managerial incentives (Alchian and Demsetz, 1972; De Alessi, 1980).

Each mechanism provides incentives for organisations to shift to improve economic efficiency but it is only the first which explicitly recognises the needs of shareholders. Thus, within a free capital market, an organisation needs to adequately compensate its shareholders for their risk otherwise their shares will be sold. The resulting fall in share price will make the company open to a potential takeover and/or will make the management's position vulnerable. The other two mechanisms actually address slightly different issues but both are based on the assumption that the privatised companies will be maximising shareholder wealth. This is demonstrated below.

An increase in competition within an industry was considered to be the best way to encourage improved performance (Beesley and Littlechild, 1983). However, due to the lack of competition within the utility industries, it was recognised that the necessary efficiency incentives were absent. Indeed it is reasonable to suggest that these industries form natural monopolies in the manner suggested by J. S. Mill (1848), whereby the most efficient provision of a good or service can be achieved through a single organisation (Foster, 1994). This does not mean that all stages of the electricity industry form a natural monopoly. On privatisation the industry in England and Wales was vertically separated as follows:

- Generation, a potentially competitive industry and therefore not requiring formal regulation.
- The National Grid, a natural monopoly as the most efficient service is provided by a single organisation (Foster, 1994) that requires regulation.
- Twelve supply and distribution companies (the RECs) which at the time of privatisation held regional monopolies. This regional separation enabled the regulator to use yardstick regulation with the intention of introducing true competition later.

The benefits of this vertical separation of the industry were seen to be the opportunity this provided to minimise regulation. For example, it was believed that electricity generation would not require regulation as it was potentially competitive, and competition was believed to provide the best incentive to efficiency.

All of the privatised utility industries in the UK are subject to industry-specific price-cap regulation as recommended by Littlechild to 'hold the fort' until competition arrives. This is not the only form of regulation used in the UK where certain public sector industries, such as elements of the National Health Service, are subject to rate of return regulation. Rate of return regulation and sliding scale regulation are often cited as the principal alternative methods of regulation (Cooper, 1998). Price-cap regulation was preferred for the utility industries as theoretically it provides the strongest incentives for economic efficiency. This form of regulation specifically targets falling real prices to consumers over time, as is evident from the RPI − X formula used. As real prices fall, so the companies need to reduce real costs at a faster rate if they are to increase their profits. The requirement to reduce real costs is the central tenet of this form of regulation (Vass, 1992) and appears to have been equated with the promotion of economic efficiency. A key feature of this regulatory regime, which distinguishes it from the others, is the fixed review periods (Helm 1994). A company will actively pursue savings only if it has time to benefit from them before the next price review incorporates them into the price cap. This whole form of regulation assumes that the privatised companies will be attempting to maximise shareholder wealth. The incentive to reduce real costs exists if the company is attempting to maximise its value to its shareholders.

Finally it is argued that a change in how management is rewarded within the private sector can provide greater incentives for management to improve efficiency. This mechanism is primarily concerned with the separation of ownership and control that was mentioned earlier. Within the private sector, managerial reward schemes have been designed and implemented with the specific aim of trying to ensure that managers are managing for shareholders. This mechanism actually presumes the primary objective of the firm should be to maximise shareholder wealth and as a result that managers should be rewarded so as to provide incentives to achieve this end.

A STAKEHOLDER ANALYSIS

The rest of this chapter will consider how the electricity industry in England and Wales has performed for each of its stakeholders in the post-privatisation period. The analysis will take into account the 15 electricity companies initially privatised; they comprise 12 regional electricity companies (RECs) responsible for the supply and distribution of electricity, the National Grid responsible for the network, and the two generating companies. This analysis therefore does not include the nuclear element of the industry. The five-year period from 1991 to 1995, from privatisation to when the government redeemed its golden share in the companies, will be considered as this can be argued to be when the effects of the change to private companies will be most pronounced. Also, since the redemption of the government's golden share, the majority of the companies have subsequently been taken over. In fact, all of the RECs have been the target of takeover bids and 11 have either merged or been taken over.

This chapter justifies the use of stakeholder theory as a means of considering the ethical validity of value-based management. Therefore, in addition to considering the wealth-creating and efficiency gains which were given primacy in the regulation of the industry, there is the complementary issue of wealth and welfare distribution. The stakeholder analysis must firstly define who the stakeholders are and how the performance of the industry has affected them. Shaoul (1998) provides evidence that the UK government justified the privatisation of the utility industries by suggesting that 'all would benefit: consumers, employees, the industry and the nation'. It is interesting to note the absence of shareholders in this list. In addition to this, other potential motivations have been identified for the privatisation programme. The most fundamental disagreement is whether the policy was designed for economic or political purposes.

Hodges (1997) and Hodges and Wright (1995) examined National Audit Office (NAO) reports that reviewed the government departments responsible for 26 privatisations and noted that the objectives have not been the same for each privatisation. It is suggested that usually they would include a combination of some or all of the following: a timely sale, maximising sale proceeds and minimising costs, widening of share ownership, and the advancement of competition and efficiency in the industry. In addition to these motivations, Vickers and Yarrow (1988) include within their perceived government objectives reduced involvement of government in the industries, reducing the public sector borrowing requirement (PSBR), the weakening of the public sector trade unions and gaining political advantage.

This chapter has so far identified several key stakeholders:

- Shareholders
- The regulator
- Consumers
- Management
- Other employees
- The environment and the future

It is now intended, for the post-privatisation period, to consider how the electricity industry in England and Wales has performed for each stakeholder group. This is of relevance to the shareholder value debate as it has been argued that one of the key mechanisms through which privatisation changes performance is via the workings of the capital market. Furthermore, Carter and Crowther (2000) noted a change in the managerial perspective in the electricity industry from primarily that of an engineering function to a more finance-based approach. Therefore, internal to the privatised companies, there has been a change in emphasis from a situation where the primary concern was to ensure that electricity was available to a situation where more emphasis is placed upon the requirements of the City and shareholders. If we accept that there has been a shift towards shareholders in the electricity industry then its performance should provide a valuable insight into the wider effects of companies following such a strategy.

SHAREHOLDERS

Before privatisation the electricity industry had been owned and managed within the public sector for decades. As such there were no shareholders and therefore this is an entirely new stakeholder group. The privatised electricity companies have made internal changes in response to threats which were not in existence while they were state owned. Since privatisation these companies have had to contend with shareholders, the regulator and the onset of competition. This is exactly as intended given that one of the key mechanisms identified by which privatisation affects the performance of organisations is via the workings of the capital market. As private sector companies they are competing with all other such organisations for finance, and the market's opinion of their performance is reflected in their share price.

The power of shareholders in the private sector is very large as they can easily withdraw their investment or have the opportunity to question and dismiss the management of the organisation. Therefore in the period from 1990 to 1995 the importance of shareholders increased dramatically, from non-existent to being a primary stakeholder, within the electricity industry. It is argued in this chapter as the power of a stakeholder group increases so they expect to receive a greater return. A brief review of the post-privatisation performance of the industry would certainly support this contention. The profitability of the electricity industry, as measured by profits attributable to shareholders as a percentage of turnover to the final consumers, increased steadily from 13.5% to 18.6% in the years ending 31 March 1992 and 31 March 1995, respectively (Cooper and Crowther, 1998). This is a 38% increase over a four-year period and reflects the ability of the privatised companies to outperform the expectations of the regulator. These results have made electricity company shares extremely attractive and therefore in the period from privatisation to 1995 the annualised total shareholder returns in the electricity industry were 41% (Cornelius and Davies, 1997). These were the highest returns provided by any industry over this time period. Perhaps unsurprisingly shareholders can definitely be considered to have benefited from the privatisation programme.

THE REGULATOR

The regulator is another new stakeholder to the electricity industry. The specific requirements of the regulator vary to a certain degree depending upon the industry structure at the time of privatisation and its perceived evolution through time. The specific responsibilities of the regulatory body of the electricity industry (OFFER) were split into primary and secondary duties. These duties have been summarised as follows:

> The primary duties comprise: ensuring that all reasonable demand for electricity is met; ensuring licence holders are able to finance their activities; and promoting competition. The secondary duties include: ensuring that consumers' interests are protected in respect of the price charged, continuity of supply and security of supply; promoting economy and efficiency in the industry and the efficient use of electricity supplied to consumers; promoting research and development; ensuring machinery established for the protection of employees' health and safety. (McGowan, 1993, pp. 76–77).

McGowan continues that the regulator has given primacy to protecting the consumer interests and promoting competition. This directly recognises there is a danger that without such regulation the consumers may well be 'gouged' by the potential for monopoly abuse of the utility companies (Veljanovski, 1991). It is also interesting to note that the regulator has a primary duty to ensure the privatised companies can finance their activities. This actually negates one of the key risks involved with investing in private companies: the risk of corporate failure. Therefore to return to the performance of the industry for shareholders, not only have they received the highest returns but it could also be argued that these returns have been made in one of the lowest-risk industries.

The role of the regulator is an interesting one when considering a stakeholder analysis of an industry. Not only is the regulatory body a stakeholder in its own right but it also has a duty to other stakeholders. This is clearly true for both consumers and the companies themselves, but in addition the regulatory process includes discussion papers which invite comments from any interested parties. Certainly political groups, trade unions and environmental groups take a keen interest in the review process and at what level the price cap for a coming period is set. Therefore part of the role of the regulator is attempting to balance the disparate needs of the different stakeholders. It is interesting to note that the *Economist* (29 July 1995) reported that 'since he became regulator of Britain's electricity industry, Stephen Littlechild has annoyed almost every part of British society'. This suggests that performing this balancing act is indeed difficult, as has been suggested by critics of stakeholder management.

Cooper et al. (1998) have argued that it is only when regulation is required and is seen to be working that there is a need for a regulator. Therefore it is assumed that if the industry becomes sufficiently competitive then the regulator, whose primary task is to provide a mechanism that 'holds the fort' until competition arrives, will no longer be required. Similarly, if the present form of regulation is, for some reason, considered to be fundamentally flawed or ineffective then the political response will undoubtedly be to close the regulatory office and introduce, if required, some new form of regulation. To date, all of the utility industries privatised in the UK are still subject to a certain degree of regulation; this is even the case in the telecommunications industry, which was the first to be privatised and has arguably the highest degree of competition.

OFFER has actually expanded in size since privatisation. According to their annual reports, OFFER staff levels were at 214 on 31 December 1991 (OFFER, 1992); by 31 December 1997 they had increased to 232 (OFFER, 1998) − an 8% increase. Similarly, the total cost of OFFER has increased from £10.6 million in 1990/91 to £13.231 million in 1996/97, an increase of 25% (as opposed to an 18% increase in the RPI). The regulatory office as a stakeholder was not required under the nationalised industry structure but has now grown, with the support of legislation, into a powerful and important stakeholder in the industry. Cooper et al. (1998) argue that the regulators need regulation to exist; it is therefore not surprising that both the performance of the privatised companies and the performance of the regulatory office itself have been publicly defended by the regulator.

CONSUMERS

Consumers would be open to abuse in an unregulated natural monopoly where the product is an essential item of modern life. Monopoly pricing would see higher prices for the product so that the producer could extract monopoly profits. In response to this, the regulator of the electricity industry has prioritised the need to protect the consumer. The price-cap regulation adopted in the UK is specifically targeting falling real prices to the consumer. The strength of the regulator and the organisation of consumer groups have made the consumer a powerful voice in the running of the electricity industry. However, this has not always been the case; when the industry was first privatised and the government set the original price cap, there were other motivations in force. They have been discussed above but they include the desire for a successful and timely sale, which is not consistent with a very strict and demanding price cap. The first price caps which were set by the government were transmission RPI − 0, distribution RPI + 1.3 (average) and supply RPI − 0. This effectively allowed an increase in the real price in electricity over the period. Therefore it could be suggested that the consumer was relatively unimportant as a stakeholder when the government set this first price cap.

As the regulator has subsequently taken over the regulation of the industry, and is now responsible for the setting of the price cap, this has changed. The regulator has interpreted his duties to be primarily to protect the consumer and has subsequently set the more recent price caps to reflect this. Each subsequent price cap has set more stringent requirements in terms of price reductions and now requires a real reduction in costs to the consumer. This is confirmed by the change in the average nominal price to the consumers, as calculated by

$$\frac{\text{Electricity supply revenue (£)}}{\text{Electricity distributed (GWh)}}$$

From privatisation until the year ended 31 March 1993, the average price increased but has subsequently declined as the stricter requirements of the regulator have been enforced (Cooper and Crowther, 1998).

A potential corollary to changes in prices is the issue of quality. It is possible to reduce costs by reducing quality and thereby externalising costs by passing them on to the consumer or to any other stakeholder group. This has been recognised by the regulator, who introduced standards of performance for the companies in 1991 (these are either guaranteed or overall standards and have been updated in 1993 and 1995) (OFFER, 1997).

The amount of payments made by the companies for failure to comply with the guaranteed standards has fallen impressively since the measures were first introduced in the year 1991/92 from 10 920 to 1911 in 1996/97. With a few exceptions it is also true that the companies have achieved the overall standards expected of them throughout the entire period since 1991/92. These results would therefore not suggest that the quality of service, as defined and measured by OFFER, has deteriorated.

Since privatisation, the price of electricity has fallen and the quality of service, as defined by OFFER, has improved. Therefore it could be argued that the consumers have benefited from privatisation and the privatised companies change in objectives. However, the question remains as to whether the consumers would have benefited as much without these changes. This is impossible to answer but we can consider how non-UK electricity consumers have fared. The Electricity Association (1999) publish comparable domestic and industrial electricity prices within the EU for the period from 1990 to 1998. The price changes in England and Wales, as opposed to other EU countries, for this period suggest that consumers in England and Wales have not benefited as much as other consumers. Over the period 1 January 1990 to 1 January 1998 nominal electricity prices to domestic consumers increased by more in England and Wales than any other EU country.

The picture is not so clear-cut for industrial prices. If we consider the published tariffs in 1998 then the nominal price has increased in England and Wales and fallen in all other EU countries. However, if we consider the 'estimated UK average contract price for 1997/98' then the UK has reduced nominal prices more quickly than six and not as quickly as five EU countries. This comparative performance raises questions as to whether consumers have truly benefited. In addition we have noted above that the electricity industry now has two extra stakeholders in the form of shareholders and the regulator. Each of these stakeholders is extracting a certain return or payment from the industry, and this is now a considerable proportion of the total cost to the consumer. In the year ended 31 March 1995 profit attributable to shareholders accounted for 18.6% of the final consumer costs and in addition there is more than £13 million per annum being spent on regulating the industry.

MANAGEMENT

On privatisation the management went from being employed by the government to having their salary levels set by the private sector. The expectation from this is that the levels of remuneration would be significantly higher within the private sector and consequently that management would be a stakeholder that benefits from the privatisation. For the purposes of this chapter, due to availability of data, management has been defined as directors. An analysis of the total directors' remuneration per the annual accounts, for 13 of the 15 companies originally privatised, has been completed. The most dramatic increase in directors' pay was noted in the year ended 31 March 1992 as compared to the year ended 31 March 1991. On average the total directors' remuneration increased by 38.8%. A large increase was reported in every company except one, where the total remuneration was identical in both years. From this it would appear that the directors were an immediate beneficiary of privatisation; however, it is possible that the remuneration for the year ending March 1991 was lower because the board of directors was still being assembled. Therefore, a comparison was also undertaken between the years ending 31 March 1995 and 31 March 1992. Over this period of three years there was an average annual increase in total remuneration, as disclosed in the annual reports of the companies, paid to the directors of 21.3%. Over the same period the retail price index has increased by 7.9% and so even after the initial readjustment the directors are gaining from the privatised industry.

A change in management remuneration of privatised companies is one of the mechanisms by which greater efficiency can be promoted. This has most clearly been achieved in the electricity industry through the use of share options. Share options have been used to a great extent in the industry and provide the directors with a clear motivation for improving share price. This recognises and may partially address the potential problems of agency theory as discussed earlier. The potential gains to the directors through share options are large and make up a significant element of their remuneration, especially when it is remembered that the total return to shareholders was 41% per annum over the period.

OTHER EMPLOYEES

So far we have identified four stakeholder groups who all, it could be argued, appear to have benefited from privatisation; however, Vickers and Yarrow (1988) suggest that one potential motivation for the privatisation programme was to reduce the power and influence of private sector trade unions. A rather conflicting view is that the privatised electricity industry will be more labour intensive than its public sector equivalent (Bunn and Vlahos, 1989). This is due to the higher rates of return required by private sector companies promoting labour-intensive rather than capital-intensive operations. It was argued that the change in ownership would result in the use of higher discount rates, in discounted cash flow project appraisal, and hence 'favour capital investments with lower capital, but higher operating costs'.

In fact, if we simply consider the levels of employment in the industry we see there has been a significant fall. The Electricity Association (1997) statistics show a 41% fall in employment levels from 1989/90 to 1995/96 and the Centre for the Study of Regulated Industries (CRI, 1998) indicate that the fall has been 38% from 1990/91 to 1995/96. Obviously these sources both indicate a huge reduction in the workforce employed by the privatised companies in the industry. The CRI (1998) also indicates that from 1990/91 to 1995/96 there has been a 31% fall in the 'total employee/staff costs'. Therefore using the CRI statistics this would indicate that the remaining employees have experienced an average salary increase of 11.8% over the five-year period as compared to a 15.3% increase in the RPI. This therefore implies that employees, as a total stakeholder group, are actually worse off in real terms, although it is recognised that this does not mean that each individual employee will necessarily be worse off.

If we reconsider the mode of regulation in the UK, it targets falling real costs. Crowther et al. (1999) argue that one of the largest and easiest costs for a company to reduce is labour, and we could anticipate a reduction in the distribution to employees. Also, as anticipated by Vickers and Yarrow (1988), the industrial relations and the role of the trade unions have changed since privatisation. Ferner and Colling (1991, 1993) examine the changes in industrial relations in the privatised utility industries and note that the effect has been 'ambiguous'. They note that one effect has been the distinction between core and non-core activities, where after privatisation non-core activities would increase in importance and would be subject to different industrial relations to those in the core.

There has also been a shift away from industry-wide negotiations to smaller and smaller groups. For example, the final national negotiations with the Amalgamated Engineering and Electrical Union (AEEU), one of the largest trade unions in the industry, occurred in 1992 and since then the trend has been to further 'reduce the size of bargaining units' (Fenelon, 1998). This division of the industry's employees effectively weakens the bargaining power of employees as a whole. Therefore a decrease in the distribution of wealth to employees may be unsurprising but in addition the welfare of the remaining employees has also been severely affected. The AEEU note plummeting staff morale being indicated by 'annual employee attitude surveys by companies' and it also cites increased levels of stress, distrust of management and a climate of fear (Fenelon, 1998). This may well appear a biased source of such information, but given the level of staff reduction in the industry noted above, it is likely that the remaining staff will feel a sense of job insecurity. Furthermore, given the fewer employees, it could be argued that at least some of the remaining employees will experience a more intense work experience. In Marxian terminology one could liken it to a greater extraction of surplus value from the labour force.

It is recognised that the above argument does not prove that employees now have reduced welfare but it questions the wisdom of the assumption that all will gain from shareholder value management. It could be argued that some of the wealth that has passed to shareholders has not been 'created' as such, but merely redistributed. In absolute terms the payments to employees have fallen from £2279 million in 1990/91 to £1580 million in 1995/96.

An annual cost reduction of £699 million in the space of five years can now be distributed to other stakeholder groups.

THE ENVIRONMENT AND THE FUTURE

The environment and the future has been included as a catch-all stakeholder group that intends to consider the longer-term effects of the privatisation. It has long been argued that the financial motivations prevalent in the United Kingdom and the United States result in a short-term view, effectively externalising costs not only outside the organisation but also temporally. That is to say, it may well be easier to pass costs onto future generations of stakeholders. It is obviously more difficult to discuss the returns or distribution of wealth to a future stakeholder, but it is still important that they should be considered. One concern for both the environment and future generations must be the reduction in the employee levels noted above. Crowther et al. (1999) report that one way in which this has been achieved has been through the discontinuation of certain practices previously performed.

Specifically mentioned is that a trade union had identified a change in risk management practices. This entails what were once routine maintenance checks no longer being performed; now a piece of machinery is repaired only if it fails. This is effectively a shift from maintenance to repair. Such practices may have very significant long-term implications for all stakeholders of the electricity industry in the future. Assets used by the industry are extremely long-lived and it is unknown what effect the less regular maintenance of, say, power stations may have on their lifespan. Also the reliability of supply in the future may well be compromised by these risk practices today. It will only be in the future that the answers to these questions will be known, but the potential problems should be acknowledged sooner rather than later. It is certainly important to remember that the management techniques deemed consistent with shareholder value principles specifically discount the future.

CONCLUSION

This chapter specifically adopted a different approach to shareholder value in that it addressed it from the perspective of its effects on different stakeholders within a society. By presenting an alternative view to shareholder value it attempts to question the assumption that shareholder value management will automatically create wealth for a society. Evidence from the last 40 years does not suggest that the more shareholder value focused economies necessarily create more wealth in terms of increasing GDP per capita. Broadening the debate from wealth creation to welfare distribution is not easy, and this chapter only marks a first attempt at considering these wider implications.

Drawing on the work of Rawls and Kant, stakeholder literature has argued that a society must, for ethical and moral reasons, consider the distributive implications of business practice. This chapter then argued that the distributive implications could be considered through the use of a case study of the electricity industry in England and Wales. It is widely agreed that one of the motivations and one of the effects of electricity privatisation was a change in the organisations' objectives to become more shareholder value oriented. The analysis attempted to identify whether stakeholder groups have benefited or lost out as a result of these changes in the industry. This is somewhat subjective, but it is argued here that shareholders, the regulators, and management have benefited from the changes whilst employees and the environment have lost out. Consumers appear to have benefited over time but not by as much as in other EU countries.

Overall it is suggested that there has been a redistribution of wealth and welfare as an effect of the change in incentives, not only a creation of wealth. Furthermore, this redistribution is dependent upon the power that a particular stakeholder group has over that company or within the society. The lack of power or attention given to these groups could result in their needs being downplayed to appease those of more pressing and powerful groups. The long-term implications of this could be serious and therefore a society and/or government should now consider whether the power relations between the different stakeholder groups are appropriate. This would specifically have implications for the precedence given to the shareholder group.

REFERENCES

Alchian, A.A. and Demsetz, H. (1972) Production, information costs and economic organizations. *American Economic Review*, **62**, 777–95.

Anon (1996) Stakeholder capitalism: unhappy families. *Economist*, Vol. **338**, issue 7952, 10 February 1996.

Atkinson, A.A., Waterhouse, J.H. and Wells, R.B. (1997) A stakeholder approach to strategic performance management. *Sloan Management Review*, Spring, 25–37.

Atkinson, A.B. (1996) Seeking to explain the distribution of income. In *New inequalities: the changing distribution of income and wealth in the United Kingdom* (ed. J. Hills). Cambridge University Press, Cambridge.

Aupperle, K.E., Carroll, A.B. and Hatfield, J.D. (1985) An empirical examination of the relationship between corporate social responsibility and profitability. *Academy of Management Journal*, **28**(2), 446–63.

Beesley, M. and Littlechild, S. (1983) Privatisation: principles, problems and priorities. Reproduced in C. Johnson (ed.) (1988) *Privatisation and Ownership – Lloyds Bank Annual Review*. Pinter, London.

Bentham, J. (1789) *Introduction to the Principles of Morals and Legislation*. Many editions.

Bunn, D. and Vlahos, K. (1989) Evaluation of the long-term effects on UK electricity prices following privatisation. *Fiscal Studies*, **10**(4), 104–16.

Carroll, A.B. (1993) *Business and Society: Ethics and Stakeholder Management*, 2nd edn. South Western Publishing, Cincinnati OH.

Carter, C. and Crowther, D. (2000) Unravelling a profession: the case of engineers in a regional electricity company. *Critical Perspectives on Accounting*, **11**(1), 23–49.

Clarkson, M.E. (1995) A stakeholder framework for analysing and evaluating corporate social performance. *Academy of Management Review*, **20**(1), 92–117.

Cooper, S. (1998) Control, accounting and value-for-money implications of utility regulation: a literature review. *Managerial Auditing Journal*, **13**(2), 117–25.

Cooper, S. and Crowther, D. (1998) Three bites of the cherry? Performance measurement in the UK electricity industry and the effects of industry structure. Paper presented at Aston Business School, Finance and Accounting Group Seminar Programme.

Cooper, S., Crowther, D. and Carter, C. (1998) Regulation – the movie: a semiotic study of the periodic review of UK regulated industry. Aston Business School Research Paper, RP9811.

Copeland, T., Koller, T. and Murrin, J. (1996) *Valuation: measuring and managing the value of companies*, 2nd edn. John Wiley, New York.

Cornelius, I. and Davies, M. (1997) *Shareholder Value*. Financial Times Publishing, London.

CRI (1998) The UK Electricity Industry Financial and Operating Review 1996/97. CIPFA, London.

Crowther, D., Cooper, S. and Carter, C. (1999) Appeasing Quetzalcoatl: accounting for ritual sacrifice. Paper presented at the 1999 Critical Perspectives on Accounting Conference, New York.

De Alessi, L. (1980) The economics of property rights: a review of the evidence. *Research in Law and Economics*, **2**, 1–47.

Donaldson, T. and Preston, L.E. (1995) The stakeholder theory of the corporations: concepts, evidence and implications. *Academy of Management Review*, **20**(1), 65–91.

Dunsire, A., Hartley, K. and Parker, D. (1991) Organizational status and performance: summary of the findings. *Public Administration*, **69** (spring), 21–40.

Electricity Association (1997) Electricity industry review. Electricity Association Services Limited, London.

Electricity Association (1999) International electricity prices: a summary of results, 1990–1998. Electricity Association Services Limited, London.

Evans, W.M. and Freeman, R.E. (1988). A stakeholder theory of the modern corporation: Kantian capitalism. In *Ethical Theory and Business* (eds T. Beauchamp and N. Bowie). Prentice Hall, Englewood Cliffs NJ.

Fenelon, B. (1998) The effects of the privatisation of the electricity industry. Amalgamated Engineering and Electrical Union.

Ferner, A. and Colling, T. (1991) Privatization, regulation and industrial relations. *British Journal of Industrial Relations*, **29**(3), 391–409.

Ferner, A. and Colling, T. (1993) Privatization of the British Utilities – regulation, decentralization, and industrial relations. In *The Political Economy of Privatization* (eds T. Clarke and C. Pitelis). Routledge, London.

Foster, C. (1994) Rival explanations of public ownership, its failure and privatization. *Public Administration*, **72** (winter), 489–503.

Freeman, R.E. (1984) *Strategic management: a stakeholder approach*. Pittman, Boston MA.

Friedman, M. (1970) The social responsibility is to increase its profits. *New York Times Magazine*, September, 32–33.

Greenley, G.E. and Foxall, G.R. (1997) Multiple stakeholder orientation in UK companies and the implications for company performance. *Journal of Management Studies*, **34**(2), 259–84.

Helm, D. (1994). British utility regulation: theory practice and reform. *Oxford Review of Economic Policy*, **10**(3), 17–33.

Hirsch, F. (1978) *Social Limits to Growth*. Routledge & Kegan Paul, London.

Hodges, R. (1997) Competition and efficiency after privatization: the role of the NAO. *Public Money and Management*, January/March, 35–42.

Hodges, R. and Wright, M. (1995) Audit and accountability in the privatisation process. The role of the National Audit Office. *Financial Accountability and Management*, **11**(2), 153–70.

Jones, T.M. (1995) Instrumental stakeholder theory: a synthesis of ethics and economics. *Academy of Management Review*, **20**(2), 404–37.

Kaplan, R.S. and Norton, D.P. (1992) The balanced scorecard – measures that drive performance. *Harvard Business Review*, January/February, 71–79.

Kaplan, R.S. and Norton, D.P. (1993) Putting the balanced scorecard to work. *Harvard Business Review*, September/October, 134–47.

Kaplan, R.S. and Norton, D.P. (1996a) Using the balanced scorecard as a strategic management system. *Harvard Business Review*, January/February, 75–85.

Kaplan, R.S. and Norton, D.P. (1996b) *The Balanced Scorecard: Translating Strategy into Action*. Harvard Business School Press, Boston MA.

Kay, J.A. and Thompson, D.J. (1986) Privatisation: a policy in search of a rationale. *Economic Journal*, March, 18-32.

L'Etang, J. (1995) Ethical corporate social responsibility: a framework for managers. *Journal of Business Ethics*, **14**, 125–32.

Litz, R.A. (1996) A resource-based view of the socially responsible firm: stakeholder interdependence, ethical awareness, and issue responsiveness as strategic assets. *Journal of Business Ethics*, **15**, 1355–63.

McGowan, F. (1993) Electricity: the experience of OFFER. In *Regulatory Review 1993* (eds T. Gilland and P. Vass). Centre for the Study of Regulated Industries, London.

Mill, J.S. (1848) *Principles of Political Economy*. Many editions.

Mill, J.S. (1863) *Utilitarianism*. Many editions.

Millward, R. and Parker, D. (1983) Public and private enterprise: comparative behaviour and relative efficiency. In *Public Sector Economics* (eds R. Millward, D. Parker, L. Rosenthal, M.T. Sumner and N. Topham). Longman, London.

Monks, R.A.G. and Minow, N. (1991) *Power and Accountability*. Harper Collins, Glasgow.

Moore, G.B. (1999) Rawls, John. In *Dictionary of Cultural Theorists* (eds E. Cashmore and C. Rojek). Edward Arnold, London.

Morris, R. (1987) *Power – A Philosophical Analysis*. Manchester University Press, Manchester.

OFFER (1992) Annual report 1991. Bentley Holland and Partners, London.

OFFER (1997) Report on customer services 1996/97. OFFER.

OFFER (1998) Annual report 1997. http://www.open.gov.uk/offer/offerhm.htm

Ogden, S. and Anderson, F. (1995) Representing consumers' interests: the case of the privatized water industry in England and Wales. *Public Administration*, **73** (winter), 535–59.

Rappaport, A. (1986) *Creating shareholder value: the new standard for business performance*. Free Press, New York.

Rawls, J. (1973) *A Theory of Justice*. Oxford University Press, Oxford.

Roberts, R.W. (1992) Determinants of corporate social responsibility disclosure: an application of stakeholder theory. *Accounting Organizations and Society*, **17**(6), 595–612.

Shaoul, J. (1998) Critical financial analysis and accounting for stakeholders. *Critical Perspectives on Accounting*, **9**(2), 235–49.

Smith, A. (1776) *The Wealth of Nations*. Many editions.

Starik, M. (1994) Essay in 'The Toronto conference: reflections on stakeholder theory'. *Business and Society*, **33**(1), 89–95.

Sternberg, E. (1997) The defects of stakeholder theory. *Corporate Governance*, **5**(1), 3–10.

Vass, P. (1992) Establishing a conceptual framework for regulated industries' accounting and accountability. *Financial Accountability and Management*, **8**(4), 299–315.

Veljanovski, C. (ed.) (1991) The regulation game. In *Regulators and the market: an assessment of the growth of regulation in the UK*. Institute of Economic Affairs, London.

Vickers, J. and Yarrow, G. (1988) *Privatisation: an economic analysis*. MIT Press, Cambridge MA.

Waddock, S.A. and Graves, S.B. (1997) Quality of management and quality of stakeholder relations. *Business and Society*, **36**(3), 250–79.

Wood, D.J. (1994) Essay in 'The Toronto conference: reflections on stakeholder theory'. *Business and Society*, **33**(1), 101–5.

Woodward, D.G. (1998) An attempt at the classification of a quarter of a century of (non-critical) corporate social reporting. Paper presented at the 1998 British Accounting Association.

6 The Dialectics of Corporate Value Measurement

DAVID CROWTHER

INTRODUCTION

Implicit within the discourse of value-based management is the concept of the primacy of the shareholder on whose behalf the firm is to be managed. Indeed so accepted is this concept that it is common to find in the objectives of the firm, as manifest explicitly in many corporate reports, a statement concerning the creation of value to shareholders. However, this concept of the creation of value for shareholders fails to satisfactorily distinguish between the actual creation of value and the redistribution of any value between the various groups of the stakeholder community (Tinker, 1985). Thus the question of value creation, despite the argument of Rappaport (1986), becomes subsumed within a more general discourse concerning value distribution.

In binary opposition to shareholders, as far as value creation and distribution for an organisation are concerned, are all others interested in the performance of the organisation, who are generally homogeneously described as 'the stakeholders'. This concept neatly distinguishes one stakeholder group, the shareholders, from all others and enables the discourse to treat amorphously all other stakeholders. It is important to remember, however, that this amorphous mass contains very discrete groupings such as employees, customers, society at large and possibly most significantly the future (Chapter 5). This future can be broadly encapsulated in the concept of the environment. In this separation of stakeholders into two distinct groupings, a dialectic is created which establishes a violent hierarchy (Laclan, 1990) between the two poles of a binary opposition by establishing the idea of a conflict of interests. The creation of this dialectic provides a legitimation for the privileging of shareholders over all other stakeholders, a task for which accounting is singularly well equipped.

At the same time the creation of this dialectic implicitly creates two dimensions to the performance of an organisation – performance for shareholders and performance for other stakeholders, with an equally implicit assumption that maximising performance for one can only be at the expense of the other.

It is in this way that a dialogue is created to consider which pole of the binarism should be dominant in the managing of corporate performance because one of the essential features of the violent hierarchy of poles established in this dialectic is that one must be privileged over the other.

The purpose of this chapter is to explore several aspects of this dialectic:

- Different perspectives on performance
- The purposes of the evaluation of performance
- Different measurements of performance

In the exploration of the dialectic, a postmodern view of organisations and their performance is adopted in order to question the needs of performance measurement from the shareholder and stakeholder perspectives. In this exploration of the dialectic it is thereby demonstrated that this oppositional construct of performance serves merely to obfuscate the organisational purposes of performance measurement and to show that the discourse of value-based management is not in conflict with stakeholder value management. Rather it is argued that the discourse disguises the potential conflict between value creation and value distribution.

PERSPECTIVES ON PERFORMANCE

The nature of the discourse regarding the measurement and evaluation of corporate performance has bifurcated in recent years with the adoption of different perspectives and this has been reflected in the changing nature of corporate reporting. Thus Beaver (1989) states there has been a shift from an economic view of corporate performance measurement to an informational perspective with a recognition of the social implications of an organisation's activities. Similarly, Eccles (1991) states there has been a shift from treating financial figures as the foundation of corporate performance measurement to treating them as part of a broader range of measures, while McDonald and Puxty (1979) maintain that companies are no longer the instruments of shareholders alone but exist within society and so have responsibilities to that society. Others (e.g. Roslender, 1996) argue for a changed basis of accounting to reflect these changes.

This part of the discourse therefore seems to have moved away from the concerns of shareholders in the firm and away from the economic rationale for accounting and towards a consideration of the wider stakeholder environment. At the same time, however, these shareholder concerns cannot be ignored and another part of the discourse has seen a return to economic values in assessing the performance of the firm. Thus Rappaport (1986) recognises some of the problems with accounting but goes on to consider the concept of shareholder value and how this can be created and sustained. Based on this work, he develops a methodology of shareholder value (Rappaport, 1992) by arguing that a shareholder value approach is the correct way of evaluating alternative company strategies. He states that the ultimate test of a corporate plan is whether it creates value for the shareholders, and according to him, this is the sole method of evaluating performance.

This return to a consideration of the importance of economic value and to the theory of the firm is based upon the assumption that maximising the value of a firm to its shareholders also maximises the value of that firm to society at large. Within the discourse, therefore, the concept of shareholder value is frequently mentioned and there is acceptance of the need to account for shareholder value within the practitioner community. Indeed the annual reports of companies regularly expound the virtue of creating value for shareholders and it is frequently cited as a corporate objective. This objective can simply be defined as being achieved when the rate of return obtained within a business exceeds the cost of obtaining funds.

The concept of shareholder value as an objective appears to be widely accepted within the accounting community but its use as a quantified evaluation is less often found in practice. This, it can be argued, is because the managers of a firm are preoccupied with other objectives, such as growth in size, turnover, market share or accounting returns, which are more easily measured. The achievement of objectives such as these is also often correlated with managerial rewards but less so with increasing shareholder value (Williamson, 1963). Indeed Jensen and Meckling (1976) use agency theory to demonstrate how following managerial interests can lead to higher rewards for those managers at the expense of a reduction in the value of the company.

A relatively recent development in the quest for a tool to measure shareholder value has been the concept of economic value added, which has been developed by Stewart (1991) as a better measure to assess corporate performance and the creation of shareholder value than conventional accounting measures. Indeed Stewart (1994, p. 73) states that 'economic value added is an estimate, however simple or precise, of a business's true economic profit'.

Economic value added is claimed to have a number of important advantages over traditional accounting measures, chiefly that economic performance is only determined after the making of a risk-adjusted charge for the capital employed in the business. Critics, however, argue that while this may be theoretically sound, the need to make arbitrary adjustments to standard accounting numbers in order to put the technique into practice makes the technique of doubtful validity. The application of the technique and the adjustments needed were evaluated by Coates et al. (1995), who suggest that simplified calculations produce satisfactorily reliable results.

Govinderajan and Gupta (1985) argue that long-run criteria contribute to organisational effectiveness rather than short-term criteria, whereas

Rappaport (1986, 1992) suggests that shareholder value analysis addresses both and maximises both. There is nevertheless a considerable body of evidence which suggests otherwise (e.g. Purdy, 1983; Child, 1984; Swieringa and Weick, 1987) and that a concern with returns to shareholders leads to a short-term focus and lack of regard for the longer term (Coates et al., 1995). Indeed some managerial actions taken to boost short-term valuations, e.g. delayering and outsourcing (D. Crowther et al., 1999), can be argued to actually reduce long-term value, particularly when the product and market development capability is externalised.

This chapter considers the way in which accounting is used as a technology to represent an organisation and its performance to its external environment through an exploration of the dialectic inherent in the discourse of value management. In doing so, it will be argued that the dialectic is spatially extant but not temporally extant, and this lack of a temporal dimension to the dialectic makes it a false dialectic which has no need of resolution.

STAKEHOLDER PERSPECTIVES ON PERFORMANCE

The dialectic outlined above indicates that organisations are attempting to polarise performance reporting into two dimensions, shareholder performance and stakeholder performance. The very survival of a business depends ultimately upon its ability to evaluate performance and select strategies which will enable it to achieve good future performance by whatever criteria are considered pertinent. Hence the evaluation of performance is not just concerned with the past but is also oriented towards the future, in the selection of alternatives which will shape the strategic direction of the business and ensure its future viability. The ability to realistically evaluate performance of the business and the ability to select suitable dimensions along which to carry out that evaluation, are therefore critically important not just to the managers of the business, nor just to the owners of the business, but to the whole stakeholder community of that business.

Evaluation of the techniques used for measuring performance has largely concentrated upon accounting techniques, although it has been recognised (Eccles, 1991) that there has been a shift from an emphasis upon financial figures as the basis of performance measurement to the use of a broader range of measures. While a consideration of the appropriateness of various techniques is vital to the mechanisms of evaluation, the approach taken by this research subsumes the crucial arguments which need to be resolved before this discussion becomes pertinent. These arguments concern the purpose of performance measurement and the determination of what can be considered good performance. Indeed the discourse of shareholder value assumes that it is only performance for shareholders which is of interest but without a consideration of these questions the evaluation of performance becomes somewhat irrelevant. This discourse, therefore, is useful but only once the fundamental rationale underpinning the measurement has been identified.

Research into the appropriateness of measures recognises that the reasons for the evaluation of performance underpin any measurement which is needed. The tendency of the research findings (Birnbeg, 1980; Kimberley et al., 1983; R. Gray et al., 1987) is to consider the effectiveness of current measures of performance in evaluating performance from a particular perspective and to find these measures inadequate. Some writers go beyond this (Rappaport, 1992; Kaplan and Norton, 1992, 1993) and suggest ways of measuring performance which will enable it to be evaluated from the particular perspective with which they are concerned. This does have merits yet there is a tendency to suggest changes in performance measurement which meet these needs, but only at the expense of neglecting other evaluation needs. Any consideration of measures suitable for evaluation needs to consider the whole purpose for which evaluation takes place in order to prevent the problems of meeting one need at the expense of others.

Besides considering the various perspectives on performance evaluation, it is important to recognise there are a variety of purposes for which performance is evaluated, purposes concerned with the actual functioning of the company, from a planning viewpoint and from an operational viewpoint. Additionally the organisation is concerned with both the present and with its future existence and so has both a short-term focus and a long-term focus. It is also concerned with its internal operations and with its external environment, so it must have both an internal focus and an external focus.

The measurement of performance is central to any consideration of performance evaluation and this resolves into two areas for consideration – why and what to measure. Measurement theory states that measurement is essentially a comparative process, and comparison provides the purpose for measurement. Measurement enables the comparison of the constituents of performance in the following areas:

- Temporally by enabling the comparison of one time period with another.
- Geographically by enabling the comparison of one business, sector or nation with another.
- Strategically by enabling alternative courses of action and their projected consequences to be compared.

One of the strengths of the techniques of value-based management is that it enables all of these comparisons to be effected but only from the perspective of the shareholder.

Performance itself is not absolute but rather comparative and it is essential in evaluating performance to be able to assess comparatively, hence a quantitative approach to performance evaluation is essential even if some aspects of performance are qualitative in nature. It is therefore necessary that measurement is a constituent of performance evaluation, so it becomes necessary to determine what should be measured in order to evaluate performance. This means it is important to select appropriate measures for the purpose of the evaluation. It is argued, however, that appropriate measures cannot be selected until the purpose of evaluation has been determined, thereby demonstrating that the foundation of performance measurement is the identification of the reasons for the evaluation of performance, and this must now be considered.

THE PURPOSE OF EVALUATION

It can be argued that the evaluation of performance takes place for several reasons: for control, and Cherns (1978) suggests that measurement equates with control; for strategy formulation; and for accountability. The discourse of shareholder value management accepts all these reasons and argues that the techniques employed address all three. There is, however, increasing concern in the discourse with accountability, rather than simply with accounting, with a greater emphasis upon the stakeholder dimension of accountability. The need for suitable measures to evaluate performance in this wider context necessitates the adoption of new measures of performance, which are not necessarily appropriate to other evaluation purposes. These measures are not necessarily always accounting based and indeed are not necessarily even quantitative, although they do need to facilitate comparison. At the same time, however, the needs of ownership accountability cannot be neglected, although Herremans et al. (1992) have suggested that a broader approach to corporate disclosure and to the evaluation of performance can lead to better economic performance by an organisation.

The evaluation of performance depends not just upon the appropriate measurement of performance but also upon the reporting of that performance. It is inevitable that each person or stakeholder grouping interested in the evaluation of the performance of an organisation needs a report, in some form, of the organisation's performance in order to undertake evaluation. The informational needs of different groups will differ considerably, depending upon their respective interests and concerns. The internal control needs, the needs of the owners, the needs of investors and potential investors, and the needs of the community as a stakeholder will all differ from each other and this poses a problem for the reporting of performance. This was recognised by Birnbeg (1980) who suggested that an organisation, through its accounting, was attempting to supply diverse groups with differing needs for information and thereby failing to communicate adequately with all the groups to meet all the reporting needs. In order to meet the reporting needs of the diverse stakeholder community, it is necessary first to identify those needs; this necessitates a consideration of the perspective of each stakeholder and a consideration of the interest in evaluation of the organisation's performance which is of importance to each stakeholder. These will be different between different groupings, which will therefore increase the reporting needs the organisation must address.

Any consideration of the varying purposes for which performance is evaluated leads to a suggestion that suitable measures for evaluation depend upon purpose and cannot necessarily be considered general to all purposes. The different perspectives and individual needs of all members of the stakeholder community must be recognised in the establishing of a system of measurement and reporting which is satisfactory to the organisation (Crowther, 1996). Any system which fails to address all such needs will inevitably be deemed unsatisfactory by some stakeholders, who will therefore exert effort to change the system. The resources of the organisation will be diluted by the internal conflict resulting from this failure to meet all needs, thereby diminishing the overall performance of the organisation. It is argued that the determination of the quality of performance therefore depends upon the person evaluating that performance, and the perspective of that person. The consideration of stakeholders is crucial to the determination of that perspective, as different stakeholder groupings are likely to have different interests and so have different perspectives upon the evaluation of that performance. In considering stakeholders, it is necessary to consider the widest definition of the stakeholder community, as all to some extent have an interest in and a perspective on the organisation. Indeed there is an increasing recognition of the need to report to all stakeholders and an increasing recognition of the accountability of the organisation not just to its owners, customers and employees but also to the community at large, and also to future constituents of that community. Thus it is recognised that the organisation operates at a local level and also at a societal level, and even at a global level, and is accountable not just for its present behaviour but also its past behaviour and also increasingly for the future effects of past and present behaviour. This is especially true when environmental effects are considered. The organisation therefore, while focusing upon the present and the future, cannot ignore the past or the unpredictable future, and while operating in the present is also operating in a juxtaposed, contiguous temporal dimension.

The analysis of stakeholders enables the perspectives of performance evaluation to be identified, which adds another dimension to the evaluation of performance. Each individual may belong to more than one stakeholder grouping (Carey and Sancto, 1998) and may therefore have more than one interest in the performance of the organisation. Thus a manager is also an employee, a member of the local community and may also be a shareholder and a customer of the organisation, and so interested in its performance from several different perspectives. Just as an individual may belong to more than one stakeholder grouping, so too may each stakeholder grouping have more than one perspective on the performance of that organisation.

The need for new measures to evaluate performance has to be set within the context of a changing external environment. Thus organisations are increasingly being concerned with a holistic approach (whereby the needs of the whole stakeholder community are considered), together with such issues as soft systems, culture and the establishment of competencies, as well as with accountability. This has created a need to evaluate performance against a set of diverse and often conflicting criteria, and this has led to the development of measures to evaluate performance for quite different purposes. These performance evaluation needs have a tendency to create tensions within the organisational performance measurement system as organisations have sought to evaluate performance against conflicting criteria. This in turn has led to tensions within the operational systems of an organisation, as organisations have sought to meet often incompatible needs.

THE OWNERSHIP OF PERFORMANCE

Agency theory suggests that the management of an organisation should be undertaken on behalf of the owners of that organisation, in other words the shareholders. Consequently, the management of value created by the organisation is only pertinent insofar as that value accrues to the shareholders of the firm. Implicit within this view of the management of the firm, as espoused by Rappaport (1986) and Stewart (1991) among many others, is that society at large, and consequently all stakeholders to the organisation, will also benefit as a result of managing the performance of the organisation in this manner. From this perspective, therefore, the concerns are focused upon how to manage performance for the shareholders and how to report upon that performance (Myners, 1998).

This view of an organisation has, however, been extensively challenged by many writers (Herremans et al., 1992; Tinker, 1985); they argue that the way to maximise performance for society at large is to manage on behalf of all stakeholders and to ensure the value thereby created is not appropriated by the shareholders but is distributed to all stakeholders. Others such as Kay (1998) argue that this debate is sterile and that organisations maximise value creation not by a concern with either shareholders or stakeholders but by focusing upon the operational objectives of the firm and assuming that value creation and equitable distribution will thereby follow.

Adherents to each of these conflicting philosophies have a tendency to adopt different perspectives on the evaluation of performance. Thus good performance for one school of thought is assumed to be poor performance for the others. Performance-maximising philosophies are polarised in the discourse and this leads to a polarisation of performance reporting and the creation of the dialectic considered earlier. Almost unquestioned within the discourse, however, is the assumption that good performance from one aspect necessitates the sacrificing of performance from the other, despite the ensuing distributional conflicts being hidden within the discourse. Indeed Kimberley et al. (1983) have argued that some areas of performance which are important to the future of the business are not even recognised let alone evaluated. It is argued that the future orientation of performance management necessitates the creation of value over the longer term for all stakeholders, and moreover, that this value creation must be manifest in how the value created in the organisation is distributed among the various stakeholders. It is only in this way that the continuing temporal existence of the organisation can be ensured.

It can readily be seen that the differing needs of different parties in the evaluation process causes tensions within the organisation as it seeks to meet its internal control, strategy formulation and accountability functions and produce a reporting structure to meet these needs. While the basic information required to satisfy these needs is the same organisational information, or at least derives from the same source data, the way in which it is analysed and used is different, which can lead to conflict within the organisation. Such conflict is exacerbated when a measure is adapted for one need but only at the expense of a deterioration in its appropriateness for another purpose. It is for this reason that accounting and information systems in organisations are in a constant state of development and enhancement as the systems are designed to meet perceived needs and adapted to meet newly identified needs. One such source of conflict in an organisation is therefore caused by the different stakeholders seeking to access and use information differently, and this conflict tends to have a dysfunctional impact upon organisational cohesiveness and ultimately performance. Performance can therefore be viewed deterministically in that it can be considered to be as good as it is evaluated to be, and Fish (1989) argues that, contextually, truth and belief are synonymous for all practical purposes.

One factor of importance in performance evaluation is the concept of sustainability as far as performance is concerned. It is therefore important for all stakeholders to be able to ascertain, or at least project, not just current performance but its implications for the future. Performance evaluation must therefore necessarily have a future orientation for all evaluations. The appropriate measures are likely to facilitate a better projection of the sustainability of performance levels and the future impact of current performance. This is because addressing the needs of all stakeholders is likely to reveal factors which will impact upon future performance and which might not be considered if a more traditional approach were taken towards performance evaluation. An example might be the degree to which raw materials from renewable resources have become significant to many industries; until recently they were not considered at all by any stakeholders of an organisation other than community and environmental pressure groups.

The proponents of VBM would argue that one of the strengths of the technique which differentiates it from traditional accounting evaluations is this ability to recognise future impacts of performance and this provides an assumed legitimation to the claimed superiority of the technique. This assumed superiority obviates the need to demonstrate this superiority. This point is elaborated by Horkheimer and Adorno (1944):

> The belief that the truth of a theory is the same as its productiveness is clearly unfounded. There are some, however, who appear to maintain the opposite: that theory has so little need of application in thinking that it should dispense with it entirely. (P. 244)

One implication of the analysis of evaluation systems is that the conflicting needs of different parties, and the different purposes for which measurements are used, are a source of tension within an organisation. Indeed it is argued that mismeasurement, by using measures for purposes for which they were not devised and are not appropriate, is itself a source of conflict within an organisation. Although it can be argued that organisations themselves are not entities but are coalitions of interest groups (i.e. stakeholders) which are held together by the tensions between the different groups, it is also argued that such tensions are not necessarily constructive but can also be destructive, wasting resources and resulting in sub-optimisation of the performance of the organisation. These tensions manifest themselves as power in the organisation, and while it is accepted that power is in the hands of the dominant coalition, it is also argued that the stakeholders who are not part of that coalition also have power which they seek to use to enable the satisfaction of their needs.

The tensions arising from this power struggle therefore make the organisation unstable and as far as performance is concerned, unless all stakeholders are involved either actively or passively in the evaluation system, the organisation wastes resources dealing with the ensuing conflict and seeking to meet the needs of excluded parties. Such needs are often met only at the expense of other needs and this itself causes tensions, with a result that the organisation tends to exist in a perpetually changing state of dynamic disequilibrium. This is deleterious to organisational performance unless the disequilibrium can be managed – by the managers. It is therefore in the managers' interests to both demonstrate the state of dynamic disequilibrium and also their ability to manage its control or resolution, in other words to create and manage the dialectic. One of the claimed strengths of VBM techniques is that they create a hierarchy of control which enables the conflicting needs of the various stakeholders to be managed, but this hierarchy exists only on the basis of the assumed legitimacy referred to by Horkheimer and Adorno (1944).

It is also apparent that the quality of performance is not absolute according to certain measures but is necessarily comparative, and it can be further argued that the same level of performance will be evaluated differently by different stakeholders according to the perspective from which they are undertaking the evaluation. It is, however, helpful to the communication process if the ensuing evaluation is broadly similar for each person. The way in which measures are used, or often misused, for a variety of evaluative purposes exacerbates the problem of differing interpretations, thereby leading to a variety of evaluations based upon the same measures for information. This problem is made worse by the use of accounting information, which can be described using Adorno's (1973) expression of 'the jargon of authenticity'. He argues that belief, or opinion, is presented as fact by the language used to express that belief and by the acceptance of this presentation as truth by its recipients.

Precision in the use of measures, and in the meaning attached to those measures, is a crucial determinant of the evaluation system used by an organisation. The failure to develop an adequate system for measuring performance will lead to an incomplete evaluation of that performance from some perspectives. More significantly it can lead to a misleading evaluation of performance as some measures are misused for evaluation in one dimension because of the lack of appropriate measures to give meaning to the evaluation. This applies not just to the measurement system but equally to the reporting system as it is this which provides the measured data to the evaluator. This flawed evaluation of performance can have serious consequences for an organisation and can lead not just to stakeholder alienation but more seriously to plans for the future of the organisation being made upon incorrect evaluations which can affect the future performance and even the viability of that organisation. Performance evaluation therefore requires the construction of adequate measures which are meaningful and appropriate. They can be financial or non-financial, quantitative or qualitative, and they are likely to combine several attributes.

Organisations exist as a loose coalition of different interest groups and power groupings which are held together by an interplay of common objectives and tensions arising from conflicting objectives. The role in which the evaluation needs of the different groups causes, exacerbates or even reduces these tensions is an area needing consideration. Horkheimer and Adorno (1944) argue that a social hierarchy is ultimately dependent upon force:

> Though it may seek a legalistic covering, the social hierarchy is ultimately dependent on force. Mastery over nature is reproduced within humanity. (P. 110)

The use of power in determining which needs are met at the expense of others is one factor which affects these tensions. Horkheimer and Adorno further argue that there is a tendency for stakeholders who have needs conflicting from those of the dominant coalition to have a tendency towards acceptance of the dominant view, as any articulation of those differences will lead towards coincidence; any irreconcilable needs will fail to be articulated. They state:

> Anyone who resists can only survive by fitting in. Once his particular brand of deviation from the norm has been noted by the industry, he belongs to it as does the land-reformer to capitalism. Realistic dissidence is the trademark of anyone who has a new idea in business. In the public voice of modern society accusations are seldom audible: if they are, the perceptive can already detect signs that the dissident will soon be reconciled. The more measurable the gap between chorus and leaders, the more certainly there is room at the top for everybody who demonstrates his superiority by well planned originality. (Ibid., p. 132)

This argues for a dynamic approach to identifying and meeting stakeholder needs and suggests that the ways in which needs are articulated determine the success of them being met. These needs will of course be reflected not in the way value is created by the firm but rather in the way it is distributed. Equally the structure of the organisation affects the tensions existing as does the extent of consensus or conflict. The evaluation system derives from the organisational structure and culture but at the same time shapes the culture of an organisation. This is perhaps reflected in the differences between the overt organisational structure and the covert structure, which is based upon the respective power of the various interest groups. The greater the divergence between the two, the greater the likelihood of tensions existing and the greater the likelihood of these tensions being unarticulated. This approach seems to provide a means of understanding the existence of tensions resulting from incompatible needs and must be considered along with more overt recognition.

One approach to the resolution of such tensions, however, is to separate their sources. Thus one objective of performance reporting is to separate the existing tensions through the creation of the dialectic. This is achieved through the representations of these two potentially conflicting priorities of performance as different and unrelated, with one (the shareholder) predominating, and this is one of the underlying assumptions of the techniques of VBM.

It has been argued earlier in this chapter that a clearer articulation of the needs of performance evaluation will not only facilitate a more meaningful evaluation of performance for all interested parties but will also lead to better performance for the organisation. This is not just because such an articulation of needs can be argued to lead to a reduction in tension within the organisational framework but also because it enables more clearly the identification of the factors which shape performance as far as meeting the objectives of the organisation is concerned, and the techniques of VBM are designed for this purpose. It is further argued, however, that successful performance, in whatever terms deemed appropriate, is not just more likely to be achieved in this manner but also is more likely to be sustainable and so shape long-term performance rather than the short-term performance of the organisation. The factors shaping performance in the long and short term are not necessarily the same and the viewpoint and time horizon of the organisation are therefore important to its approach to measurement and evaluation. An examination of this time horizon and its relationship both to the organisation's evaluation systems and its performance, both projected and actualised, is important therefore to an understanding of the operating of the organisation.

It has been proposed, using empirical evidence (Davis et al., 1992), that the financial measures used by multinational companies can lead to short-term decision making and risk-minimising behaviour rather than perfor-mance-optimising behaviour. It can therefore be argued that the measures used by an organisation depend upon the time horizon of that organisation and that short- and long-term horizons are not necessarily compatible. Conversely, it can be argued that the time horizon of the organisation is dependent upon the measures adopted for evaluating performance. This interaction will be dependent upon the power of the various stakeholders, both perceived and actual, and upon the composition of the dominant coalition and their purposes. The way in which these interactions affect performance and cause tensions within the stakeholder community need investigating and one approach is to investigate the strategic planning function and the timescales used both for planning operations and for investment appraisal. This will provide a surrogate measure leading to an understanding of the time horizons adopted within the organisation.

In the long term a successful organisation will adapt and change and will grow whereas an unsuccessful organisation will contract or even cease to exist. Historical tracking of performance can therefore be correlated with evaluation systems to help understand their interrelationship. Predictions for the future based upon the present and recent past, however, have a much lower degree of accuracy.

ACCOUNTING AND OTHER MEASUREMENTS

Traditionally performance has been measured in accounting terms, using the annual report as the reporting mechanism for external reporting and management accounting reports for internal reporting. To some extent this has been determined by legal requirements and to some extent by the easily quantifiable nature of accounting information. It has been increasingly argued, however, that accounting information does not provide a full picture of the performance of an organisation, and does not necessarily even provide an accurate picture for those areas in which it does report performance. One problem with accounting is that it lends itself to comparative analysis and has tended to be used for control purposes to track performance against budget. The purpose of doing so is to highlight problem areas for corrective action rather than to highlight areas of significance. Therefore its use has been essentially defensive rather than strategic. This use has been highlighted by Drucker (1985), who argues that strategic opportunities for organisational benefit are missed because accounting information is used defensively.

This illustrates that the evaluation of performance is dependent not just upon the perspective of those evaluating performance but also upon the measurement and reporting system. It also illustrates the danger of accepting the presentation of accounting information as truth, rather than as one representation. The increasing dissatisfaction with accounting as the sole means of measuring performance has led to the use of other measures in addition to accounting measures. They include qualitative measures as well as quantitative measures. The development of new measures of performance has largely therefore, in recent times, taken place outside the arena of accounting and has reflected the increasing concerns of both organisations and society with such issues as quality and environmental impact. There is a need, however, to view accounting measures, other quantitative measures and qualitative measures not as separate systems for measuring performance but as parts of an integrated system, and attention has turned to this.

At the same time the means by which an organisation has reported upon performance have undergone considerable change and the extent of disclosure of performance has changed from an emphasis upon minimisation to an emphasis upon maximisation. This is reflected in changes to corporate reports but also in the publication of environmental impact reports, the increasing use of press releases and general informative publicity. This arguably reflects a change from an ownership reporting stance to one of a stakeholder stance. This reflects a changing perception of the purpose of reporting performance, which at least in part has been driven by changes in the power relationships between the different stakeholders. More specifically it is argued that the extension of measures of performance tends to provide a means, through the use of such measures, for managers to shape the interpretation of performance in the way they desire, and thereby to obscure other possible interpretations of performance. This facility is enhanced when the discourse considers the measurement of performance to be a complex process.

THE SEMIOLOGY OF STAKEHOLDER PERFORMANCE MEASUREMENT

Although the discourse concerning the dialectic between stakeholder value management and shareholder value management is extensive and diverse, the semiology (i.e. the study of the signs and images created within the discourse) of such value management reporting necessitates a polarisation and the representation of one pole as the good with the other pole as the bad. Indeed the discourse of VBM automatically represents the shareholder pole as dominant through its use of terms such as 'shareholder value management', thereby creating the semiotic that the management of value for this group of stakeholders is all that is important. This has been represented in this chapter as a polarisation between the two aspects of performance and the creation of the dialectic.

The acceptance of a stakeholder approach to organisations and the existence of multiple perspectives upon the objectives of an organisation inevitably implies a rejection of such a monistic view of organisations. Thus there can be no one single view of the objectives of the organisation and consequently no one single evaluation of the performance of that organisation. It is therefore inevitable that if monism is rejected as a view of organisations then this implies that the economic rationality view of organisations and their behaviour must also be rejected. Economic rationality presupposes that organisations, and the people within those organisations, behave in a rational manner in terms of maximising utility, and the underlying assumption of such rationality is that the organisation is attempting to maximise utility for its owners, or shareholders. Under economic rationality this utility is presumed to be synonymous with wealth, perhaps because such wealth can be quantified in accounting terms and can thereby become subject to mathematical analysis. It is also assumed unquestioningly in the discourse of economic rationality that what benefits the shareholders of a business will also benefit the other stakeholders to the organisation as well as society at large. Thus the monistic viewpoint of economic rationality is based upon a stance within the discourse of modernity and accepts the philosophy of classical liberal economics. Indeed this view also accepts the tenets of classical liberalism in general.

Classical liberal philosophy places an emphasis upon rationality and reason, with society being an artificial creation resulting from an aggregation of individual self-interest, with organisations being an inevitable result of such aggregations for business purposes. Thus Locke (1689) viewed societies as existing in order to protect innate natural private rights while Bentham (1789) and J.S. Mill (1863) emphasised the pursuit of human need. Of paramount importance to all was the freedom of the individual to pursue his own ends, with a tacit assumption that maximising individual benefits would lead to the maximisation of organisational benefits and also societal benefits. In other words, societal benefits can be determined by a simple summation of all individual benefits. Classical liberal economic theory extended this view of society to the treatment of organisations as entities in their own right with the freedom to pursue their own ends. Such theory requires little restriction of organisational activity because of the assumption that the market, when completely free from regulation, will act as a mediating mechanism which will ensure that by and large the interests of all stakeholders of the organisation will be attended to by the need to meet these free-market requirements. This view resulted in a dilemma in reconciling collective needs with individual freedom. Tocqueville (1840), however, reconciled these aims by suggesting that government institutions, as regulating agencies, were both inevitable and necessary in order to allow freedom to individuals and to protect those freedoms. These utilitarian arguments can be extended into the present and are manifest in the discourse of VBM, through an assumption that any conflicts will be mediated through the operation of market forces.

Classical liberal arguments, however, recognise a limitation in the freedom of an organisation to follow its own ends without any form of regulation. Similarly, Fukuyama (1992) argues that liberalism is not in itself sufficient for continuity and that traditional organisations have a tendency to atomise in the pursuance of the ends of the individuals who have aggregated for the purpose for which the organisation was formed to fulfil. He argues that liberal economic principles provide no support for the traditional concept of an organisation as a community of common interest which is only sustainable if individuals within that community give up some of their rights to the community as an entity and accept a certain degree of intolerance. On the other hand, Fukuyama considers the triumph of liberal democracy as the final state of history, citing evidence of the break-up of the Eastern bloc as symbolising the triumph of classical liberalism.

Criticisms of the classical liberalism paradigm are essentially criticisms of modernity itself, while criticisms of the economic rationality necessitate a rejection of the view of an organisation as an entity which exists to serve the ends of its owners. In many respects the rejection of the two paradigms is inevitable when a multidimensional view of an organisation is adopted. This is recognised by Mouffe (1993), who argues that any study of organisations needs to include the political aspects of the operating of that organisation and to recognise the tensions inherent within the political processes caused by the antagonism within the power relationships of the various stakeholders, each vying to have their own agendas met. Equally J. Gray (1995) argues that the liberalism paradigm is self-defeating in its legitimation through rationality and that a pluralistic paradigm provides a better understanding of the operations of organisations within society at large. Thus, inevitably the measurement and evaluation of the performance of an organisation needs to be pluralistic also, because the different perspectives on organisational performance lead to the different purposes for which that performance is evaluated and the different time frames within which that evaluation takes place.

A further paradigm which is prevalent at present as a means of providing an interpretation of society at large and the functioning of the individual constituents of that society is founded in postmodernist theory. This theory provides a different interpretation of the functioning of organisations, of their constituent parts (i.e. the various stakeholders) and of their relationship to each other and to society at large. Indeed postmodernism not only provides a different means of interpretation but also provides a different framework, in terms of the identification of the society in which an organisation is operating, upon which that interpretation is predicated. Such an alternative interpretation can have significant consequences for an organisation in terms of its operational structures and consequently in terms of its systems for measuring and evaluating performance. These differing interpretations will also inevitably lead to different mechanisms for reporting that performance and to different structures for the reporting systems adopted.

THE IMPLICATIONS OF POSTMODERNITY

In order to consider the nature of the changed interpretation of organisational performance, and the consequent reporting of that performance, under a postmodern analysis it is first necessary to consider the nature of postmodernity itself. Postmodernism has a relatively long history and draws upon a variety of strands (Anderson, 1998). It has been defined in a number of different manners: for example as being epochal (Collins, 1989), in replacing modernity as the current time frame; or epistemological (Newton, 1996), in its relativity to other interpretations of social structures; or as a negation of modernity itself (Featherstone, 1988). The concept of postmodernity was first mentioned by Olson in 1951 (Anderson, 1998), who defined it as post-industrial and post-West. The term was brought more into public awareness by Lyotard (1984), who questioned the use of modernist metanarratives which legitimate society as existing for the good of its members with the consequent presumption that the whole unites the parts as an expression of the common good. Thus the metanarrative of economic rationality legitimates both the existence of organisations and the liberal approach which assumes that the free market provides a mediating mechanism which ensures that the freedom of organisations to pursue their own ends will inevitably become synonymous with that freedom leading to optimal benefit for both the owners of that organisation and for the other stakeholders to that organisation. On the other hand, Jameson (1991, 1998) viewed the postmodern as epochally late capitalist, marking a break with previous social forms.

A multitude of aspects exist to postmodernism but in this chapter it is the collapse of the metanarrative, as applied to organisations, which is considered in detail. This collapse of the metanarrative calls into question the existence of the organisation, as discrete from its environment, and questions therefore the maintenance of the organisational boundary, and thereby the value of VBM techniques as a way of deciding upon and operationalising organisational strategy. Furthermore, it calls into question the definitions of internal and external aspects of the organisation, its operations and its reporting as well as the polarisation of perspectives into those of share-holders and stakeholders. The reinstatement of this organisational discrete-ness through the reinstatement of its boundary, is essential to managers in order to maintain the shareholder versus stakeholder dialectic.

The collapse of the metanarrative and the consequent weakening of the macroculture of society are accompanied by the rise of an increasingly robust set of subcultures. These subcultures are operating both at a local level geographically and at a local level in terms of common interest and identity even when geographically disparate. One conclusion to be drawn from this is that, rather than universal politics, the dominance of local or regional politics becomes paramount. Thus the dominance of community as the agent of local need, as manifest by the place of people within that community and operating at a local level as an integral part of each community, assumes priority as the expression of societal organisation. This applies to organisations, as micro-societies, just as it does to society at large. Consequently, organisational and societal structures are needed which recognise this change.

A postmodernist stance therefore leads to a redefinition of locality and divorces it from spatial proximity. Indeed Harvey (1990) argues that one of the significant features of the postmodern era is the compression of space and time, brought about through developments in the technological and informational architecture of society. This compression of space and time has the effect of removing territorial boundaries from an organisation, and this has the effect of providing an opportunity for the redefinition of the concept of organisation in terms of organising local societal structures for the provision of local goods and services. The implication of this is that organisational structures need no longer be dictated solely by the need for transaction cost minimising models of service provision, and it becomes possible to define organisations for the provision of individual goods and services. Equally the question of value creation allows for multiple perspectives.

This redefinition of organisations contains within itself one of the inherent contradictions of a postmodernist view of the world, namely the contradiction between the borderlessness of any organisation within the communities within which it is seen to be operating and the extreme nationalistic inclusion/ exclusion criterion adopted for any performance evaluation and reporting systems. This criterion has the effect of polarising organisations away from an organisaional focus in their operating and reporting structures as the boundary collapses in significance, and to expand the concept to inclusion in an expanded state for some purposes while shrinking the concept of locality of operations to a local level for other purposes (Radhakrishnan, 1994). Thus postmodernity suggests that different spaces are needed for different histories and purposes and that a dominant model of the organisation has no rational meaning. When considering the question of organisations and the identity of the constituents of such an organisation, and their relationship with the macroculture and with societal structure, this suggests that the local structure has dominant importance to the individual and that their sense of community is defined circumstantially. Thus an individual considers themself to be a stakeholder to an organisation as a community for a particular purpose, and a stakeholder of other different organisational communities for different purposes, with this identity being defined in terms of commonality of interest for specific purposes rather than being an overriding part of a definition of self.

This redefinition of the relationship between self, as an organisational stakeholder for a particular purpose, and community is in perfect accord with the concept of liberal democratic pluralism which requires a separation of social spheres in order to maximise individual welfare (Du Gay, 1994). The pluralistic view of liberal democracy is not, however, extant in the economic rationality paradigm (and thereby in VBM) of societal and organisational functioning, which is predicated entirely within a monistic view of society. This definition of the relationship is, however, in perfect accordance with the concept of communitarianism (Fox and Miller, 1995), which regards the self as atomistic and aiming to maximise value (in the liberal sense of welfare) to the lonely self through acting in a community for any specific purpose.

A postmodernist view of organisations and their behaviour is that they are sustained by the rules governing their existence and by the resource appropriation mechanisms which apply to them rather than by any real need from the people who they purport to serve. Thus the legitimation of their very existence is not founded upon this redefinition of organisational identity and community need. Rather this redefinition of community suggests that a very different type of organisational structure is needed, and indeed exists, in order to cater for the needs of the individual constituents of that organisation who aggregate for one common purpose while atomising (or aggregating with different individuals) for others. Such a structure of organisations has been defined by Heckscher (1994) as a post-bureaucratic structure with its rationale for continuing existence not being through self-referential normalising mechanisms but rather through the maintenance of an interactive dialogue, based upon consensus, with the individual members of the stakeholder community which the organisation exists to serve. This view of organisational structure can be extended to also exclude a territorial basis for existence (Nohria and Berkley, 1994) whereby the organisation, through the use of informational and communicational technology, need be little more than a virtual organisation existing in a virtual environment as the need arises. Thus the continuing existence, either temporally or geographically, of any organisation, as a unit of service provision, has no meaning in its own right, as the organisation has no purpose other than the provision of the functions mandated to it by the stakeholder community, in its widest definition, which it serves. This redefinition of the organisation contains within it an implicit requirement for the redefinition of performance.

Such an instrumental view of organisations and their constituent parts would be radically different from existing paradigms and interpretations but this would be fully consistent with any postmodernist definition, based within the concept of the revised stakeholder community. It would be fully consistent with a classical liberal concept of societal structure and civilisation, provided this is based upon pluralism rather than monism. In this respect it is worth recognising that this view of societal progress is not a new concept from postmodernist theory; B. Kidd (1902, p. 8) argued that the controlling centre of evolutionary progress is in the future when he stated, 'It is the meaning, not the relation of the present to the past, but of the relation of the present to the future, to which all other meanings are subordinate'.

Such a view of historical development is in accordance with scientific rationality as well as with postmodernity insofar as it is matched by Popper's (1945) concept of the poverty of historicism by which he argues that present trends do not necessarily continue into the future and that any amount of empirical evidence and economic or sociological analysis does not change this lack of predictive power of past data.

Postmodern analysis of society and its organs is therefore fully coincidental with these views. Indeed Baudrillard (1988) claims that there is a need to break with all forms of enlightened conceptual critiques and that truth in the postmodern era is obsolete. In terms of any measurement and evaluation of organisational performance, this would suggest that the meaning of any reported performance becomes whatever it is interpreted to mean. This interpretation will depend upon the perspective of the person performing that interpretation, and the purpose for which that interpretation is undertaken. This naturally places a heavy emphasis upon the interpretative ability of the receiver of the reported information as well as presupposing that this receiver understands the language of the reporting system sufficiently well to be able to extract meaning from this information. Thus the semiotic of organisational reporting becomes central to the understanding of performance from the perspective of the reader of the corporate reporting script, when acting as an individual. It is clear therefore that, in seeking to interpret organisational performance from the multiple perspectives previously identified, there is a need to consider an organisation's performance-reporting structure from a postmodernist standpoint separately from that of the prevailing dominant hegemony. This requires a reconsideration of the purpose of an organisation within the context of this redefinition of community identity from a stakeholder perspective.

THE IMPLICATIONS FOR ORGANISATIONAL PERFORMANCE

The acceptance of such a postmodernist paradigm of organisational structure and functioning will therefore lead to a radically different interpretation of the

key determinants of organisational performance as well as a different significance being attached to these determinants for the purpose of the
evaluation of performance. Such interpretations do not, however, coexist
easily with the dominant paradigms, i.e. monism and pluralism, previously
considered. Rather than accepting postmodernism as a fresh paradigm, however, it is possible to use postmodernism simply as a means of questioning the
dominant discourse and providing fresh insights into the interpretations from
this discourse. This possibility is itself accepted from within the discourse of
postmodernity and indeed Derrida (1978) claims that this is inevitable as it is
only possible to criticise the existing institutions of any paradigm from within
the interpretative domain of that paradigm. Thus it is necessary to accept the
discourse of one of the dominant paradigms in order to provide a postmodernist interpretation of the events within that paradigm.

The argument of Derrida (1978) provides both the motivation and the
means to integrate the measures of performance necessary to the successful
operating of an organisation in this postmodern environment with the
requirements of the organisation as a whole, as manifest in the need for
traditional accounting reporting of performance. Rather than seeking to
develop two independent evaluation and reporting structures — postmodern
measures at an operational level and traditional measures at an organisational
level — it is desirable to integrate these two reporting structures into one
structure that meets all needs. This can be achieved through the extended
use of local measures to become manifest in the organisational reporting mechanism, thereby recognising that the continued existence of the
organisational boundary, deemed irrelevant to any postmodernist analysis,
is a crucial feature of any modernist interpretation of the organisational
environment. Thus one of the strengths of the techniques of VBM is the
extended use of measures which enable this integration to take place.

Probably one of the few constants in the business-related literature today is
the issue of change, and how it is manifest and affecting business organisations generally. The effects this has on traditional approaches to performance
are well documented (Howell and Soucy, 1988; P.T. Kidd, 1994; Wisner and
Fawcett, 1991). Another observable phenomenon is how this subject spans
the management disciplines; from personnel to finance, from operations to
marketing, all cannot fail to be touched in some way by this issue of change.
The clearest indication of this change phenomenon, and of the importance of
time, can be found in the imperatives that many customers are placing upon
business organisations. Whereas 20 years ago the emphasis might have been
on cost, and 10 years ago on quality, today the emphasis has swung decidedly
toward time-based issues. Stalk and Hout (1990) provide a temporal analysis
of strategy through these concepts arriving at a contemporary supposition
that time is now paramount as the competitive factor in business.

More significantly the collapse of the organisational boundary and
the displacement of temporality as a continuum would suggest that the

measurement of performance from a shareholder perspective and from a stakeholder perspective are not incompatible. Moreover, it would also imply that these two modes of performance measurement are not seeking to measure different aspects of performance and that the reporting of such performance is not seeking to address two different parts of a dialectic. Nevertheless, in the semiotic of reporting, these two aspects of performance are distinctly separated and the reporting script seeks to set the two in binary opposition to each other in terms of a separation into shareholders and investors, and other stakeholders. This can be seen from an exploration of the dialectic in terms of this binary opposition.

BINARY OPPOSITION: SHAREHOLDER VERSUS STAKEHOLDER

Accounting information is naturally used by the organisation for the internal purposes of planning, control and decision making as well as for financial reporting. Thus accounting has long been acknowledged to exist at two levels as far as an organisation is concerned, and these two levels can be broadly categorised as management accounting and financial accounting. Management accounting is essentially for internal consumption and is concerned with the internal operations of the business, with the planning and control of these operations, and with making decisions regarding the allocation of resources within the organisation. The information sources of management accounting permeate the organisation and managers throughout the organisation are concerned with the use of management accounting information. The primary focus of this information is at the level of processes within the organisation and the relationship between these individual processes and departments with each other. It is also concerned with interactions within the value chain of the organisation and so with the relationships between the various processes within the organisation and their suppliers and customers. These suppliers and customers may be other processes or departments within the organisation but may also be entities external to the organisation. Management accounting is essentially forward-looking in its concerns and can be taken to provide a representation of the organisation through representations of its individual components, without any need for a meta-representation of the organisation as a whole.

Financial accounting, on the other hand, is essentially for external consumption. It is concerned with reporting the activities of the organisation to the external world through the production of profitability statements and of annual accounts and balance sheets which are incorporated into the corporate reports, and also with the acquisition of resources from this external world in the form of borrowings and share capital. This is achieved by taking the accounting data from the organisation and structuring it to represent the activity of the organisation as a whole. It is essentially backward-looking through its emphasis upon reporting the past activities of the organisation, and is concerned with the organisation as a whole rather than the individual constituent processes within the organisation. The implicit view of the organisation, derived from using financial accounting, is that the organisation as a whole is greater than the sum of its parts and that the organisation, as represented through financial reporting, provides a metanarrative of the organisation of greater significance than the narratives obtained from the individual processes within the organisation.

In a modernist interpretation of accounting, therefore, financial accounting is superordinate to management accounting through its ability to represent the significant features of organisational performance via its external reporting function. This actuality is supported by Johnson and Kaplan's (1987) claim that the purpose of management accounting has been lost in the need to provide external financial reporting of organisational activity. Thus, as far as this binary opposition is concerned, the external consumption pole has assumed dominance and the internal consumption pole has been relegated to a secondary position. Indeed it is possible to argue that this pair of binary opposites are in fact treated as good–bad as far as the dominant coalition of managers determining the course of action of the organisation are concerned. This assumption of the dominance of external reporting, in the form of financial accounting, over internal reporting, in the form of management accounting, can be questioned from a postmodern perspective. So too can the assumption of the ability of accounting information to provide a meaningful metanarrative of the organisation, uniting the organisation through this metanarrative.

The techniques of VBM, however, recognise the imperfections of traditional accounting for performance measurement and for decision-making purposes and supplement them with a consideration of other factors such as risk. In doing so they seek to incorporate both the short-term and the long-term aspects of performance as well as creating an implicit assumption that the needs of all stakeholders are incorporated into the analysis. Given that the long-term survival of an organisation depends upon the satisfying of all stakeholder expectations, this becomes a reasonable claim but one which is implicit rather than one which can be empirically validated. Thus the semiotic of the discourse assumes paramouncy for legitimation purposes for the technique, and the shareholder versus stakeholder dialectic can be assumed to be negated.

ACCOUNTING AND THE SOCIAL CONSTRUCTION OF ORGANISATIONS

A continual reassessment of accounting in use provides a dialogue which recognises the limitations of accounting in general and fosters discussion about the way in which accounting can become more relevant to business needs. This leads to suggestions for new types of accounting such as a stakeholder approach (R. Gray et al., 1987) or a critical theory approach (Laughlin, 1987), to suggestions for new techniques such as social accounting (Fetyko, 1975) or the balanced scorecard (Kaplan and Norton, 1992, 1993), and to criticisms of techniques employed such as brand accounting (Smith, 1992). However, by its very nature and founding principles, accounting is conservative in its operation and in how it accounts for the activities of a business. It is also conservative in the pace of change to meet the perceived needs of business, this change being driven by pressure from its conservative practitioners rather than by a changing legislative framework reflecting societal needs (Lee and Parker, 1979).

The traditional use of accounting in business does, however, change over time and the function of management accounting has changed so much that Johnson and Kaplan (1987) state it is no longer relevant to managerial needs. Here is what they say about management accounting systems: 'Their original purpose of providing information to facilitate cost control and performance measurement in hierarchical organisations has been transformed to one of compiling costs for periodic financial statements' (Ibid., p. 254).

Nevertheless, accounting provides the basis for organisations to plan their operations, to measure the way in which the plan is implemented and to report upon that performance. Such reporting has an external dimension to it as far as external stakeholders are concerned but also an internal dimension (Crowther, 1996). This internal dimension is concerned with the use to which accounting data is put by the managers of the business and the way in which the data is used to make decisions for the future planning of the business. Thus accounting information is used at the same time for internal consumption, by the managers of the organisation, and for external consumption by other stakeholders, and this is inevitably reflected in the evaluation of performance. This remains true even when the traditional accounting information is supplemented through the use of the techniques of VBM.

CONCLUSION

This chapter has sought to demonstrate that in an environment of multiple interpretations there is no single interpretation of performance. Moreover, the continued existence of an organisation in a temporal framework necessitates that all stakeholders must be satisfied in the long term and this makes the dialectic a false dialectic within the temporal framework. Nevertheless, it can be seen that the dialectic exists spatially in the present but as a construction of the discourse and is therefore more apparent than real. The existence of the dialectic in this manner serves to obfuscate the central problem in value management, which is not to decide on whose behalf a firm need be managed in the creation of value but rather to address the problem of the distribution of value between the various stakeholders.

While it is clear that the techniques of VBM add to the repertoire of organisational decision-making techniques, and have merit for this alone, the claim that the use of VBM techniques leads to the creation of value for an organisation remains less clear. It has been argued in this chapter that the question of value creation depends upon the perspective of the person undertaking that evaluation. Rather the techniques of VBM, through the creation of a semiotic concerning the creation of shareholder value, actually serve to mask the central problem surrounding value, namely that of distribution. In doing so, it is argued in this chapter, the techniques provide a legitimation for redistributing that value while claiming that it is value created for shareholders. Thus it has been argued that the techniques have some merit but may not provide that panacea claimed by their proponents.

REFERENCES

Adorno, T.W. (1973) *The Jargon of Authenticity*. Routledge & Kegan Paul, London. Translated by K. Tarnowski and F. Will.

Anderson, P. (1998) *The Origins of Postmodernity*. Verso, London.

Baudrillard, J. (1988) In *Jean Baudrillard: Selected Writings* (ed. M. Poster). Polity Press, Cambridge.

Beaver, W. (1989) *Financial Reporting: An Accounting Revolution*. Prentice Hall, Englewood Cliffs NJ.

Bentham, J. (1789) *An Introduction to the Principles of Morals and Legislation*. Many editions.

Birnbeg, J.G. (1980) The role of accounting in financial disclosure. *Accounting, Organisations and Society*, **5**(1), 71–80.

Carey, A. and Sancto, J. (1998) Thinking outside the box. In *Performance Measurement in the Digital Age* (eds A. Carey and J. Sancto). ICAEW, London, pp. 6–9.

Cherns, A.B. (1978) Alienation and accountancy. *Accounting, Organisations and Society*, **3**(2), 105–14.

Child, J. (1984) *Organisation: A Guide to Problems and Practice*. Harper & Row, London.

Coates, J.B., Davies, M.L., Davis, E.W., Zafar, A. and Zwirlein, T. (1995) Adopting performance measures that count: changing to a shareholder value focus. Aston Business School Research Paper RP9510.

Collins, M. (1989) *Post-Modern Design*. Academy Editions, London.

Crowther, D., Cooper, S. and Carter, C. (1999) Appeasing Quetzalcoatl: accounting for ritual sacrifice. Paper presented at the Critical Perspectives on Accounting Conference, New York, April 1999.

Crowther, D.E.A. (1996) Corporate performance operates in three dimensions. *Managerial Auditing Journal*, **11**(8), 4–13.

Davis, E.W., Coates, J.B., Emmanuel, C.R., Longden, S.G. and Stacey, R.J. (1992) Multinational companies' performance measurement systems: international perspectives. *Management Accounting Research*, **3**, 133–49.

Derrida, J. (1978) *Writing and Difference*. Routledge & Kegan Paul, London.

Drucker, P.F. (1985) *Innovation and Entrepreneurship*. Butterworth-Heinemann, Oxford.

Du Gay, P. (1994) Colossal immodesties and hopeful monsters: pluralism and organisational conduct. *Organization*, **1**(1), 125–48.

Eccles, R.G. (1991) The performance evaluation manifesto. *Harvard Business Review*, **69**(1), 131–37.

Featherstone, M. (1988) In pursuit of the postmodern: an introduction. *Theory, Culture and Society*, **5**(2/3), 195–215.

Fetyko, D.F. (1975) The company social audit. *Management Accounting*, **56**(10), 31.

Fish, S. (1989) *Is there a text in this class? The authority to interpret communities*. Harvard University Press, Cambridge MA.

Fox, C.J. and Miller, H.T. (1995) *Postmodern Public Administration: Towards Discourse*. Sage, London,

Fukuyama, F. (1992) *The End of History and the Last Man*. The Free Press, New York.

Govinderajan, V. and Gupta, A.K. (1985) Linking control systems to business unit strategy: impact on performance. *Accounting, Organisations and Society*, **10**(1), 51–66.

Gray, J. (1995) *Enlightenment's Wake*. Routledge, London.

Gray, R., Owen, D. and Maunders, K. (1987) *Corporate Social Reporting: Accounting and Accountability*. Prentice Hall, London.

Harvey, D. (1990) *The Condition of Postmodernity*. Blackwell, Oxford.

Heckscher, C. (1994) Defining the post-bureaucratic type. In *The Post-Bureaucratic Organisation* (eds C. Heckscher and A. Donnellon). Sage, London, pp. 14–62.

Herremans, I.M., Akathaparn, P. and McInnes, M. (1992) An investigation of corporate social responsibility, reputation and economic performance. *Accounting, Organisations and Society*, **18**(7/8), 587–604.

Horkheimer, M. and Adorno, T.W. (1944) *Dialectic of Enlightenment*. Translated 1972 by J. Cumming. Herder & Herder, New York.

Howell, R.A. and Soucy, S.R. (1988) Management reporting in the new manufacturing environment. *Management Accounting*, February, 22–29.

Jameson, F. (1991) *Postmodernism, or the Cultural Logic of Late Capitalism*. Verso, London.

Jameson, F. (1998) *The Cultural Turn*. Verso, London.

Jensen, M. and Meckling, W. (1976) Theory of the firm: managerial behaviour, agency costs and ownership structure. *Journal of Financial Economics*, October, 305–60.

Johnson, H.T. and Kaplan, R.S. (1987) *Relevance lost: the rise and fall of management accounting*. Harvard Business School Press, Boston MA.

Kaplan, R.S. and Norton, D.P. (1992) The balanced scorecard – measures that drive performance. *Harvard Business Review*, January/February, 71–79.

Kaplan, R.S. and Norton, D.P. (1993) Putting the balanced scorecard to work. *Harvard Business Review*, September/October, 134–47.

Kay, J. (1998) Good business. *Prospect*, March, 25–29.

Kidd, B. (1902) *Principles of Western Civilisation*. Macmillan, London.

Kidd, P.T. (1994) *Agile Manufacturing: Forging New Frontiers*. Addison-Wesley, London.

Kimberley, J., Norling, R. and Weiss, J.A. (1983) Pondering the performance puzzle: effectiveness in interorganisational settings. In *Organisational Theory and Public Practice* (eds R.H. Hall and R.E. Quinn). Sage, Beverly Hills CA, pp. 249–64.

Laclan, E. (1990) *New Reflections on the Revolution of Our Time*. Verso, London.

Laughlin, R.C. (1987) Accounting systems in organisational contexts: a case for critical theory. *Accounting, Organisations and Society*, **12**(5), 479–502.

Lee, T.A. and Parker, R.H. (eds) (1979) *The Evolution of Corporate Financial Reporting*. Thomas Nelson, Sunbury, Middx.

Locke, J. (1689) *Essay Concerning Human Understanding*. Many editions.

Lyotard, J.F. (1984) *The Postmodern Condition*. University of Minneapolis Press, Minneapolis MN. Translated by G. Bennington and B. Massumi.

McDonald, D. and Puxty, A.G. (1979) An inducement–contribution approach to corporate financial reporting. *Accounting, Organisations and Society*, **4**(1/2), 53–65.

Mill, J.S. (1863) *Utilitarianism*. Parker & Sons, London. Many subsequent editions

Mouffe, C. (1993) *The Return of the Political*. Verso, London.

Myners, P. (1998) Improving performance reporting to the market. In *Performance Measurement in the Digital Age* (eds A. Carey and J. Sancto). ICAEW, London, pp. 27–33.

Newton, T. (1996) Postmodernism and action. *Organization*, **3**(1), 7–29.

Nohria, N. and Berkley, J.D. (1994) The virtual organisation. In *The Post-Bureaucratic Organisation* (eds C. Heckscher and A. Donnellon). Sage, London, pp. 108–28.

Popper, K.R. (1945) *The Open Society and Its Enemies*. Routledge & Kegan Paul, London.

Purdy, D.E. (1983) The enterprise theory: an extension. *Journal of Business Finance and Accounting*, **10**(4), 531–41.

Radhakrishnan, R. (1994) Postmodernism and the rest of the work. *Organization*, **1**(2), 305–40.

Rappaport, A. (1986) *Creating Shareholder Value*. Free Press, New York.

Rappaport, A. (1992) CFOs and strategists: forging a common framework. *Harvard Business Review*, May/June, 84–91.

Roslender, R. (1996) Relevance lost and found: critical perspectives on the promise of management accounting. *Critical Perspectives on Accounting*, **7**(5), 533–61.

Smith, T. (1992) *Accounting for Growth*. Century, London.

Stalk, G. and Hout, T.M. (1991) *Competing Against Time*. Free Press, London.

Stewart, G.B. III (1991) *The Quest for Value*. Harper Collins, New York.

Stewart, G.B. III (1994) EVA, fact and fantasy. *Journal of Applied Corporate Finance*, **7**(2), 71–87.

Swieringa, R.J. and Weick, K.E. (1987) Management accounting and action. *Accounting, Organisations and Society*, **12**(3), 293–308.

Tinker, T. (1985) *Paper Prophets: A Social Critique of Accounting*. Holt, Rinehart and Winston, London.

Tocqueville, A. de (1840) *Democracy in America*. Many editions.

Williamson, O.E. (1963) A model of rational managerial behaviour. In *A Behavioural Theory of the Firm* (eds R.M. Cyert and J.G. March). Prentice Hall, Englewood Cliffs NJ.

Wisner, J.D. and Fawcett, S.E. (1991) Linking firm strategy to operating decisions through performance measurement. *Production and Inventory Management Journal*, Third Quarter, 1–18.

Part III

APPLYING VALUE-BASED MANAGEMENT

7 The Cost of Capital and Shareholder Value

JANETTE RUTTERFORD

INTRODUCTION

The rise in popularity of EVA (economic value added) as an organisational performance measure has forced attention on one of its constituent elements – the cost of capital. The use of EVA is designed to enhance shareholder value, by making managers concentrate on earning more than the cost of capital in each and every division. As a result, it has become vital to make accurate measurements of the cost of capital for input into the EVA measure and other value-based metrics.

This chapter describes how firms calculate and apply the cost of capital in practice, based on in-depth interviews with 18 FTSE 100 companies, and explores how that cost of capital is used in investment decisions, performance measurement and executive pay. It concludes that, although cost of capital calculations are typically quite rigorous in terms of methods used, and consistency across firms in assumptions, the cost of capital adjustments made at divisional level are as yet too simplistic for performance measurement via EVA and other popular value-based metrics to provide meaningful results.

Economic value added (EVA) has been shown (O'Hanlon and Peasnell, 1998) to be a modern-day variant of the concept of economic or residual income (RI) put forward by such authors as Preinreich (1938) and Edwards and Bell (1961). EVA is an attempt to take a theoretically pure cash flow based measure of value added for the firm and turn it into an accounting-based measure of practical use to managers. However, in contrast to usual accounting measures, both RI and EVA measure income *after* deducting a charge for the use of financial capital to arrive at what could be considered as 'excess' income or positive net present value (NPV). The charge for financial capital is calculated as the cost of capital expressed as a percentage multiplied by the monetary value of capital employed in the business. Residual income can be estimated at the enterprise level, by considering operating income before payment of interest, or at the shareholder level, after payment of interest to debtholders. EVA measures value added at the enterprise level only. As a result, the cost of capital used in EVA estimation is the weighted average of the cost of debt and of the cost of equity, known as the weighted average cost of capital (WACC).

Stern Stewart, the main promoters of EVA, and other consultants with similar models, have strongly recommended the introduction of economic income type performance measures within organisations – whether in absolute money terms, such as EVA, or in ratio terms, such as CFROI (cash flow return on investment). In the CFROI model, the firm should earn a CFROI greater than the cost of capital. It is the IRR to EVA's NPV. The Stern Stewart approach encourages firms to concentrate on adding value for investors after allowing for the cost of capital. League tables of firms measured by EVA now appear on a regular basis in such newspapers as the UK's *Sunday Times* and finance directors of firms which do badly on such measures have felt obliged to reply publicly to such criticisms; see the *Financial Times* article by the finance director of Williams Holdings (11 November 1996).

There are a number of ways in which the use of EVA as a key performance measure can be criticised. First, the definition of EVA as net operating profit after tax (NOPAT) minus the cost of capital times capital employed requires the use of an accounting measure of income (NOPAT) instead of after-tax cash flow and of a book measure of capital employed instead of market value. This means that EVA is in practice an accounting surrogate for the more theoretically correct residual income expressed in terms of cash flows. However, in order to approximate residual income as closely as possible, Stern Stewart do suggest up to 164 accounting adjustments to book estimates of NOPAT and capital employed (Stern et al., 1995). Second, the focus on an *annual* measure of performance such as EVA can lead to sub-optimal behaviour on the part of managers, for example underinvestment in growth activities. Stern Stewart counter this by recommending management compensation plans linked to several years of EVA performance. Third, there are practical difficulties in implementing EVA measures of performance at the divisional level; the apportionment of capital employed may prove complex and the issue of transfer pricing between divisions may make EVA measures misleading (Zimmerman, 1997). Finally, there is the issue of the cost of capital itself. Paul Marsh of the London Business School has been quoted as saying that estimating the cost of capital 'is not a precise science' (*Financial Times*, 11 November, 1996) and Rene Stultz, in a keynote address to the 1995 European Financial Management Conference, admitted that 'most of what we know about the cost of capital is rather shaky'. And yet, estimates of positive and negative EVA, deemed to add or – more worryingly – to destroy value are dependent upon estimates of the cost of capital.

This chapter explores how accurately firms estimate their cost of capital in practice, based on an in-depth survey of 18 FTSE 100 firms into cost of capital estimates as reported in Gregory and Rutterford (1999). In each set of interviews with firms, I explored whether managers were theoretically correct in their methods and data inputs and whether they adjusted appropriately for divisional risk differences. I also explored how cost of capital estimates were adjusted over time, to take account of interest rate and inflation changes. I found that there is general consensus in how to estimate the cost of equity (using the capital asset pricing model) and the overall cost of capital (using the weighted average cost of capital) although the preferred method is not theoretically optimal and the data inputs were not always defensible. I also found that although there was general agreement among the firms on certain inputs, there were major differences between estimates of the equity risk premium and the choice of appropriate debt/equity ratio which made the WACC estimate a subjective one.

The WACC estimates were on the whole quite low compared to previous studies, with a mean nominal value of 11.7% and a standard deviation of 1.2%, and a mean real value of 8.8% and a standard deviation of 1.3%. (This 3.5% inflation rate assumption was consistent with the firm's forecasts, when explicit, which varied between 3% and 4.8%.) This compares for example with a mean real discount rate of 12.2% for 228 Fortune 1000 firms in the US (Poterba and Summers, 1995) and a real average hurdle rate for 438 UK manufacturing firms of 16% (Junakar, 1994).

However, the lower average WACC reported by Gregory and Rutterford (1999) is partially explained by the fact that their sample firms adjusted the WACC upwards by an average 0.93% to obtain a base hurdle rate for project appraisal. There is no theoretical rationale for this upward adjustment and managers referred to an adjustment for 'risk' or to cover unprofitable projects. It would therefore appear that firms are likely to be underinvesting in the sense that they may be rejecting some projects which have a positive NPV using the WACC but not the hurdle rate as discount rate, in particular longer-term projects (Poterba and Summers, 1995). Also, those projects which are chosen will have relatively high NPV using the WACC as discount rate and thus should lead to high levels of positive EVA.

The survey also found that five of the 18 firms referred to one or more variants of shareholder value, of which three were specifically using or looking at EVA approaches to performance measurement. However, none of the 18 firms had explicitly introduced the concept of a WACC or equity required rate of return into the board compensation schemes. The nearest equivalent was to reward senior executives on total shareholder return (TSR) achieved or TSR relative to peer group performance rather than relative to the cost of equity. Indeed, many of the sample firms were still rewarding senior managers on earnings per share.

ESTIMATING THE COST OF CAPITAL

The survey carried out by Gregory and Rutterford was a series of in-depth interviews with 18 FTSE 100 companies from a range of sectors, as shown in Table 7.1.

Table 7.1. Eighteen FTSE 100 companies
were chosen from a range of sectors

Company	Sector
A	Banking
B	Regulated utility
C	Leisure and tourism
D	Engineering
E	Materials
F	Chemicals
G	Oil
H	Food producers
I	Pharmaceuticals
J	Engineering
K	Brewing, pubs and restaurants
L	Chemicals
M	Retailing
N	Media
O	Regulated utility
P	Pharmaceuticals
Q	Regulated utility
R	Brewing, pubs and restaurants

Initially, the top 50 FTSE 100 firms by market capitalisation were approached. As this did not give a large enough sample, the remaining 50 by market capitalisation were also contacted. This resulted in a final sample size of 18 companies. The people interviewed were either finance directors or heads of corporate finance, accompanied where necessary by technical experts. Interviews were supplemented with confidential company information on detailed calculations of the cost of capital and related material. Interviews were carried out during 1996.

It is worth noting that all 18 firms chose to estimate their weighted average cost of capital. The WACC is the appropriate cost of capital for firm-level EVA in the sense that the firm is viewed as having a pool of long-term capital and being required to add value to that pool, whether provided by the debt or equity holders. This is also the appropriate cost of capital for project appraisal purposes provided that the project mirrors the firm in terms of risk and leverage. However, for divisional use, WACC estimates should be adjusted for differential risk for both EVA and project appraisal purposes; how firms allowed for this by making certain adjustments is discussed later in the chapter.

The rather restrictive assumptions underlying the use of the WACC as the best estimate of the cost of capital have been well documented (Brealey and

Myers, 1996) and include the static nature of the model as well as the use of perpetuities in order to derive the formula

$$WACC = K_d(1 - T)D/(D + E) + K_e E/(D + E)$$

where
K_d = the cost of debt
K_e = the cost of equity
T = the corporate tax rate
D = the market value of debt
E = the market value of equity

Thus, in order to estimate the WACC, managers need to estimate three things:

- Cost of equity K_e
- Cost of debt $K_d(1 - T)$
- Debt/equity ratio $D/(D + E)$

We shall look at each of them in turn.

COST OF EQUITY

Bruner et al. (1996), in a survey of US companies, financial advisers, and finance textbooks came out in favour of the capital asset pricing model (CAPM) as the 'dominant' method of estimating the cost of equity K_e. Bruner et al. (1996) surveyed 27 'highly regarded' corporations, 10 leading financial advisers and 7 finance textbooks to establish best practice. There was general agreement on using the capital asset pricing model (CAPM) as the basis for estimating the cost of equity, on using the after-tax marginal cost of debt, and on using the weighted average cost of capital with market values for debt and equity, in order to estimate the weighted average cost of capital.

However, in recent years there has been some criticism of the CAPM as an accurate estimator of the cost of equity, partly due to flaws in the testability of the model (Roll, 1977) and partly due to possible underspecification. Fama and French (1992) first suggested that a three-factor model which included price to book and price earnings factors in addition to a market factor significantly outperformed the more simply specified single-factor CAPM model in terms of explaining US equity returns. For example, they have recently shown that estimates of equity returns using their three-factor model have shown differences of up to 300 basis points with conventional CAPM estimates (Fama and French, 1997). There is also UK evidence (Strong and Xu, 1997) in support of the poor relationship between the CAPM and equity returns.

Perhaps as a result of the theoretical difficulties surrounding the CAPM, it appears that 'the practice of using the CAPM varies considerably today in the financial community. Though the model itself is widely used, and the betas are drawn from published sources, important differences exist in how the CAPM is implemented' (Bruner et al., 1996, p. 10).

In my survey, I found that 14 of the 18 companies interviewed used the CAPM, despite its flaws, to estimate the cost of equity, with none of the 18 using a more complex approach such as the Fama and French three-factor model. Five firms used the dividend discount model (DDM) of dividend yield plus estimated growth rate, and four firms used the historic real rate of return on equity. Five of the 18 firms used more than one method to estimate K_e.

The components of the cost of equity expected from the CAPM are the risk-free rate R_f, the equity beta β_e, and the equity risk premium $E(R_m) - R_f$; this is how they are related:

$$E(K_e) = R_f + \beta_e(E(R_m) - R_f)$$

where $E(K_e)$ is the expected return on equity and hence the cost of equity to the firm. We will look at how the sample firms dealt with each of these elements of the CAPM in turn.

Risk-free rate

In terms of the risk-free rate, most firms (12 out of 14 using the CAPM) preferred to use the yield on UK government bonds (choosing a maturity of between 7 and 20 years) with the remainder preferring to use a real rate of interest with an implicit or explicit inflation rate. None of the interviewees used the Treasury bill rate although there is academic support for this approach (Bruner et al., 1996, p. 9).

Beta

We found that the range of betas used by the 18 firms was from 0.7 and 1.34. The betas were either sourced from financial advisers or from databases, the most popular being the London Business School's database. However, most firms looked at more than one source and recognised the difficulties in estimating a true beta, although none made statistical adjustments to allow for this. Some managers noted that their firms' betas had probably changed over time, with one firm having recently adjusted the beta estimate to take account of a major acquisition. Another firm specifically attempted to estimate a forward beta by looking at the beta value implied in option prices. Many interviewees felt that any variation in beta estimates from different sources or assumptions would have less impact on the K_e estimate than would the choice of equity risk premium: 'The other thing is that our Beta is not that far away from the market, so although it is intellectually interesting, this question, it does not produce a huge variation in the number you end up with for your own cost of capital versus that of the market' (Company P; Gregory and Rutterford, 1999, p. 40).

Equity risk premium

There is considerable debate on how to estimate the forecast equity risk premium for input into the cost of equity equation. There are disagreements over whether to use historical averages (and if so, whether to use geometric or arithmetic averages) or forecast estimates based on current equity and risk-free asset prices, and these disagreements can lead to major discrepancies in value. For example, the telecoms regulator, Oftel, and British Telecom had a lengthy and public debate on the appropiate cost of capital for British Telecom, with Oftel arguing for a WACC of 9.2–13.4% and British Telecom arguing for a WACC of 16–18%. One element of disagreement centred around the equity risk premium which Oftel argued should be 4–6% while British Telecom preferred 7.5% (Oftel, 1995; British Telecom, 1996).

In practice, only two firms out of the 13 which estimated an equity risk premium chose what they stated to be the long-run historical average of 7.5%. (They cited the Barclays Bank Equity Gilt Survey, published annually in the UK, which reports equity, gilt and Treasury bill returns from 1918 onwards.) The remaining 11 firms chose a number in the narrow range of 4.5% to 6%. The firms concerned admitted that their estimates were a 'gut feel' choice 'that came from our planning manager. He's an MBA and a lot of his MBA work was on the cost of capital. 5% is a figure he's plucked out of the air based on his experience and knowledge' (Company O; Gregory and Rutterford, 1999, p. 43). Or they had relied on advice from their bankers that the current equity risk premium was lower than at any time in the past. Choosing a lower equity risk premium than historical analysis suggested had the effect of reducing the resulting WACC estimate by almost 2 percentage points in most cases.

COST OF DEBT

Of the 11 firms which explicitly considered the cost of debt $K_d(1 - T)$ in determining a WACC estimate, the managers used a marginal corporate tax rate for T, as recommended in Bruner et al. (1966). This varied between 30% and 33% for 8 of the 11 firms, with one at 37% and the remaining two at 13% due to surplus ACT.

The formula for the WACC derives from a US model which assumes a US corporate tax system. Under this classical tax system, the appropriate cost of debt to use is the after corporate tax rate $K_d(1 - T)$ since debt interest is deductible against corporate taxes. In the UK, until the abolition of the advance corporation tax (ACT) system in 1998, the US model needed some adjustment to allow for the tax credit on dividends available in the UK (Ashton, 1991). However, the application of the adjustment was complex since it is difficult to identify the marginal investor and the tax rate which applies in such models. In practice, only one of the 18 firms interviewed made an ACT adjustment to the cost of debt, the remainder preferring to use the US version of the WACC equation. By using the US rather than the UK version of the WACC equation, managers were able to assume a lower after-tax cost of debt and hence a lower WACC.

In terms of the cost of debt chosen, all companies restricted themselves to consideration of the cost of long-term debt. The majority chose to base the cost of debt on the cost of government debt and either take this as their cost of debt or add a credit risk premium. Three companies preferred to take the yield on their own outstanding bonds and the remainder chose a long-term bond yield based on experience. All but two firms used the gilt yield on the chosen gilt at the time the calculation was made.

There is evidence that one firm realised that shareholder value could be added not just through positive NPV physical investment but also through astute financing: 'We do not put in our real cost of debt. There are certain, for example tax driven, vehicles which give us actually quite a low cost of debt. … So we tend to ignore those. That does build up a nice margin of safety within the target (cost of capital) of course' (Company C; Gregory and Rutterford, 1999, p. 46).

DEBT/EQUITY RATIO

The WACC model assumes market values for debt and equity in the debt/equity ratio. It also assumes a constant debt/equity ratio over time; this is unlikely to be the case in practice as market values move around, even if a particular debt/equity ratio is targeted (Miles and Ezzel, 1980). Of the 15 firms which calculated the WACC as a weighted average of their cost of debt and cost of equity, 10 used a long-run target debt/equity ratio, five used the actual debt/equity ratio and one used both. Of the six firms using an actual figure, two had cash surpluses and estimated the debt/equity ratio at zero. The remaining four used the book value of debt and the market capitalisation of equity and used this estimate of an actual debt/equity ratio in the WACC equation.

In all cases where a target debt/equity ratio $D/(D + E)$ was used, this was taken as 20%, 25% or 30% and was at least as high as the current actual debt/equity ratio, in some cases substantially higher. Indeed, in one case the firm had a cash surplus but chose to use a target debt/equity ratio of 20%. The higher the debt/equity ratio input into the WACC formula, the lower the resulting WACC estimate.

WACC ESTIMATES

Figure 7.1 shows the WACC estimates for the firms in the Gregory and Rutterford survey. For the 18 firms in the Gregory and Rutterford survey, the average nominal WACC was 11.67% with a standard deviation of 1.22% and a mode of 11.70%. The average real WACC was 8.79% with a standard deviation of 1.26% and a mode of 8.00%. Of the 18 companies, ten chose to estimate a nominal WACC, five a real WACC and three both a nominal and a real WACC. Gregory and Rutterford assumed a 3.5% inflation rate to estimate the real or nominal WACC rate when not directly available. (This 3.5% inflation rate was consistent with the explicit inflation forecasts of firms, which varied between 3% and 4.8%.)

When talking to the finance professionals working for the sample firms, what was striking was the amount of consensus on methodology (with the CAPM the preferred model for estimating the cost of equity and the WACC generally accepted for the overall cost of capital). Also, the data inputs for the risk-free rate and the corporate tax rate differed little between firms. Differences in beta estimates reflected differences in actual equity return volatility. However, even with substantial consensus, differences in data inputs for the equity risk premium (from 4% to 7.5%) and the choice of debt/equity ratio (from 0% to 50%) meant that the final WACC estimate was a fairly subjective estimate for each firm.

The WACC results obtained above appear low relative to the results of other surveys. Part of this difference might be due to the timing of the surveys (as different interest rates may have prevailed). However, this seems unlikely as the Gregory and Rutterford survey was carried out in 1996, compared with 1998 for the UK Waites et al. survey, 1995 for the US Poterba and

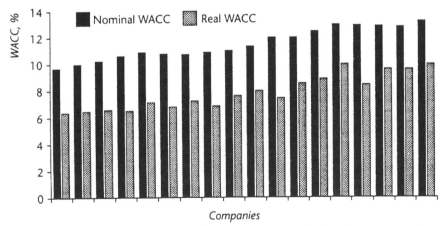

Figure 7.1 Survey companies' WACC estimates. Reproduced with permission from Gregory and Rutterford (1999).

Summers survey and 1996 for the US Bruner *et al.* survey. An alternative explanation could be due to the relative size of the firms interviewed. For example, the Junakar (1994) Bank of England survey covered 438 manufacturing firms of all sizes and the Waites et al. (1998) CBI survey mailed firms with turnover in excess of only £20 million. The Gregory and Rutterford survey covered only very large firms, which may have access to lower cost of debt and equity funding.

APPLYING THE COST OF CAPITAL

HURDLE RATES

However, one noticeable difference between the Gregory and Rutterford survey and other surveys is the fact that it looked specifically at cost of capital estimates whereas the majority of the other surveys looked at typical hurdle rates. In order to allow for this, Gregory and Rutterford also looked at how the WACC estimates of their firms were translated into hurdle rates by the firms concerned.

They found that the average *base* hurdle rate was 0.93% higher than the average WACC. The base hurdle rate is the hurdle rate firms start from when estimating NPVs for standard projects, before any adjustments for divisional differences in operating risk, financial risk or currency risk. The base hurdle rates chosen by the firms in the sample had an average value of 12.60% in nominal terms with a standard deviation of 1.51% (8.93% and 1.58% respectively in real terms). The maximum and minimum base hurdle rates for the sample were 25% and 10% respectively (21% and 6.5% in real terms).

These figures are still low when compared to the results of other surveys. For example, Poterba and Summers' 1995 survey of 228 Fortune 1000 companies revealed an average nominal hurdle rate for 'typical' projects in large divisions of 17.2% for all firms and 16.6% for manufacturing firms. Similarly, the 1998 CBI survey by Waites et al. reported an average hurdle rate of 16% for the firms which estimated in real terms, over half the sample; and 17% for the firms which estimated in nominal terms, over a third of the sample. Junakar (1994) reported an average real hurdle rate of 16% for 438 UK manufacturing firms.

Range of hurdle rates

One key point here is that most of the firms interviewed by Gregory and Rutterford had a range of hurdle rates, depending on project or other risk factors, whereas questionnaire surveys typically require companies to state an average hurdle rate. The case studies conducted by Gregory and Rutterford suggest that simple questions in mailed questionnaires about average rates are masking the richness of the processes actually used to determine individual project hurdle rates.

There was no consensus among the firms interviewed by Gregory and Rutterford on how to adjust for differential project risk. Fourteen of the 18 firms made some adjustment for different levels of risk in projects, with 9 of those 14 making some adjustment for country risk or foreign exchange risk as well as for systematic risk. However, it is worth noting that, for 17 out of 18 cases, the adjustments were made to the base hurdle rate and not to the underlying WACC estimate. In the one exception, a divisional beta and hence divisional cost of equity and WACC were estimated directly rather than by adjusting (upwards) the base case hurdle rate. The driving force for this was the recognition that one major division, property, would have a substantially lower cost of capital than the main activity, retailing, and this was made explicit by the use of separate financing, cost of capital and performance targets for the property division.

For the remaining firms, although a number of adjustments were made to the base case hurdle rate in order to adjust for project or divisional differences, the methodology used was not as sophisticated as for the underlying WACC estimate. The general view was that there was little point in getting too sophisticated in making risk adjustments: 'The comment I make in terms of the hurdle rates for investment purposes is that we do it relatively simplistically in terms of low risk, high risk, country-specific risk' (Company P; Gregory and Rutterford, 1999, p. 53).

For example, adjustments for project systematic risk varied from applying one of two hurdle rates, 15% or 20%, to increasing the base hurdle rate in steps of 2% for a number of different levels of risk. As far as allowing for country risk, this ranged from an ad hoc 5% or 10% extra for projects in Venezuela or Russia to country-by-country adjustments using country risk indicators such as those provided by the Economist Intelligence Unit. The range of hurdle rates varied but 15 firms had premiums of 0% to 8% over the base hurdle rate with the remaining three having maximum hurdle rates 10% or more above the base case. Note that most managers interviewed discussed the concept of project rather than divisional risk, although in practice different hurdle rates were applied to different divisions or different international subsidiaries.

Revision of rates

Given the volatile nature of bond yields during recent years and given that most firms in the Gregory and Rutterford survey used such yields as the source of the risk-free rate estimate, it is interesting to note how frequently the cost of capital and hurdle rate estimates are altered in practice. Of the 18 firms surveyed, one firm revised its cost of capital estimate several times a year, but most chose to do so on an ad hoc basis: 'We revise on an ad hoc basis if we believe the cost of capital has changed. It depends on the scale of the change whether we revise it or not' (Company P; ibid., p. 56).

No explicit mention was made of the impact of changing interest rates and inflation expectations on the cost of capital estimate. About half the sample changed their WACC estimate every three to four years, with four firms never having changed their WACC. However, of the firms investigating the use of shareholder value performance indicators, all were in the process of revisiting their WACC estimates.

The hurdle rates used dated in several cases from much earlier than the WACC estimates and might remain unchanged for years. A typical atttitude was: 'Our weighted average cost of capital in real terms may have declined a percentage point or two but in fact we still stick to a figure for the hurdle rate of around 10 per cent' (Company G; ibid., p. 56).

The discussion of when and how to change the WACC and hurdle rate estimates revealed a high level of pragmatism among finance managers. For those in the process of updating the estimates for input into shareholder value-related performance measures, no decisions had been made on how often to change cost of capital estimates in the future.

EXECUTIVE PAY

The interviews included discussion of how the WACC estimates fed into the financial objectives of the firm; for example, the rate of return required by investors, the mission statement and executive pay.

Five of the 18 firms interviewed referred during interviews to shareholder value. One firm was using consultants to introduce the measurement of cash flow return on investment (CFROI) with divisional and group-wide CFROI targets to be set. The CFROI targets were provided by the consultant and were not the same as the WACC calculated internally. They relied on the long-run return on equity deemed appropriate by the consultants. Within this firm, there was awareness of the role of the cost of capital in adding value for shareholders: 'All the time we are going to the investor's perception of the business ... we are competing against other large companies in the market for capital and that is why we made the change' (Company A; ibid., p. 62).

Another firm had used the idea of total shareholder return (TSR) when evaluating a recent acquisition. The TSR target was a required shareholder rate of return with an implied WACC of 8%. This was not the same as the internally determined WACC (10%) or the internal hurdle rate (12%). The TSR target was also becoming an element in determining executive pay: 'The TSR is now being incorporated into incentives. ... I am one of the people being incentivised by it ... the point being, the TSR target is supposed to put us in the top quartile of the FT-SE 100' (Company A; ibid., p. 62).

Three more firms had come across the concept of economic value added, with one firm already using divisional cost of capital estimates in measuring divisional manager (but not director) performance: 'We fell onto the Stern

Stewart models. We kept falling back to accounting matters. Where we have got to now is just cash' (Company E; ibid., p. 62).

Two firms were moving towards the implementation of EVA-style performance measures. The remaining 13 firms did not use their WACC estimates as inputs into performance measurement along residual income lines, although four firms did link WACC estimates to measures of return on capital employed or return on net assets. However, none of the 18 firms explicitly allowed for the WACC in senior executive compensation schemes. These tended to be linked to share price performance relative to the FTSE 100. Such peer group relative performance measures obviate the need for an explicit estimate of the cost of capital. The remaining firms preferred to stick to earnings-linked incentive schemes. Table 7.2 summarises the performance measurement systems in place in the Gregory and Rutterford survey firms.

CONCLUSION

This chapter has considered the results of a detailed interview survey by Gregory and Rutterford of how 18 FTSE 100 UK firms estimate their weighted average cost of capital (WACC), a vital input into the EVA calculation and other value-based metrics. It was found that the methodology used by firms to estimate the component elements of the WACC, notably the cost of equity, the after-tax cost of debt and the debt/equity ratio, was relatively consistent across firms. However, there were key variations in numerical values for WACCs due to different equity risk premium and debt/equity ratio estimates.

The WACCs estimated by the firms in the Gregory and Rutterford survey were surprisingly low compared to the results of questionnaire surveys. It would appear that firms differentiate between the cost of capital (investigated by Gregory and Rutterford) and the hurdle rate, the topic of the questionnaire surveys. Gregory and Rutterford found that, on average, firms added nearly 1% to the WACC to obtain a base hurdle rate for project appraisal with a range of from 0% to more than 10% on top for additional perceived risks. However, a striking result of the interviews was the contrast between the detailed analysis which went into the cost of capital estimates and the ad hoc nature of the add-ons to determine a set of suitable hurdle rates.

Hurdle rates were also amended less frequently than WACC estimates. Five of the firms interviewed were moving towards some kind of shareholder value analysis and, as a result, they were in the process of re-estimating their WACCs, either themselves or with the help of consultants. However, none of these firms was clear on how often WACC estimates would be changed in the future.

Table 7.2. Summary of performance evaluation measures

Company	Cost of capital used in divisional performance evaluation?	EVA/SVA used in management performance scheme?	Competitors' cost of capital calculated?	Company perceptions of investors' requirements	Comments
A banks retail	Yes. The VBM process shows value created or destroyed by individual value centres	Yes. Some share option entitlement terms are VBM based; others are EPS or RPI	Yes	Total shareholder return (TSR)	Company aim: above average growth in shareholder value over the long term
B	n/a	No	No	TSR	
C	n/a	Indirectly. For example, CEO is remunerated partly on TSR performance with FTSE 100 quartiles	No	TSR	
D	n/a	n/a	Yes	Cash flow growth to match EPS growth	
E	Yes	Yes, but divisional performance is more important	n/a	TSR	
F	Yes	EVA/SVA partly used	Yes	TSR	
G	No	No	No	n/a	
H	No	No	Yes	TSR	
I	Yes	No, but moving towards this	Yes	TSR	
J	No	No	No	EPS	
K	No, but K is considering EVA/SVA	No, but K is considering EVA/SVA	Yes	EPS and DPS	
L	Yes, a form of EVA/SVA	Not currently	Yes	TSR	
M	n/a	Yes, bonus related to economic profit created	Yes	EPS/TSR	
N	n/a	Partly	n/a	TSR	
O	n/a	Not currently	No	EPS/TSR	
P	No	No	No	Long-term EPS/DPS growth	
Q	No	No	No	Dividends	
R	No	Partly	On an ad hoc basis	ROCE	

VBM = value-based management
RPI = retail price index
Source: Gregory and Rutherford (1999), reproduced with permission

The cost of capital is clearly perceived to be a significant number at the firm level, although the range of choice available on data inputs, even when the basic model is accepted, allows for a range of WACCs to be estimated. For example, altering the choice of target debt/equity ratio or equity risk premium can have an impact of 2% or more on the resulting WACC figure. Furthermore, little work has yet been done to extend the complex analysis for the firm's WACC to the divisional level, with ad hoc hurdle rates often out of date and failing to fully take account of operational and financial risk differences. This must affect the efficacy of EVA estimates and other value-based metrics for use in performance measurement or managerial incentive schemes.

ACKNOWLEDGEMENTS

The author would like to thank Professor Alan Gregory of the University of Exeter for working with her on the cost of capital project and to thank CIMA for funding the research behind the project. The project results are reported in Gregory and Rutterford (1999).

REFERENCES

Ashton, D. (1991) Corporate financial policy: American analytics and UK taxation. *Journal of Business Finance and Accounting*, **18**(4), 465–82.

Brealey, R.A. and Myers, S.C. (1996) *Principles of Corporate Finance*, McGraw-Hill, New York.

British Telecom (1996). BT's response to OFTEL's consultative document of December 1995: BT's cost of capital. British Telecommunications plc, February 1996.

Bruner, R.F, Eades, K., Harris, R. and Higgins, R.C. (1996) 'Best practices' in estimating the cost of capital: survey and synthesis. Working Paper DSWP-96-13, Darden Graduate School of Business Administration, University of Virginia.

Edwards, E. and Bell, P. (1961) *The Theory and Measurement of Business Income*. University of California Press, Berkeley CA.

Fama, E.F. and French, K.R. (1992) The cross-section of expected stock returns. *Journal of Finance*, **47**(2), 427–66.

Fama, E.F. and French, K.R. (1997) Industry cost of equity. *Journal of Financial Economics*, **43**, 153–93.

Gregory, A. and Rutterford, J. (1999) The cost of capital in the UK: a comparison of the perceptions of industry and the city. CIMA Monograph, May.

Junakar, S. (1994) Realistic returns: how do manufacturers assess new investment? CBI Economic Situtation Report, July.

Miles, J.A. and Ezzell, J.R. (1980) The weighted average cost of capital, perfect capital markets and project life: a clarification. *Journal of Financial and Quantitative Analysis*, September, 719–30.

Oftel (1995) Pricing of telecommunications services from 1997. Annex E to the consultative document. Office of Telecommunications, December 1995.

O'Hanlon, J. and Peasnell, K. (1998) Wall Street's contribution to management accounting: the Stern Stewart EVA® financial management system. Working paper, University of Lancaster.

Poterba, J.M. and Summers, L.H. (1995) A CEO survey of US companies' time horizons and hurdle rates. *Sloan Management Review*, **37**, 43–52.

Preinreich, G. (1938) Annual study of economic theory: the theory of depreciation. *Econometrica*, July, 219–41.

Roll, R. (1977). A critique of the asset pricing theory's tests. *Journal of Financial Economics*, **4**, 129–76.

Stern, J., Stewart, G. and Chew, D. (1995) The EVA® financial management system. *Journal of Applied Corporate Finance*, Summer, 32–46.

Strong, N. and Xu, X.G. (1997). Explaining the cross-section of UK expected returns. *British Accounting Review*, March, 1–23.

Waites, C., McKelvey, K. and Barker, K. (1998) Target practice: how companies approach their key capital investment decisions. Association of Consulting Actuaries and Confederation of British Industry, July.

Zimmerman, J.L. (1997) EVA and divisional performance measurement: capturing synergies and other issues. *Journal of Applied Corporate Finance*, Summer, 000–000.

8 Value-based Metrics as Divisional Performance Measures

GRAHAM FRANCIS AND CLARE MINCHINGTON

INTRODUCTION

Much heralded in management literature, value-based metrics such as EVA (economic value added) have been promoted as financial measures that can actually determine whether shareholders' wealth is being increased. A substantial part of this literature, however, has been consultant driven. What is unclear is how many companies have implemented such measures, at a divisional level as well as a group level, and how the practical difficulties in their application are being overcome. This chapter provides empirical evidence relating to the nature and extent of the use of value-based metrics at the divisional level in practice. It also considers the range of practical and theoretical problems that an organisation might encounter when adopting an EVA-style measure.

The idea of measuring shareholder value by comparing cash flows generated by a company against the cost of capital in generating those flows first achieved widespread recognition in the work by Alfred Rappaport in the mid 1980s. Rappaport (1986) suggested seven value drivers: sales growth, operating profit margin, tax rate, working capital investment, fixed asset investment, weighted average cost of capital and the competitive advantage period. The theory is that improvement in these value drivers leads directly to an increase in shareholder value. EVA systems share this objective as Ehrbar points out:

> The mandate under an EVA® management system ... is to increase EVA as much as possible in order to maximize shareholder wealth. The arithmetic of EVA shows that companies have only four ways of doing that. (Ehrbar, 1998, p. 134)

In principle Ehrbar (1998) identified four ways of increasing EVA:

(1) Cut costs and reduce taxes to increase profitability on existing capital invested.
(2) Undertake investments earning more than the capital charge.

(3) Pull out of investments earning less than the capital charge.
(4) Structure the company's finances to minimise the capital charge.

Value-based metrics take value drivers and embody them into a single measure, be it EVA, shareholder value analysis (SVA) or a similar value-based measure. However when considering these drivers in a divisional context, which of them, if any, are controllable at the divisional level? Even a basic driver such as revenue may be difficult to control where there is an imperfect or possibly non-existent external market for the division's goods or services.

The desire to reduce performance measurement down to a single metric is not new either at the corporate level in measures such as earnings per share (EPS), or at the divisional level with the widespread use for many years of return on capital employed (ROCE); see Scapens (1979).

STUDIES ON VALUE-BASED METRICS

To date, much of the investigation of value-based metrics has centred on EVA and its correlation to share price (Dodd and Chen, 1996; Lehn and Makhija, 1996). This may tell us about its robustness as an historical measure but less has been written on value-based metrics in terms of their use as internal performance measures at the divisional level and whether they can drive performance improvement at the divisional level. Wallace (1998) undertook a survey of 76 firms in the US using EVA and found that EVA performance measures appear to shift managers' emphasis from bottom-line earnings to earning more than the cost of capital. There have been previous surveys of divisional performance measures (Bhimani, 1993; Drury et al., 1993) but these focused on traditional measures. This is to be expected as the surveys predate the widespread introduction of value-based measures. However, they did look at the use of residual income (RI) which many academics view as the forerunner of measures such as EVA (Emmanuel and Otley, 1976). The balanced scorecard approach advocated by Kaplan and Norton (1992) included only the more traditional financial measures such as profit and ROCE alongside other non-financial indicators.

There have been several studies of value-based measures by consultants such as Coopers and Lybrand (1996) and Deloitte & Touche (1996). These studies found a general lack of awareness of new measures and a relatively low level of adoption. Mills et al. (1996) undertook an investigation into the use of SVA and other techniques in valuing businesses for acquisition or divestment, but they did not explore its use as an internal performance measure. Thus, there is an absence of empirical evidence on the use of value-based metrics in organisations, particularly in relation to their use as divisional performance measures, despite widespread discussion in the literature of this potential application (Rappaport, 1986; Stewart, 1991).

Otley (1998, p. 9) sets out what he calls a performance management framework, one strand of which is EVA. However his paper asks for research to address

new financial performance measures, such as EVA^{TM}. ... How do they link with currently used measures, and how can they be integrated into an overall control system? In what circumstances do they seem appropriate and where do they need to be amended? What are the contextual factors that affect an organization's likely interest in such matters?

The findings reported here and in Spencer and Francis (1998a) seek to address this gap in the literature.

NATURE AND PREVALENCE AT DIVISIONAL LEVEL

To examine the nature and prevalence of value-based performance measures at divisional level, data was collected by means of a large-scale postal questionnaire. The questionnaires were sent to a random sample of members of the Chartered Institute of Management Accountants (CIMA) working in an accounting role in large private sector organisations across the UK. In order to reduce possible bias, and in line with the guidelines suggested by Drury et al. (1993), the questionnaire attempted to accommodate all known practices. It also provided an opportunity for respondents to enter unanticipated practices by means of open-ended qualitative questions as well as more quantitative questions. The questionnaire asked about organisational charateristics, objectives and performance measures in use and being considered for use, which ones were adopted and why. Questions were also asked about divisional autonomy and how cost of capital was established. Respondents' views on value-based measures were also sought.

As far as possible, no theoretical stance was adopted within the questionnaire as to which were the more appropriate responses to the questions. Respondents were not obliged to respond to questions where they were uncertain of the correct answer. This was felt to be a critical feature of the questionnaire design, as a number of the techniques included are new and may have been unfamiliar even to a qualified management accountant. A total of 2331 questionnaires were distributed and 258 have been returned, which represents an unadjusted response rate of 11.1%. All major industry sectors were represented.

OBJECTIVES

The first issue addressed by the questionnaire was the objectives of the division. Traditionally, organisations have focused on profit as their primary

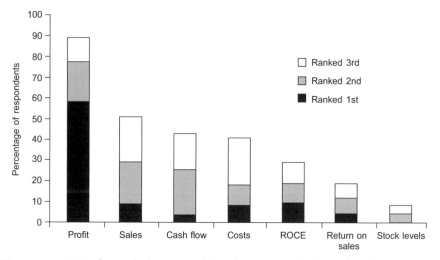

Figure 8.1. Main financial objectives of the divisions, ranked in order of importance

objective and this has been reflected down the organisation in the use of profit-based performance measures such as ROCE and divisional profit targets (Ezzamel, 1992). We would expect any move towards the more value-based metrics such as EVA to be reflected in the increasing importance of cash flow within the objectives of the division (Wallace, 1998). The respondents were asked to rank the financial objectives of their division (Figure 8.1).

Profit dominates not only as the divisional primary objective, but also when looking at the top three objectives. Cash flow came fifth in popularity as the primary objective, but when the top three objectives were considered it rose to third in the ranking. Thus despite academic criticism (Rappaport, 1986; Ezzamel, 1992), profit continues to be the dominant divisional performance target. This contrasts with work by Mills et al. (1996) on the overall corporate financial objectives of companies, where the top three objectives were earnings per share, share price and ROCE. This discrepancy between group and divisional objectives was noted by Deloitte & Touche (1996) in their financial management survey. They identified an emerging phenomenon of companies using shareholder value concepts at group level but deriving objectives for their subsidiaries expressed in more traditional measures.

When asked how the respondents established their divisional objectives, a range of approaches was expressed (Table 8.1). Involvement of the centre ranged from consultation to imposing their objectives on the division. No respondents indicated complete autonomy from the centre in setting financial objectives.

Table 8.1. How do you establish your divisional objectives?

Description given by respondent	Number of respondents
Imposed by the centre	27
Based on central targets	30
Set in consultation with the centre	24
Benchmarked against market/competitors	14
Set compared to prior year performance	4
Set to achieve continuous improvement	7
Implementation of strategic plan via annual budget	47
From annual budget	38

FINANCIAL PERFORMANCE MEASURES

The respondents were asked to specify which measures were being used or considered within their division. Table 8.2 shows the responses for measures with a greater than 5% use. Traditional accounting measures still dominate, with only 10% using EVA at divisional level. The similarities between RI and EVA have been noted and it is interesting to find the low incidence of RI in use (Spencer and Francis, 1998a; Drury et al., 1993) despite its theoretical superiority over ROCE. Like EVA, RI makes a cost of capital charge against the organisation's profit to calculate what value is being generated over and above that required by the investors. However, in the adjustments required to profit and capital figures, RI is much less sophisticated than EVA. Its lack of popularity may be explained by the absence of support by consultants for RI, contrasted with the 'new' value-based metrics such as EVA.

Table 8.2. Major financial performance measures used at divisional level

	Used (%)	Being considered (%)	Not being considered (%)	Not aware of (%)
Ability to stay within budget	99	1	0	0
Balanced scorecard approach	24	21	29	26
Economic value added (EVA)	10	18	46	26
Residual income (RI)	6	2	56	36
Return on capital employed (ROCE)	71	6	18	5
Shareholder value analysis (SVA)	15	13	53	19
Target cash flow	70	7	17	6
Target profit	94	3	2	1
Value drivers	28	18	35	19

The awareness of the new measures was surprisingly low, with 26% being unaware of EVA and a similar percentage being unaware of the balanced scorecard. Perhaps even more concerning for a sample of qualified management accountants was the lack of awareness of an established measure such as RI. This is consistent with the findings by Coopers and Lybrand (1996). In their survey of shareholder value management, they found a similarly low level of awareness of value-based techniques among finance directors of UK PLCs (Spencer and Francis, 1998b).

From the questionnaire, 41 companies (16% of all respondents) were identified who were using certain value-based metrics at group level that were not used at divisional level. Of these, 15 companies were not using or considering *any* form of value-based measure at divisional level. This is consistent with the work of Coopers and Lybrand (1996). They found that despite UK executives' increased awareness of value-based measures and a trend towards communication of group strategy and objectives in shareholder value terms, there is still a reliance on the traditional measures of profit and accounting return within the company itself. We believe that in order to achieve goal congruence throughout the organisation, performance measures must be consistent. If value-based management is being introduced centrally, then some form of value-based measure should be implemented at the divisional level as well.

The financial performance measures being used were cross-tabulated with the divisions' primary objectives (Table 8.3). The expectation was that those divisions with profit objectives would use profit-related performance measures and those with shareholder value-based objectives would use more value-based measures. This was borne out by the results in Table 8.3. EVA was used by 22% of those divisions with sales as a primary objective

Table 8.3. Performance measures cross-tabulated against objectives

	Primary financial objective (%)				
	Sales	ROCE	Profit	Costs	Cash flow
Ability to stay within budget	100	95	97	94	100
Balanced scorecard approach	22	21	21	35	38
Economic value added (EVA)	22	11	6	6	25
Residual income (RI)	0	5	2	6	13
Return on capital employed (ROCE)	67	95	65	41	75
Shareholder value analysis (SVA)	17	11	10	0	13
Target cash flow	56	68	71	29	100
Target profit	94	95	92	76	100
Value drivers	11	26	23	41	50

and 25% with a cash flow primary objective. Only 6% of the divisions with a profit primary objective used EVA. A similar pattern is seen with SVA.

A successful performance measurement system not only needs to link performance measures to the division's objectives, it also needs to motivate the managers within the organisation to work to improve the measures. EVA has been championed as the basis of a remuneration system. Hopwood (1974) described an ideal control system as one where personal goals and organisational goals are congruent due to the presence of a measurement system which is linked to rewards for individual efforts. Therefore we might expect to see performance-related pay (PRP) schemes being tied to the primary measures used to evaluate divisional performance. When asked which, if any, of the measures were linked to a performance-related scheme, 186 respondents representing 72% of the cohort indicated that they operate some form of PRP linked to financial measures.

DEVELOPMENTS IN PERFORMANCE MEASURES

Despite the dominance of traditional profit-based measures, there are indications that new measures are gaining recognition and acceptance. Table 8.4 shows the measures that have been introduced in the past three years or are being considered. This highlights the emergent nature of the new value-based measures as well as the increasing adoption of the balanced scorecard (Kaplan and Norton, 1992). A high percentage of the respondents are also considering the introduction of new measures.

The reasons for introducing new measures, given in response to an open-ended question, varied according to the measure. Justifications for the change to a balanced scorecard were mainly internally focused on gaining a better understanding of the division's overall performance and

Table 8.4. Recently introduced divisional performance measures

Performance measure	Recently introduced (%)	Being considered (%)
Balanced scorecard approach	9	21
Economic value added (EVA)	5	18
Return on capital employed (ROCE)	3	6
Cash flow return on investment (CFROI)	2	8
Economic profit	2	10
Shareholder value analysis (SVA)	2	13
Target cash flow	2	7
Target profit	2	3
Value drivers	1	18

stronger links to the division's strategy. Those implementing EVA tended to be driven by motivators external to the division, such as take-overs, 'response to City analysts' or 'desire to improve shareholder value'. Notably there was no mention of EVA helping to understand the business better.

PROBLEMS AT DIVISIONAL LEVEL

In addition to the possible lack of *awareness* of new measures, there are many difficulties in implementing value-based measures at divisional level. The barriers to implementation include *technical* difficulties such as establishing the cost of capital and capital asset base. There may be organisational barriers such as time, knowledge and resistance to change (Coopers and Lybrand, 1996). We would classify these difficulties as *cultural* and *political* in order to gain acceptance and ownership of the new measures.

These difficulties – awareness, technical, political and cultural – were illustrated by the respondents' general comments on new value-based metrics. The major criticisms addressed at the new value-based metrics were that they were 'too complicated to apply', that 'non-financial managers could not easily understand them' and they were 'possibly a fashionable short-term fad'. Those who were supportive tended to focus on the whole organisation, such as one respondent who wrote, 'EVA is very effective for top management but has limited use for operational management'. The rest of this section will concentrate on the technical difficulties associated with the implementation of value-based measures.

COST OF CAPITAL

Not least among the technical difficulties in calculating a value-based metric is that of establishing a cost of capital. In order to apply them at divisional level, these value-based metrics require calculation of the divisional cost of capital. From our questionnaire only 15% of the respondents calculated their own divisional cost of capital; 72% had their division's cost of capital determined by head office. We then asked respondents how their cost of capital was calculated. A theoretically acceptable approach to calculating a cost of capital for a division would be to calculate a weighted average cost of debt and equity.

The notional cost of equity attached to each division is calculated using the CAPM with a beta reflecting the risk of the division's activities. In this way a different cost of equity is applied to each division to reflect their different activities but the divisional cost of capital reflects the overall funding structure of the group (Emmanuel et al., 1990). Very few companies appeared to be adopting this approach. Of those who responded, 24% used a rate that reflected the cost of debt only, which would underestimate the cost of capital, and 69% did not use a different rate for different divisions to reflect their different levels of risk. These findings are consistent with the work of Mills et al. (1996), who found that 71% of companies used a company-wide rate. The requirement to calculate an accurate divisional cost of capital could be viewed as a barrier to successful implementation of value-based metrics at the divisional level. But it can lead to misleading results if an inaccurate cost of capital is used.

In adopting a performance metric that uses a cost of capital as one of its value drivers, it must be recognised that changes in this driver will result in fluctuations in perceived performance that cannot wholly or justifiably be considered as controllable by the managers of the organisation. This is the same problem that affects RI, and may explain the continued widespread use of less theoretically sound measures such as ROCE. Perhaps value-based measures would be less fashionable in times of high interest rates as more firms would be seen as destroying value, and performance-related bonuses would be significantly reduced or companies would be forced to set low or even negative targets for value added.

CAPITAL EMPLOYED

A related difficulty is establishing a value for the capital employed by the division. The most popular basis used to value fixed assets in divisional capital employed calculations is net book value (Table 8.5). This over-whelming preference for the use of the readily available net book value figure is consistent with the findings of Drury et al. (1993). But according to Stewart (1991), in order to calculate a metric such as EVA, the book value should be converted into economic book value. This includes adjustments for intangible items such as goodwill and R&D expenditure. We found no significant differences in how companies valued their assets and calculated their cost of capital between those using value-based measures and those using more traditional profit-based measures.

Table 8.5. Valuation basis used in determining divisional capital employed

Net book value	87%
Replacement cost	4%
Gross book value	3%
Current value	1%
Other	5%

DIVISIONAL INTERDEPENDENCIES

Zimmerman considered the 'conundrum of disaggregating a divisionalised firm' and the problems of using value-based measures at this level. He concluded:

> A given performance measure's degree of correlation to stock returns should not be management's sole, or even its most important, criterion in choosing to adopt a given performance measure. ... The EVA practice of 'decoupling' performance measures from GAAP while having significant incentive benefits, also has potential costs in the form of increased auditing requirements. (Zimmerman, 1997, p. 109)

There are also the difficulties of capturing the synergies among divisions. Old debates about transfer pricing may need to be revisited in order that it can be seen where within an organisation value is being created. Zimmerman (1997) concludes that 'no divisional performance measure whether it be EVA®, divisional net income or ROA is capable of capturing the synergies among divisions'.

VALUE DRIVERS

A solution to the difficulties in implementing value-based metrics at the divisional level may be to focus instead on the underlying value drivers. The measurement of selected value drivers at the divisional level could be complementary to value-based measures at group level and remove the need to calculate divisional cost of capital. Selected value drivers could be incorporated as part of a balanced scorecard approach. The balanced scorecard approach is growing in popularity, with 9% of respondents recently introducing it into their divisions and another 21% considering its introduction. Of the 41 companies who used different measures at group and divisional level, 14 companies used EVA or SVA at the group level and were using value drivers at the divisional level. We view this and the fact that 18% of our whole sample population are considering the future use of value drivers at the divisional level, as being potentially a positive development in divisional performance management.

CONCLUSION

We have shown empirical evidence of the increasing popularity of new measures at divisional level both in terms of value-based measures and the balanced scorecard. However, traditional accounting measures are still dominant in practice. We have also raised concerns over the lack of awareness of some new measures among qualified management accountants.

We believe that the current low level of adoption is due in part to the problems of implementing these new measures at divisional level. These problems could be classified as awareness, technical, political and cultural. The difficulties associated with the adoption of value-based measures may well be contingent upon organisational circumstances such as objectives, size, autonomy, corporate governance and industrial sector. Despite the difficulties in implementing such measures, we believe that divisions must adopt measures that are consistent with their organisation's overall objectives in order to achieve goal congruence. We accept that organisations having considered the new measures may not wish to adopt them. However, if an organisation is adopting a shareholder value ethos, it is our contention that the use of these new metrics in some form at divisional level is essential to create goal congruence. It is difficult to imagine how the use and reporting of value-based metrics for an organisation at the group level will produce the long-term benefits claimed by consultants if the divisions making up that organisation are not also taking decisions and being assessed against similar value-based measures.

Current value-based metrics are designed more for organisations as a whole rather than as divisional performance measures. Where objectives are stated in terms of shareholder value, then it may be more appropriate to use the underlying value drivers at the divisional level instead of the single-measure value-based metrics such as EVA. This could be within an adapted 'scorecard' framework. We therefore propose that at divisional level, if these measures are to be introduced, they may be introduced most successfully in terms of those value drivers that are consistent with maximising shareholder value for the organisation as a whole.

ACKNOWLEDGEMENTS

The authors would like to thank CIMA, Jackie Fry, Roland Kaye, Janette Rutterford, Matt Hinton, Matt Davies, Jacky Holloway, Eddie Gonsalves and Fiona Harris for their assistance with this project.

REFERENCES

Bhimani, A. (1993) Performance measures in UK manufacturing companies: the state of play. *Management Accounting*, December, 20–22.

Coopers and Lybrand (1996) *Corporate finance: international survey of shareholder value management issues*. Coopers and Lybrand, London.

Deloitte & Touche (1996) *The CIMA and Deloitte & Touche Consulting Group financial management survey: the current state of financial management in UK plc*. Deloitte & Touche Consulting Group, London.

Dodd, J.L. and Chen, S. (1996) *EVA: a new panacea? Business and Economic Review,* July–September, pp. 26–28.

Drury, C., Braund, S., Osbourne, P. and Tayles, M. (1993) A survey of management accounting practices in UK manufacturing companies. ACCA research report.

Ehrbar, A. (1998) *EVA: The Real Key to Creating Wealth.* John Wiley, New York.

Emmanuel, C.R. and Otley, D. (1976) The usefulness of residual income. *Journal of Business Finance and Accounting,* **13**(4), 201–22.

Emmanuel, C.R., Otley, D. and Merchant, K. (1990) *Accounting for Management Control.* Chapman and Hall, London.

Ezzamel, M. (1992) *Business Unit and Divisional Performance Measurement.* Academic Press, London.

Hopwood, A.G. (1974) *Accounting and Human Behaviour.* Prentice Hall, Englewood Cliffs NJ.

Kaplan, R.S. and Norton D.P. (1992) The balanced scorecard – measures that drive performance. *Harvard Business Review,* January/February, 71–79.

Lehn, K. and Makhija, A.K. (1996) EVA and MVA as performance measures and signals for strategic change. *Strategy and Leadership,* May/June, 34–38.

Mills, R., De Bono, J., De Bono, V., Ewers, D., Parker, D. and Print, C. (1996) The use of shareholder value analysis in acquisitions and divestment decisions by large UK companies. Henley Management College Working Paper 9641.

Otley, D. (1998) Performance management and strategy implementation: the role of management accounting in the modern organisation. Paper presented at the Fourth International Management Control Conference, 8 July 1998.

Rappaport, A. (1986) *Creating Shareholder Value.* Free Press, New York.

Scapens, R.W. (1979) Profit measurement in divisionalised companies. *Journal of Business Finance and Accounting,* **6**(3), 281–305.

Spencer, C. and Francis, G.A.J. (1998a) Divisional performance measures: EVA as a proxy for shareholder wealth. *Proceedings of the First International Performance Measurement Theory and Practice Conference,* Cambridge, July 1998.

Spencer, C. and Francis, G.A.J. (1998b) Quantitative skills: do we practice what we preach? *Management Accounting,* **76**(7), 64–65.

Stewart, B. (1991) *The Quest for Value: A Guide for Senior Managers.* Harper Collins, New York.

Wallace, J.S. (1998) EVA financial systems: management perspectives. *Advances in Management Accounting,* **6**, 1–15.

Zimmerman, J.L. (1997) EVA and divisional performance measurement: capturing synergies and other issues. *Journal of Applied Corporate Finance,* **10**(2), 98–109.

9 Behavioural Impediments to Value-based Management

JOHN BYRD, KENT HICKMAN AND RON AZAIR

Properly executed, VBM is an approach to management whereby the company's overall aspirations, analytical techniques, and management processes are all aligned to help the company maximize its value.

Copeland, Koller and Murrin, *Valuation*

'Properly executed' value-based management depends on rationality both within the firm and in the marketplace for the company's shares. Rationality in the market assures that managerial decisions are properly priced, so shareholders receive the value of those decisions. Rationality within the firm assures that managers are making value-enhancing decisions on behalf of shareholders. Additionally, market participants must believe that managers behave rationally in order to attribute value to their decisions. If managers make random decisions, the market cannot assign value at the announcement of a decision. Any wealth effects must wait until the results of the decision are known. For example, when a company known to pursue a strategy of random investments announces increased R&D expenditures the market does not respond. Only after the patents or products derived from that R&D are known would the market be able to assess the value of the investment. On the other hand, an identical announcement by a company known to follow a rational investment policy would generate a stock price response. The response might not completely reflect the value of the decision, but would instead rely on the firm's history of successfully developing products from R&D investments, anticipated market demand for products in this area, and so on. While this response would not be entirely accurate, it would be the best estimate that investors could make given the current information available. As more information emerges, improved estimates nudge price toward the ultimate value of the decision.

Do managers always make rational decisions, and do investors always value managerial decisions accurately? The answer to both questions is no. However, this does not negate the importance of making decisions that enhance the wealth of shareholders. Market participants, rationally acting in their self-interest, will identify companies (and managers) who make better decisions and reflect that superiority in share price. Rational self-interest also motivates investors to make an accurate as possible assessment of share value. Doing so allows them to profitably exploit errors made by other investors. Eventually the ramifications of a decision will be known and its entire value will be embedded in share price. Over the long run, better decisions will generate higher share prices.

Given incomplete information, imperfect models of consumer behaviour, and unknown responses of competitors, can decision making be improved? Yes, even in the face of these obstacles, better decisions can be made. This is not to suggest that individuals can be turned into infallible and prescient computing machines. Mistakes will still be made, and learning takes time. But decision making can be improved by recognising the types of systematic errors that people make. Behavioural economics and the psychology of decision making have articulated a variety of such systematic judgment errors. In this chapter we discuss some of these biases in judgment and how they affect corporate decisions.

OPTIMISM

Optimism (or its cousin hubris) can lead to decisions that reduce shareholder value. Auctions provide the best example of the debilitating effect of optimism. Competitive bidding in an auction setting means that the most optimistic bidder often wins, since the winner must be the person or company that places the highest value on the item. A high valuation may arise because the company has special skills or complementary assets which increase the item's value beyond the value estimated by competitors. Alternatively, a high valuation might arise because the bidder has optimistically valued the asset. The term 'winner's curse' perfectly captures this ironic situation: you get what you want, but only if you pay too much for it.

Studies examining the outcomes of auctions for oil leases find evidence consistent with a winner's curse problem (Thaler, 1988). Obviously, the winning bid must be higher than all other bids for a particular lease. However, if bidders are rational and the bids exhibit only slight differences in estimation or analysis, the winning bid will not be too far from the next highest bid. A study examining the 1969 auction of oil leases in Alaska's North Shore found that the average winning bid was nearly 2.5 times larger than the second highest bid (Capen et al., 1971). There are alternative explanations that support the winning bids as rational: collusion (competitors submit weak bids to assure that a specific bid wins at a reasonable price) or lowballing (some companies submit very low bids hoping there are no rational bids). Such explanations test one's gullibility. Surely, colluding bidders would try to make bids look competitive; and lowball strategies, while occasionally working, could not possibly be the dominant strategy in one of the most important oil-lease auctions of the century. Moreover, if winning bids tended to be too low, government regulators and public interest groups would immediately demand an investigation. More direct evidence of overbidding comes from two studies which examine the actual profits earned from oil leases in the Gulf of Mexico. One study estimates that, on average, companies bid about $200 000 too much for each lease, about 62% of leases were dry so produced no revenue, and that less than 25% of leases were profitable (Mead et al., 1983). The study also estimated that profitable leases only earned an after-tax return of about 19%, hardly enough to offset the lack of any revenue in nearly two-thirds of the leases. A second study of the same lease sales suggests that winning bidders earned profits, on average, but that bids were about 50% above the profit-maximising bid (Hendricks et al., 1987). Similar evidence of overbidding has been found in auctions for the publishing rights to potential bestsellers and in professional baseball's free agency (Dessauer, 1981; Cassin and Douglas, 1980). An interesting sidelight about bidding on oil leases is that after the publication of these articles there appears to have been a change in bidding strategy which caused the high bids for leases to drop (Helfat, 1988).

Richard Roll has applied the winner's curse or overoptimism concept to corporate takeovers (Roll, 1986). He wanted to explain the extant evidence that in takeovers the shareholders of the target firm earned large premiums while the bidder's shareholders earned nothing (and sometimes saw their wealth diminished). He argues that bidding firms analyse many potential targets, but bid only when their valuation of a target exceeds the target's current market price. For such bids to be rational, either market prices must be incorrect or managers must believe they can implement value-enhancing strategies that current management is not pursuing. Hubris or pridefulness arises if individual managers believe that their valuations are superior to the market's or they have superior ability to run the firm compared to the target's current management. Further support for the hubris explanation is that during the two years prior to bidding, the stock of bidders outperformed the market by nearly 15% (Asquith, 1983). Managers may attribute superior performance to their talent, and if so, it is a small step to believing their valuation is better than the market's. Heaton offers a somewhat kinder interpretation of the stock market evidence on takeovers. He argues that individuals' innate optimism explains why bidding firms earn such low returns (Heaton, 1998). Optimism implies that managers will assign positive value to some, but not all, acquisition targets that are in truth bad investments, so the average return to bidders will be low.

Overbidding or optimism occurs across a range of economic situations. In fact, optimism is a well-documented psychological tendency in many arenas of human behaviour (Weinstein, 1980). People assign a higher probability to their experiencing good outcomes than they assign to the population in general, and lower probabilities of bad outcomes. A survey of new entrepreneurs found that one-third were certain they would be successful and over 80% believed their chances of success to be 70% or higher (Cooper et al., 1988). These probabilities were completely independent of known indicators of entrepreneurial success such as education, experience and initial capital. These same individuals thought that other people starting businesses similar to theirs would succeed less than 60% of the time. Interestingly, all of these estimates are high. The estimated five-year survival rate for new firms is about 40% in the US (Ebert and Griffin, 1995). Optimism also pervades capital budgeting revenue and cost forecasts (Statman and Tyebjee, 1985). Costs are regularly understated. Evidence from a variety of industries finds ratios of actual-to-forecast costs ranging from 1.5 to 5.0 (a ratio of 5.0 implies costs were five times higher than forecast). A single study, which examined a large equipment manufacturing firm, found actual costs to be higher than forecasts in over half the cases (Mansfield and Brandenburg, 1966). Sales and profit forecasts were generally too high. Studies comparing actual profits (or net present values) to forecasts reported forecast errors from close to zero (i.e. no bias) to 90% below the forecast amount.

Several other decision biases accentuate or reinforce optimism. People tend to be overconfident about what they do know; that is, research shows that subjects assign a much higher than appropriate confidence level to their estimates or knowledge of a fact (Russo and Schoemaker, 1990; Lichtenstein et al., 1982). This type of overconfidence leads people to make decisions with too little information or cut short the research and investigation stage of a project. In a corporate setting, optimism combined with overconfidence will allow some poor investments to reach fruition and generate losses, when more research (and more objective research, see below) could have identified the investment as a loser. Ford's Edsel and New Coke are examples of products that more research might have saved or prevented (or saved shareholders the costs of development and roll-out). That Ford stopped doing market research on the Edsel two years prior to introduction to maintain secrecy about the car's features, is consistent with this overconfidence interpretation (Hartley, 1987).

Within the corporation, the costly nature of optimism and overconfidence is further aggravated by two other common psychological tendencies: people tend to seek out or acknowledge evidence that confirms their opinions; and optimism or overconfidence increases the more committed a person is to a particular outcome. Confirmation bias arises from the more general psychological phenomenon of cognitive dissonance. Research shows that people often become uncomfortable when presented with evidence that their basic beliefs or assumptions are wrong. The theory of cognitive dissonance suggests that people take actions to reduce this dissonance, such as avoiding new information, discrediting contradictory information, or developing contorted arguments that support their original beliefs or assumptions.

Confirmation bias applies this theory to decision making. If a manager is predisposed toward a particular decision or investment, they may only search for information that confirms that outcome and fail to consider evidence that supports alternatives or rejects their choice (Wason and Johnson-Laird, 1972; Mynatt et al., 1977; Kydd and Aucoin-Drew, 1983; Skov and Sherman, 1986). This 'selective perception' bias can also manifest itself as only remembering or acknowledging confirming evidence or devising interpretations of evidence that supports their original preference. For example, people who have just purchased a new car assiduously avoid reading advertisements for the car models they did not choose, while seeking out information on the car they bought (Erlich et al., 1957). As we discuss below, the unwillingness to accept that a decision may have been wrong or sub-optimal can affect decision making in other ways than just through confirmation bias.

Commitment to an outcome or project increases optimism about its attributes (Weinstein, 1980). Overconfidence or excessive certainty about a proposed project's profitability reduces the motivation to study the proposal thoroughly. Reduced motivation to ask hard questions about a proposed investment, combined with the other optimism-related behavioural tendencies described above, sets the stage for poor decisions. It is easy to imagine some corporate decisions (e.g. investments in new products, facilities, or programmes) suffering from optimism and commitment problems. When divisions must compete for limited investment funds, people will be highly committed to their projects. Since most corporate cultures discourage aggressive criticism of competing proposals, managers have a powerful incentive to paint as rosy a picture as possible of their projects. The decision to terminate an unprofitable project or product must often overcome the commitment of people working on the project, despite data about the project's lack of profits. Statman and Caldwell (1987) discuss the behavioural aspects of making a termination decision. They explain that commitment can turn into entrapment, with losing projects being maintained long after any potential for profit has faded.

Optimism, and its attendant behavioural biases, can severely hamper efforts to maximise corporate value. Despite the problems that people have identifying and correcting optimism in their decision processes, there are steps that companies can take to reduce the value-reducing effects of optimism. The common element among these corrective strategies is to instill objectivity into the decision process. Having an outside consultant or internal auditor examine the forecasts, marketing research data, and interpretations from the data, early in the proposal development process can help eliminate some biases. Early detection is important because as a proposal moves along it becomes more difficult to challenge its basic assumptions. Arguments such as 'You should have brought up that objection two months ago when we showed this to you' or 'We have proceeded along these lines because you approved the basic outline months ago' can be quite persuasive, even if wrong. A person with no allegiance to the project should give it a final review. Review and decision responsibilities should be separated from proposal responsibilities; that is, different people should have those assignments. At the highest level of decision making, the board of directors should include enough independent outside directors to provide an objective forum for major projects and evaluation of the value potential of business units, product lines, and so on. A board dominated by managers and their cronies will rarely have the same willingness to ask business colleagues the hard questions that a more independent board has (Byrd and Hickman, 1992). Finally, keeping records of how completed projects met or failed to meet projections can provide a database with which to identify common forecast errors.

DECISION FRAMING AND PROSPECT THEORY

The rational man model underlying much of economic theory carefully follows the standard rules of logic. The actual men and women making decisions at corporations may not. An impressive body of research shows that people reverse their choices if problems are stated in somewhat different terms. How a question is framed (or stated) can shift responders from being risk averse to risk seeking, from choosing A to choosing B in situations offering only two choices. This response to the decision frame occurs not just among college students in psychology experiments, but also among doctors, judges, and other professionals. The following problems are based on the work of Kahneman and Tversky (1979, 1981, 1984):

Problem 1

Your company has just been acquired by a large multinational corporation which has stated it may have to lay off employees at your plant. Your plant currently has 600 employees. As plant manager you may choose one of two strategies:

Plan A   Offer to cut positions in exchange for a guarantee that 200 jobs will remain.

Plan B   Let the decision be made at headquarters, where you believe there will be a 1/3 chance that all 600 jobs will be saved, and a 2/3 chance that no jobs will be saved.

Problem 2

Your company has just been acquired by a large multinational corporation which has stated it may have to lay off employees at your plant. Your plant currently has 600 employees. As plant manager you may choose one of two strategies:

Plan C   Lay off 400 people.

Plan D Let the decision be made at headquarters, where you believe there will be a 1/3 chance that no jobs will be lost, and a 2/3 chance that all 600 jobs will be lost.

Faced with problems like these, the majority of people (usually over 70%) choose plan A in the first problem and plan D in the second. Selecting plan A over plan B shows risk-averse behaviour; the certain outcome is better than the equivalent (in terms of expected value) risky alternative. In the second problem, the reverse occurs. Risky plan D is preferred over the equivalent certain outcome of plan C. Framing the problem as saving 200 of 600 jobs with certainty elicits a different response than framing it as losing 400 of 600 jobs with certainty, though they are identical outcomes. Kahneman and Tversky (1981, p. 453) explain these inconsistent choices as due to framing and 'contradictory attitudes toward risks involving gains and losses'. Framing choices in terms of gains regularly brings forth risk-averse behavior, while framing choices as losses (which cannot be avoided by taking risks) elicits risk-seeking behavior.

A number of the inconsistencies attributed to framing would vanish if people treated gains and losses similarly. Kahneman and Tversky (1979) developed prospect theory (and later, cumulative prospect theory) to explain this inconsistent behaviour. Prospect theory begins with the standard economic assumption that people have a decreasing marginal utility of wealth; that is, a person receives much more satisfaction (utility in economic terms) moving from \$10 000 to \$12 000 than from \$100 000 to \$102 000. This implies that the value a person places on a certain \$800 gain is more than 80% of the value they place on a \$1000 gain (the last \$200 has less value than any of the previous \$200 increments). This also implies that the value a person will choose a certain \$800 gain over a bet with an 80% chance of winning \$1000 and a 20% chance of winning nothing, though both have identical expected values. Kahneman and Tversky found that people also exhibit decreasing marginal utility for losses. Shifting from \$200 to \$100 (i.e. losing \$100) is more traumatic than shifting from \$2100 to \$2000. They also found that losses evoke a greater response than gains of similar magnitude. They call this attribute 'loss aversion'. Loss aversion arises, in part, from seeing problems in terms of only gains and losses rather than as changes in total wealth.

The psychological research on framing has typically looked at a fairly narrow set of decisions: comparing uncertain outcomes with stated probabilities or comparing a certain outcome to a risky outcome with similar expected value. However, the framing concept can be applied much more broadly. This broader definition of decision framing argues that good solutions cannot emerge from poorly or incorrectly framed problems. The way a problem is framed defines the range of options that will be considered, how those options will be evaluated, and how success will be judged. Here are some examples that help illustrate the importance of framing.

Apple's iMac personal computer is colourful, compact and fairly powerful. It is also the best-selling personal computer in history, and may have rescued Apple from a tragic future. The iMac appeals especially to young people, for whom computers are part of their furnishings and a centre of some social activity (Web surfing), and to neophytes who rely on ease of set-up and use to break into computing. Although we don't know for sure, we suspect that to develop the iMac, Apple must have changed its decision frame from the industry standard (more powerful computing at lower cost) to a vision that included ideas such as decoration, entertainment, and easy Internet access. Would this significant shift have occurred if Apple had not been in serious financial condition? 'If the iMac succeeds we will earn X' versus 'If we don't do this there is a $Z\%$ probability of bankruptcy or being acquired'.

Semiconductor chip manufacturing has changed dramatically in the 1990s. An industry that once could command price premiums, now produces chips that are effectively commodities. Shifting from an economic environment of tight supply and few competitors to a world where only price matters, and thereby productive efficiency, requires a serious shift in how problems are framed.

Futures and options contracts offer important risk-reducing opportunities. Will such complex strategies be implemented properly? Framing might affect the decision to use such contingent contracts. For example, your company is dependent on a particular commodity which has a moderately volatile price. With futures or options contracts you can lock in a price, but at a cost (insurance is never free). Would you be more inclined to purchase protection if one of your financial analysts posed the choice like this:

(A) We can eliminate all price uncertainty.
(B) We can reduce our total risk by $X\%$.

Most people would prefer the elimination of all risk of a particular type rather than a partial reduction of total risk, though the two could be identical in this case.

We mentioned earlier that people often behave as though a gain or loss was separate from everything else in their lives. That is, they evaluate the gain or loss from a reference point of zero. But this is almost always incorrect. The gain or loss acts as change in total wealth or income, and should be evaluated from that perspective. Here are two examples of how reference points can affect decisions.

Example 1

(A) Your company is negotiating the purchase of a piece of equipment with a base price of about $100 000. You learn that your state has just instituted an investment tax credit (ITC) programme for which the equipment purchase would qualify. The $500 after-tax saving from the ITC requires about two hours of effort to obtain and complete the necessary forms. Would you pursue this saving?

(B) Your company is buying a new computer printer that several people will share. The purchase price of the printer is $1500. You are ready to buy the printer when a colleague tells you that the identical machine is on sale for $1000 at a discounter across town. It will take you about two hours to get new purchase orders approved and travel to the discount electronics store to pick up the printer. Which printer do you buy?

Example 2

Many of us in the US refinanced our home mortgages as interest rates dropped in 1998 and 1999. At the closings there are a variety of relatively small fees that always come as a surprise. For example, $25 to overnight mail or courier the papers somewhere. When we ask if overnight service is necessary, it usually is not. But most of us see the $25 charge as such a small fraction of our mortgage that we do not quibble too much. In many other situations we would never treat giving up $25 for nothing so lightly, but the magnitude of the numbers at the mortgage closing tricks us into not seeing $25 for what it is, $25.

We are so used to thinking in terms of proportions or percentages, that we often lose track of absolute amounts. In Example 1 the two situations are identical: a two-hour investment saves the firm $500. But most people would forgo the saving in option A while collecting the saving offered in B. Their logic is that it is an incredible 33% saving in B but only a 0.5% saving in A. If shareholders were able to express their opinion, they would pursue both opportunities, as long as the employees' time was worth less than $250 per hour. It is important to remember that a 500% gain on a $1000 investment is a lot less than a 10% gain on a $1 million investment. The correct reference point is how much a decision will add to shareholder value, not its percentage return.

That prospect theory and framing emerge from psychological studies suggests that these are innate human behaviours. People naturally respond differently to losses and gains, and automatically create and respond to frames. Because they are powerful psychological phenomena, individuals cannot easily recognise and correct their decision habits. One key to overcoming these pitfalls in judgement is to build multiple perspectives into the decision process. Multiple points of view broaden the frame through which the problem is seen, allowing a richer set of solutions to be considered. Training managers in decision-making techniques and making them aware of these judgement inconsistencies can aid them in addressing these issues. The careful framing of decisions by investing more time in the development and articulation of the problem helps to ensure the analysis that follows is better targeted. Applying many sophisticated analytic tools to an ill-defined problem may sometimes produce an acceptable decision. Applying simpler tools to a well-defined problem will almost certainly produce a decision that is close to correct.

HEURISTICS OR RULES OF THUMB

Rules of thumb or decision heuristics provide people with short cuts through complex problems. Most companies have dozens of standard operating procedures (SOPs) that are followed diligently every day. Many SOPs accelerate repetitive decisions, so save time, and get to the right decision. However, if a rule of thumb is followed too slavishly, without considering if the rule applies to the particular case at hand, it can destroy value.

Example 3

In most companies managers at various levels of responsibility can sign off expenditures up to a certain amount. A group manager might have signing authority for amounts up to $3000, while a plant manager might have a limit of $10 000, and a division manager $50 000. The idea of such a system is to assure that large expenditures are examined by more and more experienced people. For the largest expenditures, the corporate board would be involved. This system also prevents someone who has not put in much time, and thereby not yet earned the trust of corporate leaders, from possibly wasting large amounts of money. The downside of such structures is that if a person at the lowest level sees an opportunity that requires more than they have authority to sign for, the opportunity may be lost before all the approvals are obtained. A rule that protects the company from unwarranted expenditures may also prevent the company from seizing short-lived opportunities.

In an extensive survey of corporate financial executives, Donaldson (1964) discovered they have developed many rules of thumb to help them make decisions about the use of debt:

(1) No long-term debt under any circumstances.
(2) Borrow the maximum available.
(3) Borrow the maximum available at the prime rate.
(4) Borrow the maximum consistent with an A rating.
(5) Limit the principal amount to $x\%$ of total capital.
(6) Use a minimum earnings coverage standard.
(7) Use debt when acquiring a cash flow generating asset (e.g. acquisition) but not for new product development.
(8) Use debt when it can be paid back quickly.

Unlike Donaldson's rules, economic theory pinpoints an optimal mix of debt and equity where the benefits of debt's tax deductibility and its disciplining effects are just offset by the potential costs that financial distress and bankruptcy can impose upon firms utilising too much debt in their capital structure. This optimal mix should be the firm's target capital structure, yet many firms utilise a 'pecking order' approach to raising capital rather than the target structure approach. The pecking order calls for the utilisation of internal equity (retained earnings), followed by debt, and finally the issuance of external equity to meet the firm's capital needs. For example, highly profitable firms' investment needs may be met solely via the use of internal equity. But doing so could overlook the possibility of issuing very low risk debt whose after-tax cost to the firm is well below the return requirements of retained earnings. The pervasiveness of the pecking order approach may be in part attributable to individual's reliance on rules of thumb as a comfortable (but perhaps not optimal) approach to a complex problem.

Another rule of thumb commonly encountered in corporate finance is the use of payback as a method of capital budgeting. The use of net present value in capital budgeting is arguably the bedrock upon which value-based management is built, but payback remains popular despite its well-known shortcomings. This rule of thumb can be traced to business practice prior to the advent of financial calculators that simplified the estimation of NPV and internal rate of return.

MENTAL ACCOUNTING

Classical economics holds that money is fungible. Fungibility implies that money will be spent on its highest-valued use, regardless of its source and whether or not the funds were initially allocated to that particular use. Yet individuals and organisations often behave as if the budgeting of money into accounts establishes sacrosanct barriers between funds which cannot be violated despite the existence of rational economic reasons for moving funds across these mental boundaries.

It is common for families earning 6% interest on children's college education savings accounts to be simultaneously paying 12% interest on their credit card balances. Economic efficiency dictates that the repayment of high-cost debt should take priority over investment at a lower rate of return. Here some funds are allocated to savings and some to debt repayment. Using money earmarked for savings to repay debt would violate the family's system of mental accounts or budgets. Similarly, funds psychologically assigned to the discretionary cash account are treated differently than funds allocated to a specific-purpose account. Consider the use of a cash machine. Many individuals tend to withdraw less than the maximum available cash when using an automated teller machine despite the fact that such a machine may charge a flat rate for the transaction. Again, efficiency would dictate a large withdrawal in order to minimise transaction costs. However, for many people having a pocketful of discretionary cash is too tempting. That is, the propensity to consume for such individuals depends on the source of the cash or whether or not it is allocated to a specific account. Here money moved from a mental 'cash reserves' account to the 'discretionary cash account' leads to greater consumption.

Sometimes being too generous in our mental budgeting can lead to wasteful behaviour. If we assign, say, $50 per day toward discretionary expenditures while we are on vacation, then we may find ourselves making extraordinary purchases that we would normally never consider. But because this mental account has a large unspent balance toward the end of the holiday, we may treat the funds differently than we otherwise would. Ironically, these extraordinary expenditures may occur in spite of a deficit balance in another of our mental accounts (e.g. lodging or meals).

Kahneman and Tversky (1981) illustrate the violation of the fungibility tenet with an interesting experiment. Individuals were told that they were going to see a play and the cost of a ticket was $10. They were then asked if, as they entered the theatre, they discovered that they had lost a $10 bill, would they still pay $10 for a ticket to the performance? Some 88% responded that they would. The problem was then reformulated so that rather than losing a $10 bill, the theatre-goer had lost a ticket to the play worth $10. The question was then asked, would they replace the $10 ticket in order to attend the theatre? Now only 46% said that they would. Classical economics makes no distinction between the two decisions, but people do.

At the business level, budgeting can inhibit value-maximising activity and also encourage wasteful behaviour. Unforeseen opportunities could be missed or delayed if, for example, the capital budget has been exhausted before the new investment project presents itself. Delaying the pursuit of a promising investment while waiting until the next budgeting cycle entails the opportunity costs associated with the time value of money and may lead to the reduction of profitability as competitors enter the market during the period of inactivity. At the other end of the spectrum is the propensity of organisational units to spend all the money in their budgets, whether or not they are wise expenditures. Not doing so, after all, could lead to a smaller budget next year, and like the family on vacation, having excess funds available tends to lead to 'excess' needs.

Too much liquidity, combined with mental accounting and overconfidence, may lead to the agency costs associated with corporate free cash flow described by Michael Jensen (1986). Jensen believes that managers tend to treat excess cash flow from profitable ventures as somehow different than other funds. He claims that internally generated funds are much easier to waste than external funds. Particularly when companies have more funds than profitable projects in which to invest, the tendency to use the money, rather than give it back to shareholders, is quite tempting. Aggravating this situation is the apparent fact that having generated excess cash signals the managers must be above average. This overconfidence can lead to a range of value-reducing decisions. In part, this free cash flow is different in that it has no contractual obligation attached to it as does debt. But the lack of direct monitoring (via covenants) or obligatory payments should not cause managers to treat internally generated cash flows with less respect than debt. Ultimately, free cash flow belongs to shareholders, so management should ask, before spending, 'Will this money be better used within the firm or by shareholders, if it is distributed via dividend or share repurchase?'

To minimise the inefficiencies associated with mental accounting, corporations can take several steps. First, zero-based budgeting can help remove the incentive for spending all of one's departmental budget. Second, reviews by independent third parties or internal auditors can help control excess expenditures associated with free cash flow. A system for funding entrepreneurial initiatives can help ensure that new, promising, and unanticipated projects can be pursued even though they may not 'fit' within the amount budgeted in the appropriate account, or though they may fall outside any account's definition.

Ironically, a form of mental accounting is often adopted to reduce the inefficiencies associated with overoptimism. Capital rationing reduces the monies available for investment, with the intended effect of eliminating the worst project proposals. However, this strategy may create incentives to further inflate already optimistic estimates. Capital rationing seems to be used as a control device when managers can think of no better way to rank projects. To quote H. Bierman Jr (1988), a financial manager: 'Rather than fighting through the assumptions in the numerator to discover the source of overoptimism, management tends to clamp on overall spending guidelines and strategy guidelines'.

STATUS QUO

Inherent in many organisations is a reluctance to change. Change threatens many well-established organisational patterns and relationships. Change also preys on 'loss aversion', the tendency of people to value losses more heavily than equivalent gains (see the earlier discussion of prospect theory). Change means that someone or some group must assume responsibility for choosing a path, and thereby be willing to accept blame if the plan fails. When faced with a changing business environment, an inability or reluctance to change reduces a company's value. Value creation depends on responding to changes in the competitive environment. In fact, the economic dominance of capitalism is based on innovation in productive efficiency and new product development. Unless a company is prepared to innovate, and thereby change, it will be left behind by more agile competitors.

A reluctance to change is not necessarily irrational. Relationships between colleagues develop over time, methods of completing tasks emerge, and links to clients or customers are built. Change can shake or shatter these relationships and procedures. We have some evidence about the importance of maintaining the status quo in both the growth of consulting and changes in corporate control.

One aspect of a consultant's job is being an agent for change. Often consultants are hired not to provide an answer – the company already has the answer – but to act as a catalyst to implement the change implied in the answer. Consultants bring more than technical expertise. They bring objectivity and, possibly most importantly, they provide someone to blame for implementing a change. When relationships shift, the consultant is at fault not a colleague. Having a common enemy helps maintain collegial cohesiveness in the face of change.

Changes in the control of corporations – takeovers and buyouts – are a more extreme reaction to the inability to change. During the 1980s in the US, and in the late 1990s in Europe, there have been 'disciplinary' or 'efficiency-increasing' control changes. Raiders and buyout artists obtained control of a company's assets by offering a substantial bid premium for a company's shares. Once in control, the acquirer sold poorly performing divisions, replaced management teams, and built stronger incentives into the company's financial and compensation structure. All of these changes could have been made by the pre-takeover managers, but they were not. The powerful inertia of the status quo made a control change the only vehicle for implementing needed changes. An outsider has fewer qualms about firing, demoting or transferring an individual or team that does not perform. Where personal ties might have prevented the original managers from making such changes, an outsider (and an outsider who just paid a premium for the company) does not have to (and cannot afford to) worry about relationships. Takeovers and buyouts are seen as evidence that some corporations do not take the necessary steps to remain competitive.

SUNK COSTS

In beginning finance courses we teach that sunk costs do not matter, but it is a lesson that is apparently difficult to learn. There are a myriad of examples of good money being thrown after bad. Always the justification is that the current infusion of funds is needed to 'save' or 'salvage' the original investment. Military procurement and large-scale public works projects provide some of the best examples of this phenomenon. Although Lockheed's L-1011 Tristar jet is an old example of the sunk cost fallacy, it is still one of the best. After spending $1 billion developing the Tristar, Lockheed wanted federal loan guarantees to continue working on the project. Its argument was that the government should provide such relief in order to save the $1 billion already invested (Reinhardt, 1973). The Teton Dam disaster provides another example. The US Bureau of Reclamation builds water projects across the US. Most of its projects up to 1990 involved building dams of various sizes.

Construction on the Teton Dam was continued despite warnings during construction of serious potential engineering problems. Congressional investigations (Thaler, 1991) revealed that, in part, the bureau had a tendency to complete all projects no matter what new information emerged during construction.

Prospect theory helps explain why sunk costs matter to people. Abandoning a project (i.e. evaluating a project without considering sunk costs) means accepting a loss. The S-shaped value curve developed by Kahneman and Tversky shows that losses elicit a large value loss relative to similar-sized gains. If a problem is framed in such a way that sunk costs are viewed as losses, then the sunk cost fallacy will emerge.

HERD BEHAVIOUR

Orleàn (1989) argues that in times of great uncertainty individuals tend to mimic other people's decisions. Not knowing what the future holds, they follow the herd. But following the herd is not harmful. If the herd knows no more than they do, they are no worse off; and if the herd is more knowledgeable, they are better off. Other economists have also recognised that contagion or herd behaviour can affect markets (Banerjee, 1992; Birkchandani et al., 1992; Shiller, 1989).

Herd behaviour has been used to explain many speculative bubbles, such as the tulip mania of the seventeenth century and the South Sea Islands in the eighteenth century. Today a similar phenomenon appears at work with companies trying to do business on the Internet. The logic seems to be: 'Since everyone else is developing an Internet presence we should too'. There is little thought about the profitability of such ventures. As Orleàn suggests, with great uncertainty about where the technology is going, imitation of those firms taking action is a dominant strategy. The ironic aspect of this surge into Internet-based business is that it almost certainly commodifies a company's product, forcing competition solely on price rather than more profitable differentiable dimensions.

OTHER DEPARTURES FROM OPTIMAL DECISION MAKING

In addition to the effects of framing, overconfidence, mental accounting and other cognitive errors discussed here, economists have documented other common behavioural traits that lead to sub-optimal decisions when judged from the perspective of classical economic thought. People tend to avoid behaviour which could lead to regret. Consequently, investors sell stocks after they have gone up and hold onto to stocks after they have declined in spite of sound tax strategies which would reward the opposite actions (Shefrin and Statman, 1985). Similar avoidance of regret may lead firms to hang on to poor projects too long in order to avoid acknowledging that sunk costs will not be recovered. Although most economists agree that a Pareto condition describes a desirable outcome, many parents would argue the point. Consider offering one child a piece of hard candy that cannot be divided but not offering similar candy to a second child. In theory, your generosity makes one child better off without making the second child worse off. Thus, Pareto conditions are met. Yet, you may be faced with an extremely unhappy second child because they may feel unfairly treated and jealous. Before offering an employee-of-the-month bonus or a similar reward which seems to satisfy the tenets of a Pareto condition, a human resource manager must carefully consider whether issues of fairness and jealousy could undermine the well-intentioned attempt to motivate employees.

AGENCY PROBLEMS

Unlike other cognitive errors that rely on less than rational behaviour, some behaviour that adversely affects business management is based on rational self-interest. Agency theory describes how employees, acting as agents of the firm's owners, may maximise their own welfare, a pursuit which at times places them at cross-purposes to the goal of shareholder wealth maximisation. Properly constructed incentive systems can help to align the interests of employees and owners, lowering agency costs (Jensen and Meckling, 1976). Executive stock options and stock appreciation rights are examples of financial methods designed to motivate management to act in the interest of shareholders. Poorly conceived incentives, on the other hand, can have unintended perverse effects. Sears found itself on the losing end of a multi-million dollar lawsuit because employees in the firm's automobile repair shops responded to the company's commission pay system by recommending unneeded repairs to customers (Brickley et al., 1996).

CONCLUSION

Behaviour that contradicts the assumptions of rational self-interest is pervasive and often predictable. Adopting a rich model of human decision making that incorporates these systematic biases and departures from the classical economic model of human action can lead to more effective management as companies pursue the maximisation of firm value. The careful framing of alternatives, well-designed incentive systems, consideration of fairness and regret, enlightened budgeting systems, caution when adopting rules of thumb, and independent review of pet projects are examples of actions that can increase the efficacy of value-based management. Managers and directors need to be aware of the behavioural characteristics that often drive the assumptions, attitudes, responses, and eventually the outcomes and effectiveness of the decisions they make.

REFERENCES

Asquith, P. (1983) Merger bids, uncertainty, and stockholder returns. *Journal of Financial Economics*, **11**, 51–83.

Banerjee, A. (1992) A simple model of herd behavior. *Quarterly Journal of Economics*, **107**(3), 797–818.

Bierman, H. Jr (1988) *Implementing Capital Budgeting Techniques*. Ballinger, Cambridge MA, p. 77.

Bikhchandani, S. Hirshleifer, D. and Welch, I. (1992) A theory of fads, fashion, custom and cultural change as informational cascades. *Journal of Political Economy*, **100**, 992–1026.

Brickley, J., Smith, C. and Zimmerman, J. (1996) *Organizational Architecture*. Irwin, Chicago IL.

Byrd, J. and Hickman, K. (1992) Do outside directors monitor managers? Evidence from tender offer bids. *Journal of Financial Economics*, **32**(2), 195–221.

Capen, E.C., Clapp, R.V. and Campbell, W.M. (1971) Competitive bidding in high-risk situations. *Journal of Petroleum Technology*, **23**, 641–53.

Cassing, J. and Douglas, R.W. (1980) Implications of the auction mechanism in baseball's free agent draft. *Southern Economic Journal*, **47**, 110–21.

Cooper, A., Woo, C. and Dunkelberg, W. (1988) Entrepreneurs perceive chances for success. *Journal of Business Venturing*, **3**, 97–107.

Copeland, T., Koller, T. and Murrin, J. (1995) *Valuation*, 2nd edn. John Wiley, New York.

Dessauer, J.P. (1981) *Book Publishing*. Bowker, New York.

Donaldson, G. (1964) *Corporate Debt Capacity*. Harvard University Press, Boston MA.

Ebert, R. and Griffen, R. (1995) *Business Essentials*. Prentice Hall, Englewood Cliffs NJ, p. 156.

Erlich, D., Guttman, J., Schonbach, P. and Mills, J. (1957) Postdecision exposure to relevant information. *Journal of Abnormal and Social Psychology*, **54**, 98–102.

Hartley, R.F. (1987) *Bullseyes and Blunders*. John Wiley, New York.

Heaton, J.B. (1998) Managerial optimism and corporate finance. Working paper, University of Chicago, April.

Helfat, C. (1988) *Investment Choices in Industry*. MIT Press, Cambridge MA, pp. 121–26.

Hendricks, K., Porter, R. and Boudreau, B. (1987) Information and returns in OCS auctions, 1954–1969. *Journal of Industrial Economics*, **35**(4), 517–42.

Jensen, M. (1986) The agency costs of free cash flow. *American Economic Review*, **76**, 323–29.

Jensen, M. and Meckling, W. (1976) Theory of the firm: managerial behavior, agency costs and ownership structure. *Journal of Financial Economics*, **34**(4), 305–60.

Kahneman, D. and Tversky, A. (1979) Prospect theory: an analysis of decision under risk. *Econometrica*, **47**(2), 263–91.

Kahneman, D. and Tversky, A. (1981) The framing of decisions and the psychology of choice. *Science*, **211**, 453–58.

Kahneman, D. and Tversky, A. (1984) Choices, values and frames. *American Psychologist*, **39**, 341–50.

Kydd, C. and Aucoin-Drew, L. (1983) Strategies for reducing cognitive bias in the design and implementation of decision support systems. *Northeast Decision Sciences Institute Proceedings*, Phildelphia, PA.

Lichtenstein, S., Fischhoff, B. and Phillips, L. (1982) Calibration of probabilities: the state of the art to 1980. In *Judgement under Uncertainty: Heuristics and Biases* (eds D. Kahneman and A. Tversky). Cambridge University Press, Cambridge, pp. 306–34.

Mansfield, E. and Brandenburg, R. (1966) The allocation, characteristics, and outcome of the firm's research and development portfolio: a case study. *Journal of Business*, **39**, 447–64.

Mead, W.J., Moseidjord, A. and Sorenson, P.E. (1983) The rate of return earned by lessees under cash bonus bidding of OCS oil and gas leases. *Energy Journal*, **4**, 37–52.

Mynatt, C., Doherty, M. and Tweney, R. (1977) Confirmational bias in a simulated research environment: an experimental study of scientific inference. *Quarterly Journal of Experimental Psychology*, **29**, 85–95.

Orleàn, F. (1989) Mimetic contagion and speculative bubbles. *Theory and Decision*, **27**, 63–92.

Reinhardt, U. (1973) Breakeven analysis for Lockheed's Tri-Star: an application of financial theory. *Journal of Finance*, **28**(4), 828–38.

Roll, R. (1986) The hubris hypothesis of corporate takeovers. *Journal of Business*, **59**, 197–216.

Russo, J.E. and Schoemaker, P.J. (1990) *Decision Traps*. Simon & Schuster, New York, pp. 70–75.

Shiller, R. (1989) Stock prices and social dynamics. In *Market Volatility* (ed. R. Shiller). MIT Press, Cambridge MA, pp. 7–48.

Shefrin, H. and Statman, M. (1995) The disposition to sell winners too early and ride losers too long. *Journal of Finance*, **XL**(3), 777–90.

Skov, R. and Sherman, S. (1986) Information-gathering processes: diagnosticity, hypothesis-confirmatory strategies, and perceived hypothesis confirmation. *Journal of Experimental Social Psychology*, **22**, 93–121.

Statman, M. and Caldwell, D. (1987) Applying behavioral finance to capital budgeting: project termination. *Financial Management*, **16**(4), 7–15.

Statman, M. and Tyebjee, T. (1985) Optimistic capital budgeting forecasts: an experiment. *Financial Management*, **14**(3), 27–33.

Thaler, R. (1988) The winner's curse. *Journal of Economic Perspectives*, **2**(1), 191–202.

Thaler, R. (1991) Congress Committee on Governmental Operations, Teton Dam Disaster, House Report No. 94-1667, September 23, 1976. Cited in *Quasi Rational Economics*, Russell Sage Foundation, New York, p. 12.

Wason, P. and Johnson-Laird, P. (1972) *Psychology of Reasoning: Stucture and Content*. Harvard University Press, Cambridge MA.

Weinstein, N. (1980) Unrealistic optimism about future life events. *Journal of Personality and Social Psychology*, **39**, 806–20.

10 Lessons from Practice: VBM at Lloyds TSB

INTRODUCTION

Since the emergence of value-based management (VBM) in the 1980s, much has been written about why and how it should be used and the benefits to be derived from doing so. Much less, however, has been written about VBM practice. Whilst examples of the 'successful' use of VBM are often cited by its advocates, such 'evidence' suffers from a potential lack of objectivity. Recent surveys, on the other hand, seem to suggest that VBM is often not applied in the manner prescribed in the literature (KPMG, 1996, 1999). Such surveys tend to interpret this as practitioners merely paying lip service to VBM and failing to understand the full requirements of adopting a 'true VBM' approach. Yet there is a lack of detailed research into the differences between VBM as prescribed and VBM as practised and why these differences arise. In short, little is known about the experiences of companies adopting VBM, what technical and behavioural issues have arisen and how they have been dealt with. Therefore, as has been argued by other writers, including O'Hanlon and Peasnell (1998) in the context of economic value added (EVA), there is a need for detailed independent research into how VBM is used in practice.

As a contribution to filling this gap, this chapter reports the experiences of Lloyds TSB, one of the largest UK companies and widely recognised as a pioneer in the adoption of VBM. The Lloyds TSB experience indicates that implementing VBM can be a difficult, time-consuming and costly process. It also demonstrates that whilst much of the emphasis of the VBM literature concerns its technical features, successful implementation may in practice depend much more upon changing managerial behaviour.

The chapter is organised into four sections. First the existing evidence on VBM in practice is briefly reviewed, and a justification for the case study research design is provided together with details of the method used in this study. Next the application of VBM in Lloyds TSB is described and analysed. The wider lessons which potentially emerge from the Lloyds TSB case are then explored, followed by some concluding comments.

THE NEED FOR CASE STUDIES

RELEVANT LITERATURE

A more detailed consideration of existing literature on VBM in practice can be found in Chapter 3 of this book. Therefore, only a summary of the issues will be presented here.

There is a general lack of empirical research into the use of VBM in practice. Evidence from surveys indicates an increasing number of companies claim to apply VBM (KPMG, 1999; PA Consulting, 1997). Such surveys also indicate, however, that often companies which have adopted VBM continue to emphasise traditional accounting measures such as earnings per share and net profit and do not meet the requirements of being a 'true VBM' company as defined by the proponents of VBM theory (KPMG, 1996, 1999; Coopers and Lybrand, 1997). Such surveys tend to conclude that practice is therefore defective.

There is, however, an alternative interpretation. It is possible that practitioners are fully aware of the VBM theory, but based on their assessment of the benefits and costs involved in its adoption and its relevance to their specific company context, conclude that it is not appropriate, or that modifications are required, or that it is not appropriate yet but will be appropriate in the future.

What is needed, therefore, is evidence on how companies apply VBM, why VBM is applied in the way it is applied, and where it is either not applied or applied in a modified form, what is done instead and for what reasons. It is argued that such evidence will only be gained through a more detailed investigation than that allowed by postal questionnaire surveys, and that the use of the case study research design is therefore essential. Such an approach is vital if we are to gain a better understanding of what doing VBM actually means in practice, what critical issues concerning the design of VBM systems are relevant, and how the use of VBM affects the adopting companies.

THE CASE STUDY APPROACH

A case study has been defined as 'an empirical inquiry that investigates a contemporary phenomenon within its real-life context when the boundaries between phenomena are not clearly evident and in which multiple sources of evidence are used' (Yin, 1994, p. 23). A number of alternative forms of case study are available. Ryan et al. (1992), for example, cite the following: descriptive, illustrative, experimental, exploratory and explanatory. In this context, they can be distilled into two main forms: descriptive case studies and explanatory case studies.

The objective of descriptive case studies is to describe the nature of existing practices. Such studies are argued to be useful in determining the extent of the potential gap between research and practice, particularly in comparison with questionnaire surveys. However, whilst descriptive case studies are often presented as examples of 'best practice', note that a case study alone cannot provide a justification for this assumption.

Explanatory case studies go beyond description and attempt to provide explanations of practice. The focus is upon theory development using an inductive, 'grounded theory' approach (Glaser and Strauss, 1967). The objective of such research is to establish a theory which provides a good explanation of what has been observed in the specific cases studied.

A criticism often levelled against the case study method is that by relying on only a small sample of subjects, the findings of a case study cannot be generalised to a wider population. This, however, ignores the potential contribution that case study research can make, particularly in areas where theory is not well developed (Ryan et al., 1992), as with VBM. A case study provides a vehicle by which theories may be developed to explain the specific circumstances of the individual case. A programme of case study research, on the other hand, will seek to generate a theory capable of explaining what has been observed in all of the cases studied, and therefore we may edge towards principles which are more widely applicable.

In the context of VBM, it is argued that case-based research is particularly relevant. VBM is a relatively new phenomenon, which in line with other recent 'initiatives' such as activity-based costing, business process re-engineering and the balanced business scorecard, have emerged from (consultancy-led) developments in practice, rather than from the work of academic researchers (Bromwich, 1998). It is argued that any meaningful consideration of VBM as a potentially useful 'management approach' must therefore include an examination of how VBM has actually been used and with what effect. Such a view is consistent with Kaplan (1984), who argues that researchers have much to learn from studying the practices of 'innovative companies' and thus advocates much greater emphasis upon field-based research.

In addition, as with any 'new approach', ambiguities arise over terminology. For example, the acronym SVA appears in the VBM literature to describe both shareholder value added and shareholder value analysis. Even the term 'shareholder value added' is open to interpretation. Rappaport (1998) uses the term to describe both the total incremental shareholder value created by a strategy and also to describe the amount of shareholder value created in a particular period. The term is also sometimes used as an alternative name for both residual income and Stern Stewart's market value added. In contrast to postal questionnaire surveys, in-depth case study research provides an opportunity for such ambiguities to be resolved.

Few VBM case studies are currently available. This is perhaps unsurprising given VBM's relatively recent rise to prominence, though it is ironic that of the three most important UK sources, two are somewhat out of date:

- Grundy (1992) reports the experiences of BP.
- Handler (1998) provides accounts of the experiences of BP, Dixons and Lloyds Bank.
- Hennell and Warner (1998) describe the VBM experiences of Unilever, Boots and an anonymous US company.

These studies tend to adopt a more descriptive as opposed to explanatory case study approach, and they also tend to lack detail. There is therefore a need for further explanatory case-based research into the use of VBM in practice.

THE CASE METHOD USED IN THIS STUDY

In the previous section it was argued that a programme of case-based research was required in order to develop theories which can help explain the use of VBM in practice. In response to this the author is currently engaged in a research study which involves an investigation into the use of VBM at more than 20 mainly UK-based companies. This chapter is based on one of these companies, Lloyds TSB, a company which is widely regarded as a champion of the VBM approach. The study offers a detailed description of the particular approach to VBM adopted by the company and an exploratory investigation into the reasons it was chosen. It thus provides an important step towards the development of a more formal explanatory model.

Regarding the specific research method employed in this study, firstly, the case material was gathered mainly via an initial semi-structured interview in 1996 with a senior manager who was directly involved in the design and implementation of the company's VBM system. This was then updated through a number of follow-up discussions over the following three-year period. This material has been supplemented by other publicly available data on the use of VBM within Lloyds Bank and Lloyds TSB.

The interview structure was as follows:

- The origins of VBM
- The process of implementation
- The application of VBM
- The impact of VBM
- Plans for the future of VBM

A summary of the interview notes was reviewed by the interviewee to check for any inaccuracies or misrepresentations. Interviewing a manager who had first-hand knowledge of the system and its conception helped to ensure that a technically competent description of VBM was obtained. It is acknowledged, however, that the interviewee's personal involvement in the implementation could also lead to a degree of personal perceptual bias.

VBM AT LLOYDS TSB

Lloyds TSB is a leading UK-based financial services group whose businesses provide a broad range of banking and financial services in the UK and overseas. The group is comprised of three main areas of business: UK retail financial services (banking, mortgages and insurance and investments), wholesale banking and international banking. Total income and profits after tax for the year ended 31 December 1998 were £7.1 billion and £2.1 billion, respectively. At 31 December 1998 the company employed over 80 000 people and had a total market capitalisation of over £46 billion, making it one of the largest companies in the UK.

As the best-known UK champion of value-based management, the Lloyds TSB experience provides some noteworthy insights into the implementation of VBM in practice. For many years the company has had a very clear and very public commitment to creating value for shareholders, as confirmed by Sir Brian Pitman's chairman's statement in the 1998 annual report: 'Maximising shareholder value – by dividend increases and share price appreciation – remains our governing objective'. But it is not merely upon such words that Lloyds TSB's reputation is founded – the company also has an impressive record in delivering value creation to shareholders. For example, according to a *Management Today* survey (Weighing up the Fat Cats, July 1999) of FTSE 350 companies, for the three-year period between 1996 to 1998, the company achieved a TSR of 215%, which is equivalent to an average annual return of 47%. This was the highest return achieved in the period of any bank, and also compares favourably with the average annual TSR performance (for those companies surveyed) for the period of 26%.

In the following section, the way in which Lloyds TSB translates shareholder value aspirations into practice through the use of VBM is explained and the company's experiences in implementing a VBM system are discussed.

THE ORIGINS OF VBM AT LLOYDS TSB

The history of the use of shareholder value principles within Lloyds TSB can be traced to the time when Sir Brian Pitman became chief executive of Lloyds Bank in 1983. At that time the company's performance, particularly its financial performance, was less than spectacular. Pitman attributed this, in part, to a lack of clarity as to what should be the company's objectives. Therefore, shortly after his appointment, he initiated a fundamental debate at the very highest level of management on the question, What does it mean to be successful? From this debate there emerged a single objective: to double shareholder value every three years.

At this time, return on equity and annual earnings were used as key measures of performance. With the new emphasis on value creation, however, came a realisation that the key measure of performance should not be return on equity per se, but rather return on equity compared with the cost of equity. Once the cost of equity for the company had been established, however, it was found that only some of the company's businesses were achieving the required level of return. This prompted a major review of the Lloyds portfolio. Businesses were ranked according to their potential for value creation and a major acquisition and divestment programme was begun.

Through a strategy of selective market leadership and through the application of net present value for decision making and planning, and return on equity against cost of equity for performance measurement, the performance of Lloyds Bank improved significantly through the 1980s.

There was a further development in 1992 when the company hired the services of the strategy consultants Marakon Associates (McTaggart et al., 1994) and started a more serious and disciplined approach to VBM. It was at this time that the concept of economic profit was introduced to Lloyds managers.

Whilst the use of shareholder value ideas at Lloyds Bank was perhaps more extensive and also perhaps had a higher profile, TSB also subscribed to a shareholder value approach. Since the late 1980s the central strategic planning department had been using VBM concepts for the evaluation of major strategic decisions, portfolio management and for communications with the investment community.

THE IMPLEMENTATION PROCESS

Following the merger in 1995, top management set out to develop a common framework which was to provide the guiding principles for the business and how it was to be managed. Although the guiding principle of shareholder wealth maximisation was agreed at a relatively early stage, the next 12 months were spent translating this into a set of parameters, measures and guidelines. The process involved extensive consultation with senior managers within the company since it was recognised that for the new approach to be successful, it would be vital to gain the support of those managers who would ultimately be required to 'sell' the ideas to their staff.

Before attempts were made to 'drive' the new approach into the business, consideration was given to how the company should be organised. The aim was to create a structure in which there was clear responsibility for value creation, at the level of the business at which it is created. As a result the company was organised into four divisions which represent the main areas of business activity, and these are regarded as value centres. In turn, each value centre is divided into a number of product-market units, which are supported by a distribution channel and a central services function.

THE APPLICATION OF VBM

Lloyds TSB applies the economic profit approach. Discounted economic profit is used for valuation and decision-making purposes and economic profit for performance evaluation. Economic profit was chosen for its perceived high correlation with market value and because it can be used not only as a means of valuing businesses and strategies but also as a measure of performance. The definition of economic profit used is the 'equity' rather than 'total business' version (McTaggart et al., 1994). In other words, from profits after deducting interest and tax, a deduction is made to reflect the cost of equity capital used in the business. The calculation is illustrated in Box 10.1. The company uses economic profit to link its key planning and control processes, from strategy development through to rewarding managerial performance, as described below.

BOX 10.1

Economic profit calculation for year ended 31 December 1998	
	£m
Profit attributable to shareholders	2120
Capital charge	(687)
(Cost of equity 10%, average equity £6865m)	
Economic profit	1433
Workings	
Equity 1 January 1988	6254
Equity 31 December 1989	7475
Average equity	6865
(Source: Lloyds TSB annual report 1998)	

Strategy, planning and budgeting

The process of strategy development and evaluation is considered to be critical to a company's ability to create value for its shareholders. The process of strategy development has therefore been subjected to much consideration and discussion. Although business units are responsible for their own strategy development, the Lloyds TSB group provides guidelines on how strategy should be developed. Units develop their own strategies in conjunction with managers of the relevant distribution and central service activities. These unit plans are then consolidated into an aggregate plan for the value centre. The process undertaken is then subjected to scrutiny by the centre. The strategic planning process consists of five stages:

(1) Position assessment. Business units are required to perform a value-based assessment of the economics of the market in which the business operates, and of the relative competitive position of the business within that market. Market attractiveness and competitive position must include a numerical rather than a purely qualitative assessment.

(2) Generate alternative strategies. Business units are required to develop a number of realistic and viable alternatives.

(3) Evaluate alternative strategies. Business units are required to perform shareholder value calculations in order to prioritise alternatives. Even if a potential strategy has a high positive net present value, this does not necessarily mean that it will be accepted. An assessment of project risk or do-ability is overlaid across the net present value calculations.

(4) Agree chosen strategy with the centre. Whilst it is perceived to be vital that the managers who best understand their business are given sufficient authority to develop strategies which they consider to be most appropriate, it is nevertheless considered equally important that there is a challenge mechanism at the centre to ensure that appropriate analyses have been performed and assumptions made are credible.

(5) The chosen strategy becomes a contract. Once the preferred strategy has been agreed with the centre, resource allocation and milestones are agreed. Budgetary performance targets are derived from the projections included within the strategic plan. Beyond this, however, business unit managers are free to choose whatever structures and performance indicators are considered to be relevant and appropriate.

Performance measurement and reporting

Economic profit is calculated down to individual product market unit level. In 1996, for a transitional period, monthly economic profit figures were calculated centrally but not reported to the unit managers concerned. Unit managers for this period were set economic profit targets but then received the conventional monthly profit and loss account statements. From 1997 onwards, economic profit has been reported monthly down to individual unit level. Beneath this level, line managers are responsible for designing appropriate measures which reflect the key value drivers for their respective businesses.

Technical features

In moving from traditional accounting measures to economic profit, perhaps the most significant additional requirement relates to the charge for employing capital. This in turn requires that both the price and the quantity of capital employed be established for each business. Lloyds TSB derive the corporate cost of equity from a CAPM-based calculation, and currently this is applied across all business units, though there are plans to move to unit-specific costs of equity in due course.

There is an awareness of the potential distortions that the use of a company-wide rate might create, but these are felt to be, in general, not as important as estimating the appropriate equity base for each business. At the time of the merger, there were a number of businesses which, for a variety of reasons, had actual book equity which exceeded what was considered appropriate to run the business. This was an issue that had also arisen within Lloyds, and the same solution was applied.

Rather than penalising managers who had inherited excess equity as a result of capital allocation decisions taken by previous management, imputed equity was used instead. Imputed equity refers to the level of capital required for a business according to regulatory standards. Although this therefore provides an objective measure, establishing imputed equity was nevertheless a time-consuming process.

Whilst the group's economic profit reported externally is calculated excluding the restructuring provision costs, the internal definition requires no significant adjustments to profit and loss account numbers. There was initially some concern over the treatment of bad debt provisions since the level of provisions for each business fluctuates widely over time, according to the different stages of its economic cycle. It was felt that this could distort economic profit calculations and so the company had considered whether to substitute an average level of provisions for the actual charge for a year. There was much debate concerning how this should be done. Some businesses are much more prone to provisions than others, so if the average group-wide level of provisions is applied, this could itself create distortions. Ultimately, however, no adjustments were made for provisions, and once the approach went live, the issue failed to generate the concerns that had been anticipated.

A further technical issue relates to transfer pricing. The way in which the costs of central services, such as those relating to the technology infrastructure, are charged out between the various operating units is recognised to be rather subjective and a source of some debate. The subjectivity inherent in transfer pricing and cost apportionment is a well-known limitation of traditional accounting-based measurements (Emmanuel et al., 1990), and the Lloyds experience provides a timely reminder that this potential problem exists within a VBM measurement system as much as any other.

It can be seen, therefore, that a reasonably pragmatic approach has been taken to the technical features of the VBM system, certainly in the early period of its use. This has been quite deliberate. There has been a conscious effort to limit the complexity of the technical financial features and instead to emphasise the strategic and management implications of VBM. The priority has been to ensure the new system is understood and accepted, and extra complexity was considered likely to have a detrimental effect in this regard. Encouraging positive behavioural and attitudinal responses have therefore been key to the successful implementation of VBM at Lloyds TSB, and this aspect is discussed further below.

Behavioural responses

Whilst the move to VBM has posed a number of technical challenges, much greater emphasis has been placed upon how to actually change managerial attitudes and decision-making behaviour. The move to VBM has been regarded as requiring significant cultural change, and this for a group which was formed out of two companies — TSB having some experience but Lloyds with several years of experience with the concepts, though admittedly the approach was not as pervasive within Lloyds Bank — has now been established within Lloyds TSB.

A number of behavioural responses have been experienced, and in this respect it is useful to distinguish between two distinct stages of the evolution of VBM within the company. The first stage relates to the evolution of VBM at Lloyds from its initial use in the early 1980s through to the TSB merger in 1995. The second stage relates to the move to a more extensive VBM approach following the creation of Lloyds TSB.

Starting with the Lloyds Bank experience, there was much initial resistance to the adoption of a shareholder value focus, particularly among middle managers. Common concerns were as follows: the approach would lead to 'short-termism'; the approach was 'just another fad'; the approach would harm the interests of other stakeholders; too much change was required. The personal commitment and enthusiasm of Sir Brian Pitman was regarded as a crucial factor in ensuring that the implementation succeeded despite these concerns. In addition, a degree of re-educating and retraining of the company's finance staff as well as external analysts, each of which were unfamiliar with the approaches used, was found to be necessary.

Difficulties were also experienced in trying to encourage some managers to switch to thinking and acting in long-term value terms. In particular, it was found that the traditional importance attached to achieving the budgeted profit and other annual targets could give rise to certain dysfunctional consequences from a shareholder value creation perspective. First, there was a temptation for unit managers to cut back on expenditures in an attempt to meet budget, without due regard for the longer-term value effect of such actions. Second, there was a tendency for budget targets to become regarded as the upper limit on performance expectations. Thirdly, there was a concern that some performance targets, including branch closure targets, were not fully aligned with the overall objective of shareholder value creation.

Before 1992 the use of shareholder value principles had largely been restricted to the corporate centre. In the period from 1992 up until the merger, however, Lloyds had started to extend the use of such ideas further into the organisation. This was achieved in two main ways. Firstly, an education process was initiated, through which the principles of shareholder value and in particular the meaning and significance of the concept of economic profit were conveyed to managers. Secondly, cash flow performance targets were introduced at the business unit level. A number of difficulties were experienced, however, with this latter initiative. First, it was felt that line managers find it difficult to relate to managing cash flows as opposed to managing earnings, and they find it very difficult to conceptualise and even harder to manage discounted cash flows. Also, the measures used were added to the existing portfolio of measures and targets already in use, with no metrics being dropped.

Following the merger, the education process was intensified as attention was focused on bringing the C&G and TSB managers' level of understanding up to a level that Lloyds managers had taken three years to develop. In addition, a fully integrated VBM system was implemented by the company, with the assistance of Marakon. The process of implementation has been difficult and time-consuming, and this despite the fact that both Lloyds and TSB had had some previous experience with the concepts.

The experience of Lloyds TSB is that the implementation of VBM requires significant cultural change. It is important to bear in mind, however, that the implementation took place shortly after the TSB merger, itself shortly after Lloyds had acquired Cheltenham and Gloucester Building Society (C&G) and Abbey Life. Thus, as well as implementing VBM, the company had to integrate these four organisations into a coherent whole. It could be argued that adopting VBM as a new and common framework may have helped in this. A key question here is the extent to which the successful introduction of VBM requires cultural change, as opposed to whether the introduction of VBM itself may help bring about a desired cultural change.

Throughout the implementation of VBM, much effort has been exerted and much time has been spent to convince managers of its logic and validity; care has been taken not to impose it from above. Internal communications and training workshops have been used to communicate the rationale and virtues, not just the methods of VBM. At the same time, the company found much enthusiasm among managers to learn about the techniques. Indeed, whilst initial training sessions emphasised the technical features of the economic profit and warranted equity value concepts, as managers realised they would soon be evaluated according to their value performance, their attention soon focused on what actions would be required to meet economic profit targets. There was far less debate over technical issues than had been expected and VBM is reported to have been well received by managers. Similarly, the rationale for the economic profit measure as a bottom-line measure of performance which requires that income is sufficient to cover all costs including shareholders' required return, this too is regarded as being well accepted and well understood.

THE IMPACT OF VBM

VBM is not used as a mechanistic, cookbook approach which can be expected to give precise answers. It is viewed as a means of balancing qualitative strategic analysis with sound economic and numerical analysis to provide a greater likelihood that value-maximising actions will be undertaken. There is a strong belief at the centre that VBM will provide Lloyds TSB with a source of competitive advantage, since it helps to improve the quality of strategic decisions. Managers focus upon how they can create value via questioning how they can change market economics and/or the competitive position of their business. There is also the conviction that using VBM is a means of developing superior managers since the challenge in terms of improvements in performance stimulates creative thought: managers are motivated to continually seek out new opportunities for creating value.

FUTURE PLANS

In summary, VBM is still evolving within Lloyds TSB, and the current practice is not treated as an end position. A sustained focus is given to resolving technical measurement problems (such as transfer pricing and unit-specific costs of equity, which are ongoing issues) and in educating management and staff on the principles of VBM. There remains the continued challenge of balancing short- and long-term business needs (faced by most if not all businesses) but there is now sufficient momentum and enthusiasm across the company to ensure that VBM becomes fully embedded into the core processes of the business.

LESSONS FROM THE LLOYDS TSB EXPERIENCE?

The Lloyds TSB case provides some noteworthy insights into how VBM can be used and some of the issues relevant to its implementation. It demonstrates that taking VBM from the centre and employing it at the business level, as a measure for decision-making and ex post evaluation, can be a major task. The implementation required the redefinition of the organisational structure to make value creation more transparent.

New information was also required. To use a residual income type measure such as economic profit requires that balance sheets must exist at the business unit level. Where they do not exist, or where the existing balance sheet information is deemed to be insufficiently reliable (as in the Lloyds TSB case) then balance sheets must be created. This can require much time and effort, and the treatment of assets which are shared among businesses can be arbitrary and subjective. This potential problem was avoided to some extent in the Lloyds TSB situation as a result of the availability of 'objective' standards by which business-level capital employed could be calculated.

Though some evidence suggests there is a perception that VBM is complex to apply (KPMG, 1996; Chapter 8), it could be argued that a relatively unsophisticated approach has been adopted by Lloyds TSB: a single corporate-wide cost of capital is used rather than business-specific rates and none of the many adjustments to accounting numbers recommended by Stern Stewart are applied. The proponents of VBM might consider these to be grounds for criticism. However, construing such features as weaknesses of the Lloyds TSB approach may well point to a misplaced emphasis on prescriptive literature.

Whilst the literature advocating the use of VBM tends to focus upon its numerical features, some writers emphasise the importance of the process of implementation of VBM and the need to change managerial behaviour, even the culture of the organisation. Often, however, the implementation issue is reduced to a prescribed series of steps that are advocated as the recipe for the successful implementation of VBM, but without being supported by a theoretical or empirical justification.

For Lloyds TSB, changing the behaviour of managers has been the single most important challenge of introducing VBM. The experience of Lloyds TSB suggests that VBM implementation requires equal understanding of change management theories and corporate finance theory. Lewin's (1958) three-step model, acknowledged as one of the classic contributions to this field, might well provide some useful insights. Lewin argued that a successful change project required three key stages:

- Unfreezing the present level
- Moving to the new level
- Refreezing the new level

This model recognises that for change to be successful, the old way must be discarded. Also, this approach is founded on the belief that the change adopter feels the need to change. It is interesting to note that one of the perceived problems with the Lloyds Bank experience of attempting to implement VBM at the business level was that the new performance measures were merely added to existing ones. Thus, it could be argued there was insufficient attention paid to unfreezing the previous system of measures in use.

With the Lloyds TSB implementation, on the other hand, significant steps were taken in unfreezing and then moving to the new approach. The merger will in itself have destabilised the previous approach and will arguably have provided a climate which facilitated the introduction of a major change programme such as VBM. In addition, there was lengthy initial consultation, the structure of the company was redefined, the new systems were introduced with much consultation and agreement with management, and extensive training was also provided.

Refreezing the new behaviour requires that the changes be reinforced, in this case the move to VBM. Lloyds TSB achieved this through, among other things, introducing economic profit as a key performance criterion for the management incentive scheme for the first year in which economic profit was reported at the business unit level. Ongoing staff training and communication programmes and the visible and unwavering commitment of top management have also contributed to this.

CONCLUSION

There are very few studies which explain in any detail how VBM is being practised in the context in which it is applied, and what issues are relevant to its successful implementation. In response to this gap in the literature, this chapter describes and explains the experiences of one of the VBM pioneers, Lloyds TSB.

The Lloyds TSB experience indicates that introducing a full VBM system is not a trivial exercise. Yet, on the other hand, the benefits from its introduction could be significant, since within Lloyds TSB the development of an integrated value-oriented planning and control system is felt to provide a major source of competitive advantage in itself.

A key lesson from the Lloyds TSB experience is that VBM need not be complicated and impenetrable to anyone other than finance specialists. Indeed, one could go further: the Lloyds TSB experience perhaps indicates that VBM must not appear to be complicated and impenetrable. Like any change management project, to be successful, VBM must be accepted and must fit the context in which it is applied. No matter how technically precise, a VBM system that is too complex or time-consuming to apply, will not be applied. For Lloyds TSB the emphasis of VBM is on promoting managerial behaviour and decisions, and this emphasis is consistent with the principles of value creation. Compared with corporate finance, it is argued that the successful implementation of VBM requires as much if not more awareness of the theories of change management.

It is worth emphasising that generalising from a single case study such as this is potentially dangerous. The purpose of the above insights is to help explain why VBM has been adopted in the way it has been adopted at Lloyds TSB. Further research is needed before a theory of VBM in practice with wider applicability can be established.

It is too early to tell whether VBM deserves the claims made on its behalf by its advocates, but at Lloyds TSB its use is regarded as fundamental to the continued success of the company.

REFERENCES

Bromwich, M. (1998) Value based financial management systems. *Management Accounting Research*, **9**, 387–89.

Coopers and Lybrand (1997) *International Survey of Shareholder Value Management Issues.*

Emmanuel, C., Otley, D. and Merchant, K. (1990) *Accounting for Management Control,* 2nd edn. Chapman and Hall, London.

Gill, J. and Johnson, P. (1997) *Research Methods for Managers,* 2nd edn. Paul Chapman, London.

Glaser, B.G. and Strauss, A.L. (1967) *The Discovery of Grounded Theory.* Aldine, Chicago IL.

Grundy, T. (1992) *Corporate Strategy and Financial Decisions.* Kogan Page, London.

Handler, S. (1998) The emphasis on value-based strategic management in UK companies. In *The Strategic Decision Challenge* (ed. D. Hussey). John Wiley, Chicheter, pp. 75–100.

Hennell, A. and Warner, A. (1998) *Financial Performance Measurement and Shareholder Value Explained.* Financial Times Management, London.

Kaplan, R.S. (1984) The evolution of management accounting. *Accounting Review,* **59**(3), 390–418.

KPMG (1996) *Value Based Management: A Survey of European Industry.*

KPMG (1999) *Value Based Management: The Growing Importance of Shareholder Value in Europe.*

Lewin, K. (1958) Group decisions and social change. In *Readings in Social Psychology* (eds G.E. Swanson, T.M. Newcomb and E.L. Hartley). Holt, Rhinehart and Winston, New York.

McTaggart, J.M., Kontes, P.W. and Mankins, M.C. (1994) *The Value Imperative.* Free Press, New York.

O'Hanlon, J. and Peasnell, K. (1998) Wall Street's contribution to management accounting: the Stern Stewart EVA® financial management system. *Management Accounting Research,* **9**, 421–44.

PA Consulting (1997) *Managing for Shareholder Value.*

Rappaport, A. (1998) *Creating Shareholder Value: A Guide for Managers and Investors.* Free Press, New York.

Ryan, B., Scapens, R.W. and Theobald, M. (1992) *Research Method and Methodology in Finance and Accounting.* Academic Press, New York.

Yin, R.K. (1994) *Case Study Research: Design and Methods,* 2nd edn. Sage, London.

11 Making Value-based Management a Way of Life

LEON KAMHI

INTRODUCTION

There is a lot of talk about shareholder value, and value-based management (VBM). Sell-side analysts such as HSBC James Capel and Credit Suisse First Boston are using value measures such as economic value added in their company reports. Buy-side fund managers including Mercury Asset Management and Gartmore are working with Holt's cash flow return on investment (CFROI) valuation approach to spot over- and undervalued companies. Companies themselves are increasingly moving in line too. In annual report after annual report, shareholder value is held up as the governing objective. Senior executive incentive schemes are linked to total shareholder return. Others have started to measure their business performance on financial indicators such as economic value added, cash flow return on investment (CFROI) and total business return.

On closer inspection, however, very few of the companies preaching the virtues of shareholder value are actually walking the talk and practising what they preach; see page 200 for some recent supporting evidence (1998). The evidence shows that whilst companies are working with VBM concepts, few have implemented VBM deeply, i.e. across all management processes. Strategic decisions continue to be made on gut feel and industry knowledge with value measures such as economic value added relegated to being used to support the decisions which would have been made anyway. Operational managers *don't understand* how they individually or as part of a team can affect the value measures which have been developed and put forward by corporate managers. With no link to compensation, not only are managers ignorant of what they practically can do to maximise shareholder value creation, they will not be incentivised to do so either. In these cases the letters VBM at best stand for value-based *measurement* not value-based *management*.

Over the last six years, working as a management consultant with Deloitte Consulting/Braxton Associates, I have been fortunate to work with close to 20 different companies each attempting VBM implementation. Some have focused their effort on *measurement*; they have provided their companies with better information but had little impact on business decisions. Others have linked value measures to specific business decisions such as resource allocation. VBM in these cases did make a partial contribution by supporting other decision-making tools already in place.

Effective VBM implementation means more than this, however, and the clients I have worked with who have been truly successful have made value a way of life in their company. They have injected value so that it becomes the lifeblood and nervous system of the company, defining its culture and most importantly becoming the focus for all business decisions which are made.

They have also focused on providing value to their customers and employees as the means to creating maximum value for shareholders. This has been demonstrated in *The Value Elite*, published by Deloitte Consulting/ Braxton Associates in 1999. The results from the research showed that there were 26 companies, dubbed 'the value elite', each of which appeared on *Fortune* magazine's list America's Most Admired Companies and its list of The 100 Best Companies to Work for in America. The list of admired companies is based on a survey of thousands of business people. Eight criteria are used to compile the ranking: quality of products or services; innovation; community or environmental responsibility; quality of management; ability to attract, develop and keep talented people; financial soundness; value as a long-term investment; and use of corporate assets. These criteria cover all three stakeholders – shareholders, customers and employees – and as *Fortune* points out, 'the companies that rise to the top exemplify precisely the qualities that people have come to admire in business: ingenuity, profitability, laser-like focus and the willingness to work hard'. The best-to-work-for list was used because it is focused specifically on companies that address the value of the employee. These companies include Cisco, Hewlett-Packard and Microsoft. Sixteen of the 26 companies in the value elite belong to the top quartile of the Fortune 500 Total Shareholder Return.

General Electric has consistently achieved superior total shareholder return for over 10 years and Jack Welch, its chief executive, has this to say:

> The three most important things you need to measure in a business are customer satisfaction, employee satisfaction and cash flow. If you are growing customer satisfaction your global market share is sure to grow too. Employee satisfaction gets you productivity, quality, pride and creativity. Cash flow is the pulse – the vital sign of life in a company.

So what is best practice? I believe making VBM a way of life in a company is about doing the following five things:

- Ensuring top management commitment to VBM
- Making value an integral part of all management processes

- Providing managers with the tools to make value-creating decisions
  - Strategy, operations
  - Training
  - Value (information) infrastructure
- Linking incentives to value
- Focusing on behavioural impacts when developing and selecting value measures

I have purposely left to last any mention of value measures, and for two reasons. Firstly, the rest of this book has spent many a page discussing the pros and cons of different measures. Secondly, because I believe there has been an excessive focus over the last 10 years on value-based *measurement* when it is the *management* which makes the difference. The rest of this chapter describes each best practice in turn.

ENSURE TOP MANAGEMENT COMMITMENT TO VBM

Any initiative of change requires *top* management commitment, otherwise the initiative doesn't happen or at best it progresses very slowly in small pockets within the organisation. Top management normally means the CEO (chief executive officer) or a strong CFO (chief finance officer) who has full support of their CEO. If the CEO manages their executives to full consensus, then the whole executive will need to provide strong support to the initiative.

Commitment is more than the CEO buying in to an initiative being led by a middle manager after a one-hour discussion at the end of a Friday afternoon. The CEO needs to own and lead the initiative. In practice this means the CEO sets aside time at business reviews and gives airtime at those reviews to the issue of whether a business is making decisions which maximise value. In addition, commitment is about the CEO fronting communications. The newsletter needs to go out from the CEO. The CEO should attend training. Value should be an important agenda item at senior manager conferences. Real commitment is a prerequisite for success, partial commitment will yield partial results.

MAKE VALUE AN INTEGRAL PART OF ALL MANAGEMENT PROCESSES

Management processes are the lifeblood of any organisation. They provide important forums for decision making and they can have a considerable influence on who are the decision makers in the organisation. The key management processes relating to VBM include monthly performance and control reporting, quarterly strategy and financial reviews, the annual

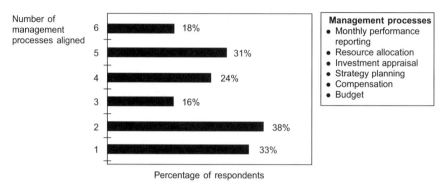

Figure 11.1. Alignment of management processes

strategy planning process, the resource allocation process, the investment appraisal process, the budget/operating plan and incentive schemes.

In surveys carried out by Deloitte Consulting/Braxton Associates, it is clear that very few companies have their management processes aligned. For example, Figure 11.1 (based on Deloitte & Touche's 1998 survey of over 40 financial controllers from top companies in the UK) demonstrates that there is little *alignment* among companies in the performance measures they use in their companies' management processes. The graph shows the percentage of respondents which said that their companies used specific performance measures for one or more of the management processes shown in the key. With the exception of 18% of respondents, performance measures are not being used consistently across management processes. Performance measures included sales growth, EPS growth, dividend growth, economic value added, ROCE, CFROI and total business return. Respondents replied on more than

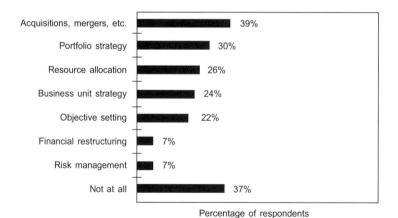

Figure 11.2. VBM concepts have received limited use in most management processes

one performance measure, so the percentage of respondents figures sum to greater than 100%.

Not only are management processes not internally aligned, they are also not aligned behind the objective of maximising shareholder value creation. Figure 11.2 from the same survey shows that 37% of companies have not implemented VBM at all. In the cases where VBM has been used, it has been to assist decisions in specific management processes only.

Making value an integral part of all management processes will encourage the business to make the right decisions. It will also have the additional advantage of aligning senior managers' agendas and actions behind value. Managers will drive the business forward in the same direction and therefore reduce the politics and emotion which can accompany corporate decision making. Here is an example of how value can be integrated into management processes and the benefits which can be achieved.

VALUE-DRIVEN STRATEGY PLANNING PROCESS

You may be wondering what strategy has to do with value. Alternatively, you may indeed believe there is at most a tenuous, intangible link between the actions taken in the commercial marketplace (i.e. strategy) with the financial returns achieved in the capital marketplace (i.e. value). Therefore, before describing a value-driven strategy planning process itself, let me provide some context and make some observations on the link between strategy and value.

Link between strategy and value

Financial returns as measured by economic value added and CFROI spread (the difference between CFROI and the cost of capital) measure a business's return relative to the investors' required return. Superior financial returns can only be achieved through competitive advantage, i.e. a winning strategy. Only if a business is offering a product or service which is more attractive to its customers and/or at lower cost than its competitors can competitive advantage and therefore superior financial returns be achieved. Michael Porter articulates this as follows: 'A company can outperform rivals only if it can establish a difference it can preserve. ... The essence of strategy is choosing to perform activities differently than rivals do' (What Is Strategy, *Harvard Business Review*, Nov/Dec 1996).

The framework in Figure 11.3 has been used for some time now by companies to assess a business's strategic position. There are two dimensions. The vertical axis indicates the attractiveness of the market (or segment) the business is operating in. Market attractiveness can be assessed based on factors such as market growth or industry profitability. Alternatively, the drivers of a market's attractiveness can be evaluated, e.g. supplier power, customer power and substitution threats. The horizontal axis provides an assessment of the business's competitive position. A business's competitive position is determined by an understanding of customers's perception of the business's product or service relative to competitors' offerings as

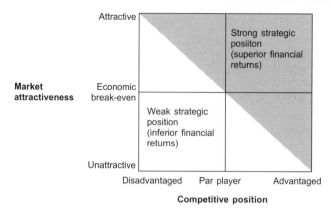

Figure 11.3. The link between strategy and value

well as the business's relative cost position. In other words, if your business has the better product and you can make it at lower cost, your business will make the sale and the profit.

If a business is in an attractive market and has a strong competitive position then it should be achieving superior financial returns, i.e. *positive* economic value added. A business in an unattractive market with a poor competitive position should be achieving inferior financial returns, i.e. *negative* economic value added. The diagonal line shows that a business can still achieve a superior return in an unattractive market if it has a strong competitive position; and a business may have inferior returns in an attractive market if its competitive position is poor.

Working in the City of London, I am continually impressed by how rapidly construction companies are able to erect the latest office block. Unfortunately, for UK construction companies, returns across the construction industry have been poor. According to Holt Value Associates, CFROI spread (a measure of financial return relative to the cost of capital) in the construction industry is very much lower (−3.5% in the UK in 1997) than the CFROI spread for the economy as a whole (+2% in the UK FTSE 350). Empirical evidence suggests that, over the long run, average CFROI is broadly consistent with the average cost of capital over a 20 year period. However, in any single year CFROI may be higher or lower than the cost of capital. In an economic boom the average CFROI will be higher; in a recession CFROI will be lower relative to the cost of capital. The reasons for poor returns become clear when we plot the average construction company on the strategic position matrix. The market is unattractive (vertical axis) due to overcapacity and a persistently flat market. Competitively (horizontal axis) there is little differentiation between players. Therefore, a typical player in the construction market will find themselves with a weak strategic position earning negative economic returns (Figure 11.4).

Many construction companies are certainly operationally effective, however. Michael Porter points out operational effectiveness is about 'performing *similar* activities better than rivals perform them ... operational effectiveness is not strategy' and therefore alone will not lead to *sustainable* superior financial returns. So strategy

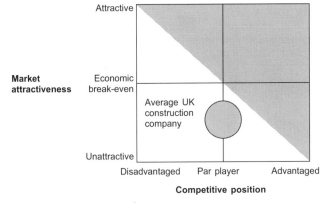

Figure 11.4. Strategic position of UK construction companies

is at the heart of value-based management and the strategy planning process needs to be integrated with value.

Integrating value into the strategy planning process

Figure 11.5 shows Deloitte Consulting/Braxton Associates' generic value-driven strategy process, StrategyPrint. This could be tailored and simplified to meet the needs of a particular company, as illustrated in Figure 11.6.

Nevertheless, the principles underlying StrategyPrint will form the basis of any value-driven strategy planning process. The overriding principle is that value needs to be fully integrated into the process. At the Issues and Options stage a financial or value position assessment as well as a strategic position assessment of the business is carried out. The strategic issues are identified from these analyses whether in the form of opportunities or threats which can then be addressed by relevant strategic options.

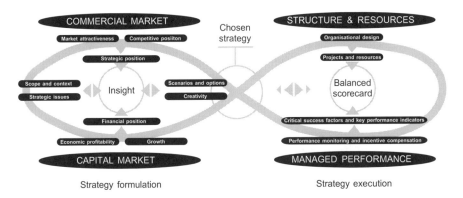

Figure 11.5. How StrategyPrint leads to a dynamic strategy

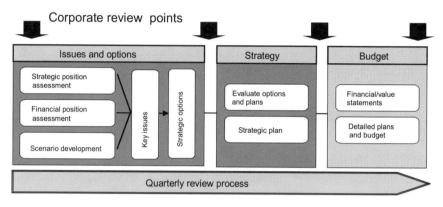

Figure 11.6. The strategic planning process

At the Strategy stage, in developing alternative strategic plans, value also has a major part to play. The evaluation of the alternative strategic plans (preferably against a number of different scenarios) on the value they will create, is a critical factor in deciding which plan to select and implement.

At the Budget stage, or performance monitoring, value also plays an important role. To judge whether the strategy is generating the results expected, value measures need to be monitored in addition to the important non-financial strategic and operational performance indicators which demonstrate whether milestones are being met and whether they are providing the desired financial returns.

In addition to making value-creating strategic decisions, other real benefits can be achieved. Firstly, integrating value into the strategy process will force teamwork across strategy and finance functions as well as alignment between the business strategy and the budget or operating plan – not too common in major companies, I have found. Secondly, if the process is staged – e.g. issues are reviewed with the corporate at one stage, the evaluation of alternative strategy plans at another – then the process will become more collaborative, less adversarial and less of a negotiation. Thirdly, in order to achieve profitable growth and creativity, measured risk taking can and should be encouraged within the process.

Theory aside, how does a value-driven strategy process work in practice? The following example comes from a global manufacturing company MFR-Co, one of whose businesses served a niche segment in the UK. To kick off the process, a position assessment was carried out. The financial position assessment showed that this business had high returns, i.e. economic value added = 20% of capital employed.

The management of the business agreed that the market was only mildly attractive since market growth was only projected to be 2–3% per year. However, they had widely different views on the business's competitive position. The managing director (MD) of the business felt that in the UK the business had a high market share in the niche segment, and by serving customers on a regional basis they were able to provide them with a localised service unmatched by competitors. The MD believed that the strategic position was good (Figure 11.7) and that this was borne out by the excellent financial returns which were being achieved.

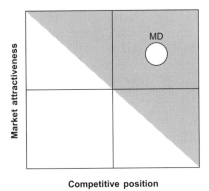

Figure 11.7. Strategic position for MFR-Co: the managing director's view

The marketing and manufacturing directors challenged this view. The marketing director observed that their major customers were increasingly purchasing on a European basis not on a UK basis, never mind a regional basis. The manufacturing director had been in discussions with suppliers of manufacturing equipment who were marketing new technologically advanced manufacturing equipment. With this equipment the manufacturing director predicted that MFR-Co's competitors would be able to close the gap in terms of product quality and cost competitiveness. Figure 11.8 shows the marketing and manufacturing directors' joint view of MFR-Co's strategic position.

Market research and further discussions with customers and equipment suppliers showed that the strategic position would worsen significantly over the next 2–3 years, more than even the marketing and manufacturing directors had believed. Customers were indeed increasingly purchasing Europe-wide. By being organised in one country in Europe on a regional basis, MFR-Co was somewhat disadvantaged against increasing European consolidation by global competitors. Furthermore, the technology in the new equipment favoured scale and would not only

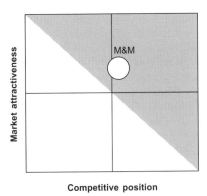

Figure 11.8. Strategic position for MFR-Co: the marketing and manufacturing view

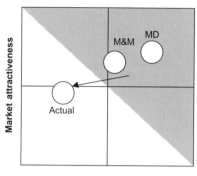

Figure 11.9. Strategic position for MFR-Co: the actual position

allow competitors to close the gap but over time it would give them distinct cost and quality advantages over MFR-Co (Figure 11.9).

The in-depth discussion, internally and with corporate executives, of MFR-Co's strategic and financial position had made managers aware of the key strategic issues which MFR-Co faced.

At the second stage of the strategic planning process, two alternative strategy plans were put forward. Strategic plan A was to consolidate manufacturing plants and provide a national UK service for UK customers. Strategic plan B was to sell the business. Evaluation of the two strategy plans was carried out by identifying the impact on the business's strategic position and then on the level of value creation.

Strategic plan A was expected to arrest the decline in competitive position; however, it was still expected that MFR-Co's competitive position would be eroded over time. The worsening of competitive position meant that the business would not be able to continue to command the prices it had historically; market share would be lost as customers switched and therefore economic value added would fall. Value would be destroyed.

Under strategic plan B the value of the business would be different depending on which competitor purchased the business. Different competitors had different motives for making the acquisition. A competitor who was purchasing the business to get a presence in the UK would gain benefits from having more of a European presence and therefore be able to serve European customers better. On the other hand, if MFR-Co's business was sold to a European competitor who already had a presence in the country, the competitor would be 'acquiring' customers and would be able to realise plant rationalisation synergies, in addition to strengthening its European presence. MFR-Co could command a high price for the business from the European competitor. This willingness to pay came from a significantly enhanced competitive position. Strategic plan B was selected. The evaluation of each strategic plan based on a cash flow valuation model which incorporated detailed strategic assumptions was key to the selection decision.

The operating plan and performance monitoring stage centred around the milestones of finding the appropriate buyer, completing the deal rapidly and achieving a good price. The key financial indicator, which measured the value creation from the strategy, was the divestment proceeds achieved, relative to the ongoing estimated value of the business.

PROVIDE MANAGERS WITH THE TOOLS TO MAKE VALUE-CREATING DECISIONS

JFK's *vision* of man walking on the moon provided the motivation for this landmark achievement in human history, but it was the technology, the ability of the scientists and ultimately the astronauts, which made JFK's vision a reality. Similarly, a football team may have the objective of winning the championship and offer to pay its players significant bonuses for achieving this objective. However, if it does not have quality players who can play well as a team and employ tactics which outmanoeuvre their competitors then the championship will not be won and the players will not receive their bonuses.

It is exactly the same with companies. Some exponents of value-based management suggest that with the right value measure as an objective and with appropriate incentive packages for managers, the company *will as a result* attain superior returns for their shareholders. I suggest this is a pipe dream. Managers need training, tools and relevant management information to enable them to make the decisions which will create value.

Training can and should take a number of forms. It is important to have interactive training, computer-based training, Q&A, etc., all placed on the company intranet or equivalent. The most valuable training is on the job, with managers using and being coached to use VBM principles to make day-to-day decisions.

What tools are available? To help make strategic decisions linking the strategic position matrix explicitly to value creation provides an extremely helpful framework, as demonstrated in the case example. In addition, there are knowledge-based software tools (StrategyPrint is one of them) which hold all the key strategic information from the position assessment through to the performance monitoring stage. In doing so, they capture the strategy, competitive intelligence, the views of key management, what was said at previous meetings, etc. This makes the process a living experience rather than simply a book gathering dust on a shelf. But software tools are not a substitute for good strategic thinking; they merely facilitate. The GIGO (garbage in, garbage out) principle still applies!

Senior management can have a large impact on value through relatively few portfolio and strategic decisions at the top of the organisation. Significantly more value can potentially be created if the whole organisation is making decisions, however small, with the objective of creating value.

To assist managers' effective operational implementation of the selected strategy, gaining an understanding of the business value drivers is important.

Business managers throughout the organisation should understand which drivers they can control, which drivers could have the greatest impact on value and how they interrelate with other business value drivers. With this information the manager can then take the operational decisions which maximise value. However, a word of caution: operational decisions need to be taken within the constraints of the selected strategy since it is the strategy which will deliver competitive advantage and sustainable superior financial returns.

VBM concepts offer great potential to an organisation but they are quite difficult to use in practice. This is because economic value added may not mean much to a sales representative, a warehouse manager or a payroll administrator. Furthermore, even if they understood the concept, they could justifiably argue that it is a measure which is out of their control.

The first challenge is therefore to identify how, at lower levels in the organisation, managers can influence value and to identify the levers they can pull to do so. Those levers are likely to be different across business functions, and indeed across businesses, reflecting the individual nature of each person's job. The second challenge is cultural. Working practices normally have a long history, as do the performance measures in place. If the cultural obstacles are to be overcome, it requires real commitment on the part of senior management and real clarity of purpose. Despite these challenges, the benefits from such a cultural transformation are well worth the effort.

IDENTIFYING AND MANAGING BUSINESS VALUE DRIVERS FOR MAXIMUM OPERATIONAL EFFECTIVENESS

Computer Sales Corp is a real-world company. Although I am unable to reveal either its identity or the precise details of the analyses, the company's experience nevertheless provides a useful illustration of how these models can be used to evaluate the value creation of alternative operational decisions.

Computer Sales Corp is the regional sales and marketing department of a multinational computer manufacturer. The strategic business unit it is a part of has recently gone through the corporate strategy process. One of the strategic options agreed by the corporate was the expansion of sales through a marketing campaign focused on large key accounts. In order to assist operational decision making, a business driver model was built to establish cause and effect.

The first step was to understand the key business drivers on the revenue and cost sides. Customer renewal rate and sales call hit rate had been identified in various customer surveys as important drivers on the demand side, so they were built into the model (Figure 11.10). On the provisioning side, the number of technical reps, etc., and their effectiveness had been identified as important drivers. The extent to which different types of staff are being utilised can be seen in the middle panel. At the top of the middle panel is the value meter, which measures the value from the business plan.

In order to focus on key accounts, Computer Sales Corp decided to appoint key account relationship managers, each of which had responsibility for no more than

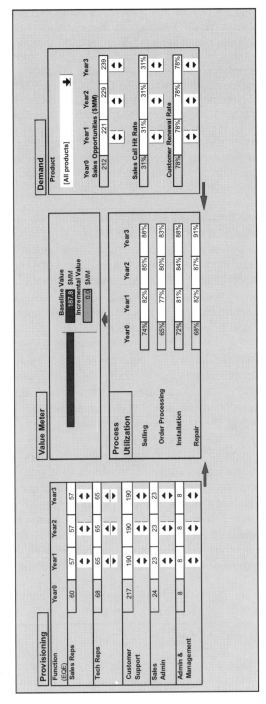

Figure 11.10. The value meter measures the value from the business plan

three key accounts. Initial piloting of this approach showed that sales call hit rate could increase from 31% to 35%. The value of this operational move would be $28 million (Figure 11.11). Increasing sales call hit rate would increase sales, which in turn would increase net cash flows and therefore value. Since margins on products sold were positive, this move would lead to an increase in value.

However, increased sales will produce close to 100% utilisation of installation and repair personnel. It this were not addressed it could lead to a very poor after-sales service and as a consequence a loss of sales. The numbers of technical and sales reps were increased, leading to higher costs. Value after this action is still positive at $19 million (Figure 11.12). The operational decision of focusing sales relationship managers on limited key accounts does create value. The ongoing challenge for business managers in Computer Sales Corp is to find other operational actions which will create further value.

With the increased functionality of software, the identification and management of business value drivers does not have to be a chore and can be easily done. No longer does an analyst have to spend a disproportionate amount of time sweating over building a model, arriving with data hot off the press for their manager who needs to use it in a board meeting an hour later. With the increasing availability of shrink-wrapped and bespoke software tools, significant time can be spent turning the data into information. The information can then be digested and informed decisions made.

Finally, to make the right decisions, managers need access to the right information. An appropriate data infrastructure is required. This could involve putting in an activity-based costing system which provides profitability information by customer, product, channel, etc. It could also entail the running of *regular* customer surveys which identify what customer needs are and how your company is meeting them, relative to competitors.

Both SAP and Oracle are increasingly cognisant of this need and (are planning to) offer a range of software applications which complement their existing enterprise resource planning (ERP) systems to allow this data to be collected in a consistent, accurate and timely manner. Their software applications will include a strategy development component as well as activity-based costing and balanced scorecard components. They are calling this new initiative strategic enterprise management (SEM). The SEM development, if successful, could transform the way all parts of business planning are carried out. However, to reiterate, the software is just an enabler. The GIGO principle still applies.

LINK INCENTIVES TO VALUE

What gets measured gets managed! This is certainly true when performance is linked to an individual's personal compensation. It is not an exaggeration to say there are some fundamental behavioural changes within a company as

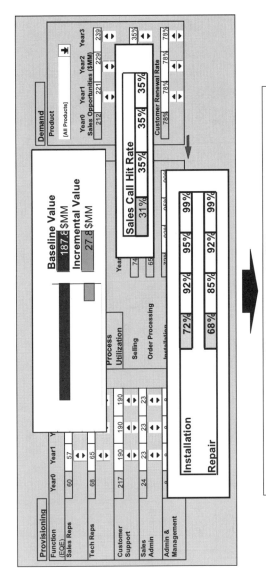

Figure 11.11. Increasing sales call hit rate from 31% to 35% increases value by $28m

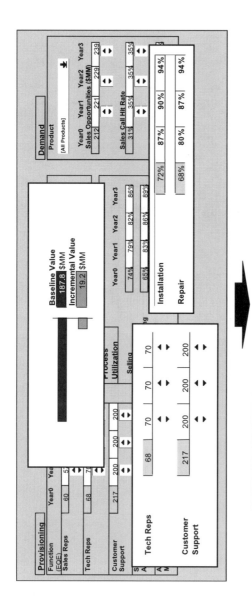

Figure 11.12. Extra technical and sales reps introduce extra costs, so the value increase falls to $19m

the incentive schemes begin to be communicated. Firstly, managers begin to focus on understanding the value measures in a way they haven't done before. The more constructive managers raise benefits and limitations; the less constructive managers begin to game the measure. Everyone pays more attention. Time spent on the VBM initiative probably quadruples and the demand for training increases. Linking incentives to value does need to be tailored to the company's needs and culture. Nevertheless, there are some principles which are common to most.

Reward superior long-term performance

Since value-based management has the objective of continuously creating shareholder value over the short and long term, managers need to be encouraged to make value-creating decisions for the long as well as the short term. This is typically done through a bank balance mechanism, where bonuses accrued from superior performance in one year cannot be cashed in until subsequent years, and then only if the performance is maintained. Alternatively or complementarily, bonuses could be paid out in shares which cannot be cashed in for a period of time. Finally, performance can be measured over a longer than annual term (say over three years).

Motivate outperforming managers with superior rewards

Achieving outperformance does provide a manager with self-satisfaction and peer respect. Normally, however, it is translating the performance into a substantially different remuneration package which really motivates managers. This can be achieved by removing or increasing the cap on bonus schemes, by increasing the amount of variable remuneration relative to fixed, and by being more generous with the payments, recognising that for every £1 of increased bonus to the manager, the shareholder will get a significant multiple.

Use measures that motivate value-creating behaviour and cannot be easily gamed

For obvious reasons, the promise of major rewards on achievement of targets on the wrong measures, this can have adverse effects and lead to the opposite of the desired results. Measures used need to be tested rigorously on their likely behavioural implications. There is unlikely to be a measure which cannot be gamed (I haven't come across one), so it is important there is a managerial process which addresses blatant gaming.

For example, business managers could game an economic value added measure of performance by *temporarily* reducing working capital at the end of the year. This could be addressed by using monthly averages in the working capital calculation. Another example: a business sees it will not achieve bonus-achieving performance levels one year, so it decides to reduce profits even further that year to make subsequent years' performance targets easier to achieve. This can be addressed by employing a bank balance mechanism, which ensures that performance shortfalls in one year are carried forward to subsequent years.

Ensure incentive schemes encourage both accountability and teamwork

Managers need to be measured on what they can control. A business unit manager whose business unit reports into a division which in turn reports into the corporate will not be strongly motivated to make the right decisions in their business unit if their bonus depends on corporate performance. Providing accountability for their actions is important. Therefore, bonuses should be paid on performance achieved in this business unit. On the other hand, the motivation of teamwork at the division and corporate levels cannot be ignored. The importance of this teamwork will differ from company to company, depending on the interrelation of the businesses. In these cases, bonuses should be paid partly on the business unit performance and partly on the division's performance.

Overall then, linking incentive schemes to value creation measures is a very powerful way of achieving the behavioural changes required. But beware, if the scheme is not thought through and the design is not sufficiently tested, the wrong behaviour may be encouraged and the incentive scheme could act as a double-edged sword.

FOCUS ON BEHAVIOURAL IMPACTS OF VALUE MEASURES

The article 'Metric Wars', published by *CFO Magazine* in October 1996, articulated the differences between economic value added and CFROI. It also described how consulting companies in particular were close to evangelical in the spreading of their particular value measure doctrine, probably thoroughly confusing most companies in the process. As the article points out, Monsanto believed that each measure had its place, using CFROI and derived measures for business decisions at corporate level and rolling out economic value added throughout the company. So what is the right measure to use?

The first observation to make is that with the right accounting adjustments it can be shown that economic value added is fully consistent with CFROI. The adjustments include inflation-adjusting assets, using economic rather than accounting depreciation and adjusting out accounting distortions, such as bad debt provisions. Secondly, what can be the crucial measurements decisions – how to treat goodwill, intangibles, provisions, exceptionals, etc. – actually apply equally to both economic value added and CFROI approaches. The key aspect is not the selection of the economic value added or CFROI framework, but rather to make the right adjustments to the framework selected to *ensure correct behaviours*. For example, the decision on whether goodwill is included or excluded should be made to motivate businesses to make profitable growth decisions. If businesses are discouraged from making profitable growth decisions *which are organic* because their return *including* goodwill is too low, then this is likely to be sub-optimal, notwithstanding that investors once paid a lot of money towards an acquisition and would have liked a return. In this case, to encourage organic growth decisions, returns should be measured excluding goodwill. On the other hand, if growth by acquisition were being contemplated, then excluding goodwill in the return measure would be inadequate.

Should exceptional items be included in the value measure? It depends. If a company wants to encourage restructuring then (at least in the short run) exceptionals should be left out otherwise essential restructuring will not occur. On the other hand, if exceptionals appear in the profit and loss account every year then they are not exceptional and should certainly be left in. Again the technical decision should be behaviour driven.

In addition, the measures used should be appropriate for the business decisions they are helping to make. CFROI (%), a measure of return on investment, is not helpful in choosing between strategy options, since based on CFROI (%) alone you may select an option which maximises profitability (in percentage terms) but not profitable growth. CFROI (%), however, is useful *as an input* into resource allocation decisions since, relative to the cost of capital, it does very clearly define which businesses are profitable and which ones are not and where investment is likely to create value. Change in economic value added or total business return can be used to choose between different strategy alternatives since they measure the level of value creation from each strategy alternative. The business decision needs to be the focus not the measure.

CONCLUSION

Making VBM a way of life in a company is more than simply an aspiration or indeed the use of value measures (economic value added, etc.), however sophisticated they are. It is about changing behaviour within the organisation. Value measures play a part for sure, providing the objectives of business performance which can be set as targets and monitored over time. However, much more important than the measures are (1) the education of managers with an understanding of how decisions influence value creation, (2) supporting them with appropriate tools, and (3) the motivation of managers through top management commitment, the ubiquitous presence of value in all key management processes and ultimately the impact on a manager's remuneration package.

The time and resources to transform a company into a value-driven organisation cannot be underestimated, but in my experience it is well worth the effort for all stakeholders: customers, managers, employees and shareholders.

12 Shareholder Value in Banking

PHIL MOLYNEUX

INTRODUCTION

The global banking market is characterised by unprecedented levels of competition and financial innovation, with technological advances and deregulation continuing to be the main forces of change. In such an environment, the distinction between banking, capital markets and other types of financial activity are becoming increasingly blurred and a level playing field is emerging for a broad range of financial products and services. In this environment banks can no longer rely on protected markets to generate quasi-monopoly rents but they must focus on minimising cost and maximising revenues if they are to compete effectively and improve overall firm performance. They also need to compete to obtain scarce capital resources. In order to obtain sufficient capital resources and in order to keep shareholders content, banks have to strategically focus on improving share-holder value – simply generating returns in excess of the cost of their capital. The larger the positive gap between the cost of funds and return on equity, the more value added or wealth created. A bank posting returns lower than the cost of capital means that it is destroying shareholder value.

This chapter provides an insight into the shareholder value concept in the banking business. The next section examines drivers of change in the banking industry and the following section outlines some of the structural and per-formance developments in European banking during the 1990s. This leads onto a section that outlines how shareholder value can be improved in bank-ing. It also provides examples of shareholder value comparisons between European universal banks and US 'bulge-bracket' investment banking firms. The final part of this chapter notes some limitations of the shareholder value approach in banking.

DRIVERS OF CHANGE

Competition is one of the most fundamental and pervasive external strategic drivers in banking. Deregulation and the resulting liberalisation of banking markets has increased competition between commercial banks, financial institutions and in the market for financial services overall. As competition between financial firms heightens, customer demands are also becoming more sophisticated and varied. This has forced banks, as well as a wide range of other financial service providers, to become much more market and customer orientated. Increased competition has created an environment where competitors and shareholders are being supplied with greater information than ever before on banks and their comparative performance. This means that banks are much more aware of their competitive position vis-à-vis their rivals and they also have to demonstrate (to shareholders) that they can add value if they are to attract increasingly scarce capital resources. In addition, customers keenly compare rival banking products and services and have become less loyal. As a consequence, banking business increasingly flows to the most competitive and efficient channels.

The major consequence of these developments is that banking markets throughout the world are now involved in a fundamental, far-reaching process of realignment and change. The strategic priority in banking has shifted away from growth and size alone towards a greater emphasis on profitability, performance and value creation. Banks are placing much greater emphasis on cost and revenue efficiency while improving the range and quality of services to their customers. Greater efficiency might be expected to lead to improved financial products and services, more innovation, a more responsive financial system and improved risk-taking capabilities if efficiency profit gains are channelled into improved capital positions.

Efficiency considerations have become more pressing as deregulation, technology and wider market developments release new competitive pressures and accelerate the capacity and need for change. Banks are under increasing pressure to use all of their resources to maximum advantage. Under these kinds of circumstances, the penalties for incorrect decisions, faulty perceptions and flawed evaluations about cost and revenue efficiency are often more immediate and severe.

Senior bank managers have become increasingly committed to efficiency in running costs and revenues; here are some of the aspects:

- Developing performance benchmarks (such as shareholder value measures) for all operational divisions.
- A continuous and relentless focus (rather than once and for all drives) on cost and revenue management.
- The ability to manage successfully the implementation of new technology.
- Greater product standardisation in areas where customer loyalty will be unaffected as well as the introduction of more innovative products and services to attract new clientele.
- Wider use of part-time staff, retail branch restructuring and an emphasis on shareholder value added solutions to a wide range of activities.

This emphasis on efficiency is being strongly motivated by increased competition between banks as well as with non-traditional suppliers of banking services such as insurance firms, finance houses, retailers and specialist (often phone-based) single-service providers like credit card and 'direct' insurance firms. Banks have to be able to price competitively as well as offer a full range of products and services if they are to retain their client base.

The aforementioned drivers of change are leading to a significant reconfiguration of many countries' banking systems. This is illustrated in the following section that examines various structural and performance developments in European banking.

STRUCTURE AND PERFORMANCE TRENDS

Increasing competition in the financial services area has had the result of reducing the number of banks operating in many countries. This trend is common to virtually all European banking markets. The same trend is also apparent across different types of banks, including the mutual savings and cooperative banks as well as for domestic commercial banks. Nevertheless, there still remain a large number of banks operating in Europe (Table 12.1). All countries (apart from Portugal) experienced a decline in the number of banks since 1989. What the table does not reveal, however, is that the number of foreign banks has increased in every banking market over the same period, reflecting the internationalisation trend and the opportunities

Table 12.1. Number of banks: banking system 1984–1996

Country	1984	1989	1992	1994	1996
Austria	1257	1240	1104	1053	1019
Belgium	165	157	157	147	141
Denmark	231	233	210	202	197
Finland	644	552	365	356	350
France	358	418	617	607	570
Germany	3025	4089	4200	3872	3674
Italy	1137	1127	1073	1002	937
Netherlands	2079	1058	921	744	658
Norway	248	179	158	153	153
Portugal	18	29	35	44	51
Spain	369	333	319	316	313
Sweden	176	144	119	125	124
Switzerland	581	631	569	494	403
UK	598	551	518	486	478

Source: Various central bank reports.

afforded by the EU's Single Market Programme (European Commission, 1997). Foreign banks constitute a significant proportion of banking sector assets in the UK (260 foreign banks with a 57% share of assets in 1996); Belgium (8 banks with 48% of banking sector assets); France (280 banks with 14% of banking sector assets); and Portugal (16 banks with 35% of banking sector assets). In all other European countries, foreign banks generally account for less than 8% of total banking sector assets.

Typically, the nationality of foreign banks operating in different countries varies enormously – London has a predominance of continental European banks, followed by US and Japanese banks. These banks are primarily investment banking/asset management/wholesale subsidiaries doing euro-currency business and under 10% of their business is sterling based. They only play a marginal role in domestic retail and corporate banking. The bulk of foreign banks tend to perform similar functions in Europe's other main financial centres: Frankfurt, Paris, Amsterdam and Zurich. Typically, the top US investment and commercial banks have a presence in every European country but only Citibank performs retail banking to any significant degree, targeted mainly at clients with high net worth. UK banks only have a small presence in continental banking markets, significantly reducing their opera-tions in the early 1990s because of poor performance. The only systems where foreign banks are strongly involved in domestic banking activities are Belgium, the Netherlands and Portugal. Recent cross-border deals reflect that, within Europe, big banks in small highly concentrated systems are increas-ingly viewing expansion in contiguous geographical markets, especially as domestic alternatives are very limited; recent examples include ING/BBL, and Merita/Nordbanken. The ING deal reflects the ability of a much larger, well-capitalised bank to acquire banks operating in markets which are familiar to them. The Nordbanken/Merita deal, between medium-sized operators, is generally regarded as defensive, protecting either from unfriendly foreign or domestic acquirers.

Despite the recent merger wave, however, Table 12.1 still indicates that in most European banking markets there are a large number of domestic and foreign banks serving the needs of domestic clients. The widespread decline in the number of banks in Europe throughout the 1990s, however, has not been exactly mirrored by a similar trend in branch numbers, as shown in Table 12.2. In fact, in many of the larger banking markets (Germany, Italy and Spain) branch numbers have proliferated during the 1990s. In Italy and Spain this has mainly been the result of the removal of branching/territorial restrictions that were in place up to the late 1980s/early 1990s. In Germany the increase in branch numbers has mainly been a reflection of expansion of the savings bank sector reflecting increased non-price competition. In Belgium, Finland, Norway, Sweden, Switzerland and the UK there has been a decline in branch numbers. The fall in branches in Scandinavian countries is mainly a consequence of the consolidation and restructuring of

Table 12.2. Number of branches 1984–1996

Country	1984	1989	1992	1994	1996
Austria	4 005	4 378	4 667	4 683	4 694
Belgium	23 502	19 211	16 405	17 040	10 441
Denmark	3 515	3 182	2 358	2 245	2 138
Finland	2 886	3 528	3 087	2 151	1 785
France	25 490	25 634	25 479	25 389	25 434
Germany	35 752	39 651	39 295	48 721	47 741
Italy	13 045	15 683	20 914	23 120	24 406
Netherlands	5 475	8 006	7 518	7 269	7 219
Norway	1 940	1 796	1 593	1 552	1 503
Portugal	1 469	1 741	2 852	3 401	3 842
Spain	31 876	34 511	35 476	35 591	37 079
Sweden	3 083	3 302	2 910	2 998	2 527
Switzerland	3 874	4 245	4 169	3 821	3 543
UK	21 853	20 419	18 218	17 362	16 192

Source: Various central bank reports.

their systems resulting from the banking crises of 1991/92. Only in Belgium, Switzerland and the UK can it be attributed mainly to the domestic consolidation processes.

This broadly indicates that European banking markets are characterised by a relatively large number of domestic banks which, in some cases, have expanded their branching presence during the 1990s. So while consolidation has undoubtedly been taking place in each banking system, the trend in branch numbers suggests that access to banking services in a range of countries, notwithstanding the introduction of new delivery systems such as phone and Internet operations, has not been dramatically reduced.

While, in most countries, access to bank branches does not appear to have been significantly adversely affected by consolidation and market restructuring during the 1990s, the fall in number of banks and increased market concentration may have adversely affected customer choice. Table 12.3 illustrates that the top five banks, especially in the smaller European banking markets, tend to dominate overall banking business. (The figure for the UK represents concentration in sterling-denominated business, because if foreign bank assets were included in the denominator the five-firm ratio would fall to around 33%.) A 1997 study by the European Commission (EC) also shows that in every EU country between 1979 and 1995, apart from France, Greece and Luxembourg, the five-firm assets concentration ratio increased. In particular, Denmark, Spain, UK, Belgium and the Netherlands experienced the largest increases during the 1990s. The EC study does not cover Finland, Sweden and Norway but all these countries experienced large increases in

Table 12.3. Concentration in European banking 1996

Country	Five-firm assets concentration (%)	Change in concentration ratio 1979–1996
Germany	17	−2
Italy	29	+5
France	47	−10
Switzerland	50	+7
UK	57	+6
Belgium	61	+10
Portugal	72	−6
Finland	74	+22
Netherlands	81	+11
Denmark	82	+25
Sweden	86	+20

Source: Bank for International Settlements (1996), central bank reports, banking associations, various others.

market consolidation resulting from restructuring after the banking crises. These trends are confirmed in Table 12.3.

Overall, European banking markets are mostly characterised by a declining number of banks, although most systems have a large number of small local and regional banks with substantial branch operations serving, together with the main commercial banks and specialist lenders, a wide range of banking customers. Market concentration, however, is increasing and in the smaller banking systems the five-firm assets ratio typically exceeds 60%. While the decline in number of banks and increased market concentration may suggest that banking service choice is declining, the growth in branch numbers in many systems may, in fact, counter this trend. In addition, increasing foreign bank presence as well as the growth of non-traditional banking service providers, such as retailers, asset-backed financing firms (leasing and factoring companies), consumer finance companies, and so forth, make it difficult to categorically state that overall customer choice is declining.

A stronger indication that consolidation and the overall decline in the number of banks has not adversely affected competitive condition in European banking is reflected in the decline in net interest margins in virtually every banking system (Table 12.4).

While margins obviously vary with the interest cycle, and there has been a convergence of money market rates to a lower level during the 1990s (especially in countries aiming to achieve the EMU criteria), the overall trend is downward. As net interest margins have been subjected to increasing competitive pressures, generally resulting in a depression of earnings streams relative to cost, banks have increasingly focused on growing other, non-interest income sources of earnings. Fees and commissions are one example of

Table 12.4. Net interest margins (%) 1984–1996

Country	1984	1989	1992	1994	1996
Austria	–	1.73	1.85	1.90	1.43
Belgium	–	1.57	1.51	1.33	1.32
Denmark	3.01	2.55	3.56	3.83	1.79
Finland	2.42	1.84	1.55	2.05	1.90
France	–	1.91	1.63	1.27	1.20
Germany	2.50	2.01	2.07	2.18	1.46
Italy	–	3.28	3.17	2.63	2.42
Netherlands	2.23	2.08	1.83	1.89	1.67
Norway	3.71	3.45	3.51	3.44	2.41
Portugal	1.86	4.12	4.11	2.78	1.95
Spain	4.15	4.05	3.59	3.00	2.54
Sweden	2.55	2.53	2.55	2.77	1.81
Switzerland	–	–	1.56	1.79	1.98
UK	3.0	3.1	2.6	2.4	2.1

Source: BankScope (1997) and various central bank reports.

an income stream arising from banks diversifying their activities. The growth of bancassurance and off-balance-sheet operations has further fuelled the potential of non-interest income in generating profitability (Molyneux and Shamroukh, 1999). Table 12.5 shows the trend to an increase in non-interest income as a proportion of total income in every European banking system.

The leading commercial banks have been generating an increasing amount of their gross income from non-interest income earning activities. In the UK nearly 45% of banking system gross income was derived from non-interest income sources as at 1996. In other European banking systems the ratio is either above or approaching 40%: Austria 38.7%, Finland 43.6%, France 39.4%, and Sweden 42%. In contrast, both Germany and Norway have a more powerful tradition of banks advancing credit to industry and customers: in these countries 20–25% of gross income comes from sources of non-interest income. In Denmark (17.7%) and Spain (24.3%) there would appear to be opportunities for banks to generate other non-interest income earning activities through diversification. Overall, giving the increasingly varied and sophisticated demands of bank customers, non-interest based income is increasingly likely to replace interest earnings on most banks' income statements.

Tables 12.4 and 12.5 also suggest that different product mixes, reflected in different margins and fee incomes, also influence the ability of various banking systems to generate income. In countries where bancassurance is well established, non-interest income tends to be higher, e.g. as in France (Genetay and Molyneux, 1998). In addition, the largest Swiss banks depended for the bulk

Table 12.5. Non-interest income/gross income (%) 1984–1996

Country	1984	1989	1992	1994	1996
Austria	–	27.9	33.4	28.7	38.7
Belgium	–	22.7	21.6	23.9	35.2
Denmark	15.5	21.8	13.1	16.7	17.7
Finland	43.2	48.5	59.6	46.9	47.7
France	–	19.7	31.3	35.7	39.4
Germany	18.0	25.6	23.9	19.4	21.5
Italy	–	22.3	18.3	23.7	30.4
Netherlands	24.7	29.4	28.6	29.0	35.0
Norway	24.2	26.1	21.1	17.9	24.7
Portugal	39.4	16.3	24.8	27.3	34.2
Spain	14.0	17.6	20.3	21.6	24.3
Sweden	46.2	45.0	39.6	35.7	42.0
Switzerland	–	–	61.3	60.8	63.8
UK	35.6	37.6	42.2	43.2	44.4

Source: BankScope (1997)

of their income (and all their profitability) in 1997 on private banking, investment banking and asset management services. The major Dutch banks also derive significant income from insurance business (half of ING's balance sheet is an insurance company) as well as international operations. Note that the data cited in Table 12.5 relates to the whole banking system. Given the large number of small local and regional banks in most markets, they most likely understate the proportion of non-interest income earned by the biggest banks, since these are usually much more involved in such things as off-balance-sheet business, trading, and so on.

While the trends in the sources of bank income are clear — a fall in interest margins compensated by an increase in non-interest income — the picture for cost levels is less clear-cut. The usual measure for bank efficiency is the cost/income ratio. It must be remembered that bank efficiency levels can be affected both by endogenous and exogenous factors. Adverse economic conditions affect the cost/income ratio in the sense that banks do not have total control over their income streams whilst restrictive labour laws in many continental European countries hinder staff reductions and productivity improvements on the cost side. In addition, M&A activity (mergers and acquisitions) can add to costs in the short term before all the efficiency savings and/or increased revenue streams are worked through. In addition, various income sources, such as those from trading activities are also notoriously volatile. Thus, recent (between 1994 and 1996) increases in the cost/income ratio are just as likely to reflect trends in earnings rather than costs. Nevertheless, the overall trend in European cost/income ratios, however, is expected to be downwards because, among other things, banks are seeking quality business against a background of improving risk controls and enhanced efficiency.

Table 12.6 shows that in the majority of countries the general trend in bank efficiency has been downwards since 1994. The only banking systems, however, which have systematically improved their efficiency levels between 1992 and 1996 are Denmark, Finland, Sweden, Switzerland and the UK. According to McCauley and White (1997) and White (1998), the UK experienced more M&A activity in its banking sector (in value terms) between 1991 and 1996 than any other European banking market, and these cost improvements could be a partial reflection of this trend. All the main UK banks have also embarked on aggressive cost-cutting strategies in terms of branch closures and staff reductions. The improved cost performance of the Scandinavian banks is (again) mainly a consequence of the forced reorganisations following the banking crises of the early 1990s. (Many continental banks, as noted earlier, are unable to generate large cost savings through rapid staff reductions because of restrictive labour laws).

The aforementioned income and cost trends feed through into profitability figures which are shown in Table 12.7. The ROE figures present a mixed picture, although in the majority of countries returns improved between 1994 and 1996; and although not shown, returns in UK and US banking have grown substantially since 1996 (Morgan Stanley Dean Witter, 1998). Given that there is no obvious downward trend in bank performance across countries, some might argue this is evidence that competition is not increasing in European banking markets. This viewpoint, however, is too simplistic.

Table 12.6. Cost/income ratios (%) 1984–1996

Country	1984	1989	1992	1994	1996
Austria	–	65.5	64.0	65.1	61.4
Belgium	–	66.8	66.9	71.3	61.1
Denmark	75.6	64.9	81.4	72.5	53.5
Finland	84.0	84.8	190.4	139.9	69.3
France	–	64.6	62.5	73.5	72.8
Germany	59.3	64.6	64.5	60.7	61.2
Italy	–	61.7	63.8	65.0	69.6
Netherlands	62.3	66.0	67.7	66.7	69.5
Norway	68.5	69.9	60.3	63.4	66.5
Portugal	67.0	46.8	53.0	58.2	56.5
Spain	64.0	60.9	60.3	59.7	63.8
Sweden	67.6	62.7	122.2	80.0	49.3
Switzerland	–	–	93.9	84.9	71.1
UK	66.9	64.8	65.9	64.1	60.3

Source: BankScope (1997)

Table 12.7. Return on equity (%) 1984–1996

Country	1984	1989	1992	1994	1996
Austria	–	10.0	6.9	7.9	9.4
Belgium	–	6.0	6.4	8.8	20.3
Denmark	1.0	3.0	−18.3	−0.9	16.4
Finland	5.1	4.0	−49.5	−25.7	11.9
France	–	9.4	4.3	−1.4	5.8
Germany	21.1	12.4	13.2	11.9	11.9
Italy	–	14.0	9.8	4.4	6.8
Netherlands	14.0	13.6	12.8	14.1	13.7
Norway	14.1	5.5	−5.8	19.3	18.0
Portugal	5.5	9.2	8.5	6.1	9.3
Spain	8.9	14.6	10.6	8.2	14.6
Sweden	4.6	5.9	18.5	19.1	23.9
Switzerland	–	–	8.2	7.8	9.6
UK	20.8	3.4	10.7	19.6	21.0

Source: BankScope (1997)

It neglects the fact that, in all banking markets, traditional margin-based business is probably more competitive than ever before. In addition, banks are increasingly building on non-interest income in areas such as investment banking, brokerage, insurance, pensions, mutual funds and other collective investment product areas (to name but a few) where there are strong established operators. So competition is likely to be intense in many of these areas. The simplistic argument also neglects the important role of technology and the role of new competitors. For instance, advances in technology allow banks to outsource non-core processing and other activities to scale efficient third-party service providers. Customer databases also make the cross-selling and delivery of new types of financial products and services more effective and profitable. Technology has promoted the development of direct banking services and so forth. Non-bank financial intermediaries, retailers and other 'brand name' firms also nowadays compete against banks in the financial services area. These are all important elements changing the economics of banking business.

ADDING SHAREHOLDER VALUE IN BANKING

The previous section identified some of the major structural and performance characteristics across various banking markets. In particular, the main themes identified were the increasing focus on non-interest income as a source of revenue growth, the greater strategic priority placed on cost and revenue efficiency and the emphasis on boosting return on equity.

Banks are having to prioritise efficiency drives as they need to be able to compete for scarce capital resources. The deregulation of international capital markets, advances in information technology and the growing importance of institutional investors have all played a role in creating substantial pools of investment capital that can flow from one market to the next practically in an instant. Banks that are unable to convince investors of their ability to deliver adequate returns are thus at a competitive disadvantage in the race for global capital resources. Managers have to learn to satisfy the demands of the capital markets else they will soon be replaced by others that can. In such an environment a growing number of banks have begun to use shareholder value techniques to measure firm (and business unit) performance.

The main premise behind the shareholder value concept is that the major goal of companies must be to maintain or increase the value of the enterprise to the suppliers of capital. Shareholder value is created by providing returns in excess of what shareholders can produce for themselves. This concept is captured in the cost of equity, which is the rate of return shareholders expect from a given company given its risk profile. Creating shareholder value in excess of what is required is done by some combination of increasing economic profits or decreasing the use of capital in a business or division. It is created when net operating income increases without a proportional increase in the use of capital. Or to put it another way, value is created when after-tax operating income is increased without a comparable increase in the use of capital, or when capital is decreased without impairing earnings.

Actions to enhance shareholder value in banks (as in other companies) therefore centre around four areas:

- Revenue creation
- Cost reduction
- Capital management
- Risk management

On the revenue side, as we have already seen, banks increasingly focus on developing non-interest income revenue streams through cross-selling and other techniques. The main objective here is to develop client relationships through multiple product offerings, especially in savings, insurance and asset management. Banks aim to create value by cross-selling as many of these types of services as possible without having to make significant capital investments. On the cost reduction side, the focus is on benchmarking best cost practices throughout the organisation, using new technology to achieve optimal scale. While the academic literature on bank efficiency suggests little evidence of substantial scale economies in the banking sector, there appears to be strong evidence of significant gains to be had through reducing inefficiencies (Molyneux et al., 1996). Banks also aim to manage their capital more effectively in order to boost returns. Shareholder wealth can be created through increased leverage and asset turnover, as well as through the reduction in excess capital – usually via share buy-backs. Given that the cost of capital is a significant component of value creation, steps taken to reduce the volatility of banks' earnings, and hence the cost of capital, will feed through into improved shareholder value.

Banks are increasingly using shareholder value concepts to evaluate the performance of their operations. One area that appears to be attracting significant attention in the banking literature is the performance features of universal banks (Walter, 1997). The stylised profile of universal banks presents shareholders with a range of more or less distinct businesses that are linked together in a complex network which uses a range of centralised financial, informational, human and organisational resources. This type of structure may be difficult to manage in a manner that achieves an optimal use of capital. The critical issue for the investor is whether shares in a universal bank represent an attractive asset allocation alternative from a perspective of both risk-adjusted return and portfolio efficiency. (For instance, it may be best for the investor to purchase shares in financial firms that specialise rather than buy universal bank shares that represent a portfolio of different businesses.)

Using shareholder value calculations one can see whether universal banks' operations add more shareholder value compared to specialist operators. This is because one can compare the added value of specialist investment banks, retail banks, insurance companies, and so on, and then compare this with the added value generated by universal banks that undertake all these operations. Such measures also allow us to see if divisions within universal banks, say the investment banking operations, perform as well as stand-alone investment banks. As an example, the next few paragraphs provide some information on the cost of capital and shareholder value for US 'bulge-bracket' investment banks, various European universal banks as well as some of their investment banking divisions. This allows us to compare whether the investment banking arms of European universal banks have performed as well as the specialist US investment banks.

For simplicity, we calculate the cost of (equity) capital and compare it with the return on equity (ROE). In order to add shareholder value, banks must generate returns exceeding their cost of capital. To calculate the cost of capital we use the capital asset pricing model (CAPM), $R_i = R_f + \beta(R_m - R_f)$ where R_i is the required rate of return on an investment, R_f is the risk-free rate and R_m refers to the market return; bear in mind the limitations of using β as the sole risk adjustment factor in CAPM calculations (Fama and French, 1992). According to Datastream, European universal banks have β ranging between 0.8 and 1.3 and the US bulge-bracket firms have β ranging between 1.0 and 1.6; median figures for the Europeans are around 1.0 with the bulge-bracket banks closer to 1.5. This means that if we take the bulge-bracket median of $\beta = 1.5$ as a proxy for global investment banks with a risk-free rate of 6%

(given by the US long-bond rate) and an equity premium of 5% $(R_m - R_f)$ then the required return for an investment bank is 13.5%. In other words, to maintain shareholder value, global investment banks have to post ROEs of 13.5% at the minimum. Returns less than 13.5% will destroy shareholder value, and vice versa. The equity market premium is usually calculated over a 20 year period and 5% is the usual benchmark for the US and UK with a slightly lower premium of around 4% for continental Europe. Values of β should also be calculated over long periods as short-term estimates may yield unreliable cost of capital estimates. Despite the limitations associated with using β, the following provides a snapshot of US investment bank and European universal bank returns for 1996.

Table 12.8 shows estimates of the cost of capital for US and European banks engaged in investment banking business. Ranges for the cost of capital

Table 12.8. Cost of capital and shareholder value for US bulge-bracket firms and European universal banks 1996

	Estimated cost of capital (%)	Return on equity (%)	Shareholder value enhancing (+) destroying (−)
Goldman Sachs	13–15	26.0	+
Salomon Bros	13–15	13.7	?
Merrill Lynch	13–15	24.8	+
Morgan Stanley	13–15	17.0	+
Bankers Trust	11	7.4	−
J.P. Morgan	11	14.4	+
SBC	8.2	10.1	+
(SBC Warburg)	13–15	16.6	+
UBS	8–8.5	−1.5	−
Credit Suisse	8	−16.0	−
(CS First Boston)	13–15	15.6	+
Deutsche Bank	9.9	7.6	−
(Deutsche Morgan Grenfell)	13–15	9.5	−
Dresdner Bank	9.1	11.5	+
Commerzbank	9.5–10	9.9	?
NatWest	13.4	6.0	−
(NatWest Markets)	13–15	9.0	−
Barclays	13.8	23.3	+
(BZW)	13–15	9.0	−
ABN AMRO	10.2	17.0	+
ING Group	10.5	13.9	+

Source: Own calculations. Note that from April 1998 Salomon Brothers became part of Citigroup; Deutsche Bank acquired Bankers Trust in December 1998; and SBC and UBC have merged to form United Bank of Switzerland.

to certain banks are provided given different values of β and the 20 year long-bond rate for the relevant countries is used as the risk-free rate. Using the cost of capital estimates for the US bulge-bracket firms as a proxy for the minimum required return on investment banking, Table 12.8 shows that returns must exceed the range 13–15% if shareholder value is to be enhanced. Note also that the table provides shareholder value calculations for European universal banks as well as their investment banking subsidiaries: Deutsche Bank and Deutsche Morgan Grenfell, NatWest and NatWest Markets, and so on. Note also that Bankers Trust ($\beta = 0.89$) and J.P. Morgan ($\beta = 0.80$) had lower estimated cost of capital given that their values of β were more in line with European commercial banks compared to the US investment banks.

Table 12.8 suggests there was substantial shareholder value destruction across European banks in 1996 and the investment banking operations of NatWest, Barclays and Deutsche Morgan Grenfell were not achieving target returns. In fact, at that time SBC Warburg and Credit Suisse First Boston appeared to be the only European investment banks creating value to shareholders. Since 1996 both NatWest and Barclays have significantly reduced their investment banking operations in the light of their poor performance in this area.

Overall, European banks probably must earn benchmark returns exceeding at least 13% if they are to be certain of increasing shareholder value. In fact, nowadays most large banks target ROE of at least 15% given that by achieving this they are more than likely to exceed their own cost of capital. Of course, different hurdle rates may be set throughout the bank's operating divisions.

CONCLUSION

While the chief executives and senior managers of the world's banks genuflect before the altar of shareholder value, one must be aware of the limitations of such metrics or measures. Firstly, these measures tend to be backward-looking and tell managers little about the future value of the firm or its operations. In addition, cost of capital calculations may be artificially boosted if managers buy back equity; in other words, these measures create an incentive to reduce equity capital. Share repurchases have been a common theme in US and UK banking over the last few years. Some have also stated that because shareholder value type calculations are increasingly being accepted by senior managers as a method for calculating their remuneration, they are bound to overstate the 'true' performance of companies.

A broader criticism, however, has been that the efficient use of capital is not the be-all and end-all for successful companies, although in banking it may be more important because of regulatory requirements. Factors such as strategy, innovation and service quality may count for more in the long run. Many banks are also using other techniques, such as balanced scorecards, where they combine numerical shareholder value measures with measures of less tangible items such as customer satisfaction and loyalty, ability to innovate, and a firm's ability to develop the skills of its employees. Most senior bankers are aware of shareholder value concepts and the target returns they generate. As such, bankers are paying greater strategic attention to measuring the less tangible (touchy-feely) areas that are believed to impact on performance and add value in the future.

REFERENCES

Bank for International Settlements (1996) Annual report. BIS, Basle.

BankScope (1997) Fitch-IBCA, London.

European Commission (1997) *The Single Market Review – Credit Institutions*. Kogan Page, London.

Fama, E.F and French, K.R. (1992) Common risk-factors in the returns on stocks and bonds. *Journal of Finance*, **47**(2), 427–65.

Genetay, N. and Molyneux, P. (1998) *Bancassurance*. Macmillan, London.

McCauley, R.N. and White, W. (1997) The euro and European financial markets. Bank for International Settlements Working Paper 41.

Molyneux, P. and Shamroukh, N. (1999). *Financial Innovation*. John Wiley, Chichester.

Molyneux, P., Altunbas, Y. and Gardener, E.P.M. (1996) *Efficiency in European Banking*. John Wiley, Chichester.

Morgan Stanley Dean Witter (1998) Consolidation and the Eurobanks: survivability and the 'selfish gene'. *UK and Europe Investment Research*, 13 October 1998, pp. 1–55.

Walter, I. (1997) Universal banking: a shareholder value perspective. *European Management Journal*, **15**(4), 344–60.

White, W. (1998) The coming transformation of continental European banking? Bank for International Settlements Working Paper 54.

Part IV

MEASURING VALUE: SOME CRITICAL PERSPECTIVES

13 A Review of Accounting and VBM Alternatives

JOHN FORKER AND RONAN POWELL

INTRODUCTION

The economic analysis of income has a long history. This chapter considers only those aspects that cast light on the characteristics of accounting and value-based metrics for the purpose of assessing managerial performance. Following Fisher's (1906) classic analysis of income, there has been an almost continuous stream of work seeking to improve our understanding of the concept of income and how it might be measured. It is possible, however, to identify sub-periods of outstanding contribution both in theoretical development and practical application. Notable among them are the analysis of the concept of income and its measurement by Lindahl (1939) and Hicks (1946). A further important phase occurred in the late 1950s to the mid 1960s. This comprised the contribution of financial economists to the valuation of the firm based on an enterprise measure of income (Modigliani and Miller, 1958) and the construction by accounting theorists of a financial accounting framework for financial planning and control (Edwards and Bell, 1961). The work of Solomons (1961) is also outstanding for highlighting the relationship between economic income and conventional accounting profit. His critical analysis of conventional accounting profit and, in particular, its unsuitability as a tool for financial planning and control, led him to conclude that 'so far as the history of accounting is concerned, the next twenty-five years may subsequently be seen to have been the twighlight of income measurement'. Solomons (1965) was also responsible for identifying the potential for control in divisionalised firms of the accounting measures of residual income and return on investment. More recently there has been a resurgence of interest in residual income techniques following the theoretical contribution of Ohlson (1989).

With the benefit of hindsight, the most significant of these contributions for the subsequent development of value-based management metrics, and also for the continuing evolution of conventional accounting practice, is the classic text *The Theory and Measurement of Business Income* (Edwards and Bell,

1961). The Edwards and Bell approach is built on two fundamental elements for value-based management metrics that are based on financial statement data. Specifically, they are the use of residual income for financial planning and control and the application of clean surplus accounting.

In the context of the practice of financial accounting, conventional accounting techniques until recently have remained largely unchanged. Significant shocks, in the form of financial scandals relating to bad accounting practice and weakness in the regulatory framework, led to the establishment of the Accounting Standards Committee (ASC) in 1970. Further financial scandals in the late 1980s resulted in a review of accounting regulation by the Dearing Committee (Dearing, 1988). As a result, the ASC was replaced in 1990 by the Accounting Standards Board and the new body was set up to be independent of the accounting profession, with improved funding, under the chairmanship of Sir David Tweedie.

Although good progress toward improving the quality of financial reporting has occurred recently, the accounting profession failed to realise the potential of financial statements to provide a basis for financial planning and control. Rather, the gap was identified and filled by the investment community. Value-based management techniques have been developed and are marketed by investment firms. Notable among them are market value added (MVA) and economic value added (EVA) marketed by Stern Stewart, total business return (TBR) promoted by Boston Consulting Group, cash flow return on investment (CRFOI), offered by Holt Value Associates, and finally shareholder value added (SVA) from the LEK/Alcar Consulting Group. This chapter focuses primarily on the links between economic income concepts and financial statement based measures of performance. The Stern Stewart metric (Stewart, 1991) is closest in construction to financial accounting measures. The opportunity is thus taken to compare the Stern Stewart measure of EVA to economic and accounting measures of per-formance. It is also the case that most of the empirical research into the relative usefulness of different metrics is confined to comparing residual income based measures with conventional accounting data.

The chapter comprises the following sections. A brief review is first undertaken of economic concepts of income and capital. The economic foundations of accounting theory, particularly as reflected in the work of Edwards and Bell, are then explained. Next the special properties of residual income and its relation to return on investment are identified. Then to provide a context for VBM metrics, relevant links between economics and finance are briefly described. Conventional financial accounting income is reviewed and recent developments in accounting regulation and practice are identified. Finally, a brief review of the empirical literature is provided to give insight into the relative usefulness of conventional accounting profit compared to residual income based metrics.

ECONOMIC CONCEPTS OF INCOME AND CAPITAL

Fisher (1906) set out the foundations for the economic analysis of income and capital in the twentieth century. He defined income as a flow of benefit in a given time period and capital as a stock of benefit at a point in time. Capital was measured as the discounted present value of future consumption. According to Fisher, the concept of income in its purest form captures the psychic satisfaction from consumption. However, the utility obtained from a given level of consumption, for example listening to a piece of music or reading a novel, differs across individuals and cannot be measured. Thus, the measurement of income as psychic satisfaction is impracticable. To operationalise the measurement of the concept of income, Fisher proceeded to identify observable alternatives. Real income, given by the cost of living in a period, was regarded as the most practical concept. Finally, money income was the money received in a period. This was viewed as an unsuitable proxy for income due to the mismatch between money income and consumption caused by either savings or dis-savings. Fisher was emphatic that income should exclude savings in order to avoid double counting on the ground that the latter represented rights to future consumption. Dis-saving in a period would, however, be included in income. The amount of spending in a period was also rejected as unsatisfactory due to the purchase and consumption of consumer durables. In Fisher's view the best income proxy was income as consumption.

Subsequent contributions from Lindahl and Hicks reinforce further the fundamental insight that a unique concept of income does not exist. Rather, there are a range of alternative concepts of economic income depending on market conditions. Lindahl devised the concept of 'income as interest' and, in the context of a world of uncertainty, differentiated between income ex ante, based on information available at the start of a period and income ex post, based on information available at the end of the period. Unexpected changes in interest rates or periodic receipts cause income ex ante to differ from income ex post. The impact of unexpected changes on wealth during the period are classified as windfalls and are excluded from the measurement of income. In this way, in a world of uncertainty, the fundamental flow characteristic of income, identified by Fisher, is retained. The measurement of 'income as interest' is obtained from the 'hindsight' value of start-of-period capital recalculated in light of the end-of-period information multiplied by the interest rate for the period. Although the concept of income as interest is unambiguous in its formulation, its measurement in practice is fraught with difficulty (Kaldor, 1955). The identification of windfall effects requires knowledge of expectations. However, these are generally unobservable so it is not practicable to identify the unexpected components of actual outcomes.

The synthesis of the economic theory of income provided by Hicks (1946) serves further to highlight the fragility of the concept and its measurement.

Hicks set his analysis of income in the context of a consideration of the purposes served by its measurement. In view of the theoretical and practical difficulties, Hicks sets the scene for his analysis by recognising the impossibility of measuring income with precision and expresses the view that, in practice, business people are best served by rough approximations to inform investment and consumption decisions. In his analysis, Hick's incorporates Lindahl's contribution for handling the resolution of uncertainty and extends the analysis to include changes in the purchasing power of income. To motivate his analysis, Hicks defined the central concept of income in terms of a guide to consumption. Income was what could be spent in a period to allow an individual to be as well off at the end of the period as they were at the start of the period.

Three proxies to the central concept were identified: capital maintenance income (Hicks 1), income maintenance (Hicks 2) and income maintenance in real terms (Hicks 3). Hicks (1) is reasonably easy to compute as consumption plus the change in asset value over the period (excluding capital contributions), but it suffers from the inclusion of windfall effects that in theory are adjustments to the stock of capital and which affect the income of subsequent periods rather than the current period. The inclusion of windfall adjustments to the stock of capital in Hicks (1) is regarded as unsatisfactory as it undermines the flow characteristic of income. A further feature of Hicks (1) is that it excludes dis-saving but includes saving, which is the opposite of Fisher's income as consumption. A basis for assessing the significance of this difference lies at the heart of Fisher's analysis and provides an important insight into the economic basis for value-based and accounting measures of performance. As highlighted in Hirshliefer's (1970) exposition of Fisher's analysis, the key insight is that, given perfect markets, the flow of benefit on which value is based is determined by the investment decision. Provided the investment decision is maintained, then any dividend policy or individual pattern of consumption can be financed by borrowing or lending. Thus, periodic income measurement, as well as the determination of value, should be independent of the dividend (consumption) decision. Saving or dis-saving decisions impact on the opening capital of the subsequent period and thus are reflected in future income. Hicks (2) and Hicks (3) exclude windfalls but Hicks (2) ignores the impact of changes in purchasing power. In principle, Hicks (3) is most satisfactory where the aim is to provide a guide to the level of consumption that would maintain the real level of welfare in perpetuity.

ECONOMICS AND ACCOUNTING

In the academic literature, Edwards and Bell (1961) provide one of the earliest and most influential expositions of the use of accounting data for the purpose of value management. In their view the primary purpose of accounting data is to allow the expectations incorporated in managerial plans to be evaluated in the light of actual outcomes. Identification of unexpected outcomes serves as the basis for either altering events for controllable errors or for altering expectations in the case of uncontrollable errors (Edwards and Bell, 1961, p. 4). The actual events of the period are highlighted as the correct basis for the identification of incorrect expectations and this serves to justify Edwards and Bell's focus on current prices as the basis for evaluating performance. The VBM credentials of Edwards and Bell's contribution are clearly identified at the outset of their classic treatise:

> If the objective of accounting is to aid in the decision-making processes within the firm, specifically to aid in the *quest for profit* ... a concept of profit which measures truly and realistically the extent to which past decisions have been right or wrong and thus aids in the formulation of new ones is required. And since rightness or wrongness must, eventually, be checked in the market place, it is changes in market values of one kind or another which should dominate accounting objectives. (Edwards and Bell, 1961, p. 25; emphasis added)

Management select among alternative investment strategies to deliver the highest expected present value of dividends for the shareholders:

$$V_t^* = E_t \sum_{\tau=1}^{N-1} \frac{(D_{t+\tau})}{(1 + k_e)^\tau} + E_t \frac{M_N}{(1 + k_e)^N} \tag{13.1}$$

where V_t^* is subjective or the fundamental value of the firm based on managerial expectations of the anticipated stream of dividends D_t, M is the market value of assets (replacement cost), E_t is the expectations operator at time t, and k_e is the cost of equity capital.

Income measurement, ex post, is based on the maintenance of the financial value of equity capital (Hicks 1) using current values. This reflects the importance attached to market values as the basis for identifying the horizon period that yields the highest present value for any given strategy. Subsequent evaluation of outcomes is then based on a comparison of expected and actual market values.

Periodic income is described as business profit and is given by

$$B_t = M_t + D_t - M_{t-1} \tag{13.2}$$

where B_t is business profit, and M_{t-1} and M_t are the current values (replacement costs) of assets at the beginning and end of the accounting period. Controlling for payments of dividends and contributions of capital, income is given by the change in the value of the accounting values of assets over the period. The final element in the Edwards and Bell approach to financial planning and control is the definition of residual or excess current income; in their book they use the term 'excess realisable income'. Subsequently, Edwards (1977, 1980) uses the term 'excess current income'. It is given by

$$R_t = M_t + D_t - (1 + k_e)M_{t-1} \qquad (13.3)$$

where in Edwards and Bell's terminology, R_t is excess current income. R_t measures the extent to which the current events of the period provide shareholders with a return in excess of the equity cost of capital employed. This serves as the basis for management to evaluate performance and strategically to revise plans and expectations with the objective of maximising value created for shareholders.

The aim of management is to maximise the present value of the stream of residual income. At any point in time the difference between the market value of equity, M_t, and the fundamental value of the firm, V_t^*, is described as subjective goodwill, G_t, and is equal to the present value of the future stream of residual income:

$$V_t^* = M_t + G_t \qquad (13.4)$$

where

$$G_t = E_t \sum_{\tau=1}^{N} \frac{R_\tau}{(1 + k_e)} \qquad (13.5)$$

Two fundamental properties and two important results underpin the measurement of business profit and excess current income. The first is that business profit satisfies the 'clean surplus' relation (CSR). Excluding dividends and contributions of equity capital, income is given by the difference between the opening and closing accounting book values of assets. The clean surplus result was first identified by Preinreich (1938). Subsequently, it figures prominently in the work of Kay (1976) and Peasnell (1982). The second is that the current market value of assets plus the discounted present value of the anticipated stream of future residual income is equal to the fundamental value of the firm. The first result is that, given the CSR, the identity between the fundamental value of the firm and the current market value of assets plus the present value of future residual income holds irrespective of the accounting basis for valuing assets. Inspection of equations (13.3) and (13.5) reveals that for a given dividend stream and the initial and horizon values for assets, all the other intermediate market values cancel out. Edwards and Bell (1961, p. 69) emphasise, however, that this does not mean they are irrelevant for decision making. Identification of the highest-value strategy entails choosing among alternative horizons for any given strategy that requires knowledge of all intermediate market values.

Second, in the context of accounting policy choice, timing differences in the recognition of costs and revenues also have no impact on the basic result that the value of the firm is given by the accounting book value of assets plus the present value of excess current income. In effect, accounting policy differences are neutralised by an equal and offsetting charge for capital employed. For example, an upward revaluation in the value of assets to reflect increased replacement costs will increase excess current profit in the year of revaluation. However, this will be exactly offset by higher depreciation and cost of capital charges in subsequent years.

Dechow et al. (1999) show that provided the CSR holds then the dividend discount model (13.1) is identical to the current book value of assets plus residual income (13.4). They point out that, in the absence of other properties, accrual accounting data compared to cash flows have no incremental information content in forecasting value. In contrast, the Edwards and Bell view, cited above, is that internal projections are framed in terms of periodic market values. Comparing expectations against outcomes is viewed as an integral part of the process driving shareholder value creation.

It is interesting to note, however, that Edwards and Bell eschew the theoretically superior approach advocated by Lindahl. In the face of errors in expectations, the resulting windfalls should be excluded from income by revising the value of capital in the light of end-of-period information to report maintainable income (Hicks 2). Rather, on the basis of full information about expectations, separate identification of windfalls is redundant in the context of internal appraisal. In this setting, management are in a position to identify the significance of the differences between expectations and outcomes and to act appropriately depending on whether the unexpected events are controllable or uncontrollable.

RESIDUAL INCOME AND RETURN ON ASSETS

Although residual income, in the form of excess current income, served a central role in Edwards and Bell's analysis, its significance was overshadowed by the attention devoted to developing a current value based framework for financial accounting to provide an appropriate comparison of outcomes against expectations. In the literature, credit for highlighting the concept of residual income belongs to Solomons (1965). In a path-breaking contribution Solomons drew attention to the relative merits of residual income and return on investment for the purpose of internal planning and control in divisionalised companies. The term 'residual income' was first coined by General Electric in the US (Solomons, 1965, p. 63) and the technique was applied by them in the 1950s, although a variant was employed as early as the 1920s by General Motors (Bromwich and Walker, 1998, p. 392). Solomons championed residual income on the grounds that it was best suited to increasing the absolute value of the company. An alternative metric, return on investment, was considered inferior as it encouraged management to underinvest by seeking to maximise the average rate of return on projects and to reject value-increasing projects that earned more than the cost of capital but less than the average for existing projects. Solomons' contribution provoked a vigorous debate in the 1970s on the strengths and, in particular, the shortcomings of residual income as a basis for motivating and apprais- ing divisional performance (Amey, 1969; Flower, 1971; Bromwich, 1973; Tomkins, 1973). Solomons' preference for residual income over return on investment emerged intact, but inconsistencies were identified between the use of residual income to control divisional performance and the objective of maximising the value of the firm. Basically, the central tenet of income measurement that a single measure of income will not be suitable for all purposes was found to apply to residual income (Amey, 1969; Flower, 1971; Bromwich, 1973; Tomkins, 1973).

An important shortcoming, in the context of residual income type VBM techniques, that forms the centrepiece of recent reviews of residual income (Bromwich and Walker, 1998; O'Hanlon and Peasnell, 1998) is that single-period residual income will not, except in special circumstances, equal the change in the fundamental value of the firm. Residual income equals $M_t + D_t - (1 - K_e)M_{t-1}$. The return to shareholders will, however, be given by the residual income plus the change in the value of subjective goodwill, where

$$V_t^* - M_t = E_t \sum_{\tau=1}^{N} \frac{R_{t+\tau}}{(1 + k_e)^\tau} \qquad (13.6)$$

and

$$V_{t-1}^* - M_{t-1} = E_{t-1} \sum_{\tau=0}^{N} \frac{R_{t+\tau}}{(1 + k_e)^{\tau+1}} \qquad (13.7)$$

then

$$V_t^* - (1 - K_e)V_{t-1}^* + D_t = M_t + D_t - (1 + K_e)M_{t-1} + G_t - G_{t-1} \qquad (13.8)$$

Thus residual income differs from the change in fundamental value where there are unexpected changes in current residual income and in the expected residual income for subsequent periods. This result also applies when the market value of the firm, reflecting investors' expectations, is substituted for fundamental value, V^*. In a climate of uncertainty the existence of windfall effects will cause reported residual income to be an unreliable performance metric when appraising single-period performance.

This criticism does not apply, in principle, to internal evaluation with knowledge of the expectations on which corporate strategy is based. For example, where start-up losses are anticipated they will be factored into plans, and reported negative residual incomes can be evaluated against expectations. Problems arise in practice, however, for external evaluation with no access to internal expectations.

The focus in Edwards and Bell is the impact of events on shareholder wealth. Alternatively, an enterprise view of the business entity extends the reporting boundary to include all interest-bearing debt in addition to shareholder equity. This perspective has many advocates among accounting theorists (Paton, 1922; Gynther, 1966; Revsine, 1973). Note, however, that the fundamental characteristics of Edwards and Bell's approach apply equally to enterprise income, namely, the CSR, residual income and the value equivalence of different intermediate accounting values for assets. For each of equations (13.1) to (13.8), enterprise income, assets and finance charges (interest plus dividends) are substituted for the equity equivalents.

ECONOMICS AND FINANCE

The literature on financial economics lacks any notable contribution to the theory and measurement of income for the purpose of performance appraisal. An enterprise model of income underpins Modigliani and Miller's (1958) classic arbitrage-based proof that the value of a firm is based on its investment policy and is independent of its financial structure. In a subsequent extension, Modigliani and Miller (1963) recognised the effect of the tax deductibility of interest as an additional element contributing to the value of levered firms. Subsequent empirical research, however, has focused on the equity value of the firm, and the ready availability of market prices for equity shares has led researchers to identify the market return, equal to dividend plus the change in share price as 'economic' income. In the family of economic income concepts, financial capital maintenance (Hicks 1) is the same as the market return. It shares the merits of Hicks (1), in that it is relatively easy to measure and it reflects how much better off the investor is in financial terms. However, it also shares its defect in that it includes the effect of incorrect expectations. As pointed out in the discussion of Edwards and Bell, for the purpose of internal appraisal, identification of errors in expectations is of central importance but these errors can only be identified given knowledge of managerial projections. They do not need to be separately identified in ex post financial reporting. In a financial markets setting, however, investors do not have access to managerial expectations. Performance evaluation and forecasting maintainable returns for valuation purposes is thus impaired in the absence of information on which to identify the effect of incorrect expectations on the market return. Thus, as is the case for residual income, observation of the market return for a single period, given uncertainty, will be an unreliable indicator of managerial achievement.

CONVENTIONAL FINANCIAL ACCOUNTING

Financial accounting practice cannot be described formally. Traditionally, it was not based on a specific income construct and preparers enjoyed considerable discretion in the choice of accounting policy. The need for a periodic account of profitability emerged in the eighteenth century in response to the funding requirements of business enterprises that were intended to run indefinitely. The arbitrary division of the trading cycle into accounting periods provides the main challenge for financial accounting. In the absence of good second-hand markets, current values are costly to obtain and there are many instances where the timing of resource consumption does not match the timing of payments. To provide a basis for fairness and comparability across firms, generally accepted conventions have evolved. The convention of matching allocates costs to the period in which the associated benefit is recognised. The allocation methods that impact most heavily on profit measurement are depreciation (fixed assets) and overhead allocation (valuation of stock in trade). Arbitrary techniques are used and they provide considerable scope for the exercise of managerial discretion. Conventionally, assets are valued at undepreciated historic cost. The concept of prudence is also applied to guard against excessive managerial optimism when recognising revenue. Gains are not recognised until realised in cash, or its equivalent, and anticipated losses are charged against profit. If assets are revalued the unrealised gain is not recognised as income, in breach of the CSR, but is taken to reserves in the balance sheet. Overall, conventional financial statements fail to reflect events of the period. Solomons (1961) summarised the relationship between accounting and economic income as follows:

Accounting income

$$
+ \left(\begin{array}{c} \text{Unrealised changes in the value of tangible assets which} \\ \text{took place during the period, over and above} \\ \text{value changes recognised as depreciation} \\ \text{of fixed assets and inventory markdowns} \end{array}\right)
$$

$$
- \left(\begin{array}{c} \text{Amounts realised this period in respect of value} \\ \text{changes in tangible assets which took place in previous} \\ \text{periods and were not recognised in those periods} \end{array}\right)
$$

$$+\left(\begin{array}{c}\text{Changes in the value of intangible assets}\\\text{during the period, i.e. goodwill}\end{array}\right)$$

$=$ Economic income

DEVELOPMENTS IN ACCOUNTING PRACTICE

The requirements of the Companies Acts are a major influence on conventional accounting practice. They are primarily designed to protect the interest of lenders in the face of the limited liability of shareholders. Before the rules in the EU Fourth Directive on distributable capacity were introduced into the 1981 Companies Act, legal guidance on the measurement of profit was confined to case law. The judiciary were generally careful not to unduly interfere with the freedom of business people. Consequently, their decisions are an inadequate guide to good accounting practice (Yamey, 1962).

In accounting practice the conventions of matching and prudence based on historic cost evolved as rough but generally accepted methods to ensure protection for lenders in the face of the interest of shareholders in dividend policy, and also to assess tax liabilities. Two other primary purposes of income measurement are the assessment of managerial performance and the use of reported income to set and revise expectations. These purposes are related. In the context of ex post reporting to external users, separate identification of permanent from transitory income effects is important for assessing the significance of periodic income (Ohlson, 1999). An earlier approach to distinguishing between exceptional and extraordinary items, adopted by the accounting profession in the 1970s (SSAP6, *Extraordinary Items and Prior Year Adjustments*, ASC, 1971) was undermined by the cosmetic manipulation of EPS by management seeking to classify gains as exceptional, and losses as extraordinary items in order to boost EPS. FRS3 then effectively abolished the classification of items as extraordinary (FRS3, *Reporting Financial Performance*, ASB, 1992). In addition, to improve the assessment and predictability of profitability, the results from continuing, discontinued and acquired operations, and the impact of exceptional items on profitability are separately identified. A further feature of FRS3 is the scope to recognise as income, in the statement of recognised gains and losses, revaluations to reflect current values of assets.

Recently, international standard setters in the G4 + 1 (this comprises members of the standard-setting bodies of Australia, Canada, New Zealand, UK and US and the IASC) have proposed a single statement that would report all recognised gains and losses as income (*Reporting Financial Performance: Proposals for Change*, ASB, 1999), whether realised or not. If implemented this would represent a significant step toward the achievement of two important characteristics of the Edwards and Bell approach. First, it opens the door to reporting business profit, provided assets are valued at current replacement cost. Second, it is consistent with clean surplus accounting.

REGULATION OF ACCOUNTING PRACTICE

Income measurement is relied upon for settlement purposes by investors, lenders, management, suppliers, employees and the government, each of whom obtains contractual entitlements in return for the provision of funds and other inputs to the firm. Where contractual entitlements depend on financial accounting data, the challenge for the financial accountant is to provide a generally acceptable basis for the resolution of these conflicts. For the purpose of this review, these conflicts can be broadly classified as those existing between preparers and users, with management in both groups.

In practice, auditors and the accounting profession respond to the relative balance of power between each group. Traditionally, in the UK the balance of influence lay with the preparers of financial statements. Over the past 30 years, however, the interests of users have been partially met by a gradual increase in information disclosed in financial statements. In recent years the increasing emphasis on linking managerial rewards to accounting profit and share price performance has, however, increased the risk of earnings management (Schipper, 1989). In the late 1980s, in the face of a gathering tide of 'creative' accounting' (Griffiths, 1995), UK accounting regulation proved inadequate. Consequently, a new framework of accounting regulation was implemented following the Dearing Report (1988). Under the chairmanship of Sir David Tweedie the ASB, with the aid of enhanced powers of enforcement, has undertaken a substantial programme of reform. There are two notable elements. First is the statement of principles published by the ASB in 1999, which stands at the heart of the ASB's strategy for the provision of neutral financial reporting. This identifies relevance and reliability as the key characteristics of financial accounting data. Accounting principles provide a framework to guide good, i.e. fair, accounting practice. The aim is that in due course all accounting standards will be consistent with these principles. Second, there has been progress toward clean surplus accounting, by the recognition in the statement of recognised gains and losses of asset revaluation as income, and by the requirement that goodwill should be amortised.

A striking omission from the ASB's agenda, however, is the failure to provide a framework to assess managerial performance that links accounting data with value created for the shareholder. One possible explanation is that the accounting profession has too readily taken the part of the preparers of financial statements by failing to adequately address users' needs for information to assess managerial performance.

The significance of the information gap in conventional accounting data is evidenced by the development and growing adoption of VBM techniques. Prominent among them is the EVA metric marketed by Stern Stewart. This technique is particularly interesting in the context of this chapter because of its derivation from fundamental accounting theories. However, it must be acknowledged that Stern Stewart have succeeded where accounting educators and the accounting profession have failed. Specifically, they identify as unacceptable the scope available for managerial manipulation of earnings. A further weakness of conventional financial data is that it takes no account of the cost of capital tied up in capital employed.

A primary feature of the Stern Stewart metric is the large number of adjustments they make to conventional measures of profit and capital. The adjustments restore the CSR and provide a measure of profit less subject to managerial manipulation. Managerial accountability is also improved by recalculating capital to reflect resources contributed by providers of capital. In particular, retaining purchased goodwill in the capital base ensures that managers are required to earn at least the cost of capital on the full cost of corporate acquisitions.

The Stern Stewart approach is based on the enterprise valuation model advanced by Modigliani and Miller (1958) and subsequently adapted to incorporate the tax shield gain from debt (Modigliani and Miller, 1963). However, the accounting counterpart of the contribution from financial economics is the 'all equities' enterprise model of the reporting entity advanced by Paton (1922). Also, as has been demonstrated in this chapter, Stern Stewart's work is remarkable for its similarity to the classic accounting contribution of Edwards and Bell. A comparison of the fundamental elements of the Edwards and Bell and Stern Stewart metrics is provided in Table 13.1, together with those for conventional accounting profit. The main differences between Edwards and Bell and Stern Stewart are (i) the choice of the boundary for the reporting entity: equity for Edwards and Bell and enterprise for Stern Stewart, and (ii) the valuation basis for assets: replacement cost for Edwards and Bell and historic cost for Stern Stewart. A further similarity is that both use interest-based methods of calculating depreciation. Edwards and Bell advocate internal rate of return depreciation (Edwards and Bell, 1961, pp. 171–98); Stern Stewart favour the cost of capital in the sinking fund or the annuity method of depreciation (Stewart, 1994, p. 80). Arguably, replacement cost accounting provides a more demanding hurdle against which to measure managerial performance. In an extension of Edwards and Bell for external reporting, Forker (1984) proposed a measurement system in which management would choose to value assets at either replacement cost or net realisable value. The resulting value of capital, and the associated cost of capital, would then serve as a commitment by management of the least amount they expected to earn on assets employed. The accounting technique was termed contract value accounting (CoVa). Note that the inclusion in

Table 13.1. Fundamental elements of financial performance methods

Characteristics	Edwards and Bell (1961)	Economic value added	Conventional accounting profit
Purpose	Internal evaluation of outcomes against plans	Internal evaluation of outcomes against plans Managerial rewards External evaluation	Dividend distribution Taxation Performance evaluation Valuation
Boundary of the reporting entity	Shareholders' equity	Enterprise: equity plus debt	Shareholders' equity
Asset valuation base	Current values (replacement cost)	Historic cost	Modified historic cost
Income construct	Business profit	NOPAT	Realised profit
Residual income/ clean surplus relation (CSR)	Business profit and CSR	NOPAT and CSR	Not applicable

financial statements of a charge for the cost of capital has been strongly advocated by Anthony (1975, 1983).

EMPIRICAL EVIDENCE

Much empirical evidence has accumulated over the years on share prices and different performance measures. Most of this earlier research centred on the relationship between earnings (or its components) and share prices versus that of cash flows and share prices; see Bowen et al. (1986) and Ali (1994) for the US, see Arnold et al. (1991) and Clubb (1995) for the UK. More recently, empirical research has examined the relationship between share prices and earnings, residual income and Stern Stewart's variant of residual income, EVA. Stern Stewart have made strong claims regarding the superiority of EVA over other performance measures such as earnings, return on equity and return on investment. The basis of these claims comes primarily from 'in-house' research. For example, Stewart (1994, p. 75) argues that 'EVA stands well out from the crowd as the single best measure of wealth creation on a con-temporaneous basis' and, furthermore, 'EVA is almost 50% better than its closest accounting-based competitor in explaining changes in shareholder wealth'. Surprisingly, little independent research has actually been published to date to test the above claims. The few studies that have been published to date are US-based, notably Biddle et al. (1997).

Biddle et al. set out to empirically test the claims made by Stern Stewart. They employ the standard relative and incremental information content methodologies to examine the association between market-adjusted returns with earnings, operating cash flows, residual income and EVA. Their findings are overwhelming in support of a simple earnings measure. For example, using the relative information content methodology for 6174 firm-years over the period 1984–93, they find earnings significantly more highly associated with market-adjusted returns ($R^2 = 12.8\%$) than with residual income ($R^2 = 7.3\%$), EVA ($R^2 = 6.5\%$) or operating cash flows ($R^2 = 2.8\%$). Furthermore, adopting the incremental information content methodology, they compared components unique to EVA (e.g. the capital charge and accounting adjustments) with components in earnings and operating cash flows, and they found that the components unique to EVA are not significant. Taken together, these results would seem to place some doubt on the claims made by Stern Stewart regarding the merits of EVA over simple earnings-based performance measures.

Arguably, however, the information content approach adopted by Biddle et al. is unsatisfactory because it fails to provide an unbiased test of the information content of the alternative accounting measures for two reasons. First, their test of the relationship between contemporaneous ex post abnormal earnings and ex post accounting performance is biased in favour of earnings because of the dominant impact of windfalls in both abnormal returns and accounting earnings. Abnormal returns, by definition, reflect the impact of unanticipated events in the current period and changed expectations about subsequent periods. Accounting earnings include windfalls for the current period and, through accruals and provisions, may serve to alter expectations about the future. Second, equity returns are compared to enterprise-based performance measures. In the light of these shortcomings, the Biddle et al. findings merit further research to identify more precisely the relative usefulness of different measures of performance.

In the UK, research on direct comparisons of EVA and other performance measures with share prices has still to be published. Replicating the Bowen et al. study, Forde (1998) found similar results using a UK dataset (the EVA dataset was purchased from Stern Stewart and comprised the top 500 firms in the UK, ranked by MVA). Several papers, published recently, have examined the link between residual income and earnings. A special issue of *Management Accounting Research*, published in 1998, contains several papers (mostly theoretical in nature) that address the issue of value-based financial management systems. Among them, Stark and Thomas (1998) examine which of residual income or earnings has a stronger relationship with market value. They estimate four cross-sectional regression models of market value on earnings and residual income. The capital charge for their residual income measure is proxied by adding back opening book value to the right-hand side of the equation. Research and development (R&D) expenditures are also included on the basis that prior research has shown them to improve the ability to explain market values. They find that although the relationship between residual income and market value may be imperfect, it has a stronger relationship with market value when R&D expenditures, opening and closing book values are included compared to earnings coupled with the same elements. This would suggest that the capital charge element of residual income has some incremental information content. Hence, in contrast to Biddle et al., their results provide some support for those who use residual income as a performance measure.

Further evidence in support of residual income based performance measures comes from Wallace (1997). He empirically tests the theory that residual income based financial management systems are more likely to encourage managers to take actions similar to owners relative to traditional accounting-based measures. A sample of firms that began using residual income measures in their compensation plans were compared to a control sample of firms that used compensation plans based on traditional accounting earnings-based measures. Compared to the control sample, residual income adopters undertook actions more in line with shareholder value maximisation and the reduction of agency costs. For example, Wallace notes that residual income adopters 'increased their payouts to shareholders through share repurchases, used their assets more intensively, increased their dispositions of assets and decreased new investment' (ibid., p. 276). Furthermore, the study finds some weak evidence of a positive response by the market to residual income adopters. As noted in the introduction, empirical research to date has been confined to the investigation of the association between accounting data and residual income-type metrics. Published empirical research into alternative VBM metrics is currently not available.

CONCLUSION

A central insight for the economic analysis of income measurement is that no single measure will satisfy the range of purposes that arise from users needs. Conventional accounting practice is easy to criticise for its arbitrary conventions. However, in the UK the Accounting Standards Board has made considerable progress in recent years to de-emphasise the importance of the 'bottom line' profit figure. Following FRS3 in 1992, the accounting profession has abandoned the earlier attempt to report maintainable earnings for the purpose of reporting earnings per share. Rather, the onus has been placed on users of accounts to form an opinion on the quality and permanency of profitability assisted by the provision of increased disclosure of the components of profit.

Following publication of the draft statement of principles by the ASB, a basis has been provided to restrict the flexibility traditionally available to management. The quality of financial reporting and the accountability of management will be further enhanced following the requirement to amortise goodwill (FRS10, *Goodwill and Intangible Assets*, ASB, 1997) and the imposition of strict rules for the recognition of provisions (FRS12, *Provisions, Contingent Liabilities and Contingent Assets*, ASB, 1998). There is, however, a growing realisation that accounting regulations and the role of auditors are an inadequate defence against the abuse of managerial flexibility in the choice of accounting policy. Following the Cadbury Report into the financial aspects of corporate governance (Cadbury Committee, 1992), the role of governance structures such as committees of the boards as instruments for internal accounting control are receiving greater attention.

It remains the case, however, that conventional accounting data is unsuitable for the purpose of financial planning and control. The gap has been filled in the investment community by the development of VBM techniques. Closest in form to financial statement data is the residual income based metric of EVA developed by Stern Stewart. The enterprise basis for EVA is attributable to the work of Modigliani and Miller on the effect of capital structure on the value of the firm. In this chapter it has been shown that while the work of these financial economists is of significance for valuation purposes, the core ideas for EVA as a tool for financial planning and control were established in the domain of accounting theory. The work of Edwards and Bell is remarkable for its similarity in spirit and construction to the EVA metric promoted by Stern Stewart. Indeed, it is arguable that the original Edwards and Bell formulation, based on current values for assets, provides a superior benchmark against which to assess performance compared to the historic cost valuation base favoured by Stern Stewart.

Value-based measurement techniques have filled a gap, particularly for internal assessment and the strategic review of managerial plans. Many claims are made by those marketing VBM techniques. However, there are dangers associated with unsophisticated interpretation. Residual income techniques have been available for many years but relatively few companies use them for internal control. One reason may be their unsuitability for use as an indicator of the value created in a single period. This criticism applies particularly to EVA. When used internally to evaluate internal projections and as a basis for managerial remuneration, as proposed by Stern Stewart, EVA would appear to be particularly appropriate. However, its use by external users to judge performance, particularly in annual league tables, is likely to be misleading. Finally, recent empirical studies provide some support for the view that residual income may have a closer association with share prices than accounting profit and that firms which link managerial remuneration to residual income generate superior performance. However, empirical research is currently only in a developmental phase. Tentative conclusions can be drawn for the residual income based metric promoted by Stern Stewart, but not for other VBM alternatives.

ACKNOWLEDGEMENT

The authors are grateful to the Research Board of the Institute of Chartered Accountants in England and Wales for funding the research on which this chapter is based.

REFERENCES

Ali, A. (1994) The incremental information content of earnings, funds flow and cash flow. *Journal of Accounting Research*, **32**, 61–74.

Amey, L. (1969) *The Efficiency of Business Enterprises*. Allen and Unwin, London.

Anthony, R. (1975) *Accounting for the Cost of Interest*. D.C. Heath, Lexington MA.

Anthony, R. (1983) *Tell It Like It Was: A Conceptual Framework for Financial Accounting*. Richard D. Irwin, Homewood IL.

Arnold, A., Clubb, C., Manson, S. and Wearing, R. (1991) The relationship between earnings, funds flow and cash flow: evidence for the UK. *Accounting and Business Research*, **22**, 12–19.

Biddle, G., Bowen, R. and Wallace, J. (1997) Does EVA® beat earnings? evidence on associations with stock returns and firm values. *Journal of Accounting and Economics*, **24**, 301–36.

Bowen, R., Burgstahler, D. and Daley, L. (1986) Evidence on the relationships between earnings and various measures of cash flow. *Accounting Review*, **61**, 713–25.

Bromwich, M. (1973) Measurement of divisional performance: a comment and extension, *Accounting and Business Research*, Spring, 123–32.

Bromwich, M. and Walker M. (1998) Residual income past and future. *Management Accounting Research*, **9**, 391–419.

Cadbury Committee, (1992) Committee on the Financial Aspects of Corporate Governance, *Report of the Committee on the Financial Aspects of Corporate Governance*, Gee & Co.

Clubb, C. (1995) An empirical study of the information content of accounting earnings, funds flows and cash flows in the UK. *Journal of Business Finance and Accounting*, **22**, 35–52.

Dearing, Sir R. (1988) *The Making of Accounting Standards*. CCAB, London.

Dechow, P., Hutton, A. and Sloan, R. (1999) An empirical assessment of the residual income valuation model. *Journal of Accounting and Economics*, **26**, 1–34.

Edwards, E. (1977) The primacy of accounting income in decisions on expansion: an exercise in arithmetic. In *Trends in Managerial and Financial Accounting* (ed. C. van Dam). Martinus Nijhoff, Amsterdam.

Edwards, E. (1980) The fundamental character of excess current income. *Accounting and Business Research*, Autumn.

Edwards, E. and Bell, P. (1961) *The Theory and Measurement of Business Income*. University of California Press, Berkeley CA.

Fisher, I. (1906) *The Nature of Capital and Income*. Macmillan, London

Flower, J. (1971) Measurement of divisional performance. *Accounting and Business Research*, Summer, 205–14.

Forde, J. (1998) EVA® – An all-purpose performance measure? Unpublished dissertation, Queen's University of Belfast.

Forker, J. (1984) Contract value accounting and the monitoring of managerial performance – a proposal based on principal agent relationships. *Accounting and Business Research*, Spring, 125–37

Griffiths, I. (1995) *New Creative Accounting*. Macmillan, Basingstoke.

Gynther, R. (1966) *Accounting for price-level changes: theory and procedures*. Pergamon, Oxford.

Hicks, J. R. (1946) *Value and Capital*, 2nd edn. Clarendon Press, Oxford.

Hirshliefer, D. (1970) *Investment, Interest, and Capital*. Prentice Hall, Englewood Cliffs NJ.

Kaldor, N. (1955) *The Concept of Income in Economic Theory: An Expenditure Tax*. Allen and Unwin, London, pp. 54–78

Kay, J. (1976) Accountants, too, could be happy in a golden age: the accountants' rate of profit and the internal rate of return. *Oxford Economic Papers*, November, 447–60.

Lindahl, N. (1939) *Studies in the Theory of Money and Capital*. Allen and Unwin, London.

Modigliani, F. and Miller, M. (1958) The cost of capital, corporation finance and the theory of investment. *American Economic Review*, June, 261–97.

Modigliani, F. and Miller, M. (1963) Corporate income taxes and the cost of capital: a correction. *American Economic Review*, June, 433–43.

O'Hanlon, J. and Peasnell, K. (1998) Wall Street's contribution to management accounting: the Stern Stewart EVA® financial management system. *Management Accounting Research*, **9**, 421–44.

Ohlson, J. (1989) Accounting earnings book values and dividends: the theory of clean surplus equation (Part 1). Unpublished Paper 59, Colombia University, New York.

Ohlson, J. (1999) On transitiory earnings. Unpublished paper, Stern School of Business, New York.

Paton, W.A. (1922), *Accounting theory: with special reference to the corporate enterprise*. Ronald Press, New York. Reprinted 1973 by Scholars Book Co., Houston TX.

Peasnell, K. (1982) Some formal connections between economic values and yields in accounting numbers. *Journal of Business Finance and Accounting*, Autumn, 361–81.

Preinreich, G. (1938) Annual study of economic theory: the theory of depreciation. *Econometrica*, July, 219–41.

Revsine, L. (1973) *Replacement Cost Accounting*. Prentice Hall, Englewood Cliffs NJ.

Schipper, K. (1989) Earnings management. *Accounting Horizons*, December, 91–102.

Solomons, D. (1961) Economic and accounting concepts of income. *Accounting Review*, July, 374–83.

Solomons, D. (1965) *Divisional Performance: Measurement and Control*. Richard D. Irwin, Homewood IL.

Stark, A. and Thomas, H. (1998) On the empirical relationship between market value and residual income in the UK. *Management Accounting Research*, **9**, 445–60.

Stewart, G. (1991) *The Quest for Value*. Harper Collins, New York.

Stewart, G. (1994) EVA®: fact or fantasy. *Journal of Applied Corporate Finance*, Summer, 71–84.

Tomkins, C. (1973) *Financial Planning in Divisionalised Companies*. Accountancy Age Books, London.

Wallace, J. (1997) Adopting residual income-based compensation plans: do you get what you pay for? *Journal of Accounting and Economics*, **24**, 275–300.

Yamey, B. (1962) The case law relating to company dividends. In *Studies in Accounting Theory*, 2nd edn (eds W.T. Baxter and S. Davidson). Richard D. Irwin, Homewood, IL.

14 Approaches to Value-based Performance Measurement

JOCHEN DRUKARCZYK AND ANDREAS SCHUELER

INTRODUCTION

This chapter is a contribution to the normative theory of finance. We assume with the great majority of academics that the maximisation of firm value is a defendable definition of the goal that managers, separated from firm owners, should try to reach.

Academic journals and finance textbooks have been discussing for over 70 years how projects or firms should be evaluated under uncertainty, different tax regimes and specified financing policies. Even if there are a number of open issues concerning the correct valuation under uncertainty, progress made so far is impressive. We know that the net present value criterion works, how financing decisions affect value, how taxes are to be incorporated in valuing projects (firms); CAPM and ICAPM taught us to understand the difficulties in measuring costs of capital.

Performance measurement of firms is closely tied to the principles governing the valuation of firms (projects). A performance measure should signal whether firm value increased or decreased in a period. Management devoted to the maximization of firm value needs performance measures linked to firm value in order to determine whether the budgeted outcomes of investment and financing strategies turn out as expected, and to trigger corrective actions if the results do not correspond to those expected. One could view value-based management as a policy of a firm which tries to enhance firm value by choosing appropriate investment, financing and dividend strategies and complements this policy by a continuous monitoring process.

Investors, creditors of firms, boards as monitors of the management need periodic performance measures related to profitability and firm value. One might argue that, if shares are listed, market price is a reliable performance measure clearly linked to firm value and that alternative measures based on accounting data are not needed. We do not support this position for the following three reasons.

First, a central problem of major firms is the overinvestment problem. Managers tend to invest in projects which do not cover their cost of capital. This behaviour is value reducing; the funds, that is the free cash flow in terms of Jensen (1986), would have been better paid out to shareholders. This feature is well known for corporations operating in mature businesses; convincing empirical support of overinvestment is available. A very partial list of references is Grabowski and Mueller (1975), Picchi (1985), Ball (1987), Jensen (1993), Blanchard et al. (1994), Shleifer and Vishny (1988), Morck et al. (1989), Mueller et al. (1993), Nowack (1997, pp. 173–201) and Schüler (1998).

The funds financing the investment outlays of firms are either generated by internal financing (primarily retentions and not cash equivalent expenses) or by external financing. On average 70% to 90% of the necessary funds are generated by internal financing. The role of funds generated by tapping the capital market is not of equal importance in different countries, but its general role is modest compared to the volume of internally generated funds in all countries. A governance structure concerning the reinvestment decision process in corporations seems therefore to be of prime importance. See Statistische Jahrbücher der Bundesrepublik Deutschland (1980–1996) and Brealey and Myers (1996, pp. 366–67). If the profitability of these funds is to be measured, one cannot rely exclusively on the rate of return shareholders have received over a given period of time (Jensen, 1993, p. 854). Assume a shareholder receives dividends and a share price increase during a ten-year period, giving them a rate of return of 12% (based on a share price of 100 at the beginning of the period), exceeding the risk equivalent cost of capital of 10%. Thus value is created, since the shareholder rate of return exceeds the cost of capital. But how would one judge the performance if the management of the firm has reinvested (besides investments corresponding to depreciation) another 200 per share? Did the reinvestment contribute to the increase in value or not? Looking only at shareholder returns does not answer this question. The periodic increases in the capital base due to additional investment outlays are to be accounted for. Recourse to accounting data is therefore necessary.

Second, value-based performance measures should be implemented at every level of the firm or the group of firms. Market prices of divisions or units cannot be observed; estimating them is often cumbersome and subject to error. Operating units are like 'private' companies owned by a publicly traded company. Accounting data is probably not an optimal starting point, but it is an objective footing upon which more acceptable performance measures could be built. And third, in all countries the majority of firms are not listed, therefore the need to define reliable performance measures based on accounting data seems convincing.

This chapter aims to develop a value-based system of performance measurement which could be implemented in the firm. It could also be used by investors and creditors without inside information. We define some (preliminary) requirements:

(1) The criterion signalling the performance of a period must be linked to (changes in) firm value.
(2) Signals should be positive (negative) at that point in time when firm value increases (decreases).
(3) Incentives to produce signals of performance corresponding to non-shareholder interest might exist. Therefore the signal should be fairly immune to manipulation.

We start with a presentation of current discounted cash flow (DCF) approaches to valuation of firms. Each of them could serve as a basis for the development of value-based performance measures. We do not discuss the interesting issue of which approach is best for the given purpose (Copeland et al., 1994, pp. 13–152; Drukarczyk, 1998, pp. 208–45). We decide in favour of the *WACC* approach, probably the best known among managers. We develop a classification of possible performance measures using as a criterion (a) whether cost of capital is charged on a capital base which is reflecting expectations or not, and (b) whether depreciation (change in the capital base) is considering expectations or not. We distinguish the problems of measuring performance at the unit level and at the corporate level. We argue that, if DCF compatibility is respected, residual income based on book value will be a defendable solution at the unit level. At the corporate level, performance measures based on book values do not meet the requirements. We develop a performance measure combining changes in market value and changes in invested capital.

VALUE OF THE FIRM AND PERFORMANCE MEASURES

APPROACHES TO THE VALUATION OF FIRMS

Ideally a (periodic) performance measure should indicate the change in value of the firm that has taken place during the period. Four approaches to valuing firms can be distinguished. Table 14.1 contains a basic description of these approaches. The notation is as follows:

$\bar{X}_t$	expected operating cash flows in period t before interest payments, repayments of debt, taxes
Dep_t	depreciation in period t
$i_D D_{t-1}$	interest payments in period t
ΔD_t	repayment of debt in period t
E_t	issuance of new equity in period t
t_c	corporate tax rate
Div_t	dividends paid in period t
Div_t^I	dividends paid in period t of a partly debt-financed firm
Div_t^{II}	dividends paid in period t of a purely equity-financed firm

Table 14.1. Different approaches to firm valuation

	Approach I Equity	Approach II APV	Approach III WACC	Approach IV Capital cash flow
(1) Cash flows to be discounted	Cash to be paid out to shareholders $\bar{X}_t - t_c(\bar{X}_t - Dep_t - i_D D_{t-1})$ $- i_D D_{t-1} - \Delta D_t + E_t$ $- I_t - \Delta NWC_t = Div_t^I$	(a) Cash to be paid out to shareholders, assuming pure equity financing of the firm $\bar{X}_t - t_c(\bar{X}_t - Dep_t)$ $+ E_t - I_t - \Delta NWC_t$ $= Div_t^{II}$ plus (b) Tax advantages due to debt financing $t_c i_D D_{t-1}$	Cash to be paid out to shareholders, assuming pure equity financing of the firm As defined in (a) of approach II	Cash to be paid out to *all* claimholders (including the benefits of tax shields) $\bar{X}_t - t_c(\bar{X}_t - Dep_t - i_D D_{t-1})$ $- i_D D_{t-1} - \Delta D_t + E_t$ $- I_t - \Delta NWC_t + i_D D_{t-1}$ $+ \Delta D_t = Div_t^{II} + t_c i_D D_{t-1}$
(2) Discount rate	k^D, containing a premium for business risk and financial risk	Cash flow (a) discounted at k Cash flow (b) discounted at i if financing policy is not linked to V^D; k if financing policy is defined by $L^* = $ constant	$WACC = i_D(1 - t_c)(D/V^D)$ $+ k^D(E/V^D)$	$WACC^* = i_D(D/V^D) + k^D(E/V^D)$
(3) Assumptions necessary if a constant discount rate is to be used	Constant business risk Constant degree of leverage $L^* = (D_t/V_t^D)$ Risk of bankruptcy and financial distress excluded Debt financing triggers tax advantages in every period	Constant business risk Constant degree of leverage L^* or autonomous financial policy, not linked to V^D Risk of bankruptcy and financial distress excluded Debt financing triggers tax advantages in every period	Constant business risk Constant degree of leverage $L^* = (D_t/V_t^D)$ Risk of bankruptcy and financial distress excluded Debt financing triggers tax advantages in every period	Constant business risk Constant degree of leverage Risk of bankruptcy and financial distress excluded Debt financing triggers tax advantages in every period

I_t investment in fixed assets in period t

ΔNWC_t investment in net working capital in period t

k cost of equity of a purely equity-financed firm

k^D cost of equity of a partly debt-financed firm

$WACC$ weighted average cost of capital

i risk-free rate of return

i_D interest rate on debt

V^D total value of the firm

E value of equity

D value of debt

The formulae are valid for a simplified taxation system; income is taxed at the corporate level only. The tax system does not discriminate between profits paid out and retained earnings. We do not pretend that income taxes are not relevant; we simply exclude them by assumption (Table 14.1).

PERFORMANCE MEASUREMENT AND VALUATION APPROACHES

In principle the performance measurement can be based on each of the above methods of valuation. Appendix 1 presents an example using the *APV* approach. This method offers some advantages: since the valuation process is decomposed into (a) the valuation of the operating activities and (b) the value effects triggered by the financing of the firm, it is made evident where the value increase (or reduction) comes from. In addition the approach adapts easily to changes in the capital structure of the firm.

In the following we will discuss performance measurement using the *WACC* approach. It is probably the approach most favoured by textbooks on finance and valuation issues, investment banks, mergers and acquisitions specialists, and other experts. We will present a concept of residual income based on the *WACC* approach. An important property of the concept is the precise compatibility with net present value. The presentation is organised as follows. We start by discussing the principle of DCF compatibility. Several performance measures are analysed, some of them based on expectations about future cash flows and some of them not. We then take a closer look at residual income based on book value. After that we discuss the role of taxes and weighted average cost of capital.

PERIODIC PERFORMANCE MEASURES AND DCF COMPATIBILITY

Basic definition of residual income

We assume value maximisation to be the managerial objective: positive *NPV* projects should be realised, negative *NPV* projects should be dropped as they do not increase the value of the firm. Therefore, performance measures should be linked to *NPV* or firm value.

First we will discuss the principle of DCF compatibility for performance measures. *NPV* is calculated by summing up the present values of cash flows, i.e. the initial capital expenditure (IC_0) and the expected net cash flows in the subsequent periods (NCF_t). We define net cash flow as operating cash flow minus capital expenditures. We call it the DCF approach:

$$NPV = -IC_0 + \sum_{t=0}^{n} NCF_t(1 + WACC)^{-t} \qquad (14.1)$$

In simple cases the residual income (RI_t) is defined by operating cash flows (OCF_t) minus depreciation (Dep_t) and a capital charge ($WACC \cdot IC_{t-1}$). If depreciation and capital charge are defined properly, the sum of discounted residual incomes is equivalent to *NPV* (Appendix 2). We call this concept the RI approach:

$$NPV = \sum_{t=0}^{n} RI_t(1 + WACC)^{-t}$$

$$= \sum_{t=1}^{n} (OCF_t - Dep_t - WACC \cdot IC_{t-1})(1 + WACC)^{-t} \qquad (14.2)$$

This concept was mentioned by Preinreich (1938, pp. 239–41) and Solomons (1965, pp. 62–66). An examination of the difference between equations (14.1) and (14.2) reveals that it is the combination of depreciation and capital charge calculated on not yet depreciated book value at the beginning of the period, which ensures the equivalence to (14.1). Depreciating an asset means a delayed expense compared to the initial outlay at time 0. This delay is exactly offset by the capital charge on the capital expenditure minus cumulated depreciations (Lücke, 1955). Before discussing the extensions of the principle, we look at an example.

Consider a project which requires an initial investment outlay of 165 and generates operating cash flows for six periods. In period 2 an additional capital expenditure of 44 occurs. The cost of capital is 7.5%. Capital expenditures are depreciated until t_6 by applying a linear depreciation schedule. We assume that operating profit plus depreciation can be paid out to owners. The *NPV* of the project is 3.7. The same result is obtained by discounting the periodic residual income (Tables 14.2 and 14.3).

The series of residual incomes based on book values (RI^{BV}) depends upon the depreciation schedule chosen. We used a linear depreciation for both the initial capital expenditure and the additional capital expenditure. A change of

Table 14.2. DCF approach

	t_0	t_1	t_2	t_3	t_4	t_5	t_6
(1) OCF before capital expenditure		40.0	40.0	50.0	50.0	45.0	40.0
(2) Initial capital expenditure	−165						
(3) Additional capital expenditure			−44				
(1) + (2) + (3) = (4) NCF	−165	40	−4	50	50	45	40

NPV = 3.7

the depreciation schedule would change the structure of residual incomes, but due to the compensating effects of the capital charge, not the *NPV*. To eliminate managerial discretion, a standard depreciation schedule could be defined. The sum of all depreciations must be equal to the initial outlay.

A positive residual income signals that the capital charge is covered, i.e. the minimum performance standard is reached. It could signal a positive conribution to *NPV*. A negative residual income could signal a negative

Table 14.3. RI approach

	t_0	t_1	t_2	t_3	t_4	t_5	t_6
(1) OCF before capital expenditure		40.0	40.0	50.0	50.0	45.0	40.0
(2) Additional capital expenditure			−44.0				
(3) Book value = invested capital	165.0	137.5	154.0	115.5	77.0	38.5	0.0
(4) Depreciation (initial capital expenditure)		27.5	27.5	27.5	27.5	27.5	27.5
(5) Depreciation (additional capital expenditure)				11.0	11.0	11.0	11.0
(4) + (5) = (6) Total depreciation		27.5	27.5	38.5	38.5	38.5	38.5
(1) − (6) = (7) Operating profit		12.5	12.5	11.5	11.5	6.5	1.5
(8) Capital charge		−12.4	−10.3	−11.6	−8.7	−5.8	−2.9
(7) + (8) = (9) RI		0.1	2.2	0.0[a]	2.8	0.7	−1.4

NPV = 3.7

[a] Rounding error.

contribution to *NPV*. It is at least interesting that the residual income of the period is linked formally to *NPV* (or firm value). One might conclude that the longer the series of positive residual incomes, the greater the probability of a positive *NPV* project.

Here are some advantages of RI^{BV}:

- DCF compatibility can be ensured.
- A well-known and readily available set of data is used.
- It is immune to manipulations caused by cash flow forecasts.
- It accounts for the past investments financed either internally or externally.

Therefore this concept deserves further attention.

Alternative approaches not using expectations

There are variations of this basic residual income. One is EVA (economic value added), as defined and marketed by Stern Stewart (Stewart, 1991). We do not cover it in detail because a number of adjustments are suggested to calculate EVA and it is not clear whether DCF compatibility is given for all adjustments (O'Hanlon and Peasnell, 1998, p. 423).

It is also possible to combine capital charge and depreciation to an annuity. Again, the sum of the depreciations contained in the annuity has to equal the invested capital over the project's lifetime. Residual income is then defined as cash flow minus this annuity, which consists of capital charge and depreciation. The sum of these residual incomes discounted at the cost of capital equals *NPV*. One might argue that the deduction of a constant annuity from the periodic cash flow does not reveal much more information than periodic cash flow itself does. It also requires separate accounting for the adjusted capital base because the periodic depreciation will not equal a regular accounting schedule. We therefore do not cover this approach in detail; see Table 14.33 (Appendix 5).

Approaches using expectations

Residual income based on market value

We defined the following requirements for a performance measurement system:

(1) The criterion signalling the performance of a period must be linked to (changes in) firm value.
(2) Signals should be positive (negative) at that point in time when firm value increases (decreases).

(3) Incentives to produce signals of performance corresponding to non-shareholder interest might exist. Therefore the signal should be fairly immune to manipulation.

Residual income based on book values can ensure DCF compatibility (requirement 1). The sum of discounted residual incomes equals *NPV*. However, periodic residual income based on book values will only accidentally coincide with value creation (or reduction). But it could signal whether value is created or destroyed and quantify approximately the value created (destroyed), if we look at a number of periods.

An ideal performance measure should signal an increase (decrease) in firm value in the same period. This is hardly possible if expectations concerning future cash flows are not allowed to enter the game; that is, as long as the capital base is defined by book values. Theoretically (at least) two possibilities emerge: (1) invested capital is defined as the market value in an efficient market; (2) superior knowledge of insiders is allowed to enter the performance measurement system.

If a market value reflecting the consequences of the strategies of the firm is used as capital base, the expected value created by a project is attributed to the starting point: the residual incomes are zero if economic depreciation (economic depreciation corresponds to the change in firm value from period $t - 1$ to period t, $Dep_t = MV_t - MV_{t-1}$) is used in calculating these targeted residual incomes and expectations are met; the *NPV* of residual incomes is zero, but periodic residual incomes are different from zero if another depreciation schedule is chosen. In both cases DCF compatibility is given. Table 14.4 shows this result for our basic example. If the economic lifespan of a project (firm) is assumed to be infinitely long, the results will not be different.

If actual residual income is different from zero, an unexpected event has occurred, which signals a change in firm value. The deviation of the actual

Table 14.4

	t_0	t_1	t_2	t_3	t_4	t_5	t_6
(1) OCF before capital expenditure		40.0	40.0	50.0	50.0	45.0	40.0
(2) Capital expenditure		−44.0					
(3) Market value[a]	168.7	141.4	156.0	117.7	76.5	37.2	0.0
(4) Economic depreciation	−	27.3	−14.6	38.3	41.2	39.3	37.2
(5) Capital charge	−	−12.7	−10.6	−11.7	−8.8	−5.7	−2.9
(1) + (2) − (4) + (5) = (6) Residual income	−	0.0	0.0	0.0	0.0	0.0	0.0

[a] The operating cash flows are paid out to shareholders.

residual income in period t from the budgeted residual income of this period, indicates a deviation of expected and/or actual cash flow of period t from budgeted cash flow. However, a positive (negative) difference between actual and budgeted market value is never certain before the end of the project. But definitive answers concerning the performance of a project which has not yet reached the end of its life are not available. It is an open question whether economic depreciation based on market prices could be implemented, and it is also an open question whether a reliance on market prices would not distort the measurement of the operating performance of firms due to factors on which managers have no impact (variations of interest rates, noise, trading, etc.). Sanctions as well as incentives based on this concept could turn out to be misspecified.

If the idea of economic depreciation is dropped, some other definition of depreciation must take its place; see Table 14.34 (Appendix 5). Then residual incomes are no longer zero, but the *NPV* of budgeted residual incomes is still zero. Such a performance measure could be called residual income using goodwill (RI^{GW}), since MV_0 could be split up into book value and economic goodwill. The depreciation schedule on goodwill does not follow economic depreciation if goodwill is not adjusted periodically. A deviation of actual residual income from budgeted residual income in period t still signals a change of firm value, even if depreciation does not reflect changes in firm value. To anyone knowing the baseline of budgeted residual incomes, the deviation of an actual residual income is a clear signal of change in value as far as period t is concerned. However, the correlation is smaller if there are accounting distortions like a change of the depreciation schedule.

The second approach mentioned above uses (assumed) superior knowledge of insiders and simulates the change in firm value attributable to a period by allowing management to capitalise its expectations concerning operating cash flows in future periods. Different sources of information are reflected in observed market values and in private projections of what a fair market value could be; nevertheless they use the same technique to calculate residual income. An approach based on market values can be implemented even if the shares of the firm are not listed.

Net economic income

Residual income based on market values (RI^{MV}) is defined by

$$RI_t^{MV} = NCF_t + (MV_t - MV_{t-1}) - WACC \cdot MV_{t-1} \qquad (14.3)$$

Given the definition of economic income (EI) as

$$EI_t = NCF_t + (MV_t - MV_{t-1}), \qquad (14.4)$$

equation (14.3) can be written as

$$RI_t^{MV} = EI_t - WACC \cdot MV_{t-1} \qquad (14.5)$$

Economic income is the sum of current cash flow and change in market value. If expectations are met, this equals the capital charge on MV_{t-1}. This is equivalent to the conclusion drawn above, that residual incomes based on market values are zero if expectations are met. Subtracting the capital charge on MV_{t-1}, as shown in (14.5), implements a benchmark. If $RI^{MV} > 0$ or $NCF_t + (MV_t - MV_{t-1}) > WACC \cdot MV_{t-1}$, current and/or future cash flows are higher than expected (budgeted).

RI^{MV} and EI are linked to market value, i.e. the NPV is included but not referred to explicitly. The capital that investors invested in the project (firm) is the benchmark for determining NPV. Of course this can be MV_{t-1} if the investor has bought the company at this price or for other reasons assumes they have done so. Because in most cases the investor has invested their capital several periods ago, the invested capital to be considered is not MV_{t-1}. Defining the capital invested in $t - 1$ by IC_{t-1}, the invested capital in t is defined by

$$IC_t = IC_{t-1}(1 + WACC) - NCF_t \qquad (14.6)$$

If t^* is the period of the initial investment and T is the current period, IC_T is defined by $IC_T = IC_{t^*}(1 + WACC)^{T-t^*} - \sum_{t=t^*+1}^{T} NCF_t(1 + WACC)^{T-t}$. Current invested capital is the invested capital of the previous period increased by cost of capital and decreased by NCF, which we assume to be paid out. We can now redefine the capital charge in (14.5) more generally by using IC. Since this measure equals economic income after a capital charge, we will call it *net* economic income (NEI):

$$NEI_t = EI_t - WACC \cdot IC_{t-1} \qquad (14.7)$$

After rearranging (14.7) by using (14.6), it becomes evident that net economic income equals the change in market value compared to the change in invested capital. This difference is the change in net present value:

$$NEI_t = (MV_t - MV_{t-1}) - (IC_t - IC_{t-1})$$
$$= NPV_t - NPV_{t-1} = \Delta NPV_t \qquad (14.8)$$

The main advantage of this measure is the combination of the change in market value with the change of invested capital, thus implementing a benchmark from the investor's perspective.

Earned economic income

Another periodic performance measure suggested by Grinyer (Grinyer, 1985, 1987, 1995; Peasnell, 1995a, 1995b; Skinner 1998) is earned economic income (*EEI*). It is defined by

$$EEI_t = NCF_t \left(1 - \frac{IC_0}{MV_0} \right) \qquad (14.9)$$

It is rather obvious that the discounted sum of *EEI* equals *NPV*:

$$\sum_{t=1}^{n} EEI_t(1 + WACC)^{-t} = \left(1 - \frac{IC_0}{MV_0} \right) MV_0 = NPV_0 \qquad (14.10)$$

This idea can be applied to our basic example, as shown in Table 14.5. *EEI* assigns *NPV* contributions to specific periods according to the time structure of periodic cash flows. We will not discuss this concept in detail here, although it seems to deserve more attention. One argument against *EEI* might be that changes in expectations lead to changes in the multiplier which require ex post adjustments of past EEI in order to ensure the precise link to *NPV*.

Shareholder value added (Rappaport)

Rappaport suggests using shareholder value added (*SVA*) for performance measurement (Rappaport, 1998). *SVA* is supposed to represent the value increase triggered by the investment decisions in period *t*. It assigns the change in net operating profit after taxes to the incremental investment, i.e. the portion of the investment which exceeds depreciation, of the same period. One might call this a 'technological explanation' of value creation: value is created in the period when investments are *made* (investment outlays are paid). *SVA* is defined by

$$SVA_t = NCF_t + RV_t - RV_{t-1}(1 + WACC) \qquad (14.11)$$

with $\quad RV_t = Residual\ Value_t = \dfrac{NCF_t + Incremental\ Investment_t}{WACC}$

or

$$SVA_t = \frac{\Delta NOPAT_t(1 + WACC)}{WACC} - Incremental\ Investment_t \qquad (14.12)$$

Appendix 6 shows the equivalence between (14.11) and (14.12). Rappaport does not consider multiplication by $(1 + WACC)$; see Rappaport (1998,

Table 14.5. Earned economic income

	t_0	t_1	t_2	t_3	t_4	t_5	t_6
(1) NCF_t	-165	40	-4	50	50	45	40
(2) MV_0	168.7						
(3) IC_0/MV_0	0.98						
(1) $* [1-(3)] = $ (4) EEI_t		0.877	-0.088	1.097	1.097	0.987	0.877
$\sum_{t=1}^{n} EEI_t (1 + WACC)^{-1} = NPV_0 = 3.7$							
(5) Capital charge: $WACC \cdot IC_{t-1}^{EEI}$		12.4	10.4	11.4	8.6	5.6	2.7
(6) Depreciation: $CF_t \dfrac{IC_0}{MV_0} - WACC \cdot IC_{t-1}^{EEI}$		26.7	-14.3	37.5	40.3	38.4	36.4
(7) IC_t^{EEI}	165.0	138.3	152.5	115.1	74.8	38.4	36.4

p. 127). This performance measure draws upon expectations about future cash flows. Of course, the assumption that incremental investment triggers an infinite stream of $\Delta NOPAT$ is quite strict. The interesting aspect is the moment when value is created: value is created when the investment is made *and* given the expectation that the rate of return of the investment exceeds the cost of capital. Due to the assumption on the infinity of $\Delta NOPAT$ the performance measure will be highly volatile.

According to Rappaport, value is not created when a new strategy is announced, even if stock prices react positively (or negatively). The value of equity reacts when the additional production capacity is realised. But why should the value of the equity not rise as soon as the investment strategy is announced? Value would then be created at time 0 instead of in little steps from, say, period 1 to 5. If one applied the residual income approach and defined the invested capital at time 0 as the market value, the expected residual incomes would be zero. Value creation then takes place at time 0, when the strategy becomes known to the market. Therefore the problem of deciding when the value was created (reduced) depends on the definition of the relevant information and on whose information is relevant.

There are several reasons why we do not pursue Rappaport's proposal here:

- If expectations about future cash flows are to be used, these expectations should not be held back until the assumed 'value trigger', i.e. incremental investment, occurs.
- The perpetuity assumption as suggested by Rappaport leads to highly volatile performance figures. This problem could be diminished by using annuities over an estimated period of time instead of perpetuities.
- Assignment of the change in *NOPAT* to the incremental investment of the period will only accidentally be consistent:
  − Other investments (of other periods) besides *incremental* investments will also cause changes in NOPAT.
  − Even if only the incremental investments cause changes in *NOPAT*, this will hardly occur in the same period and probably not in the mechanical way assumed by Rappaport.

Preliminary results

The approaches discussed so far can be classified according to their reliance on expectations. For this purpose we differentiate between depreciation of capital and capital charge (Table 14.6). We do not discuss RI^{GW} in detail; if it is adjusted periodically, RI^{GW} will be equal to RI^{MV}. Nor do we devote much detail to *EVA*, *RI* based on annuities, *EEI*, *SVA*, and *RI* on market and book values combined. This is due to the reasons mentioned above; see also Table 14.34 (Appendix 5).

Table 14.6. Capital charge and depreciation of capital for periodic performance measures

	Depreciation of capital	
Capital charge	Based on expectations	Not based on expectations
Based on expectations	RI^{MV}, RI^{GW} NEI, EEI[a] SVA[b]	RI on market and book value combined[c]
Not based on expectations		RI^{BV} EVA RI based on annuities
Not included	EI	

[a] EEI is based on expectations in t_0.
[b] SVA is based on perpetuity assumption.
[c] See Table 14.34 in Appendix 5.

The remaining measures can be classified according to their link to value creation (destruction). Value changes if expectations about future cash flows change (assuming a constant discount rate). Strong DCF compatibility is given if the periodic performance measure precisely indicates the amount of value creation (destruction) occurring in period t; the benchmark is budgeted value creation (destruction).

Weak DCF compatibility is given if the periodic performance measure indicates the change in value in the period the deviation from budgeted cash flow is occurring, but not in the period the expectations are changing. Nevertheless, weak DCF-compatible measures discounted over the project's lifetime are equivalent to *NPV* (Table 14.7).

A CLOSER LOOK AT RESIDUAL INCOME BASED ON BOOK VALUES

Extensions of the principle of DCF compatibility

Capital expenditure and depreciation represent only one difference between cash flow and income. Other differences need to be considered in order to attain DCF compatibility. Our classification is based on two criteria: Is it an incoming item or an outgoing item? Does income/expense succeed or precede cash inflow/cash outflow? It is necessary to distinguish four groups of income statement items which do not equal cash flows in the same period (Table 14.8).

Table 14.7. Selected performance measures and degrees of DCF compatibility

	DCF compatibility	
	Strong	Weak
Linked to gross present value	RI^{MV} EI	
Linked to net present value	NEI	RI^{BV}

Cases 1 and 3 contain all income/expense items which occur *later* than the corresponding cash inflow/cash outflow. As the objective is to ensure DCF compatibility, two alternative treatments are possible: either use cash flows (*CF*) or use income/expense (*IE*) combined with a compensating capital charge. The 'capital charge' is positive or negative; it is negative when income follows cash inflow. The delayed income/expense item must be exempted/ charged periodically with cost of capital in order to ensure that discounted income/expense items are equivalent to the present value of cash flow.

This principle can be expressed as follows:

$$CF_{0C1,3} = IE_{tC1,3}(1 + WACC)^{-t}$$

$$+ \sum_{j=1}^{t} WACC \cdot IE_{tC1,3}(1 + WACC)^{-j} \qquad (14.13)$$

where $C1,3$ indicates case 1 and case 3 items.

If expense follows cash outflow – case 1, depreciation (IE_{tC1}) follows capital expenditure (CF_{0C1}) – this delay is compensated by a capital charge on the portion of the capital expenditure which is not yet depreciated ($WACC \cdot IE_{tC1}$).

Table 14.8. Differences between cash flow and income/expense

Cash outflow	Case 1 Expense follows cash outflow (e.g. depreciation)	Case 2 Cash outflow follows expense (e.g. trade creditors)
Cash inflow	Case 3 Income follows cash inflow (e.g. advance payments received)	Case 4 Cash inflow follows income (e.g. trade debtors)
	Income/expense recognition succeeds cash flow	Income/expense recognition precedes cash flow

If income follows cash inflow – case 3, sales revenues for products the customer paid for in advance – the income statement signals a delay; this can be compensated by *not* charging advance payments received with cost of capital. The invested capital (IC_{t-1}) is to be reduced accordingly.

Case 2 and case 4 items *precede* the corresponding cash flows. Looking at the income statement, expense or income is signalled too early. The balance sheet entries corresponding to advanced expenses (case 2) must be exempted from cost of capital. Those items corresponding with advanced income (case 4) have to be charged with cost of capital:

$$CF_{TC2,4} = IE_{tC2,4}(1 + WACC)^{T-t}$$

$$- \sum_{j=t+1}^{T} WACC \cdot IE_{tC2,4}(1 + WACC)^{T-j} \qquad (14.14)$$

If cash outflow follows expense – case 2, a supplier's bill is paid later than it appears in the income statement – this early consideration of the expense is to be compensated by not charging trade creditors (accounts payable) with cost of capital.

If cash inflow follows income – case 4, a customer pays the bill later than the revenue appears in the income statement – this early consideration of income can be compensated by charging trade debtors (accounts receivable) with cost of capital.

In compensating timing differences between cash flow and expense/income, two *RI* versions can be distinguished. Their points of reference are different. The first version uses operating profit as a point of reference. We call this version the operating profit (OP) approach. All adjustments necessary to ensure DCF compatibility concern only the definition of the capital base. So far we have discussed this approach. Managers would probably prefer the OP approach because it is based on the well-known rules defining operating profit. We therefore focus on this approach.

The second version uses the invested capital (as shown in the balance sheet) as a point of reference. The full amount of invested capital is to be charged with cost of capital. We call this version the invested capital (IC) approach. All adjustments to ensure DCF compatibility have to be considered in defining income. The treatment of cases 1 and 4 is the same as with the OP approach. But cases 2 and 3 are treated differently. If expense is preceding cash outflow (case 2), we can charge the corresponding balance sheet item with cost of capital only if cash outflow is used instead of expense. If income recognition succeeds cash inflow (case 3), the corresponding balance sheet item can only be charged if cash inflow is used instead of income. Thus the resulting definition of income is a mixture between income

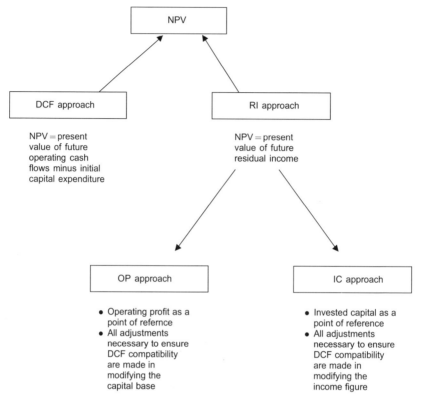

Figure 14.1. A summary of the conceptual alternatives

according to the income statement and cash flow. Since we will use the OP approach in the following, details concerning the IC approach are presented in Appendix 4. Figure 14.1 summarises the conceptual alternatives.

Modifying income and invested capital to ensure compatibility with NPV

We have presented the depreciation case. Table 14.9 shows other case 1 items with the corresponding balance sheet and income statement entries. If cash outflow follows expense (case 2), the OP approach requires us to compensate the advanced expense by not charging cost of capital on the corresponding capital. We illustrate this by extending our basic example by trade creditors (accounts payable).

Payments to suppliers (20) can be postponed from t_1 to t_3. This results in an additional cash inflow in t_1 (+20) and to an additional cash outflow in t_3 (−20) compared to the base case. Due to this delayed cash outflow, the *NPV*

Table 14.9. Treatment of case 1 items

Asset	Cash outflow	Expense	OP approach requires
Fixed assets	Capital expenditure	Depreciation	Fixed assets to be charged with cost of capital Depreciation reduces operating profit
Advance payments	Payment of bills	Costs of materials, etc.	Advance payment to be charged with cost of capital Respective costs of materials reduce operating profit
Stocks	Payment of bills	Costs of materials, etc.	Stocks to be charged with cost of capital Respective costs of materials reduce operating profit
Prepayments and accrued income	Payment of bills	Different costs	Prepayments and accrued income to be charged with cost of capital Respective costs reduce operating profit

rises to 6.2. This result can be obtained by using either the DCF approach or the OP approach (Tables 14.10 and 14.11). *NPV* is the same for cash flows and residual incomes. Table 14.12 contains further applications of case 2: cash outflow follows expense.

If income recognition follows cash inflow (case 3), income recognition is delayed and therefore cost of capital cannot be charged when the OP approach is applied. An example is an advance payment received. Since the calculations are exactly the same as for the example using trade creditors, they are not repeated here. Table 14.13 contains examples for case 3 and their treatment within a residual income framework.

If cash inflow follows income (case 4), the OP approach records income too early compared to cash inflow; it must be compensated by charging cost of capital. This case is illustrated by adding trade debtors (accounts receivable) to our basic example. Sales of 20 are not paid in t_1 but t_3, leading to a decrease in *NPV* of 2.5 to 1.2 (Tables 14.14 and 14.15).

Table 14.16 summarises our results by giving instructions how to handle each case in order to ensure DCF compatibility using the OP approach. These instructions indicate that commonly used calculations of accounting rates of return (e.g. *ROA, ROCE*) might be flawed, since they do not adjust the capital base properly. The resulting concept is quite straightforward: the capital base, consisting of debt and equity, is charged with cost of capital;

Table 14.10. DCF approach

	t_0	t_1	t_2	t_3	t_4	t_5	t_6
(1) OCF before capital expenditure		40.0	40.0	50.0	50.0	45.0	40.0
(2) Initial capital expenditure	−165.0						
(3) Additional captial expenditure			−44.0				
Trade creditors							
(4) Cash inflow[a]		20.0					
(5) Cash outflow				−20.0			
(1) + (2) + (3) + (4) + (5) NCF = (6)	−165.0	60.0	−4.0	30.0	50.0	45.0	40.0

$$NPV = 6.2$$

[a] Compared to base case.

Table 14.11. OP approach

	t_0	t_1	t_2	t_3	t_4	t_5	t_6
(1) OCF before capital expenditure		40.0	40.0	50.0	50.0	45.0	40.0
(2) Capital expenditure			−44.0				
(3) Book value	165.0	137.5	154.0	115.5	77.0	38.5	0.0
(4) Depreciation 1		27.5	27.5	27.5	27.5	27.5	27.5
(5) Depreciation 2				11.0	11.0	11.0	11.0
(4) + (5) = (6) Total depreciation		27.5	27.5	38.5	38.5	38.5	38.5
(7) Book value	165.0	137.5	154.0	115.5	77.0	38.5	0.0
(8) Trade creditors		20.0	20.0				
(7) − (8) = (9) Invested capital	165.0	117.5	134.0	115.5	77.0	38.5	0.0
(1) − (6) = (10) Operating profit		12.5	12.5	11.5	11.5	6.5	1.5
(11) Capital charge		−12.4	−8.8	−10.1	−8.7	−5.8	−1.4
(10) + (11) = (12) RI		0.1	3.7	1.5	2.8	0.7	−1.4

$$NPV = 6.2$$

Table 14.12. Treatment of case 2 items

Capital	Cash outflow	Expense	OP approach requires
Trade creditors	Payment of bills	Costs of materials, etc.	Respective costs to reduce operating profit; trade creditors to be deducted from the invested capital
Provisions	Payment	Increase in provision (expenses)	Increase in provisions to reduce operating profit; provisions to be deducted from the invested capital
Other creditors of expenses, e.g. taxes and social security	Payment of bills	Tax, employee costs, etc.	Respective costs (tax, employee costs) reduce operating profit; other creditors (for expenses) to be deducted from the invested capital

Table 14.13. Treatment of case 3 items

Capital	Cash outflow	Income	OP approach requires
Received advance payments	Received payment	Sales	Respective sales increase operating profit; received advance payments to be deducted from the invested capital
Accruals and deferred income	Received payment	Sales	Respective sales increase operating profit; accruals and deferred income to be deducted from the invested capital

operating profit minus this capital charge is the residual income. This is equivalent to the definition of residual income using profit defined according to the clean surplus rule on an entity (*WACC*) basis (Peasnell, 1982, pp. 362–67; O'Hanlon and Peasnell, 1998, pp. 423–24).

WACC AND TAXES

To specify *WACC* we need risk equivalent cost of equity, cost of debt, the relevant tax rates and the weights of debt and equity in the capital structure of

Table 14.14. DCF approach

	t_0	t_1	t_2	t_3	t_4	t_5	t_6
(1) OCF before capital expenditure		40.0	40.0	50.0	50.0	45.0	40.0
(2) Initial capital expenditure	−165.0						
(3) Additional capital expenditure			−44.0				
Trade debtors							
(4) Cash outflow[a]		−20.0					
(5) Cash inflow				20.0			
(1) + (2) + (3) + (4) + (5) NCF = (6)	−165.0	20.0	−4.0	70.0	50.0	45.0	40.0
			NPV = 1.2				

[a] Compared to base case.

Table 14.15. OP approach

	t_0	t_1	t_2	t_3	t_4	t_5	t_6
(1) OCF before capital expenditure		40.0	40.0	50.0	50.0	45.0	40.0
(2) Capital expenditure			−44.0				
(3) Cash outflow		−20.0					
(4) Cash inflow				20.0			
(5) Sales by trade debtors		20.0					
(6) Book value	165.0	137.5	154.0	115.5	77.0	38.5	0.0
(7) Depreciation 1		27.5	27.5	27.5	27.5	27.5	27.5
(8) Depreciation 2				11.0	11.0	11.0	11.0
(7) + (8) = (9) Total depreciation		27.5	27.5	38.5	38.5	38.5	38.5
(6) = (10) Book value	165.0	137.5	154.0	115.5	77.0	38.5	0.0
(11) Trade debtors		20.0	20.0				
(10) + (11) = (12) Invested capital	165.0	157.5	174.0	115.5	77.0	38.5	0.0
(1) − (3) + (5) − (9) = (13) Operating profit		12.5	12.5	11.5	11.5	6.5	1.5
(14) Capital charge		−12.4	−11.8	−13.1	−8.7	−5.8	−2.9
(13) + (14) = (15) RI		0.1	0.7	−1.6	2.8	0.7	−1.4
			NPV = 1.2				

Table 14.16. Summary of OP approach

Case	Description	Consequences
1	Expense follows cash outflow	Expense is considered too late Costs of capital compensate for that delay
2	Cash outflow follows expense	Expense is considered too early Costs of capital must not be charged
3	Income follows cash inflow	Income is considered too late Costs of capital must not be charged
4	Cash inflow follows income	Income is considered too early Costs of capital compensate for that anticipation

the firm. If these weights change, *WACC* should be adjusted. We use the CAPM in order to determine risk equivalent cost of equity. Depending on the tax system, income taxes should be considered in defining the cost of equity. The tax shield on debt financing is included in the definition of *WACC*. If other approaches to firm valuation (and performance measurement) are chosen, the tax shield will appear as part of the cash flow or residual income. See, for instance, the capital cash flow approach in Table 14.1 or the example using the *APV* approach in Appendix 1.

However, there are other tax effects of financing besides tax shields on debt, especially in a German institutional setting. Examples are provisions built up in advance of expected future cash outflows caused by pensions, losses, guarantee claims of customers, etc. They are tax deductible and thus cause tax shields. The tax reduction occurs when the provision is built up, not when the payment is to be made in a later period. Therefore one effect of the provision is to advance the tax reduction.

Several possibilities emerge to deal with this tax effect:

(1) The tax reduction is considered when the provision is built up.
(2) The tax reduction is considered when the payment occurs.
(3) The tax reduction is included in the definition of *WACC* by adding a third term containing the market value and the tax shield on provisions.

To simplify the measurement process, we suggest option 1: tax effects of other sources of capital besides debt are considered when they occur. They increase operating profit after taxes and thus residual income. Tax shields on debt financing are integrated into the definition of *WACC*.

Another issue concerning taxes is the choice of tax rates. Are standard (legal) tax rates or pragmatic tax rates to be used? Pragmatic rates are determined by the actual tax rates which the firm paid in the past. They can differ from legal tax rates since a number of international firms shift taxable earnings into countries with lower tax rates, etc. We suggest the use of standard tax rates on the divisional level, since operating managers have no impact on tax-avoiding strategies. The sum of the residual incomes reported by the units has therefore to be corrected by the influence of tax optimisation strategies adopted by top management.

OUTLINE OF A MONITORING SYSTEM

We argue that the monitoring of business units or divisions should be based on book values and residual incomes. Deviations of actual residual income from budgeted (book value based) residual income trigger positive or negative sanctions. There are several advantages:

- Additional investment outlays increase the capital base.
- Accounting rules can be modified internally to restrain creative accounting.
- Implementation costs are low.
- The measure is independent of expectations concerning future periods besides those necessary for the application of accounting rules.

One might ask whether the monitoring device should not be based directly on operating or net cash flow, since the relation of cash flow to firm value is uncontested. Residual income is a signal that has been reduced by a capital charge on invested capital and a proxy for capital consumption. This quality makes the central message of this *periodic* signal: Did the operating profit cover the cost of capital (defined on book value) and the capital consumption (measured by depreciation) or not?

These residual incomes of divisions and units have to be reported to the top management level. When deviations occur, it would be desirable to distinguish between the influence of managerial effort and bad (or good) luck. This can be achieved partly by analysing value drivers.

At the top level of the firm, market value and invested capital should be monitored. If shares are listed, the actual market value MV_t^{act} is observable. If shares are not listed or if actual market value due to thin markets, noise trading, etc., does not seem to be a reliable estimate of the value of the equity, use simulated market values based on the information of management. We call this value budgeted market value MV_t^{bud}. Since the expectations and strategies of management change over time, the valuation of the equity will be revised periodically. We call the result revised market value MV_t^{rev}. Since the

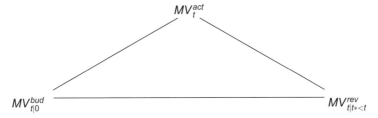

Figure 14.2. Actual, budgeted and revised market values

budgeting process and the revision of the values occur at different points in time, the notation should reflect this. Thus, we will use $MV^{bud}_{t|0}$ and $MV^{rev}_{t|t^*<t}$ (Figure 14.2).

Differences between MV^{act}_t and $MV^{rev}_{t|t^*<t}$ may be excluded only if the strong form of efficiency of the market can be assumed. Since this is not a realistic assumption, differences will probably exist:

- $MV^{rev}_{t|t^*<t}$ and MV^{act}_t could diverge due to differences in quantity and quality of information available to managers and investors. These differences affect information about markets, industries, factors affecting cash flows, targeted changes in capital structure, cost of capital and the length of the competitive advantage period.
- Besides quantity and quality it is the processing of information which leads to differences between $MV^{rev}_{t|t^*<t}$ and MV^{act}_t.

Differences between $MV^{bud}_{t|0}$ and $MV^{rev}_{t|t^*<t}$ will exist for two reasons:

- Due to new information, expectations of management could change given the strategies it decided upon.
- The strategies chosen before time t contain options which can be used or not. Using an option or not changes the strategy when time goes on.

Besides these differences, MV^{act}_t and $MV^{bud}_{t|0}$ will differ. If we assume a purely equity-financed firm for simplicity, $MV^{bud}_{t|0}$ is defined by

$$MV^{bud}_{t-1|0}(1+k) - Div_t \qquad (14.15)$$

and reflects the value expected by management given the information (expectation) at time 0. MC^{act}_t is the market estimate at time t; the reflected information in $MV^{bud}_{t|0}$ and MV^{act}_t will probably be different.

We argue that an internal monitoring system needs $MV^{bud}_{t|0}$, $MV^{rev}_{t|t^*<t}$ and invested capital (IC_t). IC_t is defined by

$$IC_t = IC_{t-1}(1+k) + \Delta IC^{EF}_t - Div_t. \qquad (14.16)$$

where $\Delta IC^{EF}_t - Div_t = NCF_t$; see equation (14.6).

The owners expect to earn cost of capital on the invested capital of the previous period and receive the net cash flows. ΔIC_t^{EF} represents the investment in fixed assets, working capital, research and development in period t financed by external (equity) funds net of depreciation. The difference between periodic market value and periodic invested capital is the periodic net present value, which equals the initial net present value plus a capital charge:

$$NPV_t = NPV_0(1+k)^t \qquad (14.17)$$

Thus, the calculation of periodic budgeted NPV becomes possible and changes in budgeted NPV triggered by changes in expectations can be shown. Table 14.17 explains the idea, based on the example in Appendix 1 and assuming a purely equity-financed firm for simplicity. The cost of equity is assumed to be 10%.

It is important for investors to know whether the invested capital defined by row (2) in Table 14.17 is at least compensated by the budgeted market value of the equity after dividend payments. Since expectations remain unchanged, IC_t is compared to $MV_{t|0}^{bud}$. The difference between rows (1) and (2) contains this information. The present value of the periodic NPV equals 129.2 for every period, since there are no changes in expectations and no external funding is to be considered.

If periodic performance measures are to be used, we suggest a monitoring system which comprises net economic income on the top level and residual income based upon book values on the unit level. Net economic income is defined as economic income, i.e. current cash flow plus change in market value, minus a capital charge on invested capital. This would lead to periodic performance measures as listed in Table 14.18, equivalent to the results shown in Table 14.17.

Net economic income equals the change in NPV which, if expectations are met, is the capital charge on the NPV. If one assumes that an investor has bought the company or shares of the company at the end of the previous period, IC_{t-1} is equal to MV_{t-1}. If there is no unexpected increase in cash flows, net economic income (residual income on market values) will be zero.

How should changes in expectations causing differences between $MV_{t|0}^{bud}$ and $MV_{t|t^*<t}^{rev}$ and IC_t be handled? Differences can occur for two reasons:

- Management's expectations concerning future cash flow changes during the current period. Other changes can occur, too: interest rates vary, tax systems change, etc. For simplicity we will focus on unexpected changes of cash flow.

Table 14.17

	0	1	2	3	4	5	6	7	8
(1) $MV_t^{bud} = MV_{t-1}^{bud}(1+k) - NCF_t$	20029.2	20141.6	20671.4	21257.2	21749.9	22306.8	22756.8	23473.5	23473.5
(2) $IC_t = IC_{t-1}(1+k) + \Delta IC_t^{EF} - Div_t$	19900.0	19999.5	20515.1	21085.3	21560.8	22098.8	22528.0	23221.7	23196.5
(1)−(2)=(3) Difference = NPV_t^{bud}	129.2	142.1	156.3	171.9	189.1	208.0	228.8	251.7	276.9
(4) PV_0 of NPV_t		129.2	129.2	129.2	129.2	129.2	129.2	129.2	129.2

Table 14.18

Periodic performance	0	1	2	3	4	5	6	7	8
Top level									
(1) NCF_t	−19 900.0	1 890.5	1 484.3	1 481.4	1 633.0	1 618.1	1 780.7	1 559.0	2 347.3
(2) Market value	20 029.2	20 141.6	20 671.4	21 257.2	21 749.9	22 306.8	22 756.8	23 473.5	23 473.5
(3) Change in market value	20 029.2	112.4	529.8	585.8	492.7	556.9	450.0	716.6	0.0
(1) + (3) = (4) Economic income	129.2	2 002.9	2 014.2	2 067.1	2 125.7	2 175.7	2 230.7	2 275.7	2 347.3
(5) Cost of capital on IC_{t-1}	0.0	1 990.0	2 000.0	2 051.5	2 108.5	2 156.1	2 209.9	2 252.8	2 322.2
(4) − (5) = (6) Net economic income	129.2	12.9	14.2	15.6	17.2	18.9	20.8	22.9	25.2
Unit level									
(1) RI_t^{act}		160.5	177.5	42.6	12.2	61.5	72.6	63.3	−61.5
(2) RI_t^{bud}		160.5	177.5	42.6	12.2	61.5	72.6	63.3	−61.5
(1) − (2) = (3) $RI_t^{act} - RI_t^{bud}$	0.0	0.0	0.0	0.0	0.0	0.0	0.0	0.0	0.0

- Budgeted performance is exceeded (or not reached) during the current period, as is revealed by the residual income of the divisions (units).

We use an example to discuss the consequences. Assume that profit after tax in year 1 is not 2150.5 as expected, but 2250.5; see Table 14.26 (Appendix 1). The budgeted residual income before tax shield of period 1 was 160.5; see Table 14.28 (Appendix 1). Residual income rises to 260.5, thus illustrating the unexpected increase of cash flow (operating profit). The operating unit would report the actual residual income to the top level. Discounting the new series of residual incomes gives the new NPV_0 of 220.1, as shown in Table 14.19.

What happens at the top level? Invested capital, shown in row (5) of Table 14.19 is 19 899.5 in period 1 and thus 100 less than budgeted due to a higher dividend payment of 100. The difference between $MV_{t|0}^{bud}$ and IC_t amounts to 242.1 and signals the improved situation. IC_t, reduced by the additional dividend payment, is the new benchmark to be compared with market values in future periods. Discounting the deviation (100) to time 0 and adding it to the budgeted NPV of 129.2 gives the revised NPV_0 of 220.1.

This can also be expressed by using periodic performance measures, as shown in Table 14.20. Both performance measures show an increase of 100 compared to the base case in period 1.

Now suppose that in period 1 management changes its expectation concerning profit after tax in period 3 — it is expected to be 2229.5 instead of 2129.5. Residual income is now *budgeted* at 142.8 instead of 42.8. Revised NPV_0 rises from 129.2 to 204.3.

At the top level, $MV_{1|0}^{bud}$ originally budgeted at 20 141.6 rises to 20 224.3 ($MV_{t|t^*<t}^{rev}$). IC_1 remains unchanged in period 1. The difference amounts to $20\,224.3 - 19\,999.5 = 224.8$, reflecting the present value of the revised expectations concerning cash flow (operating profit) of the management (82.7). Discounting this difference to time 0 and adding it to the NPV originally expected gives the revised NPV at time 0 (204.3); see Table 14.21.

These principles can be applied to any deviation that causes differences between budgeted and revised market values and adjustments of IC_t (perhaps caused by changes in dividend policy or reinvestment strategy). Table 14.22 shows the periodic performance measures. Net economic income in *period 1* shows an increase of NPV net of capital charge at 82.7 due to the changed expected performance of *period 3* ($95.6 - 12.9 = 82.7$). Residual income signals the increase when the cash flow (operating profit) occurs, i.e. in period 3. So this monitoring system can be characterised as follows:

- It combines a book value based performance measure at the unit level with a market value and invested capital based measure at the corporate level.

Table 14.19

	t_0	t_1	t_2	t_3	t_4	t_5	t_6	t_7	t_8
(1) Current increase of cash flow	100.0								
(2) $RI_t^{act} - RI_t^{bud}$	100.0								
(3) NCF_t^a		1 990.5	1 484.3	1 481.4	1 633.0	1 618.1	1 780.7	1 559.0	2 347.3
(4) $MV_t^{bud} = MV_{t-1}^{bud}(1+k) - NCF_t$	20 029.2	20 141.6	20 671.4	21 257.2	21 749.9	22 306.8	22 756.8	23 473.5	23 473.5
(5) $IC_t = IC_{t-1}(1+k) + \Delta IC_t^{EF} - Div_t$	19 900.0	19 899.5	20 405.1	20 964.3	21 427.7	21 952.4	22 366.9	23 044.6	23 001.7
(6) Difference $= NPV_t$	129.2	242.1	266.3	292.9	322.2	354.5	389.9	428.9	471.8
(7) PV_0 of NPV_t	129.2	220.1	220.1	220.1	220.1	220.1	220.1	220.1	220.1

[a] It is assumed that the dividend budgeted at 1890.5 is raised by the increase in cash flow (100) to 1990.5. If the expected investment opportunities did not change, this is a rational assumption.

Table 14.20

Periodic performance	0	1	2	3	4	5	6	7	8
Top level									
(1) NCF_t	−19 900.0	1 990.5	1 484.3	1 481.4	1 633.0	1 618.1	1 780.7	1 559.0	2 347.3
(2) Market value	20 029.2	20 141.6	20 671.4	21 257.2	21 749.9	22 306.8	22 756.8	23 473.5	23 473.5
(3) Change in market value	20 029.2	112.4	529.8	585.8	492.7	556.9	450.0	716.6	0.0
(1) + (3) = (4) Economic income	129.2	2 102.9	2 014.2	2 067.1	2 125.7	2 175.0	2 230.7	2 275.7	2 347.3
(5) Cost of capital on IC_{t-1}	0.0	1 990.0	1 990.0	2 040.5	2 096.4	2 142.8	2 195.2	2 236.7	2 304.5
(4) − (5) = (6) Net economic income	129.2	112.9	24.2	26.6	29.3	32.2	35.4	39.0	42.9
Unit level									
(1) RI_t^{act}		260.5	177.5	42.6	12.2	61.5	72.6	63.3	−61.5
(2) RI_t^{bud}		160.5	177.5	42.6	12.2	61.5	72.6	63.3	−61.5
(1) − (2) = (3) $RI_t^{act} - RI_t^{bud}$		100.0	0.0	0.0	0.0	0.0	0.0	0.0	0.0

Table 14.21

	t_0	t_1	t_2	t_3	t_4	t_5	t_6	t_7	t_8
(1) Expected increase of cash flow				100.0					
(2) NCF_t		1890.5	1484.3	1581.4	1633.0	1618.1	1780.7	1559.0	2437.3
(3) $MV_t^{rev} = \sum_{t=1}^{n} NCF_t(1+k)^{-t}$	20029.2	20224.3	20762.4	21257.2	21749.9	22306.8	22756.8	23473.5	23473.5
(4) $IC_t = IC_{t-1}(1+k) + \Delta IC_t^{EF} - Div_t$	19900.0	19999.5	20515.1	20985.3	21450.8	21977.8	22394.9	23075.3	23035.5
(5) Difference = NPV_t	129.2	224.8	247.2	271.9	299.1	329.1	362.0	398.2	438.0
(6) PV_0 of NPV_0	129.2	204.3	204.3	204.3	204.3	204.3	204.3	204.3	204.3

Table 14.22

Periodic performance	0	1	2	3	4	5	6	7	8
Top level									
(1) NCF_t	−19 900.0	1 890.5	1 484.3	1 581.4	1 633.0	1 618.1	1 780.7	1 559.0	2 347.3
(2) Market value	20 029.2	20 224.2	20 762.4	21 257.2	21 749.9	22 306.8	22 756.8	23 473.5	23 473.5
(3) Change in market value	20 029.2	195.1	538.1	494.8	492.7	556.9	450.0	716.6	0.0
(1) + (3) = (4) Economic income	129.2	2 085.6	2 022.4	2 076.2	2 125.7	2 175.0	2 230.7	2 275.7	2 347.3
(5) Cost of capital on IC_{t-1}	0.0	1 990.0	2 000.0	2 051.5	2 098.5	2 145.1	2 197.8	2 239.5	2 307.5
(4) − (5) = (6) Net economic income	129.2	95.6	22.5	24.7	27.2	29.9	32.9	36.2	39.8
Unit level									
(1) RI_t^{act}		160.5	177.5	142.6	12.2	61.5	72.6	63.3	−61.5
(2) RI_t^{bud}		160.5	177.5	42.6	12.2	61.5	72.6	63.3	−61.5
(1) − (2) = (3) $RI_t^{act} - RI_t^{bud}$		0.0	0.0	100.0	0.0	0.0	0.0	0.0	0.0

- The performance measure at the unit level is DCF compatible, but it is probably not highly correlated to changes in unit value because it does not consider expectations about future cash flows.
- Since budgeted residual incomes define a target or bottom line, financial incentives for the management could be linked to residual incomes and the deviation of actual residual incomes from budgeted residual incomes.
- The performance measure at the corporate level considers expectations and change in expectations, thus it accounts for changes in market value.
- Because IC_t and changes in IC_t are used in the definition of net economic income, investments financed by internal and external funds are written forward for performance measurement.

CONCLUSION

We defined the following requirements for a periodic performance measure:

(1) It must be DCF compatible.
(2) It should signal increases (decreases) of firm value in the period in which the increase (decrease) of firm value occurs.
(3) It should be fairly immune to manipulations.

Starting from accounting data (e.g. operating income) we develop the signal 'residual income'. We define residual income, capital base and capital charge in a way that ensures DCF compatibility. Firm value is defined by initial invested capital plus present value of residual incomes. While DCF compatibility is an important requirement, it does not seem to be sufficient, since it creates no serious restrictions on the moment when value creation (value destruction) is signalled.

But requirement 2 is difficult to achieve. Our discussion reveals that the problem of attributing value creation (value destruction) of projects (firms) to specified periods depends on the definition of the capital base (book value versus market value). If book values are used, budgeted residual incomes are different from zero and distribute the expected NPV over time. Their time structure depends on the structure of expected operating cash flows, depreciation schedules and other income statement items. If market values are used, budgeted residual incomes are zero, or at least their discounted sum is zero. The value created is attributed to time 0. Only unexpected changes in value are signalled by positive or negative residual incomes.

A second message is that invested capital as defined by (14.16) is an important element of performance measures, given the well-known risks of overinvestment. The difference between accounting data based IC_t and simulated market value is the periodic net present value. We call this performance measure net economic income.

Requirement 3 is also difficult to implement. Manipulations cannot be completely avoided. Residual income based on book value (and on internal accounting rules) seems more resistant to manipulations than performance measures based on simulated market values.

We recommend using residual income based on book values *and* net economic income. Residual income based on book values could be applied to divisions and units. For those knowing the bottom line of budgeted residual incomes, the deviations between budgeted and realised residual incomes are useful pieces of information. In addition, book values take into account the additional investment outlays irrespective of the way they are financed. At the top level, net economic income could be the basis for performance measurement. In order to monitor the reinvestment decision and to reduce the risk of overinvestment, management should analyse whether the reinvestment of internally generated funds (retained earnings) creates value to compensate the opportunity costs of shareholders included in the definition of IC_t in (14.16).

APPENDIX 1: APV APPROACH AND RESIDUAL INCOME

Data

Tax rate	$t_c = 0.45$
Interest rate	$i_D = 0.07$
Cost of equity (purely equity financed)	$k = 0.10$
Income tax is not considered	

- Not fully equited-financed firm

    Balance sheet (Table 14.23)
    Income statement (Table 14.24)

- Fully equity-financed firm

    Balance sheet (Table 14.25)
    Income statement (Table 14.26)

Table 14.23. Balance sheet

	$t = 0$	1	2	3	4	5	6	7	8+
Fixed assets	10 000.0	10 200.0	10 710.0	11 459.7	11 688.9	11 922.7	12 161.1	12 769.2	12 769.2
Working capital	9 900.0	9 960.0	10 159.2	10 057.6	10 359.3	10 773.7	11 096.9	11 318.9	11 318.9
Sum	19 900.0	20 160.0	20 869.2	21 517.3	22 048.2	22 696.4	23 258.0	24 088.0	24 088.0
Equity	11 000.0	11 707.4	12 457.6	13 145.8	13 854.4	14 644.9	15 493.2	16 379.6	16 379.6
Provisions for pension liabilities	3 000.0	3 024.0	3 048.5	3 073.6	3 099.2	3 125.4	3 152.1	3 179.5	3 179.5
Debt	5 900.0	5 428.6	5 363.1	5 297.9	5 094.6	4 926.1	4 612.8	4 528.9	4 528.9
Sum	19 900.0	20 160.0	20 869.2	21 517.3	22 048.2	22 696.4	23 258.0	24 088.0	24 088.0

Table 14.24. Income statement

	$t=1$	2	3	4	5	6	7	8+
Sales	12 000.0	12 240.0	12 117.6	12 481.1	12 980.4	13 369.8	13 637.2	13 637.2
Operating expenses	6 840.0	6 976.8	6 907.0	7 114.2	7 398.8	7 620.8	7 773.2	7 773.2
Depreciation	1 250.0	1 275.0	1 338.8	1 432.5	1 461.1	1 490.3	1 520.1	1 596.1
Increase in provisions for pension liabilities	480.0	490.4	501.2	512.2	523.6	535.3	547.3	558.1
Interest payments	413.0	380.0	375.4	370.9	356.6	344.8	322.9	317.0
Taxes	1 357.7	1 403.0	1 347.8	1 373.1	1 458.1	1 520.4	1 563.2	1 526.7
Profit after taxes	1 659.3	1 714.8	1 647.4	1 678.2	1 782.2	1 858.2	1 910.5	1 866.1
Dividends	951.9	964.6	959.2	969.6	991.7	1 010.0	1 024.0	1 866.1
Retained earnings	707.4	750.2	688.2	708.6	790.5	848.2	886.5	0.0

Table 14.25. Balance sheet

	$t = 0$	1	2	3	4	5	6	7	8+
Fixed assets	10 000.0	10 200.0	10 710.0	11 459.7	11 688.9	11 922.7	12 161.1	12 769.2	12 769.2
Working capital	9 900.0	9 960.0	10 159.2	10 057.6	10 359.3	10 773.7	11 096.9	11 318.9	11 318.9
Sum	19 900.0	20 160.0	20 869.2	21 517.3	22 048.2	22 696.4	23 258.0	24 088.0	24 088.0
Equity		20 160.0	20 869.2	21 517.3	22 048.2	22 696.4	23 258.0	24 088.0	24 088.0
Sum		20 160.0	20 869.2	21 517.3	22 048.2	22 696.4	23 258.0	24 088.0	24 088.0

Table 14.26. Income statement

	$t = 1$	2	3	4	5	6	7	8+
Sales	12 000.0	12 240.0	12 117.6	12 481.1	12 980.4	13 369.8	13 637.2	13 637.2
Operating expenses	6 840.0	6 976.8	6 907.0	7 114.2	7 398.8	7 620.8	7 773.2	7 773.2
Depreciation	1 250.0	1 275.0	1 338.8	1 432.5	1 461.1	1 490.3	1 520.1	1 596.1
Taxes	1 759.5	1 794.7	1 742.3	1 770.5	1 854.2	1 916.4	1 954.8	1 920.6
Profit after taxes	2 150.5	2 193.5	2 129.5	2 163.9	2 266.3	1 916.4	2 389.1	2 347.3
Dividends	1 890.5	1 484.3	1 481.4	1 633.0	1 618.1	1 780.6	1 559.1	2 347.3
Retained earnings	260.0	709.2	648.1	530.9	648.2	561.7	830.0	0.0

Retained earnings are defined as profit after tax + depreciation − additional investments. The firm is assumed to pursue a dividend policy following Jensen's free cash flow hypothesis.

- Cash flow to be paid to shareholders (Table 14.27)

$$V^E = 20\,028.9$$

$$\Delta V^{TS} = 5636.4 \text{ (discounted at } i_D \text{ since debt}$$
$$\text{policy does not depend on } V_t)$$

$$V^D = 25\,665.3$$

- Residual incomes and value of the firm (Table 14.28)

$$V^E = IC_0 + \sum_{t=1}^{\infty} RI_t(1 + k)^{-t}$$

$$= 19\,900 + 128.9 = 20\,028.9$$

$$\Delta V^{TS} = 5636.4$$

APPENDIX 2: DISCOUNTED RESIDUAL INCOMES AND NPV

Discounting residual income results in NPV, if invested capital is defined by book values:

$$NPV = \sum_{t=1}^{n} RI_t(1 + WACC)^{-t}$$

$$= \sum_{t=1}^{n} (OCF_t - Dep_t - WACC \cdot IC_{t-1})(1 + WACC)^{-t}$$

$$= \sum_{t=1}^{n} OCF_t(1 + WACC)^{-t}$$

$$- \sum_{t=1}^{n} (Dep_t + WACC \cdot IC_{t-1})(1 + WACC)^{-t} \tag{14.18}$$

The DCF approach is usually written as

$$NPV = -IC_0 + \sum_{t=1}^{n} OCF_t(1 + WACC)^{-t} \tag{14.19}$$

Table 14.31. Case 3: IC approach differs from OP approach

Capital	Cash inflow	Income	IC approach requires
Received advance payments	Received payment	Sales	Received advance payments to be charged with cost of capital Respective received *payment* increases operating profit
Accruals and deferred income	Received payment	Sales	Accruals and deferred income to be charged with cost of capital Respective received *payment* increases operating profit

Table 14.32. Summary of IC approach

Case	Description	Consequences
1	Expense follows cash outflow	Expense is considered too late Costs of capital compensate that delay
2	Cash outflow follows expense	Expense is considered too early Use cash outflow and cost of capital
3	Income follows cash inflow	Income is considered too late Use cash inflow and cost of capital
4	Cash inflow follows income	Income is considered too early Costs of capital compensate that anticipation

APPENDIX 5: RESIDUAL INCOME

Table 14.33. Residual income based upon book values

	Book value	EVA	Annuity
Capital consumption	Depreciation of assets at book value plus capital charge on not yet depreciated book value	Depreciation of assets at book values and change in other capitalised items and capital charge on (modified) book values	Capital consumption as an annuity
DCF compatibility	Total period: sum of discounted residual incomes equals NPV Single period: periodic NPV contribution depends upon OCF_t and depreciation schedule	Total period: sum of discounted EVA values should equal NPV Single period: periodic NPV contribution depends upon OCF_t, depreciation schedule and other items	Total period: sum of discounted residual incomes equals NPV Single period: periodic NPV contribution equals $OCF_t -$ annuity
Assigning NPV to specific periods	NPV contributions are made over total period	NPV contributions are made over total period	NPV contributions are made over total period and follow OCF
Applicability	Data available on holding level as well as on divisional and project levels	Modifications of accounting data necessary	Delivers periodic signal about NPV only if steady-state assumption holds
Remarks	Periodic residual incomes depend upon balance sheet and income statement items which might be biased Value creation possible despite negative periodic residual income, and vice versa	Final judgement about DCF compatibility cannot be made without complete information about suggested adjustments Value creation possible despite negative periodic residual income, and vice versa	Depends upon steady-state assumption Value creation possible despite negative periodic residual income, and vice versa

Table 14.34. Residual income at least partially based upon market values

	Market value	Goodwill	Market and book value combined
Capital consumption	Costs of capital are charged on market values (step 1); the remaining income equals change in market value, i.e. economic depreciation (step 2)	Cost of capital on book value and goodwill and depreciation of book values and changes of goodwill	Cost of capital on market value and depreciation of assets at book values
DCF compatibility	Total period: sum of residual incomes equals market value for step 1 or equals zero for step 2, since NPV is included in capital base Single period: residual income is change in market value (step 1) or zero (step 2)	Total period: sum of discounted residual incomes equals zero Single period: residual income depends in addition to book value approach upon development of goodwill	Total period: sum of residual income equals NPV, since it is not depreciated but charged with cost of capital Single period: periodic NPV contribution by OCF of current and future periods and depreciation schedule
Assigning NPV to specific periods	NPV is assigned to starting period	Depends upon adjustment of goodwill	NPV contributions are distributed over total period
Applicability	Applicable to corporate level, especially for listed companies Limited applicability to divisions or projects	Applicable to corporate level Goodwill can be added to book values Pragmatic approach	Applicable if periodic market values are available Limited application for divisional or project level Limited accountability to management's efforts
Remarks	Periodic market values required Distribution to business units difficult Development of market values crucial for shareholders Based upon gross present value not net present value	Practical approach for correcting book values Leaves discretionary influence to managers	Required summing up of residual incomes restricts applicability to moving performance measurement and infinite project lifetimes

APPENDIX 6: DEFINITION OF SVA

$$SVA_t = NCF_t + RV_t - RV_{t-1}(1 + WACC) \qquad (14.22)$$

with $\quad RV_t = \dfrac{NCF_t + \textit{Incremental Investment}_t}{WACC}$

Equation (14.22) can be written as

$$SVA_t = NCF_t + \Delta RV_t(1 + WACC)$$

$$- WACC \, \frac{NCF_t + \textit{Incremental Investment}_t}{WACC}$$

$$= \frac{\Delta(NCF_t + \textit{Incremental Investment}_t)(1 + WACC)}{WACC}$$

$$- \textit{Incremental Investment}_t \qquad (14.23)$$

and since $NOPAT_t = NCF_t + \textit{Incremental Investment}_t$, we have

$$SVA_t = \frac{\Delta NOPAT_t(1 + WACC)}{WACC} - \textit{Incremental Investment}_t \qquad (14.24)$$

REFERENCES

Ball, B.C. (1987) The mysterious disappearance of retained earnings. *Harvard Business Review*, **50**, 56–63.

Blanchard, O.J., Lopez de Silvanes, F. and Shleifer, A. (1994) What do firms do with cash windfalls? *Journal of Financial Economics*, **36**, 337–60.

Brealey, R.A. and Myers, S.C. (1996) *Principles of Corporate Finance*, 5th edn. McGraw-Hill, New York.

Copeland, T.E., Koller, T. and Murrin, J.F. (1994) *Valuation: Measuring and Managing the Value of Companies*, 2nd edn. John Wiley, New York.

Drukarczyk, J. (1998) *Unternehmensbewertung*, 2nd edn. Vahlen Verlag, Munich.

Grabowski, H.G. and Mueller, D.C. (1975) Life-cycle effects on corporate returns on retentions. *Review of Economic Studies*, **57**, 400–409.

Grinyer, J.R. (1985) Earned economic income – a theory of matching. *Abacus*, **21**, 130–48.

Grinyer, J.R. (1987) A new approach to depreciation. *Abacus*, **23**, 43–51.

Grinyer, J.R. (1995) Analytical properties of earned economic income – a response and extension. *British Accounting Review*, **27**, 211–28.

Jensen, M.C. (1986) Agency costs of free cash flows, corporate finance and takeovers. *American Economic Review*, **76**, 323–29.

Jensen, M.C. (1993) The modern industrial revolution, exit, and the failure of internal control systems. *Journal of Finance*, **48**, 831–80.

Lücke, W. (1955) Investitionsrechnungen auf der Grundlage von Ausgaben oder Kosten? *Zeitschrift für betriebswirtschaftliche Forschung*, **7**, 310–24.

Morck, R., Shleifer, A. and Vishny, R.W. (1989) Alternative mechanisms for corporate control. *American Economic Review*, **79**, 842–52.

Mueller, D.C. and Reardon, E.A. (1993) Rates of return on corporate investment. *Southern Economic Journal*, **60**, 430–53.

Nowack, E. (1997) On investment performance and corporate governance. Dissertation, St Gallen, Bamberg.

O'Hanlon, J. and Peasnell, K.V. (1998) Wall Street's contribution to management accounting: the Stern Stewart EVA financial management system. *Management Accounting*, **9**, 421–44.

Peasnell, K.V. (1982) Some formal connections between economic values and yields and accounting numbers. *Journal of Business Finance and Accounting*, **9**, 361–81.

Peasnell, K.V. (1995a) Analytical properties of earned economic income. *British Accounting Review*, **27**, 5–33.

Peasnell, K.V. (1995b) Second thoughts on the analytical properties of earned economic income. *British Accounting Review*, **27**, 229–39.

Picchi, B.J. (1985) The structure of the oil industry: past and future. Salomon Brothers Inc., Stock Research.

Preinreich, G. (1938) Annual survey of economic theory: the theory of depreciation. *Econometrica*, **6**, 219–41.

Rappaport, A. (1998) *Creating Shareholder Value: A Guide for Managers and Investors*, 2nd edn. Free Press, New York.

Richter, F. (1999) *Konzeption eines marktwertorientierten Steuerungs- und Monitoring-Systems*, 2nd edn. Peter Long, Frankfurt.

Schüler, A. (1998) *Performance-Messung und Eigentümerorientierung*. Peter Long, Frankfurt.

Shleifer, A. and Vishny, R.W. (1988) Value maximization and the acquisition process. *Journal of Economic Perspectives*, **2**, 7–20.

Skinner, R.C. (1998) The strange logic of earned economic income. *British Accounting Review*, **30**, 93–104.

Solomons, D. (1965) *Divisional Performance, Measurement and Control*. Richard D. Irwin, Homewood IL.

Statistische Jahrbücher der Bundesrepublik Deutschland (1980–1996) Edited by Statistischen Bundesamt.

Stewart, G.B. (1991) *The Quest for Value: A Guide for Senior Managers*. Harper Collins, New York.

15 VBM: A New Insight into the Goodwill Dilemma?

GARETH OWEN

INTRODUCTION

Value-based management (VBM), and more specifically economic value added (EVA), has been promoted by a number of contributors, as a revolutionary way of looking at corporate performance and valuation (Stewart, 1991; Rappaport, 1998). It is arguable, however, that it merely repackages existing economic and accountancy theory. It places a different emphasis on discounted cash flow techniques as a way of appraising periodic financial performance and for motivating and rewarding management. However, EVA may not achieve, even from a theoretical perspective, what it is claimed to do for a number of reasons, and it may not add anything to knowledge in the area of corporate performance measurement or management appraisal. Its main benefit, however, is that it makes a clear distinction between the balance sheet paradigm and the income approach within accounting as a reporting function. Furthermore, a close examination of market value added (MVA) as the difference between the market value and economic book values, however measured, also places a new emphasis on the seemingly intractable problem of accounting for inherent and acquired goodwill.

This chapter does not claim to break new ground in the field of corporate valuation theory, rather it attempts to synthesise economic, VBM and accounting measurement theory, in order to explore the difference between the three perspectives, and to suggest ways in which VBM may act as a bridge between the 'uncongenital twins' of economics and accounting. As VBM seems to have gained a particular kind of respectability among management consultants, now may be the right time to revisit the conflict between the economic and the accounting paradigm and to tentatively suggest some possible reforms in the area of external corporate financial reporting.

First of all in this chapter, EVA as a valuation model is critically discussed. This involves a brief exploration of the mechanics and assumptions of the model, and the accounting issues that emerge from its use as recommended. There follows a discussion of the fundamental economic theory which underlies the model. This will lead to a comparative discussion of the sharply contrasting economic and accounting perspectives on measurement and valuation, particularly with respect to generally accepted accounting and economic concepts. From this there follows a discussion of the crucial problem of goodwill, which clearly emerges as the essential timing difference arising from the use of one model or the other in their purest forms. Within this section, goodwill as a problem will also be specifically discussed from the economic and accounting perspective, referring briefly to the long-standing intellectual debate on how it should be treated in accounting terms. It is then intended to hypothesise how goodwill may be broken down into a model of its constituent elements or drivers, set firmly within the context of the VBM model and the difference between book values and market value. Finally it may be possible to hypothesise which of these drivers may be of most significance, to suggest future research opportunities that may be fruitful in this area, and to provide a lead towards a more relevant method of accounting for goodwill.

EVA AS A PERFORMANCE MEASURE

EVA as a performance measure was first advocated in 1986 by J. Stern and G.B Stewart III, and it was derived from their free cash flow concept, the fundamentals of which may be attributed to the early 1960s (Modgliani and Miller, 1961). The concept of EVA is that income should only be recognised after a charge has been made for the cost of using all sources of capital employed in generating these earnings. This concept recognises that there is an implicit opportunity cost faced by investors when they invest in a business, being the next best alternative rate of return available from another investment opportunity. Effectively the system recommends that management accept all projects which give a positive return after allowing for all costs, including the cost of capital, and rejects all projects that produce a negative return. The income which Stern Stewart recognise is known as net operating profit after tax (NOPAT). This is defined as profits from operations net of depreciation and before financing costs and non-cash bookkeeping entries. In other words, NOPAT is broadly equivalent to free cash flow less depreciation. A number of non-cash bookkeeping entries recommended by Stern Stewart (Stewart, 1991) are added to shareholder capital. These entries are known as equity equivalent reserves (EEs). Adding equity equivalents to the book value effectively undoes some of the accruals-based accounting adjustments, partially converting profit to cash flow, grossing up book value to what is known as economic book value (EBV). There are up to 164 such adjustments which may be possible, but in practice only 15 or so are considered significant in most cases (Stewart, 1994). The main adjustments considered necessary include deferred tax provisions, provisions for stock valuation, such as provisions for unrealised profits, bad debt provisions, amortised goodwill, research and development and other intangible assets, restructuring and other accounting write-offs. Stern Stewart also recommend that the present value of operating lease payments may need to be adjusted for, because this type of expenditure constitutes a recognisable asset. Stern Stewart argue that both NOPAT and EBV should be modified with respect to the above adjustments, in order to produce both income and capital numbers which are based more on economic reality than upon accounting convention. Stern Stewart then argue that if the weighted average cost of capital (WACC) is subtracted from NOPAT, an economic measure of income known as economic value added (EVA) is arrived at. They also argue, correctly, that the net present value (NPV) of all future EVAs constitutes the difference between EBV and the theoretical market value of the shares (MV).

The initial MVA calculation, however, is nothing more or less than the net present value of the company based on traditional discounting techniques. This is because, assuming that EVA is equal to free cash flow less depreciation, the net present value of all EVAs must give the MVA by a mathematical inevitability. All other things being equal, this is equivalent to the difference between the EBV and the MV of the business. In effect, the MVA is a stock measure, as is NPV. The advantage of the EVA model, according to its advocates, is that EVA is a flow measure, and is therefore useful in measuring the periodic performance of a business and its management. However, because EVA is a measure net of accounting depreciation, the undiscounted EVA figure is heavily dependent on the allocation method adopted. Therefore, although in summative terms the equivalence between MVA and NPV is irrefutable, the value of the periodic EVAs arrived at under the model may be called into question. This can be explained by using the following example.

A company is set up at time t_0 with £120m share capital, which is expected to generate net cash flows of £55m at t_1, £40m at t_2 and £50m at t_3. It is also assumed that as from t_3 the investment will be worthless. A £40m straight-line depreciation is charged against profits at t_1, t_2 and t_3. The weighted average cost of capital (K_w) for this company is 10%.

$$\text{EVAs} = (\text{net cash flow} - \text{depreciation} - \text{cost of capital})$$

$$\text{Present value of EVAs (MVA)} = 3 \times (1/1.1) - 8 \times (1/1.1^2)$$

$$+ 6 \times (1/1.1^3)$$

$$= £623\,000$$

The investment is therefore worthwhile and should be undertaken, but value is shown to be destroyed at t_2 when a negative EVA is reported (Table 15.1). Should management be held responsible? Clearly not, because the overall investment is one which has enriched the shareholders by £623 000. The negative EVA reported at t_2 is entirely due to the allocation of accounting depreciation against the cash flows realised.

Table 15.1

Time	NOPAT ($£$m)	EBV ($£$m)	Depreciation ($£$m)	K_w ($£$m) EBV $\times$ 10%	EVA ($£$m)
t_0		120			
t_1	55	80	40	12	3
t_2	40	40	40	8	-8
t_3	50	0	40	4	-6

If, for example, the sum of the digits (3/6, 2/6, 1/6) method of deprecia-tion were adopted, how would this affect reported EVAs?

$$\text{Present value of EVAs (MVA)} = -17 \times (1/1.1) - 6 \times (1/1.1^2)$$
$$+ 28 \times (1/1.1^3)$$
$$= £623\,000$$

This also equals the NPV. This time negative EVAs are reported at t_1 and t_2, and a large positive EVA at t_3 (Table 15.2), demonstrating that EVA could lead to inappropriate performance appraisal, depending on the depreciation policies adopted.

So what do the periodic EVAs actually mean? They are simply free cash flows generated in each period, but unless they are discounted, summed, referenced to a value at a single point in time and looked at as a whole, the numbers are effectively meaningless and form no legitimate basis for rewarding or sanctioning management. It is the stock not the flow figure which is all-important, and the decision to undertake such an investment can only be seen in the light of data about that project throughout its whole life not on a period-by-period basis. The counter-argument to this is that the changes in EVA are of the most importance, not the absolute numbers (Stewart, 1994, p. 78). However, by his own argument, if a sinking fund

Table 15.2

Time	NOPAT ($£$m)	EBV ($£$m)	Depreciation ($£$m)	K_w ($£$m) EBV $\times$ 10%	EVA ($£$m)
t_0		120			
t_1	55	60	60	12	-17
t_2	40	20	40	6	6
t_3	50	0	20	2	28

Table 15.3

Time	NOPAT (£m)	EBV (£m)	Depreciation (£m)	K_w (£m) EBV × 10%	EVA (£m)
t_0	−120	120			
t_1	55	100	20	12	23
t_2	40	60	40	10	−10
t_3	50	0	60	6	−16

depreciation pattern were to be taken for the above example instead of the sum of the digits pattern, the direction taken by the EVAs in the above example would simply reverse (Table 15.3).

$$\text{Present value of EVAs (MVA)} = 23 \times (1/1.1) - 10 \times (1/1.1^2)$$

$$+ 16(1/1.1^3)$$

$$= £623\,000$$

Therefore, in this situation, management would presumably be rewarded upon their performance in the first period and sanctioned for poor performance in the last two periods. Again this pattern of EVAs is determined entirely by the depreciation policy, whilst the original decision to accept the project remains unaltered.

The problem is the relationship between EVA and the EBV, due to the charging of accounting depreciation before arriving at NOPAT. The figures arrived at are highly distorting, and will nearly always underemphasise performance in the early years and overemphasise them in the later years, regardless of the kinds of usual depreciation policies adopted. The 'sinking fund' method is advocated as a method of ameliorating this distortion, but this is an artificial adjustment, and as seen above, may well simply reverse the direction in which EVAs are moving, simply because of an alternative capital reallocation pattern, without changing the overall conclusion that the initial investment was economically worthwhile.

ECONOMIC CONSIDERATIONS

If, however, EVAs are calculated on the basis of purely economic depreciation, as would be the case in the theoretical economic model, EBV or the value of the capital at each point in time is strictly based on the present value (PV) of the cash flows yet to be realised from the company or

Table 15.4

Time	NOPAT (£m)	MV (£m)	Depreciation (£m)	K_w (£m) MV × 10%	EVA (£m)
t_0		120.623 (a)			
t_1	55	77.686 (b)	42.94	12.06	nil
t_2	40	45.455 (c)	32.23	7.77	nil
t_3	50	0	45.45	4.55	nil

See text for explanation of (a), (b), (c).

project. If depreciation and asset values are chosen on this basis, the following outcome is arrived at (Table 15.4).

Present value of the cash flows =

(a) $55 \times (1/1.1) + 40 \times (1/1.1^2) + 50 \times (1/1.1^3) = £120.623m$

(b) $40 \times (1/1.1) + 50 \times (1/1.1^2) = £77.686m$

(c) $50 \times (1/1.1) = £45.455m$

In this situation, using purely economic depreciation, the resulting EVAs are
all zero. The initial £120 623 000 includes an immediate windfall gain of
£623 000 which is built into the model at the outset. This equates with the
initial MVA calculated under the EVA model. It is only this number which
has any significance for decision taking at the operational level. If an initial
positive NPV or MVA is made then the investment should be undertaken, if
not it should be rejected. Under this pure model, NOPAT should always
equate to the cost of capital. This is because the one-directional circular
relationship between the discounted value of the income and the computed
economic capital values at any point in time at the given rate of K_w, is the
result of a mathematical truism. Fisher (1930) first saw the relationship
between capital and income in this particular way, and made it quite clear
that income was the determinant of capital value. Although the generation of
income originates from a stock of physical capital goods, it isn't possible to
value the capital stock until the flow of income has itself been estimated and
a value placed upon it. Therefore, from the stock of capital goods in physical
terms is derived the flow of income, and from a meaurement of the flow of
income may be derived the value of capital:

> Income is derived from capital goods. But the value of the income is not derived
> from the value of the capital goods. On the contrary, the value of the capital is
> derived from the value of the income. (Fisher, 1930, p. 14)

The economist therefore looks at the problem of valuation from a holistic income perspective. The economist would attempt to measure the value of the business as a whole, by discounting the future stream of cash flows accruing to that entity, and wouldn't attempt to break down the income necessarily into separate parcels of capital or assets, as the accountant would traditionally need to do; although FRS 10 (ASB, 1997a), which places valuations on income-generating units (IGUs), moves the accounting model of valuation closer towards that of the economist. The economist would always have to decide whether a cash outflow is an independent event or whether that outflow was associated with other future inflows which might need to be incorporated into the overall capital calculation. This may be explained with an example. A tulip farmer plants bulbs. Each bulb paid for and planted is a cash outlay in one sense, but it is an investment in another sense. If the expected sale of each successful bloom exceeds the cost of purchase, planting and sustenance, discounted by an appropriate discount factor, then each investment yields a positive NPV or MVA at the outset, and rather than being a cost, becomes a stock of capital or an asset. However, the accountant would write off all the costs initially, and record a loss, failing to recognise the subterranean bulbs as assets, and at some later date when the blooms were sold the accountant would recognise the income, possibly in another accounting period. The economist therefore argues that measurement of assets is secondary to the measurement of income. Income is the starting point for valuation, a measure of capital is the by-product of that measurement. Fisher puts this argument in a nutshell:

> In whatever ways the ownership be distributed and symbolized in documents, the entire group of property rights are merely a means to an end — income. Income is the alpha and omega of economics. (Fisher, 1930, p. 13)

Table 15.4 would imply in theory, following the strict economic model of valuation, that there is no such thing as EVA, and by implication no MVA other than the value calculated at the beginning of the investment. This makes sense as the perspective adopted by the purely economic model assumes perfect knowledge of the future and no changes in expectations. Under these highly theoretical and prescribed conditions, EBV and the market value (MV) of the investment will inevitably coincide.

GOODWILL AND MVA

Of interest to accountants would be the nature of MVA, which might otherwise be called goodwill, and how it arises in practice. It has been shown that there is no such residual on a periodic basis in economic theory. It must therefore derive in practice from under- or overestimates of future outcomes in the economic model, or because of the inability of the accounting model to

The real value of the capital, as opposed to the nominal or monetary value, would be based on a straight comparison of the discounted cash flows expected at two different points in time. The income measure derived is known as economic income, and the relationship between it and capital is as follows:

$$Y_e = C + PV(t) - PV(t - 1)$$

where Y_e = economic income for the period
           C = net realised cash flows in the period
     $PV(t)$ = capital at the end of the period measured in terms of the present value of future cash flows expected from that time on
$PV(t - 1)$ = capital at the beginning of the period measured in terms of the present value of future cash flows expected from that time on

Therefore the individual may only consume as much of C in any one period as not to deplete $PV(t)$ as compared with $PV(t - 1)$. In order to maintain the capital at its real value, it would be necessary to reinvest any shortfall in an alternative investment which earns a rate of interest equal to the rate used as the discount factor. But as expectations change throughout the lifetime of the investment, *windfall* gains and/or losses may be experienced which need to be taken into account each period. These windfalls would mean that either additional or lesser amounts of C would need to be reinvested thereafter to maintain capital as compared with the amount expected at the beginning of the period.

Hicks drew the distinction between economic income ex ante and economic income ex post, in that economic income is calculated with information available at the beginning of the period under the ex ante model but with information available at the end of the period under the ex post model. From a pragmatic viewpoint, in order to maintain capital properly, an ex ante perspective is best taken because decisions on appropriate levels of consumption for an individual would need to be made at the beginning of a period rather than at the end. However, for a business which makes its major distribution decisions at the end of a period, the ex post perspective is quite appropriate, because in practice companies prepare their accounts at that time and do so in the light of the information they have then. This includes information available to them on the current value of their net assets and of the actual realised income earned for that period. Thus, if a company were to adopt the present value model of accounting, it would mean that the company could assess its closing capital in the light of expectations about future cash flows and cost of capital changes available to it at the end of the financial period. A company's 'economic income' would represent its realised cash profits, plus or minus any change in the capital measured at the beginning and the end of the period, with information available at the end of the period. In effect, economic income is the excess over and above the amount of money income required to be reinvested to maintain the real capital of the company. This amount would be equivalent to the cost of capital (as described in the EVA model) in a situation where the minimum requirement was to simply maintain the economic value of the capital invested. The fact that the same amount is called income under the Hicks model and cost of capital under the EVA model, merely confirms the emphasis of the economic model on the individual (i.e. shareholder) as opposed to EVA's emphasis on the entity (i.e. the company) of which the shareholder is an owner.

The Hicksian approach to income and capital valuation is illustrated using the same example as before. At time t_0 a company with equity of £120 623 000 (assuming a zero NPV or MVA), which is expected to maintain a constant cost of capital of 10%, anticipates making the following cash profits over the next three years:

- Period t_0 to t_1, £55m
- Period t_1 to t_2, £40m
- Period t_2 to t_3, £50m

However, as time, passes, the expectations about the future change as follows. At t_2 £45m profits are declared but despite this performance, and because of fears about the economy, expectations about future cash profit for t_2 to t_3 are revised downwards to £48m. In the period t_2 to t_3, however, £52m net cash flows are actually received. Under Hicks' economic income model calculated under the ex post perspective, economic income and capital valuations at the end of each period would be as shown in Table 15.6.

The capital calculations at the beginning and at the end of each period are carried out by taking the present values (PVs) of all future cash flows with information as available *at the end of each period* in accordance with the ex post perspective. The economic income is derived by taking the actual realised cash flow in the period and adjusting it by the difference between opening and closing capital. Note that this is the same as the cost of capital charge under the EVA model, being the opening capital multiplied by the cost of capital at 10%. This difference between realised cash flows in a period and the economic income must be reinvested at the prevailing rate of interest (or opportunity cost) in order to maintain the capital at its previous level. As expectations about the future change in each period, there will be a discrepancy between closing capital as worked out in the prior period, and opening capital as calculated in the current period. This difference is treated as a windfall gain or loss or 'subjective goodwill' and must be treated as a prior period adjustment to the current period's income, before arriving at the true 'economic income' for the period. The economic income in this model remains constant into perpetuity (at £12 063 000) as the total cost of capital comprises 10% of the depreciating asset value, and the 10% interest earned

Table 15.6

Time period	Net cash flow (£m) (C)	PV(t) (£m)	PV(t − 1) (£m)	PV(t − 1) × K_w (£m) (Y_e)	Windfall (£m) (w)	Total income (Y_e + w)	Reinvest C − (Y_e + w)
$t_0 - t_1$	55	77.686 (b)	120.623 (a)	12.063	nil	12.063	42.937
$t_1 - t_2$	45	43.636 (d)	80.578 (c)	8.058	2.892	10.950	34.050
$t_2 - t_3$	52		47.273 (e)	4.727	3.637	8.364	43.636
Total	152			24.848	6.529	31.377	120.623

Notes
(a) $55 \times (1/1.1) + 40 \times (1/1.1^2) + 50 \times (1/1.1^3)$
(b) $40 \times (1/1.1) + 50 \times (1/1.1^2)$
(c) $45 \times (1/1.1) + 48 \times (1/1.1^2)$
(d) $48 \times (1/1.1)$
(e) $52 \times (1/1.1)$

on the cumulative reinvested sum, which gives a constant total of 10% of the maintained market value of £120 623 000. This links directly into the REVA method (Bacidore et al., 1997), which argues that the cost of capital should be based on the market value of the investment not the expired EBV of the investment. Again it can be seen that under this pure model no EVA would ever arise. Taking the period t_1 to t_2, or the second row in Table 15.6 and expressing the values in £m:

$$NOPAT = 45$$

$$Depreciation = (80.578 - 43.636) = 36.942$$

$$K_w = (80.578 \times 0.1) = 8.058$$

therefore

$$EVA = (45 - 36.942 - 8.058) = nil$$

This model raises many questions for the treatment of gains and losses in accountancy and may give a lead in the accounting treatment of goodwill. Each capital calculation takes into account the future cash flows expected and the expected interest rate applied as a discount factor. The cash flows antici-pated would by implication include all benefits expected from the productive deployment of tangibles and intangibles, and from the synergistic benefits of their use in concert. Therefore the economic valuation model, although highly subjective, gives a pure valuation model for a business, and included in the capital valuation would by implication be the carrying value of all purchased and inherent goodwill. Although the EVA model discounts future EVAs in its determination of MVA at any point in time, the income and capital computations are different from the economic model due to the use of modified or adjusted historic cost depreciation rather than economic depre-ciation in the capital calculations. The economic model does, however, lead to a useful periodic performance yardstick by which management performance may be assessed. As stated earlier, the efficacy of taking any investment decision must be based on traditional discounted cash flow (DCF) techniques, which will yield an initial positive or negative NPV or MVA for the invest-ment as a whole. However, during the life of the investment, the management could be held responsible for subsequent windfall gains or losses arising out of changes in cash flows and expectations about such changes. For example, in Table 15.6, in the second and third periods, positive windfalls are experienced which increase the value of the original investment requiring correspondingly smaller sums for reinvestment and for capital maintenance. Management could therefore be rewarded or sanctioned upon whether windfall gains or losses were subsequently realised during the life of the investment. The only question would be whether or not these windfall gains or losses were caused by changes in cash flows, or expectations about cash flows, determined by factors within the control of management.

Having discussed the theory behind the measurement of the economic valuation paradigm, it is now necessary to discuss the accounting perspective on corporate valuation and the problem of MVA or accounting goodwill.

GOODWILL AS AN ACCOUNTING PROBLEM

Lord Eldon in the *Cruttwell v Lye* case of 1810 stipulated that:

> The goodwill that has been the subject of sale, is nothing more than the probability that the old customer will resort to the old place. (Lee, 1971)

This pithy definition encapsulates the essence of goodwill, in that it is dependent on the future cash flows (i.e. sales) as being the original source from which profit (attributable to the owner) is the residual amount. Without customers a business would be worthless, therefore valuation of a business must depend upon the anticipation of future business, and all the marketing and branding implications that go with it.

Canning also recognised the future as being critical to the value of an asset:

> An asset is any future service in money or any future service convertible into money. (Canning, 1978, p. 22)

The literature is also laden with definitions of goodwill which put forward the idea of superior earnings. Such a definition was given by Canning:

> The value of the power to earn in excess of the rate on cost that is necessary to induce men to engage in the enterprise under consideration. (Ibid., p. 188)

Proponents of this 'excess earnings' approach infer that goodwill represents an excess of returns over the normal rate of return that the identifiable net assets can earn. They state that goodwill is merely the present value of the anticipated excess earnings discounted over a number of years at an appropriate discount rate.

Ma and Hopkins also use the superior earnings perspective from which to derive their definition:

> Goodwill is viewed as the capitalised value (i.e. the present value) of the stream of superior earnings of the business to be acquired. (Ma and Hopkins, 1988, p. 26)

Lee (1971), however, tries to address the important distinction and confusion between defining the nature of goodwill and its valuation. He has argued that although identifying the superior earning power of the discounted future cash flows generated may be a starting point for valuing goodwill, it doesn't explain its nature.

Lee lists many factors which may be identified as contributing to goodwill, such as development costs, staff qualities, training, patents, etc. He goes as far as to deny that goodwill as an asset exists:

> It is a word that conveniently describes a number of business resources contributing to the overall profitability of the business. (Lee, 1971, p. 320)

This approach is known as the 'hidden assets' approach, and has been referred to by Colley and Volkan (1988, p. 36). They refer to Tearney (1973), who argues that goodwill can be fully explained away by identifying a number of identifiable intangible assets. Proponents of the 'hidden assets' approach by implication would argue that there are no 'superior earnings' to be earned, merely that they will be observed when some of the underlying assets are either undervalued or unrecognised. Therefore the true rate of return needs to be calculated by comparison of earnings to an appropriate valuation of net assets, including tangibles and all intangibles.

Lee points out that some of the 'hidden' factors he identifies are tangible in nature, some are within the control of the organisation, and others outside the control of the organisation. The question of hidden assets such as goodwill, other intangibles and unrecognised tangible assets is an admission that the accounting measurement system has its weaknesses, in that some assets are not being recognised as they should, or they are not being valued correctly.

The question of controllability of assets is an important issue in the recognition of assets or otherwise. If the business does not control a resource, is it really an asset that should be recognised? To answer that question it is necessary to refer to the Accounting Standards Board's definition of an asset in FRS 5 (ASB, 1994a), and establish whether control is a necessary element in establishing the recognition of an asset. It would seem that control of the benefits arising from rights or other access to resources is needed. However, is control of the resource itself necessary to control the future benefits which that resource yields?

According to FRS 10 (ASB, 1997a) there is a requirement to demonstrate 'control or custody' over an intangible asset before it can be recognised. For example, it may not be within the control of a retail outlet that the local council demolishes adjacent derelict houses and replaces them with a car park. However, the benefits from additional business generated by the proximity of the car park are flowing directly into the funds of the business and therefore future benefits are obtained. The problem in not recognising the asset and yet still crediting the income, is that Fisher's fundamental circular relationship between the income and its associated stock of capital is being violated, causing the immediate creation of a goodwill or MVA gap.

Chambers, like Lee, disputes the fact that goodwill is an asset and explains that the reason a company earns superior profits to another is based on the synergistic interaction of a combination of assets working in concert, and with the market. He explains goodwill within the context of a business entity:

> Goodwill subsists in its (the entity's) collection of assets and liabilities and the advantages which flow from them as they are arranged amongst themselves and in relation to the market; it does not subsist in any separable thing. (Chambers, 1966, p. 209)

Chambers argues that goodwill is not an asset because it is neither severable or measurable, but he does admit that it is capable of evaluation, although such evaluations being comparative would vary over time. However, if goodwill is capable of evaluation it surely must be capable of measurement, even if the method of measurement is crude. The objection to goodwill being an asset due to its non-severability is a weaker argument, but it is consistent with the logic of Chambers' theory of net realisable value accounting, where all assets and liabilities are valued at their separable cash equivalent exit prices. However, because exit prices for non-separable assets are difficult to establish in the marketplace, it does not mean these assets aren't valuable or capable of contributing to future economic benefits.

It is then arguable that even the measurement and proper valuation of many tangible assets is fraught with difficulties, when separate valuations are required on an item-by-item basis. This is because significant amounts of their aggregate value may be attributable to their use in concert rather than in isolation, and as they jointly contribute to future economic benefits.

Arnold et al. (1992) also discuss synergy with respect to goodwill, and classify 'jointness of activities and market imperfections' as one of the three main constituent elements of goodwill which they identify. Their paper also discusses goodwill and its nature as an asset or otherwise, referring to the economic law of synergy:

> Given the economic law that 'the whole is often greater than the sum of its parts' this process will inevitably leave a remainder which is not itself an asset or a liability of the same logical category as the assets and liabilities now identified. However, treating it as if it were another such asset is the only logical consistent and neutral way to 'undo' the transaction. (Arnold et al., 1992, p. 36)

The existence in the literature of the two fundamental perspectives on the essential nature of goodwill would suggest that little consensus exists. But is there any substantive difference in these views or are they two ways of looking at the same thing? The acceptance of superior earnings when relating anticipated income to recognised net assets, either suggests that the assets listed in the accounts from which the earnings are derived are themselves undervalued, or that the sources of those future earnings are not being recognised. That is to say, every income must have a capital, and from every capital must derive an income. This tautological argument would suggest that the notion of 'superior earnings' is flawed, and evidence of superior earnings merely reflects the existence of 'hidden' or undervalued assets, however they may be identified or disaggregated from all other assets.

ACCOUNTING FOR PURCHASED GOODWILL

Goodwill being the difference between the accounting valuation and the economic valuation, is put sharply into focus when a transaction that establishes it takes place. This is the case when one business takes over another when the price paid for the business as a whole, or a controlling proportion of that business, exceeds the fair values of the aggregate net assets acquired. In this situation it is much easier to establish goodwill as an asset, as it does substantially fall within the definition of an asset by verification through a past transaction or event, and by being measurable in monetary terms.

The explanatory note in the Accounting Standards Committee's SSAP 22 (ASC, 1984) refers to goodwill as follows:

> It is usual for the value of a business as a whole to differ from the value of its separable net assets. The difference, which may be positive or negative is described as goodwill. (P.1)

However, despite its objective measurement through a verifiable transaction, the standard goes on to say that although an amount may be attributable to goodwill in this way, this valuation is unique to the valuer and to the specific point in time at which it is measured, and is valid only at that time, and in the circumstances then prevailing. If the value and nature of goodwill are, as volatile as the standard states, then it would seem that to recognise or value it in the books of account beyond the immediate time of the transaction would be going against the measurement and recognition criteria laid down by the ASB in the draft statement of principles (ASB, 1995a).

The point about the measure of goodwill being unique to the valuer is critical to understanding the nature of the goodwill. Goodwill is based partly on a perception of value and as it is based on anticipation of future events, its valuation will depend upon how these future events will be shaped, and by whom. There may be an element of synergism in that a buyer may well see how the acquired business will fit into the business already owned, in terms of sharing common facilities and networks, etc., and will pay a premium for this that another buyer may not benefit from and would not be prepared to pay for. Ma and Hopkins (1988) state that it is frequently impossible to disentangle the flows attributable to the acquisition once it has been undertaken because of the synergy within the new group. It is therefore very difficult for an independent valuer to arrive at an objective valuation for a business, without knowing who is intending to purchase, or what their particular situation is, and their future intentions are. Any valuation that is arrived at must be recognised as only applying at that time and while plans and expectations of the future remain the same.

Lee has also made this point about the volatility of purchased goodwill and the fact that although its valuation may be established at the point of acquisition, its value at the date of disclosure may be considerably different. He argues that once the price has been paid for the goodwill it becomes like any other asset, a past capital cost, and therefore the figure loses its currency and relevance:

> It no longer remains a figure representative of current expectations of the future. Instead it is representative only of past expectations of the future. (Lee, 1971, p. 323)

Lee's view could be taken further. At worst, purchased goodwill may become representative not only of past expectations of the future, but past expectations of the past, based on misguided assumptions. However, the fact that the acquisition of goodwill is verified at a single point in time by a transaction or event requires it to be accounted for.

Having earlier stated that the pure version of the economic model seems to get around the goodwill problem, this may only be true of inherent goodwill. If a company buys another company, there may still be a difference in the price paid for the business due to differing perceptions of the net future cash flows expected, as between the existing owners with respect to their plans, and the prospective owners with respect to their own plans. Therefore, even under the economic model, a problem may still arise with respect to purchased goodwill, although these changes in expectations are allowed for in the economic model as 'subjective goodwill' or 'windfalls'. Hicks explains this disequilibrium, as he calls it, in the following way, which might as easily apply to companies:

> It remains true that income is a subjective concept dependent on the particular expectations of the individual in question. Now, as we have seen, there is no reason why the expectations of different individuals should be consistent; one of the main causes of the disequilibrium in the economic system is a lack of consistency in expectations and plans. (Hicks, 1946, p. 177)

This would bring about, within the economic model discussed in the previous section, an immediate windfall gain or loss on the investment made.

The way in which the acquired goodwill is accounted for has over the past 15–20 years been a source of intense academic debate, both in terms of selecting from available alternatives, and with respect to attaining consistency with the treatment of internally generated or inherent goodwill.

PURCHASED AND INHERENT GOODWILL: THE DEBATE

The debate between the advocates of the immediate write-off approach and those who preferred the method of capitalising and amortising goodwill has been long and drawn out. Although the original SSAP 22 preferred the immediate write-off approach, this was severely criticised by many, both within the membership of the regulatory bodies and within the accountancy firms. This opposition led initially to the issue of ED 47 (ASC, 1990). This opposition was despite the popularity and almost universal acceptance of the 'preferred approach' in SSAP 22, as evidenced by Russell et al. (1989), in Certified Research Paper 13, who found that 95% of companies then wrote off goodwill against the reserves of the consolidated group.

All the costs associated with investing in the drivers of inherent goodwill or MVA are usually charged as period costs through the profit and loss account in the year to which they appertain. As a consequence there is inevitably a time lag between the charging of the costs and the receipts of the future economic benefits. The main argument for writing off purchased goodwill directly against reserves is that it is impossible to match these costs reliably enough against the benefits received, and therefore it is best not to attempt to charge them at all (Ma and Hopkins, 1988). Russell et al. (1989) argued that this was a flawed argument. They believed it was wrong for the cost incurred in acquiring purchased goodwill to bypass the profit and loss account completely, because this means that at no time is the cost of the asset which contributes to future economic benefit charged against that benefit. This, in their view, devalued financial reports to users because costs within the control of management are not being included within the measurement criteria for assessing the performance of the company:

> If purchased goodwill is written off directly to reserves one is faced with the anomaly that increments in profit arising from that goodwill appear in the profit and loss account, while the amounts paid for such increments are not charged there, so managers are not fully accountable for their actions in acquiring other firms. (Ibid., p. 25)

Russell et al. conclude that the control issue is the key reason why purchased goodwill should be capitalised and amortised systematically; this is also consistent with the positive theory of agency (Altman and Subrahmanyam, 1985, pp. 93–131), where it is argued that accounting reports should serve to monitor the performance of management. Arguably in contrast to the current position of the ASB, Russell et al. believe that the matching approach is the most relevant for the purpose of monitoring and motivating the financial performance of management.

The main argument for the capitalisation of goodwill is that as purchased goodwill has a finite value and has a definite economic life, it must therefore be depreciated like any other fixed asset. Opponents of amortisation of purchased goodwill argue that it is a double charge on profits. Taylor (1987) argued that charging depreciation against acquired goodwill at the same time the company is building up inherent goodwill, leads to double-charging the cost of goodwill against profits, and thereby to the understatement of maintainable profits within the company. He claimed that immediate write-off 'treats purchased and non-purchased goodwill comparably by removing them both' (ibid., p. 93)

However, it can be argued that as there has been dual expenditure on the goodwill, there should in effect be a double charge against the profits. This argument can be further supported by the use of an example where a company produces its own fixed asset and then is taken over by another company. If all the expenditure in bringing the asset to its present condition and location, including attributable overheads, have all been written off directly to the profit and loss account and not capitalised, the acquired entity would by that very fact have underdeclared its profits and under-valued its net assets, according to generally accepted accounting principles. However, despite the erroneous accounting, a company wishing to acquire this entity would presumably pay the fair value for that company, including an amount to compensate the selling company's shareholders for the unrecognised fixed asset being acquired. It would be nonsense to suggest that the expenditure which had been incurred previously on the fixed asset by the acquired company, and which had been paid for by the acquiring company, should not be recognised in the acquiring company's accounts. On the contrary, the acquiring company would capitalise the asset and depreciate it accordingly.

Clearly the substance of the economic situation is that, whatever the previous accountancy treatment, an identifiable asset has been purchased, and if this asset has a finite economic life, it should be recognised under the accruals concept as a proper charge against profits. It would seem that for the sake of consistency, the same should apply to goodwill. Therefore, it must be right that any benefits which are eventually realised from expenditure on purchased and inherent goodwill, should have all the costs which originally created them charged at some point to the profit and loss account or at least to the statement of total recognised gains and losses (STRGL). The argument that profit is understated is due to the time lag between the charging of expenditure on inherent goodwill to the profit and loss account, and the eventual receipt of any future economic benefits that may be realised from that expenditure.

This is key to the problem of goodwill and MVA. At a single point in time, where a company is systematically investing in inherent goodwill, there will be an accumulated understatement of profit, but over the longer term all benefits derived from the original expenditure will eventually be received and credited to the profit and loss account. Therefore, over the economic life-time of any particular tranche of goodwill, all costs and revenues associated with that goodwill will have been matched, although not on a strict period-by-period basis.

SSAP 22 (ASC, 1984) originally recognised under point 5 that there was no difference in character between purchased goodwill and inherent goodwill, only that purchased goodwill has the attribute of being verified at a particular point in time through a market transaction. The standard stated that the preferable approach is to eliminate purchased goodwill from the accounts by immediate write-off against the acquiring company's reserves. The main argument for doing so is to maintain consistency with the treatment of costs associated with inherent goodwill, which are not capitalised (other than in exceptional circumstances, covered by accounting standards and company law). The standard also recognised the argument that goodwill, although not separately realisable as an asset, is nevertheless a capital asset, and it should be treated in the same way as any other tangible or intangible capital asset. There is a problem with this approach, in that whichever method is adopted, a clear inconsistency will arise. Where a holding company acquires a proportion of another company, it is acquiring the shares in that company, not the individual assets and liabilities of that company. If there is no material difference between the fair value of the shares acquired and the consideration given for those shares, no goodwill problem will arise in the holding company's accounts. The problem arises in the consolidated accounts, as the difference between the cost of control, and the share of capital and pre-acquisition reserves (which represent the net assets acquired) is likely to be different in most cases.

In Appendix 1 of the standard, the factors to be considered in determining the useful economic life of purchased goodwill are discussed with respect to the choice of whether to capitalise the goodwill or write it off against reserves. The appendix accepts that purchased goodwill may be gradually replaced by inherent goodwill resulting from investment expenditure undertaken by the company post-acquisition, but precludes taking account of such expenditure in determining the useful economic life of the originally purchased goodwill. This leads to the apparently perverse situation where a company's total goodwill may be growing, but goodwill write-offs continue to be made through the profit and loss account. SSAP 22 therefore accepts that it is possible to establish a valuation of an investment, based on an estimation of future cash flows, and that these estimations may provide an objective enough guide for the amortisation period to be set for purchased goodwill. This is further developed upon in the ASB's working paper on goodwill (ASB, 1995b), where 'impairment tests' are recommended for income-generating units, based on assessing the 'recoverable amount' which is a comparison of the carrying value with the greater of market value and the value in use or net present value. This technique has been gradually formalised by the ASB firstly in FRED 12 (ASB, 1996) and FRED 15 (ASB, 1997b), and finally in FRS 10 (ASB, 1997a). This method essentially allows the company to compare annually the carrying value of intangible assets with their market values. If impairment has been observed, any difference should be written off, firstly against any goodwill carried within that unit, then against the recognised intangibles within the unit, then finally pro rata against the tangible assets within the unit. The paper accepts that in some cases no write-down need take place, as long as the market value at least equals the carrying amount. The main departure from the line of SSAP 22 in FREDs 12 and 15 and in FRS 10, apart from the recommendation to reject the SSAP's 'preferred approach', is the blurring of the distinction between the value of internally generated goodwill and the value of purchased goodwill when undertaking 'impairment tests'. This was expressed in the ASB report:

> Intangible assets and goodwill having finite expected useful economic lives should be depreciated over the period of those lives. Intangible assets and goodwill having indefinite economic lives should not be depreciated. (ASB, 1995b, p. 10)

ECONOMIC LIFESPAN OF GOODWILL

Leake (1921) argued that goodwill cannot have an indefinite life. He explained that goodwill, or the level of 'super profits' expected in the future, may be thought of in terms of an annuity, which depends on the term over which the annuity is received and upon the rate of interest prevailing. Both will determine the capital value of the goodwill originally paid for. The interest rate, he argued, depends upon the risk and upon the particular circumstances facing the business in any particular case. The logic of his argument is that receipts of future super profits cannot be as valuable as those received earlier, and that therefore it is obvious the value of purchased goodwill must inevitably diminish over time. Hicks (1946) referred to periodic expectations of such future benefits as 'prospects', and as these prospects are realised, the value of capital will be diminished unless some proportion of the periodic prospect realised is reinvested in order to realise some other alternative prospect. Leake supports this point when he states that allowing for a rate of interest of 10%, no less than 95% of the present value of a perpetuity will have expired by the end of 31 years, on the grounds that beyond that time the value becomes negligible in present terms. He therefore concludes that:

> It may be safely stated that capital outlay on the purchase of goodwill inevitably expires year by year, whether the profits of an undertaking are increasing or decreasing. (Leake, 1921, p. 77)

RECOGNITION OF INHERENT GOODWILL IN THE BALANCE SHEET

For the ASB firstly in 1995 and in FRS 10 therefore, to accept that aggregate goodwill within an income-generating unit may have an indefinite life, they are making a de facto admission that any impairment test must by implication place a value upon all the goodwill within that unit, including inherent goodwill generated since the original acquisition was made. This seems to contradict both company law and generally accepted accounting practice, as previously set out.

THE CAUSES AND NATURE OF GOODWILL OR MVA

Having examined various definitions of goodwill, attempts at explaining its nature, and the accounting problems of distinguishing between inherent and purchased goodwill, several conclusions may be drawn from the accounting literature.

The first issue is whether goodwill is really an asset at all. Several commentators deny this, most notably Paton (1924), Lee (1971) and Chambers (1966). Their arguments revolve around the fact that, in their view, goodwill cannot be clearly decomposed into specific assets as a source of future income streams, nor are these assets in most cases separable from the entity as a whole. Paton saw intangible assets as measuring that part of the company's asset base which might be said to reside in the physical situation viewed as a whole, but which cannot be considered to inhere in specific units of plant, equipment, etc. Lee describes goodwill as the collection of business resources contributing to future profitability, and Chambers emphasises that the source of goodwill doesn't reside in any separable thing, but in the advantages created by the assets in combination and in relation to the market. All these views therefore imply the existence of synergy. It is clear, therefore, that some proportion of goodwill resides in relation to the earning potential of the entity as a whole, as opposed to the aggregate expected future cash flows associated with identifiable individual assets and liabilities held by the entity.

The extent to which synergy accounts for goodwill, as opposed to other identifiable intangibles, seems to require considerable additional empirical research. This appears to be recognised in much of the recent literature. It is necessary therefore to establish the extent to which goodwill comprises synergistic factors, and to what extent it comprises 'hidden assets'. These would include the undervaluation or non-recognition of tangible assets, covered by FRS 7 (ASB, 1994b), and the undervaluation and non-recognition of separable intangibles.

For too long the debate in the 1980s had revolved around the issue of whether purchased goodwill should be capitalised or immediately written off against reserves. Capitalisation is now almost universally accepted because of the very good conceptual and theoretical reasons discussed above. If the originally preferred approach had been continued with, then the goodwill or MVA gap between market values of quoted companies and their book values would have continued to widen dramatically, and the original preferred approach was one of the reasons for Stern Stewart to recommend adding back goodwill write-offs as one of their 164 recommended adjustments to accounting profit.

The key question remaining with respect to purchased goodwill is one of presentation, and whether any adjustments to the carrying value of the purchased goodwill should be charged to the profit and loss account or to the statement of recognised gains and losses, and how this should be achieved. This now arises because of the choice recently afforded by the ASB's 'all-inclusive' approach to income measurement, requiring all gains and losses to appear on the face of the profit and loss account, unless specifically exempted by company law or accounting standards.

However, a fundamental consistency problem still remains unresolved. The problem remains if inherent goodwill is not subject to 'annual impairment review', while purchased goodwill is recognised. The conclusion from this inconsistency would be that it is likely that MVA, or accounting goodwill, for companies which grow organically is likely to be greater than for those which grow predominantly through acquisition, simply as an accounting consequence of their chosen growth strategies.

The way forward therefore, in order to satisfy the theoretical framework of reporting that the ASB had set for itself in its statement of principles, may lead to questioning the 'taboo' relating to accounting for inherent goodwill in all companies, regardless of their growth strategies.

ECONOMIC DRIVERS OF GOODWILL OR MVA

What is now necessary is clear empirical research in order to establish the practical causes of goodwill, in response to the recommendations made in much of the recent literature on the subject. It is therefore important to empirically identify and explain the main constituent drivers of goodwill, to measure to what extent it can be accounted for by proper recognition and valuation of separable tangible and intangible assets, and to what extent it inheres in economic and market phenomena. In assessing the extent to which economic and market phenomena are important, a distinction will need to be established between those economic and market factors which are specific to the company and its immediate trading environment, and to those factors which have a more macro-oriented nature. Macro-oriented factors would include factors influencing the capital markets, such as economic, fiscal and political influences as they affect those markets. This distinction needs to be investigated by examining the literature on company and stock market share valuation models, and identifying the extent to which the market is concerned with individual company performance or with wider sectoral market factors.

In order to inform the more practical debate in accountancy, it is important to try to identify the sources of the MVA or goodwill gap, to hypothesise what the drivers of MVA or goodwill are, and to objectively measure their relative contributions. The factors identified in SSAP 22 as determining the economic life of purchased goodwill are as follows:

- Expected changes in products, markets, and technology.
- Expected period of future service of certain employees.
- Expected future demand for products and services.
- Expected changes in competition or other economic factors which may affect current advantages.

Canning (1978) gave examples of the kind of real situations which may bring about goodwill, such as the non-recognition or undervaluation of assets, and states that separable items of future income associated with particular assets are either ignored or undervalued. Here are some of the examples he gives:

- Services of the general manager worth more than he has agreed to accept.
- No account taken in the books of a long succession of sales orders placed but not yet filled at the time of closing the books.
- Services of land under a lease contract, the terms of which have turned out to be extremely favourable.
- Land in a location more favourable than it appeared to be at the time it was bought.
- Items of machinery, the valuations of which are based upon their cost in the marketplace, but which have a greater value for the business in the particular use to which they are put.

Synthesising the above, and including other evidence drawn from the earlier review of literature on goodwill, the probable limitations of the accounting model could be hypothesised as including the following:

- Tangible net assets may be undervalued due to inappropriate valuation systems being used.
- Identifiable intangibles may be undervalued or inappropriately valued.
- Other intangibles may not be recognised within the model.
- Synergistic effects of net assets working in concert are ignored.
- The wider impact of macroeconomic factors affecting future prospects are being ignored.
- External synergies anticipated on combination of one entity and another are ignored.

Canning (1978) explains how it is no surprise that when many components of value are either undervalued or not recognised, then returns on capital employed measured upon this basis will show higher returns than those of companies who do recognise and appropriately value such assets. It could also be argued from this that, over a period of years, expenditures on acquiring assets which have a greater value in use than the value expended upon them, will contribute to an ever increasing future stream of income. This will lead to continuously increasing returns on capital employed, as the net asset denominator figure becomes increasingly out of date in comparison with the income numerator. This is of course what is happening under the traditional accounting model, and to a lesser extent in the EVA model, due to some classes of expenditure being capitalised within equity equivalents. Each tranche of investing expenditure which is not immediately capitalised as an asset, leads to a timing difference between the expenditure itself and the fruits of that expenditure. The time gap between these events gives rise to the goodwill or MVA recognised at any point in time between those two events.

THE BRIDGE BETWEEN ACCOUNTING AND ECONOMICS

In summary, all these factors which may cause a difference between the economic and the accounting paradigm are born out of the perception problem around the relationship between capital and income. As the accountant starts, in Fisher's terms, 'downstream' and attempts to look 'upstream', it is difficult to provide a valuation of assets before consideration of income. Therefore, the accountant attempts to value his or her stock of capital, 'net assets', without reference to the measurement of future income, which Fisher explains was essential in his sequence of capital valuation (Fisher, 1930). It is this failing to take adequate account of the future income to be generated in the accounting model which is its greatest theoretical weakness, and the reason for the reporting of EVAs and MVA, and for the existence of high goodwill levels within most companies.

In order to narrow or even eliminate the 'goodwill gap' in the accounting model caused by the above theoretical weakness, it is necessary for the accounting model to address the identified limitations in turn. The first two limitations may be tackled by the adoption of a suitable systematic current value accounting model and a proper asset recognition system. In terms of proper asset and liability measurement and recognition, FRS 4 (ASB, 1993) and FRS 5 (ASB, 1994a) have made a contribution. FRS 7 (ASB, 1994b) has also helped in the proper recognition of post-acquisition 'fair values'. With respect to intangibles, FRS 10 has also made a contribution, but to some extent it has raised more questions than it answers. The last four factors require further investigation and empirical analysis to establish their relative importance before recommendations for their incorporation into any accounting model may be contemplated.

Lee emphasises the importance of making a full and complete measurement of capital and the palpable failure of the accounting system to do so:

> This means, so far as income is concerned, it is important to measure capital fully — i.e. that its value takes cognisance of all economic resources which contribute to the existence of income. However, if the historic cost and current value income models are examined, it is clearly seen that the relevant capital computations are incomplete, and that in most situations the capital of the business entity is computed on the basis of an aggregation of resource valuations which have arisen from past transactions or events. This means that significant business resources may well be omitted from the relevant capital and income computations e.g. goodwill and other intangibles, which are often created rather than acquired by the entity. (Lee, 1996, pp. 163—64)

This passage makes it abundantly clear that even if accountants were to adopt systematic current value accounting models, deemed most relevant to users, there would still exist a significant undermeasurement of the capital of an entity, not just through overconservative accounting, but due to several other factors leading to non-identification of economic resources.

With respect to identifying the relationship between the original investments and their yields, this can be very difficult in practice. The accountant has the problem of identifying and disaggregating revenues and associating them with specific assets. Paton considers that goodwill and intangibles are difficult to identify separately and defines intangibles which comprise goodwill as

> the residuum, the balance of the legitimate values attaching to an enterprise as a totality, over the sum of the legitimate values of the various tangible properties taken individually. That is, the intangibles measure that part of the company's asset total which might be said to reside in the physical situation viewed as a whole, but which cannot be considered — except upon some highly arbitrary basis — to inhere in, or have residence in, specific units of plant, equipment etc. (Paton, 1924, p. 391)

He goes further and describes the hopelessness of attempting to value a business in terms of the specific facilities or net assets held:

> The gap between enterprise income in a particular period and individual contributing factors is too wide to be bridged by any scheme of accounting, however elaborate. And even were this problem to be met successfully, it would still leave us with the difficulty of estimating the future incomes of specific factors. (Ibid., p. 391)

Canning also recognised the problem of separately valuing each asset as a component of value based on its contribution to future income as a hopeless task:

But no comprehensive analysis of this character is possible, nor are the elements capable of statistical treatment. It is as if the physicist were to attempt to write the equations for the paths in space of each molecule of gas confined in a vessel. Life is not long enough to permit success. (Canning, 1929, p. 39)

A MODEL FOR THE DECOMPOSITION OF MARKET CAPITALISATION

Despite the problems of desegregation of income flows to assets or to their originating expenditure, and the resultant gap between economic and accounting values, it may still be possible to hypothesise a model for decomposing the constituent drivers of goodwill which may be possible to test empirically. This will be done within the framework of the EVA model. It is assumed that when one company takes over another company, the post-acquisition market capitalisation of the group or its economic present value may be broken down in several ways (Figure 15.1).

Essentially the market capitalisation of the group, immediately after an acquisition has taken place, represents the economic present value of the group as a whole. This assumes an efficient market for shares, and that the markets are discounting expected future cash flows in a way consistent with the theoretical economic model. From left to right the model breaks down the group's

Breakdown (a)	Breakdown (b)	Breakdown (c)	Breakdown (d)
Group market capitalisation premium	External synergies developed through combination	Inherent goodwill generated through acquisition	Market value added (MVA) on acquisition
	Macroeconomic factors	Accumulated inherent goodwill in holding company	Market value added (MVA) in holding company
	Internal synergies developed through assets working in concert	New purchased goodwill on acquisition	
Pre-acquisition market capitalisation of the holding company	Hidden assets	Unexpired inherent and purchased goodwill within the acquired company	Economic book values (EBV)
	Fair value of separable intangible assets	Accounting fair values	
	Fair value of separable tangible assets		

Figure 15.1. Decomposition of market capitalisation

economic present values into constituents. Column (a) breaks down the present or market value of the group into two components: the market capitalisation of the holding company immediately prior to acquisition, and the amount by which the market capitalisation of the new group exceeds it, after taking into account capital repayments made to the shareholders of the acquired subsidiary. Defined in other terms, this market capitalisation premium is equivalent to the initial windfall gain or subjective goodwill in the economic model, to the positive NPV arising in capital investment appraisal, or to MVA in the EVA model. It is hypothesised that the total market value of a group of companies immediately following an acquisition could also be broken down into several constituent drivers as identified in column (b).

External synergies

External synergies are anticipated from integrating the activities and assets of the subsidiary into the new group. They can be obtained in a number of ways, but most of them revolve around strategic factors, such as possible rationalisation opportunities, or through opportunities to share distribution channels, customer bases and supply chains. In its simplest terms it would represent a figure based on the market capitalisation value of the new group *less* the market capitalisation of the holding company immediately preceding the acquisition date.

As long as the market capitalisation of the new group is greater than the market capitalisation of the holding company, immediately preceding the acquisition, net of capital payments made to subsidiary shareholders, it may be assumed that some degree of external synergy will have been recognised and discounted by the stock market, and in theory all shareholders are better off.

Macroeconomic factors

It is hypothesised that at any point in time, a proportion of the market capitalisation of any company may be due to systematic macro factors affecting the demand for equities generally and sectorally. These factors would include interest rates, exchange rates, taxation policies, and general economic and political influences. It is assumed that these factors have a general effect on a company's market capitalisation, an effect which is not in any way specific to the performance of the company or group itself.

Internal synergies

Internal synergies would be the additional values placed on separable tangible and intangible assets, hidden or visible, through working in concert within the entity.

Having established the relative significance of each of the above constituents, it may be hypothesised that the remaining residual could be attributed to the unmeasurable internal synergistic factors which the economic model accounts for holistically, which the accounting model ignores, and which would be impossible to bridge directly by empirical means.

As a separate investigation there may also be future research opportunities with respect to empirically measuring the external synergies to be obtained from acquisition as a growth strategy. It may be possible to investigate how much the market capitalisation of a company rises on anticipation of a take-over; what premiums are made on those acquisitions above the market capitalisation value of the holding company at the time of the transaction; and what are the subsequent post-acquisition effects on goodwill.

CONCLUSION

The EVA or MVA model is useful in confirming the theoretical necessity of valuing a business or investment on the basis of what will happen rather than upon what has already happened. Unfortunately, although the EVA model recommends some adjustments to accounting profit and to accounting book values, the model suffers from being a part-way house which has the disadvantages of both the traditional accounting and the economic paradigms. The calculation of periodic EVAs, and by implication the resulting MVAs, is a flawed concept as these are calculated net of depreciation which is a non-cash deduction. As a consequence, EVAs are subject to the vagaries of the accountants' subjective allocation system, rather than on pure cash flows. For this reason, management may be inappropriately motivated, rewarded and sanctioned.

Furthermore, the EVA model overlooks, albeit to a lesser extent than the traditional accounting model, the one-directional circular relationship between capital and income in the purest sense. For this reason, it too suffers from the inevitable timing differences arising from the non-recognition of assets until they are established through the receipt of income to which they are related. This is consistent with the adherence of the traditional accounting model to the realisation concept, which is difficult to abandon as a tenet. Although the EVA model attempts to bridge the goodwill gap by recommending capitalisation of some expenditures not capitalised under the traditional accounting model, it still fails to recognise the goodwill inherent in other investing expenditures such as staff costs, advertising and promotion, etc.

Finally, as an accounting model, the EVA model suffers because it attempts to identify net assets individually, and therefore cannot account discretely for synergistic factors, either internally or externally, which the purely economic model would account for holistically, and which it would have to include as part of the MVA residual.

However, as the economic model in its purest sense may be impractical to implement in accounting terms, the market capitalisation of a quoted company may be used as a surrogate for the economic present value of a company or a group. In this regard the EVA model does go some way in narrowing the gap between accounting book values and market capitalisation, and is useful from a balance sheet perspective, if not as a periodic performance measure. To narrow the gap further, without adopting the purely economic approach, it may be possible for certain defined forms of investment expenditure, currently expensed, to be capitalised. The decomposition of macro factors, internal synergies and some hidden assets may be so difficult to isolate that it may be entirely impractical to account for them separately. However, it may be perfectly feasible to monitor their combined effects as observed in changes in total goodwill determined by market capitalisation. Changes in market capitalisation (net of changes in the fair values of separable net assets) may be the most valid way of assessing the performance of the business in a holistic sense. This is because the shareholders' expectations of the future are being properly discounted into the market capitalisation of the company based on a series of ascertainable past transactions and events. The verification of goodwill can take place continuously, periodically or as a result of acquisition.

REFERENCES

Altman, E.I. and Subrahmanyam, M.G. (1985) *Recent Advances in Corporate Finance*. Richard D. Irwin, Homewood IL.

Arnold, J., Egginton, D., Kirkham, L., Macve, R. and Peasnell K. (1992) *Goodwill and Other Intangibles*. Institute of Chartered Accountants for England and Wales, London.

ASB (1993) FRS 4, *Capital Instruments*.

ASB (1994a) FRS 5, *Reporting the Substance of Transactions*.

ASB (1994b) FRS 7, *Fair Values in Acquisition Accounting*.

ASB (1995a) *Statement of Principles for Financial Reporting*.

ASB (1995b) *Goodwill and Intangible Assets (Working Paper)*.

ASB (1996) FRED 12, *Goodwill and Intangible Assets*.

ASB (1997a) FRS 10, *Goodwill and Intangible Assets*.

ASB (1997b) FRED 15, *Impairment of Fixed Assets and Goodwill*.

ASC (1984) SSAP 22, *Accounting for Goodwill*. Revised 1989, amended 1994.

ASC (1990) ED 47, *Accounting for Goodwill*.

Bacidore, J.M., Boquist, J.A., Milbourn, T.T. and Thaker, A.V. (1997) The search for the best financial performance measure. *Financial Analysts Journal*, May/June, 11–20.

Canning J.B. (1929) *The Economics of Accountancy*. Ronald Press, New York.

Canning, J.B. (1978) *The Economics of Accountancy*. Arno Press, New York (reprint).

Chambers R.J. (1966) *Accounting, Evaluation and Economic Behaviour*. Prentice Hall, Englewood Cliffs NJ.

Colley J.R. and Volkan A.G. (1988) *Accounting for Goodwill, Accounting Horizons*. American Accounting Association, Sarasota FL.

Fisher, I. (1930) *The Theory of Interest*. Macmillan, London.

Hicks, J.R. (1946) *Value and Capital*, 2nd edn. Clarendon Press, Oxford.

Keynes, J.M. (1936) *General Theory of Employment, Interest, and Money*. Oxford University Press, Oxford.

Leake, P.D. (1921) *Commercial Goodwill, Its History, Value and Treatment in Accounts*. Pitman, London.

Lee, T.A. (1971) Goodwill: an example of will-o'-the-wisp accounting. *Accounting and Business Research*, Autumn, 318–28.

Lee, T.A. (1996) *Income and Value Measurement*, ITP, New York.

Ma, R. and Hopkins, R. (1988) Goodwill: an example of puzzle solving in accounting. *Abacus*, **24**(1), 15–22.

Modigliani, F. and Miller M. (1961) Dividend policy, growth, and the valuation of shares. *Journal of Business*, October, 411–33.

Paton, W.A. (1924) *Valuation of the Business Enterprise*. Macmillan, New York.

Rappaport, A. (1998) *Creating Shareholder Value*, 2nd edn. Free Press, New York.

Russell, A., Grinyer, J.R., Walker, M. and Malton, P.A. (1989) Accounting for goodwill. Research Paper 13, Association of Certified Chartered Accountants.

Stewart, G.B. III (1991) *The Quest for Value*. Harper Collins, New York.

Stewart, G.B. III (1994) EVA, fact and fantasy. *Journal of Applied Corporate Finance*, **7**(2), 71–87.

Taylor, P.A. (1987) *Consolidated Financial Statements*. Harper & Row, New York.

Tearney, M.G. (1973) Accounting for goodwill – a realistic approach. *Journal of Accounting*, July, 41–45.

Thomas, A.L. (1979) Matching: up from our black hole. In *Accounting for a Simplified Firm Owning Depreciable Assets* (eds R.R. Sterling and A.L. Thomas). Scholars Books, Houston TX.

16 Does Accounting Practice Undermine Value-based Measurement?

MARK WHITTINGTON

INTRODUCTION

Shareholder value is the corporate catchphrase of the current day. It is a moot point whether all the users of the value jargon understand, or appreciate, the logic or the metrics, or just the marketing necessity in their pitch to their shareholders. Unless you are an insider, specifically a senior member of the management team, any attempt to calculate value will rely on the publicly available information, its fitness for purpose and the use of judgement. Published financial accounts will form a key part of the value jigsaw that the analyst is trying to piece together. Here are two key questions that need to be addressed:

- How accepting should the analyst be of the audited information that is presented?
- What degree of awareness is required of differing accounting policies that might be adopted by different companies, especially when from various countries?

When one first brushes with accounting it seems to be a science-based subject, which relies on accurate recording of data using a double-entry system that logically flows through to a profit and loss account and a balance sheet. However, whilst it may be possible to produce a set of accounts without the use of judgement, such a set would be entirely cash-based and would be unlikely to have value for a decision maker. The initial aim of accounting was the stewardship of resources, the accurate recording of the company's assets, liabilities and transactions. Such a process does not lead to an entirely useful set of numbers for other purposes. Indeed, if this were the case then the need to develop shareholder value metrics and techniques would be much reduced.

The degree of relevance of the content of published accounts to a shareholder is not consistent around the world. Some countries have given more emphasis to the economic value of the information produced for the users of accounts than others. Indeed, independent shareholders have been more important to the economic development of some nations than others. However, the attractions of adding value for shareholders crosses many boundaries, even to where the shareholder concept has still had limited impact on the information that companies are obliged to publish. Hence, as well as the frequent and accurate criticisms of accounting relevance to shareholder value, the analyst needs to recognise that the published accounts used as a data source for calculation are not of consistent usefulness.

There are many shareholder value metrics and some appear to claim they are free from the arbitrary and the 'non-value relevant' calculations of the accountant; such claims need investigation. Even if it were possible to produce a set of numbers independent from such calculations, the cultural perception of profit and value built into the analyst (or the reader of the analysis) would probably still play a role in the interpretation and the use that would follow from the metric computation.

The aim of this chapter is to highlight the likely impact of accounting and international accounting differences on the various shareholder value metrics. In order to achieve this, it begins with the importance and history of accounting differences before looking at individual metrics and then offering some hints on how to move forward given the difficulties.

WHAT WAS WRONG WITH PROFIT?

It is worth taking a moment to remind ourselves of the problems of using profit as a measure of success and as a proxy for wealth generation. Even when well intentioned, profit is misleading in the assessment of shareholder value. But the information provided in the published accounts will, of necessity, be the starting point for the outsider's assessment of value. Problems with profit measurement will inevitably cause difficulties for 'value-based' measures that draw heavily on data from a set of accounts.

Profit is a single-period assessment

Profit is an attempt to communicate the success of the organisation as a single-period assessment. Why do some biotechnology companies and internet start-ups have high share valuations when they have never generated a profit and may not do so for some years? The purchaser of shares in these entities is assessing the potential future of the company concerned; current losses reflect start-up costs or research and development costs, which are real cash outflows, but ignore the possible tremendous future such expenditures might secure. Such a future is too uncertain for an accountant to build into a single-period model where prudence is always seen to be a top priority. Indeed many of the changes in financial reporting over recent years, particularly in the UK, focus on reducing the opportunities to inflate profit.

Dividing by shareholders' funds has several flaws

One would anticipate that a successful large company would make more profit than a successful small company. Hence there is a need to take account of the cash invested in an enterprise before interpreting the profit number. The traditional answer to this was to divide the profit after tax by the shareholders' funds. The simplicity of this is appealing, but is flawed in a number of ways. Firstly, apart from countries where inflation has been extremely high, accountants have done their best to ignore it. However, if the shareholders invested in a company 50 years ago, inflation of 3% per annum would have reduced the apparent value of the investment to 23% of its original worth when compared to today's profit number. A profit of €1m on an investment of €5m would appear to give a 20% return when, if the assumptions were as above, the real return would be merely 4.6%. Secondly, the shareholders' funds segment of the balance sheet has also been treated as a balancing item. For example, writing off goodwill on the purchase of an acquisition, common practice in the UK until recently, has significantly reduced the shareholders' funds of many companies. The revaluing of properties is allowed in some countries and outlawed in others. Revaluing increases shareholders' funds, but the increase in value may not be worth anything as the asset is not held for sale. The increase in the valuation will cause shareholders' funds to rise also, further undermining the return percentage calculation. If the shareholder is a potential acquirer and asset-stripper, such valuations become more shareholder relevant.

Profit ignores risk

A further problem for profit and return is the ignoring of risk. A 10% return in a safe industry may be fine as the risk taken by investors will be low; whereas a return of 15% may be inadequate in a high-risk, volatile and cyclical industry. Return is only one part of the investor's assessment. Three-legged horses tend to be offered at long odds for a good reason! Profit is arguably an attempt at a medium-term view of how a company is doing. So when an asset is purchased, despite the cash outflow, an attempt is made to match the cost of the asset to the years in which it will be used. This issue has two problems associated with it. Firstly, the capital expenditure involves spending the shareholders' money up front, the cash outflow itself is not spread. Secondly, the commercial life of an asset is very difficult to predict; the longer the expected life, the lower the annual charge of depreciation against profit and, at least initially, the higher the profit reported. The investor is concerned over when a dividend can be paid and may be willing to wait for greater returns in the future, but will be aware that the decision to invest in buildings or equipment is a dividend forgone for now. Hence profit can overstate dividend potential.

Profits cannot be compared from company to company

Finally, one company's profit may not be directly compared with another. Some of the more boring pages of a company's annual report are those containing the accounting policies of the enterprise. Each country allows a set of acceptable policies for stock valuation, depreciation, research and development, the definition of the enterprise, etc.; a company then chooses within that set. The application of a particular policy may also be different from one company to another. The inventor of a shareholder value metric might suggest a number of adjustments to published profits to calculate value for a particular industry. However, this approach assumes a normative set of accounting policies; that is, all profits in the industry were calculated on a comparable basis. As an outsider looking in, the analyst will always wish that the company had told them rather more about the policy choices than is usually the case. Phrases such as 'equipment is depreciated over a period of between 10 and 20 years' are common but relatively unhelpful. Indeed, the problem of accounting diversity could be viewed as one of lack of disclosure rather than particular differences.

INTERNATIONAL ISSUES AND THE ASSESSMENT OF VALUE

The globalisation of markets for goods and services has been matched by the investing community, which now looks at many countries for investment opportunities. Hence an understanding of just one country's methods of calculating profit is now not sufficient if potential opportunities are not to be ignored. Profit levels differ from country to country (see below). This will be due not to superior performance of one country's companies, but rather an alternative set of accounting policy choices. There is some evidence that the announcement of financial results may not move share prices, as the content is usually predicted with reasonable accuracy; but the expectation of profit levels and the policies underlying them are of importance.

Choi and Levich (1990) investigated the decision making of players in capital markets from a number of countries and sought to discover whether international accounting differences affected their decision making; they concluded: 'One-half of those queried feel that their capital market decisions are affected by accounting diversity. This finding understates the proportion of users who feel that accounting differences matter, as it does not include second-order behavioural effects'. They examined the responses of the different groups of people involved and found some investors who thought that their understanding of accounting diversity gave them a competitive advantage over others. Hence we can conclude from this that differences in accounting appeared to matter in the days before shareholder value metrics were common, or indeed ubiquitous. If there was logic and economic understanding behind the decision making of those days and the outcomes of a country's or company's accounting policy choices mattered at the time, it may be reasonable to surmise they would be of importance now.

INTERNATIONAL ACCOUNTING: A PRIMER

Financial statements are the end result of a complex legal and quasi-legal set of rules drawn up by regulators in a particular country. These rules or traditions are often referred to as the GAAP (generally accepted accounting principles and/or practices) of the country. In order to have any claim to cogency, the rules need to be focused on a user group and their particular information requirements. So, for example, the UK and the US have a shareholder focus where the key issue to address is the reporting of the economic performance of the enterprise over the last year. Other countries may have a governmental focus that prioritises the calculation of tax or information which enables the setting or assessment of a national plan. Another country might put suppliers of goods, services and loan capital (creditors and bankers) first; their main concern will be one of adequacy of financial resource, i.e. seeking reassurance that the company is able to continue trading in the future and meet its financial obligations. Shareholder and tax requirements are likely to be focused on the profit and loss account; creditor-based systems are likely to be focused on the balance sheet. The tax-based system is likely to have clear rules with limited choice, as indeed will the tax calculations of most countries; the shareholder-focused system requires more scope for policy choice in order for company directors to choose policies that fit their economic circumstances.

Today's accounting numbers are a result of a nation's history of economic development. Nobes and Parker (1997) detail a framework that attempts to explain the approach to accounting that has been adopted by a particular country. This depends in the first instance on the importance of the capital markets, shareholder-focused information being produced where the markets are an important source of capital, otherwise the rationale for producing the annual accounts is creditor-based or tax-based. The only factor likely to override this choice of approach is the influence of a colonial power, in which case the accounting approach of the imperial power will have been introduced whether appropriate or not. If the economic system of a country has developed or changed, it is also possible that change in accounting practice may lag somewhat behind.

Certain companies, perhaps due to the international nature of their market or out of a desire to appeal to investors who might understand their products or services better, have in recent years effectively rejected the accounting policy choices of their domicile. These companies, some large, many small, have decided to produce an alternative set of accounts, usually applying US GAAP or International Accounting Standards. The most famous instance of this was the decision of DaimlerBenz to list on the Wall Street stock exchange; this required the company to comply with US reporting requirements, thereby throwing interesting light on the relative qualities and measurement bases of the German and US approaches to financial reporting.

All accounting systems have a dual requirement problem, stewardship and economic value. Arguably the different focuses that countries adopt could also be summed up by the relative importance attached to stewardship versus the economic value of the information. Accounting systems, based on double entry, report on the completeness and accuracy of the recording system, reassuring users that no material fraud or mismanagement has occurred. Such a focus works best when rules are tight and any questionable numbers, perhaps relating to intangible assets like brands or goodwill, are discarded as flawed and unreliable. The only legitimate valuation is seen to come from a transaction in the market; buildings, for example, would not be revalued over time, but left at the purchase price until sold, if ever, when a profit would be recognised.

If a set of accounts appear to be financially secure under this stewardship-prioritised system then one might reasonably assume this to be true. With the ravages of time and inflation, such a system would continue to report on the adequacy of control, but contain less and less information of economic value as the company matured and initial purchases and investments were perhaps over a century old. This problem is heightened with a greater proportion of value creation coming from knowledge- and brand-based aspects of a business and buildings and machinery reducing in importance.

A country that has a greater concern with the economic content, due to the requirement to satisfy shareholder concerns and hence to enable the capital market to work, will have looser accounting rules. This should enable company directors to choose a policy set that fits the particular economic circumstances of the firm and its competitive environment.

Hence the accounting policy set made available to the directors of a company in a particular country will have been formed over time based on an interacting mix of factors. Included in this mix will be the development of the capital market, the legal system, the development and standing of accountants and auditors and a variety of cultural factors and historical accidents. We need to bear these points in mind as we consider the calculation of shareholder value from the information made available by the company.

VBM METRICS: USERS AND INFORMATION AVAILABILITY

Value-based management (VBM) metric calculations fall into two groups: those generally used by outsiders, who we will call analysts, and those used by insiders, the management. The analysts are living in a world of limited information and rely on their skills and knowledge to understand the environment in which companies operate and also on information releases from those companies. The management team, however, have potential access to limitless internal company information, but they need to decide how to collect and organise this in order for them to best make decisions. The management have some freedom concerning the frequency and content of information releases to the analysts. In some countries, formal or legally required communication between managers and shareholders is limited; in others it may be relatively copious but perhaps of little direct relevance to the investing community. The scale and detail of the defined reporting activity may be of as much importance as the underlying differences in calculation and policy choice.

Where companies decide to make additional disclosures for shareholders in order to fill the information gap, there is a further problem. Less formal or legally defined contact by the management team has to be treated with a degree of suspicion. Lying may be uncommon, but a truthful statement may be more or less inclusive of all relevant facts and circumstances. An example of this would be the graphical content of annual reports in countries where a write-up of the year just ended and of company prospects is the norm as well as a set of financial statements. By careful choice of starting year, scale and starting point of the Y-axis, and calculation method of the statistic, a truthful yet distorting picture can be easily obtained. The choice of gearing ratio to display, whether to treat 'non-equity' shareholders (the UK term for some convertible preference shareholders) as debt or equity are all within the management's set of choices. Indeed, the most even-handed of managements are likely to show pictures of the new buildings and assets and give details of new investments whilst giving scant regard to older parts of the company portfolio. Hence the more freedom given by a country for reporting, the more likely the reason for the information release should be considered before entering upon interpretation.

Management teams who perceive either a lack of understanding, or fitness for purpose or perceived quality of the information that they are forced to produce, may respond by seeking credibility via a number of routes:

(1) They may employ auditors of international standing. For economies without a history of substantial shareholder activity, the quality or relevance of the local auditing accountant may be questioned by those from countries where the primacy of the shareholder view is taken for granted. For example, there is substantial evidence for East European firms having to use a large international audit firm before US investors will consider investing in the enterprise.

(2) They may adopt alternative accounting treatments, releasing additional information that conforms to a more widely understood or investor-relevant accounting policy set. This is usually achieved by seeking a second, foreign, listing. (For some companies there are other reasons for this over and above adopting a second accounting treatment, and indeed

some company directors complain about the extra cost of reporting in US GAAP as well as their domestic one. Some who take this route then make obtaining the extra accounting information difficult or do not publish its existence.) A listing by a foreign company in London generally requires conformity with International Accounting Standards, a listing in the US necessitates the use of US GAAP.

(3) Most dramatically, the company could seek to change domicile. This means the company ceases to be based in country A and moves to country B. The much publicised attempt of LucasVarity to cease being a UK company and become a US company was driven by a management perception (whether true or false) that UK investors did not understand or appreciate the prospects for engineering-based companies. LucasVarity had already taken the step of dual listing (the standing of the auditors not being an issue) and communicated the key features of the US accounting figures along with the UK figures. This, in their view, had not been sufficient. A number of large South African companies have also recently 'relocated' to the UK.

Annual accounts provide the only starting point for analysts to carry out a variety of predefined and judgmental adjustments that may be required for the calculation of a particular VBM metric. The concern here is the issue of whether the diversity of accounting impinges on the shareholder value calculation and therefore, at least potentially, undermines any value comparisons, especially cross-border ones. The acceptance of comparability when none exists may lead to the favouring of companies from one accounting regime compared with those of another, or to an inbuilt assumption that companies from one country generate higher shareholder values than those from another. We should recall that the problem of accounting policy diversity is not just an issue when accounting regulatory borders are crossed, but also when two companies in the same domicile decide on a different level of disclosure or the use of alternative policies or different implementations of the same policy. Each accounting regime offers a set of accounting policies that, if reasonably appropriate, may be chosen at the company's discretion. Generally, the corporate outsider will be unable to calculate the effects of an alternative policy being chosen, although educated guesses may well be possible. Having accepted there will be differences, the next question is, Does it matter?

DOES IT MATTER? A QUESTION OF MATERIALITY

Whether any particular accounting policy difference is a material difference will probably depend on the industry sector and will probably need to be considered case by case. A tendency for rapid fixed asset depreciation via the choice of seemingly short asset life, in one country this is likely to affect the accounts of capital-intensive companies to a material degree, whereas service industries may be almost unaffected. The UK's goodwill write-off policy (based on SSAP 22 until the end of 1998 and with few retrospective implications for accounts after that date) will have led to large differences in the profit levels and the balance sheet level of equity for acquisitive companies, whereas organic growth firms will be unaffected. More unusual adjustments, such as statutory reserves in the UK, may require special treatment and be crucial to the meaningful interpretation of the accounts of just a few companies.

Whittington and Steele (1998) have recently addressed the effect of international accounting on a residual income measure. They examine the previous work undertaken on estimating the average effects of cross-border accounting differences and apply it to the calculation of 'added value', a potential shareholder value metric advocated by Kay (1993). The findings,

Table 16.1. Research analysing dual-listed companies

Paper	Comparison	Year	Mean adjustment	Range
Weetman and Gray (1990)	UK to US	1985	1.17	0.5 to 5.1
		1986	1.09	0.2 to 2.9
		1987	1.25	0.6 to 11.3
Weetman and Gray (1991)	UK to US	1986	1.12	0.2 to 5.8
		1987	1.20	0.1 to 11.8
		1988	1.17	0.7 to 40.1
Weetman and Gray (1991)	Sweden to US	1986	1.03	−22.3 to 1.6
		1987	1.41	0.6 to 2.7
		1988	0.97	0.5 to 1.2
Weetman and Gray (1991)	Netherlands to US	1986	0.74	0.7 to 1.1
		1987	0.96	0.6 to 1.3
		1988	0.98	1.0 to 2.5
Norton (1995)	Australia to US	1985	0.85	0.8 to 0.9
		1986	0.93	0.7 to 1.1
		1987	−0.20	−3.5 to 1.1
		1988	0.58	0.9 to 1.1
		1989	0.64	−0.6 to 1.3
		1990	1.01	0.2 to 1.6
		1991	1.126	0.2 to 2.4
		1992	0.47	−2.9 to 2.2
		1993	0.65	−4 to 2.7
Cooke (1993)	Japan to US	1990	0.67	0.3 to 0.9
		1991	0.78	0.4 to 1.2

usually termed indices of conservatism, are then applied to a league table of companies from France, Germany, Japan, UK and US.

Table 16.1 is adapted from Whittington and Steele (1998). It first considers papers that have examined the translation of individual companies from one GAAP to another. This work is possible because of the requirement for non-US companies, which are listed on a US stock exchange, to file a document with the Securities and Exchange Commission. This filing has to convert the domestic financial reports to US GAAP.

The mean adjustment should be interpreted as follows, using the first paper as an example. Here Weetman and Gray found that the UK accounts they examined were, on average, a multiple of 1.17 times the US profit the company reported. This leads to the conclusion that the average company was some 17% less conservative (more positive) when applying UK GAAP than when applying US GAAP. Of more concern is the range, however. It is clear that for some companies the application of US GAAP means a reduced reported profit, and yet for another company the UK profit was five times the US profit. The table shows the diversity between companies and also over time. Changing economic circumstances and changes to the acceptable set of accounting choices within a country caused by new or replacement accounting standards, mean that complete consistency of adjustment is most unlikely.

Table 16.2. Conservatism indices over time

British Steel conservatism index (UK to US conversion)			Usinor conservatism index (France to US conversion)		
Year	Index value	Ignoring years with losses	Year	Index value	Ignoring years with losses
1988	0.949	0.949	1993	0.769	
1989	1.391	1.391	1994	1.032	1.032
1990	1.234	1.234	1995	0.882	0.882
1991	1.376	1.376	1996	1.521	1.521
1992	1.079		1997	1.097	1.097
1993	0.539				
1994	2.059	2.059			
1995	1.365	1.365			
1996	1.079	1.079			
1997	0.727	0.727			
1998	0.983	0.983			
Index < 0.9	2	1	Index < 0.9	2	1
0.9 < index < 1.1	4	3	0.9 < index < 1.1	2	2
Index > 1.1	5	5	Index > 1.1	1	1

Table 16.3. External analyst adjustments

Research	Japan	US	UK	France	Germany
Smithers and Co. (Economist, 1992)	1.69	0.77	0.75	0.84	1.00
Simmonds and Azieres (1989)	NA	NA	0.69	0.89	1.00

NA = not applicable

Table 16.2, from Whittington (1999), shows the conservatism indices for two European steel companies over a period of time. This highlights the volatility in such index measures over time. The final column is included as there is a problem with the calculation of this index when a loss is recorded. The volatility is caused by a number of factors, including particular accounting items or transactions that might occur in one year but not another, such as an acquisition, or changes in GAAPs of France, the UK or the US, as mentioned above.

Assuming that a 10% difference between US and domestic, UK or French GAAP here, is not material, we see a wide spread of results. One reason for this may be that some accounting differences are a question of timing, and in a mature industry it is possible that these differences may reverse over the years.

Table 16.3, adapted from Whittington and Steele (1998), shows some adjustments derived by other means. Smithers and Co. use data from national income statistics. Simmonds and Azieres derive a range of profit numbers from a theoretical accounting data set that was analysed by accountants from several European countries. Figure 16.1, drawing from the Simmonds and Azieres study, shows the range of potential choice available to a company within a particular country, with the highest, most likely and lowest possible profit numbers shown. This highlights the fact that the problem faced here is not just from one country to another, but also a question of accounting policy choice within one GAAP.

Taking conservation indices into account, the Whittington and Steele paper reworked an added value statistic for 50 companies from five countries and ranked the companies before and after attempting to allow for accounting differences. To assess the materiality of the reordering of the league table, the level of disruption from the unadjusted order was compared to the reordering caused by adjusting fixed asset life (depreciation period) and required rates of return. The change caused by international accounting was equivalent to a change in depreciation life of 80%, e.g. 10 years to 18 years, and a movement in return rate of 60%, e.g. 10% to 16%.

Whilst this provides some insight into average effect, there is no such thing as an average company. The freedom to choose reasonably realistic

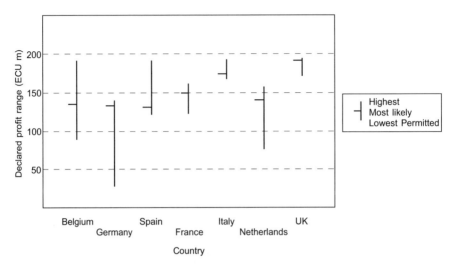

Figure 16.1 Comparison of international reporting. Reprinted, with permission, from Simmonds and Azieres (1989)

depreciation periods rather than tax-based periods, for example, only has a material effect on companies with significant tangible fixed assets.

SHAREHOLDER VALUE CALCULATIONS AND INTERNATIONAL DIFFERENCES

We can now move on to consider the consequences of accounting diversity for shareholder value calculation. The logic for VBM metrics is clear, the practical means of calculation less so. There are a variety of methods, the most popular focused on the calculation of what a traditional accountant would call residual value and an economist supernormal profit or economic rent. Profit has been derided as a measure of success for some time, though some cling to such measures as earnings per share. Precisely which metric should replace this, if any, is open to debate and, more worryingly, marketing expertise of the particular consulting organisation pushing each metric. Our concern here, however, is the impact of accounting policy differences on the calculation of shareholder value.

The relevant differences in policy depend on the particular value metric that is chosen. One might blame a lack of information more than accounting difference, as greater disclosure would increase the ability of the analyst outside the company to adjust or replace published numbers. Here we will briefly consider the main components of the most popular calculations.

ACCOUNTING EFFECTS ON CALCULATION COMPONENTS

Before considering a number of competing VBM measures, we will first consider important components of some of the metrics. Firstly, the delivery of value implies the achievement of a return above the mere compensation for risk. Of more importance to us is the measurement of the level of investment that a return needs to be made upon, the second part of this section. Thirdly, there is the issue of level of profit generated.

Required rate of return

Most methods take this from a capital asset pricing model calculation; and from a diversified shareholder and capital provider perspective, this has much to commend it. Assuming some validity in the model, the international issue here is the liquidity of the stock market in question and of the individual share being assessed, rather than differences in accounting policies. If trading is infrequent and of small quantities, then little will be learned of underlying risk assessment. One may take issue with the capital asset pricing model, but it is outside the scope of the chapter. An interested reader may wish to refer to Davies et al. (1999).

Level of investment

What we are attempting to measure here is how much have shareholders invested in order for the management team to generate current cash flow or profit? This seemingly simple question, which one might expect to answer by a quick glance at shareholders' funds in the balance sheet, is fraught with difficulty. The problems are evidenced by four issues.

Depreciation life

Any accounting policy that affects the time period in which either a sale or a cost is recognised will impact on profit recognition and therefore on profit retained in the business, the figure by which shareholders' funds rise year by year. Hence a growing company using long depreciation lives would see minimal depreciation cost whereas a stable company with shorter depreciation periods, perhaps forced on the company by the country of domicile to be in harmony with tax relief, would be recognising much more depreciation. The second company would have lower profits and lower shareholders' funds in the short term. Shareholder value created will be unrelated to such accounting choices.

Inflation

Perhaps the most obvious difficulty is inflation. If accounts are prepared under the historic cost convention, meaning that inflation is ignored, then (assuming a degree of inflation since the original investment) the balance sheet will understate the real value of the investment that the first purchaser of a share made and also the value of retained profits from earlier years. Inflation has been country-specific. Hence differences in real levels of investment from reported ones will differ enormously from one country to another. Obviously, restating the level of shareholder investment to a present value equivalent will make any company's management look worse than the standard historic cost approach.

Revaluation

Under modified historic cost, fixed assets may be revalued and any increase or decrease in value then added or subtracted from shareholders' funds. It is debatable whether a revaluation upwards is an increased investment by the shareholders, as it is likely to be unavailable for dividend payment until the revalued asset is sold and the profit is realised. Countries such as the US, Switzerland and Japan outlaw these upward adjustments, the UK and the Netherlands allow revaluation but they do not make it compulsory.

Write-offs

Some countries' GAAPs, particularly the UK, have allowed write-offs directly against shareholders' funds rather than taking all costs and changes through the profit and loss account, breaking the clean surplus accounting concept. This assumes that all changes to profit and loss reserve in the balance sheet will have been enacted through the profit and loss account. To illustrate the problems that can be caused, assume a company is acquired for £3bn, when the tangible asset base is only £1bn. This will create one of two outcomes:

(a) An intangible asset of £2bn that may or may not be written off over time by amortising through the profit and loss account. So the double entry would be cash down £3bn, tangible assets up £1bn and intangibles up £2bn.
(b) If GAAP allows it, a £2bn write-off directly against shareholders' funds, seemingly reducing the value of the shareholders' investment at a stroke. The double entry would then be as above, but also reducing shareholders' funds by £2bn to balance the goodwill write-off.

The effect of such a write-off on ratios like return on capital employed or return on equity may be large and flattering; the overstatement is caused by the reduction in the denominator of the equation. We must ensure that allegedly more meaningful calculations of performance than the traditional accounting measures are not also undermined by such adjustments. The UK allowed such write-offs up until the end of 1998, but as previous write-offs were not required to be written back, there are many UK companies with seriously depleted shareholders' funds and potentially overstated shareholder performance if the balance sheet 'value' of equity is used.

Level of profit or cash generated

There are various competing metrics for shareholder value put forward by different experts and consulting groups. Most claim to improve on the measurement of value possible from earnings per share or profit/earnings ratios. However, the extra explanatory power is limited to the materiality of improvement offered by the adjustments to published accounts that each metric suggests. The effect of accounting differences is not only on the items that might be adjusted in any particular shareholder value formula, but also on the unadjusted, therefore hidden, elements in the calculation.

VALUE METRICS

We will now consider each of the more popular metrics in turn and the potential impact of accounting differences upon them. Considered below are market value added, market to book ratio, total shareholder return, shareholder value analysis, cash flow return on investment, economic profit and economic value added. To inform our debate we will refer to a number of companies. In particular we will again refer to two competing companies from the metals sector, in order to press home the point that international comparison is a vital area for analysis. These two companies, British Steel and Usinor, are two of the largest steel companies in Europe. They both produce a broad range of steel products and compete with each other across much of their product range. Both have tapped the US capital markets and produce US GAAP compliant information as well as figures in line with their domestic GAAP.

Market value added

Stated simply, market value added (MVA) is the market value (number of shares in issue multiplied by the current share price plus the market value of debt issued) of the enterprise less the capital invested by shareholders and loanholders.

The aim of this measure is to show whether, or how much, the management has added to the funds with which they were entrusted. This is a laudable aim if it can be attained, although it is worth noting that it is assessing current share valuations against historical investment, which may have been mishandled by previous management teams. Companies who have been poor value creators in the past may have improved, but this figure could still

look bad due to the chequered past. As well as the accounting difficulties discussed, it is likely that shareholders' funds will only reflect success that has been fully achieved, rather than giving credit for such activities as the building of intellectual capital or an excellent research and development programme that will ensure future success. Indeed such investments in the company's future are likely to be treated as costs reducing current profit. When investors consider share purchases, they are concerned about what will happen next, rather than the past, although this may be an indication of the value-generating potential.

Assuming the market value and book value of debt are relatively close, we are left comparing the market capitalisation of the company's shares with the money that the shareholders have invested. Recall from the previous discussion that the shareholders' funds figure from the balance sheet is unlikely to reflect the real value of monies invested. It is fair to point out that Stern Stewart, the advocates of MVA, recommend adjusting the shareholders' funds figure for a number of potential distortions (Stewart, 1991). The attempt to adjust to 'economic book value' includes writing back any goodwill written off (has it retained its value since purchase?) and capitalising research and development (over how long should it be written off?).

Any accounting policy that affects profit will affect the MVA calculation. For example, a company that depreciates assets rapidly, due to a need or tradition of following tax rules will appear to be less value generative than a company that assumes long asset lives. It is obvious that an analyst has little chance of a sensible adjustment to achieve a number more akin to a meaningful equivalent of shareholders' stake in the company without understanding the accounting policies initially used. When a company from another country is being considered, then that implies the analyst understands the accounting structure in that country as well as his or her own.

Most international accounting research has focused on profit and loss effects of accounting policy choice rather than the balance sheet effects. Assuming historic cost accounting, the level of inflation year by year will 'cheapen' the apparent size of shareholder investment. There are other problems too, relating to legal and cultural issues. For instance, in some countries the pension provision by the company is a balance sheet component, in others it is a separate legal entity not included in the employing company's figures.

In attempting to achieve a meaningful economic value of investment, excellent knowledge of accounting in a particular country is probably required, along with an understanding of the company itself and its circumstances. The downloading of large quantities of information on numerous companies from commercial databases may lead to anomalies. To be meaningful this is going to be a thoughtful company-by-company analysis.

It is useful here to give an example of the type and potential size of such an error. In an often quoted article from the *Financial Times* (Top Companies Trip up over Value Creation, 14 May 1996), the worst-performing company out of the top 500 non-financial stocks in the UK was found to be British Steel with an MVA of −£2381m. This company had been launched on the stock market some eight years earlier with a market capitalisation of £2500m despite having a historic cost asset valuation of around £5000m. One assumes that the shareholders purchased these assets from the UK government at their perceived value in terms of future cash, profit or dividend potential, whereas much of the investment may have been carried out for alternative political motives in the past. The balance sheet was balanced by the inclusion of a statutory reserve, the majority of which was not available for distribution to shareholders as a dividend. So what is the relevant balance sheet value of the company? Is it the historic cost value of assets or the money invested by shareholders and loanholders seeking a return? A competing steel company might argue that, from their perspective, it is the size of the asset base that matters when carrying out competitor analysis, but this would not be the appropriate view of an investor.

The question for the investor is the calculation of the amount for which the company owes a continuing duty of care; this would necessarily exclude the statutory reserve which does not require servicing by dividend or by interest payments. An argument might be made for including the small proportion that is available for dividend distribution, but certainly not for the rest. Removing the statutory reserve from the investment would still leave British Steel with a poor MVA. This would place the company well down the league table, but now somewhat higher than the famous UK value destroyers of the early 1990s, such as Trafalgar House (with an MVA of −£1577).

Market to book ratio

The market to book ratio (MBR) is similar in many ways to the MVA measure above. The difference is the replacement of the subtraction by division. The balance sheet value of equity is generally a poor measure of either value or true investment by shareholders and this measure is often calculated without even the adjustments that Stern Stewart recommended for MVA. The more adjustments made to the balance sheet, the more meaningful the ratio might become, but adjusting implies that the person carrying out the task understands how the number was derived by the company in the first instance.

MVA and MBR share a further potential problem. The focus of the measures is on the retained shareholder investment rather than on the other, and complementary, shareholder reward of dividends. One may surmise that a high dividend policy will imply a lower level of retention and a reduced ability to generate further shareholder returns, or that a cash-retaining company may be spending wisely and therefore have far better prospects. If this is valid, then the measure may not be undermined. An alternative school of thought suggests that dividend policy is a long-term corporate policy, and therefore large and increasing dividends will be predictors of further such increases. If this view has some validity, then such high payers may be more highly valued by the market, given that share prices may be viewed as the present value of the future dividend stream. The 'book' value of such companies will be low and the ratio therefore high. Those who esteem large payouts and are not concerned by low dividend cover may find such a bias quite acceptable.

Dividend policy is a decision of the directors, but will be affected by the attitude of the relevant investing community. Hence if one country has a leaning to large or small dividend payouts, perhaps as a response to tax advantages or disadvantages, the companies from that country may be relatively over- or undervalued compared to others.

Total shareholder return

Total shareholder return (TSR) is market based and consists of adding the dividend to the change in share price over the period and then dividing by the opening share price.

There is no accounting information included in this statistic, so it could be claimed to be independent of accounting policy choice. However, if one assumes that accounting numbers affect share prices, or at least the level of expected profit and its increase or decrease from the previous result, then potentially there is room for accounting policy choice to undermine what might at first seem to be an accounting-neutral measure. TSR shares a common value problem with financial reporting, that is reporting the performance of the organisation without taking the level of risk into account. This problem can be addressed by comparison with the cost of capital of the enterprise or by comparing the TSR with a suitable peer group of companies.

Interestingly, one factor that is acknowledged to affect share price is liquidity. Poor liquidity, that is difficulty in buying or selling because of little active trading, leads to lower prices. Countries where stock exchanges are a relatively new phenomenon are likely to have low liquidity in most or all of the quoted stocks. Such companies are also likely to have an accounting history which is not shareholder focused as it would have been inappropriate in the past. Seeking greater liquidity, company directors look at secondary listings in London or the US, therefore producing accounts in accord with International Accounting Standards or US GAAP. Hence a new listing goes hand in hand with a data set that shareholder-focused financial analysts would feel more relaxed about interpreting.

Shareholder value analysis (free cash flow)

Shareholder value analysis (SVA) is based on deriving the free cash flow for the organisation, forecasting it forward over an appropriate period and then finding the present value of these future flows that can be released from the organisation to the providers of capital. The development of the metric, and the drivers to be examined in aiming to improve SVA, are further explained in Rappaport (1986, 1998). SVA does take risk into account, by using the cost of capital for discounting, and it also focuses on cash rather than profit, a principle advocated by most accounting textbooks when discussing long-term decision making.

At first, such a calculation again appears to be independent of accounting policy choice. However, because a cash flow statement is lacking in some countries and because some of the adjustments to calculate profit rather than tax have some relevance in predicting future cash flows, items from the profit and loss account are used in generating free cash flow forecasts. Here is a simple but useful calculation structure of the free cash flow that would be available to the capital providers:

$$\text{Sales} - \text{operating costs} = \text{operating profits}$$

$$\text{Operating profits} - \text{cash tax on profits}$$
$$= \text{operating profit after tax}$$

$$\text{Operating profit after tax}$$
$$+ \text{depreciation and amortisation}$$
$$- \text{investments in fixed assets}$$
$$- \text{working capital growth}$$
$$= \text{Free cash flow available}$$
$$\text{for providers of capital}$$

A number of these data entries are affected by local GAAP. A particular issue here is the chosen method of consolidation. Whilst the seventh European directive has considerably improved the European level of comparability, the definition of a group of companies and the inclusion of some or none of a related company's sales and profit in the parent company's accounts means

Table 16.4. Usinor's US GAAP turnover as a percentage of French GAAP turnover

1993	94%
1994	91%
1995	91%
1996	90%
1997	94%

there is still some material variation. This is generally less of a company choice, but set by the country's accounting GAAP. Table 16.4 shows the relationship between the turnover reported in the French version of Usinor's accounts and in the US GAAP version. It would be fair to add that there should be an equivalent difference in the operating costs and the operating profit should be unaffected. However, information disclosure on relevant depreciation and amortisation adjustments may be inadequate.

Some companies also disclose additional figures for sales over and above the GAAP requirement. Phrases such as 'group turnover' may refer to the inclusion of the appropriate proportion, based on percentage shareholding, of associate companies' sales in addition to the normal definition of consolidated sales. Retailers may also quote a turnover figure including sales taxes as well as the obligatory exclusive figure. Here care must be taken in using the 'correct' figure for the calculation.

Other potential sources of confusion include the need to add back any amortisation of goodwill in addition to the depreciation figure. A UK-based SVAer may, as yet, be unused to this requirement. Capitalisation of interest is another potential problem. Here the borrowing costs incurred while a fixed asset is being built can be treated as part of the cost of the asset itself. The interest can then be capitalised in the balance sheet along with the rest of the asset's cost; this amount is then depreciated over the same time period as the asset itself. Most countries allow for capitalisation as a possible accounting choice, some (US and Switzerland) expect it. There are still providers of capital that need rewarding for such an investment, so it would be better if such costs were extracted from operating costs.

The layout of the balance sheet in some countries makes it harder to distinguish between short-term and long-term debtors and creditors, hence adjustments for changes in working capital are harder to ascertain. Sometimes the cash flow statement can give assistance here; however, cash flow statements are by no means mandatory in many jurisdictions. Indeed the lack of such statements, plus the different formats and the different definitions of cash, means that this perhaps obvious route to calculating free cash flow is often unavailable or less valid than anticipated. The world is certainly moving in a cash statement direction − Japan is a recent recruit − but there are still a number of important developed economies where they are optional or unusual.

Assuming we can ascertain a reasonable estimate of free cash flow year by year for our forecast, the next issue is determining the relevant cost of capital for the enterprise to use in calculating the present value of these future flows. The temptation may well be to use a weighted average cost of capital, taking appropriate proportions of equity and debt and their relevant capital costs and deriving an average. Ascertaining the size and cost of debt will be relatively easy, and the cost of capital would normally be taken from the capital asset pricing model. The true level of shareholders' investment is most unlikely to be picked from the balance sheet without considerable pruning and cleaning. A more appropriate figure would be the market value of the shares of the company. If the balance sheet value of equity is taken instead, then the likelihood is that the weight attached to the shareholder proportion of company capital will be too small and therefore the calculated total cost of capital probably too low.

Cash flow return on investment

The calculation of cash flow return on investment is quite complex and there are several versions; see Cornelius and Davies (1997) and Madden (1999). In essence the measure has two key components: the calculation of real cash flow then the division of this number by group operating assets calculated at current prices. The real cash flow is derived by making a number of adjustments to profit after tax, mostly for non-cash items. The book value of assets is reduced by goodwill and inflated by adding back depreciation and then adjusting for inflation. The aim is to find the rate of return that the company's assets will generate, an equivalent to the internal rate of return. The subjectivity of some key assumptions, such as for asset life, should be noted.

For international consistency, knowledge of different treatments for each accounting item would need to be known and each calculation adjusted accordingly. A problem here may be lack of disclosure of policy choice or the size of the choice's impact on the profit. In particular, disclosure of the timing of asset purchase is limited and therefore difficult to adjust for inflation. As this measure does not attempt to be a valuation tool, unless used as a multi-period tool, the use of accounting practices such as the writing off of research and development may not be such a problem until it is used in this way. Note that any technique which starts with profit and attempts to work back to cash flow will be dependent on some of the accounting policies that determined the profit figure in the first place. Some policies, such as stock valuation, may occasionally prove to be important but often they are immaterial. The spotting of changes in accounting policies and treatments is crucial if one is to ascribe meaning to a higher figure in one year compared with another.

Economic profit

The key difference between profit for the shareholder and traditional economic profit (EP) is the deduction of a capital charge for equity. So the measure considers the monies left, if any, after shareholders have received an adequate reward for the risk they have undertaken.

This approach is fraught with accounting policy distortion. All the company's choices in cost recognition (depreciation period, stock valuation, research and development costs, etc.) are accepted as valid. Then a rent is charged for the use of the equity in the balance sheet, a number distorted by the same set of accounting choices and potentially wizened by the ravages of inflation over time, unless some form of inflation accounting is used.

International effects on EP-based measures can be large, as the findings from Whittington and Steele (1998) suggest. They considered average adjustments, a calculation for any particular company would need to be very careful when estimating the effects of accounting policy choice. Even the company's

choice of depreciation period cannot be taken at face value as tax life may have been more important than physical or commercial life in setting the asset's accounting longevity. Comparing the EP of companies across international boundaries is hazardous.

Economic value added

Economic value added, from Stern Stewart, effectively accepts the logic of economic profit but recognises the reliance on possibly inappropriate accounting policy choices for valuation.

Many adjustments, potentially 164, are made to profit and capital invested, but some are effectively the insertion of alternative policy choices rather than factual restatement. This is inevitable but judgmental. Should goodwill amortisation always be written back? Perhaps research in the computer industry should be written off in the year incurred as the original accounting policies would probably have decreed. There may also be a reluctance to attempt to adjust the shareholders' funds for all manipulations that are deemed unhelpful since the founding of the firm, as the time involved would be prohibitive. The need for judgement will be inescapable in any calculation of value and the reader should always be aware that the numbers presented by many of the measures are judgmental and not factual – interesting opinions but open to alternative choices in the calculation process.

COPING WITH INTERNATIONAL ACCOUNTING DIFFERENCES

One might anticipate that shareholder-dominated accounting systems would be more amenable to VBM calculations than creditor-dominated systems. Though we might also assume that the creditor-dominated systems are more factual and less interpretative by nature and therefore provide a sounder base for the judgmental stage of VBM analysis.

Different VBM metrics require different inputs from the accounts and are likely to be more or less affected by particular policy choices. Disclosure may also be a problem, particularly in countries where formal requirements are limited and, historically, companies have not had to consider shareholders' information needs. A good example of this would be the lack of a cash flow statement requirement from some countries. Indeed the disclosure issue could be viewed as the major problem rather than the differences in accounting policy. With sufficient disclosure, all material adjustments could then be made by an outsider to the company.

A country's accounting rules are part of a complex historical web of cultural, legal and tax systems and to aim at truly useful International Accounting Standards, where differences in treatment can be assumed to be immaterial, requires far greater efforts on legal and tax harmonisation than I can envisage. It may be that differences within the European Union will diminish, but it is hard to imagine that countries will give up the historical frameworks they have developed over the years. If politicians were to let the capital markets decide, then one could assume that as companies recognised their need for greater shareholder investment, they would adopt US standards. International Accounting Standards have allowed the rapid development of respectable financial reporting in many countries, but this is not the same as a global benchmark of comparability.

So how should an analyst perform a value calculation on a company from another accounting jurisdiction? They should proceed with care and caution and they should always be aware of their potential lack of knowledge. Here are some key questions to ask:

- Am I aware of all the key accounting policies the company is using?

  This question focuses on disclosure and on the policies available within the GAAP of the country in question.

- Are these the same as a comparable company from within my country?

  Finding a company of similar size from the same industry may be difficult, but the best match needs to be found. A list of the differences can then be made.

- Are the differences in policy likely to be material?

  This will depend on the industry in question. A company with substantial fixed assets may find that even a small difference on the depreciation calculation may be material. Materiality here is with reference to value calculation. Perhaps 2% of sales may seem a reasonable level of materiality in some circumstances, but for a company with a 4% sales margin that would imply a range of 2% to 6% and, probably, an equivalent range for a value calculation.

- Can I attempt to adjust the policies?

  In some instances this may be possible with some accuracy, in many others it will be a guess. The direction of change will often be known, the size may be impossible to calculate with accuracy. Here the use of sensitivity analysis may be helpful to determine the range of potential adjustment. The results of dual-listed companies may give some indication on the potential size of adjustment for some accounting policies.

● Having made these adjustments, do I believe the outcomes?

> If a company has a competitive advantage over its rivals, then one would expect outperformance in value creation. Similar companies in economies of similar levels of development with similar levels of competition might be expected to make similar value added for shareholders. Tax systems may be one cause of difference here.

We must always remember that the world is a place still rich in cultural difference. We may not wish to celebrate accounting disharmony as part of this cultural mix, but we should recognise that it is at least an outcome from historical and cultural developments. The desire for universally comparable accounting is laudable, but as European Union experience testifies, it requires more than harmonisation of layouts and words.

Awareness of difference is the first step towards a more meaningful approach to value measurement. Coming up with one number that sums up all a company's potential is most unlikely, as evidenced by the literature advocating multiple performance measures within a firm. An intelligent consideration of the issues and potential choices in calculation may lead to a likely range of value that would be more honest and reflect, to a degree, the risk involved in calculating the answer.

REFERENCES

Choi, F.D.S. and Levich, R.M. (1990) *The Capital Market Effects of International Accounting Diversity.* Dow Jones–Irwin, Homewood IL.

Cooke, T.E. (1993) The impact of accounting principles on profits: the US versus Japan. *Accounting and Business Research,* **23**(92), 460–76.

Cornelius, I. and Davies, M. (1997) *Shareholder Value.* Financial Times Publishing, London.

Davies, R., Unni, S., Drapper, P. and Paudyal, K. (1999) *The Cost of Equity Capital.* Chartered Institute of Management Accountants, London.

Economist (1992) Market focus: all the world's a ratio – the boom in international portfolio investment is stimulating new ways of comparing stock markets, 22 February.

Gray, S.J. (1980) The impact of international accounting differences from a security analysis perspective: some European evidence. *Journal of Accounting Research,* **18**(1), 65–76.

Kay, J.A. (1993) *Foundations of Corporate Success.* Oxford University Press, Oxford.

Madden, B.J. (1999) *CFROI valuation: a total systems approach to valuing the firm.* Butterworth-Heinemann, Oxford.

Nobes, C. and Parker, R. (1997) *Comparative International Accounting.* Prentice Hall, Englewood Cliffs NJ.

Norton, J. (1995) The impact of financial accounting practices on the measurement of profit and equity: Australia versus the United States. *Abacus,* **31**(2) 178–200.

Rappaport, A. (1986) *Creating shareholder value: the new standard for business performance.* Free Press, New York.

Rappaport, A. (1998), *Creating shareholder value: a guide for managers and investors*. Free Press, New York.

Simmonds, A. and Azieres, O. (1989) *Accounting for Europe: success by 2000 AD?* Touche Ross, London.

Stewart, B. (1991) *The Quest for Value: A Guide for Senior Managers*. Harper Collins, New York.

Weetman, P. and Gray, S.J. (1990) International financial analysis and comparative performance: the impact of UK versus US accounting principles on earnings. *Journal of International Financial Management and Accounting*, **2**, 111–30.

Weetman, P. and Gray, S.J. (1991) A comparative international analysis of the impact of accounting principles on profits: the USA versus the UK, Sweden and the Netherlands. *Accounting and Business Research*, **21**(84), 363–79

Whittington, M. (1999) Problems in comparing financial performance across international boundaries: a case study approach. Paper presented at Aston Business School Seminar, May 1999.

Whittington, M. and Steele, A. (1998) Still searching for excellence? International accounting and the world's most outstanding companies. *British Journal of Management*, **9**(3), 233–47.

Index

The Future of Theoretical Physics and Cosmology

Based on lectures given in honour of Stephen Hawking's sixtieth birthday, this book comprises contributions from some of the world's leading theoretical physicists. It begins with a section containing chapters by successful scientific popularisers, bringing to life both Hawking's work and other exciting developments in physics. The book then goes on to provide a critical evaluation of advanced subjects in modern cosmology and theoretical physics. Topics covered include the origin of the universe, warped spacetime, cosmological singularities, quantum gravity, black holes, string theory, quantum cosmology and inflation. As well as providing a fascinating overview of the wide variety of subject areas to which Stephen Hawking has contributed, this book represents an important assessment of prospects for the future of fundamental physics and cosmology.

GARY GIBBONS has been a Professor of Theoretical Physics in the University of Cambridge since 1997. After reading Natural Sciences, specialising in Theoretical Physics, he took Part III of the Mathematical Tripos and started research with Dennis Sciama. On the latter's move to Oxford he transferred to Stephen Hawking's supervision. Having completed his Ph.D., he continued to work in close association with Hawking on problems involving gravitational radiation, black holes, quantum field theory in curved spacetimes and quantum gravity, particularly the Euclidean approach. He has been interested in supergravity theories since their inception and pioneered a non-perturbative approach to their quantization involving ideas from soliton theory. His current interests lie mainly in the area of M Theory and String Theory and in other applications of geometrical ideas to physics.

PAUL SHELLARD received his Ph.D. from the University of Cambridge, under the supervison of Stephen Hawking. In 1985 he was awarded a research fellowship at Trinity College, Cambridge, and then spent two years as a postdoctoral fellow at the Massachusetts Institute of Technology. In 1990 he returned to Cambridge, subsequently becoming a PPARC advanced fellow in the Department of Applied Mathematics and Theoretical Physics, where he is currently a senior lecturer. In 1997 he became director of COSMOS, the UK national cosmology supercomputer. His specific research interests include early universe cosmology and theories of large-scale structure formation, cosmic strings and other topological defects (on which he has co-authored a research monograph), the cosmic microwave sky, dark matter and gravitational waves.

STUART RANKIN read mathematics at the University of Cambridge and continued his studies in the High Energy Physics group at the Department of Applied Mathematics and Theoretical Physics, going on to receive a Ph.D. Since 1995 he has worked as Administrator and System Manager for the Relativity and Gravitation group in the same Department. This post has always provided great variety, and in 1997 he took on the management of the COSMOS supercomputer facility on behalf of Stephen Hawking and the UK cosmology community, a role that (like the real Cosmos) continues to expand.

The Future of Theoretical Physics and Cosmology

Celebrating Stephen Hawking's 60th Birthday

Edited by

G. W. GIBBONS

E. P. S. SHELLARD

S. J. RANKIN

CAMBRIDGE
UNIVERSITY PRESS

012020679

PHYS

PUBLISHED BY THE PRESS SYNDICATE OF THE UNIVERSITY OF CAMBRIDGE
The Pitt Building, Trumpington Street, Cambridge, United Kingdom

CAMBRIDGE UNIVERSITY PRESS
The Edinburgh Building, Cambridge CB2 2RU, UK
40 West 20th Street, New York, NY 10011-4211, USA
477 Williamstown Road, Port Melbourne, VIC 3207, Australia
Ruiz de Alarcón 13, 28014 Madrid, Spain
Dock House, The Waterfront, Cape Town 8001, South Africa

http://www.cambridge.org

First published 2003

Printed in the United Kingdom at the University Press, Cambridge

Typeface Computer Modern 11/13pt   *System* LaTeX 2_ε [TB]

A catalogue record for this book is available from the British Library

ISBN 0 521 82081 2 hardback

Contents

Contributors

Abhay Ashtekar   Department of Physics
Pennsylvania State University
Box 25, 104 Davey Laboratory
University Park, State College
PA 16802–6300
USA

Paul Binétruy   Université Paris–XI
Bâtiment 211
F-91405 Orsay Cedex
France

Raphael Bousso   Institute for Theoretical Physics
University of California
Santa Barbara
California 93106-4030
USA

Barnard Carr   School of Mathematical Sciences
Queen Mary, University of London
Mile End Road
London E1 4NS
United Kingdom

Brandon Carter   Department d'Astrophysique Rela-
tiviste et de Cosmologie
Observatoire de Paris
5 Place J. Janssen
F-92195 Meudon Cedex
France

Peter D'Eath
Department of Applied Mathematics
and Theoretical Physics
Centre for Mathematical Sciences
Wilberforce Road
Cambridge CB3 0WA
United Kingdom

Bryce DeWitt
Center for Relativity
Department of Physics
The University of Texas at Austin
Austin Texas 78712-1081
USA

Fay Dowker
Department of Physics
Queen Mary, University of London
Mile End Road
London E1 4NS
United Kingdom

George Ellis
Department of Mathematics and Applied Mathematics
University of Cape Town
Rondebosch 7701
South Africa

Gary Gibbons
Department of Applied Mathematics
and Theoretical Physics
Centre for Mathematical Sciences
University of Cambridge
Wilberforce Road
Cambridge CB3 0WA
United Kingdom

Steve Giddings
Department of Physics
University of California
Santa Barbara
CA 93106, USA

Michael Green
Department of Applied Mathematics
and Theoretical Physics
Centre for Mathematical Sciences
University of Cambridge
Wilberforce Road
Cambridge CB3 0WA
United Kingdom

David Gross   Physics Department
University of California
Santa Barbara CA 93106
USA

Alan Guth   Center for Theoretical Physics
Massachusetts Institute
of Technology
77 Massachusetts Avenue
Cambridge MA 02139
USA

Jonathan Halliwell   Department of Physics
Blackett Laboratory
Imperial College
Exhibition Road
London SW7 2BZ
United Kingdom

James Hartle   Physics Department
University of California
Santa Barbara, CA 93106
USA

Stephen Hawking   Department of Applied Mathematics
and Theoretical Physics
Centre for Mathematical Sciences
University of Cambridge
Wilberforce Road
Cambridge CB3 0WA
United Kingdom

Gary Horowitz   Physics Department
University of California
Santa Barbara CA 93106
USA

Chris Isham   Department of Physics
Blackett Laboratory
Imperial College
Exhibition Road
London SW7 2BZ
United Kingdom

Werner Israel
Department of Physics
and Astronomy
University of Victoria
P.O. Box 3055
Victoria BC V8W 2Y2
Canada

Renata Kallosh
Department of Physics
Stanford University
Varian Building
Stanford CA 94305-4060
USA

Andrei Linde
Department of Physics
Stanford University
Varian Building
Stanford CA 94305-4060
USA

Alexander Maloney
High Energy Physics Laboratory
Harvard University
42 Oxford Street
Cambridge MA 02138
USA

Ian Moss
Department of Physics
University of Newcastle upon Tyne
Newcastle upon Tyne NE1 7RU
United Kingdom

Don Page
Department of Physics
University of Alberta
Edmonton Alberta T6G 2J1
Canada

Roger Penrose
Mathematical Institute
24–29 St Giles st, Oxford OX1 3LB
United Kingdom
and
The Center for Gravitational Physics
and Geometry
Eberly College of Science
104 Davey Lab
Penn State University
University Park PA16802-6300
USA

Malcolm Perry   Department of Applied Mathematics
                          and Theoretical Physics
                          Centre for Mathematical Sciences
                          University of Cambridge
                          Wilberforce Road
                          Cambridge CB3 0WA
                          United Kingdom

Joe Polchinski   Physics Department
                          University of California
                          Santa Barbara CA 93106
                          USA

Chris Pope   Center for Theoretical Physics
                          Texas A & M University
                          College Station TX 77843
                          USA

Martin Rees   Institute of Astronomy
                          Madingley Road
                          Cambridge CB3 0HA

Simon Ross   Department of Mathematical Sciences
                          University of Durham
                          South Road
                          Durham DH1 3LE
                          United Kingdom

Paul Shellard   Department of Applied Mathematics
                          and Theoretical Physics
                          Centre for Mathematical Sciences
                          University of Cambridge
                          Wilberforce Road
                          Cambridge CB3 0WA
                          United Kingdom

Eva Silverstein   Department of Physics
                          Stanford University
                          Varian Building
                          stanford CA 94305-4060
                          USA

Andrew Strominger   Jefferson Physical Laboratory
                        Harvard University
                        Cambridge MA 02138
                        USA

Leonard Susskind   Department of Physics
                        Stanford University
                        Varian Building
                        Stanford CA 94305-4060
                        USA

Kip Thorne   161–33, Division of Physics, Mathe-
                        matics and Astronomy
                        California Institute of Technology
                        Pasadena, CA 91125
                        USA

Paul Townsend   Department of Applied Mathematics
                        and Theoretical Physics
                        Centre for Mathematical Sciences
                        University of Cambridge
                        Wilberforce Road
                        Cambridge CB3 0WA
                        United Kingdom

Neil Turok   Department of Applied Mathematics
                        and Theoretical Physics
                        Centre for Mathematical Sciences
                        University of Cambridge
                        Wilberforce Road
                        Cambridge CB3 0WA
                        United Kingdom

Alexander Vilenkin Department of Physics
                        and Astronomy
                        Tufts University
                        Medford MA 02155
                        USA

Matt Visser   Department of Physics
                        Washington University
                        Campus Box 1105
                        One Brookings Drive
                        St. Louis MO 63130-4899
                        USA

Nick Warner   Department. of Physics and Astron-
                          omy
                          University of Southern California
                          Los Angeles CA 90089-0484
                          USA

Edward Witten   School of Natural Sciences
                          Institute for Advanced Study
                          Princeton, New Jersey 08540
                          USA

Preface

This book contains lectures delivered at the Stephen Hawking 60th Birthday Workshop and Symposium held at the Centre for Mathematical Sciences in Cambridge. They constitute the written record of what was an extremely stimulating scientific meeting of which an overview is given in the introduction. This preface is the place to recall some of the more personal aspects of the meeting and, what is more important, for the Local Organizing Committee to place on record their profound thanks to all the organizations and people who made it possible.

Meetings like this do not happen without considerable financial and logistic support. For the former we thank PPARC and its Chief Executive Ian Halliday, Denis and Sally Avery, SGI and its Chairman and Chief Executive Officer, Bob Bishop, Cambridge University Press and Simon Mitton, The London Mathematical Society and its President, J.T. Stuart, The Clay Mathematics Institute, the Master and Fellows of Trinity Hall, Gonville and Caius and St John's Colleges, and the BBC Science Unit and its head, John Lynch. The meeting was the first to be held in our new (and then only partially completed) CMS premises, for the existence of which we thank the many donors, including not least Hans and Märitt Rausing to whom we owe the building accommodating our own day-to-day activities, Pavilion B.

In addition to the scientific activities, there took place in the evenings an almost week long Birthday Party. For the immaculate arrangements and hard work involved in setting all this up over a long period we owe an enormous debt of gratitude to Jennifer Formichelli. Closer to the time of the meeting she was brilliantly assisted by Janet Bett and Claire Lambert. Hilary Bennett and her staff (James Paice, Ted Kohnke, Peter Pleasance and Xiaojing Zhao) were unfailingly helpful and courteous in the face of many challenges arising from setting up the venue for a major televised event whilst coping with on-going building work. During the meeting itself we were helped by a whole team of students and postdocs (Mohammad Akbar, Tibra Ali, Gareth Amery, Anita Barnes, Jose Blanco-Pillado, Carsten van de Bruck, Christophe Galfard, Christopher Gordon, Thomas Hertog, Yves Lemperiere, Oisin MacConamhna, Selena Ng, Ruben Portugues, James Sparks and Jochen Weller), who, with the crucial technical aid of Adrian Cullum-Hanshaw, helped ensure that the timing and recording of the lectures went with a smoothness and punctuality that evidently surprised habituées of our old site in Silver Street.

We are also grateful for logistic support from many other sources, especially the Department of Applied Mathematics and Theoretical Physics (DAMTP) and the University of Cambridge. We were pleased that both Tim Pedley, Head of DAMTP, and Sir Alec Broers, Vice Chancellor of the University, were able to be present during the final symposium. In particular, we would like to express our gratitude for the vital assistance of John Turner, the University Centre, Alison MacFarquar and the University Press and Publications Office, the University Printing Services, the Millennium Mathematics Project, Churchill College, the Møller Centre for Continuing Education, John Heppleston and University Security, the University Constables, and Cambridge Audio-Visual Services.

In drawing up the programme for the meeting we were ably assisted by our International Organizing Committee: Bruce Allen, Bernard Carr, Peter D'Eath, Fay Dowker, Jonathan Halliwell, Ian Moss, Malcolm Perry, Simon Ross and Nicholas Warner. All are former students of Stephen who hold academic positions in the field either in this country or in the US.

The work involved in a conference such as this does not stop once the meeting has finished and in particular there is an enormous effort entailed in getting the proceedings off to the press. For that and much more we are very grateful to Stefanie Wikner. For the painstaking transcription of many of the lectures from the online video record we thank Katheryn Ayres and Linda Simpkin. Finally we must express our appreciation to all the students and postdocs who voluntarily assisted with the proof-reading of the contributions to this proceedings: Mohammad Akbar, Gareth Amery, Anita Barnes, Jose Blanco-Pillado, Carsten van der Bruck, Martin Bucher, Andrew Farley, Christophe Galfard, Christopher Gordon, Marc Guilbert, Sean Hartnoll, Martin Landriau, Yves Lemperiere, Antony Lewis, James Lucietti, Oisin MacConamhna, Andrew Mennim, Christophe Patricot, Ruben Portugues, Gerasimos Rigopoulos, Frederic Schuller, Guillermo Silva, James Sparks, John Stewart, Jochen Weller, Toby Wiseman and Matthias Wohlfarth.

Gary Gibbons
Paul Shellard
Stuart Rankin   *Cambridge, November 2002*

1
Introduction

Gary Gibbons and Paul Shellard

Centre for Mathematical Sciences, University of Cambridge

Stephen's remarkable combination of boldness, vision, insight and courage have enabled him to produce ideas that have transformed our understanding of space and time, black holes and the origin of the universe.

James B. Hartle

To celebrate Stephen Hawking's 60th birthday, a workshop and symposium were held in Cambridge at the Centre for Mathematical Sciences. About two hundred colleagues, collaborators and former students, as well as younger researchers, gathered from around the world for a critical evaluation of the subjects to which Stephen has contributed with such distinction, and to assess the prospects for the future. This volume contains articles based on the lectures delivered at this remarkable event.

The title for these proceedings is adapted from Stephen's inaugural lecture as Lucasian Professor of Mathematics, 'Is the end in sight for theoretical physics?' The contributors here revisit many of the central questions raised in that lecture and which have motivated Stephen throughout his career. The recurring themes of particular importance include the endeavour to unify quantum theory with gravity and, specifically, its application to black hole evaporation, the issue of spacetime singularities and whether there was a beginning in time, and the problem of setting the special initial conditions which led to our habitable universe. We have grouped the workshop articles in this volume under eight headings, which we briefly review below; they roughly reflect the chronological order of the fields to which Stephen has contributed and in which he continues to work. The volume begins however, as the conference ended, with popular lectures from the final one-day symposium aimed at a more general audience.

1.1 Popular symposium

For any world class scientist a sixtieth birthday is sufficient cause to celebrate, but for Stephen Hawking there are particular reasons to mark the event, not just due to his personal triumph over disability but also his unique contribution to the popularization and dissemination of fundamental ideas about physics and the universe. Few could be unaware of the singular phenomenon of *A Brief History of Time*, with over ten million copies in print and now translated into 45 languages (nor is this unique, for example, with sales of *The Universe in a Nutshell* already exceeding 1.5 million). It seemed appropriate, therefore, to hold a much larger event with public lectures given by some of the foremost scientific popularizers of the present day, including Stephen himself. This symposium received worldwide media attention and BBC recordings of the event were broadcast later as a series of programmes entitled *The Hawking Lectures*.

These popular articles begin with Martin Rees, the Astronomer Royal, providing a cogent overview of our present understanding of the universe, a picture that Stephen has influenced so profoundly. Jim Hartle, Stephen's key collaborator in developing the 'no boundary' proposal for the origin of the universe, then addresses broad questions about the search for a unified

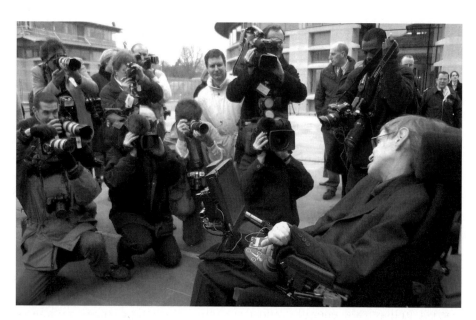

Fig. 1.1. Stephen Hawking arriving for the popular symposium which was attended by over 600 participants and attracted media interest from around the globe. [*Photograph Michael Hall*]

Fig. 1.2. Stephen Hawking at his 60th Birthday Symposium. [*Photograph Michael Hall*]

theory of everything. The challenges to be faced in such a marriage between classical general relativity and quantum mechanics is the theme continued by Roger Penrose. Next, Kip Thorne takes us on a journey from the golden age of black hole theory to the exciting prospect today of testing these theoretical predictions using a new generation of gravitational wave detectors. Finally, Stephen concludes with an account of his personal odyssey, 'sixty years in a nutshell', beginning as a Cambridge graduate student determined to tackle the big questions in cosmology. A measure of his ongoing commitment to this quest is apparent from the fact that he wrote and delivered this lecture while recovering from a broken leg, sustained less than two weeks before the conference.

1.2 Spacetime singularities

Stephen first came to the attention of the wider scientific world for his work with Roger Penrose showing that if classical general relativity is correct and certain energy conditions hold, then singularities are almost inevitable both at the beginning of the universe at the Big Bang and during the gravitational collapse inside black holes. These results were extremely influential in cosmology, as George Ellis reviews in the first of the articles in this section. He worked with Stephen to show from the cosmic microwave background that the conditions of the theorems actually hold in our universe. He also offers a masterly account of an approach to the relativistic theory of cosmological perturbations that was originally pioneered by Stephen (it prefigures articles on cosmology in the final section of the book).

The issue of closed timelike curves is another topic to which Stephen has devoted considerable attention. Classically according to general relativity it seems that they are quite possible, a point made forcibly by Kurt Goedel. However, Stephen has proposed a *chronology protection conjecture* whereby closed timelike curves are forbidden by quantum field theoretic effects. Matt Visser surveys the current evidence for the conjecture and provides a critical assessment of future prospects.

Of the classical energy conditions, the dominant energy condition is the most useful. It implies the positive mass theorem and, as pointed out by Stephen when he named it, according to classical theory it forbids the creation of matter *ex nihilo*. Brandon Carter reviews the proof. Finally, Roger Penrose points out that the singularity theorems also hold in higher dimensions and raises the question of the theoretical significance of Kaluza–Klein theory. It is interesting to note that the singularity theorems gave a powerful impetus to the search for a quantum theory of gravity because they show that classical general relativity is an incomplete theory. The obviously attractive direction in which to complete it is by passing to some quantum version. This argument is quite independent of the many other motivations for quantizing gravity such as providing a consistent marriage between quantum theory and spacetime physics or unifying gravity with the other forces of nature.

1.3 Black holes

The singularity theorems are inextricably tied up with the development of the theory of black holes and, indeed, it was from this direction that Stephen entered the field. At that time we had Werner Israel's theorem on static black holes and Brandon Carter's work on axisymmetric black holes. The main aim was to demonstrate a complete 'No Hair' or uniqueness theorem showing that the exterior of a black hole is characterized only by its mass and angular momentum. Stephen made a pivotal contribution here by giving an argument that stationary black holes must be axisymmetric, thus complementing Carter's work. About the same time he showed that the area of the event horizon cannot decrease, a fact which has come to play an essential part of our understanding of black hole thermodynamics.

Fig. 1.3. Martin Rees (left) speaking at the popular symposium and Jim Hartle (right) at the scientific workshop. [*Photographs Anna Żytkow*]

Werner Israel reviews some of this history and how he now views the problem of black hole singularities. Martin Rees points out that nowadays black holes are commonplace in astrophysics and are beginning to be used as probes of relativistic gravity, offering the exciting prospect of testing Einstein's theory in the fully non-linear regime.

One of Stephen's most striking early physical predictions, made before his work on the event horizon and its symmetry, was the possibility that very small black holes may have formed in the early universe and that they may still exist as fossil relics of the Big Bang. Bernard Carr gives a historical overview of the development of the theory of such primordial black holes and how they may also be used as experimental or observational probes for exotic physics. In many ways primordial black holes resemble very heavy elementary particles. Simon Ross describes how this similarity extends to the possibility of black hole pair creation in strong external fields. Steve Giddings concludes this section by noting that if theories with 'large' extra dimensions are correct then we should be able to make them in accelerators, a truly awesome prospect for the future.

1.4 Hawking radiation

Stephen's work on primordial black holes led him, using quantum field theory, to his most famous discovery, their thermal radiation. This raises many deep puzzles, as he has strenuously and repeatedly insisted. Among them are whether black holes can evaporate completely or must they

Fig. 1.4. In use, the black conference mug (left) transforms into white (right), revealing the Hawking temperature. [*Photographs Stefanie Wikner*]

leave relics? If the former case is true, what has happened to any conserved quantum numbers? Perhaps black hole evaporation processes and their virtual counterparts will violate any global conservation law. More puzzling still: what happens to quantum coherence during this process. Put in more popular if less helpful terms: where does all the information go?

Many of these problems cannot be solved within semiclassical general relativity and nowadays many theorists seek in string theory the answers to these puzzles. Malcolm Perry tells us what it has told us about black holes. Joe Polchinski extends the discussion to include M Theory. Gary Horowitz turns the topic around and tells us how strings can be made of black holes. Finally in this section, Lenny Susskind records his own personal journey from crisis and paradigm shift to holography.

1.5 Quantum gravity

Applying quantum mechanics to black holes might be thought to be jumping the gun if one does not yet have a quantum theory of gravity. Nevertheless one has to start somewhere. One approach much favoured by Stephen is the path integral, using a Feynman sum over positive definite metrics and Gary Gibbons describes how this may be used to elucidate many aspects of black holes, cosmology and the AdS/CFT correspondence. A key ingredient of this approach is the evaluation of functional determinants and Ian Moss reviews Stephen's suggestion that zeta function methods be used for this purpose. The article by Chris Isham, who sadly could not be present at the workshop, comes at the subject from the opposite direction pointing out that deep logical pre-conceptions may require modification. Following this, Abhay Ashtekar, who was also unable to attend, considers the changes in our geometrical notions that quantum gravity may entail. Whatever the answer to these questions, one of the things we ought to get out of a quantum theory of gravity is some account of topology change. It may be that concepts like the topology of space or of spacetime make no sense in the final formulation except as an approximate description. Nevertheless, we can try to work in a 'top-down' manner from what we know to what we don't know. Fay Dowker describes what we can expect if we retain as much of the spacetime picture as we can using Morse metrics.

1.6 M theory and beyond

In the quest for a complete quantum theory of gravity, many hopes are pinned at present on a combination of ideas from string theory and super-gravity often called M theory. The idea is that the five ten-dimensional superstring theories and eleven-dimensional supergravity should be thought of as limiting forms of a single overall structure whose precise form is at present unknown. All six theories, often envisaged as the vertices of a hexagonal space of theories, are linked by a web of dualities taking for example one theory at weak coupling to another at strong coupling or even more dramatically an eleven-dimensional theory to a ten-dimensional theory.

In his article, Ed Witten tells us about the past of string theory and how it was built up, perturbatively bit by bit, unlike general relativity: complete and beautifully-formed like Venus born from the waves. Given this unexpected turn of events he declines to make too many predictions about its future, arguing that if he had tried to do so in the past he would not have been very successful. The future may be dark and uncertain but the past is not so. David Gross and Michael Green highlight the achievements of string theory in very accessible articles. Paul Townsend describes the origin of the mysterious 'M' name and how it arose from considering membranes rather than strings.

One of the most astonishing achievements of this synthesis is the idea that supergravity in five dimensions can tell us about Yang-Mills theory in four dimensions. This is the famous AdS/CFT correspondence. Nick Warner describes how this works in practice and Chris Pope relates it to the search for metrics of special and exceptional holonomy. A striking feature of both articles is the extent to which work carried out for an entirely different purpose now takes on a new significance. Is there perhaps a lesson here for the future?

1.7 De Sitter space

The similarities between the cosmological event horizon in de Sitter space and the absolute event horizon of a black hole spacetime have long been a subject of fascination. Put in its simplest terms, black holes are regions into which one is attracted by gravity and the absolute event horizon marks the point of no return. If the cosmological constant is non-zero, as astronomers now tell us it may be and cosmologists that it probably was in the past, then we have not only to contend with Newton's universal law of gravitation but also with de Sitter's universal law of repulsion, in other words, with anti-gravity. Things are now turned inside out and every observer is surrounded by their own cosmological event horizon whose properties, including thermodynamic, closely resemble those of black holes, a point made by Stephen and Gary Gibbons long ago.

Raphael Bousso describes more recent ideas about this connection, including a formulation of the idea of holography originally proposed by Gerard t'Hooft and by Lenny Susskind, which roughly speaking implies that degrees of freedom are associated with the boundary rather than the bulk of a region of spacetime. Raphael insists that the boundary should be lightlike.

An unresolved problem here is that, unlike anti-de Sitter space, it is hard to relate de Sitter space to string theory and M theory because

Fig. 1.5. Workshop participants transfixed by a lecture on Euclidean quantum gravity. [*Photograph Anna Żytkow*]

to do so would be to violate the strong energy condition used in the Hawking–Penrose theorems and satisfied by almost all known forms of matter (except scalars with positive potentials). Andy Strominger tries to do just that and Renata Kallosh carries the discussion forward to show how extended supergravity theories are compatible with a de Sitter term and what cosmological features arise when supersymmetry is broken.

1.8 Quantum cosmology

Perhaps Stephen's most daring intellectual project has been his work on quantum cosmology and his famous proposal, developed with Hartle, that the universe has no boundary. It is motivated by the simple fact that it is not sufficient to know the dynamical laws that govern the universe, one must also specify its initial state. Jim Hartle provides a global view of what this means in practice in the context of fundamental theory and semiclassical approximations to quantum gravity. Don Page, another of Stephen's longstanding collaborators, provides his own account of the Hartle–Hawking wavefunction of the universe and how to calculate its predictions in some specific cases. Alex Vilenkin brings an alternative perspective to quantum cosmology that is not always entirely in accord with Stephen's. He concludes by arguing for the genericity of eternal inflation which may make it difficult to distinguish between competing theories of initial conditions. Quantum mechanics raises many interpretational problems of its own, as Bryce De Witt makes clear. In quantum cosmology one must add the problem of time, as Jonathan Halliwell points out, and which he tackles using the decoherent histories approach. Peter D'Eath describes what special features supersymmetry brings to a discussion of quantum cosmology.

1.9 Cosmology

Stephen began working in cosmology just before the discovery in 1965 of the cosmic microwave background (CMB). The field has since emerged from a metaphysical backwater into a truly quantitative science, a process dramatically accelerated over the last decade by the discovery and study of primordial fluctuations in the CMB. It is these observations which appear to be remarkably consistent with those predicted by inflation. The idea of the quantum origin of these inflationary fluctuations, in which Stephen played such a key role, is reviewed by Alan Guth, focusing especially on the famous 1982 Nuffield workshop in Cambridge during which their amplitude was pinned down. He then discusses the observational evidence for inflation, before turning to the implications of eternal inflation. This work suggests that even an inflationary epoch cannot avoid a singularity in the past and thus a beginning in time. Paul Shellard reviews the observational prospects for cosmology, concentrating on the role of the cosmic microwave sky in testing inflation and other early universe models. He also considers the computational effort necessary if theoretical cosmology is to keep pace with rapidly improving observations.

The endeavour to place the standard cosmology within the framework of fundamental theory has led to the concept of braneworlds, in which our universe becomes a three-dimensional membrane (or brane) within some higher dimensional space. A controversial variant of these models, in which the branes move and collide, is presented by Neil Turok as a possible alternative to inflation. Andrei Linde mounts a robust defence of the conventional viewpoint. Finally, Pierre Binetruy reviews the present status of the brave new world of branes, borrowing his title from one of Stephen's recent papers on the subject. He discusses how cosmology is modified by these extra dimensions and the potential observational signatures that might reveal their presence.

1.10 Postscript

In the short space of an introduction like this, it is not easy to summarize the enormous impact of Stephen's contributions in so many areas from cosmology to black holes to quantum gravity. It seems far better to let the articles in this volume speak for themselves in tribute of his profound influence. However, one can be left in no doubt that Stephen is a physicist of the first class, drawn, in Kip Thorne's words, 'from that small handful who repeatedly make the breakthroughs that shape research in their fields for many years'.

Stephen's close colleagues and former students have enjoyed the special privilege of knowing him personally and seeing his work at first hand. As a mentor, we are deeply indebted to him for the example he has set. He strikes at the heart of a problem using his incisive physical intuition and, out of complex mathematics, he distils the essential geometric concepts. As a friend, we have daily seen with our own eyes his unparalleled courage and his sheer determination in the face of such grave disability. He has identified what he can do well, in fact, exceptionally well, and he gets on with his life and work with such impish good humour that it is difficult to believe that he has now reached the ripe old age of sixty!

So is the end in sight for theoretical physics and cosmology? Well, who are we to presume when Stephen and so many others at the conference have exercised such wise caution in their predictions. However after a meeting like this we cannot resist voicing the optimistic sentiment that

Fig. 1.6. Stephen surrounded by current and former students at his 60th birthday party in Gonville and Caius College. [*Photograph Anna Żytkow*]

the wind looks set fair for much further progress. The unification of quantum theory and gravity will be at the centre of many theorists' attention and, given the rate of past progress and the impressive array of intellects working on the problem, we will at least learn a great deal about the nature of possible theories, even if pinning down precisely which is the correct one may prove more elusive. Experiment may come to our aid but perhaps in unexpected ways. Most important of all would be evidence for supersymmetry in accelerator experiments. That alone would go an enormous way towards vindicating the supergravity/superstring route. More serendipitously, we may see the kind of new physics associated with large extra dimensions, such as time-dependent coupling constants, a fifth force and so forth.

Regardless of the fate of the unification programme, no one can doubt that cosmology, now a fully empirical science, is on the threshold of unveiling the nature of the early universe with all the challenges that this will bring for fundamental theory. Central questions about dark matter and cosmic acceleration remain to be answered, and realistic models for the creation of primordial perturbations will need to be developed and tested. Like cosmology, the study of black holes should also become experimentally driven as the next generation of gravitational wave detectors come into full operation. A new era of gravitational wave astronomy beckons, and it may even offer insights about the moment of creation itself.

We hope that this volume gives a flavour of the tremendous advances that have been made over the last forty years since Stephen began his research, as well as the many challenges and opportunities that remain on the road ahead.

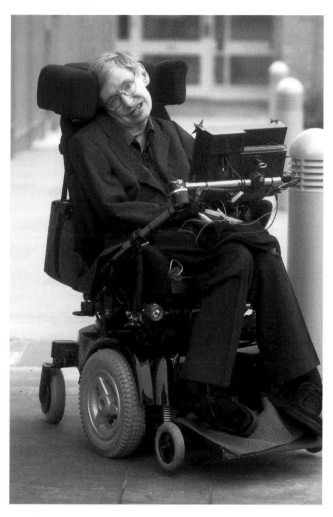

Fig. 1.7. Stephen Hawking, 60, pictured at the Centre for Mathematical Sciences, which he did so much to help create. Like Newton, his predecessor in the Lucasian Professorship, he has 'a mind forever voyaging through strange seas of thought, alone' (William Wordsworth). [*Photograph Michael Hall*]

Part 1
Popular symposium

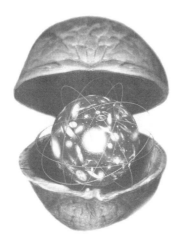

The basic ideas about the origin and fate of the universe can be stated without mathematics in a form that people without a scientific education can understand.

A Brief History of Time, 1988
[Image courtesy The Book Laboratory Inc.]

2

Our complex cosmos and its future

Martin Rees

Institute of Astronomy, University of Cambridge

2.1 Introduction

I first met Stephen Hawking when I joined Dennis Sciama's research group here in Cambridge two years after Stephen had arrived from Oxford. Astronomers are used to large numbers, but few are as huge as the odds I would then have offered against witnessing this marvellous celebration. It's a great privilege and pleasure to be speaking here.

I am going to start off with a quote not from Stephen but from Einstein. One of Einstein's best-known sayings is:

> The most incomprehensible thing about the universe is that it is comprehensible.

We are indeed starting to make some sense of the cosmos. We are learning the measure of the universe, just as ancient pioneers and 17th century navigators learnt the size and shape of our earth. I will outline these advances and then highlight two mysteries.

2.2 The universe observed

First, can we understand in some deeper sense why our universe is the way it is? And can we delineate how, from simple beginnings, it transformed itself into the complex cosmic habitat we see around us and of which we are a part?

If we could transport ourselves two million light years away and look back at our Milky Way, it would look something like the Andromeda Galaxy, a near twin of our own. It is a disc of about a hundred billion stars viewed obliquely. Modern telescopes in fact reveal billions of galaxies which are being mapped out in ever more detail. In fact, quite recently British and Australian astronomers have finished a survey showing

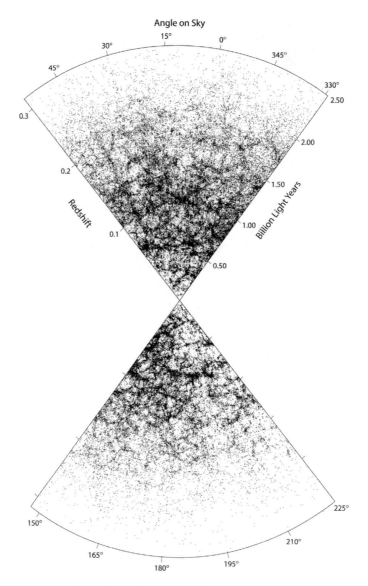

Fig. 2.1. The 2dF galaxy survey.

150,000 galaxies (Figure 2.1). It reveals the 'texture' of our universe. The galaxies are grouped into clusters, even into super-clusters. But there are not clusters of clusters of clusters *ad infinitum*. In a broad-brush sense, the universe really looks smooth. And that is a simplifying factor.

The overall motions in our universe are simple, too, as has been known since the time of Edwin Hubble. Distant galaxies recede from us with

Fig. 2.2. Lengthening rods representing an expanding universe (Escher). [*Courtesy Cordon Art*]

a speed proportional to their distance. So they all started off packed together, maybe 13 billion years ago.

But this does not imply we are in some special location. Suppose the rods in the lattice shown in Figure 2.2 were lengthened. Then the vertices would also recede from each other at a speed depending on the number of intervening rods. That is a good model for the expanding universe, except that, as Figure 2.1 shows, the galaxies are not in a regular lattice. But if you imagine clusters of galaxies all linked by rods, which all lengthen, that is a good model. There is no preferred centre, and the observer on any galaxy would see an isotropic expansion.

Because of light's finite speed, however, what we actually see as we probe deeper into space is more like this second Escher picture (Figure 2.3) 'angels and devils', because as we go out towards our horizon, we see the universe as it was when it was younger and more close-packed.

And you can now see very far back indeed. One amazing picture, taken with the Hubble space telescope, shows a small patch of sky less than a hundredth of the area covered by a full moon. Seen through a medium-sized telescope, this little patch would look quite black. But this deep exposure reveals hundreds of faint smudges of light. Each of these is an entire galaxy, thousands of light years across, which appears so small and

Martin Rees

Fig. 2.3. Angels and devils (Escher). [*Courtesy Cordon Art*]

faint because of its huge distance. And a huge span of time separates us
from these remote galaxies. They are being viewed when they had only
just formed. They have not yet settled down into the steadily spinning
pinwheels, like Andromeda. They consist mainly of glowing diffused gas.
Stars are just beginning to form in them, fuelled by nuclear fusion which
turns pristine hydrogen into the atoms of the periodic table. Indeed, all
the carbon, oxygen and silicon on Earth was forged in ancient stars in
our galaxy, These elements were made via the recycling process depicted
in Figure 2.4 before our solar system formed and are literally the nuclear
waste from the fuel that makes stars shine.

When we look at a galaxy like Andromeda, we sometimes wonder if
there might be other beings looking back at us. Maybe there are. But on
those very remote galaxies, there surely are not, because their stars have
not yet had enough time to transmute hydrogen into the building blocks
of planets, let alone of life.

Astronomers can actually look back over 90% of the time to the big
bang. In fact, the distance record is held by some newly discovered active
galaxies called quasars, whose spectra are illustrated in Figure 2.5. This
shows three spectra: the Lyman alpha line, in the far ultraviolet, 1216 Å,

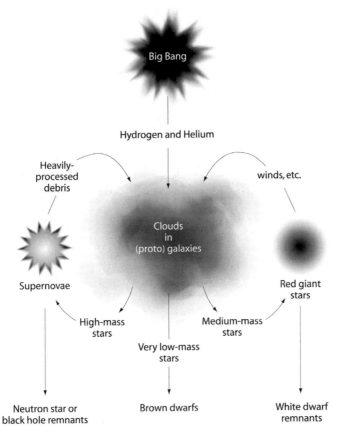

Fig. 2.4. The recycling process whereby heavy elements are synthesized in stars.

is stretched by a factor of more than 7 in this case, so it appears at 9000 Å. The light from these objects set out when the universe was about 400 times denser and 10 times younger.

But what about still more remote epochs, before any galaxies had formed at all? Our strongest clue to the early universe is the radiation that is an afterglow of our universe's dense beginning. Intergalactic space is not completely cold; it is pervaded with diffuse microwaves. In 1990 the COBE satellite showed that this radiation obeyed a black body spectrum, to a precision of 1 part in 10,000. This was just as expected, if it had come into equilibrium when everything was hot and dense. As the universe expanded, the rods in Escher's picture (Figure 2.2) lengthened, the radiation cooled and diluted, its wavelengths stretched. So it is now in the microwave band. Its temperature is only 3 degrees above absolute

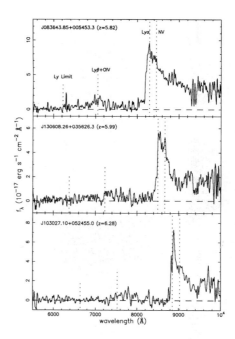

Fig. 2.5. Redshifted quasar spectra.

zero. But it is still around. It fills the universe, and has nowhere else to go.

It was the Cambridge astrophysicist Fred Hoyle who coined the name Big Bang – as a derisive description of a theory he liked much less than the Steady State that he, Hermann Bondi and Thomas Gold had proposed in 1948.

2.3 Cosmic microwave background radiation

There is another fossil of the hot beginning. During the first minute or so, everything would be hotter than the centre of a star is now. And there would be nuclear reactions. However, fortunately the universe stayed hot for such a short time that there was not time for these reactions to transmute everything into iron. Otherwise, there would be no fuel left to power the stars today. All that happened back then is that 23% of the material, according to calculations, emerges as helium, with small traces of deuterium (heavy hydrogen) as an intermediate product, and lithium. This calculation accords gratifyingly with what is observed; it corroborates the Big Bang story, because there seems to be at least 23% helium everywhere, and stellar processes cannot account for why there is so much.

Fig. 2.6. Announcement of COBE results in 1992 (*The Independent*).

Figure 2.6 shows the front page, from one day in 1992, of what was then Britain's best daily newspaper. This issue appeared on the day that NASA, with tremendous hype, announced some later results from the COBE satellite. It's an artist's impression of a cosmic time chart, right back to 10^{-43} seconds. The artist even got dinosaurs in: the only topic in popular science with as much popular appeal as cosmology. But it shows the formation of the galaxies, and right back to the first second, when the radiation and the helium were made. The details on the time chart – at least in the top half, back to one second – deserve to be taken as seriously as anything you learn from geologists or palaeontologists about the early history of our earth. Their inferences are just as indirect, and less quantitative than the cosmological evidence from the microwave background and helium.

Moreover, there were several discoveries that might have been made any time in the last 30 years, which would have invalidated the Big Bang and which have not been made. Five of them are listed in Figure 2.7. Had any of these five things been discovered, we would have had to jettison

FIVE WAYS TO REFUTE THE "HOT BIG BANG"
- Object with << 23% helium
- Millimetre-wave background below prediction
- Stable neutrino mass $100-10^6$eV
- Too much deuterium to match baryon density
- $\Delta T/T$ too small to account for present structure

Fig. 2.7. Several tests by which to invalidate the Big Bang.

the idea of the Big Bang – but none have. The Big Bang theory has lived dangerously for decades and survived. In fact, I would now place 99% confidence in the extrapolation back to one second, when the temperature was 10 billion degrees. Cosmologists are chided for being often in error but never in doubt, and that is why I prudently leave 1% for the possibility that we are as deluded in our satisfaction as a Ptolemaic astronomer who has discovered some new epicycles.

However, we have far less confidence about earlier stages – the first tiny fraction of a second, the bottom half of that time chart. You cannot believe all you read in the newspapers, and I will return to this later.

Incidentally, Fred Hoyle never came round to the Big Bang theory, although he did – towards the end of his life – compromise and develop what I might call a Steady Bang theory.

2.4 The origin of large-scale structure

People sometimes wonder how our universe can have started off as a hot amorphous fireball and ended up so intricately differentiated. This may seem contrary to a hallowed principle of physics – the second law of thermodynamics. But this development of structure is actually a natural outcome of the workings of gravity. The expanding universe turns out to be unstable to the growth of structure, in the sense that a region that starts off just very slightly overdense will suffer extra deceleration that enhances the density contrast, and so overdense regions evolve into clumps that can then be the embryos for the structures we see today.

Theorists can now follow virtual universes in their computer. These are best presented as videos, but one 'still' is shown in this written text as Figure 2.8. The simulations show how the force of gravity slowly draws matter together. The architecture of the early universe becomes apparent in a vast weblike structure of interconnected filaments. Travelling along a filament, clouds of gas and stars condense to form proto-galaxies. These complex patterns are governed by the laws of hydrodynamics, as well as gravity. Galaxies congregate into clusters at the intersections of the

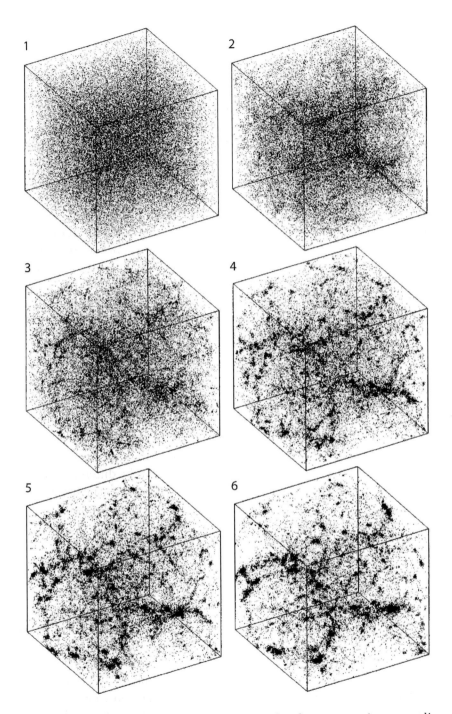

Fig. 2.8. 'Stills' from a movie showing growth of structure in expanding universe. (With permission from the Virgo Consortium).

filaments. The high density region of the cluster contains very hot gas, while the low density regions of the universe expand and cool. These processes of galaxy formation occupy several billion years. As the universe continues to evolve, clustering develops.

Galaxies sometimes collide. When two spiral galaxies are trapped by their mutual gravity they are drawn together in a fantastic collision. The violent impact produces intense shockwaves in the gas, whilst stars pass through with virtually no collisions because of the great distances between them. Along the shock fronts, huge gas clouds condense, producing explosive bursts and new star formation. The tidal forces of gravity strip long plumes of gas and stars from the galaxies. As the galactic cores approach for a second collision, a single massive structure is formed. Such a collision may be the fate of our home galaxy, the Milky Way, and its neighbour, the Andromeda Galaxy, although not for several billion years.

There is no thermodynamic paradox in evolving from an almost structureless fireball to the present cosmos, with huge temperature differences between the three degrees of the night sky and the blazing surface of the stars. Gravity amplifies linear density contrasts and then stars eventually form as gravity pulls gas clouds together, and their centres get ever hotter.

2.5 The fate of the universe

Let us now look forward rather than backwards – as forecasters rather than fossil hunters. Stars will survive the crash with Andromeda but in about 7 billion years the Sun will swell up, engulfing the inner planets, and vaporizing any remaining life on Earth before it throws off its outer layers. It will then settle down to a quiet demise as a white dwarf. But will the entire universe eventually stop expanding? Will it collapse to a big crunch? Will it go on expanding – decelerating? Will it even go on expanding and speed up in its expansion? The answer to these questions depends on how much the expansion is being decelerated by gravity. It is straightforward to calculate that the expansion can be reversed if there is on average more than about five atoms in every cubic metre. That does not sound much, but if all the galaxies were dismantled and their material was spread uniformly through space, it would make an even emptier vacuum – 0.2 atoms per cubic metre – that is like one snowflake in the volume of the earth. And it is 25 times less than the so-called critical density, which at first sight would seem to imply perpetual expansion by a wide margin.

But things are not quite so straightforward because of the famous dark matter mystery. Astronomers have discovered that galaxies and clusters would fly apart unless they were held together by the gravitational pull of at least five times more material than we actually see. There are many lines of evidence for dark matter – I will show you just one.

Fig. 2.9. Gravitationally lensed galaxies behind the cluster Abell 2218. (With permission from the Hubble Space Telescope.)

Figure 2.9 shows a cluster of galaxies about a billion light years away – the brighter galaxies belong to the cluster. But you also see lots of faint streaks and arcs – each of those is a remote galaxy several times further away still than the cluster itself. And their images are, as it were, being viewed through a distorting lens. Just as a regular pattern on wallpaper looks distorted if viewed through a poorly figured lens, so light bending, a prediction of Einstein's theory, deflects the light rays passing through or close to the cluster and distorts the images of distant galaxies. But the amount of bending and distortion which is manifest in all these arcs is much more than you would expect if there were nothing in the cluster beyond the galaxies you see. So this is evidence that these clusters contain five or ten times as much mass as we see.

So what can dark matter be? It is embarrassing that most of the universe is unaccounted for. Earlier ideas were that it might be faint stars, or dead remnants of massive stars. But most cosmologists now suspect that dark matter is not made up of atoms at all, and is exotic particles that were left over from the Big Bang. The main reason for this belief is that the amount of deuterium calculated to have emerged from the Big Bang would be discrepant with observations if the average density of atoms was 1 or 2 per cubic metre rather than 0.2. Extra exotic particles that do not participate in nuclear reactions would not scupper that concordance, but extra dark matter in atomic form would.

The nature of the dark matter may yield to a two-pronged attack in future. First, it could be detected directly. Dark matter particles pervade our entire galaxy. They are whizzing through this room at about 300 km per second. And searches for them are underway, using sensitive detectors in underground laboratories to reduce the background. There is a British effort in a mine near Whitby in Yorkshire. If the experiments succeed, then not only do we discover what most of the universe is made of, but also as a bonus some new particles.

The second line of attack is progress in particle physics. If we knew more about the types of particle that could exist in the ultra early universe, then we would calculate how many should survive from the first microsecond of the Big Bang with as much confidence as we can now calculate the helium made in the first three minutes.

Cosmologists denote the ratio of the actual density of our universe to the critical density by Ω. And it now seems that the dark matter which is inferred in galaxies and clusters still only brings Ω up to about 0.3. If that were all, we would not be in a flat universe. The geometry would be hyperbolic and distant objects would then look smaller than they do in Euclidian space.

But there is now – just within the last year or two – rather compelling evidence that our universe is flat, in the sense that if you draw a triangle in the universe, its angles add up to 180 degrees. This evidence comes from the microwave background radiation. This background radiation is not completely smooth over the sky. If you study it in detail, you find that the temperature varies by about 1 part in 10^5 from place to place over the sky. These fluctuations are the precursors of the structures in our universe today. And theory tells us that the fluctuations should be biggest on a particular linear scale, related to how far a sound wave can travel in the early universe. The angular scale corresponding to that linear scale depends however on the geometry of the universe.

At almost every cosmology conference now one sees, ad nauseam and beyond, pictures like Figure 2.10. This is a picture which shows, as a function of angular scale, how rough the universe should appear on different angular scales. If the universe had a low density, the peak would happen on a scale of about half a degree. If the universe were flat, then because the geometry is Euclidian rather than hyperbolic, the angular scale for the peak is twice as large – about 1 degree.

Just within the last year, measurements from balloons, and from ground based measurements mainly in Antarctica, have pinned down the angular scale of this so-called Doppler peak. Collecting together all the data, one finds, with 10% precision, this peak corresponds to where it should be for a flat universe. If we were in a universe where there were nothing but 0.3 of the critical density in dark matter, it would be further to the right, as shown in the dashed line.

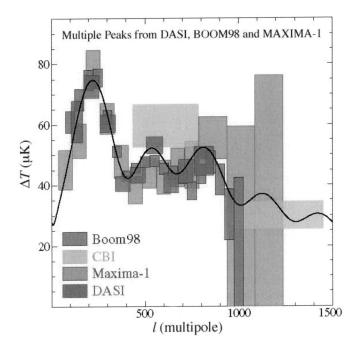

Fig. 2.10. Power spectrum of the cosmic microwave sky.

So, what is the other 70% of stuff that makes the universe flat? It is not in dark matter, but is in something which does not cluster – some kind of energy latent in space. The simplest form of this idea goes back to Einstein, in 1917. Because he then believed in a static universe, he introduced an extra term in his equations which he called the cosmological constant, or Λ. This energy latent in space (which is the way we now interpret it) leads to a repulsion, because, according to Einstein's equations, gravity depends on pressure as well as on density, and vacuum energy has to have such a large negative pressure – tension, as it were – that the net effect is repulsive, a sort of anti-gravity. So, if the extra 70% of mass-energy that makes the universe flat is latent in space, we get a flat universe, but with acceleration not deceleration. And, in fact, within the last two years a remarkable concordance has emerged, between these observations and other quite different evidence.

Distant supernovae, of type 1A (to use some technical jargon) behave like nuclear bombs, with a standard yield. We can observe how bright they are, and therefore infer their distance. From the redshift–distance relation of these distant supernovae, two independent groups of researchers have

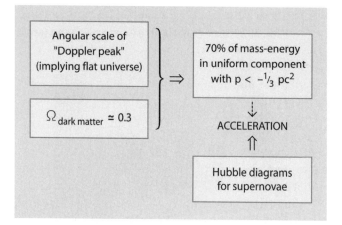

Fig. 2.11. Cosmological concordance.

found pretty good evidence that the universe is speeding up in its expansion. So we have a consistent story that leads to a preferred choice for the key parameters describing the universe, shown in Figure 2.11.

The universe is flat – gratifying to most theorists – but its mass energy is made up of a rather surprising mix of ingredients. Atoms are only about 4%, dark matter is 20–30% and the mysterious dark energy, the rest, is about 70%.

So, what is the long-range forecast? Galaxies will not merely disperse but they will get more and more redshifted as they accelerate away from us. Eventually, nothing will be in view, except the merged remnants of our galaxy and Andromeda: one amorphous galaxy formed, by then, of completely burnt out stars. In fact, even the dead remnants of stars will eventually erode as the atoms in them decay, because atoms – we believe – do not live for ever. And Stephen Hawking famously showed that black holes do not live for ever, either. But this cosmic end game is very, very slow. As Woody Allen said:

> Eternity is very long, especially towards the end!

So much, then, for the long-range forecast. Let us now go back to the beginning.

2.6 The very early universe

Calculations of cosmic structure, like the ones depicted in Figure 2.8 need to specify, at some early time such as one second, a few 'initial' numbers: the expansion rate, the proportions of all the atoms, dark matter, dark energy and radiation, the character of the fluctuations and, of course, the basic constants of physics. We do not like to leave things there – we strive to understand why those numbers have the values we observe. Any explanation must lie, if anywhere, in the first tiny fraction of a second – the still earlier universe.

Figure 2.12 depicts another version of the newspaper time chart. I was, as I said, 99% confident of tracing back to when the universe was one second old. I was confident because the matter then was still hardly denser than air. Conventional laboratory physics is applicable and is vindicated by the evidence of background radiation, helium and so forth. But the further back we extrapolate, the less foothold we have in experiment. In the first trillionth of a second, every particle would have more energy than even CERN's new LHC accelerator will reach.

But many cosmologists suspect that the expansion rates and the flatness of the universe were determined when everything in our visible universe was literally the size of a tennis ball. According to the so-called cosmic inflation theory, the universe enlarged exponentially, at an immense rate, when it was only about 10^{-35} seconds old – way down at the bottom of the figure. The inflation concept has been the front-runner ever since a classic paper of Alan Guth more than 20 years ago. But I should mention there are now rival conjectures, in particular due to Neil Turok and Paul Steinhart, who suggest that the Big Bang was triggered by the impact of another universe, separated from ours by a fourth spatial dimension.

So there are ideas to explain why the universe is so large and why it is, in the technical jargon, flat. But other features, crucial to the emergence of our complex cosmos, have as yet no clear explanation. I shall mention two.

The first concerns what I called earlier the texture of the universe – the fact that it has got a slight roughness to it, but is not so rough that cosmologists cannot use a broad-brush smooth approach. The fluctuations that are the seeds for the galaxies, which are perhaps quantum fluctuations imprinted when the universe was of microscopic size, are not fully understood. But the amplitude they need to have in order to explain the microwave background, and to give rise to the structures we see is, when measured in a natural way, one part in 100,000. This number, which I call Q, determines the roughness of the universe.

A smoother universe, with Q much smaller than 10^{-5}, would form no stars. It would remain after 10 billion years still amorphous cold hydrogen: no galaxies, no stars and no people. On the other hand, a rougher universe, where Q was much larger than 10^{-5}, would be a violent place where stars and galaxies could not form: huge black holes, much bigger in mass than a cluster of galaxies, would condense out early in the expansion and there would be no chance of galaxies and clusters forming later. So our universe,

A CHRONOLOGY OF THE UNIVERSE

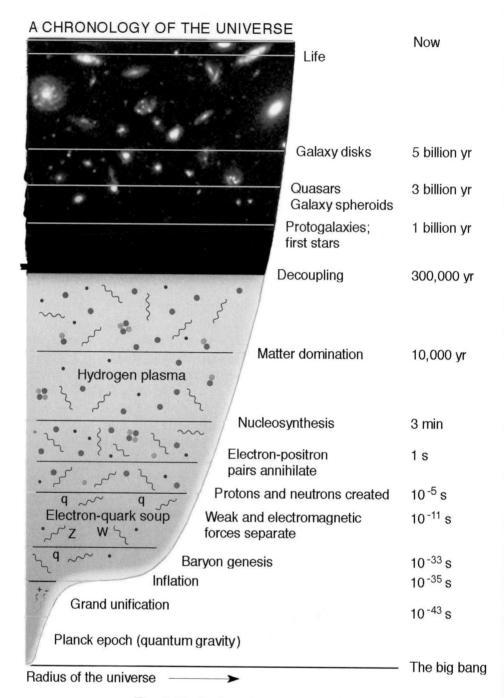

Life	Now
Galaxy disks	5 billion yr
Quasars Galaxy spheroids	3 billion yr
Protogalaxies; first stars	1 billion yr
Decoupling	300,000 yr
Matter domination	10,000 yr
Nucleosynthesis	3 min
Electron-positron pairs annihilate	1 s
Protons and neutrons created	10^{-5} s
Weak and electromagnetic forces separate	10^{-11} s
Baryon genesis	10^{-33} s
Inflation	10^{-35} s
Grand unification	10^{-43} s
Planck epoch (quantum gravity)	
	The big bang

Hydrogen plasma

q q
Electron-quark soup
Z W

q

Radius of the universe ⟶

Fig. 2.12. Early universe timescales.

to be habitable, has to have had Q in the range around 10^{-5} – we do not quite know why.

Another fundamental number, crucial for the physical world, measures the strength of gravity compared with the other natural forces. There is a sense in which gravity is very weak: if you take two protons and put them together, there is an electric force between them obeying an inverse square law; there is also a gravitational attraction between them. But the ratio of those two forces is about 36 powers of 10 – that is why chemists do not need to worry about self-gravity when they think about molecules. (A related 'large number', the reciprocal of the so-called gravitational fine structure constant, is closer to 10^{38}.) But gravity wins on large scales because all particles have a positive 'gravitational charge', whereas the positive and negative electric charges almost cancel out in any macroscopic object.

Figure 2.13 shows radius, or length, along the horizontal (on a log scale), and mass upwards. The line shown diagonally is the size of black holes –

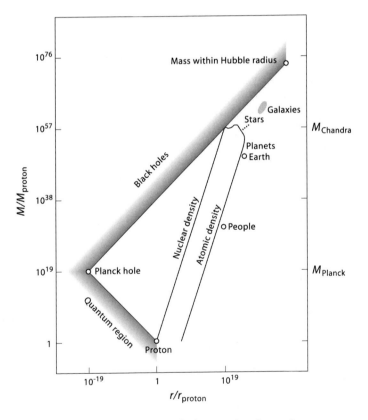

Fig. 2.13. Size vs mass of objects in the universe.

their radius is proportional to their mass. If you tried to make a miniature black hole in a laboratory that was the size of a proton, how heavy would it be? You can just read the answer off this picture – it would have to contain 10^{38} protons. That is the mass of an asteroid – several cubic miles of rock. Owing to the weakness of gravity, huge numbers of particles have to be packed into the volume occupied by one in order for gravity to compete with the micro-physical forces. These mini black holes were discussed by Stephen and have amazing properties, but it does not look as though they could ever form in our universe, which is disappointing.

Stars are gravitationally bound fusion reactors. They are of ordinary densities but they got close enough to the black hole line that gravity is important. You can see from this that the number of atoms you need to make a star is about 10^{57}, the three halves power of 10^{38}.

If gravity was not quite so weak, so that the number measuring its weakness was, say, 10^{28} rather than 10^{38}, then Figure 2.13 would look mainly the same, but stars would be small and be speeded up, and objects as big as us would be crushed by gravity. Gravity is crucial in developing structure in the universe, and holding stars and galaxies together; but the weaker it is, the grander are its consequences. Gravity must be very weak in order to allow so many powers of 10 between the microworld and the scales governed by gravity – the scale of stars and galaxies. Another way to express this (for the physicist) is that the Planck mass, which is the mass of a black hole whose Compton wavelength is equal to its gravitational radius, is about 10^{19} times larger than a proton. And another implication is that the initial quantum state of the universe is far hotter and earlier than the era when protons and anti-protons decay.

We would like to understand numbers like 10^{38} and the texture number $Q \simeq 10^{-5}$. They were imprinted at the very beginning of the universe when the role of the physics is very extreme indeed and certainly untested. This extreme physics will entail a new link between the cosmos and micro-world.

The smart money seems to be on superstrings or M theory, which involves extra dimensions wrapped up on very tiny scales. But even more excitingly – and I am just a spectator of this subject, not an expert – these extra dimensions may not all be wrapped up so tight that they cannot be observed. Some, we have heard this week, could reveal themselves by anomalies in accelerator experiments. Indeed, some extra dimensions may not be wrapped up at all. We cannot rule out the possibility that there is another universe just a few millimetres away from us. But we cannot directly see it because those millimetres are measured in a fourth spatial dimension and we are imprisoned in our three.

2.7 Multiverse?

One generic consequence of inflation (and of some other theories of the early universe) may have profound implications. It is that we may have to extend our conceptual horizon still more; what we have traditionally called our universe may not be all of physical reality; our Big Bang may not be the only one. If that is the case, how much of our Big Bang will ever be fully explained? Maybe when we understand the early universe the recipe encoded in it, which led to our actual universe, may prove to be uniquely self-consistent: no Big Bang could then produce a different kind of universe, with different values of the fundamental numbers, a different mix of atoms and dark matter, and so forth.

But a far more interesting possibility, certainly tenable in our present state of ignorance, is that some of what we call laws of nature may, in this grander perspective, be local 'by-laws', consistent with some over-arching theory governing the ensemble but not uniquely fixed by that theory. If things do turn out that way, it would remove the mystery of why our universe has the rather arbitrary seeming mix of ingredients, rather than being as simple as possible, which some people might have thought aesthetically more attractive.

I think we may be tracing a route analogous to what happened after Kepler, 400 years ago. Kepler thought the Earth was unique – its orbit was a circle, related to those of other planets, by beautiful geometry. We now realize that there are zillions of stars, many with planetary systems. Moreover, our Earth's orbit is not a circle – it is an ellipse – and it is not special at all, except insofar as it needs to be in a particular range to be compatible with life: it cannot be too eccentric; it must be at the right distance from a stable star so that water neither boils nor freezes all the time. Maybe an analogous argument applies on a far grander scale to our entire universe. If that is the case, the hope for neat explanations for some particular features of our universe may be as vain as was Kepler's numerological quest.

Firming up this kind of speculation must await a final theory that tells us whether or not there could have been many big bangs rather than just one. And even if there are many big bangs, we would have to know whether there can be variety among them, so that what we call the laws of nature may be just parochial by-laws in our cosmic patch, the only way we would ever be able to explain some features of our universe would be to assert that they lie in the range that allows us to exist.

There is a word in Figure 2.14 beginning with 'a', which I am not going to spell out. I quite like this word, and I think Stephen does as well. But it makes some physicists foam at the mouth, because they hate to feel

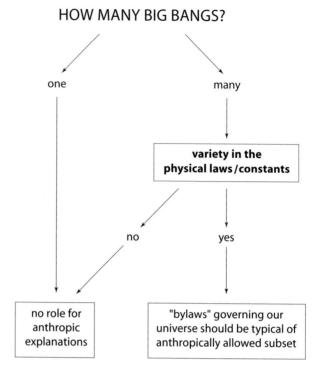

Fig. 2.14. Unique universe or multiuniverse?

that we may end up not being able to explain everything by some unique equations: they hate to think that the cosmic numbers may just be the outcome of 'environmental accidents' in the aftermath of our Big Bang.

2.8 The future of cosmology

Just to conclude: if we were to re-convene on Stephen's 70th birthday what would be the hot topics on the agenda? One strand of cosmology will, by then, probably be settled: we will know the key parameters such as the Hubble constant, Ω, Q and so forth with adequate accuracy. But the subject will then bifurcate. Sociologically this will resemble what happened in the 1970s to the field of general relativity research. By then, through the efforts to which Stephen Hawking contributed so much, the main astrophysically-interesting features of black holes were theoretically understood. Thereafter, most of the leading theorists moved either (like Stephen) closer to quantum physics, or else (like Kip Thorne, Jim Bardeen and others) closer to astrophysics.

Werner Israel distinguished two contrasting intellectual types among cosmologists: the 'chess players' and the 'mud wrestlers'. I think there will still be plenty of challenges for both of them – the intellectually refined and intellectually brutish – though there will be a sharper contrast between the two groups then than there is today, when those who model (for instance) microwave background fluctuations straddle the division.

The 'chess players' will, I hope, have replaced the boisterous variety of ideas discussed here this week, by a firmer 'best buy' theory of the ultra-early universe. They will do this perhaps by discovering internal inconsistencies in some contending theories and thereby narrowing down the field; better still, one fundamental theory may by then have earned enough credibility by explaining things we can observe, that we then gain confidence in applying it even to things we cannot observe. So we may be lucky enough to settle the two questions depicted in Figure 2.14. We would then know whether there can be one big bang, or whether there are many (and if the latter, how much variety they display).

But those of us who are not intellectually fit for chess, and who in fact rather enjoy wallowing in the mud, will still be confronted by the challenge of the more recent universe, by which I mean the last 90% of cosmic history, when it is not smooth and structureless but contains the evolving structures which are now being observationally probed and computationally simulated. For the later universe, the basic physics is known, but its manifestations are complex and non-linear, just like the weather and any other environmental phenomenon. This part of cosmology is the grandest of the environmental sciences, as well as a fundamental science. We will draw on observations and computer simulations to understand the complex feedback that governs how stars form, how galaxies evolve, and how on at least one planet and around at least one star atoms assembled into creatures that could become aware of themselves. That is the unending challenge.

Finally, a recent cosmology book – not written by anyone at this conference but I think available on the book stand – was praised in the publisher's blurb 'for its thorough coverage of the inflammatory universe'! That was a misprint, of course. But enough sparks flew here this week to make it seem a not inapt description of the lively frontiers of cosmology – frontiers where Stephen Hawking will surely inspire further advances in the coming decades.

3

Theories of everything and Hawking's wave function of the universe

James Hartle

University of California, Santa Barbara

3.1 Introduction

It is an honour, of course, to participate in this celebration of Stephen's 60th birthday and to address such a distinguished audience. But for me it is a special pleasure. I first met Stephen over thirty years ago when we were both beginning in science at the then Institute of Theoretical Astronomy here in Cambridge. I have been following his inspiration ever since and have had the privilege of working with him on several directions that he has pioneered. I want to talk to you about one of these today.

3.2 Different things fall with the same acceleration in a gravitational field

If a cat, a cannonball, and an economics textbook are all dropped from the same height, they fall to the ground with exactly the same acceleration (9.8 m/s^2) under the influence of gravity. This equality of the gravitational accelerations of different things is one of the most accurately tested laws of physics. The accelerations are known to be equal to an accuracy of a few parts in a thousand billion. That law, however, tells you very little about cats, cannonballs, or economics. That, in a nutshell, is the theme of my talk today (Figure 3.1).

Were a cat, a cannonball, and an economics text dropped from a real leaning tower, the accelerations would not be equal to an accuracy of a thousand billion. Air resistance, magnetic fields, and a host of other effects mask the purely gravitational one. Rather, the equality of accelerations is revealed to that accuracy only in delicate laboratory experiments shielded from such extraneous effects, or in the study of the accelerations of astronomical bodies for which they are not important. The record holder for

9.8 m/sec²

Fig. 3.1. The lecture in a nutshell: A cat, a cannonball, and an economics textbook all fall to the ground with exactly the same acceleration if acted upon only by gravity. The equality of accelerations of different things in a gravitational field is an example of a fundamental law of physics. But that law does not tell you much about cats cannonballs or economics. [*From a lecture transparency*]

accuracy at the moment is the lunar laser ranging demonstration that the Earth and the Moon fall with the same acceleration toward the Sun [1].

The manned and unmanned missions to the Moon in the late 1960s and early 1970s left behind arrays of corner reflectors (Figure 3.2). A corner reflector is an arrangement of three mirrors making up the sides of a cube that meet in one corner. It has the property that any light ray incident on the reflector bounces from mirror to mirror and is reflected back in exactly the direction from whence it came. Since 1969 a systematic programme to monitor the Moon's orbit using these reflectors has been carried out by the McDonald Observatory in Texas and the Observatoire de Côte d'Azur in Grasse, France [1]. High powered lasers send light pulses to the Moon that bounce off the reflectors. By measuring precisely the time it takes for the light pulse to return (about 1 second), and dividing that by the velocity of light, the distance to the Moon can be determined very accurately. About a billion, billion photons are sent out ten times a second and one returning photon is detected every few seconds. The returning photons have been detected for over 30 years, and as a consequence of this effort, we know the position of the Moon relative to the Earth to an accuracy of about a few centimetres. Study of its orbit shows it is falling towards the Sun with the same acceleration as the Earth to an accuracy of a few parts in a thousand billion.

This law of equality of accelerations of different things is a cornerstone of Einstein's general relativity – Stephen's subject. However, it is not general relativity specifically that I want to talk to you about today, but about such laws of physics more generally.

Fig. 3.2. Lunar Laser Ranging. The picture on the left shows an array of corner reflectors on the surface of the Moon left there by a manned mission decades ago. The picture on the right shows a laser pulse from the McDonald Observatory in Texas being reflected off such an array. By measuring the time between the departure of the pulse and its return, the Moon's orbit can be monitored to an accuracy of a few centimetres. Analysis of that orbit shows that the Moon and the Earth are falling toward the Sun with equal accelerations to a few parts of a thousand billion. [*NASA/McDonald Observatory*]

3.3 The fundamental laws of physics

The equality of gravitational accelerations of different things is an example of a regularity of nature. Everything falls in exactly the same way. The regularity is universal. No exceptions! There are other regularities that may apply to specific systems in similar circumstances (Figure 3.3). For example, if we drop three cats, they might all go 'meeeeow' in roughly the same way on the way down. Or perhaps there are only statistical regularities for cats – 8 out of 10 cats will go 'meeeeow' in the average drop. Other systems will do something different according to their own particular regularities. Cannonballs for example do nothing on the way down. But the equality of accelerations of different things is a special kind of law because it applies *universally* to anything falling in a gravitational field. It is an example of a fundamental law of physics.

Identifying and explaining the regularities of nature is the goal of science. Physics, like other sciences, is concerned with the regularities exhibited by particular systems. Stars, atoms, fluid flows, high temperature super-conductors, black holes and the elementary particles are just some of the many examples. Studies of these specific systems define the various subfields of physics – astrophysics, atomic physics, fluid mechanics

Fig. 3.3. Different kinds of things fall with the same acceleration in a gravitational field. That is an example of a universal regularity of nature. Different classes of things can exhibit other regularities among themselves which differ from class to class.

and so forth. But beyond the regularities exhibited by specific systems, physics has a special charge. This is to find the laws that govern the regularities that are exhibited by *all* physical systems – without exception, without qualification, and without approximation. The equality of gravitational accelerations of different things is an example. These are usually called the *fundamental* laws of physics. Taken together they are called informally a 'theory of everything'. Stephen has been a leader in the quest for these universal laws [2]. Today, I would like to ask the question: 'How much do we know about the world if we have a theory of everything?'

Ideas for the nature of the fundamental laws have changed as experiment and observation have revealed new realms of phenomena and reached new levels of precision. But since they have been studied, it has been thought that the fundamental laws consist of two parts.

- *Dynamical laws* that govern regularities in *time*. Newton's laws of motion governing the orderly progression of the planets or the trajectory of a tennis ball are examples, as is the law that different things fall with the same acceleration in a gravitational field and the Einstein equation governing the evolution of the universe.

- *Initial conditions* that govern how things started out and therefore most often specify regularities in *space*. The statistical regularities of the large scale distribution of the galaxies in the universe is a possible example (Figure 3.4).

Laplace is a name associated with this view of a theory of everything.

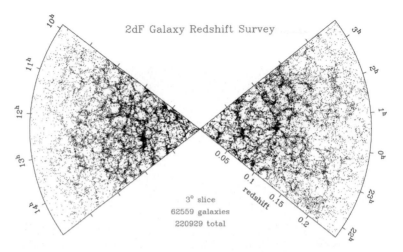

Fig. 3.4. This plot from the 2dF Galaxy Redshift Survey [3] shows the location of 62,559 distant galaxies in two angular slices of the universe approximately 90° wide and 3° thick as viewed from the Earth. A galaxy's redshift is used as a measure of its distance from our location at the centre. The statistics of the distribution of knots, filaments and voids in this picture is an example of a large scale regularity of the universe that is directly linked to its initial condition.

He wrote, famously, [4]

> An intelligence knowing, at any given instant of time, all forces acting in nature, as well as the momentary positions of all things of which the universe consists, would be able to comprehend the motions of the largest bodies of the world and those of the smallest atoms in one single formula. ... To it, nothing would be uncertain, both future and past would be present before its eyes.

That was the theory of everything circa 1820 – Newtonian determinism.

Both parts of a theory of everything are needed to make any predictions. Newton's dynamical laws by themselves don't predict the trajectory of a tennis ball you might throw. To predict where it goes, you must also specify the position from which you throw it, the direction, and how fast. In short, you must specify the ball's *initial condition*. One of Stephen's most famous achievements is just such an initial condition [2], but not for tennis balls. Stephen's no-boundary initial condition is for the whole universe.

The search for a theory of the dynamical laws has been seriously under way since the time of Newton. Classical mechanics, Newtonian gravity, Maxwell's electrodynamics, special and general relativity, quantum

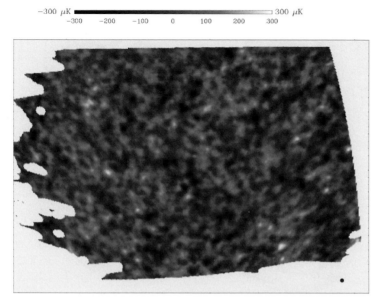

Fig. 3.5. This picture from the Boomerang experiment [5] shows the temperature distribution across a patch of sky of the cosmic background radiation. The light and dark regions differ in temperature by only a few ten millionths of a degree about a mean of 2.73 K. This is as close as one can come to a picture of the early universe some hundreds of thousands of years after the Big Bang. The temperature variations are evidence for tiny concentrations of density then which in the intervening 15 billion years grew by the action of gravitational attraction to become the galaxies we see today with the large scale distribution illustrated in Figure 3.4.

mechanics, quantum field theory and superstring theory are but some of the milestones in this search. But the search for a theory of the initial condition of the universe has been seriously under way for only the twenty years since Stephen's pioneering work on the subject. Why this difference? The examples used above to discuss regularities governed by the two parts of a theory of everything hint at the answer. The trajectory of a tennis ball was used to illustrate the regularities of dynamical laws, and the large scale distribution of galaxies was used to illustrate the regularities implied by the law of the initial condition. There is a difference in the *kind* and *scale* of regularities that the two laws predict.

Dynamical laws predict regularities in time. It is a fortunate empirical fact that the fundamental dynamical laws are local – both in space and time. The trajectory of a tennis ball depends only on conditions that are

Fig. 3.6. The equality of accelerations of different things in a gravitational field is an example of a local fundamental dynamical law. A body's acceleration depends only on the gravitational field at its location and not, say, on the arrangement of distant matter or events in the past that could not be summarized in this way. This fundamental law can therefore be discovered by experiments done locally by experimenters in their laboratories across the universe.

nearby both in space and time, and not, for example, either on what is going on in distant parts of the universe or a long time ago. This is fortunate because that means that dynamical laws can be discovered and studied in laboratories on Earth and extrapolated, assuming locality, to the rest of the universe. For example, because it is local, the law that different things fall with the same acceleration in a gravitational field can be discovered by experiments in laboratories here, and indeed all over the galaxy (Figure 3.6). Without that simplicity of the dynamical laws in the here and now it is possible that we would never have discovered them.

By contrast, the regularities governed by the law of the initial condition of the universe occur on large, cosmological scales. The universe isn't simple on small spatial scales. Look at the disorder or complexity in the room we're in right now for example. But the universe *is* simple on large, cosmological scales – more or less the same in one direction as in any other, more or less the same in one place as in any other.

The mottled map of the cosmic background radiation in Figure 3.5 illustrates this. In the beginning the universe was opaque, hot, and glowing. As it expanded it got cooler. A few hundred thousand years after the Big Bang the matter cooled to a temperature at which it was transparent. Light from that time has been propagating to us ever since, cooled to a temperature now of only a few degrees above absolute zero. This is the cosmic background radiation and a map of the temperature of the radiation in different directions, such as that in Figure 3.5, is the earliest picture we have of the universe.

The mottled map in Figure 3.5 may not look like evidence that the early universe was smooth, but the temperature difference between the light and dark regions is only 30 millionths of a degree. At the resolution of your eye the universe would look completely uniform at this time. The reason serious research on the initial condition at the Big Bang began only recently is that it is only recently that we have had cosmological observations like this that are detailed enough to reveal the regularities it governs.

3.4 Quantum mechanics

There is another way in which our vision of the fundamental laws and the nature of a theory of everything has changed since the times of Newton and Laplace. That is quantum mechanics. We don't yet know the final form the fundamental laws will take. But the inference is inescapable from the physics of the last seventy-five years that they will conform to that subtle framework of prediction we call quantum mechanics.

In quantum mechanics, any system – the universe included – is described by a wave function Ψ. There is a dynamical law called the Schrödinger equation that governs how the wave function changes in time

$$i\hbar\frac{d\Psi(t)}{dt} = H\Psi(t) \qquad \text{(dynamical law)}.$$

Here the operator H, called the Hamiltonian, summarizes the dynamical theory. There are different forms of H for Maxwell's electrodynamics, for a theory of the strong interactions, etc. Like Newton's laws of motion, the Schrödinger equation doesn't make any predictions by itself, it requires an initial condition. This is

$$\Psi(0), \qquad \text{(initial condition)}.$$

When we consider the universe as a quantum mechanical system, this initial condition is Hawking's wave function of the universe [2].

Probabilities are the key difference between classical and quantum mechanics. Let's first think about probabilities in classical physics. If I say that there is a 60% chance of hitting an audience member if I toss a ball in this room, I am not expressing a lack of confidence that its trajectory will be governed by the deterministic laws of Newtonian mechanics. Rather, the 60% reflects my ignorance of the exact initial speed I'll impart to the ball, of the influence of air on its motion, and perhaps my ability to do an accurate calculation. If I practice to control the initial condition when it's thrown, the subsequent evolution of the tennis ball becomes more certain. Probabilities in classical physics result from ignorance.

But in quantum mechanics probabilities are fundamental and uncertainty inevitable. No amount of careful determination of the present state of the tennis ball will achieve certainty for its trajectory. In quantum mechanics there is some probability that a ball will take *any* trajectory as it leaves my hand. However, in classical situations one trajectory – the one obeying Newton's laws – is much more probable than all the others. The determinism of classical physics is an approximation, but an approximation on which we can rely in many practical circumstances.

3.5 A theory of everything is not a theory of everything

My colleague Murray Gell-Mann used to ask me 'If you know the wave function of the universe, why aren't you rich?' A quantum mechanical theory of the Hamiltonian and the initial state *does* predict probabilities for every event that might happen in the universe. In that is one sense in which it is a 'theory of everything'. However, only a few things are predicted with near certainty. The vast majority of alternatives are predicted with approximately 50%–50% probabilities giving no useful information. That's the sense in which a 'theory of everything' is *not* a theory of everything.

We hope that the probability is high for the form of the effective dynamical theories that suffice to predict the outcomes of experiments done in every laboratory constructed so far. We also hope that a theory of everything predicts some large scale features of the universe with near certainty such as its approximate smoothness on large scales, the statistics of the distribution of galaxies illustrated in Figure 3.4, the vast disparity between the age of the universe and the time scales characterizing the fundamental dynamical theory, and so forth.

But it is too much to hope that an interesting probability like that for the FTSE to go up tomorrow is in this category. Since a rise tomorrow is an event in the history of the universe, a quantum mechanical probability could, in principle, be calculated for it from a theory of everything.

(Although I suspect that it is well beyond our present powers of computation.) But it's likely that, after all that work, the predicted probability would be 50% for an upward tick. That is why you can't get rich knowing the wave function of the universe, and that is why a theory of everything isn't a theory of everything.

But there is a deeper reason why a theory of everything doesn't explain everything – it's too short. Everyone with a PC knows that picture files are typically a lot longer than text files. The files for the undergraduate general relativity text that I am writing, for example, consists of roughly 1Mb of text and 100Mb of pictures. A very rough estimate is that it would take a billion, billion, billion, billion, billion, billion, billion, billion, billion (10^{81}) compact disks (CDs) to describe the visible universe at a reasonably coarse-grained level of classical description. And that is just at one moment in time! All the matter in the planets, stars, and galaxies in the visible universe would not be enough to make this number of CDs.

However, the description of the universe can be compressed because it exhibits regularities on large scales. Compression is an idea familiar from computation. When a large file exhibits regularities its length can be compressed. For instance, a string of 1000 zeros '00000000000000000000... 0000' in a file is a kind of regularity. It can be replaced by a shorter string '1000 zeros'. The regularities summarized by the laws of nature similarly permit compression. Rather than saying, 'cannonballs fall at 9.8 m/s^2, cats fall at 9.8 m/s^2, economics textbooks fall at 9.8 m/s^2, etc.', the laws of nature permit us to say '*everything* falls at 9.8 m/s^2 near the surface of the Earth'. That is shorter and therefore more useful. It is possible that everything we see, every detail of every leaf, every event in human history, every thought, is a long string which is compressible to a law implementable by a very short computer program. But there is no evidence that the universe exhibits such regularity, and even Laplace did not propose such a thing.

The initial condition of a deterministic classical theory that did not allow ignorance would have to be as detailed as a present description of the universe. It seems likely therefore that, were world governed by classical laws, it might take so many CDs to write out the law of its initial condition that we could never make the CDs to do it.

Let's contrast this situation in classical physics with Stephen's no-boundary quantum wave function of the universe. It's given by the following simple formula [2]

$$\Psi = \int \delta g \delta \phi e^{-I[g,\phi]}$$ $\begin{pmatrix} \text{The no-boundary wave} \\ \text{function of the universe} \end{pmatrix}$.

That's short! – maybe 45 LaTeX key strokes to write out. Furthermore, it's as complete a description of the initial condition as it is possible to have in quantum mechanics. It implies uncertainty but contains no ignorance. Presumably, the basic equations of the fundamental dynamical theory are similarly short.

You might think this a little misleading because I haven't said what Ψ means, what g means, and what $\int$ means, etc. But, even including the lengths of the ten or so texts that physics students read to understand what it all means, a maximum of 10 or 20 Mb would be needed to state the law – easily fitting on one CD. This means the law is the discoverable and implementable, applicable to every happening in the universe, but predicting the near certainty of only a *few* of its many regularities. A complete discoverable theory of everything is only possible in quantum mechanics where some things are predictable but not everything.

Before I left Santa Barbara to come to Cambridge, my colleague Steve Giddings asked me what I was going to talk about in this lecture. I said I would speak on the question 'What do we know if we have a theory of everything?' and answer it 'Not all that much.' He replied something like 'I hope you're going to say something more hopeful than that!' But it *is* a hopeful message. It is only because so little of the complexity of the present universe is predicted by the fundamental universal laws that we can discover them.

3.6 Reduction

Where do all the other regularities in the universe come from, those particular to specific systems – those of the behaviour of cats as they fall, those studied by the environmental sciences such as biology, geology, economics, and psychology? They are the results of chance events that occur naturally over the history of a quantum mechanical universe. As my colleague, Murray Gell-Mann puts it [6], they are *frozen accidents*: 'Chance events of which particular outcomes have a multiplicity of long-term consequences, all related by their common ancestry'.

The regularities of cats probably do depend a little bit on the fundamental physical laws, for example, an initial condition that is smooth across the universe, leads to three spatial dimensions, etc. But the origin of most of their regularities can be traced to the chance events of four billion years of biological evolution. Cats behave in similar ways because they have a common ancestry and develop in similar environments. The mechanisms that produce those chance events that led to cats are very much dependent on fundamental biochemistry and ultimately atomic physics. But the particular outcomes of those chances have little to do with the theory of everything.

Do psychology, economics, and biology reduce to physics? The answer is YES, because everything considered in those subjects must obey the universal, fundamental laws of physics. Every one of the subjects of study in these sciences – humans, market tables, historical documents, bacteria, cats, etc. – fall with the same acceleration in a gravitational field. The answer is NO, because the regularities of interest in these subjects are not predicted by the universal laws with near certainty *even in principle*. They are frozen quantum accidents that produce emergent regularities. The answer depends upon what you mean by reduce.

3.7 The main points again

I have always liked the part of the BBC news called 'The Main Points Again'. Here are my main points again:

- The fundamental laws of physics constituting a 'theory of everything' are those that specify the regularities exhibited by every physical system, without exception, without qualification, and without approximation.

- A theory of everything is not (and cannot be) a theory of everything in a quantum mechanical universe.

- If it's short enough to be discoverable, it's too short to predict everything.

- The regularities of human history, personal psychology, economics, biology, geology, etc. are consistent with the fundamental laws of physics, but do not follow from them.

But remember also, especially on this occasion, that all the beautiful regularities that we observe in the universe, certain or not, predictable or not, could be the result of quantum chances following from the fundamental dynamical theory and Hawking's no-boundary wave function of the universe.

Acknowledgement

The author's research was supported in part by the National Science Foundation under grant PHY00-70895.

References

[1] For example, see Dickey, J. O. *et al.* (1994), 'Lunar Laser Ranging: A Continuing Legacy of the Apollo Program', *Science* **265**, 482. Anderson, J. D.

and Williams, J. G. (2001), 'Long Range Tests of the Equivalence Principle', *Class. Quant. Grav.*, **18**, 2447.

[2] For example, see Hawking, S. W. (1984), 'The Quantum State of the Universe', *Nucl. Phys.* **B239**, 257.

[3] Colless, M., Dalton, G., Maddox, S., Sutherland, W. *et al.* (2001), 'The 2dF Galaxy Redshift Survey: Spectra and Redshifts', *MNRAS* **328**, 1039–1063.

[4] Laplace, P. S. (1951), *A Philosophical Essay on Probabilities*, translated from the 6th French edition, (Dover publications, New York).

[5] de Bernardis, P. *et al.* (2000), 'A Flat Universe from High-Resolution Maps of the Cosmic Microwave Background Radiation', *Nature* **404**, 955.

[6] Gell-Mann, M. (1994), *The Quark and the Jaguar* (W. Freeman, San Francisco).

4

The problem of spacetime singularities: implications for quantum gravity?

Roger Penrose

Mathematical Institute, University of Oxford

4.1 Introduction

It is certainly an honour for me to pay my respects to Stephen Hawking for his 60th birthday with this lecture. Yesterday I gave a talk at the workshop, thinking rather nervously that I would be tarred and feathered afterwards because I was going to say some things not altogether favourable about extra space dimensions – central to modern string theory. I also considered that I would rather be tarred and feathered than come to the view that people thought that these were just the ramblings of an old man and could therefore be ignored. With regard to Stephen, I am very glad to note that he has now also officially become an old man, so that he can also get away with saying such outrageous things. Of course Stephen has always done that kind of thing, but he can perhaps feel a little bolder in this even than before. And you can see I have managed to get all the tar and feathers off – plucked them out one by one and had a good bath. But what worries me now is that whereas what I said yesterday was new, in the sense that I had not said it before publicly, most of the things I want to say today I have said many times before. Yet they are perhaps even more outrageous than what I was saying yesterday.

4.2 Why quantum gravity?

I want to start by referring to the great revolutionary theories in physics of the 20th century (see Figure 4.1). First of all we have special relativity, which has to do with large velocities, giving deviations from Newtonian mechanics. And then we have quantum mechanics. Special relativity became generalized into general relativity where the spacetime, which brings space and time together into one four-dimensional framework, is

Fig. 4.1. Great theories of the twentieth century and their problems. [*From a transparency used in the lecture*]

now curved, the curvature being exactly what is required to describe gravitation. This is the amazing theory that Einstein introduced. Then one can bring special relativity and quantum mechanics together to create quantum field theory. Some of the most important fundamental contributions to this came from Dirac, and Dirac we know was one of the great physicists who previously held the chair that Stephen holds now. You see some wiggly lines going downwards in Figure 4.1. These refer to the fundamental problems encountered in these theories.

Of these, I first mention the singularities in classical general relativity; they tell us of fundamental difficulties in Einstein's classical theory. This issue arises in the Big Bang, where curvatures seem to go to infinity, and again in black holes. The natural move is to try to bring together the ideas of general relativity with those of quantum field theory, in order to make sense of physics in these extreme situations – and I am sure that this is right. However quantum field theory also has its problems and these have been around for a long time. If you do a calculation strictly according to the rules of quantum field theory, the first thing you come out with, almost always, is infinity. Infinity is not the right answer. We observe perfectly good finite answers. And this suggests that at some level, probably at some very tiny distance, the theory has to be modified. And the most popular idea about modification, whether it be string theory or ideas that go back much earlier due to Oskar Klein, is that there is in some sense a cut-off, or something more subtle, at the tiny distance referred to as the Planck scale. What we expect from the appropriate combination of general relativity with quantum field theory are changes in our very idea of space and time at these extremely tiny distances – some 20 orders of magnitude (20 powers of 10) smaller than the ordinary scales of fundamental particles.

Those of you who are perceptive will see another wiggly line going downwards in Figure 4.1. It does not come from quantum field theory but from quantum mechanics itself. It is sometimes referred to as the measurement problem – but that seems to me to be letting it off too lightly. It is the measurement paradox, and I shall be saying something about it shortly. Yet, there is the common view amongst physicists that once you have got your mind around quantum mechanics, then you can forget about the paradox. Many physicists seem to regard it as just a question of interpreting things right and that is all we need to do (although there are probably at least as many different interpretations of quantum mechanics as there are different quantum physicists – perhaps even more, because several quantum physicists have expressed contradictory views on this issue at different times in their lives, or maybe even at the same time!). But my own view that I want to try and put to you here is that not only are the first two of these problems – namely those gravitational singularities and infinities in quantum field theory – to be resolved by finding the right quantum gravity theory, but so also is the measurement paradox. Thus, once we have understood how gravity and quantum mechanics relate to each other, the measurement paradox will be resolved, but not until that time.

Am I really saying that the solution to all three problems is quantum gravity? In a sense, yes. We indeed need 'quantum gravity', but what do we mean by that term? Is quantum gravity the appropriate application of quantum field theoretic procedures to Einstein's general relativity, or perhaps to some modification of Einstein's theory? In string theory, for example, one uses higher dimensions; that is not really the original Einstein theory, but some modification of it. Moreover, although many attempts to quantize general relativity do use standard Einstein theory, the very act of quantization would involve changes to that theory. On the other hand, all these approaches take quantum field theory itself to be sacrosanct. Is this the right kind of way to think about quantum gravity or should we be looking for some more even-handed marriage, with some give on both sides? What we normally mean by 'quantum gravity' takes the rules of quantum field theory as inviolable – you do not monkey with them at all – and you apply them to some form of gravitational theory.

Almost never do people say that there should be some reaction back, altering the very structure of quantum field theory (or quantum mechanics). Of course, there is a good reason why people do not, because it is hard enough to apply even these rules to general relativity. If you have got to give up these very rules as well, where do you start? What on earth do you do? I appreciate that reason – it is a good reason. But in my view, it is not nearly a good enough reason!

4.3 The importance of singularities

I want to say a little bit more about the singularities. Figure 4.2 is my crude version of one of Martin Rees's slides, where one has the three basic models (where for simplicity I have taken the cosmological constant to be

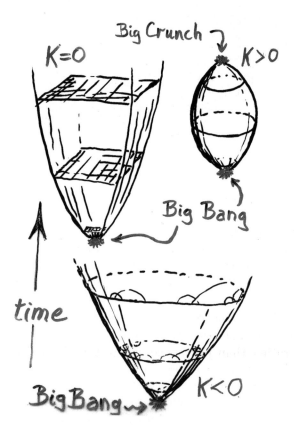

Fig. 4.2. Geometries of the three basic models of the universe and their singularities: flat $K = 0$ (upper left), positive curvature $K > 0$ (upper right) and negative curvature $K < 0$ (lower).

Fig. 4.3. Representation of hyperbolic space by M. C. Escher.

zero). There is the positive spatial curvature model with an initial Big Bang singularity, but it also has a final singularity where the universe comes back together again in what is called the big crunch. Or we might take the models with flat or negative-curvature spatial sections, which just have a singular Big Bang and then go on expanding indefinitely. Figure 4.3 is a beautiful picture due to M. C. Escher of a hyperbolic plane, which is (the two-dimensional version of) the geometry that you get for the spatial sections of the negative-curvature universe. Of course, Figure 4.3 depicts spacetime (with dimension reduced down from the actual four), rather than just space, where time is depicted as going up the picture and spatial sections (space at any given time) represented as horizontal slicings through the pictures. The Escher picture of Figure 4.3 provides one of the best ways of getting a feeling for the negatively curved spatial geometry. It is a very accurate and elegant description (in the two-dimensional case). Escher has also illustrated the spatially flat and positively curved models (see Figure 4.4), using basically the same angels and devils, as in Figure 4.3!

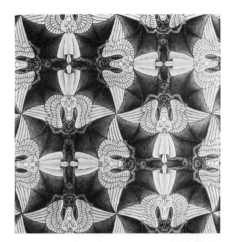 

Fig. 4.4. Escher print of flat space (left) and wood-carving of a positively curved space (right). [*Courtesy Cordon Art*]

Martin Rees was telling us that there are observations these days, which seem to indicate that we are living in a spatially flat universe. Of course we have to be very cautious about what people say in cosmology, and not only cosmology – this is true in any area – but there is another point I want to make here. Just the other day I heard people say how exciting it is that we live in an era where we shall soon actually know which of these models we are in; that is something that will only happen once, to know what the universe at its largest scales is like. But to me, this is the wrong way around. If observation tells us persuasively that we are in the closed model or the open hyperbolic model – yes, it would be an exciting time; we might well know what the universe is really like overall. But suppose that the universe is actually spatially flat on a large scale. Then, good direct observations could be consistent with that, but they could not tell us that our universe is the flat model. They could only tell us that if there is spatial curvature (which could be either positive or negative), then this curvature has less than such-and-such a value. No, we would have to wait goodness knows how long, perhaps for many centuries, until different kinds of theoretical techniques are developed that can convincingly tell us we have got to be in a flat space on the largest scales. To me this would be depressing, because it means we could not know from present-day observations which model we are in. The people saying how exciting it is to be living around now could be right, but only if the universe is actually negatively or positively spatially curved, with not too small a curvature.

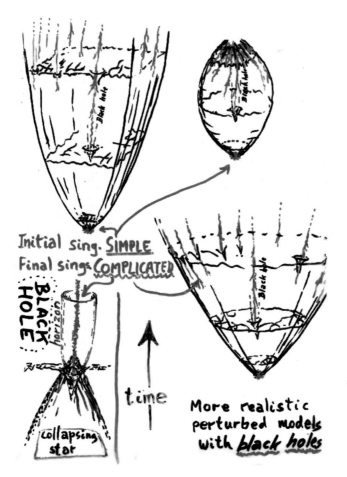

Initial sing. SIMPLE

Final sings COMPLICATED

BLACK HOLE

time

More realistic perturbed models with *black holes*

collapsing star

Fig. 4.5. The simple Friedmann models of Figure 4.2 with irregularities included. The formation of a black hole singularity is also shown (lower left).

There is another feature of this set of diagrams that I want to draw attention to now. The pictures in Figure 4.2 represent only the (zero-cosmological-constant) models of spacetime with all the irregularities removed, so one is talking about an idealized spacetime geometry without any irregularities. But if we introduce irregularities as shown in Figure 4.5 then, as Martin Rees pointed out, they will tend to clump and one eventually gets local singularities in the future of local observers. These are the singularities in black holes. So we do not just have the Big Bang singularity at the beginning but we have the singularities that come in black holes. The singularity theorems that Stephen and I found in the 1960s apply not just to the Big Bang but also to the singularities in black holes, and there seems to be no escape from them. If you take the closed recollapsing model, the singularities all come together in a great mess, but in the ever-expanding models they are more localized.

Another point I should make about the pictures in Figure 4.2 is that I have drawn them as though the Big Bang was just as in the original models of Friedmann, introduced very early in the history of cosmology and general relativity, whereas more recently people have introduced all sorts of ideas like inflationary cosmology and another theory which we have been hearing about in recent months, which has a Greek name which I always forget (ekpyrotic). Now, when I first heard about inflationary cosmology, I thought: 'Oh, well, that's all right – I do not need to understand it; that theory will have gone in a few months'. Again, I had this reaction when hearing this theory with the strange Greek name, but now perhaps I have learnt my lesson, that it will not have gone in a few months. Irrespective of what I believe about it, it will not go in that short period of time! But what I want to discuss in this talk is something that is a fundamental problem not just for conventional cosmology, it is a fundamental problem for inflationary cosmology and is, as far as I can see, an even worse problem for this new theory with the Greek name that I forget.

4.4 Entropy

Let me say something about the pictures in Figure 4.5. These pictures tell us – most blatantly in the closed recollapsing case – that we have a

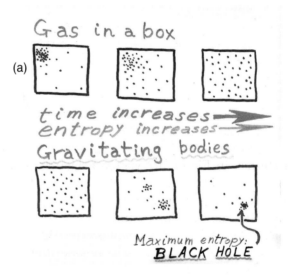

Fig. 4.6. Entropy or 'disorder' increases with time.

simple looking singularity at the beginning and a great mess at the end. It is not just that I drew these pictures myself, but they do illustrate something very fundamental about the evolution of the universe. This was also referred to in Martin Rees's talk, but let me just say it again in a slightly different way. It has to do with the second law of thermodynamics, which in rough terms says that the entropy increases with time, entropy referring in some sense to disorder. So the universe is getting more and more disordered. People used to refer to this as the 'heat death of the universe', using pictures rather like Figure 4.6a. You imagine a gas in a box. The gas may start, say, being tucked up in one corner, but as time evolves it spreads out more and more evenly, so the universe seems to get more and more boring. Time is increasing as you go from left to right in Figure 4.6, and entropy is increasing from left to right. This is consistent with the second law. But if you include gravitating bodies, then you find there is a tendency in the opposite direction. Starting with a nearly uniform distribution of bodies (where we may think of these as stars or something – gravitating bodies) we find that they start to clump and eventually they may form into a black hole. This is the way that the second law of thermodynamics works for gravitating bodies. In practice one has both tendencies going on together (Figure 4.6a and Figure 4.6b together), which I think gives us a picture of something getting more and more interesting! So I regard this as a more optimistic view.

One of the great contributions that Stephen Hawking made – building on earlier work by Bekenstein, but Hawking's argument was much more refined – is that one is able to assign an actual value to the entropy of a black hole which is directly proportional to the surface area of the horizon of the hole. This is a very remarkable formula. It tells us, in detailed terms, that the entropy that one gets when bodies collapse into black holes is enormously larger than the other entropies that we find in the universe. So, in the universe that we see today, by far the greatest entropy is in black holes. For a time, people worried about how very high the entropy was in the cosmic microwave background radiation, but it is chicken feed compared with the entropy that one finds in black holes.

Just a remark to say something about how this relates to entropy in more familiar terms, in Figure 4.7 we see a picture of the Sun and the background dark sky, and plants growing on the Earth and so on. People often say: 'Well, isn't it nice the Sun is there, because we get all this energy from it'. But energy is conserved, and as much energy goes back into space from the Earth as comes in from the Sun. Perhaps a little bit more, because the Earth produces its own heat, but basically it is the same. So we do not get energy from the Sun, but the Sun is vital to us. What we do get is energy in a low entropy form, and this has to do with

Fig. 4.7. Life on Earth exists because the Sun is a bright spot in a dark sky.

the fact that the Sun is a bright spot in an otherwise dark sky, and the energy we get from the Sun – visible light – is in the form of relatively small numbers of photons, small numbers of degrees of freedom, and the energy that feeds back into space is infrared and each individual photon is much less energetic, so there have to be many many more photons to carry this same energy away: the energy is spread over many more degrees of freedom. This is basically what is involved.

The low-entropy energy we get – basically it is what we live off – results from the entropy imbalance in the sky. If the entire sky were illuminated to the temperature of the Sun, it would be totally useless to us. We can only take advantage of a temperature imbalance. In Figure 4.7 we have the Sun as a very bright spot in a dark sky. But where does that imbalance come from? Well, where does the Sun come from? Why is the Sun there at all? The Sun is a hot spot in a dark sky ultimately because of gravitational clumping. If there were no gravity there would be no Sun and therefore no hot spot. We live off the fact that there was a very uniform distribution initially, this representing a very low entropy state (with regard to gravity). Entropy then increases via gravitational clumping. This is the key ingredient in the discussion. The creation of the Sun was just one, almost incidental, instance of this entropy raising process, albeit the crucial one that we live off.

The point I want to stress here is something I have been saying for many years. Yet I doubt that people have taken it on board sufficiently, even now. It is best illustrated by the closed model in Figure 4.5 – not that I think the universe is likely to be closed, but here we most clearly see the gross difference in singularity structure between the beginning and end. Remember what quantum gravity was 'for', in this context: we were trying to resolve the singularity problem (Figure 4.1). Indeed, this always was our main 'excuse' for wasting so much time trying to find the appropriate quantum gravity theory! Actually it is a very important reason for physics as a whole, because the past/future difference in space-time singularity structure underlies the Second Law of thermodynamics. There is a very different structure at the beginning – at the Big Bang – from the kind of structure we find in a black hole's singularity. This can be made quantitative by saying that the singularities at late times are of generic type, where the measure of curvature called Weyl curvature diverges to infinity, while on the other hand the Weyl curvature seems to be constrained to be essentially zero at the Big Bang. This initial constraint is actually enormous. Calculations show that the chance of it having arisen purely by chance is less than about 1 in $10^{(10^{123})}$. If one takes the view that the sought-for 'quantum gravity theory' is just the imposition of standard quantum field theory on standard general relativity, each being time-symmetric, one finds it very hard to see how to get this extraordinary time-asymmetry. Yet this asymmetry is an actual feature of our universe. How do we find the appropriate asymmetric theory?

4.5 Hawking radiation and information loss

As a further comment, I refer to another of Stephen's great contributions, having to do with black hole evaporation (refer to Figure 4.8). What he observed was that black holes do not just have an entropy given by a very clear geometric formula but, consistently with that, they have a temperature. This temperature is very, very tiny for black holes that we expect to arise astrophysically, but if you wait for long enough – and supposing we are in an ever-expanding universe – then there will come a time when the ambient temperature in the universe is less than even the very tiny temperature of the black hole. The hole will start to evaporate; energy will be carried away. Accordingly, it shrinks and shrinks, the Hawking temperature rising until the hole finally explodes with a 'pop' (rather than a 'bang', because by astrophysical standards it is a pretty trivial explosion) (Figure 4.8).

I am bringing this up not because I think we are going to have to contend with these things observationally; the problem is a theoretical one. What happens to the large amount of information contained in the hole (in the sense of phase space volume)? Almost all the (very considerable) information in the collapsing matter seems to get lost, with only a tiny

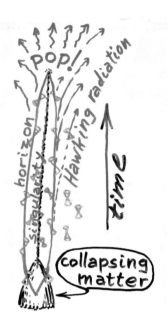

Fig. 4.8. The demise of a black hole through Hawking radiation.

pop's worth of information coming out at the end. Is the information concerning the details of the collapse lost altogether from the universe? Or is it nevertheless somehow finally retrieved in the pop? Or perhaps it is retained in some final nugget – or 'remnant', as people sometimes refer to this? I should say that this issue is an argument still going on and on among various physicists and there is no generally agreed answer.

Now, Stephen originally maintained (and I believe still does) that the information is lost. You can actually separate this 'lost' idea into two alternatives – weakly lost or strongly lost. He and I still argue about this, but we are certainly both on the 'information-lost' side, at least we used to be. (I suppose it is possible that Stephen has changed his mind since I last read something of his on this topic.) I certainly think his original reasoning is very powerful. It is very hard to see how one is going to get the information back in this final pop, and there are all sorts of problems with the nugget idea. So this suggests that the normal rules of quantum mechanics, as we understand them, have to be broadened in some way. There is the difference between the 'weakly' and 'strongly' here. Stephen has a rather minimal modification, whereas I believe we need to look for something much more drastic. The drastic thing that I believe we need to look for, in my opinion, is the same thing that is needed to resolve the measurement paradox.

4.6 The measurement paradox

I shall have to make a remark or two about how quantum mechanics is viewed. Figure 4.9 is supposed to indicate the overall picture of how our theories relate to the physical world. Either we do physics on a large scale, in which case we use classical-level physics: the equations of Newton, Maxwell, or Einstein, and these equations are deterministic, time-symmetrical and local. Or we may do quantum theory, if we are looking at small things; then we tend to use a different framework, where time-evolution is described by what is called unitary evolution. I use **C** for classical time-evolution, and **U** to describe unitary evolution. In one of the most familiar descriptions, **U** is described by the Schrödinger equation, and I have used some words to describe evolution according to the Schrödinger equation: deterministic, time-symmetrical and local. These are exactly the same words that I used for classical physics. So this might suggest that the actual evolution of the world must be like this. But there is a problem, because this is not the entire story about how we do quantum physics. In addition, we require what is called the 'reduction of the state-vector' or 'collapse of the wavefunction' to describe the procedure that is adopted when an effect is magnified from the quantum to the classical level. I use the letter **R** for that, and I have used some words for this procedure in Figure 4.9: non-deterministic, time-asymmetrical and non-local. So, although we have words for **U** and **C**, which seem to be the

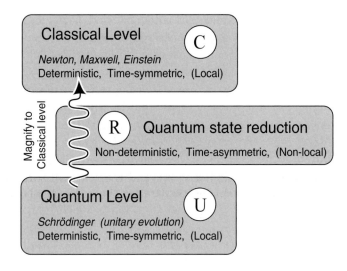

Fig. 4.9. The relationship between classical and quantum physics.

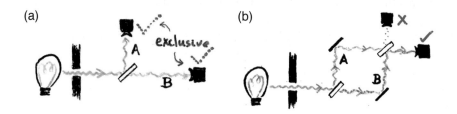

Fig. 4.10. Two configurations demonstrating wave–particle duality.

same, we have a completely different set of procedures (**R**) that we adopt for bridging from one level to the other.

Let me just give you one example, the case of a Geiger counter. Suppose the Geiger counter is entered by a quantum particle – this being a **U** object – and then there is some magnification process that carries you from the **U**-level to the **C**-level, so the Geiger counter makes a click which you can hear, the click being a **C**-level thing. It is in this process of going from the **U** level to the **C** level that you adopt this other procedure **R**, which is of a completely different nature from either **U** or **C**.

I do not have the time here to make any attempt to try and address the various viewpoints that people hold, and their ways of coming to terms with this (seeming?) discrepancy. But the measurement paradox basically is clear from this example. A Geiger counter, after all, is a physical thing made up out of atoms, molecules and this and that, and these things are individually quantum-level objects. So how can it behave in a way so different from that of the quantum-level ingredients of which it is supposed to be constructed? That is the paradox.

Now, perhaps a quick word about the details of quantum theory itself, although I do not have a great deal of time, and quantum theory you cannot explain in two minutes very well, but I am going to try. People talk about the wave–particle duality of quantum mechanics and the contradictions between the co-existing wave and particle pictures. They are illustrated here in the two very idealized experiments shown in Figure 4.10. On the left of each picture we have the source of a particle (say a photon) – think of the source as a lamp which emits photons one at a time. In the centre we have what is called a beam-splitter; think of it as a 'half-silvered mirror': half the light is reflected, half transmitted. The particle picture is illustrated (a) by having detectors at A and B, so either one or the other responds, in the idealized situation, but not both. If detector A does, then B will not. If B does, then A will not. So the photon behaves like a particle. On the other hand (b), suppose we also

have two fully silvered mirrors, at A and B, and another beam splitter on
the upper right, where detectors X and Y measure the alternatives for the
particle emerging from the beam splitter. Let us suppose that the path
lengths are all equal. Then you find that the two possible routes that the
photon might follow cancel out mysteriously at the detector X. But the
routes reinforce at the detector Y. Thus, it is always Y that receives the
photon; X never does. You could understand this if you think of waves,
with interference between waves and so on, but how do you make sense
of both these pictures (Figure 4.10a,b) at once? That is the wave-particle
duality problem.

The way we do quantum mechanics is to adopt a strange procedure
which always seems to work, that the two alternatives as illustrated in
Figure 4.10b actually co-exist in a kind of superposition. They both happen, in a sense, at once. You might try to think of these as being just
probability weighted alternatives

$$w \times (\text{alternative A}) + z \times (\text{alternative B}), \tag{4.1}$$

where w and z are numbers representing the alternative probabilities.
But we can't really look at it this way because the numbers cannot be
probabilities. Probabilities have to be real numbers between 0 and 1. Our
numbers w and z are not real numbers; they are complex numbers. (These
are numbers involving the square root of -1. The use of such numbers is an
essential ingredient of the Schrödinger equation and of many other aspects
of quantum mechanics.) They just sit there – and we can use a description
in which they do not change at all, as the **U**-evolution takes place. I will
say more about that in a moment. But then, when you magnify to the
classical level, you do the **R** thing (Figure 4.9); you take what is called
the squared moduli $|w|^2$, $|z|^2$ of these numbers, and these do give you the
relative probabilities of the two alternatives to happen. It is a completely
different process from **U**, where the (complex) numbers w and z remain
as constants 'just sitting there'.

In fact, the key to what I mean by keeping them sitting there is what
is called quantum linearity. In Figure 4.11 we have the two possible
alternatives for what might happen to a photon emerging from a beam-
splitter. In one case we have, say, the photon coming vertically from the
beam splitter and running into something and producing a whole lot of
stuff. On the other hand, it might have come out horizontally, running
into something else and producing a different lot of stuff. Quantum linearity says that if you have a superposition to start with, as the particle
emerges from the beam splitter, then this will result in the corresponding
superposition of these two 'stuffs'. And it does not matter how big these
alternatives are, you still get a superposition of the two of them.

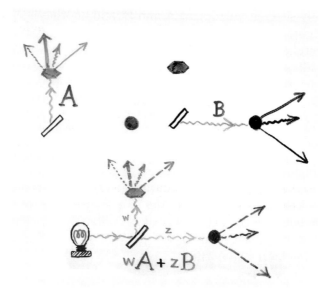

Fig. 4.11. The principle of superposition in quantum mechanics.

This leads us directly to Schrödinger's problem with his cat (Figure 4.12). The two alternatives that result from the emergence of the photon from the beam splitter are now a dead cat and the same cat alive. I should say, it was not Schrödinger's actual cat; it was only a theoretical cat, a 'thought cat' – although people sometimes accuse Schrödinger (or me) of being inhumane! I indeed wish to emphasize that this is merely a thought cat. Now the superposition of the two alternative things that individually might happen are the activating, or not, of an evil device for killing our (thought) cat. Because of the linearity just described, these two alternative things which might happen (dead cat or live cat) co-exist in superposition. That is what the **U**-evolution of quantum theory tells us; it is what the Schrödinger equation tells us. If we try to think that **U**-evolution is the only evolution that takes place in the actual world, we

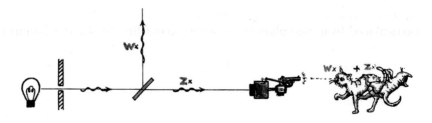

Fig. 4.12. Schrödinger's cat.

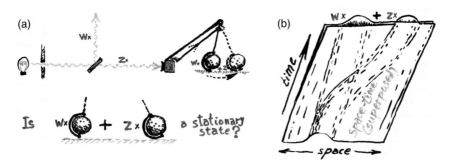

Fig. 4.13. (a) A lump put into a quantum superposition, (b) the spacetime description of this.

would indeed get the superposition of a dead cat and a live cat. But we do not see such things. Instead, we must bring in **R**. How can we get away with doing this, when systems are supposed to evolve according to **U**? This is just the measurement paradox, in a dramatic form.

My own view is that quantum theory is an approximate theory and we have to seek some new theory which supplants all three procedures – the **U**, the **R** and the **C** – that that we know today. And as I said before, there are all sorts of viewpoints on this and lots of people would not agree with me on how to resolve the measurement issue, but nevertheless it seems to me that a new theory is where we are driven. I think that this is very exciting, because it means there is a revolution in physics waiting in the wings of a quite fundamental character, more fundamental than any of the ideas that people have put forward, including things such as string theory, all these funny theories of Greek names that I cannot remember, and so on. So, is there any chance of being able to see whether this is right? Well, I think there is a good chance. In Figure 4.13a, I have mollified those people who complained of me (or Schrödinger) as being inhumane; I have now got rid of the thought cat by replacing it with a thought lump. We have a photon doing just the same as before. If it goes vertically the lump remains in its original position; if it goes the horizontally, the lump gets displaced from one place to another. According to standard quantum mechanics, the state of the object afterwards is a linear superposition of these two positions. It is just a feature of this very fundamental principle of linearity in quantum theory.

Let us consider a little more carefully what is going on in Figure 4.13b. I am now using a spacetime picture, with time going vertically upwards. The space will be initially slightly distorted by the presence of the lump, according to Einstein's theory. Time evolves and you can see the distortion caused by this initial location of the lump, and also by the alternative second location, with the lump moving off to somewhere else. You will notice that in this picture there is now a superposition between two different spacetimes – and that is what quantum gravity is all about. If you work in the subject of quantum gravity, at least according to one of those schools of thought in quantum gravity where you actually worry about these problems, then you are led to some very sophisticated types of ideas about how a space of spaces can be used to describe superpositions between spacetimes.

My own position on this is that we have to worry about the basic principles that Einstein has told us to worry about in general relativity, and one of these which Jim Hartle was very correctly emphasizing very much – is illustrated in Figure 4.14a. Here we see Galileo (or somebody) dropping a big rock and a little rock from the leaning tower of Pisa. Galileo probably did not consider an insect sitting on the bigger rock, but here I have drawn this insect looking at the smaller rock, and to this insect that rock seems to hover as though there were no gravity. This is now a

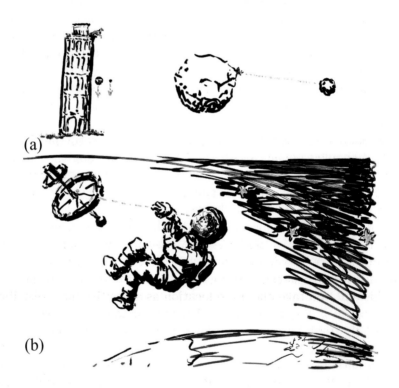

Fig. 4.14. The principles of equivalence and general covariance.

familiar feature of space travel (Figure 4.14b). Gravity seems to disappear once you fall freely with it, which is Einstein's fundamental Principle of Equivalence. I want to use something which is equally fundamental to Einstein's theory and which comes about when you try to construct a theory which takes the Principle of Equivalence as its cornerstone, namely the Principle of General Covariance. One of its implications is that no physical meaning can be attached to any particular labelling of spacetime points. In Figure 4.13b, with the quantum-superposed lumps, one has to worry about the Principle of General Covariance in the superposition. Does it make any sense to make a pointwise identification of the spaces? This is sort of question you have to ask, with this kind of situation.

I am supposing that each one of the lump positions is a stationary state, so the lump has to sit there forever, in either location, according to the rules of quantum mechanics. But is the entire superposition really going to sit there forever according to the rules of quantum mechanics? Even just to say what that means, you have to know what it means for a state to be stationary, and that refers to one of the equations that Jim Hartle did not want to tell you about. He had an operator of time-evolution in his equation $(i\partial/\partial t)$ and I will not tell you about it either. But the point about it is that to describe the physics of the superposition you need to know what the time-evolution operator means. And to know what that operator means you need to know what the spacetime is like, and here you do not have a spacetime, you have a superposition of two space-times. And to make sense of that, you are confronted with the Principle of General Covariance.

This seems to me a thing that one has to face up to: we should not identify each point in one spacetime with a corresponding one in the other spacetime, so as to get a single space. We do not have a single spacetime, so we do not really have a time-evolution operator. But suppose we say 'well, all right, let's try to do our best' and, just for the moment, we do try to identify the two spacetimes. Then we try to estimate how much error is involved in doing that. We find a certain expression for this error, which I call E_G, which can be identified with the gravitational self-energy of the difference between the mass distributions in the two states. To work this out, you take one lump location as a positive mass distribution and the other as a negative mass distribution; that is, you subtract one mass distribution from the other. Then you work out this thing called the gravitational self-energy of this difference mass distribution, and you get E_G. You find E_G is a very, very tiny energy, but this tiny energy is the crucial thing. It is the fundamental measure of energy uncertainty in the superposition.

4.7 Testing quantum gravity?

Now, usually people think that when you start to bring gravity and quantum mechanics together, the relevant quantities are going to be so tiny that it is only finicky people who are going to worry about them. Surely, such a small energy as E_G is not going to have any effect on what we see in the actual world. But there is a point that I want to emphasize in the definition of E_G. This E_G is a fundamental uncertainty in energy and I am saying that it is something like the fundamental uncertainty in the energy of a uranium nucleus. There is a thing called the Heisenberg uncertainty principle, specifically the time/energy uncertainty, which says that if you have something like an unstable particle, with a certain life-time, then the reciprocal of that, roughly speaking, is an energy uncertainty. Well, here I am reading this the other way round. I am saying that if I have an energy uncertainty which is fundamental, then the reciprocal of that, in units of $\hbar$, will be a measure of the lifetime of that state. So I am saying that this superposition will not sit there forever. It will sit there for a certain length of time. And that length of time can actually be computed, and worked out for individual systems. And although, as I said, it is a very, very tiny energy, when we work out the time scale for the superposition to decay, we find that we have Planck's constant on the top and E_G on the bottom. Each of these things is very tiny, in ordinary terms, but when we divide one by the other, we can get something of a reasonable size! When people working in quantum gravity encounter 'very tiny scales' they usually refer to the exceedingly small Planck length or Planck time, but these are small because, in effect, they come from multiplying two very small things together: Planck's constant and Newton's gravitational constant. But with the time scales considered here, these two small constants are divided rather than multiplied. So you need to be jolly careful to see whether the predicted effect is significant or not. And if you are careful, you find that you may well have to worry about it.

In fact, with some colleagues at Oxford (Dik Bouwmeester, Will Marshall, and Christoph Simon), a plausible experiment to test these ideas is being developed. So let me end by outlining the basic ideas of this experiment. (Perhaps you think it is odd that a theoretician like me should get involved with an experiment – well, perhaps it is odd, but it is all right if you have good colleagues and they can do all the real work. I just stand back and try to guess what I think might happen.) The experiment involves constructing a Schrödinger's cat or, rather, a Schrödinger's lump, but where the 'lump' is a very tiny thing in everyday terms, although huge as a quantum object. It is a little mirror about the size of a speck of dust. And you want to put this mirror into a superposition of two slightly

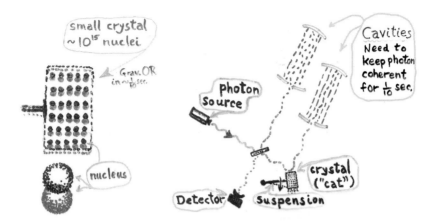

Fig. 4.15. Apparatus to test quantum mechanics.

different locations, displaced by about a nuclear diameter. I should mention that part of the idea came in discussions with Johannes Dapprich nearly ten years ago. Later Anton Zeilinger and his group in Innsbruck provided a lot of input. I initially thought that they would think the idea to be totally impractical and that they would laugh me out of court, but in fact they took it very seriously as a possibility. I would say 'What about this problem, this problem, and that problem?' They tended to reply along the lines: 'Oh yes, I think we can handle that'. Eventually I got the jargon right. When they say: 'I think we can handle that', what they mean is, maybe in about 15 years we will have the technology able to cope with this situation of yours.

I am sure it will still take quite a long time, but the proposal is to have something like that shown in Figure 4.15. I don't really want to talk about details here, but you have a photon source – very much like the sorts of things I have been talking about before – and there is a beam splitter that splits the photon into two routes. If it goes to the right, it slightly displaces the mirror, just as with my lump of material in Figure 4.13a. The displacement is only by about a nuclear diameter. Subsequently, you have to keep these two parts of the photon coherently, without losing coherence in environmental decoherence (bearing in mind all sorts of other problems that might be encountered), for the length of time that I consider you need to test whether quantum mechanics will come through unscathed or whether something like the state-reduction ideas that I am promoting will come into play. In fact you have to keep it in this superposed state for something like a tenth of a second. This might not be too bad, were it not for the fact that this photon has to be an X-ray photon in order to give the tiny crystal a sufficient kick. How do you keep an X-ray photon coherent for a tenth of a second? Well, one possibility is to do the whole thing out in space and then you can send a photon from one space platform to another, basically undisturbed. If these platforms are something like an Earth-diameter apart, it will take about a tenth of a second, there and back. A problem here is getting NASA or somebody organized to do things like that, and getting people who know about the right kind of details to do the things you want and so on, which I am not good at. There is also the more physical problem that you have to get X-ray reversing mirrors sitting an Earth-diameter apart, and you have to aim an X-ray photon, which has just been reflected off a little dust-size mirror, at another mirror, an Earth-diameter away, and that presents really fundamental problems.

Fortunately Will Marshall, Dik Bouwmeester and Christoph Simon have come up with some ingenious ideas that seem to enable the needed X-ray energies to be achieved with an ordinary visible-light photon, but reflected about a million times backwards and forwards between the crystal and much larger fixed mirror of a special kind. The problem is now converted into the issue of releasing the photon at the right moment. My colleagues have all sorts of clever ideas about how you might do this. It is very much work in progress, but the problems have now moved into areas of practical technology.

It will obviously be some years before they can get an experiment like this going at the level where the above considerations begin to come into play, but to me it would be extremely interesting. It would indicate whether quantum mechanics comes through unscathed as it always has in the past, or whether there is some modification that is going to come in when one starts to worry seriously about how general relativity and quantum mechanics actually fit together. We know that general relativity has got to be changed – small distances are not going to look exactly like what we know about at ordinary scales. But what about quantum mechanics? I think that it is very probable that there will be changes also in the structure of quantum mechanics and that these changes will enable us to resolve the measurement paradox. This is because in any measuring device, say a cat or a Geiger counter, the reduction time would be almost instantaneous. These behave like a classical objects, whereas the things which do not involve nearly as much mass displacement would behave as quantum objects. So one would have a consistent picture in which the quantum and classical levels can co-exist and where there would also be a bridging level involving quite new physical and mathematical ideas. Thus, all of **C**, **U** and **R** would be (excellent) approximations to some new, fully consistent overall scheme. As I said before, I am very optimistic. I do not know what this new theory is, but at least it could be something which somebody out there somewhere will maybe come up with in a reasonable time. I do not know when, but it would be nice to be alive when that happens.

Acknowledgements

The author is grateful to NSF for support under Contract 0090091 and to the Leverhulme Foundation for an Emeritus Fellowship.

Useful references for further reading

[1] Bell, J. S. (1966), *Speakable and Unspeakable in Quantum Mechanics* (Cambridge University Press, Cambridge; reprint 1987).

[2] Penrose, R. (1989), *The Emperor's New Mind: Concerning Computers, Minds, and the Laws of Physics* (Oxford University Press, Oxford).

[3] Penrose, R. (1996), 'On gravity's role in quantum state reduction', *Gen. Rel. Grav.* **28**, 581–600.

[4] Penrose, R. (2000), 'Wavefunction collapse as a real gravitational effect', in *Mathematical Physics 2000*, eds A. Fokas, T. W. B. Kibble, A. Grigouriou, and B. Zegarlinski (Imperial College Press, London), 266–282.

[5] Rindler, W. (2001), *Relativity: Special, General, and Cosmological* (Oxford University Press, Oxford).

5

Warping spacetime

Kip Thorne

California Institute of Technology, Pasadena

5.1 Introduction

It is a great honor and pleasure to lecture here on Stephen's sixtieth birthday. And it's a special pleasure to be sandwiched, in the speaking schedule, between Roger Penrose and Stephen, because I shall talk about plans for testing the amazing theoretical predictions that Stephen, Roger and others made about black holes during the Golden Age of black-hole research, the era from the mid 1960s to the mid 1970s.

But let me begin with an earlier era – with Albert Einstein, who in 1915 gave us general relativity. General relativity is Einstein's law of gravity, his explanation of that fundamental force which holds us to the surface of the Earth. Gravity, Einstein asserted, is caused by a warping of space and time – or, in a language we physicists prefer, by a warping of *spacetime*. The Earth's matter produces the warpage, and that warpage in turn is manifest by gravity's inward tug, toward the Earth's center.

The inward tug is not the only manifestation of spacetime warpage; the warpage is much richer than that. As we shall see, it curves space, it slows the flow of time, and it drags space into tornado-like motions – at least that is what Einstein's general relativity predicts.

In early 1916, only a few months after Einstein formulated his mathematical laws of warped spacetime, Karl Schwarzschild discovered the following mathematical solution to Einstein's general relativity equations:

$$ds^2 = -\left(1 - \frac{2M}{r}\right) dt^2 + \frac{dr^2}{1 - 2M/r} + r^2(d\theta^2 + \sin^2\theta d\phi^2). \qquad (5.1)$$

At first sight, this appears to be a rather complicated formula, but as physics formulae go, it's actually quite simple.

Fig. 5.1. Einstein a few years before formulating general relativity. [*Courtesy Albert Einstein Archives of the Hebrew University of Jerusalem*]

Physicists realized rather quickly that this formula seems to describe an object that has 'cut itself off' from the rest of the universe, an object to which John Wheeler, many decades later, would give the name *black hole*. But physicists could not believe such an outlandish interpretation of the math. For nearly fifty years the world's leading physicists, including Einstein himself, fought mightily against this concept of an object cut off from the universe. It was only in the early 1960s, as the culmination of a long intellectual struggle, that they gave in; that they finally accepted what the math seemed to be saying.

To help me explain what the math says, I have brought a black hole with me (see Figure 5.3). I normally carry my own black hole on the aeroplane when I travel, but with airline security so tight in the wake of 9/11, I've had to borrow one from Trinity College. If it really were a black hole, this Trinity black hole would be made not from matter, but entirely from a warpage of spacetime.

One way to understand that warpage is to compare the hole's circumference with its diameter. Normally, of course, the ratio of a circumference to a diameter is equal to π, which is approximately 3. But for a black hole,

Fig. 5.2. Karl Schwarzschild, who discovered the solution to Einstein's equations which describes a nonspinning black hole. [*Courtesy AIP Emilio Segrè Visual Archives*]

in fact, this ratio is much smaller than 3. The hole's circumference is tiny compared with its diameter.

We can understand this by a simply analogy. We begin with a rubber sheet (a child's trampoline) with edges held high in the air by long poles. Onto the trampoline we place a heavy rock, which stretches the trampoline's centre downward a great distance as shown in the left panel of Figure 5.4. Now, suppose that you are an ant living on this rubber sheet; the sheet is your entire universe. Suppose, moreover, that you are a blind ant, so you can't see what is warping your universe. However, you can easily measure the warpage. By marching around the rim you can measure its circumference, and by marching down through the centre you can measure its diameter. You thereby discover that the circumference is tiny compared with the diameter, in violation of Euclid's laws of plane geometry.

How is this possible? Being people outside the trampoline, and not really blind ants, we know the cause: the rock has warped the trampoline's rubber, just as something has warped the space of a black hole.

Fig. 5.3. The author holding a black hole – actually, a Trinity College bowling ball.

This, in fact, is an excellent analogy. Consider an equatorial slice through the black hole. What is the geometry of that slice? If the hole's space were 'flat' like the space that most people think we live in, the slice's geometry would be the same as that of a flat sheet of paper. But the hole's space is not flat; it is warped, so the slice must also be warped. We can visualize its warpage by pretending we are higher-dimensional beings who live in a higher-dimensional flat space, in which the warpage occurs. Science fiction writers call this higher-dimensional space *hyperspace*.

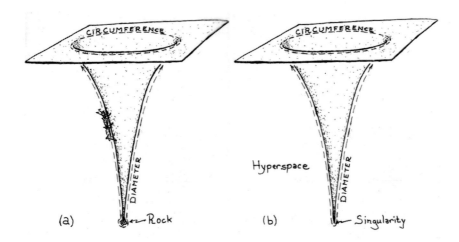

Fig. 5.4. A rubber sheet warped by a heavy stone (left) is an excellent analogy for a black hole's warped space (right).

Hypothetical hyperbeings in hyperspace could examine the hole's equatorial slice and discover it has the form shown in the right half of Figure 5.4.

Notice that the warped shape of the hole's space, as seen by a hyperbeing in hyperspace, is identical to the warped shape of the trampoline as seen by people in ordinary space. In both cases, circumferences are much smaller than diameters, and smaller by the same amount.

At the trampoline's centre there is a rock. At the hole's centre there is a *singularity* like those discussed by Roger in his lecture. It is the rock's weight that warps the trampoline. Similarly, one might suspect, it is the singularity's mass that warps the black hole's space. Not so, it turns out. The hole's space is warped by the enormous energy of its warpage. Warpage begets warpage in a *non-linear* self-bootstrapping manner that is a fundamental feature of Einstein's general relativity laws.

This does not happen in our solar system. The warpage of space throughout our solar system is so weak that the energy of warpage is miniscule, far too small to produce much self-bootstrapped warpage. Almost all the warpage in our solar system is produced directly by matter – the Earth's matter, the Sun's matter, the matter of the other planets.

Now, the most well known property of a black hole is not its warped space, but rather its trapping power, as depicted in the left panel of Figure 5.5. If I fall into a black hole carrying a microwave transmitter,

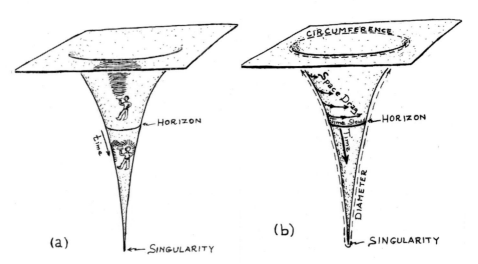

Fig. 5.5. (a) Kip falling into a black hole and trying to transmit microwave signals to you on the outside. (b) The curvature of space, the warping of time, and the dragging of space into a tornado-like motion around a spinning black hole.

say, then once I pass through a location called the hole's *horizon*, I am inexorably pulled on downward, into the singularity at its centre. Any signals that I try to transmit get pulled down with me, so nobody above the horizon can ever see the signals I send.

By 1964, when the Golden Age began, we knew that the warpage of spacetime around a black hole is actually rather complicated (right panel of Figure 5.5). There are three aspects to the warpage: first, there's the curvature of space, which I've been talking about. Second, there's a warping of time. The flow of time slows to a crawl near the horizon, and beneath the horizon time becomes so highly warped that it flows in a direction you would have thought was spatial: it flows downward towards the singularity. That downward flow, in fact, is why nothing can escape from a black hole. Everything is always drawn inexorably towards the future, and since the future inside the hole is downward, away from the horizon, nothing can escape back upward, through the horizon.

The third aspect of the warpage was discovered by Roy Kerr in 1963: black holes can spin, just as the Earth spins, and a hole's spin drags space around it into a vortex-type, whirling motion. Like the air in a tornado, space whirls fastest near the hole's center, and the whirl slows as one moves outward, away from the hole. Anything that falls toward the hole's horizon gets dragged, by the whirl of space, into a whirling motion around and around the hole, like an object caught and dragged by a tornado's wind. Near the horizon there is no way whatsoever to protect oneself against this whirling drag.

These three aspects of spacetime warpage – the curvature of space, the slowing and distortion of time, and the whirl of space – are all described by mathematical formulae. Einstein's equations, in the hands of Schwarzschild and Kerr, have predicted the curvature, distortion and whirl unequivocally. They are the essence of a black hole; they are what a black hole is made of.

As I proceed with this lecture, until nearly the end when I return to Roger's topic of singularities, I will depict only the the warped spacetime *outside the hole's horizon* (right panel of Figure 5.5). The reason is that, once anything enters the horizon, it can't send signals back out; so there is no way for us to observe or probe the inside of a hole from the outside. Since I will talk about probing black holes with solar-system-based instruments, I will be limited to probing down to the horizon, but no further.

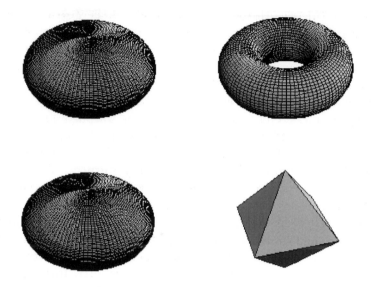

Fig. 5.6. Two of Stephen's predictions from the Golden Age. Top: the horizon of a quiescent black hole has spherical topology. Bottom: if the quiescent hole is spinning, then its horizon is circularly symmetric.

5.2 A first glimpse of the Golden Age: 1964–74

In 1964, as the Golden Age dawned, Stephen, Roger, I, and our compatriots were young, just finishing graduate school or recently finished. Roy Kerr had recently discovered that black holes can spin, John Wheeler had not yet named them, and the laws that govern them were still a mystery. The unfolding of that mystery in the Golden Age was wonderful, and Stephen and Roger were the leaders in revealing its wonders.

One of Stephen's most important contributions was to predict mathematically, using Einstein's equations, a fundamental property of every *quiescent black hole* – every hole whose shape is constant, unchanging. The horizon of a quiescent black hole, Stephen predicted, must have spherical topology; it cannot have a ring-like topology like the surface of a donut or bagel or tea cup (top half of Figure 5.6). All topologies are forbidden except that of a sphere's surface. And if the black hole is spinning but has constant, unchanging shape, Stephen predicted, then that shape must be *circularly symmetric* around its spin axis, like the shape of a spinning top. In other words, all the horizon's horizontal cross-sections must be circular, and not square or triangular or any other shape (bottom half of Figure 5.6). The reason, roughly speaking, is that, if the hole had any other shape, then as it spins, the tornado-like whirl of space would create outgoing ripples of spacetime warpage in its vicinity, just as a whirling brick in a pond of water creates ripples on the pond's surface; and those ripples would carry energy and angular momentum away from the hole, thereby changing the shape of the hole's horizon. The hole, therefore, would not be quiescent, as we insisted it be.

Among the nicest features of the Golden Age was the way we all built on each other's work. Hawking laid the foundations, and one after another his compatriots built an edifice upon them – Werner Israel,[1] Brandon Carter, David Robinson, Pavel Mazur, Gary Bunting. The final edifice was a marvelous mathematical structure, which predicted that quiescent black holes in the macroscopic, astrophysical universe have just *two hairs*, in this sense: if you know just two properties of an astrophysical black hole, then you can deduce all its other properties, uniquely. The simplest two properties to discover are a hole's *mass* (how hard its gravity pulls), and its *spin* (how fast space on its horizon whirls around and around). Having measured a hole's mass and spin, you can deduce the full details of all other features of the hole's warped spacetime – all the details of its space curvature, all the details of its slowing and distortion of time's flow, and all the details of its space's whirling motion, both near the hole and far away.

One can draw maps of these three features of the warpage (space curvature, time distortion, space whirl), and the full details of those maps are predicted by Golden-Age mathematics, once the hole's mass and spin are known.

This marvelous Hawking–Israel–Carter–Robinson–Mazur–Bunting prediction is sometimes called *black hole uniqueness*. John Wheeler has referred to it by saying *a black hole has no hair*, though it's more accurate to say that *a quiescent, astrophysical black hole has just two hairs: its mass and its spin*.

5.3 LISA: mapping black holes with gravitational waves

Since the 1970s these remarkable predictions have remained untested. They seem to be an unequivocal consequence of Einstein's general relativity laws, but relativity might be wrong or (much less likely) we might be misinterpreting its mathematics.

It is a triumph of modern technology that we are now on the verge of being able to test these predictions. I am confident they will be tested within the next decade or so, by the following means.

---

[1] Actually, Israel's contribution preceded Hawking's; Hawking shoved his foundations under it.

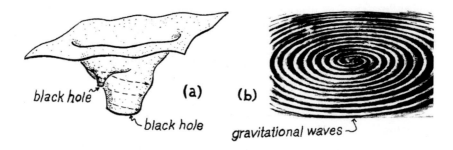

Fig. 5.7. (a) A small black hole orbiting a large black hole and gradually spiraling inward. (b) The gravitational waves produced by the small hole's inspiral.

In the distant universe there should be many 'binary' systems made of a small black hole orbiting around a much larger black hole, as illustrated in the left panel of Figure 5.7. The small hole might be about the size of Cambridge and the large hole might be a little bigger than the Sun, quite a contrast. The small hole orbits around the big one and, as it moves, it creates ripples in the fabric of spacetime that propagate outwards like ripples on a pond. These ripples are called gravitational waves.

A student of mine, Fintan Ryan, has used Einstein's equations to deduce that these ripples carry, encoded in themselves, full maps of all features of the big hole's spacetime warpage. As the small hole orbits the big hole, very gradually spiraling inward, it explores the big hole's warped spacetime, and it encodes on its outgoing waves a map of all it sees. This motivates a great challenge: detect the gravitational waves as they pass through our solar system, extract the maps that they carry, and use those maps to test the Golden Age predictions. My Caltech colleague Sterl Phinney has given the name *bothrodesy* to this enterprise, by analogy with *geodesy*, the science of measuring the shape of the Earth by probing its gravitational field. The 'geo' of geodesy means Earth; the 'bothro' of bothrodesy descends from the Greek word βοθρος (bothros) meaning 'garbage pit', a description of a black hole introduced long ago by Stephen's classmate Brandon Carter.

The physical manifestation of the small hole's gravitational waves, as they pass through the solar system, is much like ripples on the surface of a pond. Suppose two corks are floating in the pond. As the water-wave ripples go by, the corks not only bob up and down; they also are pushed back and forth relative to each other. If you were a water skeeter living on the pond's surface, you might not be aware of the up and down bobbing, but you could see the corks move back and forth; you could watch their

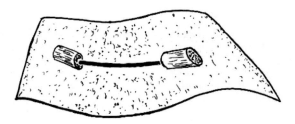

Fig. 5.8. A laser beam monitors the separation of two corks on a pond, as water waves pass by.

separation oscillate. If the waves were very weak but you were a smart water skeeter with laser technology, you might monitor the passing waves by using a laser beam – a laser-based surveying instrument – to measure the tiny oscillations of the corks' separation, as shown in Figure 5.8. This is precisely how we plan to detect and monitor gravitational waves.

A gravitational wave's ripply spacetime warpage, like the steady warpage of a black hole, is rich in its details, but the most useful feature of the wave's warpage is an oscillatory stretching and squeezing of space. The stretch and squeeze are *transverse* to the wave's propagation. During the first half of the wave's oscillation cycle, it stretches space along one transverse direction while squeezing along the other, perpendicular direction; in the next half cycle it switches, squeezing along the first direction while stretching along the second. So if the wave is passing through me from front to back, I get stretched from head to foot and squeezed from the sides, then stretched from the sides and squeezed from head to foot, and so on.

The stretch and squeeze are far too weak for you or me to feel, but we expect to detect them by monitoring the separations between 'corks' that float in interplanetary space. The 'corks' will be spacecraft, the stretch and squeeze of space will push them back and forth relative to each other, and we will use a laser-based surveying instrument to monitor their oscillating separation, as shown in the left panel of Figure 5.9.

This gravitational-wave detection system is called LISA, the Laser Interferometer Space Antenna. A joint European/American mission with launch tentatively planned for 2011, LISA will consist of three spacecraft at the corners of an equilateral triangle with 5 million kilometre sides. The laser beams will shine along the triangle's edges, linking the spacecraft. The spacecraft will travel around the Sun in approximately the same orbit as the Earth, but following the Earth by about 20 degrees as shown in the right panel of Figure 5.9. The spacecraft will be *drag-free*: they will have very special, high-precision instrumentation to prevent them

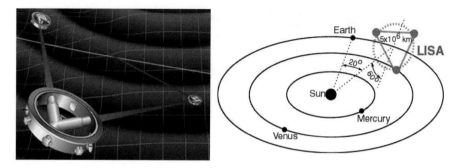

Fig. 5.9. LISA, the Laser Interferometer Space Antenna, which ESA and NASA will jointly build, launch, and use to monitor low-frequency gravitational waves. In the right panel LISA's size is exaggerated by about a factor 10 relative to the planetary orbits.

from being buffeted by the Sun's fluctuating radiation pressure and the fluctuating wind of gas that blows off the Sun – so they respond only to the steady gravitational pulls of the Sun and planets, and the waves' oscillatory stretch and squeeze of space.

The farther apart are the spacecraft, the larger will be their oscillatory displacements relative to each other; that is why we'll place them so far apart. The ratio $\Delta L/L$ of the wave-induced displacement ΔL to the separation L is equal to the *gravitational-wave field*, which we denote h. This h is one aspect of the waves' spacetime warpage, and it oscillates with time t as the wave travels through LISA, so we sometimes write it '$h(t)$'. In other words, the displacement ΔL is a fraction $h(t)$ of the separation: $\Delta L = h(t) \times L$.

Figure 5.10 gives some feeling for LISA's planned test of the Golden-Age predictions. The size of the black-hole pair, the big hole with the tiny one orbiting it, is about 5 million kilometers, so it takes about 20 seconds for light to travel across the small hole's orbit. Though the tiny hole's horizon has a circumference about the same as Cambridge's, its mass (or, more precisely, the strength of its gravitational pull on matter at some fixed distance) is enormous: about ten times the mass (or pull) of the Sun; and the big hole's mass is humongous: about a million times that of the Sun. The big hole spins rapidly, about one revolution each 66 seconds, but out at the small hole's orbit the whirl of space is somewhat slower. As the small hole gradually spirals inward toward the big hole's horizon, it samples regions of faster space whirl and stronger pull, and so precesses faster and orbits faster. This gradually changing orbital motion and precession produce the gravitational waves that we seek, waves carrying an encoded map of the large hole's warped spacetime.

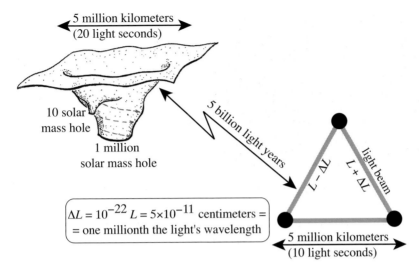

Fig. 5.10. Some numbers for LISA's bothrodesy mapping of a massive black hole.

These gravitational waves travel out from the holes, through the great reaches of intergalactic space, to our solar system, a distance of about 3 billion light years, roughly 1/5th the size of the observable universe. By the time they reach the solar system and pass through LISA, the waves have become very weak: they stretch and squeeze space by about one part in 10^{21}. In other words, the wave field h is $h \simeq 10^{-21}$.

LISA's size, $L = 5$ million kilometres, is about the same as the size of the small hole's orbit around the big hole and only a bit bigger than the big hole itself (Figure 5.10). The waves push LISA's spacecraft back and forth by an amount $\Delta L = h \times L \simeq 5 \times 10^{-11}$ centimetres, which is roughly one millionth the wavelength of the light that is used to monitor the spacecraft motions. It is a remarkable fact that modern technology is capable of monitoring such tiny motions!

The waves imprint their oscillatory pattern $h(t)$ on the stretch and squeeze ΔL that LISA measures, $\Delta L = h(t) \times L$. This oscillating pattern, called the wave's *waveform*, is depicted in Figure 5.11. With each circuit around the big hole, the small hole produces two oscillations of the waveform. The precession of the orbit, induced by the whirl of space, causes the waveform's modulation pattern (nine humps and valleys in Figure 5.11). As the small hole gradually spirals inward toward its final, catastrophic plunge, the waveform gradually changes. The full map of the large hole's warped spacetime is encoded in this gradually changing waveform. This waveform is the key to bothrodesy.

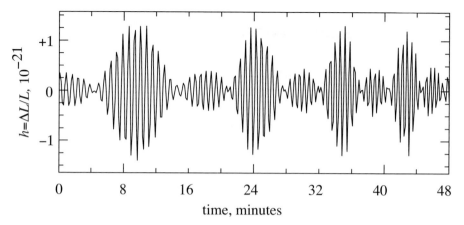

Fig. 5.11. The gravitational waveform passing LISA shortly before the small hole reaches the end of its inspiral and begins a catastrophic plunge into the big hole's horizon. This waveform was computed by Scott Hughes, a former student of mine, by solving Einstein's general relativity equations. LISA is assumed to be in the equatorial plane of the big hole, and the small hole's orbit is inclined 40 degrees to that plane.

During the entire last month of the small hole's life, it encircles the big hole 20,500 times, sending out 41,000 cycles of waves as it gradually spirals inward from a circumference three times larger than the big hole's horizon, to the horizon and its final, plunging death. The 41,000 wave cycles carry exquisitely accurate maps of all aspects of the big hole's warped spacetime, between three horizon circumferences and the horizon itself.

From these encoded maps, we can deduce with high precision the mass of the big hole and its spin, and from the mass and spin and the Hawking *et al.* Golden-Age uniqueness theorem, we can predict all the other details of the maps. If the measured maps agree with the predictions we will have a marvelous confirmation of the Golden-Age theory of black holes. If they disagree, we will struggle to understand why.

Bothrodesy will not be our only harvest from the small hole's waveforms. We will also probe other predictions from the Golden Age. For example, Stephen, working with Jim Hartle (who is also lecturing here today), predicted in 1971 that, as the small hole moves around the big one, it must raise a tide on the big hole's horizon (Figure 5.12) – a tide that is very similar to the one that the Moon and Sun raise on the Earth's oceans. This tide then pulls on the small hole, thereby changing its orbit and thence its emitted waveforms; and the small hole pulls on the tide,

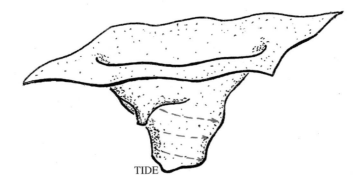

TIDE

Fig. 5.12. A small black hole orbiting a larger neighbour, raises a tide like the Moon on the Earth.

thereby changing the big hole's spin and mass. From the observed waveforms we can test, with exquisite accuracy, Stephen and Jim's predictions for how the orbit and the horizon evolve when the small hole and tide pull on each other.

5.4 The Golden Age again: colliding black holes

Let us return to the Golden Age, and turn from quiescent black holes to highly dynamical black holes – holes of similar masses and sizes that collide, vibrate wildly, and merge.

The key to understanding dynamical holes was Stephen's concept of a hole's *absolute event horizon*. Building on Roger's prior black-hole studies, Stephen realized that he would gain great predictive power by defining the horizon to be the boundary between regions of spacetime that cannot send signals to the outside universe and those that can. Regions that can't communicate with the outside universe would be in the hole's *interior*; those that can communicate would be in the *exterior*.

This definition seems obvious, but it was not. Until then, Roger, Stephen and others had used a different definition for the horizon, one with less predictive power. The immediate payoff of Stephen's new definition was his famous *second law of black-hole mechanics*: the surface area of black hole's horizon can never decrease, and in fact will generally increase, at least a little bit, when it interacts with other objects – e.g., when another hole raises a tide on it, or when something falls into it. Moreover, Stephen deduced, whenever two black holes collide and merge, as in Figure 5.13, the sum of their horizon areas will continually increase throughout the collision, throughout the wild vibrations, and throughout

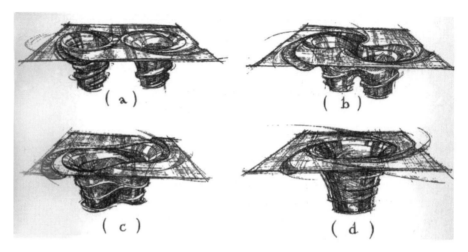

(a)

(b)

(c)

(d)

Fig. 5.13. The collision and merger of two black holes: an artist's conception. [*Courtesy the LIGO Project, California Institute of Technology*]

the merger, leaving the final, quiescent hole's surface area larger than the sum of the initial holes' areas.

Stephen's proof of the second law actually has a 'hole' in it. His proof relied on something that he was almost sure was true, but that nobody had proved as of 1970, and nobody has proved even today; it relied on Roger's *Cosmic Censorship Conjecture*: the conjecture that the laws of physics prohibit naked singularities. A singularity, as Roger has described in his lecture today, is a region of spacetime where the warpage is infinitely strong. In the Golden Age, Roger proved that the core of every black hole must harbor a singularity; such a singularity is said to be *clothed*, since it is hidden inside the hole's horizon. A singularity outside all holes, by contrast, would be 'naked'; it could be seen by anyone, humans included, in the external universe.

If naked singularities are permitted, then one they could be used to make a black hole's horizon shrink, invalidating Stephen's second law. Thus, Roger's cosmic censorship and Stephen's second law are entwined.

A dynamical hole has lots of 'hair'. One cannot predict its properties from a knowledge of its mass and its spin. Its horizon may bulge out in this manner, dimple inward in that manner, and swirl in different directions at different locations like the surface of the ocean in a storm. In the early 1970s my students Bill Press, Saul Teukolsky and Richard Price discovered the details of how a dynamical hole loses its hair. The dynamical hole can pulsate, Press discovered using computer simulations. Teukolsky, building on earlier work of others, formulated the theory of those pulsations; and

Price deduced the details of how the pulsations die out, carrying away the 'hair' and leaving the hole in its final, quiescent state.

5.5 LIGO/VIRGO/GEO: probing colliding black holes with gravitational waves

All these Golden-Age predictions – Roger's cosmic censorship, Stephen's second law, and my students' vibrational hair loss – will be tested by monitoring the gravitational waves from black-hole collisions. These waves, moreover, will show us how warped spacetime behaves when it is highly distorted and highly dynamical, vibrating in hugely nonlinear ways. We've never been clever enough to deduce this behaviour from Einstein equations. Gravitational waves are the key to learning it.

The venue for these tests and discoveries will be an international network of *earth-based* gravitational-wave detectors that is just now going into operation, and that almost certainly will watch black holes collide before the end of this decade – before LISA flies and maps quiescent holes.

LISA is the gravitational analog of a radio telescope: it will detect and study waves whose wavelengths are long, the size of the Earth–Moon separation or the Earth–Sun separation or larger. The Earth-based detectors are analogs of optical telescopes: they will detect and study waves with short wavelengths, the size of the Earth or smaller.

Figure 5.14 shows the biggest of the earth-based detectors: those of the Laser Interferometer Gravitational-Wave Observatory (LIGO). Though constructed by scientists from Caltech and MIT with American funds, LIGO has become a partnership of scientists from many nations: the

Fig. 5.14. Aerial views of the LIGO gravitational-wave detectors at Hanford, Washington (left) and Livingston, Louisiana (right). [*Courtesy LIGO Project, California Institute of Technology*]

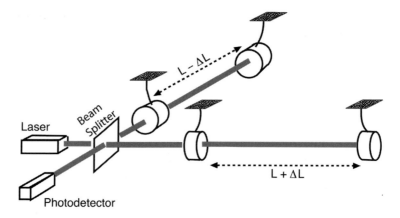

Fig. 5.15. Sketch of an Earth-based gravitational-wave interferometer.

United States, United Kingdom, Germany, Russia, Australia, Japan, India, and others. LIGO is partnered in the network with VIRGO, a French/Italian detector in PISA, Italy, and with GEO600, a much shorter UK/German detector in Hanover, Germany. The GEO600 scientists are developing and testing advanced technology for future detectors – technology that will be incorporated into LIGO when it is upgraded in 2008. If, as I expect, the advanced technology is successful in GEO600, it will permit this short detector to be a successful partner with the larger ones during the next few years, before the LIGO upgrade.

By combining the outputs of all these gravitational-wave detectors, we can watch black holes collide and test the Golden-Age predictions.

Figure 5.15 sketches how these detectors work. In place of three spacecraft moving through interplanetary space, an Earth-based detector has four heavy cylinders, made initially of quartz and later of sapphire, that hang from overhead supports and swing back and forth in response to a gravitational wave. As in LISA, we use laser beams to monitor the cylinders' relative motions, motions produced by the waves' oscillatory stretch and squeeze of space. Because these motions are detected by interfering the light from the detector's two arms (with one arm squeezed and the other stretched), the detector is called an *interferometer*; hence, LIGO's name, 'Laser Interferometer Gravitational-Wave Observatory'.

In Figure 5.16, I depict the collision of two black holes, with sketches that emphasize the whirl of space but ignore the holes' curvature of space and warping of time. Each hole drags space into a tornado-like whirl as shown, and the holes' orbital motion also creates a space whirl; so the holes are much like two tornados embedded in a third larger tornado that all come crashing together, violently. This cataclysmic collision is

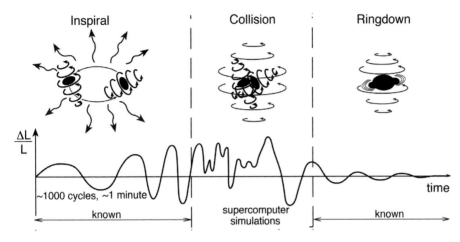

Fig. 5.16. Inspiral and merger of two black holes.

much more energetic than any other kind of event in the universe, but it involves no matter, so it cannot emit electromagnetic waves. The only waves it emits are waves made of the same stuff as the holes, waves of spacetime warpage, gravitational waves. Gravitational waves are the only means by which we can ever see such cataclysms, our only window onto them.

From the waves emitted during the holes' gradual inspiral, we can infer the two holes' masses and spins and surface areas. From the collision waves we can learn how spacetime behaves when violently, nonlinearly warped. The collision, Stephen predicted in the 1970s, will produce a single final hole; and my students showed that this final hole must be born ringing like a bell, though its ringing will quickly die out; the hole will 'ring down'. From the ringdown waves we can infer the mass and spin and surface area of the final black hole.

By adding the measured areas of the initial hole and comparing this with the measured area of the final hole, we can test Stephen's second law of black hole mechanics. If the total area does not increase, then Stephen is wrong, Einstein's general relativity laws are wrong, and we will have a great crisis in physics. By scrutinizing the ringdown waves, we will see details of how the final hole loses all its excess hairs. And we will test Roger's cosmic censorship conjecture by asking the simple question, 'Is the final object a black hole or is it a naked singularity?' If it is a black hole, then the waves will have one form; if a singularity, they will be very different.

Especially interesting, I think, will be the collision waves. To decipher the dynamical behavior of violently, nonlinearly warped spacetime from

the collision waveforms will not be easy. The key to deciphering will be
comparison with supercomputer simulations of black hole collisions. We
must go back and forth between the observed waveforms and waveforms
predicted by simulations, iterating the simulations over and over again to
get agreement, and then scrutinize the simulations to see how spacetime
was behaving during the collision. A community of scientists called 'numerical relativists' has been developing the computer-software tools for
these simulations since the mid 1970s, nearly as long as experimenters
have been developing gravitational-wave technology. The simulation tools
are extremely complex and entail numerous pitfalls, so they are not yet
finished. Much work is yet to be done, but it should be complete by the
time of LIGO's 2008 upgrade, and hopefully sooner. Figure 5.17 shows
the results of a recent simulation with partially working software tools.

5.6 Quantum behavior of human-sized objects

The upgrade of LIGO was planned from its outset. To move in one step
from the prototype interferometers of the 1980s and 1990s to LIGO's mature, big interferometers would have been too big and dangerous a leap.
An intermediate step, the 'initial interferometers' that are now beginning
to operate, was essential. With the initial interferometers we can solidify
our techniques and technology in preparation for the upgrade to the mature or 'advanced' interferometers. If we are lucky, the initial interferometers will see black hole collisions; and with the advanced interferometers
we are confident of seeing many collisions and doing rich observations.

Much of the advanced-interferometer technology is being developed
here in the UK, at the University of Glasgow, though other researchers
are making major contributions, for example in Russia and Australia and
at Caltech and MIT. This advanced technology is bringing us into the
domain where, for the first time in human history, we will watch human-
sized objects behave quantum mechanically.

We have heard about quantum mechanics in earlier talks today. For
example, Jim Hartle described his research with Stephen on applying
quantum mechanics to the entire universe, but we do not yet have the
technology to test those ideas. The only solid tests of quantum mechanics
that we humans have ever performed are in the microscopic realm of atoms
and molecules and photons and subatomic particles. But this will change
soon: LIGO's advanced interferometers, in 2008 and onward, will be able
to monitor the motions of 40-kilogramme sapphire mirrors (Figure 5.18) –
monocrystals of sapphire – to a precision about 1/10,000th the diameter
of an atomic nucleus. This precision is half the width of the quantum
mechanical wave function of what we call the 'center of mass degree of

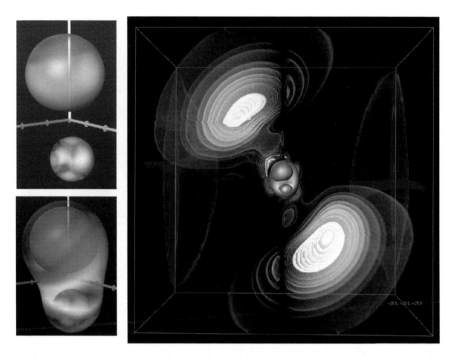

Fig. 5.17. Simulation of the glancing, but nearly head-on collision of two black holes with different sizes, as computed on a supercomputer by a group at the Albert Einstein Institute in Golm, Germany, led by Edward Seidel and Berndt Brügman. Upper left: apparent horizons (close approximations to the true horizons) of the two holes shortly before the collision. Lower left: apparent horizon of the merged hole shortly after the collision, with the individual apparent horizons inside. Right: double-lobed gravitational-wave pattern produced by the collision, with the three apparent horizons at the center. [*This visualization by Werner Begner is courtesy the Albert Einstein Institute, Max Planck Society.*]

freedom' of the mirror. This complicated phrase means that in LIGO, in 2008 and onward, we will be watching our 40-kilogramme mirrors behave quantum mechanically. We are developing a whole new branch of high technology, called *quantum non–demolition technology*, to deal with the mirrors' macroscopic, probabilistic, quantum mechanical behaviour. This effort, in fact, is my own research passion today. I have largely turned my back on relativity research, temporarily, so as to help bring quantum nondemolition technology to fruition. I'm doing this in collaboration with my students and the Russian research group of Vladimir Braginsky, who pioneered quantum non-demolition.

Fig. 5.18. A LIGO mirror, which will be seen to behave quantum mechanically in LIGO's upgraded interferometers, in 2008.

5.7 Probing the big bang with gravitational waves

Let's turn now from colliding black holes and LIGO technology to singularities in the fabric of spacetime. In 1964, Roger Penrose proved that every black hole is inhabited by a singularity. If you fall into the black hole, then its singularity will tear you apart and destroy you in a complicated way. As Roger described in his lecture today, singularities are governed by the laws of quantum gravity. This means they should be a wonderful arena in which to probe those laws.

Is there any hope ever to do experimental or observational studies of singularities? Yes, there is one singularity we can hope to study: the Big Bang singularity in which the universe was born; the singularity that created all of the material of which were are made – our bodies, the Earth, the universe. The universe got tremendously transmuted after emerging from the Big Bang; it is radically different today from at the beginning. But there is hope of penetrating those transmutations, a hope of probing all the way back through the history of the universe to the Big Bang itself and observe the Big Bang's details.

Figure 5.19 explains that hope. As we look out into the sky from the Earth (right end of Figure 5.19) we see cosmic microwave radiation, microwave photons coming from all directions. Martin Rees described these microwave photons this morning. They bring us a marvelous picture of what the universe looked like when it was 100,000 years old. We cannot use these photons study the universe when it was any younger than 100,000 years, because in the first 100,000 years of its life, the universe was filled with gas so hot and dense that photons could not propagate through

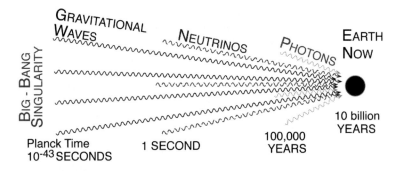

Fig. 5.19. Unlike photons and neutrinos, only gravitational waves can look back to the earliest moments of the universe.

it. The photons just got scattered or absorbed, and all the information about the Big Bang, that they might once have had, was destroyed.

There is a fundamental particle called a neutrino that is far more penetrating than a photon, and that should also have been created in the Big Bang. If and when we someday see neutrinos from the very early universe, we can use them to make pictures of the universe when it was one second old. But before then, the universe's gas was so hot and dense that neutrinos could not penetrate it. Like photons, they were scattered and absorbed, losing all the information about the Big Bang that they ever possessed.

The laws of physics tell us that the only form of radiation with enough penetrating power to emerge from the Big Bang unscathed is gravitational radiation (Figure 5.19). Any gravitational waves created in the universe's Big-Bang birth should have emerged and propagated, unscathed by any absorption or scattering by matter, from then all the way to now. However, these primordial waves were probably distorted and amplified by interacting with the universe's large-scale, dynamically changing spacetime warpage, during the first tiny fraction of a second of the universe's life. Fortunately, the amplification may have made the waves strong enough to detect, and the distortions may be decipherable; they are far less troublesome than the complete loss of information that photons and neutrinos suffer at the hands of the hot, primordial gas.

Thus, gravitational waves are our ideal tool – in fact our only tool – for directly probing the Big Bang and the first one second of our universe's life. A holy grail of gravitational wave detection over the coming decades, then, will be to study in detail this first second and the Big-Bang singularity. These studies' initial success may come from a very different kind of gravitational-wave detector from LIGO or LISA: from imprints that gravitational waves place on the polarization of the cosmic microwave photons. But time is too short for me to tell you about that.

5.8 Cosmic censorship: betting with Stephen

So the prospects are good to study one singularity – the birth of the universe. But is there any hope ever to find and study, or make and study, singularities in the present-day universe – *naked singularities?*

The physics 'establishment' is epitomised by Roger Penrose (who denies being part of the establishment) and Stephen Hawking. The establishment's viewpoint on naked singularities is firm and unequivocal: naked singularities are forbidden. You will never find them and can never make them; there is no hope of ever studying them in the laboratory. This assertion is embodied in Roger's *cosmic censorship conjecture*, which says that all singularities except the Big Bang are hidden inside black holes – that is, they are clothed by horizons.

Eleven years ago Stephen and I and John Preskill, a colleague of ours at Caltech, made a bet on this (Figure 5.20).

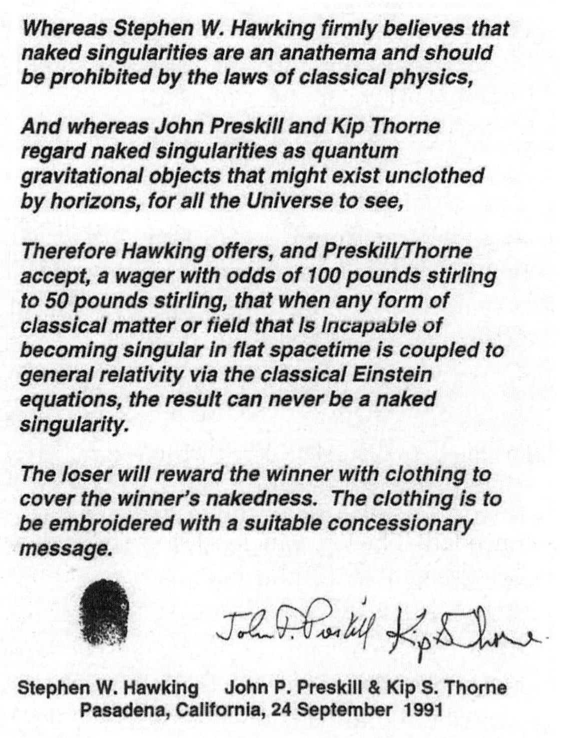

Whereas Stephen W. Hawking firmly believes that naked singularities are an anathema and should be prohibited by the laws of classical physics,

And whereas John Preskill and Kip Thorne regard naked singularities as quantum gravitational objects that might exist unclothed by horizons, for all the Universe to see,

Therefore Hawking offers, and Preskill/Thorne accept, a wager with odds of 100 pounds stirling to 50 pounds stirling, that when any form of classical matter or field that is incapable of becoming singular in flat spacetime is coupled to general relativity via the classical Einstein equations, the result can never be a naked singularity.

The loser will reward the winner with clothing to cover the winner's nakedness. The clothing is to be embroidered with a suitable concessionary message.

Stephen W. Hawking   John P. Preskill & Kip S. Thorne
Pasadena, California, 24 September 1991

Fig. 5.20. The Hawking–Preskill–Thorne bet.

Fig. 5.21. Left: Stephen concedes he has lost our cosmic-censorship bet. Right: The politically incorrect T-shirt that Stephen gave us. [*Left photo, taken at Caltech, is courtesy Irene Fertik, University of Southern California.*]

Our bet says:

> Whereas Stephen Hawking firmly believes that naked singularities are an anathema that should be prohibited by the laws of classical physics. And whereas Preskill and Thorne regard naked singularities as quantum gravitational objects that might exist unclothed by horizons for all the universe to see. Therefore Hawking offers, and Preskill and Thorne accept, a wager ...

And then there is a bunch of verbiage that was designed to protect Stephen's side of the bet, followed by our final conclusion:

> [Hawking bets that] the result can never be a naked singularity. The loser will reward the winner with clothing to cover the winner's nakedness. The clothing is to be embroidered with a suitable concessionary message.

Stephen has conceded! The left panel of Figure 5.21 shows a photograph of Stephen's concession, at a public lecture in California. You see me there, bowing with pleasure as John looks on with glee. It's not every day that Stephen gets proved wrong! With his concession, Stephen gave each of us the promised article of clothing: a T-shirt with his concessionary message. Sadly, I must tell you that Stephen's message (right panel of Figure 5.21) was not entirely gracious! He placed on the T-shirt a scantily-clad woman. (My wife and Stephen's were aghast at this, but Stephen

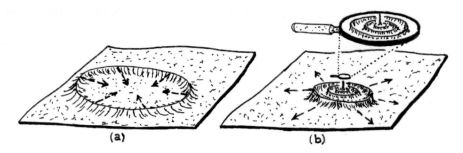

Fig. 5.22. The supercomputer simulations of imploding waves, which triggered Hawking to concede that the laws of physics permit naked singularities, at least in principle.

has never been politically correct.) As you notice, the woman's towel says *'Nature abhors a naked singularity'*. Stephen conceded, but he asserted that Nature abhors that which he concedes Nature can do. So why did he concede, and why was he so ungracious, so apparently self contradictory in his concession?

Stephen's concession was forced upon him by supercomputer simulations of imploding waves. The original, pioneering simulations were by Matthew Choptuik at the University of Texas, using the type of wave that is easiest to simulate, a so-called 'scalar wave'; but subsequent, similar simulations have been done with gravitational waves by Andrew Abrahams and Chuck Evans at the University of North Carolina. I will describe the gravitational-wave simulations.

Think of somehow creating gravitational waves, ripples in the fabric of spacetime, and sending them all inward toward a common center (left panel of Figure 5.22). Give the imploding waves almost but not quite enough energy to make a black hole at the center, through their nonlinear self-interactions. Choptuik (and Abrahams and Evans) simulated this, and their simulations revealed spacetime behaving in an amazing manner. As the waves' spacetime ripples neared the centre, they interacted with each other in a wild, nonlinear way, making spacetime 'boil' like water in a pot. The boiling created violent spacetime distortions with ever shortening wavelengths, and gravitational waves of ever shortening wavelength flowed out from the boiling centre, carrying information about the boiling. If the ingoing waves had had a bit more energy, the boiling would have made a tiny black hole. If the waves had had a bit less energy, the boiling would have been weaker and transitory, producing no object at the center at all. But with a carefully tuned wave energy, the boiling produced, right at the centre, a naked region of infinitely strong spacetime warpage –

a naked singularity. Almost all the ingoing wave energy got converted by boiling into outgoing waves, so this singularity was left with only an infinitesimal energy inside it; and we are pretty sure it could survive for only an infinitesimally short time (though the simulations were not able to tell us for certain). However, a singularity is a singularity, whether infinitesimal or note, so Stephen had to concede.

Stephen, however, was persuaded by Choptuik's simulations that Nature actually abhors naked singularities. To force Nature to make a naked singularity, Choptuik had to fine-tune the ingoing waves' energy. If the ingoing energy was slightly too small, no singularity would form at all. If slightly too large, the singularity would form clothed, surrounded by a black-hole horizon. And if tuned perfectly, the waves would produce only an infinitesimal naked singularity. What better evidence could one ask for that Nature really abhors naked singularities and does everything it can to avoid them, Stephen asked?

And so we renewed our bet with altered wording. The new bet begins:

> Whereas Stephen Hawking, having lost a previous bet by not demanding genericity [genericity means that the naked singularity should be formed without fine tuning], still firmly believes that naked singularities are an anathema and should be prohibited by the classical laws of physics, therefore ... Hawking offers, and Preskill/Thorne accept a wager that ... A dynamical evolution from generic initial conditions ... can never produce a naked singularity... . [Here I'm omitting a lot of verbiage designed, again, to protect Stephen's side of the bet.] The loser will reward the winner with clothing to cover the winner's nakedness. The clothing is to be embroidered with a suitable, *truly* concessionary message.

I'm afraid that John and I will lose this renewed bet; but we made the bet, nevertheless, as a challenge to the next generation of physicists. It is a challenge that can be probed theoretically by mathematical manipulations of Einstein's equations, and computationally by supercomputer simulations, and also observationally: we shall search for big, generic, naked singularities using gravitational-wave detectors. For example, LISA may make many maps of the warped spacetimes surrounding massive compact bodies, bodies into which smaller objects spiral, emitting gravitational waves. Each map will reveal the structure of the massive body, whether it is a black hole or something else. It is likely that all the maps will be of black holes, but among them we might find a naked singularity, or some other, unexpected type of body. What an amazing discovery that would be!

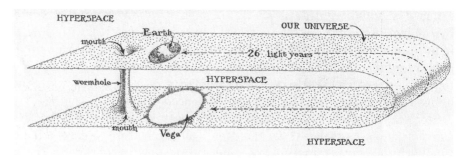

Fig. 5.23. A hypothetical wormhole connecting our solar system to the vicinity of the star Vega. [From my book *Black Holes and Time Warps: Einstein's Outrageous Legacy* (W.W. Norton, New York, 1994) [1].]

5.9 Time travel

I shall conclude with a brief history of Stephen and Kip on backward time travel, since this is something to which Stephen devotes a chapter of his new book, *The Universe in a Nutshell*. My brief history begins with wormholes.

Figure 5.23 shows a wormhole embedded in hyperspace. It is rather like two black holes (recall the right half of Figure 5.4) but without the singularities. You can go in one mouth, pass through the wormhole's throat, and and come out the other mouth. We have all seen wormholes in the film *Contact*, in *Star Trek*, and elsewhere, so I don't need to explain them any more than that.

In 1988, together with my student Michael Morris, I realized that, although general relativity permits the existence of wormholes, to hold a wormhole open, one must thread its throat with material that has negative energy. We still don't know whether the laws of physics permit the accumulation of enough negative energy in a wormhole's throat to hold the wormhole open, but I shall ignore this issue and forge onward.

In 1988, with Morris and another student Ulvi Yurstever, I realized that, if you have a wormhole, then it is very easy (in principle at least) to make a time machine. The top panel of Figure 5.24 shows me and my wife, Carolee, each holding a wormhole's mouth. To convert this wormhole into a time machine, Carolee, carrying her wormhole mouth, hops in her spaceship and zooms out through the universe at very high speed (easy in principle but not in practice!) and then zooms back to Earth. Her motion changes how time hooks up through the wormhole: if I climb into my wormhole mouth, I emerge through hers immediately, it seems to me; but I emerge long after I climbed in, as seen by anyone who stays outside

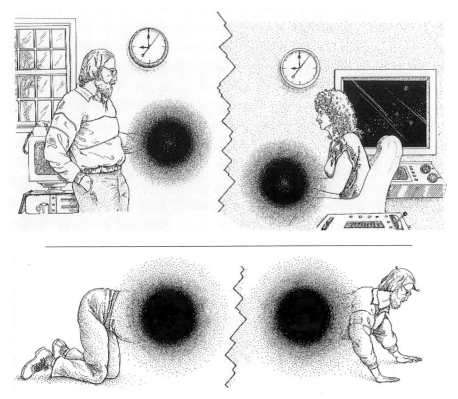

Fig. 5.24. Time travel. (Adapted from ref. [1].)

the wormhole (bottom panel of Figure 5.24); I have traveled to the future without aging. If Carolee climbs through the wormhole, she emerges much before she entered; she has traveled to the past. This is discussed in more detail in the last chapter of my book *Black Holes and Time Warps.*

Rather quickly after Morris, Yurtsever and I discovered how to convert a time wormhole into a time machine, I realized – in work with my postdoc Sung-Won Kim – that the moment one tries to activate this time machine, it might destroy itself in a massive explosion (Figure 5.25); and several other physicists independently discovered the same thing. The explosion is caused by quantum mechanical fluctuations of radiation, so-called 'vacuum fluctuations', that fly through the wormhole just when it is becoming a time machine, pile up on themselves in space at the same moment of time, and thereby become infinitely energetic. For a slower explanation, see my book.

In 1990, when Kim and I examined this explosion mathematically using the laws of physics, we found that *every* time machine, whether made from a wormhole or by some other method, must suffer a similar explosion.

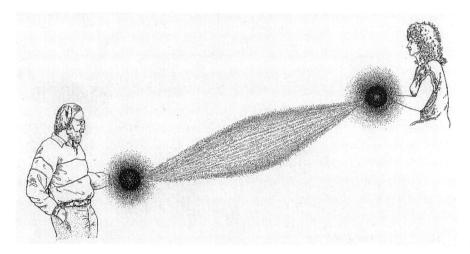

Fig. 5.25. A wormhole explodes at the moment we try to convert it into a time machine. (From [1].)

However, it appeared to us that, at least in some cases, the explosion might be weak enough for the wormhole to escape destruction. Perhaps a very advanced civilization could make a time machine after all.

We circulated a manuscript to our colleagues, describing our calculations and conclusions, and Stephen responded almost immediately. There is little politeness in our community when one of us believes the other is wrong. 'You're wrong!' Stephen said. He wrote a manuscript explaining why, and submitted it to the most prestigious of physics journals, *The Physical Review*.

The editors sent me his manuscript to referee. The refereeing took me many days because Stephen's paper, entitled 'The Chronology Protection Conjecture', was very sophisticated. In his manuscript, in a real *tour de force*, Stephen worked out the details of the theory of the creation of time machines in confined regions of space, and then argued rather convincingly that our explosion would always be so strong that it would destroy the time machine at just the moment you tried to activate it. As Stephen said, the explosion would 'keep the world safe for historians'; nobody can go back in time and try to change history. This was Stephen's *Chronology Projection Conjecture* – a conjecture, not a theorem, because both he and I were working with the laws of physics in a domain where we are uneasy about whether they really are correct, a domain where classical general relativity begins to fail and must be replaced by the ill-understood laws of quantum gravity.

Over the years since 1990, there has been much debate back and forth over whether these explosions are *always* strong enough to destroy a time machine at the moment a very advanced civilization tries to activate it. The bottom line that almost all the experts would agree on at present is that we are not absolutely sure. Probably yes, the explosion always destroys its time machine, but only the laws of quantum gravity know for sure. To be certain, we must master those laws.

On my 60th birthday, a year and a half ago, Stephen gave me a gift. His gift was a first attempt to estimate, using the laws of quantum gravity, the quantum mechanical probability that a time machine will survive the destruction, the probability that one can successfully make a time machine and go backward in time. Stephen's calculation gave an extremely small probability for time-machine survival: about 1 part in 10^{60}, that is, 0.000000000000000000000000000000000000000000000000000000000001

And so Stephen, on this, the occasion of your 60th birthday, I will give you an equally interesting gift. I'm afraid it is more in the form of a promissory note than a concrete physics result. Your birthday gift is that our gravitational-wave detectors – LIGO, GEO, VIRGO and LISA – will test your Golden-Age black-hole predictions, and they will begin to do so well before your 70th birthday. Happy Birthday, Stephen!

Acknowledgements

I thank Katheryn Ayres and Linda Simpkin for transcribing the oral version of this lecture, and Paul Shellard for ungarbling that oral prose and converting it into a readable manuscript in preparation for my final rewrite. My research on warped spacetime and gravitational waves is supported in part by National Science Foundation Grant PHY-0099568 and by NASA Grant NAG5-10707.

Useful references for further reading

[1] For a more leisurely discussion of the Golden-Age predictions, and of the basic ideas of gravitational-wave detection, see my book Thorne, K. (1994), *Black Holes and Time Warps: Einstein's Outrageous Legacy* (W.W. Norton, New York).

[2] For a leisurely and fairly up to date discussion of gravitational-wave detection, see Bartusiak, M. (2000), *Einstein's Unfinished Symphony* (National Academy Press, Washington D.C.).

[3] For a somewhat technical summary of research on gravitational-wave sources and detection as of early 2002, see Cutler C. and Thorne K. S. (2002), 'An overview of gravitational wave sources', in *Proceedings of the GR16*

Conference on General Relativity and Gravitation, ed. N. Bishop (World Scientific), in press. Available on the Web at http://xxx.lanl.gov/abs/gr-qc/0204090.

[4] For Stephen's description of his ideas and research on time travel, see Chapter 5 of his book: Hawking, S. (2001), *The Universe in a Nutshell* (Bantam Books, New York, 2001).

6

Sixty years in a nutshell

Stephen Hawking

Centre for Mathematical Sciences, University of Cambridge

6.1 Introduction

It was nearly 59.97 years in a nutshell. I had an argument with a wall a few days after Christmas, and the wall won. But Addenbrooke's Hospital did a very good job of putting me back together again.

I will skip over the first twenty of my sixty years and pick up the story in October 1962 when I arrived in Cambridge as a graduate student. I had applied to work with Fred Hoyle, the principal defender of the steady state theory, and the most famous British astronomer of the time. I say astronomer, because cosmology was at that time hardly recognized as a legitimate field, yet that was where I wanted to do my research, inspired by having been on a summer course with Hoyle's student, Jayant Narlikar.

However, Hoyle had enough students already, so to my great disappointment I was assigned to Dennis Sciama, of whom I hadn't heard. But it was probably for the best. Hoyle was away a lot, seldom in the department, and I wouldn't have had much of his attention. Sciama, on the other hand, was usually around and ready to talk. I didn't agree with many of his ideas, particularly on Mach's principle, but that stimulated me to develop my own picture.

6.2 How it began

When I began research, the two areas that seemed exciting were cosmology and elementary particle physics. Elementary particles was the active, rapidly changing field that attracted most of the best minds, while cosmology and general relativity were stuck where they had been in the 1930s. Feynman has given an amusing account of attending the conference on general relativity and gravitation in Warsaw in 1962. In a letter to his wife he said:

> I am not getting anything out of the meeting. I am learning nothing.
> Because there are no experiments, this field is not an active one, so
> few of the best men are doing work in it. The result is that there are
> hosts of dopes here (126) and it is not good for my blood pressure.
> Remind me not to come to any more gravity conferences!

Of course, I wasn't aware of all this when I began my research. But I
felt that elementary particles at that time was too like botany. Quantum
electrodynamics, the theory of light and electrons that governs chemistry
and the structure of atoms, had been worked out completely in the 1940s
and 1950s. Attention had now shifted to the weak and strong nuclear
forces between particles in the nucleus of an atom, but similar field theories didn't seem to work. Indeed, the Cambridge school, in particular,
held that there was no underlying field theory. Instead, everything would
be determined by unitarity, that is, probability conservation, and certain
characteristic patterns in the scattering.

With hindsight, it now seems amazing that it was thought this approach would work, but I remember the scorn that was poured on the
first attempts at unified field theories of the weak nuclear forces. Yet it is
these field theories that are remembered and the analytic S matrix work is
forgotten. I'm very glad I didn't start my research in elementary particles.
None of my work from that period would have survived.

Cosmology and gravitation, on the other hand, were neglected fields
that were ripe for development at that time. Unlike elementary particles,
there was a well-defined theory, the general theory of relativity, but this
was thought to be impossibly difficult. People were so pleased to find any
solution of the field equations; they didn't ask what physical significance,
if any, it had. This was the old school of general relativity that Feynman
encountered in Warsaw. But the Warsaw conference also marked the beginning of the renaissance of general relativity, though Feynman could be
forgiven for not recognizing it at the time.

6.3 General relativity and cosmology

A new generation entered the field, and new centres of general relativity
appeared. Two of these were of particular importance to me. One was
in Hamburg under Pascal Jordan. I never visited it, but I admired their
elegant papers, which were such a contrast to the previous messy work on
general relativity. The other centre was at King's College, London, under
Hermann Bondi, another proponent of the steady state theory, but not
ideologically committed to it, like Hoyle.

I hadn't done much mathematics at school or in the very easy physics
course at Oxford, so Sciama suggested I work on astrophysics. But having

been cheated out of working with Hoyle, I wasn't going to do something boring like Faraday rotation. I had come to Cambridge to do cosmology, and cosmology I was determined to do. So I read old text books on general relativity, and travelled up to lectures at Kings College, London each week with three other students of Sciama.

I followed the words and equations but I did not really get a feel for the subject. Also, I had been diagnosed with motor neurone disease, or ALS, and given to expect I did not have long enough to finish my PhD. Then suddenly, towards the end of my second year of research, things picked up. My disease was not progressing much, my work all fell into place, and I began to get somewhere.

6.4 Mach's Principle and Wheeler–Feynman electrodynamics

Sciama was very keen on Mach's principle:

> An object owes its inertia to the influence of all the other matter in the universe.

He tried to get me to work on this but I felt his formulations of Mach's principle were not well defined. However, he introduced me to something a bit similar with regard to light, the so-called Wheeler–Feynman electrodynamics. This said that electricity and magnetism were time symmetric. However, when one switched on a lamp, it was the influence of all the other matter in the universe that caused light waves to travel outward from the lamp, rather than come in from infinity and end on the lamp (Figure 6.1).

Fig. 6.1. Wheeler–Feynman electrodynamics. Light travels outward from a lamp because of the influence of all the other matter in the universe. [*From a transparency used in the lecture.*]

For Wheeler–Feynman electrodynamics to work it was necessary that all the light travelling out from the lamp should be absorbed by other matter in the universe. This would happen in a steady state universe in which the density of matter would remain constant, but not in a Big Bang universe, where the density would go down as the universe expanded. It was claimed that this was another proof, if proof were needed, that we live in a steady state universe. There was a conference on Wheeler–Feynman electrodynamics and the arrow of time in 1963. Feynman was so disgusted by the nonsense that was talked about the arrow of time, that he refused to let his name appear in the proceedings. He was referred to as Mr X, but everyone knew who X was (Figure 6.2).

I found that Hoyle and Narlikar had already worked out Wheeler–Feynman electrodynamics in expanding universes, and had then gone on to formulate a time-symmetric new theory of gravity. Hoyle unveiled the theory at a meeting of the Royal Society in 1964. I was at the lecture and, in the question period, I said that the influence of all the matter in a steady state universe would make his masses infinite. Hoyle asked why I said that, and I replied that I had calculated it.

Everyone thought I had done it in my head during the lecture but, in fact, I was sharing an office with Narlikar and had seen a draft of the paper. Hoyle was furious. He was trying to set up his own institute and threatening to join the brain drain to America if he didn't get the money. He thought I had been put up to it to sabotage his plans. However, he got his institute, and later gave me a job, so he didn't harbour a grudge against me.

Fig. 6.2. Feynman was so disgusted by the nonsense discussed about the arrow of time, that he would not allow his name to appear in the proceedings. He was referred to as Mr X.

6.5 The steady state

The big question in cosmology in the early 1960s was: did the universe have a beginning? Many scientists were instinctively opposed to the idea because they felt that a point of creation would be a place where science broke down. One would have to appeal to religion and the hand of God to determine how the universe would start off. Two alternative scenarios were therefore put forward. One was the steady state theory, in which as the universe expanded new matter was continually created to keep the density constant on average.

The steady state theory was never on a very strong theoretical basis because it required a negative energy field to create the matter. This would have made it unstable to runaway production of matter and negative energy. But it had the great merit as a scientific theory, of making definite predictions that could be tested by observations.

By 1963, the steady state theory was already in trouble. Martin Ryle's radio astronomy group at the Cavendish did a survey of faint radio sources. They found the sources were distributed fairly uniformly across the sky. This indicated that they were probably outside our galaxy because otherwise they would be concentrated along the Milky Way. But the graph of the number of sources against source strength did not agree with the prediction of the steady state theory. There were too many faint sources indicating that the density of sources was higher in the distant past.

Hoyle and his supporters put forward increasingly contrived explanations of the observations, but the final nail in the coffin of the steady state theory came in 1965 with the discovery of a faint background of microwave radiation (Figure 6.3). This could not be accounted for in the steady state theory, though Hoyle and Narlikar tried desperately. It was

Fig. 6.3. A photograph of the equipment on which the background radiation was discovered in 1965 alongside a modern simulation of the original data.

just as well I hadn't been a student of Hoyle because I would have had to have defended the steady state.

The microwave background indicated that the universe had had a hot dense stage in the past. But it didn't prove that was the beginning of the universe. One might imagine that the universe had had a previous contracting phase and that it had bounced from contraction to expansion, at a high, but finite density. This was clearly a fundamental question and it was just what I needed to complete my PhD thesis.

6.6 Gravity and the expanding universe

Gravity pulls matter together but rotation throws it apart. So my first question was: could rotation cause the universe to bounce? Together with George Ellis, I was able to show that the answer was no, if the universe was spatially homogeneous, that is, if it was the same at each point of space. However, two Russians, Lifshitz and Khalatnikov, had claimed to have proved that a general contraction without exact symmetry would always lead to a bounce with the density remaining finite. This result was very convenient for Marxist–Leninist dialectical materialism because it avoided awkward questions about the creation of the universe. It therefore became an article of faith for Soviet scientists.

Lifshitz and Khalatnikov were members of the old school in general relativity. That is, they wrote down a massive system of equations and tried to guess a solution. But it wasn't clear that the solution they found was the most general one. However, Roger Penrose introduced a new approach, which didn't require solving the field equations explicitly, just certain general properties, such as that energy is positive and gravity is attractive. Penrose gave a seminar in Kings College, London, in January 1965.

I wasn't at the seminar but I heard about it from Brandon Carter, with whom I shared an office in the then new DAMTP premises in Silver Street. At first, I couldn't understand what the point was. Penrose had showed that once a dying star had contracted to a certain radius there would inevitably be a singularity, a point where space and time came to an end. Surely, I thought, we already knew that nothing could prevent a massive cold star collapsing under its own gravity until it reached a singularity of infinite density. But, in fact, the equations had been solved only for the collapse of a perfectly spherical star. Of course, a real star won't be exactly spherical. If Lifshitz and Kalatnikov were right, the departures from spherical symmetry would grow as the star collapsed and would cause different parts of the star to miss each other and avoid a singularity of infinite density. But Penrose showed they were wrong. Small departures from spherical symmetry will not prevent a singularity.

I realized that similar arguments could be applied to the expansion of the universe. In this case, I could prove there were singularities where spacetime had a beginning. So again, Lifshitz and Khalatnikov were wrong. General relativity predicted that the universe should have a beginning, a result that did not pass unnoticed by the Church.

The original singularity theorems of both Penrose and myself required the assumption that the universe had a Cauchy surface, that is, a surface that intersects every time-like curve once, and only once. It was therefore possible that our first singularity theorems just proved that the universe didn't have a Cauchy surface. While interesting, this didn't compare in importance with time having a beginning or end. I therefore set about proving singularity theorems that didn't require the assumption of a Cauchy surface. In the next five years, Roger Penrose, Bob Geroch, and I developed the theory of causal structure in general relativity. It was a glorious feeling having a whole field virtually to ourselves. How unlike particle physics, where people were falling over themselves to latch on to the latest idea. They still are.

6.7 Collapsing stars

Up to 1970, my main interest was in the Big Bang singularity of cosmology, rather than the singularities that Penrose had shown would occur in collapsing stars. However, in 1967, Werner Israel produced an important result. He showed that, unless the remnant from a collapsing star was exactly spherical, the singularity it contained would be naked, that is, it would be visible to outside observers. This would have meant that the breakdown of general relativity at the singularity of a collapsing star would destroy our ability to predict the future of the rest of the universe.

At first, most people, including Israel himself, thought that this implied that because real stars aren't spherical, their collapse would give rise to naked singularities and the breakdown of predictability. However, a different interpretation was put forward by Roger Penrose and John Wheeler. It was that there is Cosmic Censorship. This says that Nature is a prude and hides singularities in black holes where they can't be seen. I used to have a bumper sticker, 'black holes are out of sight', on the door of my office in DAMTP (Figure 6.4). This so irritated the head of department that he engineered my election to the Lucasian professorship, moved me to a better office on the strength of it, and personally tore off the offending notice from the old office door.

My work on black holes began with a Eureka moment in 1970, a few days after the birth of my daughter, Lucy. While getting into bed, I realized that I could apply to black holes, the causal structure theory I had developed for singularity theorems. In particular, the area of the horizon,

Black holes are
out of sight

Fig. 6.4. Cosmic Censorship says that Nature is a prude, and hides singularities in black holes where they can't be seen. I used to have a bumper sticker, 'black holes are out of sight', on the door of my office in DAMTP.

the boundary of the black hole, would always increase. When two black holes collide and merge, the area of the final black hole is greater than the sum of the areas of the original holes. This, and other properties that Jim Bardeen Brandon Carter and I discovered, suggested that the area was like the entropy of a black hole. This would be a measure of how many states a black hole could have on the inside for the same appearance on the outside. But the area couldn't actually be the entropy because, as everyone knew, black holes were completely black, and couldn't be in equilibrium with thermal radiation.

There was an exciting period culminating in the Les Houches Summer School in 1972 in which we solved most of the major problems in black hole theory. This was before there was any observational evidence for black holes, which shows Feynman was wrong when he said an active field has to be experimentally driven. Just as well for M theory.

The one problem that was never solved was to prove the cosmic censorship hypothesis, though a number of attempts to disprove it, failed. It is fundamental to all work on black holes, so I have a strong vested interest in it being true. I therefore have a bet with Kip Thorne and John Preskill. It is difficult for me to win this bet, but quite possible to lose, by finding a counter example with a naked singularity. In fact, I have already lost an earlier version of the bet, by not being careful enough about the wording. They were not amused by the T-shirt I offered in settlement (Figure 6.5).

6.8 Hawking radiation

We were so successful with the classical general theory of relativity that I was at a bit of a loose end in 1973, after the publication with George Ellis,

Fig. 6.5. I lost a bet with Kip Thorne and John Preskill. They were not amused by the T-shirt I offered in settlement.

of *The Large Scale Structure Of Spacetime*. My work with Penrose had shown that general relativity broke down at singularities. So the obvious next step would be to combine general relativity, the theory of the very large, with quantum theory, the theory of the very small.

I had no background in quantum theory and the singularity problem seemed too difficult for a frontal assault at that time. So as a warm up exercise, I considered how particles and fields governed by quantum theory would behave near a black hole. In particular, I wondered can one have atoms, in which the nucleus is a tiny primordial black hole, formed in the early universe.

To answer this, I studied how quantum fields would scatter off a black hole. I was expecting that part of an incident wave would be absorbed and the remainder scattered. But to my great surprise, I found there seemed to be emission from the black hole. At first, I thought this must be a mistake in my calculation. But what persuaded me that it was real, was that the emission was exactly what was required to identify the area of the horizon, with the entropy of a black hole.

$$S = \frac{Akc^3}{4\hbar G}.$$

I would like this simple formula to be on my tombstone.

Work with Jim Hartle, Gary Gibbons and Malcolm Perry uncovered the deep reason for this formula. General relativity can be combined with quantum theory in an elegant manner if one replaces ordinary time by imaginary time. I have tried to explain imaginary time on other occasions, with varying degrees of success. I think it is the name, imaginary, that makes it so confusing. It is easier if you accept the positivist view, that a theory is just a mathematical model. In this case, the mathematical model has a minus sign whenever time appears twice. The Euclidean approach to quantum gravity, based on imaginary time, was pioneered in Cambridge. It met a lot of resistance, but is now generally accepted.

6.9 Inflation

Between 1970 and 1980, I worked mainly on black holes and the Euclidean approach to quantum gravity. But the suggestions that the early universe had gone through a period of inflationary expansion renewed my interest in cosmology. Euclidean methods were the obvious way to describe fluctuations and phase transitions in an inflationary universe. We held a Nuffield workshop in Cambridge in 1982, attended by all the major players in the field. At this meeting, we established most of our present picture of inflation, including the all important density fluctuations, which give rise to galaxy formation and so to our existence. This was ten years before fluctuations in the microwave were observed, so again in gravity, theory was ahead of experiment.

The scenario for inflation in 1982 was that the universe began with a big bang singularity. As the universe expanded, it was supposed somehow to get into an inflationary state. I thought this was unsatisfactory, because all equations would break down at a singularity. But unless one knew what came out of the initial singularity, one could not calculate how the universe would develop. Cosmology would not have any predictive power.

After the workshop in Cambridge, I spent the summer at the Institute of Theoretical Physics, Santa Barbara, which had just been set up. We stayed in student houses, and I drove in to the institute in a rented electric wheel chair. I remember my younger son, Tim aged three, watching the Sun set on the mountains, and saying, 'it's a big country'.

While in Santa Barbara, I talked to Jim Hartle about how to apply the Euclidean approach to cosmology. According to Dewitt and others, the universe should be described by a wave function that obeyed the Wheeler–DeWitt equation.

$$\left(G_{ijkl} \frac{\partial^2}{\partial h_{ij} \partial h_{kl}} - h^{3/2} R \right) \Psi = 0.$$

But what picked out the particular solution of the equation that represents our universe? According to the Euclidean approach, the wave function of the universe is given by a Feynman sum over a certain class of histories in imaginary time. Because imaginary time behaves like another direction in

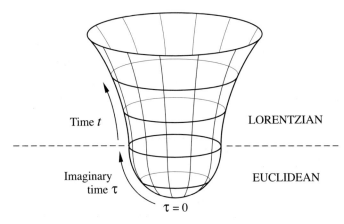

Fig. 6.6. Histories in imaginary time can be closed surfaces, like the surface of the Earth, with no beginning or end.

space, histories in imaginary time can be closed surfaces, like the surface of the Earth, with no beginning or end (Figure 6.6).

Jim and I decided that this was the most natural choice of class, indeed the only natural choice. We had side stepped the scientific and philosophical difficulty of time beginning by turning it into a direction in space.

6.10 M theory and the future

Most people in theoretical physics have been trained in particle physics, rather than general relativity. They have therefore been more interested in calculations of what they observe in particle accelerators than in questions about the beginning and end of time. The feeling was that, if they could find a theory that in principle allowed them to calculate particle scattering to arbitrary accuracy, everything else would somehow follow. In 1985 it was claimed that string theory was this ultimate theory. But in the years that followed, it emerged that the situation was more complicated, and more interesting.

It seems that there's a network called M theory. All the theories in the M theory network can be regarded as approximations to the same underlying theory in different limits. None of the theories allow calculation of scattering to arbitrary accuracy and none can be regarded as the fundamental theory, of which others are reflections. Instead, they should all be regarded as effective theories, valid in different limits.

String theorists have long used the term, effective theory, as a pejorative description of general relativity, but string theory is equally an effective

theory, valid in the limit that the M theory membrane is rolled into a
cylinder of small radius. Saying that string theory is only an effective
theory isn't very popular, but it's true.

The dream of a theory that would allow calculation of scattering to
arbitrary accuracy led people to reject quantum general relativity and
supergravity, on the grounds that they were non-renormalizable. This
means that one needs undetermined subtractions at each order, to get
finite answers. In fact, it is not surprising that naive perturbation theory
breaks down in quantum gravity. One cannot regard a black hole as a
perturbation of flat space.

I have done some work recently on making supergravity renormalizable
by adding higher derivative terms to the action. This apparently introduces ghosts, states with negative probability. However, I have found this
is an illusion. One can never prepare a system in a state of negative probability. But the presence of ghosts means that one cannot predict with
arbitrary accuracy. If one can accept that, one can live quite happily with
ghosts (Figure 6.7).

This approach to higher derivatives and ghosts allows one to revive the
original inflation model of Starobinski and other Russians. In this, the
inflationary expansion of the universe is driven by the quantum effects of
a large number of matter fields. Based on the no boundary proposal, I
picture the origin of the universe as like the formation of bubbles of steam
in boiling water. Quantum fluctuations lead to the spontaneous creation
of tiny universes out of nothing. Most of the universes collapse to nothing,

Fig. 6.7. One can live quite happily with ghosts...

but a few that reach a critical size, will expand in an inflationary manner, and will form galaxies and stars, and maybe beings like us.

6.11 Conclusion

It has been a glorious time to be alive and doing research in theoretical physics. Our picture of the universe has changed a great deal in the last 40 years, and I'm happy if I have made a small contribution (Figure 6.8).

I want to share my excitement and enthusiasm. There's nothing like the Eureka moment, of discovering something that no one knew before. I won't compare it to sex, but it lasts longer.

Fig. 6.8. One small contribution. [*Courtesy Twentieth Century Fox*]

Part 2
Spacetime singularities

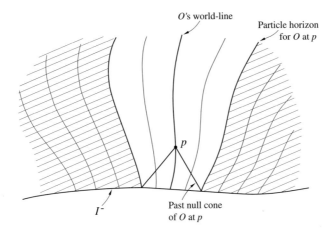

We shall therefore give an argument which indicates that the universe contains a singularity in our past, providing that the Copernican principle holds.

The Large Scale Structure of Spacetime, 1973

7

Cosmological perturbations and singularities

George Ellis

University of Cape Town

7.1 Introduction

It is a privilege to take part in these proceedings to honour Stephen Hawking's 60th birthday, and so acknowledge his major contribution to relativistic cosmology. To set the scene, I will give a Brief History of Hawking. In a nutshell, there have been four major phases of his technical work:

1. *General Relativity applied to Cosmology*: Exact properties of solutions of the Einstein field equations, perturbation solutions, singularity theorems.

2. *General Relativity applied to Black Holes*: Black hole uniqueness, thermodynamics, the area theorem.

3. *Quantum Fields in a Curved Space-Time*: Black hole particle creation, evaporation, quantum information puzzles.

4. *Semiclassical Gravity and Quantum Gravity*: Path integrals, instantons, the wave function of universe, the no boundary condition.

   A fifth significant contribution has been:

5. *Enhancing the public understanding of science*, in particular through publication of *A Brief History of Time* and *The Universe in a Nutshell*.

The topics covered in this paper relate to work done by Stephen during the first period of his career, relating to general relativity applied to cosmology, and later developments of this work by others.

Part A: Cosmological perturbations

The issue here is the formation of structure in the universe: where do galaxies and clusters of galaxies come from? This is of course crucial to our existence through eventually providing suitable habitats for life to develop, and so is important in terms of understanding our relation to the universe. Additionally, it provides the link between cosmology and astrophysics.

The physical issue is: how do inhomogeneities grow from a smooth background? The mathematical issue is: how best to handle the problem of gauge freedom. The observational issue is: how do we test the theory?

The dominant present understanding is that quantum fluctuations at the start of inflation can grow to give seeds for growth of large-scale inhomogeneities in the later hot Big Bang era and after. This provides a broadly viable picture of structure formation in the expanding universe, tested on the one hand by its predictions for the matter power-spectrum and on the other by its predictions for the cosmic background radiation (CBR) anisotropy. The conference on *The Very Early Universe* organised by Stephen and Gary Gibbons in 1982 played an important role in developing this theory, as did Stephen's own work on this theme [72]. That story is covered in other papers at this meeting. Here I will concentrate on concepts and ways of doing the perturbation calculations.

7.2 Fluids and scalar fields

Mathematically, one studies perturbations of the spatially homogeneous and isotropic Friedmann–Lemaître (FL) universe models. This involves splitting a realistic (lumpy) model of the universe into (a) a background FL model and (b) perturbations around that background, and then understanding the evolution of the universe in terms of the dynamics of the background on the one hand (independent of the perturbations, at linear order), and the dynamics of the perturbations on the other (depending crucially on the evolution of the background). Both the realistic model and the background model are required to obey the Einstein field equations[1] (EFE)

$$R_{ab} - \frac{1}{2}Rg_{ab} + \Lambda g_{ab} = \kappa T_{ab} \tag{7.1}$$

to the appropriate level of approximation (as discussed below), where R_{ab} is the Ricci tensor, R the Ricci scalar, κ the gravitational constant, T_{ab} the total matter stress-energy tensor, Λ a possibly non-zero cosmological constant, and g_{ab} the spacetime metric tensor. However, consequent on

---

[1] See e.g. [75] for a discussion.

the fact that in General Relativity there is no fixed background spacetime underlying the curved spacetime model, this splitting of a lumpy universe into a background model and its perturbations is not unique. The freedom to choose the background model in different ways, and hence change the representation of the perturbations in a given lumpy spacetime, is the gauge freedom of the problem. I will discuss four different ways of carrying out the calculations[2] and handling this issue.

7.2.1 *Special gauges and metric variables*

The first method is to deal with metric and matter perturbations represented in a particular gauge, usually specified in terms of a specific coordinate choice in the perturbed model (which implies the way the unperturbed background model is related to it). As shown in the pioneering 1946 paper by Lifshitz [88], linearizing about the EFE in this way gives the equations for the growth of inhomogeneities due to gravitational attraction, and these can usefully be analysed either by Fourier analysis [12, 99] or by use of a Green's function approach [6]. This approach has been widely used, in particular in the brilliant 1967 paper by Sachs and Wolfe [112] that first gave the relation of structure growth to CBR anisotropies. However, there are a series of problems associated with this approach. First, the metric perturbations that are the foundation of the approach are not themselves directly observable. Second, the magnitude of the density perturbation variables depends on the choice of gauge. Third, pure gauge modes arise due to the arbitrariness of splitting into background and perturbations when the gauge is not uniquely determined. There are errors and misunderstandings in a number of papers using this approach, in particular in one famous paper claiming to clear up all the previous misunderstandings. Thus it is essential to keep track of the gauge freedom associated with any particular coordinate choice in order to separate mathematical from physical perturbation modes.

Various recent investigations (e.g. [11, 12]) use this method of working in a particular gauge, handling the gauge issue by first keeping track of all gauge freedom and secondly determining strictly observational relations as their output (which must be gauge-free if properly defined). This works adequately in a pragmatic way, but is not ideal in that the basic variables used are not close representations of the physics and consequently, due to

---

[2] There are other methods possible in addition to those presented here: in particular, various tetrad-based methods are useful in some circumstances. However, they have not played such a significant role in cosmology as the four discussed here (they have been significant in studying gravitational radiation theory and perturbations of black holes), and so have not been included in this article.

the occurrence of gauge modes, one attains higher order equations than correspond to the physical degrees of freedom. The method is neither gauge-invariant nor covariant.

7.2.2 1+3 covariant approach

The second method is to use covariant variables associated with the elegant 1+3 covariant approach to fluid dynamics developed by Heckmann, Schücking, Ehlers, Kundt and Trümper (the Hamburg school) in the early 1960s. This covariant approach is summarized by Stephen Hawking in his excellent 1966 paper 'Perturbations of an expanding universe' [70]. It is based on the fact that realistic cosmological models always include at least one uniquely determined 4-velocity vector field u^a ($u^a u_a = -1$), for example that representing the average motion of mass-energy at each point, naturally associated with a preferred family of 'fundamental observers' in the universe.[3] Physically, this is the unique timelike eigenvector of the energy-momentum tensor T_{ab} ($T_{ab}u^b = -\mu u_a$, where μ is the matter energy-density). Observationally, near our own spacetime position it can be determined to high accuracy through measurement of the CBR dipole, which determines the local rest frame of matter in the universe.

Given a covariant choice of such a unique timelike vector field, it is natural to make a 1+3 split of all physical and geometrical objects and equations relative to this 4-velocity. It determines an associated covariant time derivative $\dot{T}^{ab}_{\ \ cd} \equiv T^{ab}_{\ \ cd;e}u^e$ and a local rest-frame characterized by the perpendicular projection tensor $h_{ab} = g_{ab} + u_a u_b$ ($h_a^{\ b}h_b^{\ c} = h_a^{\ c}$, $h_{ab}u^b = 0$). This is just the metric tensor of the rest spaces of u^a, and determines a spatial derivative $^{(3)}\nabla_a T^{bc}_{\ \ de}$ (projected on all indices by use of $h_a^{\ b}$). Kinematic quantities describing the flow of matter moving with 4-velocity u^a are the fluid expansion Θ, acceleration a^b, shear σ_{ab}, and vorticity ω_{ab}, together equivalent to the covariant derivative of u^a:

$$u_{a;b} = \frac{1}{3}\Theta h_{ab} + \sigma_{ab} + \omega_{ab} - \dot{u}_a u_b. \tag{7.2}$$

Here σ_{ab} is a projected symmetric trace-free (PSTF) tensor: $\sigma_{ab}u^b = 0$, $\sigma_{ab} = \sigma_{(ab)}$, $\sigma^b_{\ b} = 0$, ω_{ab} is a skew-symmetric projected tensor: $\omega_{ab}u^b = 0$, $\omega_{ab} = \omega_{[ab]}$, and a^b is orthogonal to u_b: $a^b u_b = 0$.

The spacetime curvature tensor R_{abcd} is represented first by matter variables μ, p, q_a, π_{ab} (the energy density, pressure, heat flux vector and

---

[3] The underlying theory of General Relativity is of course Lorentz invariant; the existence of this preferred velocity field and associated rest frame is yet another example of the broken symmetries that are so central to our present day understanding of fundamental physical effects.

anisotropic pressure respectively) obtained from a 1+3 decomposition of the energy-momentum tensor T_{ab} relative to u^a :

$$T_{ab} = \mu u_a u_b + p h_{ab} + 2q_{(a}u_{b)} + \pi_{ab} \tag{7.3}$$

where q_a is orthogonal and π_{ab} is a PSTF tensor. These quantities algebraically determine the Ricci tensor at each point through the EFE (7.1). The remainder of the spacetime curvature is the Weyl tensor C_{abcd} (the trace-free part of R_{abcd}), which can be characterized as the free gravitational field, determined at each point by matter at other points together with boundary conditions on the spacetime. It is decomposed relative to u^a into its electric and magnetic parts E_{ac}, H_{ac}, defined by

$$E_{ac} = C_{abcd}u^b u^d, \ H_{ac} = \frac{1}{2}\eta_{ab}{}^{ef}C_{efcd}u^b u^d, \tag{7.4}$$

where η_{abcd} is the skew-symmetric volume element. These are PSTF tensors representing both tidal forces and gravitational radiation.

The associated 1+3 decomposition of the EFE, Ricci identities for u_a, and Bianchi identities gives transparent versions of the full non-linear equations in terms of these quantities, see [41, 42, 51, 70]. The two most important cosmological equations are the energy conservation equation and the Raychaudhuri–Ehlers equation of gravitational attraction. Specifically, the energy density of a perfect fluid ($q_a = \pi_{ab} = 0$) obeys the conservation equation[4]

$$\dot{\mu} + (\mu + p)\Theta = 0, \tag{7.5}$$

which becomes determinate when a suitable equation of state relates the pressure p to the energy density μ. The time derivative of the expansion obeys the Raychaudhuri–Ehlers [37, 108] equation

$$\dot{\Theta} + \frac{1}{3}\Theta^2 - a^b{}_{;b} + 2\sigma^2 - 2\omega^2 + \frac{1}{2}\kappa(\mu + 3p) - \Lambda = 0 \tag{7.6}$$

where ω and σ are the vorticity and shear scalars respectively. This shows that shear and a positive active gravitational mass density $\mu_{grav} \equiv \mu + 3p$ cause gravitational attraction, whereas vorticity and a positive cosmological constant Λ cause gravitational repulsion. Inflation is possible when $\mu_{grav} < 0$.

In terms of these variables, the FL models [110] are characterized as irrotational and shearfree geodesic perfect fluid models ($a^b = \sigma_{ab} = \omega_{ab} = 0$,

---

[4] We are using units where $c = 1$. Note that this evolution is determined by the inertial mass density $\mu_{inertia} \equiv \mu + p$.

$q_a = \pi_{ab} = 0$) implying vanishing Weyl tensor: $E_{ab} = 0 = H_{ab}$ (and so conformal flatness) and existence of a canonical time-variable t obeying $u_a = -t_{,a}$ such that $\mu = \mu(t)$, $p = p(t)$, $\Theta = \Theta(t)$. For these models, the scale factor $S(t)$ obeys the relation $3\dot{S}(t)/S(t) = \Theta(t)$, and (7.6) becomes

$$3\ddot{S}/S = -\frac{1}{2}\kappa(\mu + 3p) + \Lambda, \tag{7.7}$$

with first integral the Friedmann equation

$$\frac{\dot{S}^2}{S^2} = \frac{\kappa\mu}{3} + \frac{\Lambda}{3} - \frac{k}{S^2}, \tag{7.8}$$

where k is the normalized spatial curvature ($k = \pm 1$ or 0).

This covariant set of equations was utilized by Hawking in his paper [70] developing a covariant approach to perturbations in cosmology. His method was to linearize the set of 1+3 covariant equations about the family of FL models. Thus regarding μ, p and Θ as zero-order quantities and a^b, σ_{ab}, ω_{ab}, E_{ab} and H_{ab} as 1st order quantities in the non-linear 1+3 covariant equations for a perfect fluid gives a clear approximation procedure leading to a set of linearized equations determining structure growth, vorticity decay, and propagation of gravitational waves in the expanding universe. Because these are tensor equations, one can write out their components in any convenient coordinate system. Choosing a suitable set of coordinates, Hawking obtained solutions to these equations showing the growth of density perturbations and the propagation of gravitational waves. This approach provides a considerable improvement over previous approaches in terms of clarity. He explains:

'Perturbations of a spatially homogeneous and isotropic universe have been investigated in a Newtonian model by Bonnor (1957), in a Newtonian approximation to a relativistic model by Irvine (1965), and relativistically by Lifshitz (1946) and Lifshitz and Khalatnikov (1963). Lifshitz' method was to consider small variations of the metric tensor. This has the disadvantage that the metric tensor is not a physically significant quantity. That is, one cannot directly measure it but only its second derivatives. It is thus not always obvious what the physical interpretation of a given perturbation of the metric is. Indeed it need have no physical interpretation at all, but merely correspond to a coordinate transformation. Instead it seems preferable to employ a method which considers small variations of the physically significant quantity, the curvature' ([70], p.544).

However, the resulting equations for the density perturbations are still not gauge-invariant, because the variables representing density inhomogeneities are defined by variation of scalar variables. They therefore depend on the choice of the spacelike surfaces of constant time in the perturbed model universes which specify the relation of the background model to the perturbed model, and hence the amplitude of the apparent density perturbations. These can be given arbitrary values by change of the fitting of the background model to the perturbed model [49].[5] Thus this method is 1+3 covariant, but not gauge-invariant.

7.2.3 Gauge-invariant coordinate based approach

The third method is to start with metric and matter perturbations defined in a particular coordinate system, work out the effect of a change of gauge on the metric components and matter variables, and so find gauge-invariant combinations of these variables. The perturbations are split into scalar, vector, and tensor parts, each of which is handled separately. The linearized field equations are written out in terms of the Fourier components of these gauge-invariant variables for each of these cases; the equations for each mode and for each wavelength decouple from each other. The variables are, however, gauge-invariant only for infinitesimal gauge transformation – 'large' transformations are not covered by this formalism.

This method was presented by Bardeen in an important paper in 1980 [4] in which he developed the general method and showed how it worked with a variety of different gauge choices. This method has been widely used, for example in a major study of perturbations of inflationary universe models by Bardeen, Steinhardt, and Turner [5]. A comprehensive review of the method is given in [97], and it is also presented by Bardeen in his contribution to this book.

This method has considerable power and utility. However, the geometric meaning of the gauge-invariant variables used is not immediately obvious; this usually has to be explained in terms of what they represent in particular gauges. Furthermore, while the splitting into scalar, vector, and tensor parts is very useful physically, it is a non-local splitting depending on how boundary conditions are chosen for the physical fields at infinity [117], and so cannot be observationally determined within our past light cone. This method is gauge-invariant, but is not 1+3 covariant.

7.2.4 1+3 covariant and gauge-invariant approach

The fourth method is to use variables and equations that are both 1+3 covariant and gauge-invariant, thus combining the advantages of the previous two methods. This can be done by using the 1+3 covariant approach

---

[5] This is true on both small and large scales, despite the claim often made that it is only relevant on large scales.

of Hawking, but introducing gauge-invariant variables to represent the density perturbations [20, 49]. In more detail, it is based on:

1. regarding the gauge choice as defining a map from the background spacetime into the realistic spacetime;

2. choosing a suitable covariantly defined 4-velocity field u^a and writing the exact non-linear 1+3 covariant equations relative to this 4-velocity field in the realistic lumpy spacetime (rather than in the background space-times, as is customary in the gauge dependent approaches); then

3. systematically approximating to obtain the linearized equations.

The key issue is variable choice that is both 1+3 covariant and gauge-invariant (CGI). These may be found by using a Lemma given by Stewart and Walker [118]: *variables that vanish in the background are necessarily gauge-invariant*. Hence CGI variables for a perturbed FL universe model are first, the first-order kinematic quantities and Weyl tensor components:

$$\sigma_{ab}, \ \omega^a, \ a^b, \ E_{ab}, \ H_{ab} \tag{7.9}$$

and secondly, the first-order inhomogeneity variables X_a, Y_a, Z_a determined from the zero-order variables $\mu(x^i)$, $p(x^i)$, $\Theta(x^i)$ by taking their spatial derivatives:

$$X_a \equiv {}^{(3)}\nabla_a \mu, \ Y_a \equiv {}^{(3)}\nabla_a p, \ Z_a \equiv {}^{(3)}\nabla_a \Theta. \tag{7.10}$$

Introducing the comoving scale factor $S(x^i)$ satisfying

$$3\dot{S} = \Theta S, \tag{7.11}$$

the vector X_a can conveniently be rescaled to give a dimensionless (fractional comoving) representation of the density variation:

$$\chi_a = \frac{S}{\mu} {}^{(3)}\nabla_a \mu \tag{7.12}$$

which is the physically useful quantity to consider when looking at structure formation.

We can get generic non-linear propagation equations for these quantities by taking the spatial gradient of the conservation equation (7.5) and Raychaudhuri equation (7.6). For the case of pressure-free matter, which moves geodesically: $a^b = 0$, this gives

$$h^a{}_c (X_a)^\cdot = -\Theta X_c - \kappa\mu Z_c - X_a(\omega^a{}_c + \sigma^a{}_c), \tag{7.13}$$

$$h^a{}_c(Z_a)^\cdot = -\frac{4}{3}\Theta Z_c - \frac{1}{2}X_c - {}^{(3)}\nabla_c 2(\sigma^2 - \omega^2) - Z_a(\omega^a{}_c + \sigma^a{}_c). \quad (7.14)$$

These are exact non-linear equations for the growth of density inhomo-geneities. We get the corresponding perturbation equations by linearizing about a FRW background, giving

$$h^a{}_c(X_a)^\cdot = -\Theta X_c - \kappa\mu Z_c, \quad (7.15)$$

$$h^a{}_c(Z_a)^\cdot = -\frac{4}{3}\Theta Z_c - \frac{1}{2}X_c. \quad (7.16)$$

Now these two equations close up: taking a time derivative of the first and substituting from the second and from the zero-order equations (7.5), (7.7) gives a second order equation for X_a. In terms of the dimensionless quantity χ_a defined in (7.12), this takes the expected form

$$(\chi_a)^{\cdot\cdot} + \frac{2}{3}\Theta(\chi_a)^\cdot - \frac{1}{2}\kappa\mu\chi_a = 0.$$

In this way, we get CGI equations for the variables (7.9), (7.10) that are true in all coordinates (they are tensor equations); these can be solved explicitly after choosing a suitable coordinate system in the perturbed model, e.g. co-moving coordinates associated with the chosen frame, and substituting the explicit background values into the coefficients of the perturbed equations. When the pressure is non-zero, pressure gradients generate a non-zero fluid acceleration, and a splitting into Fourier modes will be useful in order to separate out the behaviour for different wave-lengths [50, 53]; a Green's function approach in position space could also be used [6]. The resulting solution is then related to observational quan-tities, e.g. the covariance function and power spectra for matter and the CBR anisotropies (discussed in the next section). A splitting into scalar, vector, and tensor parts can be made (in the scalar case, for example, all the quantities in (7.9), (7.10) are gradients of scalar fields), but the basic method is not dependent on such a splitting; when such a splitting is carried out together with a Fourier mode decomposition the formalism is essentially equivalent to the Bardeen formalism [20], although obtained and expressed in a different way.

This is a clear straightforward approach which allows error estimates and non-linear developments from the linear case (because the non-linear equations are available), but depends on the choice of 4-velocity. This will be unique in simple cases (a single perfect fluid, for example), but not in realistic multifluid applications, where we need to take into account bary-onic matter, cold dark matter, neutrinos, photons, scalar fields, etc. When multiple fields are present, quantities $\chi_{(r)a}$ can be defined by (7.12) for the energy density $\mu_{(r)}$ of each separate matter component (labelled by an index r), which will generically each move with a different 4-velocity $u^a_{(r)}$. As well as equations for the evolution of the density perturbations $X_{(r)a}$, one then obtains equations for the evolution of the relative velocities $u^a_{(rs)} = u^a_{(r)} - u^a_{(s)}$ [35]. One can then choose a specific frame to simplify the dynamics, choose associated coordinates, and solve the resulting equations. Various covariant options will be available as regards the choice of the reference vector u^a, e.g. the centre of momentum choice: $q^a = 0$, baryonic or cold dark matter (pressure-free) choice, implying geodesic motion: $a^a = 0$, or (in some circumstances) a Newtonian-like choice: $\sigma_{ab} = 0$, $\omega_{ab} = 0$, each resulting in a slightly different form of the equations. Which is best depends on the application.

The equations for a generic ('imperfect') fluid give versions of the 1+3 CGI formalism that are valid in all frames for any continuous matter distribution or set of scalar fields, because choice of a specific frame (generically non-comoving) for any fluid gives a representation of its stress-tensor as a (generally imperfect) fluid [94], and this can be applied to each component in a mixture of fluids and scalar fields to give a representation of the total stress-tensor as a single fluid. For the case of a single scalar field ϕ with spacelike surfaces of constant density, on choosing u^a orthogonal to these surfaces the stress tensor has a perfect fluid form with

$$\mu = \frac{1}{2}\dot{\phi}^2 + V(\phi), \ p = \frac{1}{2}\dot{\phi}^2 - V(\phi), \tag{7.17}$$

and there exist associated conserved quantities on large (super-horizon) scales [21]. As is well known, these play a key role in the study of inflationary perturbations.

Overall, the 1+3 CGI approach to perturbations is a versatile and transparent approach with much to recommend it, with Stephen's 1966 paper as its starting point. It is described in depth in [51], which gives references to many other papers, and [28]. It can be extended to a kinetic theory approach for matter [86] and for radiation (discussed in the next section).

7.3 Cosmic background radiation

The inhomogeneous perturbed FL cosmologies result in CBR anisotropies generated first by inhomogeneities on the surface of last scattering that emits that radiation, and secondly by the propagation of the CBR to us from the surface of last scattering in the intervening inhomogeneous spacetime. To obtain predictions for the resulting CBR anisotropies, one can consider the kinetic theory description of radiation in perturbed FL space-times, with the photon distribution function $f(x,p)$ split into angular and spatial harmonics. One can then use the covariant form of the Boltzmann equation

$$L(f) = \frac{\partial f}{\partial x^i}\frac{dx^i}{dv} + \frac{\partial f}{\partial p^a}\frac{dp^a}{dv} = \mathcal{C}$$

to determine the evolution of associated energy integrals of the distribution function (a) from the end of inflation to the epoch of last scattering, and (b) from the surface of last scattering to the present day. This can be done by any of the four perturbation methods outlined above. Whichever approach is adopted, it has to relate angular scales on the sky explicitly or implicitly to spatial scales on the surface of last scattering, and should determine the angular power spectra predicted for the CBR in relation to the power spectra for matter predicted by structure formation theories (for it is these matter fluctuations that cause the CBR fluctuations), both of these being related to the spectrum of perturbations on the surface of last scattering.

There are three somewhat different methods that have been used to calculate these effects. I now discuss them in turn. Note that there is a separate literature on CBR anisotropies for the spatially homogeneous modes characterized by almost isotropic Bianchi models; these do not satisfy the Gaussian normal assumption almost universally made for the spatial distribution of inhomogeneous perturbation modes on the last scattering surface, and I will not discuss these models here.

7.3.1 Gauge dependent methods

Following the pioneering work by Sachs and Wolfe [112], there have been numerous gauge-dependent papers carrying out this programme through an analysis based on perturbed metric functions, see e.g. Wilson and Silk [130, 131], Ma and Bertschinger [91]. The same issues arise as discussed above regarding gauge-dependent analyses of perturbations: with sufficient care the method works, but it is not as straightforward as one might hope, partly because the resulting equations are higher order than is necessary to describe the physics. To be safe one should not switch gauges in mid-calculation without extreme caution, and should keep tight control of all remaining gauge freedom.

7.3.2 Gauge-invariant methods

The Bardeen gauge-invariant approach to perturbed FL models has been used to carry out this CBR programme, see [79–81], and references therein, leading to a practical approach of considerable importance. For the reasons outlined above this is a significant improvement on the gauge-dependent methods, but is still based on essentially coordinate dependent quantities.

7.3.3 1+3 covariant and gauge-invariant method

The CGI approach has also been extended to the CBR anisotropies. Developing from work of Pirani [106] and Thorne [121] on the covariant analysis of gravitational radiation, this employs a covariant harmonic analysis of the distribution function $f(x, p)$ with respect to a 4-velocity u^a [55, 60]. Relative to u^a, each photon has 4-momentum

$$p^a = E(u^a + e^a), \quad e^a e_a = 1, \quad e^a u_a = 0 \qquad (7.18)$$

where e^a is the direction of motion and E the energy measured by u^a. Relative to a suitable tetrad, $e_a = (0, \cos\theta, \sin\theta\sin\phi, \cos\theta\cos\phi)$. The distribution function is written as a function of direction in the covariant power-series form

$$f(x^i, E, e^a) = f + f_a(x^i, E)e^a + f_{ab}(x^i, E)e^a e^b + f_{abc}(x^i, E)e^a e^b e^c + \dots. \qquad (7.19)$$

that is

$$f(x^i, E, e^a) = \Sigma_{l \geq 0} f_{A_l}(x^i, E)e^{A_l} \qquad (7.20)$$

on using a collective label $A_l \equiv a_1 a_2 .. a_l$ and the product notation $e^{A_l} \equiv e^{a_1}e^{a_2}...e^{a_l}$, where the coefficients $f_{abc \cdot\cdot d}(x^i, E)$ are PSTF, i.e. they are

1. symmetric: $f_{abc \cdot\cdot d} = f_{(abc \cdot\cdot d)}$,

2. projected orthogonal to u^a: $f_{abc \cdot\cdot d} u^d = 0$,

3. trace-free: $f^a{}_{abc \cdot\cdot d} = 0$.

This representation is fully equivalent to a usual angular harmonic decomposition, but its tensorial form makes it very suitable for use in a covariant analysis. The covariant Boltzmann equation now becomes a set of exact evolution equations for the PSTF angular harmonic coefficients $f_{A_l}(x^i, E)$, [55], in general each equation linking five successive moments (l ranges over the values $L+2$, $L+1$, L, $L-1$, $L-2$ for some L).

One can integrate these coefficients over energy to define PSTF moments ('brightness multipoles')

$$\Pi_{A_l}(x^i) \equiv \int_0^\infty E^3 f_{A_l}(x^i, E)\, dE. \qquad (7.21)$$

The first three such moments are just those needed for the EFE, namely the energy density, momentum density, and anisotropic pressure of the radiation relative to u^a, with the energy density determining the isotropic pressure:

$$\mu_R = 4\Pi(x^i) = 3p_R, \quad q_R^a = \frac{4\pi}{3}\Pi^a(x^i), \quad \pi_R^{ab} = \frac{8\pi}{15}\Pi^{ab}(x^i).$$

Thus the moments $\Pi_{A_l}(x^i)$ for $0 \le l \le 2$ directly enter the EFE, but these equations are independent of all the moments for $l \ge 3$. The moments $\Pi_{A_l}(x^i)$ for $l \ge 1$ and the spatial gradients of the zero-order moments ($l = 0$) are CGI variables. Multiplying the Boltzmann equation by E^3 and integrate over all energies, using integration by parts and the fact that $E^n F_{a\cdots} \to 0$ as $E \to \infty$ for any positive n, we obtain exact evolution equations for the brightness multipoles Π_{A_l}:

$$\dot{\Pi}_{\langle A_l \rangle} + \frac{4}{3}\Theta \Pi_{A_l} + {}^{(3)}\nabla_{\langle a_l}\Pi_{A_{l-1}\rangle} + \frac{(l+1)}{(2l+3)}{}^{(3)}\nabla^b\Pi_{bA_l}$$

$$- \frac{(l+1)(l-2)}{(2l+3)}A^b\Pi_{bA_l}$$

$$+ (l+3)A_{\langle a_l}\Pi_{A_{l-1}\rangle} - l\omega^b\varepsilon_{bc(a_l}\Pi_{A_{l-1})}{}^c$$

$$- \frac{(l-1)(l+1)(l+2)}{(2l+3)(2l+5)}\sigma^{bc}\Pi_{bcA_l}$$

$$+ \frac{5l}{(2l+3)}\sigma^b{}_{\langle a_l}\Pi_{A_{l-1}\rangle b} - (l+2)\sigma_{\langle a_l a_{l-1}}\Pi_{A_{l-2}\rangle}$$

$$= K_{A_l}, \tag{7.22}$$

where $\Pi_{A_l} = 0$ if $l < 0$, see [28, 51, 55, 94] for details, where the brackets $\langle a..b \rangle$ represent the symmetric, trace-free part and K_{A_l} is an energy-integrated form of the Boltzmann collision term $\mathcal{C}$. These equations include the usual energy and momentum conservation equations for $l = 0, 1$. This is an exact result that holds for any collision term, i.e. any K_{A_l}. In realistic applications there will be many matter and radiation components present, so choice of the velocity vector becomes an issue; various covariant choices are available, as discussed above, each leading to a set of exact covariant equations.

Linearizing about a FL model, one obtains a set of linearized equations for the radiation multipoles [28, 94] which for the case of Thomson scattering with small relative velocities are

$$\dot{\mu}_R + \frac{4}{3}\Theta\,\mu_R + {}^{(3)}\nabla_a q_R^a = 0 ,$$

$$\dot{q}_R^{\langle a\rangle} + \frac{4}{3}\Theta q_R^a + \frac{4}{3}\,\mu_R\,\dot{u}^a + \frac{1}{3}\,^{(3)}\nabla^a\mu_R +\,^{(3)}\nabla_b\pi_R^{ab} = n_E\sigma_T\left(\frac{4}{3}\,\mu_R v_B^a - q_R^a\right),$$

$$\dot{\pi}_R^{\langle ab\rangle} + \frac{4}{3}\,\Theta\,\pi_R^{ab} + \frac{8}{15}\,\mu_R\,\sigma^{ab} + \frac{2}{5}\,^{(3)}\nabla^{\langle a}q_R^{b\rangle} + \frac{8\pi}{35}\,^{(3)}\nabla_c\Pi^{abc} = -\frac{9}{10}\,n_E\sigma_T\,\pi_R^{ab},$$

for $l = 0, 1, 2$, and

$$\dot{\Pi}^{\langle A_l\rangle} + \frac{4}{3}\,\Theta\,\Pi^{A_l} +\,^{(3)}\nabla^{\langle a_l}\Pi^{A_{l-1}\rangle} + \frac{(l+1)}{(2l+3)}\,^{(3)}\nabla_b\Pi^{bA_l} = -\,n_E\sigma_T\Pi^{A_l}$$

for $l \geq 3$. Here n_E is the electron density, σ_T the Thomson scattering cross-section, and v_B^a the baryon velocity. Note that these equations now link only angular multipoles of order $l - 1$, l, $l + 1$, i.e. they link *three* successive terms. This is a major qualitative difference from the full non-linear equations. There are similar equations for the electric and magnetic polarizations [25, 27].

If one now introduces a set of harmonic functions $Q(x^i)$ in the background spacetime, determining an associated set of harmonic PSTF tensors $Q_{A_l}(x^i)$, one can analyse the moments $\Pi_{A_l}(x^i)$ in terms of these spatial harmonics to obtain moments $\Pi(l, k)$ characterized by comoving wave number k as well as the angular harmonic index l. The harmonics for each k decouple from each other, leading to a full set of linearized CBR moment equations for these harmonics. They can be numerically integrated, and can also be analytically integrated in the tight-coupling (pre-decoupling) and free radiation (post-decoupling) approximations, leading to the usual predictions of the Sachs–Wolfe plateau and acoustic peaks in the angular power spectrum as discussed in other papers in this volume. This method can be used for scalar, vector, and tensor perturbations, and for polarization studies. It has been developed in detail by Maartens, Gebbie and Ellis [64, 65, 94], summarized in [51], and by Challinor, Lewis and Lasenby [25–28], leading to an efficient form of the CBR anisotropy computer codes [87].[6]

7.3.4 Almost-EGS theorem

One should note here that these analyses do not prove the universe is well represented by an almost-FL model; they assume this as their starting point, and this assumption is the cornerstone of the standard interpretation of CBR anisotropies. The best way of justifying this assumption is to use the *almost-EGS theorem*, see Stoeger, Maartens and Ellis [119], proving that if an expanding geodesically moving family of observers in an

---

[6] Available at http://camb.info/.

open set $\mathcal{U}$ all measure freely propagating radiation to be almost isotropic everywhere in $\mathcal{U}$, then[7] the universe is an almost-FL universe in $\mathcal{U}$. This theorem is applied by noting that we observe almost isotropic CBR about us, and then making *a weak Copernican assumption*: we assume we are not in a cosmologically privileged position. It follows that other co-moving observers will see similarly isotropic radiation, and the theorem applies. There are other possibilities where this Copernican assumption is not true [43], but they are not regarded as probable.

7.4 Issues

Analysis of the relation of structure formation to CBR anisotropies is at the heart of present day cosmology, and many interesting issues arise. I will briefly consider four of them.

7.4.1 Issue 1: Non-linearities

First is a thorough exploration of non-linearities associated both with structure formation and with the generation of CBR anisotropies. As regards structure formation and the associated generation of large-scale velocities, the need is for further extension of analytic approaches (such as the Zel'dovich approximation) that complement numerical studies of the non-linear regime, these approaches together providing the link between cosmological perturbation theory and observations of real astrophysical objects. As regards the CBR anisotropy, particularly because of the anticipation of much more data of much better quality becoming available in the coming decade, much work is under way on the effect of non-linearities, looking for example at the implications of the Sunyaev–Zel'dovich effect, of gravitational lensing, of slow decoupling, and of re-ionization, as well as the nature of polarization effects [34]. Other issues that need attention are:

1. mode-mixing (scalar/vector/tensor mixing, on the one hand, and mixing of different comoving wavelengths on the other) due to non-linearities;

2. the fact that five successive CBR angular modes are linked in the non-linear case, rather than three as in the linear case, and so the mode interaction is qualitatively different in the non-linear case;

---

[7] This establishes the stability of the basic result by Ehlers, Geren and Sachs [39], who showed that exact isotropy would imply an exact FL model.

3. there are non-linearities in the CBR anisotropies at high l because some terms in the Boltzmann equations are multiplied by l itself, see [94];

4. the issue of truncation of the CBR angular harmonic series (if this is done without sufficient care, the resulting equations will be consistent only if the fluid shear vanishes [55, 60]);

5. These studies should take into account the possibility of alternative spatial topologies for compact universes of all spatial curvatures, resulting in altered harmonics and CBR anisotropy patterns (see [84, 111] and references therein).

7.4.2 Issue 2: Back reaction, averaging and entropy

Second is the effect of back-reaction by the perturbations on the background model [66, 98], resulting in a change in its evolution, and inevitably arising when non-linear effects are taken into account. This is inextricably tied in to the issues of appropriately fitting the background model to the lumpy realistic model on the one hand, and the inverse procedure of averaging the latter to obtain the former on the other [23, 44, 58]. Underlying these effects is the fact that any representation of the metric and matter has an implicit averaging scale hidden in its definition, and a change of such averaging scale does not commute with evaluating the EFE [44]. Furthermore, because any such averaging procedure is a form of coarse-graining through which micro-information is hidden, this is all necessarily related to the ill-understood concept of gravitational entropy and its relation to gravitational structure formation. Because of the Second Law of Thermodynamics, this is in turn related to the issue of the gravitational arrow of time – how does the macrophysical theory have a unique arrow of time relating spontaneous structure formation (which takes place in apparent defiance of the Second Law), the generation of gravitational waves, and the expansion of the universe, even though the underlying gravitational equations (the EFE) has none? Gravitational entropy probably relates to the Weyl tensor (see [67, 103, 105] and references therein) but the way this relates to coarse-graining is quite unclear. All of this needs clarification.

7.4.3 Issue 3: Planckian effects

Third is the controversial issue of how the nature of the Planckian regime may affect the growth of inhomogeneities in the pre-inflationary era, and so influence the present day matter and CBR power spectra [19, 77, 82].

The quantum gravity regime might have a chaotic (fractal) character, as envisaged by the concept of 'spacetime foam', or a discrete or lattice-like character, as suggested by the idea that spacetime itself may be quantized at the Planck scale. Alternatively, that era may perhaps be well-described by one of the present approaches to quantum cosmology. There are many such approaches; at the time of writing, the brane cosmology scenarios are generating some excitement. In each case an appropriate generalization of the 1+3 CGI approach can be utilized to determine the evolution of perturbations. In the case of brane cosmology, the basic perturbation theory in 1+3 CGI form has been given by Maartens [92], and its development to give CBR anisotropy predictions is under way by Maartens [93] and Leong, Dunsby, Challinor, and Lasenby [85]. The key issue here is how to handle bulk modes; present approaches consider cases when they do not occur, and so consider only the subset of the full family of perturbation solutions in which physics on the brane is determinate. However, there are other approaches to quantum gravity and quantum cosmology, so a vital issue in the future is extension of structure formation and CBR anisotropy studies to these approaches also, for example loop quantum gravity [13–15] and non-commutative geometry [2, 90].

7.4.4 Issue 4: Origin of Newtonian equations

Fourth is the opposite extreme: how the relativistic theory relates at late times to the Newtonian theory of structure growth. It is known that Newtonian gravitational theory, when written in potential form with generalized boundary conditions, gives a direct analogue of the 1+3 covariant dynamical equations [41] and consequently of the 1+3 CGI perturbation theory [46], with completely analogous equations at each step of the derivation. This provides the link to important astrophysical applications, for example non-linear structure formation and the theory of peculiar velocity perturbations. But the issue now is, how do these Newtonian equations arise from the General Relativity equations when non-linearities are present?[8] The point is fundamental: Newtonian gravitational theory as generally assumed in astrophysics, with its preferred surfaces of constant time foliating spacetime, is only a valid approximation to the underlying non-linear gravitational theory in particular circumstances. Under what conditions is this a good approximation, and what consistency conditions arise? In particular, when do the ten EFE reduce to one effective Newtonian field equation?

---

[8] A frame approach to the Newtonian limit of General Relativity resulting in various exact theorems was given by Ehlers, see e.g. [38].

This first requires the occurrence of scalar perturbations only, and secondly a situation where the EFE result in a Poisson equation determining a scalar field which then guides the motion of free particles by determining spacetime geodesics. But it then, thirdly, also requires that when this equation is satisfied, that is sufficient: we do not have to satisfy a series of additional dynamic equations in addition to this one. Thus it requires that all the other EFE are valid in consequence of this Poisson equation and generally valid kinematic identities, so that when this one equation is satisfied, all the EFE are satisfied. In what gauges can this occur, and how is the analogue of the Newtonian preferred time coordinate determined then? All of this should follow in the appropriate context from the relativistic 1+3 CGI equations; the way this happens has been partly elucidated [52, 61] and needs completion. Asking this question is similar to considering how the emergence of classical theory from quantum theory occurs – an important transition in the history of the universe. It has been conjectured [48] that Newtonian theory can emerge from General Relativity only in the context of almost-FL universe models (where gravitational wave and rotational perturbations are very small), but this is not yet a rigorous theorem.

Part B: Cosmological singularities

The issue here is: is there a beginning to the universe? If so, what is its nature? This is a key question in developing our understanding of the nature of the universe. There has from time immemorial been a desire to believe in an unchanging universe or, failing that, one that even if evolving has existed for ever. The option of an unchanging ('steady state') universe has, however, been disproved by the astronomical evidence first of systematic galaxy redshifts, indicating an expanding universe, and secondly by the radio source number-counts, evidencing statistical source evolution. Taken together these imply a changing universe, and this is confirmed by the existence of the black-body CBR, physically understood as remnant radiation from the early 'Hot Big Bang' era.[9] But this does not settle the question of whether it had a beginning. Could it have existed for ever? Could it have started in an asymptotically static state, as in the Eddington–Lemaître universe, or collapsed from infinity and rebounded at a finite radius, one of Robertson's 'oscillating universes' [110], or have undergone an eternal series of bounces, as envisaged by Tolman [124]?

---

[9] And a steady state situation is in any case very hard to reconcile with the continued existence in the universe of irreversible thermodynamics and transient non-equilibrium structures, such as stars and galaxies.

It is well known that standard FL models (which we understand as obeying the energy condition $\mu + 3p > 0$) have a singular origin when $\Lambda = 0$, indeed this follows directly from equation (7.7); however, some FL models with $\Lambda > 0$ have no beginning, in virtue of the existence of a sufficiently large cosmological constant [110]. But these models cannot represent the real universe, because such a large cosmological constant is incompatible with astronomical observations. In more detail: in order to cause a turn-around or prevent a singularity, a cosmological constant Λ would have to dominate the field equations at very early times, when the density of matter was much higher than today. However, observations indicate Λ dominates matter at the present time by at most a factor of about $\Omega_\Lambda/\Omega_m = 0.7/0.3 = 2.3$, and so[10] cannot dominate at times earlier than a redshift of about $z = 0.32$ – when we know the universe was expanding. Thus matter wins, and FL models of the universe must have a singular beginning where the energy density and temperature diverge. This provides the start of the 'Hot Big Bang' epoch.

However, these are very special highly idealized models, being spherically symmetric about every point and hence also spatially homogeneous. Maybe they do not tell us whether the real universe is singular or not. The physical issue is: is the singularity in the FL models due to this very high symmetry? Will singularities remain in more realistic universe models? The mathematical issue is: is the singularity predicted by studies of the field equations in many more generic models a coordinate singularity or a physical singularity? If the latter, what is its nature? The observational issue is: can we use astronomical data to indicate whether an initial singularity exists or not?

Two major approaches have been used to study these issues. I discuss them in turn.

7.5 Analytic direct approach

The direct approach examines the field equations for specific families of models, and tries to determine if singularities occur in these cases. In the particular case of geodesic irrotational motion ($a^b = \omega_{ab} = 0$), on using definition (7.11) the Raychaudhuri equation (7.6) takes the form

$$\frac{3\ddot{S}}{S} = -2\sigma^2 - \frac{\kappa}{2}(\mu + 3p) + \Lambda. \tag{7.23}$$

---

[10] Because a cosmological constant is indeed constant, but the matter density scales at least as fast as $S^{-3} \propto (1+z)^3$.

This directly implies the fundamental:

Raychaudhuri singularity theorem [108]: *Consider a universe with matter moving geodesically and irrotationally,[11] satisfying the energy condition*

$$\mu + 3p > 0 \tag{7.24}$$

at all times, and with $\Lambda \leq 0$. Let P be an event where $H_0 \equiv \dot{S}_0/S_0 > 0$. Then there is a singularity in the family of fundamental world lines a time $t_0 < 1/H_0$ ago along the world line through P. Provided

$$\mu + p \geq \alpha\mu > 0 \tag{7.25}$$

for some constant $\alpha > 0$, this is a spacetime singularity where the energy density diverges.

Proof Consider the curve $S(t)$. By (7.23) this has curvature $\ddot{S}(t) < 0$, which implies $S \to 0$ a finite time t_0 ago. The divergence of the energy density (which is a spacetime curvature invariant) follows from the energy conservation equation (7.5) and energy condition (7.25). □

Because there is no limit to the spatial inhomogeneity involved, this covers a large class of models (including the FL models). However, rotation or acceleration might avoid the singularity, for in this case (7.6) replaces (7.23). Direct dynamic investigation of rotating spatially homogeneous (Bianchi) models failed to prove analytically that all such models are singular, because the rotation can spin up to large values in the early universe and can potentially cause a turn-around (the proof of singularities in Bianchi models is immediate from (7.23) when the matter moves orthogonally to the surfaces of homogeneity because these surfaces have geodesic normals, but in rotating Bianchi models the matter cannot move orthogonal to them). The obvious case of shear-free rotating and expanding pressure-free universes potentially provides an example of a universe where rotation does indeed cause a turn-around, but a detailed examination of their integrability conditions [40] shows that such models are not allowed by the EFE.[12] Various studies using non-comoving geodesic normal coordinates apparently show the existence of singularities [89], but these can be coordinate singularities associated with caustics of the geodesic coordinates rather than corresponding to a physical

---

[11] Raychaudhuri actually proved the theorem for the case $p = 0$, $\mu > 0$, when the energy conditions (7.24), (7.25) will both be true. When the pressure is non-zero, the acceleration-free condition of the theorem is only true when the fluid moves orthogonal to the surfaces of constant pressure (which will be true in FL models with pressure).

[12] But they can occur in Newtonian cosmological models.

singularity – indeed generically such coordinates cover only part of space-time. One can find non-singular models where the distribution of matter is bounded in some or all directions (e.g. static or oscillating star models), but these do not correspond to realistic cosmological models where the matter extends more or less uniformly at least to the Hubble radius in all directions. One can find models where a large positive cosmological constant causes singularity avoidance, but as explained above these are not realistic models of the real universe.

Overall, the attempts to prove by detailed examination of the dynamics of the field equations that all realistic cosmological models are singular have failed, but no counter examples to this conjecture have been found either. This was the case in the mid-1960s when progress on this front seemed to have ground to a halt.

7.6 Indirect method

The situation was transformed in 1965 by Roger Penrose's highly innovative paper 'Gravitational collapse and spacetime singularities' [102] showing the existence of spacetime singularities under plausible assumptions when gravitational collapse occurs. This paper, developing earlier work by Gödel, Milnor, Avez, and others, firmly introduced careful definition of causal domains, causal boundaries, and associated topological methods into General Relativity theory. It also introduced the idea of *closed trapped surfaces*, that is spacelike 2-spheres for which both the outgoing and ingoing families of orthogonal null geodesics are converging, and showed that singularities will occur in gravitational collapse once closed trapped surfaces have developed, where the existence of spacetime singularities was characterized as being equivalent to geodesic incompleteness. The theorem assumed (i) geodesic completeness and (ii) some plausible generic geometrical assumptions, together with (iii) existence of a closed trapped surface and (iv) the *weak energy condition:*

$$R_{ab}K^a K^b \geq 0 \text{ for all null vectors } K^a \tag{7.26}$$

(corresponding to $\mu + p \geq 0$ for a perfect fluid), and deduced a contradiction. The core of the theorem is the application of the null version of the Raychaudhuri equation to give a singularity theorem for null curves analogous to that for timelike curves in the Raychaudhuri theorem above. This is applied to the boundary of the future of the events inside the closed trapped surface, implying an end to this boundary within a finite affine distance, and hence causing problems for the future of the events lying inside the trapped surface. The implication was taken to be that – given the other assumptions – the spacetime considered could not be geodesically complete. The power of the theorem derives from the fact that its crucial assumptions – the energy condition and the existence of trapped surfaces – are inequalities rather than equalities, and hence are stable to perturbation.

The resulting explosion of work by Stephen Hawking, Bob Geroch, Brandon Carter, and others then clarified a range of associated concepts, specifically:

- an array of definitions of causality properties and their relation to the existence of causality violations (closed timelike or null curves) and of families of spacelike surfaces;

- the domain of influence and domain of dependence of a set, and the properties of their boundaries;

- the relation of the domain of dependence to the existence of geodesics and of focal points for families of geodesics;

- the nature of particle and event horizons and their relation to space-time conformal boundaries;

- the definition of extendibility of space-times and of singularities, regarded as boundary points of the spacetime, under various differentiability conditions;

- showing the existence of either singularities or causal violations in an extended series of circumstances.

Stephen played a major role in these developments, in particular by proving a series of theorems extending Penrose's singularity theorem to the cosmological context. A useful stepping stone was a 1965 paper we wrote jointly [73] showing the existence of singularities in spatially homogeneous world models. The problem here, also examined by Larry Shepley at about that time, was how to handle the situation when the matter moves non-orthogonally and the surfaces of homogeneity change their nature by becoming null and then timelike, so the universe changes from being spatially homogeneous to spatially inhomogeneous.[13] We were able to show that in this case too the spatially homogeneous models become singular. The study was also useful in that it showed in a very clear way the nature of the Cauchy horizon occurring at such a change of symmetry.

The prime realization underlying Stephen's series of cosmological singularity theorems was that generically, closed trapped surfaces occur in

---

[13] As happens in the maximally extended vacuum Schwarzschild solution for example, see [75].

the universe in a time-reversed sense in the past because of the refocusing of our past light cone caused by the increasing density of matter and radiation there. The resulting main theorem by Stephen is contained in his 1967 paper [71], establishing the existence of singularities in the past under a number of reasonable geometric assumptions together with the *strong energy condition*:

$$R_{ab}K^a K^b \geq 0 \qquad \text{for all non-spacelike vectors } K^a \qquad (7.27)$$

(corresponding to $\mu + 3p \geq 0$ for a perfect fluid) and the existence of a point with past-directed refocused timelike and null geodesics. The relation of this theorem to observational data is provided by the existence of the black-body CBR. In a 1968 paper [74], Stephen and I jointly showed that the presence of the CBR shows the refocusing condition of this theorem would be satisfied because either (depending on the density of matter in the universe) the radiation itself would cause such reconvergence, or the matter that had thermalized the radiation would do so; hence existence of this radiation indicates not only the existence of the Hot Big Bang era (through its thermalized spectrum) but also that there was a beginning to the universe in the sense of a spacetime singularity, if quantum effects did not intervene. The ultimate theorem applicable both to cosmology and collapse was proved by Hawking and Penrose in 1970 [76], depending on the strong energy condition and the existence of a closed trapped surface (i.e. refocusing of null geodesics only rather than both timelike and null geodesics) together with reasonable generic and causal properties, and again was related to the existence of the CBR in an appendix to that paper.

This completed the main development of these theorems. A survey of the state of the art was then written in 1973 by Stephen and myself, namely the book *The Large Scale Structure of Spacetime* [75] containing a systematic survey of the rigorous analysis of General Relativity and precise theorems resulting from this wave of activity (and see also [123, 129]). Stephen's results were a fundamental contribution to understanding the nature of cosmology: singularities are predicted to exist in the classical theory of cosmology provided the energy conditions are satisfied and no strange causal properties occur. Thus this prediction of the FL models was indeed stable: it was not just a result of the very high symmetry of the FL models.

7.7 Issues

A series of issues remain: first the further implications of the classical theory (General Relativity) for spacetime singularities, when the energy conditions are satisfied; secondly what the classical or semiclassical theory says when quantum field theory allows violation of the energy conditions; and thirdly the implications for singularities of various approaches to cosmology in the quantum gravity era.

7.7.1 Issue 1: Nature and generality of singularities

The first main issue remaining was that these theorems predict the existence of spacetime singularities in a wide variety of circumstances, but they are characterized only by geodesic incompleteness. The theorems do not make clear their physical nature. In the case of the FL models the energy density, temperature, and various spacetime curvature invariants diverge at the singularities, so this is an unavoidable spacetime singularity: a genuine beginning of space, of time, and indeed of all of physics. In this case, it does not make sense to talk of 'before the beginning' – there was no time there, there was not even any 'there' there! This isotropic singularity (it has no preferred directions) is associated with the existence of particle horizons in all directions. It was not clear which of these properties would hold more generally.

A series of investigations showed the nature of the singularity in more general contexts. Thorne [120] showed that cigar singularities would generically exist in Bianchi I spatially homogeneous universes, with pancake singularities being an exceptional possibility. Misner showed that the particle horizon is broken in the exceptional directions when pancakes occur, and that this might possibly lead to breaking of the horizon in all directions in the oscillatory Bianchi IX models [95], but this was later found not to happen. Belinskii, Khalatnikov and Lifshitz also examined these oscillatory approaches to the origin of the universe, and suggested that this behaviour is generic – it would occur in almost all inhomogeneous models as well as some spatially homogeneous ones [7, 8, 89]. An ongoing debate has examined whether these oscillatory singularities are chaotic in the strict mathematical sense [33]. Eardley, Liang and Sachs investigated velocity dominated singularities in inhomogeneous irrotational dust cosmologies, showing the existence of both timelike and spacelike singularities in these universes [36]. Ellis and King resolved the issue of what happens in Bianchi models where the surfaces of homogeneity change from spacelike to timelike [54] – non-scalar singularities occur there, with all curvature scalars finite on approaching the singularity but the curvature tensor components diverging in any parallely propagated frame. This behaviour is associated with the existence of Cauchy horizons related to the change of nature of the symmetry of these solutions, which can occur in a variety of Bianchi models. However, this kind of behaviour was shown to be non-generic by Siklos [114].

More generally, Tipler [122] defined crushing singularities as those cases where tidal forces due to the curvature tensor will cause any physical object to be crushed as it approaches the singularity. This requires not only that the curvature tensor components measured in a parallel frame diverge in a non-oscillatory way along all geodesics approaching the singularity, but also that they do so slowly enough that the object has time to respond before running into the singularity. Tipler examined properties of such singularities and showed their existence in some circumstances [122]. Clarke examined the opposite situation of locally extendible singularities, defined as singularities where the curvature tensor vanishes along all geodesics approaching the singularity. He proved a significant theorem showing that – like the conical singularities which are their canonical exemplar – in this case, spacetime is indeed locally extendible through the singular boundary points [30], and this may happen in a directionally-dependent manner [126]. Ellis and Schmidt [57] provided many examples of the various types of singularities, in particular the timelike analogue of a conical singularity (which may be useful in Regge calculus approximations to evolving cosmologies).[14] Tipler, Clarke and Ellis [123] surveyed the various kinds of singularities and the theorems concerning their existence.

Crushing scalar singularities occur inter alia in FL, Bianchi I, and velocity dominated universes. Non-crushing scalar singularities occur inter alia in Bianchi Type IX oscillatory universes and their inhomogeneous generalizations studied by Belinskiĭ, Khalatnikov and Lifshitz. These are conjectured to be generic, but the proposed proofs that this is so rely on the singularity being spacelike – while there can presumably be generic families of timelike singularities also. Non-scalar singularities occur in some tilted Bianchi Class B models, for example rotationally symmetric Type V, but are not generic. Directional non-scalar singularities may occur in brane-world models (discussed below).

Overall, this body of work gives a good overview of the variety of types of singularity, but not a complete understanding of their probability of occurrence in the cosmological context. The best progress that has been made in this direction is through dynamical systems analyses of cosmological models, developed in particular by Collins [31, 32] and by Wainwright and collaborators [128], supplemented by sophisticated analytical investigation of specific classes of models, in particular the oscillatory Bianchi type IX universes [109]. The approach of Wainwright *et al.*, using a tetrad formalism and expansion-normalized Ricci rotation coefficients as the

---

[14] Bruno, Shepley and Ellis [22] derived the null version of conical singularities, which probably is not significant in cosmology but may be useful in Regge calculus models of gravitational radiation.

basic variables, shows in a clear way how the various singularity types and their basins of attraction can be identified in phase spaces for spatially homogeneous (Bianchi) models and some inhomogeneous cases, in particular G2 cosmologies [62]. An interesting feature that arises [128] is the key role played by self-similar solutions, which are fixed points in these phase spaces (sinks, sources and saddle points) where crushing singularities can occur. Furthermore one should note that – provided the classical era extends to early enough times – both the oscillatory and self-similar anisotropic approaches to the initial singularity that occur in these phase spaces are possible states of the real universe, because many models with very anisotropic initial states later isotropize and become indistinguishable from the observable universe [127]. This can occur either at late times as they approach their asymptotic future state, or at intermediate times where they can spend very long epochs near a FL-state which is a saddle point in the phase space before becoming very anisotropic again in the far future. If one believes in generic behaviour, then these anisotropic modes will occur in the real universe. They certainly are compatible with present day observations, which can only place upper bounds on their existence, even if they dominate in the remote past.

The present need is for an extension of this kind of approach to the full space of cosmological space-times with a suitable measure defined on it, which involves a generalization of the present dynamical systems work to the infinite dimensional case. This would include extending it to the case of generic inflationary universes that include anisotropic and inhomogeneous modes.

7.7.2 Issue 2: Inflation and bounces?

It is commonly assumed that there is an inflationary phase preceding the Hot Big Bang phase.[15] This is not an inevitable conclusion, for there are some alternatives proposed [78, 116], but if it did take place the dynamics are then quite different from in the Hot Big Bang era. Thus the second issue is: can there be bounces in inflationary models, or must there be an initial singularity here too?

The key point is that in these models existence of an effective scalar field can lead to a violation of the strong energy condition (7.27), because then by (7.17)

$$\mu + 3p = 2\dot{\phi}^2 - 2V(\phi) \tag{7.28}$$

---

[15] During inflation any matter or radiation present gets rapidly diluted to zero, so the universe is very cold for most of this epoch.

which is negative when the slow-rolling approximation $\dot{\phi}^2 < V(\phi)$ holds, and hence the arguments above no longer apply. Indeed it is this violation of the energy conditions that leads to the existence of inflationary universes. The curve of $S(t)$ in inflationary FL models bends upwards because (7.24) no longer holds, thus at first sight it seems a bounce may be possible, preceding the start of the expanding inflationary era. However, a series of theorems [16–18] suggest that inflationary models cannot bounce: they are stated to be future infinite but not past infinite [69]. This is an important issue, so it is worth looking at it further. There are two major requirements to get a bounce. We look at them in turn, after setting the scene with some preliminary comments.

Irrespective of the underlying theory – a mixture of fluids, finite set of scalar fields, variable G, quadratic Lagrangian, or whatever – its effect on the standard cosmological models can be represented as follows: given a Robertson–Walker geometry, one can write the resulting dynamic equations as effective EFE, with the effective Friedmann equation

$$\frac{\dot{S}^2}{S^2} = \frac{\kappa \mu_{\text{eff}}}{3} - \frac{k}{S^2} \tag{7.29}$$

relating the scale factor $S(t)$, curvature constant k (normalized to ± 1 if it is non-zero), and the effective total energy density $\mu_{\text{eff}}(t)$, which is defined by this equation (cf. (7.8)). If there is a cosmological constant Λ, it is included by representation as perfect fluid with $\mu_\Lambda + p_\Lambda = 0$. The effective Raychaudhuri equation for this context is

$$3\frac{\ddot{S}}{S} = -\frac{\kappa}{2}(\mu_{\text{eff}} + 3p_{\text{eff}}) \tag{7.30}$$

(cf. (7.7)), which is a consequence of the effective Friedmann equation and total energy conservation equation when $\dot{S} \neq 0$. Taking all of this together we get an effective FL model. We now consider the two requirements to get a bounce.

Requirement 1: *Energy conditions and the Raychaudhuri equation*
As is discussed above, to get a bounce in an effective FL model, one needs the curve $S(t)$ of the scale factor as a function of time to bend up: that is,

$$\frac{\ddot{S}}{S} \geq 0 \Leftrightarrow (\mu_{\text{eff}} + 3p_{\text{eff}}) < 0,$$

which is just a violation of the strong energy condition. This is the case if $(\mu + p)_{\text{eff}} = 0$ (a vacuum), and indeed by (7.28) is possible for any slow-rolling scalar field. Hence as far as this condition is concerned, in an inflationary situation a bounce is possible. It is interesting to ask why the Hawking and Ellis book [75] misses this possibility in its presentation of the energy conditions underlying the singularity theorems. In fact it is included there, but is discounted in terms of astrophysical and cosmological applications. In considering the energy conditions, the authors refer to the case of a scalar field (p.95) remarking that the energy condition could be violated at a point. However, they then integrate over a region U to obtain a non-negative term plus a term that will be small compared with the first if the region U is large compared with the wavelength h/m, and then say (p.96): 'Thus although the energy-momentum tensor of π-mesons may not satisfy the strong energy condition at every point, this should not affect the convergence of timelike geodesics over distances greater than 10^{-12} cm. This might possibly lead to a breakdown of the singularity theorems in Chapter 8 when the radius of curvature of spacetime becomes less than 10^{-12} cm but such a curvature would be so extreme that it might well count as a singularity' . In effect, it is this statement that has been challenged by Guth's vision of the inflationary universe [68, 69] – which in its many varieties claims that there are indeed scalar fields that are significant and have negative energies on relevant scales, which may be less than the stated 10^{-12} cm.

Requirement 2: *Turn around and the Friedmann equation*
However, to get a turn around in an effective FL model, one also needs a time when the scale factor is a minimum. Thus there must be a time t_* such that $\dot{S}(t_*) = 0$. From the effective Friedmann equation (7.29),

$$\dot{S}^2(t_*) = 0 \Leftrightarrow \frac{\kappa \mu_{\text{eff}}(t_*)}{3} = \frac{k}{S^2(t_*)}.$$

There are two ways this can happen:

- with $k \leq 0$ (this is possible only if $\mu_{\text{eff}}(t_*) < 0$), even with a scalar field (see (7.17)) this can only be achieved by having negative potential energies, which many regard as undesirable, c.f. the debate between Turok *et al.* and Linde *et al.* [63, 116];

- with $k = +1$ (this is possible with $\mu_{\text{eff}}(t_*) > 0$ [110]), which is compatible with ordinary matter.

Thus if you want a bounce in an inflationary universe, it is sensible to look to $k = +1$ inflationary models, which indeed will turn around if a vacuum domain occurs for long enough (as curvature will eventually always win over a vacuum as we go back into the past, c.f. [56, 59]). The theorems mentioned above do not include this case, hence they only consider half the possible inflationary universe models, namely the $k = 0$

and $k = -1$ cases (and one should note here that although the scale-free $k = 0$ exponential case clearly is the model underlying the way many people approach the problem, it is highly exceptional – it is of zero measure within the space of all inflationary FL models). The situation can be restated: turnaround can't happen without major energy condition violations if $k = 0$ or $k = -1$, or equivalently if we consider only open (unbounded) models, but can happen without such violations if $k = +1$,or equivalently if we consider closed (finite) models. This is indeed just the case in the de Sitter universe, which has a bounce in the $k = +1$ frame with scale factor $S(t) = S_0 \cosh Ht$, which covers the whole spacetime and is geodesically complete [75, 113], whereas the $k = -1$ frame with scale factor $S(t) = S_0 \sinh Ht$ and the $k = 0$ frame with scale factor $S(t) = S_0 \exp Ht$ each have no bounce and each cover only half the de Sitter hyperboloid or less, and hence are geodesically incomplete – they are singular in terms of the standard understanding of spacetime singularities ([101], but c.f. [1]).

A further point has been raised: is such a bouncing inflationary model unstable in the collapse phase, and so not generic if it indeed succeeds in bouncing? Indeed Starobinsky [115] shows that with $k = +1$ and $V = m^2\phi^2/2$, there is a finite but small probability of a bounce assuming equipartition of the scalar field phase at a moment of maximal expansion. Furthermore the collapse phase is probably unstable to anisotropic and inhomogeneous modes. Thus such bouncing models can be claimed not to be probable within the set of collapsing inflationary universes, c.f. [9, 10, 125]. To investigate this properly one needs the phase plane methods discussed in the previous section, but whatever the outcome of that investigation, (a) there is some kind of fine tuning in all inflationary models, (b) one can indeed obtain a bounce if $k = +1$ in at least some cases, as evidenced for example by the de Sitter case, and (c) it does not matter if that situation is not generic if one uses Guth's argument that it does not matter how small the probability of inflation is provided it happens at least once [69]. The real universe could indeed be the child of such a bouncing inflationary model. It could, however, also be the outcome of one of the singular inflationary models, in which case the kinds of initial singularity that could occur according to the semiclassical inflationary theory presumably include all those mentioned in the previous section.

A key issue is whether $k = +1$ at the present day, for if so, as we follow the evolution of the universe back in time, the spatial curvature will eventually dominate any slow-rolling scalar field in a FL model and cause a turn around if that slow-rolling state last long enough, whereas if $k = -1$ this cannot happen. This is in principle observationally testable.

On defining the Hubble parameter $H(t) = \dot{S}(t)/S(t)$, dimensionless density parameter

$$\Omega_\mu(t) \equiv \frac{\kappa\mu(t)}{3H^2(t)},$$

and dimensionless cosmological constant parameter

$$\Omega_\Lambda \equiv \frac{\Lambda}{3H^2(t)},$$

(7.8) can be written as

$$K = H^2(\Omega_\mu + \Omega_\Lambda - 1), \tag{7.31}$$

where the spatial curvature is $K(t) = k/S^2(t)$. By (7.31), the question is simply whether the present day values $\Omega_{\mu 0}$, $\Omega_{\Lambda 0}$ of the density parameter and cosmological parameter obey the relation

$$\Omega_0 \equiv \Omega_{\mu 0} + \Omega_{\Lambda 0} > 1 \Leftrightarrow K_0 > 0 \Leftrightarrow k = +1$$

(note that K cannot change sign, irrespective of the physical transitions that take place [45], so whatever sign we determine for it today has always been its sign).

Recent observations, in particular some of the recent CBR and supernova data taken together, marginally indicate that this is indeed the case. The plethora of new astronomical data and in particular the forthcoming round of improved CBR observations will help clarify if this is really so or not. If Ω_0 is extremely close to 1, however, this question may never be observationally settled, particularly because the possibility of a time varying 'quintessence' rather than a true cosmological constant at late times may make it in principle undeterminable, the possible varieties of variation of the quintessence rendering interpretation of distant observations ambiguous. It becomes one more form of cosmological evolution rendering a unique interpretation of the data even more difficult than when a truly constant 'cosmological constant' is assumed.

7.7.3 Issue 3: Quantum gravity and bounces?

If there is indeed a bounce in the inflationary phase, then (following the expansion of the universe back in time) we may never reach the quantum gravity era. However, not all $k = +1$ models will bounce (inflation may not last long enough for the curvature to cause a turnaround) and in half the inflationary FL models, $k = -1$ and the theorems mentioned above apply: if we accept usual energy inequalities then there is a singularity in the semiclassical theory, in physical terms implying that this theory will break down and ultimately quantum gravity will dominate. Whether there is a physical singularity or not then will depend on the nature of that quantum gravity epoch.

There are a whole range of possibilities here: there may be singularities or they may be avoided; and the nature of possible singularities in these cases might include some similar to those discussed above, but includes others that are radically different. Underlying many investigations of these issues is the desire that, rather than being fixed by a choice of specific initial data from a manifold of possibilities that are all compatible with the emergent physics, the nature of the emergent classical spacetime is uniquely determined by physical theory alone – the issue of boundary conditions is resolved because there is no need for them in this cosmological context. However, a priori that attempt fails simply because multiple such prescriptions have been proposed, and it remains to be seen if any one such proposal can gain theoretical ascendancy over all the others.

Various approaches to quantum gravity and quantum cosmology are discussed in depth by others in this volume, so here I will simply list some possibilities with a few comments.[16]

1. Various approaches to quantum cosmology focus on the wave function of the universe and solution of the Wheeler–DeWitt equation, often via a path integral approach as pioneered by Stephen (discussed elsewhere in this book). However, the Wheeler–DeWitt equation is problematic in a number of ways, inter alia because of the problem of time it invokes, and is in the end untestable. Nevertheless these suggestions open up a vista of intriguing new possibilities where a classical spacetime singularity is replaced by alternatives, including the Hartle–Hawking no-boundary proposal associated with an effective change of signature, Vilenkin's tunnelling 'from nothing', the Gott and Liu proposal of the universe 'creating itself' by emergence from an epoch of causal violation, and the Hawking–Turok instanton. One related possibility is that there might be a real change of signature in the very early universe – a very weak form of singularity in the differential structure, which is not a spacetime singularity as defined above in that geodesic continuation is possible. Various classical models of this situation are available, see e.g. [29].

2. The idea of 'spacetime foam' in the quantum regime has been proposed by various authors (see e.g. [3, 96, 107]). As has been pointed

---

[16] For references and further comment, see [47].

out by Penrose, if true it can cause problems for inflation in the trans-Planckian domain for then one is amplifying by the inflationary expansion a chaotic rather than smooth substructure [104]. Because of its very nature it is difficult to formalize this concept mathematically, and in particular to characterize any associated singularities that might occur. There is, however, one theme here that could be of interest: one might suggest that one feature of such a regime at early times would be the existence of tumbling light cones, resulting at late times in the existence of gravitational kinks (see [83] and references therein) as well as the other topological defects. After inflation these would lie beyond the event horizon, but would result in a much more exotic global causal structure for the universe than is usually contemplated.

3. More recently there have been a series of string-inspired approaches to cosmology, often involving higher dimensional theories. These have included the pre-Big Bang scenario, brane cosmology, and the ekpyrotic universe, the latter approaches being discussed elsewhere in this volume. Issues of stability arise [24] and different kinds of singularities can occur in each case; as mentioned earlier, it is possible that directional locally extendible singularities occur in the ekpyrotic scenario. Penrose's extension of the topological methods and singularity theorems to these cases, reported in his public lecture at this meeting, is an important development. I would just make one comment here: whenever a FL-like model emerges from these approaches, the same issue arises as indicated above in regard to inflation: effective field equations can be defined as above, and there is a better chance of avoiding singularities if one considers the $k = +1$ class of models rather than only the $k = 0$ and $k = -1$ models (cf. [100]).

4. Loop quantum gravity provides an exciting approach to cosmology [13–15], with new kinds of issues arising because of the discrete spacetime structure underlying this theory, proving an escape from the standard singularity theorems of cosmology in the quantum gravity domain. It may also be that this approach provides the closest to the idea of having the physics determine the emergent universe uniquely.

In examining what quantum gravity may suggest for the start of the universe and the nature of any associated singularities, all these approaches need investigation before one tries to assess what is the best understanding we can attain. The implications of these approaches for the possible nature of singularities can build on and be informed by the understandings obtained for the classical regime, as outlined above.

7.8 Conclusion

The themes covered in this talk are not all that Stephen did in the first phase of his academic career, but do form a major and important part of what he did then. It was a great privilege for me to be able to collaborate with Stephen in this early part of his work.

Acknowledgment

I thank Bill Stoeger and Henk van Elst for helpful comments on an earlier version of this paper.

References

[1] Aguirrre, A. and Gratton, S. (2002), 'Steady state eternal inflation', *Phys. Rev.* **D65**, 083507.

[2] Alexander, S., Brandenberger, R. and Magueijo, J. (2001), 'Non-commutative inflation', [hep-th/0108190].

[3] Amelino-Camelia, G. (2001), 'Phenomenological description of space-time foam', [gr-qc/0104005].

[4] Bardeen, J. M. (1980), 'Gauge-invariant cosmological perturbations', *Phys. Rev.* **D22**, 1882.

[5] Bardeen, J. M., Steinhardt, P. and Turner, M. S. (1983), 'Spontaneous creation of almost scale-free density perturbations in an inflationary universe', *Phys. Rev.* **D28**, 679.

[6] Bashinsky, S. and Bertschinger, E. (2002), 'Dynamics of cosmological perturbations in position space', *Phys.Rev.* **D65**, 123008.

[7] Belinskiĭ, V. A., Khalatnikov, I. M. and Lifshitz, E. M. (1970), 'Oscillatory approach to a singular point in the relativistic cosmology', *Adv. Phys.* **19**, 525.

[8] Belinskiĭ, V. A., Khalatnikov, I. M. and Lifshitz, E.M. (1970), 'Construction of a general cosmological solution of the Einstein equations with a time singularity', *Sov. Phys. JETP* **35**, 838.

[9] Belinskiĭ, V. A. and Khalatnikov, I. M. (1987), 'On the degree of generality of inflationary solutions in cosmological models with a scalar field', *Sov. Phys. JETP* **66**, 441.

[10] Belinskiĭ, V. A., Ishihara, H., Khalatnikov, I. M. and Sato, H. (1988), 'On the degree of generality of inflation in Friedman cosmological models with a massive scalar field', *Prog. Theor. Phys.* **79**, 676.

[11] Bertschinger, E. (1996), 'Cosmological dynamics', in *Cosmology and Large-Scale Structure*, eds R Schaeffer, J Silk, M Spiro and J Zinn-Justin (Amsterdam: Elsevier), 273, [astro-ph/9503125].

[12] Bertschinger, E. (2001), 'Cosmological perturbation theory and structure formation', [astro-ph/0101009].

[13] Bojowald, M. (2001), 'Dynamical initial conditions in quantum cosmology', *Phys. Rev. Lett.* **87**, 121301.

[14] Bojowald, M. (2002), 'Isotropic loop quantum cosmology', *Class. Quantum Grav.* **19**, 2717.

[15] Bojowald, M. (2002), 'Inflation from quantum geometry', [gr-qc/0206054].

[16] Borde, A., Guth, A. H. and Vilenkin, A. (2001), 'Inflation is not past-eternal', [gr-qc/0110012].

[17] Borde, A. and Vilenkin, A. (1994), 'Eternal inflation and the initial singularity', *Phys. Rev. Lett.* **72**, 3305.

[18] Borde, A. and Vilenkin, A. (1997), 'Violations of the weak energy condition in inflating spacetimes', *Phys. Rev.* **D56**, 717.

[19] Brandenberger, R. H. (2002), 'On signatures of short distance physics in the cosmic microwave background', [hep-th/0202142].

[20] Bruni, M., Dunsby, P. K. S. and Ellis, G. F. R. (1992), 'Cosmological perturbations and the physical meaning of gauge-invariant variables', *Astrophys. J.* **395**, 34.

[21] Bruni, M., Ellis, G. F. R. and Dunsby, P. K. S. (1992), 'Gauge-invariant perturbations in a scalar-field dominated Universe', *Class. Quantum Grav.* **9**, 921.

[22] Bruno, R., Shepley, L. C. and Ellis, G. F. R. (1987), 'Quasi-regular singularities based on null planes', *Gen. Rel. Grav.* **19**, 973.

[23] Buchert, T. and Carfora, M. (2001), 'Matter seen at many scales and the geometry of averaging in relativistic cosmology', [gr-qc/0101070].

[24] Carroll, S. M., Geddes, J., Hoffman, M. B. and Wald. R. M. (2001), 'Classical stabilisation of homogeneous extra dimensions', [hep-th/0110149].

[25] Challinor, A. (1999), 'Microwave background polarization in cosmological models', [astro-ph/9911481].

[26] Challinor, A. (2000), 'The covariant perturbative approach to cosmic microwave background anisotropies', *Gen. Rel. Grav.* **32**, 1059.

[27] Challinor, A. (2000), 'Microwave background anisotropies from gravitational waves: the 1+3 covariant approach', *Class. Quantum Grav.* **17**, 871.

[28] Challinor, A. and Lasenby, A. (1999), 'Cosmic microwave background anisotropies in the CDM model: a covariant and gauge-invariant approach', *Astrophys. J.* **513**, 1.

[29] Carfora, M. and Ellis, G. F. R. (1995), 'The geometry of classical change of signature', *Int. Journ. Mod. Phys.* **D4**, 175.

[30] Clarke, C. J. S. (1973), 'Local extensions in singular spacetimes', *Commun. Math. Phys.* **32**, 205.

[31] Collins, C. B. (1971), 'More qualitative cosmology', *Commun. Math. Phys.* **23**, 137.

[32] Collins, C. B. and Ellis, G. F. R. (1979), 'Singularities in Bianchi cosmologies', *Phys. Rep.* **56**, 65.

[33] Cornish, N. J. and Levin, J. (1997), 'The mixmaster universe is chaotic', *Phys. Rev. Lett.* **78**, 998.

[34] Cooray, A. (2002), 'After acoustic peaks: what's next in CMB?', [astro-ph/0203048].

[35] Dunsby, P. K. S., Bruni, M. and Ellis, G. F. R. (1992), 'Covariant perturbations in a multi-fluid cosmological medium', *Astrophys. J.* **395**, 54.

[36] Eardley, D., Liang, E. and Sachs, R. (1972), 'Velocity-dominated singularities in irrotational dust cosmologies', *J. Math. Phys.* **13**, 99.

[37] Ehlers, J. (1961), 'Beiträge zur relativistischen Mechanik kontinuierlicher Medien', *Akad. Wiss. Lit. Mainz, Abhandl. Math.-Nat. Kl.* **11**, 793. Translated as: Ehlers, J. (1993), 'Contributions to the relativistic mechanics of continuous media', *Gen. Rel. Grav.* **25**, 1225.

[38] Ehlers, J. (1997), 'Examples of Newtonian limits of relativistic spacetimes', *Class. Quantum Grav.* **14**, A119.

[39] Ehlers, J., Geren, P. and Sachs, R. K. (1968), 'Isotropic solutions of the Einstein–Liouville equations', *J. Math. Phys.* **9**, 1344.

[40] Ellis, G. F. R. (1967), 'Dynamics of pressure-free matter in general relativity', *J. Math. Phys.* **8** 1171.

[41] Ellis, G. F. R. (1971), 'Relativistic cosmology', in *General Relativity and Cosmology (Proc. 47th Enrico Fermi Summer School)*, ed. R. K. Sachs (Academic Press, New York), 104.

[42] Ellis, G. F. R. (1973), 'Relativistic cosmology', in *Cargèse Lectures in Physics, Vol. VI*, ed. E. Schatzman (Gordon and Breach, New York), 1.

[43] Ellis, G. F. R. (1984), 'Alternatives to the Big Bang', *Ann. Rev. Ast. Ast.* **22**, 157.

[44] Ellis, G. F. R. (1984), 'Relativistic cosmology: Its nature, aims and problems', in *General Relativity and Gravitation (Invited Papers and Discussion Reports of the 10th International Conference)* eds B. Bertotti, F. de Felice and A. Pascolini (Reidel, Dordrecht), 215.

[45] Ellis, G. F. R. (1987), Note on 'Symmetry changes in Friedmann Cosmologies' by S. Bayin, *Astrophys. J.* **314**, 1.

[46] Ellis, G. F. R. (1990), 'The evolution of inhomogeneities in expanding Newtonian cosmologies', *Mon. Not. Roy. Ast. Soc.* **243**, 509.

[47] Ellis, G. F. R. (1999), 'Before the beginning: emerging questions and uncertainties', *Astrophysics and Space Science* **269–279**, 693.

[48] Ellis, G. F. R. (2001), 'Cosmology and local physics', [gr-qc/0102017].

[49] Ellis, G. F. R. and Bruni, M. (1989), 'Covariant and gauge-invariant approach to cosmological density fluctuations', *Phys. Rev.* **D40**, 1804.

[50] Ellis, G. F. R., Bruni, M. and Hwang, J. C. (1990), 'Density-gradient–vorticity relation in perfect-fluid Robertson–Walker perturbations', *Phys. Rev.* **D42**, 1035.

[51] Ellis, G. F. R. and Van Elst, H. (1999), 'Cosmological models' (Cargèse lectures 1998), in *Theoretical and Observational Cosmology*, ed. M. Lachièze-Rey. (Kluwer, Dordrecht), 1, [gr-qc/9812046].

[52] Ellis, G. F. R., Van Est, H. and Maartens, R. (2001), 'General relativistic analysis of peculiar velocities', *Class. Quantum Grav.* **18**, 5115.

[53] Ellis, G. F. R., Hwang, J. and Bruni, M. (1989), 'Covariant and gauge-independent perfect-fluid Robertson–Walker perturbations', *Phys. Rev.* **D40**,1819.

[54] Ellis, G. F. R. and King, A. R. (1974), 'Was the Big Bang a whimper?', *Commun. Math. Phys.* **38**, 119.

[55] Ellis, G. F. R., Matravers, D. R. and Treciokas, R. (1983), 'Anisotropic solutions of the Einstein–Boltzmann equations I: General formalism', *Ann. Phys.* **150**, 455.

[56] Ellis, G. F. R., McEwan, P., Stoeger, W. and Dunsby, P. (2001), 'Causality in inflationary universes with positive spatial curvature', [gr-qc/0109024].

[57] Ellis, G. F. R. and Schmidt, B. G. (1977), 'Singular space-times', *Gen. Rel. Grav.* **8**, 915.

[58] Ellis, G. F. R. and Stoeger, W. R. (1987), 'The fitting problem in cosmology', *Class. Quantum Grav.* **4**, 1679.

[59] Ellis, G. F. R., Stoeger, W., McEwan, P. and Dunsby, P. (2001), 'Dynamics of inflationary universes with positive spatial curvature', [gr-qc/0109023].

[60] Ellis, G. F. R., Treciokas, R. and Matravers, D. R. (1983), 'Anisotropic solutions of the Einstein–Boltzmann equations II: Some exact properties of the equations', *Ann. Phys.* **150**, 487.

[61] Van Elst, H. and Ellis, G. F. R. (1998), 'Quasi-Newtonian dust cosmologies', *Class. Quantum Grav.* **15**, 3545.

[62] Van Elst, H., Uggla, C. and Wainwright, J. (2002), 'Dynamical systems approach to G_2 cosmology', *Class. Quantum Grav.* **19**, 51.

[63] Felder, G., Frolov, A., Kofman, L. and Linde, A. (2002), 'Cosmology with negative potentials', [hep-th/0202017].

[64] Gebbie, T., Dunsby, P. and Ellis, G. F. R. (2000), 'Covariant cosmic microwave background anisotropies II: almost-FLRW standard model', *Ann. Phys.* **282**, 321.

[65] Gebbie, T. and Ellis, G. F. R. (2000), 'Covariant cosmic microwave background anisotropies I: algebraic relations for mode and multipole representations', *Ann. Phys.* **282**, 285.

[66] Geshnizjani, G. and Brandenberger, R. (2002), 'Back reaction and local cosmological expansion rate', [gr-qc/0204074].

[67] Grøn, O. and Hervik, S. (2002), 'The Weyl curvature conjecture', [gr-qc/0205026].

[68] Guth, A. H. (1981), 'Inflationary universe: a possible solution to the horizon and flatness problems', *Phys. Rev.* **D23**, 347.

[69] Guth, A. H. (2001), 'Eternal inflation', [astro-ph/0101507].

[70] Hawking, S. W. (1966), 'Perturbations of an expanding universe', *Astrophys. J.* **145**, 544.

[71] Hawking, S. W. (1967), 'The occurrence of singularities in cosmology II: causality and singularities', *Proc. Roy. Soc. Lond.* **A300**, 187.

[72] Hawking, S. W. (1982), 'The development of irregularities in a single bubble inflationary universe', *Phys. Lett.* **115B**, 295.

[73] Hawking, S. W. and Ellis, G. F. R. (1965), 'Singularities in homogeneous world models', *Phys. Lett.* **17B**, 246.

[74] Hawking, S. W. and Ellis, G. F. R. (1968), 'The cosmic black body radiation and the existence of singularities in our universe', *Astrophys. J.* **152**, 25.

[75] Hawking, S. W. and Ellis, G. F. R. (1973), *The Large Scale Structure of Space-Time* (Cambridge University Press, Cambridge).

[76] Hawking, S. W. and Penrose, R. (1970), 'The singularities of gravitational collapse and cosmology', *Proc. Roy. Soc. Lond.* **A314**, 529.

[77] Hogan, C. J. (2002), 'Holographic discreteness of inflationary perturbations', [astro-ph/0201020].

[78] Hollands, S. and Wald, R. M. (2002), 'An alternative to inflation', [gr-qc/0205058].

[79] Hu, W. and Dodelson, S. (2002), 'Cosmic microwave background anisotropies', [astro-ph/0110414]; Hu, W. (2000), 'CMB anisotropies: a decadal survey', [astro-ph/0002520].

[80] Hu, W. and Sugiyama, N. (1995), 'Anisotropies in the cosmic microwave background: an analytic approach', *Astrophys. J.* **444**, 489.

[81] Hu, W., Seljak, U., White, M. and Zeldarriaga, M. (1998), 'A complete treatment of CBR anisotropies in a FRW universe', *Phys. Rev.* **D57**, 3290.

[82] Hui, L. and Kinney, W. H. (2002), 'Short distance physics and the consistency relation for scalar and tensor fluctuations in the inflationary universe', *Phys. Rev.* **D65**, 103507.

[83] Kloesch, T. and Strobl, T. (1998), 'A global view of kinks in 1+1 gravity', *Phys. Rev.* **D57**, 1034.

[84] Lehoucq, R., Weeks, J., Uzan,J-P., Gausmann, E. and Luminet, J-P. (2002), 'Eigenmodes of 3-dimensional spherical spaces and their application to cosmology', [gr-qc/0205009].

[85] Leong, B., Dunsby, P., Challinor, A. and Lasenby, A. (2002), '(1+3) covariant dynamics of scalar perturbations in braneworlds', *Phys.Rev.* **D65**, 104012.

[86] Lewis, A. and Challinor, A. (2002), 'Evolution of cosmological dark matter perturbations', [astro-ph/0203507].

[87] Lewis, A., Challinor, A. and Lasenby, A. (2000), 'Efficient computation of CMB anisotropies in closed FRW models', *Astrophys. J.* **538**, 473.

[88] Lifshitz, E. M. (1946), *J. Phys. USSR* **10**, 116. Translated as: Lifshitz, E. M. (1946), 'On the gravitational instability of the expanding Universe', *Sov. Phys. JETP* **16**, 587.

[89] Lifshitz, E. M. and Khalatnikov, I. M. (1963), 'Investigations in relativistic cosmology', *Adv. Phys.* **12**, 185.

[90] Lizzi, F., Mangano, G., Miele, G. and Peloso, M. (2002), 'Cosmological perturbations and short distance physics from noncommutative geometry', [hep-th/0203099].

[91] Ma, C-P. and Bertschinger, E. (1995), 'Cosmological perturbation theory in the synchronous and conformal Newtonian gauges', *Astrophys. J.* **455**, 7.

[92] Maartens, R. (2000), 'Cosmological dynamics on the brane', *Phys. Rev.* **D62**, 084023.

[93] Maartens, R. (2001), 'Geometry and dynamics of the brane-world', [gr-qc/0101059].

[94] Maartens, R., Gebbie, T. and Ellis, G. F. R. (1999), 'Cosmic microwave background anisotropies: non-linear dynamics', *Phys. Rev.* **D59**, 083506.

[95] Misner, C. W. (1969), 'Mixmaster universe', *Phys. Rev. Lett.* **22** 1071.

[96] Misner, C. W., Thorne, K. S. and Wheeler, J. A. (1973), 'Gravitation' (Freeman, San Francisco), 1190, 1202.

[97] Mukhanov, V. F., Feldman, H. A. and Brandenberger, R. H. (1992), 'Theory of cosmological perturbations', *Phys. Rep.*, 203.

[98] Nambu, Y. (2002), 'The back reaction and the effective Einstein's equations for the Universe with ideal fluid cosmological perturbations', *Phys. Rev.* **D65** (2002) 104013.

[99] Padmanabhan, T. (1993), *Structure Formation in the Universe* (Cambridge University Press, Cambridge).

[100] Pavluchenko, S. A., Savchenko, N. Yu. and Toporensky, A. V. (2001), 'The generality of inflation in some closed FRW models with a scalar field', [gr-qc/0111077].

[101] Penrose, R. (1963), 'Conformal treatment of infinity', in *Relativity, Groups and Topology*, ed. C. DeWitt and B. De Witt (Gordon and Breach, New York), 563.

[102] Penrose, R. (1965), 'Gravitational collapse and space-time singularities', *Phys. Rev. Lett.* **14**, 57.

[103] Penrose, R. (1979), 'Singularities and time-asymmetry, in *General Relativity: An Einstein Centenary Survey*', eds S. W. Hawking and W. Israel (Cambridge University Press, Cambridge), 581.

[104] Penrose, R. (1989), 'Difficulties with inflationary cosmology', in *Proc. 14th Texas Symp. on Relativistic Astrophysics*, ed. E. J. Fergus (New York Academy of Sciences), 249.

[105] Penrose, R. (1989), *The Emperor's New Mind* (Oxford University Press).

[106] Pirani, F. A. E. (1964), 'Introduction to gravitational radiation theory.' In *Lectures on General Relativity*, ed. A. Trautmann, F. A. E. Pirani and H. Bondi (Prentice-Hall, Englewood Cliffs).

[107] Raptis, I. and Zapatrin, R. R. (2001), 'Algebraic description of spacetime foam', *Class. Quantum Grav.* **18** (2001), 4187.

[108] Raychaudhuri, A. K. (1955), 'Relativistic cosmology', *Phys. Rev.* **98**, 1123.

[109] Ringström, H. (2001), 'The Bianchi IX attractor', *Annales Henri Poincaré* **2** (2001), 405, [gr-qc/0006035].

[110] Robertson, H. P. (1933), 'Foundations of relativistic cosmology', *Proc. Nat. Acad. Sci. U.S.* **15**, 822.

[111] Rocha, G., Cayon, L., Bowen, R., Canavezes, A., Silk, J., Banday, A. J. and Gorski, K. M. (2002), 'Topology of the universe from COBE-DMR: a wavelet approach', [astro-ph/0205155].

[112] Sachs, R. K. and Wolfe, A. M. (1967), 'Perturbations of a cosmological model and angular variations of the microwave background', *Astrophys. J.* **147**, 73.

[113] Schrödinger, E. (1956), *Expanding Universes* (Cambridge University Press, Cambridge).

[114] Siklos, S. T. C. (1978), 'Occurrence of whimper singularities', *Commun. Math. Phys.* **58**, 255.

[115] Starobinsky, A. A. (1978), *Sov. Astron. Lett.* **4**, 82.

[116] Steinhardt, P. J. and Turok, N. (2001), 'A cyclic model of the universe', [hep-th/0111030; Steinhardt, P. J. and Turok, N. (2002), 'The cyclic universe: an informal introduction', [astro-ph/0204479].

[117] Stewart, J. M. (1990), 'Perturbations of Friedmann–Robertson–Walker cosmological models', *Class. Quantum Grav.* **7**, 1169.

[118] Stewart, J. M. and Walker, M. (1974), 'Perturbations of space-times in general relativity', *Proc. Roy. Soc. Lond.* **A341**, 49.

[119] Stoeger, W. R., Maartens, R. and Ellis, G. F. R. (1995), 'Proving almost-homogeneity of the universe: an almost Ehlers–Geren–Sachs theorem', *Astrophys. J.* **443**, 1.

[120] Thorne, K. S. (1967), 'Primordial element formation, primordial magnetic fields and the isotropy of the universe', *Astrophys. J.* **148**, 51.

[121] Thorne, K. S. (1980), 'Multipole expansions of gravitational radiation', *Rev. Mod. Phys.* **52**, 299.

[122] Tipler, F. J. (1977), 'Singularities in conformally flat spacetimes', *Phys. Lett.* **64A**, 8.

[123] Tipler, F. J., Clarke, C. J. S. and Ellis, G. F. R. (1980), 'Singularities and horizons: a review article', in *General Relativity and Gravitation: One Hundred Years after the Birth of Albert Einstein, Vol. 2*, ed. A. Held (Plenum Press, New York), 97.

[124] Tolman, R. C. (1934), *Relativity, Thermodynamics and Cosmology* (Oxford University Press).

[125] Toporensky, A. V. (1999), 'The degree of generality of inflation in FRW models with massive scalar field and hydrodynamical matter', *Grav. and Cosm.* **5**, 40.

[126] Vickers, J. A. G. (1992), *Rend. Sem. Mat. Univ. Politec Torino* **50**, 1.

[127] Wainwright, J., Coley, A. A., Ellis, G. F. R. and Hancock, M. (1998), 'On the isotropy of the universe: do Bianchi VIIh cosmologies isotropize?', *Class. Quantum Grav.* **15**, 331.

[128] Wainwright, J. and Ellis, G. F. R. (eds) (1997), *Dynamical Systems in Cosmology* (Cambridge University Press, Cambridge).

[129] Wald, R. M. (1984), *General Relativity* (University of Chicago Press, Chicago).

[130] Wilson, M. L. (1983), 'On the anisotropy of the cosmological background matter and radiation distribution II.', *Astrophys. J.* **273**, 2.

[131] Wilson, M. L. and Silk, J. (1981), 'On the anisotropy of the cosmological background matter and radiation distribution I.', *Astrophys. J.* **243**, 14.

8

The quantum physics of chronology protection

Matt Visser

Washington University, St. Louis

Simply put, chronology protection is the assertion that nature abhors a time machine. In the words of Stephen Hawking [1]:

> *It seems that there is a Chronology Protection Agency which prevents the appearance of closed timelike curves and so makes the universe safe for historians.*

The idea of chronology protection gained considerable currency during the 1990s when it became clear that traversable wormholes, which are not too objectionable in their own right [2–4], seem almost generically to lead to the creation of time machines [5–8]. The key word here is 'seem'. There are by now many technical discussions available in the literature (well over 200 articles), and in the present chapter I will simply give a pedagogical and discursive overview, while adding an extensive bibliography for those interested in the technical details. First: a matter of language, for all practical purposes the phrases 'time machine' and 'closed timelike curve' (or the closely related 'closed null curve') can be used interchangeably.

8.1 Why is chronology protection even an issue?

Before embarking on a discussion of chronology and how it is believed to be protected [1, 6, 7], it is useful to ask first why chronology even needs to be protected. In Newtonian physics, and even in special relativity or flat-space quantum field theory, notions of chronology and causality are so fundamental that they are simply built into the theory ab initio. Violation of normal chronology (for instance, an effect preceding its cause) is so objectionable an occurrence that any such theory would immediately be rejected as unphysical.

Unfortunately, one cannot simply *assert* that chronology is preserved, and causality respected, in general relativity without doing considerable additional work. The essence of the problem lies in the fact that the Einstein equations of general relativity are local equations, relating some aspects of the spacetime curvature at a point to the presence of stress-energy at that point. Additionally, one also has local chronology protection, inherited from the fact that the spacetime is locally Minkowski (the Einstein Equivalence Principle), and so 'in the small' general relativity respects all of the causality constraints of special relativity.

What general relativity does *not* do is to provide any natural way of imposing *global* constraints on the spacetime – certainly the Einstein equations provide no such nonlocal constraint. In cosmology this leads to the observation that the global topology of space is not constrained by the Einstein equations; spatial topology is an independent discrete variable that has to be decided by observation. (And this requires additional data over and above whatever is needed to decide the familiar $k = +1$, $k = 0$, or $k = -1$ question of the Friedmann–Robertson–Walker cosmologies [9].) Similarly, global temporal topology is not constrained by the Einstein equations themselves, and additional physical principles need to be brought into play to deal somehow with the possibility of nontrivial-temporal topology.

Without imposing additional principles along these lines, general relativity is completely infested with time machines (in the sense of closed causal curves). Perhaps the earliest examples of this pathology are the Van Stockum spacetimes [10], but the example that has attracted considerably more attention is Kurt Gödel's peculiar cosmological solution [11]. These spacetimes are exact solutions of the Einstein equations, with sources that (at least locally) look physically reasonable, which nevertheless possess serious global pathologies. If it were only a matter of dealing with these two particular examples, physicists would not be too worried – but similar behaviour occurs in many other geometries, for instance, deep inside the Kerr solution. A complete list of standard but temporally ill-behaved spacetimes is tedious to assemble, but at a minimum should include:

1. Gödel's cosmology [11];

2. Van Stockum spacetimes [10]/Tipler cylinders [12]/longitudinally spinning cosmic strings [8];

3. Kerr and Kerr–Newman geometries [13];

4. Gott's time machines [14];

5. Wheeler wormholes (spacetime foam) [15–17];

6. Morris–Thorne traversable wormholes [2, 5];

7. Alcubierre 'warp drive' spacetimes [18].

The Wheeler wormholes are included based on theorems that localized topology change implies either causal pathology or naked singularities; either possibility is objectionable [19–21]. The Morris–Thorne traversable wormholes are included based on the observation that apparently trivial manipulations of these otherwise not too objectional geometries seem to lead almost generically to the development of closed timelike curves and the destruction of normal chronology [5, 8]. For the 'warp drive' spacetimes, manipulations similar to those performed for traversable wormhole spacetimes seem to lead inevitably to time travel. (Once one has effective faster-than-light travel, whether via wormholes or warpdrives, the twin pseudo-paradox of special relativity is converted into a true paradox, in the sense of engendering various time travel paradoxes.)

Now in each of these particular cases you can at a pinch find *some* excuse for not being too concerned, but it's a different excuse in each case. The matter sources for the Gödel solution are quite reasonable, but the observed universe simply does not have those features. The Van Stockum time machines and their brethren require infinitely long cylindrical assemblages of matter rotating at improbable rates. Gott's time machines have pathological and non-physical global behaviour [22, 23]. The Kerr and Kerr–Newman pathologies are safely hidden behind the Cauchy horizon [13], where one should not trust naive notions of maximal analytic extension. (The inner event horizon is classically unstable.) The Wheeler wormholes (spacetime foam) have never been detected, and at least some authors now argue against the very existence of spacetime foam. The energy condition violations implicit in traversable wormholes and warp drive spacetimes do not seem to be qualitatively insurmountable problems [2, 8], but do certainly give one pause [24]. This multiplicity of different excuses does rather make one worry just a little that something deeper is going on; and that there is a more general underlying theme to these issues of (global) chronology protection.

8.2 Paradoxes and responses

Most physicists view time travel as being problematic, if not downright repugnant. There are two broad classes of paradox generated by the possibility of time travel, either one of which is disturbing:

1. Grandfather paradoxes: caused by attempts to 'change the past', and so modify the conditions that lead to the very existence of the entity that is trying to 'modify the timestream'.

    2. Bootstrap paradoxes: where an effect is its own cause.

Faced with the *a priori* plethora of geometries containing closed timelike curves, with the risk of these two classes of logical paradox arising, the physics community has developed at least four distinct reactions [8]:

1. Make radical alterations to our worldview to incorporate at least some versions of chronology violation and 'time travel' (the 'radical re-write' conjecture). One version of the radical re-write conjecture uses non-Hausdorff manifolds to describe 'train track' geometries where the same present has two or more futures (or two or more pasts). A slightly different version uses the 'many worlds' interpretation of quantum mechanics to effectively permit switching from one history to another [25]. More radically one can even contemplate multiple coexisting versions of the 'present'.

2. Permit constrained versions of closed timelike curves – supplemented with a consistency condition that essentially prevents any alteration of the past. (This is the essence of the Novikov consistency conditions [26–28].) The consistency conditions are sometimes summarized as 'you can't change recorded history' [29]. The central idea is that there is a single unique timeline so that even in the presence of closed timelike curves there are constraints on the possibilities that can occur. In idealized circumstances these consistency constraints can be derived from a least action principle. More complicated situations seem to run afoul of the notion of 'free will', though there is considerable doubt as to the meaning of 'free will' in the presence of time travel [30].

3. Appeal to quantum physics to intervene and provide a universal mechanism for preventing the occurrence of closed timelike curves. This, in a nutshell, is Stephen Hawking's 'chronology protection' option, the central theme of this chapter, which we shall develop in considerable detail below.

4. Agree not to think about these issues until the experimental evidence becomes overwhelming (the 'boring physics' conjecture). After all, what is the current experimental evidence? Assume global hyperbolicity and cosmic censorship and be done with it. If, for instance, one takes canonical gravity seriously as a fundamental theory then there exists at least one universal foliation by complete spacelike hypersurfaces. This automatically forbids closed timelike curves at the kinematical level, before dynamics (classical or quantum) comes into play. However, it should be noted that canonical

gravity interpreted in this strict sense has severe difficulties (for instance, in dealing with maximal analytic extensions of the Kerr spacetime).

Originally it was hoped that it would be possible to decide between these options based on classical or at worst semiclassical physics – however it it now becoming increasingly clear that the ultimate resolution of the chronology protection issue will involve deep issues of principle at the very foundations of the full theory of quantum gravity.

8.3 Elements of chronology protection

Chronology protection is at one level an attempt at 'having one's cake and eating it too' – this in the sense that it provides a framework sufficiently general to permit interesting and non-trivial topologies and geometries, but seeks to keep the unpleasant side effects under control. Chronology protection deals with the localized production and destruction of closed timelike curves: the very essence of what we might like to think of as 'creating' a time machine.

(Cosmological time machines, in the sense of Gödel, are best viewed as an example of the GIGO principle; garbage in, garbage out. Just because one has a formal solution to a set of differential equations does not mean there is any physical validity to the resulting spacetime. A differential equation without boundary conditions/initial conditions has little predictive power, and it is very easy to generate ill-posed problems. Cosmological time machines are by definition intrinsically and equally sick everywhere in the spacetime.)

In the case of a localized production of closed timelike curves the situation is more promising: the spacetime is then divided into regions of normal causal behaviour and abnormal causal behaviour, with the boundary that separates these regions referred to as the 'chronology horizon'. It is the behaviour of quantum physics at and near this chronology horizon that provides the basis for chronology protection.

Specifically, a point x is part of the chronology violating region if there is a closed causal curve (closed timelike curve) or closed chronological curve (closed null/timelike curve) passing through x. The chronology horizon is then defined as the boundary of the future of the chronology violating region. (That is, the boundary of the region from which chronology violating physics is visible.) This chronology horizon is by definition a special type of Cauchy horizon. Under reasonably mild technical conditions Hawking has argued that the chronology horizons appropriate to locally constructed time machines should be compactly generated and contain a 'fountain': essentially the first closed null curve to come into existence as the time machine is formed [1].

A classical photon placed on this fountain will circulate around the fountain infinitely many times: in effectively zero 'elapsed' time. On each circuit around the fountain there is generically a nontrivial holonomy that changes the energy of the photon. For a past chronology horizon, which expands as we move to the future (as defined by someone outside the chronology violating region) this provides a boost, a net increase in the photon energy for each circuit of the fountain. The photon energy increases geometrically, reaching infinity in effectively zero time [1]. On each circuit

$$E \to e^h\, E \to e^{2h}\, E\, \ldots; \qquad h = -2 \oint \Re(\epsilon)\, \mathrm{d}t,$$

with the size of the energy boost being controlled by a loop integration around the fountain involving the Newman–Penrose parameter ϵ. (In simple situations involving wormholes this holonomy is essentially the Doppler shift factor due to relative motion of the wormhole mouths, but when phrased in terms of $\oint \epsilon$ it can be generalized to arbitrary chronology horizons possessing a fountain.) The source of this energy must ultimately be the spacetime geometry responsible for the chronology horizon and, by extension, the stress-energy used to warp spacetime and set up the fountain in the first place. If we now let the photon (and the gravitational field it generates) back-react on the spacetime, its infinite energy will presumably alter the spacetime geometry beyond all recognition.

Unfortunately this is a classical argument, appropriate to a classical point particle following a precisely defined null curve. Will quantum physics amplify or ameliorate this effect? Real photons are wave-packets with a certain transverse size, and generically the same effect that leads to the energy being boosted leads to the wave-packet being defocused – the geometry in a tubelike region surrounding the fountain acts as a diverging lens [1].

With two competing effects, the question becomes which one wins? The answer, 'it depends'. There are geometries for which the classical defocusing effect overwhelms the boost effect, and the classical stress tensor remains finite on the fountain. There are other geometries for which the reverse holds true. But this certainly means that classical effects do not provide a *universal* mechanism for eliminating all forms of closed causal curves. Thus the search for a universal chronology protection mechanism must then (at the very least) move to the semiclassical quantum realm.

8.4 Semiclassical arguments

In semiclassical quantum gravity, one treats gravity as a classical external field, but one quantizes everything else. So far, this is just curved space quantum field theory. But then one additionally demands that the Einstein equations hold for the quantum expectation value of the stress-energy tensor,

$$G_{\mu\nu} = 8\pi G_{Newton} \langle \psi | T_{\mu\nu} | \psi \rangle.$$

Semiclassical quantum gravity seems (at first glance) to lead to a universally true statement to the effect that the renormalized expectation value of the stress-energy tensor blows up at the chronology horizon. The idea is based on the fact that in curved manifolds (modulo technical issues to be discussed below) the two-point correlation function (Green function, a measure of the mean square fluctuations) of any quantum field is of Hadamard form

$$G(x,y) = \sum_{\gamma} \frac{\Delta_{\gamma}(x,y)^{1/2}}{4\pi^2} \left\{ \frac{1}{\sigma_{\gamma}(x,y)} + \nu_{\gamma}(x,y) \ln|\sigma_{\gamma}(x,y)| + \varpi_{\gamma}(x,y) \right\}.$$

Here the sum runs over the distinct geodesics from x to y; the quantity $\Delta_{\gamma}(x,y)$ denotes the Van Vleck determinant evaluated along the geodesic γ; the quantity $\sigma_{\gamma}(x,y)$ denotes Synge's 'world function' (half the square of the geodesic distance from x to y); and the two functions $\nu_{\gamma}(x,y)$ and $\varpi_{\gamma}(x,y)$ are smooth with finite limits as $y \to x$. Provided the Green function can be put into this Hadamard form, the expectation value of the point split stress-energy tensor can be defined by a construction of the type

$$\langle T_{\mu\nu}(x,y,\gamma_0) \rangle = D_{\mu\nu}(x,y,\gamma_0) \, G(x,y).$$

Here γ_0 denotes the trivial geodesic from x to y (which collapses to a point as $y \to x$, this geodesic will be unique provided x and y are sufficiently close to each other), while $D_{\mu\nu}(x,y,\gamma_0)$ is a rather complicated second-order differential operator built up out of covariant derivatives at x and y. The covariant derivatives at y are parallel transported back to x along the geodesic γ_0 with the result that $\langle T_{\mu\nu}(x,y,\gamma_0) \rangle$ is a tensor with respect to coordinate changes at x, and a scalar with respect to coordinate changes at y. One then defines the renormalized expectation value of the stress-energy tensor by taking the limit $y \to x$ and discarding the universal divergent piece which arises from the contribution of the trivial geodesic to the Green function. In other words, the renormalized Green function is defined by

$$G(x,y)_R$$
$$= \sum_{\gamma \neq \gamma_0} \frac{\Delta_{\gamma}(x,y)^{1/2}}{4\pi^2} \left\{ \frac{1}{\sigma_{\gamma}(x,y)} + \nu_{\gamma}(x,y) \ln|\sigma_{\gamma}(x,y)| + \varpi_{\gamma}(x,y) \right\},$$

and the renormalized stress energy by

$$\langle T_{\mu\nu}(x)\rangle_R = \lim_{y\to x} D_{\mu\nu}(x,y,\gamma_0)\, G_R(x,y).$$

Other methods of regularizing and renormalizing the stress-energy could be used, the results will qualitatively remain the same. The net result is that

$$\langle T_{\mu\nu}(x)\rangle_R = \sum_{\gamma\neq\gamma_0} \frac{\Delta_\gamma(x,x)^{1/2}}{\sigma_\gamma(x,x)^2}\, t_{\mu\nu}(x) + \cdots$$

Here $t_{\mu\nu}(x)$ is a dimensionless tensor built up out of the metric and tangent vectors to the geodesic γ, while the $\cdots$ denote subdominant contributions. The key observation is that if any of the non-trivial geodesics from x to itself are null (invariant length zero), then there is an additional infinity in the stress-energy over and above the universal local contribution that was removed by renormalization. (For a slightly different way of doing things, one could just as easily choose to work with the effective action [31] instead of the stress-energy; the conclusions are qualitatively similar.)

In general, these self-intersecting null geodesics define the Nth-polarized hypersurfaces, where N is a winding number which counts the number of times the geodesic passes through the tubular region surrounding the fountain. These polarized hypersurfaces lie inside the chronology horizon and typically approach it as $N \to \infty$ [6, 7]. In particular, the fountain is a non-trivial closed null geodesic, and this argument indicates that the renormalized stress-energy tensor diverges at the fountain. But infinite stress-energy implies, via the Einstein equations, infinite curvature. The standard interpretation of this is (or rather, was) that once back-reaction is taken into account the fountain (and *ipso facto*, the entire chronology horizon) is destroyed by the (mean square) quantum fluctuations. (You do not need the stress-energy to diverge everywhere on the chronology horizon; it is sufficient if it diverges at the fountain.)

The fly in the ointment here is these same quantum fluctuations. On the one hand the quantum fluctuations are responsible for the formal infinity in the expectation value of the stress-energy at the fountain. On the other hand, does the back-reaction due to the expectation value of the stress-energy tensor become large before the quantum fluctuations in the metric completely invalidate the manifold picture? (This very question led to a spirited debate between Stephen Hawking and Kip Thorne [6, 7], with disagreement on how to define the notion of 'closeness' to the chronology horizon.)

It is now generally accepted that typically the back reaction becomes large before metric fluctuations invalidate the manifold picture, but that there are exceptional geometries where the back-reaction can be kept arbitrarily small arbitrarily close to the chronology horizon. A particular example of this phenomenon is if you take a 'ring configuration' of wormholes, where each individual wormhole is nowhere near forming a chronology horizon, but the combination is just on the verge of violating causality [32]. Then there is a closed spacelike geodesic which traverses the entire ring of wormholes whose invariant length is becoming arbitrarily small; but because the spacelike geodesic is traversing many wormhole mouths (each of which acts as a defocusing lens) the Van Vleck determinant can be made arbitrarily small in compensation.

That is, adopt the length of the shortest closed spacelike geodesic as a diagnostic for how close the spacetime is to forming a time machine. Then no matter how close one is to violating chronology, there are some geometries for which the renormalized stress-energy tensor (and the quantum-induced back reaction) can be made arbitrarily small. In a similar vein there are a number of other special case examples (for example, toy models based on variants of the Grant and Misner spacetimes [33–36]) for which the renormalized stress-energy remains finite all the way up to the chronology horizon. The upshot of all this is that the search for a universal chronology protection mechanism must (at the very least) involve issues deeper and more fundamental than the size of the quantum-induced back reaction.

8.5 The failure of semiclassical gravity

The most mathematically precise and general statements known concerning the nature of the pathology encountered at the chronology horizon are encoded in the singularity theorems of Kay, Radzikowski and Wald [37]. In a highly technical article using micro-local analysis they demonstrated the following:

Theorem 1 *There are points on the chronology horizon where the two-point function is not of Hadamard form.*

Because there are points where the two-point function is not of Hadamard form, the entire process of defining a renormalized stress-energy tensor breaks down at those points. That is:

Corollary 1 *There are points on the chronology horizon where semiclassical Einstein equations fail to hold.*

Note that the semiclassical Einstein equations,

$$G_{\mu\nu} = 8\pi G_{Newton} \langle T_{\mu\nu} \rangle_R,$$

fail for a subtle reason; they fail simply because at some points the RHS fails to exist, not necessarily because the RHS is infinite. Now typically, based on the explicit calculations of the last section, the renormalized stress-energy does blow up on parts of the chronology horizon. The significant new feature of the Kay–Radzikowski–Wald analysis is that even if the stress-energy remains finite as one approaches the chronology horizon, there will be points on the chronology horizon for which no meaningful limit exists. (For a specific example, see [38].)

The physical interpretation is that semiclassical quantum gravity fails to hold (at some points) on the chronology horizon; a fact which can be read in two possible ways:

1. If you assume that semiclassical quantum gravity is the fundamental theory (at best a minority opinion, and there are very good reasons for believing that this is not the case), then by *reductio ad absurdum* the chronology horizon must fail to form. Chronology is protected, essentially by *fiat*.

2. If you are willing to entertain the possibility that semiclassical quantum gravity is not the whole story (the majority opinion), then it follows from the above that issues of chronology protection cannot be settled at the semiclassical level. Chronology protection must then be settled (one way or another) at the level of a full theory of quantum gravity.

An attractive physical picture that captures the essence of the situation is this: sufficiently close to (but outside) the chronology violating region there are extremely short self-intersecting spacelike geodesics. The length of these geodesics can be used to develop an observer independent measure of closeness to chronology violation. Indeed let

$$\mathcal{M}(\ell) = \left\{ x \mid \exists\, \gamma \neq \gamma_0 \ : \ \sigma_\gamma(x,x) \leq \frac{\ell^2}{2} \right\}.$$

Then $\mathcal{M}(0)$ is one way of characterizing the chronology violating region, while $\mathcal{M}(L_{Planck}) - \mathcal{M}(0)$ is an invariantly defined region just outside the chronology violating region which is covered by extremely short spacelike geodesics. In a tubelike region along any one of these geodesics the metric can be put in the form

$$ds^2 = dl^2 + g_{ab}^{(2+1)}(l, x_\perp)\, dx_\perp^a\, dx_\perp^b,$$

subject to the boundary condition

$$g_{ab}^{(2+1)}(0, 0_\perp) = g_{ab}^{(2+1)}(\ell, 0_\perp).$$

If we now Fourier decompose the metric in this tubelike region the boundary conditions imply that $p_\ell = n\hbar/\ell$. For $\ell < L_{Planck}$, high-momentum trans-Planckian modes $p_\ell > n\hbar/L_{Planck} = nE_{Planck}/c$ are an unavoidable part of the analysis. That is, close enough to the chronology violating region one is intrinsically confronted with Planck scale physics; and the onset of Planck-scale physics can be invariantly characterized by the length of short but nontrivial spacelike geodesics. In particular the relevant Planck scale physics includes Planck scale fluctuations in the metric – these fluctuations in the geometry of spacetime fuzz out the manifold picture that is the essential backdrop of semiclassical gravity. Thus quantum physics wins the day, and curved space quantum field theory is simply not enough to complete the job.

Overall, this entire chain of development has led the community to a conclusion diametrically opposed to the initial hopes of the early 1990s – the hopes for a simple and universal classical or semiclassical mechanism leading to chronology protection seem to be dashed, and the relativity community is now faced with the daunting prospect of understanding full quantum gravity just to place notions of global causality on a firm footing.

8.6 Where we stand

There is ample evidence that quantum field theory is a good description of reality, and there is also ample evidence that general relativity (Einstein gravity) is a good description of reality. From the obvious statement that in our terrestrial environment gravity is well described by classical general relativity, while condensed matter physics is well described by quantum physics, it follows that semiclassical quantum gravity (curved space quantum field theory with the Einstein equations coupled to the quantum expectation value of the stress-energy) is a more than adequate model over a wide range of situations. (No-one seriously doubts the applicability of semiclassical gravity to planets, stars, galaxies, or even to cosmology itself once the universe has emerged from the Planck era.)

Nevertheless, there are apparently plausible situations in semiclassical gravity that naively seem to lead to the onset of causality violation; and attempts at protecting chronology inevitably lead one back to considerations of full quantum gravity. The situation is somewhat reminiscent of black hole physics where the infinite redshift at the black hole horizon is often interpreted as a microscope that could potentially open a window on the Planck regime [39, 40]. Similarly, in discussing chronology protection the region near the chronology horizon is subject to Planck scale physics (believed to include Planck scale fluctuations in the geometry) so that semiclassical gravity is not a 'reliable' guide near the chronology horizon [41, 42]. This opens a second window on Planck scale physics – though the chances of experimentally building a time machine (or getting close enough to forming a chronology horizon to actually see what happens) must be viewed as even somewhat less likely than the chances of experimentally building a general relativity black hole. (Black hole analogues, such as acoustic dumb holes, are another story [43–45].)

One possible response, given that we will inevitably have to face full-fledged quantum gravity, is to take chronology protection as being so basic a property that we should use it as a guide in developing our theory of quantum gravity:

1. As already mentioned, canonical gravity, whatever its limitations in other areas, does automatically enforce chronology protection by its very construction. Canonical quantum gravity certainly has serious limitations, but it does at least provide a firm kinematic foundation.

2. Lorentzian lattice quantum gravity, as championed by Ambjorn and Loll, also enforces chronology protection by construction [46–49]. It does so by summing only over a subset of Euclidean lattice geometries, a subset that is compatible with a global Wick rotation back to globally hyperbolic Lorentzian spacetime. At least in low dimensionality, large low-curvature regions of spacetime emerge (large compared with the Planck length, small sub-Planckian curvature). These regions are suitable arenas for curved-space quantum field theory. There are however many loose ends to work out – such as the details of the emergence of the Einstein–Hilbert action in the low-energy limit.

3. Quantum geometry (Ashtekar new variables) is still in a state where details concerning the emergence of a 'continuum limit' are far from settled; in particular it is not yet in a position to say anything about chronology protection one way or the other.

4. Brane models (*née* string theory) are also not yet able to address this issue. In the low-energy limit brane models are essentially a special case of semiclassical quantum gravity, with the brane physics enforcing a particular choice of low-energy quantum fields on spacetime. In this limit, brane models have nothing additional to say beyond generic semiclassical gravity. In the high-energy limit where the physics becomes 'strongly stringy' the entire manifold picture seems to lose its relevance, and there is as yet no reliable formulation of the notion of causality in the string regime. One possibility is to use string dualities. If the strongly-coupled string regime is dual to a weakly-coupled regime where the manifold picture does

make sense, then you can at least begin to formulate local notions of causality in the weakly coupled regime and then bootstrap them back to the strongly-coupled regime via duality. But then you still have to decide which class of geometries you will permit in the weakly-coupled regime (globally hyperbolic or stably causal?), and the overall situation is far from clear.

So, is chronology protected? Despite a decade's work we do not know for certain, but I think it fair to say that the bulk of physicists looking at the issue believe that something along the lines envisaged by Stephen in his 'chronology protection conjecture' will ultimately save the day, as Stephen puts it: *There is also strong experimental evidence in favour of the conjecture – from the fact that we have not been invaded by hordes of tourists from the future.* It seems to me that approaches based on Novikov's consistency condition [26–28] are now somewhat in disfavour, largely on philosophical rather than physical grounds. The same comment applies to attempts at invoking the many-worlds interpretation of quantum physics, or other ways of radically re-writing the foundations of physics. Still, despite their relative unpopularity (or maybe, because of their relative unpopularity) these more radical alternatives should also be kept in mind as exploration continues. Unfortunately, if chronology protection is the answer, we will have to wander deep into the guts of quantum gravity to know for certain.

References

[1] Hawking, S. W. (1992), 'The chronology protection conjecture'. *Phys. Rev.* **D46**, 603–611.

[2] Morris, M. S. and Thorne, K. S. (1988), 'Wormholes in space-time and their use for interstellar travel: A tool for teaching general relativity', *Am. J. Phys.* **56**, 395–412.

[3] Visser, M. (1989), 'Traversable wormholes from surgically modified Schwarzschild space-times', *Nucl. Phys.* **B328**, 203–212.

[4] Visser, M. (1989), 'Traversable wormholes: Some simple examples', *Phys. Rev.* **D39**, 3182–3184.

[5] Morris, M. S., Thorne, K. S. and Yurtsever, U. (1988), 'Wormholes, time machines, and the weak energy condition', *Phys. Rev. Lett.* **61**, 1446–1449.

[6] Thorne, K. S. (1992), 'Closed timelike curves', In *GR13: Proceedings of the 13th Conference on General Relativity and Gravitation*, eds R. J. Gleiser, C. N. Kozameh and O. M. Moreschi, (Institute of Physics, England), 295–315.

[7] Kim, S. W. and Thorne, K. P. (1991), 'Do vacuum fluctuations prevent the creation of closed timelike curves?', *Phys. Rev.* **D43**, 3929–3947.

[8] Visser, M. (1995), *Lorentzian wormholes: From Einstein to Hawking* (AIP Press, USA).

[9] Gott, J. R., III (1998), 'Topology and the universe', *Class. Quant. Grav.* **15**, 2719–2731.

[10] van Stockum, W. J. (1937), Gravitational field of a distribution of particles rotating about an axis of symmetry', *Proc. R. Soc. Edin.* **57**, 135–154.

[11] Gödel, K. (1949), 'An example of a new type of cosmological solutions of Einstein's field equations of gravitation', *Rev. Mod. Phys.* **21**, 447–450.

[12] Tipler, F. J. (1974), 'Rotating cylinders and the possibility of global causality violation', *Phys. Rev.* **D9**, 2203–2206.

[13] Hawking, S. W. and Ellis, G. F. R. (1973), *The Large Scale Structure of Space-Time* (Cambridge University Press, Cambridge).

[14] Gott, J. R., III (1991), 'Closed timelike curves produced by pairs of moving cosmic strings: exact solutions', *Phys. Rev. Lett.* **66**, 1126–1129.

[15] Wheeler, J. A. (1955), 'Geons', *Phys. Rev.* **97**, 511–536.

[16] Wheeler, J. A. (1957), 'On the nature of quantum geometrodynamics', *Ann. Phys. (NY)* **2**, 604–614.

[17] Wheeler, J. A. (1962), *Geometrodynamics* (Academic, USA).

[18] Alcubierre, M. (1994), 'The warp drive: hyper-fast travel within general relativity', *Class. Quant. Grav.* **11**, L73–L77, [gr-qc/0009013].

[19] Tipler, F. J. (1976), 'Causality violation in asymptotically flat spacetime', *Phys. Rev. Lett.* **37**, 879–882.

[20] Tipler, F. J. (1977), 'Singularities and causality violation', *Ann. Phys. (NY)* **108**, 1–36.

[21] Tipler, F. J. (1978), Energy conditions and spacetime singularities. *Phys. Rev.* **D17**, 2521–2528.

[22] Deser, S., Jackiw, R. and 't Hooft, G. (1992), 'Physical cosmic strings do not generate closed timelike curves', *Phys. Rev. Lett.* **68**, 267–269.

[23] Deser, S. and Jackiw, R. (1992), 'Time travel?', *Comments Nucl. Part. Phys.* **20**, 337–354, [hep-th/9206094].

[24] Visser, M. and Barceló, C. (1999), 'Energy conditions and their cosmological implications', In *Cosmo-99*, eds. U. Cotti, R. Jeannerot, G. Senjanović and A. Smirnov, (World Scientific) pp. 98–112, [gr-qc/0001099].

[25] Deutsch, D. (1991), 'Quantum mechanics near closed timelike lines', *Phys. Rev.* **D44**, 3197–3217.

[26] Novikov, I. D. (1992), 'Time machine and selfconsistent evolution in problems with selfinteraction', *Phys. Rev.* **D45**, 1989–1994.

[27] Carlini, A., Frolov, V. P., Mensky, M. B., Novikov, I. D. and Soleng, H. H. (1995), 'Time machines: the principle of selfconsistency as a consequence of the principle of minimal action', *Int. J. Mod. Phys.* **D4**, 557–580, [gr-qc/9506087].

[28] Carlini, A. and Novikov, I. D. (1996), 'Time machines and the principle of self-consistency as a consequence of the principle of stationary action. ii: The cauchy problem for a self-interacting relativistic particle', *Int. J. Mod. Phys.* **D5**, 445–480, [gr-qc/9607063].

[29] Various authors (1970–1990), 'Tales of the Legion of Super Heroes', Marvel Comics.

[30] Heinlein, R. A. (1959), 'All you Zombies', In *The Unpleasant Profession of Jonathan Hoag* (New English Library, USA).

[31] Cassidy, M. J. (1997), 'Divergences in the effective action for acausal space-times', *Class. Quant. Grav.* **14**, 3031–3040, [gr-qc/9705075].

[32] Visser, M. (1997), 'Traversable wormholes: The Roman ring', *Phys. Rev.* **D55**, 5212–5214, [gr-qc/9702043].

[33] Grant, J. D. E. (1993), 'Cosmic strings and chronology protection', *Phys. Rev.* **D47**, 2388–2394, [hep-th/9209102].

[34] Krasnikov, S. V. (1996), 'On the quantum stability of the time machine', *Phys. Rev.* **D54**, 7322–7327, [gr-qc/9508038].

[35] Sushkov, S. V. (1997), 'Chronology protection and quantized fields: Complex automorphic scalar field in Misner space', *Class. Quant. Grav.* **14**, 523–534, [gr-qc/9509056].

[36] Tanaka, T. and Hiscock, W. A. (1994), 'Chronology protection and quantized fields: Nonconformal and massive scalar fields in Misner space', *Phys. Rev.* **D49**, 5240–5245.

[37] Kay, B. S., Radzikowski, M. J. and Wald, R. M. (1997), 'Quantum field theory on spacetimes with a compactly generated Cauchy horizon', *Commun. Math. Phys.* **183**, 533–556, [gr-qc/9603012].

[38] Cramer, C. R. and Kay, B. S. (1998), 'The thermal and two-particle stress-energy must be ill-defined on the 2-d Misner space chronology horizon', *Phys. Rev.* **D57**, 1052–1056, [gr-qc/9708028].

[39] Stephens, C. R., 't Hooft, G. and Whiting, B. F. (1994), 'Black hole evaporation without information loss', *Class. Quant. Grav.* **11**, 621–648, [gr-qc/9310006].

[40] 't Hooft, G. (1996), 'The scattering matrix approach for the quantum black hole: an overview', *Int. J. Mod. Phys.* **A11**, 4623–4688, [gr-qc/9607022].

[41] Visser, M. (1997), 'The reliability horizon for semiclassical quantum gravity: Metric fluctuations are often more important than back- reaction', *Phys. Lett.* **B415**, 8–14, [gr-qc/9702041].

[42] Visser, M. (1997), 'The reliability horizon', In *MG8: Proceedings of the Eighth Marcel Grossmann Meeting on General Relativity*, eds T. Piran and R. Ruffini, pp. 608–610, [gr-qc/9710020].

[43] Unruh, W. (1981), 'Experimental black hole evaporation?', *Phys. Rev. Lett.* **46**, 1351–1354.

[44] Garay, L. J., Anglin, J. R., Cirac, J. I. and Zoller, P. (2000), 'Black holes in Bose–Einstein condensates', *Phys. Rev. Lett.* **85**, 4643, [gr-qc/0002015].

[45] Barceló, C., Liberati, S. and Visser, M. (2001), 'Towards the observation of Hawking radiation in Bose–Einstein condensates', [gr-qc/0110036].

[46] Ambjorn, J. and Loll, R. (1998), 'Non-perturbative Lorentzian quantum gravity, causality and topology change', *Nucl. Phys.* **B536**, 407–434, [hep-th/9805108].

[47] Ambjorn, J., Correia, J., Kristjansen, C. and Loll, R. (2000), 'On the relation between Euclidean and Lorentzian 2d quantum gravity', *Phys. Lett.* **B475**, 24–32, [hep-th/9912267].

[48] Ambjorn, J., Jurkiewicz, J. and Loll, R. (2000), 'A non-perturbative Lorentzian path integral for gravity', *Phys. Rev. Lett.* **85**, 924–927, [hep-th/0002050].

[49] Ambjorn, J., Jurkiewicz, J., Loll, R. and Vernizzi, G. (2001), 'Lorentzian 3d gravity with wormholes via matrix models', *JHEP* **09**, 022, [hep-th/0106082].

9

Energy dominance and the Hawking–Ellis vacuum conservation theorem

Brandon Carter

Observatoire de Paris-Meudon

9.1 Introduction

Although overshadowed by other more recent contributions – such as the no-boundary recipe for creation of an entire universe – one of the most obvious subjects for reminiscence on the auspicious occasion of this 60th birthday celebration for Stephen Hawking is his central role in the foundation of classical black hole theory as a mathematical discipline in the late 1960s and early 1970s. It is remarkably fortunate that it has been possible, thirty years later, to assemble so many of the other protagonists in that memorable collective enterprise, including Roger Penrose, Werner Israel, Jim Hartle, Kip Thorne, Jim Bardeen, Charles Misner, Martin Rees, Gary Gibbons, and particularly George Ellis, the co-author with Stephen of their 1973 landmark treatise *The Large Scale Structure of SpaceTime* [1], which remains unsuperseded as the definitive reference on this subject, having been published just at the time when, still under Stephen's leadership, the emergence of black hole thermodynamics diverted the main thrust of progress in black hole theory from classical to quantum aspects.

A central problem in the classical theory to which Stephen made a particularly masterly and important contribution was the question of black hole equilibrium states, as described in my recent introductory historical overview [2]. Owing to (local rather than global) limitations of both space and time I shall not attempt to take up the challenge of providing for this occasion a more general historical review of (dynamical as well as stationary) classical black hole theory and of Stephen's leading role therein. Before coming to the main point of this brief contribution I would just like to advertise the previously published personal reminiscences of some of those involved [3, 4] and to emphasize that a serious student of the

177

subject could still not do better than to start by working through the relevant sections of Hawking and Ellis [1], as reprinted in its original form, which was crafted so well that, even after all these years, no new edition or replacement has been required. (The only small point on which I am conscious of the need for any caveat concerns the questionable assumptions in a heuristic energy extraction argument invoked [1] – on p. 328 – as a step towards the important conclusion that a stationary non-rotating black hole configuration should be strictly static. As briefly described in the cited overview [2], a mathematically sound basis for this conclusion has finally been provided [5–7] by much more recent work under the leadership of Bob Wald.)

What I would like to do instead on this occasion is to draw attention to another quite distinct area (not specifically concerned with black holes) to which the treatise of Hawking and Ellis [1] made a particularly significant contribution, namely the question of energy positivity conditions and their use in establishing the stability of the vacuum against spontaneous creation processes. This question has recently become rather topical in view of the current fashionability [8] of higher dimensional theories involving what are euphemistically described as 'negative tension branes'.

Generalizing the familiar case of an ordinary membrane with a support surface having two space dimensions (as well as one dimension of time), the term 'brane' has come to be used for the limit of a system confined within a neighbourhood of relatively small thickness about a supporting worldsheet surface of arbitrary dimension, as exemplified by the special cases of a 'string' with only a single space dimension. Everyday architectural experience shows that negative tension can perfectly well be sustained by a supporting column of sufficient thickness relative to its length, but it can be shown quite generally [9] that in the small thickness limit to which the term 'brane' refers, negative tension will always be accompanied by instability against lateral – i.e. 'wiggle' type – perturbations, an effect that can be dramatically demonstrated (as I found quite inadvertently!) by pushing too hard on an ordinary thin pointing rod (such as the one rashly provided to me by Gary Gibbons on this occasion).

However it is not this ordinary destabilizing kind of negative tension that is involved in the higher dimensional brane world models of the kind considered by authors such as Gregory, Rubakov and Sibiryakov [8], but something far more exotic and dangerous. There are two reasons why the trouble with these models does not arise from ordinary wiggle instabilities. The first is that although a few authors have actually considered braneworlds having the full range [10] of lateral degrees of freedom as in ordinary branes, the majority, starting with Randall and Sundrum [11] have preferred to postulate that the relevant supporting worldsheets should be of bounding orbifold type, or subject to a reflection symmetry, which suppresses all the lateral degrees of freedom, thus making it rather misleading to use the term 'brane' at all in this context. The other reason is that, unlike the non-relativistic membranes and strings (or rods) that are familiar in everyday life, whose tensions (whatever its sign) have a magnitude that is small (in relativistic units) compared with their mass densities, the kinds of brane that occur in modern higher dimensional theories are typically of the Dirac type characterized by a tension that is approximately equal to the corresponding surface mass density. Thus, in such a brane, negativity of the tension has the alarming implication that the mass density itself should also be negative. This avoids the risk of lateral instability (which arises only when the signs are opposite) but at the expense of something that is far more frightening, namely a flagrant violation of the principle that Hawking and Ellis [1] baptized as the 'weak energy condition', and thus a fortiori of the usual 'dominant energy' condition described below.

The conventional wisdom is that admissible theories must respect this kind of energy positivity condition (at least on a classical macroscopically averaged level) in order to avoid instability of the vacuum against a runaway process of creation of positive and negative mass particles. It is perhaps conceivable that the situation might be saved by specific restrictions forbidding the excitation of the degrees of freedom that would be involved in such a runaway process, but in the recent words of Ed Witten [12], it seems more 'likely that physics with violation of the weak energy condition is unstable'. To be more specific, it is clear that in the absence of such an energy condition it would no longer be possible to invoke what Hawking and Ellis referred [1] to simply as the 'Conservation Theorem', a result that might be described more specifically as the Vacuum Conservation Theorem, whose upshot (when applicable) is effectively that, at a classical level, the vacuum must be stable against spontaneous matter creation processes.

As well as recapitulating the technical content of this noteworthy vacuum stability theorem, whose original proof sprawled over pp. 92–94 of Hawking and Ellis [1], the main objective of this brief contribution is to offer a modified derivation that is rather more concise.

9.2 The energy dominance condition

The Hawking–Ellis *vacuum conservation theorem* – to the effect that one cannot create something from nothing – applies to cases describable in terms of classical fields characterized by a stress momentum energy density tensor subject to a postulate that Hawking and Ellis [1] referred to as the 'dominant energy' condition. Following the recapitulation of the contents of this postulate immediately below in the present section, the formal statement and the proof (in a new, technically simpler version) of the theorem itself will be given in the final section of this article.

In a spacetime characterized by a time orientable pseudo-Riemannian metric with components $g_{\mu\nu}$ and Lorentz type signature such that the condition for a vector u^μ to be a timelike unit vector is

$$u^\mu u_\mu = -1 \,, \tag{9.1}$$

the meaning of the postulate that a (symmetric) stress momentum energy density tensor $T^{\mu\nu}$ satisfies the energy dominance condition in question is that for *any* future directed timelike unit vector u^μ the corresponding energy flux vector

$$\mathcal{E}^\mu = -T^{\mu\nu} u_\nu \tag{9.2}$$

should be non-spacelike, i.e.

$$\mathcal{E}^\mu \mathcal{E}_\mu \leq 0 \,, \tag{9.3}$$

with future time orientation, i.e.

$$\mathcal{E}^\mu u_\mu \leq 0 \,. \tag{9.4}$$

This latter requirement (9.4) is evidently equivalent to the requirement that the corresponding energy density scalar be non-negative, i.e.

$$T^{\mu\nu} u_\mu u_\nu \geq 0 \,. \tag{9.5}$$

It is to be observed that if t_μ is any vector that is also timelike,

$$t^\mu t_\mu < 0 \,, \tag{9.6}$$

then the condition (9.3) that the energy flux vector $\mathcal{E}^\mu$ should be non-spacelike implies that its contraction with t_μ can vanish only if the energy flux vector itself vanishes, i.e.

$$\mathcal{E}^\mu t_\mu = 0 \qquad \Rightarrow \qquad \mathcal{E}^\mu = 0 \,, \tag{9.7}$$

and that if t^μ is past directed, i.e.

$$t_\mu u^\mu > 0 \,, \tag{9.8}$$

the contraction will in any case have the non-negativity property

$$\mathcal{E}^\mu t_\mu \geq 0 \,, \tag{9.9}$$

which is equivalent to the condition that

$$T^{\mu\nu} u_\mu t_\nu \leq 0 \,, \tag{9.10}$$

for any pair of respectively future and past directed timelike vectors u^μ and t^μ.

A further almost equally obvious consequence of the energy dominance condition is that $\mathcal{E}^\mu$ cannot vanish for any particular unit vector u^μ unless it vanishes for all such unit vectors, which will happen only in a vacuum where $T^{\mu\nu}$ vanishes altogether, i.e.

$$\mathcal{E}^\mu = 0 \quad\quad \Rightarrow \quad\quad T^{\mu\nu} = 0 \,. \tag{9.11}$$

It can thus be seen, by combining (9.7) and (9.11), that according to the energy dominance condition the possibility for the contraction $T^{\mu\nu} u_\mu t_\nu$ to vanish for any timelike vectors t^μ and u^μ is excluded everywhere except in a vacuum, i.e.

$$T^{\mu\nu} u_\mu t_\nu = 0 \quad\quad \Rightarrow \quad\quad T^{\mu\nu} = 0 \,. \tag{9.12}$$

9.3 The vacuum conservation theorem

Exploiting the existence (demonstrated in Section 6.4 of their book [1]) of a globally well behaved time coordinate, τ – i.e. a field with everywhere strictly timelike gradient $\tau_{;\mu}$ – and assuming the validity of the ordinary local energy momentum conservation condition

$$T^{\mu\nu}{}_{;\nu} = 0 \,, \tag{9.13}$$

(using a semi colon for Riemannian covariant differentiation) Hawking and Ellis showed, in Section 4.3 of their book [1], how the energy dominance postulate that has just been described can be used to derive a *vacuum conservation theorem* whose purport is as follows: if the boundary of a compact causally well behaved space-time volume, $\mathcal{V}$ say, consists just of an 'initial' (but not necessarily spacelike) vacuum hypersurface $\Sigma_{(0)}$ say – i.e. a hypersurface where $T^{\mu\nu}$ vanishes – together with a future boundary hypersurface, $\Sigma_{(1)}$ say, that is *spacelike*, then the entire space-time volume $\mathcal{V}$ will be characterized by the vacuum property, $T^{\mu\nu} = 0$.

This result is obtainable as an immediate corollary of a lemma to the effect that the vacuum property will hold on the future boundary $\Sigma_{(1)}$ (and thus on the entire boundary): it evidently suffices to apply this lemma to the intersection of $\mathcal{V}$ with the past of a timelike hypersurface (given by a fixed global time τ) through any point under consideration.

It is evident from (9.10) and (9.12) that to establish the required lemma, it will be sufficient to demonstrate the non-positivity, and hence the vanishing, of an integral of the (generically positive) form

$$\mathcal{I} = \int_{\Sigma_{(1)}} \mathcal{E}^\mu t_\mu \, d\Sigma \, , \tag{9.14}$$

for some pair of respectively future and past directed timelike vector fields u^μ and t^μ on the 'final' hypersurface $\Sigma_{(1)}$ in question.

In order to do this, let us consider the case for which u^μ is taken to be the unit future (i.e. outward) directed normal to the hypersurface. The corresponding normal surface element will then be expressible as $d\Sigma_\mu = - u_\mu \, d\Sigma$, so that we shall obtain

$$\mathcal{I} = \int_{\Sigma_{(1)}} T^{\mu\nu} t_\nu \, d\Sigma_\mu \geq 0 \, . \tag{9.15}$$

If t^μ is taken to be proportional to any one of the globally well behaved past directed timelike unit vector fields that can always be constructed (see Section 2.6 of Hawking and Ellis [1]) in any time orientable space-time manifold, one can use Green's theorem to convert the surface integral (9.15) to the form

$$\mathcal{I} = \int_{\mathcal{V}} (T^{\mu\nu} t_\nu)_{;\mu} \, d\mathcal{V} \, , \tag{9.16}$$

as a consequence of the postulate that the vacuum condition should already be satisfied on the remaining 'initial' part of the boundary of the relevant space-time volume $\mathcal{V}$.

More specifically (relying on the the causal good behaviour postulate) let τ be the globally well defined time coordinate field invoked above. Then – as pointed out by Hawking and Ellis [1] in their Section 4.3 – the energy dominance condition ensures that in any compact space-time region $\mathcal{V}$ there will be some finite positive constant, $C > 0$, such that

$$|T^{\mu\nu} \tau_{;\mu\nu}| \leq C T^{\mu\nu} \tau_{;\mu} \tau_{;\nu} \, . \tag{9.17}$$

If we now choose the timelike vector in (9.16) to be the gradient of a new exponentially related time coordinate t according to a specification of the form

$$t_\mu = t_{;\mu} \, , \qquad C(t - t_\infty) = -e^{-C\tau} \, , \tag{9.18}$$

for some constant t_∞, then it can be seen from (9.13) that the expression (9.16) will reduce to the form

$$\mathcal{I} = \int_{\mathcal{V}} T^{\mu\nu} t_{;\mu\nu} \, d\mathcal{V} \, , \tag{9.19}$$

with

$$t_{;\mu\nu} = e^{C\tau}\left(\tau_{;\mu\nu} - C\tau_{;\mu}\tau_{;\nu}\right).$$ (9.20)

It then follows from (9.17) that we shall have

$$T^{\mu\nu} t_{;\mu\nu} \leq 0,$$ (9.21)

and hence

$$\mathcal{I} \leq 0,$$ (9.22)

which is compatible with the non-negative nature of the integral (9.15) only if it vanishes.

This completes the proof of the lemma (and hence of the theorem) since, as noted above, the conclusion that the integral will vanish,

$$\mathcal{I} = 0,$$ (9.23)

implies *Q.E.D*, namely that, by (9.10) and (9.12), the vacuum condition

$$T^{\mu\nu} = 0,$$ (9.24)

will indeed have to be satisfied everywhere on the 'final' hypersurface $\Sigma_{(1)}$ (and hence throughout $\mathcal{V}$).

References

[1] Hawking, S. W. and Ellis, G. F. R. (1973), *The Large Scale Structure of Space Time* (Cambridge University Press, Cambridge).

[2] Carter, B. (1999), 'Has the black hole equilibrium problem been solved?', in *The Eighth Marcel Grossman Meeting*, eds T. Piran and R. Ruffini (World Scientific) 136–155, [gr-qc/9712038].

[3] Israel, W. (1987), 'Dark stars: the evolution of an idea', in *300 Years of Gravitation*, eds S. W. Hawking and W. Israel (Cambridge University Press, Cambridge) 199–276.

[4] Thorne, K. S. (1994), *Black Holes and Time Warps* (Norton, New York).

[5] Sudarsky, D. and Wald, R. M. (1991), 'Extrema of mass, stationarity, and staticity, and solutions to the Einstein–Yang–Mills equations', *Phys. Rev.* **D46** 1453–74.

[6] Chrusciel, P. T. and Wald, R. M. (1964), 'Maximal hypersurfaces in stationary asymptotically flat spacetimes', *Comm. Math. Phys.* **163** 561–604, [gr-qc/9304009].

[7] Sudarsky, D. and Wald, R. M. (1993), 'Mass formulas for stationary Einstein–Yang–Mills black holes and a simple proof of two staticity theorems', *Phys. Rev.* **D47** 5209–13, [gr-qc/9305023].

[8] Gregory, R., Rubakov, V. A. and Sibiryakov, S. M. (2000), 'Opening up extra dimensions at ultra-large scales', *Phys. Rev. Lett.* **84** 5928–5931, [hep-th/0002072].

[9] Carter, B. (1995), 'Dynamics of cosmic strings and other Brane models', in *Formation and Interactions of Topological Defects*, NATO ASI B349, eds A. C. Davis and R. Brandenberger, (Plenum, New York) 303–348, [hep-th/9611054].

[10] Battye, R. A., Carter, B., Mennim, A. and Uzan, J. P. (2001), 'Einstein equations for an asymmetric brane-world', *Phys. Rev.* **D64** 124007, [hep-th/0105091].

[11] Randall, L. and Sundrum, R. (1999), 'A large mass hierarchy from a small extra dimension', *Phys. Rev. Lett.* **83** 4690–4693, [hep-th/9906064].

[12] Witten, E. (2000), 'The cosmological constant from the viewpoint of string theory', *Lecture at Marina del Ray*, [hep-ph/0002297 v2].

10

On the instability of extra space dimensions

Roger Penrose

Mathematical Institute, University of Oxford

10.1 The issue of functional freedom

Physical theories are common, today, in which the dimensionality of space is taken to be larger than the 3 that we directly perceive.[1] The earliest serious theory of this nature appears to be that of Kaluza (1921) and Klein (1926), in which there is a (1+4)-dimensional spacetime (i.e. 1 time and 4 space dimensions). But in this original theory, there was a $U(1)$ symmetry imposed, specified by a Killing vector pointing along the extra spatial dimension (which is curled into a tiny S^1), and electromagnetism is thereby incorporated (via the $U(1)$-gauge symmetry) along with gravity. This symmetry reduces what might have been an excessive functional freedom, down to what is usual in conventional 3-space physical theory. With the usual hyperbolic-type equations fixing the time-evolution, this freedom is specified by a finite number of free functions of three variables. In this respect, Kaluza–Klein theory provides a picture not unlike that of a conventional S^1 bundle over (1+3)-dimensional spacetime, where the extra dimension in the fibre does not increase the effective spacetime dimension, as regards functional freedom, because of the imposed fibre symmetry.

The picture presented by string theory[2] is very different, however. Here, we are provided with a (1+25)-dimensional spacetime (in the case of the original bosonic strings), a (1+9)-dimensional spacetime (in the

---

[1] This article is presented in honour of Stephen Hawking's 60th birthday, in a profoundly respectful appreciation of Stephen as a person as well as of his wonderful scientific work. I hope that he will enjoy the new use to which I have put our old singularity theorem, in section 10.3.

[2] For a classic reference on string theory, see Green *et al.* (1987); for more up-to-date accounts, see Polchinski (1998) and Green (2000).

supersymmetric version of Green–Schwarz), or a (1+10)-dimensional spacetime (more or less, in the case of M theory), where the extra space dimensions are taken to be fully dynamical. The functional freedom, in the classical versions of these theories, is enormously larger than in conventional (1+3)-dimensional physical theories, and quantum arguments need to be invoked to support the contention that such freedom will not impose itself unreasonably, at ordinary energies. The purpose of this article is to shed considerable doubt on this type of reasoning, and to argue that there are some very serious issues to be faced, which I do not believe have been at all adequately addressed in string-theoretic discussions so far.

First, let us recall the standard classical arguments about functional freedom, as made fully explicit by Élie Cartan (1945; see also Bryant *et al.* 1991). Let us first consider a manifold $\mathcal{H}$, of D real dimensions, on which is defined a C-real-component field, where it is to be taken that there are no equations to be satisfied by these components, so that they can be specified completely freely, subject only to appropriate requirements of real variable[3] smoothness (and continuity). We may imagine that $\mathcal{H}$ is a (spacelike) Cauchy hypersurface for a spacetime $\mathcal{M}$, and that all the relevant constraint equations for the initial data have been solved, thus leaving us with C free functions per point of $\mathcal{H}$. In the case of an ordinary source-free Maxwell field in (1+3)-dimensions, and also in the case of ordinary vacuum (1+3)-dimensional Einstein general relativity, we find that $C=4$ and we have $D=3$. Wheeler (1982) has used the notation

$$\infty^{C\infty^{D}}$$
(10.1)

for the functional freedom that is involved here (for a free C-component field on a space of D dimensions), so that the freedom for ordinary Maxwell electromagnetism or ordinary Einstein gravity is, in each case,

$$\infty^{4\infty^{3}}.$$
(10.2)

The justification for this notation can be understood if we think of approximating the manifold $\mathcal{H}$ by a space with a finite number N^{D} of points, where we are taking the real-number system to be 'approximated' by a

---

[3] One can also discuss these issues in the complex case. The general conclusion is that when all quantities under consideration are holomorphic (complex analytic), then the functional-freedom counting proceeds just as in the real case, where the system of Cauchy–Riemann equations do not enter explicitly into the counting. When non-holomorphic quantities are also involved, then it may be best to revert to a fully real description, and bring the Cauchy–Riemann equations explicitly in with the other (field) equations.

set of N elements, our space having D 'coordinates' taken from that set. Our space $\mathcal{F}$ of C-component fields (where a particular value of each of these C components is to be assigned to each point of $\mathcal{H}$) is likewise to be thought of as being approximated by a finite space of N^C points, the allowed values for each component being again elements of our N-element set, rather than real numbers. The number of such 'fields' on our discrete space is given by the number of maps from the discretized $\mathcal{H}$ to the discretized $\mathcal{F}$, which is simply

$$\left(N^C\right)^{\left(N^D\right)} = N^{CN^D},\tag{10.3}$$

so that taking a limit $N \to \infty$, we retrieve Wheeler's $\infty^{C\infty^D}$.

Each of the numbers C and D is an invariant, in a certain sense defined by Élie Cartan (cf. Bryant *et al.* 1991, Chapter 3) which is independent of the particular way in which the field is described. In the case of the dimension D of the space on which the fields are freely specified, there is no real argument about this (and this 'D' is what I shall be primarily concerned with in this article). Thus, there are, in a completely clear-cut and invariant sense, vastly more free finite-component fields on a $(D+k)$-dimensional space $(k > 0)$ than there would be on a D-dimensional space, whatever the respective number C' and C of components of the field might be in each case. We may express this as

$$\infty^{C'\infty^{D'}} \ggg \infty^{C\infty^D}, \qquad \text{if } D' > D,\tag{10.4}$$

irrespective of the relation between C' and C. It should be noted that this is a much more refined notion of 'size' than is obtained using Cantor's concept of cardinality, since the cardinality is, in each case, simply $\mathbf{C} = 2^{\aleph_0}$.

If the dimension D of the space is the same in each case, then we can still assert that there is, in Cartan's invariant sense, more functional freedom the larger the value of C, and we can write

$$\infty^{C'\infty^D} \gg \infty^{C\infty^D}, \qquad \text{if } C' > C.\tag{10.5}$$

A considerable amount of care must be exercised in making sure that the counting of the number C of independent components is correctly carried out, however. For example, suppose that we are counting the functional freedom in the number of solutions of the wave equation

$$\Box \varphi = 0\tag{10.6}$$

in, say, $(1+3)$ dimensions where we have

$$\Box = \frac{\partial^2}{\partial t^2} - \frac{\partial^2}{\partial x^2} - \frac{\partial^2}{\partial y^2} - \frac{\partial^2}{\partial z^2}.\tag{10.7}$$

If we use the spacelike Cauchy 3-surface $t = 0$ we would normally specify φ and $\partial\varphi/\partial t$ freely and independently at each point of the surface. These two quantities provide us with $C = 2$, and we have $D = 3$ for the dimensionality of the Cauchy surface, so the functional freedom for the space of solutions comes out as

$$\infty^{2\infty^3} \tag{10.8}$$

which is, in fact, the correct answer in Cartan's sense. However, if we choose the future null cone

$$t^2 - x^2 - y^2 - z^2 = 0, \qquad t \geq 0 \tag{10.9}$$

as our initial data surface, then we need only specify the single quantity φ on this cone, so we appear to get the answer $\infty^{1\infty^3}$. This, in Cartan's sense is an *incorrect* counting. (This has nothing to do with the fact that the region of spacetime throughout which the field is determined is only the interior of this future light cone. For this same region is obtained using the spacelike Cauchy 3-surface $t^2 - x^2 - y^2 - z^2 = 1$, $t \geq 0$ on which the *both* φ and its normal derivative would need to be specified, directly giving the correct $\infty^{2\infty^3}$ freedom.)

Cartan (1945) (see Bryant *et al.* 1991) explicitly provided an even simpler-looking example, namely the heat equation in 1 dimension

$$\frac{\partial\varphi}{\partial t} = \frac{\partial^2\varphi}{\partial x^2}. \tag{10.10}$$

One can argue that the 'general' depends on 2 functions of 1 variable (plus constants) by choosing initial data on $x = 0$, where φ and $\partial\varphi/\partial x$ are each specified independently, giving us the functional freedom

$$\infty^{2\infty^1}. \tag{10.11}$$

This is actually the correct answer, in Cartan's sense. However, one might alternatively choose to specify data on $t = 0$ (which would appear to be more natural from the physical point of view) giving merely the value of φ (and not its t-derivative), which seems to yield merely 1 function of 1 variable, leading to the apparent conclusion that the functional freedom is just $\infty^{1\infty^1}$. Cartan points out, using this example explicitly, why this second answer should be considered as 'incorrect', the above $\infty^{2\infty^1}$ beins the correct one. (The problem may be considered to be similar to that of the wave equation above, since the data on $t = 0$ is 'characteristic data' for the heat equation.)

In fact, these considerations can be greatly refined, and the 'Wheeler notation' extended to include expressions like

$$\infty^{2\infty^2 + 3\infty^1 + 5} \tag{10.12}$$

to stand for 'the general solution depends on 2 functions of 2 variables, 3 functions of 1 variable, and 5 constants'. Thus we are led to consider expressions like

$$\infty^{p(\infty)}, \tag{10.13}$$

where p denotes a polynomial with non-negative integer coefficients. The invariant nature of the functional freedom can be understood in terms of the notion of k-jets, as described in detail by Bryant *et al.* (1991). However, one must bear in mind that two systems that may *seem* to be 'equivalent' (though not in the strong sense that Cartan would require) may have functional freedoms described by differing polynomials p. One thing that is completely clear, however, is that the *degree* of p (i.e. the dimension of the manifold on which the free data is specified) cannot be changed by passing to a system that is in any reasonable sense 'equivalent' to the original one. (See the Einstein–Cartan letters, Debever (1979), where Cartan explains to Einstein just what his notion of 'general solution' means.)

10.2 Functional freedom in higher-dimensional theories

The considerations of Section 10.1 would seem to imply that a higher-dimensional physical theory, with a fully dynamical spacetime $\mathcal{M}$ of $(1+n)$-dimensions where $n > 3$, would posses vastly more degrees of freedom than is perceived in ordinary physics. Let us consider the case where our field equations are just Ricci-flatness for $\mathcal{M}$, as is the case in string theory, where one takes just the first-order term in the string constant α'. We have a hyperbolic system of partial differential equations, evolving the spacetime metric away from an n-dimensional initial spacelike hypersurface $\mathcal{H}$, so in this case we have $D = n$. The number of independent components that must be specified per point of $\mathcal{H}$ turns out to be $C = (n+1)(n-2)$, so our functional freedom (ignoring lower-order terms in our polynomial $p(\infty)$) is

$$\infty^{(n+1)(n-2)\infty^n}. \tag{10.14}$$

In the popular 10-dimensional string theory, we have $n = 9$, so Ricci-flatness leaves us with a functional freedom of

$$\infty^{70\infty^9}, \tag{10.15}$$

which of course is wildly in excess of the $\infty^{C\infty^3}$ that we would have for a conventional classical field theory, where the specific value of C would depend on the number and nature of the fields that are involved. (In fact, for *supergravity*, the '70' would be replaced by a larger number.)

It should be made clear that these considerations are essentially *local.* In certain circumstances, compactness or other topological requirements might lead to severe restrictions on the solutions of the equations (such as in the case of Maxwell's equations in a background of constant non-zero charge density ρ, where the constraint equation $\operatorname{div} \mathbf{E} = 4\pi\rho$ precludes any solution at all if the initial hypersurface $\mathcal{H}$ is compact). (In the case of the classical Einstein vacuum equations – Ricci-flatness – compactness in the initial hypersurface may not restrict the freedom, unless we demand an indefinitely extended non-singular time-evolution; see section 10.3.)

The usual string-theoretic argument for the unimportance of this excessive additional functional freedom is necessarily a quantum argument, since classically this unwanted freedom is certainly there. The picture that is presented is one in which it is assumed that the extra 6 spatial dimensions form a compact 6-manifold $\mathcal{Y}$ which is usually taken to be a Calabi–Yau space. As a starting point, we may regard the space $\mathcal{Y}$ as being essentially fixed – so that the entire spacetime $\mathcal{M}$ would have the approximate structure $\mathcal{M} = \mathbf{M}^4 \times \mathcal{Y}$ (so $\mathcal{H}$ would have the topology of $\mathbf{E}^3 \times \mathcal{Y}$), where $\mathcal{Y}$ is a definite Calabi–Yau space and $\mathbf{M}^4$ is Minkowski $(1+3)$-space. We shall be concerned with small perturbations away from this canonical structure.

To study fields on $\mathbf{M}^4 \times \mathcal{Y}$, we may think in terms of an initial value problem. We represent $\mathbf{M}^4$ as $\mathbf{M}^4 = \mathbf{E}^1 \times \mathbf{E}^3$, where the Euclidean 1-space $\mathbf{E}^1$ refers to a *time*-coordinate t and the Euclidean 3-space $\mathbf{E}^3$ refers to *space*. We then analyse these fields in terms of *normal modes* on $\mathbf{E}^3 \times \mathcal{Y}$. Because of the product metric structure of $\mathbf{E}^3 \times \mathcal{Y}$, we can represent each of these modes simply as the ordinary product of a mode on $\mathbf{E}^3$ with a mode on $\mathcal{Y}$. $\mathbf{E}^3$'s modes are just momentum states, and they form a continuous family. As for $\mathcal{Y}$'s normal modes, the *compactness* ensures that they form a discrete family, each characterized by some finite set of eigenvalues. We are to consider how one might 'excite' one of these modes.

The usual string theorist's argument that we can basically disregard perturbations of $\mathcal{Y}$, at least at the present cosmological epoch, depends upon an expectation that the *energy* needed to excite $\mathcal{Y}$'s modes would be enormously large. There are some exceptions to this, however, namely certain modes of *zero* energy which simply refer to global changes in the values of the *moduli* of the Calabi–Yau space $\mathcal{Y}$, these being parameters determining the 'shape' of $\mathcal{Y}$. This moduli freedom is considered to have importance in leading to the $SU(3) \times SU(2) \times U(1)$ symmetry of the standard model of particle physics. The moduli freedom is not regarded as problematic; on their own, the zero modes provide the ordinary $\infty^{C\infty^3}$ functional freedom that would arise in a gauge theory on $\mathbf{M}^4$, the moduli just giving 'fibre coordinates' for a bundle over $\mathbf{M}^4$. But apart from these zero modes, the energy of excitation of a $\mathcal{Y}$-mode is expected to be very large because of the very minute scale of $\mathcal{Y}$ itself. A dynamical 'standing wave' on $\mathcal{Y}$ would have a tiny wavelength, comparable to the Planck distance of $\sim 10^{-33}$ cm, and would therefore have something like a Planck frequency of $\sim 10^{-43}$ seconds. The energy required to excite such a mode would be of the general order of a Planck energy, namely around 2×10^{16} ergs, which is nearly twenty orders of magnitude larger than the largest energies involved in ordinary particle interactions. It is accordingly argued that the modes that affect $\mathcal{Y}$'s geometry will remain unexcited, in all particle-physics processes that are of relevance to physical actions available today.

The picture is presented that at the very early stages of the universe, six of its dimensions settled into the configuration described by a roughly Planck-scale $\mathcal{Y}$, whereas the remaining three spatial dimensions expanded outwards enormously to give the almost spatially flat picture of a three-dimensional universe in accordance with present-day cosmology. The $\mathcal{Y}$-spaces would, in this picture, have remained basically undisturbed from a time not long after the first Planck moments of the universe's existence. The argument is that the energies are *not* now available to excite the degrees of freedom that are potentially present in the $\infty^{70\infty^9}$ functional freedom.

To understand the argument in a little more detail, let us simplify and consider a 'hosepipe' situation where, as with the original Kaluza–Klein theory, $\mathcal{Y}$ is just a *circle* S^1, which we take to have some very small radius ρ. We can choose a real coordinate θ for S^1 (with θ identified with $\theta+2\pi$), where $\rho\theta$ measures actual distance round the circle. On $\mathbf{E}^3$ we choose ordinary Cartesian coordinates (x, y, z). We shall address the question of finding 'modes' by looking for eigenstates of the Laplacian operator. In the present context, this may be regarded as an approximation (or just a 'model') since we should, more correctly, be concerned with eigenstates of the *Hamiltonian* for the evolution of the geometry. For Ricci-flat 5-spaces we should need the appropriate Hamiltonian formulation of five-dimensional general relativity, which is complicated. The leading term of this is essentially a Laplacian, so using a Laplacian here, also, suffices as a model for the present discussion, where we are now taking $\mathcal{Y} = S^1$. The modes are now the quantities $e^{in\theta}$, where n is an integer.

Our $\mathbf{E}^3 \times S^1$ is flat, so the Laplacian is

$$\nabla^2 = \frac{\partial^2}{\partial x^2} + \frac{\partial^2}{\partial y^2} + \frac{\partial^2}{\partial z^2} + \frac{1}{\rho^2}\frac{\partial^2}{\partial \theta^2}, \tag{10.16}$$

the fourth coordinate being the $\rho\theta$ needed for S^1. To find our 'modes', we would look for eigenstates of this ∇^2. Here we shall just be concerned about the mode analysis for the S^1 part of $\mathbf{E}^3 \times S^1$ and we shall leave the $\mathbf{E}^3$-part as an ordinary field. Accordingly, we split up our fields into different contributions, each having a different integer 'n', giving a θ-dependence of the specific form $e^{in\theta}$, as described above. Thus, for an nth order S^1-mode, we can write

$$\Psi = e^{in\theta}\psi, \qquad (10.17)$$

on our initial 4-surface $\mathbf{E}^3 \times S^1$, where ψ is a function of the ordinary space coordinates x, y, z. For any such nth order mode Ψ, the term $\rho^{-2}\partial^2/\partial\theta^2$ in our above Laplacian is replaced simply by $-n^2/\rho^2$:

$$\frac{1}{\rho^2}\frac{\partial^2}{\partial\theta^2} \rightarrow -\frac{n^2}{\rho^2}. \qquad (10.18)$$

With regard to the remaining variables x, y, z, our Laplacian now reverts to the ordinary 3-space one, but we have the constant term $-n^2/\rho^2$ added to this 3-space Laplacian. An ordinary (spinless) particle of mass μ, in Minkowski spacetime $\mathbf{M}^4$, is described according to the 'Klein–Gordon' wave equation $(\square^2 + \mu^2)\psi = 0$. In the 5-space $\mathbf{M}^4 \times S^1$, however, we would have an additional term $-1/\rho^2\,\partial^2/\partial\theta^2$ in the wave operator. If we take this 5-space particle to be in an n-mode eigenstate for S^1, this term gets replaced by n^2/ρ^2, as above. Accordingly, from the ordinary Minkowski 4-space point of view, our 5-space n-mode Klein–Gordon particle satisfies the 4-space equation

$$\left(\square^2 + \mu^2 + \frac{n^2}{\rho^2}\right)\psi = 0, \qquad (10.19)$$

which is just the Klein–Gordon equation again, but with $\mu^2 + n^2/\rho^2$ in place of μ^2. Thus, we have the 4-space Klein–Gordon equation for a *new* particle, but where the mass is increased from μ to $\sqrt{\mu^2 + n^2/\rho^2}$.

Now, any of the observed particles of Nature would have a mass μ that is enormously smaller than the Planck value of roughly $1/\rho$ (for our chosen value of ρ). Assuming that $n \neq 0$, this new particle would have a mass that is at least of Planck order (n/ρ being much greater than μ) so it would lie far beyond the reach of presently feasible particle accelerators. It is accordingly reasoned by string theorists that no $n \neq 0$ mode can be accessed in any particle-physics process that is available at the present cosmological epoch!

Essentially the same argument is applied to the full Planck-sized compact 6-space $\mathcal{Y}$. It is argued that in the relatively low-energy situation we find ourselves in today, the modes of excitation of $\mathcal{Y}$ for which $n \neq 0$ are experimentally inaccessible to us, and hence there is no conflict between the hypothesis of extra space dimensions and present-day observational physics. The modes for which $n = 0$ do not cause a problem in any case, as argued above, since on their own they do not lead to excessive functional freedom.

But is this 'particle-physics' reasoning really appropriate? Leaving aside the unanswered puzzle of why, in the very early universe, three of the spatial dimensions should behave so very differently from the remaining six, we must be very cautious about this kind of argument, claiming to show that the $\mathcal{Y}$-geometry is immunized against change during the subsequent evolution of the universe. Are the positive-energy (Planck-scale) modes of vibration of the six extra dimensions *really* immune from excitation? Although the Planck energy is indeed very large when compared with normal particle-physics energies, it is still not *that* big an energy, being comparable to the energy released in a small-sized terrestrial explosion. There is, of course, enormously more energy than this available in the known universe. For example, the energy received from the Sun by the Earth in one second is *far* larger. On energy terms alone, that would be far more than sufficient to excite the lowest positive-energy $\mathcal{Y}$-mode for the *entire universe*!

In the string-theorist's reasoning, this energy is delivered in a local particle interaction, and we tend to imagine it as being administered in some tiny region of ordinary space. Yet, as noted above, the actual modes of excitation of $\mathcal{Y}$ that are supposed to be inaccessible, taken as perturbations of the initial hypersurface $\mathbf{E}^3 \times \mathcal{Y}$, being *products* of modes on $\mathbf{E}^3$ with modes on $\mathcal{Y}$, are spread uniformly (i.e. constant) over the whole of $\mathbf{E}^3$. There is nothing to say that these need (or even should) be injected at a localized region in ordinary physical space. Of course, this in itself is no argument against local particle interactions being the appropriate way to excite such modes. Momentum states, for example, *are* 'spread' over the whole of $\mathbf{E}^3$ so 'quantum particles' need in no way be spatially localized. Perhaps a better way to think of these matters is to refer to 'quanta' rather than particles. The issue to be addressed is whether or not it is reasonable to expect that a single *quantum* of Planck energy can be injected into a $\mathcal{Y}$-mode, by whatever means. It does not seem to me that we need think of such 'means' as being well described in terms of local particle interactions, rather than something *else* which is better described as a non-linear disturbance of the entire spacetime geometry.

Let us return to our hosepipe analogy, where we think of the hosepipe as being essentially *straight* in its 'large' dimension (where for visualization purposes, we can take 'ordinary space' to be a one-dimensional $\mathbf{E}^1$, as with an ordinary hosepipe, this being analogous to $\mathbf{E}^3$), and with a constant S^1 cross-section (analogous to $\mathcal{Y}$), which is a circle of tiny radius ρ. The hosepipe's modes of excitation can be composed of various waves travelling one way or the other along its length ('$\mathbf{E}^1$-modes') and of various distortions of its circular cross-sectional shape ('$\mathcal{Y}$-modes'). As we have seen, any one of these latter modes occurs *simultaneously* along the entire hosepipe. Quantum-mechanically, the energy in a single quantum of excitation of such a mode – an *exciton* – of vibrational frequency ν is $2\pi\nu$, this being *independent* of the hosepipe length!

For an *infinite* length of hosepipe, this gives a zero *density* of energy, for each individual exciton, so it may be less confusing if we imagine the pipe to be bent round into a very large circle, of radius R, say, where $R \gg \rho$. Now, think of a particular mode of vibration of $\mathcal{Y}$, with a particular frequency ν. The total energy $2\pi\nu$, in this exciton, is indeed independent of R. This may seem puzzling, because it implies that the larger we take R to be, the less the energy that exists *locally* in the vibration is, in proportion to $1/R$. This is no inconsistency, but it tells us that the *amplitude* of the vibration in an exciton, for a fixed vibrational mode of $\mathcal{Y}$, is smaller, the greater the length of the pipe. If we take the limit $R \to \infty$, the energy stored *locally* in the mode goes to zero. We learn from this that any particular way in which the hosepipe can vibrate locally, in the limit when the hosepipe length becomes infinite, must involve higher and higher numbers of quanta, the effect of each individual quantum getting less and less, so we are driven to consider that a classical rather than a quantum description of the behaviour of the hosepipe might become appropriate.

This raises the thorny issue of how the *classical limit* of a quantum system is to come about when quantum numbers get large. Strictly speaking, this is an unresolved issue even for standard quantum-mechanical systems. I do not believe that it can be fully resolved without a coherent theory of *state reduction*, which in my opinion will require us to move outside the framework of present-day quantum theory. (See for example, Penrose (1996, 2000).) Rather than getting ourselves embroiled in such issues, we can reasonably adopt the 'conventional' attitude, which would be to consider that a classical description of physical reality becomes physically appropriate when quantum numbers get excessively large. With the hosepipe, we see that the smallness of the *distance* ρ is not, in itself, an appropriate measure for telling us that a 'quantum' description is more suitable than a classical one. For fixed ρ, the description of local hosepipe vibrations seems to become more and more 'classical' the larger we take R, since for a given change in the $\mathcal{Y}$-space, we need to involve larger and larger numbers of excitons and excitons involving higher and higher vibrational quantum numbers (higher modes of $\mathcal{Y}$). We note that the excitons behave as *bosons* in a quantum-field theoretic description of the hosepipe vibrations, so there can be many quanta in any one particular $\mathcal{Y}$-mode.

Without a clear-cut theory that tells us how 'large' systems become well described classically whilst 'small' ones behave according to quantum rules, it would seem that we can come to no *definitive* conclusion concerning the alleged inaccessibility of excitations of $\mathcal{Y}$. Nevertheless, in view of the fact that actual perturbations of $\mathcal{Y}$ *do* lead us to a quantum picture of very large numbers of quanta, where each individual quantum affects the geometry of $\mathcal{Y}$ hardly at all – and to large quantum numbers – it would appear that we get more insights into how perturbations of an $\mathbf{M}^4 \times \mathcal{Y}$ universe with 'small' $\mathcal{Y}$ behave if we study these *classically*, rather than quantum mechanically. Let us consider this next.

10.3 Classical instability of extra dimensions

Suppose we consider our 10-space model as an entirely classical one. In view of the above remarks, this ought to give us some important guidance (and perhaps the *only* reliable guidance) as to how the full quantum model will actually behave. We noted above that in a classical (1+9)-spacetime there would be an unacceptable flood of excessive degrees of freedom $(\infty^{M\infty^9} \gg \infty^{N\infty^3})$, which is serious enough. But in my opinion, things are actually much *worse* than this. We shall find that a classical $\mathbf{M}^4 \times \mathcal{Y}$ universe – subject to Ricci-flatness – is highly *unstable* against small perturbations. If $\mathcal{Y}$ is compact and of a Planck-scale size, then *spacetime singularities* are to be expected to result within a tiny fraction of a second!

First consider perturbations at the initial $\mathbf{E}^3 \times \mathcal{Y}$ that disturb only the $\mathcal{Y}$-geometry and which, accordingly, do not 'leak out' into the spatial $\mathbf{E}^3$. That is to say, we examine a 'generic' Ricci-flat (1+6)-spacetime $\mathcal{Z}$ which is the perturbed evolution of $\mathcal{Y}$ alone (where the geometry of $\mathcal{Y}$ and its time derivative could be appropriately specified at time $t = 0$), and we take the entire (1+9)-spacetime to be the Ricci-flat $\mathbf{E}^3 \times \mathcal{Z}$. We consider that $\mathcal{Z}$ is the (Ricci-flat) time-evolution of some 6-space that (at $t = 0$) is 'close' to $\mathcal{Y}$, so $\mathcal{Z}$ *starts out* close to the (unchanging) 'time-evolution' $\mathbf{E}^1 \times \mathcal{Y}$ of $\mathcal{Y}$, although $\mathcal{Z}$ may deviate strongly from $\mathbf{E}^1 \times \mathcal{Y}$ at later times. (Here, I am expressing $\mathbf{M}^4$ as $\mathbf{M}^4 = \mathbf{E}^3 \times \mathbf{E}^1$, with $\mathbf{E}^1$ describing the *time* dimension and $\mathbf{E}^3$ the *space* dimensions.)

In the late 1960s Stephen Hawking and I proved a *singularity theorem* (Hawking and Penrose 1970) which shows that we must expect $\mathcal{Z}$ to be singular. The theorem was aimed at conventional (1+3)-spacetimes, but we noted in the paper that it applies equally well to $(1 + n)$-spacetimes for any $n \geq 2$, so it certainly works for (1+9)-spacetimes. As one of this theorem's consequences, any Ricci-flat spacetime which (like $\mathbf{E}^1 \times \mathcal{Y}$ or $\mathcal{Z}$) contains a compact spacelike hypersurface, which is [a] free of closed timelike curves, and which is [b] 'generic' in a certain specific sense, must indeed be *singular*. The sense of 'generic' that is used here is just the condition that each timelike or null geodesic encounters a place where $k_{[a}R_{b]cd[e}k_{f]} \neq 0$, the vector k^a being tangent to the geodesic. (A simple assessment of degrees of freedom shows that this condition is certainly satisfied in the general case.) It should be mentioned that the theorem applies in more inclusive circumstances than just Ricci-flatness. We need only that the Ricci tensor satisfies an appropriate 'non-negative energy condition' [c], expressed as the definiteness of $R_{ab}t^a t^b$, for all timelike vectors t^a. (With my own sign conventions this energy definiteness asserts $R_{ab}t^a t^b \leq 0$ for all timelike t^a, but some other writers use the opposite sign convention for R_{ab}.) The original $\mathbf{E}^1 \times \mathcal{Y}$ escapes from being singular because this generic condition fails; but a generically perturbed $\mathcal{Z}$ has to be singular.

We should recall that such 'singularity theorems' do not directly establish that the curvature diverges to an infinite value, but merely that there is an obstruction of *some* sort to timelike or null geodesics being extendable within the spacetime to infinite length (or to infinite affine extension, in the case of null geodesics). The normal expectation would be that this obstruction indeed arises because of the presence of diverging curvature, but the theorem does not directly show this. This theorem *does*, however, tell us that $\mathcal{Z}$ will become singular in this or some other way. If the perturbation away from $\mathcal{Y}$ is at all comparable with the same general scale as $\mathcal{Y}$ itself (i.e. roughly the Planck scale), then we must expect the singularities in $\mathcal{Z}$ to occur in a comparable time scale ($\sim 10^{-43}$ s), but this time scale could become somewhat longer if the perturbations are of a proportionally smaller scale than $\mathcal{Y}$ is small itself.

We conclude that if we wish to have a chance of perturbing $\mathcal{Y}$ in a finite generic way so that we obtain a *non*-singular perturbation of the full (1+9)-space $\mathbf{M}^4 \times \mathcal{Y}$, then we must turn to consideration of disturbances that significantly spill over into the $\mathbf{M}^4$ part of the spacetime. But in certain respects such disturbances are even more dangerous to our 'ordinary' picture of spacetime than those that affect $\mathcal{Y}$ alone, since the *large approaching Planck-scale curvatures*[4] that are likely to be present in $\mathcal{Y}$ will spill over into ordinary space, in gross conflict with observation. Moreover, there is good reason to believe that these will also result in spacetime singularities in very short order.

---

[4] There are exceptional cases of a *zero*-curvature $\mathcal{Y}$ with the topology of a 'hypertorus' $S^1 \times S^1 \times S^1 \times S^1 \times S^1 \times S^1$. These are not the models for $\mathcal{Y}$ favoured by today's string theorists, however. Moreover, most perturbations of the hypertorus would *not* be flat.

This last conclusion appears to be a consequence of another implication of the aforementioned singularity theorem, when this theorem is applied directly to the *entire* spacetime $\mathcal{M}$. In this application, the condition that there exist a compact spacelike hypersurface is replaced by the existence of some point p whose future light cone $\mathcal{C}$ 'curls round and meets itself' in all directions. Technically, this new condition refers to the boundary $\partial I^+(p)$ of the *future* $I^+(p)$ of p. The locus $\mathcal{C}$ is that swept out by the family of *light rays* (i.e. null geodesics), with past end-point p, and which extend indefinitely into the future. The intersection $E^+(p) = \partial I^+(p) \cap \mathcal{C}$ is swept out by light-ray segments from p, some of which extend indefinitely into the future and some of which are 'cut off' as they eventually enter $I^+(p)$. If *all* of these light rays are of the latter kind, then $E^+(p)$ is *compact*, and we say that the point p constitutes a *future-trapped set*. (This is the situation loosely referred to above as '$\mathcal{C}$ curls round and meets itself in all directions'.) The theorem asserts that (in conjunction with [a], [b] and [c]) the presence of a future-trapped set implies that the spacetime is singular (in the sense of possessing an incomplete timelike or null geodesic).

The required condition that $E^+(p)$ is compact is satisfied if every light ray, starting from p, contains a point q for which there is a strictly timelike curve into the future from p to q. In the exact $\mathbf{M}^4 \times \mathcal{Y}$ models just described, the condition fails (as expected, because $\mathbf{M}^4 \times \mathcal{Y}$ is non-singular), but it *only just fails*. Essentially what happens is that amongst the 8-dimensional family of light rays, there is only a tiny 2-dimensional sub-family that fails to wander into the '$\mathcal{Y}$-part' of the spacetime and back, thereby curling into the interior of $\mathcal{C}$. I believe that it is possible to show that with a generic but small perturbation encountered by $\mathcal{C}$, this saving property will be destroyed, so that the above-mentioned singularity theorem will indeed apply to the entire $\mathbf{M}^4 \times \mathcal{Y}$, but a fully rigorous demonstration of the appropriate statement is lacking at the moment. Details of this argument will be presented elsewhere in the event that it can be succinctly completed.

Of course, unacceptable singularities in a classical theory do not necessarily tell us that such blemishes will persist in the appropriate *quantum* version of that theory. However, the mere introduction of 'quantization procedures' will not necessarily ensure that classical singularities are removed. There are many examples (such as in most toy models of quantum gravity) where singularities persist after quantization.

We should also take note of the fact that (1+9)-dimensional Ricci-flatness is *not* 'quite' the precise requirement that string theory demands. Ricci-flatness is regarded merely as an excellent approximation to that requirement, coming about when higher-order terms in the string constant α' are ignored. One can raise the possibility that the 'exact' requirement, involving *all* orders in the string constant α', might evade the above singularity theorem. Yet, if this requirement provides us with a condition on the Ricci tensor for which the usual local energy-positivity demands are satisfied, then the singularity theorem would *still* apply. On the other hand, violations of such local energy conditions can certainly occur in quantum field theory, so these issues are far from conclusive. Nevertheless, even if all orders in α' can be fully taken into account, it is hard to imagine that the instability that we see in the first-order term could be completely nullified.

A more serious point is the fact that the *full* requirement, involving *all* orders in the string constant α', is actually an *infinite* system of differential equations of *unbounded differential order*. Accordingly, the data that would be needed on an initial 9-surface would involve derivatives of *all* orders in the field quantities (rather than just the first or second derivatives that are needed in ordinary field theories). The number of parameters per point needed on the 9-surface is then *infinite*, so we get a functional freedom *greater* than $\infty^{P\infty^9}$, for any positive integer P. This would seem to make the problem of excessive functional freedom even worse than before! I am not aware of any serious discussion of the mathematical form of this full requirement, and of what kind of initial data might be appropriate for it.

10.4 The holographic conjecture

A certain idea has gained prominence among string theorists, known as the 'holographic conjecture'. This appears to have been stimulated by the Bekenstein–Hawking formula for the entropy of a black hole, where a quantity measured on the boundary – namely the surface area of the black hole's horizon – is providing us with a measure of the total information available in the interior, i.e. of the black hole's total entropy. According to the holographic conjecture,[5] this idea is extended, suggesting that, in certain appropriate circumstances, the states of some (reasonably conventional) quantum field theory defined on the boundary $\mathcal{E} = \partial\mathcal{M}$ of a spacetime $\mathcal{M}$ can be put into direct 1-1 correspondence with the states of a string theory or M theory defined on $\mathcal{M}$. More generally (and more specifically) $\mathcal{E}$ need not actually be the boundary of $\mathcal{M}$ (although often presented as though it were), but a subspace of greater co-dimension. In the most familiar case, considered below, $\mathcal{E}$ is actually a (1+3)-dimensional timelike subspace of a conformally extended (1+9)-dimensional $\mathcal{M}$. It would seem, from the considerations of functional freedom as described

---

[5] For more information, cf. survey articles Horowitz (1998), Das and Mathur (2000).

in section 10.1, that such a conjecture has very little chance of success, unless there are some enormously strong constraints on the functional freedom in the theory that is intended to be described within $\mathcal{M}$.

The most familiar form of this 'holographic conjecture', is that referred to as the *Maldecina* conjecture, or else the ADS/CFT conjecture. Here, $\mathcal{M}$ is to be a (1+9)-dimensional product $\text{AdS}_5 \times S^5$, where AdS_5 is ('un-wrapped') (1+4)-dimensional *anti-de Sitter space*. The S^5 is a spacelike 5-sphere whose radius is of *cosmological* dimension, equal to $(-\Lambda')^{-1/2}$, where Λ' is the (negative) cosmological constant of AdS_5. The smaller space $\mathcal{E}$ is to be the four-dimensional conformal infinity (cf. Penrose 1968, p.195) of AdS_5. We note that $\mathcal{E}$, being four-dimensional (in fact, the 'un-wrapped' conformally compactified $\mathbf{M}^4$) is certainly *not* the boundary of $\mathcal{M}$ in this case, since $\mathcal{M} = \text{AdS}_5 \times S^5$ is ten-dimensional. Instead, $\mathcal{E}$ is the 'boundary' – i.e. the 'scri' – of merely the AdS_5 factor of $\mathcal{M}$. When the S^5 factor is included, we find that $\mathcal{E}$, having co-dimension 6, lies deeply within the interior of $\mathcal{M}$'s conformal extension. The Maldecina conjecture proposes that *string-theory* on $\text{AdS}_5 \times S^5$ is to be *equivalent* to a certain supersymmetric Yang-Mills theory on $\mathcal{E}$.

Here there is no chance of appealing to the type of 'quantum energy' argument outlined in section 10.2 for attempting to explain away the gross discrepancy between the functional freedom of an ordinary field on $\mathcal{M}$, namely $\infty^{M\infty^9}$ and an ordinary field on $\mathcal{E}$, namely $\infty^{E\infty^3}$. Since the extra dimensions of $\mathcal{M}$ are in no way 'small' – being of *cosmological* scale – the flood of additional functional freedom, arising not only from the 4-spatial dimensionality of AdS_5 but additionally from the fields' dependence on the five-dimensional S^5 part of $\mathcal{M}$, would spoil any possibility of an agreement between the two field theories. This would apply to ordinary quantum field theories on $\mathcal{M}$ and $\mathcal{E}$ just as well as to classical fields on these spaces, since one-particle states are themselves described simply by 'ordinary fields'. The only chance of the holographic principle being actually true for these spaces is for the quantum field theories under consideration to be *far from* 'ordinary'.

In the case the string theory on $\mathcal{M}$, it is certainly *conceivable* that there are very strong consistency conditions that drastically reduce the $\infty^{M\infty^9}$ functional freedom. But on the face of it, this seems very unlikely. For whereas the quantum state of a single particle in $(1+n)$-dimensional spacetime has the functional freedom $\infty^{P\infty^n}$, where P is some positive integer describing the number of internal or rotational degrees of freedom of the particle, the quantum state of a single string would seem to have a much *greater* functional freedom, since a *classical* string has infinitely many degrees of freedom. If the number $\infty^{P\infty^n}$ is somehow to be *reduced*, there must be huge constraints, perhaps of the type that led initially to the restrictions on spacetime dimension and curvature, but I am not aware of any such constraints having been suggested – which, in any case, would drastically affect the counting of string states in those arguments claiming to lend support to ADS/CFT (cf. Horowitz 1998).

The remaining possibility seems to be to find a way of greatly *increasing* the functional freedom in the supersymmetric Yang–Mills fields on $\mathcal{E}$. The only way that I can see of achieving this would be have to an infinite number of such fields, which could be attained by taking the limit $N \to \infty$ (N being the number of supersymmetry generators). However, in the usual form of this conjecture, one has to take a specific finite value of N, in order that there be an $SO(6)$ 'internal group' acting on the supersymmetric partners but leaving the Yang–Mills potentials unchanged. This internal symmetry is taken so as to match the $SO(6)$ symmetry of the S^5 that features in $AdS_5 \times S^5$. However, in my own view, it is fundamentally misconceived to try to match a 'spacetime symmetry' to an internal group of this kind – unless, as with the original Kaluza–Klein theory (cf. section 10.1), the spacetime symmetry is *specified as exact*, by the existence of Killing fields, and is also to be respected by all physical fields on the spacetime. The excessive functional freedom in $\infty^{M\infty^9}$ comes about precisely for the reason that there is no such specified symmetry on the S^5 part of $\mathcal{M}$, which is to be respected by fields on $\mathcal{M}$.

It is my opinion that the importance of this kind of discrepancy in functional freedom has been profoundly underrated. The functional freedom involved in the Fock spaces will be completely different whenever the functional freedom in the classical fields is completely different. It should be noted that the condition of *positive frequency*, as demanded of 1-particle states in quantum field theory, does not change the '$\infty^{C\infty^D}$' freedom for the classical fields. It simply compensates for the fact that these classical fields need to be *complexified* when we pass to a quantum-field-theoretic description.

Acknowledgements

The author is grateful to a number of colleagues for valuable discussions, most notably Abhay Ashtekar, Robert Bryant, Arvind Borde, Gary Gibbons, and Philip Candelas. He is also grateful to the Leverhulme Foundation for an Emeritus Fellowship and to the NSF for assistance under Contract 00-90091.

References

Bryant, R. L., Chern, S. -S., Gardner, R. B., Goldschmidt, H. L. and Griffiths, P. A. (1991), *Exterior Differential Systems*, MSRI publication 18 (Springer-Verlag, New York).

Cartan, É. (1945), *Les Systèmes Différentiels Extérieurs et leurs Applications Géométriques* (Hermann, Paris).

Das, S. R. and Mathur, S. D. (2000), 'The quantum physics of black holes: results from string theory', *Annual Review of Nuclear and Particle Science* **50**.

Debever, R. (ed.) (1979), *Letters on Absolute Parallelism, 1929–1932* [English translation of Cartan–Einstein correspondence], (Princeton University Press, Princeton, N.J.)

Green, M. B. (2000), 'Superstrings and the unification of physical forces', in *Mathematical Physics 2000*, eds A. Fokas, T.W.B. Kibble, A. Grigouriou, and B. Zegarlinski (Imperial College Press, London), 59–86.

Green, M. B., Schwarz, J. H. and Witten, E. (1987), *Superstring Theory*, Vols. 1 and 2 (Cambridge University Press, Cambridge).

Hawking, S. W. and Penrose, R. (1970), 'The singularities of gravitational collapse and cosmology', *Proc. Roy. Soc.* **A314**, 529–548.

Horowitz, G. T. (1998), 'Quantum states of black holes', in *Black Holes and Relativistic Stars*, ed. R. M. Wald (University of Chicago Press), pp. 241–66.

Kaluza, T. (1921), in *Sitzungsberichte* (Preussische Akademie der Wissenschaften) p. 966.

Klein, O. (1926), *Z. Phys.* **37**, 895.

Penrose, R. (1968), 'Structure of spacetime', in *Battelle Rencontres, 1967: Lectures in Mathematics and Physics*, eds. C. M. De Witt and J. A. Wheeler (Benjamin, New York).

Penrose, R. (1996), 'On gravity's role in quantum state reduction', *Gen. Rel. Grav.* 28, 581–600.

Penrose, R. (2000), 'Wavefunction collapse as a real gravitational effect', in *Mathematical Physics 2000*, eds A. Fokas, T. W. B. Kibble, A. Grigouriou, and B. Zegarlinski (Imperial College Press, London), 266–282.

Polchinski, J. (1998), *String Theory* (Cambridge University Press, Cambridge).

Wheeler, J. A. (1982), 'Geometrodynamics', in *Società Italiana Fisica: Questioni di Fisica Moderna*, Vol. 1 (Academic Press, New York), p. 177.

Part 3

Black holes

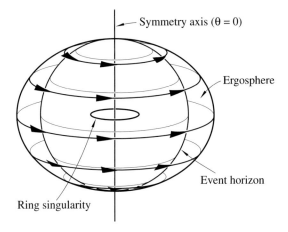

Symmetry axis (θ = 0)

Ergosphere

Event horizon

Ring singularity

The next result shows that a rotating black hole must be axisymmetric.

The Large Scale Structure of Spacetime, 1973

11

Black hole uniqueness and the inner horizon stability problem

Werner Israel

University of Victoria

11.1 Introduction

A landmark of 20th century astrophysics was the 1931 discovery by Chandrasekhar (and independently by Landau) that there is an upper limit to the mass of a cold body in equilibrium. For a star near the end of its nuclear resources and unable to lose enough weight the long-term outlook is grim. A moment will come when pressure support fails: the cooling material will crack, cave in and go into free fall.

For a spherically symmetric collapse, the ensuing course of events was described by Oppenheimer and Snyder in 1939. The imploding star will disappear inside its gravitational radius and lose all ability to influence the outside causally, leaving behind only the spherical deformation imprinted by its gravity – the Schwarzschild geometry.

However, this idealized spherical picture was expected to bear little resemblance to a realistic collapse, whose terminal state was imagined to be a forbiddingly complex object, bearing the marks of all the asymmetries, the magnetic field, and other peculiarities of its stellar progenitor. In the late 1960s it gradually became clear that this was actually not the case. Instead there emerged a picture of a very simple object, called a 'black hole' by John Wheeler, which has severed all connection with the material source that created it and settled, like a soap bubble, into the simplest configuration consistent with the external constraints. Only three characteristics of the collapsing star survive in this final state: mass, angular momentum and (in principle) charge. This circumstance – summed up in Wheeler's phrase, 'A black hole has no hair' – means that the gravitational field of a totally collapsed object is the most precisely known datum in astrophysics. It provides the basis for modelling astrophysical processes involving black holes.

Beginning in the late 1960s, the no-hair property was put on a secure footing in a series of uniqueness theorems for stationary black holes. A key result was Stephen's 1971 proof [1] that a stationary black hole must be either static or axially symmetric; it marks one of his earliest forays into black hole physics. The field has since reached an impressive level of mathematical sophistication and refinement. For instance, it emerged in the early 1990s that the no-hair property in its broadest version admits exceptions: it is possible for a black hole to support hair associated with some varieties of non-Abelian gauge fields. However, such configurations are generally unstable.

The mathematical theory is well covered in a number of excellent recent reviews [2], and there is no need to go over this again. But the job of proving theorems does not get off the ground until someone has a good hunch. In the first part of this talk, I should like to put in a word for the people who started the ball rolling – the Russian trailblazers whose bold intuition and uncanny physical instinct gave us the first broad-brush picture of a generic gravitational collapse and the nature of its endstates.

Inside a hole, gravitational waves and all other causal effects cannot propagate outwards. They are inexorably forced downwards. So one may expect hair loss to be a progressive process that eats its way inwards until it encounters the internal singularity predicted by Penrose's 1965 theorem [3]. Thus, the outer simplicity of the black hole should extend a considerable way into its interior. Recent work has confirmed these expectations and also yielded some surprises. In the second part of the talk I shall briefly summarize these developments.

11.2 The trailblazers: Moscow 1964

The first hint that there is something miraculous about the endstate of a gravitational collapse came from Vitaly Ginzburg [4] in 1964. Ginzburg believed (as it turned out, correctly) that magnetic fields as well as collapse play an essential role in the energy production of quasars and active galactic nuclei. He set out to examine how magnetic fields would build up by flux-freezing and amplification during collapse to the gravitational radius, a process similar to the one that gives rise to the large magnetic fields in neutron stars.

He modelled the collapse by a magnetized spherical mass contracting quasistatically, the only case that could be handled analytically. Moreover, this seemed to reflect quite well the viewpoint of an external observer, who sees the collapse freezing asymptotically at the gravitational radius.

Unexpectedly, he found that magnetic amplification cannot work for an unchecked collapse. His calculation showed that the magnetic field energy would grow without bound in the final stages – a manifestly unphysical result – unless the magnetic moment attenuates to zero at the gravitational radius. No physical reason for this attenuation was immediately apparent. (In this quasistatic scenario, electromagnetic radiation as the responsible mechanism would not have been the first idea to come to mind.)

To state categorically that a star in free collapse must divest itself of its magnetic field entirely would have undercut his original motivation, and such a conclusion is not blazoned forth in Ginzburg's paper. More forthright in this regard was a paper submitted ten months later (16 December 1964) by Doroshkevich, Zel'dovich and Novikov (DZN) [5], which ranks as the first frontal assault on the problem of non-spherical collapse.

DZN addressed two basic questions. First, does a generic collapse resemble the spherical case up to the stage of horizon-formation leading to self-closure? The authors answered with a clear 'Yes!', essentially on the grounds that an event horizon is not a barrier to smooth evolution of initial data (i.e., it is not what we now call a Cauchy horizon), and therefore non-spherical perturbations should evolve smoothly up to this point. This conclusion is especially noteworthy, coming at a time (before Penrose's 1965 singularity theorem [3], which DZN just managed to reference in the published version of their paper) when it was still widely believed (and apparently supported by mathematical arguments) that in at least one fundamental respect (formation of singularities) spherical and non-spherical collapse were quite different.

The next question concerned the nature of the endstate. DZN noted that a static vacuum solution representing a point mass with a quadrupole moment becomes singular at the horizon. On the other hand, no such singularity should be encountered by a collapsing non-spherical star. They inferred that quadrupole moments must somehow attenuate in the course of the collapse. They further argued that this must extend to the case where the star is rotating, though here – misled by the presence of certain off-diagonal terms in Kerr's original form of his metric (Boyer–Lindquist coordinates did not appear until 1967 [6]) – they concluded that the final state could not be Kerr.

The achievement of Ginzburg and DZN amounted to a scientific high-wire act. Held aloft by only the slenderest of clues, with sure instinct they felt their way to conclusions that were strange and startling, but in essence sound. Their work sparked and served as a basis for the next phase of black hole research: the stationary no-hair theorems and the dynamical analysis of perturbed collapse by Richard Price [7].

11.3 Cambridge 1965–71

The groundbreaking astronomical discoveries of the early 1960s – quasars in 1963, the microwave background in 1965 – opened new vistas for general relativity and cosmology. Eager to make the most of these opportunities, Dennis Sciama had by 1965 gathered a select group of research students in Cambridge that would soon rival Wheeler's group in Princeton and revolutionize the field.

While one student, Martin Rees, working in collaboration with Sciama himself, focused on quasar physics, others were encouraged in their pursuit of more mathematical questions. George Ellis and Stephen Hawking were soon engaged in extending to a cosmological setting the global methods employed in Penrose's singularity theorem. They were able to show that the mere existence of the cosmic microwave background implies, independently of any symmetries, a singular origin for the universe [8].

The mathematical study of collapsed objects was the province of Brandon Carter. His program also soon got into high gear. Carter decided to devote special attention to the Kerr family, the only non-spherical solutions representing such an object that were known at the time – in retrospect, a shrewd investment as it became increasingly plausible (around 1967) that they are the only ones that exist, a result that he himself virtually clinched with his 1971 proof [9] that vacuum black hole geometries that are stationary and axisymmetric form a two-parameter family.

Generalizing Penrose's conformal diagrammatic techniques to black holes [10], and building in part on the work of Boyer and Lindquist [6], Carter had, by 1968, successfully unravelled the intricate global structure of the Kerr–Newman manifolds, discovered that, remarkably, the orbital equations are separable and reduced them to quadratures [11]. The entire corpus of isolated black hole geometries was thus brought under mathematical control.

Stephen's active entry into this burgeoning field was held up by his work on singularity theorems, culminating in the definitive Hawking–Penrose paper of 1970 [12]. When he did enter, it was with a characteristic flourish: three landmark papers, submitted within a few months in 1971. The first dealt with primordial black holes [13], the second introduced the area theorem [14], and the third provided the missing link in the uniqueness theorems, showing that stationary but non-static black holes must be axisymmetric [1]. These were the first of a stream of contributions, culminating in the seminal quantum discoveries that reached into the heart of the black hole mystery and have made the words 'black holes' and 'Hawking' virtually synonymous.

Footnote 10 of the area paper [14] acknowledges a private communication from Roger Penrose. It refers to the area of the Kerr horizon. In those eventful days the phone lines between Cambridge and London were kept humming as the two kept each other abreast of the latest developments. One conversation must have gone somewhat like this: 'Roger, I have this neat way of getting an upper bound to the gravitational energy radiated when two spinning black holes merge: the total horizon area must grow in the process. Do you happen to know the formula for the area of the Kerr horizon?' It appears that Penrose either knew or was able to do a quick calculation. And therefore, if one needs to convey in a nutshell why Roger Penrose is newsworthy, it might be done by saying that he once told Stephen Hawking something about black holes that even Stephen didn't know!

11.4 Descent into the interior

Of course, Roger Penrose has also made other contributions to the subject! I should now like to describe recent developments in an area opened up by one of the many ideas with which he has enriched black hole physics since the 1960s: the internal structure of a generic black hole and the critical role played by the inner horizon. Again I can be brief and selective, since a number of comprehensive reviews are available [15].

What lurks inside a black hole? One's first reaction is to dismiss the question as metaphysical or hopelessly speculative. Irregularities swept inward with the collapse must be expected to grow and accumulate, producing inner chaos. The curvature deep inside the hole becomes so enormous (classically, it becomes singular) that all the known laws of physics fail. This hardly seems a fit topic for a serious scientist of sound views.

On second thought, however, the prospects are not quite so bleak. What comes to the rescue is a key property of the hole's interior: descent into a black hole is fundamentally a progression in time. (Recall, for instance, that inside a spherical hole Schwarzschild's radial coordinate r becomes timelike.) This means we are confronting an evolutionary, not a structural problem. Simple causality prevents our ignorance about the inner, high-curvature regions from affecting the description of the outer and *preceding* layers that today's well-established theories can provide.

Further, thanks to the no-hair property and the work of Richard Price [7], initial data for this evolutionary problem are known with precision (in marked contrast to the situation in cosmology). In the wake of a collapse, the external field will settle asymptotically toward a Kerr geometry. It is this geometry – perturbed by a tail of gravitational waves propagating into the hole and outward to infinity and decaying as an inverse power of external time – that forms the initial state for the internal evolution of the hole.

Exploring the inside of a hole using Einstein's equations, it thus appears, is no more problematical than following the motion of a fluid, using Euler's hydrodynamical equations, up to the onset of turbulence or a shock.

With the present limitations of physical theory, one is forced to terminate this exploration at the point where the classical Einstein equations
signal their own breakdown by predicting a curvature singularity. Penrose
noted in 1968 [16] that this first occurs (generically) not at zero radius,
but already at the hole's inner horizon. Recall that the event (or outer)
horizon (corresponding to infinite retarded time) is the last outpost from
which an infalling astronaut can still flash news to the outside.

The inner horizon (corresponding to infinite advanced time) is the last
place where he can still *receive* outside news. But then he gets *all* the
news. In the few moments remaining before he encounters this surface
and enters the core of the hole, the entire future history of the outer
universe will be flashed in fast motion before his eyes!

The blueshift accompanying this infinite time-compression has drastic
consequences. The natural power-law decay of the gravitational wave-tail
is completely swamped by the exponential blueshift, producing (classically) a curvature singularity at the inner horizon.

The advent of this singularity is not entirely unwelcome, because it saves
physics from a potential embarrassment: breakdown of predictability. The
inner horizon is also a 'Cauchy horizon', i.e., it marks the boundary of the
region where the amplitudes of physical fields can be predicted from initial
data set at the onset of collapse. Were this boundary non-singular – as,
indeed, it is for the Kerr geometry unperturbed by a gravitational wave-
tail – infalling observers crossing it could survive and enter a spacious
region where they would be subject to unpredictable influences emanat-
ing from singularities that are typically timelike. It was partly to avoid
this embarrassment that Penrose formulated his 'strong cosmic censorship' hypothesis [17], according to which the singularities formed in gravitational collapse should be generically achronal (i.e., not timelike). The
generically singular inner horizon is a lightlike surface, lending support to
this conjecture.

The Einstein equations cannot conduct us beyond the classical singularity at the inner horizon, but they do allow us to form a detailed picture
of the build-up of curvature near this horizon. This is not only of interest
for its own sake but also because this incipiently singular geometry will
eventually serve as initial state and launchpad for future studies of the
subsequent quantum phase of evolution. The following sections deal with
what has been recently learned about this geometry.

11.5 Internal evolution problem

According to Price's power law [7] for the decay of wave-tails following
a gravitational collapse, a general wavelike perturbation $\delta\Phi$ of multipole

order l (e.g., $l = 2$ for a quadrupole gravitational wave $\delta g_{\mu\nu}$) decays like

$$\delta\Phi \sim v^{-p/2+1} \qquad (v \to \infty) \qquad (11.1)$$

near the event horizon. Here, v is exterior advanced time and $p = 4l + 4$.

Thus, the initial conditions for the hole's internal evolution, which are set near the event horizon, consist of the Kerr geometry perturbed by an externally decaying wave-tail of the form (11.1).

It is found that the exterior decay of the perturbation and the convergence of the exterior field to its asymptotic Kerr form extend inside the hole. But here the convergence is non-uniform and breaks down entirely along the Cauchy horizon (CH), which appears in the Penrose–Carter conformal map as the inward extension of future lightlike infinity, i.e., it corresponds to infinite advanced time $v = \infty$.

In place of v, it is useful to introduce the Kruskal advanced time

$$V = -e^{-\kappa_0 v}, \qquad (11.2)$$

which is finite (in fact, zero) at the Cauchy horizon CH, and in terms of which the unperturbed stationary Kerr metric is manifestly regular there. (The constant κ_0 is the surface gravity of this stationary horizon.) An infalling wave $\sim \sin \omega v$ appears speeded up near CH when expressed in terms of the locally regular coordinate V, and its flux of energy is received with a diverging blueshift $e^{2\kappa_0 v}$ by interior observers falling toward CH. Acting on the wave-tail given by (11.1), this blueshift will produce an exponentially diverging stress-energy at CH.

The blueshift instability of CH was confirmed in the decade 1973–82 by a number of investigations (e.g., [18]), which studied the propagation of test fields on a *fixed* (usually Reissner–Nordström charged spherical black hole) background. Near CH, amplitudes of wave-tail perturbations typically decay like

$$\delta\Phi \sim (\ln|V|)^{-p/2+1} \qquad (V \to 0-) \qquad (11.3)$$

as one would anticipate from (11.1) and (11.2). Thus field amplitudes Φ (in particular, the metric $g_{\mu\nu}$ for gravitational-wave perturbations) stay regular on CH to first order, but their derivatives $\partial_V \Phi$ diverge.

Since the Einstein equations are quadratic in first-order gradients $\nabla\Phi$ and $\nabla g_{\mu\nu}$, it was generally expected that taking back-reaction into account would make the amplitudes themselves blow up on CH at higher orders of perturbation theory. Remarkably, however, detailed calculations have not borne out these expectations: the singularity remains relatively weak at higher orders. This is basically because the divergences at CH are lightlike: roughly speaking, terms quadratic in $\partial_V \Phi$ will be suppressed because the associated coefficient g^{VV} is zero.

It thus appears that the Cauchy horizon of a black hole formed in a generic (non-spherical) collapse is indeed singular, but this singularity may have an unexpectedly mild and orderly structure.

11.6 Spherical models

In its most general form the problem we are confronted with is formidable indeed. For a first reconnaissance it is advisable to make whatever simplifications one can, while (hopefully) not losing the essence of the physics.

Setting the angular momentum equal to zero while adding a non-zero charge makes the black hole spherical without radically changing its horizon structure. Spherical scalar waves are a reasonable simulation of quadrupole gravitational waves as far as their gravitational effects are concerned. The large blueshift near CH further suggests the use of an optical approximation, which replaces the infalling waves by a stream of lightlike particles.

The earliest models [19–21] accordingly considered the effect of radial streams of 'photons' on the interior geometry of a spherical hole with electric charge, a Reissner–Nordström black hole.

It is convenient to employ a two-dimensional reduction of the spherisymmetric Einstein field equations. Any spherisymmetric 4-metric can be expressed in the form

$$ds^2 = g_{ab}(x^c)\, dx^a\, dx^b + r^2\, d\Omega^2 \qquad (a, b, c = 0, 1) \qquad (11.4)$$

where $d\Omega^2$ is the metric on the unit 2-sphere, (x^0, x^1) are any pair of coordinates which label the privileged 2-spheres and $r(x^a)$ is a function of these coordinates. Its gradient defines a 'mass function' $m(x^a)$:

$$g^{ab}\, (\partial_a r)(\partial_b r) = 1 - \frac{2m}{r}. \qquad (11.5)$$

Physically, one may think of $m(x^a)$ as the effective gravitational mass interior to the 2-sphere labelled by x^a. More specifically, $\Psi = m/r^3$ is an invariant measure of the Weyl conformal curvature. (For spherical symmetry, the Weyl tensor has only one independent component.) The Einstein field equations $G_{\mu\nu} = 8\pi T_{\mu\nu}$ can now be reformulated as two-dimensionally covariant equations for the scalars $r(x^a), m(x^a)$. The key result is a $(1+1)$-dimensional wave equation for m, which takes the form (leaving aside some inessential terms) [20],

$$\Box m = -16\pi^2\, r^3\, T^{ab}\, T_{ab}. \qquad (11.6)$$

Effects of the non-linearity of the Einstein equations are neatly made manifest in this formula.

For an influx of radiation blueshifted near CH according to

$$T_{VV} \sim (\partial_V \Phi)^2 \sim (\ln|V|)^{-p} V^{-2} \qquad (V \to 0-), \qquad (11.7)$$

(cf. (11.3)), the right-hand side of (11.6) acts as a diverging source for m, provided some outflow is present too. (For a pure inflow, T_{ab} is lightlike, $T_{ab} T^{ab} = 0$ and m undergoes little change near CH [19].) One finds [20] that the mass function diverges at CH roughly like

$$m \sim (\ln|V|)^{-p} V^{-1}, \qquad (11.8)$$

an effect sometimes called 'mass inflation'. Of course, no trace of this drastic change of internal geometry is perceptible outside the hole.

The straightforward interpretation of (11.8) is that the Cauchy horizon increasingly appears to observers approaching it as a sphere of infinite mass, a formidable singularity indeed! However, it is spread over the surface of the inner horizon, and hence is pancake-like and locally weak in a sense which has been made precise by Amos Ori [21]. The Weyl curvature and tidal forces ($\sim m/r^3$) do become infinite, but their growth is so slow that the cumulative tidal *deformation* of bodies falling toward CH remains bounded, and indeed small, up to the very moment of crossing. Stated in a more coordinate-dependent way, the curvature blows up at CH but the metric (in suitable coordinates) does not.

(Parenthetically, it is entertaining and quite instructive to note that the gravitational effects near CH can be simulated rather well by a simple (though exotic) Newtonian model [22]. Imagine a 'planet' whose radius r_0 is the same as CH, whose mass is infinite and whose external gravity is screened by an 'atmosphere' of equal and opposite mass. Approaching the planetary surface the negative atmospheric density $\rho(r)$ is assumed to grow according to a law patterned after (11.7):

$$\rho(r) \sim -|\ln\Delta r|^{-p} (\Delta r)^{-2}, \qquad (11.9)$$

as $\Delta r \equiv (r - r_0) \to 0+$. It is then easy to check, for example, that the exterior Newtonian potential remains bounded for all $r \geq r_0$, and that falling meteorites and spacecraft are not tidally disrupted before they actually reach the surface.)

The transverse outflux which catalyses mass inflation also focuses the lightlike generators of CH, causing it to contract and eventually taper to a stronger, spacelike singularity at $r = 0$.

More general spherisymmetric models – for instance, a massless scalar field propagating into a Reissner–Nordström black hole – have been treated, both analytically [23] and numerically [24]. They confirm the general picture of a contracting, mass-inflated Cauchy horizon. Here, the outflux, originating from backscatter, is relatively unblueshifted, so the contraction of CH is relatively slow, on the order of the Schwarzschild crossing time.

11.7 The generic case

Can spherical models be trusted to provide a representative description of the real conditions inside a generic rotating black hole? From the beginning this question aroused understandable skepticism, and the issue remains unsettled. But some of the early doubts have been clarified and laid to rest.

Even in the spherical case, an early numerical study of scalar wave-tails absorbed by a charged hole suggested that the Cauchy horizon is washed away, and the $r = 0$ spacelike singularity becomes all-enveloping. But analytical work [23] and more refined numerics [24] have not confirmed this suggestion.

More serious questions arise when the restriction to spherical symmetry is relaxed. It was widely suspected that lightlike singularities cannot be generic. One line of argument runs like this. We already know of a class of singularities that are functionally generic in the sense that the geometry near a given singular hypersurface depends on eight physically arbitrary functions of three variables: six components of intrinsic 3-metric and six components of extrinsic curvature less four coordinate degrees of freedom. (Imposing definite – e.g., vacuum – field equations would subject these eight functions to four initial-value constraints.) These singularities are the BKL (Belinski–Khalatnikov–Lifshitz) or 'mixmaster' chaotic oscillatory singularities. Now the BKL singularities are *spacelike* and – presumably – they exhaust the set of generic singularities. If that is so, then lightlike singularities must be less general, and could not evolve from generic initial data. A generic perturbation should drive any such lightlike singularity into a spacelike one.

Ori and Flanagan [25] spotted a loophole in this argument. They showed that it was actually possible to construct a generic class of *weak* lightlike singularities. And one should indeed expect intuitively that the Einstein equations (which are quasi-linear) should propagate generic weak discontinuities and mild singularities along characteristic (i.e., lightlike) hypersurfaces.

It is thus not possible to rule out the presence of weak lightlike singularities inside black holes *merely* on the grounds that they are non-generic.

Of course, this should not be construed as a proof that such singularities actually do occur inside black holes!

Studies of the non-spherical case are still fragmentary, but suggest that the weak, mass-inflationary singularity persists, now overlaid with a gravitational shock wave along CH. The most detailed work along these lines, by Brady, Droz and Morsink [26], employs a double-null $(2+2)$ formalism to analyse the characteristic initial-value problem for evolution along CH, and concludes that a mass-inflationary regime is at least self-consistent. To trace the complete evolution inwards from the event horizon, much further work will be needed, probably using a combination of analytical and numerical techniques.

11.8 Conclusions

The working picture of the black hole interior suggested by recent studies is of a strong spacelike singularity preceded by a mildly singular lightlike precursor along the Cauchy horizon which is characterized by mass inflation. This classical picture only charts a coastline. To unravel what lies beyond these classically singular boundaries is a task for the physics of the new millennium.

11.9 Acknowledgements

This contribution is dedicated to Stephen with affection, admiration, and gratitude. May he continue for many more years to lead us to new insights and inspire us with his example!

I am grateful to Cecilia Tenorio and Tom Roman for their indispensable help with the preparation of the manuscript.

References

[1] Hawking, S. W. (1972), *Commun. Math. Phys.* **25**, 152.

[2] Heusler, M. (1996), *Black Hole Uniqueness Theorems* (Cambridge University Press, Cambridge); Carter, B. (1997), 'Has the black hole equilibrium problem been solved?', [gr-qc/9712038]; Chrusciel, P. T. (1994), 'No-hair theorems: folklore, conjectures, results', in *Differential Geometry and Mathematical Physics* **170**, eds J. Beem and K. L. Duggal (American Mathematical Society, Providence), [gr-qc/9402032]; Chrusciel, P. T. (2002), 'Black holes', [gr-qc/0201053]; Bekenstein, J. D. (1996), 'Black hole hair: 25 years after', [gr-qc/9605059].

[3] Penrose, R. (1965), *Phys. Rev. Letters* **14**, 57.

[4] Ginzburg, V. L. (1964), *Soviet Physics Doklady* **9**, 329.

[5] Doroshkevich, A. G., Zel'dovich, Ya. B. and Novikov, I. D. (1966), *Soviet Physics JETP* **22**, 122.

[6] Boyer, R. H. and Lindquist, R. W. (1967), *J. Math. Phys.* **8**, 265.

[7] Price, R. H. (1972), *Phys. Rev.* **D5**, 2419.

[8] Hawking, S. W. and Ellis, G. F. R. (1968), *Astrophys. J.* **152**, 25.

[9] Carter, B. (1971), *Phys. Rev. Letters* **26**, 331.

[10] Carter, B. (1966), *Physics Letters* **21**, 423.

[11] Carter, B. (1968), *Phys. Rev.* **174**, 1559.

[12] Hawking, S. W. and Penrose, R. (1970), *Proc. Roy. Soc.* **A314**, 529.

[13] Hawking, S. W. (1971), *Mon. Not. Roy. Astron. Soc.* **152**, 75.

[14] Hawking, S. W. (1971), *Phys. Rev. Letters* **26**, 1344.

[15] Burko, L. M. and Ori, A. (eds) (1998), *Internal Structure of Black Holes and Spacetime Singularities* (IOP Publishing, Bristol); Frolov, V. P. and Novikov, I. D. (1998), *Black Hole Physics* (Kluwer, Boston), Chap. 14.; Ori, A. (1997), *J. Gen. Rel. Grav.* **29**, 881; Israel, W. (1998), in *Black Holes and Relativistic Stars*, ed. R. Wald (University of Chicago Press, Chicago), Chap. 7; Brady, P.R. (1999), *Prog. Theor. Phys. Suppl.* **136**, 29.

[16] Penrose, R. (1968), in *Battelle Rencontres*, eds J. A. Wheeler and C. M. DeWitt (Benjamin, New York), p. 222.

[17] Penrose, R. (1998), in *Black Holes and Relativistic Stars*, ed. R. Wald (University of Chicago Press, Chicago), Chap. 5.

[18] Gürsel, Y., Sandberg, V., Novikov, I. D. and Starobinsky, A. A. (1979), *Phys. Rev.* **D19**, 413; Chandrasekhar, S. and Hartle, J.B. (1982), *Proc. Roy. Soc.* **A384**, 301.

[19] Hiscock, W. A. (1981), *Physics Letters* **83A**, 110.

[20] Poisson, E. and Israel, W. (1990), *Phys. Rev.* **D41**, 1796.

[21] Ori, A. (1991), *Phys. Rev. Letters* **67**, 789.

[22] Balbinot, R., Brady, P. R., Israel, W. and Poisson, E. (1991), *Physics Letters* **A161**, 223.

[23] Bonnano, A., Droz, S. and Morsink, S. M. (1994), *Phys. Rev.* **D50**, 7372; Burko, L. M. and Ori, A. (1997), *Phys. Rev.* **D57**, 7084.

[24] Brady, P. R. and Smith, J. D. (1995), *Phys. Rev. Letters* **75**, 1256; Burko, L. M. (1997), *Phys. Rev. Letters* **79**, 4958.

[25] Ori, A. and Flanagan, É. É. (1996), *Phys. Rev.* **D53**, R1754.

[26] Brady P. R., Droz, S. and Morsink, S. M. (1998), *Phys. Rev.* **D58**, 084034.

12

Black holes in the real universe and their prospects as probes of relativistic gravity

Martin Rees

Institute of Astronomy, University Cambridge

12.1 Introduction

Collapsed objects have definitely been observed: some are stellar-mass objects, the endpoint of massive stars; others, millions of times more massive, have been discovered in the cores of most galaxies. Their formation poses some still-unanswered questions. But for relativists the key question is whether observations can probe the metric in the strong-field domain, and test whether it indeed agrees with the Kerr geometry predicted by general relativity.

In a lecture in 1977, Chandrasekhar wrote:

> In my entire scientific life the most shattering experience has been the realisation that exact solutions to Einstein's theory [the Kerr solutions] provide the *absolutely exact representation* of untold numbers of massive black holes that populate the Universe.

He was of course referring to the uniqueness theorems, to which Stephen Hawking and several other participants at this conference contributed. At the time that Chandra wrote this, there was some evidence for black holes. Now the evidence is much stronger and my theme in this paper is to summarize this evidence.

I will discuss first the black holes of a few solar masses that are the remnants of supernovae, and then supermassive black holes in the mass range of a million to a billion solar masses, for which there is also good evidence. I shall also mention parenthetically that there may be a population of black holes in the range of hundreds of solar masses, relics of an earlier generation of massive stars. Bernard Carr's paper discusses primordial black holes, right down to very low masses, for which I think there is no evidence but which would be fascinating if they existed.

By the early 1970s the theoretical properties of black holes – the Kerr metric, the 'no hair' theorems, and so forth – were well established. But it took much longer for the observers to discover candidate black holes, and to recognise their nature. A fascinating review of the history has been given by Werner Israel [1]. By now, the evidence points insistently towards the presence of dark objects, with deep potential wells and 'horizons' through which matter can pass into invisibility; however, the evidence does not yet allow observers to confirm the form of the metric in the strong-gravity region. I shall briefly summarize the evidence, and then comment on the prospects for testing strong-field gravity by future observations.

12.2 Stellar mass holes

The first black hole candidates to be identified were bodies of a few solar masses, in close orbits around an ordinary companion star, emitting intense and rapidly flickering X-rays. This emission is attributed to inward-spiralling material, captured from the companion star, which swirls inward towards a 'horizon'. There are two categories of such binaries: those where the companion star is of high mass, of which Cygnus X1 is the prototype, and the low-mass X-ray binaries (LMXBs) where the companion is typically below a solar mass. The LMXBs are sometimes called 'X-ray novae' because they flare up to high luminosity: they plainly have a different evolutionary history from systems like Cygnus X1.

The X-ray emission from these objects was distinctively different from the periodic variability of a related class, which were believed to be neutron stars. The masses can be inferred from straightforward Newtonian arguments. It is gratifying that the masses inferred for the periodic sources are in all cases below 2 solar masses (consistent with the theoretically-expected mass range for neutron stars) whereas those that vary irregularly have higher masses. There are now a dozen or so strong candidates of this type. Of course, the only stellar-mass holes that manifest themselves conspicuously are the tiny and atypical fraction that lie in close binaries where mass transfer is currently going on. There may be only a few dozen such systems in our galaxy. But there are likely to be at least 10^7 black holes in our galaxy. This number is based on the rather conservative estimate that only 1 or 2 percent of supernovae leave black holes rather than neutron stars. There could be a further population of black holes (maybe in the Galactic Halo) as a relic of early galactic history [2].

Gamma ray bursts are a class of objects, of which about 3000 have been detected, which flicker on time scales of less than a second and last sometimes for only a second; sometimes for a few minutes. They are known to be at great distances: indeed they are so bright that if a gamma-ray burst went off in our galaxy it would be as bright as the Sun for a few seconds. They can be detected by X-ray or gamma-ray telescopes even at very large redshifts. These are probably a rare kind of collapsing star or merger of a compact binary which may signal the formation of a black hole. They are extremely important because they may be objects where we see a non-stationary black hole.

12.3 Supermassive holes

A seemingly quite distinct class of black hole candidates lurk in the centres of most galaxies; they are implicated in the power output from active galactic nuclei (AGNs), and in the production of relativistic jets that energize strong radio sources. The demography of these massive holes has been clarified by studies of relatively nearby galaxies: the centres of most of these galaxies display either no activity or a rather low level, but most seem to harbour dark central masses.

In most cases the evidence is of two kinds. Stars in the innermost parts of some galaxies are moving anomalously fast, as though 'feeling' the gravitational pull of a dark central mass and, in some galaxies with active nuclei, the central mass can be inferred by modelling the properties of the gas which reprocesses central continuum radiation into emission with spectral features. But there are two galaxies where central dark masses are indicated by other kinds of evidence that are far firmer.

The first, in the peculiar spiral NGC 4258, was revealed by amazingly precise mapping of gas motions via the 1.3 cm maser emission line of H_2O [3]. The spectral resolution of this microwave line is high enough to pin down the velocities with accuracy of 1 km/s. The Very Long Baseline Array achieves an angular resolution better than 0.5 milliarc seconds (100 times sharper than the HST, as well as far finer spectral resolution of velocities!). These observations have revealed, right in NGC 4258's core, a disc with rotational speeds following an exact Keplerian law around a compact dark mass. The inner edge of the observed disc is orbiting at 1080 km/s. It would be impossible to circumscribe, within its radius, a stable and long-lived star cluster with the inferred mass of $3.6 \times 10^7 \, M_\odot$.

The second utterly convincing candidate lies in our own galactic centre (see [4] for a comprehensive review). Direct evidence used to be ambiguous because intervening gas and dust in the plane of the Milky Way prevents us from getting a clear optical view of the central stars, as we can in, for instance, M31. A great deal was known about gas motions, from radio and infrared measurements, but these were hard to interpret because gas does not move ballistically like stars, but can be influenced by pressure gradients, stellar winds, and other non-gravitational influences. There is now, however, direct evidence from stellar proper motions, observed in the near infrared band, where obscuration by intervening material is less of an obstacle [5,6]. The speeds scale as $r^{-1/2}$ with distance from the centre, consistent with a hole of mass $2.6 \times 10^6\,M_\odot$. One can actually plot out the orbits of these stars. Some will make a complete circuit in little more than 100 years. Corroboration comes from the compact radio source that has long been known to exist right at the dynamical centre of our galaxy, which can be interpreted in terms of accretion onto a massive hole [7,8].

There is a remarkably close proportionality [9] between the hole's mass and the velocity dispersion of the central bulge or spheroid in the stellar distribution (which is of course the dominant part of an elliptical galaxy, but only a subsidiary component of a disc system like M31 or our own galaxy).

12.4 Scenarios for black hole formation

There is no mystery about why high-mass stars may yield gravitationally collapsed remnants of 10 solar masses or more, but the formation route for the supermassive holes is still uncertain. Back in 1978, I presented a 'flow diagram' [10] exhibiting several evolutionary tracks within a galaxy, aiming to convey the message that it seemed almost inevitable that large masses would collapse in galactic centres. There was not yet (see [1]) any consensus that active galactic nuclei were powered by black holes (despite earlier arguments by Salpeter [11], Zeldovich and Novikov [12] and, especially, Lynden-Bell [13]) We have now got used to the idea that black holes indeed exist within most galaxies, but it is rather depressing that we still cannot decide which formation route is most likely.

The main options are summarized below.

12.4.1 Monolithic formation of supermassive objects

One possibility is that the gas in a newly-forming galaxy does not all break up into stellar-mass condensations, but that some undergoes monolithic collapse. As the gas evolves (through loss of energy and angular momentum) to a state of higher densities and more violent internal dissipation, radiation pressure would prevent fragmentation, and puff it up into a single superstar. Once a large mass of gas started to behave like a single superstar, it would continue to contract and deflate. Some mass would inevitably be shed, carrying away angular momentum, but the remainder would undergo complete gravitational collapse. The behaviour of supermassive stars was studied by Bardeen, Thorne and others in the 1960s.

Because radiation pressure is overwhelmingly dominant, such objects are destabilized, in the post-Newtonian approximation, even when hundreds of times larger than the gravitational radius. Rotation has a stabilizing effect, but there has still been little work done on realistic models with differential rotation (see, however [14]).

The mass of the hole would depend on that of its host galaxy, though not necessarily via an exact proportionality: the angular momentum of the protogalaxy and the depth of its central potential well are relevant factors too.

12.4.2 Mergers of smaller holes (stellar mass or 'intermediate mass')

Rather than forming 'in one go' from a superstar that may already be a million solar masses or more, holes might grow from smaller beginnings. The first-generation stars are thought to have been more massive than those forming in galaxies today – perhaps up to hundreds of solar masses. Such stars live no more than a few million years, and leave black hole remnants if they lie in two distinct mass ranges [15]:

1. ordinary massive stars, with helium core masses up to $64\,M_\odot$; and

2. 'Very Massive Objects' (VMOs) with helium cores above $130\,M_\odot$.

Stars in between these two ranges leave no compact remnant at all, instead ending their lives by a disruptive explosion induced by the onset of electron–positron pair production.

VMO remnants could have interesting implications in the present universe [2]; such objects, captured by supermassive holes, would yield gravitational radiation signals detectable by LISA out to redshifts of order unity, possibly dominating the event rate. Could there be a link between these 'intermediate mass' holes and supermassive holes? There are two possibilities. The most obvious, at first sight, is that a cluster of such objects might merge into one. But it is not easy for a cluster of black holes to merge into a single one. To see this, note that one binary with orbital speed 10^4 km/s (with a separation of 1000 Schwarzschild radii) would have just as much binding energy as a cluster of 10000 holes with velocity dispersion 100 km/s. Thus, if a cluster accumulated in the centre of a galaxy, the likely outcome would be the expulsion of most objects, as the consequence of straightforward N-body dynamics, leaving only a few.

The prospects of build-up by this route are not quite as bad as this simple argument suggests, because the binding energy of the compact cluster could be enhanced by dynamical friction on lower-mass stars, by gas drag, or by gravitational radiation. This nonetheless seems an inefficient route towards supermassive holes.

Ordinary stars, with large geometrical cross-sections, have a larger chance of sticking together than pairs of black holes. We therefore cannot exclude a 'scenario' where a supermassive star builds up within a dense central cluster of ordinary stars. The most detailed calculations were done by Quinlan and Shapiro ([16] and other references cited therein). These authors showed that stellar coalescence, followed by the segregation of the resultant high-mass stars towards the centre, could trigger runaway evolution without (as earlier and cruder work had suggested) requiring clusters whose initial parameters were unrealistic (i.e. already extremely dense, or with implausibly high velocity dispersions). It would be well worthwhile extending these simulations to a wider range of initial conditions, and also to follow the build-up from stellar masses to supermassive objects.

12.4.3 Runaway growth of a favoured stellar-mass hole to supermassive status

Even if a large population of low-mass holes is unlikely to merge together, is it, alternatively, possible for one of them, in a specially favoured high-density environment, to undergo runaway growth via accretion? An often-cited constraint on the growth rate is based on the argument that, however high the external density was, growth could not happen on a timescale less than the classic 'Salpeter time' [11]

$$t_{\text{Sal}} = 4 \times 10^7 (\varepsilon/0.1) \, \text{yr} \tag{12.1}$$

For an efficiency ε of 0.1 this would yield an e-folding timescale of 4×10^7 years. If these holes started off with stellar masses, or as the remnants of Population III stars, there would seem to be barely enough time for them to have grown fast enough to energize quasars at $z = 6$.

This is not, however, a generic constraint; there are several suggestions in the literature for evading it [17–20].

12.5 The galactic context

12.5.1 The key issues

Physical conditions in the central potential wells of young and gas-rich galaxies should be propitious for black hole formation: such processes, occurring in the early-forming galaxies that develop from high-amplitude peaks in the initial density distribution, are presumably connected with high-z quasars. It now seems clear that most galaxies that existed at $z = 3$ would have participated subsequently in a series of mergers; giant present-day elliptical galaxies are the outcome of such mergers. Any black holes already present would tend to spiral inwards, and coalesce [21, 22] (unless a third body fell in before the merger was complete, in which case a Newtonian slingshot could eject all three: a binary in one direction; the third, via recoil, in the opposite direction).

The issues for astrophysicists are then as follows.

- How much does a black hole grow by gaseous accretion (and how much electromagnetic energy does it radiate) at each stage? Models based on semi-analytic schemes for galaxy evolution have achieved a good fit with the luminosity function and z-dependence of quasars. Less gas is available at later epochs, and this accounts for the scarcity of high-luminosity AGNs at low z.

- How far back along the 'merger tree' did this process start? A single big galaxy can be traced back to the stage when it was in hundreds of smaller components with individual internal velocity dispersions as low as 20 km/s. Did central black holes form even in these small and weakly bound systems? This issue has been widely discussed (see for instance [23–26] and references cited therein). It is important because it determines whether there is a population of high-z miniquasars.

12.5.2 Tidally-disrupted stars

When the central hole mass is below $10^8 \, M_\odot$, solar-type stars are disrupted before they get close enough to fall within the hole's horizon. A tidally disrupted star, as it moves away from the hole, develops into an elongated banana-shaped structure, the most tightly bound debris (the first to return to the hole) being at one end. There would not be a conspicuous 'prompt' flare signalling the disruption event, because the energy liberated is trapped within the debris. Much more radiation emerges when the bound debris (by then more diffuse and transparent) falls back on to the hole a few months later, after completing an eccentric orbit. The dynamics and radiative transfer are then even more complex and uncertain than in the disruption event itself, being affected by relativistic precession, as well as by the effects of viscosity and shocks.

The radiation from the inward-swirling debris would be predominantly thermal, with a temperature of order 10^5 K; however the energy dissipated by the shocks that occur during the circularization would provide an extension into the X-ray band. High luminosities would be attained – the total photon energy radiated (up to 10^{53} ergs) could be several thousand times more than the *photon* output of a supernova. The flares would, however, not be standardized – what is observed would depend on the hole's mass and spin, the type of star, the impact parameter, and the orbital orientation relative to the hole's spin axis and the line of sight; perhaps also on absorption in the galaxy. To compute what happens involves relativistic gas dynamics and radiative transfer, in an unsteady flow with large dynamic range, which possesses no special symmetry and therefore requires full 3-D calculations – still a daunting computational challenge [27–30].

The rate of tidal disruptions in our galactic centre would be no more than once per 10^5 years. But each such event could generate a luminosity several times 10^{44} erg/s for about a year. Were this in the UV, the photon output, spread over 10^5 years, could exceed the current ionization rate: the mean output might exceed the median output. The radiation emitted from the event might reach us after a delay if it reflected or fluoresced off surrounding material. Sunyaev and his collaborators have already used such considerations to set non-trivial constraints on the history of the galactic centre's X-ray output over the last few thousand years.

12.6 Do the candidate holes obey the Kerr metric?

12.6.1 Probing near the hole

The observed molecular disc in NGC 4258 lies a long way out: at around 10^5 gravitational radii. We can exclude all conventional alternatives (dense star clusters, etc); however, the measurements tell us nothing about the central region where gravity is strong – certainly not whether the putative hole actually has properties consistent with the Kerr metric. The stars closest to our galactic centre likewise lie so far out from the putative hole (their speeds are less than 1 percent that of light) that their orbits are essentially Newtonian.

We can infer from AGNs that 'gravitational pits' exist, which must be deep enough to allow several percent of the rest mass of infalling material to be radiated from a region compact enough to vary on timescales as short as an hour. But we still lack quantitative probes of the relativistic region. We believe in general relativity primarily because it has been resoundingly vindicated in the weak field limit (by high-precision observations in the Solar System, and of the binary pulsar) – not because we have evidence for black holes with the precise Kerr metric.

The emission from most accretion flows is concentrated towards the centre, where the potential well is deepest and the motions fastest. Such basic features of the phenomenon as the overall efficiency, the minimum variability timescale, and the possible extraction of energy from the hole itself all depend on inherently relativistic features of the metric – on whether the hole is spinning or not, how it is aligned, etc. But the data here are imprecise and 'messy'. We would occasionally expect to observe, even in quiescent nuclei, the tidal disruption of a star. Exactly how this happens would depend on distinctive precession effects around a Kerr metric, but the gas dynamics are so complex that even when a flare is detected it will not serve as a useful diagnostic of the metric in the strong-field domain. There are however several encouraging new possibilities.

12.6.2 *X-ray spectroscopy of accretion flows*

Optical spectroscopy tells us a great deal about the gas in AGNs. However, the optical spectrum originates quite far from the hole. This is because the innermost regions would be so hot that their thermal emission emerges as more energetic quanta. X-rays are a far more direct probe of the relativistic region. The appearance of the inner disc around a hole, taking doppler and gravitational shifts into account, along with light bending, was first calculated by Bardeen and Cunningham [31] and subsequently by several others (e.g. [32]). There is of course no short-term hope of actually 'imaging' these inner discs (though an X-ray interferometer called MAXIM, with elements separated by 500 km, is being studied). However, we need not wait that long for a probe, because the large frequency-shifts predicted in (for instance) the 6.4 keV line from Fe could reveal themselves spectroscopically – substantial gravitational redshifts would be expected, as well as large doppler shifts [33]. Until recently, the energy resolution and sensitivity of X-ray detectors was inadequate to permit spectroscopy of extragalactic objects. The ASCA X-ray satellite was the first with the capability to measure emission line profiles in AGNs. There is already one convincing case [34] of a broad asymmetric emission line indicative of a relativistic disc, and others should soon follow. The value of a/m can in principle be constrained too, because the emission is concentrated closer in, and so displays larger shifts, if the hole is rapidly rotating, and there is some evidence that this must be the case in two objects [35, 36].

The recently-launched Chandra and XMM X-ray satellites are now able to extend and refine these studies; they may offer enough sensitivity, in combination with time-resolution, to study flares, and even to follow a 'hot spot' on a plunging orbit.

The swing in the polarization vector of photon trajectories near a hole was long ago suggested [37] as another diagnostic; but this is still not feasible because X-ray polarimeters are far from capable of detecting the few percent polarization expected.

12.6.3 The Blandford-Znajek process

Back in 1969 Penrose [38] showed how energy could in principle be extracted from a spinning hole. Some years later Blandford and Znajek [39] proposed an astrophysically-realistic process whereby this might happen: a magnetic field threading a hole (maintained by external currents in, for instance, a torus) could extract spin energy, converting it into directed Poynting flux and electron–positron pairs.

Can we point to objects where this is definitively happening? The giant radio lobes from radio galaxies sometimes spread across millions of lightyears – 10^{10} times larger than the hole itself. If the Blandford–Znajek process is really going on, these huge structures may be the most direct manifestation of an inherently relativistic effect around a Kerr hole.

Jets in some AGNs definitely have Lorentz factors exceeding 10. Moreover, some are probably Poynting-dominated, and contain electron–positron (rather than electron–ion) plasma. But there is still no compelling reason to believe that these jets are energized by the hole itself, rather than by winds and magnetic flux 'spun off' the surrounding torus. The case for the Blandford–Znajek mechanism would be strengthened if baryon-free jets were found with still higher Lorentz factors, or if the spin of the holes could be independently measured, and the properties of jets turned out to depend on a/m.

The process cannot dominate unless either the field threading the hole is comparable to that in the orbiting material, or else the surrounding material radiates with low radiative efficiency. These requirements cannot be ruled out, though there has been recent controversy about how plausible they are. (The Blandford–Znajek effect could be important in the still more extreme context of gamma-ray bursts, where a newly formed hole of a few solar masses could be threaded by a field exceeding 10^{15} G.)

12.6.4 What is the expected spin?

The spin of a hole affects the efficiency of 'classical' accretion processes; the value of a/m also determines how much energy is in principle extractable by the Blandford–Znajek effect. Moreover, the orientation of the spin axis may be important in relation to jet production, etc.

Spin-up is a natural consequence of prolonged disc-mode accretion: any hole that has (for instance) doubled its mass by capturing material that is all spinning the same way would end up with a/m being at least 0.5. A hole that is the outcome of a merger between two of comparable mass would also, generically, have a substantial spin. On the other hand, if it had gained its mass from capturing many low-mass objects (holes, or even stars) in randomly-oriented orbits, a/m would be small.

12.6.5 Precession and alignment

Most of the extensive literature on gas dynamics around Kerr holes assumes that the flow is axisymmetric. This assumption is motivated not just by simplicity, but by the expectation that Lense–Thirring precession would impose axisymmetry close in, even if the flow further out were oblique and/or on eccentric orbits. Plausible-seeming arguments, dating back to the pioneering 1975 paper by Bardeen and Petterson [40], suggested that the alignment would occur, and would extend out to a larger radius if the viscosity were low because there would be more time for Lense–Thirring precession to act on inward-spiralling gas. However, later studies, especially by Pringle, Ogilvie, and their associates, have shown that naive intuitions can go badly awry. The behaviour of the 'tilt' is much more subtle; the effective viscosity perpendicular to the disc plane can be much larger than in the plane. In a thin disc, the alignment effect is actually weaker when viscosity is low. What happens in a thick torus is a still unclear, and will have to await 3-D gas-dynamical simulations.

The orientation of a hole's spin and the innermost flow patterns could have implications for jet alignment. An important paper by Natarajan and Pringle [41] shows that 'forced precession' effects due to torques on a disc can lead to swings in the rotation axis that are surprisingly fast (i.e. on timescales very much shorter than the timescale for changes in the hole's mass.)

12.6.6 Stars in relativistic orbits?

Gas-dynamical phenomena are complicated because of viscosity, magnetic fields, etc. It would be nice to have a 'cleaner' and more quantitative probe of the strong-field regime: for instance, a small star orbiting close to a supermassive hole. Such a star would behave like a test particle, and its precession would probe the metric in the 'strong field' domain. These interesting relativistic effects, have been computed in detail by Karas and Vokrouhlicky [42,43]. Would we expect to find a star in such an orbit?

An ordinary star certainly cannot get there by the kind of 'tidal capture' process that can create close binary star systems. This is because the binding energy of the final orbit (a circular orbit with the same angular momentum as an initially near-parabolic orbit with pericentre at the tidal-disruption radius) would have to be dissipated within the star, and that cannot happen without destroying it. An orbit can however be 'ground down' by successive impacts on a disc (or any other resisting medium) without being destroyed [44]: the orbital energy then goes almost entirely into the material knocked out of the disc, rather than into the star itself.

And there are other constraints on the survival of stars in the hostile environment around massive black holes – tidal dissipation when the orbit is eccentric, irradiation by ambient radiation, etc. [45, 46]. They can be thought of as close binary star systems with extreme mass ratios.

These stars would not be directly observable, except maybe in our own Galactic Centre. But they might have indirect effects: such a rapidly-orbiting star in an active galactic nucleus could signal its presence by quasiperiodically modulating the AGN emission.

12.6.7 Gravitational-wave capture of compact stars

Neutron stars or white dwarfs circling close to supermassive black holes would be impervious to tidal dissipation, and would have such a small geometrical cross-section that the 'grinding down' process would be ineffective too. On the other hand, because they are small they can get into very tight orbits by straightforward stellar-dynamical processes. For ordinary stars, the 'point mass' approximation breaks down for encounter speeds above 1000 km/s – physical collisions are then more probable than large-angle deflections. But there is no reason why a 'cusp' of tightly bound *compact* stars should not extend much closer to the hole. Neutron stars or white dwarfs could exchange orbital energy by close encounters with each other until some got close enough that they either fell directly into the hole, or until gravitational radiation became the dominant energy loss. When stars get very close in, gravitational radiation losses become significant, and tend to circularize an elliptical orbit with a small pericentre. Most such stars would be swallowed by the hole before circularization, because the angular momentum of a highly eccentric orbit 'diffuses' faster than the energy does due to encounters with other stars, but some would get into close circular orbits [47, 48].

A compact star is less likely than an ordinary star in similar orbit to 'modulate' the observed radiation in a detectable way. But the gravitational radiation (almost periodic because the dissipation timescale involves a factor M_{hole}/m^*) would be detectable.

12.6.8 Scaling laws and 'microquasars'

Two galactic X-ray sources that are believed to involve black holes generate double radio structures that resemble miniature versions of the classical extragalactic strong radio sources. The jets have been found to display apparent superluminal motions across the sky, indicating that, like the extragalactic radio sources, they contain plasma that is moving relativistically [49].

There is no reason to be surprised by this analogy between phenomena on very different scales. Indeed, the physics is exactly the same, apart from very simple scaling laws. If we define $l = L/L_{Ed}$ and $\dot{m} = \dot{M}/\dot{M}_{crit}$, where $\dot{M}_{crit} = L_{Ed}/c^2$, then for a given value of $\dot{m}$, the flow pattern may be essentially independent of M. Linear scales and timescales, of course, are proportional to M, and densities in the flow scale as M^{-1}. The physics that amplifies and tangles any magnetic field may be scale-independent, and the field strength B scales as $M^{-1/2}$. So the bremsstrahlung or synchrotron cooling timescales go as M, implying that t_{cool}/t_{dyn} is insensitive to M for a given $\dot{m}$. So also are ratios involving, for instance, coupling of electron and ions in thermal plasma. Therefore, the efficiencies and the value of l are insensitive to M, and depend only on $\dot{m}$. Moreover, the form of the spectrum, for given $\dot{m}$, depends on M only rather insensitively (and in a manner that is easily calculated).

The kinds of accretion flow inferred in, for instance, the centre of the giant galaxy M87, giving rise to a compact radio and X-ray source, along with a relativistic jet, could operate just as well if the hole mass were lower by a hundred million, as in the galactic sources. So we can actually study the same processes involved in AGNs in microquasars close at hand within our own galaxy. And these miniature sources may allow us to observe, in our own lifetimes, a simulacrum of the entire evolution of a strong extragalactic radio source, its life-cycle speeded up by a similar factor.

12.6.9 Discoseismology

Discs or tori that are maintained by steady flow into a black hole can support vibrational modes [50–52]. The frequencies of these modes can, as in stars, serve as a probe for the structure of the inner disc or torus. The amplitude depends on the importance of pressure, and hence on disc thickness; how they are excited, and the amplitude they may reach, depends, as in the Sun, on interaction with convective cells and other macroscopic motions superimposed on the mean flow. But the frequencies of the modes can be calculated more reliably. In particular, the lowest g-mode frequency is close to the maximum value of the radial epicyclic frequency k. This epicyclic frequency is, in the Newtonian domain, equal to the orbital frequency. It drops to zero at the innermost stable orbit. It has a maximum at about $9GM/c^2$ for a Schwarzschild hole; for a Kerr hole, k peaks at a smaller radius (and a higher frequency for a given M). The frequency is 3.5 times higher for $(a/m) = 1$ than for the Schwarzschild case.

Novak and Wagoner [52] pointed out that these modes may cause an observable modulation in the X-ray emission from galactic black-hole candidates. Just such quasi-periodicities have been seen. The amplitude is a few percent (somewhat larger at harder X-ray energies) suggesting that the oscillations involve primarily the hotter inner part of the disc. In one object, known as GRS 1915+105 (a galactic object that also emits relativistic jets), the fluctuation spectrum showed a peak in Fourier space at around 67 Hz. This frequency does not change even when the X-ray luminosity doubles, suggesting that it relates to a particular radius in the disc. If this is indeed the lowest g-mode, and if the simple disc models are relevant, then the implied mass is $10.2\,M_\odot$ for Schwarzschild, and $35\,M_\odot$ for a 'maximal Kerr' hole [52]. Several other X-ray sources have been found to display quasi-periodicities, and other regularities: for instance, two superimposed frequencies which change, but in such a way that the difference between them is constant. If such regularities can be understood, they offer the exciting prospect of inferring a/m for holes whose masses are independently known.

12.7 Gravitational radiation as a probe

12.7.1 Gravitational waves from newly-forming massive holes?

The gravitational radiation from black holes offers impressive tests of general relativity, involving no physics other than that of spacetime itself.

At first sight, the formation of a massive hole from a monolithic collapse might seem an obvious source of strong wave pulses. The wave emission would be maximally intense and efficient if the holes formed on a timescale as short as (r_g/c), where $r_g = (GM/c^2)$ – something that might happen if they built up via coalescence of smaller holes (cf. [21]).

If, on the other hand, supermassive black holes formed from collapse of an unstable supermassive star, then the process may be too gradual to yield efficient gravitational radiation. That is because post-Newtonian instability is triggered at a radius $r_i \gg r_g$. Supermassive stars are fragile because of the dominance of radiation pressure: this renders the adiabatic index only slightly above 4/3 (by an amount of order $10^{-1/2}$) $M_\odot$. Since = 4/3 yields neutral stability in Newtonian theory, even the small post-Newtonian corrections then destabilize such 'superstars'. The characteristic collapse timescale when instability ensues is longer than r_g/c by the 3/2 power of the collapse factor.

The post-Newtonian instability is suppressed by rotation. A differentially rotating supermassive star could in principle support itself against post-Newtonian instability until it became very tightly bound. It could then perhaps develop a bar-mode instability and collapse within a few dynamical times (cf. [14]). To achieve this tightly-bound state without drastic mass loss, the object would need to have deflated over a long timescale, losing energy at no more than the Eddington rate.

The gravitational waves associated with supermassive holes would be concentrated in a frequency range around a millihertz – too low to be accessible to ground-based detectors, which lose sensitivity below 100 Hz, owing to seismic and other background noise. Space-based detectors are needed. There are firm plans, discussed further in the papers by Shutz and Thorne, for the Laser Interferometric Space Array (LISA) – three spacecraft on solar orbit, configured as a triangle, with sides 5 million km long whose length is monitored by laser interferometry.

12.7.2 *Gravitational waves from coalescing supermassive holes*

The strongest signals are expected when already-formed holes coalesce, as the aftermath of mergers of their host galaxies. Many galaxies have experienced a merger since the epoch $z > 2$ when, according to 'quasar demography' arguments, they acquired central holes. When two massive holes spiral together, energy is carried away by dynamical friction (leading, when the binary is 'hard', to expulsion of stars from the galaxy) and also by drag on gas. Eventually the members of the binary get close enough for gravitational radiation (with a timescale proportional to the inverse 4th power of separation) to take over and drive them towards coalescence. In their final coalescence, up to ~ 10 percent of their rest mass as a burst of gravitational radiation in a timescale of only a few times r_g/c. These pulses would be so strong that LISA could detect them with high signal-to-noise even from large redshifts. Whether such events happen often enough to be interesting can to some extent be inferred from observations (we see many galaxies in the process of coalescing), and from simulations of the hierarchical clustering process whereby galaxies and other cosmic structures form. The merger rate of the large galaxies believed to harbour supermassive holes is only about one event per century, even out to redshifts $z = 4$. However, big galaxies are probably the outcome of many successive mergers. We still have no direct evidence – nor firm theoretical clues – on whether these small galaxies harbour black holes (nor, if they do, of what the hole masses typically are). However it is certainly possible that enough holes of (say) $10^5 \, M_\odot$ lurk in small early-forming galaxies to yield, via subsequent mergers, more than one event per year detectable by LISA [53].

LISA is potentially so sensitive that it could detect the nearly-periodic waves from stellar-mass objects orbiting a 10^5–$10^6 \, M_\odot$ hole, even at a range of a hundred Mpc, despite the $m^*/M_{\rm hole}$ factor whereby the amplitude is reduced compared with the coalescence of two objects of comparable mass M_{hole}. The stars in the observed 'cusps' around massive central holes in nearby galaxies are of course (unless almost exactly radial) on orbits that are far too large to display relativistic effects. Occasional captures into relativistic orbits can come about by dissipative processes – for instance, interaction with a massive disc [44]. But unless the hole mass were above 10^8 $M_\odot$ (in which case the waves would be at too low a frequency for LISA to detect), solar-type stars would be tidally disrupted before getting into relativistic orbits. Interest therefore focuses on compact stars, for which dissipation due to tidal effects or drag is less effective. As already described [47, 48], compact stars may get captured as a result of gravitational radiation, which can gradually 'grind down' an eccentric orbit with close pericentre passage into a nearly-circular relativistic orbit. The long quasi-periodic wave trains from such objects, modulated by orbital precession (cf. [22, 23]) in principle carries detailed information about the metric.

The attraction of LISA as an 'observatory' is that even conservative assumptions lead to the prediction that a variety of phenomena will be detected. If there were many massive holes not associated with galactic centres (not to mention other speculative options such as cosmic strings), the event rate would be much enhanced. Even without factoring in an 'optimism factor' we can be confident that LISA will harvest a rich stream of data.

12.7.3 Gravitational-wave recoil

Is there any way of learning, before that date, something about gravitational radiation? The dynamics (and gravitational radiation) when two holes merge has so far been computed only for cases of special symmetry. The more general problem – coalescence of two Kerr holes with general orientations of their spin axes relative to the orbital angular momentum – is a 'grand challenge' computational project being tackled at the Einstein Institute in Potsdam, and at other centres. When this challenge has been met (and one hopes it will not take all the time until LISA flies) we shall find out not only the characteristic wave form of the radiation, but the recoil that arises because there is a net emission of linear momentum.

There would be a recoil due to the non-zero net linear momentum carried away by gravitational waves in the coalescence. If the holes have unequal masses, a preferred longitude in the orbital plane is determined by the orbital phase at which the final plunge occurs. For spinning holes there may, additionally, be a rocket effect perpendicular to the orbital plane, since the spins break the mirror symmetry with respect to the orbital plane [54].

The recoil is a strong-field gravitational effect which depends essentially on the lack of symmetry in the system. It can therefore only be properly calculated when fully three-dimensional general relativistic calculations are feasible. The velocities arising from these processes would be astrophysically interesting if they were enough to dislodge the resultant hole from the centre of the merged galaxy. The recoil might even be so violent that the merged hole breaks loose from its galaxy and goes hurtling through intergalactic space. This disconcerting thought should at least impress us with the reality and 'concreteness' of the extraordinary entities to whose understanding Stephen Hawking has contributed so much.

Acknowledgements

I am grateful to several colleagues, especially Mitch Begelman, Roger Blandford, Andy Fabian and Martin Haehnelt for discussions and collaboration on topics mentioned here.

References

[1] Israel, W. (1996), *Foundations of Physics* **26**, 595.

[2] Madau, P. and Rees, M. J. (2001), *Astrophys. J.* **551**, L27.

[3] Miyoshi, K. *et al.* (1995), *Nature* **373**, 127.

[4] Melia, F. and Falcke, H. (2001), *Ann. Rev. Astr. Astrophys.* **39**, 309.

[5] Eikart, A., Genzel, R., Ott, T. and Schodel, R. (2002), *MNRAS* **331**, 917.

[6] Gehz, A. M., Morris, M., Becklin, E. E., Tanner, A. and Kremenck, T. (2002), *Nature* **407**, 349.

[7] Rees, M. J. (1982), 'The Compact Source at the Galactic Center', in *The Galactic Center*, eds G. Riegler and R. D. Blandford (AIP) pp. 166–176.

[8] Narayan, R., Yi, I. and Mahadevan, R. (1995), *Nature* **374**, 623.

[9] Merritt, D. and Ferrares, L. (2001), *Astrophys. J.* **547**, 140.

[10] Rees, M. J. (1978), *Observatory* **98**, 210.

[11] Salpeter, E. E. (1964), *Astrophys. J.* **140**, 796.

[12] Zeldovich, Y. B. and Novikov, I. D. (1964), *Sov Phys. Dok* 158, 811.

[13] Lynden-Bell, D. (1969), *Nature,* **223**, 690

[14] Baumgarte, T. W. and Shapiro, S. L. (1999), *Astrophys. J.* **526**, 941.

[15] Heger, A. and Woosley, S. (2002), *Astrophys. J.* **567**, 232.

[16] Quinlan, G. D. and Shapiro, S. L. (1990), *Astrophys. J.* **356**, 483.

[17] Begelman, M. C. (1979), *MNRAS* **187**, 237.

[18] Abramowicz, M., Jaroszynski, M. and Sikora, M. (1980), *Astron. Astrophys.* **63**, 221.

[19] Begelman, M. C. (2002), *Astrophys. J.* **568**, L97.

[20] Shaviv, N. (1998), *Astrophys. J.* **494**, L193.

[21] Ebisuzaki, T., Makino, J. and Okumura, S. K. (1991), *Nature* **354**, 212.

[22] Milosavljevic, M. and Merritt, D. (2001), *Astrophys. J.* **563**, 34.

[23] Haiman, Z. and Loeb, A. (1998), *Astrophys. J.* **499**, 520.

[24] Haehnelt, M. and Kaufmann, G. (2000), *MNRAS* **318**, 235.

[25] Menon, K., Haiman, Z. and Narayanan, V. K. (2001), *Astrophys. J.* **558**, 535.

[26] Yu, Q. and Tremaine, S. (2002), *Astrophys. J.* (in press), [astro-ph 0203082].

[27] Carter, B. and Luminet, J.-P. (1983), *Astr. Astrophys.* **121**, 97.

[28] Canizzo, J. K., Lee, H. M. and Goodman, J. (1990), *Astrophys. J.* **351**, 38.

[29] Syer, D. and Ulmer, A. (1999), *MNRAS* **306**, 35.

[30] Magorrian, J. and Tremaine, S. (1999), *MNRAS* **309**, 447.

[31] Bardeen, J. and Cunningham, J. (1972), *Astrophys. J.* **173**, L137.

[32] Rauch, K. P. and Blandford, R. D. (1993), *Astrophys. J.* **421**, 46.

[33] White, N. E. *et al.* (1989) *MNRAS* **238**, 729.

[34] Tanaka, Y. *et al.* (1995), *Nature* **375**, 659.

[35] Iwasawa, K. *et al.* (1999), *MNRAS* **306**, L191.

[36] Wilms, J. *et al.* (2001), *MNRAS* **328**, L27.

[37] Connors, P. A., Piran, T. and Stark, R. F. (1980), *Astrophys. J.* **235**, 224.

[38] Penrose, R. (1969), *Rivista del Nuivo Cimento, Numero speciale*, **1**, 252.

[39] Blandford, R. D. and Znajek, R. L. (1977), *MNRAS* **179**, 433.

[40] Bardeen, J. and Petterson, J. A. (1975), *Astrophys. J.* **195**, L65.

[41] Natarajan, P. and Pringle, J. E. (1998), *Astrophys. J.* **506**, 97.

[42] Karas, V. and Vokrouhlicky, D. (1993), *MNRAS* **265**, 365.

[43] Karas, V. and Vokrouhlicky, D. (1994), *Astrophys. J.* **422**, 208.

[44] Syer, D., Clarke, C. J. and Rees, M. J. (1991), *MNRAS* **250**, 505.

[45] Podsiadlowski, P. and Rees, M. J. (1994), in *Evolution of X-ray Binaries*, eds S. Holt and C. Day (AIP) p.403.

[46] King, A. R. and Done, C. (1993), *MNRAS* **264**, 388.

[47] Hils, D. and Bender, P. L. (1995), *Astrophys. J.* (Lett) **445**, L7.

[48] Sigurdsson, S. and Rees, M. J. (1997), *MNRAS* **284**, 318.

[49] Mirabel, F. and Rodriguez, L. F. (1999), *Ann. Rev. Astr. Astrophys* **37**, 409

[50] Kato, S. and Fukui, J. (1980), *PASJ* **32**, 377.

[51] Novak, M. A. and Wagoner, R. V. (1992), *Astrophys. J.* **393**, 697.

[52] Novak, M. A. and Wagoner, R. V. (1993), *Astrophys J.* **418**, 187.

[53] Haehnelt, M. G. (1994), *MNRAS* **269**, 199.

[54] Redmount, I. and Rees, M. J. (1989), *Comm. Astrophys. Sp. Phys* **14** 185.

13

Primordial black holes

Bernard Carr

Queen Mary and Westfield College, University of London

13.1 Preface

It seems particularly appropriate to be speaking about primordial black holes (PBHs) at this conference because Stephen Hawking might be regarded as the father of PBHs. For it was Stephen who first realized how they might form and Stephen who first discovered how they might disappear again through quantum effects. The subject is also close to my own heart because PBHs were the topic of my PhD and I have returned to study them sporadically ever since. I was particularly fortunate to be working with Stephen at the time when he discovered black-hole radiance since this enabled me to work out some of the cosmological consequences of PBH evaporations before other people and thereby make my own small contribution to the subject. Recently somebody asked me whether working with Stephen had been the heyday of my scientific career. It would be rather depressing to find that the peak of my career was at the very start, so I hope the answer is no! In any case, the period in which I worked with Stephen was a tremendously exciting one and I will always be grateful to him for getting my career off to such a good start.

Stephen's discovery in 1974 that black holes emit thermal radiation due to quantum effects was surely one of the most important results in 20th century physics. This is because it unified three previously disparate areas of physics – quantum theory, general relativity and thermodynamics – and like all such unifying ideas it was so beautiful that it almost had to be true. John Wheeler once told me that just talking about it was like 'rolling candy on the tongue'. The discovery also illustrates that studying something may be useful even if it does not exist! For even if PBHs never formed, it was only through thinking about them that Stephen was led to his remarkable insight. As we will see, their non-existence would also have interesting implications for cosmology.

Of course, the subject would be much more interesting if PBHs *did* form since their discovery would provide a unique probe of at least four areas of physics: (1) the early universe; (2) gravitational collapse; (3) high energy physics; and (4) quantum gravity. The first topic is relevant because studying PBH formation and evaporation can impose important constraints on primordial inhomogeneities, cosmological phase transitions, inflationary scenarios and varying-G models. The second topic relates to recent developments in the study of 'critical phenomena' and the issue of whether PBHs are viable dark matter candidates. The third topic arises because PBH evaporation could contribute to cosmic rays, whose energy distribution would then give significant information about the high energy physics involved in the final explosive phase of black hole evaporation. I will have very little to say about the fourth topic, because this is covered by other speakers, but in some ways this is the most exciting one of all. In particular, the talk by Steve Giddings [39] emphasizes the possibility that quantum gravity effects could appear at TeV scale leading to the intriguing possibility that small black holes could be generated in accelerators experiments or cosmic ray events, with striking observational consequences. Although such black holes are not technically 'primordial', this possibility would have radical implications for PBHs themselves.

13.2 Historical overview

It is well known that primordial black holes (PBHs) could have formed in the early universe. A comparison of the cosmological density at a time t after the Big Bang with the density associated with a black hole of mass M shows that PBHs would have of the order of the particle horizon mass at their formation epoch:

$$M_H(t) \approx \frac{c^3 t}{G} \approx 10^{15} \left(\frac{t}{10^{-23} \text{ s}} \right) g. \tag{13.1}$$

PBHs could thus span an enormous mass range: those formed at the Planck time (10^{-43}s) would have the Planck mass (10^{-5}g), whereas those formed at 1 s would be as large as $10^5 M_\odot$, comparable to the mass of the holes thought to reside in galactic nuclei. By contrast, black holes forming at the present epoch could never be smaller than about $1 M_\odot$.

Zeldovich and Novikov [115] first derived (13.1) but they were really considering 'retarded cores' rather than black holes and Hawking [51] was the first person to realize that primordial density perturbations might lead to gravitational collapse on scales above the Planck mass. His short 1971 paper on the subject contained a plethora of ideas. He argued that such black holes should be electrically charged (this was before people had considered their discharge through quantum effects) and thereby leave detectable tracks in bubble chambers. Some of them would capture particles of the opposite charge to form neutral 'atoms' and these could be accreted by stars and accumulate at their centres. By today the Sun could have captured 10^{17}g of them, giving a black hole of radius 10^{-11}cm, and Hawking invoked this to solve the solar neutrino problem. PBH atoms would also accumulate inside neutron stars and their accretion could then explain pulsar glitches. Eventually the black hole could swallow the neutron star entirely and this would generate the sort of gravitational wavebursts then being reported by Joe Weber. In 1971 the dark matter problem was beginning to rear its head, so Hawking also proposed that PBHs would be good dark matter candidates. In short, PBHs were invoked to solve almost all the major problems of astronomy at the time! Ultimately all these proposals were scuppered but for a reason that was even more exciting.

For a while the existence of PBHs seemed unlikely since Zeldovich and Novikov [115] had pointed out that they might be expected to grow catastrophically. This is because a simple Newtonian argument suggests that, in a radiation-dominated universe, black holes much smaller than the horizon cannot grow much at all, whereas those of size comparable to the horizon could continue to grow at the same rate as it throughout the radiation era. Since we have seen that a PBH must be of the order of the horizon size at formation, this suggests that all PBHs could grow to have a mass of order $10^{15} M_\odot$ (the horizon mass at the end of the radiation era). There are strong observational limits on how many such giant holes the universe could contain, so the implication seemed to be that very few PBHs ever existed. However, the Zeldovich–Novikov argument was questionable since it neglected the cosmological expansion which would presumably hinder the black hole growth. Indeed, myself and Hawking were able to disprove the notion that PBHs could grow at the same rate as the particle horizon by demonstrating that there is no spherically symmetric similarity solution which represents a black hole attached to an exact Friedmann model via a sound-wave [21]. Since a PBH must therefore soon become much smaller than the horizon, where cosmological effects become unimportant, we concluded that PBHs cannot grow very much at all. This conclusion was soon extended to more general equations of state [11, 77].

The realization that small PBHs might exist after all prompted Hawking to study their quantum properties. This led to his famous discovery [52] that black holes radiate thermally with a temperature

$$T = \frac{\hbar c^3}{8\pi GMk} \approx 10^{-7} \left(\frac{M}{M_\odot}\right)^{-1} \text{K},$$ (13.2)

and so evaporate on a timescale

$$\tau(M) \approx \frac{\hbar c^4}{G^2 M^3} \approx 10^{64} \left(\frac{M}{M_\odot}\right)^3 \text{y}.$$ (13.3)

Only black holes smaller than 10^{15}g would have evaporated by the present epoch, so eqn (refcarreqn1) implies that this effect could be important only for black holes which formed before 10^{-23} s. Despite the conceptual importance of this result, it was bad news for PBH enthusiasts. For since PBHs with a mass of 10^{15}g would be producing photons with energy of order 100 MeV at the present epoch, the observational limit on the γ-ray background intensity at 100 MeV immediately implied that their density could not exceed 10^{-8} times the critical density [98]. Not only did this render PBHs unlikely dark matter candidates, it also implied that there was little chance of detecting black hole explosions at the present epoch [100].

Despite this conclusion, it was realized that PBH evaporations could still have interesting cosmological consequences. In particular, they might generate the microwave background [116] or modify the standard cosmological nucleosynthesis scenario [95] or contribute to the cosmic baryon asymmetry [2]. PBH evaporations might also account for the annihilation-line radiation coming from the Galactic centre [96] or the unexpectedly high fraction of antiprotons in cosmic rays [70]. PBH explosions occurring in an interstellar magnetic field might also generate radio bursts [102]. Even if PBHs had none of these consequences, studying such effects leads to strong upper limits on how many of them could ever have formed and thereby constrains models of the early universe.

Originally it was assumed that PBHs would form from initial inhomogeneities but in the 1980s attention switched to several new formation mechanisms, many of which were studied by Hawking himself. Most of the mechanisms were associated with various phase transitions that might be expected to occur in the early universe and there was particular interest in whether PBHs could form from the quantum fluctuations associated with the many different types of inflationary scenarios. Indeed it soon became clear that there are many ways which PBHs serve as a probe of the early universe and, even if they never formed, their non-existence gives interesting information [19]. In this sense, they are similar to other 'relics' of the Big Bang, except that they derive from much earlier times.

In the 1990s work on the cosmological consequences of PBH evaporations was revitalized as a result of calculations by my PhD student Jane MacGibbon. She realized that the usual assumption that particles are emitted with a black-body spectrum as soon as the temperature of the hole exceeds their rest mass is too simplistic. If one adopts the conventional view that all particles are composed of a small number of fundamental point-like constituents (quarks and leptons), it would seem natural to assume that it is these fundamental particles rather than the composite ones which are emitted directly once the temperature goes above the QCD confinement scale of 250 MeV. One can therefore envisage a black hole as emitting relativistic quark and gluon jets which subsequently fragment into leptons and hadrons [80, 82] and this modifies the cosmological constraints considerably [81].

Over the last decade PBHs have been assigned various other cosmological roles. Some people have speculated that PBH evaporation, rather than proceeding indefinitely, could cease when the black hole gets down to the Planck mass [12, 29]. In this case, one could end up with stable Planck mass relics, which would provide some of the dark matter [6, 24, 79]. Although most gamma-ray bursts are now known to be at cosmological distances, it has been proposed that some of the short period ones could be nearby exploding PBHs [9, 27]. Solar mass PBHs could form at the quark-hadron phase transition and, since some of these should today reside in our Galactic halo, these have been invoked to explain the microlensing of stars in the Magellanic Clouds [61, 63, 111].

13.3 PBHs as a probe of primordial inhomogeneities

One of the most important reasons for studying PBHs is that it enables one to place limits on the spectrum of density fluctuations in the early universe. This is because, if the PBHs form directly from density perturbations, the fraction of regions undergoing collapse at any epoch is determined by the root-mean-square amplitude ϵ of the fluctuations entering the horizon at that epoch and the equation of state $p = \gamma\rho$ $(0 < \gamma < 1)$. One usually expects a radiation equation of state $(\gamma = 1/3)$ in the early universe. In order to collapse against the pressure, an overdense region must be larger than the Jeans length at maximum expansion and this is just $\sqrt{\gamma}$ times the horizon size. On the other hand, it cannot be larger than the horizon size, or else it would form a separate closed universe and not be part of our universe [21].

This has two important implications. First, PBHs forming at time t should be of the order of the horizon mass given by (13.1). Secondly, for a region destined to collapse to a PBH, one requires the fractional overdensity at the horizon epoch δ to exceed γ. Providing the density fluctuations have a Gaussian distribution and are spherically symmetric, one can infer that the fraction of regions of mass M that collapse is [17]

$$\beta(M) \sim \epsilon(M) \exp\left[-\frac{\gamma^2}{2\epsilon(M)^2}\right] \tag{13.4}$$

where $\epsilon(M)$ is the value of ϵ when the horizon mass is M. The PBHs can have an extended mass spectrum only if the fluctuations are scale-invariant (i.e. with ϵ independent of M). In this case, the PBH mass spectrum is given by [17]

$$dn/dM = (\alpha - 2)(M/M_*)^{-\alpha} M_*^{-2} \Omega_{PBH} \rho_{crit} \tag{13.5}$$

where $M_* \approx 10^{15}$g is the current lower cut-off in the mass spectrum due to evaporations, Ω_{PBH} is the total density of the PBHs in units of the critical density (which itself depends on β) and the exponent α is determined by the equation of state:

$$\alpha = \left(\frac{1 + 3\gamma}{1 + \gamma}\right) + 1. \tag{13.6}$$

$\alpha = 5/2$ if one has a radiation equation of state ($\gamma = 1/3$), as expected. This means that the density of PBHs larger than M falls off as $M^{-1/2}$, so most of the PBH density is contained in the smallest ones.

Many scenarios for the cosmological density fluctuations predict that ϵ is at least approximately scale-invariant but the sensitive dependence of β on ϵ means that even tiny deviations from scale-invariance can be important. If $\epsilon(M)$ decreases with increasing M, then the spectrum falls off exponentially and most of the PBH density is contained in the smallest ones. If $\epsilon(M)$ increases with increasing M, the spectrum rises exponentially and – if PBHs were to form at all – they could only do so at large scales. However, the microwave background anisotropies would then be larger than observed, so this possibility can be rejected.

The current density parameter Ω_{PBH} associated with PBHs that form at a redshift z or time t is related to β by [17]

$$\Omega_{\text{PBH}} = \beta \Omega_R (1 + z) \approx 10^6 \beta \left(\frac{t}{s}\right)^{-1/2} \approx 10^{18} \beta \left(\frac{M}{10^{15}g}\right)^{-1/2} \tag{13.7}$$

where $\Omega_R \approx 10^{-4}$ is the density parameter of the microwave background and we have used (13.1). The $(1 + z)$ factor arises because the radiation density scales as $(1+z)^4$, whereas the PBH density scales as $(1+z)^3$. Any limit on Ω_{PBH} therefore places a constraint on $\beta(M)$ and the constraints

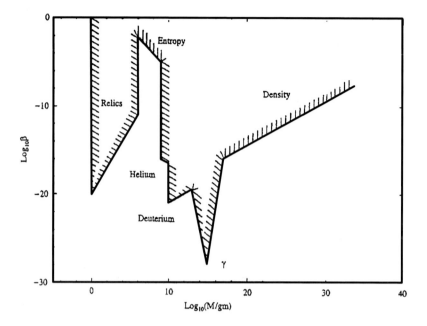

Fig. 13.1. Constraints on $\beta(M)$.

are summarized in Figure 13.1, which is taken from Carr *et al.* [24]. The constraint for non-evaporating mass ranges above 10^{15}g comes from requiring $\Omega_{PBH} < 1$ but stronger constraints are associated with PBHs smaller than this since they would have evaporated by now [18]. The strongest one is the γ-ray limit associated with the 10^{15}g PBHs evaporating at the present epoch [98]. Other ones are associated with the generation of entropy and modifications to the cosmological production of light elements [95]. The constraints below 10^6g are based on the (uncertain) assumption that evaporating PBHs leave stable Planck mass relics, in which case these relics are required to have less than the critical density [6, 24, 79].

The constraints on $\beta(M)$ can be converted into constraints on $\epsilon(M)$ using (13.4) and these are shown in Figure 13.2. Also shown here are the (non-PBH) constraints associated with the spectral distortions in the cosmic microwave background induced by the dissipation of intermediate scale density perturbations and the COBE quadrupole measurement. This demonstrates that one needs the fluctuation amplitude to decrease with increasing scale in order to produce PBHs; the lines corresponding to various slopes in the $\epsilon(M)$ relationship are also illustrated in Figure 13.2.

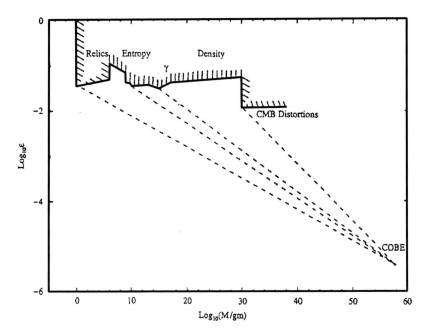

Fig. 13.2. Constraints on $\epsilon(M)$.

13.4 PBHs as a probe of cosmological phase transitions

Many phase transitions could occur in the early universe which lead to PBH formation. Some of these mechanisms still require pre-existing density fluctuations but in others the PBHs form spontaneously even if the universe starts off perfectly smooth. In the latter case, $\beta(M)$ depends not on $\epsilon(M)$ but on some other cosmological parameter.

13.4.1 Soft equation of state

Some phase transitions can lead to the equation of state becoming soft ($\gamma \ll 1$) for a while. For example, the pressure may be reduced if the universe's mass is ever channelled into particles that are massive enough to be non-relativistic. In such cases, the effect of pressure in stopping collapse is unimportant and the probability of PBH formation just depends upon the fraction of regions that are sufficiently spherical to undergo collapse; this can be shown to be [67]

$$\beta = 0.02\epsilon^{13/2}. \tag{13.8}$$

The value of β is now much less sensitive to ϵ than indicated by (13.4) and most of the PBHs will be smaller than the horizon mass at formation by a factor $\epsilon^{3/2}$. For a given spectrum of primordial fluctuations, this means that there may just be a narrow mass range – associated with the period of the soft equation of state – in which the PBHs form. In particular, this could happen at the quark–hadron phase transition since the pressure may then drop for a while [63].

13.4.2 Collapse of cosmic loops

In the cosmic string scenario, one expects some strings to self-intersect and form cosmic loops. A typical loop will be larger than its Schwarzschild radius by the inverse of the factor $G\mu$, where μ is the mass per unit length. If strings play a role in generating large-scale structure, $G\mu$ must be of order 10^{-6}. Hawking [54] showed that there is always a small probability that a cosmic loop will get into a configuration in which every dimension lies within its Schwarzschild radius and he estimated this to be

$$\beta \sim (G\mu)^{-1}(G\mu x)^{2x-2} \tag{13.9}$$

where x is the ratio of the loop length to the correlation scale. If one takes x to be 3, $\Omega_{PBH} > 1$ for $G\mu > 10^{-7}$, so he argued that one over-produces PBHs in the favoured string scenario. Polnarev and Zemboricz [99] obtained a similar result. However, Ω_{PBH} is very sensitive to x and a slight reduction could still give an interesting value [16, 38, 83]. Note that spectrum (13.5) still applies since the holes are forming with equal probability at every epoch.

13.4.3 Bubble collisions

Bubbles of broken symmetry might arise at any spontaneously broken symmetry epoch and various people, including Hawking, suggested that PBHs could form as a result of bubble collisions [31, 55, 75]. However, this happens only if the bubble formation rate per Hubble volume is finely tuned: if it is much larger than the Hubble rate, the entire universe undergoes the phase transition immediately and there is no time to form black holes; if it is much less than the Hubble rate, the bubbles are very rare and never collide. The holes should have a mass of the order of the horizon mass at the phase transition, so PBHs forming at the GUT epoch would have a mass of 10^3 g, those forming at the electroweak unification epoch would have a mass of 10^{28} g, and those forming at the QCD (quark–hadron) phase transition would have mass of around $1 M_\odot$. Only a phase transition before 10^{-23} s would be relevant in the context of evaporating PBHs.

13.4.4 Inflation

Inflation has two important consequences for PBHs. On the one hand, any PBHs formed before the end of inflation will be diluted to a negligible density. Inflation thus imposes a lower limit on the PBH mass spectrum:

$$M > M_{min} = M_{Pl}(T_{RH}/T_{Pl})^{-2} \qquad (13.10)$$

where T_{RH} is the reheat temperature and $T_{Pl} \approx 10^{19}$ GeV is the Planck temperature. The CMB quadrupole measurement implies $T_{RH} \approx 10^{16}$ GeV, so M_{min} certainly exceeds 1g. On the other hand, inflation will itself generate fluctuations and these may suffice to produce PBHs after reheating. If the inflaton potential is $V(\phi)$, then the horizon-scale fluctuations for a mass-scale M are

$$\epsilon(M) \approx [V^{3/2}/(M_{Pl}^3 V')]_H \qquad (13.11)$$

where a prime denotes $d/d\phi$ and the right-hand-side is evaluated for the value of ϕ when the mass-scale M falls within the horizon.

In the standard chaotic inflationary scenario, one makes the 'slow-roll' and 'friction-dominated' assumptions:

$$\xi \equiv (M_{Pl}V'/V)^2 << 1, \quad \eta \equiv M_{Pl}^2 V'/V << 1. \qquad (13.12)$$

Usually the exponent n characterizing the power spectrum of the fluctuations, $|\delta_k|^2 \approx k^n$, is very close to but slightly below 1:

$$n = 1 + 4\xi - 2\eta \approx 1. \qquad (13.13)$$

Since ϵ scales as $M^{(1-n)/4}$, this means that the fluctuations are slightly increasing with scale. The normalization required to explain galaxy formation ($\epsilon \approx 10^{-5}$) would then preclude the formation of PBHs on a smaller scale. If PBH formation is to occur, one needs the fluctuations to decrease with increasing mass ($n > 1$) and this is only possible if the scalar field is accelerating sufficiently fast:

$$V'/V > (1/2)(V'/V)^2. \qquad (13.14)$$

This condition is certainly satisfied in some scenarios [22] and, if it is, (13.4) implies that the PBH density will be dominated by the ones forming immediately after reheating. Since each value of n corresponds to a straight line in Figure 13.3, any particular value for the reheat time t_1 corresponds to an upper limit on n. This limit is indicated in Figure 13.3, which is taken from Carr *et al.* [24] apart from a correction pointed out by Green and Liddle [44]. Similar constraints have now been obtained by

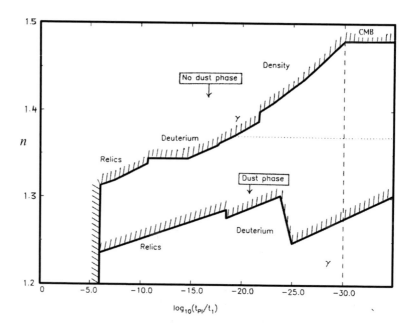

Fig. 13.3. Constraints on spectral index n in terms of reheat time t_1. [From Carr *et al.* [24]]

several other people [14, 69]. The figure also shows how the constraint on n is strengthened if the reheating at the end of inflation is sufficiently slow for there to be a dust-like phase [46]. PBHs have now been used to place constraints on many other sorts of inflationary scenarios – supernatural [101], supersymmetric [41], hybrid [37, 65], oscillating [106], preheating [8, 32, 35, 47] and running mass [76] – as well as a scenario in which the inflaton serves as the dark matter [78].

Bullock and Primack [15] and Ivanov [60] have questioned whether the Gaussian assumption that underlies (13.4) is valid in the context of inflation. So long as the fluctuations are small ($\delta\phi/\phi \ll 1$), as certainly applies on a galactic scale, this assumption is valid. However, for PBH formation one requires $\delta\phi/\phi \sim 1$ and, in this case, the coupling of different Fourier modes destroys the Gaussianity. Their analysis suggests that $\beta(M)$ is much less than indicated by (13.4) but it still depends very sensitively on ϵ.

Not all inflationary scenarios predict that the spectral index should be constant. Hodges and Blumenthal [58] pointed out that one can get any form for the fluctuations whatsoever by suitably choosing the form of $V(\phi)$. For example, (13.11) suggests that one can get a spike in the spectrum by flattening the potential over some mass range (since the fluctuation diverges when V' goes to 0). This idea was exploited by Ivanov *et al.* [61], who fine-tuned the position of the spike so that it corresponds to the microlensing mass-scale.

13.5 PBHs as a probe of a varying gravitational constant

The PBH constraints would be severely modified if the value of the gravitational 'constant' G was different at early times. The simplest varying-G model is the Brans–Dicke (BD) theory [13], in which G is associated with a scalar field ϕ and the deviations from general relativity are specified by a parameter ω. A variety of astrophysical tests currently require $|\omega| > 500$, which implies that the deviations can only ever be small [109]. However, there exist generalized scalar-tensor theories [10, 94, 108] in which ω is itself a function of ϕ and these lead to a considerably broader range of variations in G. In particular, it permits ω to be small at early times (allowing noticeable variations of G then) even if it is large today. In the last decade interest in such theories has been revitalized as a result of early universe studies. Extended inflation explicitly requires a model in which G varies [75] and, in higher dimensional Kaluza–Klein-type cosmologies, the variation in the sizes of the extra dimensions also naturally leads to this [36, 71, 85].

The behaviour of homogeneous cosmological models in BD theory is well understood [5]. They are vacuum-dominated at early times but always tend towards the general relativistic solution during the radiation-dominated era. This means that the full radiation solution can be approximated by joining a BD vacuum solution to a general relativistic radiation solution at some time t_1, which may be regarded as a free parameter of the theory. However, when the matter density becomes greater than the radiation density at $t_e \sim 10^{11}$ s, the equation of state becomes dust-like ($p = 0$) and G begins to vary again. For a $k = 0$ model, one can show [4]

$$G = G_0(t_0/t_e)^n, \quad a \propto t^{(2-n)/3} \quad (t > t_e) \tag{13.15}$$

$$G = G_e \equiv G_0(t_0/t_e)^n, \quad a \propto t^{1/2} \quad (t_1 < t < t_e) \tag{13.16}$$

$$G = G_e(t/t_1)^{-(n+\sqrt{4n+n^2})/2}, \quad a \propto t^{(2-n-\sqrt{4n+n^2})/6} \quad (t < t_1) \tag{13.17}$$

where G_0 is the value of G at the current time t_0, $n \equiv 2/(4 + 3\omega)$ and $(t_0/t_e) \approx 10^6$. Since $|\omega| > 500$ implies $|n| < 0.001$, the deviations from general relativity are never large if the value of n is always the same (as in BD itself). However, n may vary in more general scalar-tensor theories.

Such models may still have an early vacuum-dominated phase in which n is effectively constant but this value will be unconstrained by current observations.

The consequences of the cosmological variation of G for PBH evaporation depend upon how the value of G near the black hole evolves. Barrow [3] introduces two possibilities: in scenario A, G everywhere maintains the background cosmological value everywhere (so ϕ is homogeneous); in scenario B, it preserves the value it had at the formation epoch near the black hole even though it evolves at large distances (so ϕ becomes inhomogeneous). On the assumption that a PBH of mass M has a temperature and mass-loss rate

$$T \propto (GM)^{-1}, \quad \dot{M} \propto (GM)^{-2}, \tag{13.18}$$

with $G = G(t)$ in scenario A and $G = G(M)$ in scenario B, Barrow and Carr [4] calculate the evaporation time τ for various values of the parameters n and t_1 in BD theory. The results are shown in Figure 13.4a for scenario A and Figure 13.4b for scenario B. Here M_* is the mass of a PBH evaporating at the present epoch, M_e is the mass of a PBH evaporating at time t_e and M_{crit} is the mass of a PBH evaporating at the present epoch in the standard (constant G) scenario. In scenario A with $n < -1/2$, there is a maximum mass of a PBH which can ever evaporate and this is denoted by M_∞. The question of whether scenario A or scenario B is more plausible has been studied in several papers [20, 40, 49, 62] but it still remains unresolved.

13.6 PBHs as a probe of gravitational collapse

The criterion for PBH formation given in Section 13.4 is rather simplistic and is not based on a detailed calculation. The first numerical studies of PBH formation were carried out by Nadezhin *et al.* [89]. These roughly confirmed the criterion $\delta > \gamma$ for PBH formation although the PBHs could be somewhat smaller than the horizon. In recent years several groups have carried out more detailed hydrodynamical calculations and these have refined the $\delta > \gamma$ criterion and hence the estimate for $\beta(M)$ given by (13.4). Niemeyer and Jedamzik [93] find that one needs $\delta > 0.8$ rather than $\delta > 0.3$ to ensure PBH formation. They also find that there is little accretion after PBH formation, as expected theoretically [21]. Shibata and Sasaki [104] reach similar conclusions.

A particularly interesting development has been the application of 'critical phenomena' to PBH formation. Studies of the collapse of various types of spherically symmetric matter fields have shown that there is always a critical solution that separates those configurations that form a

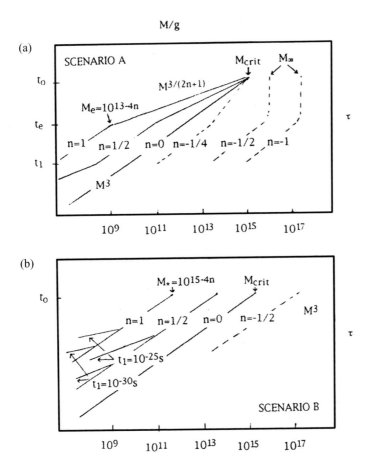

Fig. 13.4. Dependence of the PBH evaporation time τ on initial mass M in (a) BD theory with scenario A, (b) BD theory with scenario B.

black hole from those which disperse to an asymptotically flat state. The configurations are described by some index p and, as the critical index p_c is approached, the black hole mass is found to scale as $(p - p_c)^\eta$ for some exponent η. This effect was first discovered for scalar fields [25] but subsequently demonstrated for radiation [33] and then more general fluids with equation of state $p = \gamma\rho$ [72, 87].

In all these studies the spacetime was assumed to be asymptotically flat. However, Niemeyer and Jedamzik [92] have recently applied the same idea to study black hole formation in asymptotically Friedmann models and have found similar results. For a variety of initial density perturbation profiles, they find that the relationship between the PBH mass and the

the horizon-scale density perturbation has the form

$$M = KM_H(\delta - \delta_c)^\gamma \qquad (13.19)$$

where M_H is the horizon mass and the constants are in the range $0.34 < \gamma < 0.37$, $2.4 < K < 11.9$ and $0.67 < \delta_c < 0.71$ for the various configurations. Since $M \to 0$ as $\delta \to \delta_c$, this suggests that PBHs may be much smaller than the particle horizon at formation and it also modifies the mass spectrum [42, 45, 73, 113]. However, it is clear that a fluid description must break down if they are too small and recent calculations by Hawke and Stewart [50] show that black holes can only form on scales down to 10^{-4} of the horizon mass.

There has also been interest recently in whether PBHs could have formed at the quark–hadron phase transition at 10^{-5} s because of a temporary softening of the equation of state then. Such PBHs would naturally have the sort of mass required to explain the MACHO microlensing results [63]. If the QCD phase transition is assumed to be of 1st order, then hydrodynamical calculations show that the value of δ required for PBH formation is indeed reduced below the value which pertains in the radiation case [64]. This means that PBH formation will be strongly enhanced at the QCD epoch, with the mass distribution being peaked around the horizon mass. One of the interesting implications of this scenario is the possible existence of a halo population of *binary* black holes [90]. With a full halo of such objects, there could then be 10^8 binaries inside 50 kpc and some of these could be coalescing due to gravitational radiation losses at the present epoch. If the associated gravitational waves were detected, it would provide a unique probe of the halo distribution [59].

13.7 PBHs as a probe of high energy physics

We have seen that a black hole of mass M will emit particles like a black-body of temperature [53]

$$T \approx 10^{26} \left(\frac{M}{g}\right)^{-1} K \approx \left(\frac{M}{10^{13}g}\right)^{-1} \text{GeV}. \qquad (13.20)$$

This assumes that the hole has no charge or angular momentum. This is a reasonable assumption since charge and angular momentum will also be lost through quantum emission but on a shorter timescale than the mass [97]. This means that it loses mass at a rate

$$\dot{M} = -5 \times 10^{25} (M/g)^{-2} f(M) \text{ g s}^{-1} \qquad (13.21)$$

where the factor $f(M)$ depends on the number of particle species that are light enough to be emitted by a hole of mass M, so the lifetime is

$$\tau(M) = 6 \times 10^{-27} f(M)^{-1} (M/g)^3 \text{ s}. \qquad (13.22)$$

The factor f is normalized to be 1 for holes larger than 10^{17} g and such holes are only able to emit 'massless' particles like photons, neutrinos and gravitons. Holes in the mass range 10^{15} g $< M < 10^{17}$ g are also able to emit electrons, while those in the range 10^{14} g $< M < 10^{15}$ g emit muons which subsequently decay into electrons and neutrinos. The latter range includes, in particular, the critical mass for which τ equals the age of the universe. If the total density parameter is 1, this can be shown to imply $M_* = 4.4 \times 10^{14} h^{-0.3}$g where h is the Hubble parameter in units of 100 [81].

Once M falls below 10^{14}g, a black hole can also begin to emit hadrons. However, hadrons are composite particles made up of quarks held together by gluons. For temperatures exceeding the QCD confinement scale of $\Lambda_{QCD} = 250$–300 GeV, one would therefore expect these fundamental particles to be emitted rather than composite particles. Only pions would be light enough to be emitted below Λ_{QCD}. Since there are 12 quark degrees of freedom per flavour and 16 gluon degrees of freedom, one would also expect the emission rate (i.e. the value of f) to increase dramatically once the QCD temperature is reached.

The physics of quark and gluon emission from black holes is simplified by a number of factors. First, one can show that the separation between successively emitted particles is about twenty times their wavelength, which means that short range interactions between them can be neglected. Secondly, the condition $T > \Lambda_{QCD}$ implies that their separation is much less than $\Lambda_{QCD}^{-1} \approx 10^{-13}$cm (the characteristic strong interaction range), meaning that the particles are also unaffected by strong interactions. The implication of these three conditions is that one can regard the black hole as emitting quark and gluon jets of the kind produced in collider events. The jets will decay into hadrons over a distance that is always much larger than GM, so gravitational effects can be neglected. The hadrons may then decay into astrophysically stable particles through weak and electromagnetic decays.

To find the final spectra of stable particles emitted from a black hole, one must convolve the Hawking emission spectrum with the jet fragmentation function. This gives the instantaneous emission spectrum shown in Figure 13.5 for a $T = 1$ GeV black hole [82]. The direct emission just corresponds to the small bumps on the right. All the particle spectra show a peak at 100 MeV due to pion decays; the electrons and neutrinos also have peaks at 1 MeV due to neutron decays. In order to determine the

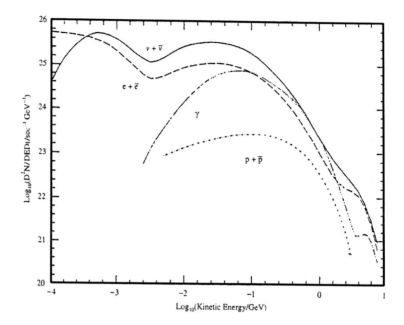

Fig. 13.5. Instantaneous emission from a 1 GeV black hole.

present day background spectrum of particles generated by PBH evaporations, one must first integrate over the life-time of each hole of mass M
and then over the PBH mass spectrum [82]. In doing this, one must allow
for the fact that smaller holes will evaporate at an earlier cosmological
epoch, so the particles they generate will be redshifted in energy by the
present epoch.

If the holes are uniformly distributed throughout the universe, the background spectra should have the form indicated in Figure 13.6. All the
spectra have rather similar shapes: an E^{-3} fall-off for $E > 100$ MeV due
to the final phases of evaporation at the present epoch and an E^{-1} tail for
$E < 100$ MeV due to the fragmentation of jets produced at the present
and at earlier epochs. Note that the E^{-1} tail generally masks any effect
associated with the mass spectrum of smaller PBHs that evaporated at
earlier epochs [18].

The situation is more complicated if the PBHs evaporating at the
present epoch are clustered inside our own galactic halo (as is most likely).
In this case, any charged particles emitted after the epoch of galaxy formation (i.e. from PBHs only somewhat smaller than M_*) will have their flux
enhanced relative to the photon spectra by a factor ξ which depends upon
the halo concentration factor and the time for which particles are trapped

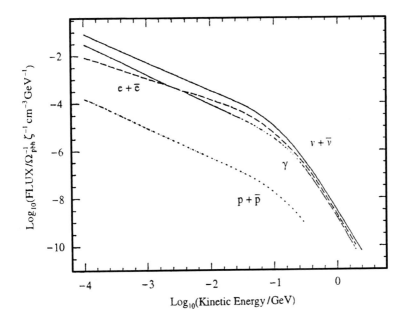

Fig. 13.6. Spectrum of particles from uniformly distributed PBHs.

inside the halo by the Galactic magnetic field. This time is rather uncertain and also energy-dependent. At 100 MeV one has $\xi \sim 10^3$ for electrons or positrons and $\xi \sim 10^4$ for protons and antiprotons. MacGibbon and Carr [81] first used the observed cosmic ray spectra to constrain $\Omega_{\rm PBH}$ but their estimates have recently been updated.

13.7.1 Gamma-rays

Recent EGRET observations [105] give a γ-ray background of

$$\frac{dF_\gamma}{dE} = 7.3(\pm 0.7) \times 10^{-14} \left(\frac{E}{100 MeV} \right)^{-2.10 \pm 0.03} {\rm cm}^{-3} {\rm GeV}^{-1} \quad (13.23)$$

between 30 MeV and 120 GeV. Carr and MacGibbon [23] showed that this leads to an upper limit

$$\Omega_{\rm PBH} \leq (5.1 \pm 1.3) \times 10^{-9} h^{-2}, \quad (13.24)$$

which is a refinement of the original Page–Hawking limit, but the form of the spectrum suggests that PBHs do not provide the dominant contribution. If PBHs are clustered inside our own galactic halo, then there should also be a galactic γ-ray background and, since this would be anisotropic, it should be separable from the extragalactic background. The ratio of the anisotropic to isotropic intensity depends on the galactic longitude and latitude, the ratio of the core radius to our galactocentric radius, and the halo flattening. Wright claims that such a halo background has been detected [110]. His detailed fit to the EGRET data, subtracting various other known components, requires the PBH clustering factor to be $(2-12) \times 10^5 h^{-1}$, comparable to that expected.

13.7.2 Antiprotons

Since the ratio of antiprotons to protons in cosmic rays is less than 10^{-4} over the energy range 100 MeV–10 GeV, whereas PBHs should produce them in equal numbers, PBHs could only contribute appreciably to the antiprotons [107]. It is usually assumed that the observed antiproton cosmic rays are secondary particles, produced by spallation of the interstellar medium by primary cosmic rays. However, the spectrum of secondary antiprotons should show a steep cut-off at kinetic energies below 2 GeV, whereas the spectrum of PBH antiprotons should increase with decreasing energy down to 0.2 GeV, hence providing a distinct signature [70].

MacGibbon and Carr originally calculated the PBH density required to explain the interstellar antiproton flux at 1 GeV and found a value somewhat larger than the γ-ray limit [81]. More recent data on the antiproton flux below 0.5 GeV comes from the BESS balloon experiment [114] and Maki *et al.* [86] have tried to fit this data in the PBH scenario. They model the galaxy as a cylindrical diffusing halo of diameter 40 kpc and thickness 4–8 kpc and then use Monte Carlo simulations of cosmic ray propagation. A comparison with the data shows no positive evidence for PBHs (i.e. there is no tendency for the antiproton fraction to tend to 0.5 at low energies) but they require the fraction of the local halo density in PBHs to be less than 3×10^{-8}, which is stronger than the γ-ray background limit. A more recent attempt to fit the observed antiproton spectrum with PBH emission comes from Barrau *et al.* [7] and is shown in Figure 13.7. A key test of the PBH hypothesis will arise during the solar minimum period because the flux of primary antiprotons should then be enhanced, while that of the secondary antiprotons should be little affected [88].

13.7.3 PBH explosions

One of the most striking observational consequences of PBH evaporations would be their final explosive phase. However, in the standard particle physics picture, where the number of elementary particle species never exceeds around 100, the likelihood of detecting such explosions is very

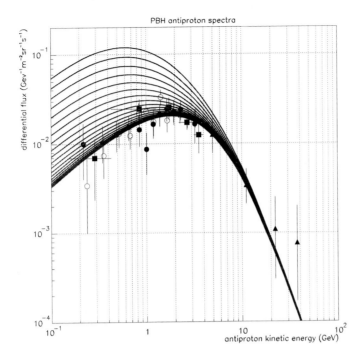

Fig. 13.7. Comparison of PBH emission and antiproton data from Barrau *et al.*

low. In this case, observations only place an upper limit on the explosion rate of 5×10^8 pc^{-3}y^{-1} [1, 103]. This compares with Wright's γ-ray halo limit of 0.3 pc^{-3}y^{-1} and the Maki *et al.* antiproton limit of 0.02 pc^{-3}y^{-1}.

However, the physics at the QCD phase transition is still uncertain and the prospects of detecting explosions would be improved in less conventional particle physics models. For example, in a Hagedorn-type picture, where the number of particle species exponentiates at the quark-hadron temperature, the upper limit is reduced to 0.05 pc^{-3}y^{-1} [34]. Cline and colleagues have argued that one might expect the formation of a QCD fireball at this temperature [26] and this might even explain some of the short period γ-ray bursts observed by BATSE [27]. They claim to have found forty-two candidates of this kind and the fact that their distribution matches the spiral arms suggests that they are Galactic. Although this proposal is speculative and has been disputed [43], it has the attraction of making testable predictions (e.g. the hardness ratio should increase as the duration of the burst decreases). Martin Rees has remarked that 'the idea isn't completely mad', which is grounds for some optimism! A rather different way of producing a γ-ray burst is to assume that the outgoing charged particles form a plasma due to turbulent magnetic field effects at sufficiently high temperatures [9].

Some people have emphasized the possibility of detecting very high energy cosmic rays from PBHs using air shower techniques [30, 48, 74]. However, recently these efforts have been set back by the claim of Heckler [56] that QED interactions could produce an optically thick photosphere once the black hole temperature exceeds $T_{crit} = 45$ GeV. In this case, the mean photon energy is reduced to $m_e(T_{BH}/T_{crit})^{1/2}$, which is well below T_{BH}, so the number of high energy photons is much reduced. He has proposed that a similar effect may operate at even lower temperatures due to QCD effects [57]. Several groups have examined the implications of this proposal for PBH emission [28, 66]. However, these arguments should not be regarded as definitive since MacGibbon *et al.* claim that QED and QCD interactions are never important [84].

13.8 Postscript

People often ask me what it was like to have Stephen as a PhD supervisor, so I will close this paper with a few personal reminiscences. Stephen has had twenty-four research students, nearly all of whom are present at this meeting. I was the third and, while Stephen's circumstances may have changed somewhat in the intervening 30 years, I'm sure what I have to say is fairly typical. Of course, Stephen was not so famous in those days and I have to confess that I'd never heard of him when I began my PhD – just as Stephen had never heard of Dennis Sciama when he began his! However, shortly after becoming his research student, I recall Jeffrey Goldstone, who was one of my tutors, telling me that he was the brightest person in DAMTP, which I found rather daunting.

The relationship between Stephen and his students is not the usual type of supervisor–student relationship, at least it wasn't for me. In those days, before he had his entourage of nurses and assistants, students would necessarily have to help Stephen in various ways on account of his disability. This was not an arduous task but it did mean that one's relationship with him became quite intimate. In my case, I shared offices with Stephen (in both DAMTP and the Institute of Astronomy), accompanied him in his invalid car on journeys between the two – rather tremulously since he would drive faster than I considered safe! – and I also lived with his family for a year in California. Many people have marvelled that Stephen has survived his illness for so long but, to my mind, the fact that he survived *me* for three years is a much greater miracle!

I was fortunate to be working with Stephen at the time when he discovered black hole radiation and for me this certainly felt like being part of history. I can well recall a tea-time conversation at the Institute of Astronomy in 1973 when he revealed that his quantum calculation was producing a strange flux. I often wish I'd had the insight to point out that it must be because black holes radiate - something which by then should have been fairly obvious – but alas I didn't. The story of how Stephen presented his result at the Second Quantum Gravity Conference at Rutherford, only to have it rubbished by the chairman, is now well known. However, my most vivid memory of the occasion was of putting my head out of the car window just as we arrived at Rutherford and being sick – a result not of nervous apprehension but of the long and winding road from Cambridge.

Accompanying Stephen as he travelled around the world, giving talks and collecting medals, was always a great adventure. As an impressionable young PhD student, it was a tremendous thrill to meet so many celebrities and renowned physicists. One of the great excitements of visiting Caltech, where Stephen was a Fairchild scholar in 1975, was meeting Richard Feynman, who was regarded almost like a God there. He used to visit our office quite often and, since Stephen's voice was already quite weak, I would act as interpreter. Shortly after arriving at Caltech, Stephen gave a physics colloquium on black hole radiation and I was sitting at the front, showing the overhead transparencies. Feynman was in the audience and afterwards I was told that he had been sketching my picture on the back of the envelope on which he was taking notes. I contacted his secretary and, although the envelope had by then been dispatched into the garbage bin, she managed to retrieve it for me. I never showed this to Stephen, because I thought he would be annoyed that Feynman had not been giving the talk his complete attention, but I still have it today and it is one of my prized possessions. As shown in Figure 13.8, it features my head, surrounded by lots of equations from the talk. I've changed quite a lot in the intervening 27 years but the equations remain the same!

Interacting with Stephen was always tremendously stimulating intellectually but it could sometimes be intimidating to work with someone so smart. Students are probably always in awe of their supervisors and with Stephen the awe was even greater. The first problem I examined for my PhD was whether there is a self-similar solution that represents a black hole growing at the same rate as the background universe. I struggled with the equations for several weeks before finally managing to prove that no such solution exists. I remember being very excited by this and rushing round to Stephen's office to tell him the good news. However, when I got there, I was disappointed to find that he had just obtained the same result and furthermore solved the problem in his head!

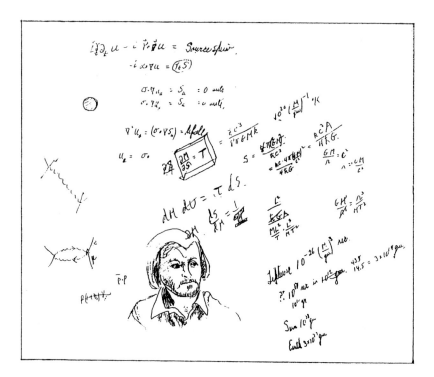

Fig. 13.8. Feynman's notes on Stephen's colloquium on black hole radiance

On matters of physics, I always regarded Stephen as an oracle and just a few words from him could yield insights which would have taken weeks of work on my own. I was therefore particularly lucky to share an office with him since this gave me privileged access to these insights. However, Stephen is only human and not all encounters led to illumination. Once, while sharing an office with him at Caltech, I asked a question about something which was puzzling me. He thought about it silently for several minutes and I was quite impressed with myself for asking something which Stephen couldn't answer immediately. His eyes then closed and I was even more impressed with myself because Stephen was clearly having to think about it very deeply. Only after ten minutes did it become clear that he had fallen asleep! Because of the circumstances I suspect Stephen has forgotten this incident but I always recall the occasion with amusement whenever I myself nod off when speaking to students!

The other human side of Stephen is that he does occasionally get annoyed. One of the myths put around is that he sometimes vents his frustration by running over the toes of students. This certainly never happened to me – he didn't have a motorized wheelchair when I was a student – but I do recall one occasion when I made a silly remark at tea, which showed that I had completely misunderstood what he'd been saying. Stephen screamed 'No' so loudly that his wheelchair shot back half way across the room under the recoil. I was most impressed that a single word from him could have such dramatic consequences!

Stories about Stephen's sense of humour are legendary but I will just relate one. At lunch one day at Caltech, we were having a conversation about the nature of fame and Stephen finally decided to define 'fame' as being known by more people than one knows. On the way back to the office we passed somebody I did not recognize who said 'Hi'. When I asked Stephen who it was, he replied with a grin 'That was fame'. Now that he has attained such public prominence, he must have many such encounters but his sense of humour still prevails. When a lady tourist recently stopped him in the street to enquire whether he was the famous Stephen Hawking, he retorted that the real one was much better looking! Actually I've often suspected that there must be more than one Stephen Hawking to have made so many important discoveries. I would like to wish all of them a very happy 60th birthday!

References

[1] Alexandreas, D. E. *et al.* (1993), *Phys.Rev.Lett.* **71** 2524.

[2] Barrow, J. D. (1980), *MNRAS* **192** 427.

[3] Barrow, J. D. (1992), *Phys. Rev.* **D46** R3227.

[4] Barrow, J. D. and Carr, B. J. (1996), *Phys. Rev.* **D54** 3920.

[5] Barrow, J. D. and Parsons, P. (1997), *Phys. Rev.* **D55** 1906.

[6] Barrow, J. D., Copeland, E. J. and Liddle, A. R. (1992), *Phys. Rev.* **D46** 645.

[7] Barrau, A. *et al.* (2002), Astron. Astrophys., in press.

[8] Bassett, B. A. and Tsujikawa, S. (2001), *Phys. Rev.* **D63** 123503.

[9] Belyanin, A. A. *et al.*, (1997), Preprint.

[10] Bergmann, P.G. (1968), *Int. J. Theor. Phys.* **1** 25.

[11] Bicknell, G. V. and Henriksen, R. N. (1978), *Ap. J.* **219** 1043.

[12] Bowick, M. J. *et al.* (1988), *Phys. Rev. Lett.* **61** 2823.

[13] Brans, C. and Dicke, R. H. (1961), *Phys. Rev.* **124** 925.

[14] Bringmann, T., Kiefer, C. and Polarski, D. (2001), preprint, [astro-ph/0109404].

[15] Bullock, J. S. and Primack, J. R. (1997), *Phys. Rev.* **D55** 7423.

[16] Caldwell, R. and Casper, P. (1996), *Phys. Rev.* **D53** 3002.

[17] Carr, B. J. (1975), *Ap. J.* **201** 1.

[18] Carr, B. J. (1976), *Ap. J.* **206** 8.

[19] Carr, B. J. (1985), in *Observational and Theoretical Aspects of Relativistic Astrophysics and Cosmology*, eds J. Sanz and L. Goicoechea (World Scientific).

[20] Carr, B. J. and Goymer, C. A. (1999), *Prog. Theor. Phys.* **136** 321.

[21] Carr, B. J. and Hawking, S. W. (1974), *MNRAS* **168** 399.

[22] Carr, B. J. and Lidsey, J. E. (1993), *Phys. Rev.* **D48** 543.

[23] Carr, B. J. and MacGibbon, J. H. (1998), *Phys. Rep.* **307** 141.

[24] Carr, B. J., Gilbert, J. H. and Lidsey, J. E. (1994), *Phys. Rev.* **D50** 4853.

[25] Choptuik, M. W. (1993), *Phys. Rev. Lett.* **70** 9.

[26] Cline, D. B. and Hong, W. (1992), *Ap. J. Lett.* **401** L57.

[27] Cline, D. B., Sanders, D. A. and Hong, W. (1997), *Ap. J.* **486** 169.

[28] Cline, J., Mostoslavsky, M. and Servant, G. (1999), *Phys. Rev.* **D59** 063009.

[29] Coleman, S., Preskill, J. and Wilczek, F. (1991), *Mod. Phys. Lett.* **A6** 1631.

[30] Coyne, D. G., Sinnis, C. and Somerville, R. (1992), in *Proceedings of the Houston Advanced Research Center Conference on Black Holes*.

[31] Crawford, M. and Schramm, D. N. (1982), *Nature* **298** 538.

[32] Easther, R. and Parry, M. (2000), *Phys. Rev.* **D62** 103503.

[33] Evans, C. R. and Coleman, J. S. (1994), *Phys. Rev. Lett.* **72** 1782.

[34] Fichtel, C. E. *et al.* (1994), *Ap. J.* **1434** 557.

[35] Finelli, F. and Khlebnikov, S. (2001), *Phys. Lett.* **B504** 309.

[36] Freund, P. G. O. (1982), *Nuc. Phys.* **B209** 146.

[37] Garcia-Bellido, J., Linde, A. and Wands, D. (1997), *Phys. Rev.* **D54** 6040.

[38] Garriga, J. and Sakellariadou, M. (1993), *Phys. Rev.* **D48** 2502.

[39] Giddings, S. (2002), this volume.

[40] Goymer, C. and Carr, B. J. (1999), preprint.

[41] Green, A. M. (1999), *Phys. Rev.* **D60** 063516.

[42] Green, A. M. (2000), *Ap. J.* **537** 708.

[43] Green, A. M. (2001), preprint, [astro-ph/0105253].

[44] Green, A. M. and Liddle, A. R. (1997), *Phys. Rev.* **D56** 6166.

[45] Green, A. M. and Liddle, A. R. (1999), *Phys. Rev.* **D60** 063509.

[46] Green, A. M., Liddle, A. R. and Riotto, A. (1997), *Phys. Rev.* **D56** 7559.

[47] Green, A. M. and Malik, K. A. (2001), *Phys. Rev.* **D64** 021301.

[48] Halzen, F., Zas, E., MacGibbon, J. and Weekes, T. C. (1991), *Nature* **298** 538.

[49] Harada, T., Carr, B. J. and Goymer, C. A. (2001), preprint, [astro-ph/0112563].

[50] Hawke, I. and Stewart, J. M. (2002), preprint.

[51] Hawking, S. W. (1971), *MNRAS* **152** 75.

[52] Hawking, S. W. (1974), *Nature* **248** 30.

[53] Hawking, S. W. (1975), *Comm. Math. Phys.* **43** 199.

[54] Hawking, S. W. (1989), *Phys. Lett.* **B231** 237.

[55] Hawking, S. W., Moss, I. and Stewart, J. (1982), *Phys. Rev.* **D26** 2681.

[56] Heckler, A. (1997), *Phys. Rev.* **D55** 840.

[57] Heckler, A. (1997), *Phys. Lett.* **B231** 3430.

[58] Hodges, H. M. and Blumenthal, G. R. (1990), *Phys. Rev.* **D42** 3329.

[59] Ioka, K., Tanaka, T. and Nakamura, T. *et al.* (1999), *Phys. Rev.* **D60** 083512.

[60] Ivanov, P. (1998), *Phys. Rev.* **D57** 7145.

[61] Ivanov, P., Naselsky, P. and Novikov, I. (1994), *Phys. Rev.* **D50** 7173.

[62] Jacobsen, T. (1999), *Phys. Rev. Lett.* **83** 2699.

[63] Jedamzik, K. (1997), *Phys. Rev.* **D55** R5871; (1998) *Phys. Rep.* **307** 155.

[64] Jedamzik, K. and Niemeyer, J. (1999), *Phys. Rev.* **D59** 124014.

[65] Kanazawa, T., Kawasaki, M. and Yanagida, T. (2000), *Phys. Lett.* **B482** 174.

[66] Kapusta, J. (2001), in *Phase Transitions in the Early Universe: Theory and Observations*, eds H. J. de Vega *et al.* (Kluwer), p. 471.

[67] Khlopov, M. Yu, and Polnarev, A. G. (1980), *Phys. Lett.* **B97** 383.

[68] Kim, H. (2000), *Phys. Rev.* **D62** 063504.

[69] Kim, H., Lee, C. H. and MacGibbon, J. H. (1999), *Phys. Rev.* **D59** 063004.

[70] Kiraly, P. *et al.* (1981), *Nature* **293** 120.

[71] Kolb, E. W., Perry, M. J. and Walker, T. P. (1986), *Phys. Rev.* **D33** 869.

[72] Koike, T., Hara, T. and Adachi, S. (1999), *Phys. Rev.* **D59** 104008.

[73] Kribs, G. D., Leibovich, A. K. and Rothstein, I. Z. (1999), *Phys. Rev.* **D60** 103510.

[74] Krennrich, F., Le Bohec, S. and Weekes, T. C. (2000), *Ap. J.* **529** 506.

[75] La, D. and Steinhardt, P. J. (1989), *Phys. Lett.* **B220** 375.

[76] Leach, S. M., Grivell, I. J. and Liddle, A. R. (2000), *Phys. Rev.* **D62** 043516.

[77] Lin, D. N. C., Carr, B. J. and Fall, S. M. (1976), *MNRAS* **177** 51.

[78] Lidsey, J. E., Matos, T. and Urena-Lopez, L. A. (2002), preprint, [astro-ph/0111292].

[79] MacGibbon, J. H. (1987), *Nature* **329** 308.

[80] MacGibbon, J. H. (1991), *Phys. Rev.* **D44** 376.

[81] MacGibbon, J. H. and Carr, B. J. (1991), *Ap. J.* **371** 447.

[82] MacGibbon, J. H. and Webber, B. R. (1990), *Phys. Rev.* **D41** 3052.

[83] MacGibbon, J. H., Brandenberger, R. H. and Wichoski, U. F. (1998), *Phys. Rev.* **D57** 2158.

[84] MacGibbon, J. H., Carr, B. J. and Page, D. N. (2002), preprint.

[85] Maeda, K. (1986), *Class. Quant. Grav.* **3** 233.

[86] Maki, K., Mitsui, T. and Orito, S. (1996), *Phys. Rev. Lett.* **76** 3474.

[87] Maison, D. (1996), *Phys. Lett.* **B366** 82.

[88] Mosalenko, I. V *et al.* (2001), in *The Outer Heliosphere: The Next Frontier*, eds. H. J. Fahr *et al.*

[89] Nadezhin, D. K., Novikov, I. D. and Polnarev, A. G. (1978), *Sov. Astron.* **22** 129.

[90] Nakamura, T., Sasaki, M., Tanaka, T. and Thorne, K. (1997). *Astrophys. J.* **487** L139.

[91] Naselsky, P.D. and Polnarev, A. G. (1985), *Sov. Astron.* **29** 487.

[92] Niemeyer, J. and Jedamzik, K. (1998), *Phys. Rev. Lett.* **80** 5481.

[93] Niemeyer, J. and Jedamzik, K. (1999), *Phys. Rev.* **D59** 124013.

[94] Nordtvedt, K. (1970), *Ap. J.* **161** 1059.

[95] Novikov, I.D., Polnarev, A. G., Starobinsky, A. A. and Zeldovich, Ya. B. (1979), *Astron. Astrophys.* **80** 104.

[96] Okeke, P. N. and Rees, M. J. (1980), *Astron.Astrophys.* **81** 263.

[97] Page, D. N. (1977), *Phys. Rev.* **D16** 2402.

[98] Page, D. N. and Hawking, S. W. (1976), *Ap. J.* **206** 1.

[99] Polnarev, A. G. and Zemboricz, R. (1988), *Phys. Rev.* **D43** 1106.

[100] Porter, N. A. and Weekes, T. C. (1979), *Nature* **277** 199.

[101] Randall, L., Soljacic, M. and Guth, A. H. (1996), *Nuc. Phys.* **B472** 377.

[102] Rees, M. J. (1977), *Nature* **266** 333.

[103] Semikoz, D. V. (1994), *Ap. J.* **436** 254.

[104] Shibata, M. and Sasaki, M. (1999), *Phys. Rev.* **D** (in press), [gr-qc/9905064].

[105] Sreekumar, P. *et al.* (1998), *Ap. J.* **494** 523.

[106] Taruya, A. (1999), *Phys. Rev.* **D59** 103505.

[107] Turner, M. S. (1982), *Nature* **297** 379.

[108] Wagoner, R. V. (1970), *Phys. Rev.* **D1** 3209.

[109] Will, C. M. (1993), *Theory and Experiment in Gravitational Physics* (Cambridge University Press, Cambridge).

[110] Wright, E. L. (1996), *Ap. J.* **459** 487.

[111] Yokoyama, J. (1997), *Astron. Astrophys.* **318** 673.

[112] Yokoyama, J. (1998), *Phys. Rev.* **D58** 083510.

[113] Yokoyama, J. (1998), *Phys. Rev.* **D58** 107502.

[114] Yoshimura, K. *et al.* (1995), *Phys. Rev. Lett.* **75** 3792.

[115] Zeldovich, Ya. B. and Novikov, I. D. (1967), *Sov. Astron. A. J.* **10** 602.

[116] Zeldovich, Ya. B. and Starobinsky, A. A. (1976), *JETP Lett.* **24** 571.

14

Black hole pair creation

Simon Ross
University of Durham

14.1 Introduction

Black hole pair creation is the process analogous to Schwinger pair creation: the creation of a real pair of black holes in some suitable background, with the energy necessary to create the black holes supplied by the background. This subject has attracted a great deal of interest for several reasons. First, it is a physically interesting non-perturbative process in quantum gravity, which can nonetheless be quantitatively studied by applying the instanton approximation in a path integral approach. It also involves topology change, a little-understood but much-discussed possibility, and a successful account of black hole pair creation may be viewed as evidence that topology change can be consistently included in quantum gravity. Finally, the pair creation rate depends on the microphysics of the black holes, allowing us to determine the number of different states in which the black hole can be pair created. A substantial part of the discussion will focus on the use of this last point to confirm the classical entropy formula $S = \mathcal{A}_{bh}/4$.

Since black hole pair creation is a topology-changing process, the only approach that we know which will allow us to study it is the path integral method [1]. As we are interested in a tunnelling process, where a background field spontaneously decays by creating a pair of black holes, we will use the instanton approximation to the path integral. That is, we look for a Euclidean metric $\bar{g}$ and matter fields $\bar{\phi}$ that are a stationary point of the action $I[g, \phi]$, and we will approximate the amplitude by the classical action,

$$\ln \Psi \approx -I[\bar{g}, \bar{\phi}]. \tag{14.1}$$

These instantons have a surface at infinity which represents a background field, which is unstable, by virtue of the existence of the instanton, and

264

a final surface represents the product of the instability. By doubling the instanton across the final surface, we construct a 'bounce', which has only the boundary at infinity, and the pair creation rate is given by $\Gamma \approx e^{-I_b}$, where I_b is the action of the bounce.

Remarkably, there are closed-form instanton solutions describing black hole pair creation. They are all constructed from the C metric, which represents a pair of charged black holes accelerating in an otherwise empty space [2] (and generalizations thereof where the black holes carry additional charges).

There are conical singularities on the axis in this solution, as there is no force to provide the acceleration. Regular solutions are constructed by adding background fields to the C metric, which provide the necessary force, thereby eliminating the conical singularities. The creation of black hole pairs by a background electromagnetic field was considered first, as the creation of electron–positron pairs or monopole pairs in background fields was familiar from field theory [3, 4]. The regular solution describing a pair of charged black holes in an electromagnetic field is the Ernst metric [5], which can be obtained by a Harrison transformation [6] of the C metric, and was used to study pair creation in [7–11]. Generalizations to include a dilaton were studied in [10–14]; A specific case of the dilaton generalization that arises by Kaluza–Klein reduction was extended to higher dimensions in [15].

One can also describe the pair creation of black holes on cosmic strings [16–18]. Here the instanton is constructed from the C metric itself, as we can regard the unavoidable conical singularities on the axis in the C metric as representing cosmic strings which drag the black holes away from each other. This is perhaps the conceptually simplest case, so we will use this as an example in discussing pair creation in detail in section 14.2.

There are two forms of pair creation which involve compact instantons: firstly, one can consider pair creation in a universe with a positive cosmological constant. This process was studied in [19–22]. Here, the relevant instantons are constructed from the C metric with a cosmological constant. When we require that the solution has no conical singularities, this C metric reduces to the Reissner–Nordström de Sitter metric, so the instantons can all be constructed from this latter metric. This discussion has been generalized to rotating black holes in [23]. Secondly, one can study the pair creation of black holes in the presence of a domain wall [24]. This case is somewhat different; the instantons are constructed by cutting and pasting vacuum black hole solutions. In this case, one can find instantons for pair creation of uncharged black holes.

14.2 Constructing instantons: the C metric

To illustrate the procedures, I will now describe the detailed construction of the instanton describing the pair creation of black holes on a cosmic string. This can be represented in an idealized fashion by the C metric, which contains a conical singularity which should be viewed as approximating the cosmic string [25]. The Lorentzian section would then be interpreted as representing a pair of black holes at the ends of two collinear pieces of cosmic string, being accelerated away from each other by the string tension. Thus, the Euclidean section of the C metric gives an instanton describing the breaking of a cosmic string, with a pair of black holes being produced at the terminal points of the string. This section will closely follow the discussion in [16].

The charged C metric solution is

$$ds^2 = A^{-2}(x-y)^{-2}\left[G(y)dt^2 - G^{-1}(y)dy^2 + G^{-1}(x)dx^2 + G(x)d\varphi^2\right],$$

$$(14.2)$$

where

$$G(\xi) = (1 + r_-A\xi)(1 - \xi^2 - r_+A\xi^3),$$

$$(14.3)$$

while the gauge potential is

$$A_\varphi = q(x - \xi_3),$$

$$(14.4)$$

where $q^2 = r_+r_-$, and $m \equiv (r_+ + r_-)/2$. To be specific, we are considering a magnetically charged case. The parameter A is an acceleration parameter; if we take the limit $A \to 0$, this solution reduces (after a change of coordinates) to a Reissner–Nordström black hole of mass m and charge q, while for $r_\pm = 0$, the solution reduces to flat space in an accelerated coordinate system.

Constrain the parameters so that $G(\xi)$ has four roots, labelled by $\xi_1 \leq \xi_2 < \xi_3 < \xi_4$. To obtain the right signature, restrict x to $\xi_3 \leq x \leq \xi_4$, and y to $-\infty < y \leq x$. The roots of $G(y)$ are interpreted as horizons: an inner black hole horizon at $y = \xi_1$, an outer black hole horizon at $y = \xi_2$, and an acceleration horizon at $y = \xi_3$. The axis $x = \xi_4$ points towards the other black hole, and the axis $x = \xi_3$ points towards infinity.

To avoid having a conical singularity between the two black holes, we must take

$$\Delta\varphi = \frac{4\pi}{|G'(\xi_4)|},$$

$$(14.5)$$

which implies that there will be a conical deficit along $x = \xi_3$, with deficit angle

$$\delta = 2\pi\left(1 - \left|\frac{G'(\xi_3)}{G'(\xi_4)}\right|\right).$$

$$(14.6)$$

Physically, we imagine that this represents a cosmic string of mass per unit length $\mu = \delta/8\pi$ along $x = \xi_3$. At large spatial distances, that is, as $x, y \to \xi_3$, the C metric (14.2) reduces to the metric for flat space with conical deficit δ, expressed in accelerated coordinates.

A useful limit of this solution is the 'point-particle' limit $r_\pm A \ll 1$. In this limit, the black hole is small on the scale set by the acceleration. Thus, the spacetime is approximately flat away from a small neighbourhood of a uniformly accelerated trajectory, which is replaced by a black hole solution. We can thus see explicitly that, in this limit, the spacetime describes a black hole accelerated by the string. In this limit, we can approximate the black hole by a point particle, and we shall exploit this later to obtain a useful check on our calculation of the black hole pair creation rate, by comparing it with the pair creation rate for monopoles.

We can obtain the Euclidean section of the C metric by setting $t = i\tau$ in (14.2). To make the Euclidean metric positive definite, we must restrict the range of y to $\xi_2 \leq y \leq \xi_3$. Then there are potential conical singularities at $y = \xi_2$ and $y = \xi_3$, which must be eliminated. The conical singularity at $y = \xi_3$ may be eliminated by taking τ to be periodic with period

$$\Delta\tau = \beta = \frac{4\pi}{G'(\xi_3)}. \tag{14.7}$$

If we assume that the black holes are extreme, that is, $\xi_1 = \xi_2$, then the spatial distance from any other point to $y = \xi_2$ is infinite, so $\xi_2 < y \leq \xi_3$ on the Euclidean section, and hence the conical singularity at $y = \xi_2$ is not part of the Euclidean section. Thus, there is always a regular Euclidean solution in the extremal case, when $\xi_1 = \xi_2$. This Euclidean section has topology $S^2 \times R^2 - \{pt\}$.

Alternatively, if we assume $\xi_1 < \xi_2$, we can avoid having a conical singularity at $y = \xi_2$ by requiring that the two horizons have the same temperature, so that both conical singularities can be removed by the same choice of $\Delta\tau$. This implies that

$$(\xi_3 - \xi_1)(\xi_3 - \xi_2)(\xi_3 - \xi_4) = (\xi_2 - \xi_1)(\xi_3 - \xi_2)(\xi_2 - \xi_4), \tag{14.8}$$

which has two solutions, $\xi_3 = \xi_2$ or

$$\xi_2 - \xi_1 = \xi_4 - \xi_3. \tag{14.9}$$

In the terminology of [12], the first of these gives the type I instanton, while the latter is the type II instanton. In fact, only the latter is related to black hole pair creation; the type I instanton is in fact just the Euclidean Reissner–Nordström solution in disguise, as shown in [22]. For the type II instanton, the Euclidean solution has topology $S^2 \times S^2 - \{pt\}$.

We can obtain an instanton by slicing the Euclidean section in half along a surface $\tau = 0, \beta/2$. This instanton will interpolate between a slice of flat space with a conical deficit and a slice of the C metric, that is, a slice containing two black holes with conical deficits running between the black holes and infinity. Thus, this instanton can be used to model the breaking of a long piece of cosmic string, with oppositely-charged black holes being created at the free ends. If $\xi_2 = \xi_1$, then the black holes are extreme, while if $\xi_2 - \xi_1 = \xi_4 - \xi_3$, then the black holes are non-extreme. In the extreme case, the topology of the spatial slice is $S^2 \times R - \{pt\}$. Since the black hole horizon is at infinite proper distance, the instanton creates a pair of infinite throats. Despite the infinite volume of these throats, the instanton gives a finite pair creation rate, as we shall see. In the non-extreme case, the topology of the spatial slice is $S^2 \times S^1 - \{pt\}$, and the black holes are created with the two horizon cross-sections identified; that is, the instanton describes the creation of a finite wormhole.

For a background electromagnetic field, one constructs instantons from the Ernst solution in a very similar way. Again, one finds instantons for extremal and non-extremal black holes. In the generalization to include a dilaton, there is always an extreme instanton, but one can only satisfy the condition that the temperatures be equal and obtain a non-extreme instanton in those cases where the charged black hole solutions of the theory approach zero temperature near extremality [12]. In particular, for the dilaton coupling arising from Kaluza–Klein reduction, there is only an extreme instanton, which describes the pair creation of Kaluza–Klein monopoles. This is the only electromagnetic instance to have a known generalization to higher dimensions [15]. For a cosmological constant, the discussion is again broadly similar; the extreme instantons have topology $S^2 \times R^2$, while the non-extreme instantons have topology $S^2 \times S^2$.

14.3 Calculation of the action

Since the bounce solution used to calculate the pair creation rate is non-compact, the action is naïvely divergent; we must perform a careful calculation of the action to avoid this divergence. This calculation has been performed in a number of different ways [9–11]. To demonstrate the relationship between the pair creation rate and horizon area, I will discuss the calculation by Hamiltonian decomposition, following [11].

The divergence in the bulk action is associated with the well-known ambiguity in the gravitational action for manifolds with boundary: one can add any function of the boundary data to the action, and its variation will still give the same equations of motion [26, 27]. This ambiguity can be fixed by the 'background subtraction' procedure, where one requires that the action of a suitable background vanish. A suitable background is one which agrees with the solution asymptotically, that is, which induces the same metric and gauge fields on a boundary 'at infinity'. This gives an action of the form

$$I = \frac{1}{16\pi} \int_M (-R + F^2) - \frac{1}{8\pi} \oint_{\partial M} (K - K_0), \qquad (14.10)$$

where R is the Ricci scalar, $F_{\mu\nu}$ is the Maxwell field, K is the trace of the extrinsic curvature of the boundary, and K_0 is the same quantity calculated for the boundary embedded in the background solution.

To isolate the effects of the horizons, it is useful to rewrite this action in Hamiltonian form. If we were interested in solutions of the form $\Sigma \times S^1$, the action could be rewritten as

$$I = \beta H, \qquad (14.11)$$

where H is the Hamiltonian, and we exploit the time-translation invariance to integrate over t. Our solutions are not of this form; foliation by surfaces of constant time breaks down at the horizons. There is therefore an extra contribution from the horizons. This arises because the surfaces of constant time meet at the horizons, and the resulting corner gives a delta-function contribution to K [1]. If both the background spacetime and the original spacetime have acceleration horizons, it is shown in [28] that the action involves the difference $\Delta\mathcal{A}$ between the area of the acceleration horizon in the physical spacetime and its area in the background. The resulting action is

$$I = \beta H - \frac{1}{4}\Delta\mathcal{A} \qquad (14.12)$$

in the extreme case, and

$$I = \beta H - \frac{1}{4}(\Delta\mathcal{A} + \mathcal{A}_{bh}) \qquad (14.13)$$

in the non-extreme case, where the Hamiltonian is

$$H = \int_\Sigma N\mathcal{H} - \frac{1}{8\pi} \int_{S^2_\infty} N(^2K - ^2K_0), \qquad (14.14)$$

$\Delta\mathcal{A}$ is the difference in area of the acceleration horizon, $\mathcal{A}_{bh}$ is the area of the black hole event horizon, Σ is a surface of constant τ, and S^2_∞ is its boundary at infinity.

Since the volume term in the Hamiltonian is proportional to the constraint $\mathcal{H}$, which vanishes on solutions of the equations of motion, the Hamiltonian is just given by the surface term. In the surface term, ^2K

is the extrinsic curvature of the surface embedded in the C metric, while $^2K_0$ is the extrinsic curvature of the surface embedded in the background, which is flat space with a conical deficit.

To calculate the differences $^2K - {}^2K_0$ and $\Delta\mathcal{A}$, we need to introduce a cut-off and work with an explicit boundary at finite position. I choose the boundary in the C metric to be at $x - y = \epsilon_c$; we will take $\epsilon_c \to 0$, returning to the full non-compact spacetime, at the end of the calculation.

To ensure that we use the same boundary when calculating the two components of the Hamiltonian, we must require that the intrinsic metrics of the boundary as embedded in the two spacetimes agree. Therefore, we want to write the flat background metric in a coordinate system in which it is easy to compare it with the C metric. In fact, the flat metric can be written as

$$ds^2 = \bar{A}^{-2}(x-y)^{-2}\left[(1-y^2)dt^2 - (1-y^2)^{-1}dy^2 \right. \tag{14.15}$$
$$\left. +(1-x^2)^{-1}dx^2 + (1-x^2)d\varphi^2\right],$$

where $\Delta\varphi = 2\pi - \delta$. Note that $\bar{A}$ represents a freedom in the choice of coordinates, and x is restricted to $-1 \leq x \leq 1$. A suitable background for the action calculation can be obtained by taking $t = i\tau$ and $y \leq -1$ in (14.15).

We now need to fix the boundary surface in this background. The boundary should obey the Killing symmetries, but there is still a family of possible embeddings. I take the boundary in the flat metric (14.15) to lie at $x - y = \epsilon_f$. It is possible that the ambiguity introduced by this choice is related to the fact that the background spacetime has an additional translational isometry along the direction of the string which is not manifest in the coordinate system (14.15).

It is easy to see that the induced metrics and gauge fields on the boundary will agree, up to second non-trivial order in ϵ_c, if

$$\bar{A}^2 = -\frac{G'(\xi_3)^2}{2G''(\xi_3)}A^2, \ \epsilon_f = -\frac{G''(\xi_3)}{G'(\xi_3)}\epsilon_c. \tag{14.16}$$

Now the two contributions to the Hamiltonian can be calculated. The contribution from the C metric is (neglecting terms which vanish as $\epsilon_c \to 0$)

$$\int_{S^2_\infty} N^2 K = \frac{8\pi}{A^2\epsilon_c|G'(\xi_4)|}\left[1 - \frac{1}{4}\epsilon_c\frac{G''(\xi_3)}{G'(\xi_3)}\right], \tag{14.17}$$

while the contribution from the flat background is

$$\int_{S^2_\infty} N^2 K_0 = \frac{4\pi}{\bar{A}^2\epsilon_f}\left|\frac{G'(\xi_3)}{G'(\xi_4)}\right|\left(1 + \frac{1}{4}\epsilon_f\right). \tag{14.18}$$

Using (14.16), we see that these two surface terms are equal to this order. Thus, in the limit $\epsilon_c \to 0$, the Hamiltonian vanishes.

Thus, the action is given by

$$I_b = -\frac{1}{4}\Delta\mathcal{A} \tag{14.19}$$

in the extreme case and

$$I_b = -\frac{1}{4}(\Delta\mathcal{A} + \mathcal{A}_{bh}) \tag{14.20}$$

in the non-extreme case.

The area of the black hole horizon is

$$\mathcal{A}_{bh} = \int_{y=\xi_2} \sqrt{g_{xx}g_{\varphi\varphi}}dxd\varphi = \frac{4\pi(\xi_4 - \xi_3)}{A^2|G'(\xi_4)|(\xi_3 - \xi_2)(\xi_4 - \xi_2)}. \tag{14.21}$$

To calculate the difference between the areas of the two acceleration horizons, calculate the area inside a circle at large radius in both the C metric and the background, and take the difference. The area of the acceleration horizon $y = \xi_2$ inside a circle at $x = \xi_3 + \epsilon_c$ in the C metric is

$$\mathcal{A}_c = \int_{y=\xi_3} \sqrt{g_{xx}g_{\varphi\varphi}}dxd\varphi \tag{14.22}$$

$$= -\frac{\Delta\varphi}{A^2(\xi_4 - \xi_3)} + \frac{\Delta\varphi}{A^2\epsilon_c}$$

$$= -\frac{4\pi}{A^2|G'(\xi_4)|(\xi_4 - \xi_3)} + \pi\rho_c^2\left|\frac{G'(\xi_3)}{G'(\xi_4)}\right|,$$

where $\rho_c^2 = 4/[A^2G'(\xi_3)\epsilon_c]$. The area of the acceleration horizon $z = 0$ inside a circle at $\rho = \rho_f$ in the flat background is

$$\mathcal{A}_f = \int \sqrt{g_{\rho\rho}g_{\varphi\varphi}}d\rho d\varphi = \pi\rho_f^2\left|\frac{G'(\xi_3)}{G'(\xi_4)}\right|. \tag{14.23}$$

To ensure that the boundary used in calculating these two components is the same, require that the proper length of the boundary be the same. This gives

$$\rho_f = \rho_c\left[1 + \frac{G''(\xi_3)}{G'(\xi_3)^2A^2\rho_c^2}\right]. \tag{14.24}$$

The difference in area is then

$$\Delta\mathcal{A} = \mathcal{A}_c - \mathcal{A}_f = -\frac{4\pi}{A^2|G'(\xi_4)|}\left[\frac{1}{(\xi_4 - \xi_3)} + \frac{G''(\xi_3)}{2G'(\xi_3)}\right] \tag{14.25}$$

$$= -\frac{4\pi}{A^2|G'(\xi_4)|}\left[\frac{2}{(\xi_3 - \xi_1)} + \frac{(\xi_2 - \xi_1)}{(\xi_3 - \xi_2)(\xi_3 - \xi_1)}\right].$$

In the extreme case, $\xi_2 = \xi_1$, so the action is

$$I_b = -\frac{1}{4}\Delta\mathcal{A} = \frac{2\pi}{A^2|G'(\xi_4)|(\xi_3 - \xi_1)}. \tag{14.26}$$

In the non-extreme case, the action is

$$I_b = -\frac{1}{4}(\Delta\mathcal{A} + \mathcal{A}_{bh}) = \frac{2\pi}{A^2|G'(\xi_4)|(\xi_3 - \xi_1)}, \tag{14.27}$$

using the condition $\xi_2 - \xi_1 = \xi_4 - \xi_3$ to cancel the second contribution from $\Delta\mathcal{A}$ with the contribution from $\mathcal{A}_{bh}$.

This calculation can be extended to the dual electrically-charged case. In considering electric charge, it is important to note that fixing the electric charge is equivalent to fixing $\sqrt{h}n_\mu F^{\mu i}$ on the boundary. To ensure that the variation of the action vanishes on solutions of the equation for an arbitrary variation satisfying these boundary conditions, we must add a boundary term to the action [29],

$$I_{el} = I - \frac{1}{4\pi}\int_{\Sigma^\infty} d^3x \sqrt{h}\, F^{\mu\nu}n_\mu A_\nu, \tag{14.28}$$

where n^μ is the unit normal to the boundary Σ^∞. Using this action, one obtains the same result for pair creation in the electrically-charged case.

The action calculation for the Ernst instanton in the electromagnetic case is very similar, but a little more complicated. In the cases involving compact instantons, the background subtraction procedure is unnecessary, because there is no boundary 'at infinity', and one simply evaluates the bulk action.

14.4 Pair creation rate

The pair creation rate for black holes is given, in the instanton approximation, by $\Gamma \sim e^{-I_b}$. Consider first the point particle limit, which provides a test of our method. In the C metric calculation above, we would expect the limit to reproduce the result of [30] on the probability for strings to break, forming monopoles at the free ends. In this limit, both the extreme and non-extreme instantons satisfy $r_+ \approx r_-$ (that is, $q \approx m$). The mass per unit length of the string in this limit is

$$\mu \approx r_+A, \tag{14.29}$$

and the action (14.26,14.27) in this limit is

$$I_b \approx \frac{\pi r_+}{A} \approx \frac{\pi m^2}{\mu}, \tag{14.30}$$

in agreement with the calculation of [30], which found that the action was $I_b = \pi M_m^2/\mu$, where M_m was the monopole mass.

We note first of all that the pair creation rate for black holes is suppressed relative to that of realistic monopoles: we do not expect this semiclassical treatment to be appropriate if the black hole mass m is less than the Planck mass, while the monopole mass is typically of the order of $10^{-2}M_{Planck}$. Furthermore, breaking to form either monopoles or black holes is extremely rare, and the effect of these tunnelling processes on cosmic string dynamics is negligible. This conclusion is more general: black hole pair creation is generally suppressed relative to other forms of pair creation by reason of the black hole's large mass, and the rate is in general too low to have practical relevance for potential sources observed in the present-day universe. Black holes can be pair created in the very early universe, but they also do not have interesting observational consequences for the present-day universe [31].

Now imagine that we had monopoles of the same mass as a black hole. Then it was observed in [9] that the pair creation rate for extreme black holes is, in the point-particle limit, the same as for monopoles, while the pair creation rate for non-extreme black holes was enhanced by $e^{\mathcal{A}_{bh}/4}$. Since the two black hole horizons are identified in the spatial slice, the black holes are created in correlated states, and this enhancement by the exponential of one black hole's entropy is exactly what we would expect if the black hole entropy really did count internal states.

The calculation of the action by Hamiltonian decomposition shows that this is not just a coincidence in the point-particle limit: there is an extra factor of precisely $\mathcal{A}_{bh}/4$ in the action of the non-extreme solution, so in this instanton approximation, the pair creation of non-extreme black holes is enhanced by precisely this factor.

The enhancement of non-extreme black holes over extreme ones is consistent with the calculation of the black hole entropy in the path integral approach. The entropy associated with a Euclidean black hole solution is given by

$$S = \left(\beta \frac{\partial}{\partial \beta} - 1 \right) I, \tag{14.31}$$

where I is the action of the black hole solution. For an extreme black hole solution, the event horizon is at infinite proper distance, so the topology is $S^1 \times R \times S^2$. Since there is an S^1 factor, the action can be written as $I = \beta H$ (the foliation does not break down at the horizon), and hence $S = 0$ [11]. By contrast, for non-extreme black holes, the topology is $R^2 \times S^2$. This means that the foliation one introduces to rewrite the action in Hamiltonian form must meet at the horizon, and the entropy is $\mathcal{A}_{bh}/4$.[1] Thus, the difference between pair creation rates is exactly the same as the difference in entropy; black hole entropy really does count states.

One of the most remarkable successes of string theory is that it has produced an explicit description of the states that the black hole entropy is counting (see, e.g., the review [33]). However, the string theory argument gives $S = \mathcal{A}_{bh}/4$ even for extreme black holes; since the solutions in question are BPS, there can be no question that they really are extreme. What should one make of the disagreement between this and the path integral result?

In fact, the path integral calculation for extreme black holes should be taken with a grain of salt. The proper size of the τ direction becomes arbitrarily small down the black hole throat, and since it is not contractible, one should expect that some kind of quantum correction to the geometry becomes important once it is sufficiently small. Indeed, in string theory, this can be made very concrete: the Euclidean extreme black hole solution is argued to be unstable, as near the black hole horizon, where the proper length of the circle is tending to zero, strings wrapped around it will become tachyonic [34]. Thus, the path integral calculation given above is not reliable for extreme black holes in string theory. However, if the true entropy of the extreme black holes can be derived from some instanton with a 'string-corrected' geometry, the action, and thus the pair creation rate, will likewise have to be calculated from the 'string-corrected' geometry, and the agreement between the entropy and pair creation rate results will be maintained.[2]

The essential point is that in the path integral approach, the contribution to the entropy and the pair creation rate from a black hole horizon is simply determined by the area of the horizon and the topology. So long as the description in terms of a smooth instanton does not break down, the pair creation rate and the entropy are both determined by the horizon area, and one can argue that black hole entropy is counting states. One can also argue on general effective field theory grounds that there should be such a connection between the thermal partition function and the pair creation rate [35].

In closing, let me mention a few more open questions and issues. The main prediction emerging from this work is that the number of

---

[1] The relation between black hole entropy and topology is discussed in more detail in [32].

[2] It would clearly be helpful to be able to give a more explicit description of the effects of strings on the extreme Euclidean solution, and determine if such a 'string-corrected' geometry exists.

microscopic states of a given black hole is precisely given by $e^{\mathcal{A}_{bh}/4}$. In one of its most impressive successes, string theory has produced an explicit description of these quantum states for a wide range of black hole solutions. However, although it correctly reproduces the Bekenstein–Hawking formula, the stringy approach offers no answer to the question of *why* the entropy is always given by $S = \mathcal{A}_{bh}/4$. This remains a key unsolved riddle of black holes, whose solution must deepen our insight into the quantum description of spacetime.

The most interesting extension of this work would be to consider the pair creation of black branes in higher dimensions in the context of string theory. The main obstacle to doing so is the absence of appropriate instantons. The instantons used in almost all the cases studied so far are based on the C metric, and with the exception of the Kaluza–Klein monopole case described in [15] (where the metric is flat from the higher-dimensional point of view), there is no analogue of the C metric in dimensions other than four. Generalizing the C metric is thus a problem of great interest.

Pair creation provides one of the few contexts where one is really concerned with the value of the action for a gravitational solution, and there are a number of subtleties in the calculation of the action which would benefit from further study. In particular, there seemed to be some arbitrariness in the choice of boundary in the background in the way we calculated the action. It might be interesting to see if this could be avoided by applying something like the counterterm subtraction procedure of [36].

Acknowledgements

I would like to once again thank all the collaborators with whom I have worked on these ideas, and most especially Stephen, for many wonderful interactions. I would also like to thank the organizers of the conference for giving me the opportunity to present this work and contribute to celebrating Stephen's 60th birthday.

References

[1] Hawking, S. W. (1979), 'The path-integral approach to quantum gravity', in *General Relativity: An Einstein Centenary Survey*, eds S. W. Hawking and W. Israel, p. 746, (Cambridge University Press, Cambridge).

[2] Kinnersley, W. and Walker, M. (1970), 'Uniformly accelerating charged mass in general relativity', *Phys. Rev.* **D2**, 1359.

[3] Affleck, I. K., Alvarez, O. and Manton, N. S. (1982), 'Pair production at strong coupling in weak external fields', *Nucl. Phys.* **B197**, 509.

[4] Affleck, I. K. and Manton, N. S. (1982), 'Monopole pair production in a magnetic field,' *Nucl. Phys.* **B194**, 38.

[5] Ernst, F. J. (1976), 'Removal of the nodal singularity of the C-metric', *J. Math. Phys.* **17**, 515.

[6] Harrison, B. K. (1968), 'New solutions of the Einstein–Maxwell equations from old', *J. Math. Phys.* **9**, 1744.

[7] Gibbons, G. W. (1986), 'Quantized flux tubes in Einstein–Maxwell theory and noncompact internal spaces', in *Fields and Geometry 1986: Proceedings of the 22nd Karpacz Winter School of Theoretical Physics*, ed. A. Jadczyk, (World Scientific, Singapore).

[8] Garfinkle, D. and Strominger, A. (1991), 'Semiclassical Wheeler wormhole production', *Phys. Lett.* **B256**, 146.

[9] Garfinkle, D., Giddings, S. B. and Strominger, A. (1994), 'Entropy in black hole pair production', *Phys. Rev.* **D49**, 958, [gr-qc/9306023].

[10] Dowker, F., Gauntlett, J. P., Giddings, S. B. and Horowitz, G. T. (1994), 'On pair creation of extremal black holes and Kaluza-Klein monopoles', *Phys. Rev.* **D50**, 2662, [hep-th/9312172].

[11] Hawking, S. W., Horowitz, G. T. and Ross, S. F. (1995), 'Entropy, area, and black hole pairs', *Phys. Rev.* **D51**, 4302, [gr-qc/9409013].

[12] Dowker, F., Gauntlett, J. P., Kastor, D. A. and Traschen, J. (1994), 'Pair creation of dilaton black holes', *Phys. Rev.* **D49**, 2909, [hep-th/9309075].

[13] Ross, S. F. (1994), 'Pair production of black holes in a $U(1) \otimes U(1)$ theory', *Phys. Rev.* **D49**, 6599, [hep-th/9401131].

[14] Ross, S. F. (1995), 'Pair creation rate for $U(1)^2$ black holes', *Phys. Rev.* **D52**, 7089, [gr-qc/9509010].

[15] Dowker, F., Gauntlett, J. P., Gibbons, G. W. and Horowitz, G. T. (1995), 'The decay of magnetic fields in Kaluza–Klein theory', *Phys. Rev.* **52**, D6929, [hep-th/9507143].

[16] Hawking, S. W. and Ross, S. F. (1995), 'Pair production of black holes on cosmic strings', *Phys. Rev. Lett.* **75**, 3382, [gr-qc/9506020].

[17] Gregory, R. and Hindmarsh, M. (1995), 'Smooth metrics for snapping strings', *Phys. Rev.* **D52**, 5598, [gr-qc/9506054].

[18] Eardley, D. M., Horowitz, G. T., Kastor, D. A. and Traschen, J. (1995), 'Breaking cosmic strings without monopoles', *Phys. Rev. Lett.* **75**, 3390, [gr-qc/9506041].

[19] Mellor, F. and Moss, I. (1989), 'Black holes and gravitational instantons', *Class. Quant. Grav.* **6**, 1379.

[20] Mellor, F. and Moss, I. (1989), 'Black holes and quantum wormholes', *Phys. Lett.* **B222**, 361.

[21] Romans, L. J. (1992), 'Supersymmetric, cold and lukewarm black holes in cosmological Einstein–Maxwell theory', *Nucl. Phys.* **B383**, 395, [hep-th/9203018].

[22] Mann, R. B. and Ross, S. F. (1995), 'Cosmological production of charged black hole pairs', *Phys. Rev.* **D52**, 2254 , [gr-qc/9504015].

[23] Booth, I. S. and Mann, R. B. (1998), 'Complex instantons and charged rotating black hole pair creation', *Phys. Rev. Lett.* **81**, 5052, [gr-qc/9806015]; *ibid* (1999) 'Cosmological pair production of charged and rotating black holes', *Nucl. Phys.* **B539**, 267, [gr-qc/9806056].

[24] Caldwell, R. R., Chamblin, A. and Gibbons, G. W. (1996), 'Pair creation of black holes by domain walls', *Phys. Rev.* **D53**, 7103, [hep-th/9602126].

[25] Achúcarro, A., Gregory, R. and Kuijken, K. (1995), 'Abelian Higgs hair for black holes', *Phys. Rev.* **D52**, 5729 , [gr-qc/9505039].

[26] Brown, J. D. and York, J. W., Jr. (1993), 'Quasilocal energy and conserved charges derived from the gravitational action', *Phys. Rev.* **D47**, 1407.

[27] Brown, J. D. and York, J. W., Jr. (1993), 'The microcanonical functional integral. 1. the gravitational field', *Phys. Rev.* **D47**, 1420, [gr-qc/9209014].

[28] Hawking, S. W. and Horowitz, G. T. (1996), 'The gravitational Hamiltonian, action, entropy and surface terms', *Class. Quant. Grav.* **13**, 1487, [gr-qc/9501014].

[29] Hawking, S. W. and Ross, S. F. (1995), 'Duality between electric and magnetic black holes', *Phys. Rev.* **D52**, 5865, [hep-th/9504019].

[30] Vilenkin, A. (1982), 'Cosmological evolution of monopoles connected by strings', *Nucl. Phys.* **B196**, 240.

[31] Bousso, R. and Hawking, S. W. (1995), 'The probability for primordial black holes', *Phys. Rev.* **D52**, 5659, [gr-qc/9506047]; Bousso, R. and Hawking, S. W. (1996), 'Pair creation of black holes during inflation', *Phys. Rev.* **D54**, 6312 , [gr-qc/9606052].

[32] Gibbons, G. W. and Kallosh, R. E. (1995), 'Topology, entropy and Witten index of dilaton black holes', *Phys. Rev.* **D51**, 2839, [hep-th/9407118].

[33] Peet, A. W. (1998), 'The Bekenstein formula and string theory (N-brane theory)', *Class. Quant. Grav.*, **15**, 3291, [hep-th/9712253].

[34] Horowitz, G. T. (1996), 'The origin of black hole entropy in string theory', [gr-qc/9604051].

[35] Giddings, S. B. (1995), 'Why aren't black holes infinitely produced?', *Phys. Rev.* **D51**, 6860, [hep-th/9412159].

[36] Balasubramanian, V. and Kraus, P. (1999), 'A stress tensor for anti-de Sitter gravity', *Commun. Math. Phys.* **208**, 413, [hep-th/9902121].

15

Black holes at accelerators

Steve Giddings

University of California, Santa Barbara

15.1 Introduction

I'd like to begin with a birthday wish for Stephen's birthday ... in 2008. It comes in the form of an email message from the future Director of CERN, dated January 8, 2008, which reads:

```
Dear Professor Hawking,

We wish to alert you to an announcement that will be made
at a press conference tomorrow.  Since the recent start up
of LHC, both ATLAS and CMS have seen numerous events with
large numbers of jets and hard leptons, large transverse
momentum, and high sphericity.  These are consistent with
TeV-scale black hole production, and in particular with
extrapolations of your predictions for black hole radiance
to higher dimensions.  The press conference is timed to
coincide with publication of the results in Phys. Rev. Lett.

With best regards,

Director General, CERN
```

It is supplemented with a present for the rest of us:

```
PS. You may also be interested to know that there appear
to be anomalous correlations and other very interesting
structure hinting at resonances at the high-energy end
of the spectrum of decay energies. Further details will
appear in the forthcoming paper.
```

The point of my talk is to explain that, with an optimistic view of TeV-scale gravity scenarios, such an amazing development could become a

278

reality. (In more pessimistic scenarios, we have to build a higher energy machine!)

What might we hope to learn from this turn of events? First, we'd be able experimentally to confront head on a profound problem that Stephen lead us to with his discovery of black hole radiance [1]: the black hole information paradox. At the same time, we might also learn a lot of other things about the quantum mechanics of gravity, and perhaps experimentally confirm the ideas of string theory. This would be more than we've ever dared to hope for.

In outline, I'll start by describing some of the basic ideas of TeV-scale gravity, which make this remarkable scenario feasible. I'll then turn to a description of black holes on brane worlds and their production in high-energy collisions. Next is a discussion of black hole decay, where Stephen's calculations come to the fore. I'll close by describing some of the other consequences of this scenario, including what appears to be the end of investigation of short-distance physics, but may be the beginning of the exploration of the extra dimensions of space. For a more in-depth treatment of the subject of black hole production in TeV-scale gravity (and more complete references), the reader should consult the original references: [2] for the overall story (see also [3]), the more recent paper [4], which treats the classical problem of black-hole formation in high-energy collisions, and [5], which serves as another review, with further discussion of black hole creation in cosmic ray collisions with the upper atmosphere [6–10].

15.2 TeV-scale gravity

The idea that the fundamental Planck scale could be as low as the TeV scale is the essential new idea that inevitably leads to black hole production at energies above this threshold. TeV-scale gravity is a novel approach to the long-standing *hierarchy problem*: we observe what appear to be two centrally important scales in physics, the weak scale $M_W \sim 1\,\text{TeV}$, and the four-dimensional Planck scale, $M_4 \sim 1/\sqrt{G} \sim 10^{19}\,\text{GeV}$, where G is Newton's gravitational constant. What explains the huge ratio between them? Traditional views invoke supersymmetry and its breaking, but the new idea is that the *fundamental* scale in physics is the TeV scale, and that the observed weakness of gravity, corresponding to the high value of M_4, results from dilution of gravitational effects in extra dimensions of space.

To explain further, suppose that there are D total dimensions of spacetime, with coordinates x^μ, $\mu = 0, 1, 2, 3$ parameterizing the ones we see, and y^m, $m = 4, \ldots, D-4$ parameterizing the small compact ones we don't. The most general spacetime metric consistent with the very nearly Poincaré invariant world we see is

$$ds^2 = e^{2A(y)}\eta_{\mu\nu}dx^\mu dx^\nu + g_{mn}(y)dy^m dy^n , \qquad (15.1)$$

where A, conventionally called the 'warp factor', is an arbitrary function of the unseen coordinates, $\eta_{\mu\nu}$ is the Minkowski metric, and g_{mn} is an arbitrary metric for the compact dimensions. Gravitational dynamics is governed by the D-dimensional Einstein–Hilbert action, and the action for four-dimensional gravity is found by inserting (15.1), with a general four-dimensional metric $g_{\mu\nu}$, into this:

$$S_D = \frac{M_P^{D-2}}{4(2\pi)^{D-4}} \int d^D x \sqrt{-g}R \rightarrow \frac{M_4^2}{4} \int d^4 x \sqrt{-g_4(x)}R_4 + \cdots . \quad (15.2)$$

Here the extra terms on the right-hand side are cancelled by whatever matter Lagrangian is necessary to make the metric (15.1) a solution to the D-dimensional Einstein equations. Define the 'warped volume' of the extra dimensions,

$$V_W = \int d^{D-4}y \sqrt{g_{D-4}}e^{2A} . \qquad (15.3)$$

The critical equation is

$$\frac{M_4^2}{M_P^2} = \frac{M_P^{D-4}}{(2\pi)^{D-4}}V_W : \qquad (15.4)$$

the ratio of the observed and fundamental Planck scales is given by the warped volume in units of the fundamental Planck length.

We now have two options. The first one is the conventional one: assume that $M_P \sim M_4 \sim 10^{19}$ GeV, which means

$$V_W \sim \frac{1}{M_P^{D-4}} . \qquad (15.5)$$

The new alternative arises if $M_P \sim 1$ TeV $\ll M_4$, and this can be attained if the warped volume is for some reason very large:

$$V_W \gg \frac{1}{M_P^{D-4}} \sim \frac{1}{\text{TeV}^{D-4}} . \qquad (15.6)$$

There are two approaches to achieving this. The first is the original idea of [11]: simply take the volume to be large. A second approach is to take the warp factor to be large; a toy model of this type was introduced in [12]. An obvious objection then arises, which is particularly clear in the large volume scenario: the size of the extra dimensions ranges from around a millimetre for $D = 6$ to $10\,\mathrm{fm}$ for $D = 10$, and gauge interactions have already been tested far past this, to around $10^{-3}\,\mathrm{fm}$, for example in the context of precise electroweak measurements. Fortunately string theory has a made-to-order solution to this problem, which is the notion of a D-brane. For example, suppose that there are six extra dimensions, but that there are some three-branes present within them: ordinary matter and gauge fields may be composed of open strings, whose ends are restricted to move in the three-dimensional space defined by the brane, whereas gravity, which is always transmitted by closed string exchange, will propagate in all of the dimensions. String theory realizations of such 'brane-world' scenarios with large volume were described in [13], and string solutions with large warping were derived in [14]. We still lack completely realistic solutions with all the features to reproduce the known physics of the Standard Model at low energies, but ideas on this subject are still developing, or it may even be that such a scenario is realized outside of string theory.

15.3 Black holes on brane worlds

Suppose, therefore, that we live on such a brane world. If we collide two quarks with sufficiently high energy, they should form a black hole. Being a gravitational object, this black hole will extend off the brane, as pictured in Figure 15.1. Study of such black holes is greatly simplified by using two approximations. The first is to assume that the size of the black hole, r_h, is much less than the size of the extra dimensions or curvature scales of the extra dimensions, denoted R_c in the figure. This is typically true since the extra dimensions are 'large'. The second is the 'probe-brane' approximation: in general the brane produces a gravitational field, but we neglect this field. This is justified if the black hole is massive as compared with the brane tension scale, which we expect to be approximately the Planck mass. So for large, but not too large, black holes, these two approximations reduce the problem to that of describing solutions in D flat dimensions.

Black holes created in particle collisions will typically have some angular momentum; spinning black hole solutions in D dimensions were first studied by Myers and Perry, in [15]. The horizon radius, Hawking temperature, and entropy of these black holes is given in terms of their mass M and spin J; in the $J \to 0$ limit, these take the form

$$r_h(M, J) \to \text{constant} \cdot M^{\frac{1}{D-3}} , \tag{15.7}$$

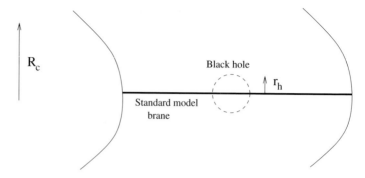

Fig. 15.1. A schematic representation of a black hole on a brane world. Gauge fields and matter are confined to the brane, but the black hole extends into all of the dimensions. We consider the approximation where the black hole size is small as compared with characteristic geometric scales.

$$T_H(M, J) \to \frac{\text{constant}}{r_h} \tag{15.8}$$

and

$$S_{BH} \to \text{constant} \cdot M^{\frac{D-2}{D-3}} . \tag{15.9}$$

We'd like to estimate the rate at which such black holes would be produced in high-energy accelerators. The energy frontier is currently at proton machines. At the fundamental level, proton collisions are collisions among their constituents, quarks and gluons, generically called partons. In order to compute a rate, we need to know the density of partons of a given energy in the proton, or *parton distribution function*, and the cross-section for a pair of partons to make a black hole. Estimates of the parton distribution function are well known, but the black hole cross-section is not.

The cross-section can, however, be estimated by making a key observation: for large centre-of-mass energies of the partons, the formation process should be essentially classical. Indeed, consider a collision of two partons, each of energy $E/2$. If they pass closely enough, we expect them to form a big black hole, with horizon radius determined by E. For $E \gg M_P$, the curvature should be very weak at the black hole horizon, quantum gravity effects should be negligible, and a classical treatment should hold.

An estimate of the cross-section follows from Thorne's hoop conjecture [16], which suggests that if energy E is concentrated in a region less than the corresponding Schwarzschild radius, $r_h(E)$, a black hole forms. If black holes form for impact parameters less than $r_h(E)$, this then indicates that

that the cross-section is given approximately by

$$\sigma \sim \pi r_h^2(E) \, . \tag{15.10}$$

Indeed, recently Eardley and I have revisited the classical problem of black hole production in high energy collisions [4], which was investigated some years ago for the case of zero impact parameter by Penrose [17] and D'Eath and Payne[18–20]. In particular, Penrose found a closed-trapped surface in the geometry describing the head-on collision of two Aichelberg–Sexl solutions, and this implies that a black hole of mass at least $E/\sqrt{2}$ forms. We extended this analysis to non-zero impact parameter. In the case of four dimensions, we explicitly found that a trapped surface forms for impact parameter $b \lesssim 1.6E$; this gives an estimated cross-section about 65% the naive value (15.10). We also find the area of the trapped surface, providing a lower bound on the mass of the resulting black hole. While the $D > 4$ problem has not been explicitly solved, we did reduce it to boundary-value problem for Poisson's equation, which corresponds to a small displacement soap bubble problem. We expect this to yield similar results to those in $D = 4$. One can also explicitly see that the trapped surface forms before the collision – and consists of two discs in the collision surface connected by a catenoid between them,[1] as well as showing that the trapped surfaces can be deformed away from the curvature singularity at the centre of the Aichelberg–Sexl solution [4]. This builds a fairly convincing case for black hole formation, with a cross-section not too far from the estimate (15.10).

Current experimental bounds [21–23] on the Planck mass place it at $M_P \gtrsim 1.1$–0.8 TeV for $D = 6$–10. The LHC has a design centre-of-mass energy of 14 TeV. Suppose we make the optimistic assumption that indeed $M_P \sim 1$ TeV (and $D = 10$). One other important point is that one does not expect to create legitimate semiclassical black holes until one is way above the Planck scale, say at a minimum mass of 5–10 TeV. The results are quite impressive [2, 3]: if the minimum mass for a black hole is 5 TeV, then LHC should produce black holes at the rate of about one *per second*. This would qualify LHC as a black hole factory, without bending standard nomenclature too far. If the minimum mass is 10 TeV, then we'd still produce black holes at the rate of about three per day.

Furthermore, from (15.10) and (15.7) we see that the cross-section for black hole production grows as

$$\sigma \sim E^{2/D-3} \, , \tag{15.11}$$

and so becomes even more dominant at higher energies.

---

[1] I thank L. Lindblom, M. Scheel, and K. Thorne for conversations on this. This construction has been subsequently rediscovered in [24].

15.4 Black hole decay and signatures

The resulting black holes will decay in several phases. When the horizon first forms, it will be very asymmetric and time dependent. The first thing that should happen is that the black hole sheds its hair, in a phase we term *balding*. It does so by classically emitting gauge and gravitational radiation. The amount of energy that can be emitted in this phase will be bounded given the bound on the minimum mass of the black hole resulting from the calculation of the area of the trapped surface. This may be improved by perturbative methods, as was done by D'Eath and Payne in [18–20]. A rough estimate is that somewhere between 15 and 40% of the initial collision energy of the partons is shed in this phase. The relevant decay time for this phase should be $\mathcal{O}(r_h)$. We expect the black hole to lose any charge rapidly as well. At the end of this phase we are left with a Kerr black hole with some mass and angular momentum.

Next quantum emission becomes relevant, and Stephen's famous calculation comes to the fore. The black hole will Hawking radiate. As shown by Page [25], it first does so by preferentially radiating particles in its equatorial plane, shedding its spin. We call the corresponding phase *spin-down*. Page's four-dimensional calculations indicate that about 25% of the original mass of the black hole is lost during spin-down; we might expect the higher-dimensional situation to be similar. However, an important homework assignment is for someone to redo Page's analysis of decay of a spinning black hole in the higher-dimensional context, and fill in the details.[2]

At the end of spindown, a Schwarzschild black hole remains, and will continue to evaporate through the *Schwarzschild phase*. This phase ends when Stephen's calculations fail, once the Schwarzschild radius becomes comparable to the D-dimensional Planck length, and quantum gravity effects become important.[3] Based on Page's analysis, roughly 75% of the original black hole mass might be emitted in this phase. As Stephen taught us, a prominent hallmark of this phase is that the emission is thermal, up to grey-body factors, at any given time. Based on this, one may estimate the resulting energy spectrum of particles in the final state, as well as estimating the ratios of different kinds of particles produced: hadrons, leptons, photons, etc.

The decay comes to an end with the *Planck phase*, the final decay of the Planck-size remnant of the black hole. This decay is sensitive to full-blown strongly coupled quantum gravity, and thus its details cannot yet

---

[2] Since the conference, some progress on this has been made in [26].

[3] In string theory there is another scale, the string length, at which the evaporation may be modified even earlier, due to effects stemming from the finite string size.

be predicted. A reasonable expectation is that the Planck-size remnant would emit a few quanta with characteristic energy $\sim M_P$. This end of the spectrum is where much of the fascination lies: we can hope for experimental input on quantum gravity and/or string theory, and may see concrete evidence for the breakdown of spacetime structure, or as Stephen has advocated [27], even of quantum mechanics.

By putting this all together, we can infer some of the signatures that would evidence black hole production if it takes place at a future accelerator. Decay of a black hole should produce of order S_{BH} primary hard particles, with typical energies given by the Hawking temperature T_H, thus ranging over roughly 100 GeV–1 TeV. Creation of primary particles is essentially democratic among species: we create an equal number of each colour, spin, and flavour of quark, of each flavour and spin of lepton, of each helicity state of the gauge bosons, etc. These ratios are then changed through QCD jet formation, or decays of the primary particles. For example, this leads to a rough estimate that we would see five times as many hadrons as leptons. Simply the presence of the hard leptons would be one notable signature. Moreover, most of the Hawking radiation is isotropic in the black hole's rest frame, which can't be highly boosted with respect to the lab frame. These events would have a high sphericity. Finally, closer study may reveal the dipole pattern characteristic of the spindown phase.

So far no one has thought of events based on standard model physics or any of its extensions that would mimic these signatures: if black holes are produced, their decays should stand out and be discovered.

Nature already provides us with particle collisions exceeding the reach of the LHC: cosmic rays hit the upper atmosphere with centre-of-mass energies ranging up to roughly 400 TeV. We might ask if we could even see black holes produced by cosmic rays. Unfortunately, the observed flux of ultra-high energy cosmic rays is believed to consist of either protons or nuclei, and even at the relevant energies, QCD cross-sections dominate the cross-section for black hole production by a factor of roughly a billion. So most of the hadronic cosmic rays will scatter via QCD processes before they can make black holes. A rough estimate is that these cosmic rays would produce 100 black holes per year over the entire surface of the Earth, which is clearly too small of a rate to measure [5].

However, it is also believed that there should be a neutrino component of the ultra-high energy cosmic ray background; this would for example arise from ultra-high energy protons scattering off the 3K photons in the microwave background to resonantly produce Δs, which produce neutrinos in their decays [28–30]. Neutrinos interact only weakly, and at ultra-high energies it turns out that black hole production is roughly competitive with rates for neutrinos to interact via standard model processes. Taking existing neutrino flux estimates at face value, this suggests that neutrinos could produce black holes at rates around [5–10]

$$\frac{\text{several black holes}}{\text{yr km}^3(\text{H}_2\text{O})} \; . \tag{15.12}$$

Detectors that are currently or soon to be operating, such as the HiRes Fly's Eye, Auger, Icecube and OWL/Airwatch, are at a level of sensitivity where they might start to see black hole events, if the assumptions about the neutrino fluxes are correct.

15.5 The future of high energy physics

High energy physics is a logical extension of a longstanding human quest to understand nature at an ever more fundamental level. Once we reach the Planck scale, things may change; shorter distances than the Planck length may well not make sense. However, physics is an experimental subject, and ultimately we might expect to address the question of shorter-distance physics experimentally. However, once black hole production commences, exploration of shorter distances seems to come to an end.

Specifically, if we want to investigate physics at a distance scale Δx that is shorter than the Planck length, the uncertainty principle tells us we should scatter particles at energies $E \sim 1/\Delta x > M_P$. But if they indeed scatter at distances Δx, they will be inside a black hole. Once a black hole forms, the outside observer cannot witness the scattering process directly – all we see is the Hawking radiation that the black hole sheds. Short distance physics is cloaked by black hole formation, and thus investigation of short distances through high energy physics comes to an end.

Some of our experimental colleagues might consider this a dismal future. However, there is another prospect that we can offer them. As they increase the energy, they will be making bigger and bigger black holes. At some distance scale, these black holes will start to become sensitive to the shapes and sizes of the extra dimensions, or to other features such as parallel branes. When black holes start extending far enough off our brane to probe these features, their properties, such as their production rate, their decay spectrum, and other properties, change. So by doing black hole physics at increasing energies, experimentalists can reach further off the brane that we are otherwise confined to, and start to explore the geography of the extra dimensions of space. This could certainly continue to yield exciting experimental discoveries!

Stephen, I hope you had a happy 60th birthday, but I'm wishing you an even more exciting 66th birthday!

Acknowledgements

I'd like to thank my collaborators D. Eardley, E. Katz and S. Thomas for the opportunity to explore these fascinating ideas together. This work was supported in part by the Department of Energy under Contract DE-FG-03-91ER40618, and was written up at Stanford University, under partial support from David and Lucile Packard Foundation Fellowship 2000-13856.

References

[1] Hawking, S. W. (1975), 'Particle creation by black holes', *Commun. Math. Phys.* **43**, 199.

[2] Giddings, S. B. and Thomas, S. (2002), 'High energy colliders as black hole factories: the end of short distance physics', *Phys. Rev.* **D65**, 056010, [hep-ph/0106219].

[3] Dimopoulos, S. and Landsberg, G. (2001), 'Black holes at the LHC', *Phys. Rev. Lett.* **87**, 161602, [hep-ph/0106295].

[4] Eardley, D. M. and Giddings, S. B. (2002), 'Classical black hole production in high-energy collisions', [gr-qc/0201034].

[5] Giddings, S. B. (2001), 'Black hole production in TeV-scale gravity, and the future of high energy physics', in *Proc. of the APS/DPF/DPB Summer Study on the Future of Particle Physics (Snowmass 2001)* eds R. Davidson and C. Quigg., [hep-ph/0110127].

[6] Feng, J. L. and Shapere, A. D. (2001), 'Black hole production by cosmic rays', [hep-ph/0109106].

[7] Dorfan, D., Giddings, S. B., Rizzo, T. and Thomas, S., unpublished.

[8] Anchordoqui, L. and Goldberg, H. (2001), 'Experimental signature for black hole production in neutrino air showers', [hep-ph/0109242].

[9] Emparan, R., Masip M. and Rattazzi, R. (2001), 'Cosmic rays as probes of large extra dimensions and TeV gravity', [hep-ph/0109287].

[10] Ringwald, A. and Tu, H. (2002), 'Collider versus cosmic ray sensitivity to black hole production', *Phys. Lett.* **B525**, 135, [hep-ph/0111042].

[11] Arkani-Hamed, N., Dimopoulos, S. and Dvali, G. R. (1998), 'The hierarchy problem and new dimensions at a millimeter', *Phys. Lett.* **B429**, 263, [hep-ph/9803315].

[12] Randall, L. and Sundrum, R. (1999), 'A large mass hierarchy from a small extra dimension', *Phys. Rev. Lett.* **83**, 3370, [hep-ph/9905221].

[13] Antoniadis, I., Arkani-Hamed, N., Dimopoulos S. and Dvali, G. R. (1998), 'New dimensions at a millimeter to a Fermi and superstrings at a TeV', *Phys. Lett.* **B436**, 257, [hep-ph/9804398].

[14] Giddings, S. B., Kachru S. and Polchinski, J. (2001), 'Hierarchies from fluxes in string compactifications', [hep-th/0105097].

[15] Myers, R. C. and Perry, M. J. (1986), 'Black holes in higher dimensional space-times', *Annals Phys.* **172**, 304.

[16] Thorne, K. S. (1972), 'Nonspherical Gravitational Collapse: A Short Review', in J. R. Klauder, (1972), *Magic Without Magic*, (W. H. Freeman, San Francisco), 231–258.

[17] Penrose, R. (1974), *unpublished*.

[18] D'Eath, P. D. and Payne, P. N. (1992), 'Gravitational radiation in high speed black hole collisions. 1. Perturbation treatment of the axisymmetric speed of light collision', *Phys. Rev.* **D46**, 658.

[19] D'Eath, P. D. and Payne, P. N. (1992), 'Gravitational radiation in high speed black hole collisions. 2. Reduction to two independent variables and calculation of the second order news function', *Phys. Rev.* **D46**, 675.

[20] D'Eath, P. D. and Payne, P. N. (1992), 'Gravitational radiation in high speed black hole collisions. 3. Results and conclusions', *Phys. Rev.* **D46**, 694.

[21] Peskin, M. E. (2001), 'Theoretical summary', [hep-ph/0002041].

[22] Giudice, G. F., Rattazzi R. and Wells, J. D. (1999), 'Quantum gravity and extra dimensions at high-energy colliders', *Nucl. Phys.* **B544**, 3, [hep-ph/9811291].

[23] Mirabelli, E. A., Perelstein, M. and Peskin, M. E. (1999), 'Collider signatures of new large space dimensions', *Phys. Rev. Lett.* **82**, 2236, [hep-ph/9811337].

[24] Yoshino, H. and Nambu, Y. (2002), 'High-energy head-on collisions of particles and hoop conjecture', [gr-qc/0204060].

[25] Page, D. N. (1976), 'Particle emission rates from a black hole. II. Massless particles from a rotating hole', *Phys. Rev.* **D14**, 3260.

[26] Kanti, P. and March-Russell, J. (2002), 'Calculable corrections to brane black hole decay. I: The scalar case', [hep-ph/0203223], and in progress.

[27] Hawking, S. W. (1976), 'Breakdown of predictability in gravitational collapse', *Phys. Rev.* **D14**, 2460.

[28] Greisen, K. (1966), 'End to the cosmic ray spectrum?', *Phys. Rev. Lett.* **16**, 748.

[29] Stecker, F. W. (1979), 'Diffuse fluxes of cosmic high-energy neutrinos', *Astrophys. J.* **228**, 919.

[30] Hill, C. T. and Schramm, D. N. (1985), 'The ultrahigh-energy cosmic ray spectrum', *Phys. Rev.* **D31**, 564.

Part 4

Hawking radiation

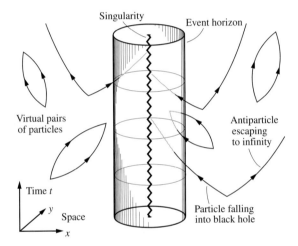

It seems that the gravitational field of a black hole will create particles and emit them to infinity at just the rate that one would expect if the black hole were an ordinary body with a temperature in geometric units of $\kappa/2\pi$, where κ is the 'surface gravity' of the black hole.

Nature, 1974

16

Black holes and string theory

Malcolm Perry

Centre for Mathematical Sciences, University of Cambridge

One of Stephen Hawking's many profound contributions to gravitational physics has been the discovery that black holes admit a thermodynamic description. One expects that a complete quantum theory of gravitation would allow one to produce a microscopic description of black hole thermodynamics. String theory produces an explanation of why there is a graviton, and enables us to calculate scattering amplitudes that include gravitons without running into the traditional difficulties of quantum gravity. In string theory one does not encounter difficulties with ultraviolet divergences or renormalizability as it is a finite theory, and also there are no apparent problems with either unitarity or causality. One should therefore hope that string theory provides a resolution to the problems of black hole physics that seem to be quantum mechanical in nature. In this article we briefly review some of the successes and puzzles of string theory as they relate to black hole physics.

Black holes were first discovered in Newtonian gravitation by John Michell in 1784 [1]. He was then rector of Thornhill in Yorkshire, although previously he had been Professor of Geology at Cambridge and a Fellow of Queen's College. He argued that it was possible for a star to become so dense that its escape velocity was greater than the speed of light. He knew a value for the speed of light as he was familiar with the book of Priestley [2] who popularized the results of Romer almost a century earlier. He computed the familiar result, that if the radius of the gravitating body of mass M was less than a critical value r_s with

$$r_s = \frac{2GM}{c^2} \tag{16.1}$$

then light could not escape from its surface. The situation in general relativity is roughly similar. Objects whose linear dimensions are less than the Schwarzschild radius given by (1) are believed to form an apparent horizon [3], and therefore the spacetime will contain regions of space that one cannot directly probe.

In gravitational collapse, one envisages a star that has exhausted its nuclear fuel and starts to undergo gravitational collapse. One possible endpoint of this process is a white dwarf, where the star is a degenerate electron gas. Such a configuration is unstable if the mass exceeds the Chandrasekhar mass [4] of around 1.4 solar masses. A second possibility is a neutron star where the material is a degenerate gas of neutrons (or possibly quarks), but again these objects cannot be stable if their mass exceeds the Oppenheimer–Volkov limit [5] of around 2 solar masses. Objects of greater mass than these must inevitably either lose mass in the collapse process or become black holes.

A black hole is characterized by a spherical event horizon that divides the spacetime into two distinct regions: the domain of outer communication, which is the region from which one can always escape to infinity along causal paths, and the black hole from which one cannot escape into the domain of outer communication. The collapsing body that forms the black hole must eventually give rise to a singularity. The existence of the singularity is guaranteed by the singularity theorems of Hawking and Penrose [6]. At a singularity one typically finds that the curvature tensor blows up, and in the context of classical general relativity, one should regard this as being the boundary of spacetime. In classical theory, one generally regards singularities as being unphysical and an indication that the theory has broken down. It is hoped that a quantum theory of gravitation would enable us to describe black holes in a way that would avoid such difficulties.

Stephen Hawking discovered that black holes are quantum mechanically unstable [7]. The event horizon produces black body radiation at a temperature

$$T = \frac{\hbar \kappa}{2\pi} \qquad (16.2)$$

where κ is the surface gravity of the horizon. (We use units here such that $G = c = 1$.) Classically, $\hbar \to 0$ and so $T \to 0$. So in the classical limit there is no radiation coming from the horizon. It should be noted that the nature of the radiation does not depend on the details of how the black hole forms, but only on the geometry of the black hole equilibrium state through κ.

Equilibrium black holes states are completely specified by a very small number of parameters. In four spacetime dimensions, a stable isolated black hole is described by a member of the Kerr–Newman metric. This is the physical content of black hole uniqueness theorems [8]. A knowledge of the mass M, electric charge Q and angular momentum J is sufficient to determine all properties of a black hole.

The first law of black hole mechanics [9] describes how the energy of a black hole characterized by M, Q and J changes as result of some process that alters these quantities infinitesimally to $M+dM, Q+dQ$ and $J+dJ$. It states that

$$dM = \frac{\kappa dA}{8\pi} + \Phi dQ + \Omega dJ, \tag{16.3}$$

where A is the geometric area of the event horizon, Φ is the electrostatic potential of the black hole and Ω is its angular velocity. This result is startlingly similar to the first law of thermodynamics. In fact, if one identifies the temperature as given by (16.2) then the first law of black hole mechanics becomes the first law of thermodynamics provided that one assumes that the entropy S of a black hole is given by

$$S = \frac{A}{4\hbar}. \tag{16.4}$$

According to the Boltzmann view of entropy as arising from a number of different microscopic states that have the same macroscopic properties, the density of states W is given by

$$W = e^S. \tag{16.5}$$

For a non-rotating uncharged black hole of mass M

$$S = \frac{4\pi M^2}{\hbar}. \tag{16.6}$$

In the limit as $\hbar \to 0$, $S \to \infty$, which reflects the fact that a classical black hole has no memory of how it was formed. Classical theory is a bad place to start to try to develop intuition about how one should explain black hole entropy. The only thing inside a black hole is the singularity itself. How can a singularity have any structure, let alone sufficient microscopic configurations to explain the entropy? It seems completely impossible and so it is to string theory that we will turn for an explanation of the entropy.

However, black hole physics has other difficulties that a quantum theory is expected to explain. Perhaps the simplest to state is the most enigmatic. Let us consider a black hole formed by the collapse of some object. Shortly after formation, the black hole will settle down to a spacetime given the Kerr–Newman metric, and will start to produce thermal radiation. For a non-rotating uncharged black hole of mass M, the temperature is given by

$$T = \frac{\hbar}{8\pi M}. \tag{16.7}$$

As the black hole radiates, it loses energy and its temperature increases. Eventually it will radiate away all of its energy and presumably disappear, leaving just thermal radiation. The initial state of the system prior to gravitational collapse can be chosen to be a pure quantum state, with zero von Neumann entropy. However, the final state being basically thermal, is a mixed state and thus will have large von Neumann entropy. In quantum mechanics, there is a unitary time evolution operator. Time evolution will therefore preserve von Neumann entropy. Thus there is a conflict between the simple picture of a black hole as a thermodynamical system, and quantum mechanics as usually presented. This is the so-called information paradox, first discussed by Hawking [10].

There are three basic types of resolution of this paradox that have been proposed. The first is to suppose that black holes do not completely disappear, but leave behind some kind of remnant. This remnant is supposed to contain all of the quantum mechanical information that is in the initial state prior to the formation of the black hole. This information most likely remains hidden from external observers. The basic difficulty with this idea is that it requires very light objects to be able to store huge amounts of information in a very tiny region of space. There is no known mechanism by which this can happen.

A second class of proposal is to suppose that the radiation from the hole is not precisely thermal, but only appears thermal in the semiclassical approximation. All of the quantum mechanical information in the initial state is encoded in the radiation. However, this type of explanation has the difficulty that it does not respect causality. The information about the initial state certainly finds itself inside the black hole together with the collapsing matter. It cannot reappear in the domain of outer communication without being able to propagate acausally. There again appears to be no theoretical framework for discussion of such processes.

A third class of proposal is to modify quantum mechanics so as to allow non-unitary time evolution. In conventional quantum mechanics, any state can be described by a density matrix ρ, and time evolution is generated by a Hamiltonian H. The Schrödinger equation describing time evolution is

$$\dot{\rho} = -\frac{i}{\hbar}[H, \rho] \tag{16.8}$$

where the dot indicates time derivative. If evolution is of this form, then the von Neumann entropy is constant and there is a conventional S-matrix. The proposal is to replace this equation by some other time evolution law that does not conserve the von Neumann entropy and gives rise to a superscattering operator $ that relates an initial density matrix

ρ_i to a final density matrix ρ_f by

$$\rho_f = \$\rho_i \qquad (16.9)$$

by analogy with the definition of the S-matrix. No satisfactory scheme to implement this suggestion has ever been proposed.

The resolution of the information paradox is one of the most important problems in gravitational physics. There have been vast number of suggestions about how to attempt to resolve it, but it is fair to say that there has been very little progress. Despite that, feelings can be very strong about how one should attempt to resolve the problem. Perhaps Stephen Hawking's only vice is that he occasionally gambles. In a celebrated bet, he and Kip Thorne reveal themselves as disbelievers in the second class of proposals. A copy of the bet can be found on a wall of the Bridge annex at Caltech, outside Kip's office. It is reproduced below.

Can it be true that the converse is also true? Perturbative string theory on a circle of radius R is equivalent to string theory on a circle of radius $1/R$. The non-perturbative dualities of M theory incorporate this idea at a deeper level and the loop expansion of string theory has long been known to render ambiguous the distinction between infrared and ultraviolet divergences, and this feature has re-emerged recently in the context of non-commutative geometry.

String theory does not yet have capability to resolve the information paradox, but in the remainder of this contribution, I will present three examples of a stringy description of entropy for gravitating systems.

The first is a description of some black holes that are supersymmetric [11, 12]. The example is five dimensional, but this restriction is just to make the model easy to explain. Low-energy type IIB string theory is described by ten-dimensional supergravity theory which contains amongst other things a graviton, a dilaton ϕ, and a Kalb–Ramond field with potential B_{ab}. Suppose that there is a time coordinate t and nine spatial coordinates $x_1, \ldots, x_9$. Five dimensions are compactified on a torus so that x_5, x_6, x_7, x_8 and x_9 are wrapped up on circles. In type IIB string theory, one finds that there can be $D1$ and $D5$ branes. The D-branes are surfaces on which strings can terminate with Dirichlet boundary conditions. Dp-branes are $(p+1)$-dimensional objects in string theory that can carry energy and momentum, and extend over p spatial dimensions and a time direction. Let us suppose that there are N_5 $D5$-branes wrapped on the five torus in the $x_5, \ldots, x_9$ directions, and N_1 $D1$-branes wrapped on the circle in the x_9 direction. Let us also suppose that there are N open strings ending on the $D1$ and $D5$ branes carrying total momentum N/R_9 in the x_9 direction, which has Kaluza–Klein radius R_9. Because the branes carry momentum in the x_9 direction, they will have a Kaluza–Klein

Whereas Stephen Hawking and Kip Thorne firmly believe that information swallowed by a black hole is forever hidden from the outside universe, and can never be revealed even as the black hole evaporates and completely disappears,

And whereas John Preskill firmly believes that a mechanism for the information to be released by the evaporating black hole must and will be found in the correct theory of quantum gravity,

Therefore Preskill offers, and Hawking/Thorne accept, a wager that:

When an initial pure quantum state undergoes gravitational collapse to form a black hole, the final state at the end of black hole evaporation will always be a pure quantum state.

The loser(s) will reward the winner(s) with an encyclopedia of the winner's choice, from which information can be recovered at will.

Stephen W. Hawking & Kip S. Thorne   John P. Preskill

Pasadena, California, 6 February 1997

Fig. 16.1. The formal bet as signed by the participants and on display at Caltech.

charge in that direction. The spacetime metric for this set up is given by the metric

$$
\begin{aligned}
ds^2 = {}& H_1^{-1/2} H_5^{-1/2} (-dt^2 + dx_9^2 + H_N (dt - dx_9)^2) \\
& + H_1^{1/2} H_5^{1/2} (dx_1^2 + dx_2^2 + dx_3^2 + dx_4^2) \\
& + H_1^{1/2} H_5^{-1/2} (dx_5^2 + dx_6^2 + dx_7^2 + dx_8^2),
\end{aligned}
\tag{16.10}
$$

with dilaton

$$
\phi = \phi_0 + \frac{1}{2} \ln H_1 - \frac{1}{2} \ln H_5
\tag{16.11}
$$

where ϕ_0 is a constant that determines the string coupling constant, and the only non-vanishing component of the Kalb–Ramond potential is

$$
B_{09} = \frac{1}{2H_1}.
\tag{16.12}
$$

H_1, H_5 and H_N are harmonic functions in the non-compact part of the space spanned by x_1, x_2, x_3 and x_4. Putting

$$x^2 = x_1^2 + x_2^2 + x_3^2 + x_4^2, \tag{16.13}$$

then

$$H_1 = 1 + \frac{c_1 N_1}{x^2}, \tag{16.14}$$

$$H_5 = 1 + \frac{c_5 N_5}{x^2}, \tag{16.15}$$

$$H_n = \frac{c_N N}{x^2} \tag{16.16}$$

where c_1, c_5 and c_N are constants. Their precise values do not concern us here. Dimensional reduction to five dimensions gives a spacetime that is a charged black hole. At $x^2 = 0$ the metric has a coordinate singularity which when resolved is in fact the black hole event horizon. The solution is supersymmetric and thus has zero temperature. Since the solution is supersymmetric, one expects the metric not to receive corrections from quantum effects. Thus we may rely on results found from this spacetime. A calculation of the entropy from the area of the event horizon gives

$$S = 2\pi \sqrt{N_1 N_5 N}. \tag{16.17}$$

This formula has a microscopic explanation in terms of counting states. The $D1$ and $D5$ branes can be regarded as heavy and fixed. The degeneracy arises from the number of light string states consistent with this configuration. In the limit as N becomes large, open strings with both ends on $D5$-branes or on $D1$-branes become massive. The only light strings are those stretching between $D1$ and $D5$-branes. One can count up the number of ways of arranging N strings to have one end on N_1 $D1$-branes and the other on N_5 $D5$-branes. For large N, after using the Hardy–Ramanujan formula for the asymptotic form of the number of partitions of an integer one finds that

$$W \sim \exp 2\pi \sqrt{N_1 N_5 N} \tag{16.18}$$

in perfect agreement with the geometric estimate.

We now move on to generalize this picture to the case of some non-extreme black holes [13]. The idea is to include both branes and antibranes in the picture. The metric we consider is

$$\begin{aligned} ds^2 &= H_1^{-1/2} H_5^{-1/2} (-dt^2 + dx_9^2 + H_N (\cosh \sigma dt + \sinh \sigma dx_9)^2) \\ &\quad + H_1^{1/2} H_5^{1/2} \left(\frac{dr^2}{(1 - r_0^2/r^2)} + r^2 d\Omega_3^2 \right) \\ &\quad + H_1^{1/2} H_5^{-1/2} (dx_5^2 + dx_6^2 + dx_7^2 + dx_8^2). \end{aligned} \tag{16.19}$$

Note that the second term on the right hand side in brackets has re-placed the flat space spanning the directions x_1, x_2, x_3 and x_4 by one that is only conformally flat and where $d\Omega_3^2$ is the line element on the unit 3-sphere. The three harmonic functions are now

$$H_1 = 1 + \frac{r_0^2 \sinh^2 \alpha}{r^2}, \tag{16.20}$$

$$H_5 = 1 + \frac{r_0^2 \sinh^2 \gamma}{r^2}, \tag{16.21}$$

and

$$H_N = \frac{r_0^2}{r^2}. \tag{16.22}$$

r_0 is a scale factor that controls the overall scale of the hole. There are three charges associated with the gauge fields of the problem, Q_1 with the electric part of the Kalb–Ramond field, Q_5 with the magnetic part. As before, we take the x_5, x_6, x_7, x_8 and x_9 directions to be wrapped up to form a five torus, so there will be a Kaluza–Klein gauge charge Q associated with the x_9 direction. In a way that is very similar to the previous example, we can regard Q_1 as arising from N_1 D1-branes and $\bar{N}_1$ anti D1-branes. Similarly Q_5 comes from N_5 D5-branes and $\bar{N}_5$ anti D5-branes. Lastly, Q comes from $N + \bar{N}$ open strings carrying N units of momentum in the positive x_9 direction and $\bar{N}$ unites in the negative x_9 direction. In terms of the variables appearing the metric,

$$Q_1 = N_1 - \bar{N}_1 = (\text{const}) \, r_0^2 \sinh 2\alpha, \tag{16.23}$$

$$Q_5 = N_5 - \bar{N}_5 = (\text{const}) \, r_0^2 \sinh 2\gamma, \tag{16.24}$$

$$Q = N - \bar{N} = (\text{const}) \, r_0^2 \sinh 2\sigma. \tag{16.25}$$

This metric is not supersymmetric and therefore may well receive quantum corrections. Nevertheless, it is certainly a superposition of various branes and tends to the previous metric when $\bar{N}_1, \bar{N}_5$ and $\bar{N}$ all vanish. If one looks at the compactified metric, then it is a black hole with temperature T given by

$$T = \frac{1}{2\pi r_0} \operatorname{sech} \alpha \operatorname{sech} \gamma \operatorname{sech} \sigma, \tag{16.26}$$

and mass M,

$$M = \text{const}(N_1 + \bar{N}_1) + \text{const}(N_5 + \bar{N}_5) + \text{const}(N + \bar{N}). \tag{16.27}$$

Lastly, the entropy takes the suggestive form

$$S = (\text{const}) \, r_0^3 \cosh \alpha \cosh \gamma \cosh \sigma$$
$$= 2\pi(\sqrt{N_1} + \sqrt{\bar{N}_1})(\sqrt{N_5} + \sqrt{\bar{N}_5})(\sqrt{N} + \sqrt{\bar{N}}). \tag{16.28}$$

There is no known microscopic derivation of this formula. However, it is exactly what one would expect if one took a thermodynamic ensemble of N_1 and N_5 branes, $\bar{N}_1$ and $\bar{N}_5$ anti-branes and N strings and $\bar{N}$ anti-strings with mass given by (16.27) and temperature (16.26). Thus the black hole looks like a system of branes in thermal equilibrium, which is rather what one might have expected given the first example. Obviously much more work needs to be done in order to see that string theory can give a complete picture of black hole entropy. Further details of these results will appear elsewhere [14].

Given the success of the brane picture, one might start to wonder if string theory can also explain the entropy of cosmological horizons. As was first shown by Gibbons and Hawking [15], de Sitter space has a cosmological event horizon that has a temperature and entropy given by (16.2) and (16.4) respectively, where κ is now the surface gravity of the horizon. In five dimensions, the metric of de Sitter space is

$$ds^2 = -dt^2 + a^2 \cosh^2 \left(\frac{t}{a}\right) d\Omega_4^2, \tag{16.29}$$

where the parameter a is the de Sitter radius and $d\Omega_4^2$ is the line element on a unit 4-sphere. The surface gravity of the cosmological horizon κ is just a^{-1}. The area of the horizon is $A = 2\pi^2 a^3$. The principal difficulty is that no non-singular compactifications of either M-theory or IIA or IIB string theories give rise to de Sitter space [16, 17]. However, one can find a rather peculiar type of string theory, so-called II^* theory. One can derive it from conventional type II string theory by compactifying the time direction on a circle, performing a T-duality, and then taking the limit as the resultant becomes infinitely large. In this way, type IIA string theory becomes type II^*B string theory, and type IIB string theory becomes type II^*A. The gauge field structure of the theories is the same as the conventional theories. However, the signs of the kinetic energy terms of the RR fields is opposite to the usual ones [18]. This change of signs might mean that the theory is pathological in some way as it appears to give rise to ghosts. However, since it is the dual of a theory that is well-defined, as such it is not so obvious that it has any type of pathology.

In type II^*B theory, there is a self-dual five-form field strength. Its sign is such that one finds a solution of the field equations of the form $H^5 \otimes dS_5$, where H^5 is hyperbolic five space (of constant negative curvature), and dS_5 is five dimensional de Sitter space. This is the analogue of $S^5 \otimes AdS_5$ in conventional type IIB theory. Like that system, the present one is also maximally supersymmetric. One therefore does not expect to find quantum corrections to leading semiclassical results. Of course, this spacetime has no compact directions. However it can be given a Kaluza–Klein interpretation by rendering the H^5 compact. One identifies H^5 under the action of some discrete group Γ that acts on H^5 without fixed points. The result is some compact space. The remaining five dimensional spacetime is just five dimensional de Sitter space.

By analogy with the AdS-CFT correspondence, it has been conjectured that there is dS-CFT correspondence [19] that relates string theory in the bulk five-dimensional de Sitter space with some conformal field theory on the boundary. By analogy with AdS-CFT correspondence, if the bulk theory is type II^*B string theory, then the boundary theory must be the statistical mechanics of a twisted $N = 4$ supersymmetric gauge theory on the boundary of de Sitter space. Five dimensional de Sitter space has two boundaries at future timelike infinity and past timelike infinity. They are both topologically S^4 and spacelike as can be seen from the form of the metric. The radius of the S^4 at timelike infinity is in fact infinite, but to do calculations, one can take it to be at finite t, and then take the limit as $t \to \infty$. A direct way to calculate the entropy of de Sitter space is to compute the gravitational action and then, using the temperature, find the entropy. The statistical field theory on the boundary has an effective action which is completely determined by the trace anomaly of the theory. Evaluating the gravitational action on $H^5/\Gamma \otimes dS_5$ gives the same result as the effective action for the supersymmetrical statistical mechanics on the boundary. Further details will appear elsewhere [20]. This result seems to indicate that the entropy of de Sitter space can be understood from string theory as long as one accepts some kind of holographic principle and the validity of II^* theories.

String theory therefore certainly provides a start in understanding some of the problems of gravitational physics. It gives us some understanding of the entropy of spacetime, for both black hole and cosmological event horizons. However, to date it does not really seem to have scratched the surface of the information paradox. We can look forward to some exciting developments in this field for which we can thank Stephen so much for starting.

References

[1] Michell, J. (1784), 'On the means of discovering the distance, magnitude &c of the fixed stars', *Phil. Trans. Roy. Soc.* **74**, 35–57.

[2] Priestley, J. (1772), *The History and Present State of Discoveries relating to Vision, Light and Colours*, (J. Johnson, London).

[3] Thorne, K. S. (1972), 'Nonspherical gravitational collapse: a short review', in *Magic without Magic*, ed. J. R. Klauder (W. H. Freeman, San Francisco).

[4] Chandrasekhar, S. (1931), 'The maximum mass of ideal white dwarf stars', *Phil. Mag.* **11**, 592–596.

[5] Oppenheimer, J. R. and Volkoff, G. M. (1939), 'On massive neutron cores', *Phys. Rev.* **55**, 374–381.

[6] Hawking, S. W. and Penrose, R. (1969), 'The singularities of gravitational collapse and cosmology', *Proc. Roy. Soc. London,* **A314**, 529–548.

[7] Hawking, S. W. (1975), 'Particle creation by black holes', *Commun. Math. Phys.* **43**, 199–220.

[8] Heusler, M. (1996), *Black Hole Uniqueness Theorems,* (Cambridge University Press, Cambridge).

[9] Bardeen, J. M., Carter, B. and Hawking, S. W. (1973), 'The four laws of black hole mechanics', *Commun. Math. Phys.* **31**, 161–170.

[10] Hawking, S. W. (1976), 'Breakdown of predictability in gravitational collapse', *Phys. Rev.* **D14**, 2460–2473.

[11] Strominger, A. and Vafa, C. (1996), 'Microscopic origin of the Bekenstein–Hawking Entropy', *Phys. Lett.* **B379**, 99–104.

[12] Callan, C. G. and Maldacena, J. (1996), 'D-brane approach to black hole quantum mechanics', *Nucl. Phys.* **B472**, 591–610.

[13] Horowitz, G. T., Maldacena, J. and Strominger, A. (1996), 'Nonextremal black hole microstates and U duality', *Phys. Lett.* **B383**, 151–159.

[14] Perry, M. J. (2002), *in preparation.*

[15] Hawking, S. W. and Gibbons, G. W. (1977), 'Cosmological event horizons, thermodynamics and particle creation', *Phys. Rev.* **D15**, 2738–2751.

[16] Gibbons, G. W. (1984), 'Aspects of supergravity theories', in *GIFT Seminar on Supersymmetry, Supergravity and Related Topics,* eds F. del Aguila, J. A. de Azcarraga and L. R. Ibanez (World Scientific, Singapore).

[17] Maldacena, J. M. and Nunez, C. (2001), 'Supergravity description of field theories on curved manifolds and a no go theorem', *Int. J. Mod. Phys.* **A16**, 822–855.

[18] Hull, C. M. (2001), 'de Sitter space in supergravity and M theory', *JHEP,* **0111**, 012.

[19] Strominger, A. (2001), 'The dS/CFT correspondence', *JHEP,* **0110**, 034.

[20] Perry, M. J. (2002), *in preparation.*

17

M theory and black hole quantum mechanics

Joe Polchinski
University of California, Santa Barbara

17.1 A story

The organizers have asked me to speak about 'M Theory,' but first I would like to tell a pertinent story. I was one of the organizers of Strings '96, and we followed an archaic system whereby speakers were actually allowed to choose *their own* titles. So at one point I received the following email, with Stephen's return address:

```
Dear Joe,
The title of my talk for the Strings conference will be:
I was wrong all along. String theory is right and
information is not lost down black holes.

Sincerely,
Stephen
```

Now this was not totally implausible: it was a few months after the Strominger–Vafa paper [1], which showed that the Bekenstein–Hawking entropy of a supersymmetric black hole could be understood in terms of that of an ordinary quantum mechanical system. However, it was still a bit surprising. I did not know Stephen very well at the time, but I understood him to be rather firm in his beliefs. The Strominger–Vafa result is very suggestive, but it leaves room for doubt: to get from the black hole to the quantum system an adiabatic continuation is needed, and one could imagine that information loss turns off exponentially in the transition.

What I was not aware of was the ease with which email headers can be forged! Within a few days the culprit confessed and then things made sense. But evidently Stephen got wind of the story, because shortly thereafter I received:

```
Dear Joe,
My title is "Why I Have Not Changed My Mind."

Stephen Hawking
```

This certainly sounds much more like the real Stephen, and indeed that is the talk that he gave.

17.2 'Finding Stephen's mistake'

What I would like to speak about is Stephen's impact from the perspective of a string/M theorist – the essential role that he has played in bringing M theory to its current state. Of course, Stephen's contributions to physics are many. For example, the idea that there is a quantitative theory of the initial conditions [2] is an important one, and an issue that string theory still needs to face. But from the rather distant perspective of a string-turned-M theorist, the work that has had the greatest impact on the direction of our field is the development of black hole quantum mechanics.

Applying quantum mechanics to black holes leads to a puzzle and a paradox. The puzzle is black hole entropy [3–6]. The paradox is black hole information loss [7]. Information loss has been a remarkable story. To discover the paradox required several deep insights:

1. Black holes evaporate.

2. Information is lost in the process of black hole formation and evaporation.

3. Number 2 is not just an artifact of the first-order treatment of Hawking radiation, but is robust against all corrections.

4. The standard laws of quantum mechanics must therefore break down, and be replaced by a different form of time evolution.

The response to this ranged from acceptance to extreme doubt. Particle physicists in particular were skeptical: if a black hole radiates thermally, then it should not be fundamentally different from a lump of hot coal, where the final thermal state is complicated but still as pure as the initial state. One after another we tried to 'find Hawking's mistake,' which was usually assumed to be somewhere around point 3. Indeed this is a subtle point, as one could imagine that tiny quantum gravitational corrections, or the effects of Planck scale physics, would encode the information in the outgoing radiation. But Stephen had gotten it right: there was no trivial resolution. Unlike a lump of coal, a black hole has a horizon, and so the information would have to travel over spacelike distances to escape.

For twenty years the situation changed little, except for the paradox being sharpened: either *quantum mechanics* had to break down (in a rather ugly, and probably inconsistent way [8]), or *spacetime locality* had to break down – not just on microscopic stringy length scales, but over the macroscopic distances characterizing the black hole horizon.[1] The paradox was so sharp that 't Hooft, Susskind and collaborators began to contemplate seriously the possibility that physics was indeed nonlocal [9–12]. This led them to formulate the 'holographic principle' and the 'principle of black hole complementarity'.

These ideas showed just how radically physics would have to change to avoid Stephen's conclusion, but within perturbative string theory there was no decisive argument in one direction or the other. Fortunately, in 1995 we acquired new tools for understanding the collective behaviours of strongly interacting strings (for a review see [13]). In a sense black holes are just balls of strongly interacting string, and so these tools should teach us something about them, and in short order Strominger and Vafa had used the new methods to give a precise statistical interpretation of the entropy of supersymmetric black holes [1]. Essentially, in string theory one can imagine reducing the gravitational coupling adiabatically, so that eventually the black hole is no longer black but becomes some weakly interacting quantum system, in this case a gas of D-branes whose spectrum is known explicitly; the state counting agrees with the black hole entropy.[2] This result, and more generally the dualities of string/M theory that relate black holes to ordinary particle states, suggest that black holes satisfy the same rules as more ordinary quantum systems. However, as I noted earlier, one can still imagine a scenario in which information is lost. In the weakly coupled D-brane or string system this loss would be exponentially small, through such effects as black hole pair production,

---

[1] There were other alternatives, such as the information remaining in a black hole remnant at the end of the decay process. This might look less radical, but the idea of a finite mass object with an arbitrarily large number of internal states seemed, and still seems, even more unattractive.

[2] There were earlier ideas for calculating the black hole entropy in string theory, for example [14, 15], but the dynamical assumptions seem to me less clear.

One can also turn off the gravitational coupling adiabatically for a non-supersymmetric Schwarzschild black hole, and it becomes a single highly excited string. Without supersymmetry one cannot follow the spectrum precisely through the transition, but an approximate matching is possible, and it agrees for the Schwarzschild and other non-supersymmetric black holes [16, 17].

but when the coupling is increased to the point that a black hole forms, these effects would become large.

In fact, we now believe that we know the answer, and it is locality that breaks down, not quantum mechanics. The new tool that we have is AdS/CFT duality: the IIB string theory, in a space that is asymptotically $AdS_5 \times S^5$, is dual to an ordinary supersymmetric gauge theory in four dimensions [18]. *Dual* means that these systems are identical, with a one-to-one mapping of the states and other observables. When the gauge coupling is weak, the gauge theory description is the useful one; when the gauge coupling is strong, the string description is weakly coupled and useful.

We have learned many surprising things about string theory in the last few years, but I think that this duality is the most remarkable: that the degrees of freedom in a four-dimensional field theory can rearrange themselves into those of a ten-dimensional string theory as the coupling is increased. From this one learns many things. First, it gives implicitly a non-perturbative definition of string theory, and thus of quantum gravity, since we believe that we know how to define precisely the dual gauge theory (if there is any doubt about the latter, one can consider instead a similar duality with a lower dimensional super-renormalizable gauge theory, where there should be no doubt). This might seem circular, using the duality to define one side of itself, but it is not: we know a great deal about the string theory independently of this, and the duality must be, and is, consistent with all that we know.

This definition of quantum gravity is explicitly holographic: the higher-dimensional spacetime locality emerges in an approximate classical description when the gauge theory variables become strongly quantum mechanical. The local observables of the gauge theory map to the boundary conditions on the string spacetime, a remarkably precise realization of the holographic idea. Also, this definition is almost background independent: the metric can fluctuate freely in the ten-dimensional interior of $AdS_5 \times S^5$, and is fixed only on the boundary. What we still lack, and it is critical, is an understanding of how to extend this to more realistic spacetimes, especially those that have an interesting cosmology.

By taking the N of the $SU(N)$ gauge theory to be large, with the string coupling fixed, one can make the dual AdS spacetime arbitrarily large and flat. A local observer can then do experiments just as in flat spacetime, such as building a black hole and then letting it decay. Since the dual gauge description is explicitly in the framework of ordinary quantum mechanics, information must be preserved: the initial state of the black hole will be encoded in the correlations of the outgoing Hawking radiation. Indeed, in the dual gauge description the black hole is just a hot ball of gas.

The sceptical reader might feel that this argument is much less direct than the original argument for information loss, and it is hard to argue with this. The weak/strong coupling dualities of string theories and supersymmetric gauge theories are deduced, they are not constructed or proven. Nevertheless, they explain so many diverse and non-trivial facts that it is very difficult to doubt them. Speaking as one who was long in the 'undecided' camp with regard to information loss, it seems that the issue is now decided.

Still, the sceptic is entitled to feel that the situation is not totally satisfactory. The prescription for calculating the final state is to translate the initial state into gauge theory language using the AdS/CFT dictionary [19, 20], evolve the state forward in time, and translate back. The time evolution is carried forward in the gauge theory variables. There are no analytic methods for doing this, it is just something that can be done in principle on a large enough computer. Further, the spacetime geometry is obscure in the gauge picture, we do not know how to 'decode the hologram' in detail. In order to say that we have 'found Hawking's mistake,' we need to be able to give a prescription for calculating the final state directly in the gravitational variables in which the Hawking calculation is done. It seems to me that such a prescription should exist, since these are the effective variables for a macroscopic black hole; I think that it is important to try harder to find this, and it may have applications elsewhere such as de Sitter space.

Now let me return to my theme, which is the influence that Stephen has had upon the development of M theory. The AdS/CFT duality (or I should say, more generally, gauge/gravity duality to cover similar examples that are not conformally invariant) is one of the deepest and most remarkable things that we know about M theory. It was discovered by considering the low energy behaviour of strings propagating in a black hole background. Thus the quantum behaviour of black holes – the subject that Stephen not only pioneered, but forced the rest of us to think about with his paradox and his audacious claim about quantum mechanics – has played an essential role in bringing us to our current understanding.

Going further, we do not yet have in M theory the central defining principle, the analogue of the equivalence principle in general relativity and the uncertainty principle in quantum mechanics. If we had to guess today what it is, the holographic principle would be the best guess: the non-locality of the fundamental degrees of freedom, and the emergence of locality as an approximation. With any scientific theory one can imagine many alternate routes to the final form, but it is difficult to see how an idea as radical as the holographic principle could have come to the fore without the black hole information paradox.

The information paradox is often seen as a conflict, between Stephen's assertion of information loss and those who don't believe it. But however the issue turns out, we should not lose sight of the fact that he was right about the most important thing: that information loss is not a trivial paradox with a simple resolution, but rather forces us to rethink and reformulate the most basic principles of physics.

17.3 The strong interaction and black holes

I would like to conclude with a few words about my own current work (for a review see [21]). This is directed at understanding the strong interaction, not gravity, but in fact it rounds the story out in a nice way. We still do not have good analytic tools for understanding quark confinement and the physics of the strong interaction at low energies. Gerard 't Hooft proposed an elegant approximation, the large-N limit [22]. Many field theories become solvable in the limit of many fields, through a sort of mean-field approximation. In QCD, going to the limit of many colours does not lead to an immediate solution, but it leads to an interesting simplification. The perturbation expansion organizes itself according to the topology of the Feynman graphs, in an exact parallel to the sum over world-sheets in string theory. Thus 't Hooft conjectured that in the large-N limit QCD could be recast as a string theory.

't Hooft's idea is very compelling. The problem is that string theories of the strong interaction were tried, and they did not work. They had some phenomenological successes, but ultimately there were some essential problems:

- String theory has a graviton; QCD does not.

- String theory has ten dimensions; QCD has four.

- Strings are smooth; QCD has pointlike partons.

- String theory does not have local observables; QCD does.

Thus it was assumed that the string theory that governs the large-N limit of QCD is very different from the one that string theorists study, and presumably uglier and more complicated.

Remarkably, we did not need a complicated new string theory, we just needed ... black holes! The string theory of large-N QCD is the same ten-dimensional theory that gives rise to gravity, but in an unusual spacetime background. Of course, I am just describing gauge/gravity duality again, but am now thinking of it in the opposite direction, as a way to solve gauge theory, rather than to understand the conceptual issues of quantum gravity. Maldacena's original duality was for highly supersymmetric gauge theories which do not confine. However, once we know such a duality we can perturb it, and so we have useful duals for various gauge theories that look like QCD at low energies, though they still become supersymmetric at high energy.[3] The duality extends *in principle* to large-N QCD itself, but not yet in a useful way: the two-dimensional quantum field theory of the string world-sheet is strongly coupled and little understood as yet. Still, it provides an 'existence proof' for a realization of 't Hooft's conjecture; the problem is to characterize the world-sheet theory more clearly.

't Hooft's large-N paper appeared in 1974, and Stephen's information loss paper two years later. As a student I studied each paper, but I had no clue that they were connected; I don't think that anyone did until very recently. But in fact, each paper poses a problem – the solution to the large-N limit of QCD, and the information paradox – and each paper has turned out to contain ideas that have been essential in solving the problem posed by the other, through gauge/gravity duality. This is an example of the tremendous richness of the structure, M theory, that we are discovering. It also shows why it has been essential to have many different approaches and perspectives, and in particular why Stephen's unique perspective has been so vital.

References

[1] Strominger, A. and Vafa, C. (1996), 'Microscopic origin of the Bekenstein-Hawking entropy', *Phys. Lett.* **B379**, 99–104, [hep-th/9601029].

[2] Hartle, J. B. and Hawking, S. W. (1983), 'Wave function of the universe', *Phys. Rev.* **D28**, 2960-2975.

[3] Bekenstein, J. D. (1973), 'Black holes and entropy', *Phys. Rev.* **D7**, 2333–2346.

[4] Bardeen, J. M., Carter, B. and Hawking, S. W. (1973), 'The four laws of black hole mechanics', *Commun. Math. Phys.* **31**, 161–170.

[5] Hawking, S. W. (1974), 'Black hole explosions', *Nature* **248**, 30–31.

[6] Hawking, S. W. (1975), 'Particle creation by black holes', *Commun. Math. Phys.* **43**, 199–220.

[7] Hawking, S. W. (1976), 'Breakdown of predictability in gravitational collapse', *Phys. Rev.* **D14**, 2460–2473.

[8] Banks, T., Susskind, L. and Peskin, M. E. (1984), 'Difficulties for the evolution of pure states into mixed states', *Nucl. Phys.* **B244**, 125.

---

[3] Again, with dualities the information flows both ways, so that the understanding of the duals to these gauge theories has taught us how string theory resolves certain spacetime singularities.

[9] 't Hooft, G. (1993), 'Dimensional reduction in quantum gravity', [gr-qc/9310026].

[10] Susskind, L., Thorlacius, L. and Uglum, J. (1993), 'The stretched horizon and black hole complementarity', *Phys. Rev.* **D48**, 3743–3761, [hep-th/9306069].

[11] Susskind, L. (1993), 'String theory and the principles of black hole complementarity', *Phys. Rev. Lett.* **71**, 2367–2368, [hep-th/9307168].

[12] Susskind, L. (1995), 'The world as a hologram', *J. Math. Phys.* **36**, 6377–6396, [hep-th/9409089].

[13] Polchinski, J. (1996), 'String duality: a colloquium', *Rev. Mod. Phys.* **68**, 1245–1258, [hep-th/9607050].

[14] Sen, A. (1995), 'Black hole solutions in heterotic string theory on a torus', *Nucl. Phys.* **B440**, 421, [hep-th/9411187].

[15] Larsen, F. and Wilczek, F. (1996), 'Internal structure of black holes', *Phys. Lett.* **B375**, 37–42, [hep-th/9511064].

[16] L. Susskind, L. (1993), 'Some speculations about black hole entropy in string theory', [hep-th/9309145].

[17] Horowitz, G. T. and Polchinski, J. (1997), 'A correspondence principle for black holes and strings', *Phys. Rev.* **D55**, 6189–6197, [hep-th/9612146].

[18] Maldacena, J. (1998), 'The large N limit of superconformal field theories and supergravity', *Adv. Theor. Math. Phys.* **2**, 231–252, [hep-th/9711200].

[19] Gubser, S. S., Klebanov, I. R. and Polyakov, A. M. (1998), 'Gauge theory correlators from non-critical string theory', *Phys. Lett.* **B428**, 105–114, [hep-th/9802109].

[20] Witten, E. (1998), 'Anti-de Sitter space and holography', *Adv. Theor. Math. Phys.* **2**, 253–291, [hep-th/9802150].

[21] Polchinski, J. (2002), 'Toward a string theory of large-N QCD', in *Strings and Gravity: Tying the Forces Together*, eds M. Henneaux and A. Sevrin (Editions Deboeck, Louvain-la-Neuve, Belgium).

[22] 't Hooft, G. (1974), 'A planar diagram theory for strong interactions', *Nucl. Phys.* **B72**, 461.

18

Playing with black strings

Gary Horowitz

University of California, Santa Barbara

18.1 Introduction

It is a real pleasure to help celebrate Stephen Hawking's sixtieth birthday. I have known Stephen for more than 20 years and had the pleasure of collaborating with him on three projects:

1. positive mass theorems for black holes [1];

2. entropy, area, and black hole pairs [2]; and

3. the gravitational Hamiltonian, action, entropy and surface terms [3].

The first arose when I was a postdoc at the Institute for Advanced Study at Princeton, and Stephen came to visit. We soon discovered that Malcolm Perry and I were working on the same problem that Stephen and Gary Gibbons were: how to generalize Witten's proof of the positive mass theorem [4] to include inner boundaries associated with black holes. We decided to join forces. I think it was because of this collaboration that Stephen invited me to visit Cambridge. I accepted and spent six weeks there in 1983. The thing I remember most about that visit was one day at tea, Stephen started to recite the names of the past Lucasian Professors of Mathematics starting with Newton. After a few names I expected him to stop. But he kept on going. He knew them all, up to the present.

I was thinking about what I could give Stephen for his birthday. Given his longstanding interest in black holes, I decided that the best present would be a new result about black holes. Since Stephen (and his colleagues) pretty much cleaned up the subject in four spacetime dimensions back in the 1970s [5], I decided to look in higher dimensions. (Motivated by string theory, there has been considerable interest in the properties of black holes in higher dimensions.) I was greatly assisted in this work

310

by my postdoc Kengo Maeda. We found something quite surprising. In fact, I was stunned when we first obtained these results. Something that I thought was true for almost ten years turns out not to be.

As you know, ordinary black holes are stable. If you perturb the Schwarzschild solution, the perturbation remains small. In fact, it either radiates to infinity or falls into the black hole and decays at a certain characteristic rate. In higher dimensions, things are not so simple. We will consider the case of one extra dimension (which is compactified to a circle of length L at infinity), but similar results hold in higher dimensions as well. In five spacetime dimensions, there is a solution which is just the product of a four dimensional Schwarzschild black hole and a circle:

$$ds^2 = -\left(1 - \frac{r_0}{r}\right)dt^2 + \left(1 - \frac{r_0}{r}\right)^{-1} dr^2 + r^2 d\Omega + dz^2 . \tag{18.1}$$

This looks like a one-dimensional extended object surrounded by a horizon, and is characterized by two parameters, the Schwarzschild radius r_0 and L. In general, we will call any object with an event horizon having topology $S^2 \times S^1$ a 'black string'. A 'black hole' will refer to an object with horizon topology S^3. (The most general topology consistent with a static horizon in five dimensions is a finite connected sum of $S^2 \times S^1$s and (homotopy) S^3s [6].) So (18.1) describes a black string. Following a suggestion by Hawking's student, Brian Whitt, Gregory and Laflamme [7] showed that this spacetime is unstable to linearized perturbations with a long wavelength along the circle. More precisely, there is a critical size L_0 of order r_0 such that black strings with $L \leq L_0$ are stable and those with $L > L_0$ are unstable. The unstable mode is spherically symmetric, but causes the horizon to oscillate in the z direction. Gregory and Laflamme also compared the total entropy of the black string with that of a five dimensional black hole with the same total mass, and found that when $L > L_0$, the black hole had greater entropy. They thus suggested that the full non-linear evolution of the instability would result in the black string breaking up into separate black holes which would then coalesce into a single black hole. Classically, horizons cannot bifurcate, but the idea was that, under classical evolution, the event horizon would pinch off and become singular. When the curvature became large enough, it was plausible that quantum effects would smooth out the transition between the black string and black holes.

This idea that long black strings will break up into black holes has been widely accepted and assumed in various arguments. However I will try to convince you that this widespread belief is incorrect: black strings do not, in fact, break up into black holes. Under very weak assumptions, one can prove that an event horizon cannot pinch off in finite time. In particular, if one perturbs (18.1), an S^2 on the horizon cannot shrink to zero size in finite affine parameter. The basic idea is the following. Hawking's famous area theorem [8] is based on a local result that the divergence θ of the null geodesic generators of the horizon cannot become negative, i.e., the null geodesics cannot start to converge. If an S^2 on the horizon tries to shrink to zero size, the null geodesics on that S^2 must be converging. The total θ can stay positive only if the horizon is expanding rapidly in the circle direction. But this produces a large shear. If the S^2 were to shrink to zero size in finite time, one can show this shear would drive θ negative. A more physical argument shows that the horizon cannot slowly pinch off, taking an infinite time to do so. The net result is that the solution must settle down to a new (as yet unknown) static black string solution which is not translationally invariant along the circle.

One can view this result as an example of spontaneous symmetry breaking in general relativity. The most symmetric solution is unstable, and the stable solution has less symmetry. Unlike the usual particle physics examples where the broken symmetry is an internal one, here the broken symmetry is spatial translations.

Once one knows that stable black strings exist, one can use them as a tool to construct a larger class of non-uniform black strings which are unrelated to any instability. For example, if one considers Einstein–Maxwell theory in five dimensions, there are translationally invariant, near extremal charged black strings which are believed to be stable. Nevertheless, we will see that there are also inhomogeneous charged black strings with the same mass and charge. In fact, the non-uniform solutions have much greater entropy. Unlike the neutral solutions, these new near extremal solutions can exist even when the size of the circle at infinity is very small.

In the next section we present the argument that stable non-uniform black strings must exist. We also discuss attempts to find these new solutions. In section 18.3, we describe some properties of the new solutions, including the transition from uniform to non-uniform configurations. In the following section we generalize to charged black strings and show that there are non-uniform solutions which are unrelated to any instability. The fifth section contains a list of open questions and future directions. We end with a brief conclusion.

18.2 Existence of new (vacuum) solutions

We first prove that horizons cannot pinch off in finite proper time [9]. Consider initial data consisting of a constant t surface in (18.1) with a spherically symmetric perturbation. We set $L > L_0$, and give the perturbation a long enough wavelength around the circle so that it grows exponentially in the linearized approximation. Now consider the full non-linear evolution of this initial data using Einstein's vacuum field equation. We will assume that naked singularities do not form away from the horizon. This would be a blatant violation of cosmic censorship in five dimensions. It would be a much more interesting conclusion than the one we will find, but also much less likely. However, we will certainly allow the possibility that singularities form on the horizon. Our goal will be to show that this cannot happen.

Since the initial data is asymptotically flat, the maximal evolution should contain at least part of future null infinity $\mathcal{I}^+$. Since the initial data contains trapped surfaces that cannot lie in the past of $\mathcal{I}^+$, there must be an event horizon. This event horizon is a four-dimensional null surface ruled by a family of null geodesics. Let λ be an affine parameter along these geodesics and set $\ell^\mu = (\partial/\partial\lambda)^\mu$. Since we have assumed that the initial data is spherically symmetric, the same will be true for the evolved spacetime. Thus, the metric on a cross-section of the horizon at constant λ can be written

$$ds^2 = e^{2\chi}dz^2 + e^{2\psi}d\Omega, \tag{18.2}$$

where z is a coordinate along the S^1, and χ, ψ are functions of λ and z. Notice that if the sphere shrinks to zero size, ψ must go to minus infinity. The divergence of the null geodesic generators is

$$\theta = \dot{\chi} + 2\dot{\psi}, \tag{18.3}$$

where a dot denotes a derivative with respect to λ. The change in the divergence along the null geodesics is given by the Raychaudhuri equation [5]. In five dimensions, this is

$$\dot{\theta} = -\frac{\theta^2}{3} - \sigma^{\mu\nu}\sigma_{\mu\nu} - R_{\mu\nu}\ell^\mu\ell^\nu, \tag{18.4}$$

where $\sigma_{\mu\nu}$ denotes the shear of the null geodesic congruence. This is a measure of how distorted a small sphere becomes when evolved along the null geodesics. For the metric (18.2) one finds

$$\sigma_{\mu\nu}\sigma^{\mu\nu} = \frac{2}{3}(\dot{\chi} - \dot{\psi})^2. \tag{18.5}$$

Since $\theta \geq 0$ and $\dot{\psi} \leq 0$, we have $\dot{\chi} \geq -2\dot{\psi}$ from (18.3) and hence $\sigma_{\mu\nu}\sigma^{\mu\nu} \geq 6\dot{\psi}^2$. Since the spacetime is Ricci flat, from (18.4) we have $\dot{\theta} \leq -6\dot{\psi}^2$. Thus if $\theta_0 > 0$ is the initial value of the divergence,

$$\theta(\lambda) \leq \theta_0 - 6\int_0^\lambda \dot{\psi}^2. \tag{18.6}$$

Using $(\dot\psi + 1)^2 \geq 0$, this implies $\theta(\lambda) \leq 12\psi(\lambda) + 6\lambda + \text{constant}$. It is now clear that if the sphere pinches off in finite affine parameter $(\psi \to -\infty)$, then θ must become negative and, in fact, go to minus infinity.

This leads to a contradiction as follows [10]. If $\theta < 0$ at some point p on the event horizon, one can deform a cross-section of the horizon through p, so that it enters the past of future null infinity and still has the outgoing null geodesics converging. This is like having a trapped surface in the past of null infinity, and can be ruled out in the same way. One considers the boundary of the future of the deformed cross-section T. This must intersect future null infinity, but (being the boundary of a future set) through every point there must exist a past directed null geodesic which stays on the boundary until it reaches T. This is impossible since $\theta < 0$ on T implies that all outgoing null geodesics have conjugate points,[1] and cannot stay on the boundary of the future of T. (Notice that even though Hawking's original argument that $\theta > 0$ [8] assumed that the null geodesic generators of the horizon were complete, this is not required in the later proofs [10].) This completes the proof that the horizon cannot pinch off in finite time.

This result can be extended in many directions. Since it is based on a local calculation, one can apply it to non-spherical perturbations, higher dimensional spacetimes, horizons extended in more than one direction (black branes), and collapsing surfaces of various dimensions. In fact, one can show that no circle on the horizon can shrink down to zero size in finite affine parameter [9].

We now argue that it is unlikely that the horizon will pinch off even in infinite affine parameter. How could this happen? Fix some late time, and consider the geometry of the horizon near its smallest cross-section. The horizon cannot stay small for a distance much larger than its width since, in that case, it would resemble a thin black string and would be unstable. One does not expect a generic perturbation to approach an unstable solution at late time. But if the horizon remains small for only a distance of order its width, it will look like two spherical black holes connected by a small 'neck'. But the spacetime near the neck would be analogous to that obtained by bringing two black holes close together, and in that case it is well known that the horizon does not form a small neck. Instead, a new trapped surface forms which surrounds both black holes. This is simply because there is now double the mass within a sphere containing both black holes so the effective Schwarzschild radius moves out. Similarly, we would expect that if the apparent horizon tried to pinch

---

[1] A conjugate point is a point where the geodesic is crossed by a nearby null geodesic originating from T.

off in an infinite affine parameter by forming a small neck, there would be another apparent horizon formed outside, and the true event horizon would not pinch off.

One might wonder if the final solution could end up independent of z, but with the proper size of the circle shrinking as one comes in from infinity, so that the horizon is stable. This is easily ruled out as follows: if the solution were independent of z, we could use a Kaluza–Klein reduction and view it as a static four-dimensional black hole coupled to χ, which acts like a massless scalar field. The usual 'no hair' theorems show that χ must be constant. So the size of the fifth dimension must be constant if the black string is translationally invariant.

Given that the horizon cannot pinch off, one can ask what the solution will approach at late time. Any oscillatory motion will probably lose energy through gravitational radiation and damp out. The most plausible outcome is that the solution settles down to a new static black string which is not translationally invariant.[2] This is similar to the standard assumption in four dimensions, that solutions with a black hole will settle down at late time to Schwarzschild (or Kerr if there is non-zero angular momentum).

What do we expect the final state to look like? If L is slightly larger than L_0, the solution will probably have a horizon with one maximum S^2 cross-section and one minimum. If $L \gg L_0$, there are two possibilities, depending on whether the size of the circle at the horizon shrinks to a value much smaller than L. (Since the solution is no longer translationally invariant, the above Kaluza–Klein reduction argument does not apply. Even though the circle can shrink, its size cannot go to zero without violating $\theta > 0$.) If the size of the circle shrinks, then one can again have a horizon with one maximum and one minimum cross-section. If the size of the circle does not shrink appreciably, it is likely that the local shape of the horizon is determined by L_0. This is because L_0 sets the scale between stable and unstable modes. We expect more or less regular oscillations on the horizon with the radii of maximum and minimum S^2s, r_{max} and r_{min}, differing from the initial Schwarzschild radius r_0 (which is of order L_0) by factors of order unity. L just imposes periodicity at a long scale, but should not affect the local structure.

---

[2] The Weyl tensor on the horizon could, in principle, diverge even though $\theta > 0$ and the horizon has not pinched off [11]. This is because θ involves only first derivatives of the metric while the Weyl tensor involves second derivatives. But there is no reason to expect that such weak curvature singularities will form from generic perturbations of the original uniform black string.

Clearly, one would like to find these new solutions and there are several methods one might try. Since they are expected to be static and spherically symmetric in five dimensions, one essentially has a set of coupled non-linear PDEs in two variables, (r, z). These equations appear to be difficult to solve explicitly, but it is possible that a clever choice of coordinates will simplify the problem. (For one attempt in this direction, see [12].) After all, in four dimensions, the analogous problem of finding that all static axisymmetric vacuum solutions can be solved completely. These are the Weyl metrics.[3] If an analytic solution cannot be found, one can always try to solve the equations numerically. This is similar to a two-dimensional elliptic problem.

Another approach is to solve the time dependent equations numerically starting with initial data corresponding to a slightly perturbed uniform black string. This is currently underway [14]. Although they have not been able to evolve reliably long enough to see the final state, their results are already quite interesting. A dimensionless measure of the inhomogeneity of the black string is the ratio of the largest radius S^2 cross-section of the horizon to the smallest, r_{max}/r_{min}. In the numerical evolution, this ratio grows rapidly to about ten. It then starts slowing down and appears to stop growing at about thirteen. There is evidence that this is not yet the final static configuration but, at the moment, further evolution is unreliable due to numerical error. Work is continuing, but it is already clear that the horizon does not simply pinch off. One advantage of this evolution approach is that once the final state is found, it is guaranteed to be stable. One never numerically evolves to an unstable configuration without fine tuning.

18.3 Properties of the new solutions

Even without explicit knowledge of the new solutions, one can deduce some of their properties. For example, the new solutions must approach the uniform black string exponentially fast at infinity. This is because at large distances from the horizon, the inhomogeneity should be washed out. It will thus resemble a perturbation of (18.1). Since z is periodic, any z-dependent perturbation satisfies a massive spin two equation and must fall off exponentially.

The surface gravity κ must be constant over the static horizon, even when it is inhomogeneous. In [9] it was argued that for the static solution,

---

[3] Unfortunately, a straightforward generalization of the Weyl ansatz does not lead to the same simplifications in five dimensions due to the fact that two-spheres have curvature while circles do not [13].

the surface gravity, mass $\hat{M}$, and horizon area A must satisfy

$$\hat{M} = \frac{\kappa A}{4\pi} . \tag{18.7}$$

The reason was the following. If ξ denotes the static Killing field, then $^*d\xi$ is closed by the vacuum Einstein equation. Consider the integral of $d^*d\xi$ over a static slice from the horizon to infinity. The surface term at infinity yields the total mass $\hat{M}$, and the surface term at the horizon yields $\kappa A/4\pi$. Since these must be equal we obtain (18.7). However this formula cannot hold for all static solutions with horizons.[4] The first law of black hole mechanics [15] (which holds in all dimensions) implies $dM = \kappa dA/8\pi$, so (if $M = \hat{M}$) we can solve for κ and obtain

$$M = 2A\frac{dM}{dA} \tag{18.8}$$

or $A \propto M^2$. This is true for Schwarzschild in four dimensions but not in higher dimensions. The problem is that the surface integral at infinity of $^*d\xi$ is the Komar mass and the mass that appears in the first law is the ADM mass. In four dimensions these two masses are the same but this is not true in higher dimensions. A simple-counter example is the product of time and the Euclidean Schwarzschild solution. This Ricci flat metric has non-zero ADM mass, but since $\xi^\mu = (\partial/\partial t)^\mu$ is covariantly constant, the Komar mass is zero. More generally, if g_{zz} has a non-zero $1/r$ contribution, the Komar mass and ADM mass will differ. In short, (18.7) will hold for all static black strings provided $\hat{M}$ represents the Komar mass.

To understand the relation between the new solutions and the original translationally invariant ones, it is convenient to introduce two dimensionless variables. In five dimensions, the ADM mass has dimensions of length squared, so M/L^2 is dimensionless, where (as usual) L is the length of the circle at infinity. This describes the overall shape of the black string. If it is large, the black string is short and fat, if it is small, the horizon is long and thin. The second parameter is the dimensionless measure of the inhomogeneity, r_{max}/r_{min}. This parameter is clearly never less than one and, when it is equal to one, there is a solution for every value of M/L^2 given by (18.1). (We previously described these solutions in terms of the two dimensionful parameters r_0, L, but to avoid trivial constant rescalings of the metric, it is convenient to use this dimensionless parameterization.)

There is a critical value of M/L^2 of order one which separates the stable and unstable uniform black strings. At this critical value, there is a nontrivial static perturbation to (18.1) [7]. This strongly suggests that

---

[4] I thank S. Gubser for pointing out this problem.

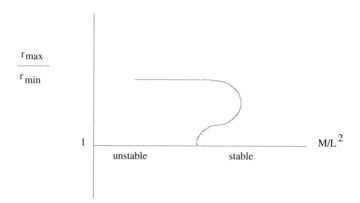

Fig. 18.1. Near the transition where the uniform black string becomes unstable, the new static solutions probably behave as shown by the curve. This is supported by both a perturbative calculation and numerical evolution.

the new inhomogeneous black strings meet the old solutions at this point. One's first thought is that the new solutions will branch off to smaller values of M/L^2 since that is where the instabilities guarantee that new solutions must exist. Surprisingly, that is not what happens. The actual behaviour is shown in the figure. The new solutions actually overlap part of the region of parameters where the uniform black string is stable. This was first found in a perturbative analysis near the critical point by Gubser [16]. He solved Einstein's equation to second order starting with the known static perturbation, and found that the inhomogeneous solution starts to increase M/L^2. This was later supported by numerical work. Starting with initial data with M/L^2 slightly below the critical value, the numerical evolution does not settle down to a slightly inhomogeneous black string [14]. Instead the inhomogeneities grow significantly, just as for smaller values of M/L^2. The main difference between the evolutions is just that when M/L^2 is slightly below the the critical value, the perturbation grows much more slowly. But eventually, the solution becomes just as inhomogeneous.

This indicates that the transition between the stable uniform black strings at large M/L^2 and stable inhomogeneous solutions at small M/L^2 involves a discontinuous jump in the horizon geometry. It is thus analogous to a first order phase transition. It also shows that there can be many solutions with the same value of M/L^2. Of the three solutions with M/L^2 slightly above the critical point, the middle one is expected to be unstable, and the other two are presumably stable. It is clear from another standpoint, that many solutions should exist. Given a stable and static black string with mass M and length L, one can always 'unwrap' it to obtain solutions with mass nM and length nL. So every solution gives rise to series of static solutions with M/L^2 reduced by $1/n$ and r_{max}/r_{min} unchanged. But the solutions with $n > 1$ need not be stable. There may be unstable modes with wavelength $L < \lambda < nL$. (This is just what happens if one starts with the stable uniform solution and unwraps it.) The existence of these different solutions with the same M and L show that the four dimensional no-hair theorems do not extend to higher dimensions, at least if one direction is compactified.

It has recently been shown that the no-hair theorems do not apply even if space is uncompactified [17]. One can take a black string and connect its ends to form a circle. This configuration would normally collapse down and form a spherical black hole, but it has recently been shown that one can stabilize it by adding rotation. In fact, Emparan and Reall [17] have found an explicit stationary axisymmetric vacuum solution in five dimensions describing this situation. It is parameterized by its total mass M and angular momentum J. It is not yet known if these solutions are stable. For large J, the black string is long and thin and is likely to be subject to the Gregory–Laflamme instability. But a rotating inhomogeneous horizon will probably radiate energy and cause the radius of the circle to shrink. When the black string is short and fat, it might be stable. For some choices of M and J there is also a rotating black hole with the same parameters. This clearly shows that the no-hair theorem does not hold in higher dimensions.

18.4 New charged black strings

So far we have talked about neutral black strings. If one adds a little charge not much changes. But near the extremal limit, one finds new phenomena. Gubser and Mitra [18] have conjectured that for a black string with a (non-compact) translational symmetry, there exists a Gregory–Laflamme instability if and only if the specific heat is negative. In other words, there is a close connection between classical stability and thermodynamic stability. Reall [19] has provided strong support for this conjecture (which was further studied in [20, 21]). Since the specific heat is often positive near extremality, one might expect that:

- there are no inhomogeneous black strings near extremality.

Also, since neutral black strings are unstable only if M/L^2 is small, one might expect:

- there are no inhomogeneous black strings with $M/L^2 \gg 1$.

We will see that both of the expectations are incorrect [22]. There exist
stable inhomogeneous near extremal black strings, even when the uniform
solution is stable. In other words, there are solutions with inhomogeneous
horizons which are not just the result of an instability in the uniform solution. Furthermore, some of these solutions have arbitrarily large M/L^2.
As an added bonus, we will see that there exist finite energy initial data
with an apparent horizon of infinite area.

   The simplest context to describe the new solutions is five-dimensional
Einstein–Maxwell theory with action

$$S = \int \sqrt{-g} \left[\frac{R}{16\pi G} - \frac{1}{4} F_{\mu\nu} F^{\mu\nu} \right] d^5 x, \qquad (18.9)$$

where G is the five-dimensional Newton constant, R is the scalar curvature and F is the Maxwell field. This theory is known to have both electrically charged black holes and translationally invariant, electrically charged
black strings. The black holes are described by the five-dimensional generalization of the Reissner–Nordström solution. We are mostly interested
in the extremal limit, which can easily be obtained as follows [23]. Let

$$ds^2 = -U^{-2}(x^i)dt^2 + U(x^i)\delta_{jk}dx^j dx^k, \qquad (18.10)$$

$$E_i = \alpha U^{-1}\partial_i U,$$

where $\alpha = \pm(3/16\pi G)^{1/2}$. Then the Einstein–Maxwell equations reduce
to just the condition that U be a harmonic function. If U is the field of a
point mass,

$$U = 1 + \frac{\mu}{x_i x^i}, \qquad (18.11)$$

where μ is a positive constant, then the solution (18.10) describes an
extremal black hole. The spatial metric has an infinite 'throat' since the
proper distance to $x^i = 0$ is stretched out infinitely, and near the origin
the area of the three-spheres of constant radius is almost independent of
the radius. In these coordinates, the event horizon is at $x^i = 0$ and has
area

$$A_{\mathrm{BH}} = 2\pi^2 \mu^{3/2}. \qquad (18.12)$$

The ADM mass M and charge Q are given by

$$M = \frac{3\pi}{4G} \mu, \qquad Q = \pm\sqrt{\frac{3\pi}{G}} \pi\mu, \qquad (18.13)$$

respectively, where we have simply normalized the charge by $Q = \oint E_i dS^i$.

Solutions describing several extremal black holes are easily constructed by letting U have several point sources. To compactify one direction, we let U be the field of a one dimensional periodic array of point masses. The resulting metric can be written [23]

$$ds_5^2 = -U^{-2}(r,z)dt^2 + U(r,z)(dr^2 + r^2 d\Omega^2 + dz^2),$$

$$U(r,z) = 1 + \frac{\pi\mu}{Lr}\frac{\sinh 2\pi\frac{r}{L}}{\cosh 2\pi\frac{r}{L} - \cos 2\pi\frac{z}{L}}, \tag{18.14}$$

where the coordinate z is periodic with period L. The black hole horizon is located at $r = z = 0$, where U diverges. Expanding U near this point yields

$$U(r,z) = 1 + \frac{\mu}{r^2 + z^2} + \frac{\pi^2}{3}\frac{\mu}{L^2} + O\left(\frac{r^2}{L^2}, \frac{z^2}{L^2}\right). \tag{18.15}$$

So the geometry near the horizon reduces to that of the isolated black hole. For $r \gg L$, we have

$$U = 1 + \frac{\pi\mu}{rL} + O(e^{-2\pi r/L}). \tag{18.16}$$

Note that the inhomogeneity in the z direction falls off exponentially for large r as expected. The ADM mass M and charge Q of the compactified solution are identical to that of the single black hole (18.13).

It is interesting to note that μ and L are independent parameters in this solution. One can fit an arbitrarily large charged black hole into a space with one direction compactified on an arbitrarily small circle (at infinity). This is possible since the size of the circle depends on U. It follows from (18.16) that when $r \sim L$ the proper length of the circle is of order $\mu^{1/2}$, independent of L.

This theory also has the charged black string solution [22]:

$$ds_5^2 = -\left(1 - \frac{r_+}{r}\right)\left(1 - \frac{r_-}{r}\right)dt^2 + \left(1 - \frac{r_+}{r}\right)^{-1}dr^2 \tag{18.17}$$

$$+ r^2\left(1 - \frac{r_-}{r}\right)d\Omega^2 + \left(1 - \frac{r_-}{r}\right)^{-1}dz^2,$$

$$F_{tr} = \pm\frac{1}{4r^2}\left(\frac{3r_+r_-}{\pi G}\right)^{1/2}. \tag{18.18}$$

The event horizon is at $r = r_+$ and has area

$$A = 4\pi r_+^2 L\left(1 - \frac{r_-}{r_+}\right)^{1/2}. \tag{18.19}$$

There is a curvature singularity at $r = r_-$. In the extremal limit, $r_+ \to r_-$, the horizon area clearly goes to zero. By a simple coordinate transformation, the extremal solution can be put into the form (18.10), where now U is the field of a line source. The total mass $\tilde{M}$ and charge $\tilde{Q}$ is given by

$$\tilde{M} = \frac{L}{4G}(2r_+ + r_-), \qquad \tilde{Q} = \pm L\sqrt{\frac{3\pi r_+ r_-}{G}}. \qquad (18.20)$$

One can check that, near extremality, (18.17) has positive specific heat and is expected to be stable.

Equating the mass of the black hole to that of the black string in the extremal limit $r_+ = r_-$, we find $\mu = Lr_+/\pi$. It then follows from (18.13) and (18.20) that the charges of the two systems are also equal. But we have seen that the horizon areas are very different.

The key question is: can one add a small amount of mass to an extreme black hole in a space with one direction compactified, so that the horizon becomes topologically $S^2 \times S^1$? The answer is yes. The basic idea is to add a thin neutral black string that goes around the circle with its ends stuck on the black hole. The mass increases roughly by $r_0 L$ and for small r_0 this is much less than the total mass M, so the configuration remains near extremal. The area of the event horizon is still of order $M^{3/2}$. This configuration will evolve since the extreme black hole wants to swallow up the black string. But, under evolution, the mass can only decrease since energy can be radiated away to infinity, and the horizon area can only increase. Since the horizon area is much greater than that of the uniform black string with the same mass and charge, it must settle down to a new inhomogeneous near extremal black string. This is true even though the uniform solution is stable.

To actually construct the initial data, it is easier to add the extreme black hole to the black string rather than vice versa. So we start with the spatial metric

$$ds_4^2 = u\left[\left(1 - \frac{r_0}{r}\right)^{-1}dr^2 + r^2 d\Omega^2 + dz^2\right], \qquad (18.21)$$

where u is a function of (r, z, θ, ϕ). z is a periodic coordinate with period L. When $u = 1$, the metric represents the spatial part of the neutral black string solution with Schwarzschild radius $r = r_0$, while the $r_0 = 0$ case reproduces a spatial slice in the extremal solution (18.10). If we assume $E = \alpha u^{-1}\nabla u$ (where α is the same constant as before), and vanishing extrinsic curvature, the time symmetric constraint equations reduce to Laplace's equation on u. So we can let u be the solution with point source at $r = r_0$, $\theta = 0$, and $z = 0$ representing a large charged black hole.

Surfaces of constant $z \neq 0$ are wormholes like the maximally extended Schwarzschild solution, and the initial data (18.21) is invariant under reflections about $r = r_0$. This shows that $r = r_0$ is an apparent horizon.

We now encounter a surprise: The area of this apparent horizon is infinite! This is because the horizon of the extreme black hole is infinitely far away in the static surface, and so the black string must be infinitely long to reach it. This does not contradict our statement that the total mass is close to that of the black hole since the mass of the black string is infinitely redshifted near the horizon. It also does not contradict our statement that the event horizon will have finite area since the event horizon will lie outside the apparent horizon and not go down the infinite throat. Nevertheless it is certainly surprising that a finite energy initial data set can contain infinite area apparent horizons.

What will the final configuration look like? A static horizon must have constant surface gravity. The initial data we have constructed has zero surface gravity on the black hole and large surface gravity on the black string. But, under evolution, we expect the black hole to swallow part of the black string and become slightly non-extremal. It is also plausible that the thin black string will acquire some charge and become near extremal. So the final configuration will probably resemble a large near extremal black hole with a near extremal black string going around the circle. This configuration would have low surface gravity everywhere. If one starts with this inhomogeneous black string and takes its extremal limit, it is plausible that the solution degenerates to an extremal black hole with a (singular) extremal black string going around the circle. This solution can be constructed explicitly. Recall the general form of static extremal solutions (18.10). The solution we want is obtained by letting U be the harmonic function with a line source and a point source superposed on the line. The line source produces the extremal black string, while the point source reproduces the extremal black hole.

The idea of adding a thin black string to initial data containing a black hole can also be applied in the vacuum case without any charges. (This requires a generalization of the gluing construction [24] to rigorously obtain time symmetric initial data.) This is of particular interest when $M/L^2 \ll 1$. Consider the evolution of initial data describing a spherical black hole of mass almost M, with a very thin black string attached going around the circle. As before, the mass can only decrease, the horizon area can only increase, and the horizon topology must remain $S^2 \times S^1$. One might wonder what the final configuration now looks like, since the surface gravity must be constant. One possibility is that the proper size of the circle at the horizon shrinks significantly. The final black string will have entropy at least as large as the initial black hole. Let us compare this with initial data describing a perturbation of a long uniform black string with $M/L^2 \ll 1$. If the radius of the circle at the horizon does not shrink, this probably evolves into an inhomogeneous black string with horizon oscillations set by the initial Schwarzschild radius. This solution would have much less entropy than the black hole with the same mass.

18.5 Open questions

Geometry of event horizon

(1) *What is the geometry of the horizon for the stable inhomogeneous black strings?*

This is clearly a key question. It cannot be answered just by looking at Einstein's equation near the horizon, since if there were a static configuration of matter outside, it would deform the horizon. One must impose the vacuum Einstein equation everywhere. A more specific question is:

(2) *Must the solution be spherically symmetric?*

As we discussed in section 18.2, the proper size of the circle at the horizon might be quite different from L when the solution is inhomogeneous. This leads us to ask:

(3) *Is the proper size of the circle at the horizon of order L, much larger, or much smaller?*

At the end of the previous section, we saw an example of a situation where it is likely that the size is much smaller.

Transitions in the space of static solutions

We have discussed the transition where the inhomogeneous black string meets the uniform solution. (See the discussion around Figure 18.1.) It is possible that there are further transitions at smaller values of M/L^2. This is because the new solutions with M/L^2 slightly below the critical value will likely have one maximum and one minimum radius of the horizon. As one decreases this parameter, there may be stable solutions with two local maxima and minima. This leads to the following question:

(4) *Are there static solutions with more than one maximum and minimum? If so, does the transition from one maximum to two proceed smoothly or discontinuously?*

For small values of M/L^2 there is another branch of solutions describing small five-dimensional spherical black holes in a space with one direction compactified. As one increases M/L^2, it is intuitively clear that this branch becomes a black string.

(5) *What is the nature of the transition from black holes to black strings? Are the first black strings formed inhomogeneous? If so, do they join onto the previously discussed solutions?*

Number of new solutions

(6) *How many static black strings are there?*

We have been implicitly assuming that for each value of M/L^2 there are at most a finite number of solutions. But a simple Newtonian analogy suggests otherwise. In (five-dimensional) Newtonian gravity, an $SO(3)$ invariant source is described by an arbitrary function $\rho(z)$ giving the line density on the axis. Of course, most of these configurations will not be static. But if one compactifies the z direction on a circle, one expects both a uniform line density and a single point mass to be static. An arbitrary linear combination would provide a continuous one parameter family of solutions, all with the same M/L^2!

This argument certainly requires some modification in general relativity. Consider the case of $M/L^2 \gg 1$. If one imagines that the horizon is located where the Newtonian potential is of order one, one obtains a small inhomogeneity on a black string that is short and fat. But the corresponding translationally invariant solution is stable. One would expect a small perturbation to decay and not remain static. Nevertheless, it is possible that there is a range of small M/L^2 for which the number of static black strings is infinite.

In the case of extreme charged black strings, this Newtonian argument can be made more precise. From the form of the solutions (18.10) it is clear that there is a static solution for any choice of the line density $\rho(z)$. Of course these solutions do not have regular horizons. It is natural to ask:

(7) *Which of the solutions (18.10) with U determined by an arbitrary line density $\rho(z)$ have non-extremal analogues with smooth event horizons?*

Black string critical phenomena

It is likely that there is a new type of black hole critical behaviour in five dimensions. Recall the situation in four dimensions involving the gravitational collapse of a spherically symmetric massless scalar field. For any initial profile, if the initial amplitude is small, the scalar field will scatter as in flat spacetime. The curvature will remain small everywhere and there will be no singularities. If the initial amplitude is large, most of the scalar field collapses down to form a large black hole. Near a critical amplitude, which separates these two phases, one finds behaviour similar to critical phenomena in condensed matter physics, including universal critical exponents [25].

This analysis of a spherically symmetric scalar field coupled to gravity in $D = 4$ can be immediately lifted to $D = 5$. This is because, if one assumes the vector potential vanishes, the standard Kaluza–Klein reduction of $D = 5$ vacuum Einstein theory is precisely Einstein gravity minimally coupled to a scalar field. More precisely, given any solution ϕ, $g_{\mu\nu}$ of $S = \int \sqrt{-g}\, d^4\, x[R - 2(\nabla\phi)^2]$, then

$$ds^2 = e^{-4\phi/\sqrt{3}}dz^2 + e^{2\phi/\sqrt{3}}g_{\mu\nu}dx^\mu dx^\nu \qquad (18.22)$$

is a vacuum metric in five dimensions. Since this solution is independent of z, Choptuik's original analysis corresponds to studying a transition between non-singular evolution and the formation of very thin black strings in $D = 5$. From the five-dimensional viewpoint, this is very unnatural. One should clearly relax the assumption of translation invariance in the extra dimension. Near the transition point, any z dependent perturbation of the initial data will probably result in the formation of small black holes (with S^3 topology) rather than a thin black string. The transition between non-singular evolution and small spherical black holes in higher dimensions is similar to four dimensions [26].[5]

However, another type of transition should occur even at non-zero horizon area. One can easily construct initial data which evolves to a black hole with S^3 horizon. One can also construct initial data which evolves to a black string with $S^2 \times S^1$ horizon. But one can continuously interpolate between these initial configurations. Since each of the final states are expected to be stable, one might expect an open set of initial data to evolve to each one. This leads to:

(8) *What happens at the transition point between the formation of black holes and black strings?*

As before, the transition can be reached by adjusting just one parameter. This dynamical question can be quite different from the static transition considered in question (5). After all, the critical solution in the four-dimensional collapse [25] cannot be found by looking at the static Schwarzschild metrics.

---

[5] This was done without compactification, but near the transition point, the compactification should not have much effect.

Generalizations

One natural generalization (especially in light of recent observations) is to add a non-zero cosmological constant. It is known that de Sitter horizons can sometimes be unstable [21, 27]. The stability of black strings in anti-de Sitter spacetime has also been investigated [28].

(9) *What is the geometry of static inhomogeneous horizons when the cosmological constant is nonzero?*

We have been treating the black strings entirely classically. When quantum matter is included, black strings will Hawking radiate just like black holes. Even though the temperature is constant over the horizon, it is not clear what happens to the inhomogeneities.

(10) *Will r_{max}/r_{min} increase, decrease, or remain the same under Hawking evaporation?*

18.6 Conclusions

Let me conclude by comparing static charged black holes in four and five dimensions (where the fifth dimension is compactified on a circle). Four-dimensional black holes are rather boring. They always have topology S^2, they are stable, have maximum symmetry (spherically symmetric), and are characterized by just their charge and mass.

In five dimensions, things are more interesting. One has static charged black holes with topology S^3. These are direct analogs of the four-dimensional case and are presumably stable and unique [29]. But, in addition, there are black strings with topology $S^2 \times S^1$. These can be unstable, can be inhomogeneous, and can have more than one stable solution with the same mass and charge.

One has the impression that the results presented here may be just the tip of the iceberg. Higher-dimensional generalizations of black holes seem to have a very rich structure that we are only beginning to explore.

Stephen has been an inspiration for me throughout my career. I wish him a very happy birthday!

Acknowledgements

It is a pleasure to thank Kengo Maeda for collaboration on all aspects of the work described here. I am grateful to V. Hubeny for extensive discussion of the Gregory–Laflamme instability and the nature of the final state. I also thank S. Gubser, J. Isenberg, and S. Ross for useful discussions. Finally, I want to thank the organizers of the Future of Theoretical

Physics and Cosmology Conference, for a very stimulating meeting. This work was supported in part by NSF grant PHY-0070895.

References

[1] Gibbons, G. W., Hawking, S. W., Horowitz, G. T. and Perry, M. J. (1983), 'Positive mass theorems for black holes', *Commun. Math. Phys.* **88** 295.

[2] Hawking, S. W., Horowitz, G. T. and Ross, S. F. (1995), 'Entropy, area, and black hole pairs', *Phys. Rev.* **D51** 4302, [gr-qc/9409013].

[3] Hawking, S. W. and Horowitz, G. T. (1996), 'The gravitational Hamiltonian, action, entropy and surface terms', *Class. Quant. Grav.* **13** 1487, [gr-qc/9501014].

[4] Witten, E. (1981), 'A simple proof of the positive energy theorem', *Commun. Math. Phys.* **80** 381.

[5] Hawking, S. W. and Ellis, G. F. R. (1973), *The Large Scale Structure of Space-Time*, (Cambridge University Press, Cambridge).

[6] Cai, M. L. and Galloway, G. J. (2001), 'On the topology and area of higher dimensional black holes', *Class. Quant. Grav.* **18** 2707, [hep-th/0102149].

[7] Gregory, R. and Laflamme, R. (1993), 'Black strings and P-branes are unstable', *Phys. Rev. Lett.* **70** 2837, [hep-th/9301052].

[8] Hawking, S. W. (1971), 'Gravitational radiation from colliding black holes', *Phys. Rev. Lett.* **26** 1344.

[9] Horowitz, G. T. and Maeda, K. (2001), 'Fate of the black string instability', *Phys. Rev. Lett.* **87** 131301, [hep-th/0105111].

[10] Wald, R. (1984), *General Relativity*, (University of Chicago Press, Chicago).

[11] Hawking, S. W., private communication.

[12] Harmark, T. and Obers, N. (2002), 'Black holes on cylinders', [hep-th/0204047].

[13] Emparan, R. and Reall, H. S. (2002), 'Generalized Weyl solutions', *Phys. Rev.* **D65** 084025, [hep-th/0110258].

[14] Choptuik, M., Lehner, L., Olabarrieta, I., Petryk, R., Pretorius, F. and Villegas, H., to appear.

[15] Wald, R. M. (1993), 'The first law of black hole mechanics', [gr-qc/9305022].

[16] Gubser, S. S. (2002), 'On non-uniform black branes', [hep-th/0110193].

[17] Emparan R. and Reall, H. S. (2002), 'A rotating black ring in five dimensions', *Phys. Rev. Lett.* **88** 101101, [hep-th/0110260].

[18] Gubser, S. S. and Mitra, I. (2001), 'Instability of charged black holes in anti-de Sitter space', [hep-th/0009126]; 'The evolution of unstable black holes in anti-de Sitter space', *JHEP* **0108** 018, [hep-th/0011127].

[19] Reall, H. S. (2001), 'Classical and thermodynamic stability of black branes', *Phys. Rev.* **D64** 044005, [hep-th/0104071].

[20] Gregory, J. P. and Ross, S. F. (2001), 'Stability and the negative mode for Schwarzschild in a finite cavity', *Phys. Rev.* **D64** 124006, [hep-th/0106220].

[21] Hubeny, V. E. and Rangamani, M. (2002), 'Unstable horizons', [hep-th/0202189].

[22] Horowitz, G. T. and Maeda, K. (2002), 'Inhomogeneous near-extremal black branes', [hep-th/0201241].

[23] Myers, R. C. (1987), 'Higher dimensional black holes in compactified space-times', *Phys. Rev.* **D35**, 455.

[24] Isenberg, J., Mazzeo, R. and Pollack, D. (2001), 'Gluing and wormholes for the Einstein constraint equations', [gr-qc/0109045].

[25] Choptuik, M. W. (1993), 'Universality and scaling in gravitational collapse of a massless scalar field', *Phys. Rev. Lett.* **70** 9.

[26] Garfinkle, D., Cutler, C. and Duncan, G. C. (1999), 'Choptuik scaling in six dimensions', *Phys. Rev.* **D60** 104007, [gr-qc/9908044].

[27] Bousso, R. and Hawking, S. W. (1998), '(Anti-)evaporation of Schwarzschild–de Sitter black holes', *Phys. Rev.* **D57** 2436, [hep-th/9709224].

[28] Gregory, R. (2000), 'Black string instabilities in anti-de Sitter space', *Class. Quant. Grav.* **17** L125, [hep-th/0004101]; Hirayama, T. and Kang, G. (2001), 'Stable black strings in anti-de Sitter space', *Phys. Rev.* **D64** 064010, [hep-th/0104213].

[29] Gibbons, G. W., Ida, D. and Shiromizu, T. (2002), 'Uniqueness and non-uniqueness of static vacuum black holes in higher dimensions', [gr-qc/0203004].

19

Twenty years of debate with Stephen

Leonard Susskind
Stanford University

19.1 Crisis and paradigm shift

Stephen, as we all know, is by far the most stubborn and infuriating person in the universe. My own scientific relation with him I think can be called adversarial. We have disagreed profoundly about deep issues concerning black holes, information and all that kind of thing. At times he has caused me to pull my hair out in frustration – and you can plainly see the result. I can assure you that when we began to argue more than two decades ago, I had a full head of hair.

I can also say that of all the physicists I have known he has had the strongest influence on me and on my thinking. Just about everything I have thought about since 1980 has in one way or another been a response to his profoundly insightful question about the fate of information that falls into a black hole [1]. While I firmly believe his answer was wrong, the question and his insistence on a convincing answer has forced us to rethink the foundations of physics. The result is a wholly new paradigm that is now taking shape. I am deeply honoured to be here to celebrate Stephen's monumental contributions and especially his magnificent stubbornness.

The new paradigm whose broad outlines are already clear involves four closely related ideas which I will call Horizon Complementarity (also known as Black Hole Complementarity) [2, 3], the Holographic Principle [4, 5], the Ultraviolet/Infrared connection [6] and the counting of black hole microstates [7–11]. Each has had strong support from the mathematics of string theory. We have also learned that certain lessons derived from quantum field theory in a fixed background can lead to totally wrong conclusions. For example quantum field theory gives rise to an ultraviolet divergent result for the entropy in the vicinity of a horizon [12, 13] and a volume's worth of degrees of freedom in a region of space. Another misleading result of quantum field theory is that increasingly large energy and momentum scales are equivalent to progressively smaller distance scales. Finally quantum field theory in a black hole background inevitably leads to the loss of quantum coherence from the vantage point of a distant observer [1].

19.2 Stephen's argument for coherence loss

Let's begin with the issue of coherence loss. Begin by drawing the Penrose diagram for black hole formation. Let us think of it as a background on which we can study conventional quantum field theory. Now let's add some additional particles which for simplicity are assumed massless. Incoming particles enter the geometry on past light-like infinity, $\mathcal{I}^-$. The initial Hilbert space of such particles is labelled $\mathcal{H}_-$. The particles interact through Feynman diagrams and some go out to $\mathcal{I}^+$ where they are seen by a distant observer. But some particles end up at the spacelike singularity. A conventional local description would have the final states live in a Hilbert space which is a product $\mathcal{H}_+ \otimes \mathcal{H}_{sing}$.

Applying ordinary rules to this system we expect the final state to be given in terms of the initial state by an S matrix,

$$|f\rangle = S|i\rangle \tag{19.1}$$

but to an observer outside the black hole the final state consists only of the particles on $\mathcal{I}^+$. It is therefore described by a density matrix

$$\rho = Tr_{sing}|f\rangle\langle f|. \tag{19.2}$$

Since black holes eventually evaporate we are left with a mixed state and a loss of quantum coherence. I have simplified some of the important parts of Stephen's argument but in the original paper he makes a very convincing case that quantum field theory in a black hole environment leads to a loss of coherence after the evaporation has occurred. The problem with this is that loss of quantum coherence violates the fundamental tenets of quantum mechanics. That of course was Stephen's point.

Historically, for a long time high energy physicists, who had other fish to fry, ignored the problem. By and large, with one or two exceptions [14], the relativity community accepted the loss of coherence without question. However, 't Hooft and I were both deeply disturbed by Stephen's conclusion. In my case I felt that loss of coherence, if it were to occur, could not be quarantined or isolated to phenomena that involved massive black holes. It would infect the rest of physics and cause dramatic disasters in ordinary situations [15]. 't Hooft also expressed similar concerns [16].

There was of course an alternative that I have not mentioned. We might suppose that instead of falling through the horizon, particles (and falling observers) encounter an obstruction, a 'brick wall' instead of the horizon. Again the trouble is that an observer, now the freely falling one, would experience a violation of a sacred law of nature, this time the equivalence principle. The horizon according to general relativity is an almost flat region that should behave like empty space, not like a brick wall. It seems that there is no way out; at least one or another observer must witness violations of the usual laws of nature.

At this point one could ask why not just assume neither observer sees a violation of sacred principles. Just assume that the infalling information is 'Xeroxed' or 'cloned' at the horizon. One copy would fall through with the infalling observer and the other copy would get scrambled and radiated with the evaporation products. Each observer would see the usual laws of nature respected. The problem is that it potentially violates another law of quantum mechanics. I call it the 'Quantum Xerox' principle. It says that quantum information stored in a single system cannot be duplicated. To illustrate the principle consider a single spin whose z component can take two values: $\sigma_z = \pm 1$. We call the two states $|+\rangle$ and $|-\rangle$. Suppose we had a quantum Xerox machine that could produce a clone of the spin in exactly the original state. Its action is defined by

$$|+\rangle \rightarrow |++\rangle$$
$$|-\rangle \rightarrow |--\rangle. \tag{19.3}$$

But now consider the action of the quantum Xerox machine on the superposition of states $|+\rangle + |-\rangle$ that represents a spin oriented along the x axis. According to the principles of quantum mechanics the result must be the superposition $|++\rangle + |--\rangle$. This is because quantum evolution is a linear process. On the other hand the QXM must clone the original state

$$(|+\rangle + |-\rangle) \rightarrow (|+\rangle + |-\rangle) \bigotimes (|+\rangle + |-\rangle) \tag{19.4}$$

or

$$(|++\rangle + |--\rangle) \rightarrow |++\rangle + |+-\rangle + |-+\rangle + |--\rangle. \tag{19.5}$$

Evidently the quantum Xerox machine is not consistent with the principle of linear quantum evolution.

The Quantum Xerox Principle was probably an implicit part of Stephen's thinking. I remember that in Aspen sometime around 1992 I gave a seminar explaining why I thought loss of coherence was a big problem and as part of the talk I introduced the QX principle. A number of people in the audience didn't believe it at first but Stephen's reaction was instantaneous: 'So now you agree with me'. I said no, that I didn't but that I was trying to explain to the high energy people why it was such a serious problem. However, it was also true that I couldn't see my way out of the paradox.

19.3 Horizon Complementarity

When you have eliminated all that is impossible, whatever remains must be the truth, no matter how improbable it is. Sherlock Holmes

The principle of Horizon Complementarity I interpret to mean that no observer ever witnesses a violation of the laws of nature. It is obvious that no observer external to the black hole is in danger of seeing the forbidden duplication of infalling information since one copy is behind the horizon. The danger, pointed out by John Preskill [17], is that the observer outside the horizon, call him B, can jump into the horizon having previously collected the relevant information in the Hawking radiation. We must now worry whether the original infalling observer (call her A) can send a signal to B so that B has witnessed information duplication albeit behind the horizon. The answer is no, it is not possible [18]. The reason is interesting and involves a fact first explained by Don Page [19] who realized that to get a single bit of information out of the evaporation products you must wait until about half the entropy of the black hole has been evaporated. This takes a time, in Planck units of order M^3, where M is the black hole mass. It is then easy to see from the black hole metric that if B waits a time of that order of magnitude before jumping behind the horizon, then A must send her signal extremely quickly after passing the horizon. Otherwise the message will not arrive at B before hitting the singularity. Quantitatively the time that B has after passing the horizon is of order $\Delta t \sim \exp(-M^2)$ where all things are given in Planck units.

Now in classical physics an arbitrary amount of information can be sent in an arbitrarily small time using an arbitrarily small energy. But in quantum theory if we want to send a single bit we must use at least one quantum. Obviously that quantum must have an energy satisfying $\Delta E \sim \exp M^2$. In other words A had to be carrying an energy vastly larger than the black hole in order that B ever witness the forbidden information cloning. This makes no sense since if A had that much energy it couldn't possibly fit inside the black hole. We see that a consistent use of quantum mechanics simultaneously allows external observations to be consistent with quantum coherence; the infalling observations to be consistent with the equivalence principle and, finally, prevents the observer who chooses to jump in after accumulating some information from ever seeing information duplication.

I can now state the principle of Horizon Complementarity. All it says is that no observer ever sees a violation of the laws of nature. More specifically it says that to an observer who never crosses the horizon, the horizon behaves like a conventional complex system which can absorb, thermalize and re-emit all information that falls on it. No information is ever lost. In essence, the world on the outside of a horizon is a closed system.

On the other hand a freely falling observer encounters nothing out of the ordinary, no large tidal force, high temperature or brick wall at the horizon. The paradox of information being at two places at the same time is apparent and a careful analysis shows that no real contradictions arise.

But there is a weirdness to it. Just to make the point, let's imagine a whole galaxy falling into a huge black hole with a Schwarzschild radius equal to a billion light years. From the outside, the galaxy and all its unfortunate inhabitants appear to be heated to Planckian temperature, thermalized and eventually emitted as evaporation products and all this takes place at the horizon! On the other hand, the infalling galactic inhabitants glide through perfectly happily. To them the trauma only happens at the singularity a billion years later. But as in the case of certain life-after-death theories, the folks on the other side can never communicate with us.

It is clear from Horizon Complementarity that a revision is needed in the way we think about information being localized in spacetime. In both classical relativity and in quantum field theory the spacetime location of an event is invariant, that is, independent of the observer. Nothing in either theory prepares us for the kind of weirdness I described above.

19.4 The Holographic Principle

The idea that information is in some sense stored at the boundary of a system instead of the bulk was called Dimensional Reduction by 't Hooft and the Holographic Principle by me [4, 5]. The simple argument for the Holographic Principle goes as follows. Imagine a ball of space Γ bounded by a spherical area $A = 4\pi R^2$. Ordinarily we would assume that the entropy in that region can be arbitrarily large. However if we introduce a cut-off in space, say at the Planck scale, and assume that within each Planckian volume only a small number of states are possible. then it is natural to assume that the maximum entropy is finite and proportional to the volume of the region. However it is easy to see that this cannot be so. Imagine an imploding spherical light-like shell with just enough energy so that the boundary of Γ gets turned into a black hole horizon. The final entropy of the system is the Bekenstein–Hawking entropy of the black hole $S_{BH} = A/4G$. By the Second Law, the entropy within Γ could not have been larger than this. But, by causality, this bound can't depend on the existence of the infalling light-like shell. Thus it follows that the largest entropy a region of space can have is given by

$$S_{max} = A/4G. \tag{19.6}$$

A further implication is that the number of degrees of freedom (binary bits) needed to describe a region is also proportional to the area. It is as though the information in the bulk of Γ can be mapped to a set of 'Holographic' degrees of freedom on the boundary. The idea that the quantum mechanics of a region can be described in terms of a theory of no more than $A/4G$ degrees of freedom is the content of the Holographic Principle. It is also very weird but it is forced on us by Bekenstein's observation about black hole entropy [20], the usual interpretation of entropy as counting states and Holmes' dictum.

19.5 The ultraviolet/infrared connection

The dominant paradigm of 20th century physics has been that small distance means high energy or more precisely high momentum. Thus to probe increasingly small (and presumably increasingly fundamental) objects, higher and higher energy accelerators have been built. Again this is a lesson learned from conventional quantum field theory. But the more we learn about the combination of gravity and quantum mechanics the clearer it becomes that this trend will eventually reverse itself. Imagine trying to probe distance scales very much smaller than the Planck scale by building the *Gedankatron*, a collider of colossal proportions, which can accelerate electrons to momenta way above the Planck scale. Well, there is no need to build it. We already know what will happen. In a head-on collision a black hole will form and the black hole will have a Schwarzschild radius of order of the centre of mass energy M in Planck units. The black hole will evaporate with a temperature of order $1/M$. Thus the collision will result in the emission of longer and longer wavelength quanta and will probe distance scales of order MG and not $1/M$. This is the simplest example of the UV/IR connection. Similar things happen in perturbative string theory where increasing energy again results in decreasing spatial resolution.

In order to clarify the mechanisms behind the UV/IR connection and show its connection with the Holographic Principle I will use the famous example of the AdS/CFT duality of Maldacena [21]. Let me quickly remind you of this duality. We begin with a stack of N D3-branes in ten-dimensional string theory. The branes fill the directions $(1, 2, 3)$. They are all placed at the origin in the $(4, 5, 6, 7, 8, 9)$ directions. We also define

$r^2 = (x^4)^2 + ... + (x^9)^2$. The geometry of the resulting stack has a horizon at $r = 0$ where the stack is located.

I will not explain in detail the so called decoupling or near-horizon limit. The literature on the subject is enormous. Suffice it to say that the D-brane stack is exactly described in two ways which are dual to one another. The first is by gravity in an AdS space with horizon at $r = 0$. The AdS also has a time-like causal boundary at $r = \infty$. Although the boundary is an infinite proper distance from any finite r, the geometry is such that light takes a finite time to travel to the boundary and back.

The dual 'Holographic' description is in terms of a 3+1 dimensional conformal gauge theory whose precise details are unimportant for our purposes. The quantum field theory is usually interpreted as residing on the boundary of the AdS, infinitely far from the horizon. On the other hand the branes that support the open string field quanta are supposedly located at $r = 0$. There seems to be some serious confusion about the location of the branes. Are they at $r = 0$ or $r = \infty$? The answer to this question is closely related to the paradox of where the information in a black hole resides.

In the field theory dual the location of the branes in the $(x^4..x^9)$ space is described by a set of six $N \times N$ matrix valued fields ϕ. The connection between the location of a brane and the corresponding field is

$$\langle r^2 \rangle = \frac{1}{N^2} \langle Tr\phi^2 \rangle. \tag{19.7}$$

Now we can see the problem in localizing the branes. The field ϕ is a canonically normalized scalar field with mass dimension 1. As such, it has zero point fluctuations which render the value of r^2 divergent. If taken at face value, this would say that the branes are located at the boundary at $r = \infty$. But this is not the most useful way to think about the problem. A better way to think about it is to introduce an ultraviolet cut-off in the gauge theory. Let the regulator frequency be called ν. Then (19.7) is replaced by

$$\langle r^2 \rangle = \frac{1}{N^2} Tr\langle \phi^2 \rangle = \nu^2. \tag{19.8}$$

Once again we see something weird. The location of the branes is not an invariantly defined quantity. It depends on the frequency resolution that the observer uses. If the branes are observed in a way that averages over high frequency oscillations then their location is near $r = 0$. On the other hand if all the ultraviolet fluctuations are included then the branes are located out near the causal boundary of AdS and the entire theory in the bulk of AdS is described by a holographic description in terms of boundary degrees of freedom. This interplay between short time cutoffs in the quantum field theory and the location of the brane degrees of freedom is called the UV/IR connection [6].

The UV/IR connection is closely related to the weirdness of Complementarity. Imagine an observer falling toward a black hole horizon while blowing a dog whistle. A dog whistle is just a whistle whose frequency is beyond the range of human hearing. The freely falling observer never hears the whistle. But to someone outside the black hole the frequency is red shifted so that after a while the whistle becomes audible. In the same way, the ultra-high frequency fluctuations of an object are invisible under ordinary circumstances. But as the object approaches the horizon the external observer becomes sensitive to them. In the example I just showed you the observed location and spread of an object depends on the visibility of the high frequency fluctuations. Thus the UV/IR connection provides a mechanism for understanding Horizon Complementarity [22]. Horizon Complementarity, the Holographic Principle and the UV/IR connection are different facets of the same weirdness that characterizes the new paradigm.

19.6 Counting black hole microstates

Ultimately the question of black hole coherence boils down to whether or not the formation and evaporation of a black hole can be described from the outside by an S-matrix. Stephen said no. 't Hooft and I said yes. Although, for years, many string theorists sat on the fence about the issue, they really had no choice. The only mathematically well defined objects in string theory, at least in a flat background, are S-matrix data. This includes the complete list of stable objects in the theory and the transition amplitudes for their scattering. Unstable objects also have meaning as resonances that can be defined as poles of the S-matrix in the complex energy plane. If the laws of quantum mechanics are not violated for a distant observer, black holes are simply such resonances. It sometimes happens that resonances become extremely densely spaced. This occurs in nuclear collisions and also in string theory. In these cases the practical tools are those of statistical mechanics and thermodynamics.

Complementarity implies that the thermodynamics of a black hole should arise from a quantum statistical mechanical origin. Consider the thermodynamic description of a bathtub of hot water. We specify a few macroscopic variables such as the volume, energy temperature, etc. Of special significance is the entropy. Entropy, as we know, is a measure of our ignorance of the precise microscopic details of the tub of water. It measures the logarithm of the number of quantum states consistent with the macroscopic description. The existence of an entropy tells us that there is a hidden set of microscopic degrees of freedom. It doesn't tell us what those degrees of freedom are but it tells us they are there and that they can store detailed information that our thermodynamic description is too coarse grained to see. The principle of Black Hole Complementarity requires the thermodynamics of black holes to originate from the coarse graining of hidden microscopic degrees of freedom and that the entropy is counting the number of microstates of the black hole.

General relativity does not tell us what those microstates are. But a theory like string theory which is supposed to be a consistent quantum theory of gravity should tell us and it does [7–11]. Let us begin with a single string in very weakly coupled string theory. If the string is excited to a high state of excitation it typically forms a random walking tangle. It is natural to describe it statistically.

Let L be the total length of string and $T = 1/\alpha'$ be the tension. The mass of the string is then

$$m = TL. \tag{19.9}$$

A good model of the string is to think of it as a series of links on a lattice. The link size is the string length $\sqrt{\alpha'}$. Lets suppose that when we follow the string and it arrives at a lattice site it can continue in n distinct directions. We can then count the number of configurations of the string. The number of links is $L/\sqrt{\alpha'}$ and the number of states is

$$N_{states} = n^{L/\sqrt{\alpha'}}. \tag{19.10}$$

Thus the entropy is

$$S = \frac{L}{\sqrt{\alpha'}} \log n \tag{19.11}$$

or, using (19.9), $S = m\sqrt{\alpha'} \log n$. The thing to abstract from this formula is that the entropy is proportional to the mass in string units. The precise coefficient is determined by the details of string theory:

$$S = cm\sqrt{\alpha'}. \tag{19.12}$$

Now imagine turning up the string coupling constant. The large ball of random walking string will begin to experience the effects of gravity. It will shrink and will gain some negative gravitational binding energy. Eventually it will turn into a black hole. This much is obvious. What is less obvious is what happens if we begin with a neutral black hole and turn off the coupling. It is clear that it must evolve into a system of free strings in this limit but how many such strings will be left at the end of the process? Surprisingly the answer is that the overwhelmingly most likely final state is a single string! The number of configurations of one long string vastly outweighs all other configurations. Thus we can go back and forth from single string states to black holes.

This suggests the following strategy [7]. Start with a black hole of a given mass M. Let us follow it while we adiabatically turn down the string coupling. The entropy will be conserved by such an adiabatic process. At the end we will get a single string of some other mass m. If we can follow the process and determine m we can use (19.12) to estimate the entropy of the original black hole.

This strategy has been used to study a large variety of black holes that occur in string theory [7–11] including Schwarzschild black holes in all dimensions, and special supersymmetric black holes where the precise coefficients can be obtained. Up to numerical coefficients of order unity, the results always agree with the universal formula

$$S = \frac{area}{4G}. \tag{19.13}$$

By now string theory has given us great confidence in the counting of black hole microstates and that there is no need to look for a new basis for gravitational entropy outside the framework of conventional quantum statistical mechanics.

19.7 De Sitter space

Let me turn now to Stephen's favorite subject, cosmology. According to the inflationary theory the universe may have started as a long lived approximation to de Sitter space with a very small radius of curvature, perhaps a couple of orders of magnitude larger than the Planck radius. Right now observations indicate that it may end as a de Sitter space of radius $\sim 10^{60} l_p$. Whether or not this will ultimately prove to be the case it clearly behoves us to study and understand the quantum nature of de Sitter space. Once again, Stephen, together with Gary Gibbons, led the way [23].

De Sitter space is another example of a spacetime that has an event horizon and therefore an entropy and temperature. Accordingly, we should expect paradoxical issues of black hole quantum mechanics to confuse and harass us in this context. The rest of my discussion will concentrate on the quantum mechanics of pure de Sitter space. However before doing so I will remind you of some facts about Schwarzschild black holes in AdS [24]. You will see why shortly. The Penrose diagram for an AdS-Schwarzschild black hole is a square bounded on top and bottom by singularities and on the sides by causal boundaries which are at an infinite proper distance. The diagonals of the square are the horizons. Note that the boundary is doubled. As usual, the diagram is divided into four regions. Region I is the exterior of the black hole. The Penrose diagram has a boost symmetry which acts in regions I and III it as time translation invariance but with the convention that in III it translates in the negative time-like direction. In regions II and IV it translates in space-like directions.

The AdS black hole has a description in the dual CFT language. It is simply the state of thermal equilibrium for the CFT above the temperature corresponding to the Hawking–Page transition [24]. Since the CFT is a conventional quantum system we can be sure that the boundary observers see nothing inconsistent with quantum theory in all possible experiments that they can perform on the black hole. In particular the region I which is in causal contact with the boundary and which is described by the CFT cannot experience anything that violates the standard quantum principles. No information can be lost across the horizon. In this respect region I is a closed quantum system.

How does black hole complementarity manifest itself in this system? To see the full implications of exact information conservation in terms of correlation functions is extremely complicated. But Maldacena has given a very useful implication [25]. Consider the correlation function of two local boundary operators at widely separated times t and t'. For example, the operators could be the gravitational field evaluated at the boundary and described by the energy-momentum tensor of the QFT. The correlation function can be computed by doing a bulk calculation of the graviton propagator in the AdS-Schwarzschild background. The answer is that it exponentially tends to zero as the time separation grows. From the CFT point of view the exponential decrease has a simple explanation. The thermal environment leads to dissipation which generally causes correlations to disappear exponentially. The coefficient in the exponential is a dissipation coefficient. However, Maldacena argues that there is something wrong with this conclusion. His claim is that the correct answer on general grounds is that the correlation decreases exponentially until it is of order exp–S where S is the finite black hole entropy. Thereafter it stops decreasing. If Maldacena is correct it means that ordinary QFT in the bulk is missing something important and that something is closely connected to conservation of information outside the black hole. The argument that the correlation has a non-vanishing limit was not spelled out in Maldacena's paper but I will derive it shortly.

Now what does all this have to do with de Sitter space? To answer this we only need to draw the Penrose diagram for de Sitter space. In fact it is identical to the AdS-Schwarzschild case! There are very big geometrical differences but the causal structure is the same. In the de Sitter case the vertical boundaries of the Penrose diagram are not spatial infinity but the 'north and south poles' of the spherical spatial sections. One of these poles we can identify as 'the observer'. The horizontal boundaries are not high-curvature singularities but are instead the infinitely inflated past I^- and the infinitely inflated future I^+.

The metric for de Sitter space is

$$ds^2 = R^2 \left(dt^2 - \cosh^2(t)d\Omega_d^2\right) \qquad (19.14)$$

where R is the radius of the de Sitter space and d is the dimension of space.

If de Sitter space exists in a quantum theory of gravity, perhaps the most urgent question is what are the mathematical objects that the theory defines. This is particularly important for string theory. In flat space the answer is S-matrix data. In AdS it is boundary correlators of the gravitational and other bulk fields. In both cases we go to the boundary of the world and define vertex operators whose correlators are the 'definables'. The obvious suggestion for de Sitter space is that we do the same thing. The boundary of de Sitter space is the union of I^- and I^+. This suggests that the definables consist of S-matrix-like elements which relate initial states on I^- to final states on I^+ [26–28]. I have used the term definables[1] and not observables for the reason that no one can ever observe them. The argument is closely connected to that of section 19.3 about why information duplication can't be detected behind a black hole horizon. In that case there was just not enough time for any observer to collect information from the observers A and B before reaching the singularity. The similarity of I^+ to the singularity of a black hole means that two observers at fixed spatial coordinates cannot transmit the results of measurements to one another once global time gets too late. Accordingly, correlators of fields at the future boundary are unobservable.

In the black hole case it is not just that quantum correlators on the singularity are un-measurable. Just their mere *mathematical* existence would require us to trace over them in defining final states. It is of obvious importance to know if the same is true in de Sitter space. In other words can similar arguments show that the existence of de Sitter space boundary correlators will lead some observer to see a violation of the laws of nature? I will argue that the answer is yes. But first we need to formulate an appropriate complementarity principle.

In the black hole case, a convenient starting point for discussing observations outside the hole is the presentation of the geometry in Schwarzschild coordinates. The distinguishing features of these coordinates are that they are static and that they only cover the region on

---

[1] Witten has used the terms computables and meta-observable for the same objects.

Leonard Susskind

the observer's side of the horizon. In de Sitter space an observer means a timelike trajectory that begins on I^- and ends on I^+. All such pairs of points are related by symmetry and it is always possible to choose them at the same spatial location. Thus we can always choose the observer to be the $r = 0$ edge of the Penrose diagram. By analogy with the AdS/Schwarzschild case the diagonals of the square Penrose diagram are horizons and the region on the observer's side of the horizon is a triangle. On this region it is possible to choose static coordinates so that the metric takes the form

$$ds^2 = R^2 \left((1 - r^2)dt^2 - (1 - r^2)^{-1}dr^2 - r^2 d\Omega_{d-1}^2 \right).　\quad (19.15)$$

This geometry has a horizon at $r = 1$ which now surrounds the observer. As usual, the horizon has an entropy

$$S = area/4G = \pi R^2/G \quad (19.16)$$

and a temperature. The proper temperature at a point r is given by

$$T(r) = \frac{1}{2\pi R\sqrt{1 - r^2}}.　\quad (19.17)$$

As for Rindler or Schwarzschild space, the temperature diverges near the horizon. The observer at $r = 0$ experiences a more modest temperature.

The statement of Horizon Complementarity is fairly obvious. An observer at $r = 0$ sees the world as a closed finite system at a non-zero temperature. Once again, closed means that no information is lost and the system obeys the rules of quantum mechanics for such closed systems [29]. What are the implications of the complementarity principle and especially the conservation of information? As in the similar AdS-Schwarzschild case there are implications for the long time behaviour of correlators. However before discussing them I want to consider the behaviour of field correlators in ordinary quantum field theory in the fixed de Sitter space background. For this purpose I return to global coordinates.

For simplicity I will use the example of a massive scalar field Φ with mass μ/R. The field equation is easily worked out and the asymptotic behavior of Φ is seen to be [26]

$$\Phi \rightarrow \exp -\gamma|t| \quad (19.18)$$

as $t \rightarrow \pm\infty$. The 'diffusion constant' γ is given by

$$\gamma = d \pm i\sqrt{\mu^2 - \frac{d^2}{4}}.　\quad (19.19)$$

The complex value of γ has a simple meaning in terms of damped oscillations. Depending of the value of μ the oscillations of the field are either under-damped or over-damped. The real part of γ is always positive.

Now let us return to static coordinates and consider the correlator at $r = 0$ and large time separation. Time translation invariance in the static patch together with (19.18) requires the correlator to behave like

$$F(t) = \langle \phi(t)\phi(t')\rangle \sim \exp -\gamma |t - t'|. \tag{19.20}$$

Thus, as in the AdS-Schwarzschild black hole the correlator evaluated by naive quantum field theory tends to zero exponentially with time. As we will see, this is inconsistent with the finite entropy of the static patch.

19.8 Correlations in finite entropy systems

Let us consider an arbitrary system described by Hamiltonian H at temperature $1/\beta$. I will not assume anything about the total number of states of the system but only that the thermal entropy is finite, $S = finite$. An immediate implication is that the spectrum is discrete and that the level spacing is of order

$$\Delta E \sim \exp -S. \tag{19.21}$$

Let's label the energy levels E_m.

Now consider a correlator of the form [30]

$$\langle \Phi(0)\Phi(t)\rangle \equiv F(t). \tag{19.22}$$

It is defined by

$$F(t) = \frac{1}{Z}Tr\, e^{-\beta H}\Phi(0)\Phi(t)$$

$$= \frac{1}{Z}\sum_{mn} e^{-\beta E_n}|\Phi_{nm}|^2 e^{it(E_m - E_n)}. \tag{19.23}$$

For simplicity I will assume that the diagonal matrix elements of Φ vanish. This implies that the time average of Φ also vanishes.

I want to determine if F tends to zero as $t \to \infty$. A simple way to do this is to compute the long-time average of F^*F.

$$L = \lim_{T\to\infty} \frac{1}{2T} \int_{-T}^{T} F^*(t)F(t). \tag{19.24}$$

If $F \to 0$ then $L = 0$.

Using (19.23) it is straightforward to compute L;

$$L = \frac{1}{Z^2} \sum_{mnrs} e^{-\beta(E_m + E_r)} |\Phi_{mn}|^2 |\Phi_{rs}|^2. \tag{19.25}$$

This is a positive definite quantity. We have therefore proved that the correlation function does not go to zero.

It is not hard to estimate L [31]. We use the fact that the level spacing is of order $\exp - S$ which implies that the matrix elements of Φ are of the same order of magnitude. The result is

$$L \sim \exp - 2S \tag{19.26}$$

indicating that at asymptotic times the average magnitude of the correlator is of order

$$|F| \sim \exp - S, \tag{19.27}$$

which agrees with Maldacena's guess.

However, this does not mean that the correlator tends smoothly to an exponentially small constant. In fact it does something quite different. It becomes 'noisy'. Typically the fluctuations are small, of order $\exp - S$. But if you wait long enough large fluctuations occur. On sufficiently long time scales the correlation function returns to close to its original value. In [30] the reader can find plots of the results of some numerical studies done by Lisa Dyson and James Lindesay [30] which show the typical behaviour. The large scale fluctuations are the quantum version of Poincaré recurrences in classical mechanics. They are just an indication that, in a closed finite system, if you wait long enough everything will eventually happen and not just once but in eternal repetition.

What is the significance of this fact and why is it missed by quantum field theory in the de Sitter space background? First of all it means that any formulation of quantum gravity in de Sitter space that relies on the existence of well defined asymptotic fields must fail. Among these I include the possibility that string theory might provide a set of scattering amplitudes relating asymptotic states on $I^{\pm}$. Another version of de Sitter space quantum gravity is the so called dS/CFT correspondence inspired by the AdS/CFT duality. This theory attempts to organize boundary correlators into a Euclidean quantum field theory.

A question that often comes up in any discussion of de Sitter space is how the static patch observer should think about objects (conventionally called elephants) that enter and leave the static patch through the diagonal past and future horizons. Such events are described by very rare fluctuations that materialize among the large number of low frequency degrees of freedom very near the horizon. In other words they are the very intermittent large fluctuations that can be see in the numerical simulations of [30]. Such elephants cannot be tossed in from I^-. To understand why, let's think about the elephant in its own frame. Because of the thermal fluctuations in de Sitter space an elephant will eventually be thermalized and turned into black body radiation. Since I^- is an infinite proper time in the past any elephants that were present in the initial conditions have long been thermalized by any finite time. Elephants in de Sitter space are thermal fluctuations that form by chance and then evaporate.

Finally, why does quantum field theory in the de Sitter space background miss these fluctuations? The answer is simply that in quantum field theory the entropy of a horizon has an ultraviolet divergence due to modes arbitrarily close to the horizon. These modes provide an infinite number of low frequency oscillators which effectively make the system open. But we know that most of these modes must be eliminated in a proper theory of quantum gravity since the entropy of horizons is finite.

If boundary correlators and S-matrix elements cannot exist in de Sitter space what then are we to base a quantum theory on? Here things are much more obscure than in AdS. A possible answer is to define a theory in the closed static patch. But, as emphasized by Bohr, the clearest use of quantum mechanics is when we can separate the world into a system and a large or classical apparatus (observer). That is just what we cannot do in a closed finite thermal system like de Sitter space. In fact the whole discussion of static patches being defined by infinitely long lived observers in de Sitter space is internally inconsistent. Like elephants, any real observer is subject to bombardment by the thermal radiation and will become degraded. Exactly how to think about quantum mechanics is far from clear. Perhaps eternal de Sitter space is just a bad idea and will go away. Perhaps not.

So you can see that Stephen and I have had much to disagree about. These disagreements have been incredibly exciting and certainly provided the high point of my own career. There is no doubt that Stephen's remarkable question about black holes has left an indelible mark on me but more importantly, on the future of physics.

Happy birthday, Stephen and best wishes for many more.

References

[1] Hawking, S. W. (1976), 'Breakdown of predictability in gravitational collapse', *Phys. Rev.* **D14** 2460.

[2] Susskind, L., Thorlacius, L. and Uglum, J. (1993), 'The stretched horizon and black hole complementarity', *Phys. Rev.* **D48** 3743–3761, [hep-th/9306069].

[3] Stephens, C. R., 't Hooft, G. and Whiting, B. F. (1994), 'Black hole evaporation without information loss', *Class. Quant. Grav.* **11** 621–648.

[4] 't Hooft, G. (1993) 'Dimensional reduction in quantum gravity', [gr-qc/9310026].

[5] Susskind, L. (1995), 'The world as a hologram', *J. Math. Phys.* **36** 6377–6396, [hep-th/9409089].

[6] Susskind, L. and Witten, E. (1998), 'The holographic bound in anti-de Sitter space', [hep-th/9805114].

[7] Susskind, L. (1993), 'Some speculations about black hole entropy in string theory', [hep-th/9309145].

[8] Sen, A. (1995), Black hole solutions in heterotic string theory on a torus', *Nucl. Phys.* **B440**, 421–440, [hep-th/9411187].

[9] Strominger, A. and Vafa, C. (1996), 'Microscopic origin of the Bekenstein–Hawking entropy', *Phys. Lett.* **379B**, 99–104, [hep-th/9601029].

[10] Callan, C. G. and Maldacena, J. M. (1996), 'D-brane approach to black hole quantum mechanics', *Nucl. Phys.* **B472**, 591–610, [hep-th/9602043].

[11] Horowitz, G. T. and Polchinski, J. (1997), 'A correspondence principle for black holes and strings', *Phys. Rev.* **D55** 6189–6197, [hep-th/9612146].

[12] 't Hooft, G. (1985), 'On the quantum structure of a black hole', *Nucl. Phys.* **B256** 727.

[13] Srednicki, M. (1993), 'Entropy and area', *Phys. Rev. Lett.* **71** 666.

[14] For an early critique of Hawking's proposal, see Page, D. N. (1980), *Phys. Rev. Lett.* **44** 301.

[15] Banks, T., Peskin, M. and Susskind, L. (1984), 'Difficulties for the evolution of pure states into mixed states', *Nucl. Phys.* **B244** 125.

[16] 't Hooft, G., 'The black hole interpretation of string theory', *Nucl. Phys.* **B335** (90) 138, and references therein.

[17] Preskill, J. (1993), Unpublished.

[18] Susskind, L. and Thorlacius, L. (1994), 'Gedanken experiments involving black holes', *Phys. Rev.* **D49** 966–974, [hep-th/9308100].

[19] Page, D. N. (1993), 'Average entropy of a subsystem', *Phys. Rev. Lett.* **71** 1291–1294, [gr-qc/9305007].

[20] Bekenstein, J. D. (1973), 'Black holes and entropy' *Phys. Rev.* **D7** 2333.

[21] Maldacena, J. (1998), 'The large N limit of superconformal field theories and supergravity', *Adv. Theor. Math. Phys.* **2**, 231, [hep-th/9711200].

[22] Susskind, L. (1993), 'String theory and the principle of black hole complementarity', *Phys. Rev. Lett.* **71** 2367–2368, [hep-th/9307168].

[23] Gibbons, G. W. and Hawking, S. W. (1977), 'Cosmological event horizons, thermodynamics, and particle creation', *Phys. Rev.* **D15** 2738–2751.

[24] Hawking, S. W. and Page, D. N. (1983), 'Thermodynamics of black holes in anti-de Sitter space', *Commun. Math. Phys.* **87** 577.

[25] Maldacena, J. M. (2001), 'Eternal black holes in AdS', [hep-th/0106112].

[26] Bousso, R., Maloney, A. and Strominger, A. (2001), 'Conformal vacua and entropy in de Sitter space', [hep-th/0112218] and references therein.

[27] Witten, E. (2001), 'Quantum gravity in de Sitter space', [hep-th/0106109].

[28] Spradlin, M. and Volovich, A. (2001), 'Vacuum states and the S-matrix in dS/CFT', [hep-th/0112223].

[29] Complementarity in the context of deSitter Space is also discussed in Banks, T. and Fischler, W. (2001), 'M-theory observables for cosmological space-times', [hep-th/0102077].

[30] Dyson, L., Lindesay, J. and Susskind, L. (2002), 'Is There Really a de Sitter/CFT Duality?', [hep-th/0202163].

[31] Srednicki, M. (1999), 'The approach to thermal equilibrium in quantized chaotic systems', *J. Phys.* **A32** 1163, [cond-mat/9809360].

Part 5
Quantum gravity

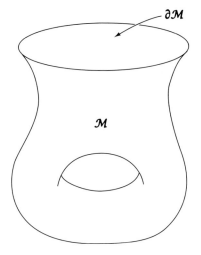

I am going to describe an approach to quantum gravity using path integrals in the Euclidean regime. The motivation for this is the belief that the topological properties of the gravitational fields play an essential role in quantum theory.

Cargese Lectures, 1978

20

Euclidean quantum gravity: the view from 2002

Gary Gibbons

Centre for Mathematical Sciences, University of Cambridge

20.1 Introduction

The organizing committee, excluding myself, have asked me to speak on 'Euclidean quantum gravity: the view from 2002'. I suspect that what they really wanted me to answer, but were too polite to ask, was:

Whatever happened to Euclidean quantum gravity?

Happily, there is an apt response:

It is alive and well and living in M Theory.

In other words, from today's standpoint, *Euclidean quantum gravity* should not be (and never should have been) viewed as a 'fundamental theory of physics' but rather an efficient and elegant means of extracting *non-perturbative* information about quantum gravity. In the terminology introduced by Fay Dowker in her talk, it should be thought of as a 'top down' rather than 'bottom up' approach. That has always been my view and since non-perturbative information is so precious it would seem churlish to ignore any that is available, regardless of its pedigree. Euclidean quantum gravity has in addition another strong point in its favour, which I personally find extremely attractive, in that it is a natural continuation of a long process in the history of our subject in which there takes place a progressive

Reduction of Physics to Geometry

It is perhaps worth fleshing out these slogans with a (in fact rather close) analogy, the theory of interfaces in what has come to be

351

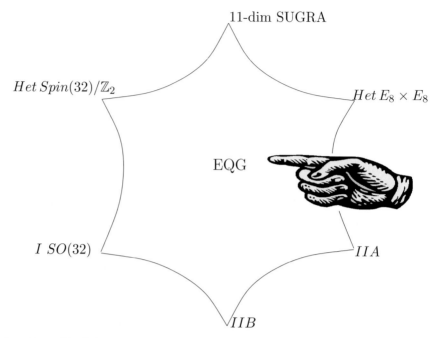

Fig. 20.1. Euclidean quantum gravity should be thought of as one of increasingly many non-perturbative methods in M theory.

called soft condensed matter physics.[1] Nobody doubts that the relevant 'fundamental' physical theory is at least as complicated as the multiparticle Schrödinger equation. Equally well, everybody recognizes that there is little real prospect of deriving in a mathematically rigorous way from that[2] equation all the wonderful properties of froths, foams, soap films, etc. that we see every day. By far the most efficient way of doing that, and this is what is done every day by experts in the field, is to capture the essential physics in the simplest geometrical model, the minimal surface equation or the equation for surfaces of constant mean curvature and proceed from there.

Considered in this light, Euclidean quantum gravity has had a number of striking successes and significant applications:

- black hole thermodynamics;

- properties of de-Sitter spacetime and inflationary perturbations;

---

[1] When I was at school this subject was called Properties of Matter, but even in DAMTP times change.

[2] Or indeed from M theory, which illustrates perhaps how meaningless is any talk of a fundamental theory, by what is meant of course is most accurate at any given time.

- pair production of charged black hole pairs and Kaluza–Klein monopoles;

- instability of certain Kaluza–Klein vacua;

- quantum cosmology and the birth of the universe;

- the AdS/CFT correspondence.

Moreover, like any other important idea in physics, Euclidean quantum
gravity has had important links with contemporary pure mathematics
(Riemannian geometry, differential geometry and topology[3]) and has led
to the discovery, for example, of explicit metrics with properties previously
unsuspected by differential geometers. In particular one should mention:

- gravitational instantons (explicit metrics, often with special or exceptional holonomy);

- index theory and L^2 cohomology for non-compact manifolds;

- the existence and enumerative properties of Einstein metrics on
  compact manifolds.

In what follows, I shall only touch on some of these topics. Others are
covered in some of the other contributions in this volume. I shall just
close this introduction with the remark that because it is essentially a
semiclassical technique, one has always hoped that the principal results
of Euclidean quantum gravity would remain at least approximately valid
independently of *whatever* turns out to be the correct microscopic theory
of gravity, even though corrections to the semiclassical approximation are
of course expected. However recent ideas on strings in $AdS_5 \times S^5$ indicate
a much deeper role for Euclidean quantum gravity in the general scheme
of things but, because of what is known as

The Infrared Ultraviolet Connection

it is *only* the semiclassical approximation which is relevant. If, as the
organizing committee requested, I were to attempt to make a prediction
for the future of theoretical physics and cosmology as a whole, I would
guess that this perennial theme, the relation between the very small and
the very large, will come to dominate our thinking. Cosmologists have
long known that living as we do at the scale of centimetres, we lie in the
midst of immensities, the immensely small at the Planck scale 10^{-33} cm
and the the immensely large at the Hubble scale 10^{28} cm. To understand
the latter one needs to understand the former. Can it be true that the

---

[3] We are all of us in the gutter, but some of us are looking at the stars (Oscar Wilde,
attrib.).

• Cosmology

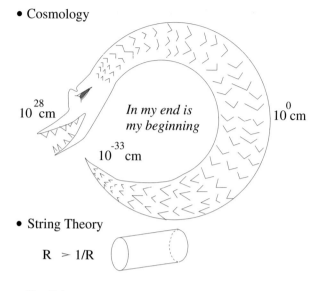

10^{28} cm

In my end is
my beginning

10^0 cm

10^{-33} cm

• String Theory

R > 1/R

• Dualities

• Loop Expansion

Fig. 20.2. The infrared ultraviolet connection: the message both from string theory and from cosmology is that to understand the very large, one, must understand the very small and conversely.

converse is also true? Perturbative string theory on a circle of radius R is equivalent to string theory on a circle of radius $1/R$. The non-perturbative dualities of M theory incorporate this idea at a deeper level and the loop expansion of string theory has long been known to render ambiguous the distinction between infrared and ultraviolet divergences, and this feature has re-emerged recently in the context of non-commutative geometry.

20.2 Some historical recollections

The story[4] begins with Stephen's discovery in 1974 of the phenomenon of black hole explosions using quantum field theory in a fixed *dynamical* spacetime background using the method of Bogoliubov transformations [2, 3]. This followed his earlier suggestion [1] that primordial black holes might have formed in the very early universe and our attempts to

---

[4] Bliss was it in that dawn to be alive but to be young was very heaven (William Wordsworth on the French Revolution).

understand whether any of them might still carry an electric charge. We began studying the spontaneous loss of charge via the Schwinger process. By the time of the Warsaw IAU meeting, where we reported some preliminary results [6], we were sure that this process would occur and lead to the emission of charged particles from charged black holes but we did not then suspect that neutral particles would be emitted thermally from neutral black holes. This was Stephen's great discovery. Afterwards it was possible to fit our earlier work on the Schwinger process into this framework [21].

Everyone who is familiar with Stephen's paper will admit that it is a technical *tour de force* but that the derivation is limited to free fields and fails to explain the *universality* of the effect and of the famous formula

$$T = \frac{1}{8\pi M} = \frac{\kappa}{2\pi}. \tag{20.1}$$

Later while Stephen was at Caltech for the year, Hartle and Hawking [8] used a 'path integral' or, more precisely, Schwinger style representation of a free scalar Green's function $G(x,y)$ in the *non-dynamical* Kruskal spacetime to derive Einstein A and B relations for the emission and absorption rates. To resolve the ambiguities in defining the Greens' function $G(x,y)$ they used a Wick rotation and began exploring the periodic

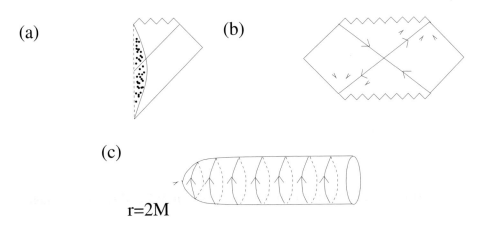

(a)   (b)

(c)

r=2M

Fig. 20.3. The end of classical spacetime: Stephen's original work used the Carter–Penrose diagram of 'realistic' classical gravitational collapse (a). Later work with Hartle on the Einstein A and B coefficients became progressively more divorced from the classical spacetime picture, starting with the unphysical Kruskal spacetime (b) and passing by analytic continuation to Euclidean spacetime (c).

geometry of the Euclidean Schwarzschild solution which they approached via the analytic properties of the Kruskal coordinates. Note that already, at this stage, the arena was moving from the simple classical dynamical spacetime to something more abstract. The era of classical spacetime was drawing to a close.

On hearing about these ideas, and after listening to a seminar given by Malcolm Perry about his and John Collins' ideas about high temperature QCD [35], Gibbons and Perry [22, 23] pointed out that Hartle and Hawking had, slightly contrary to what they had originally imagined, constructed Thermal Green's functions $G_\beta(x, y)$ for a black hole in equilibrium with its products at a temperature $T = \beta^{-1}$ given precisely by the periodicity of the Euclidean Schwarzschild solution.[5] It was then immediately apparent that the thermal equilibrium, previously envisaged by Stephen in another paper from his time at Caltech [4], was indeed universal and quite independent of any details of the interactions *including gravitational self-interactions*. In other words, together we had succeeded in extending and deepening trends already emerging in the wider field of quantum field theory at that time according to which quantum field theory could be thought of as statistical mechanics on $\mathbb{E}^4$ and finite temperature quantum field theory as statistical mechanics on $\mathbb{E}^3 \times S^1_\beta$, where S^1_β is a circle of circumference $\beta = T^{-1}$. Mathematically there is a complete equivalence. Despite some opposition at the time I think that this viewpoint is now universally accepted[6] and might be called

The Reduction of Thermodynamics to Geometry

To avoid any misunderstanding let me emphasize that this process of geometrization is not the end but rather the beginning of understanding micro-physics. Having understood the easy kinematic facts which follow without much effort, one has of course to go on and analyse the difficult things which require detailed calculations. In the surface tension analogy, having understood why all soap films independent of composition adopt the shapes they do, it still remains to investigate their microscopic atomic structure to explain, for example, why the surface tension does depend upon composition and eventually to calculate it from first principles. The theory of the catenary will not provide much help in that endeavour, as is made clear by the realization of the fact that it is governed *only* by geometry.

---

[5] I personally prefer Riemannian to Euclidean.
[6] We are all Socialists now (William Harcourt, attrib.).

20.3 The path integral

Having finished off quantum field theory in a fixed background, let us now turn to consider the Euclidean path integral for general relativity. Conceptually it is clear enough: one 'sums' over all metrics g on all manifolds M with fixed boundary Σ and which induce the same metric h on Σ. Formally one aims to calculate something like

$$Z(\Sigma, h) = \sum_M \int dg\, e^{-I(M,g)}, \qquad (20.2)$$

where $I(M, g)$ is the Einstein–Hilbert action (including boundary terms) of the metric and (if they are present) other matter. For pure gravity, the Einstein–Hilbert action is given by

$$I = -\frac{1}{16\pi} \left[\int_M (R - 2\Lambda)\sqrt{g}\, d^n x + 2 \int_{\partial M} K\sqrt{h}\, d^{n-1}x \right], \qquad (20.3)$$

where the second fundamental form K_{ij} of the boundary whose outward directed unit normal is n, is given by $K_{ij} = \frac{1}{2}\mathcal{L}_n H_{ij}$ and $K = h^{ij} K_{ij}$ is up to a factor of $n - 1$, the mean curvature of the boundary. If

$$V = \mathrm{Vol}(\partial M, h) = \int_{\partial M} \sqrt{h}\, d^{n-1}x, \qquad (20.4)$$

then

$$\frac{\partial V}{\partial n} = \int_{\partial M} K\sqrt{h}\, d^{n-1}x. \qquad (20.5)$$

Variation of the action gives

$$\delta I = -\frac{1}{16\pi} \left[\int_M \sqrt{g} \left(R^{\alpha\beta} - \frac{1}{2}Rg^{\alpha\beta} - \Lambda g^{\alpha\beta} \right) \delta g_{\alpha\beta}\, d^{n-1}x \right]$$
$$+ \frac{1}{2} \int_{\partial M} \Pi^{ij} \delta h_{ij} \sqrt{h}\, d^{n-1}x, \qquad (20.6)$$

where

$$\Pi^{ij} = -\frac{1}{8\pi}(K^{ij} - h^{ij}K) \qquad (20.7)$$

is nowadays thought of as the boundary stress tensor.

The classical saddle points of the action subject to Dirichlet boundary conditions (i.e. $\delta h_{ij} = 0$), are Einstein metrics with

$$R_{\alpha\beta} - \frac{1}{2}Rg_{\alpha\beta} = \Lambda g_{\alpha\beta}. \qquad (20.8)$$

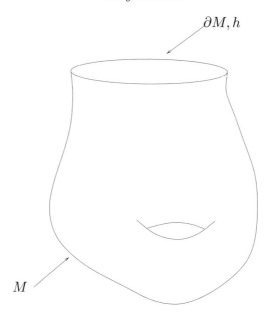

$\partial M, h$

M

Fig. 20.4. The basic set up of Euclidean quantum gravity consists of a manifold M with boundary ∂M on which a metric h is given. The partition function is a function of the boundary metric. No special significance attaches to any particular interior metric except in a semiclassical approximation.

The boundary term is necessary for the action to satisfy the composition property

$$I(M_1) + I(M_2) = I(M_1 \cup_\Sigma M_2), \tag{20.9}$$

where M_1 and M_2 are joined together along a common boundary component $\Sigma = M_1 \cap M_2$ say.

The on-shell action, i.e. the action of a classical solution is

$$I_s = \frac{1}{8\pi} \left[\frac{4\Lambda}{n-2} \mathrm{Vol}(M, g_s) + \frac{\partial V}{\partial n} \right]. \tag{20.10}$$

The following problems are immediately apparent:

- non-renormalizability – how to deal with short distance or ultraviolet divergences;

- the indefiniteness of the action;

- the on-shell action typically diverges at large distance, i.e. in the infrared, and requires boundary corrections.

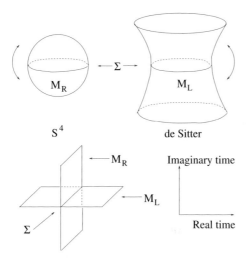

Fig. 20.5. Real tunnelling geometries such as S^4 admit a reflection map Θ and as a consequence their complexification contains both a real Riemannian section M_R and a real Lorentzian section M_L.

20.3.1 A non-problem

Leaving these problems aside for the moment, let us comment on an often repeated objection. This is the mathematically correct but physically totally irrelevant statement that 'not every Lorentzian spacetime M_L admits an analytic continuation $M_{\mathbb{C}}$ containing Riemannian section M_R'. This is also true for example of Yang–Mills connections on Minkowski spacetime, they don't always analytically continue to give real connections on Euclidean space. The answer is the same in both cases. All that is needed is the behaviour of quantities like $Z(\Sigma, h)$ as a function of boundary values. Physically the individual interior spacetimes, Riemannian or Lorentzian, that go into the functional sum have no particular significance except either in the classical limit, when one is preferred or, more interestingly in the special case when both Lorentzian and Riemannian real sections exist simultaneously in the same complex spacetime $M_{\mathbb{C}}$. An example is when $M_{\mathbb{C}}$ is the complex quadric in $\mathbb{C}^5$. This contains as real sections both the round 4-sphere $M_R = S^4$ and de-Sitter spacetime $M_L = dS_4$. They intersect in $\Sigma = S^3$, a round 3-sphere which is a totally geodesic boundary of the half-sphere and a momentarily[7] static Cauchy surface. Such solutions have come to be called real tunnelling geometries, or sometimes instantons.

---

[7] Both the spelling and the meaning are British.

20.3.2 Bulk ultraviolet divergences: rats in mazes

One view of the recent progress in theoretical physics is that, driven by the divergence problem, we have been swept along a maze in which progressively various apparently promising avenues have been blocked off.

A computational scheme, including the necessary ghosts, in which the path integral could be perturbatively implemented was first constructed by Feynman, DeWitt, and Faddeev and Popov. Although widely expected to be non-renormalizable, it wasn't until the work of 't Hooft and Veltman [39] that pure gravity (now known as $\mathcal{N} = 0$) was shown to be one-loop finite, but that this ceases to be if generic matter is included. It was not until sometime later that Goroff and Sagnotti [38] eventually showed that there was a divergence at two loops. Different people have reacted to this problem in different ways. Some, including at various times Stephen himself [42], have followed Stelle [40] in looking at higher derivative theories, despite the potential problems of ghost and loss of unitarity. Others turned to supergravity theories which pass the two loop barrier but were widely believed to crash at three loops. In Kaluza–Klein theories things are typically worse, for example the eleven-dimensional theory is divergent at one loop. After the anomaly revolution of 84 most of the community turned to super strings in ten dimensions which can be defined to all loop order, ignoring the remarkable fact discovered by Townsend and colleagues and described in his contribution to this volume that super membranes exist in eleven dimensions.[8]

The progress of string theory was only briefly slowed down by the discovery by Gross and Periwal [37] that the resulting perturbation theory is not summable. A widespread current belief is that using Polchinski's non-perturbative D-branes on the one hand and a combination of dualities one may construct a theory called M theory whose low energy limit is 11-dimensional supergravity with its super membrane. Ironically using these ideas and techniques from string theory it seems that the divergences of supergravity may not set in until five loops [41].

Whatever the final outcome, the moral as far as Euclidean gravity is concerned seems clear, the path integral can be at most approximate.

20.3.3 Indefiniteness of the action

This is the well known fact that by a conformal rescaling $g \rightarrow \Omega^2 g$ one may make the Euclidean as negative as one likes [27, 28].

---

[8] Roll up that map: it will not be wanted these ten years (William Pitt the Younger, on hearing of Napoleon's victory at Austerlitz)

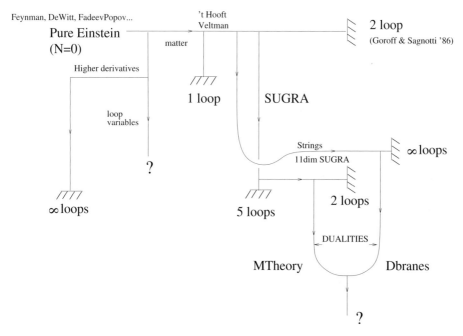

Fig. 20.6. Conventional perturbative quantization techniques appear to lead us inexorably via supersymmetry and supergravity to superstrings, and via non-perturbative D-branes to M theory.

In fact around a classical saddle point the Hessian of the action is indefinite: there are infinitely many negative directions associated with conformal deformations proportional to the metric while in the direction of deformations of the conformal structure, corresponding to transverse traceless fluctuations, the action will, except possibly for a finite number of negative and zero modes, increase. Perturbatively it is easy, as originally done by 't Hooft and Veltman, to take care of this problem by considering pure imaginary conformal perturbations. However it does serve to illustrate the point that

> The path integral for Euclidean quantum gravity can certainly not be taken, even in a formal sense, as being over all Euclidean (i.e. Riemannian) metrics.

The analogy to have in mind is the (non-uniformly) convergent integral

$$\int_{-\infty}^{+\infty} \int_{\infty}^{+\infty} e^{i(x^2 - y^2)} \, dx \, dy = \pi. \tag{20.11}$$

This oscillatory integral is like the Lorentzian path integral. We may, *if we choose*, by (Wick)-rotating the x contour through $+\pi/4$ in the complex x

plane and y by $-\pi/4$ in the complex y plane. In this analogy the variable y corresponds to the conformal modes and x to the transverse traceless modes. Thus relative to the transverse traceless modes, the conformal modes require an additional Wick rotation of $\pi/2$.

20.3.4 Instantons

The conclusion of the previous subsection again seems to be that summing over Riemannian metrics is a computational convenience to allow a saddle point evaluation rather than a fundamental feature of quantum gravity. In that light we might be interested in any classical saddle point, real or complex. It is helpful to reserve the word *gravitational instanton* for any complete non-singular positive definite Einstein manifold $\{M, g\}$. Thus Gravitational Instantons need have no Lorentzian section. However there is a distinguished class, called by James Hartle and myself, *real tunnelling geometries*, [32] which do. They are characterized by admitting an involutive isometry $\Theta : M \rightarrow M$ called a reflection map, such that $M = M^+ \cup M^-$ and $\Theta M^\pm = M^\mp$. $M^\pm$ are manifolds with totally geodesic boundary $\Sigma = M^+ \cap M^-$ stabilized by Θ, $\Theta\Sigma = \Sigma$. The hypersurface Σ serves as a momentarily stationary initial surface for the Lorentzian section. The Schwarzschild and de-Sitter solutions illustrated on the conference mug provide familiar examples.

Examples of Gravitational Instantons which do not admit a Lorentzian section are the multi-centre metrics introduced by Stephen [5] and later discussed by Stephen and myself [31]. Later, in the hands of David Gross, Malcolm Perry [43] and Raphael Sorkin [44] they turned into Kaluza–Klein monopoles. More recently they have experienced a re-incarnation in the hands of Paul Townsend as D6-branes [30]. Since the formulae are so beautiful, I cannot resist quoting them

$$ds^2 = V^{-1}(\tau + \omega.d\mathbf{x})^2 + Vd\mathbf{x}^2, \tag{20.12}$$

with

$$\operatorname{curl}\omega = \operatorname{grad}V. \tag{20.13}$$

Because the Riemann tensor is self-dual, $R_{\alpha\beta\mu\nu} = \star R_{\alpha\beta\mu\nu}$, these can have no Lorentzian section. In answer to a question posed by Bryce deWitt, as far as I know, they, unlike the real tunnelling geometries described above, have nothing to do with tunnelling.

They are however, non-trivial examples of Hyper-Kähler 4-metrics with the special holonomy group $Sp(1) \equiv SU(2) \subset SO(4)$. More about special and exceptional holonomy will be found in Chris Pope's talk, which relates recent work to its Euclidean quantum gravitational origins.

The basic example is the Taub-NUT metric on $\mathbb{R}^4$ for which $V = 1 + M/r$, where the mass parameter M is *positive*. It is a striking fact that another Hyper-Kähler 4-metric, that of Atiyah and Hitchin, is asymptotic to $\text{Taub} - \text{NUT}/CP$ but with a *negative* mass parameter and where CP, the product of charge conjugation and parity, acts as $CP : (\tau, \mathbf{x}) \rightarrow (-\tau, -\mathbf{x})$. The puzzling fact that the mass is negative has now been related to their rôle in M/string theory as *orientifold 6-planes* which are expected to have negative tension. As such, they provide an answer to a question raised by Brandon Carter during his talk at the workshop about the possibility of negative tension branes. In other words, despite admitting Killing spinor fields and hence being supersymmetric, they provide a perfectly good representation of a stable orientifold with negative tension. This is possible only because, as illustrated so graphically in Brandon's lecture, the orientifold, the dangerous negative mode, is eliminated because it is incompatible with the discrete symmetry of orientifold.

Some people, including Stephen and Neil Turok, have been tempted to turn to *singular instantons*, mainly for cosmological purposes. In my opinion there is no good reason to consider them in the stationary phase approximation, despite the fact that they may have finite action. The singularities typically mean that they are not stationary points. At this stage of theory, one cannot be dogmatic, but my feeling is that if one lets them into the game, then they lead to a completely indeterminate theory, anything goes.[9]

20.3.5 Boundary divergences

As noted above, the boundary terms is essential for the basic factorization properties of the theory to hold. However it brings problems. Consider the case when $\Lambda = 0$. The bulk contribution to the on-shell action vanishes, only the boundary term survives, but this is divergent. Consider, for example a ball of radius a in flat Euclidean 4-space $\mathbb{E}^4$. The volume of the boundary is $V = 2\pi^2 a^3$, thus $I_s = \frac{3\pi}{8} a^2$ which diverges in the infrared as $a \rightarrow \infty$.

There are two obvious stratagems:

- only compare metrics with the same boundary data, in other words introduce a fiducial comparison metric. This was our original procedure;

---

[9] I'm liberal, but to a degree. I want everybody to be free. But if you think that I'd let Barry Goldwater move in next door my daughter. You must think I'm crazy or something. I wouldn't do it for all the farms in Cuba! (Bob Dylan)

- add counter terms which are local on the boundary. This was introduced by Skenderis and Balasubramanian and Kraus in the context of the AdS/CFT correspondence;

- or try something else ...

I shall briefly review the counter-terms approach when discussing the AdS/CFT correspondence. For now I wish to comment on a possible alternative approach, sketched rather briefly in Gibbons and Pope, which is geometrically interesting and may have in it the seeds of an interesting future development. The point is that one could add to the classical boundary action

$$-\frac{1}{8\pi} \int_{\partial M} K\sqrt{h}\, d^{n-1}x \qquad (20.14)$$

a term of the proportional to

$$\left(\int_{\partial M} \sqrt{h}\, d^{n-1} \right)^{\frac{n-2}{n-1}}, \qquad (20.15)$$

with the constant of proportionality chosen so that the combination vanishes for a round ball in Euclidean space $\mathbb{E}^n$.

By a remarkable generalized iso-perimetric inequality of Minkowski, (related to the Cosmic Censorship Hypothesis), the combination, i.e. the IR regularized on-shell action of a domain in flat space, is non-positive and vanishes only for the case of a ball. In fact only by considering sufficiently spherical domains could one take the infinite limit and get a finite, and in fact zero, value for the action of flat space. The regularization can now be extended to curved asymptotically Euclidean spaces. There is perhaps a suggestion here that global geometric inequalities of Minkowski type may have an interesting rôle to play in future developments. In this connection it is worth mentioning an inequality of Reilly which states that if the Ricci tensor is non-negative, then

$$\int_{\partial M} K\sqrt{h}\, d^{n-1}x \leq \frac{(n-1)V^2(\partial M)}{nV(M)}, \qquad (20.16)$$

with equality if and only if M is Ricci flat and admits a hypersurface orthogonal homothety which is orthogonal to ∂M. In other words if M is a cone. The only regular case of equality is that of a ball in flat Euclidean space $\mathbb{E}^n$ but many singular cases exist when M is a Ricci flat cone. Such spaces are quite common and typically arise as spaces with special or exceptional holonomy (see the article by Chris Pope).

20.4 The AdS/CFT correspondence

This is not the place for a general review, for that see Nick Warner's contribution. We will just make a few points from the point of view of Euclidean quantum gravity. To set the scene, recall the conformal one-point compactification of Euclidean space. We can embed S^n in $\mathbb{E}^{n+1}$ and stereographically project $S^n \setminus \{\text{North Pole}\}$ from the north pole onto the tangent n-plane of the south pole. Under this projection, the spherical metric becomes

$$ds^2 = \frac{d\mathbf{x}^2}{(1 + \mathbf{x}^2/4)^2}. \tag{20.17}$$

The south pole maps to the origin $\mathbf{x} = 0$ and the north pole corresponds to infinity $|\mathbf{x}| \to \infty$. To exhibit the action of the conformal group, $SO(n,1)$ on S^n, one regards the sphere S^n as the intersection of the light cone of the origin in $(n+1)$-dimensional Minkowski spacetime $\mathbb{E}^{n,1}$, with a space-like n-plane which does not intersect the origin.

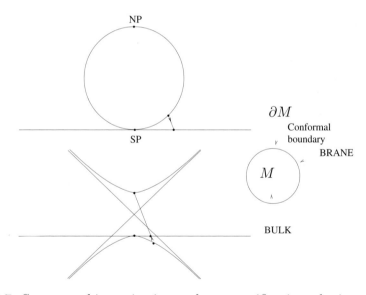

Fig. 20.7. Stereographic projection and compactification: the inverse image of projection from the north pole of a sphere onto the tangent plane of the south pole maps the plane conformally onto the complement of the north pole of the sphere. Adding the north pole gives the conformal compactification of the sphere. The analogous mapping of the lower sheet of the two sheeted hyperbola maps it conformally onto the interior of a ball in the tangent hyperplane. The conformal boundary is the intersection of the past light cone of the origin with the tangent hyperplane.

To get the correct picture for hyperbolic space H^n, which may be thought of as the Wick rotation of anti-de Sitter space AdS_n, one considers the upper sheet of the double sheeted hyperbola embedded into $\mathbb{E}^{n-1,1}$ and stereographically projects from a point on the upper sheet to the interior of a ball in a space-like n-plane which is tangent to a point on the lower sheet. Under this projection, the hyperbolic metric becomes

$$ds^2 = \frac{d\mathbf{x}^2}{\left(1 - \mathbf{x}^2/4\right)^2}. \tag{20.18}$$

The projection point on the upper sheet maps to the origin $\mathbf{x} = 0$ and infinity north pole corresponds to the S^{n-1} boundary of the ball, $|\mathbf{x}| \leq 2$. Now the key observation is that the *isometry* group $SO(n,1)$ of H^n now acts as the *conformal* group of the boundary S^{n-1}.

The AdS/CFT conjecture of Maldacena, Polyakov, Klebanov, Gubser, etc. is that Type IIB String theory on $H^5 \times S^5$ in the limit $\alpha' \to 0$ coincides with the large 't Hooft coupling constant $(g^2_{\text{Yang--Mills}})$ limit of SUSY Yang–Mills on the conformal boundary S^4. This was formulated by Witten as an identity between the infrared divergent supergravity partition function, considered as a function of boundary data, and the ultraviolet divergent partition function considered as a function of external sources

$$Z_{\text{Supergravity}}(\text{Boundary data}) = Z_{\text{Yang--Mills}}(\text{Sources}) \tag{20.19}$$

A particularly striking point of this new development was the use by Witten of some old work by Stephen and Don Page [33] in which they studied black hole thermodynamics in anti-de sitter spacetime using Euclidean techniques.

20.5 The volume canonical ensemble

At one stage Stephen advocated, in order to finesse the problem of boundary conditions, summing just over all closed manifolds, i.e. compact manifolds M without boundary $\partial M = \varnothing$. As a special case, we could fix on a particular manifold topology and just consider the no-loop partition function

$$\sum_{\text{Einstein metrics on } M} e^{-I_s(g_s)}. \tag{20.20}$$

This leads to the question

How many Einstein metrics are there on a given M with fixed scalar curvature?

Of course we also count, keeping the volume fixed. The answer is perhaps surprising, even for the simplest manifold S^n. We clearly always have the round metric but are there any others? If $n = 4$ the answer is probably not. However despite the appealing simplicity of the question in the lowest dimension for which it is non-trivial, and the efforts of many talented mathematicians, we still don't know for sure. For the most recent work see [45–47]. If $n = 4$ and the metrics are 'static', that is we have an $O(2)$ isometry group, which stabilizes an S^2 bolt, or cosmological horizon, this is essentially the Cosmic–Baldness conjecture. Work of Boucher[13] and Friedrich [14] appears to rule out this possibility. However if $4 < n < 10$, Bohm [11] has recently shown that there are infinitely many cohomogeneity one examples obtained by solving O.D.E.s, either numerically or using phase plane methods to show existence. The metrics take the form:

$$ds^2 = dt^2 + a^2(t)\, d\Omega_p^2 + b^2(t)\, d\Omega_q^2, \tag{20.21}$$

with $p+q+1 = n$, $(p-1)(q-1) \neq 0$, and $d\Omega_k^2$ the unit round metric on S^k. Choosing $a = \sin t$ and $b = \cos t$ gives the round metric on S^n. In addition there is an infinite sequence which converges to a singular double cone of on $S^p \times S^q$ with $a = \sqrt{\frac{p-1}{n-2}} \sin t$, $b = \sqrt{\frac{q-1}{n-2}} \sin t$. The limiting metric has finite volume despite the fact that it has two conical singularities at $t = 0$ and $t = \pi$. Note that the standard round metric would be obtained by replacing $S^p \times S^q$ by S^{p+q}. Note that the Bohm metrics are static, in that they admit a reversible circle action, i.e. $O(2)$ acts isometrically. This means that they have a Lorentzian analytic continuation. In other words, the Cosmic Baldness conjecture does not hold in higher dimensions [16]. Fortunately Boucher and I made no mention of higher dimensions back in 1983 when, unlike today, higher dimensions were not at the centre of many cosmologist's attention.

The on-shell action of any such metric is proportional to minus the volume

$$I_s \propto -\Lambda \mathrm{Vol}(S^n, g_s) \tag{20.22}$$

By Bishop's theorem [15] the volume is bounded above by that of the round metric. The volume of the sequence is bounded below by the volume of the limiting double cone. It follows that the zero-loop partition function must diverge for spheres with $4 < n < 10$. Note that because the sphere S^n is simply connected, there is no possibility of arguing, as Stephen has on other occasions that one may eliminate this problem by passing to a covering space. The sphere is its own covering space. The direct physical meaning of this observation is not clear. They appear to have a relation with some observations of Carlip which I will mention in a moment. Before doing so, let me mention that these have an application to the AdS/CFT correspondence. One might contemplate the replacement

$$AdS_5 \times S^5_{\text{Round}} \to AdS_5 \times S^5_{\text{Bohm}}. \tag{20.23}$$

One would find that SUSY is broken because S^5_{Bohm} admits no Killing spinors, and the global $SO(6)$ R-symmetry is broken down to $SO(3) \times SO(2)$. According to Gubser, at least in the supersymmetric case, the ratio of central charges is given in such replacements by

$$\frac{c(S^5_{\text{Round}})}{c(M,g)} = \frac{\text{Vol}(M,g)}{\text{Vol}(S^5_{\text{Round}})} < 1, \tag{20.24}$$

the last inequality coming from Bishop's theorem which tells one that the round sphere has the largest volume of any Einstein metric with the same cosmological constant.

A closer examination shows that the Bohm metrics, and other spacetimes constructed from them, are unstable [16]. Nevertheless they appear to have a number of potentially interesting further applications. Most importantly, they draw attention in the most vivid way to the fact that that if a given manifold admits an Einstein metric, it may be expected to admit very many others.

20.6 Hyperbolic 4-manifolds

A class of manifolds which were not exploited much in the early days of Euclidean quantum gravity, perhaps because of Stephen's aversion to the fundamental group, but which more recently have been applied to the question of whether our present universe may have a non-trivial topology [34], are the hyperbolic manifolds. These are of the form H^4/Γ, where Γ is a discrete subgroup of $SO(4,1) = \text{Isom}(H^4)$ such that M is a smooth compact 4-manifold without boundary and Euler number $\chi(M)$. They have constant curvature

$$R_{\alpha\beta\mu\nu} = \frac{\Lambda}{3}(g_{\alpha\mu}g_{\beta\nu} - g_{\alpha\nu}g_{\beta\mu}), \tag{20.25}$$

with negative cosmological constant Λ. A theorem of Mostow states that these metrics are rigid, there are no moduli. The Gauss–Bonnet theorem allows one to evaluate the classical action

$$I_s = \frac{3\pi}{2|\Lambda|}\chi(M). \tag{20.26}$$

Thus least action translates into least Euler number.

The hyperbolic 4-manifold with the smallest Euler number and hence least action is not known. Davis has given an example with $\chi = 23$ but it is not known whether this is the smallest possible value. The Davis example does not qualify as a real tunnelling geometry because it does not admit a reflection map Θ. However Ratcliffe and Tschantz [18] have found an example with $\chi = 46$ which does admit a reflection map. If the universe was born in some tunnelling event controlled by a negative cosmological constant, one might expect its topology to be given by this manifold.

Later [19], stimulated by some ideas of Carlip, they studied how the number of hyperbolic 4-manifolds with given Euler number $N(\chi)$ grows with Euler number, that is whether

$$\sum_\chi N(\chi)e^{-I_s} \tag{20.27}$$

converges. They found that $N(\chi)$ grows super-exponentially with χ and so convergence is not possible. Carlip had earlier argued that this type of behaviour might explain why the observed cosmological constant is not negative.

Further examples of closed Instantons with $\Lambda < 0$ are provided by Yau's solution of the Calabi conjecture in the case that the canonical bundle has negative first Chern class. These do not of course admit a reflection map Θ and so are not relevant for tunnelling but may throw light on formal aspects of the theory, such as the volume canonical ensemble.

However, so far, little has been done in this direction. Some concrete examples could be obtained by taking $H_{\mathbb{C}}^2/\Gamma$, where $H_{\mathbb{C}}^2 \equiv SU(2,1)/U(2)$ is variously called Anti $\mathbb{CP}^2$, The Bergman metric or complex hyperbolic space and Γ is a suitable discrete subgroup of $SU(2,1)$. In this case, the on-shell action is given by

$$I_s = \frac{3\pi}{4|\Lambda|}\chi(M). \tag{20.28}$$

There is an interesting example due to Mumford with $\chi = 3$ [48].

20.7 Action and complexity

The totally geodesic boundary Σ of a hyperbolic tunnelling metric is of course a hyperbolic 3-manifold of the form $\Sigma = H^3/\Gamma'$, where Γ' is a discrete subgroup of $SO(3,1)$. There is in this case a well developed concept of the *complexity* of a hyperbolic 3-manifold. For a fixed curvature, i.e. in our context of the cosmological constant, this is proportional to the volume $\text{Vol}(H^3/\Gamma')$ of the 3-manifold. Among other things, this measure of complexity measures the size of the fundamental group Γ', i,e how fast the number of words grows with the length of a word, or the entropy of the geodesics flow. It is an interesting question to ask how the complexity of the boundary grows with the action of the bulk. Remarkably, a theorem of Miyamoto states that there is a universal number c_4 such that in these circumstances at fixed Λ,

$$\text{Vol}(M) \geq c_4 \text{Vol}(\partial M). \tag{20.29}$$

In other words, the bigger the complexity of the boundary, the bigger the action of the bulk [20].

It seems difficult to believe that these facts won't find a natural home in the bigger scheme of things, possibly in the context of the AdS/CFT correspondence, possibly in some altogether different context.

20.8 Euclides ab omni naevo vindicatus?

The title of this final section comes from a book of Saccheri (1667–1733) who spent most of his life trying to justify the parallel postulate. Fortunately for us, this was almost a complete waste of time, otherwise we should not be able to talk about hyperbolic geometry, and whether we live in a $k = -1$ Friedman–Lemaitre–Robertson–Walker universe. However his work did spur on others like Gauss, Bolyai and Lobachevsky who finally made the breakthrough which liberated humankind from a prejudice of over 2000 years standing. What can we say about Euclidean quantum gravity? From the viewpoint of 2002, has it not been washed clean of every stain? Well, not exactly, and in that sense it is not the final answer, any more than Euclid's elements was the final answer, but I would like to finish by giving a final quotation which not only sums up my attitude to the subject but which also reflects Stephen's indomitable courage and daring optimism in this as in all other of his endeavours.

Ah, but a man's reach should exceed his grasp or what's a heaven for!

Robert Browning

References

[1] Hawking, S. W. (1971), *Mon. Not. Roy. Astr. Soc.* **152** 75.

[2] Hawking, S. W. (1974), *Nature* **248** 30.

[3] Hawking, S. W. (1975), *Commun. Math. Phys.* **43** 199.

[4] Hawking, S. W. (1976), *Phys. Rev.* **D 13** 191–197.

[5] Hawking, S. W. (1977), *Phys. Lett.* **A60** 81.

[6] Hawking, S. W. and Gibbons, G. W. (1974), 'Quantum aspects of accretion onto black holes in the early universe', in C. DeWitt-Morette, ed., *Gravitational Radiation and Gravitational Collapse*, D. Reidel Dordrecht, p. 185.

[7] Gibbons, G. W. and Pope, C. N. (1979) *Commun. Math. Phys.* **66** 267–290

[8] Hartle, J. B. and Hawking, S. W. (1976), *Phys. Rev.* **D13** 2188–2203.

[9] Hartle, J. B. and Hawking, S. W. (1983), *Phys. Rev.* **D28** 2960–2975.

[10] Reilly, R. C. (1980), *Archive for Rational Mechanics and Analysis* **75** 23–29.

[11] Bohm, C. (1984), *Invent. Math.* **134** 145.

[12] Boucher, W. and Gibbons, G. W. (1983), in G. W. Gibbons, S. W. Hawking and S. T. C. Siklos, eds, *The Very Early Universe* (Cambridge University Press, Cambridge).

[13] Boucher, W. (1983), in W. B. Bonnor, J. Islam and M. A. H. McCallum, eds, *Classical General Relativity* (Cambridge University Press, Cambridge).

[14] Friedrich, H. (1986), *J. Geom. Phys.* **3** 101.

[15] Bishop, R. L. (1963), *Not. Amer. Math. Soc.* **10** 364.

[16] Gibbons, G. W., Hartnoll, S. A. and Pope, C. N. (2002), [hep-th/0208031].

[17] Gibbons, G. W. (1996), *Nucl. Phys.* **B472**.

[18] Ratcliffe, J. and Tschantz, S. (1998), *Class. Quant. Grav.* **15** 2613–2627.

[19] Ratcliffe, J. and Tschantz, S. (2001), *Class. Quant. Grav.* **17** 299–3007.

[20] Gibbons, G. W. (1998), *Class. Quant. Grav.* **15** 2605–2612.

[21] Gibbons, G. W. (1975), 'Vacuum polarization and the spontaneous loss of charge by black holes', *Comm. Math. Phys.* **44** 245–264.

[22] Gibbons, G. W. and Perry, M. J. (1976), 'Black holes in thermal equilibrium' *Phys. Rev. Lett.* **36** 985–987.

[23] Gibbons, G. W. and Perry, M. J. (1978), 'Black holes and thermal Green's function', *Proc. Roy. Soc.* **A358** 467–494.

[24] Gibbons, G. W. and Perry, M. J. (1978), 'Quantizing gravitational instantons', *Nucl. Phys.* **B146** 90–108.

[25] Gibbons, G. W. and Hawking, S. W. (1977), 'Action integrals and partition functions in quantum gravity', *Phys. Rev.***D15** 2752–2756.

[26] Gibbons, G. W. and Hawking, S. W. (1977), 'Cosmological event horizons, thermodynamics and particle creation', *Phys. Rev.* **D15** 2738–2751.

[27] Gibbons, G. W. (1977), 'The Einstein action of Riemannian metrics and its relation to quantum gravity and thermodynamics' *Phys. Lett.* **A61** 3–5.

[28] Gibbons, G. W., Hawking, S. W. and Perry, M. J.,(1978), 'Path integrals and the indefiniteness of the gravitational action' *Nucl. Phys.* **B138** 141–150.

[29] Belinksi, V., Gibbons, G. W., Page, D. N. and Pope, C. N. (1978), 'Asymptotically Euclidean Bianchi IX metrics in quantum gravity' *Phys. Lett.* **B76** 433–435.

[30] Townsend, P. K. (1995), [hep-th/9507048].

[31] Gibbons, G. W. and Hawking, S. W. (1978), 'Gravitational multi-instantons', *Phys. Lett.* **B78** 430–432.

[32] Gibbons, G. W. and Hartle, J. B. (1990), 'Real tunneling geometries and the large-scale topology of the universe', *Phys. Rev.* **D42** 2458–2468.

[33] Hawking, S. W. and Page, D. N. (1983), *Comm. Math. Phys.* **87** 577.

[34] Gibbons, G. W. (1996), 'Tunnelling with a negative cosmological constant:' *Nucl. Phys.* **B 472** 683–710 [hep-th/96011075].

[35] Collins, J. C. and Perry, M. J. (1975), *Phys. Rev. Lett.* **34** 1353.

[36] Gibbons, G. W. (1998), 'Real tunnelling geometries' *Class. Quant. Grav.* **15** 2605–2612.

[37] Gross, D. and Periwal, V. (1988), *Phys. Rev. Lett.* **60** 2105–2108.

[38] Goroff, M. H. and Sagnotti, A. (1986), *Nucl. Phys.* **B 266** 709.

[39] 't Hooft, G. and Veltman, M. J. G. (1974), *Ann H Poincaré* **A20** 69–79.

[40] Stelle, K. S. (1977), *Phys. Rev.* **D16** 953.

[41] Stelle, K. S. (2002), [hep-th/0203015].

[42] Hawking, S. W. and Hertog, T. (2002), *Phys. Rev.* **d65** 103515.

[43] Gross, D. and Perry, M. J. (1983), *Nucl. Phys.* **B226** 29.

[44] Sorkin, R. (1983), *Phys. Rev. Lett.* **51** 87–90.

[45] Yang, D. (2000), *Invent. math.* **142** 435–450.

[46] Gursky, M. J. (2000), *Math. Ann.* 417–431.

[47] Singer, M. (1992), *Diff. Geom. Appl.* **2** 260–274.

[48] Mumford, D. (1979), *Amer. J. Math.* **101** 233–244.

21

Zeta functions, anomalies and stable branes

Ian Moss

University of Newcastle upon Tyne

21.1 Introduction

Stephen Hawking has made some remarkable discoveries for which he is widely known. Less well known is his uncanny ability to invent new theoretical techniques when the old ones are not up to the task in hand. An example of this came in the 1970s, when the quantum theory of black holes led to the Euclidean approach to quantum gravity. A method was needed to remove the divergences and Stephen Hawking invented the zeta function method in the form that we use today.

The ζ-function technique can be seen as a development of the proper time methods introduced by Schwinger to study vacuum polarization [1]. The proper time approach provides a fully gauge covariant regularising scheme. Bryce DeWitt extended the proper time approach to curved space [2].

Dowker and Chritchley were the first to use a zeta function for regularization in quantum field theory, but they obtained finite results by subtracting divergences [4, 5]. Stephen Hawking was interested in Euclidean formulations of quantum field theory, which leads to a ζ-function with simple analytic properties. These allowed regularization by analytic continuation [6].

ζ-function regularization is the scheme 'of choice' in Euclidean quantum field theory and string theory. One of the strengths of the ζ-function approach is that it never allows the user to overlook an anomaly, indeed most anomalies are nothing more than ζ-functions. When combined with powerful index theorems, these often reduce to purely topological terms depending on local invariants.

The status of Euclidean quantum gravity has undergone a change in recent years, and is today most often regarded as an effective theory valid at low energies. In this picture it can be valid to calculate one loop effects, and the non-renormalizability reflects some of the ambiguity caused by the neglected degrees of freedom. The present article attempts to introduce ζ-function techniques to the non-experts and bring the reader up to date with a topical application to brane cosmology.

21.2 ζ-functions

The ζ-function enters quantum field theory because of the expression for the one loop effective action

$$W = \pm\tfrac{1}{2}\log\det(\Delta/\mu_R^2) \tag{21.1}$$

where Δ is the second variation of the classical action at the chosen values of the background fields. We require a means of defining the determinant of Δ which, in Euclidean space, is a second-order elliptic operator of the form $\Delta = -D^2 + X$, where D is a covariant derivative.

The ζ-function for an elliptic operator is defined by a functional trace [7]

$$\zeta(s) = \operatorname{tr}\left(\Delta^{-s}\right). \tag{21.2}$$

If the operator has a discrete set of eigenvalues λ_n, we may write

$$\zeta(s) = \sum_{n=1}^{\infty} \lambda_n^{-s} \tag{21.3}$$

For second-order operators, the sum only converges when $2s$ is larger than the number of dimensions d, but we remove this restriction by analytic continuation to values of s in the complex plane. A crucial property of the ζ-function is that the analytic continuation is regular at $s = 0$.

Stephen Hawking introduced the ζ-function into quantum field theory by using the definition

$$\log\det(\Delta/\mu_R^2) = -\zeta'(0) - \zeta(0)\log\mu_R^2. \tag{21.4}$$

This enables us to calculate the one loop effective action in a wide range of examples, including spheres [8], balls [9], shells [10] and so on [11].

Many applications have been calculations of the vacuum energy in a static background. In these applications the eigenvalues of Δ are of the form $k^2 + w_n^2$, where k is a continuous variable. We can use a finite time interval L and take the limit $L \to \infty$ at the end, then

$$\zeta(s) = L\int\frac{dk}{2\pi}\sum_{n=1}^{\infty}(k^2 + w_n^2)^{-s} \tag{21.5}$$

The integral gives

$$\zeta(s) = \frac{L}{4} \frac{\Gamma(s-1/2)}{\Gamma(s)\Gamma(1/2)} \sum_{n=1}^{\infty} w_n^{1-2s} \tag{21.6}$$

The effective action is obtained from (21.1). The vacuum energy, E, defined by $W = LE$ in Euclidean space, becomes

$$E = \frac{1}{2}\mathrm{reg}\left(\sum_{n=1}^{\infty} w_n^{1-2s}\right), \tag{21.7}$$

where $\mathrm{reg}(f)$ denotes the regular part of the Laurent expansion of f about the origin. We recognize here the sum of the zero-point energies $\frac{1}{2}w_n$.

21.3 Heat kernel coefficients

It will prove convenient to define a smeared version of the ζ-function by

$$\zeta(s,\omega] = \mathrm{tr}\left(\Delta^{-s}\omega\right). \tag{21.8}$$

The analytic properties of the ζ-function follow from the representation

$$\zeta(s,\omega] = \frac{1}{\Gamma(s)} \int_0^{\infty} t^{s-1} \mathrm{tr}\left(\omega e^{-\Delta t}\right) dt. \tag{21.9}$$

The kernel $e^{-\Delta t}$ satisfies the heat equation, and can be analysed using WKB approximations. This was essentially the original approach of Schwinger and DeWitt, although their work used the Scrödinger equation [2]. The pure mathematicians found equivalent results using the pseudodifferential operator calculus [3, 12]. One finds that the trace has an asymptotic expansion

$$\mathrm{tr}\left(\omega e^{-\Delta t}\right) \sim t^{-d/2} \sum_{n=0}^{\infty} B_n[\omega] t^{n/2}. \tag{21.10}$$

The heat kernel coefficients $B_n[\omega]$ only depend on local combinations of covariant tensors, such as curvatures and covariant derivatives of X. When substituted into the transform (21.9) we find that

$$\zeta(0,\omega] = B_d[\omega] \tag{21.11}$$

and there are poles in the ζ-function at $s = (d-N)/2$ for $N < d$.

The properties of the heat kernel coefficients under conformal transformations often play an important role in their evaluation [17]. A conformal transformation gives a new metric $g_\epsilon = e^{2\epsilon\omega} g$. A new function X_ϵ is used in order to obtain a simple scaling of the operator,

$$-D_\epsilon^2 + X_\epsilon = e^{-2\epsilon\omega} \Delta. \tag{21.12}$$

(In a conformally invariant theory, the transformation of X to X_ϵ is automatic. In other cases the transformation is a technical device.) Differentiating the functional trace (21.2) gives,

$$\partial_\epsilon \zeta(s)|_{\epsilon=0} = 2s \operatorname{tr}\left(\omega \Delta^{-s}\right) = 2s\zeta(s,\omega). \tag{21.13}$$

From the residues at $s = (d - N)/2$,

$$\partial_\epsilon B_N = (d - N)B_N[\omega]. \tag{21.14}$$

The first thing we notice is that $B_N[\omega]$ can always be recovered from B_N by a conformal transformation. Secondly, we see that B_N is conformally invariant in N dimensions, and must be composed of conformally invariant tensors or total derivatives. Some examples are tabulated (using [13–18]), where B_N ($\equiv B_N[1]$) is written in the form

$$B_N = \frac{1}{(4\pi)^{d/2}} \int_M b_N + \frac{1}{(4\pi)^{d/2}} \int_{\partial M} c_N. \tag{21.15}$$

The total derivatives in the tables are related to the Gauss–Bonnet identity in d (even) dimensions,

$$\chi = \frac{1}{(4\pi)^{d/2}} \frac{1}{(d/2)!} \left(\int_M q_d + \int_{\partial M} q_{d-1}\right) \tag{21.16}$$

with $q_d = 2^{-d/2} d!\, R_{[\mu\nu}{}^{\mu\nu} \dots R_{\rho\sigma]}{}^{\rho\sigma}$, e.g. $q_2 = R$, in terms of the *intrinsic curvature* (see [20] for q_3).

Table 21.1 Heat kernel coefficients b_N for the operator $-D^2 + X$. The Ricci scalar is R and C is the Weyl tensor in N dimensions. See [13] for b_6. The values of $\operatorname{tr}(X)$, etc. for general spin can be found in [19].

Term	Formula
b_0	$\operatorname{tr}(1)$
b_2	$\operatorname{tr}\left(\frac{1}{6}R - X\right)$
b_4	$\operatorname{tr}\left(-\frac{1}{360}q_4 + \frac{1}{120}C^2 + \frac{1}{2}(X - \frac{1}{6}R)^2 + \frac{1}{12}F^{ab}F_{ab}\right)$

Table 21.2 Boundary heat kernel coefficients c_N. k_{ab} is the extrinsic curvature, θ its trace and $\sigma_{ab} = k_{ab} - \theta/(N-1)$. The boundary conditions are part Dirichlet $P_-\psi = 0$ and part Robin $(\psi + \partial_n)P_+\psi = 0$. For c_5 see [18].

Term	Formula
c_1	$\frac{1}{2}\pi^{1/2}\mathrm{tr}\,(P_+ - P_-)$
c_2	$\frac{1}{3}\mathrm{tr}\,(\theta - 6P_+\psi)$
c_3^D	$-\frac{1}{48}q_2 + \frac{1}{32}\sigma^2 + \frac{1}{2}(X - \frac{1}{8}R)$
c_3^R	$\frac{1}{48}q_2 + \frac{1}{32}\sigma^2 - \frac{1}{2}(X - \frac{1}{8}R) + (\psi - \frac{1}{4}\theta)^2$
c_3	$\pi^{1/2}\mathrm{tr}\,\left(P_- c_{3/2}^D + P_+ c_{3/2}^R + 48 P_{+|a}P_+{}^{|a}\right)$
c_4^D	$-\frac{1}{360}q_3 + \frac{2}{35}\sigma^3 - \frac{1}{3}(X - \frac{1}{6}R)\theta - \frac{1}{2}(X - \frac{1}{6}R)_{,n} + \frac{1}{15}C_{ancn}k^{ac}$
c_4^R	$-\frac{1}{360}q_3 + \frac{2}{45}\sigma^3 - \frac{1}{3}(X - \frac{1}{6}R)\theta + \frac{1}{2}(X - \frac{1}{6}R)_{,n} - \frac{4}{3}(\psi - \frac{1}{3}\theta)^3$
	$+2(X - \frac{1}{6}R)\psi - \frac{2}{15}(\psi - \frac{1}{3}\theta)\sigma^2 + \frac{1}{15}C_{ancn}k^{ac}$
c_4	$\mathrm{tr}(P_+ c_2^R + P_- c_2^D - \frac{2}{15}P_{+|a}P_+{}^{|a}\theta - \frac{4}{15}P_{+|a}P_{+|b}k^{ab}$
	$+\frac{4}{3}P_{+|a}P_+{}^{|a}P_+\psi - \frac{2}{3}P_+P_+{}^{|a}n^b F_{ab})$

21.4 Anomalies

Calculating anomalies and finding conditions in which they cancel is of major importance in many areas of quantum field theory and superstring theory. The ζ-function is especially good at picking out anomalies. Two simple examples are considered here. Firstly the conformal anomaly [21–23], which is important in superstring theory and plays a role in the brane world model presented later. The second example is the axial or Abelian chiral anomaly [24, 25]. This is closely related to the non-Abelian chiral anomaly which is used widely in superstring theory.

Consider the one loop effective action for a conformally rescaled theory, in the sense of the previous section,

$$W[\omega] = \frac{1}{2}\log\det(e^{2\omega}\Delta/\mu_R^2). \qquad (21.17)$$

The transformation of the ζ-function (21.13) implies

$$\partial_\epsilon W[\epsilon\omega] = -\zeta(0, \omega). \qquad (21.18)$$

In a conformally invariant theory, the conformally rescaled theory is the same as the original theory, and the ζ-function represents the change of the effective action under a conformal transformation.

The conformal anomaly can be put to a practical use. By integrating, it is possible to relate the effective action for two different backgrounds [26–28]. The integration produces a new expression,

$$W[\omega] - W[0] = C[\Delta, \omega], \qquad (21.19)$$

where $C[\Delta, \omega]$ is called the cocycle function and can be expressed in terms of local invariants [10, 27]. For example, if $d = 2$ and $\Delta = -\nabla^2 + X$,

$$C = \frac{1}{4\pi} \int_M \left\{ -\left(X - \tfrac{1}{6}R\right)\omega - \tfrac{1}{6}(\nabla\omega)^2 \right\} d\mu$$
$$+ \frac{1}{4\pi} \int_{\partial M} \left\{ -\tfrac{1}{3}\theta\omega - \tfrac{1}{2}\omega_{,n} \right\} d\mu \qquad (21.20)$$

Expressions such as this enable us to find $W[\omega]$ once $W[0]$ is known.

Similar considerations apply to the axial or Abelian chiral anomaly. Consider a Dirac operator $D = i\gamma \cdot (\nabla + A)$ and introduce a source term $\chi\nabla \cdot j_5$ for the divergence of the axial current. The one loop effective action is

$$W[A, \chi] = -\log \det \left(e^{i\gamma_5\chi} D e^{i\gamma_5\chi} \right). \qquad (21.21)$$

The expectation value of $\nabla \cdot j_5$ is then

$$\partial_\epsilon W[A, \epsilon\chi]|_{\epsilon=0} = 2i\eta(0, \chi), \qquad (21.22)$$

where

$$\eta(s, \chi] = \mathrm{tr}(D^{-2s}\chi\gamma_5). \qquad (21.23)$$

This can also be expressed in terms of local invariants. The chiral anomaly in d dimensions is related to the non-Abelian anomaly for chiral fermions in $d - 2$ dimensions [29], which plays an important role in constructing superstring theories and their low energy limits [30].

21.5 Brane worlds

In brane world models, some or all of the matter in the universe is confined to four-dimensional hypersurfaces in higher dimensions. In Randall–Sundrum I models [31] there are two hypersurfaces separated by five-dimensional anti-de Sitter space. This situation is inherently unstable, but it has been suggested that the branes can be stabilized by vacuum energy between the two branes [32, 34]. Calculation of the vacuum energy can be done with ζ-function techniques [33, 35, 36].

The full set of classical field equations for the Randall–Sundrum model can be obtained from an action

$$S = \frac{1}{8\pi G_5} \int_M (R - 2\Lambda) + \frac{1}{4\pi G_5} \int_{\partial M} \theta + \int_M \mathcal{L}_b + \int_{\partial M} \mathcal{L}_m, \qquad (21.24)$$

where the boundary $\partial\mathcal{M}$ consists of a hidden brane Σ_h and a visible brane Σ_v with extrinsic curvature scalars θ. The Lagrangian density $\mathcal{L}_m$ represents brane matter fields, and the action correctly reproduces the brane boundary conditions [37]. We shall be mostly concerned with the vacuum energies $\mathcal{V}_h$ and $\mathcal{V}_v$.

In the original Randall–Sundrum model, $\mathcal{V}_h = -\mathcal{V}_v = \mathcal{V}_0$, where $\mathcal{V}_0 = 3\kappa/(4\pi G_5)$ and $\Lambda = -6\kappa^2$. In this case the branes are neutrally stable. If $\mathcal{V}_v < -\mathcal{V}_0$, the branes accelerate towards each other.

We require boundary conditions on any bulk fields other than the graviton. Both Dirichlet or Neumann are possible, and we will distinguish the case where the boundary conditions on each brane are the same, which we call untwisted, and the case where they are different, which we call twisted.

We will consider the vacuum energy for bulk fields with conformally invariant Lagrangians in five dimensions between flat branes. The metric is

$$ds^2 = e^{-2\sigma(y)}\eta_{\mu\nu}dx^\mu dx^\nu + dy^2. \tag{21.25}$$

This metric is conformally flat,

$$ds^2 = e^{-2\sigma}(\eta_{\mu\nu}dx^\mu dx^\nu + d\tau^2) \tag{21.26}$$

where $0 \leq \tau \leq \beta$, and

$$\beta[\sigma] = \int_0^a e^\sigma dy. \tag{21.27}$$

For anti-de Sitter space, $\beta = \kappa^{-1}(e^{\kappa a} - 1)$.

The one loop effective action for conformally invariant fields can be evaluated using (21.19), which reduces the calculation to the effective action in flat space with two plane boundaries and the cocycle function. Note that we might have expanded the fields in eigenmodes along the y direction and then quantized, in which case the cocycle term would be missed. In this sense the cocycle term can be regarded as a dimensional reduction anomaly.

For untwisted fields the eigenvalues of the Laplacian in flat space are $k^2 + m_n^2$, where k is the four-dimensional wave vector and $m_n = \pi n/\beta$, where $n = 0, 1, 2 \ldots$. Twisted fields have similar eigenvalues with $m_n = (n + \frac{1}{2})\pi/\beta$.

The calculation of the ζ-function follows (21.5), now with $W = L^4 V$. For untwisted fermion fields,

$$V = \frac{3}{128\pi^2}\zeta_R(5)\beta^{-4}, \tag{21.28}$$

where ζ_R is the Riemann ζ-function. For twisted fermion fields,

$$V = -\frac{3}{128\pi^2}\frac{15}{16}\zeta_R(5)\beta^{-4}. \tag{21.29}$$

The results depend on the separation of the branes only through β given in (21.27).

If $\mathcal{V}_v < -\mathcal{V}_0$, the tendency of the branes to move together can be balanced by the vacuum energy and a stable configuration results.

An interesting variation of this theme occurs if there is a gauge symmetry in the bulk [35, 36]. We use projection operators and set $P_-\psi = 0$ and $(\psi + \partial_n)P_+\psi = 0$, but the boundary conditions on the two branes can be different:

$$\tfrac{1}{2}(1 - U_v)\psi = 0 \text{ visible brane} \tag{21.30}$$

$$\tfrac{1}{2}(1 - U_h)\psi = 0 \text{ hidden brane.} \tag{21.31}$$

From $P_-^2 = P_-$ we have $U_v^2 = U_h^2 = 1$. The boundary conditions need not commute with the gauge symmetry and the symmetry can be broken. The residual symmetry group H contains elements which commute with U_h and U_v. (This is similar to the Wilson loop symmetry breaking mechanism [38–40].)

In order to illustrate the point, consider the following example with an $SU(5)$ symmetry,

$$U_h = \begin{pmatrix} -1 & & & & \\ & -1 & & & \\ & & -1 & & \\ & & & \sigma_3 & \end{pmatrix}, \ U_v = \begin{pmatrix} -1 & & & & \\ & -1 & & & \\ & & -1 & & \\ & & & \sigma_\theta & \end{pmatrix}, \tag{21.32}$$

where $\sigma_\theta = \sigma_3 \cos 2\theta + \sigma_1 \sin 2\theta$. The boundary conditions break the gauge symmetry,

$$\theta = 0, \tfrac{\pi}{2} \quad G \to SU(4) \times U(1) \tag{21.33}$$

$$\theta \neq 0, \tfrac{\pi}{2} \quad G \to SU(3) \times U(1). \tag{21.34}$$

The vacuum energy now depends on θ. The eigenvalues are given by $k^2 + m_n^2$, as before, but now $m_n = (n \pm \theta)\pi/\beta$. The ζ-function gives

$$V = \frac{3}{128\pi^2} \sum_{n=1}^{\infty} \frac{(3 + 2\cos(2n\theta))}{n^5}\beta^{-4}. \tag{21.35}$$

This has a minimum at $\theta = \pi/2$.

The minimum of the potential picks out a particular symmetry breaking scheme. To have a physical effect, the parameters in the boundary conditions would have to evolve dynamically. This does indeed happen in this model, because kinetic terms appear in the one loop effective action. They can be seen most easily in terms involving the renormalization scale,

$$W = -\tfrac{1}{2}\zeta(0) \log \mu_R^2 + \cdots . \tag{21.36}$$

Using the known B_5 coefficient,

$$\zeta(0) = \frac{1}{4\pi^2} \int_v d^4x \left\{ -\frac{60}{5760} U_{;\mu} U_{;\nu} R^{\mu\nu} + 20 \text{ more terms} \right\}, \tag{21.37}$$

where $U = U(\theta)$. This phenomena could be described as induced dynamical symmetry breaking.

21.6 Outlook

Superstring theory has lead to renewed interest in calculations of the effective action in higher dimensions. Models such as the Horova–Witten model [30] are likely to have interesting one loop effects resembling those found in the Randall–Sundrum I model. The heat kernel coefficients play an important role in determining the renormalization group flows and the related cocycle functions can be used to find the finite parts of the effective potential. The extent of cancellations due to the supersymmetry has yet to be investigated.

One loop effects can also be calculated in the anti-de Sitter side of the AdS-CFT correspondence [41]. Comparisons of the conformal anomaly, for example, can make extensive use of heat kernel coefficients B_5 and beyond.

An interesting issue which we have not touched upon is that, with ζ-function regularization, usually $\det AB \neq \det A \det B$. A multiplicative anomaly can be defined by $a(A, B) = \log \det(AB) - \log \det A - \log \det B$. If A is a function, then the multiplicative anomaly is related to the cocycle function mentioned earlier. The multiplicative anomaly cannot be ignored, although in many cases it appears possible to absorb it into counter-terms [43, 44]. Another recent topic has been the investigation of heat kernels and ζ-functions in non-commutative spacetimes [43], where the ζ-function is not necessarily regular at the origin.

With the recent proposal that Euclidean quantum gravity is a low energy effective theory of quantum gravity it has once again become respectable to study perturbative effects and quantum fields on fixed backgrounds. These perturbative effects might be regarded as the phenomenology of quantum gravity, and include many of the most exciting areas of research: gravity waves from the early universe, black hole evaporation and quantum cosmology. Fields in which, noticeably, Stephen Hawking has made remarkable contributions.

References

[1] Schwinger, J. (1951), *Phys. Rev.* **82** 664.

[2] DeWitt, B. (1963), *Relativity Groups and Topology* (Gordon and Breach, New York).

[3] McKean, H. P. and Singer, J. M. (1971), *J. Diff. Geom.* **5** 233.

[4] Dowker, J. S. and Critchley, R. (1977), *Phys. Rev.* **D13** 3224.

[5] Dowker, J. S. and Critchley, R. (1977), *Phys. Rev.* **D16** 3390.

[6] Hawking, S. W. (1977), *Commun. Math. Phys.* **55** 133.

[7] Seeley, R. T. (1967), *Proc. Symp. Pure Math.* (Amer. Math. Soc) **10** 288.

[8] Dowker, J. S. (1994), *J Math Phys* **35** 4989.

[9] Bordag, M., Geyer, K., Kirsten, K. and Elizalde, E. (1996), *Commun. Math. Phys.* **179** 215.

[10] Dowker, J. S. and Apps, J. S. (1995), *Class. Quantum Grav.* **12** 1363.

[11] Elizalde, E., Odintsov, S. D., Romea, A., Bytsenko, A. A. and Zerbini, S. (1994) *Zeta Regularization Techniques with Applications* (World Scientific, Singapore).

[12] Gilkey, P. B. (1994), *Invariance Theory, the Heat Equation and the Atiyah-Singer Index Theorem* (CRC Press, Boca Raton).

[13] Gilkey, P. B. (1975), *J. Differential Geometry* **10** 601.

[14] Luckock, H. C. and Moss, I. G. (1989), *Class. Quantum Grav.* **6** 1993.

[15] Moss, I. G. (1989), *Class. Quantum Grav.* **6** 759.

[16] Moss, I. G. and Dowker, J. S. (1989), *Phys. Lett.* **B229** 261.

[17] Branson, T. and Gilkey, P. B. (1990), *Comm. Partial Diff. Eqns.* **15** 245.

[18] Branson, T. P., Gilkey, P. B., Kirsten, K. and Vassilevich, D. V. (1999), *Nucl. Phys.* **B563** 603.

[19] Christensen, S. M. and Duff, M. J. (1979), *Nucl. Phys.* **B154** 301.

[20] Moss, I. G. (1995), *Quantum Theory, Black Holes and Inflation* (Wiley).

[21] Capper, D. and Duff, M. (1974), *Nuovo Cimento* **23A** 173.

[22] Duff, M., Deser, S. and Isham, C. J. (1976), *Nucl Phys.* **111B** 45.

[23] Duff, M. (1994), *Class. Quantum Grav.* **11** 1387.

[24] Adler, S. L. (1969), *Phys. Rev.* **177** 2426.

[25] Bell, J. and Jackiw, R. (1969), *Nuovo Cim* **A60** 47.

[26] Brown, M. R. and Ottewill, A. C. (1985), *Phys. Rev.* **D21** 2514.

[27] Dowker, J. S. (1986), *Phys. Rev.* **D33** 3150.

[28] Dowker, J. S. and Schofield, J. P. (1989), *Nucl. Phys.* **B327** 267.

[29] Alvarez-Gaume, L. and Ginsparg, P. (1984), *Nucl. Phys.* **B243** 449.

[30] Horava, P. and Witten, E. (1996), *Nucl. Phys.* **B460** 506, (1996) *Nucl. Phys.* **B475** 96.

[31] Randall, L. and Sundrum, R. (1999), *Phys. Rev Lett* **83** 3370, (1999) *Phys. Rev Lett* **83** 4670.

[32] Toms, D. J. (2000), *Phys. Letts.* **B484** 149.

[33] Flachi, A. and Toms, D. J. (2001), *Nucl.Phys.* **B610** 144.

[34] Garriga, J., Pujolas, O. and Tanaka, T. (2001), *Nucl. Phys.* **B605** 192.

[35] Flachi, A., Moss, I. G. and Toms, D. J. (2000), Phys. Rev. **D64**.

[36] Flachi, A., Moss, I. G. and Toms, D. J. (2001), Phys. Letts **B518**, 153–156.

[37] Chamblin, H. A. and Reall, H. S. (1999), *Nucl. Phys.* **B562** 133.

[38] Hosotani, Y. (1983), *Phys. Lett.* **B309**.

[39] Ford, L. H. (1980), *Phys. Rev.* **D21** 933.

[40] Dowker, J. S. and Jadhav, S. (1989), *Phys. Rev.* **D39** 1196, *ibid* 2368.

[41] Maldacena, J. (1998), *Adv. Theor. Math. Phys.* **2** 231.

[42] Mansfield, P. and Nolland, D. (1999), *JHEP* **9907** 028.

[43] Elizalde, E., Cognola, G. and Zerbini, (1998), *Commun Math. Phys.* **194** 613.

[44] Zerbini, S. (2002), *Nucl. Phys.* (Proc. Suppl.) **B101** 224.

[45] Elizalde, E. (2002), *Nucl. Phys.* (Proc. Suppl.) **B101** 157.

22

Some reflections on the status of conventional quantum theory when applied to quantum gravity

Chris Isham

Imperial College, London

22.1 Introduction

The period in the late 1960s when I was a postgraduate student at Imperial College saw rapid changes in theoretical physics in response to data streaming from the world's particle accelerators. One consequence was that the subject matter of a student's PhD thesis sometimes changed uncomfortably rapidly during the course of his or her studies. As a result, there was a tendency for supervisors to assign a provisional thesis title like 'Topics in elementary particle physics' – a practice that was understandable, but which was finally blocked by the University of London some years ago!

When asked to speak at this Symposium in honour of Stephen Hawking, I adopted a similar tactic by choosing as the provisional title 'Prima facie questions in quantum gravity', on the grounds that this would give maximum flexibility when it came to actually write the talk. However, in the event, I have chosen to focus on one single issue, and the title of my lecture has been readjusted accordingly.

The question I wish to address is the extent to which ideas of standard quantum theory are adequate for the formulation of a quantum theory of gravity: in particular, in regard to (i) the use of continuum quantities in the mathematical foundations of quantum theory; and (ii) possible roles for topos theory. In this context it should be emphasized that all the current mainstream approaches to quantum gravity use standard quantum theory in one form or another.

Of course, it is well understood that, at a *conceptual* level, the standard interpretation of quantum theory is inadequate when, for example, applied to quantum cosmology. Specifically, the lack of any external observer of the universe 'as a whole' throws into doubt the instrumentalism of the

Copenhagen interpretation, as does any attempt to construct a quantum gravity theory with no background spacetime in which an 'observer' could be placed. The extent to which such reservations apply to quantum gravity away from the cosmological regime is still debated, but in practice most work on quantum gravity pays only lip service to these conceptual issues.

However, what I have in mind are not conceptual issues *per se* but rather certain *mathematical* ingredients in the formalism of quantum theory that are invariably taken for granted and yet which, I claim, implicitly assume certain properties of space and time that may be fundamentally incompatible with the spatio-temporal concepts needed for a successful quantum gravity theory. An example of particular interest is the use of the *continuum* (via the real or complex numbers).

More generally, one can question the almost universal assumption that spatio-temporal concepts are to be implemented mathematically using standard point-set theory: this notwithstanding the frequently-voiced objection that the literal idea of a space, or time, point is physically meaningless. In fact, there exists something – namely topos theory – that can replace set theory as the foundation of mathematics, and which could arguably be a more appropriate way of modelling spatio-temporal concepts in physical regimes where quantum gravity effects are paramount. As we shall see, topos theory is also relevant to questions concerning the status of the continuum. These considerations have motivated my focusing the lecture on two main areas: (i) the a priori status of spatio-temporal concepts in quantum theory, particularly in regard to the use of continua; and (ii) certain possible roles for topos theory in theoretical physics.

Considerations of this type are part of the general question of the role of standard spatio-temporal concepts in a theory of quantum gravity. In the current major quantum gravity programmes, most of these concepts are inserted by hand as part of the overall background structure of the theory. On the other hand, there is a school of thought that maintains that the standard ideas of space and time should 'emerge' from the theory only in some appropriate limit or physical regime; in which case, a crucial question is whether the theory contains *any* fundamental concepts/structures that can broadly identified as 'spatio-temporal', or if all such concepts or structures are emergent in some way. One of the attractions of the consistent-histories approach to quantum theory (of which more later) is that it allows for the idea of emergent structures in a natural way via the process of coarse-graining: analogous to how thermodynamical concepts arise from statistical physics when microscopic details of the system are ignored.

En passent, one might ask what else could arise from the fundamental theory in some appropriate physical limit. This might include the entire mathematical formalism of standard quantum theory, including its use of

Hilbert spaces defined over $\mathbb{R}$ or $\mathbb{C}$. Perhaps the conceptual structure of standard quantum theory is also an emergent structure: in particular, the special role for measurement, and the use of probabilities that lie in the closed interval $[0, 1]$ of the real numbers. Certainly, there is no compelling logical reason why whatever plays the role of standard quantum theory at the Planck length – if, indeed, there is *any* such theory – should possess all the features of the theory that is known to work empirically only at atomic and nuclear scales.

However, one of the key questions of interest in the present paper is not how the standard ideas of space and time (and probability) might *emerge* from a different formalism; but rather how one might proceed to construct a quantum theory *ab initio* in which whatever fundamental spatio-temporal concepts are present are definitely not the familiar continuum ones: for example, if one is given a finite causal set as a background structure. The first step, and the only one taken in the present paper, is to sound a cautionary note by emphasizing how strongly the continuum ideas of space and time are implicitly embedded in the standard formulation of quantum theory.

The plan of the paper is as follows. In section 22.2 there is a discussion of the role of continuum concepts in the formulation of quantum theory in the presence of a non-standard background (such as a causal set [2, 3]). The conclusion is that, in some appropriate sense, there may be a different *type* of quantum theory for each type of background spacetime.

If this is indeed the case, the question then arises as to how these different theories are to be 'patched' together in a true quantum gravity theory in which these backgrounds are themselves subject to quantum effects. One possibility is the use of *topos* theory. In section 22.3 we discuss other ways in which the standard notion of spacetime may change and, again, find a possible role for topos theory.

Since topos theory is an important mathematical ingredient in our considerations, one part of the subject – the theory of presheaves – is introduced in section 22.4. It is then shown in section 22.5 how this can be used in a natural way to illustrate certain key features (specifically the Kochen–Specker theorem) of standard quantum theory. The main physical idea here is a role for contextual, multi-valued logic – an idea that in itself has many possible fruitful applications in theoretical physics.

22.2 The danger of a priori assumptions

22.2.1 The use of the real and complex numbers in quantum theory

The use of the real and complex numbers is a basic feature of all approaches to quantum theory: Hilbert spaces of states, C^*-algebras of observables, quantum logic of propositions, functional integral methods, etc. These number systems have a variety of relevant mathematical properties, but the one of particular interest here is that they are *continua*, by which – in the present context – is meant not only that $\mathbb{R}$ and $\mathbb{C}$ have the appropriate cardinality, but also that they come equipped with the familiar topology and differential structure that makes them manifolds of real dimension one and two respectively.

My concern is that the use of these numbers may be problematic in the context of a quantum gravity theory whose underlying notion of space and time is different from that of a smooth manifold. The danger is that by imposing a continuum structure in the quantum theory a priori, one may be creating a theoretical system that is fundamentally unsuitable for the incorporation of spatio-temporal concepts of a non-continuum nature: this would be the theoretical-physics analogue of what a philosopher might call a 'category error'. For this reason, it is important to consider carefully the origin, and role, in standard quantum theory of this particular facet of the real (and complex) numbers.

In general terms, the real numbers arise in three ways in physical theories: (i) as the values of physical quantities; (ii) to model space and time; and (iii) as the values of probabilities. Our present task is to consider more precisely the use of real numbers in quantum theory in these terms.

As a first step, consider the simple example with which most undergraduate courses on quantum theory begin: a non-relativistic point particle moving in one dimension. The state of the system at a time t is represented by a wave function $\psi_t(x)$, and we see at once that continuum quantities are involved in three ways: (i) as the argument x in the wave function; (ii) as the value of the wave function; and (iii) as the time parameter t. Let us consider these in turn.

The x in $\psi(x)$

From one perspective, the x in $\psi(x)$ arises because we are starting with a classical theory and then 'quantizing' it. In the present example, the classical configuration space Q is identified with the real line because the system is a point particle moving in (one-dimensional) physical space, and the latter is modelled by the real numbers.

In general, the configuration space (if there is one) Q for a classical system is modelled mathematically by a differentiable manifold, and the classical state space is the cotangent bundle T^*Q. The physical motivation for using a manifold to represent Q again reduces to the fact that we represent physical space with a manifold. This is clearly so for configurations that correspond to the position of the centre-of-mass of an object in space, or its overall orientation in space, but it also applies to internal degrees of freedom of relative positions of constituent entities.

Thus, in assuming that the state space of a classical system is a manifold of the form T^*Q we are importing into the classical theory a powerful a priori picture of physical space: namely, that it is a differentiable manifold.[1] This then carries across to the corresponding quantum theory. For example, if 'quantization' is construed to mean defining the quantum states to be cross-sections of some flat[2] vector bundle over Q, then the domain of these state functions is the continuum space Q.

However, for this argument to have any force we need to consider *why* quantization is so defined, and this takes us to the issue of the space in which the wave function has its values.

The value of the function $\psi(x)$ – the role of classical physical quantities
In the example of the quantum theory of a particle moving in one dimension, the value of the state function $\psi(x)$ is a complex number: so, once again, a continuum concept arises. This particular one comes from two different sources.

On the one hand, the operator $\hat{x}$ that represents the position of the particle acts on the state function as

$$(\hat{x}\psi)(x) := x\psi(x). \tag{22.1}$$

More generally, for a system with a configuration manifold Q, a classical physical configuration quantity corresponds to a real-valued function $f : Q \to \mathbb{R}$, and this function is represented in the quantum theory by the operator

$$(\hat{f}\psi)(q) := f(q)\psi(q) \tag{22.2}$$

on sections of the appropriate vector bundle.

Although this equation does not *prove* that $\psi(q)$ is $\mathbb{C}$-valued, it does show that, for each $q \in Q$, the space in which $\psi(q)$ takes its values must be such that it admits a *multiplication* operation by real numbers.

We see that this particular source of the real numbers in quantum theory comes from the assumption that *classical* physical quantities are real-valued, which is then translated into an analogous requirement on the quantum variables.

---

[1] There may be cases where $\mathcal{S}$ is a symplectic manifold that is not a cotangent bundle; for example, $\mathcal{S} := S^2$. However, I would argue that the reason $\mathcal{S}$ is assumed to be a *manifold* is still ultimately grounded in an a priori assumption about the nature of physical space (and time).

[2] The bundle is chosen to be flat so that a covariant derivative of sections can be defined without the need to introduce extra local 'connection' variables into the theory.

A related feature is that in any quantum system the eigenvector equation for a physical quantity A is of the form $\hat{A}|a\rangle = a|a\rangle$, where a is a real number. So the state space has to be such that its elements can be multiplied by real numbers. Note that this applies even to quantum physical quantities that have no classical analogue: we still assume that their eigenvalues are real numbers. Of course, for many quantities the set of all eigenvalues will be a discrete subset of $\mathbb{R}$, but that does not detract from the point being made here.

It is thus pertinent to ask *why* physical quantities – classical or quantum – are taken to be real-valued. Many will doubtless say that the answer is obvious, or that it is even part of the definition of a physical quantity, but I would challenge these assertions as being over-hasty.

One reason why the values of physical quantities are assumed to be real numbers is undoubtedly the operational one that – at least, in the pre-digital age – physical quantities are ultimately measured with rulers and pointers, and so it is the assumed continuum nature of physical space that comes into play.

However, it is by no means obvious that physical quantities should necessarily be real-valued in, for example, a quantum gravity theory in which it is not appropriate to think of space as a smooth manifold, and where, therefore, there is no place for operational considerations that presuppose a continuum nature for space and/or time.

Of course, it is a totally open question as to what should replace $\mathbb{R}$ as the value space of a physical quantity in these circumstances – it could be something as obvious as a finite number field, but it could also be something far more radical. In any event, a key role in deciding this issue should be played by any underlying spatio-temporal concepts (albeit, non-standard) that are present.

The value of the function $\psi(x)$ – the role of probability
A different source of the $\mathbb{C}$-valued nature of the wave-function is its probabilistic interpretation. Of course, this extends outside simple wave mechanics, with the general quantum-theory result that if $\hat{E}(A \in \Delta)$ is the spectral projector onto the eigenspace of $\hat{A}$ with eigenvalues in the (Borel) set $\Delta \subset \mathbb{R}$ then, if the (normalized) state is ψ, the probability that the proposition 'the physical quantity A lies in Δ' is true is[3]

$$\text{Prob}(A \in \Delta; \psi) = \langle \psi, \hat{E}(A \in \Delta) \rangle. \tag{22.3}$$

---

[3] Of course, in the standard Copenhagen interpretation of quantum theory it would be more appropriate to say that the proposition represented by the spectral projector $\hat{E}(A \in \Delta)$ is 'if a measurement is made of A, then the value will be found to lie in Δ'.

From our present perspective, the key point is that the assumption that probabilities should lie in the interval $[0, 1]$ of the real numbers requires the field over which the Hilbert state space is defined to be such as to accommodate this assumption via the right-hand side of (22.3). So this is yet another source of the use of continuum quantities in the mathematical formulation of quantum theory.

In the context of standard physics, it is clear why probabilities are required to lie in the interval $[0, 1]$. As physicists, we most commonly employ a relative-frequency interpretation of probability in which an experiment is repeated a large number, say N, times, and the probability associated with a particular result is then defined to be the ratio N_i/N, where N_i is the number of experiments in which that result was obtained. The rational numbers N_i/N necessarily lie between 0 and 1, and if we take the limit as $N \to \infty$, as is appropriate for a hypothetical 'infinite ensemble', we get real numbers in the closed interval $[0, 1]$.

Although the relative-frequency interpretation of probability may seem natural in standard physics, it is not meaningful in situations where there is no classical spatio-temporal background in which observations could be made; or, if there is a background, it is such that there is no meaningful analogue of the relative-frequencies interpretation adapted to that background.

Under such circumstances it might be more natural to follow Aristotle, Heisenberg and Popper in adopting a *propensity* interpretation of probability, perhaps within the context of a 'post-Everett' form of quantum theory, such as consistent-histories theory.

However, if probability is viewed in this more realist way, there is no overwhelming reason for assigning its values to be real numbers lying in the interval $[0, 1]$. The minimal requirement is presumably only that the value space should be a partially ordered set $(\mathcal{V}, \leq)$ so that it makes sense to say that certain events are more, or less, probable (in the sense of the partial-ordering operation $\leq$) than others.

Note that this allows for the possibility of pairs of events whose propensities are incomparable: *i.e.*, the probability value-space $\mathcal{V}$ may not be a *totally*-ordered set. We would, however, expect there to be a unit element $1 \in \mathcal{V}$, corresponding to the probability of an event that is certain to happen (or the proposition that is identically true), and with $p \leq 1$ for all $p \in \mathcal{V}$. Similarly, there should be a null element $0 \in \mathcal{V}$, corresponding to the probability of an event that is certain not to happen (or the proposition that is identically false), and with $0 \leq p$ for all $p \in \mathcal{V}$.

It also seems natural to require that $\mathcal{V}$ has some 'semi-additive' structure so that the probability of two disjoint events is the 'sum' of the probabilities of the individual events. At the very least, if P is any proposition and $\neg P$ is its negation, we would expect the probability of $P \vee \neg P$ to be the unit[4] $1 \in \mathcal{P}$, and be equal to the 'sum' of the probabilities of P and $\neg P$.

Of course, it is an open question as to what precise mathematical structure should be used as the value-space for probabilities in the absence of any classical spatio-temporal background; or, indeed, what it should be in the presence of a non-standard background such as a causal set. But the key point is that there is no fundamental reason why this value-space has to involve the real numbers; and the form of quantum theory in such a situation should reflect this fact.

The t in $\psi_t(x)$

The time-parameter t in the wave-function is taken directly from the corresponding parameter in classical, non-relativistic physics. It is Newtonian time, and as such it is part of the background structure of standard Newtonian physics. It is represented by a real number: indeed, the full manifold structure of $\mathbb{R}$ (and of the classical state space) is invoked when defining the differential equations of motion of classical physics.

In relativistic physics, space and time are placed on a more equal footing, with a background spacetime manifold rather than just a background time. In special relativity, this background manifold has the topological and differential structure of $\mathbb{R}^4$, and is equipped with the fixed Minkowskian metric tensor.

Things change considerably when we come to the space and time of general relativity: indeed in the context of quantum gravity, time is a difficult concept – in particular, there is the well-known 'problem of time' that affects all approaches to quantum gravity in one way or another.

This problem was first explicitly encountered in the context of the canonical approach to quantum gravity, whose central feature is the constraint equations on the state vector Ψ

$$\hat{\mathcal{H}}_i(x)\Psi = 0 \tag{22.4}$$

$$\hat{\mathcal{H}}_\perp(x)\Psi = 0 \tag{22.5}$$

where $\mathcal{H}_i$ and $\mathcal{H}_\perp$ are constructed from the metric tensor g (and its conjugate variable) on an underlying 3-manifold [4, 5].

Equation (22.4) simply asserts the invariance of Ψ under (small) spatial diffeomorphisms. However, (22.5) is more problematic. In the representation in which Ψ appears as a functional $\Psi[g]$, (22.5) is the Wheeler–DeWitt

---

[4] This would not be so if for some reason the quantum propositions obeyed an intuitionistic logic (see later) where the principle of excluded middle does not necessarily apply.

equation, and – in one approach to the 'problem of time' – is interpreted as a dynamical equation with respect to an 'internal' time variable that has to be constructed from the metric tensor and its conjugate. It is always assumed that this variable will be represented by a real number: indeed, the internal time is usually sought from the perspective of *classical* canonical general relativity – which is bound to lead to a real quantity. So once again we see how a priori assumptions about the nature of time can be placed into the quantum theory from the outset. (Of course, the canonical approach already comes with an explicit background *spatial* manifold.)

22.2.2 Space-time dependent quantum theory

The main conclusion I wish to draw from the discussion above is that a number of a priori assumptions about the nature of space and time are present in the mathematical formalism of standard quantum theory, and it may therefore be necessary to seek a major restructuring of this formalism in situations where the underlying spatio-temporal concepts (if there are any at all) are different from the standard ones which are represented mathematically with the aid of differential geometry.

A good example would be to consider from scratch how to construct a quantum theory when spacetime is a finite causal set: either a single such – which then forms a fixed, but non-standard, spatio-temporal background – or else a collection of such sets in the context of a type of quantum gravity theory. In the case of a fixed background, this new quantum formalism should be adapted to the precise structure of the background, and can be expected to involve a substantial departure from the standard formalism: particularly in regard to the use of real numbers as the values of physical quantities and probabilities.

The fundamental emphasis in a causal set is on a spacetime structure as a single unit, rather than separate space and time structures, and this suggests strongly that it would be better to start *ab initio* with a *history* theory rather than one in which some type of 'temporal slicing' is introduced. It should be emphasized that the path-integral approach to standard quantum theory is *not* a history theory in the way the phrase is being used here. Indeed, a path integral generates transition amplitudes between canonical states, which implicitly requires some type of time slicing. In fact, the only genuine 'history' theory I know that can handle spacetime structures as integral entities is the consistent-histories formalism of Griffiths [6], Omnes [7] and Gell-Mann and Hartle [8].

Thus an instructive research programme would be to develop a version of consistent-history quantum theory that is appropriate for a background causal set. In this context, a particularly useful approach could be the

Gell-Mann and Hartle method as axiomatized in the language of quantum temporal logic by Isham [9], and Isham and Linden [10], together with the completely new perspective on the role of time introduced by Savvidou [16]. Here one has an orthoalgebra $\mathcal{UP}$ of propositions about the history of the system, and a space $\mathcal{D}$ of 'decoherence functions' that are maps $d : \mathcal{UP} \times \mathcal{UP} \rightarrow \mathbb{C}$ and which encode both the dynamics and the initial conditions. From a physical perspective, if a proposition $\alpha \in \mathcal{UP}$ belongs to a consistent set, then $d(\alpha, \alpha)$ is interpreted as the probability that α is true in the context of that consistent set.

It follows from the discussion above, that if there is a background causal set the quantum history formalism should be such that this structure is reflected in (i) the choice of the space $\mathcal{UP}$ of propositions about the 'universe'; and (ii) the choice of the space in which decoherence functions take their values, with an associated change in the mathematical representation of probability.

Finally, if it is indeed the case that, in some sense, to each background spacetime there is associated a corresponding type of quantum theory, then the question arises as to how these different theories can be 'patched' together to give a quantum spacetime theory in which the different backgrounds are themselves the subject of quantum effects. One possibility is the use of *topos* theory: in particular, the theory of presheaves which provides a powerful way of handling situations where there is a space of 'contexts' with respect to which individual structures are associated. For example, a context could be a causal set.

Topos theory is of potential interest in theoretical physics in a number of ways, and it will recur in much of what follows. For this reason, an introduction to some of the basic ideas is given in section 22.4.

22.3 Alternative conceptions of spacetime

22.3.1 Points or regions?

Doubts about the use of the continuum in present-day physical theories prompts one to consider more general alternative conceptions of space and time. We turn now to sketch briefly two such, both of which involve topos theory, and which raise the even more iconoclastic idea that the use of set theory itself may be inappropriate for modelling space and time in the context of quantum gravity.

From points to regions
In standard general relativity – and, indeed, in all classical physics – space (and similarly time) is modelled by a set, and the elements of that set correspond to points in space. However, it is often claimed that the notion

of a spatial (or temporal) point has no real physical meaning, and this motivates trying to construct a theory in which 'regions' are the primary concept. In such a theory, 'points' – if they exist at all – would play a secondary role in which they are determined in some way by the regions (rather than regions being collections of points, as in standard set theory).

In fact, there are axiom systems for regions, some of whose models do not contain anything corresponding to points of which the regions are composed. As an example, consider a topological space X. The family of all open sets has the algebraic operations of conjunction, disjunction and negation defined by $O_1 \wedge O_2 := O_1 \cap O_2$; $O_1 \vee O_2 := O_1 \cup O_2$; and $\neg O := \text{int}(X - O)$ respectively; and with these operations, the open sets form a complete Heyting algebra, also known as a *locale*. Here, a Heyting algebra H is defined to be a distributive lattice, with null and unit elements, that is *relatively complemented*, which means that to any pair S_1, S_2 in H, there exists an element $S_1 \Rightarrow S_2$ of H with the property that, for all $S \in H$, we have $S \leq (S_1 \Rightarrow S_2)$ if and only if $S \wedge S_1 \leq S_2$.

Heyting algebras are thus a generalization of Boolean algebras. In particular, they need not obey the law of excluded middle, and so provide natural algebraic structures for intuitionistic logic. A Heyting algebra is said to be *complete* if every family of elements has a least upper bound. Thus, when partially ordered by set-inclusion, the open sets of any topological space form a Heyting algebra. This algebra is complete since arbitrary unions of open sets are open, and the disjunction of an arbitrary family of open sets can be defined as the interior of their intersection.

However, it transpires that not every locale is isomorphic to the Heyting algebra of open sets of some topological space; and in this sense, the theory of regions given by the definition of a locale is a generalization of the idea of a topological space that allows regions that are not composed of underlying points. This might be an interesting alternative to standard topology for modelling spacetime in the context of quantum gravity.

A far-reaching generalization of this idea is given by topos theory. As we shall see in section 22.4, in any topos the idea of a 'subobject' is the analogue of the set-theoretic notion of a subset of a given set; and for any object X in a topos, the family of subobjects of X is a Heyting algebra, and hence another possible model for the regions of spacetime.

22.3.2 Synthetic differential geometry

Recent decades have seen a revival of the idea of infinitesimals: nilpotent real numbers d such that $d^2 = 0$. At first sight this seems nonsensical (apart from the trivial case $d = 0$) but it turns out that sense *can* be made of this, and in two different ways.

In the first approach, called 'non-standard analysis', every infinitesimal has a reciprocal, so that there are different infinite numbers corresponding to the different infinitesimals. There were attempts in the 1970s to apply this idea to quantum field theory: in particular, it was shown how the different orders of ultraviolet divergences correspond to different types of infinite number in the sense of non-standard analysis [11].

In the second approach, there are infinitesimals but without the corresponding infinite numbers. This is possible provided we work within the context of a *topos* rather than normal set theory: for example, a careful study of the proof that the only real number d such that $d^2 = 0$ is 0, shows that it involves the principle of excluded middle, which in general does not hold in the intuitionistic logic of a topos [12].

This approach is known as 'synthetic differential geometry' (SDG), and it is intriguing to see if our familiar physical theories can be rewritten using this structure. For example, Fearns has recently shown how some of the features of standard quantum theory can be expressed in this way [13] (see also [14]).

Of even greater importance, however, is the possibility that there may be regimes in physics, in particular involving quantum spacetime structures, where SDG is *more* appropriate than the standard approach.

One such possibility is suggested by the 'History Projection Operator' approach to consistent histories in which there are copies of the standard canonical commutation relations at each moment of time. For example, for a particle moving in one dimension we have the history algebra [15]

$$[x_t, x_{t'}] = 0 \tag{22.6}$$

$$[p_t, p_{t'}] = 0 \tag{22.7}$$

$$[x_t, p_{t'}] = i\hbar\delta(t' - t) \tag{22.8}$$

where the label t on the (Schrödinger picture) operators $\hat{x}_t$ and $\hat{p}_t$ refers to the time at which propositions about the system are asserted – the time of 'temporal logic'.

A major advance in the HPO formalism took place when time was introduced by Savvidou in a completely new way [16, 17]. It was realized that it is natural to consider time in a two-fold manner: the 'time of being' – the time at which events 'happen' (the time label t in (22.6)–(22.8) can be regarded as such), and the 'time of becoming' – the time of dynamical change, represented by a time label s. This *second* time appears in the history analogue $\hat{x}_t(s)$ of the Heisenberg picture, which is defined as $\hat{x}_t(s) := e^{is\hat{H}/\hbar}\hat{x}_t e^{-is\hat{H}/\hbar}$ where $\hat{H} := \int dt\hat{H}_t$ is the history quantity that represents the time average of the energy of the system. The notion of time evolution is now recovered for the time-averaged physical quantities, for example $\hat{x}_f(s) := e^{is\hat{H}/\hbar}\hat{x}_f e^{-is\hat{H}/\hbar}$ where $f(t)$ is a smearing function.

Associated with these two manifestations of the concept of time are two types of time transformation: the 'external' translation $\hat{x}_t(s) \mapsto \hat{x}_{t+t'}(s)$; and the 'internal' translation $\hat{x}_t(s) \mapsto \hat{x}_t(s+s')$. The external time translation is generated by the 'Liouville' operator [16]

$$\hat{V} := \int dt\, \hat{p}_t \frac{d\hat{x}_t}{dt}$$

whereas the internal time translation is generated by the time-averaged energy operator $\hat{H}$.

More importantly, it was shown in [16] that the generator of time translation in the HPO theory is the 'action' operator $\hat{S}$ defined as

$$\hat{S} := \int dt\, \hat{p}_t \frac{d\hat{x}_t}{dt} - \hat{H} = \hat{V} - \hat{H}. \tag{22.9}$$

Hence the action operator is the generator of *both* types of time translation: $\hat{x}_t(s) \mapsto \hat{x}_{t+t'}(s+s')$. It is a striking result that in the HPO theory the quantum analogue of the classical action functional is an actual operator in the formalism, and is the generator of time translations.

In the context of SDG, it is the view of Savvidou (with which I agree) that the infinitesimals of SDG are particularly well adapted to describe transformations in the external time-parameter.

If true, this has significant implications for the construction of a history theory of quantum gravity. In particular, in the context of general relativity, Savvidou has shown that the analogue of the Liouville transformations is the full spacetime diffeomorphism group [18]. Thus the intriguing possibility arises that, in a history version of general relativity, there may be a natural role for SDG, and hence for topos theory, in implementing the actions of this fundamental group.

22.4 Presheaves and related notions from topos theory

From now on we shall concentrate on topos theory itself, culminating in a particular application to standard quantum theory.

There are various approaches to the notion of a topos but the focus here will be on one that emphasizes the underlying logical structure. To keep the discussion simple, we will not develop the full definition of a topos but will concentrate on the role of a 'subobject classifier'. This involves a generalization of the set-theoretic idea of a characteristic function, and has a particularly interesting logical structure in the kind of topos to which the discussion in section 22.5 is confined: namely, a topos of presheaves [19, 20].

A topos is a type of category that behaves much like the category of sets Set.[5] In the category Set, the objects are sets and the arrows/morphisms are ordinary functions between them (set-maps). In many other categories, the objects are sets equipped with some type of additional structure, and the arrows are functions that preserve this structure. An example is the category of groups, where an object is a group, and an arrow $f : G_1 \rightarrow G_2$ is a group homomorphism from G_1 to G_2. However, a category need not have 'structured sets' as its objects. An example is given by any partially-ordered set ('poset') $\mathcal{P}$. It can be regarded as a category in which (i) the objects are the elements of $\mathcal{P}$; and (ii) if $p, q \in \mathcal{P}$, an arrow from p to q is defined to exist if, and only if, $p \leq q$ in the poset structure. Thus, in a poset regarded as a category, there is at most one arrow between any pair of objects $p, q \in \mathcal{P}$.

In any category, an object T is called *a terminal* (resp. *initial*) object if for every object A there is exactly one arrow $f : A \rightarrow T$ (resp. $f : T \rightarrow A$). Any two terminal (resp. initial) objects are isomorphic.[6] So we can fix on one such object and write 'the' terminal (resp. initial) object as **1** (resp. **0**). An arrow $1 \rightarrow A$ is called a *point*, or *global element*, of A. For example, applying these definitions to the category of sets, we see that (i) each singleton set is a terminal object; (ii) the empty set $\emptyset$ is initial; and (iii) the points of A are in one-to-one correspondence with the elements of A (in the usual sense of the word 'element' of a set).

22.4.1 Toposes and subobject classifiers

We turn now to the very special kind of category called a 'topos', concentrating on the requirement that a topos contains a generalization of the set-theoretic concept of a characteristic function.

Recall that for any set X, and any subset $A \subseteq X$, there is a characteristic function $\chi_A : X \rightarrow \{0, 1\}$, with $\chi_A(x) = 1$ or 0 according as $x \in A$

---

[5] Recall that a category consists of a collection of *objects* and a collection of *arrows* (or *morphisms*), with the following three properties: (1) each arrow f is associated with a pair of objects, known as its *domain* (dom f) and the *codomain* (cod f), and is written in the form $f : B \rightarrow A$ where $B = \text{dom} f$ and $A = \text{cod} f$; (2) given two arrows $f : B \rightarrow A$ and $g : C \rightarrow B$ (so that the codomain of g is equal to the domain of f), there is a composite arrow $f \circ g : C \rightarrow A$, and this composition of arrows obeys the associative law; and (3) each object A has an identity arrow, $\text{id}_A : A \rightarrow A$, with the properties that for all $f : B \rightarrow A$ and all $g : A \rightarrow C$, $\text{id}_A \circ f = f$ and $g \circ \text{id}_A = g$.

[6] Two objects A and B in a category are said to be *isomorphic* if there exist arrows $f : A \rightarrow B$ and $g : B \rightarrow A$ such that $f \circ g = \text{id}_B$ and $g \circ f = \text{id}_A$

or $x \notin A$. One can think of $\{0,1\}$ as truth-values, with χ_A classifying the various $x \in X$ in response to question 'Is x an element of A?'. Furthermore, $\{0,1\}$ is itself a set – i.e. an object in the category Set – and for each A, X with $A \subseteq X$, χ_A is an arrow from X to $\{0,1\}$.

These concepts extend to a general category as follows.

1. A 'subobject' is the analogue of the set-theoretic idea of a subset. More precisely, one generalizes the idea that a subset A of X has a preferred injective (i.e., one-to-one) map $A \to X$ sending $x \in A$ to $x \in X$. The categorial analogue of an injective map is called a 'monic arrow', and a subobject of any object X in a category is defined to be a monic arrow with codomain X.

2. Any topos is required to have an analogue, written Ω, of the set $\{0,1\}$ of truth-values; in particular, Ω is an *object* in the topos. Furthermore, there is a one-to-one correspondence between subobjects of an object X, and arrows from X to Ω.

3. In a topos, Ω acts as an object of generalized truth-values, just as $\{0,1\}$ does in set-theory (though Ω typically has more than two global elements). Moreover, Ω has a natural logical structure. More precisely, Ω has the internal structure of a Heyting algebra object: the algebraic structure appropriate for intuitionistic logic, mentioned in section 22.3.1. In addition, the collection of subobjects of any given object X in a topos is a complete Heyting algebra.

22.4.2 Toposes of presheaves

In preparation for the application to quantum theory discussed in section 22.5, we turn now to the theory of presheaves.[7]

First recall that a 'functor' between a pair of categories $\mathcal{C}$ and $\mathcal{D}$ is an arrow-preserving function from one category to the other. More precisely, a *covariant functor* $\mathbf{F}$ from a category $\mathcal{C}$ to a category $\mathcal{D}$ is a function that assigns (i) to each $\mathcal{C}$-object A, a $\mathcal{D}$-object $\mathbf{F}(A)$; and (ii) to each $\mathcal{C}$-arrow $f : B \to A$, a $\mathcal{D}$-arrow $\mathbf{F}(f) : \mathbf{F}(B) \to \mathbf{F}(A)$ such that $\mathbf{F}(\mathrm{id}_A) = \mathrm{id}_{\mathbf{F}(A)}$. These assignments are such that if $g : C \to B$, and $f : B \to A$ then $\mathbf{F}(f \circ g) = \mathbf{F}(f) \circ \mathbf{F}(g)$.

A *presheaf* (or *varying set*) on the category $\mathcal{C}$ is defined to be a covariant functor $\mathbf{X}$ from the category $\mathcal{C}$ to the category of sets. We want to make

---

[7] More precisely, the theory of presheaves on an arbitrary 'small' category $\mathcal{C}$ (the qualification 'small' means that the collection of objects in $\mathcal{C}$ is a genuine set, as is the collection of all arrows in $\mathcal{C}$).

the collection of presheaves on $\mathcal{C}$ into a category, and so it is necessary to define what is meant by an 'arrow' between two presheaves $\mathbf{X}$ and $\mathbf{Y}$. This is defined to be a *natural transformation* $N : \mathbf{X} \to \mathbf{Y}$, which is a family of maps (the *components* of N) $N_A : \mathbf{X}(A) \to \mathbf{Y}(A)$, where A is an object in $\mathcal{C}$, such that if $f : A \to B$ is an arrow in $\mathcal{C}$, then the composite map $\mathbf{X}(A) \xrightarrow{N_A} \mathbf{Y}(A) \xrightarrow{\mathbf{Y}(f)} \mathbf{Y}(B)$ is equal to $\mathbf{X}(A) \xrightarrow{\mathbf{X}(f)} \mathbf{X}(B) \xrightarrow{N_B} \mathbf{Y}(B)$, as shown in the commutative diagram

$$
\begin{array}{ccc}
\mathbf{X}(A) & \xrightarrow{\mathbf{X}(f)} & \mathbf{X}(B) \\
\downarrow{\scriptstyle N_A} & & \downarrow{\scriptstyle N_B} \\
\mathbf{Y}(A) & \xrightarrow{\mathbf{Y}(f)} & \mathbf{Y}(B)
\end{array}
\tag{22.10}
$$

An object $\mathbf{K}$ is said to be a *subobject* of $\mathbf{X}$ if there is an arrow in the category of presheaves $i : \mathbf{K} \to \mathbf{X}$ with the property that, for each A, the component map $i_A : \mathbf{K}(A) \to \mathbf{X}(A)$ is a subset embedding, i.e., $\mathbf{K}(A) \subseteq \mathbf{X}(A)$. Thus, if $f : A \to B$ is any arrow in $\mathcal{C}$, we get the commutative diagram

$$
\begin{array}{ccc}
\mathbf{K}(A) & \xrightarrow{\mathbf{K}(f)} & \mathbf{K}(B) \\
\downarrow & & \downarrow \\
\mathbf{X}(A) & \xrightarrow{\mathbf{X}(f)} & \mathbf{X}(B)
\end{array}
\tag{22.11}
$$

where the vertical arrows are subset inclusions.

The category of presheaves on $\mathcal{C}$, $\mathrm{Set}^{\mathcal{C}}$, forms a topos. We turn now to discussing the subobject classifier of this particular topos.

Sieves and the subobject classifier in a topos of presheaves

A key concept in presheaf theory – and something of particular importance for the quantum theory application discussed later – is that of a 'sieve', which plays a central role in the construction of the subobject classifier in the topos $\mathrm{Set}^{\mathcal{C}}$ of presheaves on a category $\mathcal{C}$.

A *sieve* on an object A in $\mathcal{C}$ is defined to be a collection S of arrows $f : A \to B$ in $\mathcal{C}$ with the property that if $f : A \to B$ belongs to S, and if $g : B \to C$ is any arrow, then $g \circ f : A \to C$ also belongs to S. In the simple case where $\mathcal{C}$ is a poset, a sieve on $p \in \mathcal{C}$ is any subset S of $\mathcal{C}$ such that if $r \in S$ then (i) $p \leq r$, and (ii) $r' \in S$ for all $r \leq r'$. Thus a sieve is just an *upper* set in the poset.

The presheaf $\mathbf{\Omega} : \mathcal{C} \to \mathrm{Set}$ is now defined as follows. If A is an object in $\mathcal{C}$, then $\mathbf{\Omega}(A)$ is defined to be the set of all sieves on A; and if $f : A \to B$, then $\mathbf{\Omega}(f) : \mathbf{\Omega}(A) \to \mathbf{\Omega}(B)$ is defined as

$$
\mathbf{\Omega}(f)(S) := \{ h : B \to C \mid h \circ f \in S \}
\tag{22.12}
$$

for all $S \in \Omega(A)$. Note that if S is a sieve on A, and if $f : A \to B$ belongs to S, then from the defining property of a sieve

$$\Omega(f)(S) := \{h : B \to C \mid h \circ f \in S\} = \{h : B \to C\} =: \uparrow B \qquad (22.13)$$

where $\uparrow B$ denotes the *principal* sieve on B, defined to be the set of all arrows in $\mathcal{C}$ whose domain is B.

A crucial property of sieves is that the set $\Omega(A)$ of sieves on A has the structure of a Heyting algebra where the unit element $1_{\Omega(A)}$ in $\Omega(A)$ is the principal sieve $\uparrow A$, and the null element $0_{\Omega(A)}$ is the empty sieve $\emptyset$. The partial ordering in $\Omega(A)$ is defined by $S_1 \leq S_2$ if and only if $S_1 \subseteq S_2$; and the logical connectives are defined as:

$$S_1 \wedge S_2 := S_1 \cap S_2 \qquad (22.14)$$

$$S_1 \vee S_2 := S_1 \cup S_2 \qquad (22.15)$$

$$S_1 \Rightarrow S_2 := \{f : A \to B \mid \forall g : B \to C \text{ if } g \circ f \in S_1 \text{ then } g \circ f \in S_2\}. \qquad (22.16)$$

As in any Heyting algebra, the negation of an element S (called the *pseudo-complement* of S) is defined as $\neg S := S \Rightarrow 0$; so that

$$\neg S := \{f : A \to B \mid \text{for all } g : B \to C, \, g \circ f \notin S\}. \qquad (22.17)$$

As remarked earlier, the main distinction between a Heyting algebra and a Boolean algebra is that, in the former, the negation operation does not necessarily obey the law of excluded middle: instead, all that be can said is that, for any element S,

$$S \vee \neg S \leq 1. \qquad (22.18)$$

It can be shown that the presheaf Ω is a subobject classifier for the topos $\mathrm{Set}^{\mathcal{C}}$. Thus subobjects of any object $\mathbf{X}$ in this topos (i.e., any presheaf on $\mathcal{C}$) are in one-to-one correspondence with arrows $\chi : \mathbf{X} \to \Omega$. This works as follows. Let $\mathbf{K}$ be a subobject of $\mathbf{X}$. Then there is an associated *characteristic* arrow $\chi^{\mathbf{K}} : \mathbf{X} \to \Omega$, whose component $\chi_A^{\mathbf{K}} : \mathbf{X}(A) \to \Omega(A)$ at each 'stage of truth' A in $\mathcal{C}$ is defined as

$$\chi_A^{\mathbf{K}}(x) := \{f : A \to B \mid \mathbf{X}(f)(x) \in \mathbf{K}(B)\} \qquad (22.19)$$

for all $x \in \mathbf{X}(A)$. That the right-hand side of (22.19) actually *is* a sieve on A follows from the defining properties of a subobject.[8]

---

[8] There is a converse to (22.19): namely, each arrow $\chi : \mathbf{X} \to \Omega$ (i.e., a natural transformation between the presheaves $\mathbf{X}$ and Ω) defines a subobject $\mathbf{K}^\chi$ of $\mathbf{X}$ via

$$\mathbf{K}^\chi(A) := \chi_A^{-1}\{1_{\Omega(A)}\} \qquad (22.20)$$

at each stage of truth A.

Thus, in each 'branch' of the category $\mathcal{C}$ going 'upstream' from the stage A, $\chi_A^{\mathbf{K}}(x)$ picks out the first member B in that branch for which $\mathbf{X}(f)(x)$ lies in the subset $\mathbf{K}(B)$, and the commutative diagram (22.11) then guarantees that $\mathbf{X}(h \circ f)(x)$ will lie in $\mathbf{K}(C)$ for all $h : B \to C$.

Thus each 'stage of truth' A in $\mathcal{C}$ serves as a possible *context* for an assignment to each $x \in \mathbf{X}(A)$ of a generalized truth-value, which is a sieve belonging to the Heyting algebra $\mathbf{\Omega}(A)$. This is the sense in which contextual, generalized truth-values arise naturally in a topos of presheaves.

Global sections of a presheaf

For the category of presheaves on $\mathcal{C}$, a terminal object $\mathbf{1} : \mathcal{C} \to$ Set can be defined by $\mathbf{1}(A) := \{*\}$ (a singleton set) at all stages A in $\mathcal{C}$; if $f : A \to B$ is an arrow in $\mathcal{C}$ then $\mathbf{1}(f) : \{*\} \to \{*\}$ is defined to be the map $* \mapsto *$. This is indeed a terminal object since, for any presheaf $\mathbf{X}$, we can define a unique natural transformation $N : \mathbf{X} \to \mathbf{1}$ whose components $N_A : \mathbf{X}(A) \to \mathbf{1}(A) = \{*\}$ are the constant maps $x \mapsto *$ for all $x \in \mathbf{X}(A)$.

A global element (or point) of a presheaf $\mathbf{X}$ is also called a *global section*. As an arrow $\gamma : \mathbf{1} \to \mathbf{X}$ in the topos $\text{Set}^{\mathcal{C}}$, a global section corresponds to a choice of an element $\gamma_A \in \mathbf{X}(A)$ for each stage of truth A in $\mathcal{C}$, such that, if $f : A \to B$, the 'matching condition'

$$\mathbf{X}(f)(\gamma_A) = \gamma_B \qquad (22.21)$$

is satisfied. As we shall see, the Kochen–Specher theorem can be read as asserting the non-existence of any global sections of certain presheaves that arises naturally in quantum theory.

22.5 Presheaves of propositions, and valuations in quantum theory

The contextual, multi-valued logic that arises naturally in a topos of presheaves has some very interesting potential applications in theoretical physics. Here, however, I shall briefly present just one particular example that has been developed in detail elsewhere [21–23]. This is the proposal to retain a 'realist flavour' in the assignment of values to quantum-theoretic quantities by using the non-Boolean logical structure of a particular topos of presheaves.

Before stating the proposal precisely, recall the Kochen–Specher theorem, which asserts the impossibility of associating real values $V(\hat{A})$ to all physical quantities in a quantum theory (if $\dim \mathcal{H} > 2$) whilst preserving the '*FUNC*' rule that $V(f(\hat{A})) = f(V(\hat{A}))$ – i.e., the value of a function f of a physical quantity A is equal to the function of the value of the quantity. Equivalently, it is not possible to assign true–false values to all the propositions in a quantum theory in a way that respects the structure of the associated lattice of projection operators. As we shall see, our topos-theoretic proposal is such that the truth value ascribed to a proposition about the value of a physical quantity need not be just 'true' or 'false'.

Thus consider the proposition '$A \in \Delta$', which asserts that the value of the quantity A lies in a Borel set $\Delta \subseteq \mathbb{R}$. Roughly speaking, our proposal is that any such proposition should be ascribed as a truth-value a set of coarse-grainings, $f(\hat{A})$, of the operator $\hat{A}$ that represents A. Exactly which coarse-grainings are in the truth-value depends in a precise way on Δ and the quantum state ψ: specifically, $f(\hat{A})$ is in the truth-value if and only if ψ is in the range of the spectral projector $\hat{E}[f(A) \in f(\Delta)]$. Note the contrast with the conventional eigenstate–eigenvalue link: our requirement is not that ψ be in the range of $\hat{E}[A \in \Delta]$, but a weaker one since, generally, $\hat{E}[f(A) \in f(\Delta)]$ is a larger spectral projector than $\hat{E}[f(A) \in f(\Delta)]$; i.e., in the lattice $\mathcal{L}(\mathcal{H})$ of projectors on the Hilbert space $\mathcal{H}$, we have $\hat{E}[A \in \Delta] \leq \hat{E}[f(A) \in f(\Delta)]$.

So the intuitive idea is that the new proposed truth-value of '$A \in \Delta$' is given by the set of weaker propositions '$f(A) \in f(\Delta)$' that are true in the old (i.e., eigenstate–eigenvalue link) sense. More precisely, the truth-value of '$A \in \Delta$' is the set of quantities $f(A)$ for which the corresponding weaker proposition '$f(A) \in f(\Delta)$' is true in the old sense. Thus the truth-value of a proposition in the new sense is given by the set of its consequences that are true in the old sense.

The first step in stating the proposal precisely is to introduce the set $\mathcal{O}$ of all bounded self-adjoint operators on the Hilbert space $\mathcal{H}$ of a quantum system. The set $\mathcal{O}$ is turned into a category by defining the objects to be the elements of $\mathcal{O}$, and saying that there is an arrow from $\hat{A}$ to $\hat{B}$ if there exists a real-valued function f on the spectrum $\sigma(\hat{A}) \subset \mathbb{R}$ of $\hat{A}$, such that $\hat{B} = f(\hat{A})$. If $\hat{B} = f(\hat{A})$, for some $f : \sigma(\hat{A}) \to \mathbb{R}$, then the corresponding arrow in the category $\mathcal{O}$ will be denoted $f_{\mathcal{O}} : \hat{A} \to \hat{B}$.

The next step is to define two presheaves on the category $\mathcal{O}$, called the *dual presheaf* and the *coarse-graining presheaf* respectively. The former affords an elegant formulation of the Kochen–Specker theorem, namely as the statement that the dual presheaf does not have global sections. The latter is at the basis of the proposed generalized truth-value assignments.

The dual presheaf on $\mathcal{O}$ is the covariant functor $\mathbf{D} : \mathcal{O} \to \mathrm{Set}$ defined as follows.

1. On objects: $\mathbf{D}(\hat{A})$ is the *dual* of W_A, where W_A is the spectral algebra of the operator $\hat{A}$ (i.e., W_A is the collection of all projectors onto the subspaces of $\mathcal{H}$ associated with Borel subsets of $\sigma(\hat{A})$).

Thus $\mathbf{D}(\hat{A})$ is defined to be the set of all homomorphisms from the Boolean algebra W_A to the Boolean algebra $\{0, 1\}$.

2. On arrows: If $f_\mathcal{O} : \hat{A} \to \hat{B}$, so that $\hat{B} = f(\hat{A})$, then $\mathbf{D}(f_\mathcal{O}) : D(W_A) \to D(W_B)$ is defined by $\mathbf{D}(f_\mathcal{O})(\chi) := \chi|_{W_{f(A)}}$ where $\chi|_{W_{f(A)}}$ is the restriction of $\chi \in D(W_A)$ to the subalgebra $W_{f(A)} \subseteq W_A$.

A global element (global section) of the functor $\mathbf{D} : \mathcal{O} \to \text{Set}$ is then a function γ that associates to each $\hat{A} \in \mathcal{O}$ an element γ_A of the dual of W_A such that if $f_\mathcal{O} : \hat{A} \to \hat{B}$ (so $\hat{B} = f(\hat{A})$ and $W_B \subseteq W_A$), then $\gamma_A|_{W_B} = \gamma_B$. Thus, for all projectors $\hat{\alpha} \in W_B \subseteq W_A$, we have $\gamma_B(\hat{\alpha}) = \gamma_A(\hat{\alpha})$.

Since each $\hat{\alpha}$ in the lattice $\mathcal{L}(\mathcal{H})$ of projection operators on $\mathcal{H}$ belongs to at least one such spectral algebra W_A (for example, the algebra $\{\hat{0}, \hat{1}, \hat{\alpha}, \hat{1} - \hat{\alpha}\}$) it follows that a global section of $\mathbf{D}$ associates to each projection operator $\hat{\alpha} \in \mathcal{L}(\mathcal{H})$ a number $V(\hat{\alpha})$ which is either 0 or 1, and is such that if $\hat{\alpha}$ and $\hat{\beta}$ are disjoint propositions then $V(\hat{\alpha} \vee \hat{\beta}) = V(\hat{\alpha}) + V(\hat{\beta})$. A global section γ of the presheaf $\mathbf{D}$ would correspond to an assignment of truth-values $\{0, 1\}$ to all propositions of the form '$A \in \Delta$', which obeyed the *FUNC* condition $\gamma_A|_{W_B} = \gamma_B$. But these are precisely the types of valuation prohibited by the Kochen–Specker theorem provided that $\dim \mathcal{H} > 2$! So an alternative way of expressing the Kochen–Specker theorem is the statement that (if $\dim \mathcal{H} > 2$) the dual presheaf $\mathbf{D}$ has no global sections.

However, we *can* use the subobject classifier $\mathbf{\Omega}$ in the topos $\text{Set}^\mathcal{O}$ of all presheaves on $\mathcal{O}$ to assign *generalized* truth-values to the propositions '$A \in \Delta$'. These truth-values will be sieves – as defined in section 22.4.2 – and since they will be assigned relative to each 'context' or 'stage of truth' $\hat{A}$ in $\mathcal{O}$, these truth-values will be contextual as well as generalized. Note that because in any topos the subobject classifier $\mathbf{\Omega}$ is unique up to isomorphism the traditional objection to multi-valued logics in quantum theory – that their structure often seems arbitrary – does not apply to these particular generalized, contextual truth-values.

The first step is to define the appropriate presheaf of propositions. The *coarse-graining presheaf* over $\mathcal{O}$ is the covariant functor $\mathbf{G} : \mathcal{O} \to \text{Set}$ defined as follows:

1. *on objects in $\mathcal{O}$:* $\mathbf{G}(\hat{A}) := W_A$, the spectral algebra of $\hat{A}$;

2. *on arrows in $\mathcal{O}$:* If $f_\mathcal{O} : \hat{A} \to \hat{B}$ (i.e., $\hat{B} = f(\hat{A})$), then $\mathbf{G}(f_\mathcal{O}) : W_A \to W_B$ is defined as[9]

$$\mathbf{G}(f_\mathcal{O})(\hat{E}[A \in \Delta]) := \hat{E}[f(A) \in f(\Delta)]. \tag{22.22}$$

---

[9] If $f(\Delta)$ is not Borel, the right-hand side is to be understood in the sense of Theorem 4.1 of [21] – a measure-theoretic nicety that we shall not discuss here.

A function ν that assigns to each object $\hat{A}$ in $\mathcal{O}$ and each Borel set $\Delta \subseteq \sigma(\hat{A})$, a sieve of arrows in $\mathcal{O}$ on $\hat{A}$ (i.e., a sieve of arrows with $\hat{A}$ as domain), will be called a *sieve-valued valuation* on **G**. We write the values of this function as $\nu(A \in \Delta)$.

From the logical point of view, a natural requirement for any kind of valuation on a presheaf of propositions such as **G** is that the valuation should specify a subobject of **G**. But subobjects are in one-one correspondence with arrows, i.e., natural transformations, $N : \mathbf{G} \to \mathbf{\Omega}$. So it is natural to require a sieve-valued valuation ν to define such a natural transformation by the equation $N_{\hat{A}}^{\nu}(\hat{E}[A \in \Delta]) := \nu(A \in \Delta)$ for all stages/contexts $\hat{A}$.

This requirement leads directly to the analogue for presheaves of the functional composition condition of the Kochen–Specker theorem, called *FUNC* above. Indeed, it transpires that a sieve-valued valuation defines a natural transformation if and only if it obeys (the presheaf version of) *FUNC*.

To spell this out, first recall that sieves are 'pushed forward' by the subobject classifier $\mathbf{\Omega}$ according to (22.12). For the category $\mathcal{O}$: if $f_{\mathcal{O}} : \hat{A} \to \hat{B}$, then $\mathbf{\Omega}(f_{\mathcal{O}}) : \mathbf{\Omega}(\hat{A}) \to \mathbf{\Omega}(\hat{B})$ is defined by

$$\mathbf{\Omega}(f_{\mathcal{O}})(S) := \{ h_{\mathcal{O}} : B \to C \mid h_{\mathcal{O}} \circ f_{\mathcal{O}} \in S \} \qquad (22.23)$$

for all sieves $S \in \mathbf{\Omega}(\hat{A})$.

Accordingly, we say that a sieve-valued valuation ν on **G** satisfies *generalized functional composition* – for short, *FUNC* – if for all $\hat{A}, \hat{B}$ and $f_{\mathcal{O}} : \hat{A} \to \hat{B}$ and all $\hat{E}[A \in \Delta] \in \mathbf{G}(\hat{A})$, we have

$$\nu(B \in \mathbf{G}(f_{\mathcal{O}})(\hat{E}[A \in \Delta])) \equiv \nu(f(A) \in f(\Delta)) = \mathbf{\Omega}(f_{\mathcal{O}})(\nu(A \in \Delta)).$$
$$(22.24)$$

It can readily be checked that *FUNC* is exactly the condition a sieve-valued valuation must obey in order to define a natural transformation – i.e., a subobject of **G** – by the equation $N_{\hat{A}}^{\nu}(\hat{E}[A \in \Delta]) := \nu(A \in \Delta)$. That is, a sieve-valued valuation ν on **G** obeys *FUNC* if and only if the functions at each context $\hat{A}$

$$N_{\hat{A}}^{\nu}(\hat{E}[A \in \Delta]) := \nu(A \in \Delta) \qquad (22.25)$$

define a natural transformation N^{ν} from **G** to $\mathbf{\Omega}$.

It turns out that with any quantum state there is associated such a sieve-valued valuation obeying *FUNC*. Furthermore, this valuation gives the natural generalization of the eigenvalue–eigenstate link described earlier. That is, a quantum state ψ induces a sieve on each $\hat{A}$ in $\mathcal{O}$ by the requirement that an arrow $f_{\mathcal{O}} : \hat{A} \to \hat{B}$ is in the sieve if and only if ψ is in the range of the spectral projector $\hat{E}[B \in f(\Delta)]$. To be precise, we define for any ψ, and any Borel subset Δ of the spectrum $\sigma(\hat{A})$ of $\hat{A}$,

$$\nu^{\psi}(A \in \Delta) := \{f_{\mathcal{O}} : \hat{A} \to \hat{B} \mid \hat{E}[B \in f(\Delta)]\psi = \psi\}$$
$$= \{f_{\mathcal{O}} : \hat{A} \to \hat{B} \mid \mathrm{Prob}(B \in f(\Delta); \psi) = 1\} \quad (22.26)$$

where $\mathrm{Prob}(B \in f(\Delta); \psi)$ is the usual Born-rule probability that the result of a measurement of B will lie in $f(\Delta)$, given the state ψ.

One can check that the definition satisfies *FUNC*, and also has other properties that it is natural to require of a valuation (discussed in [21–23]). Thus, by using topos theory we are able to assign generalized truth values to all propositions whilst preserving the appropriate analogue of the FUNC condition.

The key feature of these truth assignments is that they involve the contextual, multi-valued logic that is an intrinsic feature of a topos of presheaves. My expectation is that a similar topos structure could serve to patch together the different types of quantum theory that, as discussed earlier, I anticipate should be associated with different background space-time structures.

22.6 Conclusions

In general, the real numbers enter physical theories in three ways: as the values of physical quantities; as coordinates on a manifold model for space and time; and as the values of probabilities. The main thrust of the present paper is to argue that all three uses may become problematic in physical regimes that characterize strong quantum gravity effects.

In particular, I have argued that the assignment of real numbers as values of physical quantities and probabilities is to some extent motivated by certain a priori ideas about the continuum nature of space and time. Thus it may be fundamentally wrong to attempt to construct a quantum theory of gravity whilst using a quantum formalism in which these a priori continuum ideas are present from the beginning. My contention is that there should be a different *type* of quantum structure for each 'type' of background spacetime: in particular, the mathematical spaces in which physical quantities and probabilities take their values should reflect the structure of this background.

If this is correct, the question then arises as to how to patch together a collection of such theories in the situation where the 'background' space-times are themselves the subject of quantum effects. I have suggested that the appropriate mathematical tool for doing this is topos theory; in particular the theory of presheaves with its intrinsic contextual, multi-valued logic. As an example of the use of this theory I have briefly reviewed an application of presheaf theory to the Kocken–Specher theorem in standard quantum theory.

Topos theory is also an essential ingredient in synthetic differential geometry, and this too may have important applications in theoretical physics; particularly perhaps in the context of the two-pronged way in which time arises in the consistent history theory.

What is sketched in the first half of this paper is only a collection of ideas. It remains an outstanding challenge to implement some of these general thoughts in the context, say, of a specific non-standard spatio-temporal background, such as a causal set. This could give valuable insight into what is perhaps the hardest task of all: to construct a quantum formalism for use in situations where there are no prima facie spatio-temporal concepts at all – a situation that could well arise in a quantum gravity theory in which all of what we might want to call 'spatio-temporal concepts' emerge from the basic formalism only in some limiting sense.

Acknowledgements

Some of the material presented here is a development of earlier work [1] with Jeremy Butterfield. I am grateful to him for permission to include this material. I am also very grateful to Ntina Savvidou for detailed discussions about the present paper. Support by the EPSRC in form of grant GR/R36572 is gratefully acknowledged.

References

[1] Isham, C. J. and Butterfield, J. (2000), 'Some possible roles for topos theory in quantum theory and quantum gravity', *Found. Phys.*, **30** 1707–1735.

[2] Bombelli, L., Lee, J., Meyer, D. and Sorkin, R. D. (1987), 'Spacetime as a causal set', *Phys. Rev. Lett.*, **30** 521–524.

[3] Sorkin, R. D. (1991), 'Spacetime and causal sets', in '*Relativity and Gravitation: Classical and Quantum*', Proceedings of the SILARG VII Conference, held in Cocoyoc, Mexico, December, 1990, eds J. C. D'Olivo, E. Nahmad-Achar, M. Rosenbaum, M. P. Ryan, L. F. Urrutia and F. Zertuche, pp. 150–173, (World Scientific, Singapore).

[4] Isham, C. J. (1993) 'Canonical quantum gravity and the problem of time', in *Integrable Systems, Quantum Groups, and Quantum Field Theories*, eds L. A. Ibort and M. A. Rodriguez (Kluwer Academic Publishers), pp 157–288.

[5] Kuchař, K. V. (1992), 'Time and interpretations of quantum gravity', in *Proceedings of the 4th Canadian Conference on General Relativity and Relativistic Astrophysics*, (World Scientific), pp. 211–314.

[6] Griffiths, R. B. (1984), 'Consistent histories and the interpretation of quantum mechanics', *J. Stat. Phys.* **36** 219–272.

[7] Omnès, R. (1988), 'Logical reformulation of quantum mechanics, I. Foundations', *J. Stat. Phys.* **53** 893–932.

[8] Gell-Mann, M. and Hartle, J. (1990), 'Quantum mechanics in the light of quantum cosmology', in *Complexity, Entropy and the Physics of Information, SFI Studies in the Science of Complexity, Vol. VIII*, W. Zurek, ed., (Addison-Wesley, Reading) pp. 425–458.

[9] Isham, C. J. (1994), 'Quantum logic and the histories approach to quantum theory', *J. Math. Phys.* **35** 2157–2185.

[10] Isham, C. J. and Linden, N. (1994), 'Quantum temporal logic and decoherence functionals in the histories approach to generalized quantum theory', *J. Math. Phys.* **35** 5452–5476.

[11] Farrukh, M. (1975), 'Application of nonstandard analysis to quantum mechanics', *J. Math. Physics* **16** 177–200.

[12] Lavendhomme, R. (1996), *Basic Concepts of Synthetic Differential Geometry* (Kluwer, Dordrecht).

[13] Fearns, J. (2002), 'A physical quantum model in a smooth topos', [quant-ph/0202079].

[14] Nishimura, H. (1997), 'Synthetic Hamiltonian mechanics', *Int. Jour. Theor. Phys.* **36** 259–279.

[15] Isham, C., Linden, N., Savvidou, K. and Schreckenberg, S. (1998), 'Continuous time and consistent histories', *J. Math. Phys.* **39** 1818–1834.

[16] Savvidou, K. (1999), 'The action operator for continuous-time histories', *J. Math. Phys.* **40** 5657.

[17] Savvidou, K. (1999), 'Continuous time in consistent histories', PhD Thesis in [gr-qc/9912076].

[18] Savvidou, K. (2001), 'General relativity histories theory', *Class. Quant. Grav.* **18** 3611–3628.

[19] Goldblatt, R. (1984), *Topoi: The Categorial Analysis of Logic* (North-Holland, London).

[20] MacLane, S. and Moerdijk, I. (1992), *Sheaves in Geometry and Logic: A First Introduction to Topos Theory* (Springer-Verlag).

[21] Isham, C. J. and Butterfield, J. (1998), 'A topos perspective on the Kochen–Specker theorem: I. Quantum states as generalized valuations', *Int. J. Theor. Phys.* **37** 2669–2733,.

[22] Butterfield, J. and Isham, C. J. (1999), 'A topos perspective on the Kochen–Specker theorem: II. Conceptual aspects, and classical analogues', *Int. J. Theor. Phys.* **38** 827–859.

[23] Hamilton, J., Isham, C. J. and Butterfield, J. (2000), 'A topos perspective on the Kochen–Specker theorem: III. Von Neumann algebras as the base category', *Int. J. Theor. Phys.* **38** 827–859.

[24] Kochen, S. and Specker, E. (1967), 'The problem of hidden variables in quantum mechanics', *J. Math. and Mech.* **39** 59–87.

23

Quantum geometry and its ramifications

Abhay Ashtekar

Pennsylvania State University

23.1 Introduction

Stephen has made seminal contributions to many different areas in gravitational physics, shaping the tremendous growth the field has undergone in the last three decades. From his sustained efforts over this period, it would seem that two of these areas are particularly close to his heart: quantum cosmology and black hole physics. This is not surprising. After all, questions about the big-bang and the big-crunch – the very beginning and the very end – are among the most fascinating and challenging ones in science. On these issues, Stephen's work has provided us with those very rare glimpses of deep truths. Therefore, I thought it would be appropriate to express my admiration for Stephen's creativity by reporting on some recent advances in these two areas. Let me first set the stage by recalling the key problems.

Big Bang[10]: It is widely believed that the prediction of a singularity, such as the Big Bang of classical general relativity, is primarily a signal that the physical theory has been pushed beyond the domain of its validity. A key question to any quantum gravity theory, then, is: What replaces the Big Bang? Is the classical geometry and the continuum picture only an approximation, analogous to the 'mean (magnetization) field' of ferromagnets? If so, what are the microscopic constituents? What is the spacetime analogul of a Heisenberg quantum model of a ferromagnet? When formulated in terms of these fundamental constituents, is the evolution of the *quantum* state of the universe free of singularities? General relativity predicts that the spacetime curvature must grow as we approach the Big Bang but we expect the quantum effects, ignored by general relativity, to intervene, making quantum gravity indispensable before infinite curvatures are reached. If so, what is the upper bound on the curvature? How close to the Big Bang can we 'trust' classical general relativity? What can we say about the 'initial conditions', i.e., the quantum state of geometry and matter that correctly describes the Big Bang? If they have to be imposed externally, is there a *physical* guiding principle? To address such issues, in collaboration with Jim Hartle, Stephen put forward a bold 'no boundary' proposal and analysed its consequences in detail also with other colleagues.

Black holes[11]: In the early 1970s, using imaginative thought experiments, Jacob Bekenstein argued that black holes must carry entropy proportional to their area. About the same time, with Jim Bardeen, Brandon Carter, Stephen showed that black holes in equilibrium obey two basic laws, which have the same form as the zeroth and the first laws of ordinary thermodynamics, provided one replaces the area of the black hole horizon $a_{\rm hor}$ by a multiple of the entropy S in thermodynamics and black hole surface gravity κ by a corresponding multiple of the temperature T.[1] However, at first this similarity was thought to be only a formal analogy because the Bardeen–Carter–Hawking analysis was based on *classical* general relativity and simple dimensional considerations show that the proportionality factors must involve Planck's constant $\hbar$. This changed dramatically two years later when Stephen discovered the celebrated Hawking effect: he showed that black holes in fact radiate quantum mechanically as though they are black bodies at temperature $T = \hbar\kappa/2\pi$. Using the analogy with the first law, one can then conclude that the black hole entropy should be given by $S_{\rm BH} = a_{\rm hor}/4G\hbar$, where G is Newton's gravitational constant. This conclusion is striking and deep because it brings together the three pillars of fundamental physics – general relativity, quantum theory and statistical mechanics. However, to weave the full argument, one had to use a mixture of classical and semiclassical ideas, reminiscent of the Bohr theory of atom. A natural question then is: what is the analog of the more fundamental, Pauli–Schrödinger theory of the hydrogen atom? More precisely, what is the statistical mechanical origin of black hole entropy? What is the nature of a quantum black hole and what is the interplay between the quantum degrees of freedom responsible for entropy and the exterior curved geometry? Can one derive the Hawking effect from first principles of quantum gravity? It is widely believed that the effect provides the single definitive, detailed clue to the mysteries of quantum gravity.

---

[1] One can think of the horizon as the 'surface' of the black hole. In classical general relativity, one can not send causal signals from the region within the horizon to the region outside. Surface gravity κ is, roughly, the black hole analogue of the acceleration g due to gravity on the surface of the Earth.

Over the last 3–4 years, these issues have been revisited and analysed within a new, non-perturbative approach to quantum gravity that emphasizes the role of the *quantum nature of geometry*. Since much of the initial impetus for the development of quantum geometry came from the so-called 'loop representation' of quantum states, this approach is also referred to as 'loop quantum gravity' [3]. Developments in this area have provided a fresh perspective on how to do physics in absence of a background spacetime and resolved some of the long standing questions mentioned above. The purpose of this contribution is to summarize these advances in rather general terms and point out some directions for future work.

23.2 A bird's eye view of loop quantum gravity

In this section, I will briefly summarize the salient features and current status of quantum geometry. The emphasis is on structural and conceptual issues; details can be found in [1–9].

23.2.1 Viewpoint

In this approach, one takes the central lesson of general relativity seriously: gravity *is* geometry whence, in a fundamental theory, there should be no background metric. In quantum gravity, geometry and matter should *both* be 'born quantum mechanically'. Thus, in contrast to approaches developed by particle physicists, one does not begin with quantum matter on a background geometry and use perturbation theory to incorporate quantum effects of gravity. There *is* a manifold but no metric, or indeed any other physical fields, in the background.[2] In classical gravity, Riemannian geometry provides the appropriate mathematical language to formulate the physical, kinematical notions as well as the final dynamical equations. This role is now taken by *quantum* Riemannian geometry, discussed below. In the classical domain, general relativity stands out as the best available theory of gravity, some of whose predictions have been tested to an amazing accuracy, surpassing even the legendary tests of quantum electrodynamics. However, if one applies to general relativity the standard perturbative techniques of quantum field theory, one obtains

---

[2] In 2+1 dimensions, although one begins in a completely analogous fashion, in the final picture one can get rid of the background manifold as well. Thus, the fundamental theory can be formulated *combinatorially* [1, 3]. To achieve this goal in 3+1 dimensions, one needs a much better understanding of the theory of (intersecting) knots in 3 dimensions.

a 'non-renormalizable' theory, i.e., a theory with uncontrollable infinities. Therefore, it is natural to ask: *does quantum general relativity, coupled to suitable matter* (or supergravity, its supersymmetric generalizations) *exist as a consistent theory non-perturbatively ?* There is no a priori implication that such a theory would be the final, complete description of Nature. Nonetheless, this is a fascinating open question at the level of mathematical physics.

In the particle physics circles, the answer is often assumed to be in the negative, not because there is concrete evidence against non-perturbative quantum gravity, but because of an analogy to the theory of weak interactions, where non-renormalizability of the initial 'Fermi theory' forced one to replace it by the renormalizable Glashow–Weinberg–Salam theory. However this analogy overlooks the crucial fact that, in the case of general relativity, there is a qualitatively new element. Perturbative treatments pre-suppose that the spacetime can be assumed to be a continuum *at all scales* of interest to physics under consideration. Since this is a safe assumption for weak interactions, non-renormalizability was a genuine problem. However, in the gravitational case, the scale of interest is given by the Planck length ℓ_{Pl} and there is no physical basis to pre-suppose that the continuum picture should be valid down to that scale. The failure of the standard perturbative treatments may simply be due to this grossly incorrect assumption and a non-perturbative treatment which correctly incorporates the physical micro-structure of geometry may well be free of these inconsistencies.

As indicated above, even if quantum general relativity did exist as a mathematically consistent theory, there is no a priori reason to assume that it would be the 'final' theory of all known physics. In classical general relativity, while requirements of background independence and general covariance do restrict the form of interactions between gravity and matter fields and among matter fields themselves, they do not *determine* these interactions. Quantum general relativity would have the same limitation. Put differently, such a theory would not be a satisfactory candidate for unification of all known forces. However, just as general relativity has had powerful implications in spite of this limitation in the classical domain, quantum general relativity should have qualitatively new predictions, pushing further the existing frontiers of physics. Indeed, unification does not appear to be an essential criterion for usefulness of a theory even in other interactions. Quantum chromodynamics (QCD) for example, is a powerful theory of strong interactions even though it does not unify them with electro-weak ones. Furthermore, the fact that we do not yet have a viable candidate for the grand unified theory does not make QCD any less useful.

23.2.2 Quantum geometry

Although there is no natural unification of dynamics of all interactions in loop quantum gravity, it does provide a kinematical unification. More precisely, in this approach one begins by formulating general relativity in the mathematical language of connections, the basic variables of gauge theories of electro-weak and strong interactions. Thus, now the configuration variables are not metrics as in Wheeler's geometrodynamics, but certain spin connections; the emphasis is shifted from distances and geodesics to holonomies and Wilson loops [1]. Consequently, the basic kinematical structures are the same as those used in gauge theories. A key difference, however, is that while a background spacetime metric is available and crucially used in gauge theories, there are no background fields whatsoever now. This absence is forced on us by the requirement of diffeomorphism invariance (or 'general covariance').

This is a key difference and it causes a host of conceptual as well as technical difficulties in the passage to quantum theory. For most of the techniques used in the familiar Minkowskian quantum theories are deeply rooted in the availability of a flat back-ground metric. It is this structure that enables one to single out the vacuum state, perform Fourier transforms to decompose fields canonically into creation and annihilation parts, define masses and spins of particles and carry out regularizations of products of operators. Already when one passes to quantum field theory in *curved* space-times, extra work is needed to construct mathematical structures that can adequately capture underlying physics. In our case, the situation is much more drastic: there is no background metric whatsoever! Therefore new physical ideas and mathematical tools are now necessary. Fortunately, they were constructed by a number of researchers in the mid-1990s and have given rise to a detailed quantum theory of geometry [4–7].

Because the situation is conceptually so novel and because there are no direct experiments to guide us, reliable results require a high degree of mathematical precision to ensure that there are no hidden infinities. Achieving this precision has been a priority in the program. Thus, while one is inevitably motivated by heuristic, physical ideas and formal manipulations, the final results are mathematically rigorous. In particular, due care is taken in constructing function spaces, defining measures and functional integrals, regularizing products of field operator, and calculating eigenvectors and eigenvalues of geometric operators. Consequently, the final results are all free of divergences, well-defined, and respect the background independence and diffeomorphism invariance.

Let me now turn to specifics. Our basic configuration variable is an SU(2)-connection, A_a^i on a 3-manifold Σ representing 'space' and, as in gauge theories, the momenta are the 'electric fields' E_i^a. However, in the present gravitational context, they acquire an additional meaning: they can be naturally interpreted as orthonormal triads (with density weight 1) and determine the dynamical, Riemannian geometry of Σ. Thus, in contrast to Wheeler's geometrodynamics, the Riemannian structures, including the positive-definite metric on Σ, is now built from *momentum* variables. The basic kinematic objects are 'holonomies' of A_a^i, which dictate how spinors are parallel transported along curves, and the triads E_i^a, which determine the geometry of Σ. (Matter couplings to gravity have also been studied extensively [1, 2].)

In the quantum theory, the fundamental excitations of geometry are most conveniently expressed in terms of holonomies [3, 4]. They are thus *one-dimensional, polymer-like* and, in analogy with gauge theories, can be thought of as 'flux lines of the electric field'. More precisely, they turn out to be flux lines of areas, the simplest gauge invariant quantities constructed from E_i^a: an elementary flux line deposits a quantum of area on any 2-surface S it intersects. Thus, if quantum geometry were to be excited along just a few flux lines, most surfaces would have zero area and the quantum state would not at all resemble a classical geometry. This state would be analogous, in Maxwell theory, to a 'genuinely quantum mechanical state' with just a few photons. In the Maxwell case, one must superpose photons coherently to obtain a semiclassical state that can be approximated by a classical electromagnetic field. Similarly, here, semiclassical geometries can result only if a huge number of these elementary excitations are superposed in suitable dense configurations [13, 14]. The state of quantum geometry around you, for example, must have so many elementary excitations that $\sim 10^{68}$ of them intersect the sheet of paper you are reading. Even in such states, the geometry is still distributional, concentrated on the underlying elementary flux lines; but if suitably coarse-grained, it can be approximated by a smooth metric. Thus, the continuum picture is only an approximation that arises from coarse graining of semiclassical states.

These quantum states span a specific Hilbert space $\mathcal{H}$ consisting of wave functions of connections that are square integrable with respect to a natural, diffeomorphism invariant measure [4]. This space is very large. However, it can be conveniently decomposed into a family of orthonormal, *finite* dimensional sub-spaces $\mathcal{H} = \oplus_{\gamma,\vec{j}} \mathcal{H}_{\gamma,\vec{j}}$, labelled by graphs γ each edge of which itself is labelled by a spin (i.e., half-integer) j [5]. (The vector $\vec{j}$ stands for the collection of half-integers associated with all edges of γ.) One can think of γ as a 'floating lattice' in Σ – 'floating' because its edges are arbitrary, rather than 'rectangular'. (Indeed, since there is no background metric on Σ, a rectangular lattice has no invariant meaning.) Mathematically, $\mathcal{H}_{\gamma,\vec{j}}$ can be regarded as the Hilbert space of a spin-system. These spaces are extremely simple to work with; this is why very explicit calculations are feasible. Elements of $\mathcal{H}_{\gamma,\vec{j}}$ are referred to as *spin-network states* [5].

As one would expect from the structure of the classical theory, the basic quantum operators are the holonomies $\hat{h}_p$ along paths p in Σ and the triads $\hat{E}_i^a$ [6]. (Both sets are densely defined and self-adjoint on $\mathcal{H}$.) Furthermore, a striking result is that *all eigenvalues of the triad operators are discrete*. This key property is, in essence, the origin of the fundamental discreteness of quantum geometry. For, just as the classical Riemannian geometry of Σ is determined by the triads E_i^a, all Riemannian geometry operators – such as the area operator $\hat{A}_S$ associated with a 2-surface S or the volume operator $\hat{V}_R$ associated with a region R – are constructed from $\hat{E}_i^a$. However, since even the classical quantities A_S and V_R are non-polynomial functionals of the triads, the construction of the corresponding $\hat{A}_S$ and $\hat{V}_R$ is quite subtle and requires a great deal of care. But their final expressions are rather simple [6].

In this regularization, the underlying background independence turns out to be a blessing. For, diffeomorphism invariance constrains the possible forms of the final expressions *severely* and the detailed calculations then serve essentially to fix numerical coefficients and other details. Let us illustrate this point with the example of the area operators $\hat{A}_S$. Since they are associated with 2-surfaces S while the states are one-dimensional excitations, the diffeomorphism covariance requires that the action of $\hat{A}_S$ on a state $\Psi_{\gamma,\vec{j}}$ must be concentrated at the intersections of S with γ. The detailed expression bears out this expectation: the action of $\hat{A}_S$ on $\Psi_{\gamma,\vec{j}}$ is dictated simply by the spin labels j_I attached to those edges of γ that intersect S. For all surfaces S and three-dimensional regions R in Σ, $\hat{A}_S$ and $\hat{V}_R$ are densely defined, self-adjoint operators. *All their eigenvalues are discrete* [6]. Naively, one might expect that the eigenvalues would be uniformly spaced, given by, e.g., integral multiples of the Planck area or volume. This turns out *not* to be the case; the distribution of eigenvalues is quite subtle. In particular, the eigenvalues crowd rapidly as areas and volumes increase. In the case of area operators, the complete spectrum is known in a *closed form*, and the first several hundred eigenvalues have been explicitly computed numerically. For a large eigenvalue a_n, the separation $\Delta a_n = a_{n+1} - a_n$ between consecutive eigenvalues decreases exponentially: $\Delta a_n \leq \ell_{\rm Pl}^2 \exp -(\sqrt{a_n}/\ell_{\rm Pl})$! Because of such strong crowding, the continuum approximation becomes excellent quite rapidly just a few orders of magnitude above the Planck scale. At the Planck scale, however, there is a precise and very specific replacement. This is the arena of quantum geometry. The premise is that the standard perturbation theory fails because it ignores this fundamental discreteness.

There is however a further subtlety [2, 7]. This non-perturbative quantization has a one parameter family of ambiguities labelled by $\gamma > 0$. This γ is called the Barbero–Immirzi parameter and is rather similar to the well-known θ-parameter of QCD. In QCD, a single classical theory gives rise to inequivalent sectors of quantum theory, labelled by θ. Similarly, γ is classically irrelevant but different values of γ correspond to unitarily inequivalent representations of the algebra of geometric operators. The overall mathematical structure of all these sectors is very similar; the only difference is that the eigenvalues of all geometric operators scale with γ. For example, the simplest eigenvalues of the area operator $\hat{A}_S$ in the γ quantum sector is given by

$$a_{\{j\}} = 8\pi\gamma\ell_{\mathrm{Pl}}^2 \sum_I \sqrt{j_I(j_I+1)}, \qquad (23.1)$$

where $\{j\}$ is a collection of 1/2-integers j_I, with $I = 1, \dots N$ for some N.[3] Since the representations are unitarily inequivalent, as usual, one must rely on Nature to resolve this ambiguity: Just as Nature must select a specific value of θ in QCD, it must select a specific value of γ in loop quantum gravity. With one judicious experiment – e.g., measurement of the lowest eigenvalue of the area operator $\hat{A}_S$ for a 2-surface S of any given topology – we could determine the value of γ and fix the theory. Unfortunately, such experiments are hard to perform! However, we will see in section 23.3.2 that the Bekenstein–Hawking formula of black hole entropy provides an indirect measurement of this lowest eigenvalue of area for the 2-sphere topology and can therefore be used to fix the value of γ.

---

[3] In particular, the lowest non-zero eigenvalue of area operators is proportional to γ. This fact has led to a misunderstanding: in circles outside loop quantum gravity, γ is sometimes thought of as a regulator responsible for discreteness of quantum geometry. As explained above, this is *not* the case; γ is analogous to the QCD θ and quantum geometry is discrete in *every* permissible γ-sector. Note also that, at the classical level, the theory is equivalent to general relativity only if γ is *positive*; if one sets $\gamma = 0$ by hand, one cannot recover even the kinematics of general relativity. Similarly, at the quantum level, setting $\gamma = 0$ would lead to a meaningless theory in which *all* eigenvalues of geometric operators vanish identically.

23.2.3 Quantum dynamics

Quantum geometry provides a mathematical arena to formulate non-perturbative dynamics of candidate quantum theories of gravity, without any reference to a background classical geometry. In the case of general relativity, it provides the tools to write down quantum Einstein's equations in the Hamiltonian approach and calculate transition amplitudes in the path integral approach. Until recently, effort was focused primarily on the Hamiltonian approach. However, over the last three years, path integrals – called *spin foams* – have drawn a great deal of attention. This work has led to fascinating results suggesting that, thanks to the fundamental discreteness of quantum geometry, path integrals defining quantum general relativity may be finite. These developments will be discussed in some detail in section 23.4. In this section,[4] I will summarize the status of the Hamiltonian approach. For brevity, I will focus on source-free general relativity, although there has been considerable work also on matter couplings.

For simplicity, let me suppose that the 'spatial' 3-manifold Σ is compact. Then, in any theory without background fields, Hamiltonian dynamics is governed by constraints. Roughly, this is because, in these theories, diffeomorphisms correspond to gauge (in the sense of Dirac). Recall that, on the Maxwell phase space, gauge transformations are generated by the functional $\mathcal{D}_a E^a$ which is constrained to vanish on physical states due to Gauss law. Similarly, on phase spaces of background independent theories, diffeomorphisms are generated by Hamiltonians which are constrained to vanish on physical states. In the case of general relativity, there are three sets of constraints. The first set consists of the three Gauss equations

$$\mathcal{G}_i := \mathcal{D}_a E^a_i = 0,$$

which, as in Yang–Mills theories, generates internal SU(2) rotations on the connection and the triad fields. The second set consists of a co-vector (or diffeomorphism) constraint

$$\mathcal{C}_b := E^a F_{ab} = 0,$$

which generates spatial diffeomorphism on Σ (modulo internal rotations generated by $\mathcal{G}_i$). Finally, there is the key scalar (or Hamiltonian) constraint

$$\mathcal{S} := \epsilon^{ijk} E^a_i E^b_j F_{abk} + \ldots = 0,$$

---

[4] This section is a little more technical than the last two and can be skipped without a significant loss of continuity.

which generates time-evolutions. (The ... are extrinsic curvature terms, expressible as Poisson brackets of the connection, the total volume constructed from triads and the first term in the expression of S given above. We will not need their explicit forms.) Our task in quantum theory is three-fold: (i) elevate these constraints (or their 'exponentiated versions') to well-defined operators on the kinematic Hilbert space $\mathcal{H}$; (ii) select physical states by asking that they be annihilated by these constraints; (iii) introduce an inner-product and interesting observables, and develop approximation schemes, truncations, etc. to explore physical consequences.

This general procedure was introduced by Dirac in the 1950s and 1960s and developed further by Peter Bergmann's and John Wheeler's groups. Stephen's work on quantum cosmology lies in the broad framework of Wheeler's geometrodynamics. If we ignore fermions, one can replace triads by 3-metrics. Then we no longer have triad rotations or the Gauss constraint and are left only with the co-vector and scalar constraints. In geometrodynamics, the quantum version of the scalar constraint is called the Wheeler–DeWitt equation and the Hartle–Hawking no-boundary proposal provides a method of finding a preferred solution to this equation, called the 'wave function of the universe'. However, in geometrodynamics, mathematical issues related to the presence of an infinite number of degrees of freedom – the source of infinities and non-renormalizability – have yet to be addressed, whence the implementation of the Dirac programme has remained at a formal level. It is only in quantum cosmology where all but a finite number of degrees of freedom are frozen by symmetry requirements that concrete calculations have been made.

What is the situation in the quantum geometry approach? Here, step (i) has been completed. Since the action of the Gauss and the co-vector constraints have a simple geometrical meaning, completion of (i) in these cases is fairly straightforward. For the scalar constraint, on the other hand, there are no such guiding principles whence the procedure is subtle. In particular, specific regularization choices have to be made. Consequently, the answer is not unique. At the present stage of the programme, such ambiguities are inevitable; one has to consider all viable candidates and analyse if they lead to sensible theories. However, the availability of well-defined Hamiltonian constraint operators is by itself a notable technical success. For example, the analogous problem in quantum geometrodynamics – a satisfactory regularization of the Wheeler–DeWitt equation – is still open although the formal equation was written down some thirty five years ago. To be specific, I will focus on the procedure developed by Rovelli, Smolin, Lewandowski and others which culminated in a specific construction due to Thiemann [9].

Step (ii) has been completed for the Gauss and the co-vector constraints [8]. The mathematical implementation required a very substantial extension [1, 8] of the algebraic quantization programme initiated by Dirac, and the use of the spin-network machinery [5] of quantum geometry. Again, the detailed implementation is a non-trivial technical success. (The analogous task is yet to be completed in geometrodynamics.) Thiemann's quantum scalar constraint is defined *on the space of solutions to the Gauss and co-vector constraints*. The problem of finding a general solution to the scalar constraint has been systematically reduced to that of finding *elementary* solutions, a task that requires only analysis of linear operators on certain *finite* dimensional spaces. In this sense, step (ii) has been completed for all constraints.

This is a striking result. However, it is still unclear whether this theory is physically satisfactory; at this stage, it is in principle possible that it captures only an 'exotic' sector of quantum gravity. *A key open problem in loop quantum gravity is to show that the scalar/Hamiltonian constraint –* either Thiemann's or an alternative such as the one of Gambini and Pullin [9] – admits a 'sufficient number' of semiclassical states. Progress on this problem has been slow because the general issue of semiclassical limits is itself difficult in background independent approaches. However, as discussed in section 23.4 below, a systematic understanding has now begun to emerge and is providing the 'infra-structure' needed to analyse the key problem mentioned above. More generally, while there are promising ideas to complete step (iii), substantial further work is necessary to fully solve this problem. Recent advance in quantum cosmology, described in section 23.3.1, is an example of progress in this direction and it provides a strong support for the Thiemann scheme, but of course only within the limited context of mini-superspaces.

To summarize, the crux of dynamics in the Hamiltonian approach lies in quantum constraints. While the quantum Gauss and co-vector/diffeomorphism constraints have been solved, it is not clear if any of the proposed strategies to solve the scalar/Hamiltonian constraint incorporates the familiar low energy physics.

Technical Remark: There has been another concern about this class of regularizations of the scalar constraint which, however, is less specific. It stems from the structure of the constraint algebra. To analyse this issue, the domain of definition of the scalar constraint had to be extended to *certain* states which are not diffeomorphism invariant, so that the commutators could be meaningfully calculated. It was then found that the commutator between any two Hamiltonian constraints vanishes identically [9], while in the classical theory, the corresponding Poisson brackets vanishes only on solutions to the diffeomorphism constraint. However, it was also shown that the operator representing the right side of the classical Poisson bracket *also vanishes* on all the quantum states considered, including the ones which are not diffeomorphism invariant. Therefore, while the vanishing of the commutator of the Hamiltonian constraint was unexpected, this analysis does not reveal a clear-cut problem with these regularizations.

Furthermore, one can follow this scheme step by step in 2+1 gravity where one knows what the result should be. One can obtain the 'elementary solutions' mentioned above and show that all the standard quantum states – including the semiclassical ones – can be recovered as linear combinations of these elementary ones. As is almost always the case with constrained systems, there are *many more solutions* and the 'spurious ones' have to be eliminated by the requirement that the physical norm be finite. In 2+1 gravity, the connection formulation used here naturally leads to a complete set of Dirac observables and the inner-product can be essentially fixed by the requirement that they be self-adjoint. In 3+1 gravity, by contrast, we do not have this luxury and the problem of constructing the physical inner-product is therefore much more difficult. However, the concern here is that of weeding out unwanted solutions rather than having a 'sufficient number' of semiclassical ones, a significantly less serious issue at the present stage.

23.3 Applications of quantum geometry

In this section, I will summarize two recent developments that answer several of the questions raised in the Introduction.

23.3.1 Big Bang

Over the last three years, quantum geometry has led to some striking results of direct physical interest. The first of these concerns the fate of the Big Bang singularity.

Traditionally, in quantum cosmology one has proceeded by first imposing spatial symmetries – such as homogeneity and isotropy – to freeze out all but a finite number of degrees of freedom *already at the classical level* and then quantizing the reduced system. In the simplest case, the basic variables of the reduced classical system are the scale factor a and matter fields ϕ. The symmetries imply that spacetime curvature goes as $\sim 1/a^2$ and Einstein's equations predict a Big – Bang, where the scale factor goes to zero and the curvature blows up. As alluded to in section 23.1, this is reminiscent of what happens to ferromagnets at the Curie temperature: magnetization goes to zero and the susceptibility diverges. By analogy, the key question is: do these 'pathologies' disappear if we re-examine the situation in the context of an appropriate quantum theory? If, without any further input, one tries to solve the quantum mechanical Wheeler–DeWitt equation, one typically finds that the singularity persists. Early attempts to rectify this situation involved the introduction of artificial matter, with unphysical properties. The Hartle–Hawking [10] proposal, by contrast, provides a much more natural cure via the introduction of new boundary conditions.

What happens in the quantum geometry approach? In a series of seminal papers [10], Martin Bojowald has shown that the situation is rather different from that in the standard quantum cosmology: quantum nature of geometry makes a *qualitative* difference very near the Big Bang and naturally resolves the singularity. In the standard procedure summarized above, the reduction is carried out at the classical level and this removes all traces of the fundamental discreteness. Therefore, the key idea in Bojowald's analysis is to retain the essential features of quantum geometry by first quantizing the kinematics of the *full theory* as in section 23.2.2 and then restricting oneself to *quantum* states which are spatially homogeneous and isotropic. As a result, the scale factor operator $\hat{a}$ has *discrete eigenvalues*. Still, the continuum limit is reached rapidly. For example, the gap between an eigenvalue of $\hat{a}$ of $\sim 1\,\mathrm{cm}$ and the next one is less than $\sim 10^{-30}\,\ell_{\mathrm{Pl}}$! Nonetheless, near $a \sim \ell_{\mathrm{Pl}}$ there are surprises: predictions of loop quantum cosmology are very different from those of traditional quantum cosmology.

The first surprise occurs already at the kinematical level. Recall that, in the classical theory curvature is essentially given by $1/a^2$, and blows up at the Big Bang. What is the situation in quantum theory? Denote the Hilbert space of spatially homogeneous, isotropic kinematical quantum states by $\mathcal{H}_{\mathrm{HI}}$. A self-adjoint operator $\widehat{\mathrm{curv}}$ corresponding to curvature can be constructed on $\mathcal{H}_{\mathrm{HI}}$ and turns out to be *bounded from above*. This is very surprising because $\mathcal{H}_{\mathrm{HI}}$ admits an eigenstate of the scale factor operator $\hat{a}$ with a discrete, zero eigenvalue! At first, it may appear that this could happen only by an artificial trick in the construction of $\widehat{\mathrm{curv}}$ and that this quantization cannot possibly be right because it seems to represent a huge departure from the classical relation $(\mathrm{curv})\,a^2 = 1$. However, these concerns turn out to be misplaced. The procedure for constructing $\widehat{\mathrm{curv}}$ is natural and, furthermore, descends from full quantum theory.

Let us examine the properties of $\widehat{\mathrm{curv}}$. Its upper bound u_{curv} is finite but absolutely huge:

$$u_{\mathrm{curv}} \sim \frac{256}{81}\,\frac{1}{\ell_{\mathrm{Pl}}^2} \equiv \frac{256}{81}\,\frac{1}{G\hbar} \tag{23.2}$$

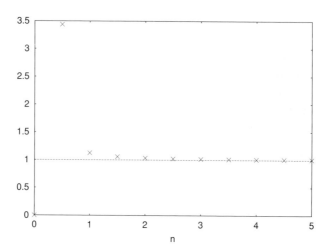

Fig. 23.1. The product $a_n \cdot b_n$ as a function of n. The corresponding classical product $a \cdot \sqrt{\text{curv}}$ equals 1.

or, about 10^{77} times the curvature at the horizon of a solar mass black hole. The functional form of the upper bound is also illuminating. Recall first the Pauli–Schrödinger treatment of the hydrogen atom in non-relativistic quantum mechanics. Because the Coulomb potential between the proton (nucleus of the atom) and the electron diverges as $-1/r$, in the classical theory the energy is unbounded from below. However, thanks to the Planck's constant $\hbar$, in the quantum theory, we obtain a finite value, $E_0 = -(me^4/\hbar^2)$. Similarly, u_{curv} is finite because $\hbar$ is non-zero and tends to the classical answer as $\hbar$ tends to zero.

At curvatures as large as u_{curv}, it is natural to expect large departures from classical relations such as $(\text{curv})\, a^2 = 1$. But is this relation recovered in the semiclassical regime? The answer is in the affirmative. In fact it is somewhat surprising how quickly this happens. As one would expect, one can simultaneously diagonalize $\hat{a}$ and $\widehat{\text{curv}}$. If we denote their eigenvalues by a_n and b_n respectively, then $a_n \cdot b_n - 1$ is of the order 10^{-4} at $n = 100$ and decreases rapidly as n increases. These properties show that, in spite of the initial surprise, the quantization procedure is viable. Furthermore, one can apply it also to more familiar systems such as a particle moving on a circle and obtain results that at first seem surprising but are in complete agreement with the standard quantum theory of these systems.

Since the curvature is bounded above in the entire Hilbert space, one might hope that the quantum evolution may be well-defined right through the Big Bang singularity. Is this in fact the case? The second surprise is that although the quantum evolution is close to that of the so-called Wheeler–DeWitt equation of standard quantum cosmology for large a, there are dramatic differences near the Big Bang which makes it well defined even *at* the Big Bang, *without any additional input.* To solve the quantum Einstein equation, Bojowald again follows, step by step, the procedure introduced (by Thiemann) in the full theory. Let us expand the full quantum state as $\mid \Psi >= \sum_n \psi_n(\phi) \mid n >$ where $\mid n >$ are the eigenstates of the scale factor operator and ϕ denotes matter fields. Then, the quantum Einstein equation takes the form:

$$c_n\psi_{n+8}(\phi) + d_n\psi_{n+4}(\phi) + e_n\psi_n(\phi) + f_n\psi_{n-4}(\phi) + g_n\psi_{n-8}(\phi)$$
$$= \gamma\ell_{\rm Pl}^2 \, \hat{H}_\phi\psi_n(\phi) \qquad (23.3)$$

where $c_n, \ldots g_n$ are fixed numerical coefficients, γ the Barbero-Immirzi parameter and $\hat{H}_\phi$ is the matter Hamiltonian. (Again, using the Thiemann regularization, one can show that the matter Hamiltonian is a well-defined operator.)

As one would expect from the phase-spaceformulation of classical general relativity, primarily, (23.3) serves to constrain the coefficients $\psi_n(\phi)$ of physically permissible quantum states. However, *if* we choose to interpret the scale factor (more precisely, the square of the scale factor times the determinant of the triad) as a time variable, (23.3) can be interpreted as an 'evolution equation' which evolves the state through discrete time steps. In a (large) neighborhood of the Big Bang singularity, this notion of time is viable. For the choice of factor ordering used in the Thiemann regularization, one can evolve in the past through $n = 0$, i.e. right through the classical singularity. Thus, the infinities predicted by the classical theory at the Big Bang are indeed artifacts of assuming that the classical, continuum spacetime approximation is valid right up to the Big Bang. In the quantum theory, the state can be evolved through the Big Bang without any difficulty. However, the classical spacetime description fails near the Big Bang; quantum evolution is well-defined but the classical spacetime 'dissolves'.

The 'evolution' equation (23.3) has other interesting features. To begin with, the space of solutions is 16 dimensional. Can we single out a preferred solution by imposing a *physical* condition? One possibility is to impose a *pre-classicality* condition, i.e., to require that the quantum state not oscillate rapidly from one step to the next at *late* times when we know our universe behaves classically. Although this is an extra input, it is not a theoretical prejudice about what should happen at (or near) the Big Bang but an observationally motivated condition that is clearly satisfied by our universe. The coefficients $c_n, \ldots g_n$ of (23.3) are such that this condition singles out a solution uniquely. One can ask what this state does at negative times, i.e., before the Big Bang. (Time becomes negative because triads flip orientation on the 'other side'.) Preliminary indications are that the state does not become pre-classical there. If this is borne out by detailed calculations, then the 'Big Bang' separates two regimes; on 'our' side, classical geometry is both meaningful and useful at late times while on the 'other' side, it is not. Another interesting feature is that the standard Wheeler–DeWitt equation is recovered if we take the limit $\gamma \to 0$ and $n \to \infty$ such that the eigenvalues of $\hat{a}$ take on continuous values. This is completely parallel to the limit we often take to coarse grain the quantum description of a rigidly spinning rotor to 'wash out' discreteness in angular momentum eigenvalues and arrive at the classically allowed continuous angular momenta. From this perspective, then, one is led to say that the most striking of the consequences of loop quantum gravity are not seen in standard quantum cosmology because it 'washes out' the fundamental discreteness of quantum geometry.

Finally, the detailed calculations have revealed another surprising feature. The fact that the quantum effects become prominent near the Big Bang, completely invalidating the classical predictions, is pleasing but not unexpected. However, prior to these calculations, it was not clear how soon after the Big Bang one can start trusting semiclassical notions and calculations. It would not have been surprising if we had to wait until the radius of the universe became, say, a few million times the Planck length. These calculations strongly suggest that few hundred Planck lengths should suffice. This is fortunate because it is now feasible to develop quantum numerical relativity; with computational resources commonly available, grids with $(10^6)^3$ points are hopelessly large but one with $(100)^3$ points are readily available.

23.3.2 Black holes

Loop quantum cosmology illuminates dynamical ramifications of quantum geometry but within the context of mini-superspaces where all but a finite number of degrees of freedom are frozen. I will now discuss a complementary application where one considers the full theory but probes consequences of quantum geometry which are not sensitive to full quantum dynamics – the application of the framework to the problem of black hole entropy. This discussion is based on joint work with Baez, Corichi and Krasnov [11] which itself was motivated by earlier work of Krasnov, Rovelli, Smolin and others.

As explained in the Introduction, since Stephen's celebrated discovery of black hole evaporation, a key question in the subject has been: what is the statistical mechanical origin of the black hole entropy $S_{\mathrm{BH}} = a_{\mathrm{hor}}/4\ell_{\mathrm{Pl}}^2$? What are the microscopic degrees of freedom that account for this entropy? This relation implies that a solar mass black hole must have $\sim (\exp 10^{77})$ quantum states, a number that is *huge* even by the standards of statistical mechanics. Where do all these states reside? To answer these questions, in the early 1990s John Wheeler suggested the following heuristic picture, which he christened 'It from Bit'. Divide the black hole horizon into elementary cells, each with one Planck unit, $\ell_{\rm Pl}^2$, of area and assign to each cell two microstates, or one 'bit'. Then the total number of states $\mathcal{N}$ is given by $\mathcal{N} = 2^n$ where $n = (a_{\rm hor}/\ell_{\rm Pl}^2)$ is the number of elementary cells, whence entropy is given by $S = \ln \mathcal{N} \sim a_{\rm hor}$. Thus, apart from a numerical coefficient, the entropy ('It') is accounted for by assigning two states ('Bit') to each elementary cell. This qualitative picture is simple and attractive. Therefore it is natural to ask if it can be made precise. Can these heuristic ideas be supported by a systematic analysis from first principles? What is the rationale behind dividing the black hole horizon into elementary cells of unit Planck area? Why are there exactly two quantum states associated with each cell? It turned out that quantum geometry could supply answers to these questions through a detailed analysis.[5]

A systematic approach requires that we first specify the class of black holes of interest. Since the entropy formula is expected to hold unambiguously for black holes in equilibrium, most analyses were confined to space-times with 'eternal' black holes admitting a global time-translation isometry, rather than the astrophysical ones which result from a gravitational collapse. From a physical viewpoint however, this assumption seems overly restrictive. After all, in statistical mechanical calculations of entropy of ordinary systems, one only has to assume that the given system is in equilibrium, not the whole world. Therefore, it should suffice to assume that the black hole itself is in equilibrium; the exterior geometry should not be forced to be time-independent. Finally, with Gary Gibbons, Stephen showed that the thermodynamical considerations apply not only to black holes but also to so-called 'cosmological horizons'. A natural question is: can these diverse situations be treated in a single stroke? Within the quantum geometry approach, the answer is in the affirmative. The idea that the black hole (or the cosmological horizon) is itself in equilibrium is captured by certain boundary conditions which ensure that the horizon itself is *isolated,* allowing time-dependent spacetime geometry and matter fields in the exterior region. Entropy associated with

---

[5] I should add, however, that this account does not follow chronology. Black hole entropy was computed in quantum geometry quite independently and the realization that the 'It from Bit' picture works so well was somewhat of a surprise.

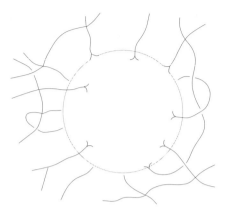

Fig. 23.2. Quantum Horizon. Polymer excitations in the bulk puncture the horizon, endowing it with quantized area. Intrinsically, the horizon is flat except at punctures where it acquires a quantized deficit angle. These angles add up to endow the horizon with a 2-sphere topology.

an isolated horizon refers to the family of observers in the exterior region for whom the isolated horizon is a physical boundary that separates the region that is accessible to them from the one that is not. (This point is especially important for cosmological horizons where, without reference to observers, one can not even define these horizons.) States which contribute to this entropy are the ones which can interact with the states in the exterior; in this sense, they 'reside' on the horizon.

In the detailed analysis, one considers space-times admitting an isolated horizon as inner boundary and carries out a systematic quantization. The quantum geometry framework can be naturally extended to this case. The isolated horizon boundary conditions imply that the intrinsic geometry of the quantum horizon is described by the so called U(1) Chern–Simons theory on the horizon. This is a well-developed, topological quantum field theory. A deeply satisfying feature of the analysis is that there is a seamless matching of three otherwise independent structures: the isolated horizon boundary conditions that come from classical general relativity; the quantum geometry in the bulk; and the Chern-Simons theory on the horizon. In particular, one can calculate eigenvalues of certain physically interesting operators using purely bulk quantum geometry without any knowledge of the Chern-Simons theory, or using the Chern–Simons theory without any knowledge of the bulk quantum geometry. The two theories have never heard of each other. Yet, thanks to the isolated horizon boundary conditions, the two infinite sets of numbers match exactly, providing a coherent description of the quantum horizon.

In this description, the polymer excitations of the bulk geometry, each labelled by a spin j_I, pierce the horizon, endowing it an elementary area a_{j_I} given by (23.1). The sum $\sum_I a_{j_I}$ adds up to the total horizon area a_{hor}. The intrinsic geometry of the horizon is flat except at these puncture, but at each puncture there is a *quantized* deficit angle. These add up to endow the horizon with a 2-sphere topology, as required by a quantum analogue of the Gauss–Bonnet theorem. For a solar mass black hole, a typical horizon state would have 10^{77} punctures, each contributing a tiny deficit angle. So, although the quantum geometry *is* distributional, it can be well approximated by a smooth metric.

The counting of states can be carried out as follows. First one constructs a micro-canonical ensemble by restricting oneself only to those states for which the total area, angular momentum, and charges lie in small intervals around fixed values $a_{\mathrm{hor}}, J_{\mathrm{hor}}, Q^i_{\mathrm{hor}}$. (As is usual in statistical mechanics, the leading contribution to the entropy is independent of the precise choice of these small intervals.) For each set of punctures, one can compute the dimension of the surface Hilbert space, consisting of Chern–Simons states compatible with that set. One allows all possible sets of punctures (by varying both the spin labels and the number of punctures), subject to the constraint that the total area a_{hor} be fixed, and adds up the dimensions of the corresponding surface Hilbert spaces to obtain the number $\mathcal{N}$ of permissible surface states. One finds that the horizon entropy S_{hor} is given by

$$S_{\mathrm{hor}} := \ln \mathcal{N} = \frac{\gamma_o}{\gamma} \frac{a_{\mathrm{hor}}}{\ell^2_{\mathrm{Pl}}} + \mathcal{O}\left(\frac{\ell^2_{\mathrm{Pl}}}{a_{\mathrm{hor}}}\right), \quad \text{where} \quad \gamma_o = \frac{\ln 2}{\sqrt{3}\pi}. \quad (23.4)$$

Thus, for large black holes, entropy is indeed proportional to the horizon area. This is a non-trivial result; for example, early calculations often led to proportionality to the square-root of the area. However, even for large black holes, one obtains agreement with the Hawking–Bekenstein formula *only* in the sector of quantum geometry in which the Barbero–Immirzi parameter γ takes the value $\gamma = \gamma_o$. Thus, while all γ sectors are equivalent classically, the standard quantum field theory in curved space-times is recovered in the semiclassical theory only in the γ_o sector of quantum geometry. It is quite remarkable that thermodynamic considerations involving *large* black holes can be used to fix the quantization ambiguity that dictates such Planck scale properties as eigenvalues of geometric operators. Note however that the value of γ can be fixed by demanding agreement with the semiclassical result just in one case – e.g., a spherical horizon with zero charge, or a cosmological horizon in the de Sitter space-time, or, ... Once the value of γ is fixed, the theory is completely fixed and we can ask: does this theory yield the Hawking–Bekenstein value of entropy of *all* isolated horizons, irrespective of the values of charges, angular momentum, and cosmological constant, the amount of distortion, or hair. The answer is in the affirmative. Thus, the agreement with quantum field theory in curved space-times holds in *all* these diverse cases.

Why does γ_o not depend on other horizon parameters such as the charges Q^i_{hor}? This important property can be traced back to a key consequence of the isolated horizon boundary conditions: detailed calculations show that only the gravitational part of the symplectic structure has a surface term at the horizon; the matter symplectic structures have only volume terms. (Furthermore, the gravitational surface term is insensitive to the value of the cosmological constant.) Consequently, in the geometric quantization procedure used in this analysis, there are no independent surface quantum states associated with matter. This provides a natural explanation of the fact that the Hawking–Bekenstein entropy depends only on the horizon geometry and is independent of electromagnetic (or other) charges.

Finally, let us return to Wheeler's 'It from Bit'. One can ask: what are the states that dominate the counting? Perhaps not surprisingly, they turn out to be the ones which assign to each puncture the smallest quantum of area (i.e., spin value $j = 1/2$), thereby maximizing the number of punctures. In these states, each puncture defines one of Wheeler's 'elementary cell' and his two states correspond to the $j_z = \pm 1/2$ states, i.e., to whether the deficit angle is positive or negative. However, in the complete theory, all values of j (and hence of j_z) must be allowed to obtain a complete description of the geometry of the quantum horizon. If one is only interested in counting states for large black holes, however, the leading contribution comes from the $j = 1/2$ states.

To summarize, quantum geometry naturally provides the micro-states responsible for the huge entropy associated with horizons. In this analysis, all black holes – including the ones of direct astrophysical interest – and cosmological horizons are treated in a unified fashion. The sub-leading term has also been calculated and shown to be proportional to $\ln a_{\text{hor}}$ [11].

23.4 Outlook

As we saw, a number of long standing questions concerning the Big Bang and black holes have been answered through quantum geometry. As is usual, these advances, in turn, raise further challenges. In this section, I will first give a few examples and then mention two other areas of focus of current research.

Let us begin with the Big Bang. It is natural to ask: how robust is Bojowald's strategy of using 'pre-classicality' to select a preferred quantum state? Work in progress on homogeneous but non-isotropic models suggests that the success of the strategy is not just an artifact of the strong isotropy assumption. Assuming the strategy is robust, is there a relation between these boundary conditions and the Hartle–Hawking 'no-boundary' proposal which also satisfies pre-classicality at late times (at least in the mini-superspace approximation)? Is the Euclidean regime in the Hartle–Hawking analysis an alternate (possibly semiclassical(?)) way to encode the effective 'dissolution' of the Lorentzian spacetime into a discrete quantum geometry very near the Big Bang? Can we repeat the Halliwell–Hawking type of analysis to address the issue of structure formation? This question is now being analysed by first embedding the state space of homogeneous cosmological models into the state space of the full theory. If the answer turns out to be in the affirmative, the program would realize the hope that the origin of the initial perturbations required for structure formation lies in non-perturbative quantum gravity effects.

Let us turn to black holes. Recall first that in the beginning of the 20th century we learnt that, although matter and radiation appear to be distinct classically, they are really two facets of the same reality; in particular, quanta of matter can be converted in to quanta of radiation. We also learnt from Einstein that geometry and matter are on the same footing; Einstein's equations provide a quantitative relation between spacetime curvature and matter stress-energy. It was therefore natural to ask whether matter and geometry can be converted into one another. Gravitational collapse can be regarded as a process of converting matter into geometry; in classical relativity, black holes are made of 'pure geometry'. What about the converse? In the Hawking evaporation process, black holes emit radiation and shrink in area, strongly suggesting that the converse does occur. However, since Stephen's original analysis assumed a classical, continuum spacetime; quanta of geometry were absent. Quantum geometry provides this missing ingredient. From this perspective, it is literally true that in the Hawking process, *quanta of area are converted into quanta of matter*. Thus, one can now hope to realize in detail Einstein's vision on the physical nature of geometry at the quantum level. Heuristically, one can regard a large black hole as a 'giant atom' in an excited but approximately stationary state which makes successive quantum transitions to lower eigenstates of area by emitting matter quanta. Can we supply more detailed calculations to support this picture? Analyse quantum processes in the near horizon region? Once the Barbero–Immirzi parameter is fixed through entropy, can we perform further checks on the resulting theory through other predictions of quantum field theory in curved spacetime? To answer these questions, we need to develop semiclassical states of quantum geometry which approximate black hole space-times. As discussed below, this is a difficult task but work has already begun.

More generally, as indicated in section 23.2.3, a major open problem is the relation between quantum geometry and low energy physics. Of necessity, a background independent description must use physical concepts and mathematical tools that are qualitatively different from those of the familiar physics formulated in flat spacetime. A major challenge then is to show that this low energy description does arise from the pristine, Planckian world in an appropriate sense. This is a central but technically difficult task because one must interpolate between regimes that differ by some 16 orders of magnitude: The characteristic length scale in the Planck regime is $\sim 10^{-33}$cm while the smallest distance we can probe with our highest energy accelerators today is $\sim 10^{-17}$cm. In this 'top-down' approach, does the fundamental theory admit a 'sufficient number' of semiclassical states? Do these semiclassical sectors provide enough of a background geometry to anchor low energy physics in? Can one pin-point why the standard 'bottom-up' perturbative approach fails? That is, what is the essential feature that makes the fundamental description mathematically coherent, but is absent in the standard perturbative quantum gravity? Over the last two years, there has been notable progress on the first set of questions and the relation between the fundamental, polymer-like excitations and the familiar Fock states has begun to emerge [14]. Furthermore, as in gauge theories, by calculating expectation values of suitable Wilson loops, one can single out the desired semiclassical states which are in the 'Coulomb phase of the theory' and thus capture the essential qualitative features of the classical theory. The current goal is to understand the physics of these states in detail. On the one hand, they should reproduce the observed low energy world, normally described by perturbative quantum field theory. On the other hand, this description must depart from the perturbative description in crucial ways by divorcing itself from over-reliance on the continuum picture. How does quantum geometry manage this delicate act?

I will conclude by mentioning another frontier, which is closely related to Stephen's path integral program: the spin-foam models [12]. Spin foams can be thought of as histories traced out by 'time evolution' of spin networks and provide a fresh path integral approach to quantum dynamics. As in Stephen's program, these path integrals can be considered as a device to extract physical states, i.e. solutions to all quantum constraints. Therefore, spin foams are expected to shed new light on the difficult issue of regularization of the Hamiltonian constraint, discussed in section 23.2.3. The well-defined quantum kinematics of section 23.2.2 has motivated specific proposals for the definition of path integrals, often called 'state sum models'. Perhaps the most successful of these is the Barrett–Crane model (modified suitably to handle a technical issue). Over the last two years, Crane, Perez and Rovelli, using earlier work of by Baez, Barrett, De Pietri, Freidel, Krasnov, Mikovič, Reisenberger and others, have made remarkable mathematical advances in showing finiteness of the (modified) Barret–Crane amplitudes . These finiteness results were quite unexpected: Although the discretization of spacetime ('topology') is kept fixed in calculating this amplitude, one still has to sum over an infinite number of spins ('geometries'). From the quantum geometry perspective, the ultraviolet finiteness is perhaps not surprising: its origin lies in the fundamental discreteness. The infrared finiteness, on the other hand, *is* surprising because there is no a priori reason for the infinite sum over spins to converge. These rigorous results have intensified the activity in the field, adding a great deal of optimism. Recently Luscher and Reuter have found some evidence for non-perturbative renormalizability of four-dimensional Euclidean quantum general relativity (stemming from the existence of a non-trivial fixed point) [12].

An outstanding open issue is to understand better the relation between Stephen's program, the Luscher–Reuter results and the spin-foam finiteness. At the present stage, it is not obvious how to extract detailed answers to any of the key *physical* questions of quantum gravity. However, this may well be an avenue to establish definitively that, in spite of the failure of perturbation theory, quantum general relativity is well defined non-perturbatively.

Acknowledgements

I would like to thank John Baez, Martin Bojowald, Rodolfo Gambini, Jerzy Lewandowski, Alejandro Perez, Jorge Pullin, Carlo Rovelli and Thomas Thiemann for numerous discussions. This work was supported in part by the NSF grant PHY-0090091 and the Eberly research funds of Penn State.

References

[1] *Books*
Ashtekar, A. (1991), *Lectures on Non-Perturbative Canonical Gravity* (World Scientific, Singapore).
Gambini, R. and Pullin, J. (1996), *Loops, Knots, Gauge Theories and Quantum Gravity*, (Cambridge University Press, Cambridge).

[2] *Classical theory*
Ashtekar, A. (1986), 'New variables for classical and quantum gravity', *Phys. Rev. Lett.* **57**, 2244–2247.

Ashtekar, A. (1987), 'New Hamiltonian formulation of general relativity', *Phys. Rev.* **D36**, 1587–1602.

Ashtekar, A., Romano, J. D. and Tate, R. S. (1989), 'New variables for gravity: inclusion of matter', *Phys. Rev.* **D40**, 2572–2587.

Barbero, F. (1996), 'Real Ashtekar variables for Lorentzian signature space-times', *Phys. Rev.* **D51**, 5507–5510.

[3] *Connections and loops*

Rovelli, C. and Smolin, L. (1988), 'Knot theory and quantum gravity' *Phys. Rev. Lett.* **61** 1155–1158. Rovelli, C. and Smolin, L. (1990), 'Loop representation for quantum general relativity', *Nucl. Phys.* **B331** 80–152.

Ashtekar, A., Husain, V., Rovelli, R., Samuel J. and Smolin, L. (1989), '2+1 quantum gravity as a toy model for the 3+1 theory', *Class. Quant. Grav.* **6**, L185–L193.

Ashtekar, A., Rovelli C. and Smolin, L. (1991), 'Gravitons and loops', *Phys. Rev.* **D44**, 1740–1755.

[4] *Quantum Geometry: Basics*

Ashtekar, A. and Isham, C. J. (1992), 'Representation of the holonomy algebras of gravity and non-Abelian gauge theories', *Class. Quant. Grav.* **9**, 1433–1467.

Ashtekar, A. and Lewandowski, J. (1994), 'Representation theory of analytic holonomy algebras', in *Knots and Quantum Gravity*, ed. J. Baez (Oxford University Press, Oxford).

Baez, J. C. (1994), 'Generalized measures in gauge theory', *Lett. Math. Phys.* **31**, 213–223.

Marolf D. and Mourão, J. (1995), 'On the support of the Ashtekar–Lewandowski measure', *Commun. Math. Phys.* **170**, 583–606.

Ashtekar A. and Lewandowski, J. (1995), 'Projective techniques and functional integration', *J. Math. Phys.* **36**, 2170–2191.

Baez, J. C. and Sawin, S. (1997), 'Functional integration on spaces of connections', *J. Funct. Analysis* **150**, 1–27.

[5] *Spin networks:*

Penrose, R. (1971), 'Angular momentum: an approach to combinatorial space-time', in *Quantum Theory and Beyond*, ed. T. Bastin (Cambridge University Press).

Rovelli, C. and Smolin, L. (1995), 'Spin networks and quantum gravity', *Phys. Rev.* **D52**, 5743–5759.

Baez, J. C. (1996), 'Spin networks in non-perturbative quantum gravity', in *The Interface of Knots and Physics*, ed. L. Kauffman (American Mathematical Society, Providence) pp. 167–203.

Baez, J. C. (1996), 'Spin networks in gauge theory', *Adv. Math.* **117**, 253–272.

Baez J. C. and Sawin, S. (1998), 'Diffeomorphism-invariant spin network states', *J. Funct. Analysis* **158**, 253–266.

[6] *Geometric operators and their properties*

Rovelli C. and Smolin, L. (1995), 'Discreteness of area and volume in quantum gravity', *Nucl. Phys.* **B442**, 593–622; Erratum: *Nucl. Phys.* **B456**, 753.

Loll, R. 'The volume operator in discretized quantum gravity', *Phys. Rev. Lett.* **75** 3048–3051.

Ashtekar A. and Lewandowski, L. (1995), 'Differential geometry on the space of connections using projective techniques', *J. Geo. Phys.* **17**, 191–230.

Ashtekar, A. and Lewandowski, J. (1997), 'Quantum theory of geometry I: Area operators', *Class. Quant. Grav.* **14**, A55–A81.

Ashtekar, A. and Lewandowski, J. (1997), 'Quantum theory of geometry II: Volume operators', *Adv. Theo. Math. Phys.* **1**, 388–429.

Loll, R. (1997), 'Further results on geometric operators in quantum gravity', *Class. Quant. Grav.* **14** 1725–1741.

Thiemann, T. (1998), 'A length operator for canonical quantum gravity', *J. Math. Phys.* **39**, 3372–3392.

[7] *Barbero–Immirzi ambiguity*

Immirzi, G. (1997), 'Quantum gravity and Regge calculus', *Nucl. Phys. Proc. Suppl.* **57**, 65–72.

Rovelli, C. and Thiemann, T. (1998), 'The Immirizi parameter in quantum general relativity', *Phys. Rev.* **D57** 1009–1014.

Gambini, R., Obregon, O. and Pullin, J. (1999), 'Yang–Mills analogs of the Immirzi ambiguity', *Phys. Rev.* **D59** 047505.

[8] *Quantum Einstein's equation I*

Marolf, D. (1995), 'Refined algebraic quantization: systems with a single constraint', [gr-qc/9508015].

Ashtekar, A., Lewandowski, J. Marolf, D., Mourão, J. and Thiemann, T. (1995), 'Quantization of diffeomorphism invariant theories of connections with local degrees of freedom', *J. Math. Phys.* **36**, 6456–6493.

Lewandowski, J. and Thiemann, T. (1999), 'Diffeomorphism invariant quantum field theories of connections in terms of webs', *Class. Quant. Grav.* **16**, 2299–2322.

[9] *Quantum Einstein's equation II*

Rovelli, C. and Smolin, L. (1994), 'The physical Hamiltonian in nonperturbative quantum gravity', *Phys. Rev. Lett.* **72**, 446–449.

Thiemann, T. (1996), 'Anomaly-free formulation of non-perturbative, four-dimensional Lorentzian quantum gravity', *Phys. Lett.* **B380**, 257–264.

Thiemann, T. (1998), 'Quantum spin dynamics (QSD)', *Class. Quant. Grav.* **15** 839–873.

Thiemann, T. (1998), 'QSD III : Quantum constraint algebra and physical scalar product in quantum general relativity', *Class. Quant. Grav.* **15**, 1207–1247.

Thiemann, T. (1998), 'QSD V : Quantum gravity as the natural regulator of matter quantum field theories', *Class. Quant. Grav.* **15**, 1281–1314.

Gambini, R., Lewandowski, J., Marolf, D. and Pullin, J. (1998), 'On the consistency of the constraint algebra in spin network quantum gravity', *Int. J. Mod. Phys.* **D7**, 97–109.

Lewandowski, J. and Marolf, D. (1998) 'Loop constraints: a habitat and their algebra', *Int. J. Mod. Phys.* **D7**, 299–330.

Di Bartolo, C., Gambini, R., Griego, J. and Pullin, J. (2000), 'Consistent canonical quantization of general relativity in the space of Vassiliev knot invariants', *Phys. Rev. Lett.* **84**, 2314–2317.

[10] *Big Bang*

Hartle, J. B. and Hawking, S. W. (1983), 'Wave function of the universe', *Phys. Rev.* **D28**, 2960–2975.

Hawking, S. W. (1984), 'Quantum cosmology', in *Relativity, Groups and Topology II*, eds B. DeWitt and R. Stora (North Holland, Amsterdam).

Halliwell, J. J. and Hawking, S. W. (1985), 'Origin of structure in the universe', *Phys. Rev.* **D31**, 1777–1991.

Bojowald, M. (2001), 'Absence of singularity in loop quantum cosmology', *Phys. Rev. Lett.* **86**, 5227–5230.

Bojowald, M. (2001), 'Dynamical initial conditions in quantum cosmology', *Phys. Rev. Lett.* **87**, 121301.

Bojowald, M. (2001), 'Inverse scale factor in isotropic quantum geometry', *Phys. Rev.* **D64** 084018.

Bojowald, M. (2001), 'Loop quantum cosmology III: Wheeler–DeWitt operators', *Class. Quant. Grav.* **18** 1055–1070.

Bojowald, M. (2001), 'Loop quantum cosmology IV: Discrete time evolution', *Class. Quant. Grav.* **18** 1071–1088.

Bojowald, M. (2001), *Quantum Geometry and Symmetry* (Saker-Verlag, Aachen).

Bojowald, M. (2002), 'The semiclassical limit of loop quantum cosmology', *Class. Quant. Grav.* **18** L109–L116.

[11] *Black holes*

Bekenstein, J. D. (1973), 'Black holes and entropy', *Phys. Rev.* **D7** 2333–2346.

Bardeen, J. W., Carter, B. and Hawking, S. W. (1973), 'The four laws of black hole mechanics', *Commun. Math. Phys.* **31** 161–170.

Bekenstein, J. D. (1974), 'Generalized second law of thermodynamics in black hole physics', *Phys. Rev.* **D9** 3292–3300.

Hawking, S. W. (1975), 'Particle creation by black holes', *Commun. Math. Phys.* **43** 199–220.

Gibbons G. and Hawking, S. W. (1977), 'Cosmological event horizons, thermodynamics, and particle creation', *Phys. Rev.* **D15** 2738–2751.

Bekenstein, J. D. and Meisels, A. (1977), 'Einstein A and B coefficients for a black hole', *Phys. Rev.* **D15**, 2775–2781.

Ashtekar, A., Baez, J., Corichi, A. and Krasnov, K. (1998), 'Quantum geometry and black hole entropy', *Phys. Rev. Lett.* **80** 904–907.

Ashtekar, A., Corichi A. and Krasnov, K. (1999), 'Isolated horizons: the classical phase space', *Adv. Theor. Math. Phys.* **3**, 418–471.

Ashtekar, A., Baez, J. and Krasnov, K. (2000), 'Quantum geometry of isolated horizons and black hole entropy', *Adv. Theo. Math. Phys.* **4**, 1–95.

Kaul, R. K. and Majumdar, P. (2000), 'Logarithmic corrections to the Bekenstein–Hawking entropy', *Phys. Rev. Lett.* **84**, 5255–5257.

[12] *Spin foams and finiteness*

Barrett, J. W. and Crane, L. (1998), 'Relativistic spin networks and quantum gravity', *J. Math. Phys.* **39**, 3296–3302.

Baez, J. (1998) Spin foam models, *Class. Quant. Grav.* **15**, 1827–1858.

Barrett, J. W. and Crane L. (2000), 'A Lorentzian signature model for quantum general relativity', *Class. Quant. Grav.* **17**, 3101–3118.

Perez, A. (2001), 'Finiteness of a spinfoam model for Euclidean quantum general relativity', *Nucl. Phys.* **B599**, 427–434.

Perez, A. and Rovelli, C. (2001), 'Spin foam model for Lorentzian general relativity', *Phys. Rev.* **D63**, 041501.

Crane, L., Perez, A. and Rovelli, C. (2001), 'Perturbative finiteness in spinfoam quantum gravity', *Phys. Rev. Lett.* **87**, 181301.

Lauscher, O. and Reuter, M. (2002), 'Is quantum Einstein gravity nonperturbatively renormalizable?', *Class. Quant. Grav.* **19**, 483–492.

[13] *Semiclassical states*

Ashtekar, A., Rovelli, C. and Smolin, L. (1992), 'Weaving a classical geometry with quantum threads', *Phy. Rev. Lett.* **69**, 237–240.

Arnsdorf, M. and Gupta, S. (2000), 'Loop quantum gravity on non-compact spaces', *Nucl. Phys.* **B577** 529–546.

Thiemann, T. (2001), 'Gauge field theory coherent states (GCS) : I. general properties', *Class. Quant. Grav.* **18** 2025–2064.

Sahlmann, H., Thiemann T. and Winkler, O. (2001), 'Coherent states for canonical quantum general relativity and the infinite tensor product extension', *Nucl. Phys.* **B606**, 401–440.

[14] *Fock states in the polymer picture*

Varadarajan, M. (2000), 'Fock representations from U(1) holonomy algebras', *Phys. Rev.* **D61**, 104001.

Varadarajan, M. (2001), 'Photons from quantized electric flux representations', *Phys. Rev.* **D64** 104003.

Ashtekar, A. and Lewandowski, J. (2001), 'Relation between polymer and Fock excitations', *Class. Quant. Grav.* **18**, L117–L127.

24

Topology change in quantum gravity

Fay Dowker

Queen Mary and Westfield College London

24.1 Introduction

The challenge facing anyone giving a talk in celebration of Stephen Hawking's contributions to physics is to convey something of the epic breadth of his work in a very short time. The subject of topology change in quantum gravity provides an opportunity to do just that. Topology change is not only a subject to which Stephen has directly made many seminal contributions but also one which, looked at from a particular point of view, weaves together several major themes of his work over the years. This is the point of view I will describe.

The framework for topology change I will set out exists in what might be called a 'top down' approach to quantum gravity. By this I mean that we take what we know – general relativity, continuum spacetime, quantum field theory and so forth – and try to put them together as best we can, preserving as much structure as possible. Most workers in the field believe that this approach will not, ultimately, be adequate for quantum gravity and that we will need a new 'bottom up' theory for which we postulate new fundamental structures and principles and in which continuum spacetime is an emergent phenomenon. Of course it may turn out that the rules we now choose to apply to our top down calculations will be shown to be wrong when we have the underlying theory of quantum gravity; there is that risk, but as a strategy it seems unavoidable. How could we hope to deduce the new principles completely unguided? We proceed in the hope that our top down calculations are giving us clues in our search for the correct bottom up theory. And contrariwise, our beliefs about the eventual form of the bottom up theory will inform the choices we must make in those top down calculations. There's a rich and complicated process of cross-influence involved in the whole endeavour.

In this spirit, we can hope that topology change will be a particularly fruitful area to study, since it is generally believed that it does not occur in classical general relativity and so would be a genuinely quantum phenomenon – one in which the underlying theory must leave its indelible mark in the realm of the continuum.

I have not attempted to give a comprehensive set of references but have tended to cite papers where more details can be found on some of the main arguments.

24.2 A top down framework for topology change

What we will mean by a topology change is a spacetime based on an n-dimensional manifold, M, with an initial spacelike $n-1$ dimensional hypersurface, Σ_0, and a final spacelike hypersurface, Σ_1, not diffeomorphic to Σ_0. For simplicity in what follows we take Σ_0 and Σ_1 to be closed and M compact so that the boundary of M is the disjoint union of Σ_0 and Σ_1. This restriction means effectively that we're studying topology changes that are localized. For example, a topology change from $\mathbb{R}^3$ to $\mathbb{R}^3$ with a handle – an $S^2 \times S^1$ – attached can be reduced to the compact case because infinity in both cases is topologically the same. On the other hand, a topology change from $\mathbb{R}^3 \times C$ to $\mathbb{R}^3 \times C'$ where C and C' are two non-diffeomorphic Calabi–Yau's, say, will not be able to be accommodated in the current scheme because it involves a change in the topology of infinity.

Following Stephen [1, 2], I prefer the Sum Over Histories (SOH) approach to quantum gravity which can be summarized in the following formula for the transition amplitude between the Riemannian metric h_0 on $(n-1)$-manifold Σ_0 and the Riemannian metric h_1 on $(n-1)$-manifold Σ_1:

$$\langle h_1 \Sigma_1 | h_0 \Sigma_0 \rangle = \sum_M \int_g [dg] \omega(g) . \tag{24.1}$$

The sum is over all n-manifolds, M, called cobordisms – whose boundary is the disjoint union of Σ_0 and Σ_1 and the functional integral is over all metrics on M that restrict to h_0 on Σ_0 and h_1 on Σ_1. Each metric contributes a weight, $\omega(g)$, to the amplitude and we'll hedge our bets for now on the type of metrics in the integral and hence the precise form of the weight.

It's clear from this that the SOH framework lends itself to the study of topology change as it readily accommodates the inclusion of topology changing manifolds in the sum. Despite the fact that we may not be able to turn (24.1) into a mathematically well-defined object within the top down approach, if even the basic form of this transition amplitude is correct then we can already draw some conclusions. We can say that a topology change from Σ_0 to Σ_1 can only occur if there is at least one manifold that interpolates between them, in other words if they are cobordant. This does not place any restriction on topology change in 3+1 spacetime dimensions since all closed 3-manifolds are cobordant, but it does in all higher dimensions: not all closed 4-manifolds are cobordant, for example. We can also say that even if cobordisms exist, there must also exist appropriate metrics on at least one cobordism and so we come to the question of what the metrics should be. There are many possibilities and just three are listed here.

1. Euclidean (i.e., positive definite signature) metrics. This choice is of course closely associated with Stephen and the whole programme of Euclidean quantum gravity [3]. It is to this tradition and to Stephen's influence that I attribute my enduring belief that topology change does occur in quantum gravity. Indeed, Euclidean (equivalently, Riemannian) metrics exist on any cobordism and it would seem perverse to exclude different topologies from the SOH.

2. Lorentzian (i.e., $(-, +, +, \ldots +)$ signature) metrics. With this choice we are forced, by a theorem of Geroch [4], to contemplate closed timelike curves (CTCs or time machines). Geroch proved that if a Lorentzian metric exists on a topology changing cobordism then it must contain CTCs or be time non-orientable. Stephen has been at the forefront of the study of these causal pathologies, formulating his famous Chronology Protection Conjecture [5] (see also Matt Visser's contribution to this volume). Stephen and Gary Gibbons also proved that requiring an $SL(2, \mathbb{C})$ spin structure for fundamental fermi fields on a Lorentzian cobordism produces a further restriction on allowed topology changing transitions [6, 7].

3. Causal metrics. By this I mean metrics that give rise to a well-defined 'partial order' on the set of spacetime events. A partial order is a binary relation, $\prec$, on a set P, with the properties:

   (i) transitivity: $(\forall x, y, z \in P)(x \prec y \prec z \Rightarrow x \prec z)$;

   (ii) irreflexivity: $(\forall x \in P)(x \not\prec x)$.

A Lorentzian metric provides a partial order via the identification $x \prec y \Leftrightarrow x \in J^-(y)$, where the latter condition means that there's a future directed curve from x to y whose tangent vector is nowhere spacelike (a 'causal curve'), so long as the metric contains no closed causal curves. (J^- is conventionally defined so that $x \in J^-(x)$, so strictly one must remove these relations before this is a partial order as we have defined.) The information contained in the order $\prec$ is called the 'causal structure' of the spacetime. By Geroch's theorem, we know there are no Lorentzian metrics on a topology changing cobordism that give rise to a well-defined causal structure. But, there are metrics on any cobordism which are Lorentzian *almost everywhere* which do [8]. These metrics avoid Geroch's theorem by being degenerate at a finite number of points but the causal structure at the degenerate points is nevertheless meaningful. Describing these metrics will be the job of the next section.

We will plump for choice 3, causal metrics, in what follows. There are many reasons to do so but the one I would highlight is that it is the choice that fits in with a particular proposal for the underlying theory, namely causal set theory, in which it is the causal structure of spacetime, over all its other properties, that is primary and will persist at the fundamental level. We will return to causal sets later. This choice, of causal spacetimes in the SOH, cannot be deduced logically from any top down considerations. It is a choice informed by a vision of what kind of theory quantum gravity will be when we have it.

24.3 Morse metrics and elementary topology changes

Morse theory gives us a way of breaking a cobordism into a sequence of elementary topology changes [8–10]. On any cobordism M there exists a Morse function, $f : M \to [0, 1]$, with $f|_{\Sigma_0} = 0$, $f|_{\Sigma_1} = 1$ such that f possesses a set of critical points $\{p_k\}$ where $\partial_a f|_{p_k} = 0$ and the Hessian, $\partial_a \partial_b f|_{p_k}$, is invertible. These critical points, or Morse points, of f are isolated and, because M is compact, there are finitely many of them. The index, λ_k, of each Morse point, p_k is the number of negative eigenvalues of the Hessian at p_k. It is the number of maxima in the generalized saddle point at p_k if f is interpreted as a height function. For spacetime dimension n, there are $n+1$ possible values for the indices, $(0, 1, \dots n)$. A cobordism with a single Morse point is called an elementary cobordism.

Three elementary cobordisms for $n = 2$ are shown in Figure 24.1. They are the $\lambda = 2$ yarmulke in which a circle is destroyed, the $\lambda = 1$ trousers in which two circles join to form a single circle and the $\lambda = 0$ time reverse of the yarmulke in which a circle is created from nothing. (The upside-down trousers is in fact also a $\lambda = 1$ elementary cobordism: locally the Morse point looks the same as the regular trousers with one maximum and one minimum.) For higher spacetime dimensions, n, the generalizations of these are easy to visualize: the index n yarmulke (or its time reverse of index 0) is half an n-sphere, the index 1 trousers (or its time reverse of index $n-1$) is an n-sphere with three balls deleted creating three S^{n-1} boundaries. For $n > 3$ qualitatively different types of Morse point exist with at least two maxima and two minima, i.e., $\lambda \neq 0, 1, n-1, n$. These are impossible to draw but we will encounter some examples in the next section.

Using a Morse function, f, on M we can construct 'Morse metrics' which are Lorentzian everywhere except at the Morse points where they are zero. The precise form is not important here, but roughly the Morse function is used as a time function as you'd expect. These Morse metrics are our candidates for inclusion in the SOH for quantum gravity.

Now, there is important counter-evidence to the claim that topology change occurs in quantum gravity. This is work that shows that the expectation value of the energy-momentum tensor of a massless scalar field propagating on a $1+1$ Morse trousers is singular along the future light cone of the Morse point [11, 12]. In addition, one can look instead at the in–out matrix element of the energy momentum tensor and one finds a singularity along both the future and past light cones of the Morse point (calculation described in [8]). This last result in particular, if it can be extended to all Morse metrics on the $1+1$ trousers, can be taken to suggest that in the full SOH expression for the transition amplitude, integrating out over the scalar field first will leave an expression for the effective action for g that is infinitely sensitive to fluctuations in g. Thus, destructive interference between nearby metrics will suppress the contribution of any metric on the trousers. To be sure, this is a heuristic argument that would need to be strengthened but suppose it is valid. Would this mean, as DeWitt has argued, that all topology change is suppressed? The answer is not necessarily, especially if the following two conjectures hold.

The first conjecture is based on the idea that it is a certain property, called 'causal discontinuity', of the causal structure of the $1+1$ trousers

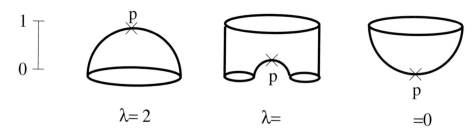

Fig. 24.1. Three elementary cobordisms for $n = 2$ and $\lambda = 2, 1, 0$: the yarmulke, trousers and time-reverse of the yarmulke.

that is the origin of the bad behaviour of quantum fields on it. So the conjecture (Sorkin) is that quantum fields will be singular on causally discontinuous spacetimes but well-behaved on causally continuous spacetimes. The second conjecture (Borde and Sorkin) is that only Morse metrics containing index 1 or $n-1$ points (trousers type) are causally discontinuous.

So what is causal discontinuity? When I was first learning about these things I was excited to discover that Stephen himself invented the concept in work with R. K. Sachs [13]. That paper is a piece of hard mathematical physics but there is a physically intuitive way of understanding the concept. Roughly, a spacetime is causally discontinuous if the causal past, or future, of a point changes discontinuously as the point is moved continuously in spacetime. We can see from Figure 24.2 that it is very plausible that the $1+1$ trousers is causally discontinuous: an observer down in one of the legs will have a causal past that is contained only in that leg, but as the observer moves up into the waist region, as they pass the future light cone of the Morse point, their causal past will suddenly get bigger and include a whole new region contained in the other leg. Interestingly, Stephen and R. K. Sachs conclude their paper by saying, '[T]here is some reason, but no fully convincing argument, for regarding causal continuity as a basic macrophysical property'. Which view ties in nicely with the first of the two conjectures.

24.4 Good and bad topology change

If we assume the two conjectures of the previous section hold, and that the argument about the consequent suppression of causally discontinuous

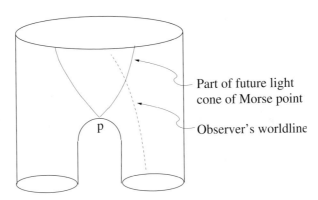

Fig. 24.2. The $1+1$ trousers with part of the future light cone of the Morse point, p. The other part goes up the back. The past light cone of the Morse point also has two parts, one down each leg.

metrics in the SOH is valid, the implication is that cobordisms which admit only Morse metrics containing index 1 and/or $n - 1$ points will be suppressed in the sum over manifolds. We can use this to draw conclusions about many interesting topology changing processes in quantum gravity. They divide into 'good' ones that can occur and 'bad' ones that do not. The results in this section and the next are taken from a series of papers on topology change [14–17].

Good processes include the pair production of black holes of different sorts in a variety of scenarios worked on by many people including Stephen (see the contribution by Simon Ross in this volume). For example, in 4 spacetime dimensions, the manifold of the instanton that is used to calculate the non-extremal black hole pair production rate [18] admits a Morse function with a single index 2 Morse point. The pair production of Kaluza–Klein monopoles [19] is also good, as is the nucleation of spherical bubbles of Kaluza–Klein $(n-5)$-branes in magnetic fluxbrane backgrounds [20]. The decay of the Kaluza–Klein vacuum [21] is good, which is slightly disappointing: one might have hoped that it would be stabilized by these considerations. We know, however, that the cobordism for KK vacuum decay is the same as that for pair production of KK monopoles [22] and so if the latter is a good process so must the former be.

The Big Bang, or creation of an $(n - 1)$-sphere from nothing via the yarmulke, is good. Notice that in this way of treating topology change as a sequence of elementary changes, the universe, if created from nothing, must start off as a sphere. No other topology is cobordant to the empty set via an elementary cobordism. The conifold transition in string theory [23] where a three-cycle shrinks down to a point and blows up again as a two-cycle is good. Indeed, the shrinking and blowing up process traces out the seven-dimensional cobordism (each stage of the process is a level surface of a corresponding Morse function) and the fact that it is a three-cycle that degenerates and a two-cycle that blows up tells us that the index of the cobordism is three.

Bad topology changes include spacetime wormholes where an S^3 baby universe is born by branching off a parent universe, the epitome of a trousers cobordism. Stephen founded the study of baby universes and spacetime wormholes [24] within the Euclidean quantum gravity framework where our present considerations do not apply. However, if one takes the view that Euclidean solutions – instantons – are to be thought of as devices for calculating transition amplitudes which are nevertheless defined as sums over real, causal, spacetimes, then the badness of the trousers would be counterevidence for the relevance of spacetime wormholes.

Another bad topology change is the pair production or annihilation of topological geons, particles made from non-trivial spatial topology. This deals a serious blow to the hope that the processes of pair production and annihilation of geons could restore to geons the spin-statistics correlation that they lack if their number is fixed [25].

In $1 + 1$ and $2 + 1$ spacetime dimensions, all topology changes except for the yarmulkes and their time-reverses are bad ones. This raises the question, is this not in conflict with string theory and the finiteness of topology changing amplitudes in $2 + 1$ quantum gravity [26]? For the former, Lenny Susskind has argued that the the infinite burst of energy when a loop of string splits into two can be absorbed as a renormalization of the string coupling constant [27]. Martin Roček takes an alternative view, that in first quantized string theory, choosing to integrate over causal metrics on the world sheet would be analogous to choosing paths in the SOH for relativistic quantum mechanics that move only forward in time which would be inconsistent [28]. In the latter case, it seems that in the first order, frame-connection formalism suitable for $2+1$ gravity, topology change can occur even as a classical process since the relationship between the frame and connection is an equation of motion and can hold even at points where the frame is degenerate [29]. In this case, it is no surprise that quantum amplitudes for topology changing processes in $2+1$ gravity are non-zero. In fact, it becomes something of a puzzle why we do not see topology change on macroscopic scales all the time if it is an allowed classical process. It would seem that the first order formalism and the metric formalism are genuinely different theories of gravity and distinguishing between them might be an observational issue.

24.5 Progress on the Borde–Sorkin conjecture

Having looked at some of the consequences of the conjectures, we can ask how plausible they are. There is fragmentary evidence for the conjecture that causal discontinuity leads to badly behaved quantum fields but causally continuous topology changes allow regular quantum field behaviour [8, 30]. A key investigation that needs to be done is of quantum field theory on a four-dimensional spacetime with an index 2 point, which is conjectured to be regular.

On the other hand we are well on the way to proving the Borde–Sorkin conjecture that Morse spacetimes are causally continuous if and only if they contain no index 1 or $n - 1$ points. I will sketch the basic ideas involved in the progress made to date.

If we think about the causal structure around the Morse point, p, of the $1 + 1$ trousers, it seems intuitive that the causal past of p should contain two separate parts, one down each 'leg' of the trousers. And the causal future of the Morse point also divides into two lobes, one up the front and one up the back of the trousers. It's also intuitive that the causal discontinuities of the $1+1$ trousers should be related to the disconnectedness of the causal past and future of p in the neighbourhood of p. Flattening out the crotch region, we should obtain a causal structure that looks like that shown in Figure 24.3. There is a special metric for the $1+1$ trousers in which the causal structure can be proved to be exactly as shown: the past (future) of the Morse point p consists of the two regions P_1 and P_2 (F_1 and F_2).

There are two types of causal discontinuity here. The first type is when an observer starting in P_1, say, crosses the past light cone of p into S_1, say. As it does so the causal future of the observer, which at first contains regions in both F_1 and F_2, jumps so that it no longer contains any points in F_2. The second type is when an observer in S_1, say, crosses the future light cone of p into F_1. As this happens, the causal past of the observer which contained no points in P_2 suddenly grows to contain a whole new region in P_2.

The special metric in which this behaviour can be demonstrated exactly generalizes to higher dimensions and all Morse indices. For dimension n and index $\lambda \neq 0, n$ (no yarmulkes for now), the causal past and future of p are obtained from Figure 24.3 by rotating it around the x-axis by $SO(n-\lambda)$ and around the y-axis by $SO(\lambda)$. We see that when $\lambda = 1$ the past of p remains in two disconnected pieces and when $\lambda = n-1$ the

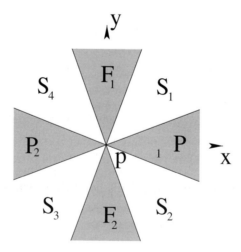

Fig. 24.3. The causal structure in the neighbourhood of the Morse point, p, of the $1+1$ trousers. The past (future) of p consists of the two regions P_1 and P_2 (F_1 and F_2). The 'elsewhere' of p divides into four regions $S_1, \ldots S_4$.

future of p remains in two pieces. But when $\lambda \neq 1, n-1$ then both the future and past of p become connected sets.

These suggestive pictures can be turned into a proof that, for these special metrics, index 1 and $n-1$ Morse points produce causal discontinuities and the other indices do not. We can further show that, not just these special metrics, but any index 1 and $n-1$ Morse metric is causally discontinuous. It is also true that any Morse metric on the yarmulke is causally continuous. It remains to be proved that any Morse metric on a $\lambda \neq 0, 1, n-1, n$ elementary cobordism is causally continuous.

24.6 Looking to the future

I will end by speculating on possible implications that these results might have for a particular proposal for quantum gravity, namely causal set theory, the approach championed by Rafael Sorkin [31–33]. The basic hypothesis is that the underlying fundamental substructure of spacetime is a discrete object called a causal set, which is, roughly, a Planck density random sampling of the causal structure of spacetime. Mathematically, a causal set, C, is a partial order (thus it satisfies the conditions of transitivity and irreflexivity given previously) which is also 'locally finite' meaning that the set $\{z \in C : x \prec z \prec y\}$ has finite cardinality for all pairs of points x and y in C.

How could a causal set hope to be the basic stuff of spacetime? How could such a truly discrete entity, with not a real number in sight, underlie a continuum spacetime with its topology, differential structure and metric? The answer lies in work by Stephen and others that shows that for Lorentzian manifolds satisfying a certain causality condition (marginally stronger than the absence of closed causal curves) the causal structure determines the metric up to an overall conformal factor. Since this result is not as well known as it should be, I'll give a few details here. Stephen proved that if (M, g) and (M', g') are Lorentzian spacetimes and $f : M \rightarrow M'$ is a homeomorphism where f and f^{-1} preserve future directed continuous null geodesics then f is a smooth conformal isometry [34]. Malament used this result to show that if (M, g) and (M', g') are past and future distinguishing spacetimes (this condition means that distinct points have non-equal pasts and futures) and $F : M \rightarrow M'$ is a bijection such that $x \in I^+(y)$ if and only if $F(x) \in I^+(F(y))\ \forall x, y \in M$, then F is a smooth conformal isometry [35]. Finally one can show that a bijection that preserves the causal structure, J^+ (*i.e.* $F : M \rightarrow M'$ such that $x \in J^+(y)$ if and only if $F(x) \in J^+(F(y))\ \forall x, y \in M$) also preserves the chronological structure I^+ when the spacetimes are distinguishing [36]. Notice that in the final form of the result, the bijection is not required even to be continuous or have any properties apart from being causal structure preserving.

Given this powerful result, it seems plausible, even reasonable to suppose that a Planck scale 'discretization' of the causal structure should encode all information about a spacetime at length scales above the Planck length. The missing conformal factor, or volume information, is fixed by making the correspondence that the volume of a region counts the number of causal set elements contained in the region.

The causal set hypothesis is both conservative and radical. It is conservative in that it takes the belief that many workers in quantum gravity hold that spacetime is discrete at the fundamental level and the theorem that causal structure is nearly all the metric and puts them together in the most obvious way: the underlying structure is a discretization of the causal structure. The hypothesis then ties up, in a most satisfying way, the question of how the remaining spacetime information is provided, because the correspondence of Volume $\sim$ Number can only be made due to the discreteness of the causal set. The details of the hypothesis include the prototype of a solution to the knotty problem of how to discretize spacetime whilst maintaining local Lorentz invariance, which solution – roughly that the discretization is random – is conjectured by Sorkin to be essentially unique. Causal set theory is nevertheless radical because it proposes that, fundamentally, there is only a local finitude with a partial order. Dimension, manifold, topology, differentiable structure, spacetime metric, spacetime causal structure, perhaps also matter, would all be unified in terms of order. To whet the appetite even further, let me mention that causal set theory was used to make a surprising prediction which has subsequently been verified by observation: namely a prediction of the current order of magnitude of a non-zero cosmological constant [32, 33, 37].

Could the picture of topology change I have sketched tell us anything about causal set calculations or vice versa? To see how it could, I will discuss two examples.

One is the process of black hole evaporation which Stephen discovered, the understanding of which is going to play a key role in the development of any successful theory of quantum gravity. As far as the continuum theory goes, the nearest we can come to a spacetime description of black hole formation and evaporation is the conjectured Carter–Penrose diagram shown in Figure 24.4. What could be the description in quantum gravity of this crucial process? One motivation for Stephen's study of baby universes was that a spacetime wormhole, or trousers, was the most obvious candidate for a spacetime description in the Euclidean approach, with the matter falling into and the radiation emitted from the black hole residing in the baby universe. The approach we have taken here, however,

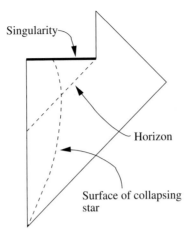

Fig. 24.4. The Carter–Penrose conformal diagram of the formation and evaporation of a black hole.

suggests that trousers cannot occur and so we must look for a different description.

According to the causal set hypothesis, the underlying reality is a causal set, we know that much. Where we have a continuum description, the causal set must be manifold-like and where the continuum description breaks down, close to the singularity, the causal set will have no continuum approximation and only the causal set itself will be a good description of what is happening there. We don't yet have a quantum dynamics for causal sets but we do have a family of physically motivated 'warm up' dynamical models to play with. These are classical, stochastic models in which a causal set grows, element by element, in a probabilistic way that respects (the discrete versions of) general covariance and classical causality, the 'Rideout-Sorkin' (RS) models [38]. Joe Henson has proved that in these RS models every element in a causal set almost surely has an element to its future, with the corollary that every point has an infinite future set [39]. This result might be called, 'Causal Immortality'.

If this prediction persists in the quantum theory of causal sets we will then know what to expect in a causal set description of black hole formation and evaporation. The causal set will have a continuum approximation corresponding to almost all of the Carter–Penrose conformal diagram but close to the singularity the causal set will cease to be manifold-like. It won't, however, end there: the causal set will extend on into the future. It's possible that the part of the causal set that is 'born' in the singularity will continue to be non-manifold-like forever but, alternatively, it may become manifold-like again. (Note, these words 'continue', 'forever' and 'become' are merely suggestive, they are not supposed to imply a physically meaningful background 'time'.) In the latter case it would then be a 'baby universe', disconnected from the region in which the black hole formed and evaporated, though not a baby universe created by a continuum wormhole.

It is tempting to speculate yet further that this might realize something like Smolin's idea of cosmological natural selection [40], with new universes with different coupling constants being created, not inside black holes but when black holes evaporate. The causal structure of the black hole singularity in the formation-evaporation spacetime would be the following. If the singularity represents a single causal set point s and if $F(s) = \{x \in C : s \prec x\}$ is the future set of s, then any point $x \in F(s)$ would have the property that a point related to x must be related to s. This says that nothing can influence the future of s except through s and means that s is a so-called 'partial post' as far as $F(s)$ is concerned (a 'post' is a point in a causal set to which all points in the set are related). Now, posts are responsible for a cosmological renormalization of the coupling constants which characterize the dynamics of causal sets, at least in the classical RS models [41, 42] and it seems that a similar renormalization would take place when there's a partial post.

The second example is an investigation into how causal discontinuity might be ruled out by causal set dynamics. First we need a characterization of causal discontinuity in terms of the causal order alone. This might be done by looking at the various equivalent conditions for causal discontinuity in the continuum that Stephen and R. K. Sachs have provided [13]. Alternatively, thinking about causal sets that arise by randomly sampling causally discontinuous spacetimes, it seems that one possible characteristic that they share is the existence of an element x, which has a (past or future) relation, which if severed would make a big change in the size of the past or future set of x. One would have to make this more precise but intuitively it seems to make sense. Then one would hope to be able to predict that causal sets with such a property do not occur. This would have to be done in the, as yet unknown, quantum theory of causal sets but to see broadly how it might work we could ask whether we are able make such a prediction in the RS models. In these models, one can prove things like Henson's result that every point has a future relation. Graham Brightwell has also shown that an infinite antichain (an antichain is a totally unordered subset) almost surely doesn't occur [39]. It seems possible that one could prove something like 'the probability that a point x will have a future set which has a large subset which will be cut off from x by the severing of a single relation is zero'.

So, for the future, there is much to be done on the specific conjectures mentioned, in order to put this whole approach to topology change on a firmer footing. And for the broader picture, I think that things look very interesting and promising for the causal set approach to quantum gravity. Although Stephen has not worked directly on this area, his work on global causal analysis is one of the crucial underpinnings of the programme. His work is central to the proof that the causal structure of a spacetime encodes most of the information about that spacetime. He has also been one of the main proponents of the Sum Over Histories approach to quantum gravity that will be at the heart of developments on a quantum dynamics for causal sets. This is because a causal set has an essentially 'spacetime' character: it's hard to see how one could make any headway with an attempt at the space+time split required for a canonical quantization for example. In a sense, causal sets provide an explanation for Stephen's Chronology Protection Conjecture because one can 'predict' that there will be no CTCs (this is slightly more than a case of simply assuming what we want to prove – the irreflexivity condition on the causal set can be dropped but a spacetime with CTCs will nevertheless never be an approximation to a transitive digraph even when it has closed loops [43]). Of course, Stephen's work on black hole thermodynamics will have a major role to play in any proposed theory of quantum gravity but it is particularly important in causal set theory since one of the main motivations for believing in an underlying screte structure at all is the finiteness of the black hole entropy [37]. Altogether, it wouldn't be going too far to say that the influence of Stephen's work can be seen in the very foundations of the causal set approach. I hope there will be some successes of causal set theory to report for Stephen's 70th birthday.

References

[1] Hawking, S. W. (1978), 'Quantum gravity and path integrals', *Phys. Rev.* **D18** 1747–1753.

[2] Hawking, S. W. (1978), 'Space-time foam', *Nucl. Phys.* **B144** 349–362.

[3] Gibbons, G. W. and Hawking, S. W. eds (1993) *Euclidean Quantum Gravity* (World Scientific, Singapore).

[4] Geroch, R. (1967), 'Topology in general relativity', *J. Math. Phys.* **8** 782.

[5] Hawking, S. W. (1992), 'The chronology protection conjecture', *Phys. Rev.* **D46** 603–611.

[6] Gibbons, G. W. and Hawking, S. W. (1992), 'Selection rules for topology change', *Commun. Math. Phys.* **148** 345–352.

[7] Gibbons, G. W. and Hawking, S. W. (1992), 'Kinks and topology change', *Phys. Rev. Lett.* **69** 1719–1721.

[8] Sorkin, Rafael D. (1990), 'Consequences of space-time topology', in A. Coley, F. Cooperstock, and B. Tupper, eds, *Proceedings of the third Canadian Conference on General Relativity and Relativistic Astrophysics, Victoria, Canada, May 1989* (World Scientific, Singapore) pp. 137–163.

[9] Yodzis, P. (1973), Lorentz cobordisms. *Gen. Rel. Grav.* **4** 299.

[10] Alty, L. J. (1995), 'Building blocks for topology change', *J. Math. Phys.* **36** 3613–3618.

[11] Anderson, A. and Dewitt, B. (1986), 'Does the topology of space fluctuate?', *Found. Phys.* **16** 91–105.

[12] Manogue, C. A., Copeland, E. and Dray, T. (1988), 'The trousers problem revisited', *Pramana* **30** 279.

[13] Hawking, S. W. and Sachs, R. K. (1974), 'Causally continuous spacetimes', *Comm. Math. Phys.* **35** 287–296.

[14] Dowker, H. F. and Garcia, R. S. (1998), A handlebody calculus for topology change. *Class. Quant. Grav.* **15** 1859–1879.

[15] Dowker, F. and Surya, S. (1998), 'Topology change and causal continuity', *Phys. Rev.* **D58** 124019.

[16] Borde, A., Dowker, H. F., Garcia, R. S., Sorkin, R. D. and Surya, S. (1999), 'Causal continuity in degenerate spacetimes', *Class. Quant. Grav.*, **16** 3457–3481.

[17] Dowker, H. F., Garcia, R. S. and Surya, S. (2000), 'Morse index and causal continuity: A criterion for topology change in quantum gravity', *Class. Quant. Grav.* **17** 697–712.

[18] Garfinkle, D. and Strominger, A. (1991), 'Semiclassical wheeler wormhole production', *Phys. Lett.* **B256** 146–149.

[19] Dowker, F., Gauntlett, J. P., Giddings, S. B. and Horowitz, G. T. (1994), 'On pair creation of extremal black holes and Kaluza–Klein monopoles', *Phys. Rev.* **D50** 2662–2679.

[20] Dowker, F., Gauntlett, J. P., Gibbons, G. W. and Horowitz, G. T. (1996), 'Nucleation of *p*-branes and fundamental strings', *Phys. Rev.* **D53** 7115–7128.

[21] Witten, E. (1982), 'Instability of the Kaluza–Klein vacuum', *Nucl. Phys.* **B195** 481.

[22] Dowker, F., Gauntlett, J. P., Gibbons, G. W. and Horowitz, G. T. (1995), 'The decay of magnetic fields in Kaluza–Klein theory', *Phys. Rev.* **D52** 6929–6940.

[23] Greene, B. R., Morrison, D. R. and Strominger, A. (1995), 'Black hole condensation and the unification of string vacua', *Nucl. Phys.* **B451** 109–120.

[24] Hawking, S. W. (1988), 'Wormholes in space-time', *Phys. Rev.* **D37** 904–910.

[25] Dowker, H. F. and Sorkin, R. D. (1998), 'A spin-statistics theorem for certain topological geons', *Class. Quant. Grav.* **15** 1153–1167.

[26] Witten, Edward (1989), 'Topology changing amplitudes in (2+1)-dimensional gravity', *Nucl. Phys.* **B323** 113.

[27] Susskind, L. (2002), Comment at this meeting, Cambridge.

[28] Roček, M. (2002), Private communication, Cambridge.

[29] Horowitz, G. T. (1991), 'Topology change in classical and quantum gravity', *Class. Quant. Grav.* **8** 587–602.

[30] Louko, J. and Sorkin, R. D. (1997), 'Complex actions in two-dimensional topology change', *Class. Quant. Grav.* **14** 179–204.

[31] Bombelli, L., Lee, J.-H., Meyer, D. and Sorkin, R. (1987), 'Space-time as a causal set', *Phys. Rev. Lett.* **59** 521.

[32] Sorkin, R. D. (1991), 'First steps with causal sets', in *Proceedings of the Ninth Italian Conference on General Relativity and Gravitational Physics, Capri, Italy, September 1990*, R. Cianci, R. de Ritis, M. Francaviglia, G. Marmo, C. Rubano and P. Scudellaro, eds, (World Scientific, Singapore) pp. 68–90.

[33] Sorkin, R. D (1991), 'Space-time and causal sets', in *Relativity and Gravitation: Classical and Quantum, Proceedings of the SILARG VII Conference, Cocoyoc, Mexico, December 1990*, J. C. D'Olivo, E. Nahmad-Achar, M. Rosenbaum, M. P. Ryan, L. F. Urrutia, and F. Zertuche, eds, (World Scientific, Singapore) pp. 150–173.

[34] Hawking, S. W. King, A. R. and McCarthy, P. J. (1976), 'A new topology for curved space-time which incorporates the causal, differential, and conformal structures', *J. Math. Phys.* **17** 174–181.

[35] Malament, D. B. (1977), 'The class of continuous timelike curves determines the topology of spacetime', *J. Math. Phys.* **18** 1399–1404.

[36] Levichev, A. V. (1987), 'Prescribing the conformal geometry of a Lorentz manifold by means of its causal structure', *Soviet Math. Dokl.* **35** 452–455.

[37] Sorkin, R. D. (1997), 'Forks in the road, on the way to quantum gravity', *Int. J. Theor. Phys.* **36** 2759–2781.

[38] Rideout, D. P. and Sorkin, R. D. (2000), 'A classical sequential growth dynamics for causal sets', *Phys. Rev.* **D61** 024002.

[39] Brightwell, G., Dowker, H. F., Garcia, R. S., Henson, J. J. and Sorkin, R. D. (2002), 'Generalized percolation', in preparation.

[40] Smolin, Lee (1992), 'Did the universe evolve?' *Class. Quant. Grav.* **9** 173–192.

452 Fay Dowker

[41] Sorkin, R. D. (2000), 'Indications of causal set cosmology', *Int. J. Theor. Phys.* **39** 1731–1736.

[42] Martin, X., O'Connor, D., Rideout, D. P. and Sorkin, R. D. (2001), 'On the 'renormalization' transformations induced by cycles of expansion and contraction in causal set cosmology', *Phys. Rev.* **D63** 084026.

[43] Sorkin, R. D. (1997), 'The causal set approach to quantum gravity'. Talk given at the Santa Fe Workshop, *New Directions in Simplicial Quantum Gravity, 28th July–8th August 1997*, [http://t8web.lanl.gov/people/emil/Slides/sf97talks.html].

Part 6

M theory and beyond

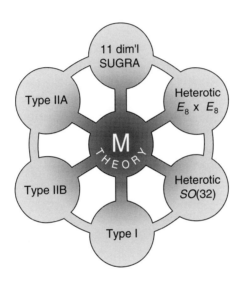

What are the prospects of obtaining a quantum theory of gravity and of unifying it with the other three categories of interactions? The best hope seems to lie in an extension of general relativity called supergravity.

Inaugural Lecture as Lucasian Professor, 1980

25

The past and future of string theory

Edward Witten

Institute for Advanced Study, Princeton

Once upon a time, there was the Fermi theory of weak interactions. The interaction Lagrangian contained four-fermi interactions such as the familiar interaction

$$L_{int} = \frac{G_F}{\sqrt{2}} \bar{e} \gamma_\alpha (1 - \gamma_5) \nu_e \bar{\nu}_\mu \gamma^\alpha (1 - \gamma_5) \mu$$

responsible for muon decay. In the tree level, it gave an excellent approximation. But the quantum corrections were infinite – the theory is 'unrenormalizable'.

One might have wondered if perturbative renormalizability was the right question. Might the Fermi theory makes sense non-perturbatively, even though in perturbation theory it has problems? But it turned out that making sense of perturbation theory was the right question. The answer was to modify the theory with a key new ingredient – non-Abelian gauge symmetry – and to incorporate a new physical idea – spontaneous symmetry breaking. With these plus important technical advances in quantization, it was possible to achieve perturbative renormalizability and to construct the modern theory of the electroweak interactions.

In the case of the strong interactions, there was a wealth of experimental data, much of it of high precision. Hadronic masses and magnetic moments, nuclear binding energies and transition rates, many things were measured with great accuracy. But the strongly interacting world was so complicated that most of the experimental data was hard to interpret. Only a fraction of the experimental knowledge of strong interactions, such as the scaling behaviour in deep inelastic electron–nucleon scattering, gave simple clues about the underlying quark–gluon world. As a result, experimental clues alone did not suffice. Finding the right theory – QCD – depended on interpreting the relatively few clear clues coming from experiment in the right theoretical framework. The key ingredients that were combined to construct QCD were

- experimental hints of quarks and color and simple short distance behavior;

- perturbative renormalizability;

- the newly recognized role of non-Abelian gauge symmetry.

The last point is worthy of some note. The effort to replace the Fermi theory of weak interactions with a renormalizable theory was not only necessary for understanding weak interactions. It also led to the uncovering of a new ingredient in nature – non-Abelian gauge symmetry – that was needed for further progress.

While helping find the right theory, was perturbation theory adequate for understanding it? For the weak interactions, the answer is 'yes' for most purposes, precisely because the weak interactions are weak. The most notable exception is the 't Hooft process of baryon number violation by weak instantons. This (or at least its high temperature analogue, which proceeds much faster) may conceivably eventually play a role in cosmology, together with other ingredients, in understanding the baryon asymmetry of the universe. Even here, to be able to perform this non-perturbative computation, a proper understanding of perturbation theory is a prerequisite.

In any event, regardless of how computations are done, for understanding and appreciating the electroweak theory, perturbation theory is not enough. The perturbative Feynman rules are a complicated looking contrivance if one does not understand where they come from. The beauty and understanding of the theory come from the underlying non-Abelian gauge theory Lagrangian with spontaneous symmetry breaking.

For the strong interactions, the answer is more complex. Perturbation theory, extended by 'asymptotic freedom', is adequate for understanding 'hard scattering', and thus convincing ourselves that the theory is right. But many of the most obvious observables – particle masses and magnetic moments, nuclear binding energies, scattering amplitudes – require non-perturbative methods.

One important non-perturbative method – lattice gauge theory with Monte Carlo integration – was developed relatively quickly. This has made it possible to demonstrate quark confinement rather convincingly, and to perform moderately accurate computations of particle masses and some other static properties. It has not yet led to precision computations of masses, or to computations of less accessible observables such as particle scattering amplitudes and nuclear binding energies.

Another presumably important non-perturbative method – the $1/N$ expansion, which might one day lead to an *understanding* of surprising properties of QCD such as quark confinement, and not just a silicon-based computation – remains out of reach 28 years after it was first proposed. The closest we have come to being able to implement the $1/N$ expansion is in the AdS/CFT correspondence, which is one of the most exciting recent themes in string theory. It has led to an understanding of the $1/N$ expansion for certain strongly coupled four-dimensional gauge theories. Still, we are far from understanding how to do this for QCD.

So in practice, after over a quarter century, because of the difficulty in developing non-perturbative methods, we are still unable to use QCD to answer many of the most obvious questions about hadrons. This is a case study in the need to be pragmatic in physics. One can well go astray if one has too much of a preconceived notion of where progress should come. One might, back in the 1950s, for example, have felt that the deuteron binding energy was such a fundamental strong interaction observable that one would evaluate a theory of strong interactions based on its success in computing the deuteron binding energy. But here we are in 2002; an attractive and convincing strong interaction theory emerged nearly three decades ago, and we still do not know how to compute the deuteron binding energy.

What about gravity? General relativity is a wonderful theory classically. One can well argue that it is our finest classical theory; for example, it is the only classical theory to which we devote conferences! But quantum mechanically, it is perturbatively unrenormalizable, like the Fermi theory of weak interactions.

It seems that this story partly replayed itself in the 1970s. It was found, unexpectedly and without anyone really having the concept for it, that the rules of perturbation theory can be changed in a way that makes relativistic quantum gravity inevitable rather than impossible. The change is made by replacing point particles by strings. Then Feynman graphs are replaced by Riemann surfaces, which are smooth – unlike the graphs, which have singularities at interaction vertices. The Riemann surfaces can degenerate to graphs in many different ways.

In field theory, the interactions occur at the vertices of a Feynman graph. By contrast, in string theory, the interaction is encoded globally, in the topology of a Riemann surface, any small piece of which is like any other. This is reminiscent of how non-linearities (in problems such as the self-dual Yang–Mills equations) are encoded globally in twistor theory.

Replacing particles by strings is a naive-sounding step, from which many other things follow. In fact, replacing Feynman graphs by Riemann surfaces has numerous consequences:

1. It eliminates the infinities from the theory. In fact, the infinities of perturbative quantum field theory arise when different interaction vertices in a Feynman graph coincide in spacetime. But the Riemann surface that substitutes for a Feynman graph in string theory has no interaction vertices, and so generates no infinities.

2. It greatly reduces the number of possible theories. Ordinary quantum field theories are distinguished from each other to a large extent by the choice of which interaction vertices one postulates, but in string theory there is no interaction vertex, and the interactions are determined once the free string is introduced. As a result, the various string theories have certain things in common; they generate gravity (which in this context means a theory that at long distances looks like general relativity), non-Abelian gauge symmetry, and supersymmetry. Of these, gravity and non-Abelian gauge symmetry were understood and found to be important in physics independently of their role in string theory. But supersymmetry was conceived partly because of its role in string theory, and we still do not know if it is right. About this, I will say more later.

3. It gives the first hint that string theory will change our notions of spacetime. In field theory, the interaction occurs at a distinguished spacetime event, the interaction vertex in the Feynman diagram. But in string theory the interaction vertex – and with it the notion of a spacetime event – is gone. String theory is a new kind of theory, based on new concepts of spacetime that we still do not really understand.

Just as in QCD, so also in gravity, many of the interesting questions cannot be answered in perturbation theory. In string theory, to understand the nature of the Big Bang, or the quantum fate of a black hole, or the nature of the vacuum state that determines the observed properties of the elementary particles, requires information beyond perturbation theory – information that is hard to come by, and that for the most part we still do not have. Perturbation theory is not everything. It is just the way the theory was discovered!

The limitation of the applicability of perturbation theory does not come from the fact that it might not converge, but from the fact that the asymptotic expansion that it furnishes might not be useful in the regime of interest. In fact, perturbation theory ordinarily does not converge. Even for the anharmonic oscillator, with Hamiltonian $H = p^2 + x^2 + \lambda x^4$, perturbation theory (with respect to λ) does not converge: it furnishes an asymptotic expansion. When, as is ordinarily the case, perturbation theory does not converge, it is interesting to ask whether it can be resummed, for example by a Borel resummation, to give the right answer. But even when this is the case, one never in practice carries out a computation for which perturbation theory is inadequate by computing and resumming the perturbation series. This is never feasible. When perturbation theory is inadequate, in other words when one is not in the realm of usefulness of the asymptotic expansion in question, one generally needs to find a different method. And this, as I have explained in the case of QCD, is often easier said than done.

Regardless of what it is useful for, where does the perturbation series of string theory come from? This is one of the big mysteries. For field theory, the Feynman diagrammatic expansion is obtained by perturbatively quantizing an underlying classical theory, which in the case of gravity would correspond to general relativity and the Einstein–Hilbert action. For string theory, we know the perturbation expansion, but we do not have the analogue of the Einstein–Hilbert action or the principle of equivalence that led Einstein to it. We can reasonably suspect that the stringy analogue of the Einstein–Hilbert action is even more subtle and beautiful than the Einstein–Hilbert action itself, by analogy with the fact that the stringy perturbation expansion is much more subtle and beautiful (and more interesting mathematically) than the field theory perturbation expansion. But we do not know what it is.

The fact that thirty years later, we still do not know where it all comes from is a clear statement of how far beyond anyone's conception string theory was when it began to fall from the sky around 1970.

Once again, we see the need to be pragmatic in physics. It is very surprising that humans stumbled on a method to generalize the perturbation expansion of relativistic quantum field theory without understanding how to generalize the underlying theory. This certainly seems like an unlikely event. But when good fortune comes our way, we have to take advantage of it, no matter how unlikely the source.

We can see how this story began, but it is very hard to guess where it may end. In thinking about the future, we almost inevitable think of the latest clues. The high points of the last decade were:

- the role of branes as non-perturbative excitations of string theory;

- the extension of the power of perturbative string theory via the idea of D-branes, and the role of D-branes in connecting gauge theory to gravity;

- the discovery of non-perturbative spacetime dualities unifying the string theories and describing their strong coupling behaviour;

- the recovery of Stephen Hawking's black hole entropy formula from microscopic counting of quantum states;

- the non-perturbative descriptions of string theory in some situations, via matrix models and the AdS/CFT correspondence.

There is certainly some redundancy in this list, as the different items are closely linked up. I suppose that if I had to isolate one item that might be particularly significant for the future, I might point to the links between gauge theory and gravity, and perhaps to the notion of holography, which enters in some of the known non-perturbative descriptions.

A decade earlier, the highlights (of the previous decade) had been:

- Green–Schwarz anomaly cancellation;

- the construction of the heterotic string;

- the exploration of conformal field theory as the basis of string perturbation theory;

- the emergence of semi-realistic, finite, elegant models of particle physics plus quantum gravity;

- non-perturbative 'worldsheet' dualities like T-duality and mirror symmetry, giving our first glimpses of non-classical phenomena that occur as a result of replacing Riemannian geometry by the new and little-understood stringy geometry.

A decade before, a summary of the highlights (again, of the previous decade) certainly would have to focus largely on the emergence of the Standard Model of particle physics. But looking at things more narrowly in terms of string theory, the highlights, apart from the discovery of the basics of the string, were the discovery and exploration of supersymmetry and supergravity. They were discovered at least in part because of their role in making it possible (originally in the Ramond model) to have fermions in string theory. Supergravity, in particular, was understood in the late 1970s and early 1980s as a long distance semiclassical limit of the string. Supergravity is a remarkably rich subject in its own right and was the subject of intense study in the decade following its discovery.

Looking ahead, I do not think I would have much more luck now in guessing where theoretical progress will come from in the next decade than I would have had ten or twenty years ago in anticipating those decades.

One could list the problems one would like to solve. But we do not usually get our druthers. As always, we have to take progress where it comes. If I would try to make any detailed theoretical predictions for the next decade, I would probably be wrong not only about the answers, but even about the questions! That is, I would probably be unable to guess the questions where important progress would be made.

There is only one big discovery that I can point to as having a reasonably big chance for this decade. That discovery is not in theory, but may be something we need even more. I do not know whether this discovery will be made, either, but at least I can say that there is a reasonable chance.

There probably will be big discoveries in theory, but I cannot guess where they may come from. However, because of clues such as the measured value of the weak mixing angle θ_W – which agrees very well with the prediction based on supersymmetric Grand Unified Theories – it is reasonable to hope that the coming decade may see the discovery of supersymmetry. The discovery will probably be made at Fermilab with the Tevatron (which should soon be running with significantly higher luminosity) or at CERN with the LHC (which should be operating after 2006, with significantly higher energy than we now have and with very high luminosity).

Experimental discovery of supersymmetry would be wonderful for all of us, and especially for Stephen – since in the last 20 years, no one has been more enthusiastic about supersymmetry than he has!

Discovery of supersymmetry would give string theory a big boost, since it would complete the triad of structures – gravity, gauge theory and supersymmetry – that emerge from perturbative string theory in much the same way. And it would put experimentalists back in the lead – maybe for an extended period – because the fact is that we do not have any convincing model of what the TeV superworld would look like in detail. The general idea of supersymmetry is very simple and clear, but the possible details of the TeV superworld are quite involved and unclear.

If we had a unique and convincing model of the TeV superworld, we would be more sure that supersymmetry is right, but we would have less to learn by exploring it.

If supersymmetry is discovered, the details of the masses and interactions of the supersymmetric particles will give priceless clues about physics at yet higher energies, maybe all the way back to, or near, the string scale. There will be so many new particles and interactions to explore that it will take decades, and it will not all be done at Fermilab, or the LHC.

To carry out this exploration, we will need the interest and support of society. To maintain this support, we will need to learn yet again from Stephen, who has done such a marvelous job of popularizing our science.

The search for and exploration of supersymmetry – 'a modification of Einstein's theory of spacetime to include quantum variables' – can definitely interest many people. But so far, for the most part, they do not know about it.

Acknowledgements

This work was supported in part by NSF Grant PHY-0070928. I also wish to thank the theory group at Caltech for its hospitality.

26

String theory

David Gross
University of California, Santa Barbara

26.1 Motivations for quantum gravity

The organizers of this wonderful conference asked me to give a critical review of the current status and the future prospects for progress in string theory and related areas of quantum gravity. A tall order, which is why the talk was announced for many months as 'TBA'. Then they changed it to string theory. Of course, all I want to do is give a few brief and general remarks aimed at the relativists in the crowd.

As I was a particle physicist, I first met Stephen rather late, in 1973. He does not remember because I did not meet him in person but rather in print. I remember it very well. I was at FermiLab during the summer of 1973 finishing a large version of a paper with Frank Wilczek on asymptotic freedom and QCD. I was very engrossed in that effort but someone told me there was a fascinating preprint in the preprint library entitled 'Black hole explosions'. It was indeed exciting, even though at that point I had not much interest in quantum gravity. This was really an enormously wonderful paper, which has indeed proved to be influential for all of us. That is the first time I met Stephen but I did not have much contact with him for many years. After all I was a particle physicist and particle physicists at the time did not think that thinking about quantum gravity made any sense at all. There was this enormous gap of 10^{19}GeV between quantum gravity and the physics we were interested in, where experiments were churning out marvelous things. Although gravity was a beautiful classical theory, quantum gravity seemed totally beyond reach.

I remember well a talk given by Johnny Wheeler when I first came to Princeton in 1969 or 1970. It was a presentation that rivals today's Powerpoint presentations, because he would give these colloquia with 70 different kinds of coloured chalk. It was a marvelous talk about quantum gravity and he said in no uncertain terms that the fundamental physics is at the Planck scale and all these particles that particle physicists were playing with are just long wavelength manifestations of Planck scale physics. My colleagues and I thought he was totally nuts!

Our attitude, in retrospect, I like to believe was quite sane. We were developing the Standard Model and there were tons of experimental data right in our immediate energy range of 10 GeV. The prospects were there, in fact were realized, of gaining a complete understanding of all the interactions that one could directly probe. This as you all know changed dramatically in the late 1970s, because we completed the Standard Model and we were being put in the exactly the same position that the general relativists had been for a long time; there were no interesting experiments.

There were other intellectual reasons why we ended up in the same camp. One of them has to do with the great success of thinking about unification and extrapolating the strength of the forces of nature to high energy. That extrapolation led to the prediction that the next scale of high energy physics was close to the Planck scale, and remains our strongest guide to the fact that the next threshold is likely to involve quantum gravity. So those of us who began to think about unification beyond the Standard Model could no longer ignore quantum gravity.

The second reason had more to do with Stephen. Particle physics in some sense stands halfway between relativity and condensed matter physics. In the cube of theories (see Figure 26.1), classical relativity occupies the front face, particle physics the upper face, condensed matter physics just one edge, which, as shown, has almost no intersection with relativity. Condensed matter physicists and relativists never talk, but we

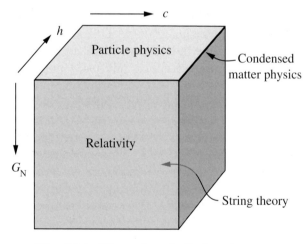

Fig. 26.1. The cube of all theories.

particle physicists talk to both communities. In fact, during the time when I grew up in the 1960s and early 1970s there were two main intellectual currents that influenced enormously the development of the Standard Model and its consequences. One was the concept of gauge symmetry, which turned out to underlie all the interactions of the Standard Model, and which provided the dynamical basis of electroweak and the strong interactions. The other idea came from condensed matter physics. It was the renormalization group, and the whole set of phenomenon connected with it, that profoundly affected particle physics as well as condensed matter physics. These are very different approaches and the attitude of these two communities to our left and to our right are quite different. I like to summarize these differing attitudes by the following descriptions:

> Particle physicists believe that from beauty there shall emerge garbage.

In other words, the basic laws of physics are based on symmetry principles, are simple and beautiful, and then all the complicated phenomena at large distances, the garbage, is messy and hard to calculate. At the other end of the spectrum we have the opposite viewpoint:

> Condensed matter physicists believe that from garbage there shall emerge beauty.

In this case, you start out with some complicated ugly system and then at a critical point at large distances, sometimes, you discover beautiful systems. This attitude still pervades and indeed there are condensed matter physicists who are alive who still believe in this and even believe that gravity will emerge from the critical behavior of some messy non-gravitational system. But most particle physicists fall into the first group and have much more intellectual companionship with general relativity than they do with condensed matter physics. In that respect, Stephen played an enormously important role in attracting a whole bunch of field theorists to think seriously about quantum gravity. His work on quantum gravity, for example the various techniques that Gary Gibbons reviewed so nicely a few days ago on the Euclidean path integral, meant that some of us could use the techniques that we had been playing around with in quantum field theory to address what were clearly important conceptual issues in gravity. We started to work on quantum gravity and, with the advent of string theory (which covers all the cube), the connections started getting stronger and stronger.

I got to know Stephen particularly well during a tour that I carried out with him in Japan about ten years ago as guests of NEC. They sponsored some public lectures that we delivered, and as a bonus gave us a fancy tour of Japan. It was interesting because when you travel with Stephen

you get to meet all sorts of people you would never meet otherwise –
he opens all sorts of doors for you. We didn't get to meet the Emperor,
which I regret, but we did get to meet somebody who I gather in Japan is
even more popular and more famous, that is, the Green Tea Master, and
we got to meet geisha girls, etc. But the most interesting experience was
once when Stephen, who as you know insists on experiencing everything,
insisted we all go to a karaoke bar one evening. He actually got us to get
up there and sing 'Yellow Submarine' which, if I were to try to reproduce,
you would run screeching from the room. Every time the chorus came up
Stephen would pipe in 'Yellow Submarine'; he probably still has a 'Yellow
Submarine' button that he can push!

26.2 The achievements of string theory

Now for the (perhaps) serious part–string theory. What has string theory
achieved? We do believe that string theory provides us with a real extension of the conceptual framework of physics. It is clearly an extension
in the sense that it is not encompassed by the conceptual framework we
use for the Standard Model including general relativity, which is based on
local quantum field theory. Some of us really do believe that this is not
just a small extension but a profound extension that is similar to other
ones we have experienced in the last century, but involving now the basic
unit of length. This is *the* extension that, when completed, will lead to a
full understanding of the physics at distances of order the Planck length.

From the point of view of general relativity the most important contribution of string theory is that it provides a consistent perturbative
theory of quantum gravity. Ed Witten yesterday stressed in great detail
the importance and limitations of the perturbative formulation of the theory. Although perturbation theory might not be sufficient for describing
all properties of the theory, the consistency and finiteness of the perturbative expansion is a major, major achievement. It is necessary for any
quantum theory of gravity to have a consistent asymptotic expansion,
otherwise both Einstein and Newton would be turning in their graves. So
this is an incredible achievement, but it's more than that. As we heard
and we'll hear more, string theory is now in the position based on that
very firm, consistent, and finite foundation to start to address some of the
tough conceptual issues that Stephen and his colleagues have brought so
forcefully to our attention, such as the properties of black holes.

Finally, of course, string theory does offer a structure that has all the
ingredients to complete the cube, to describe the world in all of its glory. In
recent years we have made a lot of progress in fleshing out the theory into
the non-perturbative domain and perhaps have made some progress in

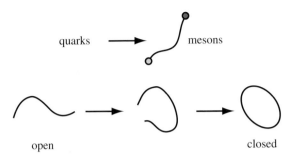

quarks → mesons

open ~ → closed

Fig. 26.2. A theory with open strings leads inevitably to one with closed strings.

completing the framework. Here, as for general relativity, the fact that we have so few experimental clues is a real handicap, but one that might be cured in the near future. Also the completion of the conceptual framework might be ultimately necessary to make contact with experiment in the absence of experimental clues.

I want to stress one very important aspect of string theory that has become more and more clear in the last few years, due to ideas of holography. That is the fact that string theory can be thought of as a theory of open strings. Originally when string theory was discovered, as Mike Green explained, people were trying to understand mesons, which behave as if they were flux tubes that look like strings. That's why string theory was discovered by doing hadronic phenomenology. However, even in the early days of string theory, closed strings were deduced by noticing that open strings could curl back and become closed (Figure 26.2). Technically, a quantum correction to open string physics, involving a loop of open strings, namely a diagram where an open string goes around in a loop, can be equally viewed as a closed string propagator. Thus, once one calculates quantum mechanical corrections to the propagation of open strings one finds closed strings. In this sense, people were led to closed strings and one can say that string theory predicts gravity.

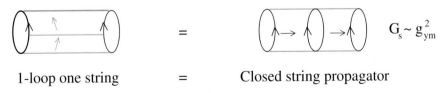

$$G_s \sim g_{ym}^2$$

1-loop one string = Closed string propagator

Fig. 26.3. Infrared–ultraviolet connection between closed and open strings.

This is the famous connection between the ultraviolet behaviour of open strings and the infrared presence of closed strings singularities or gravitons. From the very beginning, string theory could be thought of, and in fact developed that way, as a theory of open strings in which closed strings came out in the one-loop approximation. Not as bound states of some kind, but rather as due to this ultraviolet–infrared connection. In some sense the closed string particles, low energy particles like the graviton, are manifestations of the ultraviolet behaviour of the quantum mechanics of open strings.

This duality – this ultraviolet–infrared connection – has been made quite explicit in a holographic sense in the famous AdS/CFT correspondence (should we call it a theorem now?). Here there is a strict duality between a string theory, which at low energy is described by supergravity on AdS5 times an internal space and a four-dimensional gauge theory which, in a sense, lives on the boundary of the AdS5. Here one has a complete duality between a closed string theory or supergravity and a four-dimensional gauge theory, which is the low energy form of a theory of open strings. Open strings contain all the information you want about the closed string theory. There is one-to-one correspondence between the observable correlation functions of operators in the gauge theory in four-dimensions and the observables, the S-matrix say, of gravity in the bulk. This correspondence has proven to be of enormous value to us, because it allows us to learn a lot about gauge theories by using classical string theory; but also to learn a lot about string theory or gravity by using ordinary gauge theories, for example to count the number

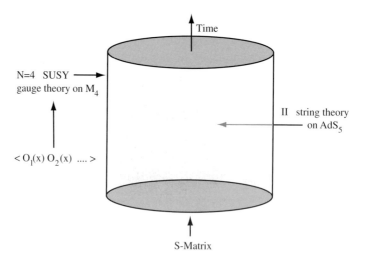

Fig. 26.4. The AdS-CFT correspondence.

of microstates of black holes, thus explaining the Beckenstein–Hawking entropy.

This ability to reformulate gravity(closed string theory) in terms of an underlying theory (gauge theory or open string theory), which is a lot easier to understand conceptually, is the beginning of a profound set of consequences, most of which have not yet been worked out. The advantages of the open string formulation or, if you want, the gauge theory formulation, is that the conceptual foundations and the nature of observables are absolutely clear. We are familiar with gauge theories, we have no doubt that they are unitary and described by Hamiltonian time evolution and that they are consistent; they are theories you could calculate to arbitrary precision if you had enough time and money.

The time evolution of black holes, for example, is now clearly resolved. You throw things into black holes and out comes Hawking radiation and information seems to be lost (Figure 26.5). One of Stephen's most influential mistakes was to insist that this meant that the laws of quantum mechanics are violated. This certainly motivated a lot of particle physicists, me as well, to work very hard to show that he was wrong. I think that it is fair to argue that string theory is beginning to succeed in that respect. In the case of AdS5 we can describe quantum gravity in terms of the theory on the boundary, which is an ordinary local quantum field theory governed by a unitary S-matrix. The information loss problem, once translated into this language, clearly will have a unitary solution. The precise details are hard to work out in detail and remain to be done for realistic black holes (or for any black hole for that matter). However,

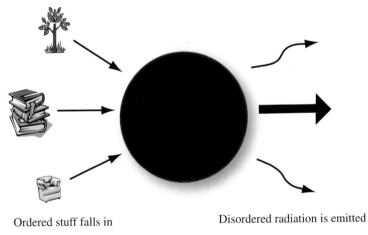

Ordered stuff falls in   Disordered radiation is emitted

Fig. 26.5. During black hole radiation, information appears to be lost.

there is a price to be paid. We have to give up something and that is the locality of bulk physics, which from my point of view is no big deal, though some people seem to be quite disturbed by it.

Thinking about quantum gravity in terms of the open string picture will undoubtedly look very different in other non-AdS backgrounds – we don't even know how to imitate the AdS5/CFT duality in flat space, not to speak of cosmological backgrounds. This is one of the big directions of study in the string theory and it will hopefully lead to an understanding of many of the paradoxes of general relativity.

26.3 The future of string theory

To predict the future of string theory is rather difficult. To predict what will happen in the next decade in string theory, as Ed Witten argued forcefully, is probably impossible, especially given the past surprises. But to predict very general things that will happen is not so difficult, and is somewhat trivial. I think there are perhaps three areas where many of us feel there will be conceptual revolutions. Revolutions that are hinted by string theory, but have not yet been fully realized. The first is the nature of spacetime, the second has to do with cosmology and the initial conditions of the universe, and the third has to do with quantum mechanics.

The nature of spacetime is the most likely place where we believe that a revolution in our concepts is about to take place. Even before string theory, many people believed that spacetime had to be modified at short distances. String theory gives us many clues as to why and how that might happen, but we are still far from truly understanding what can replace the classical picture of spacetime. There are a number of phenomena in string theory that strongly suggest that we have to give up our traditional notions of spacetime: the fact that you can change the number of dimensions by varying a coupling; the fact that that you can change topology continuously at the classical level in string theory; the fact that in string theory there is no way of probing arbitrarily short distances. Strings are large non-local objects themselves, therefore they cannot be used to probe short distances with arbitrary accuracy. The same is true if you try to squeeze small volumes to zero size, you just get back (via T-duality) to spaces of large size again.

All of these and many other aspects of string theory strongly suggest that space, at least, is not a primary concept. Indeed we have hints that space can be replaced by other degrees of freedom, based on holographic formulations of the theory (such as Matrix theory) in which space plays no fundamental role. Time, so far, continues to play the role it has always played, but we all know that if space goes, then time is not far behind.

The idea that closed strings (gravitons) are just an emergent feature of open string theory that appears at a quantum level, suggests that the whole notion of a dynamical spacetime manifold is not one that is primary in string theory, but rather an emergent concept. But how to replace spacetime by something else, and in a background independent setting, is one of the main problem of the field. I like to phrase this by paraphrasing Democritus who said, two and a half millennia, ago that:

> By convention there is color,
> by convention sweetness,
> by convention bitterness,
> but in reality there are atoms and space.

What we will eventually say is:

> By convention there is space,
> by convention there is time,
> but in reality there is ...

The initial conditions and the history of the universe are clearly an issue that faces any theory of quantum gravity, as Stephen and his colleagues have taught us. This is the place where string theory has a real chance of making contact with an important conceptual problem and maybe even conceivably with observation. String theory has a hope of dealing with the Big Bang and perhaps in explaining the initial conditions of the universe, because string theory is notoriously good at avoiding singularities. It does not tolerate singularities, it finds ways to reformulate the theory, in a dual non-singular description. The study of string theory in cosmological backgrounds is a hard problem, but clearly one in which much work will be done in the next few years. Whether progress will be made is more of an open question, but it is an obvious route forward and eventually should succeed.

Finally, I have a suspicion that unlike traditional physics, where there is a sharp distinction between kinematics and dynamics, this will not be so in string theory. In a traditional theory, such as quantum field theory, you have a kinematical framework, quantum mechanics and relativity, and you formulate specific laws within this kinematical framework, such as Yang–Mills theory and other aspects of the Standard Model. However, this is unlikely to be the case in the full background-independent and non-perturbative formulation of string theory. The reason I believe this is partly because once you really do away with time as a fundamental concept, it is very hard to imagine a framework like quantum field theory or quantum mechanics in the usual sense. My intuition is not really very precise at this stage, but one of the most specific things that we have been led to in string theory – what I regard as a particular corner of the

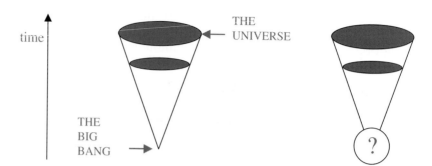

Fig. 26.6. String theory might allow us to understand the principle that fixes the initial conditions of the universe.

theory which might open up into a big room called M theory – is that corner of string theory that at low energies is described by 11-dimensional supergravity. For the first time, this corner shows no indication of free parameters that one can tune to yield a semiclassical approximation. This, of course, is one of the difficulties in understanding that corner. It is a regime where it does not look as if you are quantizing anything. It is not as if you are given a classical theory which you then quantize, you just have the whole thing, the kinematics and dynamics together. It is hard to deal with such a situation; we are not used to thinking about such theories. What quantum mechanics means in a theory where time is an emergent concept is beyond me, but I firmly believe that it will not turn out to be deterministic. If we need to change or amplify our notion of quantum mechanics in this scenario its only going to be weirder.

So that's all I have to say, except: Happy Birthday Stephen!

27

A brief description of string theory

Michael Green

Centre for Mathematical Sciences, University of Cambridge

27.1 Introduction

This talk is intended to illustrate the way that string theory combines classical general relativity with the other physical forces in a manner that is quantum mechanically consistent. This provides persuasive evidence that the theory is on the right track even if our understanding of its detailed physical implications is still very crude. The success or failure of string theory will ultimately depend on whether it explains observed physics.

Given the nature of this occasion I will start with some reminiscences, which are shared by anyone in this community who is old enough to remember the state of theoretical physics around thirty years ago – quite old but not ancient.

These comments refer particularly to Cambridge, where I was a research student and postdoc. Although I was in the physics department I spent much of my time in DAMTP. There was a sharp division between the particle physicists group and the general relativity group and I was most definitely amongst the particle physicists, whereas Gary Gibbons and Malcolm Perry, for example, were in the relativity group with Stephen. In those days gravity was not considered to be a force worth considering in particle physics. Indeed to many it was irrelevant because it was too weak to be measured and the only physics worth discussing was physics observed in accelerator experiments. Actually, the sub-text was that general relativity was too difficult for various reasons, the main one being that a quantum field theory of gravity was inconsistent. Cosmology was even worse – it was considered a sub-branch of astrology and was not discussed at all!

On the other hand the general relativity group had developed historically through the study of Einstein's equations, describing gravity coupled to Maxwell theory. The sub-nuclear forces were more or less ignored. Furthermore, quantum mechanics was considered to be a nuisance because nobody knew what to do with it in the context of gravity. Of course, there were one or two very special people who were around then and who are in the audience who were seriously involved in trying to resolve the incompatibility of quantum field theory and general relativity. The most dramatic development that bridged the research interests of the two groups was the work of Stephen in 1974 where he understood some of the extraordinary consequences of combining quantum mechanics and gravity. His later work on quantum cosmology opened up other important avenues of research. Thank you, Stephen for giving such impetus to the unification of particle physics, cosmology and quantum general relativity.

Another profound influence on bridging the gap between particle physics and general relativity at that time was string theory, which was developing from its early beginnings in the dual resonance model to a theory which also bridges the divide between particle physics and general relativity. As a result in the present Department, the separation between the two groups is largely for administrative convenience. We no longer have separate activities in terms of seminars and assignment of graduate students. We are now one group of theoretical physicists and that has been a major change.

This talk will concentrate on string theory, which evolved directly out of issues in particle physics and particularly out of the confusing experimental state of the strong interactions in the late 1960s. One of the most bizarre features of string theory, which appears to be a rather mathematical subject, is the way in which it evolved directly out of the study of experimental data.

27.2 Historical background

Let me go back to around 1900 when particle physics had its origins. J. J. Thomson had discovered the first elementary particle, the electron, in 1897. This was followed by Rutherford's discovery of the positively charged atomic nucleus in 1911 that lead to the identification of the proton. These particles appeared to be point-like but that was obviously inconsistent since classical point particles have singular electric and gravitational fields. Despite great efforts, no consistent model for an extended electron was found. The assumption that particles are point-like was therefore taken as the paradigm for subsequent developments in quantum mechanics and quantum field theory. In the end, it was understood how to live with these problems – they are part and parcel of the structure of renormalizable quantum field theory which has been immensely successful in the context of the standard model.

So the history of the development of particle physics has been based on patching up theories in which particles are point-like and have no extension. That is curious, because just after the discovery of the electron there was a huge effort put into trying to understand extended particles with unsuccessful models by Abraham, Lorentz and others. It might have been expected that a theory of a relativistically extended particle would have been constructed following the formulation of special relativity in 1905. But this did not happen. One of the puzzles of string theory is why it took so long before a mathematically consistent theory of an extended particle was developed.

There were a couple of notable exceptions to the pursuit of a point-like description of the elementary particles. In 1934 Born and Infeld constructed a non-linear extension of electromagnetism expressed by the well-known Born–Infeld action

$$S_{BI} = \frac{1}{l^4} \int d^4x \sqrt{\det(G_{\mu\nu} + l^2 F_{[\mu\nu]})}, \qquad (27.1)$$

where G is the spacetime metric ($\mu, \nu = 0, 1, 2, 3$) and F is the Maxwell field strength tensor. At distances much larger than the length parameter l the theory approximates to Maxwell's theory. However, the non-linearity of the theory gives rise to solitonic solutions which Born and Infeld wanted to identify with electrons (which still have singular charge densities). Although this idea did not influence the later developments in electrodynamics, the Born–Infeld theory plays an important rôle in the recent developments in string theory, as I will describe later.

Another key idea, which was developed by Dirac in 1962, has also entered into string theory in recent years. Dirac considered the idea that the electron and muon might be excitations of an extended membrane-like object, like a soap bubble. He developed the mathematical formalism for describing a relativistic extended object embedded in an ambient space-time. This is the prototype for modern description of p-branes in string theory, which are objects that are extended in p spatial directions. The Dirac action, when generalized to an object with extension in p spatial directions embedded in d-dimensional spacetime, has the form

$$S_{Dirac} = T_p \int d^{p+1}\xi \sqrt{\det \partial_\alpha X^\mu \partial_\beta X^\nu G_{\mu\nu}(X)}, \qquad (27.2)$$

where ξ^α ($\alpha = 0, 1, \ldots, p$) are the world-volume coordinates and T_p is the surface tension. This action is the square root of the determinant of the pull-back of the metric from d-dimensional spacetime onto the

$(p+1)$-dimensional world-volume of the membrane. So it took from 1905 to 1962 before a relativistically consistent extended particle theory was formulated. The case $p = 1$ corresponds to a string, and in this case Dirac's action degenerates into the Nambu–Goto action, although this came along later, in 1969.

The motivation for the Nambu–Goto string action emerged directly out of theoretical ideas that were based on experimental hadronic physics. The late 1960s was an era in which a subset of particle physicists were very pessimistic about the relevance of quantum field theory to the strong and weak forces, despite the obvious successes of quantum electrodynamics. Ironically, this was also the period in which others were laying the foundations of the hugely successful Standard Model, based on Yang–Mills quantum field theory. The systematics of the spectrum of hadronic resonances and of high energy scattering at fixed momentum transfer culminated in 1968 with Veneziano's remarkable guess for the four-particle scattering amplitude of mesons (originally for the scattering process $\pi\pi \to \pi\omega$). The Veneziano model was interpreted as a Born term for some novel perturbation approximation, in which an infinite tower of massive particles is exchanged. Over the next four years it was understood how this amplitude arises from the scattering amplitude of relativistic open strings.

This original string theory based on Veneziano's observation was in striking qualitative agreement with both the spectrum of meson resonances and the high energy scattering encompassed by the Regge pole model. The open string was supposed to represent a meson with a quark and antiquark at each endpoint. Consistency of the theory also required the presence of closed strings which were identified with the 'pomeron' trajectory of Regge theory – now identified with the glueball states of QCD. This agreement with the data indicates very clearly that hadronic particles really are string-like.

However, there were various drawbacks to understanding hadrons as strings. One of the most severe, was that hadrons have point-like substructure. The data on deep inelastic scattering, the analogue of Rutherford scattering with hadrons, indicates the presence of point-like substructure, whereas strings as originally formulated had no point-like substructure. They are very diffuse objects – there is no suppression of the have infinitely high frequencies – and very different from the hadrons seen experimentally for that reason. There also seemed to be no way of coupling strings to external currents, whereas hadrons obviously couple to electromagnetism and to the weak interactions. The absence of point-like substructure and the absence of off-shell currents meant that string theory failed to be a sensible model of hadrons. Nevertheless QCD – the field theory of the strong interactions that evolved around 1973 – does seem to describe hadrons as strings. This is particularly clear in the 't Hooft limit where the gauge group is $SU(N)$ with $N \to \infty$ and $g^2 N$ fixed, where g is the Yang–Mills coupling constant.

There were other profound problems for string theory as a theory of hadrons, notably, that in the original bosonic theory the dimension of spacetime was required to be 26 and the theory was unstable since there was a tachyonic mode. Adding fermionic world-sheet coordinates ultimately led to a supersymmetric theory which was consistent in ten spacetime dimensions and free of tachyons. Another difficulty was the fact that the spectrum of states in all string theories contained massless states with spin one and spin two which did not correspond to any hadrons. These states are now interpreted as Yang–Mills and graviton states, respectively, and the strings now represent fundamental particles rather than the effective strings of QCD. Nevertheless, one of the most curious themes of current developments is the understanding of how a consistent string theory of hadrons might arise from fundamental string theory.

27.3 String theory today

I will skip thirty years and turn to the present status of string theory. The degrees of freedom in perturbative string theory are still open and closed strings, although the open strings are not interpreted as mesons and the closed strings are not interpreted as glueballs. A closed string now describes the massless graviton together with an infinite set of massive excitations. So the theory is a generalization of general relativity in which a string-like graviton moves through ten-dimensional spacetime. An open string describes a massless vector gauge particle together with an infinite set of massive excitations. Since the endpoints of an open string can join together to form a closed string we see that Yang–Mills and gravity are unified, which is the most profound insight that string theory has to offer.

27.3.1 Open strings and D-branes

An open string has endpoints that satisfy boundary conditions that generally localize them on a $(p+1)$-dimensional hyper-plane. The string fluctuates in the ten-dimensional bulk between the endpoints. Such open strings contain massless states that describe Yang–Mills particles propagating in a $(p+1)$-dimensional world-volume. They also describe massless scalar states that correspond to the displacement of this hyper-plane in transverse directions. In other words the hyperplane, or Dp-brane, is a dynamical object that can fluctuate and which has a world-volume in which gauge particles propagate. Objects of this type are solitonic solutions to string theory and the description I have given is one that is valid in the regime in which string perturbation theory is valid. They can also be discovered in a different limit in which string theory reduces to classical supergravity. Theories of this type are classical theories of gravity that contain a variety of massless gauge fields, including rank-$(p + 1)$ tensor potentials that are generalizations of the rank-1 Maxwell vector potential. These theories possess solitonic solutions that are generalizations of black holes known as 'black p-branes', which are extended objects carrying a charge that couples minimally to a rank $(p + 1)$ tensor potential. These classical solutions correspond to the Dp-branes seen in a very different limit in string perturbation theory.

So nowadays we think of string theory as not simply being a theory of strings which move through the bulk, but it also contains extended massive objects, whose excitations are described by Yang–Mills or electromagnetic-type modes living in the world volume. There are also further massive solitonic states in string theory which carry other kinds of charges that are not easily seen from the open string point of view.

D-branes have been used to describe the quantum properties of black holes within string theory. A simple quantum description of Hawking radiation follows – an open string excitation of one of these black brane type objects shakes off a closed string which then moves into the bulk and is interpreted as Hawking radiation. This string picture is valid in the near-extremal limit where the approximation can be controlled by keeping the string coupling constant small. This is similar to the situation with a Reissner–Nordstrom black hole where the black p-brane possesses a non-zero conserved charge associated with a $(p + 1)$-form potential.

At long wavelengths these Dp-branes have an effective description in terms of the massless open string modes propagating in the $(p + 1)$-dimensional world volume. The action describing their dynamics is a combination of Dirac's action for the relativistic embedding and the Born–Infeld action for the world-volume electromagnetic potential that appears here as a massless mode of an open string. So here we see two of the more obscure early developments of the last century united into a description of the effective action of D-branes. The Dp-brane generalizes the Dirac membrane, to a $(p + 1)$-dimensional object embedded in ten spacetime dimensions, with a $(p + 1)$-dimensional Born–Infeld–Maxwell world-volume field. These objects also carry a conserved charge associated with a $(p + 1)$th rank tensor potential that couples minimally to the world-volume. Supersymmetry also requires the presence of world-volume fermion fields. The D-brane world-volume theory is therefore a supersymmetric generalization of the Dirac–Born–Infeld version of supersymmetric Maxwell theory.

Many beautiful things happen when D-branes are combined. For example, if N Dp-branes coincide there is an enhancement of the Maxwell gauge symmetry to a $U(N)$ gauge group since there are $N^2 - 1$ extra massless open strings that join the different Dp-branes. When these D-branes are separated the gauge symmetry is broken via a Higgs mechanism. In fact, the moduli space of maximally supersymmetric $U(N)$ $(p+1)$-dimensional Yang–Mills can be identified with the parameter space of the positions of N Dp-branes. These statements have very many generalizations obtained by considering arrays of Dp-branes with different values of p and at different angles, and embedded in space-times of non-trivial topology. This has lead to many insights into supersymmetric quantum field theories in various dimensions.

27.3.2 Closed strings and supergravity

The closed string sector describes the gravitational part of the theory. Although this is equivalent to general relativity at long distances, it differs radically at short distances associated with the string scale l_s. This can be illustrated by the explicit expression for the tree-level scattering amplitude of four gravitons, $h_{(r)\,\mu\nu}$ (which are the fluctuations of the metric tensor around flat spacetime). Let the two incoming strings in their graviton ground states with momenta k_1 and k_2 scatter into the two outgoing graviton strings with momenta k_3 and k_4. The amplitude is given by

$$A_4^{tree} = e^{-2\phi} \frac{\tilde{K}}{stu} \frac{\Gamma(1 - l_s^2 s)\Gamma(1 - l_s^2 t)\Gamma(1 - l_s^2 u)}{\Gamma(1 + l_s^2 s)\Gamma(1 + l_s^2 t)\Gamma(1 + l_s^2 u)} \qquad (27.3)$$

$$= e^{-2\phi} \frac{\tilde{K}}{stu} \exp\left(\sum_{n=1}^{\infty} \frac{l_s^{4n+2} 2\zeta(2n+1)}{2n+1} (s^{2n+1} + t^{2n+1} + u^{2n+1}) \right),$$

where the second equality follows from elementary properties of Γ functions. In these expressions $s = -(k_1 + k_2)^2$, $t = -(k_1 + k_4)^2$ and $u = -(k_1 + k_3)^2$ are the Mandelstam invariants (satisfying $s + t + u = 0$) and the overall kinematic factor $\tilde{K}$ is the linearized approximation to $\mathcal{R}^4$, where $\mathcal{R}$ is the Riemann curvature tensor. This contains the dependence on the polarization states of the four gravitons, $h_{(r)\,\mu\nu}$ ($r = 1, 2, 3, 4$). The overall factor of $e^{-2\phi}$, where ϕ is the scalar dilaton field, is characteristic of string tree-level amplitudes. In perturbation theory ϕ is a constant and $e^{\phi} = g$ is the string coupling constant that governs the string perturbative loop expansion. Every term in the exponent of (27.3) can be expressed as a polynomial in s and t multiplied by stu where $n \geq 1$. Each power of the string scale l_s is associated with one derivative, or one power of momentum, in the amplitude. Expanding in a power series on derivatives gives

$$
\begin{aligned}
A_4^{tree} \sim e^{-2\phi}\tilde{K} \Bigg(&\frac{1}{stu} + 2\zeta(3)(l_s)^6 + 2\zeta(5)(s^2 + st + t^2)(l_s)^{10} \\
&+ 2\zeta(3)^2 stu(l_s)^{12} + 2\zeta(7)(s^4 + 2s^3t + 3s^2t^2 + 2st^3 + t^4)(l_s)^{14} \\
&+ 2\zeta(3)\zeta(5)stu(s^2 + st + t^2)(l_s)^{16} + \cdots \Bigg).
\end{aligned}
\tag{27.4}
$$

The first term in this expansion, $\tilde{K}\frac{1}{stu}$, reproduces the sum of the Born diagrams with poles in the s, t and u channels that would be obtained from an expansion of the Einstein–Hilbert field theory action,

$$
S_{EH} = \frac{1}{l_s^8} \int d^{10}x \sqrt{-\det g}\, e^{-2\phi}\, R.
\tag{27.5}
$$

The term with coefficient $\zeta(3)$ in (27.4) has four extra derivatives and is identified with a correction to the Einstein–Hilbert theory of the form $\mathcal{R}^4$ where the contractions between the curvature tensors are such that only the Weyl tensor contributes. Similarly, the higher order terms in (27.4) correspond to an infinite sequence of terms in the effective action with higher derivatives acting on the curvatures. This simple example already exhibits the richness of string theory. There are many other bosonic and fermionic fields in the theory, so the complete effective action contains many more terms. The full string theory, even at tree level, cannot be captured simply from this low energy effective action since the excited string states play an essential part in the high energy description of the theory.

A particularly important feature of the version of the Einstein–Hilbert action (27.5) that comes out of string theory, is the presence of the dilaton factor, $e^{-2\phi}$. This means that the (ten-dimensional) Newton constant, G_N, depends on the string coupling. As a result the Planck length is given by $l_P \sim l_s^4 g^{1/4}$ and can be tuned to an arbitrarily small scale by choosing the coupling to be small enough. This means that it is possible to discuss the physics of a collection of black p-branes and therefore black holes in a sensible perturbative approximation. This has led to the impressive calculations of quantum effects of black holes discussed by others at this workshop.

The quantum loop corrections to string theory are free of the problematic ultraviolet divergences of conventional perturbative quantum gravity. This is related to non-local features of string theory that are encoded in the infinite series of terms in the tree-level effective action. If the theory is cut off at any finite number or terms, ghosts (negative norm states) will arise and the finiteness properties of loop amplitudes are lost. Although it seems as though Stephen is willing to tolerate ghosts, we string theorists think it is rather wonderful that they are absent in string theory! This makes the theory distinct from any local quantum field theory – the string is a very diffuse non-local object.

More generally, the theory might depend on a number of scalar fields that correspond to moduli that parameterize the spacetime geometry. One of the great advances of the last few years, is the understanding that has developed of the dependence of the theory on these scalar fields. The mapping out of these moduli spaces makes strong use of various dualities that have been discovered which relate various very different approximations to string theory.

27.4 Duality and M theory

Until the mid-1990s there appeared to be a variety of distinct superstring theories. We now know that these apparently different theories are really different perturbative approximations to the same underlying theory. The strings that are the fundamental excitations in one string perturbation expansion theory appear as solitonic strings in another. The variety of p-branes play an important rôle in the consistency of this picture. These relationships between different descriptions of the same theory are dualities, or discrete transformations, which act on the moduli space. These dualities typically relate one theory at weak coupling to another at strong coupling. Supersymmetry is an important element in understanding the strong coupling limit since 'BPS' states are protected from renormalization and therefore do not depend on the value of the coupling.

Many of these identifications are made by considering the solitonic solutions of the classical supergravity field theories that approximate to string theory in the low energy limit. In addition to the many interconnections between different string theories, the dualities also relate string theory to eleven-dimensional supergravity, which does not correspond to the low energy limit of any string theory. Since the quantum version is not understood in this limit, all we know about eleven-dimensional supergravity is based on its classical field theory formulation. The theory possesses a solitonic membrane (or two-brane) and when this is compactified on a circle one direction on the membrane can be wrapped, resulting in a string moving in the non-compact directions. So in some sense the eleven-dimensional theory gives rise to a string theory in ten dimensions–although this is a very classical argument. The alternative way of understanding the connection is to start with the ten-dimensional string theory, and obtain eleven-dimensional supergravity as an effective theory arising from highly quantum effects in string theory. More precisely, strong-coupling quantum mechanical effects involving D-particles (or $D0$-branes) in string theory give rise to the extra dimension that is present in the eleven-dimensional theory. In fact the string theory coupling constant is identified with the radius of the eleventh dimension, which therefore becomes sizeable in the strong coupling limit of string theory.

This dual way of looking at the interconnections between the ten and eleven-dimensional theories is just one of very many dualities that interconnect all of the apparently different theories. In each case a perturbative approximation is known in some limit or other – the weak coupling limit in the case of the various string perturbation theories or the low energy limit in the case of the derivative expansion of classical supergravity. The set of such limits defines the boundary of moduli space of non-perturbative string theory. The way in which progress has been made is by exploiting the symbiosis between, on the one hand, classical supergravity and supersymmetric Yang–Mills (which are low energy approximations to string theory) and, on the other hand, the quantum properties deduced from string theory in the presence of D-branes. The underlying theory that gives rise to the non-perturbative moduli space has not been formulated convincingly but it has been given the name 'M theory'. I worry that this is such a bad name that it cannot describe what we're looking for! Since we all use TeX maybe we do not need to give it a name, just a compellingly beautiful symbol, which we can all admire.

27.5 Future perspective

I will end this talk without trying to make predictions. There are various obvious questions. For example, it is important to understand to what extent string theory avoids the singularity problems associated with general relativity. We already know string theory avoids certain types of singularities, but it would be good to have a much deeper understanding of that. Understanding how string theory might avoid the kinds of singularities associated with cosmological solutions would be particularly interesting. Other obvious questions concern the black hole information paradox raised by Stephen all those years ago We obviously want a theory of elementary particles that describes observed accelerator physics. Somewhat ironically we would also really like to understand in what sense string theory describes QCD , which was the original motivation for string theory – we would then have come full circle. And there is a host of other such obvious questions.

Although most of these and other key physical questions seem far from being answered, string theory does give a compelling qualitative description of the forces and particles that are observed in accelerator experiments. At the same time it embodies all of the theoretical features that are essential for a quantum theory that contains gravity, which makes it particularly interesting as a subject for further study.

An extreme optimist might hope that the present state of string theory is analogous to the situation with quantum theory in the early 1920s. By then there had been amazing developments in quantum theory backed up by experimental data over a period of twenty years or more. But even by 1924 the greatest experts could not have imagined what was about to happen the very next year. This is a salient lesson to anyone trying to predict the future of string theory, which is already more than thirty years old and is much less firmly based on detailed experiment.

Once again, happy birthday to Stephen.

28

The story of M

Paul Townsend

Centre for Mathematical Sciences, University of Cambridge

'They were learning to draw', the doormouse went on, '... and they drew all manner of things – everything that begins with M'.

'Why with an M?', said Alice.

'Why not?', said the March Hare.

28.1 Introduction

Shakespearean actors are traditionally averse to pronouncing the name of the play 'Macbeth', preferring to call it 'the Scottish play'. Presumably it was only distaste for cryptic abbreviations that prevented it from becoming known as the 'M-play'. M theory acquired its name from a similar aversion, in this case of string theorists to the word 'Membrane'. The *story of M* is thus the story of membranes, supermembranes in particular. The occasion of Stephen Hawking's sixtieth birthday is an appropriate one for me to put on record some recollections of this story because Stephen was exceptional in giving his support and encouragement to work on supermembranes during the years in which the 'M word' could not be pronounced. Thank you, Stephen, and happy sixtieth birthday.

A membrane is of course just a special case of a brane and, as the reader will probably know, M theory is really an Orwellian democracy in which there are many equal branes but with some being more equal than others. Strings are more equal for all the usual reasons, but membranes are more equal too, for a different set of reasons. In the light-front gauge, membranes are equivalent to the large n limit of $SU(n)$ gauge theories, dimensionally reduced to a quantum mechanical model. The M(atrix) model formulation of M theory could have been, and nearly was, found from the 11-dimensional supermembrane in this way. But this is all well-known and, given my spacetime limitations, I prefer to reminisce on the (pre)history of the 11-dimensional supermembrane.

This will be a selective history, chosen to motivate discussion of a surprising, and little-known, fact:[1] the field theory limit of a supermembrane in certain hyper-Kähler backgrounds is a three-dimensional sigma-model with $N = 4$ supersymmetry, but the supermembrane itself generically has only $N = 3$ supersymmetry [5]. This is a sigma-model analogue of the breaking of $N = 4$ to $N = 3$ supersymmetry in three-dimensional gauge theories by the addition of a Chern–Simons term [6].

28.2 The supermembrane

It is well known that string theory arose from attempts to understand the physics of hadrons. What is less well-known is that M theory has roots in hadron physics too. In 1978, the same year that 11-dimensional supergravity appeared [7], a 'classical' bag model for hadrons was proposed by Aurilia, Christodoulou and Legovini [8]; this was based on the idea that the closed QCD 4-form $Tr(F \wedge F)$ should be replaced, in an effective description of hadrons, by an Abelian 4-form field strength $G = dC$. Hadrons were identified as those regions in which G acquires a non-zero expectation value; these regions would be separated from the vacuum by a membrane coupled to the 3-form potential C. I heard about this model from Antonio Aurilia in 1980 and realized that the 4-form field strength G of 11-dimensional supergravity could be similarly used, after reduction on T^7, to introduce a positive cosmological constant into N=8 D=4 supergravity. This supergravity theory had recently been constructed by Cremmer and Julia [9] but they had eliminated the surviving four-dimensional 4-form field strength as if it were a non-dynamical auxiliary field. If one instead uses the field equation of the 3-form potential C then a positive cosmological constant appears as the square of an integration constant.[2] We enlisted Hermann Nicolai to help construct the new N=8 supergravity theory, which turns out to have a positive scalar

---

[1] In the talk I explained how a tubular but axially *asymmetric* supermembrane, supported against collapse by angular momentum, can be both stable and supersymmetry-preserving [1]. This did surprise some members of the audience, although I discovered that the stability issue had been previously addressed in a non-supersymmetric context [2]. As a full discussion is available in [1] and subsequent papers [3, 4], I have chosen to discuss another surprising fact about supermembranes in this write-up.

[2] This idea occurred independently to Duff and Van Nieuwenhuizen [10] but without the connection to 11-dimensional supergravity.

potential rather than a cosmological constant [11]. As this potential has
no critical points it was unclear what use it might have.[3] We should have
continued this research by considering whether a non-vanishing 4-form in
D=4 could be combined with compactifications on spaces other than T^7.
We did not, but Freund and Rubin did [13] and their demonstration that
D=11 supergravity could be compactified on a 7-sphere sparked off the
revival of interest in Kaluza-Klein theory.

It was somehow forgotten, in all the Kaluza-Klein excitement, that the
3-form potential C could couple to membranes (although Bernard Julia
was aware of the possibility [14]). I think that the main reason for this
collective amnesia was the fact that 11-dimensional supergravity was being promoted as a candidate unified field theory, so the apparent absence
of anything to which it could couple was viewed as an advantage. This
attitude discouraged thinking about membranes, which did not resurface
until after the superstring revolution of 1984. Following the construction
by Green and Schwarz of a covariant superstring action [15], it was natural to reconsider the possibility of an 11-dimensional supermembrane.
During the summer of 1986, Luca Mezincescu and I attempted to construct a supermembrane generalization of the Green–Schwarz (GS) action
but the attempt did not succeed because we were unable to generalize
the self-dual worldsheet vector parameter of the GS 'κ-symmetry'; this
made the two-dimensionality of the string world-sheet seem an essential feature of the construction. In fact, it is not; there is an alternative,
but equivalent, form of the κ-symmetry transformation with a world-
sheet *scalar* parameter. This was found by Hughes, Liu and Polchinski in
their construction of an action for a super-3-brane in a D=6 Minkowski
background [16]; they were motivated by the observation that a vortex
of the D=6 supersymmetric Abelian-Higgs model is a supersymmetry-
preserving 3-brane for which the effective action must be of GS-type. I
saw this paper the day before I was to travel to Trieste to continue a
collaboration with Eric Bergshoeff and Ergin Sezgin, and soon after my
arrival we succeeded in constructing an 11-dimensional supermembrane
action that is consistent in any background that solves the field equations of 11-dimensional supergravity [17]. For unit tension the action takes
the form

$$S = -\int [\text{Vol} \pm C] \tag{28.1}$$

---

[3] Stephen Hawking used the idea of a dynamical cosmological constant in his suggestion
that the 'cosmological constant is probably zero' [12] but it now seems that it probably
is not zero.

where Vol is the (appropriately defined) induced volume 3-form, and $\mathcal{C}$ is the worldvolume 3-form induced by the *superspace* 3-form potential of 11-dimensional supergravity (of which C is the bosonic truncation). The choice of relative sign corresponds to the choice between a supermembrane and an anti-supermembrane, or an $M2$-brane and an $\overline{M2}$-brane in modern terminology.

A feature of all GS-type super-brane actions is that the fermions are (apparently) worldvolume scalars. If this were really true then, for example, the GS superstring action could not be equivalent to the world-sheet supersymmetric NSR superstring action. In fact, the GS fermions are *not* scalars because they are subject to the κ-symmetry gauge transformation; it is for a similar reason that the 4-vector potential of electrodynamics is not really a 4-vector field. To determine the transformation properties of the GS fermions under any symmetry of the action (which would include spacetime Lorentz transformations for a Minkowski background) one must first fix the κ-symmetry gauge; the transformation is then a superposition of the 'naive' transformation with whatever compensating κ-symmetry transformation is needed to maintain the gauge choice. The gauge fixing must break the spacetime Lorentz group but can be chosen to preserve the worldvolume Lorentz subgroup, under which the gauge-fixed GS fermions turn out to transform as worldvolume spinors.

This transformation from spacetime spinor to worldvolume spinor is clearly necessary if any spacetime supersymmetries are to be interpreted as worldvolume supersymmetries after gauge-fixing, but it is not obviously sufficient. In fact, initially it was far from clear that spacetime supersymmetry would imply worldvolume supersymmetry of the supermembrane, partly because the supermembrane has no NSR formulation, and Achúcarro, Gauntlett, Itoh and I went to great lengths to verify it directly [18]; our article was originally entitled *Supersymmetry on the brane* but we had to change the title to accommodate a referee who insisted that use of the word 'brane' would bring the physics community into disrepute.[4]

Nowadays, the connection between spacetime supersymmetry and worldvolume supersymmetry is considered obvious. However, as I hope the following discussion will show, surprises are still possible.

---

[4] Possibly this referee had in mind the earlier use of the word in the 1954 essay *Akquire culture and keep the brane clean* by Nigel Molesworth [19]. As this essay's subtitle is *How to be Topp in Latin* it is regrettable that it fails to provide the modern translation of *mens sana in corpore sano* which is *clean brane in clean bulk*, otherwise known as the braneworld cosmological principle.

28.3 Backgrounds of reduced holonomy

The $G \wedge G \wedge C$ term of 11-dimensional supergravity preserves spacetime parity if C is taken to be parity-odd, and with this parity assignment the coupling of G to fermion bilinears also preserves parity because of the peculiar way that fermion bilinears behave under parity in odd dimensions [20]. Thus 11-dimensional supergravity preserves parity. It follows that solutions breaking parity must come in parity doublets, each of which will preserve the same fraction of supersymmetry because parity commutes with supersymmetry. We shall be interested in solutions with vanishing G and product 11-metric of the form

$$ds_{11}^2 = ds^2(\mathbb{E}^{(1,2)}) + g_{IJ}(X)dX^I dX^J \tag{28.2}$$

where g_{IJ} ($I, J = 1, \ldots, 8$) is the metric of some Ricci-flat eight-dimensional manifold $\mathcal{M}_8$, or its orientation reversal $\overline{\mathcal{M}}_8$. Any submanifold with fixed position on $\mathcal{M}_8$ is a minimal surface that we may identify as the Minkowski vacuum of an infinite planar supermembrane. In the gauge in which the worldvolume coordinates ξ^i are identified with coordinates for $\mathbb{E}^{(1,2)}$, the physical bosonic worldvolume fields of the $M2$-brane are maps $X^I(\xi)$ from the worldvolume to $\mathcal{M}_8$, and the bosonic action is

$$I = -\int d^3\xi \sqrt{-\det(\eta_{ij} + g_{ij})} \tag{28.3}$$

where η is the 2+1 Minkowski metric and

$$g_{ij}(\xi) = \partial_i X^I \partial_j X^J g_{IJ}(X). \tag{28.4}$$

To incorporate the fermions one may begin by noting that the gauge choice breaks the 11-dimensional Lorentz group to the product of the three-dimensional Lorentz group $Sl(2; \mathbb{R})$ with $SO(8)$. A 32-component spinor of $SO(1, 10)$ decomposes into the sum of the $(\mathbf{2}, \mathbf{8}_s)$ and $(\mathbf{2}, \mathbf{8}_c)$ irreps of this product group, where $\mathbf{8}_s$ is the spinor representation of $SO(8)$ and $\mathbf{8}_c$ is the conjugate spinor representation. Only one of these two irreps of $Sl(2; \mathbb{R}) \times SO(8)$ survives the κ-symmetry gauge-fixing, which one depends on whether the covariant action is the one for the $M2$-brane or the one for the $\overline{M2}$-brane. By convention, we shall take the physical fermion fields of the $M2$-brane to be in the $(\mathbf{2}, \mathbf{8}_c)$ representation and those of the $\overline{M2}$-brane to be in the $(\mathbf{2}, \mathbf{8}_s)$ representation. The spacetime parity transformation that interchanges $\mathcal{M}_8$ with $\overline{\mathcal{M}}_8$ will also interchange the $\mathbf{8}_s$ and $\mathbf{8}_c$ representations of $SO(8)$, and hence will interchange $M2$ with $\overline{M2}$. Thus, an $M2$-brane in $\mathbb{E}^{(1,2)} \times \mathcal{M}_8$ is equivalent to an $\overline{M2}$-brane in $\mathbb{E}^{(1,2)} \times \overline{\mathcal{M}}_8$. In the case that $\mathcal{M}_8$ has an orientation reversing isometry

Table 28.1.

H	$\mathcal{M}_8$	N	N'
G_2	$M_7 \times \mathbb{E}^1$	1	1
$SU(3)$	$CY_3 \times \mathbb{E}^2$	2	2
$SU(2)$	$HK_4 \times \mathbb{E}^4$	4	4

we have $\mathcal{M}_8 \cong \overline{\mathcal{M}}_8$ and the $M2$-brane action will be equivalent to the $\overline{M2}$-brane action.

Note that the field content of the gauge-fixed supermembrane is bose-fermi balanced, as would be required for worldvolume supersymmety. Whether the supermembrane *is* worldvolume supersymmetric will depend on the choice of $\mathcal{M}_8$. This follows from the fact that (super)symmetries of the supermembrane action arise from (super)isometries of the background that leave invariant the superspace 4-form field strength. In particular, for bosonic backgrounds of the type under consideration, supersymmetries arise from Killing superfields whose spinor component is a Killing spinor of M, and these exist only if $\mathcal{M}_8$ has special holonomy.

Let $H \subset SO(8)$ be the holonomy group. The number N of linearly-realized supersymmetries of the supermembrane is the number of singlets in the decomposition of the spinor representation $\mathbf{8}_s$ of $SO(8)$ into irreps of H. The number N' of *non-linearly* realized supersymmetries is the number of singlets of the $\mathbf{8}_c$ representation of $SO(8)$ in its decomposition into irreps of H. For the anti-supermembrane the numbers N and N' are interchanged. The groups H for which $N > 0$ fall into one of two nested sequences. One sequence is

$$G_2 \supset SU(3) \supset SU(2). \tag{28.5}$$

The corresponding types of 8-manifold, and the values of N and N' are given in Table 28.1. (where CY_n is a $2n$-dimensional Calabi–Yau n-fold and HK_{4n} is a hyper-Kähler manifold of quaternionic dimension n).

In each of these cases the 8-manifold $\mathcal{M}_8$ takes the form $\mathcal{M}_8 = \mathcal{M}_{8-k} \times \mathbb{R}^k$ ($k = 1, 2, 4$) for some irreducible $(8 - k)$-dimensional manifold $\mathcal{M}_{8-k}$. Such 8-manifolds have an orientation-reversing isometry, so the $M2$-brane in these backgrounds is equivalent to the $\overline{M2}$-brane. In fact, they are identical because an anti-membrane can be obtained from a membrane by a rotation in some $\mathbb{E}^3$ subspace of $\mathbb{E}^{2+k}$. The reason that the $M2$ and $\overline{M2}$ actions can be identical is that their κ-symmetry transformations differ and this difference can compensate for the different sign in (28.1).

Note that fixing the position in $\mathcal{M}_{8-k}$ yields a supermembrane in a Minkowski spacetime of dimension $D = 4, 5$ or 7, according to whether

Table 28.2.

H	$\mathcal{M}_8$	N	N'
$Spin(7)$	$Spin(7)$	1	0
$SU(4)$	CY_4	2	0
Sp_2	HK_8	3	0
$Sp_1 \times Sp_1$	$HK_4 \times HK_4$	4	0

$k = 1, 2$ or 4, respectively; as it happens, these are precisely the other dimensions for which the supermembrane action is classically consistent [17], so the existence of these lower-dimensional supermembrane actions is explained by the existence of the 11-dimensional supermembrane.

The other sequence of holonomy groups is

$$Spin(7) \supset SU(4) \supset Sp_2 \supset Sp_1 \times Sp_1. \qquad (28.6)$$

The corresponding types of 8-manifold, and the values of N and N' are given in Table 28.2.. In each of these cases there are no non-linearly-realized supersymmetries, so replacing the $M2$-brane by the $\overline{M2}$-brane breaks all supersymmetries. Equivalently, replacing the 8-manifold $\mathcal{M}_8$ by its orientation reversal $\overline{\mathcal{M}}_8$ breaks all N supersymmetries of the $M2$-brane action.[5]

28.4 The sigma model limit

The action (28.3) can be expanded as a power series in ∂X. Discarding a constant and terms with more than two derivatives we arrive at the field theory action

$$S = -\frac{1}{2} \int d^3\xi \sqrt{-\det \eta}\, \eta^{ij} \partial_i X^I \partial_j X^J g_{IJ}(X). \qquad (28.7)$$

This is a D=3 sigma-model with the 8-manifold $\mathcal{M}_8$ as its target space. If the supermembrane preserved N supersymmetries then an analogous expansion yields a supersymmetric sigma-model with at least N super-symmetries. In most cases one can easily see that it can have no more than N supersymmetries because of the constraints imposed on the target space of a sigma-model by extended supersymmetry; specifically, a

---

[5] Note that the background solutions preserve N supersymmetries irrespective of the orientation of $\mathcal{M}_8$; it is only the rigid worldvolume supersymmetries on the super-membrane that are broken when $\mathcal{M}_8$ is replaced by $\overline{\mathcal{M}}_8$. This is in contrast to the related phenomenon of supergravity solutions with non-zero G that are supersym-metric for one orientation but non-supersymmetric for the other orientation [21].

supersymmetric D=3 sigma model with an irreducible target space has $N = 2$ supersymmetry if the target space is Kähler and $N = 4$ if it is hyper-Kähler [22]. For example, because $Spin(7)$ manifolds are not Kähler we know that the sigma-model obtained from the supermembrane action can have at most $N = 1$ supersymmetry. The same is true for the G_2 case, although the conclusion is less immediate in this case because the 8-manifold is not irreducible. Note that for the $N = 2$ case of either table the target space is Kähler, as consistency requires, but not hyper-Kähler, so the sigma-model has $N = 2$ supersymmetry. Similarly, for both $N = 4$ cases the target space is hyper-Kähler, as required for consistency. This leaves only the case of Sp_2 holonomy of Table 28.2. to consider, and here we find a surprise. As one sees from Table 28.2., the gauge-fixed supermembrane action has only $N = 3$ supersymmetry but, as its target space is hyper-Kähler, the sigma model obtained from the field theory limit has $N = 4$ supersymmetry. Thus, in this one case, the low-energy sigma-model has *more* supersymmetries than the supermembrane action from which it was derived!

From the sigma-model perspective, the supermembrane just adds higher-dimension terms to the action. An interaction term that breaks $N = 4$ supersymmetry to $N = 3$ must also break worldvolume parity. Majorana mass terms break parity in three dimensions [23] and although the supermembrane has no mass terms it does have a mass parameter, determined by the membrane tension. Higher dimension fermion interactions in the supermembrane must involve this parameter and so may break parity. For example, if ψ is the 8-plet of real two-component $Sl(2; \mathbb{R})$ spinor fields then a term of the form

$$(\bar{\psi}\psi)(\bar{\psi}\gamma \cdot \partial\psi) \tag{28.8}$$

breaks parity for the same reason that Majorana mass terms break parity. The supersymmetric completion of this term will not include any purely bosonic term, consistent with parity preservation of the bosonic truncation of the supermembrane, and it will not survive in the field theory limit, consistent with parity preservation of the supersymmetric sigma model. Moreover, it can occur only when there are no non-linearly realized supersymmetries, and hence must be absent in the cases of Table 28.1.. Thus, a term of the above type is a candidate for a parity-violating interaction that will break $N = 4$ to $N = 3$ supersymmetry when the hyper-Kähler target space has Sp_2 holonomy, although it must be absent if the holonomy is contained in the $Sp_1 \times Sp_1$ subgroup of Sp_2.

There is a gauge theory precedent for all this. The addition of a Chern–Simons to a three-dimensional gauge theory with $N = 4$ supersymmetry can preserve at most $N = 3$ supersymmetry, in which case its supersymmetric completion will include parity-violating fermion mass terms [6]. In fact, this phenomenon is an M theory dual of the one discussed here, at least for the class of toric hyper-Kähler 8-manifolds, because the M2-brane in such a background is dual to a D3-brane suspended between (p, q)-fivebranes and the effective field theory on the intersection is precisely a three-dimensional $N = 3$ gauge theory with a Chern–Simons term [5, 24].

Acknowledgements

I thank Jerome Gauntlett, Gary Gibbons, Paul Howe, Chris Pope and Kellogg Stelle for helpful discussions.

References

[1] Mateos, D., Ng, S. and Townsend, P. K. (2002), 'Tachyons, supertubes and brane-antibrane systems', *JHEP* **0203** 016.

[2] Carter, B. and Martin, X. (1993), 'Dynamic instability criterion for circular string loops', *Ann. Phys* **227** 151.

[3] Mateos, D., Ng, S. and Townsend, P. K. (2002), 'Supercurves', [hep-th/0204062].

[4] Kruczenski, M., Myers, R. C., Peet, A. W. and Winters, D. J. (2002), 'Aspects of supertubes', [hep-th/0204103].

[5] Gauntlett, J. P., Gibbons, G. W., Papadopoulos, G. and Townsend, P. K. (1997), 'Hyper-Kähler manifolds and multiply intersecting branes', *Nucl. Phys.* **B500** 133.

[6] Kao, H-C. and Lee, K. (1992), 'Self-dual Chern–Simons Higgs systems with $N = 3$ extended supersymmetry', *Phys. Rev.* **D46** 4691.

[7] Cremmer, E., Julia, B. and Scherk, J. (1978), 'Supergravity theory in eleven dimensions', *Phys. Lett.* **76B** 409.

[8] Aurilia, A., Christodoulou, D. and Legovini, F. (1978), 'A classical interpretation of the bag model for hadrons', *Phys. Lett.* **B73** 429.

[9] Cremmer, E. and Julia, B. (1970), 'The $SO(8)$ supergravity', *Nucl. Phys.* **B159** 141.

[10] Duff, M. J. and Van Nieuwenhuizen, P. (1980), 'Quantum inequivalence of different field representations', *Phys. Lett.* **B94** 179.

[11] Aurilia, A., Nicolai, H. and Townsend, P. K. (1980), 'Hidden constants: the theta parameter of QCD and the cosmological constant of N=8 supergravity', *Nucl. Phys.* **B176** 509.

[12] Hawking, S. W. (1984), 'The cosmological constant is probably zero', *Phys. Lett.* **B134** 403.

[13] Freund, P. G. O. and Rubin, M. A. (1980), 'Dynamics of dimensional reduction', *Phys. Lett.* **B97**, 233.

[14] Julia, B. (1979), 'Extra dimensions: recent progress using old ideas', in *proceedings of the 2nd Marcel Grossman Meeting*, Trieste, Italy, 1979.

[15] Green, M. B. and Schwarz, J. H. (1984), 'Covariant description of superstrings', *Phys. Lett.* **B136**, 367.

[16] Hughes, J., Liu, J. and Polchinski, J. (1986), 'Supermembranes', *Phys. Lett.* **B180** 370.

[17] Bergshoeff, E., Sezgin, E. and Townsend, P. K. (1987), 'Supermembranes and 11-dimensional supergravity', *Phys. Lett.* **B189** 75.

[18] Achúcarro, A., Gauntlett, J., Itoh, K. and Townsend, P. K. (1989), 'Worldvolume supersymmetry from spacetime supersymmetry of the four dimensional supermembrane', *Nucl. Phys.* **B314** 129.

[19] Williams, G. and Searle, R. (1954), *How to be Topp* (Max Parish & Co.).

[20] Gavela, M. B. and Nepomechie, R. I. (1984), 'Discrete symmetries in Kaluza-Klein theories', *Class. Quant. Grav.* **1** L21.

[21] Duff, M. J., Nilsson, B. E. W. and Pope, C. N. (1983), 'Spontaneous symmetry breaking by the squashed seven-sphere', *Phys. Rev. Lett.* **50** 2043.

[22] Alvarez-Gaumé, L. and Freedman, D. Z. (1981), 'Geometrical structure and ultraviolet finiteness in the supersymmetric sigma model', *Commun. Math. Phys.* **80** 443.

[23] Deser, S., Jackiw, R. and Templeton, S. (1982), 'Topologically massive gauge theories', *Ann. Phys.* **140** 372.

[24] Kitao, T. and Ohta, N. (2000), 'Spectrum of Maxwell–Chern–Simons theory realized on type IIB brane configurations, *Nucl. Phys.* **B578** 215.

29

Gauged supergravity
and holographic field theory

Nick Warner

University of Southern California, Los Angeles

29.1 Gauged supergravity and a thesis project

I became one of Stephen's students a little over 20 years ago. At the time, Stephen was formulating and developing many of his ideas of Euclidean quantum gravity, and was also greatly interested in, and supportive of, other approaches to quantum gravity. Most particularly, he was an enthusiastic advocate of supergravity theories. Supergravity theories grew out of particle physics[1] and were not the standard fare of Relativists. It is a testament to Stephen's broad interests and the atmosphere in the Cambridge Relativity Group that the lines between these disciplines were completely blurred and that it was possible – indeed encouraged – for me as a student to move from my first work in relativity and Euclidean quantum gravity to the study of symmetry breaking in gauged supergravity. I remain very grateful to Stephen and to the Relativity Group for this opportunity and, most particularly, for the excitement, interest and enthusiasm with which they pursued the 'Grand Enterprise' of looking for a viable quantum theory of gravity.

The primary problem of quantum gravity is the infinite number of different kinds of divergences in the perturbation theory of pure quantum gravity. It was well known that divergences caused by fermions generically have the opposite sign to similar divergences caused by bosons. In a supersymmetric theory, bosons are paired with fermions in just such a manner that these divergences have the same structure and tend to cancel one another in the quantum theory. In a supergravity theory, the

---

[1] I would like to apologize in advance to the large number of people who made huge contributions to the development of supergravity and string theory, but my allotted space makes it impossible to reference them all adequately and correctly.

graviton is paired with one, or more, fermionic partners, called gravitini. The number of gravitini, $\mathcal{N}$, denotes the amount of (extended) supersymmetry. The more supersymmetry the larger the spectrum of the theory: $\mathcal{N} = 1$ supergravity has simply a graviton and one gravitino, and the maximal supergravity in four dimensions has $\mathcal{N} = 8$, with a spectrum of one graviton, eight gravitini, 28 vector bosons, 56 spin-1/2 particles and 70 scalar fields. One cannot go beyond $\mathcal{N} = 8$ since the spectrum would then have to include particles whose spin is higher than that of the graviton and, as far as we know, non-stringy higher spin theories appear to be inconsistent. The important point is that, in general, the more supersymmetry there is, the more the divergences are cancelled. The crucial question of the early 1980s was whether $\mathcal{N} = 8$ supergravity was finite. It was ultimately shown that even maximal supergravity very probably had divergences at higher orders [1–3], but despite this difficulty, it was clear that supergravity was a very important step in the right direction and that it had to be part of the right answer. Subsequent history has born this prejudice out in that supergravity is the low energy limit of string theory, which *is* (as far as we can tell) a finite quantum theory of gravity.

In the early 1980s, when we were still trying to turn supergravity into the *Theory of Everything*, there was another important issue: maximal supergravities contained vector bosons, but in the original formulations all these vector bosons in these theories were Abelian. To describe the real world one needs non-Abelian gauge symmetry, and many people painstakingly constructed the so-called gauged supergravity theories, that is, theories with non-Abelian gauge symmetry mediated by the vector bosons. This work culminated in the eventual construction of gauged, maximal ($\mathcal{N}=8$) supergravity theory [4]. This theory also had the maximal possible gauge group of $SO(8)$.

It is a remarkable and rather attractive feature of these gauged supergravity theories that the joint requirements of gauge symmetry and supersymmetry also requires a non-linear potential in the scalar sector. Moreover, the more the supersymmetry, the more rigid the potential, and indeed the potential is completely fixed in the maximal theory. Thus, the maximal gauged theory determines its own symmetry breaking structure completely; there are no choices and no arbitrary parameters to be fixed.

In the early days of supergravity the focus, for obvious reasons, was primarily upon supergravity in four spacetime dimensions. However, it became very important to study supergravity in every possible dimension. There are several reasons for this (some of which will be described later), but one of the primary reasons was that the higher dimensional maximal theories are generically simpler, and thus easier to construct. Indeed

the lower dimensional maximal theories were often first constructed by
dimensionally reducing the higher dimensional theories (see, for example [5, 6]). Here I will be concerned mainly with the gauged maximal
supergravities in four dimensions and in five dimensions; both of these
theories have $\mathcal{N} = 8$ supersymmetry. The latter theory has a spectrum
of one graviton, eight gravitini, 15 vector bosons, 12 tensor gauge fields,
48 'spin-1/2' particles and 42 scalar fields; the gauge group is $SO(6)$. The
five-dimensional theory was also the last gauged maximal supergravity
to be constructed [7–9]. This was, to some extent, because of technical
issues, but also because it seemed of the least phenomenological interest.
It is thus a wonderful irony that this situation is now reversed.

As I walked home with him one wet winter's day, Stephen suggested
that I should study the four-dimensional, maximal gauged $\mathcal{N} = 8$ theory
and try to understand its symmetry breaking structure. This was to be
the last project of my PhD. At the time, neither I nor Stephen remotely
suspected that, rather than finding its most important application directly
within quantum gravity, this work would prove important 20 years later
in determining part of the phase diagram of strongly coupled, large N,
$\mathcal{N} = 4$ Yang–Mills theory: a theory that is a distant relative of QCD,
which describes the force that underpins the strong nuclear interaction.
It is the purpose of this talk to outline how all of this came about, and
describe how the ideas of gravity and supergravity can be used to give
beautiful and remarkable insights into field theory via the idea holography
on branes.

29.2 The ups and downs of maximal gauged supergravity

In any supergravity theory, or string theory, one wants to find interesting,
and hopefully viable, ground states for the theory. In gauged supergravity
one is thus naturally led to study the scalar fields and their potential.
Both the four- and five-dimensional maximal gauged supergravity theories
have a completely determined scalar potential, and these potentials have
somewhat similar structural features. Thus, while my remarks in this
section will be directed toward the four-dimensional theory, many of the
results have five-dimensional parallels that will be important later.

29.2.1 The universe is not anti-de Sitter

It is a fundamental property of the superalgebra underlying gauged supergravity that if a ground state preserves supersymmetry, and that supersymmetry transforms under a non-Abelian gauge symmetry, then the
ground state must necessarily have a negative cosmological constant. This

cosmological constant, Λ, is of order $-g^2$ in Planck units, where g is the gauge coupling constant in the supergravity.

This fact means that the easiest (i.e., most symmetric) ground states to find will generically be associated with anti-de Sitter (AdS) space with Planck scale Λ. In particular, this includes the maximally supersymmetric ground state, in which all the scalars vanish. An optimist would note that $\mathcal{N} = 0, 1$ or $\mathcal{N} = 2$ supersymmetric vacua with zero cosmological constant are still allowed since such theories have either no gauge symmetry action, or an (Abelian) $U(1)$ action on the residual supersymmetry generators. Thus a phenomenologically interesting ground state is not excluded by the AdS superalgebra. But there is still the problem of explaining the transition from the maximally supersymmetric AdS vacuum to the (hopefully) flat vacuum.

29.2.2 Stability of ground states

There was also the more immediate problem that all the ground states appeared to be pathologically unstable, even the maximally supersymmetric ground state. Figure 29.1 shows a contour map of a typical two-parameter section through the maximally supersymmetric critical point. This point is a local *maximum* of the potential, and is thus naively unstable.

It turns out that any supersymmetric critical point is completely classically (and semi-classically) stable [10]. One can prove this by establishing an AdS positive mass theorem. The key physical insight is that

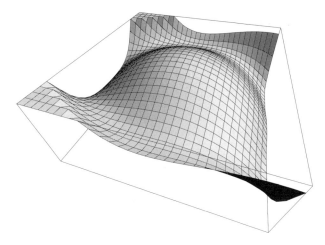

Fig. 29.1. A generic contour map of a two-dimensional section through the maximally symmetric critical point of a supergravity potential. The hump in the middle is the maximally supersymmetric local maximum.

because the potential is Planck scale, the gravitational back-reaction is very strong. Indeed Breitenlohner and Freedman showed very generally that in AdS space, a scalar field was perturbatively stable so long as its mass-squared is not 'too negative' [11]. This bound in an anti-de Sitter space, AdS_d, of dimension d and radius R is [11, 12]:

$$m^2 \geq -\frac{(d-1)^2}{4\,R^2}. \tag{29.1}$$

29.2.3 The standard model and chiral fermions

The maximal possible gauge symmetry of maximal supergravity is $SO(8)$, and this group is not large enough to contain the gauge groups of the standard model: $SU(3) \times SU(2) \times U(1)$. There were suggestions that the physical gauge groups might emerge through some composite mechanism, or via a large $SU(8)$ local composite symmetry of the supergravity theory. These ideas have remained just that, and were not given substance in four dimensions.

The other problem was that the fermions come in real representations of the $SO(8)$ gauge symmetry, and even if one could break to $SU(3) \times U(1)$ (hoping that $SU(2)$ would emerge somehow at low energy) then the fermions would still be in non-chiral (real) representations of these groups. Thus $SO(8)$ seemed to be fairly hopeless in terms of phenomenology (in spite of some remarkable numerology that originated with Gell-Mann. See [13] for details).

Thus the 'real-world' possibilities were very remote for this most divergence-free theory of all supergravities. Moreover, by this time, a consensus emerged that this theory was also most probably not finite. Thus the gauged maximal supergravity slowly faded from notice and interest.

29.3 Exploring higher dimensions

Parallel to the development of maximal supergravity in four dimensions was the development and construction of supergravity in higher dimensions. As I remarked earlier, the ungauged maximal theories were first obtained by 'trivial' (i.e., on tori) dimensional reduction of the eleven-dimensional supergravity. It was one of the major industries of the early 1980s to see what low-dimensional theories might be obtained by compactifying higher-dimensional maximal theories on other manifolds.

Initially the focus was upon Kaluza–Klein methods, in which gauge symmetries in lower dimensions emerged via isometries of the compactifying manifold. As with gauged supergravity, there were huge phenomenological problems with this. First, isometries on the compactifying manifold tended to lead to AdS space-times. Furthermore, it was finally shown [14–16] that one could never get chiral fermions though Kaluza–Klein without having chiral fermions *ab initio*.

In the mid 1980s string theory emerged from a long hibernation, and with the invention of the heterotic string it appeared that one could finally get a finite theory of quantum gravity with large enough gauge groups, chiral fermions and no anomalies. The focus thus turned to the compactification of string theory, some of which entailed finding compactifications of the corresponding low-energy supergravity theories (often coupled to supersymmetric matter).

29.3.1 Sphere compactifications

One particular focus of supergravity was the compactification of eleven-dimensional supergravity on S^7 down to AdS_4. It was believed, and indeed subsequently proven, that the low energy sector (i.e., essentially the lowest Fourier modes on S^7) of this theory is, in fact, maximal gauged $\mathcal{N} = 8$ supergravity in four dimensions. The complete set of Fourier modes of the S^7 compactification would thus extend maximal gauged $\mathcal{N} = 8$ supergravity by infinite towers of massive states.

A variant of this idea is of particular relevance today. There is a maximal supergravity theory, called IIB supergravity, in ten dimensions that has two chiral fermions [17] (and so is not a trivial dimensional reduction of eleven-dimensional supergravity). This theory is a low-energy limit of the ten-dimensional, IIB superstring. This supergravity, and the corresponding string theory theory have a compactification on S^5 down to five dimensional AdS_5, and this almost certainly (though it was never fully proven) yields, in the massless sector, the maximal gauged $\mathcal{N} = 8$ theory in five dimensions.

This string background also arises in another very interesting manner.

29.3.2 Brane backgrounds

A very important class of stringy backgrounds are *p*-branes, which are the higher dimensional analogues of the extreme Reissner–Nordström black holes. That is, they are $(p, 1)$-dimensional objects that minimally couple to a $(p+1)$-form gauge potential. If the gauge field is a Ramond–Ramond (RR) field of the string then they are called *Dp*-branes, and most significantly, in a closed string theory there can also be open strings that end on the *D*-branes [18]. The lowest modes of the closed string generically describe the graviton supermultiplet, and the lowest modes of the open string generically describe a vector supermultiplet. The directions

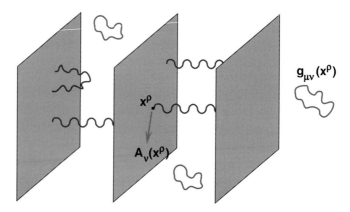

Fig. 29.2. Open strings can end on the *D*-branes, while only closed strings appear in the bulk. The lowest modes of the closed string describe the graviton supermultiplet, while the lowest modes of the open strings describe vector supermultiplets localized on the *D*-branes.

of the oscillations of the string give rise to the polarization tensors (see figure 29.2).

The consequence of this is that a closed string in the presence of *Dp*-branes will induce a Yang–Mills theory on the *D*-branes. If there are N coincident *D*-branes then the Yang–Mills theory has an $SU(N)$ gauge group, and the amount of supersymmetry on the brane is half of that of the bulk theory. Thus IIB superstrings induce $\mathcal{N} = 4$ supersymmetric, $SU(N)$ Yang–Mills theory on a stack of N coincident *D*3-branes (whose world-volume is four dimensional). This particular Yang–Mills theory is also a conformal field theory (CFT), even as a strongly coupled quantum theory.

The extreme Reissner–Nordström black hole has a 'near-horizon' limit that is essentially an infinitely long throat described by $AdS_2 \times S^2$. In the same manner, the near-brane limit of the *D*3-brane background is $AdS_5 \times S^5$. The metric in this near-brane limit may be written:

$$ds_{10}^2 = e^{2 A(r)} \left(\eta_{\mu\nu} \, dx^\mu \, dx^\nu \right) + dr^2 + ds_5^2, \qquad (29.2)$$

where $A(r) = r/L$ and ds_5^2 is the metric of an S^5 of radius L. The factor $\eta_{\mu\nu} \, dx^\mu \, dx^\nu$ is the flat metric on the $\mathbb{R}^{3,1}$ slices parallel to the *D*3-branes. The first two terms in (29.2) combine to make the AdS_5 metric in which $L = (4\pi g_s \alpha' N)^{\frac{1}{4}}$ is the AdS radius. Here N is the number of *D*3 branes, g_s is the string coupling and α' is the string tension parameter. Thus, as depicted in Figure 29.3, this maximally supersymmetric background of

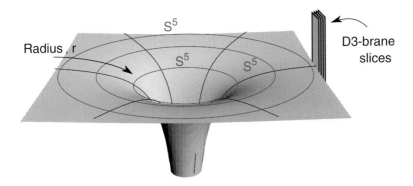

Fig. 29.3. The near-brane limit of $D3$-branes. The circles denote the S^5s around the branes in the core of the solution, while the radial coordinate and the slices parallel to the $D3$-branes combine to make an AdS_5.

the IIB superstring emerges as an infinitely long throat as one tries to approach the horizon of the $D3$-brane background.

The next leap forward was made by Maldacena [19] in the late 1990s, and it was to conjecture a deep relationship between the physics of the closed IIB superstring theory (and hence IIB supergravity) in the 'near-brane' background and the physics of the Yang–Mills theory on the $D3$-branes.

29.4 Holographic field theory and AdS/CFT correspondence

As discussed by other speakers at this meeting, the basic idea in holographic field theory is that, in the presence of gravity, physics in a region of spacetime can be encoded on a lower-dimensional surface surrounding that region. In particular, the quantum properties of matter that has formed a black hole can be (and have been) holographically encoded on its horizon [20, 21]. The Maldacena Conjecture[2] makes precise computational proposals for several such holographic encodings. One of these states that there is a precise quantum duality between IIB superstring theory in an $AdS_5 \times S^5$ background and the CFT on $D3$-branes, that is, $\mathcal{N} = 4$ Yang–Mills theory. The holographic principle was originally intended as a way of studying gravity by looking at a holographic field theory on a surface, but here I will be using the holographic principle in reverse to derive field theory results on the brane using IIB string theory, or more precisely supergravity.

---

[2] By now it is sufficiently widely believed and tested that we should probably call it a theory or principle.

The heart of this AdS/CFT correspondence is to realize that a gauge invariant operator, $\mathcal{O}(x)$, in the Yang–Mills theory on the brane will act as a source for closed strings in the bulk. In particular, conserved currents on the brane must couple to local gauge fields in the string background. For example, the energy-momentum tensor of the Yang–Mills theory couples to (or is dual to) the graviton in the string theory, and the currents of the global $SO(6)$ R-symmetry of Yang–Mills are dual to the vector bosons of the gauged supergravity. This idea extends, via supersymmetry, to a complete correspondence of fields in the Yang–Mills energy-momentum supermultiplet with the fields in the graviton supermultiplet. The latter are precisely the massless fields that constitute the spectrum of maximal gauged $\mathcal{N} = 8$ supergravity in five dimensions. In particular, the 42 scalar fields of the gauged supergravity are dual to bilinears of fundamental Yang–Mills fields, or roughly the Yang–Mills gauge coupling, θ-angle, and all the mass terms for the Yang–Mills fermions and scalar fields.

More generally, if one introduces a generating function for correlation functions of gauge invariant Yang–Mills operators, then the AdS/CFT correspondence states that [19, 22, 23]:

$$\left\langle \exp\left(-\int \varphi_j^{(0)} \, \mathcal{O}_j(x_j) \, d^4x\right)\right\rangle\Bigg|_{\text{brane}} = \mathcal{Z}_{\text{string}}[\varphi_k]$$
$$\to \mathcal{Z}_{\text{supergravity}}[\varphi_k]$$
$$\to \exp\left(-\mathcal{S}[\varphi_k]\right) . \qquad (29.3)$$

In this equation the left-hand side is the generating function with operators integrated against arbitrary density functions, $\varphi_j^{(0)}$, on the branes. The function $\mathcal{Z}_{\text{string}}[\varphi_k]$ is the string path integral evaluated in the AdS background fields, φ_k, that satisfy boundary conditions

$$\varphi_k(x^\mu, r) \to \varphi_j^{(0)}(x^\mu) \quad \text{as} \quad r \to \infty, \qquad (29.4)$$

where r is AdS_5 radial coordinate transverse to the branes, and is defined in (29.2). The first limit in (29.3) reduces the string theory to its supergravity limit, and this may be done by a combination of taking the string tension to infinity ($\alpha' \to 0$) and sending $g_s N \to \infty$. The second limit in (29.3) is obtained by making the saddle-point approximation ($g_s \to 0$) of the supergravity path integral, $\mathcal{Z}_{\text{supergravity}}[\varphi_k]$, and thus one simply evaluates the supergravity action on the classical supergravity solution that satisfies the boundary conditions (29.4). The strongest form of the correspondence is, of course, the string theory expression, but, in practice, it is much easier to work with supergravity actions, and it is in this context that most (but not all) of the testing has been done.

The 'bottom line' is that the classical action of IIB supergravity in ten dimensions should holographically capture the large-N limit of strongly coupled quantum Yang–Mills theory. Moreover, if one restricts it to the operators of the energy-momentum tensor supermultiplet (mass insertions, gauge coupling and θ angle) then the behaviour of this large-N strongly quantum theory on the brane, under such perturbing operators, should be captured entirely by gauged, $\mathcal{N} = 8$ supergravity in five dimensions.

29.5 Bulk gravity and brane renormalization: where are the branes?

From the gravitational perspective the branes must be at the core of the solution, that is, at the bottom of the infinitely long throat. Therefore, the boundary condition (29.4) as $r \to \infty$ seems very counterintuitive: the branes are at $r = -\infty$ and not at $r = +\infty$. However, locating the branes is not so simple in the holographic perspective: In holography one considers the field theory on any of the $(3+1)$-dimensional Poincaré invariant slice of the spacetime. The idea is that one is then 'sampling' the field theory on a brane located at some radius, r, in the metric (29.2), and the choice of the radius represents a choice of the renormalization scale in the field theory. I want to illustrate this in several ways since this idea is central to some of the more remarkable tests and applications of the AdS/CFT correspondence.

First, one should recall that AdS_5 is invariant under $SO(4,2)$, and that this is the conformal group in $(3+1)$ dimensions. If one takes a general $D3$-brane slice of (29.2) then fixing a finite value of r breaks $SO(4,2)$ down to the Poincaré invariance on the slice, and in particular, scale invariance has been broken. However, the slice at $r = \infty$ is special: it is fixed under the action of $SO(4,2)$, and so the field theory induced on this slice is conformally invariant. Thus we associate the brane at infinity with a conformal, ultraviolet fixed point of the brane field theory, and a brane at finite r with the theory at some cut-off scale set by r. Indeed, to implement many computations using (29.3) one has to regulate the Green functions, and this can be done explicitly by setting $r = 1/\epsilon$ and sending $\epsilon \to 0$. (See, for example [22–24].) As one might expect, the true physical scale on the brane is set by the cosmological scale factor, $e^{A(r)}$, in (29.2), and not so much by r itself.

29.5.1 Coarse-graining and redshifts

The foregoing is a rather formal justification, and other more physical arguments can be given (see, for example, Lenny Susskind's contribution

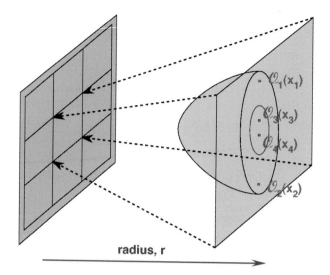

radius, r

Fig. 29.4. The ultraviolet–infrared duality of holography: large-distance behaviour on the brane depends upon details at small radii, r, while short-distance behaviour depends only upon large r. Alternatively, gravitational redshifts generate Wilsonian coarse graining on the brane.

to these proceedings). One way that one can see this rather clearly is to consider two parallel slices at different values of r, as depicted in Figure 29.4. If one considers the correlator of two operators on a brane then the correlator is only sensitive to the region of the spacetime that is relatively near both operators. If the operators are widely separated, as are $\mathcal{O}_1$ and $\mathcal{O}_2$ in Figure 29.4, then they sample deeply into the interior of the spacetime (down to lower values of r). If the operators are close together like $\mathcal{O}_3$ and $\mathcal{O}_4$ then they are only sensitive to details of the spacetime at large r. Thus we see the ultraviolet–infrared duality of holography: short distance behaviour on the brane depends upon large r, while large distance behaviour on the brane depends upon small values of r.

One can take a more active view of the same process. Consider a fixed volume, say $1m^3$, on the $D3$-brane measured in the Poincaré metric, but consider this volume at two different values of r. This is depicted in Figure 29.4 by the large squares on the left and right. If one uses supergravity to evolve data from large r to smaller r then it will be blueshifted. Thus if one uses supergravity equations to determine evolution in r, studying physics on a Poincaré scale of $1m^3$ at smaller r will involve averaging over data from several regions of size $1m^3$ at the larger value of r. This is precisely Wilsonian coarse-graining and it comes out of holography via gravitational red (blue)-shifts. The evolution to smaller values of r is thus renormalization group flow to the infrared.

29.5.2 Central charge and cosmological entropy

There are several ways in which one can put computational flesh on these ideas, but one of the simplest and most beautiful is the the holographic c-theorem.

In a conformal field theory the central charge essentially counts the number of massless degrees of freedom in the theory. It may be defined in terms of the leading singularity in the correlator, or operator product, of two energy-momentum tensors. In d dimensions the energy-momentum tensor, $T(z)$, has dimension d, and so to leading order one has

$$T(x)\, T(y) \sim \frac{C}{|x-y|^{2d}}. \tag{29.5}$$

(I am suppressing all the details of tensor indices.) If $T(x)$ is canonically normalized then the constant C is essentially the central charge, and it is proportional to the number of degrees of freedom within the theory: it simply counts the ways in which energy can be transmitted.

In a holographic theory one can argue that the central charge is dual to a power of the 'effective cosmological constant', that is,

$$C(r) \sim \frac{1}{A'(r)^{d-1}}, \tag{29.6}$$

where $A(r)$ is the function in (29.2). The central charge thus depends upon the scale r. Moreover, it can shown [25] that if the matter in the supergravity theory obeys a weak energy condition, then $C(r)$ monotonically decreases as r decreases, and is only stationary in an AdS vacuum, and hence at a conformal fixed point on the brane. In other words, the number of dynamical degrees of freedom monotonically decreases as one flows to the infrared, unless the flow reaches a conformal fixed point and then the number of degrees of freedom remains constant. This is precisely what one should expect as a result of coarse-graining: a gradual loss of non-scale invariant degrees of freedom.

In cosmology, where the evolution is over time, the quantity analogous to $A'(r)^{d-1}$ is the entropy density of the universe, and this is monotonically increasing. Thus there is at least a formal link between the entropy in cosmology and the central charge in holographic renormalization group flows. Moreover, both the flow of entropy and the flow of the central charge reflect a loss of information about the detailed finer structure of the matter within the spacetime.

29.5.3 *Universality and black branes*

The foregoing shows that there are remarkable links between classical results of relativity and quantum properties of field theory on the brane. Much has been done to develop this, but given that this meeting is to celebrate Stephen's contributions to science, there is one speculation that seems very appropriate.

In quantum field theory the idea of universality loosely states that the (infrared) end-point of a renormalization group flow does not depend upon ultraviolet details. In low dimensions one can go further and argue that infrared renormalization group fixed points do not depend upon details of interactions, but merely depend upon the symmetries of, and number of degrees of freedom in the physical system. If one thinks holographically, then this says that the supergravity solution for small values of r does not depend upon the details of the matter at large values of r. This begins to sound like a 'no hair' theorem, particularly when one thinks of the stronger low-dimensional idea of universality. If the flow solution evolves (as many of them do) to a black brane in the core, then indeed universality of the field theory on brane, and a 'no hair' theorem for the black brane are trying to capture exactly the same physical ideas.

It should, of course, be remembered that in holography of four-dimensional field theories we are interested in radial evolution in five, or even ten, dimensions. As Gary Horowitz's talk illustrates, the collapse of black-branes in higher dimensions can lead to rather exotic end-states. There is, however, a very interesting convergence. One would like to know all the infrared fixed points of Yang–Mills theories, and it is intriguing to think that (at least for large N) it might rest upon understanding the possible end-states of collapse of black branes.

29.6 Holographic renormalization group flows: an example

One of the simplest ways to exhibit a holographic renormalization group flow is to take a conformally invariant holographic theory and perturb it by a relevant operator and then use supergravity to study the flow. One may also seek out fixed points of such a flow by looking for new, non-trivial AdS vacua that might be approached in the infrared ($r \to -\infty$).

Gauged $\mathcal{N} = 8$ supergravity in five dimensions provides a powerful tool for analysing a sub-class of flows in $\mathcal{N} = 4$ Yang–Mills theory [25–27]. The 42 scalars of the supergravity are dual to bilinear operators in the Yang–Mills theory, and thus by choosing the appropriate supergravity scalar one can introduce a gauge invariant mass term for any field in the Yang–Mills theory. The flow to the infrared will then correspond to integrating the massive field out of the Yang–Mills action, leaving a reduced number of degrees of freedom, and perhaps some new, non-trivial interactions. In the supergravity theory the scalars corresponding to the mass terms must be Poincaré invariant, but will depend upon r, and their evolution will be determined by the supergravity equations of motion. The potential in the supergravity will thus determine the flow, and critical points of the potential will, in principle, determine non-trivial conformal fixed points of a flow. Therefore, the (rigidly-determined) supergravity potential represents and characterizes the phase diagram and flows of $\mathcal{N} = 4$ Yang–Mills theory under mass perturbations.

29.6.1 Stability and unitarity

There are several subtleties involved in holographic duality, and the identification of flows, and one of these involves the stability issue. There are several known critical points of the gauged $\mathcal{N} = 8$ supergravity potential [28], and several of them fail the Breitenlohner–Freedman stability condition (29.1). They are thus not even perturbatively stable supergravity vacua.

It turns out that the holographic correspondence yields a direct relationship between the mass of small oscillations in the supergravity and the dimension of conformal operators on the brane [22, 23]. If a supergravity scalar fails the Breitenlohner–Freedman condition then the corresponding operator has imaginary conformal dimension, and the field theory cannot be unitary. Moreover, if one carefully examines a flow from the maximally symmetric critical point to an unstable critical point one can see that it appears to correspond to an infinite energy deformation involving a mass and a vacuum expectation value for the same operator.

This raises the question as to what critical points and flows are physically sensible. The general belief is that if the critical point is stable then it is a physical vacuum for both the supergravity and the theory on the brane, but there is a further issue. It should always be remembered that the supergravity description is really only valid at large N, and so it may be that a flow, or a critical point might represent a 'large N pathology' that may not be physical for finite N. Fortunately string theory gives us an answer. At finite N one must use the full string path integral, and so a flow solution in supergravity will be valid at finite N if we can demonstrate that it is a good string vacuum. The latter is not so easy to do, but based upon experience in string compactification in the late 1980s we know that supergravity vacua are usually good approximations to string vacua if they are supersymmetric. Such vacua also have the virtue of being completely semi-classically stable.

We are thus led to the following proposal. Any supersymmetric supergravity flow solution will reflect a real physical flow at finite N for the theory on the brane. This proposal has passed several very non-trivial tests, and I will now outline one of them.

29.6.2 A supersymmetric flow

In $\mathcal{N} = 4$ Yang–Mills theory there is one gauge field, A_μ, four fermions, λ^a, and six scalars, X^I, all in the adjoint of $SU(N)$. Consider the following mass perturbation on the brane:

$$\Delta \mathcal{L} \; = \; m_1 \, \text{Tr} \, (\lambda^1 \, \lambda^1) \; + \; m_2^2 \, \text{Tr} \, ((X^1)^2 + (X^2)^2) \,. \tag{29.7}$$

If $m_1 = m_2$ then this perturbation preserves $\mathcal{N} = 1$ supersymmetry on the brane. Moreover, in field theory at finite N, this particular flow is known to lead to a non-trivial, $\mathcal{N} = 1$ supersymmetric fixed point [29].

In supergravity the perturbation (29.7) is represented by two scalars, $\varphi_1 = m_2^2$ and $\varphi_2 = m_1$. On this sub-sector the supergravity potential is easily computed, and it is in fact shown in Figure 29.1. The contours of this potential are shown in Figure 29.5.

The supergravity equations of motion are, of course, second order and involve the potential, $\mathcal{V}$. However, if one seeks the supersymmetric flow then this is given by solving a first-order system involving a superpoten-

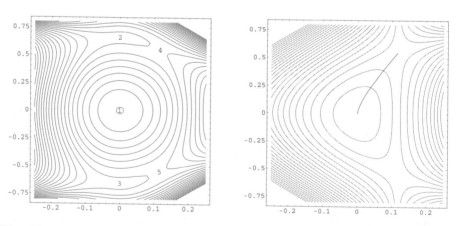

Fig. 29.5. The contour diagrams of part of the supergravity potential and superpotential. The mass parameters $\varphi_1 = m_2^2$ and $\varphi_2 = m_1$ are plotted along the horizontal and vertical axes respectively. Critical points are numbered on the plot of the potential, and the line on the second contour plot shows the steepest descent between critical points of the superpotential.

tial. That is one solves:

$$\frac{d\varphi_j}{dr} = \frac{1}{L}\frac{\partial \mathcal{W}}{\partial \varphi_j}, \qquad \frac{dA(r)}{dr} = -\frac{2}{3L}\mathcal{W}, \qquad (29.8)$$

where L is the AdS radius as $r \to \infty$, and

$$\mathcal{W} \equiv \frac{1}{4\rho^2}\left[\cosh(2\varphi_2)\,(\rho^6 - 2) - (3\rho^6 + 2)\right], \qquad \rho \equiv e^{\frac{1}{\sqrt{6}}\varphi_1}. \quad (29.9)$$

The supergravity potential is then given by:

$$\mathcal{V} = \frac{1}{2\,L^2}\sum_{j=1}^{2}\left|\frac{\partial \mathcal{W}}{\partial \varphi_j}\right|^2 - \frac{4}{3\,L^2}\,|\mathcal{W}|^2. \qquad (29.10)$$

The contour diagrams in Figure 29.5 show several critical points. The central one is the maximally supersymmetric vacuum in which all the supergravity scalars vanish. The other vacua come in pairs related by a trivial reflection. The vacua labelled 2 and 3 are unstable, while the vacua labelled by 4 and 5 are $\mathcal{N} = 2$ supersymmetric in the bulk ($\mathcal{N} = 1$ super-symmetric on the brane) and preserve $SU(2) \times U(1) \subset SO(6)$. Only the supersymmetric vacua show up on the contour plot of the superpotential, $\mathcal{W}$. Thus there is a good candidate supergravity vacuum state for the field theory fixed point of [29]. Indeed it is easy to verify that the unbroken supersymmetry and R-symmetry at the non-trivial critical point exactly matches that found in [29].

Equations (29.8) show that the flow is a given by steepest descent on $\mathcal{W}$, and that the cosmological function, $A(r)$, is completely determined by the steepest descent. This steepest descent is shown in Figure 29.5. One can see that near the central critical point one has $\varphi_1 \sim \varphi_2^2$, which is consistent with $m_1 = m_2$ as required by supersymmetry. At the non-trivial critical point one can examine the linearized supergravity spectrum and one finds that it matches perfectly with holographically dual operators that one expects to find in the field theory [25]. Most significantly, the supergravity predicts the following ratios of central charges:

$$\frac{C_{IR}}{C_{IR}} = \left(\frac{A'(-\infty)}{A'(+\infty)}\right)^3 = \frac{27}{32}. \qquad (29.11)$$

This can be checked against a direct, and rather non-trivial, anomaly computation within the field theory, and there is perfect agreement.

29.6.3 An important open problem

One does not have to restrict one's attention to flows to non-trivial fixed points. There are many physically interesting families of flows that

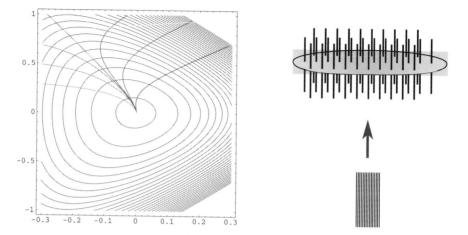

Fig. 29.6. Half-maximal supersymmetric flows appear as steepest descents on a supergravity superpotential. The physically most interesting flow follows the ridge line. This flow is singular at finite r, and corresponds to a 'disc-like' smearing out of the D3-brane distribution.

approach singular metrics at finite values of r. Among the most interesting of these are the half-maximal supersymmetric flows ($\mathcal{N} = 2$ on the brane $\mathcal{N} = 4$ in the bulk). These are particularly important because part of the quantum effective action is exactly known [30, 31], and thus one can perform some extremely non-trivial tests of such holographic flows.

Rather surprisingly, only a little is known about this class of solutions in IIB supergravity. Indeed only one such flow solution is known, and this was constructed again using the techniques of gauged $\mathcal{N} = 8$ supergravity, and the result was then lifted to the full ten-dimensional theory [32]. Physically one again looks at steepest descents on another supergravity superpotential, as shown in Figure 29.6. In the corresponding ten-dimensional solution the branes are now located at finite r and are spread apart over a uniform 'disc-like' distribution. The asymptotic behaviour of this solution can be studied in detail [33] and one does indeed find results that are beautifully consistent with those of the quantum field theory.

The solution of [32] represents only one fixed (in fact, the most uniform) distribution of smeared out D3-branes. The quantum field theory results of [30, 31] allow, and give exact results, for an arbitrary two-dimensional distribution of the D3-branes. Thus the solution of [32] is but a single point in an infinite moduli space of half-maximally supersymmetric solutions. No other solutions in this class are known.

For this reason, and for several others it would be very nice to find general results for half-maximal supersymmetric backgrounds. There are theorems about hyper-Kähler manifolds leading to such backgrounds in the absence of branes, and so the open question is to find the analogue of the hyper-Kähler condition for half-maximal supersymmetry in the presence of branes and the Ramond–Ramond fluxes that they generate.

29.7 Final comments

In the late 1980s an eminent particle physicist publicly compared string theory to President Reagan's rather misguided Strategic Defence Initiative, commonly called 'Star Wars'. The suggestion was that both programmes were making extravagant claims based upon little, or no experimental evidence. While this commentary probably grew out of some closed-mindedness on one side and a certain amount of hubris on the other, it serves to underscore some much broader issues that concern string theory and string theorists.

First, the problem of quantum gravity is very unusual in science: the usual methodology is that one develops theories and chooses between them based on experimental data. In quantum gravity we have the problem that there are fundamental inconsistencies between two classes of well tested theory, and the problem has been to find *any* theory that solves the most basic of theoretical constraints. Stephen's work on black hole radiance and upon information loss has been extremely important in making us aware of some central aspects of what happens when quantum mechanics meets gravity. In particle physics, supergravity was a very important step in addressing the problem of divergences, and string theory is almost certainly finite. String theory remains the *only* viable theory of quantum gravity that we have found after 50 years of trying. This is a remarkable achievement, but it is has remained rather esoteric, and perhaps not as widely appreciated as it might, and should be.

This is further complicated by the fact that research in string theory does not fit the classical 'scientific method': predict and then experimentally test. Instead we test string theory in as many ways as we can computationally, and we study it in many, many limits. What is remarkable is that when we do this we often get new and deeper insights not just into quantum gravity but into particle physics and mathematics: String theory created the field of mirror symmetry in algebraic geometry; it has given new methods of computing multi-gluon amplitudes in QCD; it has spun-off a whole industry on 'braneworlds' and as, other speakers at this meeting have described, string theory and *D*-branes have given new insight into the apparent information loss in black holes. In this talk I have tried to describe how string theory has given us a new way of looking

at and analysing strongly coupled quantum field theories via holography. There are beautiful dualities between renormalization group flows,
coarse graining and cosmological redshifts and entropy. There are simple
classical calculations from which one obtains insight into the phase structure of strongly coupled quantum field theory. This, and all the other
developments, are not experimental confirmation, but they do represent
major progress in theoretical understanding. I believe that over the last
few years the physics community has begun to appreciate the remarkable
list of string theory spin-offs because there currently seems to be a more
broadly based enthusiasm for string theory than there was in the 1980s.

This still leaves open the issue of experimental confirmation. It should
be remembered that a quantum theory of gravity only becomes important
at energy scales vastly above the reach of any conceivable particle accelerator. So, to a purist, the experimental confirmation of string theory many
take a very, very long time. On the other hand, supersymmetry is one
of the foundational components of string theory, and current experimental data slightly favours the minimal *supersymmetric* standard model. At
this meeting Edward Witten predicted that within the next decade we
will see supersymmetry at the LHC. In terms of a solution to quantum
gravity it is by no means essential that this happens, but I think it is very
important to further strong support of string theory within the research
community.

Finally, it is worth remembering that for about a decade after they
were first invented, supersymmetric theories were considered by many to
be mathematical freaks with particle spectra that are obviously ridiculous.
Today, the study of supersymmetric field theories is not only respectable,
but it lies at the core of particle physics phenomenology. In 1980 it was
not very clear what the future of supersymmetry would be, but it was
obviously a very important, new theoretical idea. Stephen has always had
a very good sense for the important issues and the right questions to
ask. I am therefore very grateful to Stephen for his interest, support and
encouragement in the pursuit of a body of ideas that has grown into one
of the most exciting theoretical fields of the last, and hopefully the next,
twenty years.

References

[1] Howe, P. S. and Lindstrom, U. (1981), 'Higher order invariants in extended
     supergravity', *Nucl. Phys.* **B181** 487.

[2] Kallosh, R. E. (1981), 'Counterterms in extended supergravities', *Phys. Lett.*
     B99 122.

[3] Howe, P. S., Stelle, K. S. and Townsend, P. K. (1981), 'Superactions', *Nucl. Phys.* **B191**, 445.

[4] de Wit, B. and Nicolai, H. (1982), '$\mathcal{N} = 8$ supergravity', *Nucl. Phys.* **B208** 323.

[5] Cremmer, E., Julia, B. and Scherk, J. (1978), 'Supergravity theory in 11 dimensions', *Phys. Lett.* **B76** 409.

[6] Cremmer, E. and Julia, B. (1979), 'The SO(8) supergravity', *Nucl. Phys.* **B159** 141.

[7] Gunaydin, M., Romans, L. J. and Warner, N. P. (1985), 'Gauged $\mathcal{N} = 8$ supergravity in five-dimensions', *Phys. Lett.* **B154** 268.

[8] Gunaydin, M., Romans, L. J. and Warner, N. P. (1986), 'Compact and non-compact gauged supergravity theories in five-dimensions', *Nucl. Phys.* **B272** 598.

[9] Pernici, M., Pilch, K. and Van Nieuwenhuizen, P. (1985), 'Gauged $\mathcal{N} = 8$ D = 5 supergravity', *Nucl. Phys.* **B259** 460.

[10] Gibbons, G. W., Hull, C. M. and Warner, N. P. (1983), 'The stability of gauged supergravity', *Nucl. Phys.* **B218** 173.

[11] Breitenlohner, P. and Freedman, D. Z. (1982), 'Stability in gauged extended supergravity', *Annals Phys.* **144** 249.

[12] Townsend, P. K. (1984), 'Positive energy and the scalar potential in higher dimensional (super)gravity theories', *Phys. Lett.* **B148** 55.

[13] Nicolai, H. and Warner, N. P. (1985), 'The $SU(3) \times U(1)$ invariant breaking of gauged $\mathcal{N}=8$ supergravity', *Nucl. Phys.* **B259** 412.

[14] Witten, E. (1981), 'Search for a realistic Kaluza–Klein theory', *Nucl. Phys.* **B186** 412.

[15] Wetterich, C. (1983), 'Chirality index and dimensional reduction of fermions' *Nucl. Phys.* **B223** 109.

[16] Witten, E. (1985), 'Symmetry breaking patterns in superstring models', *Nucl. Phys.* **B258** 75.

[17] Schwarz, J. H. (1983), 'Covariant Field Equations Of Chiral $N = 2 D = 10$ supergravity', *Nucl. Phys.* **B226** 269.

[18] Polchinski, J. (1995), 'Dirichlet–Branes and Ramond–Ramond charges', *Phys. Rev. Lett.* **75** 4724, [hep-th/9510017].

[19] Maldacena, J. (1998), 'The large N limit of superconformal field theories and supergravity', *Adv. Theor. Math. Phys.* **2** 231 (*Int. J. Theor. Phys.* **38** (1998) 1113), [hep-th/9711200].

[20] 't Hooft, G. (1993), 'Dimensional reduction in quantum gravity', [gr-qc/9310026].

[21] Susskind, L. (1995), 'The world as a hologram', *J. Math. Phys.* **36** 6377, [hep-th/9409089].

[22] Gubser, S. S., Klebanov, I. R. and Polyakov, A. M. (1998), 'Gauge theory correlators from non-critical string theory', *Phys. Lett.* **B428** 105, [hep-th/9802109].

[23] Witten, E. (1998), 'Anti-de Sitter space and holography', *Adv. Theor. Math. Phys.* **2** 253, [hep-th/9802150].

[24] Henningson, M. and Skenderis, K. (1998) 'The holographic Weyl anomaly', *JHEP* **9807** 023, [hep-th/9806087].

[25] Freedman, D. Z., Gubser, S. S., Pilch, K. and Warner, N. P. (1999), 'Renormalization group flows from holography supersymmetry and a c-theorem', *Adv. Theor. Math. Phys.* **3** 363, [hep-th/9904017].

[26] Distler, J. and Zamora, F. (1999), 'Non-supersymmetric conformal field theories from stable anti-de Sitter spaces', *Adv. Theor. Math. Phys.* **2** 1405, [hep-th/9810206].

[27] Girardello, L., Petrini, M., Porrati, M. and Zaffaroni, A. (1998), 'Novel local CFT and exact results on perturbations of $N = 4$ super Yang–Mills from AdS dynamics', *JHEP* **9812** 022, [hep-th/9810126].

[28] Khavaev, A., Pilch, K. and Warner, N. P. (2000), 'New vacua of gauged $N = 8$ supergravity in five dimensions', *Phys. Lett.* **B487** 14, [hep-th/9812035].

[29] Leigh, R. G. and Strassler, M. J. (1995), 'Exactly marginal operators and duality in four-dimensional $N = 1$ supersymmetric gauge theory', *Nucl. Phys.* **B447** 95, [hep-th/9503121].

[30] Seiberg, N. and Witten, E. (1994), 'Electric–magnetic duality, monopole condensation, and confinement in $N = 2$ supersymmetric Yang–Mills theory', *Nucl. Phys.* **B426** 19, [Erratum-ibid. B **430** (1994) 485], [hep-th/9407087].

[31] Seiberg, N. and Witten, E. (1994), 'Monopoles, duality and chiral symmetry breaking in $N = 2$ supersymmetric QCD', *Nucl. Phys.* **B431** 484, [hep-th/9408099].

[32] Pilch, K. and Warner, N. P. (2001), '$N = 2$ supersymmetric RG flows and the IIB dilaton', *Nucl. Phys.* **B594** 209, [hep-th/0004063].

[33] Buchel, A., Peet, A. W. and Polchinski, J. (2001), 'Gauge dual and non-commutative extension of an $N = 2$ supergravity solution', *Phys. Rev.* **D63** 044009, [hep-th/0008076].

30

57 Varieties in a NUTshell

Chris Pope

Center for Theoretical Physics, Texas A & M University

30.1 Introduction

Supersymmetry has proved to be one of the most important ideas in high-energy physics and the search for unification in the last few decades. In this article, contributed as part of the celebration of the sixtieth birthday of one of the most remarkable theoretical physicists of any decade, I shall review some connections between supersymmetry and holonomy, which is itself a fascinating topic in differential geometry. To do this, I shall focus on some areas where I have worked myself, starting with my time as a PhD student of Stephen Hawking in the late 1970s.

Difficult though it may be to believe these days, there was a time when the world was thought to be four dimensional. In the mid-1970s, exciting developments in gauge theories had led to the realization that topology had an important role to play, in the shape of Yang–Mills instantons. These topologically non-trivial solutions of the Yang–Mills equations are complex if written in Minkowski spacetime, but they are real if time is Wick rotated so that the four-dimensional space becomes Euclidean. Around the same (Minkowskian) time, Stephen Hawking had astonished the physics community with his demonstration that black holes are not after all black, but that they radiate a thermal spectrum of particles at a temperature inversely proportional to their mass [1]. Shortly after that, Hartle and Hawking [2] showed that Green functions in the black hole background are periodic in imaginary time, with a periodicity given by the inverse temperature. This established a connection with statistical thermal physics, and led on to the idea that a Wick-rotated or 'Euclideanized' description of the black hole spacetime might be more appropriate. Shortly afterwards, Stephen, Gary Gibbons and Malcolm Perry developed the idea further, leading to a one-line derivation of the

515

Hawking temperature of a black hole. Taking Schwarzschild as an example, one sends $t \longrightarrow i\tau$, giving the Euclideanized metric

$$ds^2 = \left(1 - \frac{2M}{r}\right)^{-1} dr^2 + \left(1 - \frac{2M}{r}\right) d\tau^2 + r^2 \left(d\theta^2 + \sin^2\theta \, d\phi^2\right), \quad (30.1)$$

defines a new radial coordinate ρ by $(1 - 2M/r) = \rho^2/(16M^2)$ and notes that near $r = 2M$, corresponding to $\rho = 0$, the metric takes the form

$$ds^2 \sim d\rho^2 + \rho^2 \left(\frac{d\tau}{4m}\right)^2 + 4M^2 \left(d\theta^2 + \sin^2\theta \, d\phi^2\right). \quad (30.2)$$

The first two terms look like $\mathbf{R}^2$ in polar coordinates, and so the metric can be extended to include $\rho = 0$ provided that τ has the period $8\pi M$. Thus the celebrated Hawking temperature $T = 1/(8\pi M)$ is obtained, with a minimum of calculation.

The Schwarzschild metric has the feature of admitting real Lorentzian and Euclidean sections, but the experience with Yang–Mills instantons had already emboldened physicists to allow the inclusion in the functional integral of solutions that are real only in the Euclidean section. With these examples pointing the way, Stephen took the bolder step of proposing that quantum gravity should properly be studied in the Euclidean regime, where the functional integral is better defined, and so the idea of 'Euclidean Quantum Gravity' was born.

30.2 Four-dimensional self-dual metrics

A particular feature of the Yang–Mills instantons is that they have field strengths that are *self-dual*, $F = *F$, and indeed it is because of this that they cannot be real in Minkowski spacetime. This is because $*^2 = -1$ on 2-forms in four Minkowski dimensions, whereas $*^2 = +1$ in four Euclidean dimensions. For many reasons self-duality is a nice condition to impose, not least because the Yang–Mills equations $D*F = 0$, which are second-order in derivatives of the potential A that gives rise to the field strength $F = dA + [A, A]$, are replaced by the much simpler first-order equations $F = *F$. It became natural therefore to look for gravitational analogues, where the Riemann curvature tensor is self-dual[1], $R_{abcd} = \frac{1}{2}\epsilon_{abef} R^{ef}{}_{cd}$. In terms of the curvature 2-forms $\Theta^a{}_b \equiv d\omega^a{}_b + \omega^a{}_c \wedge \omega^c{}_b$, this reads $\Theta_{ab} = \frac{1}{2}\epsilon_{abcd} \Theta^{cd}$, or, assuming torsion vanishes, $\Theta^a{}_b = *\Theta^a{}_b$. At first sight this still looks to be second-order in derivatives of the metric, since the spin connection $\omega^a{}_b$ is constructed from first derivatives of the vielbein,

---

[1] In general, the term *self-dual* will be taken to embrace both self-dual and anti-self-dual curvature.

$de^a = -\omega^a{}_b \wedge e^b$. However, the first-order 'self-duality' equations $\omega_{ab} = \frac{1}{2}\epsilon_{abcd}\,\omega^{cd}$ for the spin-connection imply the curvature self-duality equations, and conversely one can show that there exists a local frame in which the spin connection for any self-dual curvature satisfies these first-order equations. A further consequence of the self-duality of the Riemann tensor is that the metric is automatically Ricci-flat.

30.3 Non-compact self-dual 4-metrics

An early application of the first-order self-duality equations was in [3], where the Eguchi–Hanson metric

$$ds^2 = \left(1 - \frac{\ell^4}{r^4}\right)^{-1} dr^2 + \tfrac{1}{4}r^2 \left(1 - \frac{\ell^4}{r^4}\right)\sigma_3^2 + \tfrac{1}{4}r^2\left(\sigma_1^2 + \sigma_2^2\right) \tag{30.3}$$

was obtained. The σ_i here are (locally) the left-invariant 1-forms of $SU(2)$, satisfying $d\sigma_i = -\frac{1}{2}\epsilon_{ijk}\,\sigma_j \wedge \sigma_k$. In terms of Euler angles they can be written as $\sigma_1 + i\,\sigma_2 = e^{-i\psi}\,(d\theta + i\sin\theta\,d\phi)$, $\sigma_3 = d\psi + \cos\theta\,d\phi$. The Eguchi–Hanson metric has striking parallels with the Yang–Mills instantons in Euclidean space, in that it has curvature that reaches a maximum at the 'origin' $r = \ell$, falling away to zero in all four directions as the radius r increases. The apparent singularity in (30.3) at $r = \ell$ was analysed in [4], and shown to be only a coordinate singularity, provided that ψ is assigned the period 2π. This can be seen by performing a coordinate transformation analogous to the one for Schwarzschild discussed above. Since the radial coordinate runs down only as far as $r = \ell$, there is a minimal 2-sphere of radius ℓ there, described by the metric $\ell^2\,(\sigma_1^2 + \sigma_2^2) = \ell^2\,(d\theta^2 + \sin^2\theta\,d\phi^2)$. This degeneration of the generic three-dimensional orbits to the two-dimensional sphere is known as a 'Bolt', a term coined by Stephen Hawking and Gary Gibbons that parallels the 'NUT' at the origin of the Euclidean Taub-NUT metric, where the three-dimensional orbits degenerate to a point.

Since ψ has period 4π in $SU(2) \sim S^3$, this means that the principal orbits (the level sets $r = \text{constant}$) are $S^3/\mathbf{Z}_2 = \mathbf{RP}^3$ rather than S^3, and so the metric at large distance looks like $\mathbf{R}^4/\mathbf{Z}_2$ rather than Euclidean $\mathbf{R}^4$ [4]. Thus the Eguchi–Hanson instanton is not asymptotically Euclidean, but instead *Asymptotically Locally Euclidean*, or ALE.[2]

---

[2] Again a term coined by Stephen Hawking. At the time, in the late 1970s, several of his students and postdocs were enthusiastic practising supporters of the *Campaign for Real Ale*, which was waging a battle to replace the industrially-produced liquids then prevalent in pubs by real beer. This was Stephen's contribution to the highly successful campaign. Regrettably, although ALE spaces quickly migrated across the Atlantic, the taste for beer of flavour has been slower to develop in the US.

An equivalent statement to the self-duality of the Riemann tensor in four dimensions is that the holonomy group is $SU(2)$, corresponding to either the left-handed or right-handed factor in the tangent-space group $SO(4) \sim SU(2)_L \times SU(2)_R$. Which factor one has depends on whether the Riemann tensor is self-dual or anti-self-dual. In general the holonomy group is generated, locally, by the Riemann tensor. It characterizes the subgroup of tangent-frame rotations $SO(n)$ in n dimensions that a vector field will suffer if it is parallel transported around all possible infinitesimal closed paths:

$$\delta V^a = V^b \, R^a{}_{bcd} \, d\Sigma^{cd} \,. \tag{30.4}$$

The concept of self-duality is sometimes known as 'half-flatness', since the Riemann curvature resides in one or other half of the $SO(4) \sim SU(2) \times SU(2)$ group of tangent-frame rotations of a generic 4-manifold. A particular consequence of this is that spinors of one handedness or the other do not see any curvature at all if the Riemann tensor is self-dual, and so for such spinors we can have $\nabla_a \eta = 0$ since their integrability condition $[\nabla_a, \nabla_b] \eta = \frac{1}{4} R_{abcd} \Gamma^{cd} \eta$ will be identically satisfied. If a supergravity theory is put in a background of a metric with self-dual Riemann tensor, then such covariantly-constant spinors will be associated with unbroken supersymmetries that leave the vacuum invariant.

Yet another way of expressing the self-duality of the Riemann tensor is that the four-dimensional metric is Ricci-flat and Kähler. In general, in $n = 2m$ real dimensions, a Kähler manifold is one where there is an almost complex structure tensor $J_a{}^b$ such that $J_a{}^b J_b{}^c = -\delta_a^c$, the metric g_{ab} is almost-Hermitian, meaning that $J_{ab} \equiv J_a{}^c g_{cb}$ is antisymmetric, and J_{ab} is covariantly-constant with respect to the Christoffel connection, $\nabla_a J_{bc} = 0$. These conditions imply that the holonomy group is $U(m) \subset SO(2m)$. If in addition the metric is Ricci-flat, then the $U(1)$ factor in $U(m)$ will be absent, and the holonomy group becomes $SU(m)$.

The Eguchi–Hanson metric (30.3) is one example of a Bianchi IX metric with self-dual Riemann tensor. More generally, one can consider the triaxial Bianchi IX class

$$ds_4^2 = dt^2 + a_i^2 \, \sigma_i^2 \,, \tag{30.5}$$

where a_i are functions of the radial coordinate t. The principal orbits are three-dimensional 'squashed' 3-spheres, with a transitive $SU(2)$ isometry corresponding to the left translations that leave the 1-forms σ_i invariant. In the orthonormal frame $e^0 = dt$, $e^i = a_i \sigma_i$, the spin connection is given by

$$\omega_{01} = \beta_1 \, e^1 \,, \qquad \omega_{23} = \gamma_1 \, e^1 \,, \qquad \text{and cyclic}\,, \tag{30.6}$$

where

$$\beta_1 = -\frac{\dot{a}_1}{a_1}, \qquad \gamma_1 = \frac{a_1^2 - a_2^2 - a_3^2}{2 a_1 a_2 a_3}, \qquad \text{and cyclic}. \qquad (30.7)$$

By introducing a new radial coordinate ρ such that $dt = (a_1 a_2 a_3) \, d\rho$, and defining $\alpha_i \equiv \log a_i$, it is a straightforward exercise to show that the equations for Ricci-flatness are

$$2\alpha_1'' = a_1^4 - (a_2^2 - a_3^2)^2, \qquad \text{and cyclic}, \qquad (30.8)$$

where a prime means $d/d\rho$. In this Bianchi IX example it is rather easy to spot first integrals of these equations by inspection, namely [5]

$$2\alpha_1' = a_2^2 + a_3^2 - a_1^2 - 2\lambda_1 a_2 a_3, \qquad \text{and cyclic}, \qquad (30.9)$$

where the constants λ_i satisfy $\lambda_1 = \lambda_2 \lambda_3$ and cyclically. There are two inequivalent solutions, modulo orientation-reversals, in which $(\lambda_1, \lambda_2, \lambda_3)$ are given by $(0, 0, 0)$ or $(1, 1, 1)$. Reverting to the original radial coordinate t, the first-order systems in the two cases are

$$\text{Case 1: } \dot{a}_1 = \frac{a_2^2 + a_3^2 - a_1^2}{2 a_2 a_3}, \qquad \text{and cyclic}, \qquad (30.10)$$

$$\text{Case 2: } \dot{a}_1 = \frac{(a_2 - a_3)^2 - a_1^2}{2 a_2 a_3}, \qquad \text{and cyclic}. \qquad (30.11)$$

Referring back to (30.6) and (30.7), we see from (30.10) that in Case 1, the spin connection satisfies $\omega_{01} = \omega_{23}$ and cyclically, which means that it is self-dual in the sense discussed earlier, and so the Riemann tensor will necessarily be self-dual. Thus the Eguchi–Hanson metric is a special case within the Case 1 metrics, which is biaxial with $a_1 = a_2$. The general triaxial Case 1 solution was found in [4], and can be written, after a change of radial coordinate, as

$$ds_4^2 = F^{-1/2} \, dr^2 + \tfrac{1}{4} r^2 \, F^{1/2} f_i \, \sigma_i^2, \qquad (30.12)$$

where

$$f_i \equiv 1 - \frac{\ell_i^4}{r^4}, \qquad F \equiv \frac{1}{f_1 f_2 f_3}. \qquad (30.13)$$

Unfortunately this metric has genuine curvature singularities unless two of the three constants ℓ_i are set equal, in which case one gets back the Eguchi–Hanson metric. There is an extra $U(1)$ isometry in the Eguchi–Hanson metric, making $U(2)$ in all, since a $U(1)$ subgroup of the right-acting $SU(2)$, which transforms the σ_i into one another, leaves $\sigma_1^2 + \sigma_2^2$ invariant.

Case 2 is somewhat harder to solve in general, but the rewards are higher because one obtains a nice metric that extends globally to a smooth manifold. The solution, the Atiyah–Hitchin metric, was found in [6], and it is given by

$$ds_4^2 = w_1 \, w_2 \, w_3 \, (u^{-4} \, d\tau^2 + w_i^{-1} \, \sigma_i^2) , \qquad (30.14)$$

where

$$
\begin{aligned}
w_1 &= -u \, u' - \tfrac{1}{2} u^2 \, \csc \tau , \\
w_2 &= -u \, u' + \tfrac{1}{2} u^2 \, \cot \tau , \\
w_3 &= -u \, u' + \tfrac{1}{2} u^2 \, \csc \tau ,
\end{aligned} \qquad (30.15)
$$

a prime means $d/d\tau$, and u satisfies

$$u'' + \tfrac{1}{4} u \, \csc^2 \tau = 0 . \qquad (30.16)$$

The solution is taken to be

$$u = \frac{1}{\pi} \sqrt{\sin \tau} \, K(\sin^2 \tfrac{1}{2}\tau), \qquad K(k) \equiv \int_0^{\pi/2} \frac{d\phi}{(1 - k \, \sin^2 \phi)^{1/2}} . \qquad (30.17)$$

The radial coordinate ranges from $\tau = 0$, where there is a bolt described by $\sigma_2^2 + \sigma_3^2$, to an infinity at $\tau = \pi$, where the coefficients of σ_1 and σ_2 grow linearly, while the coefficient of σ_3 grows to a limiting value $-2/\pi$. The regularity at $\tau = 0$ requires that in suitably chosen Euler angles $(\tilde{\theta}, \tilde{\phi}, \tilde{\psi})$ where $\sigma_1 = d\tilde{\psi} + \cos \tilde{\theta} \, d\tilde{\phi}$, the coordinate $\tilde{\psi}$ must have period π, and hence the principal orbits are $SO(3)/\mathbf{Z}_2$. A careful analysis shows that the bolt at $\tau = 0$ is, in consequence, an $\mathbf{RP}^2 \sim S^2/\mathbf{Z}_2$. The asymptotic infinity is not ALE like Eguchi–Hanson, because a circle is splitting off and stabilizing to a fixed radius. Thus the metric looks asymptotically like a cylinder $\mathbf{R}^3 \times S^1$; this is sometimes known as *Asymptotically Flat*.

There is a much simpler biaxial specialization of the Case 2 solutions. If we set $a_1 = a_2$ it is easily seen that the solution to (30.11) can be written as

$$ds_4^2 = \left(\frac{r + m}{r - m}\right) dr^2 + 4m^2 \left(\frac{r - m}{r + m}\right) \sigma_3^2 + (r^2 - m^2) \, (\sigma_1^2 + \sigma_2^2) . \qquad (30.18)$$

This is the self-dual Taub-NUT metric, first written down as a Euclidean-signature solution by Stephen Hawking in [9]. It extends to a non-singular metric on $\mathbf{R}^4$, with r running from a NUT (the origin of hyperspherical polar coordinates) at $r = m$ to an asymptotic region at $r = \infty$. Like Atiyah–Hitchin, the Taub-NUT metric is asymptotically flat, with a circle described by σ_3 splitting off and stabilizing at large distance.

30.4 Compact self-dual 4-metrics: K3

The art of finding explicit solutions of Einstein's equations is to restrict attention to some subclass of metrics that have continuous symmetries. By this means, one can reduce the number of independent metric components, and also restrict their dependence on the coordinates. In the previous discussion we considered four-dimensional metrics of the Bianchi IX type. These have cohomogeneity one, meaning that the metric is described as a foliation of homogeneous surfaces (S^3 in the Bianchi IX case), with functions that parameterize the shape of the homogeneous surfaces, but which depend only on the remaining, radial, coordinate. By this means the Einstein equations were reduced to coupled ordinary differential equations. All the solutions that were found were non-compact, with the radial coordinate ranging between a bolt or NUT at one end to an asymptotic infinity at the other.

In the case of Ricci-flat metrics on compact spaces, there cannot be any continuous isometries at all, except in trivial cases with circle factors. This follows from a simple argument. A Killing vector K^a satisfies $\Box K_a + R_{ab} K^b = 0$, where $\Box \equiv \nabla_a \nabla^a$ is the scalar Laplacian. Multiplying by K^a and integrating over the compact manifold M, we obtain

$$\int_M (-|\nabla_a K_b|^2 + R_{ab} K^a K^b) \sqrt{g}\, d^n x = 0. \tag{30.19}$$

If $R_{ab} = 0$ it follows that $\nabla_a K_b = 0$, and this can only be satisfied by a non-vanishing K_a if it lies along a totally flat direction, with vanishing Riemann tensor components along K_a. Thus unless there is a trivial direct-product S^1 factor in M, there cannot be any Killing vector in a Ricci-flat metric on M. As a consequence, it is more or less hopeless to obtain explicit Ricci-flat metrics on non-trivial compact manifolds.

There is known to be one simply-connected Ricci-flat compact manifold in four dimensions, namely the celebrated K3 surface. Its Riemann tensor is self-dual, and so, as discussed previously, it has holonomy $SU(2)$, it is Ricci-flat Kähler, and it admits covariantly-constant spinors of one chirality. The existence of the metric is guaranteed by Yau's proof [7] of the Calabi conjecture [8], but, in line with the observations above, its explicit form is not, and probably never will be, known. It is an intriguing space, and because of the existence of the covariantly-constant spinors, Stephen and I became interested in studying it as a supersymmetric background in supergravity [10]. Since we could not work with an explicit metric, we investigated to see how far one could go without knowing the metric.

One of the interesting questions in quantum field theory, and one of the few that can be tackled directly in a non-renormalizable theory such as gravity or supergravity, is to study the quantum functional integral at the one-loop level. Evaluating this in non-trivial backgrounds can be reduced to the problem of calculating the spectrum of eigenvalues of the Laplacian operators for the various fields in the theory. In a supergravity theory, one is therefore interested in the spectra of Laplacians for fields of integer and half-integer spins $s \leq 2$. We realized that the covariantly-constant spinors in any metric with a self-dual Riemann tensor would provide an invertible mapping between the non-zero modes of the Laplacians for the various spins [10].

The idea can be seen most easily in the 2-component spinor formalism, where we can take the covariantly-constant spinors to be u_A^i (right-handed, say), which, for $i = 1$ and 2 span the space of undotted $SU(2)$ spinors. Given a scalar eigenfunction ϕ, one can then form two right-handed spin-1/2 eigenfunctions $\psi_A^i = \phi u_A^i$, and two left-handed spin-1/2 eigenfunctions $\psi_{A'}^i = \nabla^A{}_{A'} \phi u_A^i$. One then constructs four vector eigenfunctions $V_{AA'}^{ij} = u_A^i \psi_{A'}^j$, and so on for all the higher spins, using multiplication by u_A^i to add undotted indices, and applying derivatives $u_A^i \nabla^A{}_{A'}$ to add dotted indices. The covariant-constancy of the u_A^i, together with the generation of curvature terms when $u_A^i \nabla^A{}_{A'}$ passes through the preceding Laplacian, implies that the higher-spin modes all satisfy the correct Laplacian equations. The eigenvalues of the various spin-s modes related by this construction are all equal.

An application of these eigenfunction relations is to calculate the zero-point amplitude itself. This is expressible, at one loop, as a certain ratio of determinants of the various Laplacians. Since the determinants are the products of the eigenvalues, this means that in a self-dual background the zero-point amplitude is expressible purely in terms of the eigenvalues of the scalar Laplacian (together with contributions from the zero-modes, which are not all related to the constant scalar because the derivative $u_A^i \nabla^A{}_{A'}$ annihilates it). Taking proper care of the Fadeev–Popov ghost contributions, it turns out that the net power in the numerator from fermionic contributions exactly cancels the net power in the denominator from bosonic contributions, and so the non-zero modes cancel exactly in the one-loop result on a self-dual background [10].

The zero-mode sector is a special case in the analysis, and one might at first have thought that no relations could be found for these. However, it turns out that enough can be deduced purely from topological properties of the manifold to allow one to determine all the relevant zero modes in a self-dual space. In particular, one knows that K3 has Euler number $\chi = 24$ and Hirzebruch signature $\tau = -16$. Now $\chi = 2 + b_2$ and $\tau = b_2^+ - b_2^-$, where $b_2 = b_2^+ + b_2^-$ is the second Betti number, counting the number of harmonic 2-forms, and $b_2^\pm$ are the numbers of self-dual and anti-self-dual harmonic 2-forms. Thus we conclude that $b_2^+ = 3$ and $b_2^- = 19$.

In fact the three self-dual harmonic 2-forms must therefore be the three covariantly-constant self-dual 2-forms that we can construct from the two covariantly-constant spinors u^i_A; in 2-component spinor language they are $J^{ij}_{AA'BB'} = u^i_{(A} u^j_{B)} \epsilon_{A'B'}$. The 19 anti-self-dual harmonic 2-forms correspond, in 2-component spinor language, to symmetric bispinors $\omega^\alpha_{A'B'}$, for $1 \leq \alpha \leq 19$.

A problem of particular interest is to calculate the dimension of the modulus space of Ricci-flat metrics on K3. (The more conventional term 'moduli space' has always struck me as sounding about as grammatical as apples pie.) Ricci-flat volume-preserving perturbations correspond to transverse traceless zero modes of the Lichnerowicz operator for spin-2 fluctuations. In 2-component language, these zero-modes are written as $h_{AA'BB'}$, symmetric in the indices AB and in $A'B'$. It was shown in [10] that the $h_{AA'BB'}$ could be expressed in terms of the self-dual and anti-self-dual harmonic 2-forms, as $J^{ij}_{AB} \omega^\alpha_{A'B'}$. This at first puzzled us, because a question we had asked Nigel Hitchin before we worked this out had suggested that the modulus space would be 38-dimensional, whereas we were getting $3 \times 19 = 57$. Accordingly, we wrote a letter (as one did in those days) to Nigel, explaining our procedure and pointing out the apparent discrepancy. I well remember writing the letter; Stephen dictating, I and the scribe. The body of the letter comprised the bare mathematical details. As he reached the punchline, Stephen's face broke into a mischievous smile as he dictated '...and so we have *57 Varieties*'. It would have made a nice advertisement for baked beans.

The resolution to the puzzle was that Nigel Hitchin had been counting the moduli that preserved the complex structure, whereas Stephen and I were counting all the Ricci-flat deformations, which included 19 that deform the complex structure.

Another way to think about K3 is via an orbifold limit. A construction due to Kummer begins by taking a 4-torus, and dividing out by a $\mathbf{Z}_2$ under which each circle in $T^4 = S^1 \times S^1 \times S^1 \times S^1$ is identified under a mirror reflection across a diameter. There will be $2^4 = 16$ fixed points, and so to make a non-singular space one excises a small ball, of radius r_0 say, around each of these. Were it not for the identification, the boundary of each ball would be S^3, but because of the $\mathbf{Z}_2$ it is instead $S^3/\mathbf{Z}_2$. This is precisely the topology of the boundary of the Eguchi–Hanson metric at large distance [4] and, using this fact, it was observed in [5] that one could make the Kummer construction a bit more concrete, by taking 16 copies of Eguchi–Hanson, cut off at radius $r = r_0$, and plugging them into the 16 holes. The resulting metric will have gradient discontinuities, and hence delta-function curvature singularities, at the joins, but these can be made arbitrarily small by taking the scale sizes ℓ of the Eguchi–Hanson metrics to be very small compared with r_0.

This approximate construction of K3 was pushed further by Don Page, in a paper he called 'A physical picture of the K3 gravitational instanton' [11]. In particular, he showed that one can also count the 57 moduli by heuristic arguments. To do this, one notes that each of the 16 Eguchi–Hansons has a scale size ℓ, and two parameters required to specify its angular orientation. Furthermore, the flat T^4 from which the Kummer construction begins has 10 Ricci-flat moduli, specifying the sizes and angles between the four circles; of these, 1 is the overall volume modulus. Thus one gets $(1+2) \times 16 + 10 - 1 = 57$ volume-preserving moduli.

When I described this in my talk at Stephen's 60th birthday conference, I remarked that Don had probably done this calculation, in his minute and uniquely characteristic font, on the back of one of the many envelopes that he saves for the purpose. He added the information that he had in fact been visiting Scotland at the time, hiking in the Cuillin Hills on the Isle of Skye. This is particularly appropriate for two reasons. First, although they are called hills, the Cuillins are about as rugged and mountainous as any landscape to be found in Britain, and hence an excellent setting for pondering on the complexities of the mountainous K3. Secondly, Don had a reputation for economical living during his holidays, scoffing at the extravagance of *Europe on 10 Dollars a Day*, and often finding it unnecessary to change any foreign currency at all during some of his European trips, since he could live quite happily for a few days on the peanuts and tinned fish that he would carry in his rucksack. It is quite likely, therefore, that Don was enjoying one of the *57 Varieties* as his staple diet during his trip to the Isle of Skye.

30.5 Special holonomy in higher dimensions

When the results that I have described above were being obtained, the principal reason for physicists to study four-dimensional self-dual metrics was because they could be viewed as stationary points in the functional integral over Euclideanized four-dimensional spacetimes. Since then, there have been numerous developments in supergravity, string theory and M theory. One of the common threads in much of this has been the emergence of higher dimensions as an inevitable part of the story. Thus ten is the fundamental dimension for perturbative superstring theory, and eleven is the fundamental dimension of M theory. There are close connections, via their low-energy limits, with the various supergravity theories in ten and eleven dimensions.

As a consequence of these developments, another natural application for Euclidean-signature metrics of special holonomy arose. If one starts from string theory in ten dimensions, and wants eventually to describe four-dimensional physics, then it is necessary to find a mechanism whereby six of the ten dimensions become effectively unobservable at low energies. The most natural way to do this is to wrap up the extra six dimensions into a small compact space, whose dimensions are of the order of the Planck scale. Then, in a fashion similar to the Kaluza–Klein procedure developed originally for toroidal reductions, one can study the effective four-dimensional theory that results from expanding the ten-dimensional fields in harmonics on the internal space. At some level of approximation, one can hope that the massive modes in the expansion can be neglected, and that the observable particles are described by the fields in the zero-mode sector.

Unlike a circle or torus reduction where an exact calculation can be performed, in a reduction on an inhomogeneous space such as K3 or a higher-dimensional analogue, one is effectively restricted to performing a small-fluctuation analysis around a chosen 'vacuum' or ground-state solution. The most natural vacuum to choose is one that takes the form $(\text{Minkowski})_4 \times Y_n$, where Y_n would be chosen to be an appropriate 6-manifold Y_6 if reducing from $D = 10$, or a 7-manifold Y_7 if reducing from $D = 11$. The vacuum should solve the string or M theory equations, and the simplest way to achieve this is to take Y_6 or Y_7 to be Ricci-flat. Since we would like some of the supersymmetry of the string theory or M theory to survive in the vacuum solution, this means that Y_n should admit covariantly-constant spinors.

Having covariantly-constant spinors in fact implies that the metric must be Ricci flat. It also implies that the metric must have *special holonomy*, since the existence of a covariantly-constant spinor means that if it is parallely-propagated around any closed path, it cannot suffer any rotation. The possible special holonomy groups for Ricci-flat metrics were classified by the mathematician Berger in the 1950s. There are generic possibilities $SU(m) \subset SO(2m)$ in $n = 2m$ dimensions, and $Sp(m) \subset SO(4m)$ in $n = 4m$ dimensions. These are Ricci-flat Kähler, with two covariantly-constant spinors, and hyper-Kähler, with $(m + 1)$ covariantly-constant spinors, respectively. There are also exceptional cases $G_2 \subset SO(7)$ in seven dimensions, and $\text{Spin}(7) \subset SO(8)$ in eight dimensions. In each case there is one covariantly-constant spinor.

30.6 Ricci-flat Kähler 6-metrics and the conifold

The natural candidates for Kaluza–Klein compactification of string theory are the so-called Calabi–Yau 6-manifolds, which are compact Ricci-flat Kähler manifolds. There has been an enormous amount of research done on these, and the physical implications for four-dimensional physics, starting with the work of [12]. Like K3, these have no continuous isometries, and so there is no prospect of obtaining explicit Ricci-flat metrics. However, as with K3, an enormous amount can be learned by means of orbifold constructions, and by making use of topological properties of the manifolds. There are many more examples than the lone K3 of four dimensions, and estimates run into the tens of thousands.

One feature that is especially interesting in the Calabi–Yau manifolds is the question of what happens when a singularity develops. Each Calabi–Yau space will have Ricci-flat moduli, analogous to the 57 varieties for K3. As the moduli are adjusted, one can push them to boundaries of the modulus space, where the curvature of the Calabi–Yau metric will become peaked and singular at some point in Y_6. These singularities will generically be of some orbifold type. It can be shown that for many purposes, the relevant type of singularity that develops [13] will be one in which the metric near to the singular point looks like the cone over $T^{1,1} \equiv (S^3 \times S^3)/U(1)$, where the $U(1)$ denominator in this five-dimensional coset space sits diagonally in the two S^3 factors. It has an Einstein metric ds_5^2, and assuming this is normalized so that $R_{ab} = 4g_{ab}$ (like the unit 5-sphere), the metric

$$ds_6^2 = dr^2 + r^2\, ds_5^2 \qquad (30.20)$$

on the cone over $T^{1,1}$ will be Ricci-flat. It is singular at the apex of the cone $r = 0$, and in fact the Riemann tensor has a power-law divergence there. Properties of the metric ds_5^2 mean that the cone metric ds_6^2 has special holonomy $SU(3)$, as it must since it is arising in a singular limit of a Calabi–Yau metric. The space described by the metric (30.20) is usually referred to as the *conifold*.

If the moduli are adjusted so that the metric on Y_6 has not quite developed the singularity near which it is approximated by (30.20), it must be that the metric close to the nearly-singular point can be approximated by a non-compact Ricci-flat Kähler metric that is a smoothed-out version of the conifold (30.20). The way in which this works is analogous to the way in which the Eguchi–Hanson metric smooths out the cone over $\mathbf{RP}^3$.

If we take (30.3) and set the scale parameter $\ell = 0$, the metric looks locally like flat Euclidean $\mathbf{R}^4$ in hyperspherical polar coordinates, except for the fact that we identified the Euler angle ψ with period 2π rather than 4π. This means that the principal orbits are $\mathbf{RP}^3$ rather than S^3, and so the $\ell = 0$ metric is the cone over $\mathbf{RP}^3$, with a singularity at the apex $r = 0$. The Eguchi–Hanson metric smooths out, or *resolves*, the singularity, by blowing it up into an S^2 bolt. At large distance the metric looks more and more like the cone metric, and for this reason it is often referred to as being *asymptotically conical*, or AC.

Going back to the conifold, one is interested in studying the smooth metric or metrics that 'blow up' the conifold point $r = 0$ and resolve the singularity. It turns out in this case that there are two distinct ways this can occur. In one, the point is blown up to an S^2, giving the *small resolution* of the conifold, whilst in the other it is blown up to an S^3, giving the *deformed conifold*. The Ricci-flat Kähler metrics in these two cases were first obtained in [14].

A convenient description, for our purposes, is given in [15]. One considers a metric ansatz

$$ds_6^2 = dt^2 + a^2 \left[(\Sigma_1 + g\,\sigma_1)^2 + (\Sigma_2 + g\,\sigma_2)^2\right] + b^2 \left[(\Sigma_1 - g\,\sigma_1)^2 + \right.$$
$$\left. + (\Sigma_2 - g\,\sigma_2)^2\right] + c^2 \left(\Sigma_3 - \sigma_3\right)^2. \tag{30.21}$$

where a, b, c and g are functions only of the radial variable t, and σ_i and Σ_i are left-invariant 1-forms of $SU(2) \times SU(2)$. In the vielbein basis

$$e^0 = dt\,, \quad e^1 = a\,(\Sigma_1 + g\,\sigma_1)\,, \quad e^2 = a\,(\Sigma_2 + g\,\sigma_2)\,, \tag{30.22}$$
$$e^3 = c\,(\Sigma_3 - \sigma_3)\,, \quad e^4 = b\,(\Sigma_1 - g\,\sigma_1)\,, \quad e^5 = b\,(\Sigma_2 - g\,\sigma_2)\,,$$

an invariant choice for an almost complex structure is

$$J = e^0 \wedge e^3 + e^1 \wedge e^5 - e^2 \wedge e^4\,. \tag{30.23}$$

From this, a natural choice for a complex holomorphic vielbein is $\epsilon^0 = e^0 + i\,e^3$, $\epsilon^1 = e^1 + i\,e^5$, $\epsilon^2 = e^2 - i\,e^4$. One then defines the holomorphic 3-form

$$\epsilon_{(3)} \equiv \epsilon^0 \wedge \epsilon^1 \wedge \epsilon^2\,. \tag{30.24}$$

It can be shown that the metric will have special holonomy $SU(3)$ if and only if $dJ = 0$ and $d\epsilon_{(3)} = 0$. These conditions imply [15]

$$2(a\,b)^{\cdot} + c = 0\,, \quad 2(a\,b\,g^2)^{\cdot} + c = 0\,, \quad \left[(a^2 - b^2)\,c\right]^{\cdot} = 0\,,$$
$$2(a\,b\,c\,g)^{\cdot} + (a^2 + b^2)\,g = 0\,, \quad \left[(a^2 - b^2)\,c\,g^2\right]^{\cdot} = 0\,,$$
$$\left[(a^2 + b^2)\,c\,g\right]^{\cdot} + 2a\,b\,g = 0\,, \quad c\,(a^2 - b^2)\,(1 - g^2) = 0\,. \tag{30.25}$$

Note that the last equation is purely algebraic, allowing one of the metric functions to be solved for, while the rest give three first-order equations for the remaining three metric functions.

The algebraic equation in (30.25) implies a bifurcation when we solve the equations since we have (modulo orientation choices that need not concern us) either $a = b$ or $g = 1$. Taking $a = b$, the solution gives the small resolution, which can be written as

$$ds_6^2 = \frac{r^2 + 2\ell^2}{r^2 + 3\ell^2} \, dr^2 + \tfrac{1}{6}r^2 \left(\sigma_1^2 + \sigma_2^2\right) + \tfrac{1}{6}(r^2 + 2\ell^2)\left(\Sigma_1^2 + \Sigma_2^2\right)$$
$$+ \tfrac{1}{9}r^2 \left(\frac{r^2 + 2\ell^2}{r^2 + 3\ell^2}\right)\sigma_3^2 . \tag{30.26}$$

The radial coordinate runs from the S^2 bolt at $r = 0$ to the asymptotic region at $r = \infty$, where the metric approaches the cone over $T^{1,1}$.

Taking $g = 1$ instead, the solution gives the deformed conifold, which can be written as

$$ds_6^2 = R^{-2/3} \sinh^2 2r \, (dr^2 + (\Sigma_3 - \sigma_3)^2) + 3R^{1/3} \, [\coth r \, ((\Sigma_1 + \sigma_1)^2$$
$$+ (\Sigma_2 + \sigma_2)^2) + \tanh r \, ((\Sigma_1 - \sigma_1)^2 + (\Sigma_2 - \sigma_2)^2)], \tag{30.27}$$

where $R \equiv \tfrac{1}{8}(\sinh 4r - 4r)$. For simplicity this is written in a form where the S^3 bolt at $r = 0$ has radius $6^{1/3}$, but a scale size ℓ can of course easily be introduced. The two metrics (30.26) and (30.27) are both asymptotically conical, approaching the same conifold metric at large distance.

The fact that there are two inequivalent smoothed-out versions of the conifold is interesting because we can consider adjusting the moduli of the Calabi–Yau manifold so that a metric singularity is approached via a collapsing S^2 bolt, and then we can come out on the other side in modulus space via a growing S^3 bolt, or *vice versa*. This conifold transition is especially interesting in string theory, since in the Kaluza–Klein reduction on Y_6 the modulus parameters acquire the interpretation of massless scalar fields in the effective four-dimensional theory. As they evolve to values where a conifold transition occurs, the collapsing S^2 or S^3 can be wrapped by branes whose volume goes to zero, leading to additional massless states in the theory [13].

The fact that the small resolution and the deformation of the conifold could both be obtained from the first-order system (30.25) resulting from requiring $SU(3)$ holonomy for (30.21) is nice, but a slightly inelegant feature is that one has a bifurcation on account of the algebraic equation in (30.25). It turns out that an arguably more unified description of the two metrics can be obtained by going to seven dimensions, and studying the special holonomy G_2 [16].

30.7 Seven-dimensional metrics of G_2 holonomy

It was quite a while after the results of Berger on the possible special holonomy groups before explicit non-singular examples of metrics with the exceptional cases of G_2 and Spin(7) holonomy were found. They first appeared in a paper by Bryant and Salamon [17], and shortly afterwards in a paper by Gary Gibbons, Don Page and myself [18]. Our interest had initially been in constructing broader classes of Ricci-flat metrics and Einstein metrics on $\mathbf{R}^3$, $\mathbf{R}^4$ and S^4 bundles over quaternionic-Kähler base manifolds, but as a by-product we stumbled upon the same examples of special holonomy metrics that had, somewhat to our chagrin, been found already in [17]. There were three examples of complete non-singular G_2 metrics, on an $\mathbf{R}^3$ bundle over S^4 or $\mathbf{CP}^2$, and an $\mathbf{R}^4$ bundle over S^3; and one example of a complete non-singular Spin(7) metric, on an $\mathbf{R}^4$ bundle over S^4 [17, 18]. They are all AC, being asymptotic to cones over certain Einstein manifolds of dimension 6 and 7. Here I shall just describe the G_2 holonomy metric on the cone over $S^3 \times S^3$, since it is the one that is relevant to the previous discussion of the conifold.

The construction of the AC special holonomy metrics in [18] was a little roundabout, in that we first found them as Ricci-flat solutions of the second-order Einstein equations, and only showed *post facto* that they in fact had special holonomy. The result for the G_2 metric with $S^3 \times S^3$ principal orbits is

$$ds_7^2 = \left(1 - \frac{\ell^3}{r^3}\right)^{-1} dr^2 + \tfrac{1}{9}r^2 \left(1 - \frac{\ell^3}{r^3}\right)(\Sigma_i - \tfrac{1}{2}\sigma_i)^2 + \tfrac{1}{12}r^2 \sigma_i^2. \quad (30.28)$$

The radial variable runs from an S^3 bolt at $r = \ell$ to an asymptotic region at $r = \infty$, where the metric approaches the cone over $S^3 \times S^3$. It should be emphasized that the $S^3 \times S^3$ at infinity does not have the usual direct-product metric, but rather the 'twisted' one that can be read off from (30.28). The AC metric is clearly closely analogous to Eguchi–Hanson metric (30.3) of four dimensions.

As well as obtaining examples of complete non-singular metrics of G_2 and Spin(7) holonomy, it was also shown in [18] that certain eigenfunction relations, analogous to the ones found in [10] for self-dual 4-metrics, could be obtained. In particular it was shown that the number of volume-preserving moduli for Ricci-flat metrics on a compact G_2 manifold is given by $b_3 - 1$, where b_3 is the third Betti number, and that the number of such moduli for compact Spin(7) metrics is equal to b_4^-, the number of anti-self-dual harmonic 4-forms [18].

Interest in metrics of exceptional holonomy has increased in recent times because of their significance in string theory and M theory. Especially, compact 7-manifolds Y_7 with G_2 holonomy are natural spaces to consider in the context of M theory, since they provide supersymmetric vacua of the form (Minkowski)$_4 \times Y_7$.

Here, we shall just present one recent development, which makes contact with the previous discussion of the resolved and deformed conifolds. It is described in detail in [16]. We consider a more general ansatz for metrics of cohomogeneity one with $S^3 \times S^3$ principal orbits, given by

$$ds_7^2 = dt^2 + a^2 \left[(\Sigma_1 + g\,\sigma_1)^2 + (\Sigma_2 + g\,\sigma_2)^2 \right] + \tilde{b}^2 \left[(\Sigma_1 - g\,\sigma_1)^2 \right. $$
$$\left. + (\Sigma_2 - g\,\sigma_2)^2 \right] + c^2 \left(\Sigma_3 - \sigma_3 \right)^2 + f^2 \left(\Sigma_3 + g_3\,\sigma_3 \right)^2 . \quad (30.29)$$

In the orthonormal basis

$$ e^0 = dt , \quad e^1 = a \left(\Sigma_1 + g\,\sigma_1 \right), \quad e^2 = a \left(\Sigma_2 + g\,\sigma_2 \right), $$
$$ e^3 = c \left(\Sigma_3 - \sigma_3 \right), e^4 = b \left(\Sigma_1 - g\,\sigma_1 \right), $$
$$ e^5 = b \left(\Sigma_2 - g\,\sigma_2 \right), \quad e^6 = f \left(\Sigma_3 + g_3\,\sigma_3 \right); \quad (30.30)$$

there is a natural candidate for an invariant associative 3-form, namely

$$ \Phi = e^0 \wedge (e^1 \wedge e^4 + e^2 \wedge e^5 + e^3 \wedge e^6) - (e^1 \wedge e^2 - e^4 \wedge e^5) \wedge e^3 $$
$$ + (e^1 \wedge e^5 - e^2 \wedge e^4) \wedge e^6 . \quad (30.31)$$

Requiring the closure and co-closure of this 3-form gives a set of first-order equations for G_2 holonomy [16],

$$ \dot{a} = \frac{c^2 (a^2 - b^2) + [4a^2 (a^2 - b^2) - c^2 (5a^2 - b^2) - 4a\,b\,c\,f]\,g^2}{16a^2\,b\,c\,g^2} , $$

$$ \dot{b} = -\frac{c^2 (a^2 - b^2) + [4b^2 (a^2 - b^2) + c^2 (5b^2 - a^2) - 4a\,b\,c\,f]\,g^2}{16a\,b^2\,c\,g^2} , $$

$$ \dot{c} = \frac{c^2 + (c^2 - 2a^2 - 2b^2)\,g^2}{4a\,b\,g^2} , \quad (30.32)$$

$$ \dot{f} = -\frac{(a^2 - b^2)\,[4a\,b\,f^2\,g^2 - c\,(4a\,b\,c + a^2\,f - b^2\,f)\,(1 - g^2)]}{16a^3\,b^3\,g^2} , $$

$$ \dot{g} = -\frac{c\,(1 - g^2)}{4a\,b\,g} , $$

together with an algebraic equation for g_3:

$$ g_3 = g^2 - \frac{c\,(a^2 - b^2)(1 - g^2)}{2a\,b\,f} . \quad (30.33)$$

The general solution of the first-order equations (30.32) is not known. Of course the asymptotically conical G_2 metric (30.28) is a solution. Another exact solution is known, which was found in [19];

$$ ds_7^2 = \frac{(r^2 - \ell^2)}{(r^2 - 9\ell^2)}\,dr^2 + \tfrac{1}{12}(r - \ell)(r + 3\ell)[(\Sigma_1 - \sigma_1)^2 + (\Sigma_2 - \sigma_2)^2] $$
$$ + \tfrac{1}{9}r^2 \left(\Sigma_3 - \sigma_3 \right)^2 + \tfrac{1}{12}(r + \ell)(r - 3\ell)[(\Sigma_1 + \sigma_1)^2 $$
$$ + (\Sigma_2 + \sigma_2)^2] + \tfrac{4}{9}\ell^2\,\frac{r^2 - 9\ell^2}{r^2 - \ell^2}\,(\Sigma_3 + \sigma_3)^2 . \quad (30.34)$$

The radial coordinate runs from an S^3 bolt at $r = 3\ell$ to an asymptotic region as r approaches infinity. The metric is asymptotically locally conical, with the radius of the circle with coordinate $(\psi + \tilde{\psi})$ stabilizing at infinity. The metric is closely analogous to an ALC Spin(7) metric on an $\mathbf{R}^4$ bundle over S^4 that had been found previously [20, 21].

Although explicit solutions to the first-order system (30.32) are not in general known, it is nevertheless possible to study the system by a combination of approximation and numerical methods. Specifically, one can perform a Taylor expansion around the bolt at minimum radius where the $S^3 \times S^3$ orbits degenerate, and use this to set initial data just outside the bolt for a numerical integration to large distance. The criterion for having a complete non-singular metric is then that the metric functions should be well-behaved at large distances, either growing linearly with distance as in an AC metric such as (30.28), or else with one or more metric coefficients stabilizing to fixed values asymptotically, as in an ALC metric such as (30.34). This method is discussed in detail in [16, 22, 23], and it is established that there exist three families of non-singular ALC metrics, each with a non-trivial parameter λ that adjusts the size of a stabilizing circle at infinity relative to the size of the bolt at short distance. The metrics, denoted by $\mathbf{B}_7$, $\mathbf{D}_7$ and $\widetilde{\mathbf{C}}_7$, have bolts that are a round S^3, a squashed S^3 and $T^{p,q} = S^3 \times S^3/U(1)_{(p,q)}$ respectively. The radius of the stabilizing circle ranges from zero at $\lambda = 0$ to infinity at $\lambda = \infty$. As one takes the limit $\lambda \longrightarrow 0$, the ALC G_2 metric approaches the direct product of a six-dimensional Ricci-flat Kähler metric and a vanishing circle. This limit is known mathematically as the Gromov–Hausdorff limit.

The cases of most immediate interest are $\mathbf{B}_7$ and $\mathbf{D}_7$. Their Gromov–Hausdorff limits are a vanishing circle times the deformed conifold, and a vanishing circle times the resolved conifold, respectively [16, 23]. On the other hand, as λ goes to infinity, they both approach the original AC metric (30.28). If, therefore, we begin with a solution (Minkowski)$_4 \times Y_7$ in M theory, with Y_7 being a $\mathbf{B}_7$ or $\mathbf{D}_7$ metric, then we can dimensionally reduce it on the circle that stabilizes at infinity, thereby obtaining a solution of the type IIA string. The radius of the M theory circle, R, is related to the string coupling constant g_{str} by $g_{str} = R^{3/2}$. This means that taking the Gromov–Hausdorff limit in $\mathbf{B}_7$ or $\mathbf{D}_7$ corresponds to the weak-coupling limit in the type IIA string, and the ten-dimensional solution becomes the product of (Minkowski)$_4$ with the deformed or resolved conifold. In the strong-coupling domain, where λ goes to infinity, these two ten-dimensional solutions become unified via the $\mathbf{B}_7$ and $\mathbf{D}_7$ solutions in M theory.

30.8 Spin(7) holonomy

The remaining dimension where there exist Ricci-flat metrics of special holonomy is eight. Here, one can have metrics whose holonomy group is Spin(7)$\in$ $SO(8)$. An example of a non-singular such metric, which is asymptotically conical, was found in [17, 18]. It is again a metric of cohomogeneity one, with principal orbits that are 7-spheres. It can be written as

$$ds_8^2 = \left[1 - \left(\frac{r_0}{r}\right)^{10/3}\right]^{-1} dr^2 + \tfrac{9}{100} r^2 \left[1 - \left(\frac{r_0}{r}\right)^{10/3}\right] (\sigma_i - A^i)^2 + \tfrac{9}{20} r^2 \, d\Omega_4^2 ,$$

(30.35)

where, $d\Omega_4^2$ is the metric on the unit 4-sphere, and A^i is the single-instanton self-dual $SU(2)$ Yang–Mills solution on S^4. It is asymptotic to the cone over the squashed Einstein metric on S^7.

Generalizations of this Spin(7) metric were found recently, by considering a more general class of metrics with S^7 orbits. The easiest way to describe them is by introducing the left-invariant 1-forms $L_{AB} = L_{[AB]}$ of $SO(5)$, and describing the 7-sphere as the coset $SO(5)/SO(3)$, where the $SO(3)$ is one of the factors in the $SO(4) \sim SO(3) \times SO(3)$ subgroup of $SO(5)$. This can conveniently be done by taking the fundamental $SO(5)$ index A to range over $0 \le A \le 4$, and writing $R_i = L_{0i} + \tfrac{1}{2}\epsilon_{ijk} L_{jk}$, $P_a = L_{a4}$, where $1 \le i \le 3$ and $0 \le a \le 3$. The exterior algebra of the R_i and P_a follow from the $SO(5)$ exterior algebra $dL_{AB} = L_{AC} \wedge L_{CB}$.

The Spin(7) metrics found in [20, 21] arise by considering principal orbits described by the 7-sphere metric $ds_7^2 = 4a^2 (R_1^2 + R_2^2) + 4b^2 R_3^2 + c^2 P_a^2$. The first-order equations that follow by requiring that the 8-metric

$$ds_8^2 = dt^2 + 4a^2 (R_1^2 + R_2^2) + b^2 R_3^2 + c^2 P_a^2 \qquad (30.36)$$

have Spin(7) holonomy are derived in [20, 21]; the easiest way to do this is by writing down the natural invariant self-dual 4-form, and requiring that it be closed. This gives the equations

$$\dot{a} = 1 - \frac{b}{2a} - \frac{a^2}{c^2}, \qquad \dot{b} = \frac{b^2}{2a^2} - \frac{b^2}{c^2}, \qquad \dot{c} = \frac{a}{c} + \frac{b}{2c}. \qquad (30.37)$$

The AC metric (30.35) in this description corresponds to $(\sigma_i - A^i)^2 = 4R_i^2$, $d\Omega_4^2 = P_a^2$.

Remarkably, it turns out that these equations can be solved exactly. The upshot [20, 21] is that the general Spin(7) metrics in this class are given by

$$ds_8^2 = \frac{v\,f\,dz^2}{4z\,(1-z^2)(1-z)\,(v-2)} + \frac{4(v-2)\,z\,f}{(1+z)\,v}\,(R_1^2 + R_2^2)$$
$$+ \frac{16(v-2)\,z\,f}{(1+z)\,v^3}\,R_3^2 + f\,P_a^2, \tag{30.38}$$

with v defined by

$$v = \frac{2k\,\sqrt{z}}{(1-z^2)^{1/4}} - 2z\, {}_2F_1[1, \tfrac{1}{2}; \tfrac{5}{4}; 1 - z^2]. \tag{30.39}$$

and f defined by

$$f = \left(\frac{1+z}{1-z}\right)^{1/2} \exp\left[\int^z \frac{d\tilde{z}}{v(\tilde{z})\,(1-\tilde{z}^2)}\right]. \tag{30.40}$$

It is shown in [20, 21] that this gives non-singular solutions, denoted by $\mathbf{B}_8$, that are asymptotically locally conical, with a non-trivial parameter that determines the ratio of the radius of the stabilizing circle at infinity divided by the radius of the S^4 bolt at short distance.

30.9 Conclusion

We have reviewed a number of examples of metrics of special holonomy, starting from examples of self-dual Ricci-flat 4-metrics that were first studied in the days when Euclidean gravity in four dimensions was regarded as a candidate for a consistent quantum theory in its own right. Times have changed, and now we usually view the four-dimensional world as an effective low-energy description of a more fundamental theory of strings or extended objects in ten or eleven dimensions. Many of the ideas that were first explored in the 1970s have survived, with transmutations that were not dreamed of in the earlier philosophy. It is still true today that many of the insights into string theory and M theory, especially the non-perturbative aspects, are derived from considerations of the supergravities that describe the low-energy limits. Supergravity, Killing spinors and holonomy are as important today as they were 20 years ago.

Acknowledgements

I am indebted to all my collaborators in the work described in this paper, including Volodya Belinsky, Mirjam Cvetič, Gary Gibbons, Hong Lü and Don Page. Most of all, I am indebted to Stephen Hawking, for his help, guidance and inspiring encouragement. Happy Birthday Stephen!

References

[1] Hawking, S. W. (1974), 'Black hole explosions', *Nature* **248** 30.

[2] Hartle, J. B. and Hawking, S. W. (1976), 'Path integral derivation of black hole radiance', *Phys. Rev.* **D13** 2188.

[3] Eguchi, T. and Hanson, A. J. (1978), 'Asymptotically flat selfdual solutions to Euclidean gravity', *Phys. Lett.* **B74**, 249.

[4] Belinsky, V. A., Gibbons, G. W., Page, D. N. and Pope, C. N. (1978), 'Asymptotically Euclidean Bianchi IX metrics in quantum gravity', *Phys. Lett.* **B76**, 433.

[5] Gibbons, G. W. and Pope, C. N. (1979), 'The positive action conjecture and asymptotically Euclidean metrics in quantum gravity', *Commun. Math. Phys.* **66**, 267.

[6] Atiyah, M. F. and Hitchin, N. J. (1985), 'Low-energy scattering of nonabelian monopoles', *Phys. Lett.* **A107**, 21.

[7] Yau, S.-T. (1978), 'On the Ricci curvature of a compact Kähler manifold and the complex Monge–Ampère equations, I', *Comm. Pure and Appl. Math.* **31**, 339.

[8] Calabi, E. (1957), *On Kähler Manifolds with Vanishing Canonical Class, Algebraic Geometry and Topology*, A symposium in honor of S. Lefschetz, (Princeton University Press, Princeton, N.J.), pp. 78–89.

[9] Hawking, S. W. (1977), 'Gravitational instantons', *Phys. Lett.* **A60**, 81.

[10] Hawking, S. W. and Pope, C. N. (1978), 'Symmetry breaking by instantons in supergravity', *Nucl. Phys.* **B146**, 381.

[11] Page, D. N. (1978), 'A physical picture of the K3 gravitational instanton', *Phys. Lett.* **B80**, 55.

[12] Candelas, P., Horowitz, G. T., Strominger A. and Witten, E. (1985), 'Vacuum configurations for superstrings', *Nucl. Phys.* **B258**, 46.

[13] Strominger, A. (1995), 'Massless black holes and conifolds in string theory', *Nucl. Phys.* **B451**, 96, [hep-th/9504090].

[14] Candelas, P. and de la Ossa, X. C. (1990), 'Comments on conifolds', *Nucl. Phys.* **B342**, 246.

[15] Cvetič, M., Gibbons, G. W., Lü, H. and Pope, C. N. (2002), 'Almost special holonomy in type IIA and M theory', [hep-th/0203060], to appear in *Nucl. Phys.* **B**.

[16] Cvetič, M., Gibbons, G. W., Lü, H. and Pope, C. N. (2001), 'A G_2 unification of the deformed and resolved conifolds', to appear in *Phys. Lett.* **B**, [hep-th/0112138].

[17] Bryant, R. L. and Salamon, S. (1989), 'On the construction of some complete metrics with exceptional holonomy', *Duke Math. J.* **58**, 829.

[18] Gibbons, G. W., Page, D. N. and Pope, C. N. (1990), 'Einstein metrics on S^3, $\mathbf{R}^3$ and $\mathbf{R}^4$ bundles', *Commun. Math. Phys.* **127**, 529.

[19] Brandhuber, A., Gomis, J., Gubser, S. S. and Gukov, S. (2001), 'Gauge theory at large N and new G_2 holonomy metrics', *Nucl. Phys.* **B611**, 179, [hep-th/0106034].

[20] Cvetič, M., Gibbons, G. W., Lü, H. and Pope, C. N. (2002), 'New complete non-compact Spin(7) manifolds', *Nucl. Phys.* **B620**, 29, [hep-th/0103155].

[21] Cvetič, M., Gibbons, G. W., Lü, H. and Pope, C. N. (2001), 'New cohomogeneity one metrics with Spin(7) holonomy', math.DG/0105119.

[22] Cvetič, M., Gibbons, G. W., Lü, H. and Pope, C. N. (2002) 'Cohomogeneity one manifolds of Spin(7) and G_2 holonomy' *Phys. Rev.* **D65**, 106004, [hep-th/0108245].

[23] Cvetič, M., Gibbons, G. W., Lü, H. and Pope, C. N. (2002), 'M-theory conifolds', *Phys. Rev. Lett.* **88**, 121602, [hep-th/0112098].

Part 7
De Sitter space

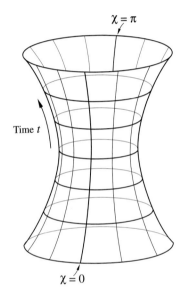

An observer in a cosmological model with a positive cosmological constant ... will detect an isotropic background of thermal radiation with temperature $\kappa/2\pi$ coming, apparently, from the event horizon.

Physical Review, 1977

31

Adventures in de Sitter space

Raphael Bousso

University of California, Santa Barbara

31.1 Introduction

It is a pleasure to help celebrate Stephen Hawking's 60th birthday (not least because Stephen knows how to party). I am grateful for the good fortune I had in working with him, and for the physics I learned from him as his student from 1997 to 2000. But what I am most thankful for is the homework. Stephen's discoveries amount to a formidable problem set. I'm afraid we're late turning it in. Without question, it will keep us happily occupied for years to come.

Stephen and I have published five journal articles together (Bousso and Hawking, 1995, 1996b, 1997c, 1998b, 1999a), as well as a number of proceedings (Bousso and Hawking, 1996a,c, 1997a,b, 1999b). Most of these papers, and much of my subsequent work, are concerned in one way or another with aspects of quantum gravity in de Sitter space. In my contribution to this Festschrift I should therefore like to survey some of the results, problems, and speculations surrounding this topic.

Stephen's contributions to black hole physics and cosmology find a synthesis in his semiclassical treatment of de Sitter space. Gibbons and Hawking (1977) demonstrated that the de Sitter horizon, like a black hole, is endowed with entropy and temperature. Thus, the quantum properties of black holes will extend to the universe as a whole, if the vacuum energy is positive.

More than ever, the implications of this work are under active investigation. The Bekenstein–Hawking entropy of the spacetime, in particular, has been taken either as a starting point, or alternatively, as a crucial test, of various approaches to a full quantum gravity theory for de Sitter space.

A brief description of the de Sitter geometry is given in section 31.2. In section 31.3.1, I summarize the concepts of black hole entropy and the generalized second law of thermodynamics (Bekenstein, 1972, 1973, 1974), as well as Hawking's (1974, 1975) results on black hole temperature and radiation. This will provide a context for a review of the main conclusions of Gibbons and Hawking (1977), in section 31.3.2.

The generalized second law has been used to infer universal bounds on the entropy of matter systems. In section 31.4.1, I describe how the Bekenstein (1981) bound, $S \leq 2\pi ER$, is obtained from a gedankenexperiment involving a black hole. When this kind of argument is extended to the de Sitter horizon, one obtains analogous bounds in various limits (Schiffer, 1992; Bousso, 2001). In section 31.4.2, I discuss one of these bounds, the D-bound, whose good agreement with the Bekenstein bound is non-trivial.

Roughly speaking, the Bekenstein–Hawking entropy of empty de Sitter space is the largest entropy attainable in any asymptotically de Sitter spacetime (Fischler, 2000a,b; Banks, 2000). In section 31.5, I make this absolute entropy bound more precise. One must distinguish between spacetimes that are de Sitter in the past, in the future, or both. Moreover, it is natural to include at least some spacetimes with positive cosmological constant but no asymptotic de Sitter region. The more carefully one characterizes the spacetime *portions* whose entropy need be considered, the broader the *class* of spacetimes obeying the bound. It is argued that only the entropy contained in causal diamonds is observable (Bousso, 2000). However, even with this restriction, one can find some $\Lambda > 0$ universes with unbounded entropy (Bousso, DeWolfe and Myers, 2002).

The formulation of a quantum gravity theory describing de Sitter space remains an open problem. In section 31.6, I outline some of the strategies that can be adopted and the difficulties they face. In particular, asymptotic regions, which are conventionally used to define observables, are not globally accessible to any de Sitter observer; quantum mechanical obstructions may be even more severe. I also discuss the possibility that a new class of theories, with a manifestly finite number of states, may play a role in the description of de Sitter space.

Section 31.7 is most closely related to my joint work with Stephen. It discusses the largest possible black hole in de Sitter space. This spacetime, the Nariai solution, exhibits a remarkable set of instabilities. Small perturbations can lead to an infinite variety of global structures, including the fragmentation of the spatial geometry into disconnected de Sitter universes (Bousso, 1998). I place these results in the context of present approaches to de Sitter space.

This article is by no means an attempt to review the subject. It touches upon a small portion of the literature, whose selection is biased by my current interests and by some of my own adventures in de Sitter space.

Many of these were shared with Stephen and with other collaborators: Andrew Chamblin, Oliver DeWolfe, Andrei Linde, Alex Maloney, Rob Myers, Jens Niemeyer Joe Polchinski and Andy Strominger. I would like to thank them, and I emphasize that the shortcomings of this article, for which I apologize, are mine.

Planck units are used throughout. For definiteness, the number of space-time dimensions is taken to be $D = 4$ unless noted otherwise. The discussion generalizes trivially to higher dimensions except where special cases are pointed out. For a review of de Sitter space, see, e.g., Spradlin, Strominger and Volovich (2001). Extensive lists of references are also given by Balasubramanian, de Boer and Minic (2001); Spradlin and Volovich (2001).

31.2 De Sitter space

This section summarizes a number of the classical properties of de Sitter space that are used below. A more extensive discussion is found in Hawking and Ellis (1973).

De Sitter space is the maximally symmetric solution of the vacuum Einstein equations with a positive cosmological constant, Λ. It is positively curved with characteristic length

$$\ell = \sqrt{\frac{3}{\Lambda}}. \tag{31.1}$$

Globally, de Sitter space can be written as a closed FRW universe:

$$\frac{ds^2}{\ell^2} = -d\tau^2 + \cosh^2 \tau \, d\Omega_3^2 \tag{31.2}$$

The spacelike slices are 3-spheres. The space-time can be visualized as a hyperboloid (Figure 31.1). The smallest S^3 is at the throat of the hyperboloid, at $\tau = 0$. For $\tau > 0$, the 3-spheres expand exponentially without bound. The time evolution is symmetric about $\tau = 0$, so 3-spheres in the past are arbitrarily large and contracting.

The Penrose diagram of de Sitter space is a square (Figure 31.1). The spatial 3-spheres are horizontal lines. As usual, every point represents a 2-sphere, except for the points on the left and right edge of the square, which represent the poles of the 3-sphere. The top and bottom edge are future and past infinity, $\mathcal{I}^+$ and $\mathcal{I}^-$, where all spheres become arbitrarily large.

In the static coordinate system,

$$\frac{ds^2}{\ell^2} = -V(r) \, dt^2 + \frac{1}{V(r)} dr^2 + r^2 d\Omega_2^2, \tag{31.3}$$

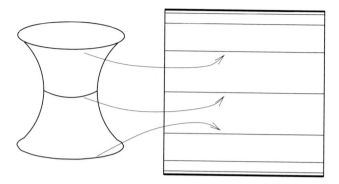

Fig. 31.1. De Sitter space as a hyperboloid. Time goes up. Right: Penrose diagram. Horizontal lines represent three-spheres.

where

$$V(r) = 1 - r^2,\qquad\qquad(31.4)$$

it becomes manifest that an observer at $r = 0$ is surrounded by a cosmological horizon at $r = 1$. These coordinates cover only part of the space-time, namely the interior of a cavity bounded by $r = 1$ (Figure 31.2). This is precisely the operationally meaningful portion of de Sitter space, i.e., the region that can be probed by a single observer. The upper and lower triangles contain exponentially large regions that cannot be observed; in particular, they contain the conformal boundaries $\mathcal{I}^+$ and $\mathcal{I}^-$.

An object held at a fixed distance from the observer is redshifted. The redshift, $V(r)^{1/2}$, diverges near the horizon. If released, the object will accelerate towards the horizon. Once it crosses the horizon, it can no longer be retrieved. In short, the cosmological horizon acts like a black

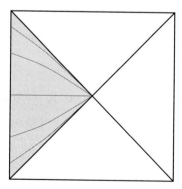

Fig. 31.2. Past and future event horizon (diagonal lines). The static slicing covers the interior of the cosmological horizon (shaded).

hole 'surrounding' the observer. Note that the symmetry of the space-time implies that the location of the cosmological horizon is observer-dependent. The black hole analogy carries over to the semiclassical level; this is discussed further in section 31.3.2.

31.3 Entropy and temperature of event horizons

31.3.1 Black holes

The entropy of an ordinary object is lost to an outside observer when the object falls into a black hole. However, the black hole's horizon area increases in this process. (Indeed, Hawking (1971) showed that it never decreases in any classical process.) In order to salvage the second law of thermodynamics, Bekenstein (1972, 1973, 1974) proposed that a black hole carries an entropy on the order of its horizon area, A, in Planck units. Moreover, he conjectured a generalized second law of thermodynamics: the sum of ordinary entropy and horizon entropy never decreases.

The analogy between the laws of thermodynamics and classical proper-ties of black hole spacetimes – with the surface gravity, κ, playing the role of temperature, and the horizon area, A, mimicking entropy – was soon understood in great detail. Still, Bekenstein's proposal met with scepti-cism (Bardeen, Carter and Hawking, 1973), because it appeared to lead to a contradiction. If A represented an actual entropy, the temperature ($\sim \kappa$) had to be a physical effect as well. But how could black holes radiate?

Using Bogolibov transformation techniques, Hawking (1974, 1975) dem-onstrated that black holes emit radiation by a quantum process, at a temperature

$$T_{\text{hor}} = \frac{\kappa}{2\pi}. \tag{31.5}$$

For a Schwarzschild black hole of mass M, $\kappa = (4M)^{-1}$. Via the first law of thermodynamics,

$$\frac{1}{T_{\text{hor}}} = \frac{\partial S_{\text{hor}}}{\partial M}, \tag{31.6}$$

Hawking's calculation confirmed Bekenstein's entropy formula (up to an additive constant which can be argued to vanish) and determined its numerical coefficient:

$$S_{\text{hor}} = \frac{A}{4}. \tag{31.7}$$

31.3.2 De Sitter space

In spacetimes which are asymptotically de Sitter in the future, any ob-server is surrounded by an event horizon. At late times, its area is given by

$$A_0 = 4\pi\ell^2, \tag{31.8}$$

where

$$\ell = \sqrt{\frac{3}{\Lambda}} \tag{31.9}$$

is the curvature radius, and Λ is the cosmological constant. Gibbons and Hawking (1977) noted that this horizon possesses surface gravity $\kappa = 1/\ell$ and satisfies analogues to the classical laws of black hole mechanics (Bardeen, Carter and Hawking, 1973).

This suggests that the horizons of black holes and of de Sitter space share quantum properties as well. In analogy to Hawking's (1974) result, one would expect the horizon to be at a non-zero temperature according to (31.5). Moreover, ordinary matter entropy is lost when systems cross the de Sitter horizon. In analogy to Bekenstein's (1972) argument, one would expect that the de Sitter horizon must have non-zero entropy according to (31.7).

Using Euclidean techniques, Gibbons and Hawking (1977) demonstrated that an observer in de Sitter space does detect thermal radiation at a temperature

$$T_{\mathrm{dS}} = \frac{1}{2\pi\ell}, \tag{31.10}$$

in agreement with expectation. The presence of thermal Green functions had been noticed previously in 1+1 dimensional de Sitter space (Figari, Hoegh-Krohn and Nappi, 1975).

One would like to infer the cosmological horizon entropy from the Gibbons–Hawking temperature by the first law of thermodynamics (31.6). The mass of a cosmological horizon is not defined a priori. However, only a mass differential is needed. Hence, let us express the first law in an alternate form, which refers to the change in matter energy rather than the change in 'horizon energy'.[1]

Leaving de Sitter space aside for a minute, consider a closed system consisting of a black hole initially well separated from ordinary matter. The total energy is conserved in any process whereby energy is exchanged between the components. Hence, $dM = -dE$, where M is the black hole mass and E is the energy of matter, and (31.6) becomes

$$\frac{1}{T_{\mathrm{hor}}} = -\frac{\partial S_{\mathrm{hor}}}{\partial E}. \tag{31.11}$$

---

[1] Gibbons and Hawking (1977) formally assign a negative mass to the cosmological horizon, but this is a mere convenience. The differential treatment of energy-momentum flux across the horizon makes reference only to the matter stress tensor.

In this form, the first law makes no reference to the 'energy of the horizon'. It can be adapted to the de Sitter case, where the matter energy M is perturbatively defined in terms of the timelike Killing vector field in the interior of the cosmological horizon. By studying black hole solutions in de Sitter space,[2] one finds that

$$\frac{\partial A_{\text{hor}}}{\partial E}\bigg|_{A_{\text{hor}}=A_0} = 8\pi\ell \tag{31.12}$$

for the derivative of the cosmological horizon area [see also (31.18) below]. With the Bekenstein ansatz, $S_{\text{hor}} = \eta A_{\text{hor}}$, for the entropy of the cosmological horizon, the usual coefficient, $\eta = 1/4$, follows from (31.10)–(31.12). Up to an additive constant, which is taken to vanish, (31.7) thus applies both to cosmological and to black hole horizons. In particular, the total entropy of empty de Sitter space is given by its horizon entropy, which is

$$S_0 = \frac{A_0}{4} = \frac{3\pi}{\Lambda}. \tag{31.13}$$

Thus, Gibbons and Hawking (1977) showed that the de Sitter horizon is endowed with the same quantum properties as a black hole horizon: a temperature and an entropy. They noted that the de Sitter horizon, unlike a black hole horizon, is observer dependent. They interpreted their results as an indication that quantum gravity may not admit a single, objective and complete description of the universe. Rather, its laws may have to be formulated with reference to an observer – no more than one at a time. These insights foreshadow more radical assertions of the need for complementary descriptions (Susskind, Thorlacius and Uglum, 1993), which eventually arose from considerations of unitarity in the presence of black holes.

31.4 Entropy bounds from horizons

31.4.1 Black holes and the Bekenstein bound

When a matter system falls into a black hole, the matter entropy disappears. At the same time, the horizon area (and hence, the black hole entropy) increases. Bekenstein's generalized second law *may* hold, but

---

[2] By finding the zeros of $V(r)$ in (31.26) as a function of E, one estimates the horizon area as a function of enclosed energy. Unlike Gibbons and Hawking (1977), this argument is quick and dirty. It assumes that a small Schwarzschild–de Sitter black hole with mass parameter E in (31.26), and a perturbative Killing mass $E = \int d^3x \sqrt{h} T_{\mu\nu} \chi^\mu n^\nu$, have equal cosmological horizon area after back-reaction is taken into account. (Here $\chi = \partial/\partial t$ and $n = \chi/|\chi|$.)

only if the horizon entropy increases by enough, i.e., if

$$\frac{\Delta A_{\text{hor}}}{4} \geq S_{\text{matter}}. \tag{31.14}$$

Bekenstein (1981) estimated a lower bound on ΔA_{hor} based on the 'Geroch process', by which a the system of mass E is added to the black hole only after first extracting a maximum amount of work. This minimizes the increase in the black hole mass, and hence, in its area.

One finds that $\Delta A_{\text{hor}} \leq 8\pi ER$, where R is the largest[3] dimension of the system. Hence,

$$S_{\text{matter}} \leq 2\pi ER. \tag{31.15}$$

Remarkably, this conclusion does not depend on microscopic properties of matter and thus betrays a fundamental aspect of nature. However, the bound applies only to matter systems that can actually be added to black holes. In particular, one must assume that gravity is not the dominant force in the system.

31.4.2 De Sitter space and the D-bound

Analogous arguments can be made for matter systems crossing the de Sitter horizon. One possibility is to study matter systems that are very small compared with the cosmological horizon (Schiffer, 1992). In this case the cosmological constant is exploited only to provide a horizon; its effect on spatial curvature is negligible over the scale of the system. One finds agreement with the Bekenstein bound. The Unruh–Wald analysis can also be generalized in this limit (Davies, 1984).

A different possibility is to consider systems whose size is comparable to the horizon radius. The resulting entropy bound is called the D-bound. The cosmological curvature is significant in large systems, and it is not obvious that the D-bound will agree with Bekenstein's bound, which applies to systems which perturb flat space weakly. With reasonable definitions of mass and 'largest dimension' of the system, however, one finds precise agreement. This section follows Bousso (2001).

---

[3] This is an empirical choice. Classical analysis of the Geroch process would suggest that R can be the smallest dimension, which would lead to contradictions. However, Unruh (1976) radiation must be taken into account for very flat systems. More generally, the proper quantum treatment of the Geroch process is under debate (see, for example, Bekenstein, 1999; Wald, 2001; Marolf and Sorkin, 2002). Independently of its logical status, there is empirical evidence that Bekenstein's bound holds for all weakly gravitating matter systems that can actually be constructed (Schiffer and Bekenstein, 1989; Wald, 2001). See Bekenstein (2001) and Wald (2001) for reviews; further references are also given in Bousso (2002).

Consider a matter system in an asymptotically de Sitter spacetime, i.e., a spacetime in which an observer's causal domain agrees well with empty de Sitter space at late times. The total initial entropy is the sum of the matter entropy, S_{matter}, and the horizon entropy, (31.7). The total final entropy is $A_0/4$, the entropy of empty de Sitter space. By the generalized second law,

$$S_{\text{matter}} \leq \frac{A_0 - A_{\text{hor}}(\text{initial})}{4}. \tag{31.16}$$

This is the D-bound. It holds for any matter system that can be contained in a causal domain of an asymptotically de Sitter universe; no assumptions about weak gravity are necessary. In particular, the D-bound predicts that the cosmological horizon will have area $A_{\text{hor}} < A_0$ as long as matter is present. This can be verified explicitly for many solutions, e.g., for the Schwarzschild–de Sitter spacetimes. For light matter systems within the cosmological horizon, the D-bound is more stringent than the holographic bound, $S_{\text{matter}} \leq A_{\text{hor}}/4$. This can be seen readily in the limit of empty de Sitter space, for which $A_{\text{hor}} \to A_0$ and the D-bound vanishes.

Equation (31.16) is not always the most useful form of the D-bound. One would like to evaluate the right-hand side in terms of intrinsic characteristics of the matter system. Let us assume that the matter system is light, i.e., it does not affect the de Sitter horizon much:

$$A_0 - A_{\text{hor}}(\text{initial}) \ll A_0. \tag{31.17}$$

Next, suitable quantities must be defined. We seek a definition of 'mass' in de Sitter space that makes reference only to the causally accessible region (which prevents us from using the definition of Abbott and Deser, 1982), but does not assume a fixed background (which precludes the use of a timelike Killing vector). A convenient definition makes use of the cosmological horizon area.

The mass E of a system in asymptotically flat space could be alternatively written as a 'gravitational radius' R_{g}, the radius[4] of the Schwarzschild black hole with the same mass. In this vein, let us define the mass of a matter system in de Sitter space to be the radius of the particular Schwarzschild–de Sitter black hole that leads to the same value of the cosmological horizon area.

By substituting $\partial A_{\text{hor}} \to 4S_{\text{matter}}$ and $\partial E \to R_{\text{g}}/2$ in (31.12), the D-bound can be expressed in the form

$$S_{\text{matter}} \leq \pi R_{\text{g}} R_{\text{c}}, \tag{31.18}$$

---

[4] This refers to the area radius of a horizon, defined as the root of the proper horizon area divided by the area of a unit sphere. R_{g} and R_{c} are physical lengths, unlike the coordinate r used in (31.3) and (31.25).

That is, the entropy of a spherical system in de Sitter space cannot be larger than π times the product of its gravitational radius and the radius of the cosmological horizon, R_c.

In order to compare this result with the Bekenstein bound, it is useful to express (31.15) in terms of the gravitational radius $R_g = 2E$:

$$S_{\text{matter}} \leq \pi R_g R. \tag{31.19}$$

The 'largest dimension', R, plays a role comparable to R_c, at least in the sense that the horizon size in de Sitter space places an upper bound on the extent of the system. Hence, the two bounds agree for large dilute systems in de Sitter space. This is not trivial as the spacetime background differs significantly. For smaller systems, the Bekenstein bound is more stringent. Of course, in the limit of very small systems, one expects the Bekenstein bound to hold, since the deviations from flat space will be negligible.

Both the Bekenstein bound and the D-bound can be extended to $D > 4$ spatial dimensions. They continue to agree exactly in the limit of large dilute systems. However, surprisingly, one finds that black holes saturate the Bekenstein bound only for $D = 4$.

31.5 Absolute entropy bounds in spacetimes with $\Lambda > 0$

The generalized second law states, loosely speaking, that the final entropy is the largest entropy. In any spacetime which asymptotes to de Sitter space this implies that the maximal entropy is given by (31.13). This statement was used to derive the D-bound in the previous section. However, de Sitter space has two conformal boundaries, one in the past, and one in the future. At fixed value of Λ, one can demand the presence of both boundaries, only one, or neither.

Interestingly, there are in fact several different statements of the type $S \leq S_0$ for $\Lambda > 0$ universes, depending on asymptotic conditions. With liberal conditions on the asymptotic structure, S must be rather restrictively defined for $S \leq S_0$ to obtain. With stringent boundary conditions, $S \leq S_0$ holds more broadly.

All of these bounds are *absolute* in the sense that they refer to the maximal entropy that can be contained (or probed) in a spacetime. They are a consequence of (but not as general as) the holographic bound ('t Hooft, 1993; Susskind, 1995; Bousso, 1999a,b), which limits entropy in the neighborhood of arbitrarily chosen codimension two spatial surfaces, relative to the surface area.

31.5.1 dS⁺ and the second law

Let us begin with the class of universes familiar from the previous section. The set $\mathbf{dS}^+(\Lambda)$ is defined to contain all spacetimes which possess an asymptotic de Sitter region in the future, with cosmological constant Λ. I will not make specific assumptions about matter content either here or below, except to demand that reasonable energy conditions are satisfied, e.g., the dominant energy condition (Wald, 1984).

At least for those observers who reach the asymptotic region, the second law argument can be completed, and one may conclude that the D-bound holds, and moreover, that the entropy of empty de Sitter space provides an upper bound on the total matter and horizon entropy at any prior time.

The reference to an observer is crucial, however. The $\mathbf{dS}^+$ class contains, for example, a spatially flat Friedmann–Robertson–Walker universe that starts with a Big Bang singularity, is radiation or matter dominated initially, and dominated by a cosmological constant at late times. (This may be a good approximation to our own universe.) The spatial extent of this universe is infinite at all times, and the entropy on a global time slice is clearly unbounded. However, the cosmological horizon shields all but a finite portion of the universe from any single observer.

The statement $S \leq S_0$ refers only to the entropy of matter inside the observer's horizon (that is, matter in the observer's causal past), plus the horizon entropy. Otherwise, it would obviously be violated. This restriction is implicit in the generalized second law argument. The growth of the de Sitter horizon to its asymptotic value at late times can only be a response to the matter that actually crosses that horizon. The horizon has no knowledge of the entropy of matter that was already beyond it to start with.

In a $\mathbf{dS}^+$ universe, the generalized second law thus implies the following result. *Consider an observer whose worldline approaches $\mathcal{I}^+$, the future de Sitter infinity, and let P be the causal past of the point where the worldline meets $\mathcal{I}^+$. Let Σ be any (suitably smooth and complete) timelike hypersurface. The spatial region $\Sigma' \equiv \Sigma \cap P$ corresponds to a particular instant of time in the observer's causal past, and the boundary of Σ' in Σ, $\partial\Sigma'$, is the event horizon at that time. Let S_{matter} be the entropy of matter in the region Σ', and let A_{hor} be the area of $\partial\Sigma'$. Then*

$$S_{\text{matter}} + \frac{A_{\text{hor}}}{4} \leq S_0. \tag{31.20}$$

Note that this argument applies to any observer who reaches $\mathcal{I}^+$, but not to observers who fail to do so, for example because they fall into a black hole. With suitable energy conditions preventing the formation of large regions in the interior of a black hole, one still expects that the entropy in the causal past of such observers will be bounded as in (31.20). However, I will not give a detailed argument.

31.5.2 $dS^{\pm}$ and global entropy

Next, consider a subset of $\mathbf{dS^{+}}$. Rather than demanding an asymptotic de Sitter region only in the future ($\mathcal{I}^{+}$), let us insist on a similar region in the past as well ($\mathcal{I}^{-}$). The spacetimes that possess both infinities define the set $\mathbf{dS^{\pm}}$.

The Penrose diagram of empty de Sitter space, Figure 31.2, is exactly a square, because a light-ray starting in the infinite past will barely reach the opposite end of the universe in an infinite time. If de Sitter space is not completely empty, the Penrose diagram will be deformed. An example is the Big Bang universe described earlier; it corresponds to a diagram whose width exceeds its height. Following Leblond, Marolf and Myers (2002), I will call such diagrams 'short'. This shape reflects the property that no complete Cauchy surface is contained in any observer's past. Examples of this type preclude a bound on global entropy in the $\mathbf{dS^{+}}$ class of universes.

However, if a universe is in $\mathbf{dS^{\pm}}$, i.e., if it also has a past asymptotic de Sitter region, one can use a theorem of Gao and Wald (2000) to argue that its Penrose diagram is necessarily 'tall', except for the exact vacuum de Sitter solution. Hence, the observer's event horizon will cross the entire diagram. Its area at late times will be A_0; at some finite earlier time t_{form}, its area will vanish. Hence, there will be early time ($t \leq t_{\mathrm{form}}$) Cauchy surfaces that are completely contained ($\Sigma = \Sigma'$) in an observer's causal past P. Simply put, an observer in a $\mathrm{dS}^{\pm}$ universe can see what the *whole* universe looked like it did in its early days.

Cauchy surfaces that precede the formation of the event horizon do not intersect the horizon and hence have $A_{\mathrm{hor}} = 0$. Then (31.20) reduces to $S_{\mathrm{matter}} \leq S_0$, where S_{matter} refers to the global entropy on a sufficiently early Cauchy surface (Bousso, 2002). The existence of such surfaces is guaranteed by the Gao–Wald result for all $\mathrm{dS}^{\pm}$ spacetimes (except for the exact de Sitter solution, in which the matter entropy classically vanishes at all times).[5]

To summarize, (31.20) and the theorem of Gao and Wald (2000) imply the following statement. *Consider a spacetime in* $\mathbf{dS^{\pm}}$, *and let* S_{matter} *be*

---

[5] The result of Gao and Wald (2000), and hence, our conclusion, relies on a number of technical requirements. In particular, the spacetime must be geodesically complete. The presence of both infinities is not sufficient to guarantee geodesic completeness even with reasonable smoothness requirements, because black holes can form. However, one would not expect the geodesic incompleteness due to black hole singularities to invalidate the above conclusions (Susskind, Thorlacius and Uglum, 1993).

the total matter entropy on a sufficiently early Cauchy surface. Then

$$S_{\text{matter}} \leq S_0. \tag{31.21}$$

The boundedness of the global entropy may seem a surprising result, since the early-time Cauchy surfaces have divergent volume. Hence, an arbitrary amount of entropy can be placed on them without significant local back-reaction. However, with this choice of coordinates, the space-time will be collapsing initially. The characteristic scale it will reach before it can re-expand is set by the value of the cosmological constant. However, if the matter density becomes larger than the energy density of the cosmological constant during the collapsing phase, it begins to dominate the evolution, and the universe will collapse to a big crunch.[6] Then there will be no future infinity, in contradiction to our assumption.

31.5.3 General $\Lambda > 0$ universes and the covariant entropy bound

Beginning with the set $\mathbf{dS}^+(\Lambda)$ in section 31.5.1, an absolute bound was derived on the entropy in an observer's causal past. Specializing to the $\mathbf{dS}^\pm(\Lambda)$ subset in section 31.5.2, this result was see to imply a bound on global entropy. Let us now explore the opposite direction and try to generalize to larger set of spacetimes. Can the $\mathbf{dS}^+(\Lambda)$ set be augmented non-trivially while retaining an absolute entropy bound of the type $S \leq S_0$?

Let us define $\mathbf{all}(\Lambda)$ to be the set of all spacetimes with positive cosmological constant Λ. Let's further assume that matter satisfies the dominant energy condition and that the number of species is not exponentially large. Note that Λ must be taken to be the lowest accessible vacuum energy. (For example, if there are scalar fields, Λ will refer to the cosmological constant at the minimum of their potential.)

$\mathbf{dS}^+(\Lambda)$ is a proper subset of $\mathbf{all}(\Lambda)$, that is, there are spacetimes with $\Lambda > 0$ that do not asymptote to de Sitter space in the future. Consider, for example, a closed universe which begins with an initial singularity (a big bang). If the density of ordinary matter is sufficiently high, the universe will cease its expansion before the cosmological constant can begin to dominate the evolution. The universe will then recollapse to a big crunch. Another example is the time-reversal of our own universe (supposing that it started with a big bang and is about to be dominated by a cosmological constant, as some observations suggest).

---

[6] Weakly perturbed de Sitter space is protected from singularity theorems (Hawking and Ellis, 1973; Wald, 1984) only because the strong energy condition is violated by a positive cosmological constant. If matter satisfying the strong energy condition dominates while the universe contracts, one expects this protection to break down.

It is more difficult to obtain an absolute entropy bound in $\Lambda > 0$ space-times without a future de Sitter region, because the second law is no longer of any use. Indeed, it turns out that **all**(Λ) contains spacetimes with unbounded observable entropy (Bousso, DeWolfe and Myers, 2002). The significance of these examples will be discussed later.

Nevertheless, it is possible to prove an entropy bound for an interesting subset of **all**(Λ) which includes certain spacetimes without $\mathcal{I}^+$. The place of the generalized second law is taken by the covariant entropy bound (Bousso, 1999a; Fischler and Susskind, 1998), which states that the en-tropy on any *light-sheet* (a contracting null hypersurface) will not exceed a quarter of its largest area (see Bousso, 2002, for a review). We will now summarize this argument.

In order to prove an entropy bound in this context, one must take great care to determine which parts of the spacetime are accessible to an observer. In order to show (31.20) for **dS**$^+$, it sufficed to restrict to the portion of the spacetime in the observer's past. However, it is not really enough for information to be present in our past; for it to have operational meaning, it has to get to us – or, at the very least, it has to enter a spacetime region that we can actively probe. Such a region has the shape of a *causal diamond* (Bousso, 2000).

Given an observer's worldline between two points p and q, the causal diamond $C(p,q)$ is defined by the intersection of the past of q with the future of p (Figure 31.3):

$$C(p,q) \equiv J^-(q) \cap J^+(p). \tag{31.22}$$

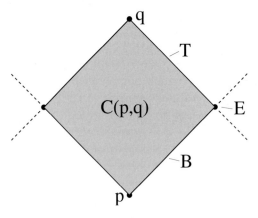

Fig. 31.3. Causal diamond $C(p,q)$, bounded by top (T) and bottom (B) cone, which intersect on the edge (E). A spatial region that fails to fit into *any* causal diamond cannot be probed in any experiment.

In order to determine the largest amount of information available to any observer in a spacetime $\mathcal{M}$, it suffices to find an upper bound on the entropy in the causal diamond $C(p, q)$, for all p and q in $\mathcal{M}$.[7] To demonstrate an absolute entropy bound for a whole set of spacetimes, one has to repeat this argument for each spacetime in the set (or, more efficiently, show that it applies to all).

The set considered in Bousso (2000) is a subset of **all**(Λ), namely the spherically symmetric spacetimes with cosmological constant Λ. Moreover, not all observers will be considered (i.e., not all p and q), but only the observers that are central (i.e., respect the spherical symmetry). The entropy seen by such observers, including horizon entropy if horizons are present near $C(p, q)$, will not exceed S_0.

This is shown as follows. At the top (the 'future end'), the causal diamond $C(p, q)$ is bounded by a kind of past light-cone (the boundary of the past of q). Let us call this the top cone, $T(p, q)$. By the second law, the entropy captured on $T(p, q)$ is an upper bound on the entropy on any other time slice of the causal diamond. Hence it suffices to consider $T(p, q)$.

The cone $T(p, q)$ can be thought of as consisting of one light-like direction and $D - 2$ spatial directions. The latter span cross-sectional spatial surfaces whose area depends on the position along the light-like direction. The focusing theorem implies that this cross-sectional area takes on precisely one maximal value, A_{max}. This can be a local maximum along $T(p, q)$ (an apparent horizon), or it can be reached on the edge, E, of the cone, where T meets a similar cone, B, extending from p to the future (Figure 31.3).

In either case, one can show that the surface of maximal area is either *normal* (that is, it is neither properly trapped nor properly anti-trapped), or that its area is smaller than the area of some normal surface. Hence, A_{max} must be smaller than the largest possible normal sphere in any spherically symmetric $\Lambda > 0$ universe. By Birkhoff's theorem, it must be possible to match such a normal sphere to a portion of a Schwarzschild–de Sitter solution. One easily verifies that no Schwarzschild–de Sitter solution contains any normal spherically symmetric surfaces with area greater than $4S_0$. It follows that

$$A_{max} \leq 4S_0. \tag{31.23}$$

---

[7] Causal diamonds may well play a rather general role in quantum gravity. Restriction to regions of the form $C(p, q)$ may alleviate various problems. For example, classically, no more than one point of any spacelike singularity can be contained in a causal diamond. Thus it is not clear that a quantum treatment of the vicinity of a spacelike singularity will need to address the singularity globally.

Then a rough argument shows immediately that the maximal entropy will be of the order of S_0. Namely, the surface $A_{\max}$ divides the top cone into one or two portions. On each portion, the cross-sectional area decreases in the direction away from $A_{\max}$. Hence, each portion is a light-sheet of $A_{\max}$ and contains entropy no greater than $A_{\max}/4 = S_0$. Therefore, $S_{\text{matter}} \leq 2S_0$. One also has to take into account the potential presence of a quasistatic event horizon. Its area, however, will not exceed $A_{\max}$. Hence, the total observable entropy, $S_{\text{matter}} + (A_{\text{hor}}/4)$, will not exceed $3S_0$.

A more detailed analysis shows that the D-bound, (31.16), applies to portions of the top cone in some cases, yielding tighter inequalities (Bousso, 2000). Moreover, the presence of a quasistatic event horizon can be excluded in many cases. Overall, these considerations allow a tightening of the above inequality by a factor of 3. This leads to the following conclusion.

Observable matter entropy must be contained in a causal diamond. Let $C(p, q)$ be an arbitrary spherically symmetric causal diamond in a spacetime with positive cosmological constant Λ. Let $S_{\text{matter}}[C(p, q)]$ be the total matter entropy contained in $C(p, q)$. Define the total observable entropy $S[C(p, q)]$ to be $S_{\text{matter}}[C(p, q)]$ plus the horizon entropy $A_{\text{hor}}/4$ of any quasistatic horizons in the vicinity of the boundary of $C(p, q)$. Then

$$S[C(p, q)] \leq S_0. \tag{31.24}$$

The assumption of spherical symmetry was necessary in order to apply Birkhoff's theorem. This assumption is most relevant for the spacetimes in **all**$(\Lambda)-$**dS**$^+(\Lambda)$, where other arguments for an absolute entropy bound are lacking. For observers which reach $\mathcal{I}^+$ in a dS$^+$ spacetime, the bound 31.24 holds generally. We expect that (31.24) holds for all observers in **dS**$^+$, but this has not been proven.

Yet, the fact that (31.20) is independent of spherical symmetry in **dS**$^+$ suggests that its validity in **all**(Λ) is more generic than the preceding proof. It would be surprising if (31.24) could be violated by small deviations from spherical symmetry. Hence, it was conjectured in Bousso (2000) that (31.24), the 'N-bound', holds generally in **all**(Λ).

However, the N-bound is in fact violated for some spacetimes in **all**(Λ) (Bousso, DeWolfe and Myers, 2002). The known counter-examples are topologically different from spherically symmetric solutions. Thus, the possibility remains that a set of spacetimes larger than **dS**$^+(\Lambda)$ but smaller than **all**(Λ) can be identified for which the N-bound holds generally. The existence of such a set may be of some significance for the prospects of quantum gravity theories with a finite number of states. This will be discussed at the end of the next section.

31.6 Quantum gravity in de Sitter space

There is evidence that we possess a quantum theory of gravity for certain asymptotically anti-de Sitter (AdS) spacetimes, which are negatively curved. String theory is known to admit spacetimes of the form $AdS_m \times M_n$ where M_n is a suitable compact Euclidean manifold, for some dimensions (m, n). In these backgrounds, a non-perturbative definition of the theory (and thus, of quantum gravity) has been found in terms of a conformal field theory (Maldacena, 1998; Gubser, Klebanov and Polyakov, 1998; Witten, 1998). String theory (and non-perturbatively, M(atrix)-theory; Banks *et al.*, 1997) also defines S-matrix amplitudes in some asymptotically flat geometries and in other backgrounds.

Rather than attacking the problem of quantum gravity in complete generality, these successes suggest that progress can be made by restricting to suitable classes of spacetimes, characterized by asymptotic boundaries which are protected from quantum fluctuations. After addressing flat and negatively curved geometries, a natural step is to consider a positive cosmological constant next. This case is of particular interest because it might include the universe we inhabit (Riess *et al.*, 1998; Perlmutter *et al.*, 1999).

However, twenty-five years after the semiclassical results of Gibbons and Hawking (1977), a full quantum gravity theory for asymptotically de Sitter spacetimes is still lacking. In particular, it has turned out very difficult to realize de Sitter space in string theory (for recent approaches, see, e.g., Hull, 2001; Silverstein, 2001; Gutperle and Strominger, 2002; and the contribution by Maloney, Silverstein and Strominger in Chapter 32, this volume).

31.6.1 To drop infinity or to keep infinity

It is not clear how broad a set of spacetimes would be described by a 'quantum theory of de Sitter space'. From the experience with string theory, one expects that a particular matter content, presumably compatible with reasonable energy conditions, will arise from the theory. But what about asymptotic conditions? Should both asymptotic regions be demanded ($\mathbf{dS}^{\pm}$)? Will the theory describe the broader class $\mathbf{dS}^{+}(\Lambda)$, requiring only that the spacetime asymptote to de Sitter space in the future? Or should we abandon asymptotic conditions entirely and seek a theory of $\mathbf{all}(\Lambda)$, spacetimes characterized merely by a particular positive value of the cosmological constant?

No such confusions arise for asymptotically AdS and flat universes, because their asymptotic boundaries have only one connected component.

Moreover, in the AdS and flat cases, the presence of the asymptotic region is not affected by continuous changes to Cauchy data. For spacetimes with positive cosmological constant, however, small changes in the stress tensor at one time may affect the presence of asymptotic de Sitter regions in the past or future (Bousso, 2000; Bousso, DeWolfe, and Myers, 2002). Of course, it is conceivable that a non-perturbative quantum theory will preclude variations of Cauchy data that would classically change the asymptotic structure. However, at least from a low-energy perspective, this would seem unnatural.

Classically, one must keep in mind that even in a dS$^+$ universe, not all observers reach future infinity; some fall into black holes. Moreover, an observer's causal diamond contains at most one point each of $\mathcal{I}^+$ and $\mathcal{I}^-$, so that physical observables cannot be defined in the asymptotic regions. At the quantum level, one expects all structures to be thermalized by Gibbons–Hawking radiation within finite time, which prevents observers from reaching $\mathcal{I}^+$ altogether. Together with the difficulty mentioned in the previous paragraph, this makes it desirable to seek a theory which ultimately does not require or make use of asymptotic de Sitter regions (for example a theory of **all**(Λ), with suitable matter restrictions).

However, one has no control over metric fluctuations in the spacetime interior, and no symmetries can be assumed. This impedes concrete progress without some reference to asymptotic regions. Moreover, whether or not it will ultimately survive in the formulation, the structure of the de Sitter infinities may well provide clues to properties of a quantum gravity theory. This has been the subject of numerous studies, especially in the context of the correspondence between de Sitter space and a Euclidean conformal field theory recently conjectured by Strominger (2001a).[8]

31.6.2 A theory with finite-dimensional Hilbert space?

Reproduction of the entropy S_0 of de Sitter space provides a key test for any formulation of quantum gravity. For dS$^\pm$ spacetimes, Witten (2001) has argued that a Hilbert space of dimension e^{S_0} might arise from a larger space of states via a non-standard inner product. In the context of the dS/CFT correspondence, the entropy of de Sitter and Kerr–de Sitter spacetimes has been numerically reproduced (e.g., Balasubramanian, de Boer and Minic, 2001; Bousso, Maloney and Strominger, 2001).

---

[8] I will not attempt to survey the literature on this approach. Extensive lists of references may be found in Balasubramanian, de Boer, and Minic (2001), and in Spradlin and Volovich (2001). In viewing cosmological evolution as inverse RG flow, Strominger (2001b) has also outlined a possible approach to understanding the apparent increase in the number of available degrees of freedom with time.

However, this was done by methods whose justification from the CFT point of view is still incomplete.

Fischler (2000a,b) and Banks (2000) have proposed that the finiteness of the de Sitter entropy should be elevated to a defining principle for the theory. The bound on observable entropy in all dS^+ universes, (31.20), implies that a finite number of states suffices to describe completely all of physics in such universes. It would be most economical, therefore, to seek a quantum gravity theory with Hilbert space of finite dimension e^{S_0}. Conversely, perhaps a positive cosmological constant should be regarded as nature's way of ensuring that entropies greater than S_0 simply cannot occur – an essential cut-off if our Hilbert space is really finite.

The Banks–Fischler proposal suggests that a positive cosmological constant should not be regarded as a consequence of complicated quantum corrections and cancellations. Rather, $\Lambda > 0$ constitutes a direct and fundamental reflection of the size of the Hilbert space of quantum gravity. A correspondence between the value of the cosmological constant and the number $\mathcal{N}$ of states in the Hilbert space is thus implied. Thus, the proposal offers a fresh perspective on the cosmological constant problem. (This is called the 'Λ-N correspondence', where $N = \log \mathcal{N}$, in Bousso, 2000.)

It must be stressed that this proposal goes beyond what is necessary to explain de Sitter entropy. It exploits the fact that a cosmological constant can be regarded as a fixed property of a theory, rather than a variable parameter associated with a solution. The finite entropy of a black hole, by contrast, reflects only those states (of a larger or infinite Hilbert space) that actually correspond to the black hole. As the mass of the black hole is usually considered a variable parameter, it cannot possibly constrain the dimension of the full Hilbert space, which ought to be infinite for asymptotically flat or AdS spacetimes.

The Banks–Fischler proposal asserts that the de Sitter entropy will not arise from a subset of states, but represents the complete Hilbert space of a theory. In particular, there would be no possibility of describing de Sitter by a theory with infinitely many states. This would be a remarkable constraint. For example, a single harmonic oscillator has an infinite-dimensional Hilbert space, not to speak of quantum field theory or string theory.

The Banks–Fischler proposal assigns a crucial role to theories with Hilbert space of finite dimension $\mathcal{N}$ for the description of certain cosmological spacetimes. The physics of asymptotically flat or AdS universes (e.g., string theory) would be recovered only in the limit $\mathcal{N} \to \infty$. Conversely, this would explain why de Sitter space has not been found in string theory.

For $D > 4$, the Λ-N correspondence suffers from the shortcoming that the specification of a positive cosmological constant alone does not guarantee the entropy bound (31.24). As discussed at the end of the previous section, explicit counterexamples are known (Bousso, DeWolfe and Myers, 2002). In other words, **all**(Λ) contains spacetimes with observable entropy greater than S_0. Such spacetimes cannot possibly be described by a theory with only $\mathcal{N} = e^{S_0}$ states. Some $\Lambda > 0$ spacetimes must be excluded from the 'gravity dual' of any finite-$\mathcal{N}$ theory.

Thus, a simple relation between the size of Hilbert space and the cosmological constant cannot hold unless additional conditions are specified. Clearly, the demand of a future asymptotic de Sitter region is a sufficient condition. However, as discussed in section 31.6.1, it is both artificial and operationally questionable to distinguish spacetimes in $\mathbf{dS}^+$ from at least some of the closely related spacetimes in **all**$(\Lambda) - \mathbf{dS}^+(\Lambda)$.

The search for a suitable completion of the set $\mathbf{dS}^+(\Lambda)$, in which (31.24) would hold, has not yet succeeded. Such a completion would give support to the Banks–Fischler proposal. It would provide a concrete candidate set of spacetimes that might be described by quantum gravity theories with finite $\mathcal{N}$, if such theories exist.

31.6.3 Other questions

There are many other open questions about de Sitter space. If the region near $\mathcal{I}^+$ cannot be observed, then what are the observables? Is the evolution of matter fields and horizon in de Sitter space unitary or is information lost?

Hawking (1976) claimed that black holes convert pure states to mixed states. The debate continues despite recent results in support of unitarity (Strominger and Vafa, 1996; Maldacena, 1998). For a de Sitter horizon, it is not clear whether the question is even well-posed. One can attempt to extend black hole complementarity (Susskind, Thorlacius and Uglum, 1993) to de Sitter space (Dyson, Lindesay and Susskind, 2002) and restrict to a causal diamond region (Bousso, 2000). However, asymptotic states cannot be defined, and it is not clear how unitary evolution would be verified in any experiment.

In particular, a black hole can evaporate completely; in principle, it can return information in correlations of the Hawking radiation. On the other hand, the cosmological horizon never disappears completely except in the catastrophic collapse of the entire spacetime. No more than a third of the degrees of freedom are available in matter form (this limit arises from the largest black hole in de Sitter space). Thus, if the whole system, consisting of matter and the cosmological horizon, were in a pure state, the matter subsystem would be unlikely to contain any information at all (Page, 1993). Finite observer lifetimes further complicate this problem.

Yet, whether or not we live in de Sitter space, many of the above conceptual problems arise in any attempt at a quantum treatment of cosmology. De Sitter space offers a relatively simple arena for their investigation.

31.7 Instabilities of the Nariai solution

31.7.1 Schwarzschild-de Sitter and Nariai

Black holes in de Sitter space cannot be larger than the de Sitter horizon. Small Schwarzschild–de Sitter black holes are much hotter than the cosmological horizon, and the geometry in their neighbourhood is a good approximation of a Schwarzschild black hole in flat space. Their evolution will not differ much from their flat space cousins.

In this section I will discuss quantum aspects of black holes that are of a size comparable to the cosmological horizon. These 'large' Schwarzschild–de Sitter black holes have no flat space analogue. They constitute interesting physical systems in their own right. The interplay between the two horizons leads to novel effects. Instabilities arise that can complicate the global structure of asymptotically de Sitter spacetimes.

The Schwarzschild–de Sitter solution is given by the metric

$$\frac{ds^2}{\ell^2} = -V(r)dt^2 + \frac{dr^2}{V(r)} + r^2 d\Omega_2^2, \qquad (31.25)$$

where

$$V(r) = 1 - \frac{2E}{r} - r^2. \qquad (31.26)$$

This metric is static and covers only a portion of the maximally extended spacetime, as seen in the Penrose diagram of Figure 31.4.

The mass parameter E grows monotonically with the size of the black hole. For $E = 0$ one recovers empty de Sitter space. If $0 < E < E_{max} \equiv 3^{-3/2}$, $V(r)$ has two positive zeros, corresponding to the black hole and the cosmological horizon. The fully extended spatial geometry at $t = 0$ has topology $S^1 \times S^2$. The size of the S^2 varies as a function of the coordinate on the S^1; it is minimal on the black hole horizon and maximal on the cosmological horizon.

The cosmological horizon decreases as E is increased. For $E = E_{max}$, both horizons are at the same value of r, at $r = 3^{-1/2}$. In the metric (31.25) it would appear that there is no space left in the geometry. In fact, however, only the coordinate r becomes degenerate and ceases to be useful. A proper limiting procedure (Ginsparg and Perry, 1983)

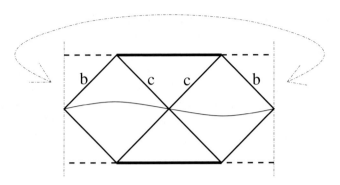

Fig. 31.4. Penrose diagram of a Schwarzschild–de Sitter spacetime. The curved line is a slice of equal time in the static coordinates; its geometry is a warped product of S^1 and S^2. The S^2 directions are suppressed in this diagram; the S^1 arises because the left and right ends are identified. The black hole (b) and cosmological (c) horizons are indicated. The static coordinates, (31.25), cover one of the diamond-shaped regions. The black hole singularity and the de Sitter infinity are shown as dashed and bold lines, respectively. The Nariai solution has the same Penrose diagram except for the nature of the boundaries. The Penrose diagram for a multiple Schwarzschild–de Sitter solution is obtained by joining several copies of this diagram before identifying the ends.

shows that the geometry of the $t = 0$ slice remains perfectly regular as $E \to E_{\mathrm{max}}$ and becomes the geometry of the Nariai solution. This space is the direct product of an S^1 and an S^2, both with radius $r = 3^{-1/2}$.

31.7.2 First-mode instability

Although the Nariai and Schwarzschild–de Sitter geometries nearly agree at an instant of time, they differ markedly in their temporal evolution. The S^1 factor of the Nariai solution expands exponentially, forming a 1+1 dimensional de Sitter spacetime. The S^2 factor remains constant. In global coordinates, the Nariai metric is given by

$$\frac{ds^2}{\ell^2} = \frac{1}{3}\left(-dT^2 + \cosh^2 T \, dx^2 + d\Omega_2^2\right). \tag{31.27}$$

Unlike all of the Schwarzschild–de Sitter solutions, the Nariai spacetime is homogeneous. It does not possess any singularity, nor does it possess four-dimensional asymptotic de Sitter regions.[9]

---

[9] The singularities as well as the asymptotic boundaries of the Schwarzschild–de Sitter spacetimes lie in the far future or past. They are not places in space. Hence the different boundary structure of the Nariai solution does not contradict the similarity

These properties make a classical instability of the Nariai solution manifest. Consider a small perturbation of the $T = 0$ slice, such that the two-sphere area is not constant but instead is given by $(\ell^2/3)(1+\epsilon \cos x)$. That is, the two-sphere size oscillates once as a function of the angular variable on the S^1. To leading order, this will revert the geometry to a nearly maximal Schwarzschild–de Sitter metric (Ginsparg and Perry, 1983). The 2-spheres that are smaller than the Nariai value will collapse to form the black hole interior. The larger 2-spheres expand exponentially to generate an asymptotic de Sitter region.

A nearly maximal Schwarzschild–de Sitter black hole is classically stable. Quantum mechanically one expects Hawking radiation to be emitted both by the black hole, and by the cosmological horizon that surrounds it. In the Nariai solution, the two horizons would be in equilibrium at a temperature $T = 3^{1/2}/(2\pi\ell)$ (Bousso and Hawking, 1996b). The black hole and the cosmological horizon emit and receive equal amounts of radiation.

One expects perturbations of the Nariai geometry to disturb this equilibrium. This question was studied by Bousso and Hawking (1998b). The quantum radiation was included in the s-wave approximation at the level of a one-loop effective action. (Different actions were employed by Nojiri and Odintsov, 1999a,b, 2001). We found that large Schwarzschild–de Sitter black holes are unstable to radiation.

Because of the interplay between the two nearly equal horizons, the dynamics of the evaporation can be more involved than it is for small black holes. For some perturbations, the black hole horizon grows towards the Nariai value at early times. However, the shrinking mode is expected to dominate at late times.

Our analysis was carried out perturbatively about the Nariai solution. This did not amount to a conclusive argument that the evaporation of black holes will continue well into the small black hole regime, where the effect of the cosmological horizon can be neglected and one can be sure that the evaporation process will in fact complete. Later this was demonstrated by a non-linear numerical analysis (Niemeyer and Bousso, 2000). Schwarzschild–de Sitter black holes evaporate, be they large or small.

31.7.3 Higher modes and fragmentation

So far, I have discussed only a first-mode perturbation. The Nariai solution has more in store. A constant mode perturbation[10] makes the

---

of the spatial metrics at one instant of time [the $T = 0$ slice of (31.27) and the $E \to E_{\max}$ limit of (the full extension of) the $t = 0$ slice of (31.25)].

[10] Classically, the perturbations in vacuum must satisfy certain constraint equations. In the one-loop model studied by Bousso and Hawking (1998b) this becomes a con-

Nariai

2 x Schwarzschild
de Sitter

2 x de Sitter

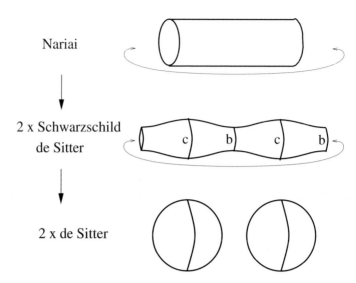

Fig. 31.5. Fragmentation. Nariai space is a product $S^1 \times S^2$. The S^2 is represented as an S^1 here; the time direction is suppressed in the drawings and indicated only through the arrows evolving the snapshots of the spatial geometry. Upon a higher-mode perturbation (here, $n = 2$), Nariai space can evolve into a sequence of Schwarzschild–de Sitter universes. Black hole (b) and cosmological (c) horizons are indicated. When the black holes evaporate, the geometry pinches in several places, and only disconnected de Sitter portions remain.

two-sphere area everywhere smaller, or everywhere larger, than the value $\ell^2/3$. The former case is like trying to make a black hole that doesn't fit into de Sitter space; the spacetime collapses globally in a big crunch. The latter case will lead to a solution in which all regions are locally de Sitter but the global topology is non-trivial.

Higher-mode perturbations of the Nariai solution give rise to rather drastic global effects (Bousso, 1998). Consider the nth mode ($n > 1$), which perturbs the two-sphere radius as $(\ell^2/3)(1 + \epsilon \cos nx)$. If this fluctuation dominates, one finds the following classical evolution. The mode is oscillatory at first, increasing in proper wavelength as the S^1 expands. When the S^1 has expanded by a factor n, the wavelength becomes larger than the horizon scale, and the mode grows exponentially. This marks the beginning of the formation of n black hole interiors and n asymptotically de Sitter regions (Figure 31.5).

straint on the initial distribution of the radiation, which can be satisfied for all metric perturbations at leading order.

The geometry then resembles a sequence of Schwarzschild–de Sitter solutions. In the ordinary Schwarzschild–de Sitter solution ($n = 1$), the black hole connects opposite ends of a single asymptotic de Sitter region (Figure 31.4). There are two black hole horizons, but only one black hole interior. In the solutions obtained for $n > 1$, however, each black hole connects two different de Sitter regions; after traversing[11] n such regions and n black holes, one is back at the first region.

The higher-mode instabilities of the Nariai solution become even more interesting when Hawking radiation is taken into account (Bousso, 1998). Perturbatively, each of the black holes is found to evaporate, much like a large Schwarzschild–de Sitter black hole in a single asymptotic region. At the non-linear level, the evaporation was again found to continue until the black holes are much smaller than the cosmological horizons (Niemeyer and Bousso, 2000); then nothing can stabilize them, and one expects that they will disappear altogether.

If $n = 1$, the complete evaporation of a Schwarzschild–de Sitter black hole can be visualized as a deformation and eventual topological transition of the $S^1 \times S^2$ spatial sections. The direct product metric (Nariai) becomes a warped product (Schwarzschild–de Sitter), in which the two-sphere size varies along the S^1. Eventually the S^2 vanishes at one point; the $S^1 \times S^2$ geometry pinches off and reverts to an S^3 topology (empty de Sitter space). If $n > 1$, however, the S^2 size decreases at n points on the S^1, as all n black holes evaporate. Hence, the spatial geometry is pinched in several places, leaving behind n disconnected spatial manifolds, each of topology S^3.

Thus, the spacetime fragments. Notice that this is not an off-shell Planckian quantum fluctuation of the metric by which some kind of baby universe is created. The process is slow and under good semiclassical control. Planckian curvatures enter only at the endpoint of the evaporation, which is usually assumed to correspond to the disappearance of the black hole. The fragments can be arbitrarily large.

31.7.4 Global structure, black hole creation, and proliferation

The instability of the Nariai solution is remarkable in that arbitrarily small variations in the spatial geometry can lead to an unlimited variety of causal structures. The mode number of the dominant perturbation determines the number of copies of $\mathcal{I}^+$; upon inclusion of Hawking radiation, it determines the number of disconnected components of space at late times. This can be regarded as a generalization of an effect discussed

---

[11] This is a description of spacelike surfaces, not of causal paths through the spacetime.

in section 31.6 above. There it was noted that small changes in Cauchy data can determine whether or not $\mathcal{I}^+$ is present at all.

In this section, I have described the decay of the Nariai solution, not the decay of de Sitter space. However, it is possible for black holes to nucleate spontaneously in de Sitter space. A number of arguments lead to this expectation and yield mutually compatible estimates of the nucleation rate. For example, black holes can be assumed to lie in the exponential tail of the thermal radiation emitted by the cosmological horizon. However, the gravitational instanton approach has been most commonly used (Ginsparg and Perry, 1983; Bousso and Hawking, 1995, 1996b, 1999a; Mann and Ross, 1995; Chao, 1997; Bousso and Chamblin, 1999). In this picture, the formation of black holes is regarded as a tunnelling event, much like the Schwinger pair creation of charged particles in a strong electric field. One finds at leading order that the rate of black hole formation is suppressed by the difference between the de Sitter entropy and the Schwarzschild–de Sitter entropy:

$$\Gamma \sim \exp(S_{\text{SdS}} - S_0). \tag{31.28}$$

In particular, a Nariai black hole might nucleate, at a rate of $\exp(-\pi/\Lambda)$. Thus, the possibility arises that de Sitter space proliferates (Bousso, 1998) by the iterated production, evaporation, and fragmentation of Nariai geometries. However, it is not clear whether a global description of the nucleation process, suggested by the instanton approach, is adequate (section 31.5.3). In fact, the repeated nucleation of black holes at different times, which occurs naturally in a single causal region from a statistical mechanics point of view, faces global obstructions in the instanton picture, as the nucleation surfaces would mutually intersect (Jacobson, unpublished). For the purpose of generating an unlimited number of components of $\mathcal{I}^+$, at least, those obstructions can be circumvented by considering black holes of sufficient charge (Bousso, 1999c).

31.7.5 Discussion

The work reported in this section precedes the current surge of interest in de Sitter space and accelerating universes. Many of the present approaches are guided by the desire to apply string theory, or at least some of the lessons learned from recent developments in string theory, to the problem of de Sitter quantum gravity. The study of the Nariai solution might add some useful perspectives to these endeavors.

It is possible to explore the vacuum structure of string theory by identifying certain unstable configurations (e.g., the vacuum of bosonic string theory, or a D-brane/anti-D-brane pair). The idea is to study their evolution and try to describe the structure of the decay product (see, e.g., Sen, 1999). In this sense, the Nariai solution may offer a way of circumventing the difficulty of incorporating de Sitter space in string theory. If a Nariai solution could be constructed, its decay would naturally lead to de Sitter space, and perhaps to the more complicated configurations obtained by the fragmentation process. Though there is no guarantee that a Nariai solution can be implemented in string theory, the possibility of this approach should be noted.

In some of the present approaches to de Sitter quantum gravity (section 31.6), asymptotic boundaries play a central role, and the presence of a single copy each of $\mathcal{I}^+$ and $\mathcal{I}^-$ is often assumed (e.g., Strominger, 2001a; Witten 2001). We noted earlier that the presence of these boundaries is by no means guaranteed and is sensitive to small variations of Cauchy data. The present section has shown that the conformal boundary can become arbitrarily complicated in de Sitter-like spacetimes. There can be an unlimited number of disconnected components of $\mathcal{I}^+$. Moreover, spacetimes with a large variety of different asymptotic structures can be obtained from small variations of topologically identical initial conditions. It is conceivable that this additional structure might play a role in the formulation of a quantum gravity theory in de Sitter space.

Acknowledgement

This work was supported in part by the National Science Foundation under Grant No. PHY99-07949.

References

Abbott, L. F. and Deser, S. (1982), 'Stability of gravity with a cosmological constant', *Nucl. Phys.* **B195**, 76.

Balasubramanian, V., de Boer J. and Minic, D. (2001), 'Mass, entropy and holography in asymptotically de Sitter spaces', [hep-th/0110108].

Banks, T. (2000), 'Cosmological breaking of supersymmetry or little Lambda goes back to the future II', [hep-th/0007146].

Banks, T., Fischler, W., Shenker, S. H. and Susskind, L. (1997), 'M theory as a matrix model: a conjecture', *Phys. Rev.* **D55**, 5112, [hep-th/9610043].

Bardeen, J. M., Carter, B. and Hawking, S. W. (1973), 'The four laws of black hole mechanics', *Commun. Math. Phys.* **31**, 161.

Bekenstein, J. D. (1972), 'Black holes and the second law', *Nuovo Cim. Lett.* **4**, 737.

Bekenstein, J. D. (1973), 'Black holes and entropy', *Phys. Rev.* **D7**, 2333.

Bekenstein, J. D. (1974), 'Generalized second law of thermodynamics in black hole physics', *Phys. Rev.* **D9**, 3292.

Bekenstein, J. D. (1981), 'A universal upper bound on the entropy to energy ratio for bounded systems', *Phys. Rev.* **D23**, 287.

Bekenstein, J. D. (1999), 'Non-Archimedean character of quantum buoyancy and the generalized second law of thermodynamics', [gr-qc/9906058].

Bekenstein, J. D. (2001), 'Quantum information and quantum black holes', [gr-qc/0107049].

Bousso, R. (1998), 'Proliferation of de Sitter space', *Phys. Rev.* **D58**, 083511, [hep-th/9805081].

Bousso, R. (1999a), 'A covariant entropy conjecture', *JHEP* **07**, 004, [hep-th/9905177].

Bousso, R. (1999b), 'Holography in general space-times', *JHEP* **06**, 028, [hep-th/9906022].

Bousso, R. (1999c), 'Quantum global structure of de Sitter space', *Phys. Rev.* **D60**, 063503, [hep-th/9902183].

Bousso, R. (2000), 'Positive vacuum energy and the N-bound', *JHEP* **11**, 038, [hep-th/0010252].

Bousso, R. (2001), 'Bekenstein bounds in de Sitter and flat space', *JHEP* **04**, 035, [hep-th/0012052].

Bousso, R. (2002), 'The holographic principle', [hep-th/0203101].

Bousso, R. and Chamblin, A. (1999), 'Patching up the no-boundary proposal with virtual Euclidean wormholes', *Phys. Rev.* **D59**, 084004, [gr-qc/9803047].

Bousso, R. and Hawking, S. W. (1995), 'The probability for primordial black holes', *Phys. Rev.* **D52**, 5659, [gr-qc/9506047].

Bousso, R. and Hawking, S. W. (1996a), 'Pair creation and evolution of black holes during inflation', *Helv. Phys. Acta* **69**, 261, [gr-qc/9608008].

Bousso, R. and Hawking, S. W. (1996b), 'Pair creation of black holes during inflation', *Phys. Rev.* **D54**, 6312, [gr-qc/9606052].

Bousso, R. and Hawking, S. W. (1996c), 'Primordial black holes: tunneling vs. no boundary proposal', [gr-qc/9608009].

Bousso, R. and Hawking, S. W. (1997a), 'Black holes in inflation', *Nucl. Phys. Proc. Suppl.* **57**, 201.

Bousso, R. and Hawking, S. W. (1997b), 'Trace anomaly of dilaton-coupled scalars in two dimensions', *Phys. Rev.* **D56**, 7788, [hep-th/9705236].

Bousso, R. and Hawking, S. W. (1998a), in *COSMO 97: 'Proceedings of the 1st International Workshop on Particle Physics and the Early Universe'*, ed. L. Roszkowski (World Scientific, Singapore).

Bousso, R. and Hawking, S. W. (1998b), '(Anti-)evaporation of Schwarzschild–de Sitter black holes', *Phys. Rev.* **D57**, 2436, [hep-th/9709224].

Bousso, R. and Hawking, S. W. (1999a), 'Lorentzian condition in quantum gravity', *Phys. Rev.* **D59**, 103501, [hep-th/9807148].

Bousso, R. and Hawking, S. W. (1999b), 'Primordial black holes: Pair creation, Lorentzian condition, and evaporation', *Int. J. Theor. Phys.* **38**, 1227.

Bousso, R., DeWolfe, O. and Myers, R. C. (2002), 'Unbounded entropy in spacetimes with positive cosmological constant', [hep-th/0205080].

Bousso, R., Maloney, A. and Strominger, A. (2001), 'Conformal vacua and entropy in de Sitter space', [hep-th/0112218].

Chao, W.-Z. (1997), 'Quantum creation of a black hole', *Int. J. Mod. Phys.* **D6**, 199, [gr-qc/9801020].

Davies, P. C. W. (1984), 'Mining the universe', *Phys. Rev.* **D30**, 737.

Dyson, L., Lindesay, J. and Susskind, L. (2002), 'Is there really a de Sitter/CFT duality', [hep-th/0202163].

Figari, R., Hoegh-Krohn, R. and Nappi, C. R. (1975), 'Interacting relativistic boson fields in the de Sitter universe with two space-time dimensions', *Commun. Math. Phys.* **44**, 265.

Fischler, W. (2000a) unpublished.

Fischler, W. (2000b) 'Taking de Sitter seriously' Talk given at *Role of Scaling Laws in Physics and Biology*, (celebrating the 60th Birthday of Geoffrey West), Santa Fe, December 2000.

Fischler, W. and Susskind, L. (1998), 'Holography and cosmology', [hep-th/9806039].

Gao, S. and Wald, R. M. (2000), 'Theorems on gravitational time delay and related issues', *Class. Quant. Grav.* **17**, 4999, [gr-qc/0007021].

Gibbons, G. W. and Hawking, S. W. (1977), 'Cosmological event horizons, thermodynamics, and particle creation', *Phys. Rev.* **D15**, 2738.

Ginsparg, P. and Perry, M. J. (1983), 'Semiclassical perdurance of de Sitter space', *Nucl. Phys.* **B222**, 245.

Gubser, S. S., Klebanov, I. R. and Polyakov, A. M. (1998), 'Gauge theory correlators from noncritical string theory', *Phys. Lett.* **B428**, 105, [hep-th/9802109].

Gutperle, M. and Strominger, A. (2002), 'Spacelike branes', *JHEP* **04**, 018, [hep-th/0202210].

Hawking, S. W. (1971), 'Gravitational radiation from colliding black holes', *Phys. Rev. Lett.* **26**, 1344.

Hawking, S. W. (1974), 'Black hole explosions', *Nature* **248**, 30.

Hawking, S. W. (1975), 'Particle creation by black holes', *Commun. Math. Phys.* **43**, 199.

Hawking, S. W. (1976), 'Black holes and thermodynamics', *Phys. Rev.* **D13**, 191.

Hawking, S. W. and Ellis, G.F.R. (1973), *The Large Scale Stucture of Space-Time* (Cambridge University Press Cambridge).

Hull, C. M., (2001), 'de Sitter space in supergravity and M theory', *JHEP* **11**, 012, [hep-th/0109213].

Leblond, F., Marolf, D. and Myers, R. C. (2002), *'Tall tales from de Sitter space. I: Renormalization group flows'*, [hep-th/0202094].

Maldacena, J. (1998), 'The large N limit of superconformal field theories and supergravity', *Adv. Theor. Math. Phys.* **2**, 231, [hep-th/9711200].

Mann, R. B. and Ross, S. F. (1995), 'Cosmological production of charged black hole pairs', *Phys. Rev.* **D52**, 2254, [gr-qc/9504015].

Marolf, D. and Sorkin, R. (2002), 'Perfect mirrors and the self-accelerating box paradox', [hep-th/0201255].

Niemeyer, J. C. and Bousso, R. (2000), 'The nonlinear evolution of de Sitter space instabilities', *Phys. Rev.* **D62**, 023503, [gr-qc/0004004].

Nojiri, S. and Odintsov, S. D. (1999a), 'Effective action for conformal scalars and anti-evaporation of black holes, *Int. J. Mod. Phys.* **A14**, 1293, [hep-th/9802160].

Nojiri, S. and Odintsov, S. D. (1999b), 'Quantum evolution of Schwarzschild-de Sitter (Nariai) black holes', *Phys. Rev.* **D59**, 044026' [hep-th/9804033].

Nojiri, S. and Odintsov, S. D. (2001), 'De sitter space versus Nariai black hole: Stability in d5 higher derivative gravity', *Phys. Lett.* **B523**, 165, [hep-th/0110064].

Page, D. N. (1993), 'Expected entropy of a subsystem', *Phys. Rev. Lett.* **71**, 1291, [gr-qc/9305007].

Perlmutter, S. *et al.* (1999), 'Measurements of Omega and Lambda from 42 high-redshift supernovae', *Astrophys. J.* **517**, 565, [astro-ph/9812133].

Riess, A. G. *et al.* (1998), 'Observational evidence from supernovae for an accelerating universe and a cosmological constant', *Astron. J.* **116**, 1009, [astro-ph/9805201].

Schiffer, M. (1992), 'The possible role of event horizons in quantum gravity', *Gen. Rel. Grav.* **24**, 705.

Schiffer, M. and Bekenstein, J. D. (1989), 'Proof of the quantum bound on specific entropy for free fields', *Phys. Rev.* **D39**, 1109.

Sen, A. (1999), 'Descent relations among bosonic D-branes', *Int. J. Mod. Phys.* **A14**, 4061, [hep-th/9902105].

Silverstein, E. (2001), '(A)dS backgrounds from asymmetric orientifolds', [hep-th/0106209].

Spradlin, M. Strominger, A. and Volovich, A. (2001), 'Les Houches lectures on de Sitter space', [hep-th/0110007].

Spradlin, M. and Volovich, A. (2001), 'Vacuum states and the S-matrix in dS/CFT', [hep-th/0112223].

Strominger, A. (2001a), 'The dS/CFT correspondence', *JHEP* **10**, 034, [hep-th/0106113].

Strominger, A. (2001b), 'Inflation and the dS/CFT correspondence', *JHEP* **11**, 049, [hep-th/0110087].

Strominger, A. and Vafa, C. (1996), 'Microscopic origin of the Bekenstein–Hawking entropy', *Phys. Lett.* **B379**, 99, [hep-th/9601029].

Susskind, L. (1995), 'The world as a hologram', *J. Math. Phys.* **36**, 6377, [hep-th/9409089].

Susskind, L. Thorlacius, L. and Uglum, J. (1993), 'The stretched horizon and black hole complementarity', *Phys. Rev.* **D48**, 3743, [hep-th/9306069].

't Hooft, G. (1993), 'Dimensional reduction in quantum gravity', [gr-qc/9310026].

Unruh, W. G. (1976), 'Notes on black hole evaporation', *Phys. Rev.* **D14**, 870.

Wald, R. M. (1984), *General Relativity* (The University of Chicago Press, Chicago).

Wald, R. M. (2001), 'The thermodynamics of black holes', *Living Rev. Rel.* **4**, 6, [gr-qc/9912119].

Witten, E. (1998), 'Anti-de Sitter space and holography', *Adv. Theor. Math. Phys.* **2**, 253, [hep-th/9802150].

Witten, E. (2001), 'Quantum gravity in de Sitter space', [hep-th/0106109].

32

De Sitter space in non-critical string theory

Andrew Strominger

with Alexander Maloney and Eva Silverstein
Harvard University and Stanford University

32.1 Introduction

The purpose of this talk is to discuss recent attempts to embed de Sitter space in string theory and understand its quantum properties. The ultimate goal is to resolve the puzzles raised by Hawking's seminal discovery with Gibbons [1] that de Sitter space has an entropy. It is a tribute to the depth of Stephen's insights that, a quarter century later, they are still driving the forefront of theoretical physics research.

Recent progress in string theory has led to deep conceptual insights into the quantum nature of a number of spacetime geometries, including black holes and AdS. dS (de Sitter) has so far been largely left out of the fun. A key reason for this is that so far no fully satisfactory dS solution of string theory has been found.[1] The problem is intrinsically difficult because there can be no unbroken supersymmetry in dS [2]. Hence the solutions are likely to be isolated with no massless scalars or moduli.

A recent approach [3] employs supercritical superstring theory. Although they do not have flat space as a solution, non-critical string theories are of intrinsic interest for a wide variety of reasons. They are implicated in tachyon decay processes in compact closed string backgrounds [4], and in attempts to obtain the QCD string [5]. Their precise place in the M theory duality web remains an outstanding question. New cosmological solutions (with a strongly coupled singularity) of supercritical string theory were discussed in [6]. The recent application to de Sitter space [3] utilizes an asymmetric orientifold construction in non-critical twelve-dimensional string theory which has no moduli. The supercriticality introduces a leading-order cosmological term (dilaton potential)

---

[1] However there are a number of interesting constructions which may not have been fully exploited [7–13].

which aids in fixing the dilaton. By turning on RR fluxes it is possible to arrange for the dilaton to have a non-trivial minimum with a positive cosmological constant. The string coupling at the minimum is numerically, but not parametrically, small. However, as stressed in [3], the true expansion parameter about the minimum – and the nature of string perturbation theory about a minimum which balances dilaton tadpoles from non-criticality against RR fluxes – are not understood. For both of these reasons the existence of a string perturbation expansion about the minimum is in question, and strong coupling effects could in principle eliminate the dS solution. A second issue in this model is that the dS minimum is unstable to decay to flat space. This implies that not every point on the asymptotic boundary of the space is dS. One of the recent lessons of string theory is that the nature of the boundary can be quite important, so a theory which asymptotically decays to flat space may be very different from a 'stable' dS.

In this talk we report on work in progress which improves on this construction. A generalized asymmetric orientifold construction is introduced with a new parameter: the number of dimensions D. By making the number of dimensions large and employing the Bousso–Polchinski mechanism [14] with the RR fluxes we are able to make the cosmological constant at the minimum parametrically small, the higher-dimensional string coupling parametrically weak, and the effective barrier to the linear dilaton regime parametrically large. Despite this improvement we have not understood the true expansion parameter about the minimum, which could therefore in principle be eliminated by strong coupling effects.

In particular, as a function of the dimensionality D, the number of RR fields is $n_{RR} = 2^D$, which dominates the spectrum at large D. This is potentially both a liability and an asset: on the one hand, the 2^D RR species threaten to render the effective coupling uncontrollably large; on the other hand, the large number of RR fluxes facilitate the construction of vacua with small cosmological constant and weak D-dimensional string coupling. As one increases D, the naive number of degrees of freedom increases and, as we will see, one can obtain a larger and larger de Sitter space. It is tempting to speculate that the 2^D RR degrees of freedom pertain to the entropy; this will be interesting to explore in the future. In particular, since a large de Sitter space requires a large number of states (to account for the large entropy), the large number of degrees of freedom intrinsic to supercritical string theory may play a natural role.

We also consider, in a more general setting, the issue of the decay of dS space to flat space. When the barrier is small such decays clearly occur via flat space bubble nucleation and are described by gravitational instantons. However, the required bubble size grows with the barrier height, and eventually the bubble wall crosses the horizon. We will argue that the inclusion of such superhorizon processes has bizarre consequences. Causality and unitarity appear to be violated, and for very large height the process describes the tunnelling of the entire universe to a Planckian region! The proper rules for dS quantum gravity are not well understood, and this casts doubt on the assertion that such instantons should be included in the first place. We further note that the tunnelling time exceeds the Poincaré recurrence time for dS [15] for exactly the same parameter range that the instanton becomes superhorizon sized. (It also exceeds the (shorter) time for all of de Sitter space to tunnel into a maximal black hole [16].) Hence both the observable significance and the validity of the semiclassical approximation are in question for the superhorizon decay processes.[2] If the superhorizon instantons are excluded, a 'false' dS vacuum may be stable against decay to flat space (or to the linear dilaton regime in the case of the supercritical models), or equivalently the decay time may become so long as to be meaningless.

In the supercritical models, one can in this way potentially forbid decays from a large range of dS minima to the linear dilaton regime, since as we will see the domain wall tension is too large for a sub-horizon size bubble. However, we also find decays between different flux vacua proceeding via nucleation of D-branes (as in [14],[17],[18]), including transitions from dS to AdS. The model thus is a stringy construction sharing features with those studied in [14], [17–19] exhibiting a dynamical relaxation of the cosmological constant. Among the different flux vacua, there are many more choices of flux configuration yielding larger values of the cosmological constant than smaller values, and in our system there are large degeneracies among different flux vacua due to the highly symmetric structure of the internal dimensions.

This contribution is organized as follows. Subsection 32.2.1 presents the asymmetric orientifold construction. Section 32.2.2 describes the de Sitter minima, and 32.2.3 discusses the lower limit on the cosmological constant implied by flux quantization. Section 32.3.1 reviews the instantons which describe the tunnelling from de Sitter to flat space. Section 32.3.2 questions the conventional wisdom that this tunnelling occurs (or is even well-defined) for arbitrarily high barriers. Section 32.3.3 relates this to Poincaré recurrence and the breakdown of the semiclassical approximation. Finally, in subsection 32.3.4 we address the stability of the asymmetric orientifold models.

---

[2] As discussed in subsection 32.3.4 and alluded to in [18], this is a de Sitter analogue of the breakdown of the semiclassical approximation for black holes discussed in [20]. Related discussions can be found in [21],[22].

32.2 De Sitter compactifications of super-critical string theory

In this section we generalize the construction of [3] to large numbers D of dimensions and describe de Sitter solutions of the low energy action. We compute the contributions to the dilaton potential from non-criticality, orientifold planes and RR fluxes. We demonstrate that by taking the number of dimensions to be large, one can find potentials having minima at a parametrically small value of the D-dimensional string coupling. Finally, we consider flux quantization and show that at large D the cosmological constant can be made parametrically small.

32.2.1 Asymmetric orientifolds in non-critical string theory

In D (more than 10) dimensions, we start with the string frame low energy effective theory for the graviton, dilaton and Ramond–Ramond fields

$$S_D =$$

$$\frac{1}{2\kappa_D^2} \int d^D x \sqrt{-G} \left(e^{-2\phi} \left(R - \frac{2(D-10)}{3\alpha'} + 4\nabla_\mu \phi \nabla^\mu \phi \right) - \frac{1}{2} \sum_p (F_p)^2 \right),$$

$$(32.1)$$

where the sum runs over the various RR fields F_p in the theory.

We will be interested in asymmetric orientifold models obtained from this D-dimensional theory in which the dilaton is fixed. Let us begin by noting a few salient points regarding the spectrum in these relatively unfamiliar theories. Note from the action (32.1) (and as discussed in [23] and reviewed in [3]), the graviton, dilaton, and RR fields in D dimensions are massless. However, if one calculates using free field theory the putative zero-point energy of these fields in flat (string-frame) space, i.e. in the linear dilaton background, one finds in the NS sector a vacuum energy of $-(D-2)/16$. As explained in [23], this reflects the effective tachyonic behaviour of the fields in the linear dilaton background (obtained from (32.1) by expanding in small fluctuations about the linear dilaton solution). In order to obtain the effective mass squared of the fields in the Lagrangian expanded around a putative extremum with constant dilaton (such as those we are studying herein) one must therefore cancel the contribution from the linear dilaton from the zero point energy. This amounts to the statement that, in the NS sector, the effective vacuum energy E is off from the free field result E_0 by

$$E = E_0 + \frac{D-10}{16}.$$

$$(32.2)$$

Let us now proceed to the models of interest here, which are compactifications from D down to $d = D - r$ dimensions. We will eventually be interested in the case of large D with d held fixed, and in particular how various quantities depend on D. Because, as we will see, the quantities relevant to our conclusions scale exponentially with D, some numerical factors that are order one will not be explicitly computed.

We begin with a self-dual torus T^r. The zero modes on the torus are given by

$$p_L^i = \frac{1}{\sqrt{\alpha'}}(m^i + n^i)$$

$$p_R^i = \frac{1}{\sqrt{\alpha'}}(m^i - n^i)$$

(32.3)

and the dimensions of the corresponding worldsheet operators are $(\frac{\alpha'}{4}p_L^2, \frac{\alpha'}{4}p_R^2)$. Mod out by the orientifold group generated by

$$g_1 \equiv (0, s^2)_{d+1} \ldots (0, s^2)_{d+r},$$

(32.4)

$$g_2 \equiv (-1, 1)_{d+1} \ldots (-1, 1)_{d+r},$$

(32.5)

$$g_3 \equiv \Omega I_r,$$

(32.6)

$$g_4 \equiv (-1)^F (s, s)_{d+1} \ldots (s, s)_{d+r}.$$

(32.7)

As in [3], we adopt the following notation. $(0, s^2)_i$ is an asymmetric shift on the ith coordinate, and acts as $(-1)^{n^i + m^i}$. $(s, s)_i$ is a geometric shift on the ith coordinate by half the circle radius, and acts as $(-1)^{m^i}$. Ω is an orientation reversal, I_r a reflection on all r coordinates of the T^r. $(-1, 1)_i$ is a reflection on the ith left-moving coordinate only, and is at the heart of the moduli-fixing effect of this model, since it projects out all the untwisted NS NS moduli.

In order to check level-matching (for modular invariance) and to check for twisted moduli, we must compute the vacuum energy in all inequivalent sectors, taking into account (32.2). Let us start with the shifts. In the $(0, s^2)^r$ twisted sector, the momentum and winding lattice (32.3) is shifted so that $(m, n) \to (m + 1/2, n + 1/2)$, while in the (s, s) sector it is shifted by $(m, n) \to (m, n + 1/2)$. Each $(0, s^2)$ shift (per direction) has a right-moving energy of $1/4$, while each (s, s) shift (per direction) gives left and right moving energies of $1/16$. For the element $g_2 = (-1, 1)^r$, we have ground state energies

$$\left(E_L = \frac{r}{8} - \frac{1}{2}, E_R = -\frac{1}{2}\right).$$

(32.8)

This level-matches if $r = 4k$ for integer k. In order to avoid any massless modes (potential moduli) in this sector, we must take $k > 1$. For the element $g_2 g_4$ we have

$$\left(E_L = \frac{r}{8} - \frac{1}{2} = \frac{k-1}{2}, E_R = \frac{r}{16} - \frac{1}{2} = \frac{k-2}{4}\right),$$

(32.9)

requiring that $k \equiv 2N$ be even for level-matching. As discussed in [23], in order to have a standard GSO projection, one requires $D = d + r \equiv 8j + 2$ for integer j. Altogether, in order to have a consistent orientifold group we need

$$r = 8N, \tag{32.10}$$

for integer $N \geq 1$, and to have an ordinary GSO projection we need

$$d = D - 8N = 8j + 2 - 8N. \tag{32.11}$$

This model has two sets of orientifold planes – O-$(d-1)$-planes generated by the element g_3 and spacefilling O-$(D-1)$-planes generated by the T-dual element $g_2 g_3 g_2 = \Omega$. We also have anti-orientifold planes, which are necessary to cancel the RR tadpoles – these are generated by the elements $g_3 g_4$ and $g_2 g_3 g_4 g_2$. The total contribution to the action due to these orientifold planes is

$$S_{\text{Orientifold}} = \sum_i T_{O_i} \int d^{p_i+1} x \sqrt{-G} e^{-\phi}, \tag{32.12}$$

where i runs over the orientifolds – here the orientifold group acting on the r dimensions of our torus introduces 2^{r-1} O-$(d-1)$ planes, 2^{r-1} $\bar{O}$-$(d-1)$ planes, as well as the T-dual objects, an O-$(D-1)$ plane, and an $\bar{O}$-$(D-1)$ plane. These T-dual pairs are identified under the action of g_2, so (32.12) is just 2^r times the action for a single O_{d-1} plane:

$$S_{\text{Orientifold}} = 2^r T_{O_{d-1}} \int d^d x \sqrt{-G} e^{-\phi}$$
$$= -\frac{2^{7/2+D/4} \pi^{1/2}}{\kappa_D \ell_s^{1-D/2+d}} \int d^d x \sqrt{-G_d} e^{-\phi}. \tag{32.13}$$

Here we have defined the string length

$$\ell_s = 2\pi \sqrt{\alpha'} \tag{32.14}$$

and are using the generalized formula for the tension of an orientifold p-plane in D dimensions derived in [3] with the assumptions listed there (which consist essentially of the procedure (32.2) for the closed-string channel modes applied to the annulus diagram),

$$2^{D-(p+1)} T_{O_p} = -\frac{2^{7/2+D/4} \pi^{1/2}}{\kappa_D \ell_s^{p+2-D/2}}. \tag{32.15}$$

The action of the orientifold group projects out the NS-NS moduli of the T^r, so the d-dimensional action for the untwisted NS-NS sector reduces to

$$S_{NS} = \frac{1}{2\kappa_d^2} \int d^d x \sqrt{-G_d} e^{-2\phi} \left(R_d - \frac{2(D-10)}{3\alpha'} + 4\nabla_\mu \phi \nabla^\mu \phi \right), \quad (32.16)$$

where the d-dimensional gravitational coupling is

$$\kappa_d^2 = \frac{\kappa_D^2}{v\ell_s^r} = v^{-1}\ell_s^{d-2}. \quad (32.17)$$

v here is the dimensionless effective volume of the compactification space given by

$$\left(\int_{T^r} d^{4m} x \sqrt{-G_r} \right)_{eff} = v\ell_s^r, \quad (32.18)$$

and is of order one. We have taken the D-dimensional coupling to be $\kappa_D^2 = \ell_s^{D-2}$.[3]

Note that one could also consider multiple copies of this orientifold group acting on subtori of T^r. Each ΩI_p action reduces the RR spectrum by half, so this has the virtue of reducing the number of species which contribute to the effective coupling. However, there is a danger of also reducing the effective volume and thus v in (32.18), thereby increasing the effective coupling. It would be interesting to determine the winner of the competition between these two effects, but for now we will stick to a single copy of the orientifold group (32.4–32.7).

We now turn on some RR fluxes along the compact directions (see, e.g. [24–30]). In D dimensions, a p-form field strength wrapped on a cycle of volume V_p will be quantized as

$$\frac{1}{2\kappa_D} \int_{V_p} F_p = \sqrt{\pi} \ell_s^{\frac{2p-D}{2}} Q, \quad (32.19)$$

where Q is an integer. Let us use a basis of cycles given by the square subtori $\subset T^r$. We will label these by $i = 1, \ldots, 2^r$. Turning on RR fluxes adds a dilaton independent piece to the d dimensional string frame action. Before orientifolding, there are $\binom{r}{k}$ possible k-form fluxes to choose from, for a total of 2^r. Although some of the internal fluxes will be projected out by the orientifold action, certain flux configurations will be left invariant. These invariant combinations of fluxes from the untwisted sector of the orbifold, which involve fluxes of different rank related to each other by T-duality, will also be subject to the quantization condition inherited from

---

[3] In making this choice, we are tacitly assuming that high-order terms in the perturbation series will be $\leq$ order one with respect to this choice of coupling. See the discussion in [3] for more details.

the parent theory. Because our orbifold is of finite order independent of r, the number of invariant fluxes still scales like 2^r for large r after taking into account the reduction in the RR spectrum effected by the orientifold action. Chern–Simons couplings among the many RR fields at large D may also affect the spectrum in a given flux background, and the set of consistent choices of flux configuration; this would be interesting to work out in detail.

Going to d-dimensional Einstein frame

$$G_{d\mu\nu} \to \tilde{G}_{\mu\nu} = G_{d\mu\nu} e^{\frac{4\phi}{2-d}}, \qquad (32.20)$$

the low energy action becomes

$$S = \frac{1}{2\kappa_d^2} \int d^dx \sqrt{-\tilde{G}} \left(\tilde{R} - \left(\frac{4}{(d-2)} \right) \partial_\mu \phi \partial^\mu \phi - \frac{1}{v\ell_s^2} U(\phi) \right). \qquad (32.21)$$

The Einstein frame dilaton potential is

$$U(\phi) = e^{\frac{4}{d-2}\phi}(a - be^\phi + ce^{2\phi}), \qquad (32.22)$$

where

$$a = v4\pi^2 \left(\frac{2(D-10)}{3} \right),$$

$$b = 2 \, 2^{7/2+D/4} \pi^{1/2} v_O, \qquad (32.23)$$

$$c = \sum_{i=1} \frac{\pi}{v_{p_i}} Q_i^2 \ell_s^{2p_i - D} + \Lambda_1 \equiv \pi \sum_{i=1} \tilde{Q}_i^2 + \Lambda_1.$$

Here in the expression for b, v_O is a dimensionless volume associated with the orientifold planes on our orbifold similar to v; again this is of order 1 in our model and we will not keep track of such factors in our analysis. In the expression for c, i labels the fluxes in the square basis discussed above, and we consider only invariant combinations of these basic fluxes. p_i is the degree of the field strength and v_{p_i} is an order one dimensionless volume associated to the ith flux. (Before the orientifolding, these volumes are self-dual, but as in (32.21) the effective volumes may be reduced by the action of the orientifold group.)

Λ_1 is the one-loop dilaton potential. It will be proportional to $n_{RR} \sim 2^D$ times $\xi(D)$ where $\xi(D)$ is an unknown D-dependent constant, which is related to the effective loop-counting parameter in our theory. (For some insight into the scaling of loop effects in gravitational field theory as a function of dimension D, see [31], where factors of $1/D!$ appear with additional loops, providing enhanced control at large D.) Because the 2^D RR bosons dominate the spectrum, Λ_1 is likely to be negative in the string theoretically regulated theory, similarly to the situation in, for example, Scherk-Schwarz compactifications [32] and many other non-supersymmetric orbifold examples that have been analysed in critical string theory, in which one finds the sign of Λ_1 to be the same as that of the difference between the number of massless fermions and bosons in the tree-level spectrum. Below, we will analyse the potential assuming conservatively that $\Lambda_1 \sim -2^D$ for definiteness but, as will become clear, the qualitative results apply for a large range of possible values of Λ_1 including those with smaller magnitude.

In principle, we should also include a renormalization of Newton's constant at the same order; this will not affect the perturbative stabilization in what follows in this section, but non-perturbatively may adjust the instanton actions in Section 32.3.

32.2.2 De Sitter solutions

Let us write the potential as

$$U(\phi) = \left(a - be^\phi + \frac{b^2}{4a}(1 + \delta)e^{2\phi} \right) e^{\frac{4\phi}{d-2}}. \tag{32.24}$$

There is a de Sitter solution if $U(\phi)$ has a stable minimum at positive energy. This requires that the solutions of $U'(\phi) = 0$,

$$e^{\phi_\pm} = \frac{a}{db} \left(\frac{d + 2 \pm \sqrt{(d-2)^2 - 8d\delta}}{1 + \delta} \right) \tag{32.25}$$

are real – here $\phi_\pm$ is the local minimum (maximum). In addition the effective cosmological constant

$$\Lambda = U(\phi_+), \tag{32.26}$$

should be greater than zero. These two conditions require that

$$0 < \delta < \frac{(d-2)^2}{8d}. \tag{32.27}$$

As δ increases from the lower bound to the upper bound, $U(\phi_+)$ increases from 0 to $(a^{\frac{d+2}{d-2}} 8^{\frac{4}{d-2}} (d-2)^2)/(b^{\frac{4}{d-2}} d(d+2)^{\frac{d+2}{d-2}})$ and the string coupling decreases from $2a/b$ to $8a/b(d+2)$. Near $\delta = 0$, the cosmological constant goes like

$$U(\phi_+) = a \left(\frac{2a}{b} \right)^{\frac{4}{d-2}} \delta + \mathcal{O}(\delta^2). \tag{32.28}$$

If we wish to minimize the string coupling we must take $\delta \sim (d-2)^2/8d$. For example, in the original scenario of [3] ($D = 12$, $d = 4$) this gives

$$a = \frac{8\pi^2}{3}, \qquad b = \pi^{1/2}2^{15/2}, \qquad \Lambda \sim \frac{1}{(2\pi\alpha^{1/2})^4}(0.05), \qquad e^{\phi_+} \sim 0.11.$$

$$(32.29)$$

This has the disadvantage that Λ is only a couple orders of magnitude above string scale. Also, the potential barrier separating the local minimum from the global minimum at $\phi \to -\infty$ is small, so the vacuum is not very stable against tunnelling effects. Let us instead try to minimize Λ by taking $\delta \to 0$. We find that (modulo issues of flux quantization, which we will consider in the next section) we can make Λ as small as we like, with

$$\Lambda \sim 0, \qquad e^{\phi_+} \sim 0.16. \qquad (32.30)$$

We have found that Λ can be made arbitrarily small, at the cost of a small increase in the string coupling. In addition, this solution is much more stable, since the potential barrier is high.

A solution with small D-dimensional string coupling is found by taking $a/b \to 0$. From the expressions (32.23) it is clear that this can always be accomplished by taking D large. However, it is not clear that this implies a small true effective string coupling after compactification. The latter may, for example, be enhanced by the enormous multiplicity ($\sim 2^D$) of RR fields. (On the other hand, if things work as in [31], there may in fact be overcompensating loop-suppression factors as a function of D that preserve the smallness of the effective coupling.)

32.2.3 Solutions with small Λ

In order to get a small cosmological constant we must take $\delta \to 0$. However, flux quantization constrains how small we can get δ, and thus how small we can get Λ. We see from Section 32.2.2 that for $\Lambda \sim 0$ and large D, c approaches a large value

$$c = \pi \sum_i \tilde{Q}_i^2 + \Lambda_1 \sim\to\sim \frac{b^2}{4a} \sim \frac{2^{D/2}}{4a}. \qquad (32.31)$$

For example, this is $3072/\pi$ in the scenario in [3]. Since $\Lambda_1 \sim -2^D$, we have

$$\pi \sum_i \tilde{Q}_i^2 \sim 2^D. \qquad (32.32)$$

By taking linear combinations of many different fluxes we can tune c quite accurately – this is similar to the mechanism of Bousso and Polchinski [14], though in our case we have large degeneracies in the set of flux configurations. The allowed charges Q_i lie on a $q \sim 2^r \sim 2^D$-dimensional lattice. Because of the flux quantization condition, the smallest jumps we can have in c are of order 1. Because of (32.32) and the fact that we have 2^D independent fluxes $\tilde{Q}_i$ to pick, there will always be some $\tilde{Q}_i$ which are of order 1 (or smaller), so order 1 jumps are indeed possible. Using (32.28), this gives for the scale of the lowest-lying de Sitter minima

$$\Delta c \sim \frac{b^2}{4a}\delta \sim 1,$$

$$\Lambda = U(\phi_+) \sim \left(\frac{a}{b}\right)^{\frac{2d}{d-2}} \sim 2^{-\frac{Dd}{2(d-2)}}. \tag{32.33}$$

Since $b \sim 2^{D/4}$, this vacuum energy is exponentially small for large D.

32.3 Metastability of the De Sitter vacuum

In addition to the de Sitter minimum, the dilaton potential (32.22) has a global minimum with vanishing cosmological constant at $\phi \to -\infty$. Our system also has a multitude of different dS and AdS vacua obtained from different configurations of flux in the internal space. This raises the issue of whether or not the de Sitter minimum is only metastable. This question arises generically in any string construction of a de Sitter solution involving a potential which vanishes at weak coupling, and/or containing many flux vacua.

Instantons have been described [17, 19, 33]which might be related to this tunnelling. However, as we will see in this section, when the barrier between the minima is sufficiently large, the instanton degenerates and no longer describes tunnelling of a de Sitter horizon volume to a comparably sized-region of flat space. The instanton describes a rather unphysical process in which the visible universe disappears altogether. Such 'super-horizon' instantons occur in the parameter range for which the bubble wall lies behind the horizon.

Whether or not such processes actually occur, and whether or not such de Sitter vacua can be stable, are questions that cannot be definitively settled with our present understanding of quantum gravity in de Sitter space. In ordinary field theory, instantons provide saddle point approximation to a functional integral with fixed boundary conditions. The instantons that describe the decay/disappearance of de Sitter space have no boundary at all, and so it is not clear if they should be included. We will argue that the super-horizon instantons in a sense violate both causality and unitarity and should be omitted altogether. We will also discuss other potential mechanisms for mediating vacuum decay.

32.3.1 The instantons

For simplicity we work in the thin wall approximation, in which case the relevant instanton solutions are rather simple. They have been described in detail in [17] and will now be reviewed.

The Euclidean solutions are characterized by the tension T of the bubble wall and the dS cosmological constant Λ. The solutions are determined by simply matching the extrinsic curvatures on the two sides of the bubble wall to the tension T in accord with the Israel junction condition. The instanton looks like a portion of a round sphere glued to a portion of flat space. The spherical portion is

$$ds^2 = R_{dS}^2(d\theta^2 + sin^2\theta d\Omega_3^2), \qquad 0 \le \theta \le \arcsin\frac{R_B}{R_{dS}}, \qquad (32.34)$$

where $d\Omega_3^2$ is the metric on the unit three sphere, $R_{dS} = \sqrt{3/\Lambda}$ is the dS radius, and R_B is the radius of the S^3 boundary. The flat space portion is

$$ds^2 = dr^2 + r^2 d\Omega_3^2, \qquad 0 \le r \le R_B. \qquad (32.35)$$

The full instanton is then obtained by gluing together (32.34) and (32.35) along the S^3 bubble wall at radius R_B. This is depicted in Figure 32.1. The Israel junction condition

$$\frac{1}{R_B^2} = \frac{1}{R_{dS}^2} + \left(\frac{1}{TR_{dS}^2\kappa^2} - \frac{T\kappa^2}{4}\right)^2, \qquad (32.36)$$

where M_P, the Planck mass, determines R_B in terms of T. Note that R_B increases with T for small T but then decreases for T greater than the critical value

$$T_C = \frac{2}{\kappa^2 R_{dS}}. \qquad (32.37)$$

R_B approaches zero for very large T.

It is straightforward to generalize these euclidean solutions to the dS→dS and dS→AdS cases. In general dimension d, the relation (32.36) becomes [17]

$$\frac{1}{R_B^2} = \frac{2\Lambda_o}{(d-2)(d-1)} + \left(\frac{\kappa_d^2 T}{2(d-2)} + \frac{\Lambda_i - \Lambda_o}{(d-1)T\kappa_d^2}\right)^2. \qquad (32.38)$$

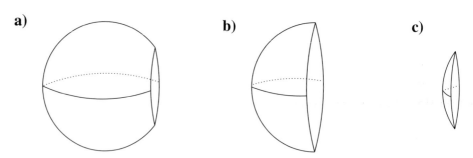

a) **b)** **c)**

Fig. 32.1. The Euclidean instanton solutions matching the sphere (Euclidean de Sitter) to flat space. The cases $T < T_C$, $T = T_C$ and $T > T_C$ are shown in (a), (b) and (c) respectively.

Here, Λ_o is the initial dS cosmological constant (outside the bubble) and Λ_i is the final cosmological constant Λ_i (inside the bubble). In general dimension d, the critical tension is

$$T_C^2 = \frac{2(\Lambda_o - \Lambda_i)(d - 2)}{(d - 1)\kappa_d^4}. \tag{32.39}$$

The instanton purportedly describes tunnelling from one classical geometry to another. We are interested in an initial dS geometry. The final geometry is then given by the analytic continuation of the instanton, which describes an expanding bubble of flat space inside dS. The two geometries are glued together along the moment of time symmetry. This is depicted in Figure 32.2a–c. The tunnelling rate is purportedly given by the action of the instanton minus the background action of Euclidean dS without a bubble. This is

$$\Delta S = 2\pi^2 R_B^3 T + \frac{2\pi^2}{R_{dS}^2 \kappa^2} \left[2R_{dS}^4 \mp \left\{ 3R_{dS}^3 (R_{dS}^2 - R_B^2)^{1/2} \right. \right.$$
$$\left. \left. - R_{dS}(R_{dS}^2 - R_B^2)^{3/2} \right\} \right]. \tag{32.40}$$

The upper and lower signs correspond to $T < T_C$ and $T > T_C$, respectively. Again, the expression for general d was worked out in [17] (equations (6. 4)–(6. 7)).

32.3.2 *Causality*

The tunnelling process depicted for small tensions in Figure 32.2a approaches the usual flat space false vacuum decay in the limit $M_P \to \infty$

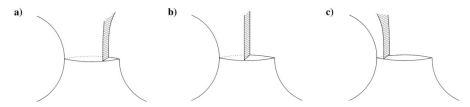

Fig. 32.2. The Lorentzian instanton geometry describing the nucleation of a bubble of flat space (the shaded region) inside de Sitter space. The cases $T < T_C$, $T = T_C$ and $T > T_C$ are shown in (a), (b) and (c) respectively.

with T held fixed. The rate according to (32.40) also approaches the correct flat space value. The instanton of Figure 32.1a surely describes this tunnelling process for sufficiently small but finite T/M_P^3.

The process depicted in Figure 32.2c on the other hand has a bizarre interpretation. The entire universe tunnels to a small dime, with one flat and one dS face! Furthermore for $T \to \infty$ the rate from (32.40) approaches a constant. Hence the tunnelling rate can be enhanced by adding a large number of ultra-Planckian domain walls. In fact, the action 32.40 is not monotonically increasing in the regime $T > T_C$; for certain ranges of parameters, the tunnelling rate *increases* as the tension increases! This conflicts with the notion of decoupling in low-energy field theory, as well as the general fact that tunnelling effects are suppressed as the size of the barrier increases.

This process also appears in conflict with causality. An observer in dS should be insensitive to any physics behind the horizon. In particular there should be no consequences of placing boundary conditions on the fields along a timelike surface behind the horizon. It is easy to find boundary conditions that forbid the super-horizon instanton. Therefore the observer can learn about physics behind the horizon by waiting to see whether or not the tunnelling occurs.

There is also an issue with unitarity. In the benign process of Figure 32.2a, an observer at the South Pole finds him or herself, after the tunnelling, in the middle of a bubble of flat space. However for the superhorizon case of Figure 32.2c, his or her entire southern causal diamond – the entire observable universe – disappears. It has been advocated by many (see for example [34] and the contribution [35] to these proceedings) that the causal diamond should be viewed as a closed unitary system (whose microstates compute the entropy). Surely this process – in which the diamond disappears altogether – violates unitarity in the worst possible manner!

Based on these observations, our conclusion is that when the tension T exceeds T_C, the superhorizon instantons simply should not be included in the semiclassical description of dS. At the same time we wish to stress that, with our current level of understanding of dS quantum gravity, no such conclusions can be drawn with certainty.

The above arguments apply equally well to tunnelling from de Sitter to de Sitter or anti-de Sitter, with the critical tension given by (32.39). We should note that the criterion

$$T > T_C \qquad (32.41)$$

in the case $\Lambda_o = 0$, $\Lambda_i < 0$ reproduces the well known Coleman and DeLuccia condition for the stability of flat space against tunnelling to anti de Sitter [33]. We may thus regard the stability criterion (32.41) as a generalization of the Coleman–DeLuccia mechanism.

Even if such instantons are not to be included, there may be other processes which mediate the decay of the dS to flat space when the barrier is very high. For example if de Sitter space is viewed as a thermal ensemble[4], thermal fluctuations could eventually push the value of ϕ over the top (see e.g., [36, 37] for a discussion of this mechanism). This however is also not obviously possible. There appears to be a maximum energy allowed in dS given by the largest black hole which can fit inside the observer horizon. If the energy required to cross the barrier to flat space exceeds this value, it may be suppressed. Furthermore if the appealing notion [38–40] that dS has a finite number of states given by the area law is accepted, there must be a highest energy state. Again if this is less than the barrier height decay to flat space is suppressed.

32.3.3 Breakdown of the semiclassical approximation

There is yet another way to interpret the condition $T^2 > T_C^2 \sim \Lambda$, which involves a further assumption about de Sitter quantum gravity. Following [38], we assume that de Sitter gravity has a finite number of degrees of freedom which determine the de Sitter quantum entropy. Imagine in this context a detector sitting on a timelike geodesic for a very long time. The detector must be built out of a subset of the finite number of degrees of freedom, all of which will eventually be thermalized by de Sitter radiation from the horizon. This thermalization process sets a maximum timescale in de Sitter space, intervals longer than which can never be measured by a geodesic observer. (See also [21, 22].) The precise value of the thermalization time depends on the structure of the detector, but it is certainly

---

[4] with temperature conjugate to the energy defined by the timelike Killing vector which preserves the causal diamond

less than the Poincaré recurrence time, which is a timescale on which *all* degrees of freedom have been thermalized. This recurrence time is related to the de Sitter entropy by [15] [5]

$$t_{\text{recurrence}} \sim \exp\{S\} = \exp\left\{\frac{8\pi^2 R_{dS}^2}{\kappa^2}\right\}. \qquad (32.42)$$

Another time scale in de Sitter is the typical time for the entire space to tunnel to a maximal sized black hole. This has been estimated using instantons in [16] as

$$t_{\text{blackhole}} \sim (t_{\text{recurrence}})^{1/3}. \qquad (32.43)$$

Hence the entire space tunnels into a maximal black hole exponentially many times before the Poincaré recurrence time.

We wish to compare these times with the expected lifetime of de Sitter space due to vacuum decay. When the tension equals the critical value T_C, the lifetime for the putative instanton decay is (omitting a prefactor which is polynomial in R_{dS})

$$t_{\text{decay}} \sim \exp\{\Delta S\} = \exp\left\{\frac{8\pi^2 R_{dS}^2}{\kappa^2}\right\}. \qquad (32.44)$$

This is precisely the Poincaré recurrence time! Thus as T approaches the critical value T_C the life-time becomes comparable to the recurrence time, and no observer will ever live long enough to see the vacuum decay.[6] Moreover, at $T = T_C$ the lifetime is much longer than the time (32.43)

$$
\begin{aligned}
t_{\text{decay}} &\sim t_{\text{recurrence}} \\
&\sim t_{\text{black hole}}^3 \sim.
\end{aligned}
\qquad (32.45)
$$

Hence in order to observe the decay of de Sitter space when $T = T_C$ one needs a detector capable of passing through a black hole exponentially many times. We regard the existence of such detectors doubtful!

Let us state this in yet another way. The semiclassical approximation describes the de Sitter horizon as a hot wall in contact with a heat

---

[5] The authors of [15] considered several different types of recurrence phenomena. Here we quote the time scale for two point fluctuations proportional to the thermal background value of the Green function – so called 'relative' fluctuations – as opposed to fluctuations of some fixed size independent of S.

[6] Given that the action (32.40) *decreases* at $T \gg T_C$ one might worry that naively applying the instanton methods for very large tensions would lead to decay timescales shorter than the recurrence time. This turns out not to be the case: as $T \to \infty$ the decay time precisely approaches (32.44).

reservoir with *infinite* heat capacity. In this approximation no correlations ever appear in the radiation emitted from the horizon. In the exact theory, it is plausible that the horizon has a finite heat capacity as determined from the finite de Sitter entropy. This means that, if we watch long enough, correlations will be seen in the radiation.[7] A typical time required to see those correlations is the Poincaré recurrence time. Hence this time scale signals the breakdown of the semiclassical approximation. A semiclassical instanton which involves a longer time scale therefore cannot be trusted.

Phrased in this way, our argument parallels a similar one give for black holes in [20], and alluded to in the de Sitter context in [18]. In [20], it was argued that the semiclassical approximation for near-extremal black holes breaks down as the temperature goes to zero very near extremality. The breakdown occurs when the energy of a typical thermal Hawking quantum exceeds the excitation energy of the black hole above extremality. Clearly the Hawking emission cannot proceed under these circumstances because it would leave a subextremal black hole with a naked singularity.

This is a close analogy to the situation we have described in the de Sitter context. The hot horizon emits a thermal spectrum of bubbles of flat space. When the energy of these bubbles (as determined in part by the tension of the bubble walls) exceeds the energy of de Sitter space above flat space, the semiclassical approximation breaks down.

In the black hole case, it was eventually quantitatively understood [41] in the context of string theory that this breakdown of the semiclassical approximation signals the appearance of a gap. Presumably similarly interesting and yet-to-be understood phenomena appear in the de Sitter context.

In conclusion, superhorizon tunnelling processes from dS to flat space do not appear to be meaningful or consistent. The stability and correct quantum description of a dS vacuum separated by a very high barrier from flat space is an open question.

32.3.4 Instantons in the orientifold model

In the asymmetric orientifold model the tension of the domain wall separating the de Sitter from the flat vacuum at $\phi \to -\infty$ is determined by the shape of $U(\phi)$; for example in $d = 4$ it is roughly

$$T \sim \frac{a^{3/2}}{b}. \tag{32.46}$$

---

[7] Of course, as mentioned above, no one can live that long. However this only underscores the unphysical nature of a tunnelling process which takes such a long time.

Using the criterion of the previous subsection, we conclude that many of the de Sitter minima discussed in section 32.2 are stable against decay to the linear dilaton regime.[8] The maximum-energy de Sitter minimum stable under this decay is at $c \sim (b^2/4a) + \mathcal{O}(b^2)$, i.e. at $\delta \sim 1$. (Here we are only keeping track of exponential dependence on D, i.e. factors of b but not a.) This corresponds to an energy of the order

$$U_+^{max} \sim \frac{1}{b^2} \sim 2^{-D/2}. \tag{32.47}$$

The minimum-energy de Sitter minima possible with our quantization condition on the charges and thus on c (which are of course also stable under this decay) have $c \sim (b^2/4a) + \mathcal{O}(1)$, i.e. at $\delta \sim a/b^2$. This corresponds to an energy of the order

$$U_+^{min} \sim \frac{1}{b^4} \sim 2^{-D}. \tag{32.48}$$

In addition to the instanton decays to the linear dilaton regime discussed above, there is also the possibility of transitions among the different flux vacua, as in [14, 17, 18, 42]. D-branes extended along $d-1$ of the d de Sitter dimensions constitute domain walls separating vacua with different flux configurations. More specifically, D-branes of charge Q connect vacua of flux Q_1 and $Q_1 - Q$ on the dual cycle to the D-brane on the compactification. In order to determine the (in)stability of our solutions, we must apply the results reviewed in section 18.3.1 to such D-brane induced decays in addition to the dilatonic domain wall we considered above.

At our de Sitter minima for $d = 4$, the string coupling is

$$g_s \sim 1/b \tag{32.49}$$

and the energy is

$$U_+ \sim (a^4/b^4)(c - (b^2/4a)). \tag{32.50}$$

As we just discussed, the lowest-lying dS vacua have c tuned to cancel $b^2/(4a)$ to within order 1, so that

$$U_+^{min} \sim 1/b^4 \tag{32.51}$$

The highest-lying dS minima that are stable against decay to the linear dilaton background have, from our earlier calculation, c tuned such that $c - (b^2/4a) \sim b^2$, i.e.

$$U_+^{max} \sim a^2/b^2. \tag{32.52}$$

---

[8] We should note that when D is large, the thin wall approximation breaks down for the potentials (32.22); in this limit the width of the domain wall interpolating between the de Sitter and flat vacua scales as T^{-1}. However, this subtlety does not affect the causality considerations of subsection 32.3.2.

Recall from (32.39) that

$$T_C^2 \sim \Lambda_o - \Lambda_i .$$ (32.53)

The D-brane tension is, in Einstein frame, from [3] and the above scaling of g_s at the minimum,

$$T \sim (1/b^2)2^{-D/4}.$$ (32.54)

This formula will apply for a transition in which the bubble wall is a single D-brane; the tension of multiple D-branes will be subject to appropriate binding energy contributions.

If we allow the instanton, i.e. if $T < T_C$, then its action B is given by equation (6.4) in [17]. One should keep in mind that the renormalization of Newton's constant may affect the overall scaling of the action. In addition to the contribution of exp(-action) to the probability for decay, there will also be significant degeneracy factors from the large multiplicity of vacua in our large-D system. Here we will confine ourselves to checking whether the transitions occur at all according to the criterion we have developed herein, assuming that the semiclassical instanton analysis applies (i.e. that the action is large enough in renormalized Planck units).

For example, consider decays from $U_+^{max} \to U_+^{max} - a^4/b^4$. This occurs if $c \sim \sum(\tilde{Q}_i)^2$ changes by order 1 and, in, particular can proceed via a bubble consisting of a single D-brane . In this case, the D-brane tension is

$$T_{(i)} \sim 2^{-D/4}(1/b^2),$$ (32.55)

while the critical tension in this case is

$$T_{C(i)} \sim 1/b^2.$$ (32.56)

So $T_{(i)} << T_{C(i)}$, and the decay proceeds according to our criterion developed above.

Similarly, there are decays from dS to AdS. Consider for example a transition $U_+^{min} \to -U_+^{min}$. Here again

$$T_{(iii)} \sim 2^{-D/4}1/b^2$$ (32.57)

and

$$T_{C(iii)} \sim 1/b^2,$$ (32.58)

so the decay is again allowed.

As we mentioned above, there will be large factors in the transition rates associated with the relative multiplicity of different decay endpoints. In particular, the smaller the value of $\sum \tilde{Q}_i^2 \equiv R^2$ coming into the coefficient c, the fewer choices of flux configuration there are in the window between R and $R + \Delta R$ for a fixed ΔR. So although decays to AdS are possible, it is reassuring that this degeneracy factor prefers the less negative Λ_i values. (In fact these factors also prefer higher dS vacua to lower ones, which may act to suppress the decays depending on the scaling of the renormalized instanton action.)

Acknowledgements

We are grateful to M. Aganagic, T. Banks, R. Bousso, S. Kachru, A. Karch, A. Linde, S. Minwalla, L. Motl, L. Susskind, N. Toumbas and A. Vilenkin for useful conversations. This work was supported in part by DOE grant DE-FG02-91ER40654 and contract DE-AC03-76SF00515 and by the A. P. Sloan Foundation.

References

[1] Gibbons, G. W. and Hawking, S. W. (1977), 'Cosmological event horizons, thermodynamics and particle creation' *Phys. Rev* **D15** 2738–2751

[2] Pilch, K., Van Nieuwenhuizen, P. and Sohnius, M. F. (1985), 'De Sitter Superalgebras and supergravity,' *Commun. Math. Phys.* **98**, 105 .

[3] Silverstein, E. (2001), '(A)dS backgrounds from asymmetric orientifolds,' [hep-th/0106209].

[4] De Alwis, S. P., Polchinski, J. and Schimmrigk, R. (1989), 'Heterotic strings with tree level cosmological constant,' *Phys. Lett.* **B218**, 449.

[5] Polyakov, A. M. (1999), 'The wall of the cave,' *Int. J. Mod. Phys.* **A14**, 645, [hep-th/9809057].

[6] Craps, B., Kutasov, D. and Rajesh, G. (2002), 'String Propagation in the Presence of Cosmological Singularities,' [hep-th/0205101].

[7] Gates, S. J. and Zwiebach, B. (1983), 'Gauged N=4 supergravity theory with a new scalar potential,' *Phys. Lett.* **B123**, 200.

[8] Chamblin, A. and Lambert, N. D. (2001), 'de Sitter space from M-theory,' *Phys. Lett.* **B508**, 369, [hep-th/0102159].

[9] Kallosh, R. (2001), 'N = 2 supersymmetry and de Sitter space,' [hep-th/0109168].

[10] Gibbons, G. W. and Hull, C. M. (2001), 'de Sitter space from warped supergravity solutions,' [hep-th/0111072].

[11] Hull, C. M. (2001), 'de Sitter space in supergravity and M theory,' *JHEP* **0111**, 012, [hep-th/0109213].

[12] Berglund, P., Hubsch, T. and Minic, D. (2001), 'de Sitter spacetimes from warped compactifications of IIB string theory,' [hep-th/0112079].

[13] Fre, P., Trigiante, M. and Van Proeyen, A. 'Stable de Sitter Vacua from N=2 Supergravity,' [hep-th/0205119].

[14] Bousso, R. and Polchinski, J. (2000), 'Quantization of four-form fluxes and dynamical neutralization of the cosmological constant,' *JHEP* **0006**, 006, [hep-th/0004134].

[15] Dyson, L., Lindesay, J. and Susskind, L. (2002), 'Is there really a de Sitter/CFT duality,' [hep-th/0202163].

[16] Ginsparg, P. and Perry, M. J. (1983), 'Semiclassical perdurance of de Sitter space,' *Nucl. Phys.* **B222**, 245.

[17] Brown, J. D. and Teitelboim, C. (1988), 'Neutralization of the cosmological constant by membrane creation,' *Nucl. Phys.* **B297**, 787.

[18] Feng, J. L., March-Russell, J., Sethi, S. and Wilczek, F. (2001), 'Saltatory relaxation of the cosmological constant,' *Nucl. Phys.* **B602**, 307.

[19] Abbott, L. F. (1985), 'A mechanism for reducing the value of the cosmological constant,' *Phys. Lett.* **B150**, 427.

[20] Preskill, J., Schwarz, P., Shapere, A. D., Trivedi, S. and Wilczek, F. (1991), 'Limitations on the statistical description of black holes,' *Mod. Phys. Lett.* **A6**, 2353.

[21] Bousso, R. 'Adventures in de Sitter space', [hep-th/0205177].

[22] Bousso, R., DeWolfe, O. and Myers, R. C. 'Unbounded entropy in spacetimes with positive cosmological constant,' [hep-th/0205080].

[23] Chamseddine, A. H. (1992), 'A study of noncritical strings in arbitrary dimensions,' *Nucl. Phys.* **B368**, 98.

[24] Dasgupta, K., Rajesh, G. and Sethi, S. (1999), 'M theory, orientifolds and G-flux,' *JHEP* **9908**, 023, [hep-th/9908088].

[25] Kachru, S., Schulz, M. and Trivedi, S. (2002), 'Moduli stabilization from fluxes in a simple IIB orientifold,' [hep-th/0201028].

[26] Frey, A. R. and Polchinski, J. (2002), 'N = 3 warped compactifications,' [hep-th/0201029].

[27] Gukov, S., Vafa, C. and Witten, E. (2000), 'CFT's from Calabi–Yau four-folds,' *Nucl. Phys.* **B584**, 69, [Erratum-ibid. (2001), **B608**, 477], [hep-th/9906070].

[28] Giddings, S. B., Kachru, S. and Polchinski, J. 'Hierarchies from fluxes in string compactifications,' [hep-th/0105097].

[29] Becker, K. and Becker, M. (1996), 'M-Theory on eight-manifolds,' *Nucl. Phys.* **B477**, 155, [hep-th/9605053].

[30] Polchinski, J. and Strominger, A. (1996), 'New vacua for Type II string theory,' *Phys. Lett.* **B388**, 736, [hep-th/9510227].

[31] Strominger, A. (1981), 'The inverse dimensional expansion in quantum gravity,' *Phys. Rev.* **D24**, 3082.

[32] Rohm, R. (1984), 'Spontaneous supersymmetry breaking in supersymmetric string theories,' *Nucl. Phys.* **B237**, 553.

[33] Coleman, S. R. and De Luccia, F. (1980), 'Gravitational effects on and of vacuum decay,' *Phys. Rev.* **D21**, 3305.

[34] Maldacena, J. M. and Strominger, A. (1998), 'Statistical entropy of de Sitter space,' *JHEP* **9802**, 014, [gr-qc/9801096].

[35] Susskind, L. (2002), 'Twenty years of debate with Stephen,' [hep-th/0204027].

[36] Linde, A. D. (1992), 'Hard art of the universe creation (stochastic approach to tunnelling and baby universe formation),' *Nucl. Phys.* **B372**, 421.

[37] Garriga, J. and Vilenkin, A. (1998), 'Recycling universe,' *Phys. Rev.* **D57**, 2230, [astro-ph/9707292].

[38] Banks, T. (2001), 'Cosmological breaking of supersymmetry?,' *Int. J. Mod. Phys.* **A16**, 910.

[39] Bousso, R. (2000), 'Positive vacuum energy and the N-bound,' *JHEP* **0011**, 038, [hep-th/0010252].

[40] Fischler, W. unpublished.

[41] Maldacena, J. M. and Susskind, L. (1996), 'D-branes and fat black holes,' *Nucl. Phys.* **B475**, 679, [hep-th/9604042].

[42] Kachru, S., Pearson, J. and Verlinde, H. (2001), 'Brane/flux annihilation and the string dual of a non-supersymmetric field theory,' [hep-th/0112197].

33

Supergravity, M theory and cosmology

Renata Kallosh
Stanford University

33.1 Introduction

Stephen Hawking has played an exceptional role in the lives and scientific careers of many people and I am one of them. My first encounter with Stephen was back in 1978 in Moscow. He told me that he knew my work on supergravity and would like to invite me to Cambridge for a supergravity workshop. Since at that time I was never allowed to travel abroad, I did not believe that I would be able to do so. However Stephen Hawking's word carried much weight in the Academy of Sciences of the USSR, and efforts of Academician M. Markov made my visit to England possible. It is not clear to me how my career would have evolved if not for this miracle.

Stephen Hawking's ability to be deeply involved in studies of gravity, cosmology as well as fundamental high-energy physics is extraordinary. We can see it clearly at this conference dedicated to his sixtieth birthday. We see people from several different scientific communities who mostly do not talk to each other because the tools and lores are different. But all of us who came here have some deep connection through various aspects of Stephen's work, as he has made a strong impact on all of these fields.

At present it is difficult to continue with traditional developments in supergravity and string/M theory. If any of these theories, to a large extent based on supersymmetry, is underlying a fundamental theory of gravity, one cannot ignore experimental facts established during the last few years. Recent cosmological observations based on the study of the anisotropy of the cosmic microwave background radiation (see [1] for the most recent data) as well as supernova suggest that soon after the Big Bang our universe experienced a stage of very rapid accelerated expansion (inflation). Moreover, observations indicate that a few billion years after the Big Bang the universe entered a second stage of accelerated expansion. The rate of acceleration now is many orders of magnitude smaller than during the stage of inflation in the early universe.

On the other hand, significant progress in cosmology may require some input from supersymmetric M/string theory which at low energies is described by supergravity. It is plausible that supersymmetric particles will be discovered at high-energy accelerators. If this happens, general relativity and cosmology will have to accommodate these facts.

In the meantime, as long as the results of the current cosmological experiments are not proven wrong and there is a hope that supersymmetry is present in nature, we may try to reconcile cosmology with supergravity and M/String theory.

De Sitter (dS) spaces relevant to cosmological issues are extremely unnatural for any supersymmetric theory. On the contrary, anti-de Sitter spaces are natural spaces in fundamental theories with supersymmetry: in string theory, in M theory and in most supergravity theories. Anti-de Sitter spaces have unbroken supersymmetry; dS spaces always break supersymmetry.

It is difficult [2] to construct dS vacua by compactification from ten or eleven dimensions, where the string theory and M theory reign. The basic problem seems to originate from the compactification of M/string theory on an internal space with finite volume. Still some 4d extended gauged supergravity theories are known to have dS solutions with the spontaneous breaking of supersymmetry. The first model of this kind was discovered in [3] and many more were found later. These versions of 4d supergravity are related to 11d supergravity with a non-compact internal 7d space [4].

In this paper I will discuss topics on which I have worked or which are closely related. I will not be able to cover all attempts to construct viable cosmological theories in supergravity and M theory, see however, other contributions in this volume.

In the first part of this paper I will discuss extended supergravities $N \geq 2$ with dS vacua[1] and their properties. My main statement is that in all known extended supergravities *masses of scalars in dS vacua are quantized in terms of the cosmological constant*. The quantization condition is of the form

$$\frac{m^2}{H^2} = k. \tag{33.1}$$

---

[1] Unextended N=1 supergravities have been studied in the cosmological context before. They are much less restrictive and more difficult to relate to M/string theory.

Here $\Lambda = 3H^2$ (in units with $M_P = 1$) is a cosmological constant equal to the value of the potential in dS extremum, *k are some integers of order unity, completely independent of all parameters of the theory.* They may take negative values in models with tachyons. I will point out here that m^2/H^2 is an eigenvalue of the Casimir operator in dS space. Therefore the mass quantization condition described above has a geometric group-theoretic interpretation: *in extended supergravities with dS vacua eigenvalues of the Casimir operator take integer values.*

This part of the paper is based on work performed with Linde, Prokushkin and Shmakova [5] where a large class of N=8,4,2 supergravities with dS vacua were studied. Our purpose was to study the properties of the potentials near dS vacua which would be interesting either for early universe inflation or for the present day acceleration. We have found two important features of dS vacua:

- in all theories of 4d extended supergravities which were known at that time, there are *tachyons in dS vacua*;

- in all these theories *masses of scalars in dS vacua are quantized in terms of the cosmological constant.* We have found that $k = 3m^2/\Lambda$ is an integer.

In [5] we had examples[2] with $k = 12, 6, 4, -6$, see equations (52–53) in [5]. Quite recently new models of N=2 supergravity were constructed which have dS vacua without tachyons, $m^2 \geq 0$ [7]. A surprising feature of these theories is that again near dS extremum all masses of scalar particles are quantized in terms of the cosmological constant with $k = 6, 4,$ $3, 2, 0$.

In application to the present cosmological constant this leads to the immediate conclusion that there are ultra-light scalars with a mass of the order

$$m \sim H \sim 10^{-33} \text{eV}.$$

The significance of this fact and the possibility of using these supergravity models in cosmology still has to be understood. The existence of such ultra-light fields may be a desirable feature for a description of an accelerated universe [8]. The presence of ultra-light scalars signals that the corresponding potentials are very shallow. As we will see, in extended supergravities ultra-light fields necessarily come in a package with an ultra-small cosmological constant. Supersymmetry in dS vacua is broken

---

[2] It was pointed to us by A. Van Proeyen that one class of N=2 supergravity models [6] was not analysed in [5]. We have checked now that these models also have integer values of Casimir operator, $k = 12, -2, -6$.

spontaneously due to the presence of the cosmological constant, the scale of SUSY breaking here is $\sim 10^{-3}$eV. In this model, before it is coupled to a 'visible sector', both the small value of the cosmological constant as well as the ultra-light masses of scalars are protected from large quantum corrections. The major problem is of course how to couple these theories to the rest of the world. If they play the role of a 'hidden sector', one may wonder whether its properties, the tiny cosmological constant and masses of the order of a Hubble constant, will be preserved after coupling to the 'visible sector'. We see now that the preservation of the small cosmological constant may imply preservation of small scalar masses. Thus, extended supergravities suggest a new perspective for the investigation of the *cosmological constant problem, intertwined with ultra-light scalars.*[3]

In the second part of the paper, based on the work done in collaboration with Dasgupta, Herdeiro and Hirano [9, 10], we will pursue another strategy to reconcile superstring theory with cosmology. We suggest a particular possibility of using the D-branes of string theory in a cosmological context. The main feature of this development is the possibility of reinterpreting various stages of hybrid inflation [11–15] in a string theory context.

We start with familiar and well-understood BPS objects, like D4 and D6 branes or D3 and D7 branes placed at some distance from each other. Each of them separately is supersymmetric and stable. Some *instability of the initial state of these branes is introduced via a small deviation of supersymmetry for the system of two such objects.* For example, for a D4/D6 model we use a *small angle between BPS branes* as a source of instability. Alternatively, in the dual model one can allow a *small magnetic field* to live on the D7 brane so that the D3 brane is attracted to it. This generates an expansion of the universe in a nearly dS state, when the brane configuration is coupled to gravity. At some distance between the branes, the masses of the open strings become tachyonic and the process of symmetry breaking, resembling tachyon condensation in string theory [16], brings the system towards the exit of inflation. The final stage in all the cases that we study is supersymmetric. In a D4/D6 model the branes reconfigure and restore supersymmetry. The final stage is particularly nicely described in the D3/D7 model: there is a bound state D3/D7 system in which the D3 dissolves on the D7 as an instanton. The embedding of the cosmological D-brane construction into 11d M theory will be also discussed.

---

[3] These considerations were stimulated by discussions with Kaloper and Linde.

33.2 Extended supergravities with dS vacua

The observation in [5] that there are tachyons in all supergravity models with $N \geq 2$ with dS vacua was made a while ago. I reported the results about tachyons and about mass quantization at the conferences dedicated to the sixtieth birthday of John Schwarz and the twenty-fifth birthday of supergravity. The mass quantization observed in [5] (with models [6] added), that is,

$$\frac{m^2}{H^2} = k, \qquad k = 12, 6, 4, -2, -6 \tag{33.2}$$

remained a mystery. After intensive discussions with practically all experts in the field we concluded that there is no reason to believe that the presence of tachyons in dS vacua is necessary in extended supergravities. Therefore one could expect that new versions of supergravity without tachyons in dS space could be found. The art of constructing gauged supergravities is rather complicated. However new developments in cosmology urge us to find new gauged supergravities. Only when extended supergravities are gauged, will they have non-trivial potentials.

Recently new studies of gauged supergravities were performed [17] and it was also shown that one may find new types of gaugings not studied before [18]. More importantly, new classes of N=2 models with dS vacua without tachyons were constructed by Fré, Trigiante and Van Proeyen, [7]. A fascinating property of scalar masses quantized in terms of the cosmological constant in dS vacuum remains true for all models constructed so far. One finds that

$$\frac{m^2}{H^2} = k, \qquad k = 6, 4, 3, 2, 0. \tag{33.3}$$

Here we would like to describe this quantization rule for models discussed in [5, 7] in geometric and group-theoretic terms.

The dS hypersurface embedded in 5d space with the flat metric is

$$\eta_{\alpha\beta} X^\alpha X^\beta = -H^{-2}, \qquad \eta_{\alpha\beta} = \mathrm{diag}(1, -1, -1, -1, -1). \tag{33.4}$$

The Casimir operator C_2 is given by

$$C_2 = -\frac{1}{2} M^{\alpha\beta} M_{\alpha\beta} \qquad \alpha = 0, i; \quad i = 1, 2, 3, 4, \tag{33.5}$$

where the ten generators

$$M_{\alpha\beta} = -i \left(X_\beta \frac{\partial}{\partial X_\alpha} - X_\alpha \frac{\partial}{\partial X_\beta} \right) \tag{33.6}$$

form the $SO(1,4)$ algebra and C_2 commutes with all of them. Therefore C_2 is a constant in each representation. Our quantization means that it has integer eigenvalues in extended supergravities.

$$\langle C_2 \rangle = \langle -\frac{1}{2} M^{\alpha\beta} M_{\alpha\beta} \rangle = \frac{m^2}{H^2} = k. \tag{33.7}$$

To explain this we will employ the dS studies used before by Dixmier [19] to classify the representations in dS space. For $k \geq 9/4$ the representations are called principal series. For $0 < k < 9/4$ the representations are called complementary series. Finally $k = 0$ belongs to a discrete series of representations. The meaning of k is nicely explained in [20]. One starts with dS space with bounded global coordinates describing a compactified version of dS space, a Lie sphere. The metric is

$$ds^2 = \frac{1}{H^2 \cos^2 \rho} \left(d\rho^2 - d\alpha^2 - \sin^2 \alpha d\theta^2 - \sin^2 \alpha \sin^2 \theta d\phi^2 \right). \tag{33.8}$$

Here ρ is a timelike coordinate $-\pi/2 < \rho < \pi/2$ and the rest of the coordinates describe a S^3 part of the Lie sphere.[4]

The massive scalar field equation in dS background is

$$(\Delta_{LB} + m^2)\phi = 0, \tag{33.9}$$

where the Laplace–Beltrami operator on dS space in coordinates specified above is proportional to the Casimir operator C_2

$$\Delta_{LB} = \frac{1}{\sqrt{g}} \partial_\nu \sqrt{g} g^{\mu\nu} \partial_\mu = H^2 \cos^2 \rho (\Delta_1 - \Delta_3) = -H^2 C_2. \tag{33.10}$$

Here $\Delta_1 = \cos^2 \rho \frac{\partial}{\partial \rho} \left(\frac{1}{\cos^2 \rho} \frac{\partial}{\partial \rho} \right)$ and Δ_3 is the Laplace operator on the hypersphere S^3. Thus the second-order differential operator C_2 is

$$C_2 = \cos^2 \rho (\Delta_3 - \Delta_1) = \sum_i (M_{0i})^2 - \sum_{i>j} (M_{ij})^2. \tag{33.11}$$

The scalar field equation of motion (33.9) can now be rewritten as[5]

$$\frac{1}{H^2} (\Delta_{LB} + m^2)\phi = 0, \quad \Rightarrow \quad C_2 \phi = \frac{m^2}{H^2} \phi \tag{33.12}$$

---

[4] The metric in (33.8) is the standard one in the textbook [21], equation (5.67) with $\rho = \eta - \pi/2$.

[5] The standard equation for the scalar field in [21], equation (5.68), is for a scalar field $\tilde{\phi} = \Omega^2 \phi$ after a conformal transformation to a frame with $d\tilde{s}^2 = d\eta^2 + \dots$. In this frame the interpretation of k as an eigenvalue of the Casimir operator is lost since the second-order differential operator C_2 does not commute with the conformal transformation and therefore $C_2 \tilde{\phi} \neq k\tilde{\phi}$.

This group-theoretical basis for quantization sheds light on the universality of the quantization condition (33.1). We still do not have a derivation of the quantization condition (33.1) in extended supergravity but only the observation that it takes place in all known models at present.

Here we will present a truncated version of all the models described in [7], so that only axion-dilaton scalars are present. This will give us an opportunity to explain the mechanism for the appearance of the ultra-light axions and dilatons in dS vacua with ultra-small cosmological constant. The axion-dilaton system in string theory and ungauged supergravity has $SL(2, R)$ or $SL(2, \mathbf{Z})$ symmetry. The action is given by

$$g^{-1/2}L = \frac{g^{\mu\nu}\partial_\mu \tau \partial_\nu \bar{\tau}}{(2\mathrm{Im}\,\tau)^2}. \tag{33.13}$$

This action is invariant under linear fractional transformations of the complex modular parameter $\tau = a - ie^{-\varphi}$. These include in particular the shift of an axion $a \to a + \mathrm{const}$. The relevant part of the new gauged N=2 supergravity action is

$$-\frac{1}{2}R + \frac{1}{4}[(\partial\varphi)^2 + e^{2\varphi}(\partial a)^2] - V(a, \varphi), \tag{33.14}$$

where the potential is:

$$V = \Lambda\left[\cosh(\varphi - \varphi_0) + \frac{1}{2}e^{(\varphi+\varphi_0)}(a - a_0)^2\right]. \tag{33.15}$$

We have presented the axion-dilaton potential as a function of the cosmological constant Λ and the critical values of the axion-dilaton field $\tau_0 = a_0 - ie^{-\varphi_0}$. At the minimum where $V' = 0$,

$$\varphi = \varphi_0, \qquad a = a_0, \qquad V(a_0, \varphi_0) = \Lambda > 0. \tag{33.16}$$

The solution of the equations of motion is a dS space with axion-dilaton field fixed at constant values τ_0. It is clear from the action that near dS vacuum the mass of the dilaton as well as the mass of the axion fields are equal and given by

$$m_\varphi^2 = m_a^2 = 6\frac{\Lambda}{3} = 2\Lambda. \tag{33.17}$$

Note that the global axion shift symmetry $a \to a + \mathrm{const}$ is broken by the potential with a fixed value of a_0.

The original parameters used in [7] are some particular combinations of the gauge coupling e_0, Fayet–Iliopoulos term e_1 and magnetic rotation angles θ, such that

$$\Lambda = e_0 e_1 \sin\theta, \qquad a_0 = \cot\theta, \qquad e^{-\varphi_0} = \frac{e_0}{e_1 \sin\theta}. \tag{33.18}$$

In the presence of other scalars there are also a few additional values $k = 4, 3, 2$, as there are some flat directions with $m^2 = 0$. This means that all of these scalars have a mass of the order 10^{-33} eV.

To the best of our knowledge, no other theory so far has made such a prediction. Interestingly, these ultra-light masses occur in all newly discovered extended gauged supergravities with a dS minimum. It is also interesting that this is the only model known to us of supergravity where dilaton-axion stabilization naturally takes place, instead of the more familiar run-away behaviour.

This result could have interesting cosmological implications. Indeed, in the early universe the light scalar fields may stay away from the minima of their potentials; they begin moving only when the Hubble constant determined by cold dark matter decreases and becomes comparable to $|m|$. A preliminary investigation shows that for $0 < m^2 < 6H^2$, the fields move down very slowly and do not reach the minimum of the effective potential at the present stage of the evolution of the universe. This may result in noticeable changes of the effective cosmological constant during the last 10 billion years. The existence of this effect can be verified by observational studies of the acceleration of the universe. In addition, a slow drift of the fields to the minima of the effective potential may lead to a time-dependence of effective coupling constants.

33.3 Hybrid inflation with D-branes

In the previous section I described properties of de Sitter state that can emerge in extended supergravity. Now we will try to see what may happen in M theory describing interacting branes. But before we turn to M theory, we will describe an N=2 supersymmetric P-term hybrid inflation model [15]. Two different M theory constructions that we have suggested in [9, 10] are based on this model.

33.3.1 The potential of P-term hybrid inflation

Hybrid inflation scenario [11] can be naturally implemented in the context of supersymmetric theories [12, 13]. The basic feature of hybrid inflation is the existence of two phases in the evolution of the universe: a slow-roll inflation in the dS valley of the potential (the Coulomb phase of the gauge theory) and a tachyon condensation phase, or 'waterfall stage', towards the ground state Minkowski vacuum (a Higgs phase in gauge theory).

In $\mathcal{N} = 1$ supersymmetric theories, hybrid inflation may arise as F-term inflation [12] or D-term inflation [13]. In $\mathcal{N} = 2$ supersymmetric theories there is a triplet of Fayet–Iliopoulos (FI) terms, ξ^r, where $r = 1, 2, 3$.

Choosing the orientation of the triplet of FI terms, ξ^r, in directions 1,2, F-term inflation was promoted to $\mathcal{N} = 2$ supersymmetry [14]. The more general case with $\mathcal{N} = 2$, when all three components of the FI terms are present, called *P-term inflation*, was suggested in [15]. When ξ^3 is non-vanishing, a special case of D-term inflation with Yukawa coupling related to gauge coupling is recovered. In this fashion, the two supersymmetric formulations of hybrid inflation are unified in the framework of $\mathcal{N} = 2$ P-term inflation. This gauge theory has the potential [15]

$$V = \frac{g^2}{2}\Phi^\dagger \cdot \Phi \, |\Phi_3|^2 - \left[\frac{1}{2}(P^r)^2 + P^r \left(\frac{g}{2}\Phi^\dagger \sigma^r \Phi + \xi^r\right)\right], \qquad (33.19)$$

where P^r is a triplet of auxiliary fields of the $\mathcal{N} = 2$ vector multiplet, Φ is a doublet of 2 complex scalars, Φ_1 and Φ_1, forming a charged hypermultiplet, Φ_3 is a complex scalar from the $\mathcal{N} = 2$ vector multiplet and g is the gauge coupling. The auxiliary field satisfies the equation $P^r = -(g\Phi^\dagger \sigma^r \Phi/2 + \xi^r)$ and the potential for the choice $\xi^3 = \xi$ simplifies to [15]

$$V = \frac{g^2}{2} \left[(|\Phi_1|^2 + |\Phi_2|^2)|\Phi_3|^2 + |\Phi_1|^2|\Phi_2|^2 \right.$$
$$\left. + \frac{1}{4}\left(|\Phi_1|^2 - |\Phi_2|^2 + \frac{2\xi}{g}\right)^2 \right], \qquad (33.20)$$

which is depicted in Figure 33.1. The potential (33.20) has a local minimum, corresponding to a dS space when coupled to gravity, with $|\Phi_3|$ being a flat direction. This vacuum breaks all supersymmetries spontaneously; here, the vev of the hypers vanishes, $\langle\Phi_1\rangle = \langle\Phi_2\rangle = 0$, and the vev of the scalar from the vector multiplet, which is the inflaton field, is non-vanishing, $\langle\Phi_3\rangle \neq 0$. The masses of hypermultiplets in the dS valley are split:

$$M_2^2 = g^2|\Phi_3|^2 - g\xi, \quad M_\psi = g|\Phi_3|, \quad M_1^2 = g^2|\Phi_3|^2 + g\xi. \quad (33.21)$$

Here ψ is the hyperino, Φ_1 (Φ_2) are positively (negatively) charged scalars of the hypermultiplet. The value of the potential at this vacuum is $V = \xi^2/2$. This is the cosmological constant driving exponential expansion of the universe. The presence of the FI term breaks supersymmetry spontaneously, which is imprinted in the fact that the supertrace of the mass spectrum vanishes, $\mathrm{STr}\, M^2 \equiv \sum_j (-1)^{2j}(1+2j)M_j^2 = 0$. The point where one of the scalars in the hypermultiplet becomes massless,

$$M_2^2 = g^2|\Phi_3|_c^2 - g\xi = 0 \quad \Leftrightarrow \quad |\Phi_3|_c = \sqrt{\frac{\xi}{g}} \qquad (33.22)$$

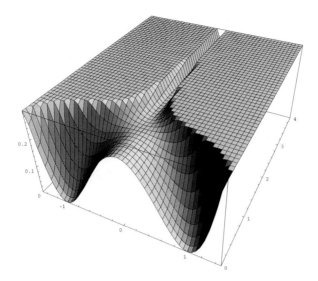

Fig. 33.1. Cosmological potential with Fayet–Iliopoulos term; notice that the dS valley is classically flat; it is lifted by a one-loop correction, corresponding to the one-loop potential between branes. In this figure the valley is along the $|\Phi_3|$ axis; the orthogonal direction is a line passing through the origin of the complex Φ_2 plane and we have put $|\Phi_1| = 0$. Notice there is no $\mathbf{Z_2}$ symmetry of the ground state, it is just a cross-section of the full $U(1)$ symmetry corresponding to the phase of the complex Φ_2 field.

is a bifurcation point. At $|\Phi_3|^2 \leq \xi/g$, the dS minimum becomes a dS maximum; beyond it, such scalars become tachyonic. The system is unstable and the waterfall stage of the potential leads it to a ground state. Finally, the system gets to the absolute minimum with vanishing vev for the scalars in the vector multiplet, $\langle \Phi_3 \rangle = 0$, and non-vanishing vev for the scalars in the hypermultiplet, $\langle \Phi_2 \rangle^2 = 2\xi/g$: supersymmetry is unbroken. The gauge theory one-loop potential lifts the flat direction, via a logarithmic correction

$$V = \frac{1}{2}\xi^2 + \frac{g^2}{16\pi^2}\xi^2 \ln \frac{|\Phi_3|^2}{|\Phi_3|_c^2}. \tag{33.23}$$

This is precisely what is necessary to provide a slow roll-down for the inflaton field, since this is an attractive potential. We would like to stress that in the absence of the FI term ξ, none of the interesting things takes place. The potential with $\xi = 0$ is plotted in Figure 33.2. There is a Minkowski valley with the flat direction.

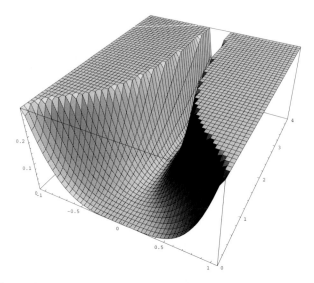

Fig. 33.2. Cosmological potential without Fayet–Iliopoulos term.

33.3.2 D4/D6 model

In our first attempt[6] to link string theory to a gauge model with a hybrid potential [9], we used a system with a D4-brane attached to heavy NS5-branes, having a small angle ϕ relative to a supersymmetric position with regard to the D6-brane. The initial state is slightly non-supersymmetric and forces D4 to move towards the D6-brane (see also [24]). This setup reproduces accurately the properties of the non-supersymmetric dS vacuum of P-term inflation. In particular, the mass splitting of the scalars in the hypermultiplet is reproduced by the low-lying string states. Notice that the inflaton Φ_3 is the distance in the $4, 5$ direction between D4 and D6 in the brane model.

The most important dynamical effect is the attractive potential between $D4$ and $D6$. In open string theory one-loop potential V is given by

$$-\int_0^\infty \frac{dt}{t} \int_{-\infty}^\infty \frac{d^4p}{(2\pi)^4} \left[\mathrm{Tr}_{NS} \frac{1 + (-1)^F}{2} e^{-2\pi t L_0^{NS}} - \mathrm{Tr}_R \frac{1 + (-1)^F}{2} e^{-2\pi t L_0^R} \right],$$

which results in

$$V = \left(\frac{1}{8\pi^2\alpha'} \right)^2 \frac{\sin^2\phi}{\cos\phi} \int_{\alpha'/\Lambda^2}^\infty \frac{dt}{t} \exp\left[-2\pi t \frac{(\Delta s)^2}{\alpha'} \right] + \mathcal{O}(e^{-2\pi/t}),$$

$$\sim \frac{g_{YM}^2}{16\pi^2} \left(\frac{\tilde\phi}{2\pi\alpha'} \right)^2 \log \frac{(\Delta s)^2}{\Lambda^2}. \tag{33.24}$$

---

[6] Earlier studies of brane inflation were performed in [22, 23].

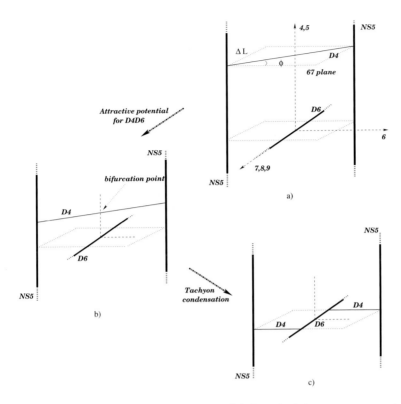

Fig. 33.3. Brane configuration evolution. (a) For $\phi \neq 0$, supersymmetry is broken and D4–D6 experience an attractive force. (b) At the bifurcation point, a complex scalar in the hypermultiplet becomes massless; when we overshoot a tachyon instability forms, taking the system to a zero energy ground state shown in (c).

Here $(\Delta s)^2$ is proportional to $(x^4)^2 + (x^5)^2$, the distance between branes. The string theory potential reproduces the one-loop correction in the field theory (33.23), including the numerical coefficient, in the small angle and large separation approximation. Therefore the motion of the D4 towards the D6 is the slow roll down of the inflaton.

When the distance between the branes becomes smaller than the critical distance the spectrum of D4–D6 strings develops a tachyon. The tachyon condensation is associated with a phase transition. A final Higgs phase with unbroken $\mathcal{N} = 2$ supersymmetry is described in this model by a reconfiguration of branes: D6 cuts D4 into two disconnected parts, so that $\mathcal{N} = 2$ supersymmetry is restored.

One attractive feature of the D4/D6/NS5 model is that the deviation from supersymmetry in the Coulomb stage can be very small and supersymmetry is spontaneously broken. Nevertheless, a large number of e-foldings can be produced within a D-brane.

The main difference between our model [9] and other models of brane inflation [22–26] is that our model provides the brane description of the full potential of hybrid P-term inflation. This includes both the logarithmic quantum corrections to the Coulomb branch potential and the exit from inflation with the corresponding supersymmetric Minkowski vacuum.

33.3.3 D3/D7 model

The model suggested in [10] describes a D3-brane parallel to a D7-brane at some distance. The distance again plays the role of the inflaton field. The supersymmetry breaking parameter is related to the presence of the anti-symmetric $\mathcal{F}_{mn}$ field on the world volume of the D7-brane, but transverse to the D3-brane. When this field is not self-dual in this four-dimensional space, the supersymmetry of the combined system is broken. This is (to some extent) a type IIB dual version of the cosmological model proposed in [9].

The Higgs stage with

$$P^r = -(g\Phi^\dagger \sigma^r \Phi/2 + \xi^r) = 0 \tag{33.25}$$

can be associated with the Atiyah–Drinfeld–Hitchin–Manin construction of instantons. The moduli space of one instanton is the moduli space of vacua of a $U(1)$ gauge theory with N hypermultiplets and (33.25) is the corresponding ADHM equation. We find an Abelian non-linear instanton solution on the world-volume of the brane in the Higgs phase with the associated ADHM equation (33.25).

One other nice feature of the D3/D7 cosmological model is that it is well explained in terms of κ-symmetry of the D7-brane action, both in the Coulomb phase and in the Higgs phase. We use in both cases the BPS condition on the world-volume given by [27]

$$(1 - \Gamma)\,\epsilon = 0.$$

Here, $\Gamma(X^\mu(\sigma), \theta(\sigma), A_i(\sigma))$ is a generator of κ-symmetry and it should be introduced into the equation for unbroken supersymmetry with a vanishing value of the fermionic world-volume field $\theta(\sigma)$. The existence or absence of solutions to these equations fits naturally with the two stages of our cosmological model.

A perturbative analysis of the string spectra is performed for a type IIB system with $D3$ and $D7$-branes plus a constant world-volume gauge field $\mathcal{F}$. This is illustrated in Figure 33.4. There is a constant world-volume

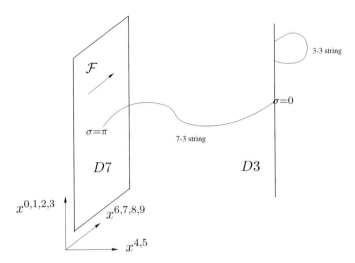

Fig. 33.4. The D3/D7 'cosmological' system. The 3–3 strings give rise to the $\mathcal{N} = 2$ vector multiplet, the 7–3 strings to the hypermultiplet and the world volume gauge field $\mathcal{F}$ to the FI terms of the $D = 4$ gauge theory.

gauge field $\mathcal{F} = dA - B$ present on D7:

$$\mathcal{F}_{67} = \tan \theta_1, \qquad \mathcal{F}_{89} = \tan \theta_2, \tag{33.26}$$

responsible for spontaneous breaking of supersymmetry. Note that if $\mathcal{F}$ is self-dual, supersymmetry would be unbroken. This can be explained via κ-symmetry. The lowest lying multiplet of states of open strings consist of bosons whose masses are given by

$$M_{\pm}^2 = \frac{d^2}{(\pi \alpha')^2} \pm \frac{\theta_1 - \theta_2}{2\pi \alpha'}, \tag{33.27}$$

where we observe that the boson of mass M_-^2 becomes tachyonic at the critical distance.

The $\mathcal{F}$ field plays the role of the Fayet–Iliopoulos term, from the viewpoint of the field theory living on the D3-brane. It creates an instability in the system driving the D3-brane into the D7-brane; this is the de Sitter stage. When the critical distance is reached a tachyon will form and the system will end in a supersymmetric configuration.

D3/D7 bound state and unbroken κ-symmetry is specified by a solution of the equation $\Gamma \epsilon = \epsilon$. It has an interpretation of a D3-brane dissolved into a D7-brane. The BPS condition requires that

$$\frac{\mathcal{F}_{ik}^-}{1 + \mathrm{Pf}\,\mathcal{F}} = -\frac{B_{ik}^-}{1 + \mathrm{Pf}\,B}. \tag{33.28}$$

Here $\mathcal{F}^-$ is the anti self-dual 2 form field on the world volume of the D7 brane and B is the anti self-dual 2 form of the background. This is the non-linear instanton equation with known properties.

In the presence of the non-commutative parameter θ^- or equivalently the B^- field, the singularity of the $U(1)$ instanton is improved. In particular the solution has a finite instanton number. Thus the endpoint vacuum is described by a non-marginal bound state of D3 and D7-branes. The D3-branes on the D7-branes can be thought of as instantons on the D7-branes due to the Chern–Simons coupling, $\frac{1}{16\pi^2}\int_{D7}C_4\wedge F\wedge F = N\int_{D3}C_4$. The Higgs phase of the D3/D7 system is actually identical to the non-commutative generalization of the ADHM construction of instantons. One may argue therefore that our Minkowski vacuum is described by the non-commutative instanton [28, 29]. Thus we have found a possible link between the cosmological constant in spacetime (0123-space) and the non-commutativity of internal space (6789-space).

33.4 M theory on a four-fold with G-fluxes

In addressing compactification of a D-brane cosmological model to four dimensions, to recover four-dimensional gravity, one is faced with the issue of anomalies. In many cases this is associated to the requirement that the overall charge in a compact space must vanish. Our D3/D7 model can be considered within a more general set-up, related to F-theory [30] where the D7-brane charge is cancelled by orientifold 7-planes or (p,q) 7-branes. This seems to provide a setup where, in string theory, the compactification could be consistently performed.[7]

The above set-up can be further simplified by lifting it to M theory. Supersymmetry is broken by choosing a non-primitive G-flux [31]. We may summarize the situation in the following table.

Type IIB	M theory
$T^2/(\Omega\cdot(-1)^{F_L}\cdot\mathbb{Z}_2)\times K3$	$T^4/\mathbb{Z}_2\times K3$
$4(O7+4\ D7)$	4 orbifold fixed points
$D3$	$M2$
$\mathcal{F}$ on $D7$	Localized G-flux at fixed-points
Coulomb phase	Non-primitive G-flux
Higgs phase	Primitive G-flux
Away from orientifold limit	$T^4/\mathbb{Z}_2\ \rightarrow\ $ Smooth $K3$

---

[7] Some recent papers that also consider orientifold planes to describe the inflationary scenario are [26].

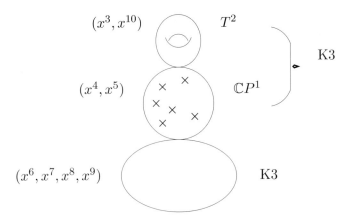

Fig. 33.5. The 'snowman' fibration of the $K3 \times K3$ four-fold. The crosses indicate points on the $\mathbb{C}P^1$ base at which the fibre tori degenerate. In the orbifold limit of the 'top' K3 there will be four such points.

The model that we are going to use is M theory compactified on a four-fold with G-fluxes switched on. To get a $\mathcal{N} = 2$ theory we have to compactify M theory on $K3 \times K3$. We shall take one of the $K3$, to be a torus fibration over a $\mathbb{C}P^1$ base (see Figure 33.5).

To go to type IIB theory we have to shrink the fibre torus to zero size. We assume the orbifold limit of K3 is the initial stage of our dynamical process. In terms of type IIB language, we place a D3-brane at the centre of mass of the $4 \times (4D7/O7)$ set-up on one side of the 'pillow' $T^2/\mathbb{Z}_2$ and another on its diametrically opposite side, as in Figure 33.6. We turn on the same gauge fluxes on all of the four fixed points. The logarithmic potential creates a force between each pair of D3 and D7 branes, if we assume the size of the $T^2/\mathbb{Z}_2$ to be large enough. However in this config-uration the total force between D3 and D7 branes is balanced, and the logarithmic potential being approximately flat leads to a nearly de Sitter evolution. Quantum fluctuations will destabilize the system allowing both

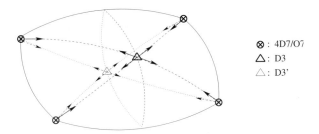

⊗ : 4D7/O7
△ : D3
△ : D3'

Fig. 33.6. The initial brane configuration on the 'pillow' $T^2/\mathbb{Z}_2$.

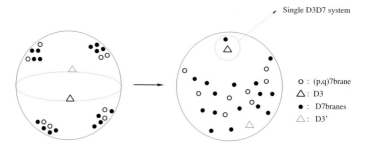

Fig. 33.7. The Coulomb branch. As the system is driven away from the unstable point of Figure 33.2, $T^2/\mathbb{Z}_2 \rightarrow \mathbb{C}P^1$, the orientifold planes split into (p,q) 7-branes, and the D3-brane will eventually fall into one D7-brane as an instanton.

the D3-brane to move towards some D7-brane and the D7-branes to move away from the orbifold fixed points. This is the beginning of the Coulomb phase or equivalently the inflationary stage (Figure 33.7). The whole system eventually moves away from the orientifold limit, which in M theory language means we have a generic K3. Finally, we expect the D3 to fall into one particular D7-brane as a non-commutative instanton. This is the supersymmetric configuration that has been studied in M theory.

The 4-fold vacua has a tadpole anomaly given by $\chi/24$ where χ is the Euler characteristics of the 4-fold. If $\chi/24$ is integral, then the anomaly can be cancelled by placing a sufficient number of spacetime filling M2-branes n on points of the compactification manifold. There is also another way of cancelling the anomaly and this is through G-flux. The G-flux contributes a C tadpole through the Chern–Simons coupling $\int C \wedge G \wedge G$. When $\chi/24$ is not integral then we need both the branes and the G-flux to cancel the anomaly. The anomaly cancellation formula becomes $\frac{\chi}{24} = \frac{1}{8\pi^2}\int G \wedge G + n$, which must be satisfied for type IIA or M theory. The anomaly cancellation condition will now become, $\frac{\chi}{24} = n + \int H_{RR} \wedge H_{NSNS}$, in type IIB theory, where n is the number of D3 branes [32]. Thus we have suggested here a compactified picture in M theory on $K3 \times K3$ manifold with a choice of G-flux on it related to a cosmological D-brane model of P-term inflation.

We have presented above an attempt to use in the context of cosmology the structures developed over the years in M/string theory. Mostly they were used before in the BPS context with unbroken supersymmetry. Even the non-BPS branes were not used much for time-dependent cosmological evolution. Our analysis suggests that all of these tools that have been developed in M/string theory can be very useful for finding realistic models of hybrid inflation.

In the list of open questions in the context of supergravity, M theory and cosmology, those of foremost importance are: Are these theories compatible? Can we learn from the fundamental M/string theory and supergravity about cosmology? There is no clear answer yet. In this paper I have described some early attempts in which I have participated, to address these issues. One may expect much more to come in the near future. Hopefully, the cosmological experiments as well as the high-energy experiments will help to direct the developments of the theory.

Happy birthday, Stephen!

Acknowledgements

It is a pleasure to thank J. Gates, G. Gibbons, B. de Wit, S. Ferrara, P. Fré, D. Freedman, C. Hull, N. Kaloper, L. Kofman, M. Roček, M. Trigiante, A. Tseytlin, A. Van Proeyen and N. Warner for useful discussions of supergravity-cosmology issues, and my collaborators on projects described above, K. Dasgupta, C. Herdeiro, S. Hirano, A. Linde, S. Prokushkin, M. Shmakova. Also I want to thank the organizers of the Future of Theoretical Physics and Cosmology conference, for a very stimulating meeting. This work was supported by NSF grant PHY-9870115.

References

[1] Sievers, J. L. *et al.* (2002), 'Cosmological parameters from cosmic background imager observations and comparisons with BOOMERANG, DASI, and MAXIMA', [astro-ph/0205387].

[2] Gibbons, G. W. (1985), 'Aspects of supergravity theories', in *Supersymmetry, Supergravity and Related Topics*, eds F. del Aguila, J. A. de Azcárraga and L. E. Ibañez (World Scientific) pp. 346–351; Maldacena, J. and Nuñez, C. (2001), 'Supergravity description of field theories on curved manifolds and a no-go theorem', *Int. J. Mod. Phys.* **A16**, 822.

[3] Gates, S. J. and Zwiebach, B. (1983), 'Gauged N=4 supergravity theory with a new scalar potential', *Phys. Lett.* **B123**, 200.

[4] Hull, C. M. and Warner, N. P. (1988), 'Noncompact gaugings from higher dimensions', *Class. Quant. Grav.* **5**, 1517.

[5] Kallosh, R., Linde, A. D., Prokushkin, S. and Shmakova, M. (2002), 'Gauged supergravities, de Sitter space and cosmology', *Phys. Rev.* **D65**, 105016, [hep-th/0110089].

[6] de Wit, B. and Van Proeyen, A. (1984), 'Potentials and symmetries of general gauged N=2 supergravity – Yang–Mills Models', *Nucl. Phys.* **B245**, 89.

[7] Fré, P., Trigiante, M. and Van Proeyen, A. (2002), 'Stable de Sitter vacua from N=2 supergravity,' [hep-th/0205119].

[8] Carroll, S. M. (1998), 'Quintessence and the rest of the world', *Phys. Rev. Lett.* **81**, 3067, [astro-ph/9806099].

[9] Herdeiro, C., Hirano, S. and Kallosh, R. (2001), 'String theory and hybrid inflation/acceleration', *JHEP* **0112** 027, [hep-th/0110271].

[10] Dasgupta, K., Herdeiro,C., Hirano S. and Kallosh, R. (2002), 'D3/D7 inflationary model and M theory', [hep-th/0203019].

[11] Linde, A. D. (1991), 'Axions in inflationary cosmology', *Phys. Lett.* **B259**, 38; Linde, A. D. (1994), 'Hybrid inflation', *Phys. Rev.* **D49**, 748, [astro-ph/9307002].

[12] Copeland, E. J., Liddle, A. R., Lyth, D. H., Stewart, E. D. and Wands, D., (1994), 'False vacuum inflation with Einstein gravity', *Phys. Rev.* **D49**, 6410, [astro-ph/9401011]; Dvali, G. R., Shafi Q. and Schaefer, R. (1994), 'Large scale structure and supersymmetric inflation without fine tuning', *Phys. Rev. Lett.* **73**, 1886, [hep-ph/9406319]; Linde, A. D. and Riotto, A. (1997), 'Hybrid inflation in supergravity', *Phys. Rev.* **D56**, 1841, [hep-ph/9703209].

[13] Binetruy, P. and Dvali, G. (1996), 'D-term inflation', *Phys. Lett.* **B388**, 241, [hep-ph/9606342]; Stewart, E. D. (1995), 'Inflation, supergravity and superstrings', *Phys. Rev.* **D51**, 6847, [hep-ph/9405389]; Halyo, E. (1996), 'Hybrid inflation from supergravity D-terms', *Phys. Lett.* **B387**, 43, [hep-ph/9606423].

[14] Watari, T. and Yanagida, T. (2001), 'N=2 supersymmetry in a hybrid inflation model', *Phys. Lett.* **B499**, 297, [hep-ph/0011389].

[15] Kallosh, R. (2001), 'N=2 supersymmetry and de Sitter space', [hep-th/0109168].

[16] Sen, A. (1998), 'Stable non-BPS states in string theory', *JHEP* **9806**, 007, [hep-th/9803194]; Sen, A. and Zwiebach, B. (2000), 'Stable non-BPS states in F-theory', *JHEP* **0003**, 036, [hep-th/9907164].

[17] Gibbons, G. W. and Hull, C. M. (2001), 'de Sitter space from warped supergravity solutions', [hep-th/0111072]; Gates, S. J. (2002), 'Is stringy-supersymmetry quintessentially challenged?', [hep-th/0202112].

[18] Andrianopoli, L., D'Auria, R., Ferrara, S. and Lledo, M. A. (2002), 'Gauging of flat groups in four dimensional supergravity,' [hep-th/0203206]; Hull, C. M. (2002), 'New gauged N=8, D=4 supergravities', [hep-th/0204156].

[19] Dixmier, J. (1961), 'Représentations intégrables du groupe de de Sitter', *Bull. soc. math. France* **89**.

[20] Gazeau, J. P., Renaud, J. and Takook, M. V. (2000), 'Gupta–Bleuler quantization for minimally coupled scalar fields in de Sitter space', *Class. Quant. Grav.* **17**, 1415, [gr-qc/9904023].

[21] Birrell, N. D. and Davies, P. C. (1982), Quantum fields in curved space, (Cambridge University Press, Cambridge), 340p.

[22] Dvali, G. R. and Tye, S. H. (1999), 'Brane inflation', *Phys. Lett.* **B450**, 72, [hep-ph/9812483]; Halyo, E. 'Inflation from rotation', [hep-ph/0105341].

[23] Alexander, S. H. (2001), 'Inflation from D – anti-D brane annihilation', [hep-th/0105032]; Burgess, C. P., Majumdar, M., Nolte, D., Quevedo, F., Rajesh G. and Zhang, R. J. (2001), 'The inflationary brane–antibrane universe', *JHEP* **0107**, 047, [hep-th/0105204]; Dvali, G. R., Shafi, Q. and Solganik, S. (2001), 'D-brane inflation', [hep-th/0105203]; Mazumdar, A., Panda, S. and Perez-Lorenzana A. (2001), 'Assisted inflation via tachyon condensation', *Nucl. Phys.* **B614**, 101, [hep-ph/0107058].

[24] Kyae, B. S. and Shafi, Q. (2001), 'Branes and inflationary cosmology', [hep-ph/0111101].

[25] Garcia-Bellido, J., Rabadan, R. and Zamora, F. (2001), 'Inflationary scenarios from branes at angles', [hep-th/0112147]; Jones, N., Stoica, H. and Tye, S. H. (2002), 'Brane interaction as the origin of inflation', [hep-th/0203163].

[26] Burgess, C. P., Martineau, P., Quevedo, F., Rajesh G. and Zhang, R. J. (2001), 'Brane–antibrane inflation in orbifold and orientifold models', [hep-th/0111025]; Blumenhagen, R., Kors, B., Lust, D. and Ott, T. (2002), 'Hybrid inflation in intersecting brane worlds', [hep-th/0202124].

[27] Bergshoeff, E., Kallosh, R., Ortin, T. and Papadopoulos, G. (1997), 'κ-symmetry, supersymmetry and intersecting branes', *Nucl. Phys.* **B502**, 149, [hep-th/9705040].

[28] Nekrasov, N. and Schwarz, A. (1998), 'Instantons on noncommutative R**4 and (2,0) superconformal six dimensional theory', *Commun. Math. Phys.* **198**, 689, [hep-th/9802068].

[29] Seiberg N. and Witten, E. (1999), 'String theory and noncommutative geometry', *JHEP* **9909**, 032, [hep-th/9908142].

[30] Vafa, C. (1996), 'Evidence for F-theory', *Nucl. Phys.* **B469** 403, [hep-th/9602022]; Sen, A. (1996), 'F-theory and orientifolds', *Nucl. Phys.* **B475**, 562, [hep-th/9605150]; Banks, T., Douglas, M. R. and Seiberg, N. (1996), 'Probing F-theory with branes', *Phys. Lett.* **B387**, 278, [hep-th/9605199].

[31] Becker, K. and Becker, M. (2001), 'Supersymmetry breaking, M-theory and fluxes', *JHEP* **0107**, 038, [hep-th/0107044].

[32] Dasgupta, K., Rajesh, G. and Sethi, S. (1999), 'M theory, orientifolds and G-flux', *JHEP* **9908**, 023, [hep-th/9908088].

Part 8
Quantum cosmology

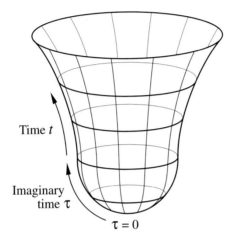

Time t

Imaginary
time τ

$\tau = 0$

*There ought to be something very special about the boundary
conditions of the universe and what can be more special than
the condition that there is no boundary.*

Vatican papers, 1982

34

The state of the universe

James Hartle

University of California, Santa Barbara

34.1 Introduction

The universe has a quantum state. What is it? That is the central question of quantum cosmology – the subject to which Stephen Hawking has contributed so many seminal ideas.

To ask this question is to assume that the universe is a quantum mechanical system. We perhaps have little direct evidence of peculiarly quantum mechanical phenomena on large and even familiar scales, but there is no evidence that the phenomena that we do see cannot be described in quantum mechanical terms and explained by quantum mechanical laws. Further, every major candidate for a fundamental dynamical law from the standard model to M theory conforms to the quantum mechanical framework for prediction. If this framework applies to the whole thing, there must be a quantum state of the universe.

It would be even more interesting if quantum mechanics broke down on cosmological scales. But there is not a shred of evidence for that, and my guess is that, even if it does, we will only find out by pursuing the assumption that quantum mechanics is the framework for a final theory of cosmology.

My talk will not review any of the current ideas for a quantum state of the universe – even Stephen's no-boundary wave function [1]. The articles of Don Page and Alex Vilenkin in this volume do that. Rather, in the limited time available, I want to concentrate on explaining why a theory of the quantum state of the universe must be part of any final theory. I am also not going to discuss the generalizations of usual quantum theory that are required for quantum cosmology [2]. For the essential points of this talk you can just imagine that the universe is a vast number of particles in a very large expanding box.

34.2 Final theories

The final theory (to use Steve Weinberg's term) predicts the regularities that are exhibited by all physical systems – without exception, without qualification, and without approximation. Much of this conference has been concerned with the search for the final theory. A possible view at present is that it consists of two parts:

- a universal dynamical law such as string theory or its successors;

- a law for the quantum state of the universe such as Hawking's no-boundary wave function of the universe.

In a model universe in a box these two parts are represented by the Hamiltonian specifying the form of the Schrödinger equation

$$i\hbar \frac{d|\Psi(t)\rangle}{dt} = H |\Psi(t)\rangle \tag{34.1}$$

and the initial quantum state

$$|\Psi(0)\rangle. \tag{34.2}$$

Both of these pieces are necessary for prediction. The Schrödinger equation makes no predictions by itself. The probabilities p_α predicted by quantum mechanics for a set of alternatives represented by projection operators $\{P_\alpha\}$ are

$$p_\alpha = \|P_\alpha|\Psi(t)\rangle\|^2. \tag{34.3}$$

To compute these the quantum state is needed at least at one time. No state, no predictions.

To put this in a different way, if the state is arbitrary, the predictions are arbitrary. Pick any probabilities p_α you like for the alternatives P_α. There is some state that will reproduce them. For example, you can take

$$|\Psi(t)\rangle = \sum_\alpha p_\alpha^{\frac{1}{2}}|\Psi_\alpha\rangle \tag{34.4}$$

where the $|\Psi_\alpha\rangle$ are any set of eigenstates of the P_αs

$$P_\alpha|\Psi_\beta\rangle = \delta_{\alpha\beta}|\Psi_\beta\rangle. \tag{34.5}$$

The $|\Psi(t)\rangle$ constructed according to (34.4) will reproduce the pre-assigned probabilities p_α.

Neither is ignorance bliss. If you assume you know nothing about the state of the universe in a box then you should make predictions with a density matrix proportional to unity

$$\rho = \frac{I}{Tr(I)} \tag{34.6}$$

reflecting that ignorance. But this density matrix corresponds to equilibrium at infinite temperature and its predictions are nothing like the universe we live in. In particular, there would be no evolution since $[H, \rho] = 0$. There would be no second law of thermodynamics since the entropy $-Tr[\rho \log \rho]$ is already at its maximum possible value. There would be no classical behaviour since, although the expected value of a field averaged over a spacetime volume R might be finite, its fluctuations, $\langle \phi(R)^2 \rangle$, would be infinite.

The search for a unified fundamental dynamical law has been seriously under way at least since the time of Newton with string theory or its generalizations being the most actively investigated direction today. By contrast, the search for a theory of the quantum state of the universe has only been actively under way since the time of Hawking, let us say on this occasion. Why this difference?

Dynamical laws govern regularities in time and it is an empirical fact that the basic dynamical laws are local in space on scales above the Planck length. The laws that govern regularities in time across the whole universe are therefore discoverable and testable in laboratories on Earth. By contrast many of the regularities predicted with near certainty by the quantum state of the universe are mostly in space on large cosmological scales. Only recently has there been enough data to confront theory with observation. That difference in the nature of the predicted regularities, or their difference in scales, should not obscure the fact that the state is just as much a part of the final theory as is its Hamiltonian.

Given these differences, what grounds do we have to hope that we can discover the quantum state of the universe? There are two: the first is the simplicity of the early universe revealed by observation – more homogeneous, more isotropic, more nearly in thermal equilibrium than the universe is today. It is therefore possible that the universe has a simple, discoverable initial quantum state and that all of the complex universe of galaxies, stars, planets and life today arose from quantum accidents that have happened since and the action of gravitational attraction. The second reason is the idea that the quantum state and the dynamical theory may be naturally connected as in Hawking's no-boundary theory.

34.3 Effective theories

We are used to the idea of effective dynamical theories that accurately describe limited ranges of phenomena. The Navier–Stokes equations, non-relativistic quantum mechanics, general relativity, quantum electrodynamics, and the standard model of particle physics are all familiar examples. To construct an effective theory we typically assume a coarse-grained description (restricting attention to energies below the Planck scale for instance) and assume some simple property that the state might predict there (classical spacetime, for example).

Cosmology too has its effective theory and its standard model. This is summarized neatly by the following list of Martin Rees [3]. I reproduce it here with unauthorized additions:

- spacetime is classical, governed by the Einstein equation,

- our universe is expanding,

- from a hot big bang,

- in which light elements were synthesized,

- there was a period of inflation,

- which led to a flat universe today,

- structure was seeded by Gaussian irregularities,

- which are relics of quantum fluctuations,

- the dominant matter is cold and dark,

- but a cosmological constant (or quintessence) is dynamically dominant.

Possibly all current observations in cosmology, at least the large scale ones, can be compressed into an effective 'standard model' based on this list of ten assumptions and a few cosmological parameters. That is not unlike the situation in particle physics where most observations can be compressed into the Lagrangian of the standard model and its eighteen or so parameters.

However, the success of such effective theories which operate in limited ranges of phenomena should not obscure the need to find fundamental ones which apply to all phenomena without qualification and without approximation. It would be inconsistent, I believe, to pursue a fundamental dynamical theory in the face of a successful effective, standard dynamical model, and not pursue a fundamental theory of the state of the universe because of the success of *its* effective, standard cosmological model. That not least because the fundamental theory could provide a unified explanation of its assumptions.

It must be said, however, that when the natural domains of fundamental theories are as far from controllable experiments as string theory and the quantum initial condition the possibility of definitive tests seems to recede. It could be that the predictions of string theory are limited to general relativity, gauge theories, supersymmetry, and the parameters of the standard particle model. In a similar way the predictions of the state of the universe could be limited to classical spacetime, the initial conditions for inflation, and the quantum fluctuations that satisfy large scale structure. Perhaps that is prediction enough.

34.4 Directions

The instructions of the organizers were to discuss 'future directions in theoretical physics and cosmology'. Continuing the search for a final theory incorporating dynamics and the initial quantum state is certainly one direction. But I would like to mention three questions that might lead to different approaches to the main one.

34.4.1 What's environmental?

Which features of the observed universe follow entirely from the dynamical theory (H) and which follow entirely from the initial condition $(|\Psi(0)\rangle)$, and which are the result of quantum accidents that occurred over the course of the universe's history with probabilities specified by the combination of H and $|\Psi(0)\rangle$. Those that depend significantly on $|\Psi(0)\rangle$ are called 'environmental'. Some version of this question was number one on the list of top ten questions for the next millennium prepared by string theorists at the Strings 2000 conference [4].

Take the coupling constants in effective dynamical theories for instance. The viscosities and equation-of-state in the Navier–Stokes equation are certainly environmental. They vary with system, place, and time. But at a given energy do the coupling constants of the standard model of the elementary particle interactions vary with place and time or with the possible history of the universe? If so then the initial quantum state is central to determining their probabilities.

34.4.2 Why quantum mechanics?

The founders of quantum mechanics thought that the inherent indeterminacy of quantum theory 'reflected the unavoidable interference in measurement dictated by the magnitude of the quantum of the action' (Bohr). But why then do we live in a quantum mechanical universe which, by definition, is never measured from the outside?

The most striking general feature of quantum mechanics is its exact linearity – the principle of superposition. But why should there be a principle of superposition in quantum cosmology which has only a single quantum state?

34.4.3 Why a division into dynamics and initial condition?

The schema for a final theory which I have been describing posits a separate theory of dynamics and quantum state. Could they be connected? They already are in Hawking's no-boundary wave function [1]

$$\Psi = \int \delta g \, \delta \phi \, e^{-I[g,\phi]} \tag{34.7}$$

where the action for metric $g_{\alpha\beta}(x)$ coupled to matter $\phi(x)$ determines both the state and quantum dynamics. Is there a principle that determines both? Is there a connection between superstring theory and its successors and a unique quantum state?

A unified quantum theory of state and dynamics would be truly a final theory. Pursuing that vision is surely a direction for theoretical physics and cosmology.

Acknowledgements

This paper was supported in part by NSF Grant PHY00-70895.

References

[1] Hawking, S. W. (1984), *Nucl. Phys. B*, **239**, 257.

[2] Isham, C. J. (1994), *J. Math. Phys.*, **35**, 2157; Isham, C. J. and Linden, N. (1995), *J. Math. Phys.*, **35**, 5452 (1994); *ibid.*

[3] Rees, M. J. (1997), 'The state of modern cosmology', in *Critical Dialogues in Cosmology*, ed. N. G. Turok, (World Scientific, Singapore).

[4] Duff, M. J., Liu, J. T. and Lu, J., eds (2001), *Strings: Proceedings of the 2000 International Superstrings Conference* (World Scientific, Singapore).

35

Quantum cosmology

Don Page
University of Alberta

35.1 Motivation for a quantum state of the cosmos

A complete model of the universe needs at least three parts:

1. A complete set of physical variables (e.g., the arguments of the wavefunction) and dynamical laws (e.g., the Schrödinger equation for the wavefunction, the algebra of operators in the Hilbert space, or the action for a path integral). Roughly speaking, these dynamical laws tell how things change with time. Typically they have the form of differential equations.

2. The correct solution of the dynamical laws (e.g., the wavefunction of the universe). This picks out the actual quantum state of the cosmos from the set of states that would obey the dynamical laws. Typically a specification of the actual state would involve initial and/or other boundary conditions for the dynamical laws.

3. The connection with conscious experience (e.g., the laws of psychophysical experience). These might be of the form that tells what conscious experience occurs for a possible quantum state for the universe, and to what degree each such experience occurs (i.e., the measure for each set of conscious experiences [1, 2]).

Item 1 alone is called by physicists a TOE or 'theory of everything,' but it is not complete by itself. In this chapter I shall focus on Item 2, but even Items 1 and 2 alone are not complete, since by themselves they do not logically determine what, if any, conscious experiences occur in a universe. For example, suppose we have a unique quantum state for a TOE that consists of some completion of string/M theory. If this completion is anything like our present partial knowledge of string/M theory or of

621

other dynamical laws in physics, it will not by itself answer the question of why most alert humans are usually consciously aware of their visual sensations but not of their heartbeats.

(Of course, one might postulate some principle whereby one would most of the time be consciously aware of visual sensations but not of one's heartbeat, but I do not see how such a principle would be directly derivable from the quantum state and a full set of dynamical laws that are at all similar to our presently known incomplete approximations to these laws. One might propose that awareness of visual sensations would be more useful in the survival of the fittest than awareness of one's heartbeat, but it is not obvious to me how conscious awareness contributes to survival, even though it may be correlated with some physical information processing that is useful for survival. When Fermilab Director Robert Wilson was asked by a Congressional committee what Fermilab contributes to the defence of the nation, he is reported to have responded, 'Nothing. But it helps make the nation worth defending'. Similarly, consciousness may contribute nothing to the survival of an organism, but it may make the organism worth surviving and may be the selection mechanism that makes us aware of being conscious organisms.)

But even before we attack the difficult question of the relationship between conscious experience and the rest of physics, it is clear that much of what we try to describe in physics depends not only on the dynamical laws but also on some features of the quantum state of the cosmos [3]. For example, the observation that the universe has far less entropy than one might imagine, so that the entropy tends to increase (the second law of thermodynamics), cannot be purely a consequence of the familiar types of dynamical laws but must also depend on the quantum state of the cosmos.

35.2 The Hartle–Hawking proposal for the quantum state

Here I shall focus on Item 2, the quantum state of the cosmos, and in particular focus on a proposal by Hawking [4, 5] and by Hartle and Hawking [6] for this quantum state. They have proposed that the quantum state of the universe, described in canonical quantum gravity by what we now call the Hartle–Hawking wavefunction, is given by a path integral over compact four-dimensional Euclidean geometries and matter fields that each have no boundary other than the three-dimensional geometry and matter field configuration that is the argument of the wavefunction.

(Thus this proposal is sometimes called the 'no-boundary' proposal. However, just as in this volume my main Ph.D. advisor Kip Thorne has rebelled against his advisor John Wheeler in relabelling Wheeler's 'no-hair' conjecture as the 'two-hair' conjecture, to count the mass and angular momentum of a Kerr black hole, so I am emboldened to rebel half as much against my other Ph.D. advisor, Stephen Hawking, by relabelling his 'no-boundary' proposal as the 'one-boundary' proposal, to count the one boundary of the path integral that is the argument of the wavefunction.)

In particular, the wavefunction for a three-geometry given by a three-metric $g_{ij}(x^k)$, and for a matter field configuration schematically denoted by $\phi^A(x^k)$, where the three-metric and the matter field configuration are functions of the three spatial coordinates x^k (with lower-case Latin letters ranging over the three values $\{1, 2, 3\}$), is given by the wavefunction

$$\psi[g_{ij}(x^k), \phi^A(x^k)] = \int \mathcal{D}[g_{\mu\nu}(x^\alpha)]\mathcal{D}[\phi^\Omega(x^\alpha)]e^{-I[g_{\mu\nu}, \phi^\Omega]}, \qquad (35.1)$$

where the path integral is over all compact Euclidean four-dimensional geometries that have the three-dimensional configuration $[g_{ij}(x^k), \phi^A(x^k)]$ on their one and only boundary. Here a four-geometry are given by a four-metric $g_{\mu\nu}(x^\alpha)$, and four-dimensional matter field histories are schematically denoted by $\phi^\Omega(x^\alpha)$, both functions of the four Euclidean spacetime coordinates x^α (with lower-case Greek letters ranging over the four values $\{0, 1, 2, 3\}$).

The Hartle–Hawking 'one-boundary' proposal is incomplete in various ways. For example, in quantum general relativity, using the Einstein–Hilbert-matter action, the path integral is ultraviolet divergent and non-renormalizable [7]. This non-renormalizability also occurs for quantum supergravity [8]. String/M theory gives the hope of being a finite theory of quantum gravity (at least for each term of a perturbation series, though the series itself is apparently only an asymptotic series that is not convergent). However, in string/M theory it is not clear what the class of paths should be in the path integral that would be analogous to the path integral over compact four-dimensional Euclidean geometries without extra boundaries that the Hartle–Hawking proposal gives when general relativity is quantized.

Another way in which the Hartle–Hawking 'one-boundary' proposal is incomplete is that conformal modes make the Einstein–Hilbert action unbounded below, so the path integral seems infinite even without the ultraviolet divergence [9]. If the analogue of histories in string/M theory that can be well approximated by low-curvature geometries have actions that are similar to their general-relativistic approximations, then the string/M theory action would also be unbounded below and apparently exhibit the same infrared divergences as the Einstein–Hilbert action for general relativity. There might be a uniquely preferred way to get a finite answer by a suitable restriction of the path integral, but it is not yet clear what that might be.

A third technical problem with the Hartle–Hawking path integral is that one is supposed to sum over all four-dimensional geometries, but the sum over topologies is not computable, since there is no algorithm for deciding whether two four-dimensional manifolds have the same topology. This might conceivably be a problem that it more amenable in string/M theory, since it seems to allow generalizations of manifolds, such as orbifolds, and the generalizations may be easier to sum over than the topologies of manifolds.

A fourth problem that is likely to plague any proposal for the quantum state of the cosmos is that even if the path integral could be uniquely defined in a computable way, it would in practice be very difficult to compute. Thus one might be able to deduce only certain approximate features of the universe from such a path integral.

Despite the difficulties of precisely defining and evaluating the Hartle–Hawking 'one-boundary' proposal for the quantum state of the universe, it has had a certain amount of partial successes in calculating certain approximate predictions for highly simplified toy models:

1. Lorentzian-signature spacetime can emerge in a WKB limit of an analytic continuation [5, 6].

2. The universe can inflate to large size [5].

3. Models can predict near-critical energy density [5, 10].

4. Models can predict low anisotropies [11].

5. Inhomogeneities start in ground states and so can fit cosmic microwave background data [12].

6. Entropy starts low and grows with time [13–15].

35.3 Zero-loop quantum cosmology and FRW-scalar models

One can avoid many of the problems of the Hartle–Hawking path-integral, and achieve some partial successes for the 'one-boundary' proposal, by taking

$$\psi[g_{ij}(x^k), \phi^A(x^k)] \approx \psi_{0-\text{loop}} = \sum_{\text{some extrema}} e^{-I[g_{\mu\nu}, \phi^\Omega]}, \qquad (35.2)$$

summing over a small set of extrema of the Euclidean action I, generally complex classical solutions of the field equations.

Even at this highly simplified approximation to the path integral, there is the question of which extrema to sum over, since typically there are infinitely many.

A simple class of models that has often been considered is the $k = +1$ Friedmann–Robertson–Walker-scalar model, in which the three-geometry boundary is an S^3 with radius $\sqrt{2G/3\pi}\, a_b$ and the (real) scalar field takes the homogeneous value $\sqrt{3/4\pi G}\, \phi_b$ on the boundary, where Newton's constant is G and I have set $\hbar$ and c equal to unity. (The numerical factors used to define the physical radius and scalar field value in terms of rescaled values a_b and ϕ_b enable one to dispense with similar factors in the expressions involving a_b and ϕ_b.)

Then the zero-loop approximation gives

$$\psi(a_b, \phi_b) \approx \psi_{0-\text{loop}}(a_b, \phi_b) = \sum_{\text{some extrema}} e^{-I(a_b, \phi_b)}, \qquad (35.3)$$

where $I(a_b, \phi_b)$ is the Euclidean action of a classical solution that is compact and has the S^3 geometry and homogeneous scalar field as its one and only boundary.

'One-boundary' FRW-scalar histories have a time parameter t that can be taken to run from 0 (at a regular 'centre') to 1 (at the boundary), and then to have $\phi = \phi(t)$ and four-metric

$$ds^2 = \left(\frac{2G}{3\pi}\right)\left[N^2(t)dt^2 + a^2(t)d\Omega_3^2\right], \qquad (35.4)$$

where $N(t)$ is the Euclidean lapse function and $d\Omega_3^2$ is the metric on a unit round S^3. The boundary conditions of regularity at the centre are $a(0) = 0$, $\dot{a}(0)/N(0) = 1$, and $\dot{\phi}(0)/N(0) = 0$, and the match to the boundary at $t = 1$ gives $a(1) = a_b$ and $\phi(1) = \phi_b$.

If the scalar field potential is $[9/(16G^2)]V(\phi)$ (with the coefficient again chosen to simplify the formulae below in terms of the rescaled potential $V(\phi)$), then the Euclidean action of the history is

$$I = -iS = \int dt \left[\frac{1}{2N}(-a\dot{a}^2 + a^3\dot{\phi}^2) + \frac{1}{2}N(-a + a^3 V)\right]$$

$$= -\frac{1}{2}\int dt \left[\tilde{N}^{-1}\tilde{G}_{AB}\dot{X}^A\dot{X}^B + \tilde{N}\right] = -\int d\tilde{s}, \qquad (35.5)$$

where

$$\tilde{N} = a\left(1 - a^2 V\right)N \equiv e^\alpha\left(1 - w\right)N, \qquad (35.6)$$

with

$$\alpha \equiv \ln a, \tag{35.7}$$

$$w \equiv a^2 V, \tag{35.8}$$

and $d\tilde{s}$ is the infinitesimal proper distance in the auxiliary two-metric

$$\begin{aligned}
d\tilde{s}^2 &= \tilde{G}_{AB} dX^A dX^B \\
&= a^4 \left(1 - a^2 V\right) \left(\frac{da^2}{a^2} - d\phi^2\right) = e^{4\alpha} \left(1 - w\right) \left(d\alpha^2 - d\phi^2\right) \\
&= e^{2u+2v} \left(1 - w\right) du\, dv = \frac{1}{4} \left(1 - w\right) dX\, dY.
\end{aligned} \tag{35.9}$$

The auxiliary metric (35.9) has null coordinates

$$u \equiv \alpha - \phi \equiv \ln a - \phi, \quad v \equiv \alpha + \phi \equiv \ln a + \phi, \tag{35.10}$$

or alternate null coordinates

$$X \equiv e^{2u} \equiv e^{2\alpha - 2\phi}, \quad Y \equiv e^{2v} \equiv e^{2\alpha + 2\phi}. \tag{35.11}$$

The zero-loop or classical histories are those that extremize the Euclidean action (35.5). Define the rescaled proper Euclidean time (or, for short, 'Euclidean time')

$$\tau = \int_0^t N(t')dt' = \sqrt{\frac{3\pi}{2G}} \text{(proper radius or Euclidean 'time')}, \tag{35.12}$$

which is gauge invariant, invariant under reparameterizations of the original time coordinate t when the lapse function $N(t)$ is properly adjusted, though its value at the boundary depends upon the particular history chosen. Then extremizing the action with respect to $N(t)$ leads to the constraint equation

$$\left(\frac{da}{d\tau}\right)^2 - a^2 \left(\frac{d\phi}{d\tau}\right)^2 = 1 - a^2 V \equiv 1 - w. \tag{35.13}$$

Extremizing with respect to $\phi(t)$ leads to the scalar field equation

$$\frac{d^2\phi}{d\tau^2} + \frac{3}{a}\frac{da}{d\tau}\frac{d\phi}{d\tau} = \frac{1}{2}\frac{dV}{d\phi}, \tag{35.14}$$

and extremizing with respect to $a(t)$ leads to the other field equation,

$$\frac{1}{a}\frac{d^2a}{d\tau^2} + 2\left(\frac{d\phi}{d\tau}\right)^2 = -V, \tag{35.15}$$

though either of these last two equations is redundant if one uses the other along with the constraint equation.

Alternatively, zero-loop or classical histories (extrema of the action) are geodesics of the auxiliary two-metric (35.9), with this metric giving the proper distance along an extremum as

$$d\tilde{s} = -dI = \tilde{N}dt = a\left(1 - a^2 V\right)d\tau. \qquad (35.16)$$

The Euclidean action I is then simply the negative of the proper distance from the centre to the boundary along a geodesic of the auxiliary metric. If the centre has $\tau = 0$ and the boundary (where the wavefunction is being evaluated) has

$$\tau = \tau_b = \int_0^1 N(t)dt, \qquad (35.17)$$

then the Euclidean action for the classical history is

$$I = -\int_0^1 \tilde{N}dt = -\int_0^{\tau_b} a\left(1 - a^2 V\right)d\tau. \qquad (35.18)$$

35.4 Real classical solutions for the FRW-scalar model

Therefore, a classical or extremal history $(a(\tau), \phi(\tau))$ for the FRW-scalar model obeys the regularity conditions $a = 0$, $da/d\tau = 1$, and $d\phi/d\tau = 0$ at the centre, $\tau = 0$, and so is uniquely determined, for a given rescaled potential function $V(\phi)$, by the value of ϕ at the centre, $\phi_0 \equiv \phi(0)$, and by the value of τ at the boundary, τ_b, where the wavefunction is being evaluated. (One could alternatively have $da/d\tau = -1$ at the centre, but this would give a negative value for the volume of the Euclidean geometry, and the opposite sign of the Euclidean action, so I shall reject this possibility.)

Let us for simplicity restrict attention to analytic potentials that for all real finite ϕ are real finite convex functions that are bounded below by non-negative values (which can be considered to be non-negative cosmological constants). Since the action and extrema are invariant under replacing ϕ by $\phi' = -\phi$ if $V(\phi)$ is replaced by $V'(\phi') = V(\phi)$, without loss of generality we can consider the case in which the convex $V(\phi)$ is non-decreasing as ϕ is increased from ϕ_0, so $dV/d\phi \geq 0$ for $\phi \geq \phi_0$. (We shall not need any further the condition that $V(\phi)$ be convex and non-negative for real ϕ, but only that $V(\phi)$ be real, finite, positive, differentiable and monotonically increasing for $\phi > \phi_0$.)

Then the scalar field equation (35.14), rewritten as

$$\frac{d}{d\tau}\left(a^3 \frac{d\phi}{d\tau}\right) = \frac{1}{2}a^3 \frac{dV}{d\phi}, \qquad (35.19)$$

implies that ϕ cannot decrease with τ. Furthermore, it can stay constant only if ϕ_0 is at the minimum value of $V(\phi)$, say V_0, in which case ϕ does stay at ϕ_0, and one gets $a = V_0^{-1/2} \sin(V_0^{1/2}\tau)$, giving a 4-metric (35.4) that is part or all of a round 4-sphere of radius $(1.5\pi V_0/G)^{-1/2}$, depending on whether τ_b is less than or equal to its maximum value of $\pi V_0^{-1/2}$, where a returns to zero.

But if $dV/d\phi$ is positive at $\phi = \phi_0$ (and hence, by assumption, remains positive for all larger ϕ), then (35.16) has its right-hand side become positive as soon as $a(\tau)$ becomes positive, and so $a^3 d\phi/d\tau$ increases monotonically with real increasing τ. It thus follows that ϕ and V also increase monotonically with τ.

The field equation (35.15) with real a, ϕ and τ and with positive V implies that a is a concave function of τ. With V not only positive but also increasing with τ, $a(\tau)$ necessarily reaches a finite maximum, say $a_m = a_m(\phi_0)$ at the Euclidean time $\tau_m = \tau_m(\phi_0)$, with the functions $a_m(\phi_0)$ and $\tau_m(\phi_0)$ depending on the function $V(\phi)$, and then a returns to 0 at finite τ, say $\tau_s = \tau_s(\phi_0)$, with the function $\tau_s(\phi_0)$ also depending on the function $V(\phi)$.

Since $a^3 d\phi/d\tau$ increases monotonically with τ under the assumptions above, $d\phi/d\tau$ becomes infinite at $\tau = \tau_s$ as a returns to zero, giving a curvature singularity there, and one can further show that ϕ goes to infinity there as well.

Given a particular fixed rescaled potential $V(\phi)$ obeying the assumptions above for all real ϕ (real, finite, differentiable, and either monotonically increasing with ϕ for all ϕ or else monotonically increasing in both directions away from a single minimum), we thus see that a choice of the two real parameters ϕ_0 and τ_b leads to a unique classical solution, if $\tau_b < \tau_s(\phi_0)$, and uniquely gives the boundary values $a_b = a(\phi_0, \tau_b)$ and $\phi_b = \phi(\phi_0, \tau_b)$, as well as the action $I = I(\phi_0, \tau_b)$.

Of course, we are really interested in evaluating $\psi(a_b, \phi_b)$ by the zero-loop approximation and hence want the action, for each of a suitable set of extrema, as a function of a_b and ϕ_b instead of as a function of ϕ_0 and τ_b. To do this, we need to solve for values of the parameters (ϕ_0, τ_b) that give the desired boundary values (a_b, ϕ_b). Because the number of parameters matches the number of boundary values, we expect a discrete set of solutions, but the number of solutions may not be precisely one for each (a_b, ϕ_b).

For example, consider the case in which $V(\phi)$ is a slowly varying function of ϕ. In this case the scalar field (35.14) implies that ϕ does not change much during the evolution, so as a zeroth-order approximation one can take $\phi \approx \phi_0$ and hence also $\phi_b \approx \phi_0$. Then if one restricts to real values of τ_b, one sees that there are two solutions for (ϕ_0, τ_b) given (a_b, ϕ_b) if $a_b < a_m(\phi_0) \approx a_m(\phi_b)$, because the real classical Euclidean solution that starts at the centre, $a = 0$, with real ϕ_0 there, has a increasing from 0 to its maximum $a_m(\phi_0)$ at $\tau = \tau_m(\phi_0)$ and then decreasing to 0 again at $\tau = \tau_s(\phi_0)$, so there are two solutions for τ_b, one with $\tau_b < \tau_m$ in which a crosses a_b while increasing with τ, and the second with $\tau_b > \tau_m$ in which a crosses a_b while decreasing with τ.

On the other hand, if $a_b > a_m(\phi_0) \approx a_m(\phi_b)$, there are no real solutions for (ϕ_0, τ_b), because all of the real solutions that match ϕ_b have maxima for a that are smaller than a_b.

One proposal would be simply to say that the zero-loop approximation gives a wavefunction that is the sum of the e^{-I}s when there are one or more real classical solutions matching the real boundary data that are the arguments of the wavefunction, and that the zero-loop approximation gives zero when there are no real classical solutions. However, then one would simply get zero for most large universes with non-trivial matter, such as $\psi_{0-\text{loop}}(a_b, \phi_b) = 0$ when ϕ_b is not at the minimum of the potential that is zero there (or is at the minimum if the potential is positive there) and when a_b is sufficiently large (e.g., larger than $V_0^{-1/2}$ if the rescaled potential has a positive minimum of V_0).

Furthermore, even for potentials allowing large classical Euclidean universes, the action for each of them would be real, and so the zero-loop approximate wavefunction would be purely real and not have the oscillatory behaviour apparently necessary to describe our observations of an approximately Lorentzian universe.

Therefore, it is not adequate to restrict the zero-loop approximation to real classical Euclidean histories.

35.5 Complex classical solutions for the FRW-scalar model

To get a potentially adequate zero-loop approximation, we shall consider complex classical solutions (though still with real boundary values that are the arguments of the wavefunction). That is, we shall take the classical field equations (35.13)–(35.15) as complex analytic equations for complex quantities a, ϕ, τ and $V(\phi)$. We shall assume that $V(\phi)$ is a complex analytic function that for real values of ϕ has the properties assumed above (real, finite, differentiable, and either monotonically increasing with ϕ for all ϕ or else monotonically increasing in both directions away from a single minimum). The monotonicity property of $V(\phi)$ for real ϕ is not really important but shall continue to be assumed here to simplify some of the discussion.

For a complex classical or extremal history $(a(\tau), \phi(\tau))$ for the FRW-scalar model, we shall continue to assume the regularity conditions $a = 0$, $da/d\tau = 1$, and $d\phi/d\tau = 0$ at the centre, $\tau = 0$, as complex analytic equations that are the essential input from the 'one-boundary' proposal when it is extended to allow complex solutions in the zero-loop approximation. Again the classical history is uniquely determined, for a given rescaled potential function $V(\phi)$, by the value of ϕ at the centre, $\phi_0 \equiv \phi(0)$, and by the value of τ at the boundary, τ_b, where the wavefunction is being evaluated. The only difference is that both ϕ_0 and τ_b may be complex, though we shall only be interested in solutions that give real values for $a_b(\phi_0, \tau_b)$ and $\phi_b(\phi_0, \tau_b)$.

For example, let us return to the case in which $V(\phi)$ is slowly varying so that ϕ remains close to ϕ_0 throughout the classical history. Then $\phi_b \approx \phi_0$, so for the desired real ϕ_b, we can take ϕ_0 to be approximately real. Now let us take a_b to be much larger than $a_m(\phi_b)$, so there is no real classical solution matching (a_b, ϕ_b) on the boundary. However, we can find a complex classical solution matching the boundary data in the following way.

First, relative to the small variation of $V(\phi)$, take the zeroth-order approximation that $\phi_0 = \phi_b$. Then the history is given by a contour in the complex τ plane from its value of 0 at the centre to some complex value τ_b at the boundary. Consider the contour in which τ starts off real and increasing. The rescaled S^3 size a begins increasing as τ, but as a concave function of real τ, it eventually reaches a maximum, $a_m(\phi_0)$, at $\tau = \tau_m(\phi_0)$, and then would decrease if τ continued to increase along its real axis. Thus, to lowest non-trivial order, $a(\tau)$ varies quadratically with $\tau - \tau_m$ when this quantity is small, with a negative coefficient.

Therefore, after reaching τ_m on the real axis, make a right-angled bend in the contour for τ so that now $\tau - \tau_m$ takes on an imaginary value and a continues to increase. One can then follow a contour for τ so that a stays real and increases up to the desired boundary value a_b.

If $V(\phi)$ were positive and precisely constant, having no variation at all and thus being equivalent to a cosmological constant, the classical solution would have $\phi = \phi_0$ everywhere and so would match the boundary condition if one chose $\phi_0 = \phi_b$. In this case the part of the contour with τ increasing along the real axis from 0 to τ_m would give the geometry of a Euclidean 4-hemisphere, and then the part of the contour with $\tau - \tau_m$ changing in the imaginary direction would give a Lorentzian de Sitter universe expanding from its time-symmetric throat at $\tau = \tau_m$ (to be discussed more below).

If $V(\phi)$ is not precisely constant but has a slow variation with ϕ, and if ϕ_0 is taken to be precisely real, then along the part of the contour in which τ increases along the real axis from 0 up to τ_m, ϕ will develop a small positive derivative, $d\phi/d\tau$, and will increase slightly over its initial value of ϕ_0 to become, say, ϕ_m at $\tau = \tau_m$, still real. But when one turns the corner in the contour for τ, although a had zero time derivative there and so could remain real, ϕ has a small positive time derivative and so picks up a small imaginary contribution as $\tau - \tau_m$ increases (or decreases) in the imaginary direction, hence becoming slightly complex at τ_b where a matches the boundary value a_b.

(The fact that ϕ becomes slightly complex implies that the varying $V(\phi)$ also becomes slightly complex, making the geometry slightly complex. This would make $a(\tau)$ slightly complex, and hence never reaching the real boundary value a_b, if one kept τ on a contour with $\tau - \tau_m$ purely imaginary, though that contour would keep the time-time part of the metric, proportional to $d\tau^2$, purely real and negative or Lorentzian. However, one can instead, at least if $V(\phi)$ is slowly varying, distort the contour for τ slightly to keep $a(\tau)$ precisely real, and hence reaching a_b, but at the cost of making $d\tau^2$, and hence the time-time part of the geometry, slightly complex.)

However, just as one can compensate for a slightly complex $a(\tau)$ along the simple-minded contour by distorting the contour slightly, one can also compensate for a slightly complex value of $\phi(\tau_b)$ by distorting the initial value ϕ_0 slightly into the complex, as several of us realized independently but which Lyons [16] was the first to write down; see also [17, 18] for more recent work in this area. To the lowest order in the slow variation of $V(\phi)$, one can see how much error there is in $\phi(\tau_b)$ when one starts with the trial value $\phi_0 = \phi_b$ and then evolves along the contour for τ that keeps $a(\tau)$ real and positive until one reaches $a = a_b$ at $\tau = \tau_b$, and then correct that trial value of ϕ_0 by the opposite of that error. One can take this first-corrected ϕ_0 as a second trial value for ϕ_0, follow a contour that goes from $a = 0$ to $a = a_b$ at a suitable $\tau = \tau_b$, find the error in $\phi(\tau_b)$, and make a second correction. In this way one can in principle iterate until one presumably finds, to sufficient accuracy, the correct complex ϕ_0 that leads to $\phi = \phi_b$ at $a = a_b$.

For a sufficiently rapidly varying $V(\phi)$, this iteration procedure may not converge. For example, there may be no contour that keeps a real all the way from 0 to a_b and also allows $\phi = \phi_b$ there. An example of this for an exponential potential will be given below. However, there can be other complex solutions that can match the boundary values (a_b, ϕ_b), even if there are none that have a stay purely real along some contour. Of course, this also highlights the possibility that even when the iterative procedure above leads to a unique complex solution (up to complex conjugation; see immediately below) matching the boundary values, there may be other complex solutions that also match the boundary values, and finding the criterion for which to include in the zero-loop approximation may be problematic.

The complex histories that lead to the desired real boundary values will have complex Euclidean action I, with the imaginary part depending on the boundary values that are the argument of the wavefunction, so the contribution that they give to the zero-loop wavefunction, e^{-I}, will be complex and have complex oscillations as a function of the boundary values. (This is true even if $V(\phi)$ is precisely constant and positive.)

When $V(\phi)$ is an analytic function that is real for real ϕ, and when the boundary values a_b and ϕ_b are real, as I am always assuming, then for any complex initial data (ϕ_0, τ_b) that leads to these real boundary values, the complex conjugate data will lead to the same real boundary values and thus also represent a history that matches the boundary values, by the analyticity of the classical equations. Therefore, complex classical histories always occur in pairs. Since the actions of the two histories in each pair will also be the complex conjugates of each other, when in the zero-loop approximation one adds up the two complex conjugate values of e^{-I}, one will always get a real sum. No matter how many pairs of complex conjugate contributions one adds (or whether one adds individual real contributions from real classical solutions), one always gets a real wavefunction (in this configuration representation), though it can be negative and hence oscillate with the boundary values in a way that the contributions of the purely real classical solutions could not.

Of course, one would expect that this feature would persist even if one multiplied the zero-loop contributions by prefactors (say to incorporate one-loop determinants) or otherwise went beyond the one-loop approximation, but this discussion shows that a real oscillating wavefunction can arise simply out of the zero-loop approximation if one allows the contributions from complex conjugate pairs of classical solutions.

35.6 FRW-scalar models with an exponential potential

To illustrate some of these ideas quantitatively, it is helpful to consider the case of an exponential potential,

$$V(\phi) = e^{2\beta\phi}, \tag{35.20}$$

where β is a real parameter that characterizes how fast the potential varies as a function of ϕ.

In terms of the quantities defined by (35.7), (35.8), (35.10) and (35.11), one then gets

$$w \equiv a^2 V = e^{2\alpha + 2\beta\phi} = e^{(1-\beta)u + (1+\beta)v} = X^{\frac{1-\beta}{2}} Y^{\frac{1+\beta}{2}}. \tag{35.21}$$

The auxiliary two-metric (35.9) is then

$$d\tilde{s}^2 = e^{4\alpha} (1 - w) \left(d\alpha^2 - d\phi^2 \right)$$
$$= e^{2u+2v} \left(1 - e^{(1-\beta)u+(1+\beta)v} \right) du\,dv$$
$$= \frac{1}{4} \left(1 - X^{\frac{1-\beta}{2}} Y^{\frac{1+\beta}{2}} \right) dX\,dY. \tag{35.22}$$

This metric has a scaling symmetry, exhibited by the homothetic Killing vector

$$\mathbf{K} = (1 + \beta) \frac{\partial}{\partial u} - (1 - \beta) \frac{\partial}{\partial v}, \tag{35.23}$$

whose action is to multiply $a^2 \equiv e^{2\alpha} \equiv e^{u+v}$ by a constant while keeping w (or $\alpha + \beta\phi$) fixed, thereby multiplying the metric (35.22) by the square of this constant. This is a symmetry that maps geodesics (which represent classical solutions) onto geodesics, though multiplying the lengths of the geodesics, and hence the actions of the solutions they represent, by the same constant by which a^2 is multiplied. It is this symmetry that allows one to reduce the two non-trivial parameters of a generic two-metric to one non-trivial parameter for the metric (35.22) and to reduce the generic second-order geodesic equation to a single first-order differential equation below.

For the exponential potential (35.20), the constraint equation (35.13) becomes

$$\left(\frac{d\alpha}{d\tau} \right)^2 - \left(\frac{d\phi}{d\tau} \right)^2 - e^{-2\alpha} + e^{2\beta\phi} = 0. \tag{35.24}$$

The scalar field equation (35.14) becomes

$$\frac{d^2\phi}{d\tau^2} + 3\frac{d\alpha}{d\tau}\frac{d\phi}{d\tau} - \beta e^{2\beta\phi} = 0, \tag{35.25}$$

and the field equation (35.15) becomes

$$\frac{d^2\alpha}{d\tau^2} + \left(\frac{d\alpha}{d\tau} \right)^2 + 2\left(\frac{d\phi}{d\tau} \right)^2 + e^{2\beta\phi} = 0. \tag{35.26}$$

As before, these two second-order field equations are not independent of each other if one uses the constraint (35.15).

The symmetry action of the homothetic Killing vector upon these classical field equations with an exponential potential is to multiply the rescaled Euclidean time τ, the rescaled S^3 size $a = e^\alpha$ and the inverse square root of the rescaled potential, $V^{-1/2} = e^{-\beta\phi}$, all by the same constant.

If we take out the scaling behaviour represented by the homothetic Killing vector of the auxiliary two-metric (35.22), we can represent the non-trivial behaviour of the classical solutions by using two scale-invariant quantities. For one of them it is convenient to use w defined by (35.21) above. When $\beta \neq 0$, for the other it is convenient to use

$$u \equiv -\frac{1}{\beta}\frac{d\phi}{d\alpha}. \tag{35.27}$$

I shall henceforth use this definition of u rather than the previous (different) use of u for the null coordinate defined in (35.10). The non-trivial behaviour of a classical solution is then given by the relation between u and w, say $u(w)$ in a regime where this function is single-valued.

One can readily find that the relation between u, w, and α is given by the following two equations:

$$\frac{du}{d\alpha} = -\left(\frac{1 - \beta^2 u^2}{1 - w}\right)(2u + w - 3uw), \tag{35.28}$$

$$\frac{dw}{d\alpha} = -2w(1 - \beta^2 u). \tag{35.29}$$

The relation with the Euclidean time τ is then given by the constraint equation

$$\left(\frac{da}{d\tau}\right)^2 = \frac{1 - w}{1 - \beta^2 u^2}. \tag{35.30}$$

Now we see that we can divide (35.28) by (35.29) to get a single first-order differential equation relating the two scale invariant quantities, u and w:

$$\frac{du}{dw} = -\left(\frac{1 - \beta^2 u^2}{1 - \beta^2 u}\right)\frac{2u + w - 3uw}{2w(1 - w)}. \tag{35.31}$$

There is a one-parameter set of solutions of (35.31), say labelled by the initial condition $u(w_0)$ for some w_0. In the FRW-scalar model, the centre of the FRW geometry has, if V is finite there, $w = 0$. This is a singular point of (35.31), but one can readily show that the regularity of the geometry there implies the 'one-boundary' condition

$$u(w) = -\frac{1}{4}w + O(w^2). \tag{35.32}$$

Analogous to what was done above, one should also take the positive square root of the constraint equation (35.30), so that $da/d\tau = +1$ at the centre and hence that the Euclidean volume is positive near there for positive real τ.

Once one solves (35.31) for $u(w)$ with the 'one-boundary' condition (35.32), one can start at the boundary value

$$w_b = a_b^2 V(\phi_b) \tag{35.33}$$

and choose a complex contour for w to go to the centre, $w = 0$. Along this contour, one can start at the boundary with the boundary values $\alpha_b \equiv \ln a_b$ and ϕ_b and integrate

$$d\alpha = \frac{dw}{2w(1 - \beta^2 u)} \tag{35.34}$$

and

$$d\phi = -\beta u \, d\alpha = \frac{-\beta u \, dw}{2w(1 - \beta^2 u)} \tag{35.35}$$

to get $\alpha(w)$ and $\phi(w)$ along the contour. One can also evaluate the action of this classical history as

$$I(a_b, \phi_b) = - \int a^2 \sqrt{1 - w} \sqrt{d\alpha^2 - d\phi^2}$$
$$= -\frac{1}{2} \int_0^{w_b} dw \, e^{-2\beta\phi} \sqrt{1 - w} \, \frac{\sqrt{1 - \beta^2 u^2}}{1 - \beta^2 u}. \tag{35.36}$$

However, one can also find that once $u_b \equiv u(w_b)$ is determined, the action is given algebraically by

$$I(a_b, \phi_b) = -\frac{1}{2} a_b^2 (1 - u_b) \sqrt{\frac{1 - w_b}{1 - \beta^2 u_b^2}}. \tag{35.37}$$

This may be derived by considering the fact that as a function of the coordinates of the auxiliary two-metric (35.9) for a general FRW-scalar model, the action obeys the Hamiltonian–Jacobi equation

$$1 = (\nabla I)^2 = G^{AB} I_{,A} I_{,B} = \frac{e^{-4\alpha}}{1 - w} \left[\left(\frac{\partial I}{\partial \alpha} \right)^2 - \left(\frac{\partial I}{\partial \phi} \right)^2 \right]. \tag{35.38}$$

When one restricts to the exponential potential so that $w = e^{2\alpha + 2\beta\phi}$, one gets the auxiliary two-metric (35.22) with its homothetic Killing vector, and one may look for solutions of the Hamilton–Jacobi equation (35.38) of the form

$$I = -\frac{1}{2} a^2 g(w), \tag{35.39}$$

where $g(w)$ obeys the differential equation

$$\left(g + w \frac{dg}{dw} \right)^2 - \beta^2 \left(w \frac{dg}{dw} \right)^2 = 1 - w. \tag{35.40}$$

One can then readily check that if $u(w)$ obeys the differential equation (35.31), then

$$g(w) = (1 - u) \sqrt{\frac{1 - w}{1 - \beta^2 u^2}} \tag{35.41}$$

obeys the differential equation (35.40).

In terms of a classical solution of the field equations (35.24)–(35.26), say written as $e^\alpha = a(\tau)$ and $\phi = \phi(\tau)$, the action may alternatively be written as

$$I = -\frac{1}{2}a^2 \left(\frac{da}{d\tau} + \frac{a\, d\phi}{\beta\, d\tau}\right). \tag{35.42}$$

So far I have written as if there were a unique $u(w)$, obeying the differential equation (35.31) with the 'one-boundary' regularity condition (35.32) at the centre, for each point of the complex w-plane. Indeed it is true that if one starts with the regularity condition (35.32) at the centre and integrates (35.31) outward along some contour in the complex w-plane that avoids the singular points of that differential equation, one gets a unique answer for $u(w)$ along that contour, and the analyticity of the differential equation (away from its singular points) guarantees that the result for $u(w)$ is independent of deformations of the contour that do not cross any of the singular points. However, because the differential equation (35.31) does have singular points (at $w = 0$, $w = 1$, and $w = \infty$, and at $u = 1/\beta^2$ if β^2 is neither 0 nor 1; in the latter case the zero in the denominator of the right-hand side of (35.31) is cancelled by the zero in the numerator), the result for $u(w)$ generically depends upon the topology of the contour relative to the singular points. Thus one gets different Riemann sheets in which $u(w)$ has different values. In particular, when one goes to the boundary value w_b and evaluates $u_b = u(w_b)$ and then the action $I(a_b, \phi_b)$ by (35.37), the action will, generically, depend upon the topology of the contour in the complex w-plane from the centre at $w = 0$ to the boundary at $w = w_b$.

For example, if one contour leads to a complex value of $u(w_b)$ (even though we are restricting to w_b real), there will be a complex conjugate contour that leads to the complex conjugate value of $u(w_b)$ and hence to the complex conjugate value of the action $I(a_b, \phi_b)$. However, generically there will be far more than a single pair of topologically inequivalent contours leading from $w = 0$ to $w = w_b$. Typically there will be an infinite number of such pairs, corresponding to winding around the various singularities arbitrarily many times. Because there is more than one singularity, one could presumably wind around one singularity an arbitrary (integer) number of times, then around another an arbitrary number of times, then around another, and so on ad infinitum, which would give an uncountably infinite number of infinite contours. However, if one is restricted to finite contours, there would be merely a countable infinity of them.

One might also allow both signs for the square root in (35.37) for the action, but I would argue that one should not do that for a given contour in the complex w-plane. For a contour that stays at small real w in going from 0 to a small real w_b with a real Euclidean geometry, one would want the four-volume to be positive and hence for the action to be negative, $I \approx -a_b^2/2$. This requires that one take the positive square root when $1 - w$ and $1 - \beta^2 u^2$ are both real and near unity, thus determining which branch of the square root to choose in the part of a contour when it just leaves the centre, $w = 0$. For any contour emerging from the center (so long as it does not pass through the singular point $w = 1$ and also avoids $\beta^2 u^2 = 1$), one can follow the sign of the square root continuously as one goes from $w = 0$ to $w = w_b$ to get a unique answer there.

However, this consideration does show that if one deforms a contour to wrap once around a point with $\beta^2 u^2 = 1$, this continuity requirement on the branch choice for the square root will cause it to switch sign relative to the undeformed contour that did not wrap around the $\beta^2 u^2 = 1$ point. Thus the value of the action will depend not only on the topology of the contour relative to the singular points $w = 0$, $w = 1$, $w = \infty$, and, generically, $u = 1/\beta^2$ of the differential equation (35.31), but its sign will also depend upon its topology relative to the points $u = 1/\beta$ and $u = -1/\beta$.

35.6.1 $\beta = 0$ deSitter example, $V = $ const.

There are two values of β^2 for which one can explicitly solve the differential equation (35.31) and get the classical solutions and their action, $\beta^2 = 0$ and $\beta^2 = 1$. (Reversing the sign of β is equivalent to reversing the sign of the scalar field and has no effect on the differential equation (35.31) or on the action.)

When $\beta = 0$, the potential is independent of ϕ. For the exponential potential $V(\phi) = e^{2\beta\phi}$ given by (35.20), this would give $V = 1$, but one can easily generalize the result to any constant V.

It is convenient to define

$$x \equiv \sqrt{1 - w} = \sqrt{1 - Va^2} \qquad (35.43)$$

as a useful replacement for w in certain equations. I shall choose the positive sign at the centre, so there $x = 1$. However, for real $a > 1/\sqrt{V}$, x will be purely imaginary and can have either sign, depending on which side of the singular point $w = 1$ the contour is taken, and whether it wraps around that point an even or odd number of times.

The 'one-boundary' solution for constant V is

$$\phi = \phi_b, \qquad (35.44)$$

$$a = \frac{1}{\sqrt{V}} \sin\left(\sqrt{V}\tau\right), \qquad (35.45)$$

$$w = \sin^2 (\sqrt{V}\tau), \tag{35.46}$$

$$x = \cos (\sqrt{V}\tau). \tag{35.47}$$

For real τ ranging up to $\pi/\sqrt{V}$, one gets part of a round Euclidean S^4 with equatorial S^3 of rescaled radius

$$a_m = a(\tau_m) = \frac{1}{\sqrt{V}} \tag{35.48}$$

at

$$\tau_m = \frac{\pi}{2\sqrt{V}}. \tag{35.49}$$

If τ ranges all the way from 0 to $2\tau_m$, one gets a complete Euclidean S^4. On this S^4, define the latitudinal angle

$$\theta = \sqrt{V}(\tau_m - \tau), \tag{35.50}$$

so

$$a = a_m \cos \theta, \ x = \sqrt{1 - w} = \sin \theta. \tag{35.51}$$

Now to get to real $a > a_m$, as discussed above for a general slowly varying positive potential, have τ go along its real axis from $\tau = 0$ to $\tau = \tau_m$ but then make a right-angled bend in the complex τ-plane, so that $\tau - \tau_m$ becomes henceforth imaginary. In particular, analytically continue θ to $\theta = \pm i\psi$ with ψ real to get

$$a = a_m \cosh \psi, \ x = \sqrt{1 - w} = \pm i \sinh \psi. \tag{35.52}$$

Then the four-metric (35.4) becomes

$$ds^2 = \left(\frac{2G}{3\pi V} \right) \left(-d\psi^2 + \cosh^2 \psi d\Omega_3^2 \right), \tag{35.53}$$

which is the real Lorentzian de Sitter spacetime.

Although strictly speaking u as defined by (35.27) is not well defined when $\beta = 0$, as both the numerator and the denominator are zero, it is well defined when one starts with $\beta \neq 0$ and then takes the limit of β going to zero. In particular its differential equation (35.31), and its 'one-boundary' regularity condition (35.32) at the centre, are both well-defined when $\beta = 0$ and lead to the solution

$$u = \frac{1}{3} \left(1 - \frac{2}{1 - w + \sqrt{1 - w}} \right) = \frac{(x - 1)(x + 2)}{3x(x + 1)}, \tag{35.54}$$

one example of an equation that is simpler in terms of $x \equiv \sqrt{1 - w}$ than in terms of $w \equiv 1 - x^2$.

Unlike the case of generic β, for $\beta = 0$ there is only the two-fold ambiguity in u(w), depending on the choice of the sign of the square root of $1 - w$ for $x = \sqrt{1 - w}$.

When one uses this $u(w)$ or $u(x)$ in (35.37) for the Euclidean action, one gets

$$I = \frac{x_b^3 - 1}{3V} = \frac{(1 - w_b)^{3/2} - 1}{3V} = \frac{\sin^3 \theta_b - 1}{3V} = \frac{\pm i \sinh \psi_b - 1}{3V}. \quad (35.55)$$

Thus the Euclidean action is real (and negative) for $w_b < 1$ (or $a_b < 1/\sqrt{V}$) but is complex (but still with a negative real part) for $w_b > 1$ (or $a_b > 1/\sqrt{V}$).

In the special case of $\beta = 0$, there also seems to be no possibility of different topologies of the contour relative to the points that are at $\beta^2 u^2 = 1$ for non-zero β, so in this special case there does not seem to be the possibility to reverse the overall sign of the action, assuming that one always starts the contour from $w = 0$ and the choice of the sign of the square root in (35.37) or (35.41) so that the four-volume starts off becoming positive.

For $a_b \geq 1/\sqrt{V}$, one gets

$$|e^{-I}|^2 = e^{+\frac{2}{3V}}, \quad (35.56)$$

the famous Hartle–Hawking enhancement of the relative probabilities that is greater for smaller positive V [5].

35.6.2 $\beta = 1$ example, $V = e^{2\phi}$

This special exponential potential has been discussed by [19], who give the solutions in terms of different variables, but here I shall follow my previous notation to show how they fit into my scheme for a general exponential potential.

For $\beta = 1$, the auxiliary two-metric (35.22) becomes the flat metric

$$d\tilde{s}^2 = \frac{1}{4}(1 - Y)dXdY = \frac{1}{4}(1 - w)dXdw = dXdZ, \quad (35.57)$$

where now $X = a^2/V = a^4/w$ and $Y = a^2V = w$, and I have defined $Z = (2w - w^2)/8$ to get the metric into the explicitly flat form with null coordinates X and Z.

One can show that only for an exponential potential, and then only for $\beta = \pm 1$, is the general auxiliary two-metric (35.9) flat for the general FRW-scalar model.

The generic geodesic of the flat auxiliary two-metric (35.57) has the form

$$X = CZ + D, \qquad (35.58)$$

where C and D are arbitrary constants. The 'one-boundary' condition of regularity at the centre, $a = 0$, implies that the exponential potential V must be finite and non-zero there, so both X and Z should vanish there, giving $D = 0$ [19, 20]. Then

$$X \equiv \frac{a^2}{V} \equiv \frac{a^4}{w} \equiv \frac{w}{V^2} = CZ \equiv \frac{C}{8}(2w - w^2) = \frac{C}{8}(2a^2V - a^4V^2), \quad (35.59)$$

so

$$C = \frac{8a_b^4}{w_b^2(2 - w_b)} = \frac{8e^{-4\phi_b}}{2 - a_b^2 e^{2\phi}}, \qquad (35.60)$$

$$V^2 = \frac{8}{C(2 - w)} = \frac{V_b^2(2 - a_b^2 V_b)}{2 - w}, \qquad (35.61)$$

$$a^4 = \frac{C}{8}w^2(2 - w) = a_b^4 \frac{w^2(2 - w)}{w_b^2(2 - w_b)}$$
$$= \frac{1}{V^2}\left(2 - \frac{8}{CV^2}\right)^2 = \left(\frac{a_b^2 V_b^3 - 2V_b^2}{V^3} + \frac{2}{V}\right)^2. \qquad (35.62)$$

One can further show that the differential equation (35.31), with the 'one-boundary' regularity condition (35.32) at the centre, leads to the solution

$$u = \frac{-w}{4 - 3w} = \frac{1}{3}\left(1 - \frac{4}{4 - 3w}\right) = \frac{x^2 - 1}{3x^2 + 1}. \qquad (35.63)$$

In this case (only) there is no branch-cut ambiguity at all in $u(w)$, though there is a two-fold ambiguity in the action when it is complex, as there must be, since for any 'one-boundary' regular classical solution with real boundary values (a_b, ϕ_b), its complex conjugate, with a complex conjugate action, must also be a regular classical solution by the analyticity properties of the field equations and the regularity conditions.

As the negative of the geodesic path length in the the flat auxiliary two-metric (35.57), the Euclidean action can easily be evaluated to be

$$I = -\sqrt{X_b Z_b} = -\frac{1}{2}a_b^2\sqrt{1 - \frac{1}{2}a_b^2 V_b}. \qquad (35.64)$$

For $0 < w_b < 2$, one gets $C > 0$ and a real Euclidean solution with real (negative) action. Unlike the case of $\beta = 0$, for which the action approached the negative value $-1/(3V)$ at the boundary of the Euclidean region, there at $w_b = 1$ or $x_b = 0$, here at the boundary of the Euclidean region (now at $w_b = 2$ or $x_b = \pm i$) the Euclidean action approaches zero. Along any real Euclidean classical solution, the action becomes negative and decreases as w increases from 0 to 1, and then the action increases back to zero as w further increases from 1 to 2. (It is interesting that the turning point for the action, at $w = 1$, does not coincide with the turning point for a, which increases from zero to a maximum as w increases from 0 to 4/3 and then decreases back to zero as w further increases from 4/3 to 2.)

For $2 < w_b$, one gets $C < 0$, and the geodesic in the (X, w) coordinates has, if one follows a contour of real w, X starting off zero at zero w and then goes negative, decreasing as w increases from 0 to 1 and then increasing back to zero again as w increases from 1 to 2. In this region (35.61) and (35.62) show that V^2 and a^4 and are both negative, so the geometry is complex. Although the complex a returns to 0 at $w = 2$, the purely imaginary V goes to infinity there, giving a singularity in the metric, though one that could be avoided by choosing the contour in the complex w-plane to avoid the point $w = 2$.

It is interesting that this singular point in the geometry at $w = 2$ is not a singular point, when $\beta^2 = 1$, of the differential equation (35.31), which then has singular points only at $w = 0$, $w = 1$ and $w = \infty$. Conversely, $w = 0$ is not a singularity of the geometry when the regularity condition (35.32) is imposed, $w = 1$ is just a coordinate singularity in the flat auxiliary metric (35.57) that also gives no physical singularity, and $w = \infty$ simply gives a universe that has expanded to infinite size and zero potential (if $w_b > 2$ and if w is taken to ∞ along the positive real axis).

If one continues to follow a contour of real w for $w_b > 2$, when $w > 2$ one gets a precisely real Lorentzian four-metric,

$$ds^2 = \left(\frac{2G}{3\pi}\right)(-C)^{1/2}\frac{\sin 2\eta}{\cos^3 2\eta}\left(-d\eta^2 + d\Omega_3^2\right), \qquad (35.65)$$

for conformal time η in the range $0 < \eta < \pi/4$, and defined, up to sign and up to shifts by arbitrary multiples of $\pi/2$, by

$$w = 2\sec^2 2\eta. \qquad (35.66)$$

During the expansion of this universe from a big bang at $\eta = 0$ to infinite size at $\eta = \pi/4$, the rescaled potential is given by

$$V = e^{\pm 2\phi} = 2(-C)^{-1/2}\cot 2\eta \qquad (35.67)$$

and thus drops from an infinite value at the Big Bang to a value of zero at infinite expansion.

Unlike the case in which the potential $V(\phi)$ is slowly varying, the exponential potential $V = e^{2\beta\phi}$ with $\beta^2 = 1$ does not allow one to follow a contour that keeps a real as one goes from the regular centre to an asymptotic region where the geometry is asymptotically real and Lorentzian (in this case precisely real and Lorentzian). This one can see from (35.62) for $a^4(w)$ with $C < 0$. If one starts from $w = 0$ along a contour that keeps a real (initially having w depart from 0 in the purely imaginary direction), then if one follows the contour with a real, one will for large w have it asymptotically become a large (and growing) real number multiplied by one of the two complex cube roots of unity, rather than having it join the real axis where the metric is real and Euclidean.

From purely looking at this Lorentzian big-bang solution, which is singular at $a = 0$, one would hardly guess that it also obeys the 'one-boundary' regularity condition at $a = 0$, but from the analysis above we see that it does, having both a singular big bang singularity with $a = 0$ and infinite V at $w = 2$ or $\eta = 0$, and also having a regular centre with $a = 0$ and finite (though complex) $V = V_b\sqrt{1 - w_b/2}$ at $w = 0$ or $\eta = \pm i\infty$.

Thus we see that for a constant potential ($\beta = 0$), an analytic continuation of the 'one-boundary' condition of regularity at $a = 0$ leads to a precisely real and Lorentzian geometry, the de Sitter four-metric (35.53), which is non-singular everywhere and has no big bang or big crunch. For the exponential potential with $\beta^2 = 1$, $V = e^{\pm 2\phi}$ for the rescaled scalar field ϕ, one also gets that an analytic continuation of the 'one-boundary' condition of regularity at $a = 0$ leads to a precisely real and Lorentzian geometry, the four-metric (35.65), but this time it is a singular metric with a big bang in which both the potential energy and the kinetic energy densities of the scalar field are infinite.

35.6.3 Generic β in the exponential potential $V = e^{2\beta\phi}$

For β^2 different from 0 or 1, the singularities of the differential equation (35.31) generically lead to non-trivial branch cuts, except for the one at $w = 1$, which is typically accompanied by having u pass through $\pm 1/\beta$ so that all quantities behave regularly there. The singular point at $w = 0$ is also generically accompanied by having u pass through $\pm 1/\beta$ (except at the beginning of a contour for which one imposes the 'one-boundary' regularity condition to avoid a singularity there), but if indeed $u = \pm 1/\beta$ at $w = 0$, this represents a curvature singularity, and going around it in different ways in the complex plane can lead to different results for

$u(w)$ (being on different Riemann sheets). The singular point at $w = \infty$ cannot be accompanied by $u = \pm 1/\beta$ but is accompanied by $u = 1/3$ and represents a universe that has expanded to infinite size. It is also a branch-cut singularity, so that one gets different results for $u(w)$ depending on the topology of the contour relative to that singularity, as well as to the one at $w = 0$.

For $\beta^2 < 3$, a solution for $u(w)$ can be analytically continued to give an asymptotically real Lorentzian solution with large real w and nearly real a, ϕ, and rescaled proper Lorentzian time $t_L = -i\tau$, with

$$u \sim \frac{1}{3} + \frac{2}{9}\left(\frac{9-\beta^2}{3+\beta^2}\right)\frac{1}{w} + O\left(\frac{1}{w^3}\right) + C_1(\beta^2)\left(-\frac{1}{w}\right)^{\left(\frac{9-\beta^2}{6-2\beta^2}\right)}\left[1 + O\left(\frac{1}{w}\right)\right],$$

(35.68)

where $C_1(\beta^2)$ is some function of β^2. One can then use this to find that the Euclidean action at large $|w|$ asymptotically goes as

$$I \sim \frac{1}{\sqrt{9-\beta^2}V}\left[(-w)^{\frac{3}{2}} + \frac{3}{2}A(-w)^{\frac{1}{2}} - AC_2(\beta^2)(-w)^{-\frac{\beta^2}{3-\beta^2}} - \frac{3}{8}A^2(-w)^{-\frac{1}{2}}\right],$$

(35.69)

where

$$A \equiv \left(\frac{\sqrt{9-\beta^2}}{3+\beta^2}\right).$$

(35.70)

For simplicity I have dropped the subscripts b on the boundary values, but what is written here as V and w should actually be V_b and w_b. Here $C_2(\beta^2)$ is another function of β^2, derivable from $C_1(\beta^2)$. $C_2(0) = C_2(1) = 1$, and according to a preliminary approximate equation I have obtained for $C_2(\beta^2)$ [18], apparently it lies between approximately 0.94 and 1 for $0 \le \beta^2 \le 1$.

Equation (35.69) gives the behaviour of the action 'near' the singular point $w = \infty$ (i.e., for $|1/w| \ll 1$), with the Euclidean action being purely real (and positive) if one takes the contour in the complex w-plane to run along the negative real axis (which of course is a rather unphysical region with $w \equiv a^2V < 0$). Then to get to positive w, one can follow $1/w$ around 0 in its complex plane from its negative axis to its positive axis. Let us define the integer n to be zero if one takes $1/w$ counterclockwise half way around its zero, from the negative real axis to the positive real axis for $1/w$ in the sense that goes below 0 in the complex plane. Then let non-zero n represent the number of excess times the contour is taken counterclockwise around $1/w = 0$. For example, if the contour were then taken once clockwise around after reaching the positive real axis from the counterclockwise half-rotation, so that the net effect would be a clockwise half-rotation, passing once above 0 in going from the negative axis to the positive axis for $1/w$, then $n = -1$.

As a result of this, after reaching the positive w axis with some integer n representing the integer part of the winding number, one can make the replacement

$$\left(-\frac{1}{w}\right) = e^{(2n+1)\pi i}\left(\frac{1}{w}\right) \tag{35.71}$$

in the asymptotic formula (35.69) for the action, giving

$$I \sim \frac{1}{3V}\left(\frac{\sqrt{9-\beta^2}}{3+\beta^2}\right)C_2(\beta^2)w^{-\frac{\beta^2}{3-\beta^2}}\left[\cos\frac{(2n+1)\pi\beta^2}{3-\beta^2}+i\sin\frac{(2n+1)\pi\beta^2}{3-\beta^2}\right]$$
$$\frac{i(-1)^n}{\sqrt{9-\beta^2}\,V}\left[w^{3/2}-\frac{3}{2}Aw^{1/2}+\frac{3}{8}A^2w^{-1/2}+O(w^{-3/2})\right]. \tag{35.72}$$

This formula represents only a tiny class of possible contours for w in going from the regular centre at $w = 0$ to the asymptotically Lorentzian regime of a large universe with $w \gg 1$, with only the single integer n, representing how many times around the singularity at $w = \infty$ the contour wraps. Thus this class of contours does not include the possibility of wrapping around the singularity at $w = 0$ an arbitrary number of times between each possible wrapping around the singularity at $w = \infty$. That much larger class, though still not including the possibility of going around the singularity at $u = 1/\beta^2$ (which seems to give merely a two-fold square-root ambiguity and so may have less effect than the other singularities), would be parametrized by an arbitrary sequence of integers and signs (with each integer in the sequence being the number of times wrapping around the singularity at $w = 0$ between each time of wrapping once around the singularity at $w = \infty$, and with each sign being the sign of the wrapping around the singularity at $w = \infty$). However, here we are not wrapping around the singularity at $w = 0$ at all, so the small subclass being considered is characterized by the single integer n.

The first term in the Euclidean action above is the real part of the Euclidean action, I_R, which gives the magnitude of the zero-loop approximation to the wavefunction if only that history contributes, $|e^{-I}|^2 = e^{-2I_R}$. If $n = 0$ or $n = -1$, the two simplest contours, then I_R is negative for $\beta^2 < 1$ (assuming that $C_2(\beta^2)$ remains positive) and vanishes for $\beta^2 = 1$, this last fact being consistent with the exact solution given above for $\beta^2 = 1$. Presumably these simplest contours then make I_R positive when β^2 is increased beyond 1. If $C_2(\beta^2)$ remains positive for all β^3 up to 3, then the simplest contours would make I_R oscillate an infinite number of times as β^2 is increased to 3, the maximum value it can have and still lead to an approximately Lorentzian universe that can expand to arbitrarily large size. For example, if the asymptotic formula (35.72) were accurate for the real part of the action, I_R, that quantity would oscillate and pass through zero at

$$\beta^2 = \frac{6N - 3}{2N + 1} \tag{35.73}$$

for each positive integer N (unrelated to n, which is being set equal to 0 or -1 to give the simplest possible contours), assuming that $C_2(\beta^2)$ does not pass through infinity at any of those points to prevent I_R from passing through zero.

If the winding number n can take on arbitrary integer values, then for values of β^2 other than those given by (35.73), I_R can take on both positive and negative values. This highlights the question of what classical histories are to be included if the zero-loop approximation is supposed to be a reasonable approximation to the 'one-boundary' wavefunction.

In models in which $Re\sqrt{g}$, the real part of the proper four-volume per coordinate four-volume, has a fixed sign, Halliwell and Hartle [21] proposed that one should include only classical histories in which the sign is positive. The most conservative interpretation of this in models such as those being considered here, in which the sign of $Re\sqrt{g}$ can vary along a contour, is that one should choose the square root of this metric determinant g to give a real value in the part of the contour near the centre, which is the same as my choice of the sign of the square root in (35.41) to make my $g(w)$ (not the determinant of the metric) positive for small w in the part of the contour near its beginning at the centre, $w = 0$.

But one might also interpret the Halliwell–Hartle proposal as requiring that, for a monotonically increasing real time coordinate t along the complex contour for w, one have $Re\sqrt{g} \propto Re(a^3 d\tau/dt)$ be positive along the entire contour. It remains to be seen whether this can always be satisfied for the models considered above. (It does have the ugliness of depending on the details of the contour even within the same topological class of how it winds around the various singularities, whereas one would prefer simply a restriction to a particular topological class.) But if it can, one might conjecture that it might be satisfied only for the contours given above with $n = 1$ and $n = -1$ (which are a complex-conjugate pair).

Alternatively, one might simply postulate that for the FRW-scalar model with an exponential potential, for large w_b one should just use the simplest single complex-conjugate pair of contours, those given above with $n = 0$ and $n = -1$. Both of these have the same real part, I_R, and opposite imaginary parts, say I_I for $n = 0$, so $n = 0$ gives $I = I_R + iI_I$ and $n = -1$ gives the complex conjugate $I' = I^\star = I_R - iI_I$. (In general the action for some n is the complex conjugate of the action with a new integer $n' = -n-1$, e.g., $n' = -1$ for $n = 0$.) Then if we take the zero-loop approximation to be given by those two contributions, we get

$$\psi_{0-\text{loop}}(a_b, \phi_b) = e^{-I} + e^{-I'} = 2e^{-I_R} \cos I_I. \tag{35.74}$$

However, it would be highly desirable to have some physically motivated principles for selecting a suitable set of complex classical solutions for the zero-loop approximation.

35.7 Summary

- The Hartle–Hawking 'one-boundary' proposal is one of the first attempts to say which wavefunction, out of all those satisfying the dynamical equations, correctly describes our universe.

- There are severe problems doing the path integral for which it calls.

- At the zero-loop level it makes a number of remarkable predictions (large nearly flat Lorentzian universe, second law of thermodynamics, etc.)

- However, even here there are generically an infinite number of complex extrema to choose from, and it is not quite clear how to do this properly. Certainly one important goal of this approach to quantum cosmology would be to give a specification of which extrema to use, and then of course one would like to compare the results with as many observations as possible.

Acknowledgements

I am deeply indebted to Stephen Hawking for being an excellent mentor for me as a graduate student, postdoc, and professor. His courage in tackling physical challenges has been personally inspiring, and his courage in tackling physics challenges has been academically inspiring. He has opened up a whole new approach to physics and cosmology in seeking to find the quantum state of the universe, and I am certain that the path he has begun will become an integral part of our understanding of the world.

For the particular work summarized here, I am not only indebted to Hawking's work but have also benefited from recent discussions with Jonathan Halliwell and Bill Unruh. This work was financially supported in part by the Natural Sciences and Engineering Council of Canada.

References

[1] Page, D. N. (1995), 'Sensible quantum mechanics: are only perceptions probabilistic?', [http://arXiv.org/abs/quant-ph/9506010].

[2] Page, D. N. (2001), 'Mindless sensationalism: a quantum framework for consciousness', to be published in *Consciousness: New Philosophical Essays*, eds. Q. Smith and A. Jokic (Oxford University Press, Oxford), [quant-ph/0108039].

[3] Hartle, J. B. (2001), 'Quantum cosmology: Problems for the 21st century', in *Physics 2001*, ed. M. Kumar, and in *Proceedings of the 11th Nishinomiya-Yukawa Memorial Symposium on Physics in the 21st Century: Celebrating the 60th Anniversary of the Yukawa Meson Theory, Nishinomiya, Hyogo, Japan, 7-8 Nov 1996*, pp. 179–199, [gr-qc/9701022].

[4] Hawking, S. W. (1982), 'The boundary conditions of the universe', in *Astrophysical Cosmology: Proceedings of the Study Week on Cosmology and Fundamental Physics, September 28–October 2, 1981*, eds H. A. Brück, C. V. Coyne and M. S. Longair (Pontificiae Academiae Scientiarum Scripta Varia, Vatican).

[5] Hawking, S. W. (1984), 'The quantum state of the universe', *Nucl. Phys.* **B239**, 257–276.

[6] Hawking, S. W. and Hartle, J. B. (1983), 'Wave function of the universe', *Phys. Rev.* **D28**, 2960–2975.

[7] Goroff, M. H. and Sagnotti, A. (1986), 'The ultraviolet behavior of quantum gravity', *Nucl. Phys.* **B266**, 709–744.

[8] Deser, S. (1999), 'Nonrenormalizability of (last hope) D=11 supergravity, with a terse survey of divergences in quantum gravities', [hep-th/9905017].

[9] Gibbons, G. W. Hawking, S. W. and Perry, M. J. (1978), 'Path integrals and the indefiniteness of the gravitational action', *Nucl. Phys.* **B138**, 141–154.

[10] Hawking, S. W. and Page, D. N. (1986), 'Operator ordering and the flatness of the universe', *Nucl. Phys.* **B264**, 185–196.

[11] Hawking, S. W. and Luttrell, J. C. (1984), 'The isotropy of the universe', *Phys. Lett.* **B143**, 83–86.

[12] Halliwell, J. J. and Hawking, S. W. (1985), 'The origin of structure in the universe', *Phys. Rev.* **D31**, 1777–1791.

[13] Hawking, S. W. (1985), 'The arrow of time in cosmology', *Phys. Rev.* **D32**, 2489–2495.

[14] Page, D. N. (1985), 'Will entropy decrease if the universe recollapses?' *Phys. Rev.* **D32**, 2496–2499.

[15] Hawking, S. W., Laflamme, R. and Lyons, G. W. (1993), 'The origin of time asymmetry', *Phys. Rev.* **D47**, 5342–5356.

[16] Lyons, G. W. (1992), 'Complex solutions for the scalar field model of the universe', *Phys. Rev.* **D46**, 1546–1550.

[17] Unruh, W. G. and Jheeta, M. (1998), 'Complex paths and the Hartle Hawking wave-function for slow roll cosmologies', [gr-qc/9812017].

[18] Page, D. N. (2002), 'Hartle–Hawking wavefunctions with exponential potentials', in preparation.

[19] Garay, L. J. Halliwell, J. J. and Marugán, G. A. M. (1991), 'Path integral quantum cosmology: a class of exactly soluble scalar field minisuperspace models with a exponential potentials', *Phys. Rev.* **D43**, 2572–2589.

[20] Unruh, W. G. (2001), Private communication.

[21] Halliwell, J. J. and Hartle, J. B. (1990), 'Integration contours for the no boundary wavefunction of the universe', *Phys. Rev.* **D41**, 1815–1856.

36

Quantum cosmology and eternal inflation

Alexander Vilenkin

Tufts University

36.1 Introduction

Stephen and I at times disagreed about minor things, like the sign in the wave function of the universe, $\psi \sim e^{\pm S}$. But for me Stephen has always been a major source of inspiration. I will mention just one episode, when I talked to Stephen at a conference and was telling him why I thought my wave function was better than his. To which Stephen replied: 'You do not have a wave function'.

Talking to Stephen is a little like talking to the Oracle of Delphi: you are likely to hear something as profound as it is difficult to decipher. But in that particular case I knew immediately what he meant. He was pointing to the lack of a general definition for the tunneling wave function, which at the time was defined only in a simple model. My talk was scheduled for the next morning, so I spent the night working out a general definition and rewriting my transparencies. I ended up giving a very different talk from what was initially intended. I can thus say with some justification that Stephen contributed to the development of the tunnelling approach, although he may not be very pleased with the result.

My contribution here will consist of two parts. In the first part, I will review the tunnelling approach to quantum cosmology and will briefly comment on the alternative approaches. In the second part, I will discuss the relation between quantum cosmology and eternal inflation. After a brief review of eternal inflation, I will discuss whether or not we need quantum cosmology in the light of eternal inflation, and then whether or not quantum cosmology makes any testable predictions.

36.2 Quantum cosmology

If the cosmological evolution is followed back in time, we are driven to
the initial singularity where the classical equations of general relativity
break down. There was initially some hope that the singularity was a
pathological feature of the highly symmetric Friedmann solutions, but this
hope evaporated when Stephen and Roger Penrose proved their famous
singularity theorems. There was no escape, and cosmologists had to face
the problem of the origin of the universe.

Many people suspected that in order to understand what actually happened in the beginning, we should treat the universe quantum-mechanically and describe it by a wave function rather than by a classical
spacetime. This quantum approach to cosmology was initiated by DeWitt
[1] and Misner [2], and after a somewhat slow start received wide recognition in the last two decades or so. The picture that has emerged from
this line of development [3–9] is that a small closed universe can spontaneously nucleate out of nothing, where by 'nothing' I mean a state with
no classical space and time. The cosmological wave function can be used
to calculate the probability distribution for the initial configurations of
the nucleating universes. Once the universe nucleates, it is expected to go
through a period of inflation, driven by the energy of a false vacuum. The
vacuum energy is eventually thermalized, inflation ends, and from then
on the universe follows the standard hot cosmological scenario. Inflation
is a necessary ingredient in this kind of scheme, since it gives the only
way to get from the tiny nucleated universe to the large universe we live
in today.

The wave function of the universe ψ satisfies the Wheeler–DeWitt
equation,

$$\mathcal{H}\psi = 0, \tag{36.1}$$

which is analogous to the Schrödinger equation in ordinary quantum mechanics. To solve this equation, one has to specify some boundary conditions for ψ. In quantum mechanics, the boundary conditions are determined by the physical set-up external to the system. But since there is
nothing external to the universe, it appears that boundary conditions for
the wave function of the universe should be postulated as an independent
physical law. The possible form of this law has been debated for nearly
20 years, and one can hope that it will eventually be derived from the
fundamental theory.

Presently, there are at least three proposals on the table: the Hartle–
Hawking wave function [5, 10], the Linde wave function [6], and the tunnelling wave function [8, 11].

36.3 The tunnelling wave function

To introduce the tunnelling wave function, let us consider a very simple model of a closed Friedmann–Robertson–Walker universe filled with a vacuum of constant energy density ρ_v and some radiation. The total energy density of the universe is given by

$$\rho = \rho_v + \epsilon/a^4, \tag{36.2}$$

where a is the scale factor and ϵ is a constant characterizing the amount of radiation. The evolution equation for a can be written as

$$p^2 + a^2 - a^4/a_0^2 = \epsilon. \tag{36.3}$$

Here, $p = -a\dot{a}$ is the momentum conjugate to a and $a_0 = (3/4)\rho_v^{-1/2}$.

Equation 36.3 is identical to that for a 'particle' of energy ϵ moving in a potential $U(a) = a^2 - a^4/a_0^2$. For sufficiently small ϵ, there are two types of classical trajectories. The universe can start at $a = 0$, expand to a maximum radius a_1, and then recollapse. Alternatively, it can contract from infinite size, bounce at a minimum radius a_2 and then re-expand (see Figure 36.1). But in quantum cosmology there is yet another possibility. Instead of recollapsing, the universe can tunnel through the potential barrier to the regime of unbounded expansion. The semiclassical tunnelling probability can be estimated as

$$\mathcal{P} \sim \exp\left(-2 \int_{a_1}^{a_2} |p(a)| \mathrm{d}a\right). \tag{36.4}$$

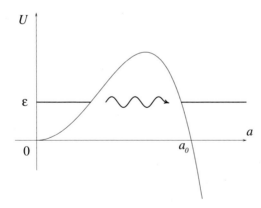

Fig. 36.1. The potential for the scale factor in (36.3). Instead of recollapsing, the universe can tunnel through the potential barrier to the regime of unbounded expansion.

It is interesting that this probability does not vanish in the limit of $\epsilon \to 0$, when there is no radiation and the size of the initial universe shrinks to zero. We then have tunnelling from *nothing* to a closed universe of a finite radius a_0; the corresponding probability is

$$\mathcal{P} \sim \exp\left(-2\int_0^{a_0} |p(a)|da\right) = \exp\left(-\frac{3}{8\rho_v}\right). \qquad (36.5)$$

The tunnelling approach to quantum cosmology assumes that our universe originated in a tunnelling event of this kind. Once it nucleates, the universe immediately begins a de Sitter inflationary expansion.

The Wheeler–DeWitt equation for our simple model can be obtained by replacing the momentum p in (36.3) by a differential operator[1], $p \to -id/da$,

$$\left(\frac{d^2}{da^2} - a^2 + \frac{a^4}{a_0^2}\right)\psi(a) = 0. \qquad (36.6)$$

This equation has outgoing and ingoing wave solutions corresponding to expanding and contracting universes in the classically allowed range $a > a_0$ and exponentially growing and decaying solutions in the classically forbidden range $0 < a < a_0$. The boundary condition that selects the tunnelling wave function requires that ψ should include only an outgoing wave at $a \to \infty$. The under-barrier wave function is then a linear combination of the growing and decaying solutions. The two solutions have comparable magnitudes near the classical turning point, $a = a_0$, but the decaying solution dominates in the rest of the under-barrier region.

The tunnelling probability can also be expressed in the language of instantons. The nucleated universe after tunnelling is described by de Sitter space, and the under-barrier evolution can be semiclassically represented by the Euclideanized de Sitter space. This de Sitter instanton has the geometry of a four-sphere. By matching it with the Lorentzian de Sitter at $a = a_0$ we can symbolically represent [4] the origin of the universe as in Figure 36.2. For 'normal' quantum tunnelling (without gravity), the tunnelling probability $\mathcal{P}$ is proportional to $\exp(-S_E)$, where S_E is the instanton action. In our case,

$$S_E = \int d^4x\sqrt{-g}\left(-\frac{R}{16\pi G} + \rho_v\right) = -2\rho_v\Omega_4 = -3/8G^2\rho_v, \qquad (36.7)$$

where $R = 32\pi G\rho_v$ is the scalar curvature, and $\Omega_4 = (4\pi^2/3)a_0^4$ is the volume of the four-sphere. Hence, I concluded in [4] that $\mathcal{P} \propto \exp(3/8G^2\rho_v)$.

---

[1] Here and below I disregard the ambiguity associated with the ordering of noncommuting factors a and d/da. This ambiguity is unimportant in the semiclassical domain, which we shall be mainly concerned with in this paper.

Fig. 36.2. A schematic representation of the birth of inflationary universe.

I resist the temptation to call this 'the greatest mistake of my life', but I did change my mind on this issue [8]. I now believe that the correct answer is given by (36.5). In theories with gravity, the Euclidean action is not positive-definite and the naive answer no longer applies. Similar conclusions were reached independently by Linde [6], Rubakov [7] and by Zeldovich and Starobinsky [9]. But the story does not end there. Not everybody believes that my first answer was a mistake. In fact, Stephen and his collaborators believe that I got it right the first time around and that it is now that I am making a mistake. I shall return to this ongoing debate later in this paper.

In the general case, the wave function of the universe is defined on superspace, which is the space of all three-dimensional geometries and matter field configurations, $\psi[g_{ij}(\mathbf{x}), \varphi(\mathbf{x})]$, where g_{ij} is the 3-metric, and matter fields are represented by a single field φ. The tunnelling boundary condition can be extended to full superspace by requiring that ψ should include only outgoing waves at the boundary of superspace, except the part of the boundary corresponding to vanishing 3-geometries (see [11, 12] for more details).

Alternatively, the tunnelling wave function can be defined as a path integral

$$\psi_T(g, \varphi) = \int_\emptyset^{(g,\varphi)} e^{iS}, \qquad (36.8)$$

where the integration is over paths interpolating between a vanishing 3-geometry $\emptyset$ ('nothing') and (g, φ). I argued in [12] that this definition is equivalent to the tunnelling boundary condition in a wide class of models.

Note that according to the definition (36.8), ψ_T is strictly not a wave function, but rather a propagator

$$\psi_T(g, \varphi) = K(g, \varphi|\emptyset), \tag{36.9}$$

where $K(g, \varphi|g', \varphi')$ is given by the path integral (36.8) taken over Lorentzian histories interpolating between (g', φ') and (g, φ). One expects, therefore, that ψ_T should generally be singular at $g = \emptyset$. In simple mini-superspace models this singularity was noted in my paper [11] and also by Kontoleon and Wiltshire [13] (who regarded it as an undesirable feature of ψ_T).

I should also mention an interesting issue raised by Rubakov [7, 14] who argues that cosmic tunnelling of the type illustrated in Fig. 36.1 results in a catastrophic particle production and in a breakdown of the semiclassical approximation. This conclusion is reached using a Euclidean formalism in which particles are defined by an instantaneous diagonalization of the Hamiltonian. This is a rather unconventional approach and I am not convinced that 'particles' defined in this way are the same particles that observers will detect when the universe emerges from under the barrier. If Rubakov is right, then the tunnelling wave function cannot be obtained as a limit of tunnelling from a small initial universe in a generic quantum state when the size of that universe goes to zero. (There is no dispute that for a particular quantum state, corresponding to the de Sitter invariant Bunch–Davis vacuum, there is no catastrophic particle production and the semiclassical approximation is well justified [14, 15].) This issue requires further study.

At present, the general definitions of the tunnelling wave function remain largely formal, since we do not know how to solve the Wheeler-DeWitt equation[2] or how to calculate the path integral (36.8), except for simple models (and small perturbations about them), or in the semiclassical limit. A promising recent development is the work by Ambjorn, Jurkiewicz and Loll [16] who developed a Lorentzian path integral approach to quantum gravity. It would be interesting to see an application of this approach to the tunnelling problem.

---

[2] Note that the Wheeler–DeWitt equation applies assuming that the topology of the universe is fixed. Possible modification of this equation accounting for topology change have been discussed in [12]. Here, I have disregarded topology change, assuming the simplest S_3 topology of the universe. For a discussion of topology-changing processes in quantum gravity, see Fay Dowker's contribution to this volume.

36.4 Alternative proposals for the wave function

I shall now comment on the other proposals for the wave function of the universe.

36.4.1 The DeWitt wave function

I should first mention what I believe was the first such proposal, made by DeWitt in his 1967 paper [1]. DeWitt suggested that the wave function should vanish for the vanishing scale factor,

$$\psi_{DW}(a = 0) = 0. \tag{36.10}$$

The motivation for this is that $a = 0$ corresponds to the cosmological singularity, so (36.10) says that the probability for the singularity to occur is zero.

The boundary condition (36.10) is easy to satisfy in a mini-superspace model with a single degree of freedom, but in more general models it tends to give an identically vanishing wave function. No generalizations of the DeWitt boundary condition (36.10) have yet been proposed.

36.4.2 The Hartle–Hawking wave function

The Hartle–Hawking wave function is expressed as a path integral over compact Euclidean geometries bounded by a given 3-geometry g,

$$\psi_{HH}(g, \varphi) = \int^{(g,\varphi)} e^{-S_E}. \tag{36.11}$$

The Euclidean rotation of the time axis, $t \to i\tau$, is often used in quantum field theory because it improves the convergence of the path integrals. However, in quantum gravity the situation is the opposite. The gravitational part of the Euclidean action S_E is unbounded from below, and the integral (36.11) is badly divergent. One can attempt to fix the problem by additional contour rotations, extending the path integral to complex metrics. However, the space of complex metrics is very large, and no obvious choice of integration contour suggests itself as the preferred one [17].

In practice, one assumes that the dominant contribution to the path integral is given by the stationary points of the action and evaluates ψ_{HH} simply as $\psi_{HH} \sim e^{-S_E}$. For our simple model, $S_E = -3/8\rho_v$ and the nucleation probability is $\mathcal{P} \sim \exp(+3/8\rho_v)$. The wave function $\psi_{HH}(a)$ for this model has only the growing solution under the barrier and a superposition of ingoing and outgoing waves with equal amplitudes in the classically allowed region. This wave function appears to describe a contracting and re-expanding universe.

It is sometimes argued [10, 14] that changing expansion to contraction does not do anything, as long as the directions of all other physical processes are also reversed. So if the ingoing and outgoing waves are CPT conjugates of one another, they may both correspond to expanding universes, provided that the internal direction of time is determined as that in which the entropy increases. I would like to note that this issue is clarified in models where the universe is described by a brane propagating in an infinite higher-dimensional bulk space [18–20]. The nucleation of the universe then appears as bubble nucleation from the point of view of the bulk observer. In such models, there is an extrinsic bulk time variable, and the interpretation of incoming and outgoing waves is unambiguous [21]. The tunnelling wave function appears to be the only correct choice in this case.

36.4.3 The Linde wave function

Linde suggested that the wave function of the universe is given by a Euclidean path integral like (36.11), but with the Euclidean time rotation performed in the opposite sense, $t \to +i\tau$, yielding

$$\psi_L = \int^{(g,\varphi)} e^{+S_E}. \tag{36.12}$$

For our simple model, this wave function gives the same nucleation probability (36.23) as the tunnelling wave function.

The problem with this proposal is that the Euclidean action is also unbounded from above and, once again, the path integral is divergent. If one regards (36.12) as a general definition that applies beyond the simple model (something that Linde himself never suggested), then the divergence is even more disastrous than in the Hartle–Hawking case, because now all integrations over matter fields and over inhomogeneous modes of the metric are divergent. This problem of the (extended) Linde's wave function makes it an easy target, and I suspect it is for this reason that Stephen likes to confuse ψ_L and ψ_T and refers to both of them as 'the tunnelling wave function'. In fact, the two wave functions are quite different, even in the simplest model [22]. The Linde wave function includes only the decaying solution under the barrier and a superposition of ingoing and outgoing modes with equal amplitudes outside the barrier.

Using Stephen's expression, I think it would be fair to say that at present none of us 'has a wave function'. All four proposals are well defined only in simple mini-superspace models or in the semiclassical approximation. So they are to be regarded only as prototypes for future work in this area, and not as well defined mathematical objects.

36.5 Semiclassical probabilities

Quantum cosmology is based on quantum gravity and shares all of its problems. In addition, it has some extra problems which arise when one tries to quantize a closed universe. The first problem stems from the fact that ψ is independent of time. This can be understood [1] in the sense that the wave function of the universe should describe everything, including the clocks which show time. In other words, time should be defined intrinsically in terms of the geometric or matter variables. However, no general prescription has yet been found that would give a function $t(g_{ij}, \varphi)$ that would be, in some sense, monotonic.

A related problem is the definition of probability. Given a wave function ψ, how can we calculate probabilities? There was some debate about this in the 1980s, but now it seems that the only reasonable definition that we have is in terms of the conserved current of the Wheeler–DeWitt equation [1, 2, 23]. The Wheeler–DeWitt equation can be symbolically written in the form

$$(\nabla^2 - U)\psi = 0, \tag{36.13}$$

which is similar to the Klein–Gordon equation. Here, ∇^2 is the superspace Laplacian and the 'potential' U is a functional of g_{ij} and φ. (We shall not need explicit forms of ∇^2 and U.) This equation has a conserved current

$$J = i(\psi^* \nabla \psi - \psi \nabla \psi^*), \qquad \nabla \cdot J = 0. \tag{36.14}$$

The conservation is a useful property, since we want probability to be conserved. But one runs into the same problem as with the Klein–Gordon equation: the probability defined using (36.14) is not positive-definite. Although we do not know how to solve these problems in general, they can both be solved in the semiclassical domain. In fact, it is possible that this is all we need.

Let us consider the situation when some of the variables $\{c\}$ describing the universe behave classically, while the rest of the variables $\{q\}$ must be treated quantum-mechanically. Then the wave function of the universe can be written as a superposition

$$\psi = \sum_k A_k(c) e^{iS_k(c)} \chi_k(c, q) \equiv \sum_k \psi_k^{(c)} \chi_k, \tag{36.15}$$

where the classical variables are described by the WKB wave functions $\psi_k^{(c)} = A_k e^{iS_k}$. In the semiclassical regime, ∇S is large, and substitution of

(36.15) into the Wheeler–DeWitt equation (36.13) yields the Hamilton–Jacobi equation for $S(c)$,

$$\nabla S \cdot \nabla S + U = 0. \tag{36.16}$$

The summation in (36.15) is over different solutions of this equation. Each solution of (36.16) is a classical action describing a congruence of classical trajectories (which are essentially the gradient curves of S). Hence, a semiclassical wave function $\psi_c = Ae^{iS}$ describes an ensemble of classical universes evolving along the trajectories of $S(c)$. A probability distribution for these trajectories can be obtained using the conserved current (36.14). Since the variables c behave classically, these probabilities do not change in the course of evolution and can be thought of as probabilities for various initial conditions. The time variable t can be defined as any monotonic parameter along the trajectories, and it can be shown [1, 23] that in this case the corresponding component of the current J is non-negative, $J_t \geq 0$. Moreover, one finds [24–26] that the 'quantum' wave function χ satisfies the usual Schrödinger equation,

$$i\partial\chi/\partial t = \mathcal{H}_\chi\chi \tag{36.17}$$

with an appropriate Hamiltonian $\mathcal{H}_\chi$. Hence, all the familiar physics is recovered in the semiclassical regime.

This semiclassical interpretation of the wave function ψ is valid to the extent that the WKB approximation for ψ_c is justified and the interference between different terms in (36.15) can be neglected. Otherwise, time and probability cannot be defined, suggesting that the wave function has no meaningful interpretation. In a universe where no object behaves classically (that is, predictably), no clocks can be constructed, no measurements can be made, and there is nothing to interpret. It would be interesting, however, to investigate the effects of small corrections to the WKB form of the wave functions and of non-vanishing interference.

36.6 Comparing different wave functions

To see what kind of cosmological predictions can be obtained from different wave functions, one needs to consider an extension of the mini-superspace model (36.6). Instead of a constant vacuum energy ρ_v, one introduces an inflation field φ with a potential $V(\varphi)$. The Wheeler–DeWitt equation for this two-dimensional model can be approximately solved assuming that $V(\varphi)$ is a slowly-varying function and is well below the Planck density.

After an appropriate rescaling of the scale factor a and the scalar field φ, the Wheeler–DeWitt equation can be written as

$$\left[\frac{\partial^2}{\partial a^2} - \frac{1}{a^2}\frac{\partial^2}{\partial \varphi^2} - U(a, \varphi) \right] \psi(a, \varphi) = 0, \qquad (36.18)$$

where

$$U(a, \varphi) = a^2[1 - a^2 V(\varphi)]. \qquad (36.19)$$

With the above assumptions, one finds [27] that Hartle–Hawking and tunnelling solutions of this equation are given essentially by the same expressions as for the simple model (36.6), but with ρ_v replaced by $V(\varphi)$. The only difference is that the wave function is multiplied by a factor $C(\varphi)$, such that $\psi(a, \varphi)$ becomes φ-independent in the limit $a \to 0$ (with $|\varphi| < \infty$).

The initial state of the nucleating universe in this model is characterized by the value of the scalar field φ, with the initial value of a given by $a_0(\varphi) = V^{-1/2}(\varphi)$. The probability distribution for φ can be found using the conserved current (36.14). For the tunnelling wave function one finds

$$\mathcal{P}_T(\varphi) \propto \exp\left(-\frac{3}{8G^2 V(\varphi)} \right). \qquad (36.20)$$

This is the same as (36.5) with ρ_v replaced by $V(\varphi)$.

Equation (36.20) can be interpreted as the probability distribution for the initial values of φ in the ensemble of nucleated universes. The highest probability is obtained for the largest values of $V(\varphi)$ (and smallest initial size). Thus, the tunnelling wave function 'predicts' that the universe is most likely to nucleate with the largest possible vacuum energy. This is just the right initial condition for inflation. The high vacuum energy drives the inflationary expansion, while the field φ gradually 'rolls down' the potential hill, and ends up at the minimum with $V(\varphi) \approx 0$, where we are now.

The Hartle–Hawking wave function gives a similar distribution, but with a crucial difference in sign,

$$\mathcal{P}_H(\varphi) \propto \exp\left(+\frac{3}{8G^2 V(\varphi)} \right). \qquad (36.21)$$

This is peaked at the smallest values of $V(\varphi)$. Thus the Hartle–Hawking wave function tends to predict initial conditions that disfavour inflation. There has been much discussion of this point in the literature [27–31], but as I will explain in section 36.8, the eternal nature of inflation makes this distinction between the wave functions rather irrelevant.

36.7 Do we need quantum cosmology?

The status of quantum cosmology is closely related to that of eternal inflation, and I am going to discuss this relation in the rest of the paper.

A very generic feature of inflation is its future-eternal character [32–34]. The evolution of the inflaton field φ is influenced by quantum fluctuations, and as a result thermalization does not occur simultaneously in different parts of the universe. One finds that, at any time, the universe consists of post-inflationary, thermalized regions embedded in an inflating background. Thermalized regions grow by annexing adjacent inflating regions, and new thermalized regions are constantly formed in the midst of the inflating sea. At the same time, the inflating regions expand and their combined volume grows exponentially with time. It can be shown that the inflating regions form a self-similar fractal of dimension somewhat smaller than 3 [35, 36].

Given this picture, it is natural to ask if the universe could also be past-eternal. If it could, we would have a model of an infinite, eternally inflating universe without a beginning. We would then need no initial or boundary conditions for the universe, and quantum cosmology would arguably be unnecessary.

This possibility was discussed in the early days of inflation, but it was soon realized [37, 38] that the idea could not be implemented in the simplest model in which the inflating universe is described by an exact de Sitter space. The reason is that in the full de Sitter space, exponential expansion is preceded by an exponential contraction. If thermalized regions were allowed to form all the way to the past infinity, they would rapidly fill the space, and the whole universe would be thermalized before the inflationary expansion could begin.

More recently, general theorems were proved [39], using the global techniques of Penrose and Hawking, where it was shown that inflationary spacetimes are geodesically incomplete to the past. However, it is now believed [40, 41] that one of the key assumptions made in these theorems, the weak energy condition, is likely to be violated by quantum fluctuations in the inflating parts of the universe. This appears to open the door again to the possibility that inflation, by itself, can eliminate the need for initial conditions. Now I would like to report on a new theorem, proved in collaboration with Arvind Borde and Alan Guth [42], which appears to close that door completely. (For a more detailed discussion of the theorem and an outline of the proof, see Alan Guth's contribution to this volume.)

The theorem assumes that (i) the spacetime is globally expanding and (ii) that the expansion rate is bounded below by a positive constant,

$$H > H_{min} \geq 0. \tag{36.22}$$

The theorem states that any spacetime with these properties is past geodesically incomplete. Both of the above conditions need to be spelled out.

It is important to realize that expansion and contraction are not local properties of spacetime. Rather, they refer to the relative motion of comoving observers filling the spacetime, with observers being described by a congruence of timelike geodesics. The global expansion condition requires that the spacetime can be filled by an expanding congruence of geodesics.[3] This condition is meant to exclude spacetimes like de Sitter space (which can be said to have a globally contracting phase).

The Hubble expansion rate H is defined as usual, as the relative velocity divided by the distance, with all quantities measured in the local comoving frame. Since we do not assume any symmetries of spacetime, the expansion rates are generally different at different places and in different directions. The bound (36.22) is assumed to be satisfied at all points and in all directions. This is a very reasonable requirement in the inflating region of spacetime.

The theorem is straightforwardly extended to higher-dimensional models. For example, in Bucher's model [19], brane worlds are created in collisions of bubbles nucleating in an inflating higher-dimensional bulk spacetime. Our theorem implies that the inflating bulk cannot be past-eternal. Another example is the cyclic brane world model of Steinhardt and Turok [43]. One of the two branes in this model is globally expanding and thus should have a past boundary.

This is good news for quantum cosmology. It follows from the theorem that the inflating region has a boundary in the past, and some new physics (other than inflation) is necessary to determine the conditions at that boundary. Quantum cosmology is the prime candidate for this role. The picture suggested by quantum cosmology is that the universe starts as a small, closed 3-geometry and immediately enters the regime of eternal inflation, with new thermalized regions being constantly formed. In this picture, the universe has a beginning, but it has no end.

36.8 Is quantum cosmology testable?

There is also some bad news. In the course of eternal inflation, the universe quickly forgets its initial conditions. Since the number of thermalized

---

[3] This formulation of the global expansion condition may be somewhat too restrictive. Congruences of geodesics tend to develop caustics and often cannot be globally defined. A weaker form of the condition, which is still sufficient for the proof of the theorem, requires that an expanding congruence satisfying (36.22) can be continuously defined along a past-directed timelike or null geodesic. Members of the congruence may cross or focus away from that geodesic.

regions to be formed in an eternally inflating universe is unbounded, a typical observer is removed arbitrarily far from the beginning, and the memory of the initial state is completely erased. This implies that any predictions that quantum cosmology could make about the initial state of the universe cannot be tested observationally. All three proposals for the wave function of the universe are therefore in equally good agreement with observations, as well as a wide class of other wave functions – as long as they give a non-vanishing probability for eternal inflation to start [44].[4]

The only case that requires special consideration is when there are some constants of nature, α_j, which are constant within individual universes, but can take different values in different universes of the ensemble. (One example is the cosmological constant in models where it is determined by a four-form field.) In this case, the memory of the initial state is never erased completely, since the values of α_j are always equal to their initial values. One might hope that probabilistic predictions for the values of α_j could be derived from quantum cosmology and could, in principle, be tested observationally. Unfortunately, this prospect does not look very promising either.

Quantum cosmology can give us the probability distribution $P_{nucl}(\alpha)$ for a universe to nucleate with given values of α_j. In other words, this is the probability for a universe arbitrarily picked in the ensemble to have this set of values. To get the probability of observing these values, it should be multiplied by the average number of independent observers, $N(\alpha)$, that will evolve in such a universe [46],

$$P_{obs}(\alpha) \propto P_{nucl}(\alpha)N(\alpha). \tag{36.23}$$

The number of observers in each eternally inflating universe grows exponentially with time,

$$N(\alpha; t) = B(\alpha) \exp[\chi(\alpha)t]. \tag{36.24}$$

The prefactor $B(\alpha)$ depends on the details of the biochemical processes, and at present we have no idea how to calculate it. But the rate of growth χ is determined by the growth of thermalized volume and can be found as an eigenvalue of the Fokker–Planck operator, as discussed in [34, 44]. It is independent of biology, but generally depends on α_j. This suggests that the most probable values of α_j should be the ones maximizing the expansion rate $\chi(\alpha)$. As time goes on, the number of observers in universes with this preferred set of α_j gets larger than the competition by an arbitrarily

---

[4] There is, arguably, a much wider class of wave functions which describe highly excited states of the fields, but these will generally exhibit no quasi-classical behaviour and will not, therefore, allow for the existence of observers [45].

large factor. In the limit $t \to \infty$, this set has a 100% probability, while the probability of any other values is zero,

$$P_{obs}(\alpha) \propto \delta(\alpha - \alpha_*), \qquad (36.25)$$

where $\chi(\alpha_*) = \max$. We thus see that the probability of observing the constants α_j is determined entirely by the physics of eternal inflation and is independent of the nucleation probability $P_{nucl}(\alpha)$ – as long as $P_{nucl}(\alpha_*) \neq 0$.

The situation I have just described is somewhat clouded by the problem of gauge-dependence. The problem is that the expansion rate $\chi(\alpha)$ and the values of α_j maximizing this rate depend on one's choice of the time coordinate t [44]. Time in General Relativity is an arbitrary label, and this gauge dependence casts doubt on the meaningfulness of the probability (36.25). We now have some proposals on how this problem can be resolved in a single eternally inflating universe [47, 48], but comparing the numbers of observers in disconnected eternally inflating universes still remains a challenge.

I can think of two possible responses to this situation. (i) There may be some preferred, on physical grounds, choice of the time variable t, which should be used in this case for the calculation of probabilities. For example, one could choose the proper time along the worldlines of comoving observers. (ii) One can take the point of view that no meaningful definition of probabilities is possible for observations in disconnected, eternally inflating universes. While this issue requires further investigation, the important point for us here is that, in either case, an observational test of quantum cosmology does not seem possible.

Thus, the conclusion is that, sadly, quantum cosmology is not likely to become an observational science. However, without quantum cosmology our picture of the universe is incomplete. It raises very intriguing questions of principle and will, no doubt, inspire future research. I wish that Stephen continues to lead and challenge us in this adventure.

References

[1] DeWitt, B. S. (1967), 'Quantum theory of gravity. I. The canonical theory', *Phys. Rev.* **160**, 1113.

[2] Misner, C. W. (1972), 'Minisuperspace', in *Magic without Magic* (Freeman, San Francisco).

[3] Grishchuk, L. P. and Zeldovich, Ya. B. (1982), 'Complete cosmological theories', in *Quantum Structure of Space and Time*, eds M. Duff and C. Isham (Cambridge University Press, Cambridge).

[4] Vilenkin, A. (1982), 'Creation of universes from nothing', *Phys. Lett.* **B117**, 25.

[5] Hartle, J. B. and Hawking, S. W. (1983), 'Wave function of the universe', *Phys. Rev.* **D28**, 2960.

[6] Linde, A. D. (1984), 'Quantum creation of the inflationary universe', *Lett. Nuovo Cimento* **39**, 401.

[7] Rubakov, V. A. (1984), 'Quantum mechanics in the tunnelling universe', *Phys. Lett.* **148B**, 280.

[8] Vilenkin, A. (1984), 'Quantum creation of universes', *Phys. Rev.* **D30**, 509.

[9] Zeldovich, Ya. B. and Starobinsky, A. A. (1984), 'Quantum creation of a universe in an nontrivial topology', *Sov. Astron. Lett.* **10**, 135.

[10] Hawking, S. W. (1986), 'Quantum cosmology', in *300 Years of Gravitation*, eds S. W. Hawking and W. Israel (Cambridge University Press, Cambridge).

[11] Vilenkin, A. (1986), 'Boundary conditions in quantum cosmology', *Phys. Rev.* **D33**, 3560.

[12] Vilenkin, A. (1994), 'Approaches to quantum cosmology', *Phys. Rev.* **50**, 2581.

[13] Kontoleon, N. and Wiltshire, D. L. (1999), 'Operator ordering and consistency of the wave function of the universe', *Phys. Rev.* **D59**, 063513.

[14] Rubakov, V. A. (1999), 'Quantum cosmology', [gr-qc/9910025].

[15] Vachaspati, T. and Vilenkin, A. (1988), 'On the uniqueness of the tunnelling wave function of the universe', *Phys. Rev.* **D37**, 898.

[16] Ambjorn, J., Jurkiewicz, J. and Loll, R. (2001), 'Dynamically triangulating Lorentzian quantum gravity', *Nucl. Phys.* **B610**, 347.

[17] Halliwell, J. J. and Hartle, J. B. (1990), 'Integration contours for the no boundary wave function of the universe', *Phys. Rev.* **D41**, 1815.

[18] Davidson, A., Karasik, D. and Lederer, Y. (1999), 'Wave function of a brane-like universe', *Class. Quant. Grav.* **16**, 1349.

[19] Bucher, M. (2001), 'A braneworld universe from colliding bubbles', [hep-th/0107148].

[20] Dvali, G., Gabadadze, G. and Porrati, M. (2000), '4D gravity on a brane in 5D Minkowski space', *Phys. Lett.* **B484**, 112.

[21] Cordero, R. and Vilenkin, A. (2001), 'Stealth branes', *Phys. Rev.* **D65**, 083519.

[22] Vilenkin, A. (1998), 'Wave function discord', *Phys. Rev.* **D58**, 067301.

[23] Vilenkin, A. (1989), 'Interpretation of the wave function of the universe', *Phys. Rev.* **D39**, 1116.

[24] Lapchinsky, V. and Rubakov, V. A. (1979), 'Canonical quantization of gravity and quantum field theory in curved space-time', *Acta Phys. Polon.* **B10**, 1041.

[25] Halliwell, J. J. and Hawking, S. W. (1995), 'The origin of structure in the universe', *Phys. Rev.* **D31**, 1777.

[26] Banks, T. (1985), 'TCP, quantum gravity, the cosmological constant and all that ...' *Nucl. Phys.* **B249**, 332.

[27] Vilenkin, A. (1988), 'Quantum cosmology and the initial state of the universe', *Phys. Rev.* **D37**, 888.

[28] Hawking, S. W. and Page, D. N. (1986), 'Operator ordering and the flatness of the universe', *Nucl. Phys.* **B264**, 185.

[29] Grishchuk, L. P. and Rozhansky, L. V. (1988), 'On the beginning and the end of classical evolution in quantum cosmology', *Phys. Lett.* **B208**, 369.

[30] Barvinsky, A. O. and Kamenshchik, A. Y. and Mishakov, I. V. (1997), 'Quantum origin of the early inflationary universe', *Phys. Lett.* **B332**, 270.

[31] Page, D. N. (1997), 'Space for both no-boundary and tunnelling quantum states of the universe', *Phys. Rev.* **D56**, 2065.

[32] Vilenkin, A. (1983), 'Birth of inflationary universes', *Phys. Rev.* **D27**, 2848.

[33] Linde, A. D. (1986), 'Eternally existing selfreproducing chaotic inflationary universe', *Phys. Lett.* **B175**, 395.

[34] Starobinsky, A. A. (1986), 'Stochastic de Sitter (inflationary) stage in the early universe', in *Field Theory, Quantum Gravity, and Strings*, eds H. J. de Vega and N. Sanchez, Lecture Notes in Physics Vol. 246 (Springer, Heidelberg).

[35] Aryal, M. and Vilenkin, A. (1987), 'Fractal dimension of inflationary universe', *Phys. Lett.* **B199**, 351.

[36] Winitzki, S. (2002), 'The eternal fractal in the universe', *Phys. Rev.* **D65**, 083506.

[37] Steinhardt, P. J. (1983), 'Natural inflation', in *The Very Early Universe*, eds G. W. Gibbons and S. W. Hawking (Cambridge University Press, Cambridge).

[38] Linde, A. D. (1983), 'The new inflationary universe scenario, in *The Very Early Universe*', eds G. W. Gibbons and S. W. Hawking (Cambridge University Press, Cambridge).

[39] Borde, A. and Vilenkin, A. (1994), 'Eternal inflation and the initial singularity', *Phys. Rev. Lett.* **72**, 3305; (1996), 'Singularities in inflationary cosmology: a review', *Int. J. Mod. Phys.* **D5**, 813.

[40] Borde, A. and Vilenkin, A. (1997), 'Violation of the weak energy condition in inflating spacetimes', *Phys. Rev.* **D56**, 717.

[41] Winitzki, S. (2001), 'Null energy condition violations in eternal inflation', [gr-qc/0111109].

[42] Borde, A., Guth, A. H. and Vilenkin, A. (2001), 'Inflation is past-incomplete', [gr-qc/0110012].

[43] Steinhardt, P. J. and Turok, N. (2001), 'A cyclic model of the universe', [hep-th/0111030].

[44] Linde, A. D., Linde D. A. and Mezhlumian, A. (1994), 'From the big bang to the theory of a stationary universe', *Phys. Rev.* **D49**, 1783.

[45] Hartle, J. B. (1994), 'Quasiclassical domains in a quantum universe', [gr-qc/9404017]; (1997), 'Sources of predictability, in *Complexity*', **3**, 22.

[46] Vilenkin, A. (1995), 'Predictions from quantum cosmology', *Phys. Rev. Lett.* **74**, 846.

[47] Vilenkin, A. (1998), 'Unambiguous probabilities in an eternally inflating universe', *Phys. Rev. Lett.* **81**, 5501.

[48] Garriga, J. and Vilenkin, A. (2001), 'A prescription for probabilities in eternal inflation', *Phys. Rev.* **D64**, 023507.

37

Probability in the deterministic theory known as quantum mechanics

Bryce DeWitt

Center for Relativity, The University of Texas at Austin

37.1 Quantum measurement

When a macroscopic apparatus makes a measurement of an observable s of a quantum system it needs to be coupled to the quantum system. The coupling produces a change in the combined state vector $|\Psi\rangle$ of system and apparatus given by a unitary transformation of the form

$$|\Psi\rangle \longrightarrow e^{ig\mathcal{X}} |\Psi\rangle \qquad (37.1)$$

where $\mathcal{X}$ is an Hermitian operator that depends on the observables of both system and apparatus and g is an adjustable constant that controls the strength of the coupling.

The result of the measurement is typically stored in an apparatus observable $\mathbf{P}$. This is accomplished by choosing the operator $\mathcal{X}$ to satisfy the commutation relations

$$[\mathcal{X}, \mathbf{P}] = i\mathbf{s}, \qquad [\mathcal{X}, \mathbf{s}] = 0 \qquad (\hbar = 1), \qquad (37.2)$$

(for example by choosing $\mathcal{X} = \mathbf{Xs}$ where $\mathbf{X}$ is any observable conjugate to $\mathbf{P}$). The coupling then produces the following change in $\mathbf{P}$:

$$\mathbf{P} \longrightarrow e^{-ig\mathcal{X}} \mathbf{P} e^{ig\mathcal{X}} = \mathbf{P} + g\mathbf{s}. \qquad (37.3)$$

Moreover, the coupling defines a preferred basis in the state vector space, namely the simultaneous eigenvectors of $\mathbf{s}$ and $\mathbf{P}$:

$$|s, P\rangle = |s\rangle |P\rangle, \qquad \mathbf{s}|s\rangle = s|s\rangle, \qquad \mathbf{P}|P\rangle = P|P\rangle. \qquad (37.4)$$

The measurement begins with the system and apparatus in uncorrelated states described by vectors $|\psi\rangle$ and $|\Phi\rangle$:

$$|\Psi\rangle = |\psi\rangle|\Phi\rangle = \sum_s \int |s\rangle|P\rangle c_s \Phi(P) dP, \qquad (37.5)$$

$$c_s = \langle s | \psi \rangle, \qquad \Phi(P) = \langle P | \Phi \rangle. \tag{37.6}$$

(Here we are, for simplicity, assuming the spectrum of $\mathbf{s}$ to be discrete and the spectrum of $\mathbf{P}$ to be continuous.) The unitary transformation (37.1) produced by the coupling between system and apparatus induces a correlation between the two:

$$|\Psi\rangle \longrightarrow e^{ig\mathbf{X}} \, |\Psi\rangle = \sum_s \int |s\rangle |P + gs\rangle c_s \Phi(P) dP. \tag{37.7}$$

Expression (37.7) can be rewritten in the form

$$e^{ig\mathbf{X}} \, |\Psi\rangle = \sum_s c_s |s\rangle |\Phi[s]\rangle \tag{37.8}$$

where

$$|\Phi[s]\rangle = \int |P + gs\rangle \Phi(P) dP \tag{37.9}$$

$|\Phi[s]\rangle$ is known as a *relative state*. Equation (37.8) shows that, as a result of the measurement coupling, the system-apparatus state becomes a state in which, for each possible outcome of the measurement, i.e., for each possible eigenvalue s, the apparatus 'goes into' a corresponding relative state, in which the apparatus 'observes' that eigenvalue. The measurement is said to be *good* if the variance of P in the state $|\Phi\rangle$ satisfies

$$\triangle P << g \triangle s \tag{37.10}$$

where $\triangle s$ is the minimal spacing between those eigenvalues of $\mathbf{s}$ that are contained in the support of the function c_s. When the measurement is good the relative states are orthogonal to one another:

$$\langle \Phi[s] | \Phi[s'] \rangle = \delta_{ss'} . \tag{37.11}$$

37.2 Reality

If the formalism of quantum mechanics is regarded as providing a faithful representation of reality then quantum mechanics becomes a completely deterministic theory and all the possible measurement outcomes appearing in the superposition (37.8) must be regarded as *there*. All must be regarded as being part of a globally deterministic reality. Each outcome must be regarded as corresponding to a different 'world', and by further elaborating the quantum theory of measurement one may easily show that these worlds are unaware of one another.

Up to this point the quantum formalism implies the following:

1. An apparatus that measures an observable never records anything but an eigenvalue of the operator that represents the observable, at least if the measurement is good.

2. The operator represents not the value of the observable, but rather *all* the values that the observable can assume under various conditions, the values themselves being the eigenvalues.

3. The dynamical variables of a system, being operators, do not represent the system other than generically. That is, they represent not the system as it really is, but rather all the situations in which the system might find itself.

4. Which situation a system is actually in is specified by the state vector. Reality is therefore described jointly by the dynamical variables and the state vector. This reality is not the reality we customarily think of, but is a reality composed of many worlds.

This list is unfortunately not yet sufficient to tell us how to apply the formalism to practical problems. The symbols that describe a given system, namely the state vector and the dynamical variables, describe not only the system as it is observed in one of the many worlds comprising reality, but also the system as it is seen in all the other worlds. We, who inhabit only one of these worlds, have no symbols to describe our world alone. Because we ordinarily have no access to the other worlds we are unable to make rigorous predictions about reality as we observe it. Although reality as a whole is completely deterministic, our own little corner of it suffers from indeterminism. The interpretation of the quantum formalism is complete only when we show that this indeterminism is nevertheless governed by rigorous statistical laws.

37.3 Signalling by permutations

Suppose, in the superposition (37.8), that a particular eigenvalue of s fails to appear, i.e., that $c_s = 0$ for that eigenvalue. Then in none of the many worlds represented by the superposition does the apparatus observe the value in question. It is natural to say that the apparatus will not observe that value, or that the value has *zero likelihood* of being observed. But what significance must one ascribe to the nonvanishing coefficients?

David Deutsch[1] has given the best answer to this question, an answer that is free from a priori statistical notions and is based solely on factual

---

[1] D. Deutsch, Oxford preprint, 1989 (unpublished). See also *Proc. Roy. Soc.* (*London*) **A455**, 3129 (1999).

physical properties of the system. Denote by $\mathcal{S}$ the set of eigenvalues s. Let $\mathcal{F}$ be a finite subset of $\mathcal{S}$ contained in the support of the function $c : \mathcal{S} \to \mathbf{C}$. That is

$$s \epsilon \mathcal{F} \quad \Rightarrow \quad c_s \neq 0. \tag{37.12}$$

Denote by $\mathcal{P}$ the set of all one-to-one maps

$$\Pi : \mathcal{S} \to \mathcal{S} \quad \text{such that} \quad \Pi(s) = s \text{ if } s \notin \mathcal{F}. \tag{37.13}$$

$\mathcal{P}$ is a group, its elements Π being permutations of the eigenvalues in $\mathcal{F}$. Let $\mathcal{A}$ be the operator algebra of the system S and let $\mathbf{U} : \mathcal{P} \to \mathcal{A}$ be a mapping that satisfies

$$\mathbf{U}(\Pi_1)\mathbf{U}(\Pi_2) = \mathbf{U}(\Pi_1 \circ \Pi_2), \tag{37.14}$$

$$\mathbf{U}(\Pi)|s\rangle = |\Pi(s)\rangle, \tag{37.15}$$

for all $\Pi_1, \Pi_2, \Pi \epsilon \mathcal{P}$ and all $s \epsilon \mathcal{S}$. It is easy to see that $\mathbf{U}(\Pi)$ is a unitary operator for each Π. Moreover, since $\mathbf{U}(\Pi)\mathbf{U}(\Pi^{-1}) = \mathbf{U}(Id) = 1$, it follows that

$$\mathbf{U}(\Pi^{-1}) = \mathbf{U}(\Pi)^*, \tag{37.16}$$

$$\mathbf{U}(\Pi)^*|s\rangle = |\Pi^{-1}(s)\rangle. \tag{37.17}$$

Let $\mathcal{T}$ be an external agent that can act on the system S in such a way that the state vector, whatever it is, undergoes the change

$$|\psi\rangle \longrightarrow \mathbf{U}(\Pi)|\psi\rangle, \tag{37.18}$$

and suppose $\mathcal{T}$ can choose to do this for any Π in $\mathcal{P}$. We do not inquire here about the practical feasibility of producing such an agent. We merely remark, as is well known, that dynamical changes in quantum systems correspond to the unfolding-in-time of unitary transformations. The problem is therefore one of finding the dynamical agent that will produce the unitary transformation (37.18).

Let $\mathcal{R}$ be a second agent that can make arbitrary measurements on the system S, after $\mathcal{T}$ has acted on it and permuted the eigenvectors of $\mathbf{s}$. One may conveniently speak of $\mathcal{T}$ as a *transmitter* and $\mathcal{R}$ as a *receiver*. Thus, if $\mathcal{R}$ knows that the state vector of S, before $\mathcal{T}$ acts on it, is $|\psi\rangle$, and if $\mathcal{T}$ sends a *signal* to $\mathcal{R}$ by choosing a particular permutation in (37.18), then $\mathcal{R}$ may first of all try to determine whether anything other than a null signal has been sent by checking whether there has been a change in

$|\psi\rangle$. $\mathcal{R}$'s best strategy for checking whether a change has occurred is to measure the projection operator $|\psi\rangle\langle\psi|$. If $\mathcal{R}$ obtains the value 1 for this operator, he cannot tell whether $|\psi\rangle$ has been changed, but if he obtains the value 0 then he knows then he knows that it has.

37.4 Equal likelihood

Suppose $|\psi\rangle$ has the property that, no matter what permutation $\mathcal{T}$ chooses to perform, $\mathcal{R}$ cannot detect the change in $|\psi\rangle$ by any measurement whatever. That is, the permutations themselves are undetectable and hence leave the physics of the system unchanged. It is natural, under these circumstances, to say that if a measurement of $\mathbf{s}$ *were* to be made then all those outcomes s that lie in $\mathcal{F}$ are *equally likely*. Note that although this terminology is probabilistic the statement itself is purely factual, concerning the impossibility of using permutations to send signals, and has no probabilistic antecedents.

When all the outcomes in $\mathcal{F}$ are equally likely it is impossible for $\mathcal{R}$ to obtain the value 0 when he measures $|\psi\rangle\langle\psi|$. But this means that the projection operator is unchanged and hence that

$$\mathbf{U}(\Pi)|\psi\rangle = e^{i\chi(\Pi)}|\psi\rangle \quad \text{for all} \quad \Pi\epsilon\mathcal{P}. \tag{37.19}$$

for some $\chi : \mathcal{P} \to \mathbf{R}$. From (37.17) it follows that

$$\langle s|\psi\rangle = e^{-i\chi(\Pi)}\langle s|\mathbf{U}(\Pi)|\psi\rangle = e^{-i\chi(\Pi)}\langle\psi|\mathbf{U}(\Pi)^*|s\rangle^*$$

$$= e^{-i\chi(\Pi)}\langle\psi|\Pi^{-1}(s)\rangle^* = e^{-i\chi(\Pi)}\langle\Pi^{-1}(s)|\psi\rangle \tag{37.20}$$

and hence

$$|\langle s|\psi\rangle| = |\langle\Pi^{-1}(s)|\psi\rangle| \quad \text{for all} \quad \Pi\epsilon\mathcal{P}. \tag{37.21}$$

Conversely, if (37.21) holds then the eigenvectors of $\mathbf{s}$ can be altered by phase factors so that all the $\langle s|\psi\rangle$ with $s\epsilon\mathcal{F}$ are equal, and the operator

$$\mathbf{U}(\Pi) = \sum_s |\Pi(s)\rangle\langle s| \tag{37.22}$$

will satisfy (37.14), (37.15) and (37.19) with $\chi(\Pi) = 0$. This means that all the members of a finite subset $\mathcal{F}$ of eigenvalues of $\mathbf{s}$ are equally likely to be observed in a measurement if and only if $|\langle s|\psi\rangle|$ is constant over the subset.

Suppose $\mathcal{F}$ has n members and happens to coincide with the support of the function c. Then no eigenvalues will be observed other than those contained in $\mathcal{F}$, and it is natural to push the probabilistic terminology one step further by saying that each of the eigenvalues in $\mathcal{F}$ has *probability* $1/n$ of being observed. When this happens one has

$$1 = \langle\psi|\psi\rangle = \sum_{s'}\langle\psi|s'\rangle\langle s'|\psi\rangle = n|\langle s|\psi\rangle|^2, \quad s\epsilon\mathcal{F}, \tag{37.23}$$

so this probability can be expressed in the form

$$1/n = |\langle s|\psi\rangle|^2, \quad s\epsilon\mathcal{F}. \tag{37.24}$$

We stress again that although the terminology of probability theory is now being used, the words themselves have no probabilistic antecedents. They are defined neither in terms of an a priori metaphysics nor in terms of the mathematical properties of the state vector, but in terms of factual physical properties of the system in the state that the state vector represents. However, once the terminology of probability theory has been introduced there need be no hesitation in using it in exactly the same way as it is used in the standard probability calculus. That is, the probability calculus, in particular the calculus of *joint probabilities*, may be freely used to motivate further definitions.

37.5 The case of degeneracy

Up to this point we have been tacitly assuming that the eigenvalues s constitute a complete set of state-vector labels for the system S. It is more frequently the case that such eigenvalues are degenerate. The case of degeneracy actually presents no difficulty for the above arguments. One simply introduces the projection operators on the eigenvalues s:

$$\mathbf{P}_s = \sum_{\alpha}|s,\alpha\rangle\langle s,\alpha| \tag{37.25}$$

where α denotes the other labels needed to complete the state specification. The unitary operators $\mathbf{U}(\Pi)$ continue to permute the eigenvalues s (leaving the other labels alone), but this is now expressed by

$$\mathbf{U}(\Pi)\mathbf{P}_s\mathbf{U}(\Pi^{-1}) = \mathbf{P}_{\Pi(s)} \tag{37.26}$$

instead of by (37.15). Undetectability of the permutations is still expressed by (37.19), but this now implies

$$\langle\psi|\mathbf{P}_{\Pi(s)}|\psi\rangle = \langle\psi|\mathbf{P}_s|\psi\rangle, \tag{37.27}$$

and when $\mathcal{F}$ coincides with the support of c, (37.24) gets replaced by

$$\langle\psi|\mathbf{P}_s|\psi\rangle = \frac{1}{n}, \quad s\epsilon\mathcal{F}. \tag{37.28}$$

37.6 Unequal probabilities

When $|\langle s|\psi\rangle|^2$ is not constant over the support of the function c, the elucidation of its meaning requires a more elaborate, nonetheless firmly physically-based, argument. Introduce two auxiliary physical systems, Q and R, in addition to S, together with their state vectors $|\phi\rangle$ and $|\chi\rangle$. Let $\mathcal{A}$ be a subset of m distinct eigenvalues q of an observable $\mathbf{q}$ of Q and let $\mathcal{B}$ be a subset of $n-m$ distinct eigenvalues r of an observable $\mathbf{r}$ of R. Let the rs in $\mathcal{B}$ be all different from the qs in $\mathcal{A}$ so that the set $\mathcal{A}\cup\mathcal{B}$ has n distinct elements.

Suppose $|\phi\rangle$ and $|\chi\rangle$ are such that all the qs in $\mathcal{A}$ are equally likely and all the rs in $\mathcal{B}$ are equally likely. Suppose, furthermore, that $\langle q|\phi\rangle = 0$ when $q \notin \mathcal{A}$ and $\langle r|\chi\rangle = 0$ when $r \notin \mathcal{B}$. Then each q in $\mathcal{A}$ has probability $1/m$ of being observed and each r in $\mathcal{B}$ has probability $1/(n-m)$ of being observed. In mathematical language

$$|\langle q|\phi\rangle|^2 = 1/m, \qquad q\epsilon\mathcal{A}, \qquad\qquad (37.29)$$

$$|\langle r|\chi\rangle|^2 = 1(n-m), \qquad r\epsilon\mathcal{B}, \qquad\qquad (37.30)$$

In the combined state-vector space of the systems Q, R and S, consider the operator

$$\mathbf{u} = \mathbf{q}\otimes 1\otimes |s\rangle\langle s| + 1\otimes\mathbf{r}\otimes(1-|s\rangle\langle s|). \qquad (37.31)$$

This operator, which is an observable of the combined system, can be measured as follows. First measure $\mathbf{s}$. If s is obtained then measure $\mathbf{q}$. If s is not obtained measure $\mathbf{r}$ instead. The final outcome in either case is the measured value of $\mathbf{u}$. Note that $\mathbf{u}$ has n distinct eigenvalues lying in the set $\mathcal{A}\cup\mathcal{B}$, and these are the only eigenvalues that can turn up when the state vector of the combined system is

$$|\Psi\rangle = |\phi\rangle|\chi\rangle|\psi\rangle. \qquad\qquad (37.32)$$

Now suppose that the state of S (state vector $|\psi\rangle$) is such that, when $\mathbf{u}$ is measured, all the n outcomes u lying in $\mathcal{A}\cup\mathcal{B}$ are equally likely, as defined by the permutation-signaling prescription. Then each u in $\mathcal{A}\cup\mathcal{B}$ has probability $1/n$ of being observed. Given the prescription for measuring $\mathbf{u}$, it follows from the calculus of joint probabilities that

$$\frac{1}{n} = p\times\frac{1}{m} \quad\text{or}\quad (1-p)\frac{1}{n-m} \qquad (37.33)$$

where p is *the probability that s will be observed when* $\mathbf{s}$ *is measured*. Note that p is defined *via* the calculus of joint probabilities and that both possibilities in (37.33) lead to

$$p = \frac{m}{n}. \tag{37.34}$$

Although the derivation of this result refers to hypothetical measurements made on the hypothetical auxiliary systems Q and R, it nevertheless refers only to factual properties of S.

To relate p to $|\langle s|\psi\rangle|^2$, consider the projection operator on the eigenvalue u of $\mathbf{u}$:

$$\mathbf{P}_u = \sum_q \delta_{uq}|q\rangle\langle q| \otimes 1 \otimes |s\rangle\langle s| + \sum_r \delta_{ur}1 \otimes |r\rangle\langle r| \otimes (1 - |s\rangle\langle s|). \tag{37.35}$$

If $u \epsilon \mathcal{A} \cup \mathcal{B}$ then

$$\frac{1}{n} = \langle\Psi|\mathbf{P}_u|\Psi\rangle$$

$$= \sum_{q\epsilon\mathcal{A}} \delta_{uq}|\langle q|\phi\rangle|^2|\langle s|\psi\rangle|^2 + \sum_{r\epsilon\mathcal{B}} \delta_{ur}|\langle r|\chi\rangle|^2(1 - |\langle s|\psi\rangle|^2)$$

$$= \frac{1}{m}|\langle s|\psi\rangle|^2 \quad \text{or} \quad \frac{1}{n-m}(1 - |\langle s|\psi\rangle|^2), \tag{37.36}$$

in which (37.29) and (37.30) are used in passing to the last line. Comparing (37.36) with (37.33), one sees immediately that

$$p = |\langle s|\psi\rangle|^2 = |c_s|^2. \tag{37.37}$$

Note that this result does not require the support of the function c to be a finite subset of $\mathcal{S}$.

The above analysis gives a factual meaning to all rational probabilities. One can extend it to irrational probabilities by introducing the notion 'at least as likely' and making a kind of Dedekind cut between those states in which the eigenvalue s is at least as likely to be observed as in the given state and those in which it is not. It is essential that one prescribe a specific class of *physical* processes for carrying out the state comparison. Although this can be done, we shall not do it here. The Dedekind-cut method of defining irrational probabilities is, at best, unnecessarily pedantic and, at worst, unrealistic and hence unphysical, for the following reasons. First, probabilities themselves are physically measurable only when viewed as frequencies, and physically measured numbers are always rational. Secondly, the set of comparison states in the Dedekind cut definition is infinite in number, so the definition is a non-operational one. It cannot be checked by any physical process.

38

The interpretation of quantum cosmology and the problem of time

Jonathan Halliwell

Imperial College, London

38.1 Introduction

It is a truly great pleasure to be part of Stephen Hawking's 60th birthday celebrations. It is now almost twenty years since I commenced my PhD studies with Stephen, and I recall that exciting time very fondly. Numerous researchers were just beginning to address the conceptual and technical difficulties of quantum cosmology, and the confusion and controversy at that time led to some very lively debates in which Stephen played a very central role. The atmosphere of this conference has reminded me very pleasantly of those early days.

The work described here concerns some generally interesting issues in quantum cosmology. This is the area I started working on with Stephen, and its intriguing problems and difficulties have been the inspiration for much else I have pursued in physics. Quantum cosmology was born in the 1960s with the work of Bryce DeWitt, Charles Misner, John Wheeler and others [5, 27, 35], but it really took off in the early 1980s with Hartle and Hawking's seminal paper, *The Wave Function of the Universe* [18]. This development was very pertinent since the appearance of the inflationary universe scenario at about that time underscored the urgency to acquire an understanding of cosmological initial conditions. The new ingredients of quantum cosmology, compared with its older 1960s version, were two-fold. First, there was the use of Euclidean path integral methods which had grown out of their very successful application to black hole physics. Secondly, and perhaps more importantly, there was the Hartle–Hawking 'no-boundary' proposal. This gave, perhaps for the first time, a genuinely quantum gravitational proposal which implied cosmological initial conditions. In this proposal, wave functions satisfying the

Wheeler–DeWitt equation

$$\mathcal{H}\Psi[h_{ij}] = 0 \tag{38.1}$$

are given by a sum over histories expression of the form

$$\Psi[h_{ij}] = \int_C \mathcal{D}g_{\mu\nu} \exp\left(-I[g_{\mu\nu}]\right) \tag{38.2}$$

where the sum is over closed four-geometries whose only boundary is the three-surface on which the three-metric h_{ij} is specified. (Note also that the functional integral is taken to be over a *complex* contour C [11]).

There were two questions of particular interest in these early days. First, what sort of picture can quantum gravity give about the initial singularity? And secondly, what initial conditions does the theory imply for classical cosmological solutions? In simple, somewhat heuristic models, the answer to the first question is that the initial singularity is replaced by some kind of quantum tunnelling situation. That is, the classical singularity can (at least in some models) become a classically forbidden region. The second question can be answered by showing how quantum cosmology produces, in a quasiclassical limit, an approximate probability distribution on the space of classical cosmological solutions.

The most pressing questions in those days were to do with cosmological issues. Does the no-boundary proposal predict initial conditions which produce inflationary solutions and subsequent structure formation [13, 19]? The interpretation associated with these models was heuristic [8, 10, 19, 24]. For example, one considered the Klein–Gordon flux

$$J = i\left(\Psi^*\nabla\Psi - \Psi\nabla\Psi^*\right) \tag{38.3}$$

associated with the wave functions of the WKB type,

$$\Psi = Ce^{iS}. \tag{38.4}$$

These heuristic methods appeared to be adequate for the questions considered at the time.

Now, however, in 2002, far more is known about the foundations and interpretation of quantum theory. Moreover, there has also been a considerable amount of activity in the experimental tests of foundational ideas. As a result of this, the foundations of quantum theory is now more in the mainstream of physics, when previously it was regarded as the domain of the philosophers. Perhaps as a result of this, there has been a secondary wave of much slower activity in quantum cosmology that aims to look more deeply into a whole variety of mathematical and conceptual issues related to the application of quantum theory to the universe as a whole. In particular, it is now reasonable to ask, how can the heuristic ideas used earlier be derived or reconciled with a properly defined interpretational structure for quantum theory of models described by a Wheeler–DeWitt equation? For example, in standard quantum theory, probabilities generally have the form

$$\mathrm{Tr}\,(P\rho) \tag{38.5}$$

where ρ is the density operator, P is a projection operator and the trace is over a complete set of states (and so assumes a Hilbert space of states with a suitably defined inner product). How can the predictions of quantum cosmology be reconciled with a formula of this type?

Related to these issues is the notorious problem of time [3, 21, 24]. The Wheeler–DeWitt equation, in simple minisuperspace models, has the form,

$$H\Psi = \left(-\nabla^2 + U\right)\Psi = 0 \tag{38.6}$$

where ∇^2 is a d'Alembertian type operator. The equation is of the form of a Klein–Gordon equation in a general curved spacetime background with a spacetime dependent mass term. There is no single variable to play the role of time, nor is there the possibility of splitting the solutions into positive and negative frequency. In the usual Klein–Gordon equation one then resorts to second quantization, but the Wheeler–DeWitt equation is in some sense already the second quantized theory, so one has to face the issue of the lack of a time coordinate more squarely.

In this contribution to the conference, I will describe how the decoherent histories approach may be used to provide a quantization of simple mini-superspace models, perhaps avoiding some of the serious difficulties outlined above, and agreeing with the heuristic methods used earlier on.

I begin by making two simple observations about the Wheeler–DeWitt equation that are generally relevant to the discussion. The first is that, at least classically speaking, the constraint equation,

$$H = f^{ab}p_a p_b + V = 0 \tag{38.7}$$

is related to reparameterization invariance. (This is the leftover of four-dimensional diffeomorphism invariance after the restriction to minisuper-space.) In keeping with Dirac's general ideas about quantizing constrained systems, we therefore look for *observables* – quantities which commute with the constraint. There has been a certain amount of debate about this issue in the context of general relativity, but this will not affect us here [6, 33].

Second, as observed by Barbour [1, 2], by analogy with Mott's 1929 calculation of tracks in a cloud chamber [29], there is a natural association between the Wheeler–DeWitt equation and the emergence of classical trajectories. Mott asked why the outgoing spherical wave associated with alpha decay produced a straight line track in a cloud chamber. By considering the Hamiltonian of the decaying atom interacting with ionizing particles in the cloud chamber he showed that the ionized particles with high probability lie along a straight line. Interestingly, and as Barbour observed, Mott actually solved the time-independent Schrödinger equation,

$$H\Psi = E\Psi \tag{38.8}$$

rather than the time-dependent one, to obtain the tracks. This is therefore an interesting analogy for the Wheeler–DeWitt equation where, in the quasi-classical limit one expects to obtain emergent classical trajectories. (In fact, a model of the Wheeler–DeWitt equation including explicit detectors, and exhibiting these features has been constructed [9]. Some related approaches to timeless models are [28, 31, 32].)

With these preliminaries out of the way, we now focus on the following simple question: Suppose we have an n dimensional configuration space with coordinates $\mathbf{x} = (x_1, x_2, \cdots x_n)$, and suppose the wave function of the system is in an eigenstate of the Hamiltonian,

$$H\Psi(x_1, x_2, \cdots x_n) = E\Psi(x_1, x_2, \cdots x_n). \tag{38.9}$$

What is the probability of finding the system in a series of regions of configuration space $\Delta_1, \Delta_2, \cdots \Delta_N$ *without reference to time?*

This question will form the main focus of the rest of this paper. We first consider the classical case, and then the decoherent histories analysis.

38.2 The classical case

We begin by considering the classical case which contains almost all the key features of the problem. (We follow the treatment of [15] quite closely.) For simplicity we will concentrate on the case of a single region of configuration space Δ.

We will consider a classical system described by a $2n$-dimensional phase space, with coordinates and momenta $(\mathbf{x}, \mathbf{p}) = (x_k, p_k)$, and Hamiltonian

$$H = \frac{\mathbf{p}^2}{2M} + V(\mathbf{x}). \tag{38.10}$$

More generally, we are interested in a system for which the kinetic part of the Hamiltonian has the form $g^{kj}(\mathbf{x})p_k p_j$, where $g^{kj}(\mathbf{x})$ is an inverse metric of hyperbolic signature. Most mini-superspace models in quantum cosmology have a Hamiltonian of this form. However, the focus of this paper is the timelessness of the system, and the form of the configuration space metric turns out to be unimportant. So for simplicity, we will concentrate on the form (38.10).

We assume that there is a classical phase space distribution function $w(\mathbf{p}, \mathbf{x})$, which is normalized according to

$$\int d^n p \, d^n x \, w(\mathbf{p}, \mathbf{x}) = 1 \tag{38.11}$$

and obeys the evolution equation

$$\frac{\partial w}{\partial t} = \sum_k \left(-\frac{p_k}{M} \frac{\partial w}{\partial x_k} + \frac{\partial V}{\partial x_k} \frac{\partial w}{\partial p_k} \right) = \{H, w\} \tag{38.12}$$

where $\{ \ , \ \}$ denotes the Poisson bracket. The interesting case is that in which w is the classical analogue of an energy eigenstate, in which case $\partial w / \partial t = 0$, so the evolution equation is simply

$$\{H, w\} = 0. \tag{38.13}$$

It follows that

$$w(\mathbf{p}^{cl}(t), \mathbf{x}^{cl}(t)) = w(\mathbf{p}(0), \mathbf{x}(0)) \tag{38.14}$$

where $\mathbf{p}^{cl}(t), \mathbf{x}^{cl}(t)$ are the classical solutions with initial data $\mathbf{p}(0), \mathbf{x}(0)$, so w is constant along the classical orbits. (The normalization of w then becomes an issue if the classical orbits are infinite, but we will return to this in the quantum case discussed below.)

Given a set of classical solutions $(\mathbf{p}^{cl}(t), \mathbf{x}^{cl}(t))$, and a phase space distribution function w, we are interested in the probability that a classical solution will pass through a region Δ of configuration space. We construct this as follows. First of all we introduce the characteristic function of the region Δ,

$$f_\Delta(\mathbf{x}) = \begin{cases} 1, & \text{if } \mathbf{x} \in \Delta; \\ 0 & \text{otherwise.} \end{cases} \tag{38.15}$$

To see whether the classical trajectory $\mathbf{x}^{cl}(t)$ intersects this region, consider the phase space function

$$A(\mathbf{x}, \mathbf{p}_0, \mathbf{x}_0) = \int_{-\infty}^{\infty} dt \, \delta^{(n)}(\mathbf{x} - \mathbf{x}^{cl}(t)). \tag{38.16}$$

(In the case of periodic classical orbits, the range of t is taken to be equal to the period.) This function is positive for points $\mathbf{x}$ on the classical trajectory labelled by $\mathbf{p}_0, \mathbf{x}_0$ and zero otherwise. Hence intersection of the classical trajectory with the region Δ means,

$$\int d^n \mathbf{x} \, f_\Delta(\mathbf{x}) \int_{-\infty}^{\infty} dt \, \delta^{(n)}(\mathbf{x} - \mathbf{x}^{cl}(t)) > 0. \tag{38.17}$$

Or equivalently, that

$$\int_{-\infty}^{\infty} dt \; f_\Delta(\mathbf{x}^{cl}(t)) > 0. \tag{38.18}$$

This quantity is essentially the amount of parameter time the trajectory spends in the region Δ. We may now write down the probability for a classical trajectory entering the region Δ. It is

$$p_\Delta = \int d^n p_0 d^n x_0 \; w(\mathbf{p}_0, \mathbf{x}_0) \; \theta \left(\int_{-\infty}^{\infty} dt \; f_\Delta(\mathbf{x}^{cl}(t)) - \epsilon \right). \tag{38.19}$$

In this construction, ϵ is a small positive number that is eventually sent to zero, and is included to avoid possible ambiguities in the θ-function at zero argument. The θ-function ensures that the phase space integral is over all initial data whose corresponding classical trajectories spend a time greater than ϵ in the region Δ.

The classical solution $\mathbf{x}^{cl}(t)$ depends on some fiducial initial coordinates and momenta, $\mathbf{x}_0$ and $\mathbf{p}_0$, say. In the case of a free particle, for example,

$$\mathbf{x}^{cl}(t) = \mathbf{x}_0 + \frac{\mathbf{p}_0 t}{M}. \tag{38.20}$$

The construction is independent of the choice of fiducial initial points. If we shift $\mathbf{x}_0$, $\mathbf{p}_0$ along the classical trajectories, the measure, phase space distribution fun ction w and the θ-function are all invariant. Hence the integral over $\mathbf{x}_0$, $\mathbf{p}_0$ is effectively a sum over classical trajectories. The shift along the classical trajectories may also be thought of as a reparameterization, and the quantity (38.19) is in fact a reparameterization-invariant expression of the notion of a classical trajectory. This means that the probability (38.19) has the form of a phase space overlap of the 'state' with a reparameterization-invariant operator.

It is useful also to write this result in a different form, which will be more relevant to the results we get in the quantum theory case. In the quantum theory, we generally deal with propagation between fixed points in configuration space, rather than with phase space points. Therefore, in the free particle case, consider the change of variables from $\mathbf{x}_0, \mathbf{p}_0$ to $\mathbf{x}_0, \mathbf{x}_f$, where

$$\mathbf{x}_f = \mathbf{x}_0 + \frac{\mathbf{p}_0}{M} \tau. \tag{38.21}$$

Hence $\mathbf{x}_f$ is the position after evolution for starting from $\mathbf{x}_0$ for parameter time τ. The probability then becomes

$$p_\Delta = \frac{M}{\tau} \int d^n x_f d^n x_0 \; w(\mathbf{p}_0, \mathbf{x}_0) \; \theta \left(\int_{-\infty}^{\infty} dt \; f_\Delta(\mathbf{x}_0^f(t)) - \epsilon \right), \tag{38.22}$$

where $\mathbf{p}_0 = M(\mathbf{x}_f - \mathbf{x}_0)/\tau$ and

$$\mathbf{x}_0^f(t) = \mathbf{x}_0 + \frac{(\mathbf{x}_f - \mathbf{x}_0)}{\tau}t. \qquad (38.23)$$

The parameter τ may in fact be scaled out of the whole expression, hence the probability is independent of it.

The result now has the form of an integral over 'initial' and 'final' points, analogous to similar results in quantum theory. The result is again essentially a sum over classical trajectories with the trajectories now labelled by any pair of points $\mathbf{x}_0$, $\mathbf{x}_f$ along the trajectories, and is invariant under shifting $\mathbf{x}_0$ or $\mathbf{x}_f$ along those trajectories. Naively, one might have thought that the restriction to paths that pass through Δ is imposed by summing over all finite length classical paths which intersect Δ as they go from the 'initial' point $\mathbf{x}_0$ to 'final' point $\mathbf{x}_f$, that is, Δ lies *between* the initial and final points. This is also what one might naively expect in the quantum theory version. However, one can see from the above construction that the correct answer is in fact to sum over *all* classical paths (which can be of infinite length) passing through $\mathbf{x}_0$ and $\mathbf{x}_f$ that intersect Δ at *any* point along the entire trajectory, even if Δ does not lie between the two points (see Figure 38.1). This feature is related to the reparameterization invariance of the system.

The above point turns out to be quite crucial to what follows in the rest of this paper, so it is worth saying it in an alternative form. Loosely speaking, the statement is that only the entire classical path respects the reparameterization invariance associated with the constraint equation. A section of the classical path does not. This may be expressed more precisely in terms of the function $A(\mathbf{x}, \mathbf{p}_0, \mathbf{x}_0)$ introduced in (38.16). This function is concentrated on the entire classical trajectory, and is zero when $\mathbf{x}$ is not on the trajectory. It is easy to see that it has vanishing Poisson bracket with the Hamiltonian $H = H(\mathbf{p}_0, \mathbf{x}_0)$, since we have

$$\begin{aligned}
\{H, A(\mathbf{x}, \mathbf{p}_0, \mathbf{x}_0)\} &= \int_{-\infty}^{\infty} dt \, \{H, \delta^{(n)}(\mathbf{x} - \mathbf{x}^{cl}(t))\} \\
&= -\int_{-\infty}^{\infty} dt \, \frac{d}{dt}\delta^{(n)}(\mathbf{x} - \mathbf{x}^{cl}(t)) \\
&= 0.
\end{aligned} \qquad (38.24)$$

This is the precise sense in which the entire trajectory is reparameterization invariant, and the phase space function A may be regarded as an observable – a quantity that commutes with the constraint H [25, 33]. By way of comparison, consider a second phase space function similarly

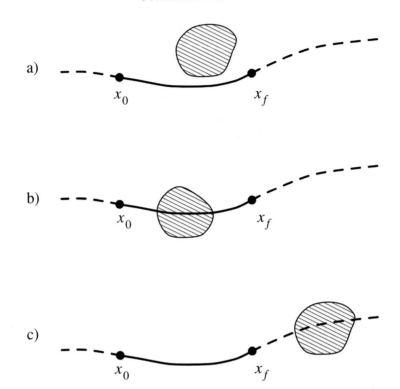

a)

x_0 x_f

b)

x_0 x_f

c)

x_0 x_f

Fig. 38.1. The rewritten classical probability (38.22) in terms of a sum over initial and final points x_0 and x_f. The probability for not entering Δ is a sum over paths as in case (a). The probability for entering Δ includes a sum over classical paths in which Δ lies between the initial and final points, as in case (b). But, to agree with the phase space form of the result (38.19), it must also include a sum over initial and final points for which Δ does not lie between them, as in case (c). This figure also applies to the semiclassical propagator in the quantum case.

defined, but on only a finite section of trajectory,

$$B(\mathbf{x}, \mathbf{p}_0, \mathbf{x}_0) = \int_0^T dt \, \delta^{(n)}(\mathbf{x} - \mathbf{x}^{cl}(t)). \tag{38.25}$$

It is easily seen that

$$\{H, B(\mathbf{x}, \mathbf{p}_0, \mathbf{x}_0)\} = -\delta(\mathbf{x} - \mathbf{x}^{cl}(\tau)) + \delta(\mathbf{x} - \mathbf{x}^{cl}(0)). \tag{38.26}$$

Hence B 'almost' commutes with H, failing only at the end points, and it is in this sense that a finite section of trajectory does not fully respect reparameterization invariance.

A third version of the classical result is also useful. It is of interest to obtain an expression for the probability for intersecting an $(n-1)$-dimensional surface Σ. Since the result (38.19) involves the parameter time spent in a finite volume region Δ it does not apply immediately. However, suppose that the set of trajectories contained in the probability distribution w intersect the $(n-1)$-dimensional surface Σ only once. Then we may consider a finite volume region Δ obtained by thickening Σ along the direction of the classical flow. If this thickening is by a small (positive) parameter time Δt, then the quantity appearing in the θ-function in (38.19) is

$$
\int dt \int_\Delta d^n x \, \delta^{(n)}(\mathbf{x} - \mathbf{x}^{cl}(t)) = \Delta t \int dt \int_\Sigma d^{n-1}x \, \mathbf{n} \cdot \frac{d\mathbf{x}^{cl}(t)}{dt}
$$
$$
\times \, \delta^{(n)}(\mathbf{x} - \mathbf{x}^{cl}(t))
$$
$$
= \Delta t \, I[\Sigma, \mathbf{x}^{cl}(t)], \tag{38.27}
$$

where $\mathbf{n}$ is the normal to Σ, and we suppose that the normal is chosen so that $\mathbf{n} \cdot d\mathbf{x}^{cl}/dt$ is positive. The quantity $I[\Sigma, \mathbf{x}^{cl}(t)]$, in a more general context, is the intersection number of the curve $\mathbf{x}^{cl}(t)$ with the surface Σ, and takes the value 0 for no intersections, or ± 1 (depending on whether there is an even or odd number of intersections). In this case we have assumed that the trajectories intersect at most once, hence $I = 0$ or 1. We then have

$$
\theta(\Delta t I - \epsilon) = \theta(I - \epsilon') = I \tag{38.28}
$$

(where $\epsilon = \Delta t \, \epsilon'$) and the probability for intersecting Σ may be written

$$
p_\Sigma = \int dt \int d^n p_0 d^n x_0 \, w(\mathbf{p}_0, \mathbf{x}_0) \int_\Sigma d^{n-1}x \, \mathbf{n} \cdot \frac{d\mathbf{x}^{cl}(t)}{dt} \, \delta^{(n)}(\mathbf{x} - \mathbf{x}^{cl}(t)) \tag{38.29}
$$

At each t, we may perform a change of variables from $\mathbf{p}, \mathbf{x}$ to new variables $\mathbf{p}' = \mathbf{p}^{cl}(t)$, $\mathbf{x}' = \mathbf{x}^{cl}(t)$, and using (38.14), we obtain the result

$$
p_\Sigma = \frac{1}{M} \int dt \int_\Sigma d^n p' \, d^{n-1}x' \, \mathbf{n} \cdot \mathbf{p}' \, w(\mathbf{p}', \mathbf{x}') \tag{38.30}
$$

Finally, the integrand is now in fact independent of t, so the t integral leads to an overall factor. (This might be infinite but is regularized as discussed below.) We therefore drop the t integral.

This result is relevant for the following reason. In the heuristic 'WKB interpretation' of quantum cosmology, one considers WKB solutions to the Wheeler–DeWitt equation of the form

$$
\Psi = C e^{iS}. \tag{38.31}
$$

It is usually asserted that this corresponds to a set of classical trajectories with momentum $\mathbf{p} = \nabla S$, and with a probability of intersecting a surface Σ given in terms of the flux of the wave function across the surface [8, 10, 19]. As we shall show, from the decoherent histories analysis, the quantum theory gives a probability for crossing a surface Σ proportional to (38.30) with w replaced by the Wigner function of the quantum theory. The Wigner function of the WKB wave function is, approximately [10],

$$W(\mathbf{p}, \mathbf{x}) = |C(\mathbf{x})|^2 \, \delta(\mathbf{p} - \nabla S). \tag{38.32}$$

Inserting in (38.30), we therefore obtain, up to overall factors, the probability distribution,

$$p_\Sigma = \int_\Sigma d^{n-1}x \, \mathbf{n} \cdot \nabla S \, |C(\mathbf{x})|^2 . \tag{38.33}$$

We therefore have agreement with the usual heuristic analysis.

38.3 The decoherent histories approach to quantum theory

Our aim is to analyse the quantum case using the decoherent histories approach to quantum theory [7]. We first give a very brief review of the formalism.

In non-relativistic quantum mechanics, quantum histories are represented by so-called class operators $C_{\underline{\alpha}}$, which are given by time-ordered sequences of projection operators

$$C_{\underline{\alpha}} = P_{\alpha_n}(t_n) \cdots P_{\alpha_1}(t_1) \tag{38.34}$$

(or more generally, by sums of terms of this form), where $\underline{\alpha}$ denotes the string of alternatives $\alpha_1, \alpha_2 \cdots \alpha_n$, and $P_{\alpha_k}(t)$ are projection operators in the Heisenberg picture. The central object of interest is then the decoherence functional,

$$D(\underline{\alpha}, \underline{\alpha}') = \mathrm{Tr} \left(C_{\underline{\alpha}} \rho C_{\underline{\alpha}'}^\dagger \right). \tag{38.35}$$

Intuitively, the decoherence functional is a measure of the interference between pairs of histories $\underline{\alpha}, \underline{\alpha}'$. When its real part is zero for $\underline{\alpha} \neq \underline{\alpha}'$, we say that the histories are consistent and probabilities

$$p(\underline{\alpha}) = D(\underline{\alpha}, \underline{\alpha}) \tag{38.36}$$

obeying the usual probability sum rules may be assigned to them. Typical physical mechanisms which produce this situation usually cause both the real and imaginary part of $D(\underline{\alpha}, \underline{\alpha}')$ to vanish. This condition is usually called decoherence of histories, and is related to the existence of so-called generalized records.

In the non-relativistic case, for histories characterized by projections onto configuration space, a path integral version of the decoherence functional is available, and can be very useful. It has the form

$$D(\underline{\alpha}, \underline{\alpha'}) = \int_{\underline{\alpha}} \mathcal{D}x \int_{\underline{\alpha'}} \mathcal{D}y \exp\left(\frac{i}{\hbar}S[x(t)] - \frac{i}{\hbar}S[y(t)]\right) \rho(x_0, y_0), \quad (38.37)$$

where the sum is over pairs of paths $x(t)$, $y(t)$ passing through the pairs of regions $\underline{\alpha}$, $\underline{\alpha'}$. This is equivalent to the form (38.34), (38.35), when the histories are strings of projections onto ranges of positions. Equation(38.37) is a useful starting point for the generalization to timeless theories.

The power of the decoherent histories approach is that it readily generalizes to a variety of different situations in which time plays a non-trivial role [4, 36, 37]. In particular, it may be generalized to the question of interest here, in which the system is in an energy eigenstate and we would like to answer questions that do not refer to time in any way. This generalization requires, however, specification of the inner product used to construct the decoherence functional, and a prescription for the construction of the class operators. We consider each in turn.

38.4 The induced inner product

For many situations, and especially for the analogous situation in quantum cosmology, the Hamiltonian has a continuous spectrum so the energy eigenstates are not normalizable in the usual inner product,

$$\langle \Psi_1 | \Psi_2 \rangle = \int d^n x \; \Psi_1^*(\mathbf{x}) \Psi_2(\mathbf{x}). \quad (38.38)$$

A way to deal with this has been developed, and goes by the name of the induced inner product, or Rieffel induction [17, 30]. Consider the eigenvalue equation

$$H|\Psi_{E\lambda}\rangle = E|\Psi_{E\lambda}\rangle \quad (38.39)$$

where λ denotes the degeneracy. These eigenstates will typically satisfy

$$\langle \Psi_{E'\lambda'} | \Psi_{E\lambda} \rangle = \delta(E - E')\delta_{\lambda\lambda'} \quad (38.40)$$

from which it is clear that the inner product diverges when $E = E'$. The induced inner product on a set of eigenstates of fixed E is defined, loosely speaking, by discarding the δ-function $\delta(E - E')$. That is, the induced or physical inner product is then defined by

$$\langle \Psi_{E\lambda'} | \Psi_{E\lambda} \rangle_{phys} = \delta_{\lambda\lambda'}. \quad (38.41)$$

This procedure can be defined quite rigorously, and has been discussed at some length in [17, 30]. We will use it here to construct the decoherence functional. A simple prescription for using it in the decoherence functional is to regularize each propagator and energy eigenstate by using a different energy for each. The final answer will then involve a number of δ-functions in energy, as in (38.40), which are simply dropped.

Applied to the Klein–Gordon equation in flat space, where solutions may be split into positive and negative frequency parts, $\phi = \phi^+ + \phi^-$, the induced inner product may be expressed in terms of the Klein–Gordon inner product (which is negative on the negative frequency solutions):

$$(\phi, \phi)_I = (\phi^+, \phi^+)_{KG} - (\phi^-, \phi^-)_{KG}. \tag{38.42}$$

This is clearly positive definite. That is, the induced inner product effectively changes the sign of the negative frequency solutions to make the overall expression positive definite. Importantly, the induced inner product does *not* require a split into positive and negative frequency solutions, and so is generally applicable in quantum cosmological models.

Although the induced inner product has been around for a long time (in the Klein–Gordon case it was noted by Henneaux and Teitelboim [20]), it is only comparatively recently that it made an appearance in quantum cosmology.

38.5 The class operators

The most important part of the construction of the decoherence functional for our timeless model is the construction of the class operators. On the face of it, a natural prescription for constructing these is the following expression:

$$C_\Delta(\mathbf{x}_f, \mathbf{x}_0) = \int_{-\infty}^{\infty} d\tau \, e^{-iE\tau} \int \mathcal{D}\mathbf{x}(t) \exp\left(iS[\mathbf{x}(t)]\right)$$
$$\times \, \theta\left(\int_0^\tau dt \, f_\Delta(\mathbf{x}(t)) - \epsilon\right). \tag{38.43}$$

This expression consists of a functional integral between the initial and final points in fixed parameter time τ over paths constrained to enter the region Δ (enforced by the θ-function as in the classical case), followed by a sum over all possible parameter times τ [16]. In keeping with the general ideas of Dirac quantization, we expect that, in order that the reparameterization invariance of the theory is fully respected, a properly constructed class operator should be annihilated by the constraint,

$$HC_\Delta = 0. \tag{38.44}$$

It is straightforward to show that this is indeed the case in the limit that Δ becomes the entire configuration space. However, as shown in [15], this is not in fact the case when the region Δ is finite: one obtains δ-functions on the boundary of Δ on the right-hand side of (38.44).

This is a serious difficulty since it means that reparameterization invariance is in some sense violated. It is due to the fact that, as the end-points move from inside Δ to outside, the class operator changes discontinuously. This in turn is related to the fact that a projection operator onto the region Δ does not commute with the constraint equation.

Because of this difficulty, it is necessary to replace the class operator C_Δ with a modified class operator C'_Δ which is as much as possible defined by a sum over paths passing through Δ but satisfies the constraint equation everywhere [17]. At present, there does not appear to be a universally agreed way to do this, but some suggestions and discussion of this point were given in [14, 15, 17].

Fortunately, in the semiclassical approximation, it seems clear how to construct the modified propagator. It is

$$C'_\Delta(\mathbf{x}_f, \mathbf{x}_0) = \theta \left(\int_{-\infty}^\infty dt \; f_\Delta(\mathbf{x}_0^f(t)) - \epsilon \right) P(\mathbf{x}_f, \mathbf{x}_0) \; e^{iA(\mathbf{x}_f, \mathbf{x}_0)}. \quad (38.45)$$

Here Pe^{iA} is the usual unrestricted semiclassical propagator, so $A(\mathbf{x}_f, \mathbf{x}_0)$ is the classical action between initial and final points, and P is a prefactor. The θ-function here is the same as in the (rewritten) classical case (38.22) in terms of 'initial' and 'final' points, where $\mathbf{x}_0^f(t)$ denotes that classical path from $\mathbf{x}_0$ to $\mathbf{x}_f$. (This is exactly as in the classical case depicted in Fig. 38.1.) Note also that

$$\nabla A \cdot \nabla \; \theta \left(\int_{-\infty}^\infty dt \; f_\Delta(\mathbf{x}_0^f(t)) - \epsilon \right) = 0 \quad (38.46)$$

as may be shown by shifting the t integration. It follows that the modified class operator is a semiclassical solution to the constraint equation, as required.

It is important that t is integrated over an infinite range in the quantity inside the θ-function, otherwise the modified class operator would not in fact satisfy the constraint. Recall that the originally defined class operator (38.43) contained a similar θ-function, with a finite range of time integration, which one might have been tempted to use in the semiclassical approximation, but this class operator does not in fact satisfy the constraint.

Hence we see that the difference between the modified and original class operators in the semiclassical approximation is the difference between using the entire classical trajectory or using finite segments of it in the θ-functions. We also see that these modified class operators are the correct ones to use in order to be consistent with the discussion of the classical case and (38.22). There, we saw that it is appropriate to sum over classical paths intersecting Δ even if Δ does not lie on the segment of classical trajectory *between* $\mathbf{x}_0$ and $\mathbf{x}_f$. This feature therefore appears to be necessary for the particular type of reparameterization invariance used here. Only the entire trajectory is reparameterization-invariant notion. A finite section of trajectory is not. (See [12] for a further discussion of reparameterizations in this sort of context.)

38.6 Decoherence and the decoherence functional

In terms of the class operators C_α and an 'initial' state $\Psi(\mathbf{x})$ (an eigenstate of H), the decoherence functional is

$$D(\alpha, \alpha') = \int d^n x_f d^n x_0 d^n y_0 \ C_\alpha(\mathbf{x}_f, \mathbf{x}_0) C_{\alpha'}(\mathbf{x}_f, \mathbf{y}_0) \ \Psi(\mathbf{x}_0) \Psi^*(\mathbf{y}_0). \tag{38.47}$$

Here, α denotes the two sets of histories that either pass through Δ or not. The decoherence functional will generally not be diagonal except for special initial states, so a decoherence mechanism is necessary.

The details of the decoherence mechanism are somewhat lengthy and may be found in [15]. Briefly, one may couple the system to a generic environment consisting of large number of degrees of freedom, and then trace out the environmental coordinates. We do not address the more physical question of what the environment actually is for mini-superspace models, but it is sufficient to observe that there are very many fields that are unobserved in cosmological models, and so may serve as an environment. The overall result is that, in the semiclassical approximation, the decoherence functional (38.47) becomes

$$D(\alpha, \alpha') = \int d^n x_f d^n x_0 d^n y_0 \ C_\alpha(\mathbf{x}_f, \mathbf{x}_0) C_{\alpha'}(\mathbf{x}_f, \mathbf{y}_0)$$
$$\times \ F(\mathbf{x}_f, \mathbf{x}_0, \mathbf{y}_0) \ \Psi(\mathbf{x}_0) \Psi^*(\mathbf{y}_0), \tag{38.48}$$

where $F(\mathbf{x}_f, \mathbf{x}_0, \mathbf{y}_0)$ is the influence functional in the semiclassical approximation. As shown in [15], it typically has the form,

$$F = \exp\left(iv^a \Gamma_a - \frac{1}{2} v^a v^b \sigma_{ab} \right), \tag{38.49}$$

where $\mathbf{v} = \mathbf{x} - \mathbf{y}$, and Γ_a and σ_{ab} are real coefficients (and depend only on $\mathbf{x} + \mathbf{y}$), and σ_{ab} is a non-negative matrix. The form of the influence functional broadly indicates that interference between different values of $\mathbf{x}$ (or more generally, different semiclassical trajectories) is suppressed, as expected. (The matrix σ_{ab} may develop a zero eigenvalue, but this corresponds to the fact that interference between points along the same trajectory is not suppressed, i.e., that the influence functional is sensitive only to different trajectories, reflecting the underlying reparameterization invariance.)

Given decoherence, we may therefore compute the probability for passing through the region Δ. Introducing the variable $\mathbf{X}_0 = \frac{1}{2}(\mathbf{x} + \mathbf{y})$, and introducing the Wigner function,

$$W(\mathbf{p}, \mathbf{X}) = \frac{1}{(2\pi)^n} \int d^n v \; e^{-i\mathbf{p}\cdot\mathbf{v}} \; \rho\left(\mathbf{X} + \frac{1}{2}\mathbf{v}, \mathbf{X} - \frac{1}{2}\mathbf{v}\right), \qquad (38.50)$$

it is readily shown that the probability is

$$p_\Delta = \int d^n p_0 d^n X_0 \; \theta\left(\int_{-\infty}^{\infty} dt \; f_\Delta(\mathbf{X}^{cl}(t)) - \epsilon\right) \tilde{W}(\mathbf{p}_0, \mathbf{X}_0). \qquad (38.51)$$

Here, $\mathbf{X}^{cl}(t)$ is the classical path with initial data $\mathbf{X}_0, \mathbf{p}_0$, and we have defined the smeared Wigner function

$$\tilde{W}(\mathbf{p}_0, \mathbf{X}_0) = \int d^n p \; \exp\left(-\frac{1}{2}(\mathbf{p}_0 - \mathbf{p} - \Gamma)^a \sigma_{ab}^{-1}(\mathbf{p}_0 - \mathbf{p} - \Gamma)^b\right)$$
$$\times W(\mathbf{p}, \mathbf{X}_0). \qquad (38.52)$$

Equation (38.51) is the main result. It shows that the decoherent histories analysis very nearly produces the classical result (38.19), except that instead of a classical phase space probability distribution, we get a smeared Wigner function. We also see that the coefficient Γ_a from the influence functional produces a small modification in the classical equations of motion, and that there are fluctuations about the classical motion governed by σ_{ab}^{-1}. (A possible zero eigenvalue for σ_{ab}^{-1} simply means that the exponential in (38.52) becomes a δ- function in one particular direction, so there are no fluctuations in that direction.)

38.7 Summary and discussion

The present work shows that it is possible to carry out a decoherent histories quantization of simple quantum cosmological models. This quantization method reproduces, approximately, heuristic methods based on essentially classical ideas. These models have the key property of not possessing a time parameter, but this does not appear to present an insurmountable obstruction to the application of the approach.

Central to both the classical and quantum problems is the notion of an entire trajectory. At the classical level it appears to be the appropriate reparameterization-invariant notion for the construction of interesting probabilities. At the quantum level, the decoherent histories approach appears to handle the problem in a natural way, perhaps because it readily incorporates the notion of trajectory.

This approach to quantizing cosmological models in this way is certainly only a first bite at the problem, and a list of further topics and related issues is described at some length in [15]. Whilst it is gratifying that quantum cosmological models may be successfully quantized using the decoherent histories approach, what has been particularly interesting for me is the observation that this area appears to be a point of confluence for a number of different fields. As indicated at the beginning of this article, for example, quantum cosmology puts severe pressure on the foundations of standard quantum theory. There has also been an interesting interplay going on between quantum cosmology and the question of time in standard, non-relativistic quantum mechanics [34], and this is likely to prove fruitful for quantum cosmology. In the long run, quantum cosmology may or may not be able to provide useful, testable cosmological predictions. But what is pretty certain is that work in this area is likely to remain a source of stimulus for a long time to come.

Acknowledgements

I am very grateful to Gary Gibbons, Paul Shellard and Stuart Rankin for organizing such a wonderful meeting. Particular gratitude goes to Stephen Hawking for giving us something to have a meeting about.

References

[1] Barbour, J. (1994) *Class. Quant. Grav.* **11**, 2853.

[2] Barbour, J. (1994), *Class. Quant. Grav.* **11**, 2875.

[3] Butterfield, J. and Isham, C. J. [gr-qc/9901024].

[4] Craig, D. and Hartle, J. B. (1998), preprint UCSBTH-94-47.

[5] DeWitt, B. S. (1967), *Phys. Rev.* **160**, 1113.

[6] DeWitt, B. (1962), in *Gravitation: An Introduction to Current Research*, ed. L. Witten (John Wiley and Sons, New York).

[7] Gell-Mann, M. and Hartle, J. B. (1990), in *Complexity, Entropy and the Physics of Information, SFI Studies in the Sciences of Complexity*, Vol. VIII, ed. W. Zurek (Addison Wesley, Reading, ; and in *Proceedings of the Third International Symposium on the Foundations of Quantum Mechanics*

in the Light of New Technology, eds S. Kobayashi, H. Ezawa, Y. Murayama and S. Nomura (Physical Society of Japan, Tokyo, 1990); (1993), *Phys. Rev.* **D47**, 3345; Griffiths, R. B. (1984), *J. Stat. Phys.* **36**, 219; (1993), *Phys. Rev. Lett.* **70**, 2201; (1987) *Am. J. Phys.* **55**, 11; Omnès, R. (1988), *J. Stat. Phys.* **53**, 893; (1988), **53**, 933; (1988), **53**, 957; (1989), **57**, 357; (1991), **62**, 841; (1990) *Ann. Phys.* **201**, 354; (1992) *Rev. Mod. Phys.* **64**, 339; Hartle, J. B. (1991), in *Quantum Cosmology and Baby Universes*, eds S. Coleman, J. Hartle, T. Piran and S. Weinberg (World Scientific, Singapore; Halliwell, J. J. (1994), in *Fundamental Problems in Quantum Theory*, eds D. Greenberger and A. Zeilinger, Annals of the New York Academy of Sciences, Vol 775, 726. For further developments in the decoherent histories approach, particularly adpated to the problem of spacetime coarse grainings, see Isham, C. (1994), *J. Math. Phys.* **23**, 2157; Isham, C. and Linden, N. (1994), *J. Math. Phys.* **35**, 5452; (1995), **36**, 5392.

[8] Halliwell, J. J. (1992), in, *Proceedings of the 13th International Conference on General Relativity and Gravitation*, eds R. J. Gleiser, C. N. Kozameh and O. M. Moreschi (IOP Publishers, Bristol). (Also available as the e-print gr-qc/9208001.)

[9] Halliwell, J. J. (2001), *Phys. Rev.* **D64**, 044008.

[10] Halliwell, J. J. (1987), *Phys. Rev.* **D36**, 3626 .

[11] Halliwell, J. J. and Hartle, J. B. (1990), *Phys. Rev.* **D41**, 1815.

[12] Halliwell, J. J. and Hartle, J. B. (1991), *Phys. Rev.* **D43**, 1170 .

[13] Halliwell, J. J. and Hawking, S. W. (1985), *Phys. Rev.* **D31**, 1777.

[14] Halliwell, J. J. and Thorwart, J. (2001), *Phys. Rev.* **D64**, 124018.

[15] Halliwell, J. J. and Thorwart, J. (2002), [gr-qc/0201070], accepted for publication in Physical Review D.

[16] Hartle, J. B. (1995), in *Proceedings of the 1992 Les Houches School, Gravity and its Quantizations*, eds B. Julia and J. Zinn-Justin (Elsevier Science B. V.).

[17] Hartle, J. B. and Marolf, D. (1997), *Phys. Rev.* **D56**, 6247.

[18] Hartle, J. B. and Hawking, S. W. (1983), *Phys. Rev.* **28**, 2960.

[19] Hawking, S. W. and Page, D. N. (1986), *Nucl. Phys.* **B264**, 185; **B298**, 789 (1988).

[20] Henneaux, M. and Teitelboim, C. (1982), *Ann. Phys. N.Y.* **143** 127.

[21] Isham, C. J. [gr-qc/9210011].

[22] Kazama, Y. and Nakayama, R. (1985), *Phys. Rev.* **32**, 2500.

[23] Kiefer, C. (1988), *Phys. Rev.* **D38**, 1761.

[24] Kuchar, K. (1991), in *Conceptual Problems of Quantum Gravity*, eds A. Ashtekar and J. Stachel (Birkhäuser, Boston); and in *Proceedings of the 4th Canadian Conference on General Relativty and Relativistic Astrophysics*,

eds G. Kunstatter, D. E. Vincent and J. G. Williams (World Scientific, New Jersey, 1992). See also the e-print gr-qc/9304012, 'Canonical quantum gravity'.

[25] Marolf, D. (1995), *Class. Quant. Grav.* **12**, 1199.

[26] Marolf, D. (1996) *Phys. Rev.* **D53**, 6979; (1995) *Class. Quant. Grav.* **12**, 2469; (1995) *Class. Quant. Grav.* **12**, 1441.

[27] Misner, C. W. (1972), in *Magic Without Magic: John Archibald Wheeler, a Collection of Essays in Honor of his 60th Birthday*, ed. J. Klauder (Freeman, San Francisco).

[28] Montesinos, M., Rovelli, C. and Thiemann, T. (1999), *Phys. Rev.* **D60**, 044009; Montesinos, M. (2001), *Gen. Rel. Grav.* **33**, 1; Montesinos, M. and Rovelli, C. (2001), *Class. Quantum Grav.* **18**, 555.

[29] Mott, N. F. (1929), *Proc. Roy. Soc* **A124**, 375, reprinted in *Quantum Theory and Measurement*, eds Wheeler, J. and Zurek, W. (1983), (Princeton University Press, Princeton, New Jersey). For further discussions of the Mott calculation see also, Bell, J. S. (1987), *Speakable and Unspeakable in Quantum Mechanics* (Cambridge University Press, Cambridge); Broyles, A. A. (1993), *Phys. Rev.* **A48**, 1055 ; Castagnino, M. and Laura, R. (2000) [gr-qc/0006012].

[30] Ashtekar, A., Lewandowski, J., Marolf, D., Mourao, J. and Thiemann, T. (1995), *J. Math. Phys.* **36**, 6456; Higuchi, A. (1991), *Class. Quant. Grav.* **8**, 1983; Giulini, D. and Marolf, D. (1999), *Class. Quant. Grav.* **16**, 2489; (1999), *Class. Quant. Grav.* **16**, 2479; Embacher, F. (1998), *Hadronic J.* **21**, 337; Landsmann, N. (1995), *J. Geom. Phys.* **15**, 285; Marolf, D. (2000), [gr-qc/0011112].

[31] Rovelli, C. (1990), *Phys. Rev.* **42**, 2638.

[32] Rovelli, C. (1991), *Phys. Rev.* **43**, 442.

[33] Rovelli, C. (1991), *Class. Quant. Grav.* **8**, 297; **8**, 317.

[34] An extensive list of references to the issue of time in quantum mechanics may be found in [15]. See also Muga, J. G. Sala Mayato, R. and Egusquiza, I. L. (eds) (2002), *Time in Quantum Mechanics*, (Springer).

[35] Wheeler, J. A. (1968), in *Batelles Rencontres*, eds C. DeWitt and J. A. Wheeler (Benjamin, New York).

[36] Whelan, J. (1994), *Phys. Rev.* **D50**, 6344.

[37] Yamada, N. and Takagi, S. (1991), *Prog. Theor. Phys.* **85**, 985; (1991), **86**, 599; (1992), **87**, 77; Yamada, N. (1992), *Sci. Rep. Tôhoku Uni., Series 8*, **12**, 177; (1996) *Phys. Rev.* **A54**, 182; Halliwell, J. J. and Zafiris, E. (1998), *Phys. Rev.* **D57**, 3351–3364; Hartle, J. B. (1991), *Phys. Rev.* **D44**, 3173; Micanek, R. J. and Hartle, J. B. (1996), *Phys. Rev.* **A54**, 3795.

39

What local supersymmetry can do for quantum cosmology

Peter D'Eath

Centre for Mathematical Sciences, University of Cambridge

39.1 Introduction

In all approaches to quantum gravity, one makes vital use of the classical theory, with the knowledge and intuition which this carries, in conjunction with the quantum formulation. When, in addition, the theory possesses local supersymmetry, this generally has profound consequences for the nature of classical solutions, as well as for the quantum theory.

We are used to the procedure in which a bosonic field, such as a massless scalar field ϕ in flat four-dimensional space-time, obeying the wave equation

$$\Box \phi = 0 \tag{39.1}$$

is paired with a fermionic field taken to be (say) an unprimed spinor field ϕ^A, using 2-component language [66]. The corresponding Weyl equation,

$$\nabla_{AA'}\phi^A = 0, \tag{39.2}$$

is a system of two coupled first-order equations, which further imply that each component of ϕ^A obeys the massless wave equation (39.2). These bosonic and fermionic fields may be combined (with an auxiliary field) into a multiplet under (rigid) supersymmetry [81]. The classical fermionic field equation (39.2) may be viewed as a 'square root' of the original second-order bosonic equation (39.1).

There is a further relation here, which will be examined in the following sections. This is with the possibility of curvature being *self-dual* in four-dimensional Riemannian geometry [11]. Only in four dimensions, and only for signature $+4$ (Riemannian), 0 (ultra-hyperbolic) and -4 (equivalent to Riemannian) is this property defined [62]. It applies both to the curvature or field strength $F_{\mu\nu}^{(a)}$ of Yang–Mills or Maxwell theory on a (possibly curved) Riemannian background geometry [66], and to the conformally invariant Weyl curvature tensor $W_{\alpha\beta\gamma\delta}$ of the geometry, which contributes 10 of the 20 algebraic degrees of freedom contained in the Riemann curvature tensor $R_{\alpha\beta\gamma\delta}$. The other 10 degrees of freedom reside in the Ricci tensor $R_{\alpha\gamma} = g^{\beta\delta}R_{\alpha\beta\gamma\delta}$, where $g^{\beta\delta}$ describes the inverse metric. In Einstein's theory, the Ricci tensor corresponds to the matter source for the curvature. The Weyl tensor $W_{\alpha\beta\gamma\delta}$ may be thought of as describing the 'vacuum' part of the gravitational field in general relativity.

In both the Yang–Mills and the Weyl-tensor cases, one can describe the curvature simply in two-component spinor language [66]. The Yang–Mills field-strength tensor $F^{(a)}_{\mu\nu} = F^{(a)}_{[\mu\nu]}$ corresponds to the spinor field

$$F^{(a)}_{AA'BB'} = \phi^{(a)}_{AB}\varepsilon_{A'B'} + \tilde{\phi}^{(a)}_{A'B'}\varepsilon_{AB}, \tag{39.3}$$

where $\phi^{(a)}_{AB} = \phi^{(a)}_{(AB)}$ and $\tilde{\phi}^{(a)}_{A'B'} = \tilde{\phi}^{(a)}_{(A'B')}$ are symmetric. Here, ε_{AB} is the unprimed alternating spinor, and $\varepsilon_{A'B'}$ its primed counterpart. In the present Riemannian case, the fields $\phi^{(a)}_{AB}$ and $\tilde{\phi}^{(a)}_{A'B'}$ are independent complex quantities. If the field strength $F^{(a)}_{\mu\nu}$ is real, arising (say) from real Yang–Mills potentials $v^{(a)}_{\mu}$, then each of $\phi^{(a)}_{AB}$ and $\tilde{\phi}^{(a)}_{A'B'}$ is subject to a condition which halves the number of real components of each. [But in the Lorentzian case, for real $F^{(a)}_{\mu\nu}$, $\tilde{\phi}^{(a)}_{A'B'}$ will be replaced by $\bar{\phi}^{(a)}_{A'B'}$, the complex conjugate of $\phi^{(a)}_{AB}$.]

In the Riemannian case, the Yang–Mills field strength is said to be *self-dual* if

$$\phi^{(a)}_{AB} = 0. \tag{39.4}$$

Similarly, an anti-self-dual field has $\tilde{\phi}^{(a)}_{A'B'} = 0$. In the case (say) of a Maxwell field in flat Euclidean 4-space, the (anti-)self-dual condition can be written in terms of the electric and magnetic fields as $\mathbf{E} = \pm\mathbf{B}$. Generally, if a Yang–Mills field is anti-self-dual, then the Yang–Mills field equations reduce to the set:

$$D^{B}{}_{A'}\phi^{(a)}_{AB} = 0, \tag{39.5}$$

where $D_{AA'}$ is the covariant derivative [66]. This set of equations is, of course, a generalization of the Weyl (massless Dirac) equation (39.2).

Regular real solutions of the anti-self-dual Yang–Mills equations (39.5) on the four-sphere S^4 are known as instantons [29]. Since (39.5) is conformally invariant [11], such a solution corresponds to a 'localized' region of Yang–Mills curvature in flat Euclidean $\mathbb{E}^4$, with suitable asymptotic behaviour at large four-dimensional radius. For the simplest non-trivial gauge group SU(2), Atiyah *et al.* [10] have, remarkably, given a construction of the general Yang–Mills instanton. Yang–Mills instantons can also be described in terms of twistor theory [79].

In section 39.2, motivated by the Hartle–Hawking proposal in quantum cosmology [44, 46], we shall be led to consider Riemannian Einstein gravity, including possibly a negative cosmological constant Λ, in the case that the Weyl tensor is (anti-)self-dual [13]. The Einstein field equations

$$R_{\mu\nu} = \Lambda g_{\mu\nu} \tag{39.6}$$

are the conditions for an *Einstein space*. The (anti-)self-duality condition then gives a further set of equations, closely related to the (anti-)self-dual Yang–Mills equations (39.5) in the SU(2) case. But in the case of quantum cosmology, the boundary conditions are usually specified on a compact connected three-surface, such as a three-sphere S^3, in contrast to the Yang–Mills instanton case, where they are specified at infinity. This gravitational version is therefore more complicated. Note that a treatment of the related boundary-value problem for Hermitian Yang–Mills equations over complex manifolds has been given by Donaldson [28]. In the case of 2-complex-dimensional manifolds with Kähler metric [29], this leads to anti-self-dual Yang–Mills connections.

The corresponding purely gravitational solutions, in the case where the boundary is at infinity (with suitable fall-off) or where the manifold is compact without boundary, are known as gravitational instantons [29, 45]. The (anti-)self-dual condition on the Weyl tensor $W_{\alpha\beta\gamma\delta}$ (in the Riemannian case) may again be described in spinor terms [66]: $- W_{\alpha\beta\gamma\delta}$ corresponds to

$$W_{AA'BB'CC'DD'} = \Psi_{ABCD}\varepsilon_{A'B'}\varepsilon_{C'D'} + \tilde{\Psi}_{A'B'C'D'}\varepsilon_{AB}\varepsilon_{CD}, \tag{39.7}$$

where the *Weyl spinors* $\Psi_{ABCD} = \Psi_{(ABCD)}$ and $\tilde{\Psi}_{A'B'C'D'} = \tilde{\Psi}_{(A'B'C'D')}$ are again totally symmetric. The Weyl tensor is *self-dual* if

$$\Psi_{ABCD} = 0, \tag{39.8}$$

and *anti-self-dual* if

$$\tilde{\Psi}_{A'B'C'D'} = 0. \tag{39.9}$$

Thus, in the anti-self-dual case (say) arising in quantum cosmology, the Ricci tensor is restricted by (39.6) and the Weyl tensor by (39.9). The Bianchi identities [66] then imply further that the remaining Weyl spinor Ψ_{ABCD} obeys

$$\nabla^{AA'}\Psi_{ABCD} = 0. \tag{39.10}$$

These equations are again a generalization of the Weyl equation (39.2).

Thus, at least at the formal level, there are clear resemblances concerning supersymmetry and (anti-)self-dual classical Yang-Mills or Einstein theory. More detail will be given in sections 39.4–39.6.

Turning now to the quantum theory, one has an apparent choice in quantum cosmology between the Feynman path-integral approach [44] and the differential approach given by Dirac's theory of the quantization of constrained Hamiltonian systems [23–27]. Loosely speaking, the latter may be thought of as a description of quantum theories with local invariance properties, such as gauge invariance and/or invariance under local coordinate transformations, although in fact it is more general than that. Historically, a large amount of work on quantum cosmology was carried out by relativists following the pioneering work of DeWitt [21] and Wheeler [82] based on the Dirac approach. The eponymous (Wheeler–DeWitt) equation is central to the resulting quantum treatment of spatially-homogeneous cosmologies, possibly containing bosonic matter, in which the classical dynamics involves a (typically small) number of functions of a time-coordinate t only, and the resulting quantum field theory reduces to a quantum-mechanical theory, with a finite number of coordinate variables [71]. However, it has not been possible to make sense of the second-order functional Wheeler–DeWitt equation in the non-supersymmetric case of Einstein gravity plus possible bosonic fields, when the gravitational and any other bosonic fields are allowed to have generic spatial dependence.

The path-integral approach of relevance here is that of Hartle and Hawking [44]. There is, formally speaking, a 'preferred quantum state' for the quantum theory of (say) a spatially-compact cosmology, where typically the coordinate variables, which become the arguments of the wave functional, are taken to be the Riemannian three-metric h_{ij} of the compact three-manifold, together with (say) any other bosonic fields on the three-manifold, denoted schematically by ϕ_0. One then considers all possible Riemannian metrics $g_{\mu\nu}$ and all other fields ϕ on all possible four-manifolds $\mathcal{M}$, such that the original three-manifold is the boundary $\partial\mathcal{M}$ of $\mathcal{M}$, and such that the 'interior' $\mathcal{M}$ together with its boundary $\partial\mathcal{M}$, namely $\mathcal{M} \cup \partial\mathcal{M}$ or $\bar{\mathcal{M}}$, is a compact manifold-with-boundary. The three-metric and other fields inherited from $(g_{\mu\nu}, \phi)$ on the boundary must agree with the originally prescribed (h_{ij}, ϕ_0). For visualization, the simplest example is the compact manifold S^3 (the three-sphere), with interior the four-ball B^4. The *Hartle–Hawking state* Ψ_{HH}, also known as the '*no-boundary state*', is then (formally) described by

$$\Psi_{HH}(h_{ij}, \phi_0) = \int \mathcal{D}g_{\mu\nu}\mathcal{D}\phi \exp[-I(g_{\mu\nu}, \phi)/\hbar]. \qquad (39.11)$$

Here the functional integral is over all suitable infilling fields $(g_{\mu\nu}, \phi)$, and I is the corresponding Euclidean action [19, 44]. Since the integrand is an analytic (holomorphic) function of its arguments, this path integral may be regarded as a giant contour integral, with the set of suitable infilling fields deformed into the complex. The question of finding a suitable contour for which the integral is meaningful (convergent) is a major problem in this approach to quantum cosmology; in the above Riemannian case, the Euclidean action I is unbounded below [37], so that the integrand in (39.11) can become arbitrarily large and positive.

The Feynman-path-integral and Dirac-quantization approaches are *dual* integral and differential attempts to describe the same quantum theory, here 'quantum gravity'. As shown in the book of Feynman and Hibbs [32], for non-relativistic quantum mechanics, the path integral gives a wave function or quantum amplitude for a particle to go from initial position and time (x_a, t_a) to final (x_b, t_b), with $t_b > t_a$, which obeys the Schrödinger equation and also satisfies the boundary conditions as $t_b \rightarrow t_a$. Similarly for the converse. Indeed Feynman's Princeton Ph.D. thesis evolved from his continuing thought about the paper by Dirac [22], which in effect derived the path integral for propagation in a short time-interval Δt. Similar dual relations even hold, somewhat schematically, for the path-integral and differential versions of quantum gravity [44].

Given the above difficulties, which of these two approaches (if any) should we use and, perhaps, trust? The bad convergence properties of the gravitational path integral seem, at present, very difficult to overcome. Similarly for the question of defining the second-order Wheeler–DeWitt operator in the non-supersymmetric case. But the Hartle–Hawking path integral provides a powerful conceptual, indeed visual, *schema*. And when local supersymmetry is included, the Wheeler–DeWitt equation is replaced by its fermionic 'square root' [76], the quantum supersymmetry constraints [19], which allow more sense to be made of the quantum theory. One should expect to use both approaches together, so far as is possible. Richard Feynman himself certainly attended to the Dirac constrained-quantization approach, notably in his last substantial paper [31], on Yang–Mills theory in 2+1 dimensions, on which he worked for three years. Indeed, when Feynman gave the first of the annual Dirac lectures in Cambridge, in June 1986, he remarked 'How could I refuse the invitation? – Dirac was my hero'. Pragmatically, anyone who has to teach a first undergraduate course in quantum mechanics will usually base it on the Schrödinger equation (the differential approach). But, of course, there is nothing to stop them from inducting the students *via* the path-integral approach. Maybe this has been tried, at least at CalTech!

39.2 No-boundary state

To expand on the description (39.11) of the Hartle–Hawking state, we will need later to be able to include fermions with the gravitational and other bosonic fields, in the Riemannian context. This requires the introduction of an orthonormal tetrad $e^a{}_\mu$ of one-forms; here $a = 0, 1, 2, 3$ labels the four orthonormal co-vectors $e^a{}_\mu$, while μ is the 'space-time' or 'world' index. One has, by orthogonality and completeness:

$$g^{\mu\nu} e^a{}_\mu e^b{}_\nu = \delta^{ab}, \quad \delta_{ab} e^a{}_\mu e^b{}_\nu = g_{\mu\nu}. \tag{39.12}$$

Thus $e^a{}_\mu$ is a 'square root' of the metric $g_{\mu\nu}$, non-unique up to local SO(4) rotations acting on the internal index a.

In this case, instead of specifying the intrinsic three-metric h_{ij} on the boundary $(i, j, \ldots = 1, 2, 3)$, one would specify the four spatial one-forms $e^a{}_i$, with

$$h_{ij} = \delta_{ab} e^a{}_i e^b{}_j. \tag{39.13}$$

This seems a redundant description, since only three co-vectors $e^a{}_i$ are needed to take the 'square root' of h_{ij} in (39.13). On and near the boundary surface, it is valid to work in the 'time gauge' [65], using a *triad* $e^a{}_i$ $(a = 1, 2, 3)$ to obey (39.13). Equivalently, one imposes $e^0{}_i = 0$ as a gauge condition. Instead of integrating over all Riemannian four-metrics $g_{\mu\nu}$ in (39.11), one integrates over all $e^a{}_\mu$, each of which corresponds to a Riemannian metric by (39.12).

The gravitational part of the Euclidean action I in (39.11) is [34]

$$I_{grav} = -\frac{1}{2\kappa^2} \int_{\mathcal{M}} d^4x \, g^{\frac{1}{2}} (R - 2\Lambda) - \frac{1}{\kappa^2} \int_{\partial\mathcal{M}} d^3x \, h^{\frac{1}{2}} tr K. \tag{39.14}$$

Here $\kappa^2 = 8\pi$, $g = det(g_{\mu\nu}) = [det(e^a{}_\mu)]^2$, R is the four-dimensional Ricci scalar, Λ is the cosmological constant and $tr K = h^{ij} K_{ij}$, where K_{ij} is the second fundamental form (or extrinsic curvature) of the boundary [19, 64].

In the path integral (39.11), one expects to sum over all four-manifolds $\mathcal{M}$, of different topology, which have the prescribed three-manifold as boundary $\partial\mathcal{M}$; for each topologically different $\mathcal{M}$, one then integrates over metrics $g_{\mu\nu}$ or tetrads $e^a{}_\mu$. For each choice of $\mathcal{M}$, one can ask whether there are any solutions of the classical field equations, for the given boundary data h_{ij} or $e^a{}_i$, other bosonic data ϕ_0 and possible fermionic data. In the simplest case of gravity without matter (for definiteness), there may be zero, one, two, ... real Riemannian solutions of (39.6) for a given topology $\mathcal{M}$. Of course, for the same $\mathcal{M}$ and real boundary data h_{ij}, there may be a larger number of *complex* classical solutions $g_{\mu\nu}$.

Suppose, again for definiteness, that we again have gravity without matter, and that there is a unique classical solution $g_{\mu\nu}$ (up to coordinate transformation) which is Riemannian (and hence real) on a particular four-manifold $\mathcal{M}_0$, corresponding to the boundary data $h_{ij}(x)$. Further, suppose that there are no other classical solutions on any other manifold $\mathcal{M}$. Then, were the path integral (39.11) to be meaningful, one would expect to have a *semiclassical expansion* of the Hartle–Hawking state, of the form

$$\Psi_{HH}[h_{ij}(x)] \sim (A_0 + \hbar A_1 + \hbar^2 A_2 + ...) \exp(-I_{class}/\hbar). \qquad (39.15)$$

Here the wave function Ψ_{HH}, the 'one-loop factor' A_0, 'two-loop factor' A_1, ... and the Euclidean action I_{class} of the classical solution [as in (39.14)] are all functionals of $h_{ij}(x)$. Technically, one might expect that such an expansion, if it existed, would only be an asymptotic expansion valid in the limit as $\hbar \to 0_+$. Even in non-relativistic quantum mechanics, semiclassical expansions are typically only asymptotic but not convergent [49]. Note also that, if well-posed fermionic boundary data are included, and there is a unique corresponding coupled bosonic-fermionic classical solution, then one expects again a semiclassical wave function Ψ_{HH} of the boundary data, of the form (39.15), except that each of I_{class}, A_0, A_1, A_2,... will be a functional of the complete bosonic and fermionic boundary data.

39.3 The classical Riemannian boundary-value problem

39.3.1 The general boundary problem

As follows from section 39.2, it is important to understand the nature of the Riemannian boundary-value problem for Einstein gravity, possibly including a Λ-term, matter fields and local supersymmetry. Only very partial results are available in the generic case for which the boundary data has no symmetries. Reula [68] proved an existence theorem for the vacuum Riemannian Einstein equations ($\Lambda = 0$) on a slab-like region, where suitable data on two parallel planes enclosing a slab of Euclidean $\mathbb{E}^4$ are slightly perturbed. For weak perturbations of a suitable known compact manifold-with-boundary, the case $\Lambda \leq 0$ was studied by Schlenker [75]. To fix one's intuition, consider the case in which the unperturbed boundary is a metric three-sphere S^3, bounding part of flat $\mathbb{E}^4$ (if $\Lambda = 0$) or of a hyperbolic space $\mathbb{H}^4$ (if $\Lambda < 0$). Then any sufficiently weak perturbation of the boundary metric h_{ij} yields a corresponding (perturbed but non-linear) interior solution $g_{\mu\nu}$ for the 4-metric, obeying $R_{\mu\nu} = \Lambda g_{\mu\nu}$.

Boundary-value problems 'at infinity' have also been studied, for $\Lambda < 0$, when a four-dimensional Riemannian geometry can be given a conformal infinity [39]. The canonical example is hyperbolic space $\mathbb{H}^4$, with its metric of constant curvature, here normalized such that $\Lambda = -12$. Let ds_b^2 denote the flat Euclidean metric on $\mathbb{R}^4$, expressed in terms of Cartesian coordinates x^μ ($\mu = 0, 1, 2, 3$); then define the conformal function $\rho = \frac{1}{2}(1 - |x|^2)$ on the unit ball $B^4 \subset \mathbb{R}^4$. The *conformal metric* $ds^2 = \rho^{-2}ds_b^2$ is the hyperbolic metric on the open set B^4, and the 'conformal metric at infinity ($|x| = 1$)' can be taken to be the standard metric H_{ij} on S^3. Graham and Lee [39] have shown that this 'conformal Einstein' problem is also well-behaved for small perturbations of the unit-sphere metric H_{ij} on the *conformal boundary* S^3. As in the previous paragraph, for 3-metrics h_{ij} sufficiently close to H_{ij}, there is a corresponding conformal metric on the interior B^4, close to the unperturbed hyperbolic metric.

The case with conformal infinity, imposing the Einstein condition $R_{\mu\nu} = \Lambda g_{\mu\nu}$ with $\Lambda < 0$, has also been studied subject to the additional requirement of (say) self-duality of the Weyl tensor, $\Psi_{ABCD} = 0$ [(39.5.2)]. LeBrun [58] has shown that, when the conformal infinity $\partial\mathcal{M}$ is a real-analytic 3-manifold with conformal metric h_{ij}, then, in a neighbourhood of $\partial\mathcal{M}$, there is a conformal 4-metric $g_{\mu\nu}$ on a real-analytic 4-manifold $\mathcal{M}$, satisfying the Einstein equations with $\Lambda < 0$ and self-dual Weyl curvature. The real-analytic condition on the conformal boundary $\partial\mathcal{M}$ is essential, since the Einstein-space condition $R_{\mu\nu} = \Lambda g_{\mu\nu}$ together with self-duality imply that the 4-manifold must be real-analytic [11]. Further, LeBrun [59] has shown that there is an infinite-dimensional space of conformal metrics h_{ij} on S^3 which bound *complete* Einstein metrics on the 4-ball, with (anti-)self-dual Weyl curvature; that is, S^3 is again conformal infinity, but now the result is not just local, in a neighbourhood of the S^3 boundary, but extends smoothly across the interior, the 4-ball.

Finally, note that LeBrun [58] also proved a local result in which the conformal infinity $\partial\mathcal{M}$ is taken to be a suitable complex 3-manifold with given holomorphic metric [80], and a complex 4-manifold $\mathcal{M}$ in a neighbourhood of $\partial\mathcal{M}$ is then guaranteed to exist, with holomorphic metric obeying $R_{\mu\nu} = \Lambda g_{\mu\nu}$ and $\Lambda \neq 0$ (possibly complex), together with self-duality of the Weyl tensor. This is of potential interest in quantum gravity, since, as in section 39.1, the Hartle–Hawking path integral is a contour integral, and there may be stationary points (classical solutions) with holomorphic 4-metrics; further, one would expect to be able to continue the boundary data, such as h_{ij}, into the complex (i.e., holomorphically).

39.3.2 Example – biaxial Riemannian Bianchi-IX models

As an example, consider the family of Riemannian 4-metrics with isometry group $SU(2) \times U(1)$, given (locally in the coordinate r) by:

$$ds^2 = dr^2 + a^2(r)(\sigma_1^2 + \sigma_2^2) + b^2(r)\sigma_3^2. \tag{39.16}$$

Here, $a(r)$ and $b(r)$ are two functions of the 'radial' coordinate r, and $\{\sigma_1, \sigma_2, \sigma_3\}$ denotes the basis of left-invariant 1-forms (co-vector fields) on the three-sphere S^3, regarded as the group $SU(2)$, with the conventions of [29]. The more general triaxial Bianchi-IX metric [56] – see below – would have three different functions multiplying σ_1^2, σ_2^2 and σ_3^2 in (39.16).

In the biaxial case, the boundary data at a value $r = r_0$ are taken to be the intrinsic 3-metric

$$ds^2 = a^2(r_0)(\sigma_1^2 + \sigma_2^2) + b^2(r_0)\sigma_3^2, \tag{39.17}$$

determined by the positive numbers $a^2(r_0)$ and $b^2(r_0)$. This gives a 'squashed 3-sphere' or *Berger sphere*. Thus one wishes to find a regular solution of the Einstein-Λ field equations (39.6) in the interior $\mathcal{M}$ of the boundary $\partial\mathcal{M} \cong S^3$ (denoting '$\partial\mathcal{M}$ is diffeomorphic to S^3'), subject to the boundary data (39.17). There are two possible ways in which such a 4-geometry could close in a regular way as r is decreased from r_0, to give a compact manifold-with-boundary $\mathcal{M} \cup \partial\mathcal{M} = \bar{\mathcal{M}}$. Either $\mathcal{M}$ is (diffeomorphically) a 4-ball B^4, with standard polar-coordinate behaviour

$$a(r) \sim r, \quad b(r) \sim r \text{ as } r \to 0 \tag{39.18}$$

near the 'centre' $r = 0$ of the 4-ball. Or $\mathcal{M}$ has a more complicated topology, still with boundary $\partial\mathcal{M} \cong S^3$, such that

$$a(r) \to c(\text{constant} > 0), \quad b(r) \sim r \text{ as } r \to 0. \tag{39.19}$$

Here the 4-metric degenerates to the metric of a round 2-sphere S^2, as $r \to 0$. The first case is described as *NUT behaviour* as $r \to 0$, and the second as *BOLT behaviour* [29, 35]. In both cases, the apparent singularity at $r = 0$ is a removable coordinate singularity.

The general Riemannian solution of the Einstein field equations $R_{\mu\nu} = \Lambda g_{\mu\nu}$ for biaxial Bianchi-IX metrics can be written in the form [35, 36]

$$ds^2 = \frac{(\rho^2 - L^2)}{4\Delta}d\rho^2 + (\rho^2 - L^2)(\sigma_1^2 + \sigma_2^2) + \frac{4L^2\Delta}{(\rho^2 - L^2)}\sigma_3^2, \tag{39.20}$$

where

$$\Delta = \rho^2 - 2M\rho + L^2 + \frac{1}{4}\Lambda(L^4 + 2L^2\rho^2 - \frac{1}{3}\rho^4). \tag{39.21}$$

This 2-parameter family of metrics, labelled (for given Λ) by the constants L, M, is known as the Taub–NUT–(anti)de Sitter family.

It was found by Jensen *et al.* [53] that a 4-geometry in this family has NUT behaviour (near $\rho^2 = L^2$) precisely when one of the relations

$$M = \pm L\left(1 + \frac{4}{3}\Lambda L^2\right) \tag{39.22}$$

holds. Further [36], these are the conditions for (anti-)self-duality of the Weyl tensor. In the classical NUT boundary-value problem, positive values of $A = a^2(r_0), B = b^2(r_0)$ are specified on the boundary $\partial\mathcal{M}$, and the geometry must fill in smoothly on a 4-ball interior, subject to the Einstein equations $R_{\mu\nu} = \Lambda g_{\mu\nu}$. As remarked by Jensen *et al.* [53], NUT regularity corresponds to one further requirement, given by a cubic equation, beyond (39.22). This is investigated further in [1]; see also Chamblin *et al.* [16]. Taking (say) the anti-self-dual case in (39.22), assuming also $\Lambda < 0$ for the sake of argument, and given positive boundary values (A, B), the cubic leads to three regular NUT solutions (counting multiplicity). Depending on the values (A, B), from zero to three of these are *real* Riemannian solutions of the type (39.20). The remaining NUT solutions are inevitably complex (holomorphic) geometries. In the physically interesting limit, where both 'cosmological' (radii)^2 A and B are large and comparable, all three solutions are real. In the Hartle–Hawking path integral (39.11) and its semiclassical expansion (39.15), with Euclidean action $I_{grav}(\ )$, this would give an estimate, say for the isotropic case $A = B$:

$$I_{class} \sim -\frac{\pi}{12|\Lambda|}A^2 \text{ as } A \to \infty, \tag{39.23}$$

with

$$\Psi_{HH} \sim (\text{slowly varying prefactor}) \times \exp(-I_{class}/\hbar). \tag{39.24}$$

In such an Einstein-negative-Λ model, without further matter, the relative probability of finding a universe with a given A would increase enormously with A.

If instead $\Lambda = 0$, the solution (39.20,6) reduces to the Euclidean Taub–NUT solution [45]. For $\Lambda > 0$, one may visualize the isotropic case $A = B$, with a metric 4-sphere S^4 as Riemannian solution, the radius being determined in terms of Λ. When the (radii)^2 A and B become too large relative to Λ^{-1}, there will be no real Riemannian solution [53], but only complex (holomorphic) geometries.

The alternative regular BOLT solutions are studied in [2], particularly in the case $\Lambda < 0$, for given positive boundary data (A, B). These solutions *do not* have an (anti-)self-dual Weyl tensor. Further, their topology is more complicated than that of the 4-ball B^4 – the simplest way of filling in an S^3. This difference can be seen, for example, by computing the topological invariants χ, the Euler invariant, and τ, the Pontryagin number, each of which is given by a volume integral quadratic in the Riemann tensor, together with a suitable surface integral [29]. For the 4-ball, one has $\chi = 1, \tau = 0$; for a BOLT solution, $\chi = 2, \tau = -1$. The problem of finding BOLT solutions depends on studying a seventh-degree polynomial! The number of *real* regular BOLT solutions, for given positive boundary data (A, B), must be twice a strictly positive odd number; other solutions are necessarily complex. When the boundary is not too anisotropic, i.e., when A and B are sufficiently close to one another, there are exactly two regular BOLT solutions.

Of course, one could in principle study the corresponding much more elaborate triaxial boundary-value problem. This has at least been done for the case of a conformal boundary at infinity, as in section 39.3.1, with conformal 3-metric of triaxial Bianchi-IX type [48]. The solutions involve Painlevé's sixth equation [62]; see also [77].

39.4 Self-duality

39.4.1 Hamiltonian approach; Ashtekar variables

Consider now a Hamiltonian treatment of Einstein gravity with a Λ-term, modified for use in the Riemannian or 'imaginary-time' case. Since we shall later include fermions, a tetrad (or triad) description of the geometry must be used, as in (39.12, 39.13), except that we shall use spinor-valued one-forms $e^{AA'}{}_\mu$ instead of the tetrad $e^a{}_\mu$. Here

$$e^{AA'}{}_\mu = \sigma_a^{AA'} e^a{}_\mu, \tag{39.25}$$

where $\sigma_a^{AA'}$ are appropriate Infeld-van der Waerden translation symbols [66]. The spatial 3-metric h_{ij} is given by

$$h_{ij} = -e_{AA'i} e^{AA'}{}_j, \tag{39.26}$$

where the spinor-valued spatial one-forms $e^{AA'}{}_i$ are regarded as the coordinate variables in a 'traditional' Hamiltonian treatment. The *Lorentzian normal vector* n^μ has spinor version $n^{AA'}$, which is determined once the $e^{AA'}{}_i$ are known [19]. In our Riemannian context, the corresponding *Euclidean normal vector* ${}_en^\mu$ corresponds to

$${}_en^{AA'} = -in^{AA'}. \tag{39.27}$$

In the 'time gauge' of section 39.2, one has only a triad $e^a{}_i (a = 1, 2, 3)$, and the remaining one-form $e^0{}_\mu$ is constrained by $e^0{}_i = 0$; equivalently

$en^\mu = \delta_0^a$. The local invariance group of the theory becomes SO(3) in the triad version.

For Riemannian 4-geometries, the torsion-free connection is given by the *connection 1-forms* $\omega^{ab}{}_\mu = \omega^{[ab]}{}_\mu$ [19]. In spinor language, these correspond to

$$\omega^{AA'BB'}{}_\mu = \omega^{AB}{}_\mu \varepsilon^{A'B'} + \tilde{\omega}^{A'B'}{}_\mu \varepsilon^{AB}, \qquad (39.28)$$

where $\omega^{AB}{}_\mu = \omega^{(AB)}{}_\mu$ is a set of 1-forms taking values in the Lie algebra $\mathfrak{su}(2)$ of the group SU(2); similarly for the independent quantity $\tilde{\omega}^{A'B'}{}_\mu = \tilde{\omega}^{(A'B')}{}_\mu$, with a different copy of SU(2). Then the curvature is described by the 2-forms $R^{AB}{}_{\mu\nu} = R^{(AB)}{}_{[\mu\nu]}$, defined by

$$R^{AB}{}_{\mu\nu} = 2(\partial_{[\mu}\omega^{AB}{}_{\nu]} + \omega^A{}_{C[\mu}\omega^{CB}{}_{\nu]}), \qquad (39.29)$$

and a corresponding $\tilde{R}^{A'B'}{}_{\mu\nu}$. In the language of forms [29], the spinor-valued 2-form R^{AB} is defined equivalently as

$$R^{AB} = d\omega^{AB} + \omega_A{}^C \wedge \omega_C{}^B \qquad (39.30)$$

and corresponds to the anti-self-dual part of the Riemann tensor. Similarly, $\tilde{R}^{A'B'}$ corresponds to the self-dual part.

In the Hamiltonian formulation of Ashtekar [4–7], one defines the spatial spinor-valued 1-forms $\sigma^{AB}{}_i = \sigma^{(AB)}{}_i$ as

$$\sigma^{AB}{}_i = \sqrt{2}ie^A{}_{A'i}n^{BA'}. \qquad (39.31)$$

These can equally be described, in the time gauge, in terms of the spatial triad $e^a{}_i$, the translation symbols $\sigma_a^{AA'}$ and the unit matrix $\delta^{AA'}$. Then, with $\sigma^{ABi} = h^{ij}\sigma^{AB}{}_j$, one defines the density

$$\tilde{\sigma}^{ABi} = h^{\frac{1}{2}}\sigma^{ABi}, \qquad (39.32)$$

where $h = det(h_{ij})$. The *Ashtekar canonical variables* are then $\tilde{\sigma}^{ABi}$ and ω_{ABi}, the spatial part of the unprimed connection 1-forms with spinor indices lowered. It can be verified that these are canonically conjugate. Of course, since they contain only unprimed spinor indices, they are very well adapted for a description of (anti-)self-duality. For this purpose, we shall also need the spinor-valued 2-form

$$\Sigma_{AB} = e_A{}^{A'} \wedge e_{BA'}, \qquad (39.33)$$

obeying $\Sigma_{AB} = \Sigma_{(AB)}$.

In the Hamiltonian approach [4–6, 13, 51], the action can be decomposed in terms of the spatial 'coordinate variables' $\omega_{ABi} = \omega_{(AB)i}$ and 'momentum variables' $\tilde{\sigma}^{ABi} = \tilde{\sigma}^{(AB)i}$, together with the Lagrange multi-pliers N (lapse), N^i (shift) and ω_{AB0} [specifying local SU(2) transformations]. The (Lorentzian) action S has the form

$$S = \int Tr[\tilde{\sigma}^i \dot{\omega}_i + (N\tilde{\sigma}^i \tilde{\sigma}^j (R_{ij} - \frac{1}{3}\Lambda\Sigma_{ij}) + N^i \tilde{\sigma}^j Rij + \omega_0 D_i \tilde{\sigma}^i)]. \quad (39.34)$$

Here, all spinor indices have been suppressed, but spatial indices are left explicit. The conventions $(MN)_A{}^C = M_A{}^B N_B{}^C$ and $Tr(M_A{}^B) = M_A{}^A$ are being used. The spatial curvature 2-forms $R^{AB}{}_{ij} = R^{(AB)}{}_{[ij]}$ are constructed as in (39.29) from the spatial connection 1-forms $\omega^{AB}{}_i$, and D_i denotes the spatial covariant derivative. From variation of the Lagrange multipliers, one finds as usual that each of their coefficients vanish, giving the *constraint equations* which restrict the form of the allowed data $(\omega_{ABi}, \tilde{\sigma}^{ABi})$ for classical solutions (whether anti-self-dual or more general). Further, the spatial 2-forms $\Sigma^{(AB)}{}_{[ij]}$ of (39.33) are related to the variables $\tilde{\sigma}^{ABi}$ by

$$\tilde{\sigma}^{ABi} = \varepsilon^{ijk}\Sigma^{AB}{}_{jk}. \quad (39.35)$$

The generalization of Ashtekar's approach to supergravity was given by Jacobson [51], and will be used in section 39.6.

39.4.2 Non-zero Λ: the anti-self-dual case and the Chern–Simons functional

It was shown in [14, 72] that the anti-self-dual Einstein field equations (39.6,39.39), with a *non-zero cosmological constant* Λ, can be re-expressed in terms of the (four-dimensional) 2-form $\Sigma^{AB} = \Sigma^{(AB)}$. Note first that, for any set of orthonormal 1-forms $e^{AA'}{}_\mu$, the 2-forms Σ^{AB} defined in (39.33) automatically obey

$$\Sigma^{(AB} \wedge \Sigma^{CD)} = 0. \quad (39.36)$$

Equivalently, for a *real* SO(3) triad $e^a{}_\mu$, where $a = 1, 2, 3$ here, the conditions (39.36) read

$$\Sigma^a \wedge \Sigma^b - \frac{1}{3}\delta^{ab}\Sigma^c \wedge \Sigma_c = 0. \quad (39.37)$$

In the case of self-dual Weyl curvature ($\Psi_{ABCD} = 0$), the Einstein field equations reduce to

$$R^{AB} = \frac{1}{3}\Lambda\Sigma^{AB}. \quad (39.38)$$

Conversely, these authors show that, given any $\mathfrak{su}(2)$-valued unprimed connection 1-form $\omega^{AB} = \omega^{(AB)}$, with corresponding curvature 2-forms

$R^{AB} = R^{(AB)}$ defined by (39.30), it is sufficient (locally) that the R^{AB} further obey the *algebraic conditions*

$$R^{(AB} \wedge R^{CD)} = 0, \tag{39.39}$$

or the equivalent of (39.37), with R^a replacing Σ^a, in the real SO(3) triad case. Then, defining Σ^{AB} by the inverse of (39.39):

$$\Sigma^{AB} = 3\Lambda^{-1} R^{AB}, \tag{39.40}$$

it is shown that (locally) this defines, *via* (39.33), a metric which obeys the Einstein-Λ equations, with self-dual Weyl curvature.

The Hamiltonian approach with $\Lambda \neq 0$, taking canonical variables $(\omega_{ABi}, \tilde{\sigma}^{ABi})$ with action S given by (39.34), has been further discussed by [55]. A necessary and sufficient condition for an initial-data set to correspond locally to a solution of the Einstein equations with self-dual Weyl curvature is that

$$\tilde{\sigma}^{ABi} = \frac{-3}{\Lambda} \tilde{B}^{ABi}. \tag{39.41}$$

Here, $\tilde{B}^{ABi}$ is a densitized version of the magnetic part of the Weyl tensor [64], defined by

$$\tilde{B}^{ABi} = \frac{1}{2} \varepsilon^{ijk} R^{AB}{}_{jk}, \tag{39.42}$$

where ε^{ijk} is the alternating symbol in three dimensions, and $R^{AB}{}_{jk} = R^{(AB)}{}_{[jk]}$ gives, as usual, the spatial part of the curvature 2-form, following (39.29).

The evolution equations are most easily described in terms of the equivalent variables $(\omega_{ai}, \tilde{\sigma}^{ai})$, where $a = 1, 2, 3$ is a local SO(3) index. Recall that ω_{ai} and $\tilde{\sigma}^{ai}$ are defined by $\omega_{ai} = \Sigma_a^{AB} \omega_{ABi}$, $\tilde{\sigma}^{ai} = \Sigma_{AB}^a \omega^{ABi}$, where Σ_a^{AB} and Σ_{AB}^a are the triad Infeld–van der Waerden translation symbols. Then, in the self-dual Riemannian case, the normal derivative of ω_{ai} is given by

$$\dot{\omega}_{ai} = \left(\frac{3}{4\Lambda}\right) N \varepsilon_{ijk} \varepsilon_{abc} \tilde{B}^{bj} \tilde{B}^{ck}. \tag{39.43}$$

Here, in the language of (39.34), only the 'lapse' Lagrange multiplier N is taken non-zero. Hence, if ω_{ai} is specified on a hypersurface, then, assuming self-duality, the conjugate variable $\tilde{\sigma}^{ai}$ is determined by (39.41). The evolution of ω_{ai} away from the hypersurface is then determined by solving the set of partial differential equations (39.43), which involves no more than first derivatives of ω_{ai}, in the form $\dot{\omega}_{ai}$ and $\varepsilon^{ijk} \partial \omega_{aj} / \partial x^k$, the latter quadratically. Away from the bounding hypersurface, the conjugate variables $\tilde{\sigma}^{ai}$ continue to be given in terms of ω_{ai} by (39.41).

As usual for Hamiltonian systems with first-order evolution for the 'coordinates' alone (here ω_{ai}), the classical action $I[\omega_{ai}]$, regarded as a functional of the boundary data ω_{ai}, is the principal generating function [3, 38, 57], with (in spinor language):

$$\frac{\delta I}{\delta \omega_{ABi}} = \tilde{\sigma}^{ABi}, \tag{39.44}$$

together with the correct evolution equations. Up to an additive constant, the classical action $I[\omega_{ai}]$ is precisely the *Chern–Simons action*

$$I_{CS}[\omega_{ai}] = \frac{-3}{2\Lambda}\int \varepsilon^{ijk}[\omega^{AB}{}_i(\partial_j\omega_{ABk}) + \frac{2}{3}\omega^{AB}{}_i\omega_B{}^C{}_j\omega_{CAk}], \tag{39.45}$$

as studied in this general context by [8, 54] and others. Here, for comparison, we again assume that the bounding hypersurface $\partial\mathcal{M}$ is diffeomorphic to S^3. Note further that the value of I_{CS} for a particular classical solution does not change as one evolves the boundary data ω_{ai} in (say) the normal direction, because of the Hamiltonian (normal) constraint $\tilde{\sigma}^i\tilde{\sigma}^j R_{ij} = 0$, arising from (39.15). In the case of Bianchi-IX symmetry, for Einstein-Λ gravity, the corresponding *Chern–Simons quantum states*

$$\Psi_{CS}[\omega_{ai}] = \exp(\pm I_{CS}[\omega_{ai}]/\hbar) \tag{39.46}$$

in quantum cosmology have been further studied by [17, 40, 60]. For $N = 1$ (simple) supergravity, including a non-zero positive cosmological constant Λ [51], this state has been studied in the case of $k = +1$ cosmology (round S^3) by [74]; see also [73]. In all of these mini-superspace treatments, it is clear that the Chern–Simons state(s) are at least WKB or semiclassical approximations to exact quantum states; similarly in the full theory [8]. An excellent review of Yang–Mills theory in Hamiltonian form, the Yang–Mills Chern–Simons action and its *rôle* in topology and the quantum theory, is given by Jackiw [50].

There has been some discussion as to whether the Chern–Simons state Ψ_{CS} with the minus sign in (39.46) is also the Hartle–Hawking state [17, 60], at least within the context of Bianchi-IX symmetry. I doubt whether the last word has been said on this subject, despite the definite tone of the latter paper. The argument involves the stability of the SO(4)-spherically symmetric solution of the evolution equation (39.43) for ω_{ai}; for definiteness, assume here that $\Lambda < 0$, giving a hyperboloid $\mathbb{H}^4$ as the maximally symmetric solution. The corresponding self-dual evolution has the form $\omega_{ai} = A(t)(\sigma_a)_i$, where σ_a ($a = 1, 2, 3$) denotes the orthonormal basis of left-invariant 1-forms on S^3, as used in section 39.3.2, and [17]

$$A(t) = \frac{1}{2}[1 + \cosh(4mt)]; \quad \Lambda = -12m^2. \tag{39.47}$$

Here t is a 'Euclidean time coordinate', with its 'origin' chosen to be at $t = 0$. Correspondingly, the form of the resulting $\tilde{\sigma}^{ai}$ shows that the intrinsic radius $a(t)$ of the S^3 at 'time' t is given by

$$a^2(t) = \frac{1}{8m^2} \sinh^2(4mt), \tag{39.48}$$

as it should be for a 4-space of constant negative curvature. Small gravitational perturbations of $\mathbb{H}^4$, whether of Bianchi-IX type or generic inhomogeneous distortions, give a linearized unprimed Weyl spinor Ψ_{ABCD}, obeying the linearized Bianchi identity (39.10) in the background $\mathbb{H}^4$. The appropriate spherical harmonics X_{ABCD} and $\bar{Y}_{ABCD}$ on S^3 are, respectively, of positive and of negative frequency with respect to the spatial first-order (Dirac-like) projection of $\nabla_{AA'}$. The linearized t-evolution of such a harmonic is regular at $t = 0$ for positive frequency, but singular for negative frequency. As was seen in section 39.3.2, there is a one-parameter family of regular anti-self-dual Einstein metrics, containing the reference $\mathbb{H}^4$, of biaxial Bianchi-IX type. When linearized about $\mathbb{H}^4$, they give for ω_{ai} or Ψ_{ABCD} a lowest-order (homogeneous) positive-frequency harmonic, multiplying a function of t, with regular behaviour near the 'origin' $t = 0$ [60]. But generic linearized data on a bounding S^3, in the ω_{ai} description, will give perturbations of ω_{ai} away from the background value $A(t)(\sigma_a)_i$, diverging as $t \to 0$ within a linearized approximation.

Hence, the linear regime does not give enough information, and one must confront the full non-linear (but first-order) evolution equation (39.43) for ω_{ai}. This partial differential equation is somewhat reminiscent of the heat-like equation for the Ricci flow on Riemannian manifolds, studied by Hamilton [41–43], and it is possible that it might be susceptible to related techniques. This is under investigation; see also [62]. Of course, there are also descriptions of the general solution of the Riemannian self-dual Einstein equations, for $\Lambda \neq 0$, in terms of twistor theory [78, 79] and in terms of $\mathcal{H}$-space [58].

At least, in the much simpler case of (Abelian) Maxwell theory, when one takes the (anti-)self-dual part of the spatial connection (vector potential) A_i to be the 'coordinate variables', the normalizable Chern–Simons state Ψ_{CS} *is* the ground state [9]. This corresponds to the *wormhole state* in quantum cosmology [19, 47]. Similarly, one expects that the non-normalizable 'state' Ψ_{CS}, corresponding to the opposite sign in (39.46), gives the Maxwell version of the Hartle–Hawking 'state'. Note here that, when the Maxwell field in this representation is split up into an infinite sum of harmonic oscillators, the description of each oscillator is that of the *holomorphic representation* [30]; this recurs in supergravity.

In gravity, the ubiquitous Chern–Simons action I_{CS} of (39.45) reappears (naturally) as the generating function in the transformation from 'traditional' coordinates $e^{AA'}{}_i$ and conjugate momenta $p_{AA'}{}^i$ to Ashtekar variables $(\omega_{ABi}, \tilde{\sigma}^{ABi})$ [63]. The corresponding property for N=1 (simple) supergravity is described by Macías [61].

One might then ask whether, for further generalizations containing Einstein gravity and other fields, corresponding (Euclidean) actions I_{CS} can be found from descriptions of Ashtekar type. This requires (first) a suitably 'formal' geometric treatment of the Lagrangian. Robinson [69, 70] has done this for, respectively, Einstein–Maxwell and Einstein–Yang–Mills theory, both with Λ-term; see also Gambini and Pullin [33]. For relations between self-dual Yang–Mills theory and self-dual gravity, see, for example, [12]. It would be extremely interesting if the generality could be increased to include, for example, N=1 supergravity with gauged supermatter, with gauge group SU(2), SU(3), ... [19, 81] – see the following sections 39.5 and 39.6.

39.5 Canonical quantum theory of N=1 supergravity: 'traditional variables'

39.5.1 Dirac approach

Turning back to supergravity, consider the Dirac canonical treatment of simple N=1 supergravity, using the 'traditional variables' $(e^{AA'}{}_i, p_{AA'}{}^i, \psi^A{}_i, \tilde{\psi}^{A'}{}_i)$, [18, 19] which are the natural generalization of the 'traditional' variables $(e^{AA'}{}_i, p_{AA'}{}^i)$ for Einstein gravity, based on the spatial tetrad components $e^a{}_i$ and their conjugate momenta $p_a{}^i$ $(a = 0, 1, 2, 3)$. In the supergravity version, the fermionic quantities $(\psi^A{}_i, \tilde{\psi}^{A'}{}_i)$ are the spatial projections of the spin-3/2 potentials $(\psi^A{}_\mu, \tilde{\psi}^{A'}{}_\mu)$. As classical quantities, they are odd Grassmann quantities, anti-commuting among themselves, but commuting with bosonic quantities such as $e^{AA'}{}_i$ and $p_{AA'}{}^i$. The bosonic quantities, such as $e^{AA'}{}_i, p_{AA'}{}^i$, are not necessarily Hermitian complex (in Lorentzian signature, say), but are generally even elements of a Grassmann algebra; that is, they are (schematically) of the form (complex) + (complex)×(bilinear in $\psi, \tilde{\psi}$)+ analogous fourth-order terms +.... The bosonic fields $e^{AA'}{}_i(x)$, $p_{AA'}{}^i(x)$ are canonical conjugates, and the canonical conjugate of $\psi^A{}_i(x)$, in the fermionic sense of Casalbuoni [15], is

$$\pi_A{}^i = -\frac{1}{2}\varepsilon^{ijk}\tilde{\psi}^{A'}{}_j e_{AA'k}. \tag{39.49}$$

In the quantum theory, one can, for example, consider wave-functionals of the 'traditional' form:

$$\Psi = \Psi[e^{AA'}{}_i(x), \psi^A{}_i(x)], \tag{39.50}$$

living in a Grassmann algebra over the complex numbers $\mathbb{C}$. Following the Dirac approach, a wave function Ψ, describing a physical state, must obey the *quantum constraints*, corresponding to the classical constraints appearing in a Hamiltonian treatment of a theory with local invariances, as seen in section 39.4.1 for Ashtekar variables. Taking the case of Lorentzian signature, for definiteness, the only relevant quantum constraints to be satisfied are the *local Lorentz constraints*

$$J^{AB}\Psi = 0, \qquad \bar{J}^{A'B'}\Psi = 0, \tag{39.51}$$

together with the *local supersymmetry constraints*

$$S^A\Psi = 0, \qquad \bar{S}^{A'}\Psi = 0, \tag{39.52}$$

The local Lorentz constraints (39.51) simply require that the wavefunctional Ψ be constructed in a locally Lorentz-invariant way from its arguments; that is, that all unprimed and all primed spinor indices be contracted together in pairs. Classically, the fermionic expression $\tilde{S}_{A'}$ is given by

$$\tilde{S}_{A'} = \varepsilon^{ijk} e_{AA'i}(^{3s}D_j\psi^A{}_k) + \frac{1}{2}i\kappa^2\psi^A{}_i p_{AA'}{}^i, \tag{39.53}$$

with $\kappa^2 = 8\pi$, where $^{3s}D_j()$ denotes a suitable torsion-free spatial covariant derivative [18, 19]. The classical S^A is given formally by Hermitian conjugation of (39.53).

In the quantum theory, the operator $\bar{S}_{A'}$ contains only a first-order bosonic derivative:

$$\bar{S}_{A'} = \varepsilon^{ijk} e_{AA'i}(^{3s}D_j\psi^A{}_k) + \frac{1}{2}\hbar\kappa^2\psi^A{}_i \frac{\delta}{\delta e^{AA'}{}_i}. \tag{39.54}$$

The resulting constraint, $\bar{S}_{A'}\Psi = 0$, then has a simple interpretation in terms of the transformation of Ψ under a local primed supersymmetry transformation, parametrized by $\tilde{\varepsilon}^{A'}(x)$, acting on its arguments. One finds [18, 19] that, under the supersymmetry transformation with

$$\delta e^{AA'}{}_i = i\kappa\tilde{\varepsilon}^{A'}\psi^A{}_i, \qquad \delta\psi^A{}_i = 0, \tag{39.55}$$

the change $\delta\Psi$ is given by

$$\delta(\log \Psi) = \frac{-2i}{\hbar\kappa}\int d^3x\, \varepsilon^{ijk} e_{AA'i}(^{3s}D_j\psi^A{}_k)\tilde{\varepsilon}^{A'}. \tag{39.56}$$

The quantum version of S^A is more complicated in this representation, involving a mixed second-order functional derivative, schematically

$\delta^2 \Psi / \delta e \delta \psi$. However, one can move between the $(e^{AA'}_{\ i}, \psi^A_{\ i})$ representation and the $(e^{AA'}_{\ i}, \tilde{\psi}^{A'}_{\ i})$ representation, by means of a suitable functional Fourier transform. In the latter representation, the operator S^A appears simple, being of first order, while the operator $\bar{S}_{A'}$ appears more complicated. Finally, note that in N=1 supergravity, there is no need to study separately the quantum constraints $\mathcal{H}^{AA'} \Psi = 0$, corresponding to local coordinate invariance in four dimensions, and summarized classically in the Ashtekar representation by the vanishing of the quantities multiplying the Lagrange multipliers in (39.52). This is because the anti-commutator of the fermionic operators S^A and $\bar{S}^{A'}$ gives $\mathcal{H}^{AA'}$, in a suitable operator ordering, plus quantities multiplying J^{AB} or $\bar{J}^{A'B'}$; hence, the annihilation of Ψ by $S^A, \bar{S}^{A'}, J^{AB}$ and $\bar{J}^{A'B'}$ implies further that $\mathcal{H}^{AA'} \Psi = 0$.

39.5.2 The quantum amplitude

Consider, within N=1 simple supergravity, the 'Euclidean' quantum amplitude to go from given asymptotically flat initial data, specified by $(e^{AA'}_{\ iI}(x), \psi^{A'}_{\ iI}(x))$ on $\mathbb{R}^3$, to given final data $(e^{AA'}_{\ iF}(x), \psi^A_{\ iF}(x))$, within a Euclidean time-separation $\tau > 0$, as measured at spatial infinity. Formally, this is given by the path integral

$$K(e_F, \psi_F; e_I, \tilde{\psi}_I; \tau) = \int \exp(-I/\hbar) \mathcal{D}e \mathcal{D}\psi \mathcal{D}\tilde{\psi}, \qquad (39.57)$$

where I denotes a version of the Euclidean action of supergravity, appropriate to the boundary data [18, 19], and Berezin integration is being used for the fermionic variables [30]. Of course, this is very close to being a Hartle–Hawking integral, as in (39.11), except that part of the boundary has been pushed to spatial infinity, and that the fermionic data have been taken in different forms on the initial and final $\mathbb{R}^3$.

As in any theory with local (gauge-like) invariances, when treated by the Dirac approach, the quantum constraint operators at the initial and final surfaces annihilate the quantum amplitude K above. In particular, on applying (say) the supersymmetry constraint $\bar{S}_{A'} K = 0$ at the final surface, one obtains

$$\varepsilon^{ijk} e_{AA'iF} \left({}^{3s}D_j \psi^A_{\ kF} \right) K + \frac{1}{2} \hbar \kappa^2 \psi^A_{\ iF} \frac{\delta K}{\delta e^{AA'}_{\ iF}} = 0. \qquad (39.58)$$

As in section 39.5.1, this describes how K changes (in a simple way) when a local primed supersymmetry transformation (39.55) is applied to the final data $(e^{AA'}_{\ iF}, \psi^A_{\ iF})$. One then considers the semiclassical expansion of this 'Euclidean' quantum amplitude, by analogy with (39.15). However, one should first note that, in general, there is no classical solution

$(e^{AA'}{}_\mu, \psi^A{}_\mu, \tilde{\psi}^{A'}{}_\mu)$ of the supergravity field equations, agreeing with the initial and final data as specified above, and corresponding to a Euclidean time interval τ at spatial infinity. This was not appreciated in [18], but was later corrected in [19]. The difficulty resides in the classical $\tilde{S}^{A'} = 0$ constraint at the final surface [(39.53)], and similarly $S^A = 0$ at the initial surface; it is precisely related to the primed supersymmetry behaviour of (39.55,8) finally, and similarly for unprimed supersymmetry initially.

Suppose now that we start from a purely bosonic (Riemannian) solution $e^{AA'}{}_\mu$ of the vacuum Einstein field equations, while $\psi^A{}_\mu = 0$, $\tilde{\psi}^{A'}{}_\mu = 0$. Then, for the corresponding bosonic boundary data $e^{AA'}{}_{iI}$ and $e^{AA'}{}_{iF}$, we expect there to exist a semiclassical expansion of $K(e_F, 0; e_I, 0; \tau)$, as in (39.15). By studying (say) the quantum supersymmetry constraint $\bar{S}_{A'} K = 0$ of (39.58) at the final surface, and allowing the variable $\psi^A{}_{iF}(x)$ at the final surface to become small and non-zero, while still obeying the *classical* $\tilde{S}_{A'} = 0$ constraint (39.53) at the final surface, one finds:

$$A_0 = const., \quad A_1 = A_2 = \ldots = 0, \tag{39.59}$$

for the loop prefactors $A_0, A_1, A_2, \ldots$ in the expansion (39.15). Thus, in N=1 supergravity, for purely bosonic boundary data, the semiclassical expansion of the 'Euclidean' amplitude K is *exactly semiclassical*; that is,

$$K \sim A_0 \exp(-I_{class}/\hbar), \tag{39.60}$$

where A_0 is a constant. The symbol $\sim$ for an asymptotic expansion, has been used in (39.60), rather than equality $=$, as there will sometimes be more than one inequivalent *complex* solution of the vacuum Einstein equations joining $e^{AA'}{}_{iI}$ to $e^{AA'}{}_{iF}$. In that case, there will be more than one classical action I_{class}, but only the leading contribution, corresponding to the most negative value of Re$[I_{class}]$, will appear in (39.60). Since there has been some disagreement in the past about the result described in this paragraph, it should be noted that no published paper, since the publication of the revised argument in [19], has given a substantive contrary argument.

Finally, one might ask whether more general amplitudes

$$K(e_F, \psi_F; e_I, \tilde{\psi}_I; \tau)$$

in N=1 supergravity share some of the simplicity of the purely bosonic amplitude above. Here, non-trivial fermionic data $\psi^A{}_F$ and $\tilde{\psi}^{A'}{}_I$ should be chosen such that there is a classical solution joining the data in Euclidean time τ, whence a semiclassical expansion of K should exist, by analogy with (39.15). By considering the possible form of locally supersymmetric counterterms, formed from volume and surface integrals of various curvature invariants, at different loop orders, one is led to expect that the full amplitude K might well be finite on-shell; certainly, the purely bosonic part of each invariant must be identically zero, by the property (39.59), and it would then be odd if some of its partners, which are quadratic, quartic, ... in fermions, managed not to be zero identically. A more detailed investigation of fermionic amplitudes, at one loop in N=1 supergravity with gauged supermatter, is given in [20].

39.5.3 N=1 supergravity with gauged supermatter

Gauge theories of 'ordinary matter', with spins $0, 1/2, 1$, can be combined with N=1 supergravity (say) in a very geometrical way, to give a theory with *four types of local invariance*: local coordinate, local tetrad rotation, local N=1 supersymmetry, and (say) local $SU(n)$ invariance [81]. The resulting theory is uniquely defined once the coupling constant g is specified (with $g^2 = 1/137.03\ldots$), except for an analytic potential $P(a^I)$, where the a^I are complex scalar fields, which live on complex projective space $\mathbb{C}P^{n-1}$ (for $n \geq 2$). In the simplest non-trivial case, with $SU(2)$ gauge group, there is one complex scalar field a, with complex conjugate $\bar{a}$. There is a natural *Kähler metric* on $\mathbb{C}P^1$, or the Riemann sphere, parametrized by a (provided one includes the point $a = \infty$ at the North pole, while $a = 0$ corresponds to the South pole). The *Kähler potential* is

$$K = \log(1 + a\bar{a}), \tag{39.61}$$

giving the *Kähler metric*

$$g_{11^*} = \frac{\partial^2 K}{\partial a \partial \bar{a}} = \frac{1}{(1 + a\bar{a})^2}. \tag{39.62}$$

Equivalently, this metric reads as

$$ds^2 = \frac{da\,d\bar{a}}{(1 + a\bar{a})^2}, \tag{39.63}$$

which is the metric on the unit round 2-sphere (really, $\mathbb{C}P^1$). Not surprisingly, the isometry group for this geometry is just the original gauge group $SU(2)$.

The other fields in the $SU(2)$ theory may be summarized as follows. There is a spin-1/2 field $(\chi_A, \tilde{\chi}_{A'})$, which has no Yang–Mills index in this case, and which is the partner of $(a, \bar{a})$. The Yang–Mills potential(s) $v_\mu^{(a)}$, with $(a) = 1, 2, 3$, have fermionic spin-1/2 partners $(\lambda_A^{(a)}, \tilde{\lambda}_{A'}^{(a)})$; thus there is a distinction between two different types of underlying spin-1/2 field – the χs and the λs. As usual, gravity is described by the tetrad $e^{AA'}{}_\mu$, with spin-3/2 supersymmetry partner $(\psi^A_\mu, \tilde{\psi}^{A'}_\mu)$. The relevant Lagrangian may be found in [81].

This model can be extended to the group SU(3), for example, by using the corresponding Kähler metric given in [36]. A suitable basis of eight generators of the Lie algebra $\mathfrak{su}(3)$, as employed in the Lagrangian of [81], is given by the Gell-Mann matrices in [49].

Perhaps the most immediately striking feature of the resulting Lagrangian is the enormous *negative cosmological constant* Λ, with

$$\Lambda = -\frac{g^2}{8} \tag{39.64}$$

in Planck units, for SU(2) and SU(3). However, at least in the case of zero potential $[P(a) = 0]$, when the theory is written out in Hamiltonian form, and the Dirac approach to canonical quantization is taken [19, 20], then the N=1 local supersymmetry again implies that quantum amplitudes K to go between initial and final *purely bosonic configurations* in a Euclidean time-at-infinity τ are *exactly semiclassical:*

$$K \sim const. \exp(-I_{class}/\hbar). \tag{39.65}$$

Correspondingly, one might again expect some related simplification in amplitudes K for which there are non-trivial *fermionic* boundary data, in addition to gravity, Yang–Mills and scalars. Some evidence of this has been found in an investigation of one-loop corrections in the SU(2) theory, where the 'background' purely bosonic classical solution is taken to be a suitable hyperboloid $\mathbb{H}^4$, corresponding to the negative value of Λ, and the 'unperturbed' initial and final boundaries are taken to be two round 3-spheres S^3 at different radii from the 'centre' of the $\mathbb{H}^4$ [20]. Consistent weak-field fermionic boundary data are put on the spheres, and the one-loop corrections to the quantum amplitude are studied with the help of *both* (local) quantum supersymmetry constraint operators S^A and $\bar{S}^{A'}$. The Dirac approach to the computation of loop terms in such a locally supersymmetric theory was found to be extremely streamlined by comparison with the corresponding path-integral calculation. Typically, fermionic one-loop examples of this type are often very simple, sometimes not even involving an infinite sum or integral. In non-trivial examples, the amplitudes appear to be exponentially convergent [20], and the structure suggests that this will continue at higher loop order.

Since the loop behaviour of this SU(2) model appears reasonable, it would seem worthwhile to investigate this and other SU(n) models further, to understand better their physical consequences, and to try to predict effects which are observable at accelerator energies.

39.6 Canonical quantization of N=1 supergravity: Ashtekar–Jacobson variables

Now consider the canonical variables introduced by Jacobson [51] for N=1 supergravity, following Ashtekar's approach, possibly including a *positive cosmological constant* written as $\Lambda = 12\mu^2$ [cf. (39.47) for negative Λ]. For consistency, the fermionic variables have been renormalized as in D'Eath [19]. The bosonic variables are again taken to be the connection 1-forms $\omega_{ABi} = \omega_{(AB)i}$, together with the canonically-conjugate variables $\tilde{\sigma}^{ABi} = \tilde{\sigma}^{(AB)i}$. The fermionic variables are taken to be the unprimed spatial 1-forms ψ_{Ai} and their conjugate momenta $\tilde{\pi}^{Ai}$. Once again, all variables only involve unprimed spinor indices, and so are well adapted to a treatment of (anti-)self-duality. Note that $\tilde{\pi}^{Ai}$ is given in terms of the 'traditional' variables of section 39.5 by

$$\tilde{\pi}^{Ai} = \frac{i}{\sqrt{2}}\varepsilon^{ijk}e^{AA'}{}_j\tilde{\psi}_{A'k}. \tag{39.66}$$

The classical supersymmetry constraints involve

$$\begin{aligned} S^A &= \mathcal{D}_i\tilde{\pi}^{Ai} + 4i\mu(\tilde{\sigma}^k\psi_k)^A \\ &= 0, \end{aligned} \tag{39.67}$$

where $\mathcal{D}_i$ is a spatial covariant derivative involving the connection ω_{ABi}, and

$$\begin{aligned} S^{\dagger A} &= (\tilde{\sigma}^j\tilde{\sigma}^k\mathcal{D}_{[j}\psi_{k]})^A - 4i\mu(\tilde{\sigma}_k\tilde{\pi}^k)^A \\ &= 0. \end{aligned} \tag{39.68}$$

Note here that $\tilde{\sigma}^{AB}{}_k = (1/\sqrt{2})\varepsilon_{kmn}\tilde{\sigma}^{ACm}\tilde{\sigma}_C{}^{Bn}$ [19, 51]. Quantum-mechanically, for a wave-functional $\Psi[\omega_{ABi}, \psi_{Ai}]$, the constraint $S^A\Psi = 0$ is a first-order functional differential equation, namely:

$$\mathcal{D}_i\left(\frac{\delta\Psi}{\delta\psi_{Ai}}\right) - 4\mu\psi^B{}_k\left(\frac{\delta\Psi}{\delta\omega_{ABk}}\right) = 0. \tag{39.69}$$

This simply describes the invariance of the wave-functional Ψ under a local unprimed supersymmetry transformation, parametrized by $\varepsilon^A(x)$, applied to its arguments $\omega_{ABi}(x), \psi_{Ai}(x)$. Note that the unprimed transformation properties of 'traditional' variables include

$$\delta e_{AA'i} = -i\tilde{\psi}_{A'i}\varepsilon_A, \quad \delta\psi_{Ai} = 2\mathcal{D}_i\varepsilon_A, \quad \delta\tilde{\psi}_{A'i} = 0. \tag{39.70}$$

One further deduces, following [14], the variation

$$\delta\omega_{ABi} = \mu\psi_{(Ai}\varepsilon_{B)}.$$ (39.71)

However, the quantum constraint $S^{\dagger A}\Psi = 0$ is described by a complicated second-order functional differential equation. One can (say) transform from 'coordinate' variables $(\omega_{ABi}, \psi_{Ai})$ to the opposite 'primed' coordinates $(\tilde\omega_{A'B'i}, \tilde\psi_{A'i})$, via 'traditional' coordinates $(e_{AA'i}, \psi_{Ai})$ [61], using functional Fourier transforms [19], with Berezin integration over fermionic variables [30]. In the 'primed' coordinates $(\tilde\omega_{A'B'i}, \tilde\psi_{A'i})$, the quantum constraint operator S^A will appear complicated and second-order, while the operator $S^{\dagger A}$ becomes simple and first-order.

In the unprimed representation $(\omega_{ABi}, \psi_{Ai})$, in the case $\Lambda = 12\mu^2 > 0$, one can again define the Chern–Simons action I_{CS} for N=1 supergravity [73, 74] as:

$$I_{CS}[\omega_{ABi}, \psi_{Ai}] = \frac{3}{2\Lambda}\int W,$$ (39.72)

$$W = \omega_{AB} \wedge d\omega^{AB} + \frac{2}{3}\omega_{AC} \wedge \omega^C{}_B \wedge \omega^{AB} - \mu\psi^A \wedge \mathcal{D}\psi_A.$$ (39.73)

Here, we assume that the integration is over a compact (boundary) 3-surface. The notation $\mathcal{D}\psi_A$ denotes the covariant exterior derivative of ψ_{Ai}, using the connection ω_{ABi} [19]. It should be noted that the functional $I_{CS}[\omega_{ABi}, \psi_{Ai}]$ is *invariant under unprimed local supersymmetry transformations* (39.70), (39.71) applied to its arguments, with parameter $\varepsilon^A(x)$.

Correspondingly, the *Chern–Simons wave function*,

$$\Psi_{CS} = \exp(-I_{CS}[\omega_{ABi}, \psi_{Ai}]/\hbar),$$ (39.74)

obeys the first quantum supersymmetry constraint

$$S^A\Psi_{CS} = 0.$$ (39.75)

But, by symmetry, when one transforms this wave function into the opposite primed $(\tilde\omega_{A'B'i}, \tilde\psi_{A'i})$ representation, it will have the same form, and hence is also annihilated by the $S^{\dagger A}$ constraint operator. Hence, since Ψ_{CS} is automatically invariant under local tetrad rotations, this Chern–Simons wave function obeys all the quantum constraints, and so defines a physical 'state'. Here inverted commas have been used, since it is not clear whether or not Ψ_{CS} is normalizable.

The classical action $I_{CS}[\omega_{ABi}, \psi_{Ai}]$ is the generating function for self-dual evolution of boundary data $(\omega_{ABi}(x), \psi_{Ai}(x))$ given on the compact spatial boundary, just as $I_{CS}[\omega_{ABi}]$ generated the classical evolution for Einstein gravity with a non-zero Λ term in section 39.4.2. This certainly justifies further investigation.

39.7 Comments

Dirac's approach to the quantization of constrained Hamiltonian systems can be applied to boundary-value problems, whether the Hartle–Hawking path integral of quantum cosmology, or the transition amplitude to go from given initial to final asymptotically-flat data in Euclidean time τ. When the crucial ingredient of local supersymmetry is added, the main quantum constraints to be satisfied by the wave-functional Ψ become the supersymmetry constraints $S^A \Psi = 0$ and $\bar{S}^{A'} \Psi = 0$, each of which is only of first order in bosonic derivatives. Using 'traditional' canonical variables, one finds that, both for N=1 simple supergravity and for N=1 supergravity with gauged SU(n) supermatter (at least in the simplest case of zero potential), transition amplitudes to go from initial to final purely bosonic data are exactly semiclassical, without any loop corrections. This, in turn, strongly suggests that quantum amplitudes including fermionic boundary data are also finite in these theories.

Ashtekar's different (essentially spinorial) choice of canonical variables, for Einstein gravity with cosmological constant Λ, allows a very efficient treatment of (anti-)self-dual Riemannian 'space-times'. For $\Lambda \neq 0$, self-dual evolution arises from the Chern–Simons generating functional I_{CS} of section 39.4.2. Jacobson's extension of Ashtekar canonical variables to include N=1 supergravity for $\Lambda \geq 0$ is again adapted to the study of self-dual supergravity in the Riemannian case. For $\Lambda > 0$, self-dual evolution in N=1 supergravity similarly arises from the Chern–Simons functional I_{CS} of section 39.6. Further, when Ashtekar–Jacobson variables are used, the Chern–Simons wave function $\Psi_{CS} = \exp(-I_{CS})$, of N=1 supergravity with $\Lambda > 0$, gives an exact solution of all the quantum constraints. (In contrast, it is not clear whether such a statement is meaningful in the non-supersymmetric case of section 39.4.2.) There remains the difficult question of the relation between Ψ_{CS} and the Hartle–Hawking state.

Such inter-connections between (anti-)self-duality in Riemannian geometry and meaningful states in quantum cosmology may well provide an enduring Union (or, possibly, an Intersection) between Oxford and Cambridge and other such Centres of Gravity.

Acknowledgements

I am very grateful to Andrew Farley, Gary Gibbons, Ted Jacobson, John Thompson and Pelham Wilson for valuable discussions.

References

[1] Akbar, M. M. and D'Eath, P. D. (2002a). 'Classical boundary-value problem in Riemannian quantum gravity and self-dual Taub–NUT–(anti)de Sitter geometries'. DAMTP preprint 2002-26, [gr-qc/0202073].

[2] Akbar, M. M. and D'Eath, P. D. (2002b), 'Classical boundary-value problem in Riemannian quantum gravity with a negative cosmological constant: BOLT case', Paper in preparation.

[3] Arnold, V. I. (1980), *Mathematical Methods of Classical Mechanics* (Springer, Berlin).

[4] Ashtekar, A. (1986), 'New variables for classical and quantum gravity', *Phys. Rev. Lett.* **57**, 2244–7.

[5] Ashtekar, A. (1987), 'New Hamiltonian form of general relativity', *Phys. Rev.* **D35**, 1587–1602.

[6] Ashtekar, A. (1988), *New Perspectives in Canonical Gravity* (Bibliopolis, Naples).

[7] Ashtekar, A. (1991), *Lectures on Non-Perturbative Canonical Gravity* (World Scientific, Singapore).

[8] Ashtekar, A., Balachandran, A. P. and Jo, S. (1989), 'The CP problem in quantum gravity', *Int. J. Mod. Phys.* **A4**, 1493–1514.

[9] Ashtekar, A., Rovelli, C. and Smolin, L. (1992), 'Self-duality and quantization', *J. Geom. Phys.* **8**, 7–27.

[10] Atiyah, M., Hitchin, N. J., Drinfeld, V. G. and Manin, Yu. I. (1978a), 'Construction of instantons', *Phys. Lett.* **65A**, 185–7.

[11] Atiyah, M., Hitchin, N. J. and Singer, I. M. (1978b), 'Self-duality in four dimensional Riemannian geometry', *Proc. Roy. Soc. London* **A362**, 425–64.

[12] Bengtsson, I. (1990), 'Self-dual Yang–Mills fields and Ashtekar's variables', *Class. Quantum Grav.* **7**, L223–7.

[13] Capovilla, R., Jacobson, T. and Dell, J. (1990), 'Gravitational instantons as SU(2) gauge fields', *Class. Quantum Grav.* **7**, L1–3.

[14] Capovilla, R., Dell, J., Jacobson, T. and Mason, L. (1991), 'Self-dual 2-forms and gravity', *Class. Quantum Grav.* **8**, 41–57.

[15] Casalbuoni, R. (1976), 'On the quantization of systems with anticommuting variables', *Nuovo Cimento* **33A**, 115–25.

[16] Chamblin, A., Emparan, R., Johnson, C. V. and Myers, R. C. (1999), 'Large N phases, gravitational instantons, and the nuts and bolts of AdS holography', *Phys.Rev.* **D59**, 0640101–9.

[17] Cheng, A. D. Y. and D'Eath, P. D. (1997), 'Relation between the Chern–Simons functional and the no-boundary proposal', *Phys.Lett.* **B398**, 277–80.

[18] D'Eath, P. D. (1984), 'Canonical quantization of supergravity' *Phys. Rev.* **D29**, 2199–2219.

[19] D'Eath, P. D. (1996), *Supersymmetric Quantum Cosmology* (Cambridge University Press, Cambridge).

[20] D'Eath, P. D. (1999), 'Loop amplitudes in supergravity by canonical quantization', in *Fundamental Problems in Classical, Quantum and String Gravity*, ed. N. Sanchez (Observatoire de Paris), [hep-th/9807028].

[21] DeWitt, B. S. (1967), 'Quantum theory of gravity I. The canonical theory', *Phys. Rev.* **160**, 1113–48.

[22] Dirac, P. A. M. (1933), 'The Lagrangian in quantum mechanics', *Physikalische Zeitschrift der Sowjetunion*, **3**, 1, 64–72.

[23] Dirac, P. A. M. (1950), 'Generalised Hamiltonian dynamics', *Canad. J. Math.* **2**, 129–48.

[24] Dirac, P. A. M. (1958a), 'Generalised Hamiltonian dynamics', *Proc. Roy. Soc. London* **A246**, 326–32.

[25] Dirac, P. A. M. (1958b), 'The theory of gravitation in Hamiltonian form', *Proc. Roy. Soc. London* **A246**, 333–43.

[26] Dirac, P. A. M. (1959), 'Fixation of coordinates in the Hamiltonian theory of gravitation', *Phys. Rev.* **114**, 924–30.

[27] Dirac, P. A. M. (1965), *Lectures on Quantum Mechanics* (Academic Press, New York).

[28] Donaldson, S. K. (1992), 'Boundary value problems for Yang–Mills fields', *J. Geom. Phys.* **8**, 89–122.

[29] Eguchi, T., Gilkey, P. B. and Hanson, A. J. (1980), 'Gravitation, gauge theories and differential geometry', *Phys. Rep.* **66**, 214–393.

[30] Faddeev, L. D. and Slavnov, A. A. (1980), *Gauge Fields: Introduction to Quantum Theory* (Benjamin Cummings, Reading, Mass.).

[31] Feynman, R. P. (1981), 'The qualitative behavior of Yang–Mills theory in 2+1 dimensions', *Nucl. Phys.* **B188**, 479–512.

[32] Feynman, R. P. and Hibbs, A. R. (1965), *Quantum Mechanics and Path Integrals* (McGraw-Hill, New York).

[33] Gambini, R. and Pullin, J. (1993), 'Quantum Einstein–Maxwell fields: A unified viewpoint from the loop representation' *Phys. Rev.* **D47**, R5214–8.

[34] Gibbons, G. W. and Hawking, S. W. (1977), 'Action integrals and partition functions in quantum gravity', *Phys. Rev.* **D15**, 2752–56.

[35] Gibbons, G. W. and Hawking, S. W. (1979), 'Classification of gravitational instanton symmetries', *Commun. Math. Phys.* **66**, 291–310.

[36] Gibbons, G. W. and Pope, C. N. (1978), '$\mathbb{C}P^2$ as a gravitational instanton', *Commun. Math. Phys.* **61**, 239–48.

[37] Gibbons, G. W., Hawking, S. W. and Perry, M. J. (1978), 'Path integrals and the indefiniteness of the gravitational action', *Nucl. Phys.* **B138**, 141–50.

[38] Goldstein, H. (1980), *Classical Mechanics* (Addison-Wesley, Reading, Mass.).

[39] Graham, C. R. and Lee, J. M. (1991), 'Einstein metrics with prescribed conformal infinity on the ball', *Adv. Math.* **87**, 186–225.

[40] Graham, R. and Paternoga, R. (1996), 'Physical states of Bianchi type IX quantum cosmologies described by the Chern–Simons functional', *Phys.Rev.* **D54**, 2589–2604.

[41] Hamilton, R. S. (1982), 'Three-manifolds with positive Ricci curvature' *J. Diff. Geom.* **17**, 255–306.

[42] Hamilton, R. S. (1986), 'Four-manifolds with positive curvature operator', *J. Diff. Geom.* **24**, 153–79.

[43] Hamilton, R. S. (1988), 'The Ricci flow on surfaces', in *Mathematics and General Relativity* (Contemporary Mathematics **71**), ed. J. A. Isenberg (American Mathematical Society, Providence, Rhode Island).

[44] Hartle, J. B. and Hawking, S. W. (1983), 'Wave function of the universe', *Phys. Rev.* **D28**, 2960–75.

[45] Hawking, S. W. (1977), 'Gravitational instantons', *Phys. Lett.* **60A**, 81–3.

[46] Hawking, S. W. (1982), In *Astrophysical Cosmology*, eds. H. A. Brück *et al.* (Pontificia Academiae Scientarium, Vatican City) **48**, 563–80.

[47] Hawking, S. W. (1988), 'Wormholes in space-time', *Phys. Rev.* **D37**, 904–10.

[48] Hitchin, N. J. (1995), 'Twistor spaces, Einstein metrics and isomonodromic deformations', *J. Diff. Geom.* **42**, 30–112.

[49] Itzykson, C. and Zuber, J.-B. (1980), *Quantum Field Theory* (McGraw-Hill, New York).

[50] Jackiw, R. (1984), 'Topological investigations of quantized gauge theories', in *Relativity, Groups and Topology II*, eds. B. S. DeWitt and R.Stora (North-Holland, Amsterdam), 221–331.

[51] Jacobson, T. (1988), 'New variables for canonical supergravity', *Class. Quantum Grav.* **5**, 923–35.

[52] Jacobson, T. and Smolin, L. (1988), 'Covariant action for Ashtekar's form of canonical gravity', *Class. Quantum Grav.* **5**, 583–94.

[53] Jensen, L. G., Louko, J. and Ruback, P. J. (1991), 'Biaxial Bianchi type IX quantum cosmology', *Nucl. Phys.* **B351**, 662–78.

[54] Kodama, H. (1990), 'Holomorphic wave function of the universe', *Phys. Rev.* **D42**, 2548–65.

[55] Koshti, S. and Dadhich, N. (1990), 'On the self-duality of the Weyl tensor using Ashtekar's variables', *Class. Quantum Grav.* **7**, L5–7.

[56] Kramer, D., Stephani, H., MacCallum, M. and Herlt, E. (1979), *Exact Solutions of Einstein's Field Equations* (Cambridge University Press).

[57] Landau, L. D. and Lifshitz, E. M. (1976), *Mechanics* (Pergamon Press, Oxford).

[58] LeBrun, C. R., (1982), '$\mathcal{H}$-Space with a cosmological constant', *Proc. Roy. Soc. London* **A380**, 171–85.

[59] LeBrun, C. R. (1991), 'On complete quaternionic-Kähler manifolds', *Duke Math. J.* **63**, 723–43.

[60] Louko, J. (1995), 'Chern–Simons functional and the no-boundary proposal in Bianchi-IX quantum cosmology', *Phys. Rev.* **D51**, 586–590.

[61] Macías, A. (1996), 'Chiral (N=1) supergravity', *Class. Quantum Grav.* **13**, 3163–74.

[62] Mason, L. J. and Woodhouse, N. M. J. (1996), *Integrability, Self-Duality, and Twistor Theory* (Oxford University Press, Oxford).

[63] Mielke, E. W. (1990), 'Generating function for new variables in general relativity and Poincaré gauge theory', *Phys. Lett.* **A149**, 345–50.

[64] Misner, C. W., Thorne, K. S. and Wheeler, J. A. (1973), *Gravitation* (Freeman, San Francisco).

[65] Nelson, J. E. and Teitelboim, C. (1978), 'Hamiltonian formulation of the theory of interacting gravitational and electron fields', *Ann. Phys. N.Y.* **116**, 86–104.

[66] Penrose, R. and Rindler, W. (1984), *Spinors and Space-time, Vol.1: Two-Spinor Calculus and Relativistic Fields* (Cambridge University Press, Cambridge).

[67] Penrose, R. and Rindler, W. (1986), *Spinors and Space-time, Vol.2: Spinor and Twistor Methods in Space-time Geometry* (Cambridge University Press, Cambridge).

[68] Reula, O. (1987), 'A configuration space for quantum gravity and solutions to the Euclidean Einstein equations in a slab region', Max-Planck-Institut für Astrophysik, preprint **MPA** 275.

[69] Robinson, D. C. (1994), 'A $\mathcal{G}L(2,\mathbb{C})$ formulation of Einstein-Maxwell theory', *Class. Quantum Grav.* **11**, L157–61.

[70] Robinson, D. C. (1995), 'Lagrangian formulation of the Einstein–Yang–Mills equations', *J. Math. Phys.* **36**, 3733–42.

[71] Ryan, M. P. and Shepley, L. C. (1975), *Homogeneous Relativistic Cosmologies* (Princeton University Press).

[72] Samuel, J. (1988), 'Gravitational instantons from the Ashtekar variables', *Class. Quantum Grav.* **5**, L123–5.

[73] Sano, T. (1992), 'The Ashtekar formalism and WKB wave functions of N=1,2 supergravities', University of Tokyo preprint **UT**-621.

[74] Sano, T. and Shiraishi, J. (1993), 'The non-perturbative canonical quantization of the N=1 supergravity', *Nucl. Phys.* **B410**, 423–47.

[75] Schlenker, J.-M. (1998), 'Einstein manifolds with convex boundaries', Orsay preprint.

[76] Teitelboim, C. (1977), 'Supergravity and square roots of constraints', *Phys. Rev. Lett.* **38**, 1106–10.

[77] Tod, K. P. (1994), 'Self-dual Einstein metrics from the Painlevé VI equation', *Phys. Lett.* **A190**, 221–4.

[78] Ward, R. S. (1980), 'Self-dual space-times with cosmological constant', *Commun. Math. Phys.* **78**, 1–17.

[79] Ward, R. S. and Wells, R. O. (1990), *Twistor Geometry and Field Theory* (Cambridge University Press, Cambridge).

[80] Wells, R. O. (1980), *Differential Analysis on Complex Manifolds* (Springer, Berlin).

[81] Wess, J. and Bagger, J. (1992), *Supersymmetry and Supergravity* (Princeton University Press).

[82] Wheeler, J. A. (1968), 'Superspace and the nature of quantum geometrodynamics', in *Battelle Rencontres 1967*, eds. C.M.DeWitt and J. A. Wheeler (Benjamin, New York).

Part 9

Cosmology

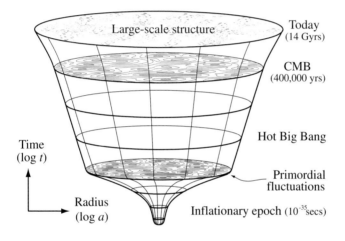

Large-scale structure

Today
(14 Gyrs)

CMB
(400,000 yrs)

Hot Big Bang

Primordial
fluctuations

Inflationary epoch (10^{-35}secs)

Time
($\log t$)

Radius
($\log a$)

These would lead to fluctuations in the rate of expansion which would have the right spectrum to account for the existence of galaxies.

Physics Letters, 1982

40

Inflation and cosmological perturbations

Alan Guth

Center for Theoretical Physics, Massachusetts Institute of Technology

40.1 The origin of inflationary fluctuations

Since the topic of inflation and density perturbations pretty much came to fruition at the Nuffield Workshop [15] almost 20 years ago, and since I was one of the attendees, I thought I would spend about half my talk reminiscing about the history of those events. The three-week period of the Nuffield meeting was certainly among the most exciting times of my life. I will always cherish the memories of those events, and I will always be grateful to Stephen for the important role that he played in making them happen.

When 'old inflation' [17] was first invented, we knew at once that we could identify at least one possible source of density perturbations: namely, the random nucleation of bubbles. In that model the phase transition was assumed to be strongly first order, so it ended with bubbles of the new phase nucleating and colliding, producing some kind of inhomogeneous froth similar to boiling water. But it was of course not clear immediately whether these density perturbations would have the right properties to serve as the seeds for structure formation. Stephen played an important role in sorting out this question, as one of the key papers was that of Hawking, Stewart and Moss [29]. Once the issue was understood, the answer was clear. The density perturbations created in the old inflationary model were ridiculously large – colossal – so there was absolutely no hope of getting a universe from it that looked like ours.

Fortunately, inflation was resurrected by the invention of 'new inflation' by Linde [33], and Albrecht and Steinhardt [2], and it was in that context that the question of density perturbations could first be intelligently addressed. For new inflation, however, the question of density perturbations was much more subtle.

The first I remember hearing about this was at a meeting at Moriond in March of 1982. I chatted with Michael Turner, and I guess he had been in touch with Jim Bardeen. As far as I know, Jim was one of first people to really worry about this issue. Jim had realized that in the context of the new inflationary model, any density perturbations present before inflation would be suppressed by an enormous exponential factor as they evolved through the inflationary regime. This meant that if the model was to have any chance of viability, some mechanism would have to be found to allow the density perturbations to survive. According to Michael, Jim was exploring the possibility that there might be some mechanism at the very end of inflation that would amplify the density perturbations which had been suppressed out of sight by the process of inflation itself. At about the same time I had a conversation with Dave Schramm, who was also aware of this problem, and who thought that maybe we would have to learn about turbulence to understand how density perturbations could survive.

In May 1982, there was a chance meeting in Chicago of three physicists interested in these questions: Michael Turner, Paul Steinhardt and Stephen Hawking. Michael was of course based in Chicago, as he still is, Paul was visiting to give a colloquium, and Stephen was by chance visiting at the same time to collaborate with Jim Hartle. It had been five years since Stephen had written his famous paper [14] with Gary Gibbons on quantum field theory in de Sitter space, so Stephen was well-versed in the role that quantum fluctuations can play in an exponentially expanding space. In that paper Gary and Stephen had shown the now-classic result that quantum fluctuations in de Sitter space produce thermal radiation with a temperature

$$T_{\text{GH}} = \frac{H}{2\pi} \, , \tag{40.1}$$

where H is the Hubble constant of the de Sitter space, and I use units for which $\hbar = c = k_{\text{Boltzmann}} = 1$. Stephen was of course also one of the world's experts on cosmological density fluctuations, going back to his seminal work on the evolution of density perturbations in 1966 [25]. I was of course not part of this meeting, but I learned about it from Michael and Paul while I was gathering material for my popular level book [18][1] of which the Nuffield Workshop was one of the highlights. Apparently not much in the way of details was discussed at this meeting, but the three physicists discussed a crucially important new idea: the possibility that the structure of the cosmos originated in quantum fluctuations. From

---

[1] In the book I erroneously stated that the meeting took place in April. This was based on some early discussions, but later Paul checked his travel records and discovered that his trip extended from May 5 to 7, 1982.

the point of view of unity in physics, this is a truly breathtaking idea, proposing that the same quantum phenomena that are central to the study of atoms and subatomic physics are also responsible for the largest structures known to humans. The meeting reportedly ended when Stephen left to shop at F.A.O. Schwarz, the famous toy store.[2]

Later in May, I learned from Paul Steinhardt that he and Michael had come up with a plausible way of estimating the effects of quantum fluctuations, in the context of what was then the universally favoured grand unified theory, the minimal SU(5) model. They concluded that the spectrum would be scale-invariant, which is what cosmologists favoured [23, 56], but that $\delta\rho/\rho$, the fractional perturbations in the mass density, would be about 10^{-16}. The answer that we all wanted was about 10^{-4}, so they knew they were not there yet, but they were still trying.

On June 7, 1982, Stephen gave a seminar in Princeton about his density perturbation calculations. I was not there either, but Paul Steinhardt was. The day after the talk, Paul and I had a long telephone conversation in which he gave me a detailed summary of what Stephen had said. I took notes while on the phone, and I still have them. In contrast to Paul's and Michael's result of 10^{-16}, Stephen's calculations gave the result of $\delta\rho/\rho \sim 10^{-4}$, exactly what was wanted. Shortly afterward Stephen circulated a preprint [26] summarizing these calculations. I learned from Stephen that his preprint was actually written before his trip to the U.S. at the beginning of May, although its date is listed as June, when the typing was completed. The abstract of that preprint explained that irregularities would be produced in inflationary models by quantum fluctuations in the scalar field as it ran down the hill of an effective potential diagram. The abstract continued:

> These would lead to fluctuations in the rate of expansion which would
> have the right spectrum and amplitude to account for the existence
> of galaxies and for the isotropy of the microwave background.

So it was a big success! Inflation actually worked, accounting not only for the large-scale uniformity of the universe, but also for the spectrum of density fluctuations needed to explain the tapestry of cosmic structure.

When Paul and I were discussing Stephen's Princeton seminar on the telephone, Paul relayed to me essentially all the equations that Stephen had presented. These began with equations relating the perturbations during inflation to the quantum fluctuations of the scalar field, as described

---

[2] While the idea that the large-scale scale structure of the universe originated from quantum fluctuations was, so far as I know, new in the West, the idea had been explored in the Soviet Union more than a year earlier, when Mukhanov and Chibisov [40] studied quantum fluctuations in the Starobinsky [48, 49] version of inflation.

by the scalar field two-point function. We did not quite understand what Stephen was talking about, but we assumed he was probably right. Stephen also described – in a couple of lines – how density perturbations would evolve from the beginning of inflation up to the present day. These were the sort of calculations that Stephen had done long before; he knew the answers, so he just wrote them down. Again Paul and I assumed that Stephen must have known what he was talking about. There was one step in the calculation, however, where Stephen calculated the time derivative of the scalar field, as it rolled down the hill of the potential energy diagram. That was really the only step in the calculation that I was capable at the time of understanding, but as far as Paul and I could tell, Stephen got it wrong. If we did this calculation our way, the answer became larger by about a factor of 10^4, giving $\delta\rho/\rho$ about equal to one. So Paul and I were very skeptical of Stephen's result, although, since we did not understand the rest of the calculation, we were not really sure what Stephen was thinking, or whether we were correctly interpreting his equations. From our point of view Stephen's result looked wrong, but we were not absolutely sure.

I then began working on this in detail with So-Young Pi. We closely followed the pattern of Stephen's calculation, trying to make sure that we understood each step. A key element in Stephen's approach was to think of the primary driving force behind the density fluctuations as the fluctuation $\delta t(\vec{x})$ in the time at which inflation ends in different places. The description of density perturbations depends very much on the coordinate system (i.e., the choice of gauge) in which they are described, so the papers on this subject that came out of the Nuffield meeting [3, 19, 27, 50] do not all look the same. While all of these papers got the same answer, the calculations are difficult to compare. The papers by Stephen, Starobinsky, and the one by So-Young and me all focused on the time delay function $\delta t(\vec{x})$, but they still used somewhat different ways of connecting this function to the final result. The paper by Bardeen, Steinhardt and Turner used a more complete integration of the full set of equations from perturbative general relativity. I have always found that the time-delay approach, which we learned from Stephen, is the clearest way to understand density fluctuations, as long as one is interested in models with a single scalar field that rolls slowly, so that the Hubble parameter H can be treated as a constant during the period when the perturbations of the relevant wavelengths are generated. The models that interested us in 1982 fell within these restrictions, although the generality of the Bardeen–Steinhardt–Turner approach (and further elaborations – see for example [41]) is needed to analyse the wider range of models that have since become relevant.

By the way, Stephen's paper on density perturbations [27] turns out to be his third most cited paper of all time, so I am personally rather proud to have been vaguely involved in Stephen's third most cited paper! I made a list of Stephen's most cited papers from yesterday's listings on SPIRES (http://www.slac.stanford.edu/spires/hep/), and I was flabbergasted to see that Stephen has 33 papers that have more than a hundred cites; I think this is really astounding. Cites do not mean everything, of course, but when you see this many, you can be sure they mean something!

40.2 The 1982 Nuffield workshop

Chronologically, the next event – the big event – was the Nuffield Workshop, which began on Monday, June 21, 1982. I still have my original invitation from the organizers of the meeting, Gary Gibbons and Stephen (see Figure 40.1). I, of course, didn't care about Gary, but I was so impressed that I received a letter that was actually signed by the famous Stephen Hawking (or at least by someone authorized to use his signature) that I saved it for 20 odd years. The key paragraph in the letter stated the premise of the meeting, which with historical hindsight seems very impressive. It is a really good description of where cosmology was at then, and some of these problems are still problems that we are talking about now:

> The standard model seems to provide a satisfactory account of the evolution of the universe after 1 sec but it assumes certain initial conditions such as thermal equilibrium, spatial homogeneity and isotropy with small fluctuations, spatial flatness, and the baryon to entropy ratio. The aim of the workshop would be to discuss how these conditions could have arisen from physical processes in the very early universe on the basis of grand unified theories and quantum gravity. Topics covered would include phase transitions, the generation of baryon number, the production of monopoles, primordial black holes and other long lived particles, the existence and nature of the initial singularity, particle creation and the origin of fluctuations.

What I want to talk about today is the success of this conference in making real progress on the issue of the primordial density perturbations.

I still have the transparencies from the talk I gave at the very end of the conference, which summarizes what I knew then about density fluctuations. Figure 40.2 shows my opening transparency from that talk. I have to confess that the very first thing on the transparency is the potential energy diagram of the minimal $SU(5)$ grand unified theory with a Coleman–Weinberg potential, which at that time we all knew was the correct theory. Its amazing that after 21 years of research we now know so much less – but I guess that is a form of progress, too.

UNIVERSITY OF CAMBRIDGE

Department of Applied Mathematics and Theoretical Physics
Silver Street, Cambridge CB3 9EW
Telephone: Cambridge (0223) 51645

Dr. A. H. Guth,
Center for Theoretical Physics,
Laboratory for Nuclear Science and
   Department of Physics,
M.I.T.
Cambridge – Massachusetts, 02139,
United States of America.   14 October, 1981.

Dear Dr. Guth,

   As you may know, the Nuffield Foundation has provided funds for a series
of workshops on Quantum Gravity and related topics.   Next year we are
planning to hold a workshop here in Cambridge on the very early Universe
(< 1 sec).   The dates envisaged are June 21st to July 9th 1982.

   The standard model seems to provide a satisfactory account of the evolution
of the universe after 1 sec but it assumes certain initial conditions such as
thermal equilibrium, spatial homogeneity and isotropy with small fluctuations,
spatial flatness, and the baryon to entropy ratio.   The aim of the workshop
would be to discuss how these conditions could have arisen from physical processes in the very early universe on the basis of grand unified theories and
quantum gravity.   Topics covered would include phase transitions, the
generation of baryon number, the production of monopoles, primordial black
holes and other long lived particles, the existence and nature of the initial
singularity, particle creation and the origin of fluctuations.   As in previous
years the aim would be to limit the formal programme to about two seminars a
day to leave time for informal discussion.

   We would like to invite you to take part in the workshop.   We could pay
your airfare and subsistence, but we would be grateful if you could take
advantage of any cheap fares that are convenient to enable us to stretch our
limited funds as far as possible.

   Please let us know whether you will be able to come.   We would be grateful
for any comments you may have on the organization of the workshop or of topics
to be discussed.

                         Yours sincerely,

                         Gary Gibbon

                         Stephen Hawking

                         Stephen W. Hawking
                         Gary W. Gibbons

Fig. 40.1. Invitation to the Nuffield workshop on the Very Early Universe.

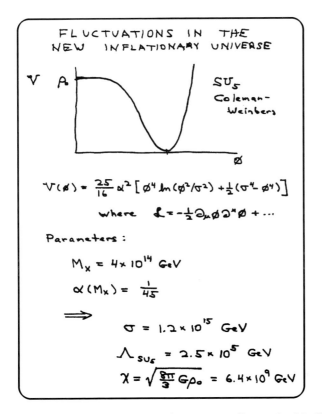

Fig. 40.2. The opening transparency from my talk at the Nuffield Workshop on *Fluctuations in the New Inflationary Universe.*

In that same talk, I tried to describe the flow of thoughts on the subject, so I made a transparency to summarize the evolution of our thinking on the values of $\delta\rho/\rho$ as a function of time in 1982 (see Figure 40.3). We were evaluating $\delta\rho/\rho$ for each mode at 'second Hubble crossing', labelled on the chart as $2t = \ell$. Here ℓ is the wavelength in physical (as opposed to comoving) units, and $2t$ in the radiation-dominated era is equal to H^{-1}, the Hubble length. (This is the second Hubble crossing, because for each mode there was also a time during inflation when the physical wavelength, which grows exponentially during inflation, crosses the Hubble length, which is approximately constant during inflation.) The scale-invariant Harrison–Zeldovich spectrum is the spectrum for which $\delta\rho/\rho$ at second Hubble crossing has the same value of each mode, and although we were disagreeing on the amplitude, we were all getting approximately scale-invariant spectra.

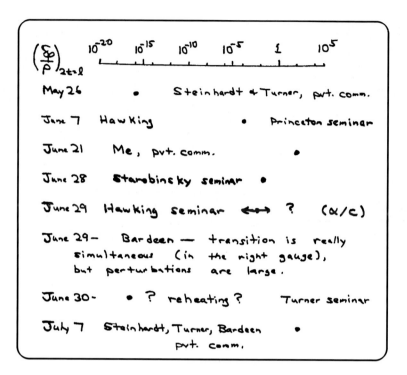

Fig. 40.3. From my Nuffield Workshop talk: evolution of theoretical predictions for the amplitude of the density fluctuations from inflation.

The chart starts at May 26, 1982, when Paul Steinhart told me that he and Michael Turner were getting $\delta\rho/\rho \sim 10^{-16}$. The second line refers to Stephen Hawking's seminar in Princeton on June 7, when he announced the result that $\delta\rho/\rho \sim 10^{-4}$. The following line shows my own answer, $\delta\rho/\rho \sim 50$, listed as a private communication from me to me, on June 21. Now I'll admit that showing this transparency may have been a bit egotistical on my part, but after all, these were the days when Stephen and I were both young.

I was working with So-Young Pi, and as I said we started from Hawking's work, struggling to fill in all the details that we needed to get from one line of Stephen's preprint to the next. But we evaluated the time-derivative of the scalar field differently from Stephen, and concluded that in the minimal SU(5) model the perturbations would be far too large, with $\delta\rho/\rho \sim 50$. So-Young and I had started these calculations together, but we didn't have the final answer until I completed the calculations the day after I arrived here in Cambridge. Cambridge is a great place to do calculations. They gave us rooms in Sidney Sussex College with thick walls

Fig. 40.4. Photograph of the participants at the Nuffield Workshop.

and thick doors and no telephones, so I worked late into the night and finished the calculation the next morning, after breakfast, behind those thick doors. I have always thought Cambridge is a fantastic place to do physics. Anyway I got the answer shown in the third line of the chart, $\delta\rho/\rho \sim 50$, which means that the model did not work. It is interesting to wonder whether I was disappointed with my result, since inflation was my baby. The answer is that, since inflation had not really caught on yet in 1982, I was absolutely thrilled to find an answer that I was pretty sure corrected a calculation of Stephen's, which to me was more of a victory than if inflation had worked! In the end I have had some of the benefits of both options, since the minimal SU(5) grand unified theory is now ruled out by the absence of observed proton decays, and we can construct other particle theory models that allow the density perturbation amplitude to turn out right.

Continuing, the next line shows the first seminar on density fluctuations at the Nuffield Workshop, by Alexei Starobinski, on Monday June 28, at the beginning of the second week. My chart shows him at $\delta\rho/\rho \sim 10^{-2}$, but he later clarified that he found that the perturbations were of order unity, and hence the real conclusion is simply that perturbation theory could not be trusted.

Then Stephen gave his seminar, on Tuesday June 29, a little more than a week into the conference. Before this time I had had one conversation with Stephen about density perturbations, but that conversation was cut off by the start of the next seminar; I remember that this was my seminar so I did not think I should miss it! Stephen was continuing to argue that his original preprint was correct, but Paul Steinhardt and I were having trouble understanding Stephen's line of reasoning. Stephen's seminar was impishly titled 'The End of Inflation', which of course could have meant that he was going to discuss how the inflationary era would end, or it could have meant that he was going to argue that the inflationary theory is dead. Stephen always liked to generate surprises. When Stephen began his seminar, Paul and I were prepared to pounce at the point where we thought he had made a mistake, hoping that the ensuing discussion could settle the issue. But when Stephen reached this point in the seminar, very near the end, he jolted us by not using the argument we expected, but instead substituted a new calculation which in fact agreed with our calculation for the time derivative of the scalar field. He then agreed with our answer, that the density perturbations were indeed far too large. He expressed his answer as α/C, where α is the fine-structure constant of the grand unified theory, and C was a dimensionless constant that was not calculated, which he referred to in his talk as a 'fudge factor'. In his talk, Stephen concluded that we would need $C \sim 100$, or else the inflationary scenario would have to be abandoned. In the published version of Stephen's paper [27], the abstract began identically but ended differently:

> These [irregularities in the scalar field] would lead to fluctuations in the rate of expansion which would have the right spectrum to account for the existence of galaxies. However the amplitude would be too high to be consistent with observations of the isotropy of the microwave background unless the effective coupling constant of the Higgs scalar was very small.

'Very small', as we now know, means about 10^{-13} or something close to that. I have never known when it was that Stephen changed his mind, or whether he circulated this preprint just to tease us from the beginning. He certainly did not change his mind while he was giving his talk, so he must have decided earlier that his original preprint had the wrong answer. But he did not tell any of us. Stephen recently told me that he initially calculated the time derivative of the scalar field when it was halfway down the hill, but talking to people at the workshop made him realize that it should be evaluated at first Hubble crossing, which gives much larger perturbations. When Stephen gave the talk, he proceeded without a pause, with no suggestion that the result he was presenting was in contradiction of his own preprint.

As my chart shows, by the time of my talk Bardeen, Steinhardt and Turner had invented a more accurate way to solve their equations, and found an answer in agreement with the rest of us. The result that we all found was roughly

$$\left(\frac{\delta\rho}{\rho}\right)_{2t=\ell} = C\,\frac{H\,\delta\phi}{\dot{\phi}_{\mathrm{cl}}}\,, \tag{40.2}$$

where $\delta\phi \sim H$ is the quantum fluctuation in ϕ, C is a constant of order unity which depends on detailed normalization conventions, and $\dot{\phi}_{\mathrm{cl}}$ is the proper time-derivative of the function that describes the classical evolution of the inflaton field. The right-hand side is evaluated at first Hubble crossing, the instant during the inflationary era when the physical wavelength of the mode under consideration is equal to H^{-1}.

40.3 Observational evidence for inflation

At the time of the Nuffield meeting, I thought it was great fun and excitement to try to calculate the predictions for the density perturbations resulting from inflation, but I never believed that anyone would actually measure these density perturbations. I guess I am speaking mainly for myself, but I suspect that the others felt the same way. I knew that we had some idea of what density perturbations were needed to explain galaxy formation, and I'm sure I believed that such estimates would improve with time. But I never thought we would have direct measurements of the density perturbations coming from the microwave background. The radiation itself is incredibly weak; it is, we should keep in mind, thermal radiation at $3\,\mathrm{K}$, which is about $100,000,000$ times weaker than thermal radiation at room temperature, which is itself pretty weak. And the non-uniformities that we are talking about are at the level of only about one part in $100,000$. So I found it absolutely astounding when the COBE results were published in 1992, and I was even more astounded by the recent results of Boomerang, Maxima, DASI, and CBI.

Today the measurements of the cosmic microwave background (CMB) and the perturbations that they exhibit are truly extraordinary. Figure 40.5 is a graph of the most recent data that was released by the Boomerang group [42], the Maxima group [32], the DASI group [22], and the CBI group [43]. These experiments measure the non-uniformities $\Delta T(\theta,\phi)$ of the CMB radiation, which are described by their expansion in spherical harmonics:

$$\Delta T(\theta,\phi) = \sum_{\ell m} a_{\ell m} Y_{\ell m}(\theta,\phi). \tag{40.3}$$

For each ℓ one defines

$$C_{\ell} \equiv \left\langle |a_{\ell m}|^2 \right\rangle, \tag{40.4}$$

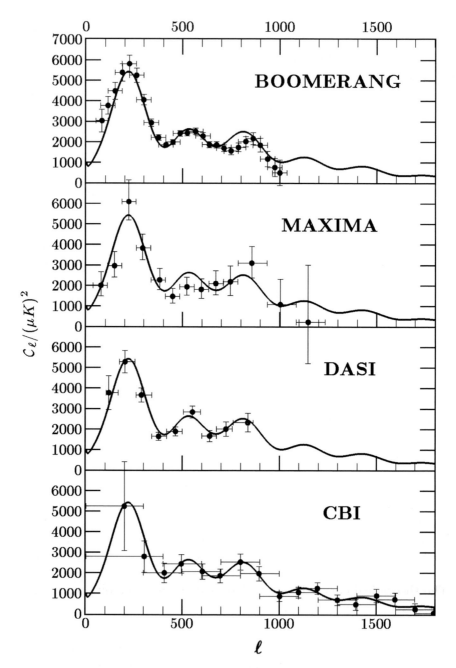

Fig. 40.5. Angular power spectrum of the CMB compared with an inflationary model. The theoretical model is the best fit to all the data obtained by the CBI group ([43]), described by the parameters $\Omega_{\text{tot}} = 1.0$, $\Omega_\Lambda = 0.7$, $\Omega_{\text{CDM}} = 0.257$, $\Omega_b h^2 = 0.020$, $h = 0.68$, $n_s = 0.95$, $\tau_c = 0$.

and then

$$\mathcal{C}_\ell \equiv \frac{1}{2\pi}\ell(\ell+1)C_\ell. \tag{40.5}$$

The graphs show the measurements of the $\mathcal{C}_\ell$s in microkelvin^2, as a function of multipole ℓ. The graph also shows a theoretical prediction, corresponding to the 'Joint model' of [43], which was computed using the computer code of Seljak and Zaldarriaga, CMBFAST [47].

The curves show a series of well-defined 'acoustic' peaks, caused by the oscillations of the cosmic fluid of photons, neutrinos, electrons, protons and dark matter. Roughly speaking, the image of the cosmic background radiation on the sky is a snapshot of what the universe looked like at the time of last scattering, a time about 400,000 years after the Big Bang, at which the plasma of the early universe neutralized to form a transparent gas. Although the fluctuations of all wavelengths are imprinted on the CMB at the same time, it is nonetheless a conceptually useful approximation to think of the graph of $\mathcal{C}_\ell$s versus ℓ as if it were a graph of the fluctuations of the early universe as a function of time. The shorter wavelength (i.e., higher ℓ) fluctuations evolve faster, so at the time of last scattering they have undergone more oscillations and are therefore in a later stage of their evolution than their longer wavelength cousins. The lower amplitude at higher ℓ is partly due to the damping of these oscillations, and partly due to the fact that the time of last scattering is not unique, since the transition from opacity to transparency is actually somewhat gradual. Thus the CMB image has some similarities to a photographic time exposure, and the small scale details are therefore blurred.

The probability distribution for the time of last scattering is shown in Figure 40.6, calculated[3] for exactly the same parameters as the curves in Figure 40.5. The median time of last scattering is 388,000 years, the peak of the curve is at 367,000 years, and the full width at half maximum is 113,000 years. (The mean was computed as 475,000 years, but the calculation was influenced significantly by a long late-time tail of the probability distribution, extending to billions of years; it is not clear if this calculation is reliable or relevant.)

The theoretical curve shown in Figure 40.5 has an amplitude which is normalized to the data; in practice inflationary models do not make any

---

[3] The visibility function shown here was calculated using CMBFAST, but the program had to be modified to print out this information, which normally is used internally. I also modified the code slightly to keep track of proper time, as opposed to conformal time. The ionization evolution was calculated using the RECFAST subroutine distributed with CMBFAST, which was written by D. Scott, based on calculations by Seager, Sasselov and Scott [46].

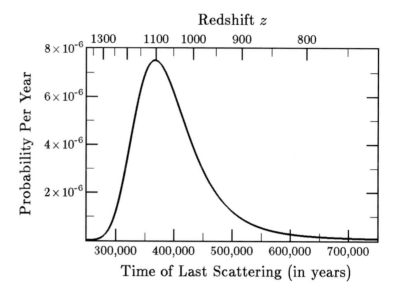

Fig. 40.6. The probability distribution for the time of last scattering of the CMB photons. The curve was computed using the same parameters as in Figure 40.5.

prediction for the overall amplitude of the fluctuations, though we could in principle make a prediction if we really knew the potential energy function of the inflaton field, the scalar field that drives inflation.

However, everything else about this curve is pretty well fixed either by inflation, or by astronomical determinations of cosmological parameters. For example, the curves depend sensitively on $\Omega_{tot} = \rho_{tot}/\rho_c$, where ρ_{tot} is the total mass density, and the critical mass density ρ_c is defined to be that density which corresponds to a flat spatial geometry.[4] ρ_c is related to the Hubble constant H by $\rho_c = 3H^2/(8\pi G)$, where G is Newton's gravitational constant. Inflation predicts that $\Omega_{tot} = 1$, and the curves are drawn for $\Omega_{tot} = 1$. If Ω_{tot} were decreased from 1, all the peaks would

---

[4] Until recently it was common to say that the critical density was that density which put the universe just on the borderline between eternal expansion and eventual collapse. This definition was never generally accepted as a technical definition, but was nonetheless often used in lectures, especially those intended for a non-technical audience. If the only materials present are normal matter, dark matter, and radiation, then the two definitions are equivalent. However, since we now believe that the universe contains a large amount of 'dark energy' with negative pressure, these definitions are no longer equivalent. We must therefore keep in mind that the critical density is defined in terms of the spatial geometry of the universe.

shift to the right. If Ω_{tot} were 0.3, as was widely believed five years ago, the first peak would be at about $\ell = 400$.

The curve also depends on the present value of the Hubble constant, which was taken to be $H \equiv 100\,h \cdot \text{km} \cdot \text{s}^{-1} \cdot \text{Mpc}^{-1}$, with $h = 0.68$. This value is completely consistent with the Hubble Key Project value [13], $h = 0.72 \pm 0.08$. An increase in h would push all the peaks downward and toward the left.

The density of baryons in the universe also affects the predicted curves. This density is usually quantified by the product $\Omega_b h^2$. (Note that $\Omega_b h^2 \equiv \rho_b h^2 / \rho_c$, so the explicit factor of h^2 cancels the h-dependence of ρ_c, and consequently $\Omega_b h^2$ is really just an indirect way of describing ρ_b.) A high density of baryons suppresses the second peak, and indeed when the first Boomerang results [4] were released in 2000, the absence of an apparent second peak led some to speculate (see, for example, [31]) that the universe might contain 50% more baryons than expected on the basis of Big Bang nucleosynthesis. This problem soon dissolved with the appearance of new data, and the fit shown in Figure 40.5 uses $\Omega_b h^2 = 0.020$, in perfect agreement with nucleosynthesis-based estimate of Burles, Nollett and Turner [11], $\Omega_b h^2 = 0.020 \pm 0.002$ (95% confidence).

The scalar power law index n_s is predicted to be very near one for simple inflationary models, corresponding to a scale-invariant Harrison–Zeldovich [23, 56] spectrum; the data is fit with $n_s = 0.95$. $\tau_c = 0$ means that no re-ionization of the intergalactic medium is assumed, and the values used for the densities of cold dark matter ($\Omega_{\text{CDM}} = 0.257$) and 'dark energy' ($\Omega_\Lambda = 0.7$) are consistent with the supernova observations [44, 45].

So, except for the height of the curve, the data shown in Figure 40.5 can be essentially predicted on the basis of other measurements and on the inflationary model. I consider this a spectacular success. I am amazed that this data can be measured, and that it agrees so well with what we predicted back in 1982. It seems to show not only that inflation is correct, but that the simplest form of slow-roll inflation is correct. Given the amount of flexibility that inflationary models allow, and also the uncertainties that exist in the data, I suspect that probably it is fortuitous that the agreement is as good as what we see. My guess is that we are going to see some disagreements before things really fit together tightly, but nonetheless we are currently seeing a very spectacular agreement which strongly suggests that we are on the right course.

40.4 Eternal inflation

For the remaining half of my talk, I want to discuss an issue related to the eternal nature of inflation. This may be only vaguely related to the topic that I was asked to talk about, inflation and cosmological perturbations, but there is a connection. The density perturbations arising from inflation are never truly scale invariant, but typically grow slowly at large wavelengths. Eternal inflation is really a consequence of the very long wavelength, high amplitude tail of the density perturbation spectrum of inflation. At extremely long wavelengths these perturbations are usually so large that they prevent inflation from ending at all in some places, leading to what is called eternal inflation.

My main goal is to describe a singularity theorem that I recently proved in collaboration with Alex Vilenkin and Arvind Borde [5]. But first, I would like to give a brief explanation of how eternal inflation works.

There are basically two versions of inflation, and consequently two answers to the question of why inflation is eternal (see Figure 40.7). In the case of new inflation, the exponential expansion occurs as the scalar field rolls from the peak of a potential energy diagram down to a trough. (I refer to the state for which the scalar field is at the top of the hill as a *false vacuum*, although this is a slight change from the original definition of the phrase.) The eternal aspect occurs while the scalar field is hovering around the peak. The first model of this type was constructed by Steinhardt [52] in 1983, and later that year Vilenkin [54] showed that new inflationary models are generically eternal. The key point is that, even though classically the field would roll off the hill, quantum-mechanically there is always an amplitude, a tail of the wave function, for it to remain

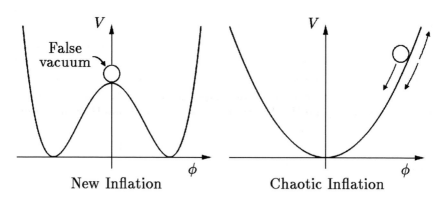

Fig. 40.7. Eternal inflation from both a new inflationary potential (left) and a chaotic inflationary potential (right).

at the top. If you ask how fast does this tail of the wave function fall off with time, the answer in almost any model is that it falls off exponentially with time, just like the decay of most metastable states [20]. The time scale for the decay of the false vacuum is controlled by

$$m^2 = -\left.\frac{\partial^2 V}{\partial \phi^2}\right|_{\phi=0}, \qquad (40.6)$$

the negative mass-squared of the scalar field when it is at the top of the hill in the potential diagram. This is an adjustable parameter as far as our use of the model is concerned, but m has to be small compared with the Hubble constant or else the model does not lead to enough inflation. So, for parameters that are chosen to make the inflationary model work, the exponential decay of the false vacuum is slower than the exponential expansion. Even though the false vacuum is decaying, the expansion outruns the decay and the total volume of false vacuum actually increases with time rather than decreases. Thus inflation does not end everywhere at once, but instead inflation ends in localized patches, in a succession that continues ad infinitum. Each patch is essentially a whole universe – at least its residents will consider it a whole universe – and so inflation can be said to produce not just one universe, but an infinite number of universes. These universes are sometimes called bubble universes, but I prefer to use the phrase 'pocket universe', to avoid the implication that they are approximately round. (While bubbles formed in first-order phase transitions are round [12], the local universes formed in eternal new inflation are generally very irregular, as can be seen for example in the two-dimensional simulation by Vanchurin, Vilenkin and Winitzki in Figure 2 of [53].)

In the context of chaotic inflationary models, as developed by Andrei Linde (who both proposed the models [35, 36] and showed that they are eternal [16, 37–39]), the situation is slightly more complicated. Inflation is occurring as the scalar field rolls down a hill of the potential energy diagram, starting high on the hill. As the field rolls down the hill, quantum fluctuations will be superimposed on top of the classical motion. The best way to think about this is to ask what happens during one time interval of duration $\Delta t = H^{-1}$ (one Hubble time), in a region of one Hubble volume H^{-3}. Suppose that ϕ_0 is the average value of ϕ in this region, at the start of the time interval. By the definition of a Hubble time, we know how much expansion is going to occur during the time interval: exactly a factor of e. (This is the only exact number in today's talk, so I wanted to emphasize the point.) That means the volume will expand by a factor of e^3. One of the deep truths that one learns by working on inflation is that e^3 is about equal to 20, so the volume will expand by a factor of 20. Since correlations typically extend over about a Hubble length, by the end of one Hubble time, the initial Hubble-sized region grows and breaks up into 20 independent Hubble-sized regions.

As the scalar field is classically rolling down the hill, the classical change in the field $\Delta\phi_{cl}$ during the time interval Δt is going to be modified by quantum fluctuations $\Delta\phi_{qu}$, which can drive the field upward or downward relative to the classical trajectory. For any one of the 20 regions at the end of the time interval, we can describe the change in ϕ during the interval by

$$\Delta\phi = \Delta\phi_{cl} + \Delta\phi_{qu} \ . \tag{40.7}$$

In lowest order perturbation theory the fluctuation is treated as a free quantum field, which implies that $\Delta\phi_{qu}$, the quantum fluctuation averaged over one of the 20 Hubble volumes at the end, will have a Gaussian probability distribution, with a width of order $H/2\pi$ [34, 50, 51, 55]. There is then always some probability that the sum of the two terms on the right-hand side will be positive – that the scalar field will fluctuate up and not down. As long as that probability is bigger than 1 in 20, then the number of inflating regions with $\phi \geq \phi_0$ will be larger at the end of the time interval Δt than it was at the beginning. This process will then go on forever, so inflation will never end.

Thus, the criterion for eternal inflation is that the probability for the scalar field to go up must be bigger than $1/e^3 \approx 1/20$. For a Gaussian probability distribution, this condition will be met provided that the standard deviation for $\Delta\phi_{qu}$ is bigger than $0.61|\Delta\phi_{cl}|$. Using $\Delta\phi_{cl} \approx \dot{\phi}_{cl}H^{-1}$, the criterion becomes

$$\Delta\phi_{qu} \approx \frac{H}{2\pi} > 0.61 \,|\dot{\phi}_{cl}|\, H^{-1} \iff \frac{H^2}{|\dot{\phi}_{cl}|} > 3.8 \ . \tag{40.8}$$

Comparing with (40.2), we see that the condition for eternal inflation is equivalent to the condition that $\delta\rho/\rho$ on ultra-long length scales is bigger than a number of order unity.

The probability that $\Delta\phi$ is positive tends to increase as one considers larger and larger values of ϕ, so sooner or later one reaches the point at which inflation becomes eternal. If one takes, for example, a scalar field with a potential

$$V(\phi) = \frac{1}{4}\lambda\phi^4 \ , \tag{40.9}$$

then the de Sitter space equation of motion in flat Robertson–Walker coordinates ($ds^2 = -dt^2 + e^{2Ht}d\vec{x}^2$) takes the form

$$\ddot{\phi} + 3H\dot{\phi} = -\lambda\phi^3 \ , \tag{40.10}$$

where spatial derivatives have been neglected. In the 'slow-roll' approximation one also neglects the $\ddot{\phi}$ term, so $\dot{\phi} \approx -\lambda\phi^3/(3H)$, where the Hubble constant H is related to the energy density by

$$H^2 = \frac{8\pi}{3}G\rho = \frac{2\pi}{3}\frac{\lambda\phi^4}{M_p^2} , \qquad (40.11)$$

where $M_p \equiv 1/\sqrt{G}$ is the Planck mass. Putting these relations together, one finds that the criterion for eternal inflation, (40.8), becomes

$$\phi > 0.75\,\lambda^{-1/6}\,M_p . \qquad (40.12)$$

Since λ must be taken very small, on the order of 10^{-12}, for the density perturbations to have the right magnitude, this value for the field is generally well above the Planck scale. The corresponding energy density, however, is given by

$$V(\phi) = \frac{1}{4}\lambda\phi^4 = 0.079\lambda^{1/3}M_p^4 , \qquad (40.13)$$

which is actually far below the Planck scale.

So for these reasons we think inflation is almost always eternal. I think the inevitability of eternal inflation in the context of new inflation is really unassailable – I do not see how you could possibly avoid it, assuming that the rolling of the scalar field off the top of the hill is slow enough to allow inflation to be successful. The argument in the case of chaotic inflation is a bit more approximate, and some people have questioned it, but I still believe it has to work because the criterion that has to be satisfied is so mild. For eternal inflation to set in, all one needs is that the probability for the field to increase in a given Hubble-sized volume during a Hubble time interval is larger than $1/20$.

40.5 A new singularity theorem

Eternal inflation implies that once inflation starts, it never stops. This leads to the question: can inflation by itself be the complete theory of cosmic origins? Can inflation be eternal into the past as well as the future, allowing a model which on very large scales is steady state, eliminating the need for a beginning? The answer I believe is no, although I would not claim that we have a rock-solid proof. Borde, Vilenkin and I [5] have proven a rigorous theorem, which I will describe, and this theorem certainly shows that the simplest type of inflationary models still require a beginning, even though they are eternal into the future. The difficulty is that we have no way of discussing the class of all possible inflationary models, so we cannot say that our theorem applies to all cases. Our singularity theorem was certainly inspired by Stephen's famous work on singularity theorems, which established the value of such theorems, so it is very fitting that I describe this theorem at a symposium in honour of Stephen's 60th birthday. And I am sure that our conclusions fall on the side that Stephen would prefer, since Stephen has put much effort into studying the quantum origin of the universe, a subject which could have been bypassed if inflationary models could avoid a beginning.

I will not try to state the theorem immediately, since it will be easier later, after some definitions have been put forward.

An unusual feature of the new singularity theorem is that it avoids any mention of things such as energy conditions, which are crucial assumptions for other formulations of singularity theorems. In particular, in the context of eternal inflation, the key papers by Borde and Vilenkin [6–9] proved several different theorems, all of which invoked the weak energy condition. This is the condition that $n_\mu n_\nu T^{\mu\nu} \geq 0$, where $T^{\mu\nu}$ is the energy-momentum tensor and n_μ is any timelike vector. For a perfect fluid, the condition is equivalent to assuming that $\rho \geq 0$ and $\rho + p \geq 0$, where ρ is the energy density and p the pressure. The weak energy condition is always valid classically, but it is nevertheless violated by quantum fluctuations. In particular, in a perfect de Sitter space the quantity $\rho+p$ is identically equal to zero. In a quantum description, however, the vacuum is never an eigenstate of $\rho+p$, so the quantity must fluctuate, but it must still average to its classical value of zero. It therefore fluctuates both positively and negatively, thereby violating the weak energy condition about half the time [10, 21]. The nice thing about the new theorem is that it is purely kinematical; it really depends in no way on the dynamics of general relativity, but only on the redshifting of velocities in an expanding universe. It seems rather amazing, however, that we can learn something useful by considering only relativistic kinematics. Crudely speaking, the theorem says that if the universe expands fast enough, then it cannot possibly be geodesically complete to the past. In a few minutes I will be able to define what it means for the universe to expand fast enough.

We wish to prove a theorem that will apply to any universe, no matter how inhomogeneous or anisotropic, so we want to think of the expansion as a local phenomenon. To describe this expansion, we need to adopt a local definition of the Hubble parameter. One way to define a local Hubble parameter would be to imagine measuring the velocities of particles moving with the Hubble flow within some small neighbourhood, and then one could define a local Hubble parameter in terms of the divergence of the velocity field. For the purpose of our theorem, however, we have found it

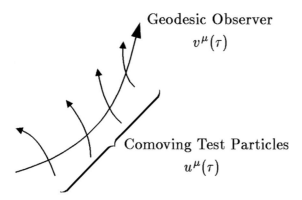

Fig. 40.8. An observer measures the velocity of passing test particles to infer the Hubble parameter.

useful to consider an even more local definition of the Hubble parameter, one that can be measured by a single geodesic observer travelling through the universe. Our hypothetical observer would never get a job at the Keck because he does not know how to use a telescope. He is completely myopic, able to measure the velocity only of those particles that intersect his own trajectory. If he is at rest relative to the local Hubble expansion he will not be able to measure anything, but if he is moving relative to the Hubble expansion he will pass a succession of particles, and will infer a Hubble expansion parameter from the rate at which those particles are separating from each other. We will call the particles that the observer passes 'comoving test particles', but for the purpose of the theorem it is not really necessary that these particles exist. All that is necessary is that the worldlines of these hypothetical particles can be defined on the background spacetime, and that each worldline has zero acceleration at the instant that it intersects the observer's trajectory. The observer will be assumed to be travelling on a geodesic, either timelike or null. As illustrated in Figure 40.8, the four-velocity of the observer will be called $v^\mu(\tau)$, where τ will denote proper time for the case of a timelike observer, and an affine parameterization for the case of a null observer. In either case $v^\mu(\tau) \equiv dx^\mu/d\tau$. The comoving test particle passed by the observer at time τ will be moving at a four-velocity called $u^\mu(\tau)$.

To define the Hubble parameter that the observer measures at time τ, the observer focuses on two particles, one that he passes at time τ, and one at $\tau + \Delta\tau$, where in the end he takes the limit $\Delta\tau \to 0$. The Hubble parameter is defined by

$$H \equiv \frac{\Delta v_{\text{radial}}}{\Delta r} , \tag{40.14}$$

where Δv_{radial} is the radial component of the relative velocity between the two particles, and Δr is their distance, where both quantities are computed in the rest frame of one of the test particles, not in the rest frame of the observer. Note that this definition reduces to the usual one if it is applied to a homogeneous isotropic universe, but it can be defined for any spacetime in which one has identified a geodesic observer and a family of comoving test particle trajectories. We will also be interested in the relative velocity between the test particles and the observer, which can be measured by

$$\gamma \equiv u_\mu v^\mu . \tag{40.15}$$

For the case of timelike observers, γ corresponds to the usual Lorentz factor of special relativity

$$\gamma = \frac{1}{\sqrt{1 - v_{\text{rel}}^2}} . \tag{40.16}$$

Now the key point is that the observer, if H is positive, will see himself redshifting in an expanding universe, which means that his velocity relative to the test particles will be slowing down. Looking into the past, however, the velocity will become blueshifted, becoming faster and faster as one follows the trajectory further into the past. We will find that under many circumstances this velocity reaches the limiting speed of light in a finite proper time, and then the trajectory can be continued no further.

We are accustomed to calculating the redshifting of particle velocities by writing the metric for the background spacetime and then solving the geodesic equations. However, the slowdown is a kinematical effect that is much simpler than one might infer from seeing the standard calculation. To understand the logic, it is useful to begin with a simple one-dimensional non-relativistic analogy. Consider a stream of cars travelling on a straight road, and imagine that they are moving apart from each other, so the cars are the comoving test particles of an expanding universe of cars. You will play the role of the geodesic observer in this thought experiment, and to simplify the description we can imagine that the rest frame of the road coincides with your rest frame; i.e., you are standing at rest just alongside the road. Suppose that one car goes by and you measure its speed relative to you as 40 miles per hour. When the next car comes by, you know that its speed is *not* going to be 50 mph, because that would mean it was catching up to the first car, and we already said that the cars were getting further apart. If they are getting further apart, then the second car has to be moving slower than the first, and the rate that they are getting further apart is directly proportional to the difference between the speeds. So the Hubble expansion rate that you would measure for the stream of cars is directly proportional to the rate at which the relative speed between you and the cars is decreasing.

When one increases the number of space dimensions from one to three, one might expect that the simple relationship would break down. Now the velocity of the comoving test particles relative to the observer can change both in magnitude and direction, so the result is less obvious. However, if one remembers that the Hubble parameter is defined in terms of the radial component of the relative velocity, a short calculation shows that the one-dimensional result is still valid: the Hubble parameter is directly proportional to the rate of change of the relative speed between the observer and the comoving test particles, with changes in direction giving no contribution. Finally, one wants to generalize the calculation to allow for relativistic velocities. As Borde, Vilenkin and I showed in our paper, one finds again that the Hubble parameter as defined by (40.14) can be related directly to the rate of change of the relative velocities. Specifically, in our paper we defined a quantity

$$
F(\gamma) = \begin{cases} \gamma^{-1} & \text{for null observers} \\ \frac{1}{2}\ln\left(\frac{\gamma+1}{\gamma-1}\right) & \text{for timelike observers,} \end{cases} \tag{40.17}
$$

which I like to call the slowness parameter. Note that for the timelike case, a relative velocity of zero ($\gamma = 1$) corresponds to infinite slowness ($F(\gamma) = \infty$), and that in both cases the limiting relative velocity $\gamma \to \infty$ corresponds to zero slowness ($F(\gamma) = 0$). The existence of a maximum possible relative velocity corresponds to a minimum possible slowness. The definition (40.17) has been chosen so that the minimum value is zero.

In our paper we showed that the Hubble parameter is related to the slowness by the simple relation,

$$
H = \frac{\mathrm{d}F(\gamma)}{\mathrm{d}\tau} . \tag{40.18}
$$

That is, the Hubble parameter is equal to the rate of change of the slowness. If $H > 0$ the universe expands, and the slowness increases, which means that the velocity of the geodesic observer relative to the comoving test particles is redshifted. If one looks backwards along the geodesic, however, one sees a blueshift. The velocity of the geodesic observer relative to the comoving test particles increases as one looks backwards, and the slowness decreases. However, the slowness cannot fall below zero. Once the slowness reaches zero it cannot get any lower, so according to (40.18) it is impossible to continue the geodesic any further if H continues to be positive.

The verbal argument of the previous paragraph can be translated into a rigorous inequality by integrating (40.18) over proper time, and using the fact that the value of $F(\gamma)$ at the lower limit of integration is always non-negative. For timelike geodesics, this leads to the result

$$\int^{\tau_f} H \, d\tau \le \frac{1}{2} \ln \left(\frac{\gamma + 1}{\gamma - 1} \right) \, , \tag{40.19}$$

where γ refers to the value of $u_\mu v^\mu$ at the final time τ_f, and the inequality holds for any value of the lower limit of integration. Thus, the integral of H along a backwards-going geodesic is limited by an expression that depends only on the final value of the relative velocity between the geodesic observer and the comoving test particles. The limit disappears only for the case in which the geodesic observer is at rest (relative to the comoving test particles) at the final time, in which case the right-hand-side of (40.19) is infinite. The right-hand-side of (40.19) can be algebraically rewritten as

$$\int^{\tau_f} H \, d\tau \le \ln \left(\frac{1}{v_{\rm rel}} \right) + \ln \left(1 + \gamma^{-1} \right) \, , \tag{40.20}$$

where the first term dominates for low velocities, and the second term dominates for large velocities.

For null observers the result looks even simpler, but it depends on the normalization chosen for the affine parameter. If we normalize it by the convention that $\gamma = dt/d\tau = 1$ at the final time τ_f, where t is the time measured by comoving observers, then the bound is simply

$$\int^{\tau_f} H \, d\tau \le 1 \, . \tag{40.21}$$

Equations (40.19) and (40.21) are technically our final results, but I would like to say a few words about what we think these results mean.

One illustration of the theorem is its application to de Sitter space, especially as described in flat Robertson–Walker coordinates:

$$ds^2 = -dt^2 + e^{2\bar{H}t} d\vec{x}^2 \, , \tag{40.22}$$

where $\bar{H}$ is a constant. Using the worldlines $\vec{x} = constant$ as comoving test particle trajectories, this spacetime would give $H = \bar{H}$ at all points in the coordinate system, independent of the geodesic observer worldine used to define the measurement. As is well-known, however, at least to readers of Hawking and Ellis [28], these coordinates cover only half of de Sitter space. The locus $t = -\infty$ describes a null hypersurface that forms the boundary of the two halves. The comoving geodesics ($\vec{x} = constant$)

have infinite length within the half of de Sitter space described by these coordinates, but our theorem implies (as can be verified by direct calculation) that any other backwards-going timelike geodesic reaches $t = -\infty$ in a finite amount of proper time. In fact, any non-comoving backwards-going timelike geodesic reaches the $t = -\infty$ hypersurface with $\gamma = \infty$, and therefore just saturates the bound implied by our theorem. If we follow such a backwards-going geodesic, it is of course possible to continue it into the other half of the de Sitter space, since de Sitter space as a whole is geodesically complete. Such an extended geodesic would have infinite proper length. Furthermore, since de Sitter space is homogeneous, at any location along the infinite backwards-going geodesic it would be possible to construct a neighbourhood containing comoving test particle trajectories that would make the universe appear to be expanding, with $H = \bar{H}$. Our theorem guarantees, however, that it is not possible to define such comoving test particle trajectories globally, so that $H = \bar{H}$ everywhere along the backwards-going geodesic. In fact, since the bound is saturated as the trajectory reaches the $t = -\infty$ hypersurface, the theorem guarantees that H must turn negative beyond this hypersurface, no matter how the comoving test particle trajectories might be chosen. Thus, comoving test particle trajectories can be chosen so that $H = \bar{H}$ anywhere in the de Sitter space, but this condition cannot be enforced everywhere at once.

One simple description of the entire de Sitter space is the closed universe description,

$$ds^2 = -dt^2 + \cosh^2(\bar{H}t) \left\{ \frac{dr^2}{1-r^2} + r^2 \left[d\theta^2 + \sin^2\theta \, d\phi^2 \right] \right\} . \quad (40.23)$$

For the comoving test particle trajectories $(r, \theta, \phi) = constant$, $H = \bar{H}\tanh(\bar{H}t)$, and thus the space is contracting at early times and expanding only at late times. This is geodesically complete, but does not constitute a model of inflation that is eternal into the past, since in the past the model is contracting and not inflating. If the false vacuum that supports the de Sitter space is only metastable, it would decay completely during the infinite period of contraction, so inflation would never take place.

To describe the implications of our theorem succinctly, it is useful to define a concept that we call *uniformly bounded expansion*. A region of spacetime is said to be undergoing uniformly bounded expansion if it is possible to define a congruence of comoving test particle trajectories with the property $H > H_{min}$ everywhere in the region, for some $H_{min} > 0$. The half of de Sitter space described by (40.22) provides an example of a spacetime with uniformly bounded expansion throughout. The bounds of (40.19) and (40.21) imply that any spacetime that contains at least one non-comoving past-directed geodesic exhibiting uniformly bounded expansion cannot be geodesically complete in the past.

40.6 The origin of the universe

Now what does this say about the universe? First let me point out a few disclaimers, to make it clear what the theorem does not say. It does not imply that an eternally inflating model must have a unique beginning, and it also does not imply that there is an upper bound on the length of all backward-going geodesics from a given point. Our theorem places no bound on the length of the comoving trajectories, and we know from the de Sitter space example of (40.22) that such trajectories really can be infinite. Furthermore, our theorem allows for the possibility of models that have regions of contraction interspersed among regions of expansion, so that (40.19) and (40.21) can perhaps be satisfied for infinitely long backwards-going geodesics. I should also mention here for completeness that Aguirre and Gratton [1] responded to our paper by suggesting a geodesically complete model which uses the full de Sitter space, but proposes that the thermodynamic arrow of time is reversed in the two halves, so that both halves appear to be expanding. This successfully evades our theorem, but for my taste it seems like an extravagant assumption.

In summary, the theorem by Borde, Vilenkin and me does show that any inflating model that is globally expanding must be geodesically incomplete in the past. This theorem certainly applies to the simplest models of eternal inflation, in which an approximately de Sitter region grows exponentially, with pieces of it breaking off and decaying to form pocket universes. Geodesic incompleteness of the inflating region implies that there must be some other physics introduced at the beginning, to explain what happens at the past boundary of the inflating region. The most likely possibility, from my point of view, is some kind of quantum origin, which of course touches on Stephen's work. This means that even in eternally inflating models, a beginning is necessary. I would expect that the details of this beginning would be washed out by the inflationary evolution, but nonetheless the model still requires a beginning of some sort, something like the Hartle–Hawking [24] or Hawking–Turok [30] wave function of the universe.

References

[1] Aguirre, A. and Gratton, S. (2002), 'Steady state eternal inflation', *Phys. Rev.* **D65**, 083507, [astro-ph/0111191].

[2] Albrecht, A. and Steinhardt, P. J. (1982), 'Cosmology for grand unified theories with radiatively induced symmetry breaking', *Phys. Rev. Lett.* **48**, 1220–1223.

[3] Bardeen, J. M., Steinhardt, P. J. and Turner, M. S. (1983), 'Spontaneous creation of almost scale-free density perturbations in an inflationary universe', *Phys. Rev.* **D28**, 679–693.

[4] de Bernardis, P. *et al.* (2000), 'A flat Universe from high-resolution maps of the cosmic microwave background radiation', *Nature* **404**, 955–959.

[5] Borde, A., Guth, A. H. and Vilenkin, A. (2001), 'Inflation is not past eternal', [gr-qc/0110012].

[6] Borde, A. (1994), 'Open and closed universes, initial singularities and inflation', *Phys. Rev.* **D50**, 3692–3702, [gr-qc/9403049].

[7] Borde. A. and Vilenkin, A. (1994), 'Eternal inflation and the initial singularity', *Phys. Rev. Lett.* **72**, 3305–3309, [gr-qc/9312022].

[8] Borde, A. and Vilenkin, A. (1995), 'The impossibility of steady state inflation', in *Relativistic Astrophysics: The Proceedings of the Eighth Yukawa Symposium*, ed. M. Sasaki (Universal Academy Press, Japan), [gr-qc/9403004].

[9] Borde, A. and Vilenkin, A. (1996), 'Singularities in inflationary cosmology: a review', *Int. J. Mod. Phys.* **D5**, 813–824, [gr-qc/9612036].

[10] Borde, A. and Vilenkin, A. (1997), 'Violations of the weak energy condition in inflating space-times', *Phys. Rev.* **D56**, 717–723, [gr-qc/9702019].

[11] Burles, S., Nollett, K. and Turner, M. S. (2001), 'Big bang nucleosynthesis predictions for precision cosmology', *Astrophys. J.* **552**, L1–L6, [astro-ph/0010171].

[12] Coleman, S. and De Luccia, F. (1980), 'Gravitational effects on and of vacuum decay', *Phys. Rev.* **D21**, 3305–3315.

[13] Freedman, W. L. (2001), 'Final results from the Hubble Space Telescope Key Project to measure the Hubble constant', *Astrophys. J.* **553**, 47–72, [astro-ph/0012376].

[14] Gibbons, G. W. and Hawking, S. W. (1977), 'Cosmological event horizons, thermodynamics, and particle creation', *Phys. Rev.* **D15**, 2738–2751.

[15] Gibbons, G. W., Hawking, S. W. and Siklos, S. T. C., eds (1983), *The Very Early Universe*, Proceedings, Nuffield Workshop, Cambridge, UK, June 21–July 9, 1982 (Cambridge University Press, Cambridge).

[16] Goncharov, A. S., Linde, A. D. and Mukhanov, V. F. (1987), 'The global structure of the inflationary universe', *Int. J. Mod. Phys.* **A2**, 561–591.

[17] Guth, A. H. (1981), 'The inflationary universe: a possible solution to the horizon and flatness problems', *Phys. Rev.* **D23**, 347–356.

[18] Guth, A. H. (1997), *The Inflationary Universe: The Quest for a New Theory of Cosmic Origins* (Addison-Wesley, Reading, Mass.).

[19] Guth, A. H. and Pi, S.-Y. (1982), 'Fluctuations in the new inflationary universe', *Phys. Rev. Lett.* **49**, 1110–1113.

[20] Guth, A. H. and Pi, S.-Y. (1985), 'The quantum mechanics of the scalar field in the new inflationary universe', *Phys. Rev.* **D32**, 1899–1920.

[21] Guth, A. H., Vachaspati, T. and Winitzki, S. (2002), In preparation.

[22] Halverson, N. W. *et al.* (2002), 'DASI first results: A measurement of the cosmic microwave background angular power spectrum', *Astrophys. J.* **568**, 38–45, [astro-ph/0104489].

[23] Harrison, E. R. (1970), 'Fluctuations at the threshold of classical cosmology', *Phys. Rev.* **D1**, 2726–2730.

[24] Hartle, J. B. and Hawking, S. W. (1983), 'Wave function of the universe', *Phys. Rev.* **D28**, 2960–2975.

[25] Hawking, S. W. (1966), 'Perturbations of an expanding universe', *Astrophys. J.* **145**, 544–554.

[26] Hawking, S. W. (1982), 'The development of irregularities in a single bubble inflationary universe', unpublished preprint, June 1982.

[27] Hawking, S. W. (1982), 'The development of irregularities in a single bubble inflationary universe', *Phys. Lett.* **B115**, 295–297.

[28] Hawking, S. W. and Ellis, G. F. R. (1973), *The Large Scale Structure of Space-Time* (Cambridge University Press, Cambridge), 125–126.

[29] Hawking, S. W., Moss, I. G. and Stewart, J. M. (1982), 'Bubble collisions in the very early universe', *Phys. Rev.* **D26**, 2681–2693.

[30] Hawking, S. W. and Turok, N. (1998), 'Open inflation without false vacua', *Phys. Lett.* **B425**, 25–32, [hep-th/9802030].

[31] Hu, W. (2000), 'Ringing in the new cosmology', *Nature* **404**, 939–940.

[32] Lee, A. T. *et al.* (2001), 'A high spatial resolution analysis of the MAXIMA-1 cosmic microwave background anisotropy data', *Astrophys. J.* **561**, L1–L6 [astro-ph/0104459].

[33] Linde, A. D. (1982), 'A new inflationary universe scenario: a possible solution of the horizon, flatness, homogeneity, isotropy and primordial monopole problems', *Phys. Lett.* **B108**, 389–393.

[34] Linde, A. D. (1982), 'Scalar field fluctuations in expanding universe and the new inflationary universe scenario', *Phys. Lett.* **B116**, 335.

[35] Linde, A. D. (1983), 'Chaotic inflating universe', *Zh. Eksp. Teor. Fiz.* **38**, 149–151 [*JETP Lett.* **38**, 176–179].

[36] Linde, A. D. (1983), 'Chaotic inflation', *Phys. Lett.* **B129**, 177–181.

[37] Linde, A. D. (1986), 'Eternal chaotic inflation', *Mod. Phys. Lett.* **A1**, 81.

[38] Linde, A. D. (1986), 'Eternally existing selfreproducing chaotic inflationary universe', *Phys. Lett.* **B175**, 395–400.

[39] Linde, A. D. (1990), *Particle Physics and Inflationary Cosmology* (Harwood Academic Publishers, Chur, Switzerland) Sections 1.7–1.8.

[40] Mukhanov, V. F. and Chibisov, G. V. (1981), 'Quantum fluctuation and 'nonsingular' universe', *Pisma Zh. Eksp. Teor. Fiz.* **33**, 549–553, [*JETP Lett.* **33**, 532–535].

[41] Mukhanov, V. F., Feldman, H. A. and Brandenberger, R. H. (1992), 'Theory of cosmological perturbations', *Phys. Rept.* **215**, 203–333.

[42] Netterfield, C. B. *et al.* (2002), 'A measurement by BOOMERANG of multiple peaks in the angular power spectrum of the cosmic microwave background', *Astrophys. J.* **571**, 604–614, [astro-ph/0104460].

[43] Pearson, T. J. *et al.* (2002), 'The anisotropy of the microwave background to $\ell = 3500$: Mosaic observations with the Cosmic Background Imager', submitted to *Astrophys. J.* on May 23, 2002, [astro-ph/0205388].

[44] Perlmutter, S. *et al.* (Supernova Cosmology Project) (1999), 'Measurements of Ω and Λ from 42 high-redshift supernovae', *Astrophys. J.* **517**, 565–586, [astro-ph/9812133].

[45] Riess, A. *et al.* (High Z Supernova Search Team) (1998), 'Observational evidence from supernovae for an accelerating universe and a cosmological constant', *Astron. J.* **116**, 1009–1038, [astro-ph/9805201].

[46] Seager, S., Sasselov, D. and Scott, D. (1999), 'A new calculation of the recombination epoch', *Astrophys. J.* **523**, L1–L5.

[47] Seljak, U. and Zaldarriaga, M. (1996), 'A line of sight approach to Cosmic Microwave Background anisotropies', *Astrophys. J.* **469**, 437–444, [astro-ph/9603033]. The program can be accessed at http://www.physics.nyu.edu/matiasz/CMBFAST/cmbfast.html.

[48] Starobinski, A. A. (1979), 'Relict gravitation radiation spectrum and initial state of the universe', *Pisma Zh. Eksp. Teor. Fiz.* **30**, 719–723 [*JETP Lett.* **30**, 682–685].

[49] Starobinski, A. A. (1990), 'A new type of isotropic cosmological models without singularity', *Phys. Lett.* **B91**, 99–102.

[50] Starobinski, A. A. (1982), 'Dynamics of phase transition in the new inflationary universe scenario and generation of perturbations', *Phys. Lett.* **B117**, 175–178.

[51] Starobinsky, A. A. (1986), 'Stochastic de Sitter (inflationary) stage in the early universe', in *Field Theory, Quantum Gravity and Strings*, eds H. J. de Vega and N. Sánchez (Springer Verlag, Berlin) pp. 107–126.

[52] Steinhardt, P. J. (1983), 'Natural inflation', in Ref. [15], 251–266.

754 Alan Guth

[53] Vanchurin, V., Vilenkin, A. and Winitzki, S. (2000), 'Predictability crisis in inflationary cosmology and its resolution', *Phys. Rev.* **D61**, 083507, [gr-qc/9905097].

[54] Vilenkin, A. (1983), 'The birth of inflationary universes', *Phys. Rev.* **D27**, 2848–2855.

[55] Vilenkin, A. and Ford, L. H. (1982), 'Gravitational effects upon cosmological phase transitions', *Phys. Rev.* **D26**, 1231–1241.

[56] Zeldovich, Ya. B. (1972), 'A hypothesis, unifying the structure and the entropy of the Universe, *Mon. Not. Roy. Astron. Soc.* **160**, 1P–3P.

41

The future of cosmology: observational and computational prospects

Paul Shellard

Centre for Mathematical Sciences, University of Cambridge

41.1 Empirical cosmology

The important role of observation and experiment in constraining cosmological theories has always been one of Stephen Hawking's central concerns. Not content with some of the most dramatic conceptual leaps in recent physics, whether black hole evaporation or quantum cosmology, Stephen invariably has followed up these with publications investigating their direct observational consequences. It is appropriate, therefore, that we spend some time at this conference reflecting on the flood of observational data now becoming available about our universe, as well as the computational effort required to confront it with theoretical predictions of comparable precision.

Cosmology is one of the most exciting and rapidly advancing fields in the physical sciences at the present time. The observational effort is vast, ranging from automated telescope surveys of over a million galaxies, providing information about the recent universe, through to satellite and other probes of the cosmic microwave sky which tell us about the state of the universe at around 0.01% of its present age. New windows are being prised open at higher energies, whether X-ray, gamma ray or even cosmic ray surveys, and ultimately there is the real prospect of detecting gravitational waves which might conceivably unveil the universe in the first moments after its creation.

This progress has been matched by growing confidence in the standard hot big bang cosmology extended into the early universe using the inflationary paradigm [1]. Almost all recent observations of the universe on the largest scales have been seamlessly absorbed into this framework, while improving and modifying a so-called 'cosmic concordance' model. It might even be tempting to think that the end is in sight for cosmology, were not the unanswered questions so obvious. Just to mention the composition of the universe: What is the dark energy that apparently dominates the universe today? What is the dark matter that makes up most of the remainder? In what dark form is the ordinary baryonic matter primarily hiding? Why is the energy density of these constituents so coincident today? What is the origin of the matter–antimatter asymmetry? And the list goes on, even when restricting attention to questions about the homogeneous background cosmology.

There is clearly no hope that I can do justice to the over-ambitious title in the short time available, so I am going to concentrate not on the background cosmology, but on the perturbations about it, that is, the density fluctuations which led to the formation of large-scale structures. In particular, I want to focus on the science that can be extracted from the cosmic microwave background (CMB) because it is one of the cleanest and clearest tests of early universe models. This is all the more pertinent here because, as Alan Guth has reminded us [2], we are all aware of Stephen's pioneering role in proposing the quantum origin of inflationary fluctuations [3]. The properties of these fluctuations are the most testable predictions of inflation and they will continue to be the subject of observational scrutiny into the foreseeable future.

41.2 The cosmic microwave sky

41.2.1 Sources of CMB anisotropy

In order briefly to review the origin of CMB fluctuations, consider an observer situated on the Earth in the centre of Figure 41.1. At early times, photons scatter efficiently off free electrons so that the universe remains opaque to electromagnetic radiation until these electrons are captured to form neutral hydrogen at about 400,000 years after the Big Bang. Subsequent to recombination, the photons propagate freely to the observer today, who is able to reconstruct the surface of last scattering (and any irregularities on it) along the different lines of sight. In a direction $\hat{\mathbf{n}}$, the possible sources of these temperature irregularities are given by the Sachs–Wolfe formula [4]:

$$\frac{\Delta T}{T}(\hat{\mathbf{n}}) = \frac{1}{4}\delta_\gamma(t_{\text{dec}}) - \hat{\mathbf{n}} \cdot \mathbf{v}(t_{\text{dec}}) - \frac{1}{2}\int_{t_{\text{dec}}}^{t_0} \dot{h}_{ij}\hat{n}^i\hat{n}^j dt. \tag{41.1}$$

Here, the first term represents the effect of variations in the photon density $\delta_\gamma = \delta\rho_\gamma/\rho_\gamma$ (causing a temperature change through $\rho_\gamma \approx 0.2T^4$), the second comes from Doppler shifts due to coherent velocities on the surface

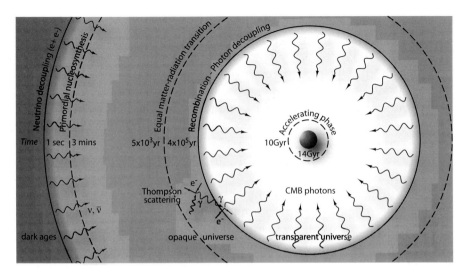

Fig. 41.1. The cosmic microwave sky. An observer on Earth today sees the surface of last scattering in every direction, a linear 'snapshot' of the primordial fluctuations in our universe at $t \approx 400,000$ years.

of last scattering, and the third represents the gravitational effect of small metric fluctuations h_{ij} about the background FRW metric.[1]

If the perturbations are primordial in origin (that is, like inflation they are all created before t_{dec}), then the last gravitational term can be integrated along the line of sight so that (41.1) simplifies to

$$\frac{\Delta T}{T}(\hat{\mathbf{n}}) = \frac{1}{4}\delta_\gamma(t_{\mathrm{dec}}) - \hat{\mathbf{n}} \cdot \mathbf{v}(t_{\mathrm{dec}}) - \Phi(t_{\mathrm{dec}}) + 2\int_{t_{\mathrm{dec}}}^{t_0} \dot{\Phi}\, dt\,, \qquad (41.2)$$

where Φ is the (conformal) Newtonian potential. The second last term is due to the gravitational redshift on the surface of last scattering and the last is due to late-time variations in the gravitational potential, for example, due to the acceleration of the universe.

To a first approximation, then, the temperature anisotropies represent an accurate and linear 'snapshot' of the primordial perturbations only 400,000 years after the Big Bang, that is, well before the complex non-linear processing that occurs in the late universe as structures form. (This is true but for the last term in (41.2) which only has a benign effect on

---

[1] In (41.1) we define the metric fluctuations $h_{\mu\nu}$ in synchronous gauge (the condition $h_{0\mu} = 0$) about a flat FRW line element $ds^2 = dt^2 - a^2(t)[\delta_{ij} - h_{ij}]$. Note that the second expression (41.2) is in Newtonian gauge (altering δ_γ and $\mathbf{v}$) and, again, we neglect monopole and dipole terms.

large angular scales relative to others.) However, there are two important caveats here. First, the actual measured signal is muddied by debris
from the late universe, such as point sources and foregrounds of galactic
dust, which must be systematically removed during data analysis (often
making some implicit assumptions about the primordial signal which is
being sought). And, secondly, alternative paradigms for structure formation with active sources such as cosmic strings create gravitational perturbations in the CMB after last scattering and through to the present
day. In this case, we must solve the Sachs–Wolfe formula in the original
form (41.1), calculating the effect of these sources along the line of sight.
Temperature alone may not be able to differentiate between pre-existing
perturbations and those being continuously created, but fortunately there
is further information in the polarization of the CMB signal.

Polarization is created at the surface of last scattering because photons
which scatter off moving electrons become linearly polarized; this depends
on the relative alignment of the electron velocity with respect to the
radiation wavefront. It is a fairly inefficient process so the polarization
signal is only about 10% of the temperature anisotropy. The polarization
can be described by two Stokes paramenters Q, U which in turn represent
an electric-type polarization due to gradient effects (labelled 'G') and
magnetic-type due to the curl of the velocities (labelled 'C'). Purely scalar
perturbation models (such as inflation without tensor modes) can only
source electric-type polarization.

Apart from Thompson scattering by electrons at photon decoupling,
it is very difficult to create polarization by any other means in the late
universe. In principle, re-ionization at relatively recent redshifts can cause
some further polarization, but it has a clear signature which should not
be easily confused with that imprinted at last scattering. So, unlike the
temperature anistropy, the CMB polarization signal *is* necessarily primordial in origin. An active or 'causal' theory will only be able to create
correlations on scales up to the horizon at photon decoupling, whereas
a primordial theory such as inflation should exhibit polarization also on
superhorizon scales.

41.2.2 *The cosmic microwave sky observed*

CMB anisotropy experiments measure data on a sphere, the last scattering surface, so it is natural to decompose this in spherical harmonics
$Y_{\ell m}(\theta, \phi)$ as

$$\frac{\Delta T}{T}(\theta, \phi) = \sum_{\ell m} a_{\ell m} Y_{\ell m} \qquad (41.3)$$

and analogously for the electric- and magnetic-type polarization signal with corresponding expansion coefficients $a_{\ell m}^{G}$ and $a_{\ell m}^{C}$ respectively. Given that inflationary perturbations are Gaussian and therefore completely specified by their variance, they can be represented as

$$\langle a_{\ell m} a_{\ell' m'} \rangle = C_{\ell} \delta_{\ell' \ell} \delta_{mm'}, \qquad (41.4)$$

where the C_{ℓ}s represent the angular power spectrum. The experimental task then is to extract the C_{ℓ}s from a noisy CMB sky. As well as the autocorrelators of the temperature and polarization there are also the cross-correlators which contain further useful information, $C_{\ell}^{X,X'} = \langle a_{\ell m}^{X} a_{\ell' m'}^{X'} \rangle$ ($X = $ T, G, C). Since the polarization signal is related to the magnitude of the velocities it should be out of phase with temperature contributions from the density contrast.

With the level of activity in CMB experiments such as it is, any summary of the present status will inevitably become dated in the near future. Nevertheless, Figure 41.2 represents a condensation of observations over the last few years, including COBE [6], the recent experiments by

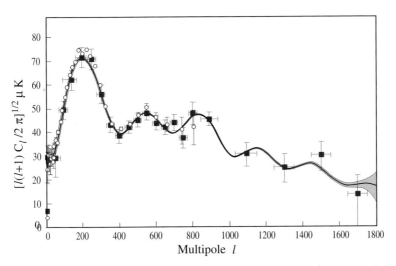

Fig. 41.2. Observational status of CMB observations (as compiled in late 2002 in [5]) as well as results from the 2003 WMAP satellite (circles). To the pre-2003 data is fitted a 'concordance model' with the following parameters $\Omega_{\text{tot}} = 1$, $\Omega_{\Lambda} = 0.7$, $\Omega_{\text{cdm}} h^2 = 0.14$, $\Omega_{\text{b}} h^2 = 0.02$, $n = 0.975$. The anticipated sensitivity of the Planck satellite measurements is indicated by the grey shaded area (below about $\ell \leq 1500$ the limit is dominated by sample variance).

Boomerang [7], Maxima [9], DASI [8], CBI [10], VSA [11] and Archeops [12]. This is compared with the first year's data from the WMAP satellite [55]. A single compilation of all CMB experiments produces a messy picture from which it is difficult to discern a clear trend. However, the more recent data dominate the overall statistical significance, and various authors (see, for example, [5, 14]) claim that the data can be self-consistently combined into a weighted sum of bandpowers to yield the cleaner view offered in Figure 41.2. (This procedure exploits calibration uncertainties in particular.) What appears to be emerging is excellent evidence for a strong primary peak around $\ell \approx 200$, followed by growing evidence for some further acoustic oscillations at higher multipoles.

Figure 41.2 already provides an indication of the high precision future for CMB science. Even with a preliminary analysis from its first year, the WMAP data already exceeds the significance of the other currently available data in the range $\ell \leq 600$. The data should continue to improve with further results at higher $\ell \leq 1000$ over the mission lifetime. The last word for CMB temperature anisotropies on large to intermediate scales will come from the Planck Surveyor satellite due for launch in 2007, for which the anticipated sensitivity is also shown in Figure 41.2. Because of its improved sensitivity and resolution, as well as a greater number of frequency channels, Planck should be able to measure primary CMB anisotropies down to the cosmic variance limits for multipoles $\ell \leq 1500$. If one compares this with the data provided by COBE for $\ell \leq 30$ back in 1992, then there can be little doubt about the orders of magnitude of further information we are about to learn about our universe.

There are two other areas of CMB science in which neither WMAP nor Planck will be the last word: first, in mapping the polarization signal and, secondly, in measuring very small-angle anisotropies at high resolution ($\ell \gg 1000$). The DASI experiment made the first formal announcement of the discovery of a polarization signal [13], which was soon followed by a significant detection over a much broader range by WMAP (providing, for example, a clear signature of the reionization history of the universe). Ultimately, however WMAP's sensitivity should be far exceeded by Planck and numerous other experiments in between. This is a focus of observational effort at the present time and, over the next few years, we are sure to accumulate an unambiguously primordial snapshot of the universe at 400,000 years.

There are also very high resolution, high sensitivity CMB experiments planned which are mainly targeted at studying clusters of galaxies, but which will have implications for early universe cosmology. One example is AMI, the Arcminute Microkelvin Imager (led here in Cambridge by the Cavendish Astrophysics group). This is an interferometer which will have a resolution of 1.5′, far smaller than Planck ($2500 \leq \ell \leq 6000$), and a sensitivity as low as 8μK after integration for a month.

Of course, there are many other observational surveys underway apart from the CMB which will reveal important information about the nature of density fluctuations. Important examples include weak lensing, the Lyman α forest and galaxy clustering, though their interpretation is complicated by the greater influence of non-linear processes in the late universe. These are complementary to the CMB data in different regimes and can be used, for example, to break a number of cosmological parameter degeneracies (see, for example, [5, 14, 15]).

41.3 Cosmological perturbations and cosmic concordance?

A powerful consensus has emerged that the CMB anisotropies and large-scale structures we observe are remarkably consistent with the predictions of inflation. The latest CMB data appear to confirm this conclusion spectacularly, as Alan Guth has emphasized [2]. Some surprises have occurred, such as an inferred baryon density inconsistent with primordial nucleosynthesis [16] or evidence for a cosmological constant [17], but this has either vanished through data reanalysis or it has been readily absorbed into the 'concordance model'. Indeed, so pervasive are inflation's successes that CMB researchers, in particular, appear to be lining up to join the National Standards Laboratory, content to estimate cosmological parameters to that next decimal place rather than worrying about testing the underlying early universe models.

Fortunately, there are several good reasons why such a narrowed perspective remains premature. First, the simple form of the perturbations currently being delineated by observations may also be consistent with models other than inflation. Secondly, inflation itself is not so much a testable theory as a paradigm in search of a realistic physical context. Thirdly, observations will continue to improve dramatically for the foreseeable future, with the possibility of new windows on the universe opening up, such as gravitational waves. Interesting new phenomena and even radical surprises may still be in store, so let us briefly discuss these three motivations further.

41.3.1 The nature of cosmological perturbations

If you were to ask what current observations are telling us about the fluctuations that led to large-scale structure formation, then few would argue with the following four key properties:

1. primordial;
2. scale-invariant;

3. adiabatic;

4. Gaussian.

Spelt backwards these words form a useful acronym because there would
be a collective 'gasp' if any were disproved (though some may need to be
qualified with 'very nearly' or 'predominantly'). Note also that here we
focus on the properties of the fluctuations themselves, leaving aside the
background cosmology (since *flatness* is often added to this list).

The *primordial* nature of the perturbations means that there is evidence that they were laid down on all relevant lengthscales long before
photon decoupling or galaxy formation. Unlike actively sourced perturbations (such as cosmic defects), primordial perturbations necessarily exist
on scales larger than the Hubble radius; they are loosely termed 'superhorizon'. They are consistent, therefore, with the large-angle anisotropy
measurements made by COBE and Archeops (that is, for $\theta > 2°$ or $\ell \leq 200$
in Figure 41.2). Implicit also, here, is the assumption that the primordial
fluctuations were 'well-behaved' in the past, that is, they were small (and
linear) and the only significant late contributions could come from the
growing mode. Their primordial nature also means that as they cross
the Hubble radius they set up coherent oscillations in the radiation fluid
which can be observed as a set of acoustic peaks in the CMB angular
power spectrum. Primordial perturbations also have an inevitable and
corresponding effect on the polarization of the CMB signal.

There have been persuasive arguments since the 1970s indicating that
perturbations must be approximately 'flat' or *scale-invariant* [18]; this has
always been the first hurdle for any viable structure formation theory. Too
much tilt towards small scales causes unacceptable black hole formation
and *vice versa* for large-scale inhomogeneity. Combining the CMB angular
power spectrum with other data sets and fitting with a power law (spectral
index n) provides good evidence for near scale-invariance [55]:

$$n = 0.93 \pm 0.03. \qquad (41.5)$$

The WMAP data taken alone is even closer to the scale-invariant value
$n = 1$. This result already depends on a number of 'weak priors' and the
errors can be reduced further by assuming flatness.

Observations also point to the primordial seeds for structure formation
being *adiabatic* scalar perturbations. The evidence for this is threefold:
First, the consistency of the normalization of the CMB (which potentially includes scalar, vector and tensor mode contributions) and large-
scale structure (which includes only a scalar density mode) indicates that
the CMB has a predominantly scalar contribution. Secondly, the phase of
the acoustic peaks observed in the CMB power spectrum indicates that

the scalar modes are adiabatic (true curvature fluctuations) rather than isocurvature (entropy fluctuations). In the adiabatic case in a flat background, these start with the highest amplitude primary peak at $\ell \approx 220$ and are followed by nearly periodic secondary peaks of lower amplitude at higher multipoles (as shown in Figure 41.2). Thirdly, WMAP has observed the temperature-polarization expected from adiabatic perturbations. Modelling of the effects of these different modes also provides a constraint on the relative amplitude of any tensor contribution (see, for example, [5])

$$r \equiv \frac{\mathcal{A}_T}{\mathcal{A}_S} \leq 0.5, \tag{41.6}$$

where $\mathcal{A}_S$ and $\mathcal{A}_T$ are the scalar and tensor power spectra amplitudes respectively.

Finally, there is every indication that the observed perturbations are *Gaussian* or nearly Gaussian. The CMB fluctuations from COBE, Maxima, Boomerang, CBI and WMAP all have a one-point temperature distribution for which a Gaussian is a good fit. Analysis of all these data sets has failed to find non-Gaussian signals in a variety of statistics which can be unambiguously attributed to primary CMB anisotropy. However, the present constraints are relatively weak and can be expected to continue to improve.

Up until this point, the observational evidence for these four simple fluctuation properties has been discussed without reference to inflation. This is in contrast to elsewhere where these properties are described as the 'pillars of inflation' (or similar). Such an identification is appropriate only to the extent that they are exclusive to inflation and no other theory. However, alternative contexts have been proposed which, in principle, could exhibit these properties, with recent examples including:

- *Bouncing scenarios*: Primordial perturbations can be set up during a 'collapsing' phase in pre-Big Bang [19] and ekpyrotic models [20].

- *Bi-metric or varying speed-of-light theories*: A larger causal horizon (or two) allows for fluctuation creation on large lengthscales [21].

- *Pre-Planckian physics*: It may be possible that quantum fluctuations are 'born' in their ground state before the Planck time [22].

- *Active 'mimic' models*: The days are numbered for actively-sourced models which may be able to mimic inflationary predictions [23].

No doubt it can be argued that each of these speculative alternatives is disreputable to some degree (if not entirely!) but they may be difficult

5-dimensional assisted inflation	extended open inflation	late-time mild inflation	pre-Big-Bang inflation
anisotropic brane inflation	extended warm inflation	low-scale inflation	primary inflation
anomaly-induced inflation	extra dimensional inflation	low-scale supergravity inflation	primordial inflation
assisted inflation	F-term inflation	M-theory inflation	quasi-open inflation
assisted chaotic inflation	F-term hybrid inflation	mass inflation	quintessential inflation
boundary inflation	false vacuum inflation	massive chaotic inflation	R-invariant topological inflation
brane inflation	false vacuum chaotic inflation	moduli inflation	rapid asymmetric inflation
brane-assisted inflation	fast-roll inflation	multi-scalar inflation	running inflation
brane gas inflation	first order inflation	multiple inflation	scalar-tensor gravity inflation
brane-antibrane inflation	gauged inflation	multiple-field slow-roll inflation	scalar-tensor stochastic inflation
braneworld inflation	generalised inflation	multiple-stage inflation	Seiberg-Witten inflation
Brans-Dicke chaotic inflation	generalized assisted inflation	natural inflation	single-bubble open inflation
Brans-Dicke inflation	generalized slow-roll inflation	natural Chaotic inflation	spinodal inflation
bulky brane inflation	gravity driven inflation	natural double inflation	stable starobinsky-type inflation
chaotic hybrid inflation	Hagedorn inflation	natural supergravity inflation	steady-state eternal inflation
chaotic inflation	higher-curvature inflation	new inflation	steep inflation
chaotic new inflation	hybrid inflation	next-to-minimal supersymmetric	stochastic inflation
D-brane inflation	hyperextended inflation	hybrid inflation	string-forming open inflation
D-term inflation	induced gravity inflation	non-commutative inflation	successful D-term inflation
dilaton-driven inflation	induced gravity open inflation	non-slow-roll inflation	supergravity inflation
dilaton-driven brane inflation	intermediate inflation	nonminimal chaotic inflation	supernatural inflation
double inflation	inverted hybrid inflation	old inflation	superstring inflation
double D-term inflation	isocurvature inflation	open hybrid inflation	supersymmetric hybrid inflation
dual inflation	K inflation	open inflation	supersymmetric inflation
dynamical inflation	kinetic inflation	oscillating inflation	supersymmetric topological inflation
dynamical SUSY inflation	lambda inflation	polynomial chaotic inflation	supersymmetric new inflation
eternal inflation	large field inflation	polynomial hybrid inflation	synergistic warm inflation
extended inflation	late D-term inflation	power-law inflation	TeV-scale hybrid inflation

Fig. 41.3. Proliferation of inflationary models: excerpts from a recent archive search. The most difficult model to rule out may well be super-natural inflation.

to preclude, especially in a higher-dimensional context. And, although inflation remains the most attractive and economical paradigm, it too is not without its own shortcomings, as we shall discuss. So, while we await compelling observational confirmation of more specific inflationary signatures, the search for alternative explanations of these four simple fluctuation properties remains a legitimate enterprise and will continue to prove lively and controversial.

41.3.2 'Standard' inflation and the profusion problem

Certain scientific fields of study (such as dinosaur extinction) are routinely criticized for having as many theories as there are researchers. For inflation the number of available models far exceeds the number of active theorists, as can be easily demonstrated by an archive search (see Figure 41.3). With most participants staying in Churchill College, an appropriate summary of the situation might be:

> Never in cosmic history
> have so many models
> been created by so few
> and to which physics owes so little ...

The heart of the problem is the last line; inflation entails an extrapolation into the early universe using ad hoc scalar fields in effective theories which

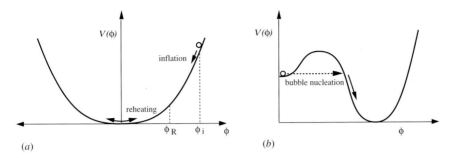

Fig. 41.4. Two inflationary potentials. (a) The 'simplest' forms of inflation have a single real scalar field slowly rolling down a 'smooth' potential. (b) False vacuum decay at the end of extended inflation could lead to violent first-order bubble collisions, producing a signature of gravitational waves.

do not at present sit happily in a broader fundamental framework.[2] To address this confusing situation it seems clear that a more disciplined approach to model-building will be necessary with improved criteria by which to judge relative credibility. However, putting these questions aside, one can still ask if it is possible to identify any generic predictions of inflation from this wide range of options?

It is common in the literature to discuss the consistency between the simplest models of inflation and observation, as illustrated by the cosmic concordance in Figure 41.2. It is not always clear what these simplest models are (so-called 'vanilla' inflation), but it certainly means those with a single real scalar field ϕ with an inflationary potential $V(\phi)$ including at least those with a power law $V(\phi) \propto \phi^n$, $n = 2, 3, 4\ldots$ (Figure 41.4). A broader definition usually encompasses a much wider range of potentials satisfying the slow-roll condition V', $V'' \ll V$ during inflation (a sufficient condition for inflation if $V(\phi)$ dominates but not a necessary one). Now the behaviour of any single field model can be approximated using a Taylor expansion of the Hubble parameter $H(\phi)$ about the value of the inflaton field relevant for structure formation $\phi = \phi_s$. In the slow-roll case, the first two coefficients in the expansion reduce to [27]

$$\epsilon \approx \frac{m_{\rm pl}^2}{16\pi}\left(\frac{V'}{V}\right)^2, \qquad \eta \approx \frac{m_{\rm pl}^2}{8\pi}\frac{V''}{V}. \qquad (41.7)$$

---

[2] For example, pure eleven-dimensional supergravity and its compactifications (along with Type IIA and IIB string theory) exclude the violations of the strong energy condition required for the acceleration of the universe (inflation) [24, 25]. But whether this is a problem for inflation or for M theory is not clear, because even the present universe appears to be accelerating! For some recent views on inflation's failings refer to [22, 26].

One can then use ϵ and η to calculate the amplitudes $\mathcal{A}_S$, $\mathcal{A}_T$ and spectral indices n, n_T of the power spectra of the density fluctuations and the gravitational waves respectively. The COBE normalization of the density fluctuations yields the relation,

$$\frac{V^{1/4}}{\epsilon^{1/4}} \approx 0.005\, m_{pl} \approx 7 \times 10^{16} \text{ GeV}, \tag{41.8}$$

and the scalar spectral index is shifted slightly away from scale-invariance

$$n \approx 1 - 6\epsilon + 2\eta. \tag{41.9}$$

Unlike the scalar modes, the amplitude of the tensor modes measures the energy scale of inflation directly $\mathcal{A}_T \sim V/m_{pl}^4$ with the tensor spectral index given simply by

$$n_T \approx -2\epsilon. \tag{41.10}$$

Finally, for slow-roll inflation, there is a consistency condition between the tensor index and the relative amplitudes of the scalar and tensor modes:

$$r \equiv \frac{\mathcal{A}_T}{\mathcal{A}_S} \approx -\frac{200}{9} n_T. \tag{41.11}$$

Together these three results make a distinct and testable prediction of slow-roll inflation. For definiteness, the simplest case with a massive scalar field predicts approximately

$$V(\phi) = m^2 \phi^2 : \quad m \approx 10^{13} \text{ GeV}, \quad n \approx 0.96, \quad n_T \approx -0.02, \quad r \approx 0.35, \tag{41.12}$$

which is consistent with present observations (see previous section).

Beyond the subset of slow-roll inflation models, it is possible to use the same expansion of the Hubble parameter to describe the behaviour of more general single field inflationary models. Choosing a point in a suitably truncated expansion of the parameters ϵ, η, ... is equivalent to selecting a particular model. One then needs to study the flow of these models to investigate the 'generic' predictions of inflation [28, 29], because the simple slow-roll relations (41.9–41.11) break down. Monte Carlo simulations of 'reasonable' initial conditions with strongly suppressed higher derivatives produced some interesting results. Most models with sufficient inflation were not scale-invariant, producing a large spectral index $n > 1.5$ which is already observationally excluded. Restricting to models with $0.9 \leq n \leq 1.0$ indicated that it was likely there would be some tensor contribution in the range $0.05 \leq r \leq 0.5$.[3] However, for the allowed initial

---

[3] Of course, this assertion has no real statistical significance because no invariant measure has been provided either on the space of inflation models or those of the initial conditions (see the discussions in [22, 31]).

conditions, inflation models populated all the available observational parameter space for the spectral index n and the scalar-tensor ratio r (modulo an excluded region at large n and r). So even before the Planck satellite flies we can rest assured that a single field inflation model will match almost any possible observation of the scalar and tensor power spectra!

This simple example illustrates the significance of the profusion problem for inflation. There seem to be two possible strategies in response. On the one hand, there is a phenomenological approach in which one assumes inflation a priori then employs the power spectra data to learn more about the properties of the model. This underlies the 'inflaton potential reconstruction' programme [30] for which – setting aside issues of uniqueness – even the most optimistic outcomes are hardly inspirational. On the other hand, one can pin one's colours to the mast at the outset by specifying a realistic inflationary model on the basis of more general physical considerations. Stephen Hawking clearly prefers the latter, since he has had the courage to wager that tensor modes will be observed at a level equal to or above that predicted for the massive scalar field model (41.12). It would seem an opportune time for other leading inflation proponents to accept the challenge and to do likewise.

41.3.3 Competing structure formation paradigms

With Tom Kibble as session chairman it would be amiss not to make some mention of cosmic defects, out of which arose a structure formation scenario which predated inflation [32, 33]. Elsewhere this proceedings contains an extensive debate about colliding braneworlds [34, 35], a more recent pretender to inflation's throne, so I will confine myself here only to cosmic strings and other topological defects [36]. I do so with some hesitation because of their current disfavour,[4] but there are lessons to be learnt from the unambiguous and falsifiable signatures of defects and they could still play a subdominant, but significant, role in structure formation.

Unlike monopoles and domain walls, cosmic strings and other global defects are not cosmologically pathological; as the universe expands their evolution rapidly becomes scale-invariant with a constant number of defects per horizon volume (see Figure 41.5). Hence, throughout cosmic history, they continuously source scale-invariant gravitational perturbations on 'causal' subhorizon scales. The one parameter in these models is

---

[4] Back in 1997, Hawking predicted: 'I expect the observations will be consistent with inflation and rule out defects. But we will have to wait and see. Inflation is such a neat solution, I'm sure that God would have chosen it.'

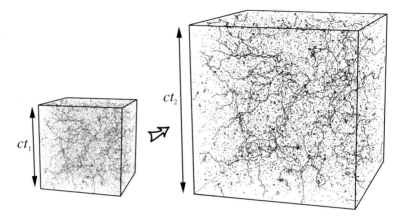

Fig. 41.5. Could precision cosmology reveal anomalies such as cosmic strings? The string network evolves in a scale-invariant manner with about 40 strings crossing any horizon volume throughout the history of the universe (from [37]). The long string network is diluted by the creation of small closed loops which oscillate and decay into a stochastic background of gravitational waves.

the energy scale of the phase transition at which the topological defects are created, which needs to be around the grand unification scale if they are to seed structure formation. While this is a natural scale at which to form these generic objects, it was originally thought to be incompatible with inflation. However, more recent models of hybrid inflation and pre-heating, for example, provide mechanisms by which to produce defects at high energy scales.

Apart from scale-invariance, defect-induced fluctuations appear to be the antithesis of inflation because they are 'causal' or active (not primordial), the scalar density mode is isocurvature (there are also large vector and tensor contributions), and they are non-Gaussian. These characteristics leave clear signatures in the CMB angular power spectrum, chief of which is a much broader primary peak and little evidence of secondary oscillations; unlike inflation, active defect sources act incoherently with extra large-scale power from the vectors and tensors. Moreover, their isocurvature nature provides a partial explanation for why the broad primary peak ends up at much larger multipoles $\ell \geq 300$ (though this can be shifted back towards $\ell \approx 200$ in a closed cosmology [38]). The poor fit between defect models and current observations is apparent in Figure 41.6.

On the basis of knowledge from present simulations, therefore, cosmic defects alone are very unlikely to have been the seeds for large-scale structure formation. However, they cannot be ruled out entirely. For ex-

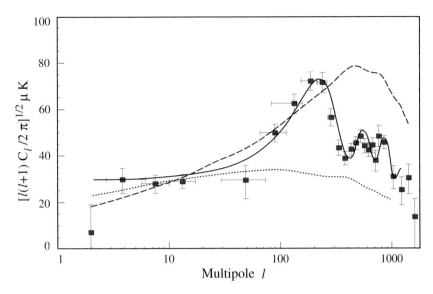

Fig. 41.6. Hybrid models with an admixture of inflation and cosmic defects can provide a good fit to current data (here the solid line has an 18% global defect contribution [39]). The poor fit of cosmic defect models alone is indicated by that for global textures [40] (dotted line) and cosmic strings (dashed line) [41].

ample, admixtures of inflationary power spectra with significant cosmic defect contributions (around 20%) do provide a satisfactory fit to present data (see Figure 41.6 again). This is the sort of level at which the non-Gaussian signatures of cosmic strings should still be discernible (see Figure 41.7), although their distinct line-like discontinuities [42] are only clearly identifiable on small angular scales around a few arc minutes. The serendipitous discovery of cosmic defects or other exotic phenomena in forthcoming cosmological surveys would have profound implications for our understanding of the early universe and fundamental theory.

41.4 Critical observational tests

So what are the distinguishing observational tests which are going to tell us if what we see is actually from inflation? Over the next few years, the inexorable progress of CMB experiments towards improved coverage, sensitivity and resolution will have a corresponding effect on our understanding of cosmological perturbations. First, will be to establish the fundamental properties of cosmological perturbations; all doubt will be removed about whether or not we are dealing with a 'gasp' theory

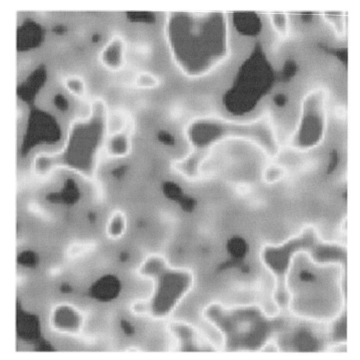

Fig. 41.7. Small-angle anistropies from cosmic strings [43].

(primordial, scale-invariant, adiabatic and Gaussian). Secondly, specific theories will be subjected to tests for their characteristic signatures, for example, determining whether particular slow-roll inflation models are adequate or other alternatives are required. A clear confirmation of distinct slow-roll inflationary predictions would underpin the reliability of cosmological parameter estimation. New CMB polarization data will play a very influential role in this confrontation as the following important examples illustrate.

41.4.1 Primordial vs 'causal' theories

The CMB polarization signal from the surface of last scattering is truly primordial because, unlike the temperature signal, it is unaffected by intervening gravitational effects. Primordial theories, therefore, must reveal a polarization signature on superhorizon scales at photon decoupling $(\theta \geq 2°)$, though being a velocity effect it will decay on large scales. In contrast, actively-sourced or causal theories should reveal no correlations in the signal on these superhorizon scales. The differences between inflation and a causal toy model are illustrated in Figure 41.8. The presence

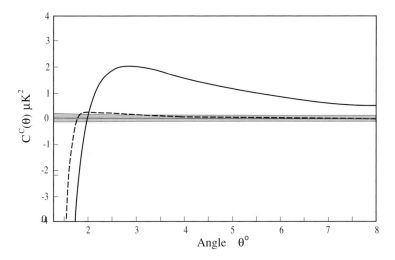

Fig. 41.8. Cross-correlation of the CMB temperature and polarization signals, showing MAP sensitivity as the grey shaded area. The superhorizon signal above $\theta \approx 2°$ for an inflationary model (solid line) contrasts starkly with an actively-sourced or 'causal' model (dashed line) [44].

of an anticorrelated superhorizon polarization signal in the WMAP data means inflation has passed this important test.

Primordial models produce acoustic peaks in the CMB angular power spectrum which will be clearly delineated by satellite experiments. One consequence is that it should be possible to establish if there are significant departures from scale-invariance as predicted by specific slow-roll inflation models such as (41.12).

41.4.2 Scalar, vector and tensor modes

One of the most exciting prospects is the discovery of magnetic-type CMB polarization (B-modes) as this would reveal the presence of vector and/or tensor modes. Cosmic defect models may be further constrained in the near future because B-modes are predicted to have amplitudes comparable to the electric-type E-modes (for $\ell \leq 200$). At high resolution, one could also hope to observe defects directly through the B-mode signal, against a relatively unperturbed background. Conversely, the detection of vector modes would provide strong evidence against inflation.

Inflation models are already constrained to have a relative tensor contribution below about $r \leq 0.5$. Although polarization experiments will require sensitivities as low as $0.1\ \mu K$, it is possible that B-modes from tensors could be detected around $r \approx 0.1$, corresponding to inflationary energy scales near 10^{15}GeV. If it were possible also to measure the tensor mode spectral index n_T – an even more formidable task – then it would provide a real test of the slow-roll prediction (41.10). Such a concordance of n, n_T and r would certainly buttress inflation against quests for alternative primordial theories.

Polarization data will also strongly constrain a significant isocurvature contribution to the mainly adiabatic density fluctuations. Isocurvature modes can be a signature of more complicated physics during inflation, such as the effects of two or more scalar fields.

41.4.3 Gaussian vs. non-Gaussian

Future CMB experiments, especially at high resolution, will probe the degree of Gaussianity of the primordial fluctuations. The detection of significant and unambiguous non-Gaussianity in the primary CMB signal would be inconsistent with simple slow-roll inflation. More general inflationary models can accommodate certain types of non-Gaussianity, such as two-field models with a χ^2 contribution, and one can also envisage non-Gaussianity from excited initial states for inflation.

It is interesting to note that current CMB experiments do not have the sensitivity or resolution to detect cosmic string signatures directly. Boomerang and Maxima, for example, have sensitivities of only about 60 to 70 μK while GUT scale strings predict jumps of around 20 μK. However, with high resolution sensitivities below 10 μK in the near future, direct constraints (or detection) will be possible. This is just one example of the interesting new science that future high resolution CMB experiments might uncover in the years ahead.

41.5 Primordial gravitational waves

While I have completely neglected cosmological surveys other than the CMB, it is difficult to resist some mention of the search for gravitational waves which is now well underway (see Kip Thorne's contribution [45]). After all, gravitational wave astronomy may prove to be the ultimate probe of the very early universe (Figure 41.9). Gravitational radiation effortlessly penetrates the electromagnetic surface of last scattering at $t = 400,000$ years, propagating freely towards us from times as early as the Planck epoch at 10^{-43} seconds.

The next generation of detectors – LIGO, VIRGO and LISA – may be able to observe a stochastic background of gravitational waves produced by violent processes during the earliest moments after the creation of the universe (for a review, see [46]). Possible scenarios within detector sensitivity include strongly first-order phase transitions, possibly at

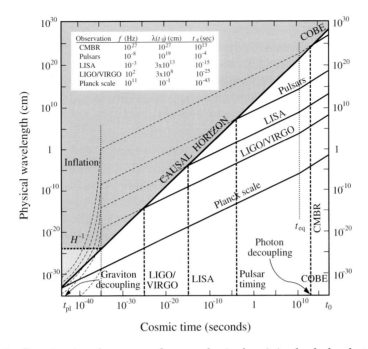

Fig. 41.9. Gravitational waves of cosmological origin look back to the earliest fractions of a second of the history of our universe, many orders of magnitude earlier than the CMB.

the end of inflation, and networks of cosmic strings. The stochastic backgrounds from these sources are illustrated in Figure 41.10. Perhaps more easily distinguishable above the expected astrophysical backgrounds will be specific waveforms from exotic sources such as cosmic strings [47, 48]. Other backgrounds from superstring-inspired pre-Big Bang models might also be accessible [19]. At this stage, other primordial backgrounds from slow-roll inflation, global topological defects and the standard electroweak phase transition appear to be out of range of the present experiments. Apart from technological limitations, a key constraint is due to stochastic backgrounds of astrophysical origin, though a possible window on the early universe at 0.1–1 Hz has been identified [49].

41.6 Computational prospects

In 1997 Stephen Hawking said that *something* (and this is where you have to fill in the gap)

> [...] will enable us to calculate what our theories of the early universe predict and test them against the new observational results that are now coming in.

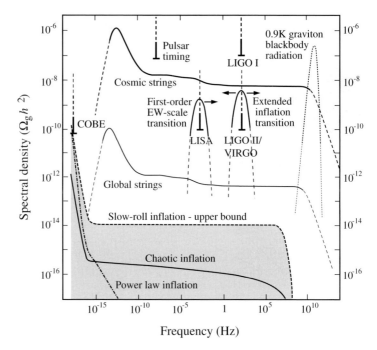

Fig. 41.10. Possible backgrounds of primordial gravitational waves and the anticipated sensitivities of forthcoming detection experiments.

The most credible wrong alternative is probably graduate students! But the correct answer is COSMOS, the UK National Cosmology Supercomputer of which Stephen is principal investigator (see Figure 41.11). Its inception marked a new quantitative threshold in cosmology in which theorists recognized that it was no longer adequate to echo Zel'dovich's old adage: 'What's a factor of two in cosmology?'. The universe is a large, complex and non-linear system, terms usually associated with analytically intractable problems. In order for theoretical predictions to match the growing precision of observations, large-scale computational resources must be deployed. In fact, this is pivotal to the ongoing fruitful interaction between the theoretical and observational communities. In terms of the CMB, apart from the enormous data analysis task which requires improved numerical techniques and algorithms, the quest to measure cosmological parameters to ever higher precision requires vast fine-grained searches through the available model parameter space. And if we are to test for signatures beyond that of the simplest inflation models, the computational challenge is very much greater.

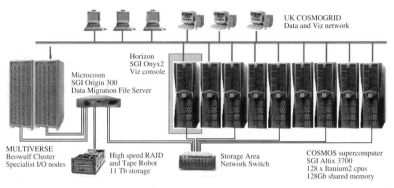

Fig. 41.11. COSMOS, the UK National Cosmology Supercomputer (early 2003 upgrade), of which Stephen Hawking is principal investigator. It is supported by HEFCE, PPARC and SGI. The primary consortium institutions are Cambridge, Portsmouth and Sussex Universities and Imperial College; Oxford, Durham and Manchester are also members.

Cosmology has entered the realm of big science with experimental projects like the Planck Surveyor satellite costing the better part of a billion dollars or euros. While the theoretical community has responded with enthusiasm, the personnel and computational resources actually deployed at the hard numerical interface remain relatively meagre. For example, it is interesting to observe the dependence of CMB data analysis projects on the single Boltzmann code, CMBFAST [50]. While this important and pioneering code has been extensively tested and there is now a second (partially independent) code CAMB [51] for comparison, its validation would be unlikely to meet commercial quality standards for projects of such enormous cost, nor is it a model of design integrity. Research councils and funding bodies will have to make more substantial contributions towards both hardware and programming personnel to exploit the anticipated data flow effectively. The reliable extraction of science from these high precision cosmological observations presents both an exciting challenge and opportunity, particularly for those newly entering the field.

Now, turning to a more personal note, it might seem somewhat surprising that Stephen has lent such full support to the COSMOS supercomputer project; he is perhaps an unlikely numerical afficionado! But it derives from more than his belief in the importance of furthering the confrontation between theory and observation, it comes from direct experience of the unique and quantitative insight that can be gained from numerical simulations.[5] Stephen, for example, is the first person I know who attempted to study cosmic defects numerically in more than one dimension; he worked on this in collaboration with his son Robert on a BBC microcomputer back in 1982. And he has written many collaborative papers in which numerical simulations have been the primary result, whether demonstrating the problems of old inflation or calculating the wave function of the universe [52]. There can be little doubt that without his direct involvement and support, COSMOS would not be what it is today, a successful and fruitful project dedicated particularly to the study of the early universe and the cosmic microwave sky. Indeed, it is the primary computational platform for the Cambridge Planck Analysis Centre a key data analysis centre that is actively preparing for the launch of the Planck satellite. And at this point, it is appropriate to acknowledge, not only my personal indebtedness to Stephen for his support and encouragement over the years, but I think all UK cosmologists can be grateful that we have such an exceptional champion for our cause.

41.7 Afterword

An impressive array of cosmological observations and experiments promise to advance the understanding of our universe and the origin of its large-scale structure. It is possible to envisage the ongoing harmony between these new observations and a cosmic concordance model based around slow-roll inflation. Such a scenario might enable cosmological parameters to be pinned down to an extra decimal place or even two, but it would still not spell the end for theoretical cosmology. Too many questions remain outstanding about the basic constituents of the universe – its dark energy, dark matter and baryons – let alone about its perturbations. To what extent were the seeds for structure formation primordial, scale-invariant, adiabatic and Gaussian? Can unique signatures of a specific inflationary model be identified? Can inflation be placed in a self-consistent fundamental framework? And, there will always remains the unavoidable problem of specifying the initial conditions of the universe, one of Stephen's primary goals in recent years [53].

On the other hand, one might also hope that anomalies in this coherent picture will emerge, perhaps some relics or other clues from the very early universe which might advance our understanding of fundamental

---

[5] In his 1980 inaugural lecture, Stephen suggested that the end might be in sight for theoretical physicists (if not for theoretical physics) because computers would begin to take their place!

theory. In many ways, it would be disappointing if the rich two- and three-dimensional information about our universe which new observations are about to reveal, were all to collapse into a one-dimensional power spectrum characterized by an amplitude and a spectral index (and perhaps its slope)! While Stephen could be pleased by the observational confirmation of his ideas, a dark inflationary curtain would descend over the very early universe. It would be far more interesting if this veil did not close completely, leaving gaps for the discovery of signatures of extra dimensions, cosmic strings or other phenomena as yet unimagined. One of the most exciting possibilities is the prospect of detecting primordial gravitational waves that have travelled direct to us from the moment of creation.

Martin Rees [54] presents a future for cosmology in which the community bifurcates into environmental cosmologists, those exploring details of the emergence of structure in the universe, and the rest who venture into ever earlier and more speculative regimes; perhaps, it could be loosely summarized as the 'technicians' vs the 'magicians'. This seems to me somewhat pessimistic, because our primary hope must be that the anticipated observations will provide cosmological theories with a firmer empirical grounding on which to develop in future. Inflationary model-building has already provided a clear enough picture (Figure 41.3) of the fruits of the lightly constrained imagination, a feat now being repeated in five dimensions (and more)! Instead, we might do well to heed that early string theorist, Robert Hooke, who in 1665 warned:

> The truth is, the Science of Nature has been already too long made only a work of the Brane and the Fancy: It is now high time that it should return to the plainness and soundness of Observations.

After all, the future looks bright for cosmology and there can be little doubt that many real scientific advances in the understanding of our universe will take place over the next few years.

References

[1] Guth, A. H. (1981), 'The inflationary universe: a possible solution to the horizon and flatness problems', *Phys. Rev.* **D23**, 347–356. See also Linde, A. D. (1982), *Phys. Lett.* **B108**, 389–393; Albrecht, A. and Steinhardt, P. J. (1982), *Phys. Rev. Lett.* **48**, 1220–1223.

[2] Guth, A. (2003), 'Inflation and cosmological perturbations', this proceedings.

[3] Hawking, S. W. (1982), 'The development of irregularities in a single bubble inflationary universe', *Phys. Lett.* **B115**, 295–297. See also Mukhanov, V. F. and Chibisov, G. V. (1981), *Pisma Zh. Eksp. Teor. Fiz.* **33**, 549–553 [*JETP Lett.* **33**, 532–535]; Guth, A. H. and Pi, S.-Y. (1982), *Phys. Rev. Lett.* **49**,

1110–1113; Bardeen, J. M. Steinhardt, P. J. and Turner, M. S. (1983), *Phys. Rev.* **D28**, 679–693; Starobinski, A. A. (1982), *Phys. Lett.* **B117**, 175–178. Hawking, S. W. and Moss, I. G. (1983), *Phys. Rev.* **D26**, 2681–2693.

[4] Sachs, R. K. and Wolfe, A. M. (1967), *Astrophys. J.* **147**, 73.

[5] Wang, X. Tegmark, M. and Zaldarriaga, M. (2002), 'Is cosmology consistent?', *Phys. Rev.* **D65**, 083002.

[6] Smoot, G. F. *et al.* (1992), *Ap.J.* **395**, L1.

[7] Netterfield, C. B. *et al.*(2002), 'A measurement by BOOMERANG of multiple peaks in the angular power spectrum of the cosmic microwave background', *Astrophys. J.* **571**, 604–614

[8] Halverson, N. W. *et al.* (2002), 'DASI first results: A measurement of the cosmic microwave background angular power spectrum', *Astrophys. J.* **568**, 38–45.

[9] Lee, A. T. *et al.* (2001), 'A high spatial resolution analysis of the MAXIMA-1 cosmic microwave background anisotropy data', *Astrophys. J.* **561**, L1–L6.

[10] Pearson, T. J. *et al.* (2002), 'The anisotropy of the microwave background to $\ell = 3500$: Mosaic observations with the Cosmic Background Imager', submitted to *Astrophys. J.*, [astro-ph/0205388].

[11] Scott, P. F. *et al.* (2002), 'First results from the VSA - III. The CMB power spectrum', submitted to *Mon. Not. R. Astron. Soc.*, [astro-ph/0205380].

[12] Benoit, A. *et al.* (2002), 'The cosmic microwave background anisotropy power spectrum measured by ARCHEOPS', [astro-ph/0210305].

[13] Kovac, J. *et al.* (2002), 'Detection of polarization in the cosmic microwave background using DASI', [astro-ph/0209478].

[14] Bond, R. B. *et al.* (2002), 'The cosmic microwave background and inflation, then and now', [astro-ph/0210007].

[15] Efstathiou, G. (2001), 'Principal component analysis of the cosmic microwave background anisotropies: revealing the tensor degeneracy', submitted to *Mon. Not. Roy. Astron. Soc.*, [astro-ph/0109151].

[16] de Bernardis, P. *et al.* (2000), 'A flat universe from high-resolution maps of the cosmic microwave background radiation', *Nature* **404**, 955–959.

[17] Perlmutter, S. *et al.* (Supernova Cosmology Project) (1999), 'Measurements of Ω and Λ from 42 high-redshift supernovae', *Astrophys. J.* **517**, 565–586; Riess, A. *et al.* (High Z Supernova Search Team) (1998), 'Observational evidence from supernovae for an accelerating universe and a cosmological constant', *Astron. J.* **116**, 1009–1038.

[18] Harrison, E. R. (1970), 'Fluctuations at the threshold of classical cosmology', *Phys. Rev.* **D1**, 2726–2730; Zeldovich, Ya. B. (1972), 'A hypothesis, unifying the structure and the entropy of the universe, *Mon. Not. Roy. Astron. Soc.* **160**, 1P–3P.

[19] Buonnano, A. Damour, T. and Veneziano, G. (1999), *Nucl. Phys.* **B543**, 275 and references therein.

[20] Steinhardt, P. J., and Turok, N. (2002), *Science,* **296**, 1436.

[21] See, for example, Moffat, J. W. (2002), 'Variable speed of light cosmology: an alternative to inflation', [hep-th/0208122]; Albrecht, A. and Magueijo, J. (1998), 'A time varying speed of light as a solution to cosmological puzzles', *Phys. Rev.* **D59**, 043516; Avelino, P. P. and Martins, C.J.A.P. (2000), 'Primordial adiabatic fluctuations from cosmic defects', *Phys. Rev. Lett.* **85**, 1370.

[22] Hollands, S. and Wald, R. M. (2002), 'Comment on inflation and alternative cosmology', [hep-th/0210001], and references therein.

[23] Turok, N. G. (1996), *Phys. Rev. Lett.* **77**, 4138 and references therein.

[24] Gibbons, G. W. (1984), 'Aspects of supergravity theories', in *GIFT Seminar on Supersymmetry, Supergravity and Related Topics*, eds F. del Aguila, J. A. Azcarraga and L. E. Ibanez (World Scientific).

[25] Maldacena, J. and Nunez, C. (2001), *Int. J. Mod. Phys.* **A16**, 822.

[26] Turok, N. (2002), 'A critical review of inflation', *Class. Quantum Grav.* **19**, 3449–67.

[27] Liddle, A. R. and Lyth, D. H. (2000), *Cosmological Inflation and Large-Scale Structure* (Cambridge University Press, Cambridge).

[28] Hoffman, M. B. and Turner, M. S. (2001), *Phys. Rev.* **D64**, 023506.

[29] Kinney, W. H. (2002), Inflation: flow, fixed points and observables to arbitrary order in slow roll', [astro-ph/0206032].

[30] Lidsey, J. *et al.* (1997), *Rev. Mod. Phys.* **69** 373.

[31] Hawking, S. W. and Page, D. N. (1988), 'How probable is inflation?', *Nucl. Phys.* **B298**, 789.

[32] Zel'dovich, Ya. B. (1980), 'Cosmological fluctuations produced near a singularity', *Mon. Not. Roy. Astron. Soc.* **192**, 663.

[33] Vilenkin, A. (1981), 'Cosmological density fluctuations produced by vacuum strings', *Phys. Rev. Lett.* **46**, 1169. Erratum: **46**, 1496.

[34] Turok, N. (2003), 'The ekpyrotic universe and its cyclic extension', this proceedings.

[35] Linde, A. (2003), 'Inflationary theory versus the ekpyrotic/cyclic scenario', this proceedings.

[36] Vilenkin, A. and Shellard, E.P.S. (2000), *Cosmic Strings and other Topological Defects* (Cambridge University Press, Cambridge).

[37] Allen, B. and Shellard, E.P.S. (1990), 'Cosmic string evolution – a numerical simulation', *Phys. Rev. Lett.* **64**, 119.

[38] Pogosian, L. (2001), 'Cosmic defects and CMB anisotropy', *Int. J. Mod. Phys.* **A16S1C**, 1043.

[39] Bouchet, F. R. Peter, P., Riazuelo, A. and Sakellariadou, M. (2001), 'Evidence against or for topological defects in the Boomerang data?', [astro-ph/0005022].

[40] Durrer, R. Kunz, M. and Melchiori, A. (1999), 'Cosmic microwave background anisotropies from scaling seeds: global defect models', *Phys. Rev.* **D59**, 123005.

[41] Battye, R. Albrecht, A. and Robinson, J. (1998), 'Structure formation by cosmic strings with a cosmological constant', *Phys. Rev. Lett.* **80**, 4847.

[42] Kaiser, N. and Stebbins, A. (1984), 'Microwave anisotropy due to cosmic strings', *Nature* **310**, 391.

[43] Landriau, M. and Shellard, E.P.S. (2002), 'Small-angle CMB anisotropies from cosmic strings', in preparation.

[44] Spergel, D., and Zaldarriaga, M. (1997), *Phys. Rev. Lett.*

[45] Thorne, K. (2003), 'Warping spacetime', this proceedings.

[46] Battye, R. A. and Shellard, E.P.S. (1996), 'Relic gravitational waves', GRG essay, [astro-ph/9610196].

[47] Vilenkin, A. and Damour, T. (2000), 'Gravitational wave bursts from cosmic strings', *Phys. Rev. Lett.* **85** 3761.

[48] Allen, B. and Ottewell, A. (2002), 'Waveforms for gravitational radiation from cosmic string loops', *Phys. Rev.* **D65** 122000.

[49] Ungarelli, C. and Vecchio, A. (2001), 'High energy physics and the very early universe', *Phys. Rev.* **D63**, 064030.

[50] Seljak, U. and Zaldarriaga, M. (1996), 'A line of sight approach to cosmic microwave background anisotropies', *Astrophys. J.* **469**, 437–444.

[51] Lewis, A. Challinor, A. and Lasenby, A. (2000), *Ap.J.* **538**, 473.

[52] For example, Hawking, S. W. Moss, I. G. and Stewart, J. M. (1982), 'Bubble collisions in the very early universe', *Phys. Rev.* **D26**, 2681–2693.

[53] Hawking, S. W. (1982), 'The boundary conditions of the universe', in *Astrophysical Cosmology: Proceedings of the Study Week on Cosmology and Fundamental Physics, September 28–October 2, 1981*, eds H. A. Brück, C. V. Coyne, and M. S. Longair (Pontificiae Academiae Scientiarum Scripta Varia, Vatican).

[54] Rees, M. (2000), 'Introductory lecture' in *Proceedings of NATO-ASI Workshop on Large-scale Structure Formation*, eds R.G. Crittenden and N.G. Turok (Kluwer).

[55] Bennett, C.L. et al., 'First year WMAP observations: preliminary maps and basic results', astro-ph/0302207.

42

The ekpyrotic universe and its cyclic extension

Neil Turok

Centre for Mathematical Sciences, University of Cambridge

42.1 Introduction

It is both a pleasure and an honour to speak at Stephen's 60th birthday conference. Through his work connecting cosmology with fundamental theory, Stephen helped create a field now acknowledged to be amongst the most challenging and interesting in modern science.

As an undergraduate at Cambridge, I attended Stephen's inaugural lecture entitled 'Is the end of theoretical physics in sight?' His answer was 'yes', and he claimed supergravity was the final theory. Although sceptical, I was impressed by the directness and clarity of his vision. And indeed he was right to the extent that supergravity, now extended to M theory, is still our best hope for an ultimate theory.

When I returned to join the faculty here, one of the great pleasures was being able to collaborate with Stephen, and gain an insider's view of his intellectual power. But also of his iconoclastic sense of humour and his terrific sense of fun. As Lou Reed would have said, he's got a real 'Lust for Life', which keeps him going against all the odds, and which is another great inspiration to the rest of us. The topic of my lecture today is orthogonal to Stephen's favourite approach to cosmology. Nonetheless I hope he will enjoy it, if only as a challenging diversion.

Many cosmologists have hailed the discoveries [1] of the acoustic peaks in the cosmic microwave anisotropy as the final confirmation of the inflationary universe scenario [2], which has dominated theoretical cosmology for two decades. Stephen played a key role in predicting the form of the density perturbations from inflation, and I think he like others tends to find the new evidence compelling.

I believe this interpretation is premature. In spite of two decades of theoretical effort, there is still no real theory of inflation. All inflationary

781

predictions depend on the assumed form of the inflaton potential, not yet derivable from fundamental theory. Simple models include an arbitrary potential, which must be fine tuned to obtain agreement with observation. Worse, they are quantum mechanically inconsistent (non-renormalizable) beyond leading order when gravity is included. At best, the models are a 'stand-in' effective theory for a fundamental approach still to be developed (for a critical review of inflation, see [3]).

Second, most of the detailed features of the cosmic microwave data (specifically, the presence of acoustic peaks and the damping at high l) are not a consequence of inflation but of far more mundane and well understood plasma physics. All that is really required to fit the observations is primordial fluctuations which are:

(A) linear, growing mode, adiabatic, Gaussian;

(B) scale invariant, in a flat Universe.

The characteristics listed in (A) might reasonably be expected from *any* simple mechanism operating only in the early universe (hence not including cosmic defects). Decaying mode perturbations would have rapidly disappeared. Local thermal equilibrium re-establishes adiabaticity, so as long as no extra information survived from the early, fluctuation-generation phase (e.g. fluctuations in a light scalar field or a conserved particle number), adiabatic perturbations result. Linearity and Gaussianity are generic consequence of amplifying free field quantum fluctuations. So none of these features are really very specific to inflation.

Flatness and scale invariance are arguably more specific successes. The simplest approaches to inflation, assuming a nearly smooth initial patch with high inflaton field, predict a flat universe. More spectacularly, as Hawking showed [4], such models produce a nearly scale-invariant spectrum of fluctuations as an automatic side-effect of quantum mechanics [4]. The amplitude remains problematic (fitting observation requires fine tuning to 10^{-12}–10^{-14}). But embarrassment over this faded with time as the main rivals to inflation (such as cosmic defects) were disproved, and alternatives failed to emerge.

It is hard to prove or disprove inflation scientifically using the above observational signatures. Open or closed inflationary universes are possible, either through non-monotonic potentials [5], or with instantons of the type discussed by Hawking and me, even for monotonic potentials [6, 7]. It is possible to construct inflationary models producing non-adiabatic, non-scale invariant and non-Gaussian perturbations. Strictly speaking, it is only specific models of inflation which are testable, not the idea of inflation itself.

In my view, the main successes of simple inflation models may be attributed more to their simplicity (adiabaticity, Gaussianity, scale invariance, flatness) rather than to inflation itself. The strongest argument for inflation is just that there is no other viable alternative. But that situation may be starting to change with the emergence of the ekpyrotic and cyclic scenarios, which are (with some assumptions) able to match all of the successes of simple inflation models, to the same exquisite accuracy. But the new models are also distinguishable from simple inflation models via specific observations which, if we are lucky, will be made in the coming few years.

A period of inflation would have generated a nearly scale-invariant spectrum of long wavelength gravitational waves [8], in simple models such as ϕ^2 inflation, the amplitude of a 'curl' component of the polarization of the cosmic microwave sky (which cannot be produced by scalar perturbations). The ekpyrotic and cyclic models predict a very small gravitational wave amplitude on large scales, so the observation of a 'curl' component would disprove the models [9]. Non-observation would disprove the simplest inflation models, but not inflation itself, because it is easy to construct models of inflation (especially two-field models, which are more flexible) in which the gravitational wave amplitude may be made unobservably small.

Rather than retreat into a corner of parameter space, in typical style Stephen made a public bet with me that (assuming foregrounds allow it) Planck will confirm the presence of long wavelength gravitational waves at least at the level expected from ϕ^2 inflation. Stephen has a habit of making interesting bets, and he does not always win. But his willingness to stick his neck out is a credit to him, and stimulating for the science. We shall see!

Of course, of equal significance to observations, we must try through theoretical investigations to establish or disprove the consistency of inflation or ekpyrosis with M theory or other approaches to quantum gravity. Both theories must face up to cosmology's other basic puzzles: did the universe 'begin'? what happened at the initial 'singularity'? what determined the puzzling parameters of today's universe? – especially the cosmological constant, but also the abundances of different forms of matter and radiation. Here, the ekpyrotic and especially the cyclic model have the potential to offer more than inflationary theory, as I will explain.

42.2 Homage to the Ancients

The work 'ekpyrotic' means 'out of fire', and describes the cosmology of the ancient Greek philosophers around 500 BC. Anaximander, an early exponent of these ideas, was a very interesting individual. He is credited with having invented two-dimensional maps, with having proposed that fish evolved from plants in the sea, and that all matter arose from one primordial substance (i.e., the ancient version of string theory!). He also argued that the Earth floated in empty space rather than rested on anything, and is credited with inventing the notion of an infinite universe. A very remarkable thinker!

Anaximander's ideas were developed by Heraclitus, who famously held that change in the universe must come from a tension between opposites. Heraclitus had a fierce debate with Parmenides, one of the other great thinkers of the time, who argued instead that all change was an illusion, it being logically impossible for something, or a new state of something, to come into being when it did not exist before. This debate prefigured (by over two millennia) the modern debate between Hartle and Hawking's no boundary proposal and our ekpyrotic/cyclic Universe model. According to Hawking, the only 'real' time is Euclidean time, which is a spatial dimension hence Lorentzian time is not a fundamental notion. According to the ekpyrotic and cyclic models, real Lorentzian time exists forever. It is a fun and exciting state of affairs that we are now discussing these profound philosophical questions in the context of definite mathematical models, which are furthermore observationally distinguishable thanks to technological progress.

42.3 The ekpyrotic universe model

The ekpyrotic universe model proposed by Khoury, Ovrut, Steinhardt and me was inspired by brane world constructions in M theory, combined with a naive physical intuition. The basic construction in M theory models of realistic particle physics, due to Horava and Witten [10], involves parallel branes (technically, orientifold planes) separated by a gap (Figure 42.1). The simplest case, with two boundary branes, is illustrated in Figure 42.1. Z_2-symmetric boundary conditions are imposed so that in the covering space picture the configuration is mirrored infinitely many times through each of the two boundary branes. Whilst most of the work on particle physics assumes a static set-up, for the real world of cosmology, the branes must be allowed to expand. In general this corresponds to their moving across the bulk, and relative to one another. For example, in the Horava–Witten picture the branes may be only a few thousands of Planck lengths apart. They do not have to be moving very fast in order to collide once within the age of the universe, as in the cyclic model.

The collision between two brane worlds is a most remarkable event. For example, the effective gauge symmetry and the number of light degrees

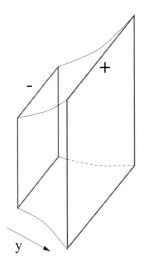

Fig. 42.1. Positive and negative tension orientifold planes (which I shall loosely call branes) separated by a warped extra dimension. Motion of the branes along the extra dimension corresponds to an expansion or contraction of their transverse dimensions.

of freedom typically change suddenly when branes merge or separate. The idea behind the ekpyrotic model was that if such a collision occurred at finite speed, particle production would occur due to the non-adiabatic nature of the changes involved. Such a collision could therefore have been the origin of the radiation and matter in our hot big bang. In the first version of the model, we considered the collision between a third, bulk brane, with one of the two 'boundary' branes. However, as noted in our original paper, it is hard to avoid a subsequent collision between the two boundary branes. This being so, one may as well simply consider the two brane case. In which case, the opportunity arises for a cyclic model in which the two boundary branes repeatedly attract, collide and rebound. Each cycle represents a big bang (brane separation) followed by a big crunch (brane collision), and the cycles might repeat indefinitely.

Most workers in cosmology have got used to the notion that time must have 'begun', even though this is a truly paradoxical notion. For justification, most would refer to the classic singularity theorems of the 1970s, when Hawking and Penrose proved under mild assumptions that classical general relativity implied the existence of a cosmic singularity at a finite time in our past. However, these theorems do not at all imply a beginning of time. All they prove is that general relativity broke down. But this is hardly surprising: we know a more complete theory of quantum gravity is needed, and that corrections to general relativity will be large in the vicinity of a singularity. Which part of general relativity is likely to be wrong there? The most conservative guess is that the assumption of a smooth three geometry fails. We already know this is allowed in orbifold constructions of string theory. But it is not at all necessary that time began: and there is no evidence from string theory for a 'beginning of time'. Since string theory is an S matrix theory, for every 'out' state there is an 'in' state. So, even if time is only a classical notion there would seem to be no way for it to 'begin' or 'end' [11].

Was there time before the cosmic singularity? Again, this is an old question dating back at least as far as Tolman's classic book [13]. Tolman considered closed universe models with zero cosmological constant and pointed out a physical objection to the continuation of time back into the infinite past. Since a bounce from crunch to bang would undoubtedly be a violent process, he argued it would inevitably produce entropy (radiation). But each crunch/bang transition would then add to the total amount of radiation present, and each subsequent cycle would be longer and longer. Tracing time back into the past, the accumulated age would converge as the cycle length shrank. Thus, even Tolman's bouncing model failed to allow time to be extended back infinitely into the past.

Our cyclic universe model provides a way around this. First, the universe is flat and infinite rather than closed. Second, there is dark energy (quintessence) component which dominates at late times in each cycle. The flat, infinite geometry means that it is only the density of radiation which matters, not the total number of photons. A brane collision produces a finite density of radiation. The subsequent expansion, eventually driven by dark energy, dilutes the radiation away to negligible levels, before it is replenished by the next collision. Each cycle may be almost identical to the one before it, and the presence of the cosmological constant allows for a stably periodic solution in which the cycles continue forever [12].

42.4 The main problem

The main obstacle to such a cyclic model is the passage across the singularity which occurs when the two boundary branes collide. Clearly, the geometry changes from being D dimensional to $D - 1$ dimensional, and the classical spacetime can no longer be described by a smooth manifold. This is a form of singularity, but much milder than the usual cosmological big bang singularity. The D, D component of the metric vanishes but at any finite time away from the singularity the spacetime curvature is small (and may be zero). Since the $D - 1$ dimensional geometry on the branes is non-singular at the collision, the density of brane-world matter remains finite there.

Even if such a singularity is mild, can one really pass through it? In our paper with Seiberg [14], we outlined a continuation. Namely, when two boundary branes collide, they could simply pass through, with the bulk re-appearing after the collision. Steinhardt and I subsequently showed [12] that if one imposes the equation of state for the branes (i.e. how much matter and radiation there is) after the collision, then the outcome is essentially uniquely determined by total energy and momentum conservation. But this is only enough to determine the background evolution. Propagating the perturbations across the boundary brane collision is harder, and no completely satisfactory prescription yet exists. I will return to this crucial issue later.

Recently (subsequent to this talk), several detailed investigations have occurred of this type of time-dependent, singular spacetime within the context of string theory. Some of these results are negative, showing that in one approach ('Lorentzian orbifolding'), string theory amplitudes diverge in an unacceptable way, even at tree level [15].

I believe it is too early for pessimism, however. In the ekpyrotic/cyclic model, it was most natural to consider the extra dimension separating the colliding branes to be the M theory dimension, i.e. the eleventh dimension of supergravity. At least two special features are associated with the collapse of this dimension, which are not properly represented in the string theory calculations just mentioned, First, as the eleventh dimension shrinks to zero, the theory becomes a weakly coupled string theory, with the string coupling constant tending to zero as the eleventh dimension vanishes. Hence it is reasonable to suspect that the behaviour will be different (and perhaps better) than that found in the string theory calculations performed so far. Second, the most obvious obstacle to a transition from D to $D - 1$ dimensions and back is that there would seem to be no way to represent the initial D dimensional degrees of freedom faithfully in the intermediate $D - 1$ dimensional state. But this isn't the case for the collapse of the eleventh dimension. Witten argued some time ago that eleven-dimensional supergravity (with two boundary branes carrying appropriate matter fields) is the strong coupling limit of ten-dimensional heterotic string theory [16]. Thus the degrees of freedom required to describe the eleven-dimensional world of supergravity must be describable as non-perturbative excitations of ten-dimensional string theory. Therefore it should be possible for the degrees of freedom of the original eleven-dimensional configuration to be faithfully represented in an intermediate, ten-dimensional state.

42.5 Flatness

As mentioned above, the two most significant successes for inflation were the flatness of the universe and the scale invariance of the perturbations. In the ekpyrotic model, we imposed the flatness of the universe with an assumption of symmetry ('BPS-ness') in the initial state. This was a mathematical prescription rather than a dynamical mechanism, and I think it is fair to argue that the explanation of flatness is weaker in that model than in the inflationary model.

But in the cyclic extension of the ekpyrotic model, flatness really is a dynamical consequence of today's dark energy, operating in the previous cycle. Since the existence of dark energy is an observational fact, this seems a more economical explanation of flatness than that offered by inflation.

42.6 Density perturbations

The discovery of an alternate mechanism for generating scale invariant fluctuations, without inflation, was really the key stimulus for our first paper on the ekpyrotic model. The physical picture we had in mind was that some mechanism (e.g. the exchange of virtual massive states) led to an attractive force between branes, falling off rapidly with separation. In this situation, as the branes approach, ripples are amplified. Where the branes are closer, the attractive force is greater, and the gap shrinks faster. Remarkably, in this situation, the vacuum fluctuations initially present on the branes are amplified into scale invariant fluctuations, as needed for structure formation in the universe.

As I shall derive in a moment, the separation between the two branes (or the length of the extra dimension) is a four-dimensional scalar, and in a four-dimensional effective description it may be written in terms of a four-dimensional scalar field ϕ. We are interested in the power spectrum of fluctuations acquired by this field as the branes approach.

We assume that the scalar field fluctuation modes start in the ordinary Minkowski vacuum. This assumption is precisely analogous to that usually made in inflationary theory, that on short wavelengths field modes should be in the adiabatic vacuum state. In inflation, it is conventional to argue that as long as inflation proceeds for a long time, then short wavelength excitations are quickly damped away so the adiabatic vacuum is an attractor state. In the cyclic model, the same argument holds but it is much stronger because the universe has been expanding for an infinite period of time In each cycle, the branes expand by an exponentially large amount, in the transverse dimensions. The fluctuation modes amplified in each cycle are new modes, never previously excited.

We further assume that the scalar field potential tends to zero rapidly with increasing ϕ. A simple model for such a potential is a negative exponential,

$$V(\phi) = -V_0 e^{-c\phi}. \tag{42.1}$$

The initial conditions for the field are that it is large, and has very little kinetic energy. Thus the energy

$$E = \frac{1}{2}\dot{\phi}^2 + V(\phi) \approx 0. \tag{42.2}$$

Because the energy density is small, one might expect gravitational effects to be small, and this is confirmed by a detailed analysis [17]. So let us ignore gravity from now on. For zero energy, the solution is

$$\phi = \frac{2}{c}\ln(-t), \tag{42.3}$$

where I have absorbed an integration constant into the definition of the time. The time t is negative, and tends to zero as ϕ runs off to minus infinity.

The equation of motion for the scalar field Fourier modes, $\delta\phi(\vec{x}) = \sigma_{\vec{k}}\delta\phi_{\vec{k}}e^{i\vec{k}.\vec{x}}$ is:

$$\ddot{\delta\phi}_{\vec{k}} + k^2\delta\phi_{\vec{k}} = -V_{,\phi,\phi}\delta\phi_{\vec{k}} = +\frac{2}{t^2}\delta\phi_{\vec{k}}, \tag{42.4}$$

where we keep only linear terms in the fluctuation. (A detailed analysis of the non-linear terms shows them to be very small for the long wavelength modes of interest [20].)

We are interested in starting with the quantum field in the incoming adiabatic Minkowski vacuum state. The normalized field modes therefore behave as

$$\delta\phi_{\vec{k}} \sim \frac{e^{-ikt}}{\sqrt{2k}}, \qquad t \to -\infty. \tag{42.5}$$

Equation (42.4) can be solved exactly, but the qualitative evolution may simply be read off. At large negative t, the right-hand side is negligible. But as $|t|$ falls below k^{-1}, the right-hand side dominates over the k^2 term, and the solution tends to the growing mode $\delta\phi_{\vec{k}} \propto t^{-1}$. Since $\delta\phi_{\vec{k}} \sim k^{-1\frac{1}{2}}$ when $k|t| \sim 1$, it follows that for modes which are in the growing mode,

$$\delta\phi_{\vec{k}} \sim k^{-\frac{3}{2}}t^{-1}. \tag{42.6}$$

Since the real space variance of the scalar field, $\langle \delta \phi^2 \rangle$ receives an equal contribution from each logarithmic interval in k, it follows that the field $\delta \phi$ has acquired a scale invariant spectrum of classical, growing fluctuations.

The time dependence of the fluctuations also has a simple interpretation. The classical background solution is (42.3). The classical field background equation is invariant under time translations, but a time shift corresponds to a perturbation $\delta \phi \sim t_0 \frac{d}{dt} \ln(-t) \sim -t_0/t$, $|t_0| << |t|$. This allows us to predict the form of the $\delta \phi_{\vec{k}}$ power spectrum for the case where the potential bends upwards to zero, for negative *phi*. As long as we evolve for times shorter than k^{-1}, then the modes we have amplified via the potential (42.1) are effectively frozen in, and they will have fluctuations given by $\delta t \dot{\phi}$ where $\dot{\phi}$ is the background solution and δt equals $\delta \phi_{\vec{k}}$ given in (42.6).

As we shall now see, the branes collide when $\phi \to -\infty$, which is reached in finite time. The scale invariant time delay just computed is then imprinted on the initial conditions for the hot big bang.

42.7 Brane collisions

The basic set-up assumed in the ekpyrotic and cyclic models is illustrated in Figure 42.1. An extra dimension (parameterised by y) is bounded by a positive, and a negative tension brane. The simplest case consists of two empty branes separated by a region of anti-de Sitter spacetime with line element

$$dy^2 + e^{\frac{2y}{L}}(-dt^2 + d\mathbf{x}^2),\qquad\qquad(42.7)$$

where $\mathbf{x}$ parameterize the three uncompactified dimensions, t is the time, and L is the AdS radius (related to the value of the negative bulk cosmological constant). If the tension of the two branes is $\pm 6/L$, the configuration exhibited in Figure 42.1 is a static solution of the field equations, for arbitrary locations y_+ and y_- of the two orbifold branes. Equivalently, we can describe the set of static solutions in terms of the *scale factors* on the two branes, $a_0 \equiv e^{y_+/L}$, and $a_1 \equiv e^{y_-/L}$ (the reason for the notation will become clear in a moment).

The dynamical evolution of this system can be described with a four-dimensional effective field theory including a four-dimensional metric a and a scalar field ϕ. To compute the action, we use the following argument. First, we assume the branes are perfectly parallel and flat. In this case, the motion may be described by computing the action for a configuration with time dependent moduli $a_0(t)$ and $a_1(t)$. If the velocities are slow, a computation of the full Einstein-brane action yields [9]

$$S = 3M_5^3 L \int dt d^3\mathbf{x} (-\dot{a}_0^2 + \dot{a}_1^2). \tag{42.8}$$

Now, it is clear that the moduli a_0 and a_1 transform as scale factors under rescaling the $\mathbf{x}$ coordinates. However, their ratio a_0/a_1 is a scalar under such transformations. If we change variables using $a_0 = a\cosh(\phi/\sqrt{6})$, $a_1 = -a\sinh(\phi/\sqrt{6})$, with a a scale factor, then (42.8) becomes

$$S = M_4^2 \int dt d^3\mathbf{x} (-\dot{a}^2 + \frac{1}{2}a^2\dot{\phi}^2). \tag{42.9}$$

which is just the action for Einstein gravity (with metric $a^2(t)(-dt^2+d\mathbf{x}^2)$) coupled minimally to a scalar field ϕ. The four-dimensional Planck mass squared is given by $M_4^2 = M_5^3 L$.

The map from the brane scale factors a_0 and a_1 to the Einstein frame scale factor is surprising in two respects:

- The Einstein gravity scale factor is given by the formula $a^2 = a_0^2 - a_1^2$. Thus when the two branes coincide, $y_+ = y_-$ so $a_0 = a_1$ with both scale factors finite even though the Einstein scale factor vanishes. What looks like the standard cosmic singularity ($a = 0$) in Einstein frame appears far less singular in the brane picture. For example, the density of matter or radiation, or the spacetime curvature on either brane is finite as the branes collide.

- The distance between the two branes is given by

$$d = L\log(\coth(-\phi/\sqrt{6})). \tag{42.10}$$

  The range $0 < d < \infty$ is mapped to $-\infty < \phi < 0$, so that d tends to zero as ϕ tends to minus infinity, and d tends to ∞ as ϕ tends to zero.

Now, if we want to describe more general brane configurations, including branes with 'ripples' on them as we will need for the density perturbation mechanism, we must generalize the action (42.9) to that describing branes which are not perfectly planar. Four-dimensional covariance allows us to do this trivially. That is, whatever the low energy effective theory is, it should be invariant under Four-dimensional coordinate transformations. But the only such action, involving gravity and a scalar field, and which agrees with the action (42.9) we have just calculated, is the Einstein-scalar action

$$S = M_4^2 \int d^4x \sqrt{-g^{(4)}} (\frac{1}{2}R - \frac{1}{2}(\partial\phi)^2). \tag{42.11}$$

From this almost trivial calculation, we have inferred the low energy effective action for arbitrary non-planar-symmetric brane configurations, a very powerful result. Matter localized on the positive tension brane couples to the metric on that brane, given by the four-dimensional Einstein frame metric $g_{\mu\nu}^{(4)}$ times some function $\beta^2(\phi)$ of the scalar field ϕ. For example in the simple AdS model, we have for matter on the positive and negative tension branes respectively, $\beta_0(\phi) = \cosh(\phi/\sqrt{6})$, and $\beta_1(\phi) = -\sinh(\phi/\sqrt{6})$. (I note in passing that this derivation yields the correct couplings between the scalar field ϕ and matter localized on the branes [21], a rather complicated calculation by other methods [22]).

Evidently, higher-dimensional gravity with branes yields four-dimensional gravity plus a scalar field (the 'radion'). This is the putative origin of the scalar field in the ekpyrotic and cyclic models. Before continuing, we should ask whether such a scalar field is detectable through its effect on the gravitational couplings of matter. Since the variation of the matter action with respect to the conformal factor of the metric yields the trace of the stress energy tensor, one finds the equation

$$\Box\phi \sim (\beta(\phi))_{,\phi} T^{\mu}_{\mu}. \tag{42.12}$$

From this it is clear that conformally coupled matter (for example classical radiation) does not source ϕ whereas non-relativistic matter (with zero pressure) does. Non-relativistic matter should therefore possess a 'fifth force' field, which in general violates the equivalence principle. Solar system tests now yield the constraint $\Delta a/a < 10^{-12}$ for the fractional difference in acceleration between the Moon (mostly silicon) and the Earth (mostly iron). This translates into a constraint $\beta_{,\phi}/\beta < 10^{-3}$, for our brane, which is not hard to satisfy in the Randall–Sundrum model if the matter we are considering is on the positive tension brane. The observational constraint is set to improve strongly with the STEP satellite measurement, which may take the constraint to $\beta_{,\phi}/\beta < 10^{-6}$.

A second potential problem for brane world cosmology is that, in general, all the low energy couplings in the theory (such as the gauge couplings) may depend on the scalar field ϕ, more specifically on the brane separation which is a function of ϕ/M_4 where M_4 is the four-dimensional (reduced) Planck mass. But this turns out to be a rather mild constraint. The point is that as the universe expands, the kinetic energy in ϕ redshifts away like a^{-6}. At early times ϕ kinetic energy dominates, and one finds, $a \propto t_P^{1/3}$ where t_P is the proper (Einstein frame) time. The scalar field moves logarithmically in time in this era. However, at some time $t_{P,rad}$ radiation (which scales as a^{-4}) comes to dominate and the scale factor then grows as $a \propto t_P^{1/2}$. The the integrated change in ϕ after some time $t_{P,i} > t_{P,rad}$ is then seen to be $\sim M_4(t_{P,rad}/t_{P,i})^{1/2}$ which is very small as long as $t_{P,i} \gg t_{P,rad}$. For example, if nucleosynthesis occurs well after radiation dominance, there is very little subsequent variation in coupling constants and the standard predictions remain unaffected.

42.8 The inter-brane potential

The inter-brane potential performs many roles in the cyclic model (see Figure 42.2). The positive region causes exponential expansion of the branes, 'cleaning up' the universe after each big bang, and making the branes parallel and flat. It also causes ϕ to roll back to negative values, pulling the branes towards each other and thereby causing the next big bang. The region of strong negative curvature generates scale invariant density perturbations as explained above. Finally, the negative region causes the Einstein frame scale factor a to contract towards zero, and this part of the cycle regenerates (through the usual blue-shifting effect of cosmic contraction) the energy density required to fuel the next big bang.

In the papers published so far, we have just imposed the potential by hand. This is unsatisfactory, and we would like to derive the potential from fundamental theory. Let me mention one idea for how the potential might arise. Consider a scalar field ψ on a circle, with a symmetry breaking potential (e.g. $-\frac{1}{2}m^2\psi^2 + \lambda\psi^4$). Recall, we are really interested in an orbifolded circle, which means we identify y with $L - y$. Assume ψ is odd under this identification. When the circle is small, the ground state for the scalar field is $\psi = 0$. But as the circle grows, the ground state changes to become a kink–antikink configuration, with one at 0 and the other at $L/2$. For large L the energy is approximately $2E_K - (\text{const} e^{-mL/2})$ where E_K is the energy of a kink. Now, recall that the length of the circle is $L \propto e^{\phi/\sqrt{6}}$ where ϕ is measured in reduced Planck units. At large ϕ we have a potential which depends on ϕ as a double exponential. This is extremely flat, even at modest ϕ, and would in the density perturbation calculation, give very accurately scale invariant perturbations. Of course, the constant $2E_K$ term must be cancelled by hand (this is the cosmological constant puzzle), so the model needs further development. It is also important to check whether a mechanism like this can work in supergravity theories, once supersymmetry breaking effects are included.

42.9 The cyclic universe

The cyclic universe scenario proposed by Steinhardt and me is summarized in Figure 42.2. It is very surprising that a cosmology with this form of potential can work at all – one might easily be forgiven for assuming that the field would settle at the minimum of the potential, which is large and negative, and that the universe would find itself in a highly curved anti-de Sitter state. What we realised is that instead the state of the Universe is one of 'hovering' over the potential minimum, with an energy density that never goes negative.

The caption to Figure 42.2 describes a complete cycle in Einstein frame. Einstein frame is convenient because we have good intuition as to the motion of ϕ, and how it is damped in an expanding universe, or anti-damped in a contracting universe, in this frame. However, the brane scale factors a_0 and a_1 defined above provide a more physical description, and one in which all variables of interest (matter density, spacetime curvatures on the branes) are finite at the bounce. Finiteness of a_0 and a_1 allows us to match across the bounce, revealing that the universe actually expands nearly continuously from cycle to cycle. (There is a brief episode of slight contraction of the positive tension brane before collision, and of the negative tension brane after collision, but this is an almost negligible effect.) A sketch of the behaviour of a_0 and a_1 over several cycles is shown in Figure 42.3.

A simple example of a potential which works for the cyclic model takes the form

$$V(\phi) = V_0(1 - e^{-c\phi}), \tag{42.13}$$

where V_0 is chosen to match the currently observed dark energy density, contributing $\Omega_\Lambda \sim 0.7$. When gravitational back-reaction is included, the perturbation spectral index is given by $1 - 4/c^2$. This is in good agreement with observational constraints provided c is greater than 10 or so. Constraints on more general potentials are derived in [9].

42.10 Back to the singularity

Clearly, the linchpin of the cyclic model is the safe passage through the collision of the two boundary branes. Let me make a few further comments about this.

As we approach the singularity, the D dimensional metric may be approximated by

$$-dt^2 + H_5^2 t^2 dy^2 + d\vec{x}^2, \quad 0 \le y \le L, \tag{42.14}$$

which is a wedge of Minkowski spacetime in two-dimensional Milne coordinates. The circle $0 < y < L$ is Z_2-identified so that the branes are located at $y = 0$ and $L/2$ (see Figure 42.4).

The compactified Milne solution to the vacuum Einstein equations $R_{\mu\nu} = 0$ is special because it is just Minkowski spacetime in disguise:

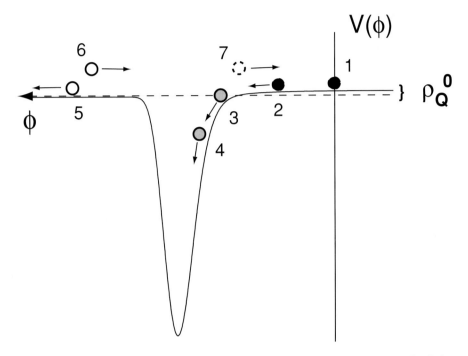

Fig. 42.2. The cyclic scenario corresponds to motion in a potential of the form shown. (1) Today, the potential energy is positive, and driving the recently detected cosmic acceleration. (2) The tiny positive slope of the potential causes the field ϕ to roll down towards the region of negative potential. (3) Soon after the potential crosses zero, the energy density hits zero and the Einstein-frame expansion ceases and turns into contraction. Scale invariant perturbations in ϕ are being generated at this point, on macroscopic length scales. (4) End of generation of scale invariant perturbations as potential curves upwards. Contraction of Einstein frame scale factor results in blueshifting of kinetic energy of ϕ, ensuring that rather than settling at the potential minimum, it speeds up and leaves the potential with large positive kinetic energy. (5) The scalar field runs off to $-\infty$ in finite time as the Einstein frame scale factor tends to zero. (6) As the branes collide and recoil (or equivalently, pass through), the scalar field rebounds from $-\infty$. If more radiation is produced on the negative tension brane, the speed of ϕ at each ϕ is greater in the big bang than it was in the big crunch. The collision fills the universe with radiation and matter: as radiation comes to dominate, its effect is to slow the motion of the field as it crosses the potential. (7) Before nucleosynthesis, the field approaches its final resting state so that it moves very little (in Planck units) from then until today, so coupling constants depending on ϕ typically change very little.

the Riemannian curvature is zero everywhere away from the singularity (where the space is non-Hausdorff). A more general class of solutions is obtained by allowing the non-compact directions parameterized by $\vec{x}$ to expand or contract too: these are the Kasner solutions,

$$-dt^2 + H_5^2 t^{2p} dy^2 + t^{2q} dx_1^2 + t^{2r} dx_2^2 + ..., \qquad (42.15)$$

which solve the Einstein equations provided $p + q + r + ... = 1$ and $p^2 + q^2 + r^2 + ... = 1$. In the Milne solution, $p = 1$ and $q = r = ... = 0$. We can perturb the solution by setting $p = 1$ and $q = \epsilon$, $r = -\epsilon$, with $\epsilon << 1$, to obtain a solution to the linearized Einstein equations. Clearly, the metric perturbation $h_{11} \sim t^{2\epsilon} - 1 \sim \epsilon \log t^2$, to first order in ϵ, which diverges logarithmically as $t = 0$ is approached. This behaviour is in fact that found for all metric perturbations in linear perturbation theory in synchronous gauge [17]. So within conventional D-dimensional Einstein gravity, the Milne solution, and the behaviour shown in Figure 42.4, is

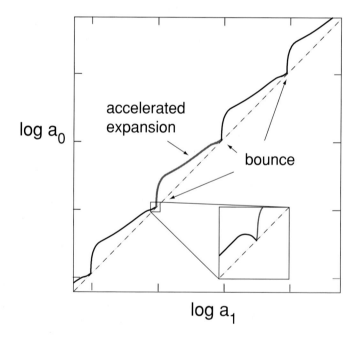

Fig. 42.3. The evolution of the scale factors a_0 and a_1 (the brane scale factors) over several cycles of the cyclic universe. Matter couples to these scale factors, and in consequence all quantities are finite at the big crunch/big bang transition.

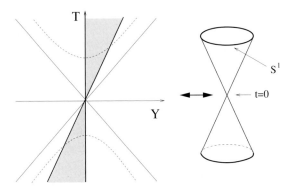

Fig. 42.4. The compactified Milne universe. On the left is two-dimensional Minkowski space. The Lorentz invariant coordinate t satisfying $t^2 = T^2 - Y^2$ is constant on the dashed surfaces, which provide a spacelike foliation of the causal future and past of the origin. These surfaces are parameterized by a coordinate y. Identifying y with $y + L$ compactifies space to produce the spacetime on the right, consisting of two Lorentzian cones joined tip-to-tip at $t = 0$. If the circular sections of these cones are orbifolded by a Z_2, then the two fixed points of the Z_2 are two tensionless branes which collide and pass through one another at $t = 0$.

very special. It requires passage through 'the eye of a needle', because a generic perturbation diverges as one approaches $t = 0$. This does does not prove that there is necessarily a problem in M theory. The point at which the divergence sets in is also the point where higher-order corrections to the Einstein equations become significant, and these corrections do not vanish for the Kasner solution (whereas they do for the Milne solution).

How are we to match across $t = 0$? Ultimately, the full power of string and M theory, and the inclusion of all the relevant degrees of freedom will be needed. The strongest argument that a matching rule should exist is simply that the alternative, for time to 'end', seems unacceptable. Can we anticipate the form of the matching rule within the low energy effective theory? In [17] an approach was proposed based upon a gauge invariant variable (the comoving energy density perturbation) which is finite at $t = 0$. However, this is not an unambiguous choice, and other choices lead to different results. An improved approach has been developed by Durrer and Vernizzi [19], which involves applying Israel matching across the bounce with an assumed contribution to the stress energy in the form of a 'space-like brane'. If the matching is performed on shear-free hypersurfaces, and the stress energy of the brane is isotropic in the noncompact dimensions, one obtains a similar result to that of [17]. Other approaches are being developed and I believe these will be useful guides (although not substitutes for) full string and M theory calculations.

42.11 Conclusions

The ekpyrotic and cyclic universe models represent new approaches to old cosmological puzzles. If the postulated transition from big crunch to big bang is allowed, cyclic models offer the promise of solving puzzles well beyond the scope of conventional inflationary cosmology.

Consider the explanation offered by the conventional model for the current constitution of the universe. There are at least five forms of energy present in today's universe (dark energy, dark matter, baryonic matter, neutrinos and photons) with cosmologically significant densities. Why should this be so? The traditional view is that the ratios were determined from fundamental particle physics, which at high energies knows nothing of the future evolution of the universe. It is really a surprise that these very different forms of matter are each present in an abundance which significantly influences cosmic evolution. It could have easily have been otherwise. A similar puzzle concerns the ultimate future of the universe. Positive dark energy implies a future for our universe in which exponential expansion will take hold, redshifting away all of the interesting structures and leading to an empty, pointless future.

In the cyclic model, a new viewpoint on these puzzles emerges. The composition of the universe at late times in a cycle (in particular the presence of dark energy) determines the state of the universe at the start of the next cycle. If a periodic cyclic solution is to be an attractor, it is essential that positive dark energy be present to redshift away the density inhomogeneities present from the previous cycle so they do not accumulate and make the universe more and more inhomogeneous with every cycle. Likewise, since all forms of energy present play a role in the history of a cycle, there is the possibility of explaining their relative abundances today in terms of their influence on the attractor property. This is an entirely new approach to a deep questions with which standard approaches seem incapable of dealing.

References

[1] Miller, A. D. *et al.* (1999), *Astrophys.J.* **524** L1; De Bernardis, P. *et al.* (2000), *Nature*, **404**, 955, Hanany, S. *et al.* (2000), [astro-ph/0005123].

[2] Guth, A. (1981), *Phys. Rev* **D23**, 347; Linde, A. D. (1982), *Phys. Lett.* **108B**, 389; Albrecht, A. and Steinhardt, P. (1982), *Phys. Rev. Lett.* **48**, 1220.

[3] Turok, N. (2002), *Class. Quantum Grav.* **19** 3449.

[4] Hawking, S. W. (1982), *Phys. Lett.* **115B**, 295; Guth, A. H. and Pi, S.-Y. (1982), *Phys. Rev. Lett.* **49**, 1110; Starobinsky, A. A. (1982), *Phys. Lett.* **117B**, 175; Bardeen, J., Steinhardt, P. and Turner, M. (1983), *Phys. Rev.* **D28,** 679; Harrison, E. R. (1970), The requirement of scale invariance was anticipated in *Phys. Rev.* **D1**, 2726; Zeldovich, Ya. B. (1972), *M.N.R.A.S.*, **160**, 1.

[5] Bucher, M., Goldhaber, A. and Turok, N. (1995), *Phys. Rev.* **D52**, 3314.

[6] Hawking, S. W. and Turok, N. (1998), *Phys. Lett.* **B425** 25–30.

[7] Gratton, S., Lewis, A. and Turok, N. (2002), *Phys.Rev.* **D65** 043513, [astro-ph/0111012].

[8] Kamionkowski, M., Kosowsky, A. and Stebbins, A. (1997), *Phys. Rev. Lett.* **78**) 2058, [astro-ph/9611125]; Zaldarriaga, M. and Seljak, U. (1997), *Phys. Rev. Lett.* **78** 2054, [astro-ph/9609170]; for a recent discussion see Lewis, A., Challinor, A. and Turok, N. (2002), *Phys. Rev.* **D65** 023505.

[9] Khoury, J., Ovrut, B. A., Steinhardt, P. J. and Turok, N. (2001) *Phys.Rev.* **D64** 123522.

[10] Horava, P. and Witten, E. (1996), *Nucl. Phys.* **B460** 506; (1996), **B475** 94.

[11] I thank D. Kutasov for a discussion on this point.

[12] Steinhardt, P. J. and Turok, N. (2002), *Science* **296**, 1436; (2002), *Phys. Rev.* **D65**, 126003.

[13] Tolman, R. C. (1934), *Relativity, Thermodynamics and Cosmology* (Oxford University Press, Clarendon Press).

[14] Khoury, J., Ovrut, B. A., Seiberg, N. and Steinhardt, P. J. (2002), *Phys. Rev.* **D 65** 086007, [hep-th/0108187].

[15] Cornalba, L., Costa, M. S. and Kounnas, C., [hep-th/0204261]; Craps, B., Kutasov, D. and Rajesh, G., [hep-th/0205101]; Liu, H., Moore, G. and Seiberg, N., [hep-th/0206182]; Horowitz, G. T. and Polchinski, J., [hep-th/0206228]; Fabinger, M. and McGreevy, J., [hep-th/0206196]; Elitzur, S., Giveon, A., Kutasov, D. and Rabinovici, E., [hep-th/0204189].

[16] Witten, E. (1995), *Nucl. Phys.* **B443** 85, [hep-th/9503124].

[17] Khoury, J., Ovrut, B. A., Steinhardt, P. J. and Turok, N. (2002), *Phys. Rev.* D, in press, [hep-th/0109050].

[18] Lyth, D. H. (2002), *Phys. Lett.* **B524** 1; (2002), *ibid.* **B526** 173; Brandenberger, R. and Finelli, F. 0111 (2001), *JHEP* 056; Finelli, F. and Brandenberger, R. **D65** (2002), *Phys. Rev.* 103522; Hwang, J-C. (2002), *Phys. Rev.* **D65** 063514; Hwang, J-C. and Noh, H. (2002), *Phys. Rev.* **D65** 124010; Martin, J., Peter, P., Pinto-Nieto, N. and Schwarz, D. J. (2002), *Phys. Rev.* **D65** 123513; Peter, P. and Pinto-Nieto, N., [hep-th/0203013].

[19] Durrer, R., [hep-th/0112026]; Durrer, R. and Vernizzi, F., [hep-ph/0203275].

[20] Rajantie, A. and Turok, N. in preparation (2002).

[21] Bucher, M. and Turok, N. in preparation (2002).

[22] Garriga, J. and Tanaka, T. (2000), *Phys. Rev. Lett.* **84** 2778, [hep-th/9911055].

43

Inflationary theory versus the ekpyrotic/cyclic scenario

Andrei Linde

Stanford University

43.1 Introduction

My first encounter with Stephen Hawking was related to inflationary theory. It was quite dramatic. In the middle of October 1981 there was a conference on Quantum Gravity in Moscow. This was the first conference where I gave a talk on the new inflation scenario [1]. After my talk many participants of the conference from the USA and Europe came up to me, asked questions, and even suggested smuggling my paper abroad to speed up its publication. (The paper was written in July 1981, but in accordance with Russian rules I spent three months getting permission for its publication.)

Somehow I did not have a chance to discuss it with Stephen at the conference, but I did the next day, under rather unusual circumstances. He was invited to give a talk at the Sternberg Astronomy Institute of Moscow State University. His talk, based on his work with Moss and Stewart [2], was about the problems of the old inflationary theory proposed by Alan Guth [3]. The main conclusion of their work [2], as well as of the subsequent paper by Guth and Weinberg [4], was that it is impossible to improve the old inflation scenario.

Rather unexpectedly, I was asked to translate. At that time Stephen did not have his computer, so his talks were usually given by his students. He would just sit around and add brief comments if a student would say something wrong. This time, however, they were not quite prepared. Stephen would say one word, his student would say one word, and then I would translate this word, so in the beginning the talk progressed very slowly. Since I knew the subject, I started adding lengthy explanations in Russian. Thus, Stephen would say one word, his student would say one word, and then I would talk for few minutes. Then Stephen would talk again, etc. Everything went smoothly during the first part of the talk when we were explaining the problems of the old inflationary theory.

Then Stephen said that recently Andrei Linde had suggested an interesting way to solve the problems of inflationary theory. I happily translated this. The best physicists of Russia are here to listen to Stephen, my future depends on them, and now he is going to explain my work to them; what could be better? But then Stephen said that the new inflationary scenario cannot work, and I translated. For the next half hour I was translating for Stephen and explaining to everyone the problems with my scenario and why it does not work.

I do not remember ever being in any other situation like that. What shall I do, what shall I do? When the talk was over I said that I translated but I disagreed, and explained why. Then I suggested to Stephen that we discuss it privately. We found an empty office and for almost two hours the authorities of the Institute were in a panic searching for the famous British scientist who had miraculously disappeared. Meanwhile I was talking to him about various parts of the new inflationary scenario. From time to time Stephen would say something and his student would translate: 'But you did not say that before'. This was repeated over and over again. Then Stephen invited me to his hotel where we continued the discussion. Then he started showing me photos of his family and invited me to Cambridge. This was the beginning of a beautiful friendship.

After that event the story developed at a rapid pace. In October I sent my paper to *Physics Letters* and I also sent my preprints to many places in the USA. After returning to England, Stephen started working on new inflation together with Ian Moss [5]. Three months later, Paul Steinhardt and Andy Albrecht wrote a paper on new inflation with results very similar to mine [6]. In Summer 1982 Stephen organized a workshop in Cambridge dedicated to new inflation. This was the best and most productive workshop I have ever attended.

In a certain sense, this was the first and the last workshop on new inflation. The theory of inflationary perturbations of scalar fields [7, 8], as well as the theory of post-inflationary density perturbations [9–11], were to a large extent developed at this workshop [10]. Calculations using these theories showed that the coupling constant of the scalar field in new inflation had to be smaller than 10^{-12}. Such a field could not be in a state of thermal equilibrium in the early universe. This means, in particular, that the theory of high-temperature phase transitions [12], which served as the basis for old and new inflation, was in fact irrelevant for inflationary cosmology. Thus, some other approach was necessary. The assumption of thermal equilibrium requires many particles interacting with each other. This means that new inflation could explain why our universe was so large only if it was very large from the beginning. Finally, inflation in this theory begins very late, and during the preceding epoch the universe could easily have collapsed or become so inhomogeneous that inflation could never happen. In addition, this scenario could work only if the effective potential of the field ϕ had a very flat plateau near $\phi = 0$, which is somewhat artificial. Because of all of these difficulties, no realistic versions of the new inflationary universe scenario have been proposed so far.

From a more general perspective, old and new inflation represented a substantial but incomplete modification of the big bang theory. It was still assumed that the universe was in a state of thermal equilibrium from the very beginning, that it was relatively homogeneous and large enough to survive until the beginning of inflation, and that the stage of inflation was just an intermediate stage of the evolution of the hot universe. In the beginning of the 1980s these assumptions seemed natural and practically unavoidable. That is why it was so difficult to overcome a certain psychological barrier and abandon all of these assumptions. This was done with the invention of the chaotic inflation scenario [13]. This scenario resolved all the problems mentioned above. According to this scenario, inflation can occur even in theories with the simplest potentials such as $V(\phi) \sim \phi^n$. Inflation can begin even if there was no thermal equilibrium in the early universe, and it can even start close to the Planck density, in which case the problem of initial conditions for inflation can be easily resolved [14].

Stephen was the first person (apart from my Russian colleagues) to whom I spoke about chaotic inflation. Since that time in his work on inflation he has used only this model, as well as some modifications of the Starobinsky scenario [15]. Let me describe the basic features of chaotic inflation.

43.2 Chaotic inflation

Consider the simplest model of a scalar field ϕ with a mass m and with the potential energy density $V(\phi) = \frac{m^2}{2}\phi^2$. Since this function has a minimum at $\phi = 0$, one may expect that the scalar field ϕ should oscillate near this minimum. This is indeed the case if the universe does not expand, in which case the equation of motion for the scalar field coincides with the equation for harmonic oscillator, $\ddot{\phi} = -m^2\phi$.

However, because of the expansion of the universe with Hubble constant $H = \dot{a}/a$, an additional term $3H\dot{\phi}$ appears in the harmonic oscillator equation:

$$\ddot{\phi} + 3H\dot{\phi} = -m^2\phi. \tag{43.1}$$

The term $3H\dot{\phi}$ can be interpreted as a friction term. The Einstein equation for a homogeneous universe containing scalar field ϕ appears as follows:

$$H^2 + \frac{k}{a^2} = \frac{1}{6}\left(\dot{\phi}^2 + m^2\phi^2\right). \tag{43.2}$$

Here $k = -1, 0, 1$ for an open, flat or closed universe respectively. We work in units $M_p^{-2} = 8\pi G = 1$.

If the scalar field ϕ initially was large, the Hubble parameter H was large too, according to the second equation. This means that the friction term $3H\dot{\phi}$ was very large, and therefore the scalar field was moving very slowly, like a ball in a viscous liquid. Therefore at this stage the energy density of the scalar field, unlike the density of ordinary matter, remained almost constant, and expansion of the universe continued with a much greater speed than in the old cosmological theory. Due to the rapid growth of the scale of the universe and a slow motion of the field ϕ, soon after the beginning of this regime one has $\ddot{\phi} \ll 3H\dot{\phi}$, $H^2 \gg k/a^2$, $\dot{\phi}^2 \ll m^2\phi^2$, so the system of equations can be simplified:

$$H = \frac{\dot{a}}{a} = \frac{m\phi}{\sqrt{6}}, \qquad \dot{\phi} = -m\sqrt{\frac{2}{3}}. \tag{43.3}$$

The first equation shows that if the field ϕ changes slowly, the size of the universe in this regime grows approximately as e^{Ht}, where $H = m\phi/\sqrt{6}$. This is the stage of inflation that ends when the field ϕ becomes much smaller than $M_p = 1$.

This is as simple as it could be. Inflation does not require supercooling and tunnelling from the false vacuum [3], or rolling from an artificially flat top of the effective potential [1, 6]. It appears in the theories that can be as simple as a theory of harmonic oscillator [13]. Only after I realized it, I started to believe that inflation is not a trick necessary to fix problems of the old big bang theory, but a generic cosmological regime.

In realistic versions of inflationary theory the duration of inflation could be as short as 10^{-35} seconds. When inflation ends, the scalar field ϕ begins to oscillate near the minimum of $V(\phi)$. As any rapidly oscillating classical field, it looses its energy by creating pairs of elementary particles. These particles interact with each other and come to a state of thermal equilibrium with some temperature T [17–19]. From this time on, the universe can be described by the usual big bang theory.

The main difference between inflationary theory and the old cosmology becomes clear when one calculates the size of a typical inflationary domain at the end of inflation. Investigation of this question shows that even if the initial size of an inflationary universe were as small as the Plank size

$l_P \sim 10^{-33}$ cm, after 10^{-35} seconds of inflation the universe acquires a huge size of $l \sim 10^{10^{12}}$ cm! This number is model-dependent, but in all realistic models the size of the universe after inflation appears to be many orders of magnitude greater than the size of the part of the universe which we can see now, $l \sim 10^{28}$ cm. This immediately solves most of the problems of the old cosmological theory [13, 14].

Our universe is almost exactly homogeneous on large scale because all inhomogeneities were exponentially stretched during inflation. The density of primordial monopoles and other undesirable 'defects' becomes exponentially diluted by inflation. The universe becomes enormously large. Even if it was a closed universe of a size $\sim 10^{-33}$ cm, after inflation the distance between its 'South' and 'North' poles becomes many orders of magnitude greater than 10^{28} cm. We see only a tiny part of the huge cosmic balloon. That is why nobody has ever seen how parallel lines cross. That is why the universe looks so flat.

If our universe initially consisted of many domains with a chaotically distributed scalar field ϕ (or if one considers different universes with different values of the field), then domains in which the scalar field was too small never inflated. The main contribution to the total volume of the universe will be given by those domains which originally contained a large scalar field ϕ. Inflation of such domains creates huge homogeneous islands out of initial chaos. Each homogeneous domain in this scenario is much greater than the size of the observable part of the universe.

Now let us make another simple step and add a small constant term $V_0 > 0$ to the potential $m^2\phi^2/2$, see Figure 43.1. If one does not take gravity into account, this term does not change equations for the scalar field, i.e. we still consider a simplest harmonic oscillator theory. However,

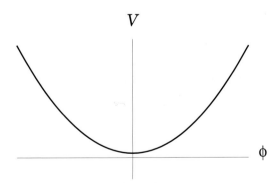

V

ϕ

Fig. 43.1. The harmonic oscillator scalar field potential $V(\phi) = V_0 + m^2\phi^2/2$ in a simplest version of chaotic inflation.

the term V_0 acts as a cosmological constant that does not vanish even at $\phi = 0$. As a result, the simplest theory with $V(\phi) = V_0 + m^2\phi^2/2$ will describe *two stages of inflation*. The first stage occurs in the early universe, when the scalar field was large. The second stage occurs right now; it corresponds to the recently discovered accelerated expansion of the universe.

The first models of chaotic inflation were based on the theories with polynomial potentials, such as $V(\phi) = \pm\frac{m^2}{2}\phi^2 + \frac{\lambda}{4}\phi^4$. But the main idea of this scenario is quite generic. One should consider any particular potential $V(\phi)$, polynomial or not, with or without spontaneous symmetry breaking, and study all possible initial conditions without assuming that the universe was in a state of thermal equilibrium, and that the field ϕ was in the minimum of its effective potential from the very beginning [13]. This scenario strongly deviated from the standard lore of the hot big bang theory and was psychologically difficult to accept. Therefore during the first few years after the invention of chaotic inflation many authors claimed that the idea of chaotic initial conditions is unnatural, and made attempts to realize the new inflation scenario based on the theory of high-temperature phase transitions, despite numerous problems associated with it. Some authors even introduced so-called 'thermal constraints' which were necessary to ensure that the minimum of the effective potential at large T should be at $\phi = 0$ [20], even though the scalar field in the models they considered was not in a state of thermal equilibrium with other particles. Gradually, however, it became clear that the idea of chaotic initial conditions is most general, and it is much easier to construct a consistent cosmological theory without making unnecessary assumptions about thermal equilibrium and high temperature phase transitions in the early universe.

43.3 Hybrid inflation

In the previous section we considered the simplest chaotic inflation theory based on the theory of a single scalar field ϕ. The models of chaotic inflation based on the theory of two scalar fields may have some qualitatively new features. One of the most interesting models of this kind is the hybrid inflation scenario [21]. The simplest version of this scenario is based on chaotic inflation in the theory of two scalar fields with the effective potential

$$V(\sigma, \phi) = \frac{1}{4\lambda}(M^2 - \lambda\sigma^2)^2 + \frac{m^2}{2}\phi^2 + \frac{g^2}{2}\phi^2\sigma^2. \qquad (43.4)$$

The effective mass squared of the field σ is equal to $-M^2 + g^2\phi^2$. Therefore for $\phi > \phi_c = M/g$ the only minimum of the effective potential $V(\sigma, \phi)$

is at $\sigma = 0$. The curvature of the effective potential in the σ-direction is much greater than in the ϕ-direction. Thus at the first stages of expansion of the universe the field σ rolled down to $\sigma = 0$, whereas the field ϕ could remain large for a much longer time.

At the moment when the inflaton field ϕ becomes smaller than $\phi_c = M/g$, the phase transition with the symmetry breaking occurs. If $m^2\phi_c^2 = m^2M^2/g^2 \ll M^4/\lambda$, the Hubble constant at the time of the phase transition is given by $H^2 = M^4/12\lambda$ (in units $M = 1$). If one assumes that $M^2 \gg \lambda m^2/g^2$ and that $m^2 \ll H^2$, then the universe at $\phi > \phi_c$ undergoes a stage of inflation, which abruptly ends at $\phi = \phi_c$.

One of the advantages of this scenario is the possibility of obtaining small density perturbations even if coupling constants are large, $\lambda, g = O(1)$. This scenario works if the effective potential has a relatively flat ϕ-direction. But flat directions often appear in supersymmetric theories. This makes hybrid inflation an attractive playground for those who want to achieve inflation in supergravity.

Another advantage of this scenario is a possibility of having inflation at $\phi \sim M/g \ll 1$. (This happens because the slow rolling of the field ϕ in this scenario is supported not by the energy of the field ϕ as in the scenario described in the previous section, but by the energy of the field σ.) This helps to avoid problems which may appear if the effective potential in supergravity and string theory blows up at $\phi > 1$. Several different models of hybrid inflation in supergravity have been proposed during the last few years (F-term inflation [22], D-term inflation [23], etc.). A detailed discussion of various versions of hybrid inflation in supersymmetric theories can be found in [24]. Recent developments in this direction have been reported by Kallosh at this conference [25].

43.4 Quantum fluctuations and density perturbations

The vacuum structure in the exponentially expanding universe is much more complicated than in ordinary Minkowski space. The wavelengths of all vacuum fluctuations of the scalar field ϕ grow exponentially during inflation. When the wavelength of any particular fluctuation becomes greater than H^{-1}, this fluctuation stops oscillating, and its amplitude freezes at some non-zero value $\delta\phi(x)$ because of the large friction term $3H\dot{\phi}$ in the equation of motion of the field ϕ. The amplitude of this fluctuation then remains almost unchanged for a very long time, whereas its wavelength grows exponentially. Therefore, the appearance of such a frozen fluctuation is equivalent to the appearance of a classical field $\delta\phi(x)$ that does not vanish after averaging over macroscopic intervals of space and time.

Because the vacuum contains fluctuations of all wavelengths, inflation leads to the creation of more and more new perturbations of the classical field with wavelengths greater than H^{-1}. The average amplitude of such perturbations generated during a typical time interval H^{-1} is given by [7, 8]

$$|\delta\phi(x)| \approx \frac{H}{2\pi} . \qquad (43.5)$$

These fluctuations lead to density perturbations that later produce galaxies. The theory of this effect is very complicated [9, 10], and it was fully understood only in the second part of the 1980s [11]. Here we will only give a rough and oversimplified idea of this effect.

Fluctuations of the field ϕ lead to a local delay of the time of the end of inflation, $\delta t = \delta\phi/\dot\phi \sim H/2\pi\dot\phi$. Once the usual post-inflationary stage begins, the density of the universe starts to decrease as $\rho = 3H^2$, where $H \sim t^{-1}$. Therefore a local delay of expansion leads to a local density increase δ_H such that $\delta_H \sim \delta\rho/\rho \sim \delta t/t$. Combining these estimates together yields the famous result [9–11]

$$\delta_H \sim \frac{\delta\rho}{\rho} \sim \frac{H^2}{2\pi\dot\phi} . \qquad (43.6)$$

This derivation is oversimplified; it does not tell, in particular, whether H should be calculated during inflation or after it. This issue was not very important for new inflation where H was nearly constant, but it is of crucial importance for chaotic inflation.

The result of a more detailed investigation [11] shows that H and $\dot\phi$ should be calculated during inflation, at different times for perturbations with different momenta k. For each of these perturbations, the value of H should be taken at the time when the wavelength of the perturbation becomes of the order of H^{-1}. However, the field ϕ during inflation changes very slowly, so the quantity $H^2/2\pi\dot\phi$ remains almost constant over an exponentially large range of wavelengths. This means that the spectrum of perturbations of the metric is flat.

In a detailed calculation in our simplest chaotic inflation model the amplitude of perturbations gives [24] $\delta_H \sim m\phi^2/5\pi\sqrt{6}$. The perturbations on scale of the horizon were produced at $\phi_H \sim 15$ [14]. This, together with COBE normalization $\delta_H \sim 2 \times 10^{-5}$ gives $m \sim 3 \times 10^{-6}$, in Planck units, which is approximately equivalent to 7×10^{12} GeV. Exact numbers depend on ϕ_H, which in its turn depends slightly on the subsequent thermal history of the universe.

The magnitude of density perturbations $\delta\rho/\rho$ in our model depends on the scale l only logarithmically. The flatness of the spectrum of $\delta\rho/\rho$

together with the flatness of the universe ($\Omega = 1$) constitute the two most robust predictions of inflationary cosmology. It is possible to construct models where $\delta\rho/\rho$ changes in a very peculiar way, and it is also possible to construct theories where $\Omega \neq 1$, but it is difficult to do so.

43.5 From the Big Bang to eternal inflation

The next step in the development of inflationary theory that I would like to discuss here is the discovery of the process of self-reproduction of the inflationary universe. This process was known to exist in the old inflationary theory [3] and in the new one [26], but it is especially surprising and leads to most profound consequences in the context of the chaotic inflation scenario [27, 28]. It appears that a large scalar field during inflation produces large quantum fluctuations which may locally increase the value of the scalar field in some parts of the universe. These regions expand at a greater rate than their parent domains, and quantum fluctuations inside them lead to production of new inflationary domains that expand even faster. This surprising behaviour leads to an eternal process of self-reproduction of the universe.

To understand the mechanism of self-reproduction, remember that the processes separated by distances l greater than H^{-1} proceed independently of one another. Indeed, during exponential expansion the distance between any two objects separated by more than H^{-1} grows with a speed exceeding the speed of light. As a result, an observer in the inflationary universe can see only the processes occurring inside the horizon of the radius H^{-1}. An important consequence of this general result is that the process of inflation in any domain of radius H^{-1} occurs independently of any events outside it. In this sense any inflationary domain of initial radius exceeding H^{-1} can be considered as a separate mini-universe.

To investigate the behaviour of such a mini-universe, taking account of quantum fluctuations, let us consider an inflationary domain of initial radius H^{-1} containing a sufficiently homogeneous field with initial value $\phi \gg 1$. Equation (43.3) implies that during a typical time interval $\Delta t = H^{-1}$ the field inside this domain will be reduced by $\Delta\phi = V'/V = 2/\phi$. By comparison of this expression with $|\delta\phi(x)| \approx H/2\pi = m\phi/2\pi\sqrt{6}$ one can easily see that if ϕ is much greater than $\phi^* \sim 5/\sqrt{m}$, then the decrease of the field ϕ due to its classical motion is much smaller than the average amplitude of the quantum fluctuations $\delta\phi$ generated during the same time. Because the typical wavelength of the fluctuations $\delta\phi(x)$ generated during the time is H^{-1}, the whole domain after $\Delta t = H^{-1}$ effectively becomes divided into $e^3 \sim 20$ separate domains (mini-universes) of radius H^{-1}, each containing almost homogeneous fields $\phi - \Delta\phi + \delta\phi$. In almost a half of these domains the field ϕ grows by $|\delta\phi(x)| - \Delta\phi \approx |\delta\phi(x)| = H/2\pi$, rather than decreases. This means that the total volume of the universe containing a *growing* field ϕ increases ten times. During the next time interval $\Delta t = H^{-1}$ the situation repeats. Thus, after two time intervals H^{-1} the total volume of the universe containing the growing scalar field increases 100 times, etc. The universe enters the eternal process of self-reproduction. Note that this process begins at $V(\phi) \sim m \ll 1$, i.e. at a density that is still much smaller than the Planck density. In a more general case, the criterion for self-reproduction is $12\pi^2 V'^2 \ll V^3$ [27, 28].

Until now we have considered the simplest inflationary model with only one scalar field, which had only one minimum of its potential energy. Meanwhile, realistic models of elementary particles describe many kinds of scalar fields. The potential energy of these scalar fields may have several different minima. This means that the same theory may have different 'vacuum states', corresponding to different types of symmetry breaking between fundamental interactions, and, consequently, to different laws of low-energy physics. As a result of quantum jumps of the scalar fields during inflation, the universe may become divided into infinitely many exponentially large domains that have different laws of low-energy physics. Note that this division occurs even if the whole universe originally began in the same state, corresponding to one particular minimum of potential energy.

Note that this process occurs only if the Hubble constant during inflation is much greater than the masses of the field Φ in the minima of the effective potential. In the new inflation scenario the Hubble constant H was about three orders of magnitude smaller than M_{GUT} and six orders of magnitude smaller than the Planck mass. The transitions of the type discussed above would be impossible or at least very improbable. This was one of the reasons why the realization that new inflation is eternal did not attract much interest and for a long time remained essentially forgotten by everyone including those who found this effect [26].

The situation changed completely when it was found that eternal inflation occurs in the chaotic inflation scenario [27]. Indeed, in this case an eternal process of self-reproduction of the universe is possible even at $H \sim M_p$. This allows the transitions between all vacua, even if the masses of the corresponding scalar fields approach the Planck mass. In such a case the universe can probe all possible vacuum states of the theory. This for the first time provided physical justification of the anthropic principle.

If this scenario is correct, then physics alone cannot provide a complete explanation for all the properties of our part of the universe. The same physical theory may yield large parts of the universe that have diverse properties. According to this scenario, we find ourselves inside a four-dimensional domain with our kind of physical laws, not because domains with different dimensionality and with alternate properties are impossible or improbable, but simply because our kind of life cannot exist in other domains.

43.6 Inflation and observations

Inflation is not just an interesting theory that can resolve many difficult problems of the standard Big Bang cosmology. This theory made several predictions that can be tested by cosmological observations. Here are the most important predictions.

1. The universe must be flat. In most models $\Omega_{total} = 1 \pm 10^{-4}$.

2. Perturbations of metric produced during inflation are adiabatic.

3. Inflationary perturbations have a flat spectrum. In most inflationary models the spectral index $n = 1 \pm 0.2$ ($n = 1$ means totally flat).

4. These perturbations are Gaussian.

5. Perturbations of metric could be scalar, vector or tensor. Inflation mostly produces scalar perturbations, but it also produces tensor perturbations with a nearly flat spectrum, and it does *not* produce vector perturbations. There are certain relations between the properties of scalar and tensor perturbations produced by inflation.

6. Inflationary perturbations produce specific peaks in the spectrum of CMB radiation.

It is possible to violate each of these predictions if one makes this theory sufficiently complicated. For example, it is possible to produce vector perturbations of metric in the models where cosmic strings are produced at the end of inflation, which is the case in some versions of hybrid inflation. It is possible to have open or closed inflationary universes and it is possible to have models with non-Gaussian isocurvature fluctuations with a non-flat spectrum. However, it is extremely difficult to do so, and most of the inflationary models satisfy the simple rules given above.

It is not easy to test all of these predictions. The major breakthrough in this direction was achieved due to the recent measurements of the CMB anisotropy. These measurements revealed the existence of two (or perhaps even three) peaks in the CMB spectrum. The position of these peaks is consistent with predictions of the simplest inflationary models with adiabatic Gaussian perturbations, with $\Omega = 1 \pm 0.03$, and $n = 1.03 \pm 0.06$ [30].

The inflationary scenario is very versatile, and now, after 20 years of persistent attempts of many physicists to propose an alternative to inflation, we still do not know any other way to construct a consistent cosmological theory. But maybe we did not try hard enough?

Since most of inflationary models are based on 4D cosmology, it would be natural to venture into the study of higher-dimensional cosmological models. In what follows we will discuss one of the recent attempts to formulate an alternative cosmological scenario.

43.7 Alternatives to inflation?

There were many attempts to suggest an alternative to inflation. However, in order to compete with inflation, a new theory should offer an alternative solution to many difficult cosmological problems. Let us look at these problems again before starting a discussion.

1. Homogeneity problem. Before even starting an investigation of density perturbations and structure formation, one should explain why the universe is nearly homogeneous on the horizon scale.

2. Isotropy problem. We need to understand why all directions in the universe are similar to each other, why there is no overall rotation of the universe, etc.

3. Horizon problem. This one is closely related to the homogeneity problem. If different parts of the universe have not been in a causal contact when the universe was born, why do they look so similar?

4. Flatness problem. Why is $\Omega = 1 \pm 0.03$? Why do parallel lines not intersect?

5. Total entropy problem. The total entropy of the observable part of the universe is greater than 10^{87}. Where did this huge number come from? Note that the lifetime of a closed universe filled with hot gas with total entropy S is $S^{2/3} \times 10^{-43}$ seconds [14]. Thus S must be huge. Why?

6. Total mass problem. The total mass of the observable part of the universe is $\sim 10^{60} M_p$. Note also that the lifetime of a closed universe filled with non-relativistic particles of total mass M is $M/M_P \times 10^{-43}$ seconds. Thus M must be huge. But why?

7. Structure formation problem. If we manage to explain the homogeneity of the universe, how can we explain the origin of inhomogeneities required for the large scale structure formation?

8. Monopole problem, gravitino problem, etc.

This list is very long. That is why it was not easy to propose any alternative to inflation even before we learned that $\Omega \approx 1$, $n \approx 1$, and that the perturbations responsible for galaxy formation are mostly adiabatic, in agreement with predictions of the simplest inflationary models.

Despite this difficulty (or maybe because of it) there has always been a tendency to announce that we have eventually found a good alternative to inflation. This was the ideology of the models of structure formation due to topological defects or textures. Of course, even 10 years ago, everybody knew that these theories at best could solve only one problem (structure formation) out of the eight problems mentioned above. The true question was whether inflation with cosmic strings/textures is any better than inflation without cosmic strings/textures. However, such a formulation would not make the headlines. Therefore the models of structure formation due to topological defects or textures were sometimes announced in the press as the models that 'match the explanatory triumphs of inflation while rectifying its major failings' [31].

Recently the theory of topological defects and textures as a source of the large scale structure was essentially ruled out by observational data, but the tradition of advertising various 'successful' alternatives to inflation is still flourishing. A recent example is given by the ekpyrotic/cyclic scenario [32, 33]. The 50-page long paper on the ekpyrotic scenario [32] appeared in hep-th in April 2001 and, ten days later, before any experts could make their judgement, it was already being enthusiastically discussed on the BBC and CNN as a viable alternative to inflation. The reasons for the enthusiasm can be easily understood. We were told that finally we have a cosmological theory that is based on string theory and that is capable of solving all major cosmological problems without any use of inflation; this was called 'superluminal expansion' [32].

However, a first look at this scenario revealed several minor problems and inconsistencies, then we found much more serious problems, and eventually it became apparent that the original version of the ekpyrotic scenario [32] did not live up to its promise [34, 35]. In particular, instead of expanding, the ekpyrotic universe collapses to a singularity [35, 36]. The theory of density perturbations in this scenario is very controversial [37–42]. More importantly, this scenario offers no solution to major cosmological problems such as the homogeneity, flatness and entropy, so it is not a viable alternative to inflation [34]. Let me explain this first, before we turn our attention to the cyclic scenario [33].

43.8 Ekpyrosis

43.8.1 Basic scenario

According to the ekpyrotic scenario [32], we live at one of the two 'heavy' 4D branes in a 5D universe described by the Hořava–Witten (HW) theory [43]. Our brane is called visible, and the second brane is called hidden. There is also a 'light' bulk brane at a distance Y from the visible brane in the fifth direction. The three brane configuration is assumed to be in a nearly stable BPS state. The bulk brane has potential energy $V(Y) = -ve^{-m\alpha Y}$, where m is some constant. It is assumed that at small Y the potential suddenly vanishes.

The bulk brane moves towards our brane and collides with it. Due to the slight contraction of the scale factor of the universe, the bulk brane carries some residual kinetic energy immediately before the collision with the visible brane. After the collision, this residual kinetic energy transforms into radiation which will be deposited in the three-dimensional space of the visible brane. The visible brane, now filled with hot radiation, somehow begins to expand as a flat FRW universe. Quantum fluctuations of the position of the bulk brane generated during its motion from $Y = R$ to $Y = 0$ will result in density fluctuations with a nearly flat spectrum. The spectrum will have a blue tilt. It is argued that the problems of homogeneity, isotropy, flatness and horizon do not appear it this model because the universe, according to [32], initially was in a nearly BPS state, which is homogeneous.

43.8.2 Ekpyrotic scenario versus string theory

It would be great to have a realistic brane cosmology based on string theory. However, ekpyrotic theory is just one of the many attempts to do so, and its relation to string theory is rather indirect.

One of the central assumptions of the ekpyrotic scenario is that we live on a negative tension brane. However, the standard HW phenomenology [43] is based on the assumption that the tension of the visible brane is positive. There were two main reasons for such an assumption. First of all, in practically all known versions of the HW phenomenology, with few exceptions, a smaller symmetry group (such as E_6) lives on the positive tension brane and provides the basis for GUTs, whereas the symmetry E_8 on the negative tension brane may remain unbroken. It is very difficult to find models where E_6 or $SU(5)$ live on the negative tension brane [44, 45].

There is another reason why the tension of the visible brane is positive in the standard HW phenomenology [43]: the square of the gauge coupling constant is inversely proportional to the Calabi–Yau volume [43]. On the negative tension brane this volume is greater than on the positive tension one, see e.g. [32]. In the standard HW phenomenology it is usually assumed that we live on the positive tension brane with small gauge coupling, $g_{GUT}^2/4\pi \sim 0.04$. On the hidden brane with negative tension the gauge coupling constant becomes large, $g_{hidden}^2/4\pi = O(1)$, which makes the gaugino condensation possible [43]. It is not impossible to have a consistent phenomenology with the small gauge coupling on the hidden brane, but this is an unconventional and not well explored possibility [44]. Therefore the original version of the ekpyrotic scenario was at odds with the standard HW phenomenology as defined in [43].

Another set of problems is related to the potential $V(Y)$ playing a crucial role in this scenario. This potential is supposed to appear as a result of non-perturbative effects. However, it is not clear whether the potential with the required properties may actually emerge in the HW theory. Indeed, the potential $V(Y)$ must be very specific. It should vanish at $Y = 0$, and it must be negative and behave as $-e^{-\alpha m Y}$ at large Y. One could expect terms like that, but in general one also obtains terms such as $\pm e^{-\alpha m(R-Y)}$, where $R - Y$ is the distance between the bulk brane and the second 'heavy' brane [46]. Such terms, as well as power-law corrections, must be forbidden if one wants to obtain density perturbations with a flat spectrum [34]. The only example of a calculation of the potential of such type was given in [46]. In this example the 'forbidden' terms $\pm e^{-\alpha m(R-Y)}$ do appear, and the sum of all terms is not negative, as assumed in [32], but strictly positive [46].

An additional important condition is that near the hidden brane the absolute value of the potential must be smaller than e^{-120}, because otherwise the density perturbations on the scale of the observable part of the universe will not be generated [34]. Also, if one adds a positive constant suppressed by the factor $\sim e^{-120}$ to $V(Y)$, inflation may begin. This is something the authors of the ekpyrotic scenario were trying to avoid.

But if the non-perturbative effects responsible for $V(Y)$ are so weak, how can they compete with the strong forces which are supposed to stabilize the positions of the visible brane and the hidden brane in Hořava–Witten theory? Until the brane stabilization mechanism is understood, it is very hard to trust any kind of 'derivation' of the miniscule non-perturbative potential $V(Y)$ with extremely fine-tuned properties.

After we made these comments [34], the authors of the ekpyrotic scenario have changed it. In the cyclic scenario [33] the potential $V(Y)$ is supposed to approach a small *positive* value at large Y. This leads to inflation that is supposed to solve the homogeneity problem. Thus, the cyclic scenario is no longer an alternative to inflation. Also, the branes in the cyclic scenario are not stabilized. Therefore this scenario is no longer related to the standard string phenomenology.

43.8.3 Singularity problem

The discussion of brane collision in the ekpyrotic scenario was based on the static 5D solution describing non-moving branes in the absence of the potential $V(Y)$ [32]. However, the action as well as the solution for the static 3-brane configuration given in [32] was not quite correct. The corrected version of the action and the solution was given in [35].

More importantly, the solution discussed there was given for branes that were not moving. It was assumed in [32] that in order to study 5D cosmological solutions it is sufficient to take the static metric used in [32] and make its coefficients time-dependent. However, we have found that the 5D cosmological solution given in [32] was incorrect. The ansatz for the metric and the fields used in [32] does not solve the time-dependent 5D equations [35]. Moreover, we have shown that if one uses effective 4D theory in order to describe the brane motion, as proposed in [32], the universe after the brane collision can only collapse [35]. Thus, instead of the Big Bang one gets a Big Crunch! This conclusion later was confirmed in [36].

Since that time, the singularity problem has become an unavoidable part of the ekpyrotic/cyclic scenario. This problem is very complicated. In this respect, various authors have rather different opinions. Those who have tried to solve this problem in general relativity are more than skeptical. The authors of the ekpyrotic scenario hope that experts in string theory will solve the problem of the cosmological singularity very soon. Meanwhile, the experts in string theory study toy models, such as the 2+1 dimensional model with a null singularity rather than with a space-like cosmological singularity [48]. Even in these models the situation is very complicated because of certain divergent scattering amplitudes. Therefore, at present, string theorists do not want to make any speculations about the resolution of the singularity problem in realistic cosmological theories [49, 50].

43.8.4 Density perturbations

The problems discussed above are extremely complicated. But let us take a positive attitude and assume for a moment that all of these problems eventually will be solved.

Now let us discuss the mechanism of the generation of density perturbations in the ekpyrotic scenario. As was shown in [34], this mechanism is based on the tachyonic instability with respect to generation of quantum fluctuations of the bulk brane position in the theory with the potential $V(Y) \sim -e^{-\alpha mY}$. One may represent the position of the brane $Y(x)$ by a scalar field ϕ, and find that the long wavelength quantum fluctuations of this field grow exponentially because the effective mass squared of this field, proportional to $V''(Y)$, is negative. A detailed theory of such instabilities was recently developed in the context of the theory of tachyonic preheating [19].

Inhomogeneities of the brane position lead to the x-dependent time delay of the Big Crunch, i.e. of the moment when the 'brane damage' occurs and matter is created. In inflationary theory, a position-dependent delay of the moment of reheating leads to density perturbations [9, 10]. Simple estimates based on a similar idea lead to the conclusion [34] that in the scenario with $V(Y) \sim -e^{-\alpha mY}$ one obtains a nearly flat spectrum of perturbations δt. If one naively multiplies δt by H after the brane collision, these perturbations translate into density perturbations $\delta\rho/\rho \sim H\delta t$. These perturbations have a flat spectrum with a small red tilt [34].

However, this approach is oversimplified. Just as in the case of inflationary theory, one should specify when the Hubble constant is to be evaluated. In the ekpyrotic theory this question is crucial, because during the process of production of the perturbations δt the Hubble constant is vanishingly small, and it was rapidly changing. Therefore if one multiplies δt by H at the time of the production of fluctuations $\delta\phi$, as we did for inflationary theory, one will get extremely small perturbations with a non-flat spectrum.

In order to obtain an unambiguous result, one should use the methods developed in [11]. There have been several attempts to do so. The authors of the ekpyrotic theory, as usual, are very optimistic and claim that they are obtaining perturbations with a flat spectrum [37]. Meanwhile everybody else [38–41], with the exception of [42], insist that adiabatic perturbations with a flat spectrum are not generated in this scenario, or, in the best case, we simply cannot tell anything until the singularity problem in this theory is resolved.

I share this point of view, and I would like to add something else. In order to obtain perturbations of desirable magnitude, the absolute value of the effective potential $V(Y)$ should be greater than the Planck density, $|V(Y)| > 1$ [33, 37], see below. But in this case the perturbation theory is expected to fail, quite independently of the singularity problem.

I believe that a complete analysis of this problem could be possible only in the 5D theory rather than in the effective 4D theory. This brings additional complications described in [35, 51].

43.8.5 And the main problem is...

If adiabatic density perturbations with a flat spectrum are not produced [38–41], one may stop any further discussion of this scenario. However, let us be optimistic again and assume that the singularity problem is resolved and the theory of density perturbations developed in [32, 34, 37] is correct. In this case one has a new problem to consider.

Tachyonic instability, which is the source of these perturbations, amplifies not only quantum fluctuations, but also classical inhomogeneities [34]. These inhomogeneities grow in exactly the same way as the quantum fluctuations with the same wavelength. Therefore to avoid cosmological problems *the initial classical inhomogeneities of the branes must be below the level of quantum fluctuations.* In other words, the universe on the large scale must be *ideally homogeneous* from the very beginning.

To understand the nature of the problem one may compare this scenario with inflation. Inflation removes all previously existing inhomogeneities and simultaneously produces small density perturbations. Meanwhile in the ekpyrotic scenario even very small initial inhomogeneities become exponentially large. Therefore instead of resolving the homogeneity problem, the ekpyrotic scenario makes this problem much worse.

Now let us assume for a moment that we were able to solve the homogeneity problem without using inflation. But we still have the flatness/entropy problem to solve. Suppose that the universe is closed, and initially it was filled with radiation with total entropy S. Then its total lifetime is given by $t \sim S^{2/3} M_p^{-1}$, after which it collapses [14]. In order to survive until the moment $t \sim 10^{34} M_p$, where the inhomogeneities on the scale of the present horizon are produced in the ekpyrotic scenario, the universe must have a total entropy greater than 10^{50} [34]. Thus in order to explain why the total entropy (or the total number of particles) in the observable part of the universe is greater than 10^{88} one must assume that it was greater than 10^{50} from the very beginning. This is the entropy problem [14]. If the universe initially has the Planckian temperature, its total initial mass must be greater than $10^{50} M_p$, which is the mass problem. Also, such a universe must have very large size from the very beginning, which is the essence of the flatness problem [14].

In comparison, in the simplest versions of the chaotic inflation scenario the homogeneity problem is solved if our part of the universe initially was relatively homogeneous on the smallest possible scale $O(M_p^{-1})$ [13]. The whole universe could have originated from a domain with total entropy $O(1)$ and total mass $O(M_p)$. Once this process begins, it leads to eternal self-reproduction of the universe in all its possible forms [14, 27]. Nothing like that is possible in the ekpyrotic scenario.

Thus, the original version of the ekpyrotic scenario does not represent a viable alternative to inflation. Independently of all other troublesome features of the ekpyrotic scenario, it does not solve the homogeneity, flatness and entropy problems. Apparently, the authors of this scenario realized it, because their new model, cyclic scenario [33], includes *an infinite number of stages of inflation.* Each new stage of inflation is supposed to ensure homogeneity of the universe at the subsequent cycle. The main difference between this version of inflationary theory and the usual one is that inflation in a cyclic universe occurs before the singularity rather than immediately after it. I will describe this scenario following our recent paper with Felder, Frolov and Kofman [52].

43.9 Cyclic universe

43.9.1 Basic scenario

In [34] it was pointed out that avoiding inflation in the ekpyrotic scenario requires incredible fine-tuning. If one adds a small positive constant V_0 to $V(Y) \sim -e^{-\alpha mY}$, the universe at large Y becomes inflationary. In the beginning, the authors of the ekpyrotic scenario claimed that they do not need this stage of 'superluminal expansion' to solve all major cosmological problems, but eventually they did exactly what we suggested in [34]: they added a small constant $V_0 \sim 10^{-120}$ (in Planck units) to $V(Y) \sim -e^{-\alpha mY}$, which leads to inflation at large Y.

Since the cyclic scenario is formulated mainly in terms of the effective 4D theory with the brane separation Y represented by a scalar field ϕ, we will follow the same route. In this language, the cyclic scenario, unlike the ekpyrotic scenario, assumes, in accordance with [34], that the potential $V(\phi)$ at large ϕ behaves as $V_0(1 - e^{-c\phi})$ [33]:

$$V(\phi) = V_0 \left(1 - e^{-c\phi}\right) F(\phi) . \tag{43.7}$$

In the particular example studied in the last paper of [33] one has $F(\phi) = e^{-e^{-\gamma\phi}}$, $V_0 = 10^{-120}$, $c = 10$, $\gamma \approx 1/8$. This potential is shown in Figure 43.2. At $\phi = 0$ this potential vanishes. It approaches its asymptotic value $V_0 = 10^{-120}$ at $\phi > 1$.

Inflation in this scenario is possible at $\phi > 1$. The potential has a minimum at $\phi \approx -36$; the value of the potential in this minimum is $V_{\min} \approx -3$ in units of Planck density [33].

Let us try to understand the origin of the parameters $c = 10$, $\gamma \approx 1/8$ and $V_{min} \sim 3$ used in [33]. According to [37], the amplitude of density perturbations can be estimated as $\delta_H < 10^{-7} \xi^4 v_0^{-2/3} \sqrt{|V_{min}|}$. Here $\xi \ll 1$ and v_0 is a ratio of Calabi–Yau volume to M_{GUT}^{-6}. That is why in order to obtain $\delta_H \sim 2 \times 10^{-5}$ for $v_0 = O(1)$ [53] one should have $|V_{min}| \gg 1$. The spectrum of density perturbations obtained in [37] is not blue, as in [32], but red, in the simplest versions of chaotic inflation. The spectral index is $n \approx 1 - 4/c^2$. Observational data suggest that $n = 1.03 \pm 0.06$ [30], which implies that $c > 10$. If one takes $c \gg 10$, and $V_{min} > 1$, one finds that the curvature of the effective potential in its minimum becomes much greater than 1, i.e. the scalar particles there have mass that is much greater than M_p.

Once one takes $V \sim -3$ in the minimum of the potential with $c = 10$ [33], the parameter γ can be determined numerically: $\gamma = 0.1226$. It would be hard to provide explanation of the numerical value of this parameter. If one takes, for example, $\gamma = 1/8 = 0.125$, one finds $V \sim -3 \times 10^{-3}$ in the minimum of the potential. This would reduce δ_H by a factor of 30. Thus, in order to have density perturbations with a correct magnitude one should fine-tune the value of $\gamma = 0.1226$ with accuracy better than 1%.

According to the cyclic scenario, right now the scalar field is large, $\phi > 1$, so that $V(\phi) \approx V_0 \sim 10^{-120}$. This corresponds to the present stage of accelerated expansion of the universe. Gradually the field ϕ begins drifting to the left and falls towards the minimum of $V(\phi)$. On the way there the curvature of the potential becomes negative, and therefore small perturbations of the field ϕ are generated by the mechanism explained

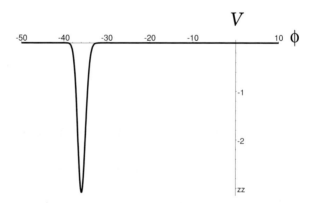

Fig. 43.2. Cyclic scenario potential used in [33]. The potential at $\phi > 1$ approaches a very small constant value $V_0 \sim 10^{-120}$. At $\phi \ll -40$ the potential vanishes.

in [19, 32, 34]. These are the fluctuations that are supposed to produce density perturbations after the singularity.

Then the field reaches the region with $V(\phi) < 0$. At some point the total energy (including kinetic energy) vanishes. At that time, according to the Friedmann equation for a flat universe $\dot{a}^2/a^2 = \rho/3$, the universe stops expanding and begins to contract to a singularity. Collapse leads to negative friction coefficient $3H$ in the term $3H\dot{\phi}$, which accelerates the evolution of the field ϕ. A numerical investigation of the motion of the field moving from $\phi > 0$ in a theory with this potential shows that its kinetic energy at the moment when ϕ reaches the minimum of the effective potential is $O(10^2)M_p^4$. When the field approaches $\phi \sim -39$, where the effective potential becomes flat, the kinetic energy of the field ϕ becomes $\sim 10^6 M_p^4$, i.e. a million times greater than the Planck density!

At this stage a weaker soul could falter, but we must proceed because we have not described the complete scenario yet.

The subsequent evolution develops very fast. When the field accelerates enough it enters the regime $\dot{\phi}^2 \gg V(\phi)$ and continues moving to $-\infty$ with a speed practically independent of $V(\phi)$: $\phi \sim \ln t$, $\dot{\phi} \sim t^{-1}$, where t is the time remaining until the Big Crunch singularity. For all potentials $V(\phi)$ growing at large ϕ no faster than some power of ϕ one has $\dot{\phi}^2/2$ growing much faster than $V(\phi)$ (a power law singularity versus a logarithmic singularity). This means that one can neglect $V(\phi)$ in the investigation of the singularity, virtually independently of the choice of the potential at large $|\phi|$ [52]. This regime corresponds to a 'stiff' equation of state $p = \rho$.

Usually, the Big Crunch singularity is considered the end of the evolution of the universe. However, in the cyclic scenario it is assumed that the universe goes through the singularity and re-appears. When it appears, in the first approximation it looks exactly as it was before, and the scalar field moves back exactly by the same trajectory by which it reached the singularity [50].

This is not a desirable cyclic regime. Therefore it is assumed in [33] that the value of the kinetic energy of the field ϕ *increases* after the bounce from the singularity. This increase of energy of the scalar field is supposed to appear as a result of particle production at the moment of the brane collision (even though one could argue that usually particle production leads to an opposite effect). It is very hard to verify the validity of this crucial assumption since the consistency of the 5D picture proposed in [33] is questionable, see e.g. [51]. But let us just assume that this is indeed the case because otherwise the whole scenario does not work and we have nothing to discuss. If the increase of the kinetic energy is large enough, the field ϕ rapidly rolls over the minimum of $V(\phi)$ in a state with a positive total energy density, and continues its motion towards $\phi > 0$. The kinetic energy of the field decreases faster than the energy of matter produced at the singularity. At some moment the energy of matter begins to dominate. Eventually the energy density of ordinary matter becomes smaller than $V(\phi)$ and the present stage of inflation (acceleration of the universe) starts again. This happens if the field ϕ initially moved fast enough to reach the plateau of the effective potential at $\phi \gg 1$.

Because the potential at $\phi \gg 1$ is very flat, the field may stay there for a long time and inflation will make the universe flat and empty. Eventually the field rolls towards the minimum of the potential again, and the universe enters a new cycle of contraction and expansion.

As we see, this version of the ekpyrotic scenario is not an alternative to inflation anymore. Rather it is a very specific version of inflationary theory. The major cosmological problems are supposed to be solved due to exponential expansion in a vacuum-like state, i.e. by inflation, even though it is a low-energy inflation and the mechanism of production of density perturbations in this scenario is non-standard. Let us remember that Guth's first paper on inflation [3] was greeted with so much enthusiasm precisely because it proposed a solution to the homogeneity, isotropy, flatness and horizon problems due to exponential expansion in a vacuum-like state, even though it didn't address the formation of large scale structure.

In fact, the stage of acceleration of the universe in the cyclic model is *eternal inflation*. Eternal inflation occurs if $V'^2 \ll V^3$ [27, 28]. For the potential $V(\phi)$ used in the cyclic model this condition is satisfied at large ϕ since $V = const.$ in the limit $\phi \to \infty$, whereas $V' \to 0$ in this limit. Thus the universe at large ϕ (at $\phi > 15$ in the model of [33]) enters the stage of eternal self-reproduction, quite independently of the possibility of going through the singularity and re-appearing. In other words, the universe in the cyclic scenario is not merely a chain of eternal repetition, as expected in [33], but a growing self-reproducing inflationary fractal of the type discussed in [26–28].

One may wonder, however, whether this version of inflationary theory is good enough to solve all major cosmological problems. Indeed, inflation in this scenario may occur only at a density 120 orders of magnitude smaller than the Planck density. If, for example, one considers a closed universe filled with matter and a scalar field with the potential used in the cyclic model, it will typically collapse within the Planck time $t \sim 1$, so it will not survive until the beginning of inflation in this model at $t \sim 10^{60}$. For consistency of this scenario, the overall size of the universe at the Planck time must be greater than $l \sim 10^{30}$ in Planck units, which constitutes the usual flatness problem. The total entropy of a hot universe that may survive until the beginning of inflation at $V \sim 10^{-120}$ should be greater than 10^{90}, which is the entropy problem [14]. An estimate of the probability of quantum creation of such a universe 'from nothing' gives [54]

$$P \sim e^{-|S|} \sim \exp\left(-\frac{24\pi}{V_0}\right) \sim e^{-120}. \tag{43.8}$$

There are many other unsolved problems related to this theory, such as the origin of the potential $V(\phi)$ [34] and the 5D description of the process of brane motion and collision [35, 51]. In particular, the cyclic scenario assumes that the distance between the branes is not stabilized, i.e. the field ϕ at present is nearly massless. This may lead to a strong violation of the equivalence principle. This is one of the main reasons why it is usually assumed that the branes in Hořava–Witten theory must be stabilized. To avoid this problem, the authors of [33] introduce the function $\beta(\phi)$ describing interaction of the scalar field with matter. The violation of the equivalence principle can be avoided if $(\ln \beta(\phi))_{,\phi} \ll 10^{-3}$. However, in the Kaluza–Klein limit, in which the 4D approximation used in [33] could be valid, one has $\beta(\phi) \sim e^{\phi/\sqrt{6}}$ [33]. In this approximation, one has $(\ln \beta(\phi))_{,\phi} = 1/\sqrt{6}$, and the equivalence principle is strongly violated.

We will not discuss these problems any longer here. Instead, we will concentrate on the phenomenological description of possible cycles using the effective 4D description of this scenario. This will allow us to find out whether the cyclic regime is indeed a natural feature of the scenario proposed in [33].

43.9.2 Are there any cycles in the cyclic scenario?

As we have seen, the existence of the cyclic regime requires investigation of particle production in the singularity. This subject was intensely studied more than 20 years ago. The main results can be summarized as follows. Since $H \sim t^{-1}$ in the standard big bang theory, the curvature scalar R in the universe dominated by a kinetic energy of a scalar field behaves as t^{-2}. Scalar particles minimally coupled to gravity, as well as gravitons and helicity 1/2 gravitinos [55], are not conformally invariant; their frequencies thus experience rapid non-adiabatic changes induced by the changing curvature. These changes lead to particle production due to non-adiabaticity with typical momenta $k^2 \sim R \sim t^{-2}$. The total energy-momentum tensor of such particles produced at a time t after (or before) the singularity is $T_{\mu\nu} \sim O(k^4) \sim R^2 \sim t^{-4}$ [56, 57]. Comparing the density of particles produced with the classical matter or radiation density of the universe $\rho \sim t^{-2}$, one finds that the density of created particles produced at the Planck time $t \sim 1$ is of the same order as the total energy density in the universe. Moreover, if one bravely attempts to describe the situation near the singularity, at $R > 1$, then one may conclude that the contribution of particles produced near the singularity (as well as the contribution of quantum corrections to $T_{\mu\nu}$) is always greater than the energy momentum tensor of the classical scalar field.

This argument will be very important for us. The existence of even a small amount of particles created near the singularity may have a significant effect on the motion of the field. Indeed, the kinetic energy of the scalar field $\dot{\phi}^2/2$ in the regime $\dot{\phi}^2/2 \gg V(\phi)$ decreases as a^{-6}. Meanwhile, the density of ultra-relativistic particles decreases as a^{-4}. Therefore at some moment t_0 the energy density of ultra-relativistic particles eventually becomes greater than $\dot{\phi}^2/2$. In this regime (and neglecting $V(\phi)$) one can show that $\dot{\phi} = \dot{\phi}_0(a_0^3/a^3) = \dot{\phi}_0(t_0/t)^{3/2}$. Even if this regime continues for an indefinitely long time, the total change of the field ϕ during this time remains quite limited, $\Delta\phi = \int \dot{\phi} dt = 2 \dot{\phi}_0 t_0$. If t_0 is the very beginning of radiation domination ($\dot{\phi}_0^2/2 \sim \rho_{\text{total}}$), then $H_0 \sim t_0^{-1} \sim \dot{\phi}_0$. Therefore $\Delta\phi < 1$ in Planck units (i.e. $\Delta\phi < M_p$).

This simple result has several important implications. In particular, if the motion of the field in a matter-dominated universe begins at $|\phi| \gg 1$, then it can move only by $\Delta\phi < 1$. Therefore in theories with flat potentials the field always remains frozen at $|\phi| \gg 1$. It begins moving again only when the Hubble constant decreases and $|3H\dot{\phi}|$ becomes comparable to $|V_{,\phi}|$. But in this case the condition $3H\dot{\phi} \approx |V_{,\phi}|$ automatically leads to inflation in such theories as $m^2\phi^2/2$ for $\phi \gg 1$. This means that even a small amount of matter or radiation may increase the chances of reaching a stage of inflation, see [52, 58].

In application to the cyclic scenario this result implies that the scalar field in the presence of ultra-relativistic matter created near the singularity should immediately loose its kinetic energy and freeze to the left of the minimum of the effective potential in Figure 43.2. Then it slowly falls to the minimum. If the field moved rapidly, as expected in [33], it would roll to positive ϕ without triggering the collapse of the universe. But a slow motion leads to a collapse of the universe [52], instead of the inflationary stage anticipated in [33].

But what if we are wrong, and for some reason particle production near the singularity was inefficient [59]? Independently of it, a later stage of efficient particle production is unavoidable. Indeed, at $\phi < -40$ the mass squared of the scalar field $m^2 = V''$ vanishes. Near the minimum one has $m > O(1)$ in Planck units, and at $\phi > -32$ the mass almost exactly vanishes again. The transition from $m \ll 1$ to $m \sim 1$ and back to $m \ll 1$ occurs within the time $\Delta t \sim 1$. Thus, the change of mass was strongly non-adiabatic, with typical frequency ~ 1. This should lead to the production of ultra-relativistic particles ϕ with Planckian density [18].

These particles, in their turn, should immediately freeze the motion of the field ϕ near $\phi \sim -30$. The field never reaches the region $\phi > 1$, and inflation never begins. Instead of this, the field slowly falls again to the minimum of $V(\phi)$ and the universe collapses.

Thus, unless one makes some substantial modification to the scenario proposed in [33], it does not work in the way anticipated by its authors.

43.9.3 Cycles and epicycles

Of course, one could save this scenario by adding new epicycles to it. For example, if particle production near the singularity at $\phi = -\infty$ freezes the field to the left of the minimum of $V(\phi)$, then the universe collapses for the second time when the field runs to $\phi = +\infty$. If the field bounces back from the singularity at $\phi = +\infty$ and then freezes at $\phi > 0$ due to efficient particle production at the singularity, a stage of low-energy inflation begins. This scenario is quite different from the one proposed in [33], but it might work. Density perturbations in this scenario will be produced due to tachyonic instability in the potential with the shape determined by the term $e^{-e^{-\gamma\phi}}$.

Also, one may consider effects related to non-relativistic particles produced at the singularity. These particles contribute to the equation of motion for the field ϕ by effectively increasing its potential energy density [33]. They may push the field towards positive values of the field ϕ despite the effects described above. However, this would add an additional complicated feature to a scenario that is already quite speculative.

But one can do something simpler. For example, instead of the asymmetric potential shown in Figure 43.2, one may consider a symmetric potential, as in Figure 43.3. As a toy model, one may consider, e.g., a potential $V(\phi) = V_0(1 - A\cosh^{-1}(\phi - \phi_0))$, where $A > 1$ and ϕ_0 are some constants.

In the beginning, the scalar field is large and positive and it slowly moves towards the minimum. When it falls to the minimum the universe begins to contract and the field is rapidly accelerated towards the singularity at $\phi = -\infty$. As we already mentioned, the structure of the singularity is not sensitive to the existence of the potential, especially if it is as small as $V_0 \sim 10^{-120}$.

Now let us assume, as in [33], that the field ϕ bounces from the singularity and moves back. The kinetic energy of the field rapidly drops down because of radiation, so it freezes at the plateau to the left of the minimum of $V(\phi)$. At this stage the energy density is dominated by particles produced near the singularity. Then the universe cools down while the field is still large and negative and the late-time stage of inflation

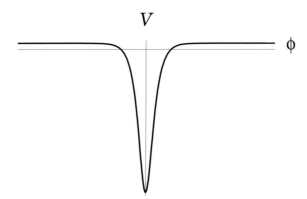

Fig. 43.3. Symmetric scalar field potential in the bicycling scenario. At large values of $|\phi|$ one has $V(\phi) \approx V_0 \sim 10^{-120}$ and there is a minimum at $\phi = \phi_0$.

begins. During this stage the field slowly slides towards the minimum of the effective potential and then rolls towards the singularity at $\phi \to \infty$. When it bounces from the singularity, a new stage of inflation begins. The universe in this scenario enters a cyclic regime with twice as many cycles as in the original cyclic scenario of [33]. The same regime will appear even if the potential is asymmetric but positive both at $\phi \ll 0$ and at $\phi \gg 0$. We have called it the *bicycling scenario* [52].

An advantage of this scenario is that it may work even if, as we expect, a lot of radiation is produced at the singularity and the field ϕ rapidly loses its kinetic energy. However, if in order to have density perturbations of a sufficiently large magnitude one needs to have a potential with a super-Planckian depth $V(\phi) < -1$, as in [33, 37], then this scenario has the same problem as the scenario considered in the previous section. The kinetic energy of the field ϕ becomes greater than the Planck density as soon as it rolls to the minimum of $V(\phi)$. It becomes even greater when the field rolls out of the minimum, and the 4D description fails.

Thus, the bicycling scenario is more robust than the original version of the cyclic scenario [33], but it is still very problematic.

43.9.4 Cycles with inflationary density perturbations

Even though it may not be easy to solve the singularity problem, the old idea that the Big Bang is not the beginning of the universe but a point of a phase transition is quite interesting, see e.g. [60–67]. However, the more assumptions about the singularity one needs to make, the less trustworthy are the conclusions. In this respect, inflationary theory provides us with a unique possibility of constructing a theory largely independent of any assumptions about the initial singularity. According to this theory, the structure of the observable part of the universe is determined by processes at the last stages of inflation, at densities much smaller than the Planck density. As a result, observational data practically do not depend on the unknown initial conditions in the early universe.

Since the cyclic scenario does require repeated periods of inflation anyway, it would be nice to avoid the vulnerability of this scenario with respect to the unknown physics at the singularity by placing the stage of inflation before the stage of large scale structure formation rather than after it.

In order to do so [52], one may consider a toy model with a potential

$$V(\phi) = V_0(1 - A \cosh^{-1}(\phi - \phi_0)) \qquad \text{for} \quad \phi < 0, \qquad (43.9)$$

$$V(\phi) = V_0(1 - A \cosh^{-1}(\phi - \phi_0)) + \frac{m^2}{2}\phi^2 \quad \text{for} \quad \phi > 0.$$

Thus, for $m = 0$ this is the same potential as in the bicycling scenario proposed in the previous section. If one takes $\phi_0 \ll -1$, then the potential at $\phi < 0$ looks very similar to the potential of the original cyclic model, see Figure 43.2, but it is positive everywhere except in a small vicinity of ϕ_0, see Figure 43.4. Also, we will not need to have a very deep minimum of the effective potential because density perturbations will be produced by the standard inflationary mechanism. Therefore one can take A just a bit greater than 1. At $\phi > 0$ the potential coincides with the simplest chaotic inflation potential $V_0 + (m^2/2)\phi^2$ considered at the beginning of

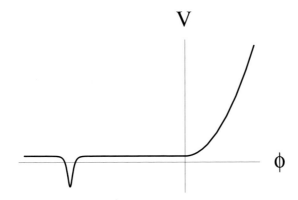

Fig. 43.4. Scalar field potential in the cyclic scenario incorporating a stage of chaotic inflation. The potential has a minimum at $\phi_0 < 0$. Inflationary perturbations are generated and the large-scale structure of the universe is produced at $\phi > 0$.

this paper.

Now let us assume that initially the universe was slowly inflating in a state with $\phi < \phi_0$. Then the scalar field started moving towards the minimum of the effective potential, as in the cyclic scenario (though in an opposite direction). When the field approaches the minimum, the universe begins to collapse. After that moment, the field begins growing with an increasing speed. Let us assume that one can ignore the effective potential $(m^2/2)\phi^2$ that appears only at $\phi > 0$. According to the investigation performed in [52], for $A = O(1)$ the kinetic energy of the field ϕ will reach the Planck value $\dot\phi^2/2 \sim 1$ at $\phi - \phi_0 \sim 100$. Meanwhile, for $m = 3 \times 10^{-6}$ (COBE normalization), the effective potential $(m^2/2)\phi^2$ reaches the Planck value only at $\phi \sim 10^5$, where the kinetic energy of the field ϕ would be much greater than 1. Thus, if one takes $A = O(1)$, $\phi_0 \sim 100$, one can completely ignore $V(\phi)$ during the investigation of the development of the singularity, as well as during the first stages of the motion of the field ϕ bounced back from $+\infty$.

However, according to our discussion of particle production and its effect on the motion of the scalar field, one may expect that, after bouncing from the singularity, the scalar field immediately freezes and does not move (or moves relatively slowly) until its potential energy begins to dominate. But this creates ideal initial conditions for the beginning of a long stage of chaotic inflation!

An important advantage of this scenario is that the density perturbations produced at the end of the inflationary stage have the desirable magnitude $\delta_H \sim 2 \times 10^{-5}$ independently of any assumptions about the behaviour of perturbations passing through the singularity. Also, one no longer needs to trust calculations of perturbations at $|V(\phi)| > 1$.

Chaotic inflation ends at $\phi \sim 1$. At that time the kinetic energy of the scalar field is $\dot\phi^2/2 \sim m^2$ [14]. The energy density of particles produced at the singularity vanishes during inflation. However, new particles with energy density $H^4 \sim m^4$ are produced at the end of inflation because of the gravitational effects [56, 57, 69] and because of the non-adiabatic change of the mass of the field ϕ. These particles in turn freeze the rolling field ϕ. This field freezes even more efficiently if it interacts with any other particles and give them mass $\sim g|\phi|$. In this case the mechanism of instant preheating leads to production of these particles, which freezes the motion of the field ϕ at $\phi \sim -\ln g^{-2}$, [70, 71]. The new particles created at that stage and the products of their interactions constitute the matter contents of the observable universe.

After many billions of years the density of ordinary matter decreases, and the energy density of the universe becomes determined by $V(\phi) \approx V_0$. The universe enters the present stage of low energy inflation. This stage

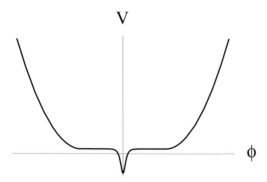

Fig. 43.5. Scalar field potential in the cyclic scenario incorporating a stage of chaotic inflation. Inflationary perturbations are generated and the large-scale structure of the universe is produced both at $\phi < 0$ and at $\phi > 0$.

lasts for a very long time. During this time the field ϕ slowly rolls towards $\phi = \phi_0$. Then it falls to the minimum, runs to $-\infty$, bounces back after the singularity, slows down due to radiation, experiences low-energy inflation at $\phi < \phi_0$, rolls down to the minimum of $V(\phi)$ again, runs to $+\infty$, bounces back, and a new stage of chaotic inflation begins.

In this model inflationary perturbations are generated only every second time after the universe passes the singularity (at $\phi < 0$, but not at $\phi > 0$). The model can be further extended by making the potential rise both at $\phi \to \infty$ and at $\phi \to -\infty$, see Figure 43.5. In this case the stage of high-energy inflation and large-scale structure formation occurs each time after the universe goes through the singularity.

Thus we see that it is possible to propose a scenario describing an oscillating inflationary universe without making any assumptions about the behaviour of non-inflationary perturbations near the singularity [52]. Another important advantage of this scenario is that inflationary cycles may begin in a universe with initial size as small as $O(1)$ in units of the Planck length, just as in the standard chaotic scenario [13].

Even though this scenario is free of many problems that plagued the old cyclic scenario [33], it still remains complicated and speculative. The main problem of this model is that one must still assume that somehow the universe can go through the singularity. However, now this assumption is no longer required for the success of the scenario since the large scale structure of the observable part of the universe in this scenario does not depend on processes near the singularity. This allows us to remove the remaining epicycles of this model.

Indeed, the main source of all the problems in this model is the ex-

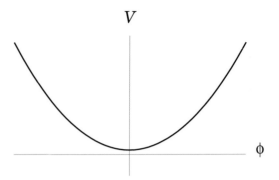

Fig. 43.6. The scalar field potential that appears after the step-by-step simplification of the cyclic scenario. It coincides with the simplest version of the chaotic inflation scenario, Figure 43.1.

istence of the minimum of the effective potential with $V(\phi) < 0$. Once one cuts off this minimum, the potential becomes extremely simple, see Figure 43.6, and all problems mentioned above disappear. In particular, one may use the simplest harmonic oscillator potential $(m^2/2)\phi^2 + V_0$ with $V_0 \sim 10^{-120}$ considered at the beginning of our paper. This theory describes an eternally self-reproducing chaotic inflationary universe, as well as the late stage of accelerated expansion (inflation) of the universe driven by the vacuum energy $V_0 > 0$.

43.10 Conclusions

In this paper I have briefly reviewed the basic principles of inflationary cosmology. During the last 20 years this theory has changed considerably and gradually become the standard framework for the investigation of the early universe. Recent observational data has brought us additional reasons to believe that we might be on the right track. It is quite encouraging that so far the simplest versions of inflationary cosmology seem to be in good agreement with observations. Still there are many things to do. We do not know which version of inflationary theory is the best. We do not even know whether the inflaton field is a scalar field, as in old, new and chaotic inflation, or something related to the curvature scalar, as in the Starobinsky model, or something else entirely like the logarithm of the radius of compactification or a distance between branes. It is possible to have several different stages of inflation; one could solve the homogeneity and isotropy problems while another could produce density perturbations. This latter stage may look like exponential expansion in all directions, or it may be viewed as exponential expansion on some particular hypersurface in a higher-dimensional space.

Thus, there exist many different versions of inflationary cosmology, and many new ones will certainly appear with every new development in the theory of fundamental interactions. But one may wonder whether these new developments will eventually allow us to find a consistent non-inflationary cosmological theory? While we cannot give a general answer to this question, we hope that our investigation of the ekpyrotic/cyclic scenario demonstrates how difficult it is to construct a consistent cosmological theory without using inflation.

The original version of the ekpyrotic scenario [32] contained many incorrect and unproven statements [34, 35]. In particular, instead of expansion of the colliding branes described in [32], one has contraction to a singularity [35, 36]. Despite the optimistic statements of the authors of [32], the singularity problem in this scenario remains unsolved. The theory of density perturbations in this scenario is controversial; most authors believe that the mechanism of generation of density perturbations proposed in [32, 36] does not lead to adiabatic perturbations with a flat spectrum [38–41]. Most importantly, this scenario offers no solution to major cosmological problems such as the homogeneity, flatness and entropy problems. In fact, the homogeneity problem in this scenario is even more complicated than in the usual non-inflationary big bang theory [34].

As for the cyclic scenario [33], its authors recently issued a paper announcing this scenario in the popular press [72] and another one aimed at astrophysicists [73]. These new papers, which were supposed to give a summary of the state of the cyclic universe theory, omitted any mention of the criticisms of the ekpyrotic/cyclic scenario contained in [52] and in [34, 35, 38–41, 51]. It was claimed in [73] that the cyclic scenario:

> ... is able to reproduce all of the successful predictions of the consensus model [i.e. of inflationary cosmology – A.L.] with the same exquisite detail.

They continued by saying that:

> All of the differences between the two paradigms harken back to the disparate assumptions about whether there is a 'beginning' or not.

Then they said that:

> ... if the big bang were not a beginning, but, rather, a transition from a pre-existing contracting phase, then the inflationary mechanism would fail.

I cannot agree with these statements, for the reasons explained in [52] and in this paper. First of all, the cyclic scenario uses an infinite number of stages of inflation to solve the homogeneity problem, and therefore it is not an alternative to inflation. These stages of inflation are possible only if the universe is always huge. Thus, the flatness and entropy problems remain unsolved. This scenario is plagued by the singularity problem, and the situation with density perturbations is as obscure as in the ekpyrotic scenario. Finally, as was shown in [52], the simplest version of this scenario does not work in the way anticipated in [33] because of effects related to particle production. Just as in the ekpyrotic scenario [32], where the universe collapses instead of expanding [35], in the cyclic model of [33] the universe collapses instead of inflating [52].

In this paper, following [52], I described several ways to modify the cyclic model of [33] in order to avoid this problem. The simplest way is to make the potential positive both at $\phi \gg 0$ and at $\phi \ll 0$. This doubles the number of inflationary cycles but still leaves the scenario vulnerable with respect to the unknown physics at the singularity and to the problem of density perturbations.

One can resolve these problems by adding a stage of chaotic inflation after the singularity [52]. Indeed, contrary to the statement in [73], there is no reason to believe that the existence of a stage of contraction prior to the singularity should disallow inflation after the singularity. One should not represent inflation and the existence of the universe prior to the singularity as two incompatible possibilities.

The addition of an inflationary stage after the singularity allows one to use the standard inflationary mechanism of generation of density per-turbations and makes all observational consequences of the theory indis-tinguishable from those in the usual chaotic inflation. However, in this scenario one still needs to assume that the universe can pass through the singularity, and one should use a non-standard mechanism of reheating after inflation.

But once we agree that one needs inflation in one way or another to solve the major cosmological problems, then why should one suffer with such complicated versions of inflationary theory? All of the problems discussed above completely disappear if one removes the minimum of the potential with $V(\phi) < 0$. This final simplification reduces the theory to the stan-dard chaotic inflation scenario describing an eternally self-reproducing inflationary universe, as well as the late stage of accelerated expansion of the universe.

This paper is dedicated to Stephen Hawking celebrating his 60th birth-day, and therefore I would like to finish it on a positive note. So here it is:

> The ekpyrotic/cyclic scenario is the best alternative to inflation that I am aware of.

I really mean it. I think that we should be very grateful to its authors.

Indeed, if a model speculating about an infinite number of inflationary stages separated by an infinite number of singularities is the best alternative to inflation invented during the last 20 years, this means that inflationary theory is in very good shape.

References

[1] Linde, A. D. (1982), 'A new inflationary universe scenario: a possible solution of the horizon, flatness, homogeneity, isotropy and primordial monopole problems', *Phys. Lett.* **B108**, 389.

[2] Hawking, S. W., Moss, I. G. and Stewart, J. M. (1982), 'Bubble collisions in the very early universe', *Phys. Rev.* **D26**, 2681.

[3] Guth, A. H. (1981), 'The nflationary universe: a possible solution to the horizon and flatness problems', *Phys. Rev.* **D23**, 347.

[4] Guth, A. H. and Weinberg, E. J. (1983), 'Could the universe have recovered from a slow first order phase transition?', *Nucl. Phys.* B **212**, 321.

[5] Hawking, S. W. and Moss, I. G. (1982), 'Supercooled phase transitions in the very early universe', *Phys. Lett.* **B110**, 35.

[6] Albrecht, A. and Steinhardt, P. J. (1982), 'Cosmology for grand unified theories with radiatively induced symmetry breaking', *Phys. Rev. Lett.* **48**, 1220.

[7] Vilenkin, A. and Ford, L. H. (1982), 'Gravitational effects upon cosmological phase transitions', *Phys. Rev.* **D26**, 1231.

[8] Linde, A. D. (1982), 'Scalar field fluctuations in expanding universe and the new inflationary universe scenario', *Phys. Lett.* **B116**, 335.

[9] Mukhanov, V. F. and Chibisov, G. V. (1981), 'Quantum fluctuation and 'nonsingular' universe', *JETP Lett.* **33**, 532 [(1981), *Pisma Zh. Eksp. Teor. Fiz.* **33**, 549].

[10] Hawking, S. W. (1982), 'The development of irregularities in a single bubble inflationary universe', *Phys. Lett.* **B115**, 295; Starobinsky, A. A. (1982), 'Dynamics of phase transition in the new inflationary universe scenario and generation of perturbations', *Phys. Lett.* **B117**, 175; Guth, A. H. and Pi, S. Y. (1982), 'Fluctuations in the new inflationary universe', *Phys. Rev. Lett.* **49**, 1110; Bardeen, J. M., Steinhardt P. J. and Turner, M. S. (1983), 'Spontaneous creation of almost scale-free density perturbations in an inflationary universe', *Phys. Rev.* **D28**, 679.

[11] Mukhanov, V. F. (1985), 'Gravitational instability of the universe filled with a scalar field', *JETP Lett.* **41**, 493. [(1985), *Pisma Zh. Eks. Teor. Fiz.* **41**, 402]; Mukhanov, V. F., Feldman, H. A. and Brandenberger, R. H. (1992), 'Theory of cosmological perturbations', *Phys. Rept.* **215**, 203.

[12] Kirzhnits, D. A. and Linde, A. D. (1976), 'Symmetry behavior in gauge theories', *Annals Phys.* **101**, 195.

[13] Linde, A. D. (1983), 'Chaotic inflation', *Phys. Lett.* **B129**, 177.

[14] Linde, A. D. (1990), *Particle Physics and Inflationary Cosmology* (Harwood, Chur, Switzerland).

[15] Starobinsky, A. A. (1980), 'A new type of isotropic cosmological model without singularity', *Phys. Lett.* **B91**, 99.

[16] Dolgov, A. D. and Linde, A. D. (1982), 'Baryon asymmetry in inflationary universe', *Phys. Lett.* **B116**, 329.

[17] Dolgov, A. D. and Linde, A. D. (1982), 'Baryon asymmetry in inflationary universe', *Phys. Lett.* **B116**, 329; Abbott, L. F., Farhi, E. and Wise, M. B. (1982), 'Particle production in the new inflationary cosmology', *Phys. Lett.* **B117**, 29.

[18] Kofman, L., Linde A. D. and Starobinsky, A. A. (1994), 'Reheating after inflation', *Phys. Rev. Lett.* **73**, 3195, [hep-th/9405187]; Kofman, L., Linde, A. D. and Starobinsky, A. A. (1997), 'Towards the theory of reheating after inflation', *Phys. Rev.* **D56**, 3258, [hep-ph/9704452].

[19] Felder, G., Garcia-Bellido, J., Greene, P. B., Kofman, L., Linde, A. and Tkachev, I. (2001), 'Dynamics of symmetry breaking and tachyonic preheating', *Phys. Rev. Lett.* **87**, 011601, [hep-ph/0012142]; Felder, G., Kofman, L. and Linde, A. (2001), 'Tachyonic instability and dynamics of spontaneous symmetry breaking', [hep-th/0106179].

[20] Ovrut, B. A. and Steinhardt, P. J. (1983), 'Supersymmetry and inflation: a new approach', *Phys. Lett.* **B133**, 161; Ovrut, B. A. and Steinhardt, P. J. (1984), 'Inflationary cosmology and the mass hierarchy in locally supersymmetric theories', *Phys. Rev. Lett.* **53**, 732; Ovrut, B. A. and Steinhardt, P. J. (1984), 'Locally supersymmetric cosmology and the gauge hierarchy', *Phys. Rev.* **D30**, 2061.

[21] Linde, A. D. (1991), 'Axions in inflationary cosmology', *Phys. Lett.* **B259**, 38; Linde, A. D. (1994), 'Hybrid inflation', *Phys. Rev.* **D49**, 748, [astro-ph/9307002].

[22] Copeland, E. J., Liddle, A. R., Lyth, D. H., Stewart, E. D. and Wands, D. (1994), 'False vacuum inflation with Einstein gravity', *Phys. Rev.* **D49**, 6410, [astro-ph/9401011]; Dvali, G. R., Shafi, Q. and Schaefer, R. (1994), 'Large scale structure and supersymmetric inflation without fine tuning', *Phys. Rev. Lett.* **73**, 1886, [hep-ph/9406319].

[23] Binetruy, P. and Dvali, G. (1996), 'D-term inflation', *Phys. Lett.* **B388**, 241, [hep-ph/9606342]; Halyo, E. (1996), 'Hybrid inflation from supergravity D-terms', *Phys. Lett.* **B387**, 43, [hep-ph/9606423].

[24] Lyth, D. H. and Riotto, A. (1999), 'Particle physics models of inflation and the cosmological density perturbation', *Phys. Rept.* **314**, 1, [hep-ph/9807278].

[25] Kallosh, R. (2001), 'N = 2 supersymmetry and de Sitter space', [hep-th/0109168], Herdeiro, C. Hirano S. and Kallosh, R. (2001), 'String theory and hybrid inflation/acceleration', *JHEP* **0112** 027, [hep-th/0110271]; Dasgupta, K., Herdeiro, C. Hirano, S. and Kallosh, R. (2002), 'D3/D7 inflationary model and M-theory', [hep-th/0203019].

[26] Steinhardt, P. J. (1982), 'Natural Inflation', UPR-0198T *Invited talk given at Nuffield Workshop on the Very Early Universe, Cambridge, England, Jun 21–Jul 9, 1982*; Linde, A. D. (1982), 'Nonsingular regenerating inflationary universe', Cambridge University preprint Print-82-0554; Vilenkin, A. (1983), 'The birth of inflationary universes', *Phys. Rev.* **D27**, 2848.

[27] Linde, A. D. (1986), 'Eternally existing selfreproducing chaotic inflationary universe', *Phys. Lett.* **B175**, 395.

[28] Linde, A. D., Linde, D. A. and Mezhlumian, A. (1994), 'From the Big Bang theory to the theory of a stationary universe', *Phys. Rev.* **D49**, 1783, [gr-qc/9306035].

[29] Borde, A., Guth, A. H. and Vilenkin, A. (2001), 'Inflation is not past-eternal', [gr-qc/0110012].

[30] Sievers, J. L., Bond, J. R., Cartwright, J. K., Contaldi, C. R., Mason, B. S., Myers, S. T., Padin, S., Pearson, T. J., Pen, U.-L., Pogosyan, D., Prunet, S., Readhead, A. C. S., Shepherd, M. C., Udomprasert, P. S., Bronfman, L., Holzapfel, W. L. and May J. (2002), 'Cosmological parameters from Cosmic Background Imager observations and comparisons with BOOMERANG, DASI, and MAXIMA', (u. de Chile), [astro-ph/0205387].

[31] Spergel, D. and Turok, N. (1992), 'Textures and cosmic structure', *Scientific American* **266**, 52.

[32] Khoury, J., Ovrut, B. A., Steinhardt, P. J. and Turok, N. (2001), 'The ekpyrotic universe: colliding branes and the origin of the hot big bang', *Phys. Rev.* **D64**, 123522, [hep-th/0103239].

[33] Steinhardt, P. J. and Turok, N. (2001), 'A cyclic model of the universe', [hep-th/0111030]; Steinhardt, P. J. and Turok, N. (2001), 'Cosmic evolution in a cyclic universe', [hep-th/0111098]; Steinhardt, P. J. and Turok, N. (2001), 'Is vacuum decay significant in ekpyrotic and cyclic models?', [astro-ph/0112537].

[34] Kallosh, R., Kofman, L. and Linde, A.D. (2001), 'Pyrotechnic universe', *Phys. Rev.* **D64**, 123523, [hep-th/0104073].

[35] Kallosh, R., Kofman, L., Linde, A. D. and Tseytlin, A. A. (2001), 'BPS branes in cosmology', *Phys. Rev.* **D64**, 123524, [hep-th/0106241].

[36] Khoury, J., Ovrut, B. A., Seiberg, N., Steinhardt, P. J. and Turok, N. (2002), 'From big crunch to big bang', *Phys. Rev.* **D65**, 086007, [hep-th/0108187].

[37] Khoury, J., Ovrut, B. A., Steinhardt, P. J. and Turok, N. (2001), 'Density perturbations in the ekpyrotic scenario', [hep-th/0109050].

[38] Lyth, D. H. (2002), 'The primordial curvature perturbation in the ekpyrotic universe', *Phys. Lett.* **B524**, 1, [hep-ph/0106153]; Lyth, D. H. (2002), 'The failure of cosmological perturbation theory in the new ekpyrotic scenario', *Phys. Lett.* **B526**, 173, [hep-ph/0110007].

[39] Brandenberger, R. and Finelli, F. (2001), 'On the spectrum of fluctuations in an effective field theory of the ekpyrotic universe', *JHEP* **0111**, 056, [hep-th/0109004]; Finelli, F. and Brandenberger, R. (2001), 'On the generation of a scale-invariant spectrum of adiabatic fluctuations in cosmological models with a contracting phase', [hep-th/0112249].

[40] Hwang, J. c. (2002), 'Cosmological structure problem in the ekpyrotic scenario', *Phys. Rev.* **D65**, 063514, [astro-ph/0109045]; Hwang, J. c. and Noh, H. (2001), 'Non-singular big-bounces and evolution of linear fluctuations', [astro-ph/0112079]; Hwang, J. and Noh, H. (2002), 'Identification of perturbation modes and controversies in ekpyrotic perturbations', [hep-th/0203193].

[41] Martin, J., Peter, P., Pinto-Neto, N. and Schwarz, D. J. (2001), 'Passing through the bounce in the ekpyrotic models', [hep-th/0112128]; Martin, J., Peter, P., Pinto-Neto N. and Schwarz, D. J. (2002), 'Comment on "Density perturbations in the ekpyrotic scenario"', [hep-th/0204222]; Peter, P., Martin, J., Pinto-Neto, N. and Schwarz, D. J. (2002), 'Perturbations in the ekpyrotic scenarios', [hep-th/0204227].

[42] Durrer, R. and Vernizzi, F. (2002), 'Adiabatic perturbations in pre big bang models: Matching conditions and scale invariance', [hep-ph/0203275].

[43] Hořava, P. and Witten, E. (1996), *Nucl. Phys.*, **B475** 94, [hep-th/9603142]; Witten, E. (1996), *Nucl. Phys.* **B471**, 135, [hep-th/9602070]; Banks, T. and Dine, M. (1996), *Nucl. Phys.* **B479**, 173, [hep-th/9605136]; Nilles, H. P. (2000), [hep-ph/0004064].

[44] Benakli, K. (1999), 'Scales and cosmological applications of M-theory', *Phys. Lett.* **B447**, 51, [hep-th/9805181]; Lalak, Z., Pokorski, S. and Thomas, S. (1999), 'Beyond the standard embedding in M-theory on S^1/Z_2', *Nucl. Phys.* **B 549**, 63, [hep-ph/9807503].

[45] Donagi, R. Y., Khoury, J., Ovrut, B. A., Steinhardt, P. J. and Turok, N. (2001), 'Visible branes with negative tension in heterotic M-theory', *JHEP* **0111**, 041, [hep-th/0105199].

[46] Moore, G. W., Peradze, G. and Saulina, N. (2001), 'Instabilities in heterotic M-theory induced by open membrane instantons', *Nucl. Phys.* **B607**, 117, [hep-th/0012104].

[47] Lukas, A., Ovrut, B. A. and Waldram, D. (1998), *Nucl. Phys.* **B532**, 43, [hep-th/9710208]; *Phys. Rev.* **D57**, 7529, [hep-th/9711197]; Lukas, A., Ovrut, B. A., Stelle, K. S. and Waldram, D. (1999), *Phys. Rev.* **D59**, 086001, [hep-th/9803235]; Lukas, A., Ovrut, B. A., Stelle, K. S. and Waldram, D. (1999), *Nucl. Phys.* **B552**, 246, [hep-th/9806051].

[48] Liu, H., Moore, G. and Seiberg, N. 'Strings in a time-dependent orbifold', [hep-th/0204168].

[49] Nekrasov, N. A. (2002), 'Milne universe, tachyons, and quantum group', [hep-th/0203112].

[50] Seiberg, N. (2002), *String Theory on a Time Dependent Orbifold*, a seminar at the UCSC, 29 April 2002; Polchinski, J., private communication.

[51] Rasanen, S. (2002), 'On ekpyrotic brane collisions', *Nucl. Phys.* **B626**, 183, [hep-th/0111279].

[52] Felder, G., Frolov, A., Kofman, L. and Linde, A. (2002), 'Cosmology with negative potentials', [hep-th/0202017]; to be published in *Phys. Rev. D*

[53] Banks, T. and Dine, M. (1996), 'Phenomenology of strongly coupled heterotic string theory', [hep-th/9609046].

[54] Linde, A. D. (1984), 'Quantum creation of the inflationary universe', *Lett. Nuovo Cim.* **39**, 401; Vilenkin, A. (1984), 'Quantum creation of universes', *Phys. Rev.* **D30**, 509.

[55] Kallosh, R., Kofman, L., Linde, A. D. and Van Proeyen, A. (2000), 'Superconformal symmetry, supergravity and cosmology', *Class. Quant. Grav.* **17**, 4269, [hep-th/0006179].

[56] Ford, L. H. (1987), 'Gravitational particle creation and inflation', *Phys. Rev.* **D35**, 2955.

[57] Zel'dovich, Ya. B. and Starobinsky, A. A. (1971), 'Particle production and vacuum polarization in an anisotropic gravitational field', *Zh. Exp. Theor. Fiz.* **61**, 2161; (1972) *Sov. Phys. JETP*, **34**, 1159; Grishchuk, L. P. (1975), 'The amplification of gravitational waves and creation of gravitons in the isotropic universes', *Lett. Nuovo Cim.* **12**, 60; *Sov. Phys. JETP* **40**, 409; Grib, A. A., Mamaev, S. G. and Mostepanenko, V. M. (1988), *Vacuum Quantum Effects in Strong Fields* (Energoatonizdat, Moscow).

[58] Toporensky, A. V. (1999), 'The degree of generality of inflation in FRW models with massive scalar field and hydrodynamical matter', *Grav. Cosmol.* **5**, 40, [gr-qc/9901083].

[59] Tolley, A. J. and Turok, N. (2002), 'Quantum fields in a big crunch/big bang spacetime', [hep-th/0204091].

[60] Tolman, R. C. (1931), *Phys. Rev.* **38**, 1758; Lemaître, G. (1933), *Ann. Soc. Sci. Bruxelles* **A53**, 51, translated in (1997), *Gen. Rel. Grav.* **29**, 935 (1997); Dicke, R. and Peebles, P. J. E. (1979), in: *General Relativity*, eds S. W. Hawking and W. Israel (Cambridge University Press, Cambridge), 504p.

[61] Tolman, R. C. (1934), *Relativity, Thermodynamics and Cosmology*, (Oxford University Press, London).

[62] Peebles, P. J. E. (1993), *Principles of Physical Cosmology* (Princeton University Press, Princeton).

[63] Markov, M. A. (1984), 'Problems of a perpetually oscillating universe', *Annals Phys.* **155**, 333.

[64] Linde, A. D. (1984), 'The inflationary universe', *Rept. Prog. Phys.* **47**, 925, Appendix 1.

[65] Brandenberger, R. H. and Vafa, C. (1989), 'Superstrings in the early universe', *Nucl. Phys.* **B316**, 391.

[66] Brandenberger, R. H., Mukhanov, V. and Sornborger, A. (1993), 'A cosmological theory without singularities', *Phys. Rev.* **D48**, 1629, [gr-qc/9303001].

[67] Veneziano, G. (1991), 'Scale factor duality for classical and quantum strings', *Phys. Lett.* **B265**, 287; Gasperini, M. and Veneziano, G. (1993), 'Pre-big bang in string cosmology', *Astropart. Phys.* **1**, 317, [hep-th/9211021].

[68] Turner, M. S. and Weinberg, E. J. (1997), 'Pre-big-bang inflation requires fine tuning', *Phys. Rev.* **D56**, 4604, [hep-th/9705035]; Kaloper, N., Linde, A. D. and Bousso, R. (1999), 'Pre-big-bang requires the universe to be exponentially large from the very beginning', *Phys. Rev.* **D59**, 043508, [hep-th/9801073]; Buonanno, A. and Damour, T. (2001), 'The fate of classical tensor inhomogeneities in pre-big-bang string cosmology', *Phys. Rev.* **D64**, 043501, [gr-qc/0102102].

[69] Spokoiny, B. (1993), 'Deflationary universe scenario', *Phys. Lett.* **B315**, 40, [gr-qc/9306008]; Peebles, P. J. and Vilenkin, A. (1999), 'Quintessential inflation', *Phys. Rev.* **D59**, 063505, [astro-ph/9810509].

[70] Felder, G. N., Kofman, L. and Linde, A. D. (1999), 'Instant preheating', *Phys. Rev.* **D59**, 123523, [hep-ph/9812289].

[71] Felder, G. N., Kofman, L. and Linde, A. D. (1999), 'Inflation and preheating in NO models', *Phys. Rev.* **D60**, 103505, [hep-ph/9903350].

[72] Steinhardt, P. J. and Turok, N. (2002), 'A cyclic model of the universe', *Science*, published online April 25, 2002; 10.1126/science.1070462 (Science Express Research Articles).

[73] Steinhardt, P. J. and Turok, N. 'The cyclic universe: An informal introduction', [astro-ph/0204479].

44

Brane (new) worlds

Pierre Binétruy

Université Paris-XI

44.1 Why study brane cosmology?

There seems to be a deep connection between the unification of gravity
with other fundamental interactions and the presence of extra spatial dimensions. The first realization of such a possibility was the attempt by
Th. Kaluza [1] (and later O. Klein [2]) in the 1920s to unify electrodynamics with gravitation by introducing a fifth spacetime (fourth spatial)
dimension. Indeed, a higher-dimensional metric tensor (which Einstein
had taught us a few years earlier to consider as the central object in
the theory of gravity) has components which are naturally interpreted as
four-dimensional gauge fields (as well as four-dimensional scalars). Thus
gauge theories naturally appear in the low-energy four-dimensional effective theory.

Such ideas were dramatically revived in the 1980s with the advent of
string theories as unifying theories of all known interactions. In this case,
consistency at the quantum level imposes the choice of a number of (spacetime or internal) dimensions larger than four: 10 (resp. 11) in the case of
the weakly (resp. strongly) coupled superstring. The recent realization
that objects known as branes play a central rôle in some string theories
has opened up new possibilities of understanding the status of our own
four-dimensional world. Branes can be thought as surfaces where energy
and matter is localized. In string theory, they appear as the locus of the
ends of open strings.

In the context of higher-dimensional theories, one may thus envisage
two extreme possibilities:

1. A standard Kaluza–Klein picture: our own four-dimensional universe is obtained through the compactification of the higher-
   dimensional spacetime. Such a picture relies heavily on the dynamics

of compactification which is not well under control. And many difficult questions remain open: why four dimensions? are all the moduli fields, which describe the shape or radii of the compact manifold, dynamically determined?

2. A brane-universe picture: our four-dimensional world is a 3-brane (3 for the number of spatial dimensions) [3]. From the point of view of string theory, the main questions revolve around the time evolution of such objects since, until recently, they were considered in a static configuration. This has led recently to a surge of activity in the study of time-dependent set-ups.

We will pursue in what follows the second possibility from the point of view of cosmology. Indeed, we realized a few years ago that the cosmology of such universes may be somewhat different from the standard cosmology. Ultimately, this may provide cosmological tests to discriminate such models from the standard picture.

Needless to say that intermediate models where a higher-dimensional ($p > 3$) brane universe undergoes standard Kaluza–Klein compactification also exist. For example, a model which has served as a reference set-up for many of the ideas that follow is Hořawa–Witten supergravity [4]: our 3-brane universe is obtained by compactification on a six-dimensional Calabi-Yau manifold of a 9-brane which is the boundary of the 11-dimensional spacetime. Matter and gauge interactions are localized on the brane.

Moreover, because of the attractiveness of the brane scenario, many have been tempted to push it beyond the strict string framework where it was defined, and to generalize it to topological defects on which matter is localized. The dimensions orthogonal to the brane are compact in order to recover four-dimensional gravity in the effective low energy theory. Or alternatively, four-dimensional gravity is itself localized on the brane, as in the original proposal of Rubakov and Shaposhnikov [5] recently developed by Randall and Sundrum [6–8].

Since brane universes are new set-ups, they may provide new twists to old problems. Indeed, whereas most of fundamental physics seems to be well understood (as LEP collider precision measurements indicate), a certain number of problems tend to indicate that we are missing part of the picture:

- Large hierarchies of scales: Why are they stable under radiative corrections (naturalness problem)? Why are they large (hierarchy problem)?

- Baryogenesis: What is the mechanism that generates the baryon–antibaryon asymmetry observed in the universe? Is the source of CP violation necessary for this mechanism connected with the observed CP violation?

- Cosmological constant: What is the cosmological status of vacuum energy? What is the origin of the extinction of most sources of vacuum energy? What is the source of the presently (?) observed vacuum or dark energy?

Low energy supersymmetry solves the first problem (naturalness) but does not seem to provide a clue to some of the other problems. Would the brane set-up lead to new solutions? We may note that the last two sets of problems are of a cosmological nature.

44.2 Life on the brane

We start by illustrating brane cosmology on a five-dimensional toy model which consists of a 3-brane with tension σ. Matter with pressure p and energy density ρ is localized on the brane. Away from the brane, the bulk of five-dimensional spacetime (from now on referred to as the 'bulk') is empty but has vacuum energy Λ_B:

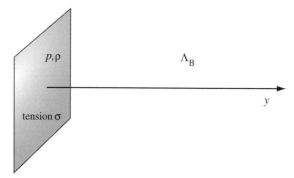

The fact that the brane is a hypersurface of codimension 1 allows us to solve the system completely. Using the five-dimensional Einstein equations and the Israel junction conditions which express the discontinuities of the metric coefficients (or more precisely of their derivatives in the fifth direction orthogonal to the brane) due to the localization of matter on the brane, one may obtain a generalized Friedmann equation on the brane. This equation [9–12] gives the evolution of the cosmic scale factor $a_0(t)$ on the brane through the Hubble parameter $H \equiv \dot{a}_0(t)/a_0(t)$:

$$H^2 = \frac{1}{6M_5^3}\Lambda_B + \frac{1}{36M_5^6}\sigma^2 + \frac{1}{18M_5^6}\sigma\rho + \frac{1}{36M_5^6}\rho^2 + \frac{\mathcal{C}}{a_0^4} - \frac{k}{a_0^2} \qquad (44.1)$$

with the five-dimensional Newton's constant given by $8\pi G_5 \equiv M_5^{-3}$.

This should be compared with the standard Friedmann equation

$$H^2 = \frac{\lambda}{3} + \frac{1}{3M_P^2}\rho - \frac{k}{a^2} \tag{44.2}$$

where λ is the cosmological constant and k the spatial curvature ($k = 0, \pm 1$ if space is flat, closed or open).

Comparing (44.1) with (44.2), one may make several remarks.

First, the four-dimensional cosmological constant λ receives contributions both from the bulk vacuum energy Λ_B and from the string tension σ (squared).

Comparing the linear terms in ρ allows a cosmological determination of the four-dimensional Planck scale M_P

$$M_P^2 = 6\frac{M_5^6}{\sigma}. \tag{44.3}$$

In the brane universe case (44.1), there is a new contribution which is quadratic in ρ, the energy density of matter on the brane. This shows that the cosmology of a four-dimensional brane universe is generically different from the cosmology of a four-dimensional universe. An important difference is the notion of extrinsic curvature, i.e. the way the brane is curved within the higher-dimensional spacetime; the presence of localized energy induces extrinsic curvature.

We note that, because the energy density of the universe increases as one goes back in time, the importance of the non-conventional ρ^2 term increases as well. Such a term may have an important role in the early universe, for example at the outcome of inflation.

Finally, the dark radiation term $\mathcal{C}/a_0^4$ represents the effect of the gas of bulk gravitons on the cosmological evolution of the brane. Its presence is a clear sign that the evolution on the brane cannot be decoupled from the evolution in the bulk. The brane does not represent a closed system.

A generalization of Birkhoff's theorem, valid in the set-up described here, allows us to choose the general solution for the bulk metric as static. In general relativity, Birkhoff's theorem states that a spherically symmetric gravitational field in empty space must be static, with a metric given by the Schwarzschild solution. Similarly here a generalized Birkhoff's theorem [13] ensures that, for a bulk with three-dimensional surfaces of homogeneity and isotropy, the metric is static: the cosmological evolution on the brane is only due to its motion in the static bulk. Then, the five-dimensional metric in the bulk has the form of the AdS-Schwarzschild metric:

$$ds^2 = -h(y)dt^2 + y^2 d\Sigma_k^2 + \frac{1}{h(y)}dy^2,$$

$$h(y) = k - \frac{C}{y^2} + \frac{y^2}{\ell^2}, \tag{44.4}$$

where

$$\ell \equiv \sqrt{\frac{6M_5^3}{|\Lambda_B|}} \tag{44.5}$$

is called the AdS_5 curvature radius. Thus C may be interpreted as the mass of the five-dimensional black hole that is formed in the bulk because of graviton radiation from the brane.

But when do we expect to recover on the brane the four-dimensional evolution described by (44.2)? In principle, whenever the physics on the brane is four-dimensional. One may distinguish three different situations:

- The extra dimension is compact and its radius is stabilized. An example is Hořava–Witten supergravity where the 11th dimension radius is fixed [14]. Another is a two brane system with stabilized distance between them [15].

- The extra dimension is non-compact but the four-dimensional graviton is localized. For example, in the Randall–Sundrum (RS-II) model [8], the extra dimension is warped, i.e. the cosmic scale factor has a dependence in the fifth coordinate:[1]

$$a(\tilde{y}) = e^{-|\tilde{y}|/\ell}. \tag{44.6}$$

Spacetime is Minkowski (M_4) under the constraint that the cosmological constant vanishes, i.e. using (44.1) and (44.2),

$$\frac{1}{3}\lambda = \frac{1}{6M_5^3}\Lambda_B + \frac{1}{36M_5^6}\sigma^2 = 0. \tag{44.7}$$

This is known as the Randall–Sundrum constraint. Then the Planck scale of the effective theory is computed to be

$$M_P^2 = M_5^3 \int_{-\infty}^{+\infty} e^{-2|\tilde{y}|/\ell}d\tilde{y} = M_5^3\ell. \tag{44.8}$$

The fact that the integral converges is directly connected with the presence of a normalizable graviton zero mode (the four-dimensional

---

[1] This may be seen from (44.4) with $k = C = 0$ and $y = \ell e^{-\tilde{y}/\ell}$.

graviton). We note that, even though the distance from the brane is allowed to be infinitely large in the bulk, the volume of the extra dimension is finite (and equal to ℓ). Indeed, (44.8) agrees with the standard expression for the Planck scale of the low energy four-dimensional effective theory:

$$M_P^2 = M_5^3 L, \tag{44.9}$$

for a five-dimensional theory with one compact dimension of size L.

The expression (44.8) agrees with the cosmological evaluation (44.3): using the Randall–Sundrum condition (44.7) we have

$$M_P^2 = M_5^3 \ell = M_5^3 \left(\frac{6M_5^3}{|\Lambda_B|}\right)^{1/2} = \frac{6M_5^6}{\sigma}.$$

It should be stressed however that the determination of the Planck scale using the effective low energy and the Friedmann equation may differ [16]. This is for example what happens in the case of dS_4 or AdS_4 branes.

- The extra dimension has infinite size. In this case, (44.9) can no longer apply, even in an approximate way. Concurrently, there is no normalizable graviton zero mode. It is however possible [48] that the continuum of bulk zero modes produces a metastable state which reproduces the four-dimensional graviton. Since this state is metastable, one expects that at large (cosmological) distances, it decays and one recovers the five-dimensional law of gravity. We will return to this possibility in section 44.7.

Finally, let us conclude this section with the geometric formulation of Shiromizu, Maeda and Sasaki [17] which gives an additional viewpoint on the issues discussed above. The effective four-dimensional equations read, in terms of the usual four-dimensional Einstein tensor $G_{\mu\nu}^{(4)} = R_{\mu\nu}^{(4)} - \frac{1}{2}g_{\mu\nu}R^{(4)}$

$$G_{\mu\nu}^{(4)} = -\lambda\, h_{\mu\nu} + \frac{\sigma}{6M_5^6}\, \tau_{\mu\nu} + \frac{1}{M_5^6}\, \pi_{\mu\nu} - E_{\mu\nu}, \tag{44.10}$$

where $h_{\mu\nu}$ is the induced metric on the brane, $\tau_{\mu\nu}$ is the brane energy-momentum tensor on the brane; $\pi_{\mu\nu}$ is quadratic in this energy-momentum tensor:

$$\pi_{\mu\nu} = -\frac{1}{4}\,\tau_{\mu\alpha}\tau_\nu{}^\alpha + \frac{1}{12}\,\tau_\alpha{}^\alpha\tau_{\mu\nu} + \frac{1}{8}\,h_{\mu\nu}\,\tau_{\alpha\beta}\tau^{\alpha\beta} - \frac{1}{24}\,h_{\mu\nu}\,(\tau_\alpha{}^\alpha)^2. \tag{44.11}$$

Finally $E_{\mu\nu}$ is the projection ('electric part') of the five-dimensional Weyl tensor $C_{\mu\nu\rho\sigma}$[2]:

$$E_{\mu\nu} = C_{\mu\alpha\nu\beta}\, n^\alpha n^\beta .\qquad(44.12)$$

This term corresponds to the radiation term $\mathcal{C}/a_0^4$ in (44.1).

44.3 AdS/CFT correspondence

According to the AdS/CFT correspondence [18], the theory of gravity in a slice of AdS space bounded by a cut-off brane is equivalent to a conformal field theory (CFT) on the boundary with an ultraviolet cut-off related to the position y_b of the boundary. This is summarized in the following equation:

$$\int_{g|_b=h} \mathcal{D}g\, e^{iS_5} = e^{iS_{\text{c.t.}}} \left\langle e^{i\int d^4x\, h_{\mu\nu}T^{\mu\nu}} \right\rangle_{CFT},\qquad(44.13)$$

where a set of counterterms denoted $S_{\text{c.t.}}$ must be added on the CFT side. They include higher derivative terms quadratic in the Ricci tensor.

There has been an extensive literature on the AdS/CFT correspondence in the context of the Randall–Sundrum model [19–24] Regarding the cosmological evolution described in the previous section, we have the following results.

- The dark radiation term in the generalized Friedmann equation (44.1) may be understood as bulk degrees of freedom heated at the black hole temperature [20], $T_{BH} = \mathcal{C}^{1/4}\ell^{-3/2}/\pi$ or locally at position y [25], $T(y) = T_{BH}/\sqrt{h(y)}$. The conformal field theory which represents the bulk degrees of freedom as seen from the brane is heated at $T(y_b)$ and its energy density is

$$\rho = \frac{3\pi^2}{2} c\, [T(y_b)]^{1/4} .\qquad(44.14)$$

  where c is the trace anomaly coefficient.

- The ρ^2 term has been found to be associated with the presence of higher derivative terms quadratic in the Ricci tensor [26, 27]. In four dimensions, this may be related to the CFT trace anomaly [28].

This has been used by Hawking, Hertog and Reall [29, 30] to do a quantum treatment of a model where inflation is driven by the trace anomaly

---

[2] We recall that the Weyl tensor is the part of the Riemann tensor which is not in the Ricci tensor, hence not determined by the Einstein's equations.

[31]. Let us take the Randall–Sundrum set-up and add a strongly coupled (large N) CFT theory to the brane. This provides a new contribution to the tension on the wall which yields a de Sitter (dS_4) geometry. The Euclidean no-boundary initial conditions provide a computation of quantum fluctuations tensor correlator. The effect on the tensor spectrum is a suppression of small scale fluctuations. In this model, the trace anomaly induces curvature square terms and ghosts which turn out to be harmless here because they do not cause runaways [32].

44.4 Moduli fields. Moduli space approximation

In an AdS_5 background, we have seen earlier that one may choose static coordinates. Generically, in a static background, the cosmological evolution on the brane is purely due to its motion in the bulk [33]. This has been called *mirage cosmology* by Kehagias and Kiritsis [34].

Let us indeed consider the following set-up where the position of the brane is $\mathcal{R}(t)$.

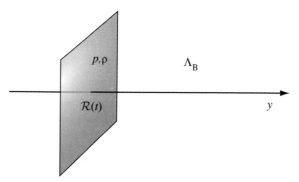

Solving Einstein equations in the bulk yields the explicit form (44.4) of the static metric. The induced metric on the brane at $y = \mathcal{R}(t)$ is then simply

$$ds^2\big|_{\text{ind}} = -\left[h(\mathcal{R}) - \frac{1}{h(\mathcal{R})} \left(\frac{d\mathcal{R}}{dt} \right)^2 \right] dt^2 + \mathcal{R}^2 d\Sigma_k^2$$

$$\equiv -d\tau^2 + \mathcal{R}^2(\tau) d\Sigma_k^2 . \tag{44.15}$$

$\mathcal{R}(t)$ is thus the cosmic scale factor on the brane. Its evolution is fixed by the junction conditions on the brane. We note that the corresponding modulus field provides the semiclassical notion of time on the brane.

In the set-up with two branes, the interbrane distance is described by a scalar field or radion. One may choose bulk coordinates such that one of the two branes sits at $y = 0$; they are known as Gaussian normal coordinates.

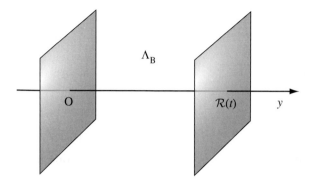

In the case of Randall–Sundrum (M_4 branes), the radion field corresponds to a flat direction of the scalar potential. It is easy to check that the AdS-Schwarzschild bulk metric (44.4) has in this case ($k = 0$) the following symmetry [26]:

$$
\begin{aligned}
t &\to t' = e^{-\alpha}t \\
x^i &\to x'^i = e^{-\alpha}x^i \\
y &\to y' = e^{\alpha}y \\
\mathcal{C} &\to \mathcal{C}' = e^{4\alpha}\mathcal{C} .
\end{aligned}
\tag{44.16}
$$

We note that this may be understood from the four-dimensional point of view as a dilatation symmetry: $y = \mathcal{R}(t)$ scales as a scalar field (modulus) and $\mathcal{C}$ as an energy density.

Alternatively, one may choose static coordinates in the bulk: the two branes have time-dependent positions, resp. $\mathcal{R}_1(t)$ and $\mathcal{R}_2(t)$.

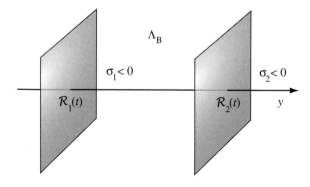

In order to obtain the four-dimensional effective action, one may integrate over y in the full action:

$$S = M_5^3 \int dy d^4x \sqrt{-g} \left(\frac{1}{2} R^{(5)} - \Lambda_B \right) - \sum_i \int d^4x \sqrt{-h_i} \, \sigma_i$$

$$+ \; M_5^3 \sum_i \int d^4x \sqrt{-h_i} \, K \,, \tag{44.17}$$

where the last term is the Gibbons–Hawking term (K is the extrinsic curvature) [35, 36].

The moduli space approximation for the low energy theory is valid for:

- $H\ell \ll 1$, which ensures the validity of the Kaluza–Klein reduction [14];

- $\dot{\mathcal{R}} \ll 1$ which ensures the validity of the moduli space approximation.

Then [37]

$$S = \frac{\ell M_5^3}{2} \int d^4x \, \frac{6}{N} \left(a'(\mathcal{R}_1)^2 - a'(\mathcal{R}_2)^2 \right) \,, \tag{44.18}$$

where N is the lapse function and a' denotes the derivative of a with respect to conformal time. We note that the corresponding equation of motion is simply

$$a'(\mathcal{R}_1)^2 = a'(\mathcal{R}_2)^2 = \mathcal{C} \tag{44.19}$$

with $\mathcal{C}$ constant. Since $H^2 = \dot{a}^2/a^2 = a'^2/a^4$, this gives on each brane:

$$H^2 = \frac{\mathcal{C}}{a^4} \,. \tag{44.20}$$

Thus, in this approximation, we recover (as an integration constant) the dark radiation term.

44.5 Cosmological constant

The braneworld set-up provides new twists to the cosmological constant problem.

It may for example allow us to use the old argument of supersymmetry for a vanishing vacuum energy. The weakness of this argument is that supersymmetry is obviously broken in our four-dimensional world. But, in a brane set-up, this just means that supersymmetry is broken on our brane (in technical jargon, it is non BPS). Supersymmetry could still be a reason for the bulk to be asymptotically flat, as in the models with infinite dimensions discussed in a later section.

Generally speaking, as we have seen in (44.7), the cosmological constant measured on the brane receives a contribution of the vacuum energies from the bulk and from the brane:

$$\lambda = \frac{1}{2M_5^3}\Lambda_B + \frac{1}{12M_5^6}\sigma^2.$$

(44.21)

This has the advantage of decoupling somewhat the cosmological constant from the brane vacuum energy, i.e. the tension σ.

Of course, the problem remains. It requires a delicate fine-tuning between the brane and bulk vacuum energies. Various attempts have been made to relieve this fine-tuning through some dynamics in the bulk.

In the scenario of self-tuning [38, 39], one introduces a bulk scalar field ϕ which couples conformally to the matter on the brane. Let us illustrate this on the simple case where there is only vacuum energy σ on the brane:

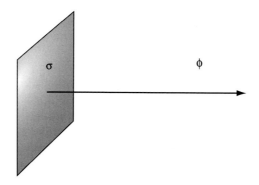

The action reads:

$$\mathcal{S} = \mathcal{S}_{bk} + \mathcal{S}_{br} = \frac{1}{2}\,M_5^3 \int d^5 x \sqrt{|g_5|}\left[R^{(5)} - \frac{4}{3}\,\partial^m \phi\,\partial_m \phi - \mathcal{V}(\phi)\right]$$
$$+ \int_{\text{brane}} d^4 x \sqrt{|g_4|}\,f^2(\phi)\,(-\sigma),$$

(44.22)

where $f(\phi)$ describes the conformal coupling of the bulk scalar field ϕ to matter on the brane (here only vacuum energy).

It turns out that Minkowski spacetime, i.e. static spatially flat spacetime, is a solution to the classical equations of motion *for any value of the brane tension.* Let us illustrate this on the simple case of a vanishing scalar potential $(\mathcal{V}(\Phi) = 0)$ and a conformal coupling of the form $f^2(\phi) = e^{\mp\frac{4}{3}\phi}$. Einstein equations have a solution with a Minkowski spacetime metric and warping in the fifth dimension:

$$ds^2 = e^{2A(y)}\eta_{\mu\nu}dx^\mu dx^\nu + dy^2,$$

$$A(y) = \frac{1}{4}\ln\left(1 - \frac{|y|}{y_c}\right), \tag{44.23}$$

$$\phi(y) = \phi_0 \pm \frac{3}{4}\ln\left(1 - \frac{|y|}{y_c}\right). \tag{44.24}$$

Matching conditions at the brane position $y = 0$ yield the condition

$$\sigma = \frac{3M_5^3}{2y_c}e^{\mp\frac{4}{3}\phi_0}, \tag{44.25}$$

which corresponds to an adjustment of an integration constant, and no longer to a fine tuning between parameters of the theory.

We note the presence in the solution of a naked singularity at $|y| = y_c > 0$. The choice $y_c > 0$ is related to the fact that we want to have four-dimensional gravity localized on the brane and thus a finite Planck scale, just as in (44.8): $M_P^2 = M_5^3 \int e^{2A(y)}dy$. In the case $y_c > 0$, we choose to cut spacetime at the singularity $|y| = y_c$ and thus

$$M_P^2 = M_5^3 \int_{-y_c}^{+y_c} e^{2A(y)}dy = M_5^3 y_c. \tag{44.26}$$

An infinite Planck mass $M_5^3 \int_{-\infty}^{+\infty}(1 + |y|/|y_c|)\,dy$ results from a negative value for y_c.

It has been argued [40] that there remains a severe fine tuning which has been put 'under the rug' of the singularity. For example, one may cure the singularity by adding a second brane but the content of the second brane is then fine-tuned as badly as in the original cosmological constant problem.

We [41] have shown recently that including the one-loop corrections to gravity in the bulk may lead to solutions with no naked singularity. Let us consider the following actions, inspired by string theory at one loop,

$$S_{\text{bulk}} = \frac{M_5^3}{2}\int d^4x\,dy\sqrt{-g}\left\{R - \zeta(\nabla\phi)^2\right.$$

$$\left. + \alpha e^{-\zeta\phi}\left[\mathcal{L}_{GB} + c_2(\nabla\phi)^4\right] - 2\Lambda_B e^{\zeta\phi}\right\}, \tag{44.27}$$

$$S_{\text{brane}} = -\int d^4x\sqrt{|g_4|}\,\sigma e^{\chi\phi}, \tag{44.28}$$

where ϕ is the string dilaton, ζ and χ are constants and the Gauss–Bonnet combination $\mathcal{L}_{GB}$ reads

$$\mathcal{L}_{GB} = R^2 - 4R_{ab}R^{ab} + R^{abcd}R_{abcd}. \tag{44.29}$$

There exist solutions with no naked singularity at finite distance from the brane:

$$A(y) = A_0 + x \ln\left(1 + \frac{|y|}{y_c}\right),$$

$$\phi(y) = \phi_0 - \frac{2}{\zeta} \ln\left(1 + \frac{|y|}{y_c}\right), \qquad (44.30)$$

where x is a parameter which can be determined in terms of $\alpha\Lambda_B$. The constraint of a finite four-dimensional Planck scale

$$M_P^2 = M_5^3 \int_0^\infty dy\, e^{2A(y)} \left(1 + 4\alpha e^{-\zeta\phi(y)}(3A'^2(y) + 2A''(y))\right)$$

$$\propto \left[\frac{y_c}{2x+1}\left(1 + \frac{y}{y_c}\right)^{2x+1}\right]_0^\infty \qquad (44.31)$$

imposes $x < -1/2$. One may however check that, now that the singularity is absent, one recovers an unwanted fine tuning among the parameters.

One may alternatively replace the bulk scalar field by a black hole configuration in the bulk. Indeed, it is possible [42] to find flat brane solutions without naked singularities, with enough parameters to avoid fine tuning of the theory. For example, in the case of an AdS–Reissner–Nordstrom black hole which is a charged black hole, the singularity is protected by two horizons. There are enough parameters (mass M, charge Q) so that they can be tuned to take into account variations of the brane vacuum energy.

44.6 Bulk scalars

Bulk scalar fields are considered in various contexts: they may help stabilizing the radion field [43–45] and the self-tuning approach to the cosmological constant makes use of the conformal coupling of a bulk scalar to matter on the brane. Does the presence of scalars in the bulk modify the cosmology?

We note that the presence of a scalar field in the bulk leads to a violation of Birkhoff's theorem: one may expect non-static background solutions.

Let us consider the simple set-up

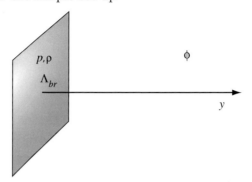

with the corresponding action

$$S = S_{bk} + S_{br} = \frac{1}{\kappa^2} \int d^5x \sqrt{|g_5|} \left[\frac{1}{2} R^{(5)} - \frac{3}{2} \partial^m \phi \, \partial_m \phi - 3\mathcal{V}(\phi) \right]$$

$$+ \int_{\text{brane}} d^4x \sqrt{|g_4|} \, f^2(\phi) \left[\mathcal{L}_{\text{mat.}}(\psi^{(m)}, g_{\mu\nu} f(\phi)) - \Lambda_{br} \right].$$

Using Einstein equations in five dimensions and the junction conditions on the brane, one obtains, in the Einstein frame:

$$\frac{dH}{d\tau} + 2H^2 = \mathcal{V}(\phi) + \frac{\kappa^4}{36} \Lambda_{br} f^2 (f^2 - f'^2) \left[\rho - 3p + 2\Lambda_{br} \right] \qquad (44.32)$$

$$- \frac{1}{2} \left(\frac{d\phi}{d\tilde{\tau}} \right)^2 - \frac{\kappa^4}{36} f^4 \rho(\rho + 3p) - \frac{\kappa^4}{288} f^2 f'^2 (3p - \rho)^2.$$

This should be compared with scalar-tensor cosmology

$$S = \int d^4x \sqrt{g} \left[\frac{1}{2} F(\phi) R - \frac{1}{2} K(\phi) \partial^\mu \phi \partial_\mu \phi - V(\phi) \right]$$

$$+ S_{\text{Matter}}$$

where we have

$$\frac{dH}{d\tau} + 2H^2 = \frac{1}{6F^2} \left[(\rho - 3p) - \left(K + \frac{3}{2} F'^2 \right) F \left(\frac{d\phi}{d\tilde{\tau}} \right)^2 + 4V(\phi) \right].$$

$$(44.33)$$

In (44.32), we identify:
- a bulk potential term $\mathcal{V}(\phi)$ and a kinetic term for ϕ;
- quadratic terms in p and ρ, important in the very early universe;
- in the late evolution, quadratic terms become negligible and comparison with (44.33) yields

$$F^2 \sim \frac{1}{f^2(f^2 - f'^2)}.$$

once ϕ has stabilized, $F (<\phi>)$ fixes M_{Pl};

- a four-dimensional cosmological constant [46] $\Lambda(\phi) = \mathcal{V}(\phi) + \frac{\kappa^4}{18}\Lambda_{br}^2 f^2 \left(f^2 - f'^2\right)$ In the case of the original self-tuning solution, i.e. $\mathcal{V}(\phi) = 0$, $f^2 = f'^2$, we conclude that all cosmological evolution is flushed with the cosmological constant.

44.7 Infinite dimensions

We have seen earlier that in a class of brane models, the extra dimension may be of infinite size. A collection of massive graviton modes contribute to form a four-dimensional unstable massless graviton bound state on the brane. Because of this instability, five-dimensional gravity (i.e. a gravitational force in r^{-3}) is recovered at large distance. The first model of this class was proposed by Gregory, Rubakov and Sibiryakov [48]. It involves two slices of AdS_5 separated by a positive tension branes and isolated by two negative tension branes from the ambient infinite flat five-dimensional spacetime.

The problems of this precursor model are:

(i) a violation of the weak energy conditions which leads to an instability (negative tension branes);

(ii) a five-dimensional massive graviton (5 degrees of freedom) yields in four dimensions a massless graviton (2 degrees of freedom), a massless graviphoton (2 degrees of freedom) and a real scalar field (1 degree of freedom). The latter contributes to one-particle exchange which it dominates at large distances.

In the general class of models with a very light graviton, the latter problem seems to be more serious, if not disastrous. It is connected with the so-called van Dam–Veltman–Zakharov (vDVZ) discontinuity [49, 50]. A massive graviton propagator

$$G_m^{\mu\nu\alpha\beta}(p) = \frac{\frac{1}{2}\left(g^{\mu\alpha}\,g^{\nu\beta} + g^{\mu\beta}\,g^{\nu\alpha}\right) - \frac{1}{3}\,g^{\mu\nu}\,g^{\alpha\beta} + O(p^2/m^2)}{p^2 - m^2 - i\varepsilon} \qquad (44.34)$$

has a different tensor structure from a massless graviton propagator

$$G_0^{\mu\nu\alpha\beta}(p) = \frac{\frac{1}{2}\left(g^{\mu\alpha}\,g^{\nu\beta} + g^{\mu\beta}\,g^{\nu\alpha}\right) - \frac{1}{2}\,g^{\mu\nu}\,g^{\alpha\beta}}{p^2 - i\varepsilon}n, \qquad (44.35)$$

in other words, the limit $m \to 0$ cannot be taken smoothly. This has measurable physical effects, for example, the gravitational bending of light by a massive source is $3/4$ the Einstein prediction.

This discontinuity is however not really generic. In AdS background, one-graviton amplitude is continuous in the limit $m^2/\Lambda \to 0$: an

AdS graviton may become massive if coupled to conformal matter [51–53].[3]

Moreover, it has been argued that the vDVZ discontinuity may be due to the perturbative treatment [55–57]. For example [56], let us consider the Schwarzschild solution of the Pauli–Fierz action [58]:

$$S = M_P^2 \int d^4x \left(R + \frac{m^2}{4} [h_{\mu\nu}^2 - (h_\mu^\mu)^2] - \frac{1}{2M_{Pl}^2} h_{\mu\nu} T^{\mu\nu} \right), \qquad (44.36)$$

and denote by $r_M \equiv 2G_N M$ the Schwarzschild radius of a source of mass M (say the Sun).

If we perform a perturbative expansion in the gravitational coupling G_N, the next to leading corrections are of order $r_M/(m^4 r^5)$, which is singular and thus breaks down in the limit of vanishing mass. But we can also perform a mass expansion in m: the next to leading corrections are then of order $m^2 r^{5/2}/r_M^{1/2}$ and there is obviously no mass discontinuity. In the case of the Sun ($r_M = 3 \cdot 10^3$ m), this is valid for $r < r_M^{1/5}/m^{4/5} = 10^{19}$ m if we take the largest allowed value for the graviton mass $m = (10^{23}$ m$)^{-1}$.

Models of this class include the multi-brane models of Kogan, Mouslopoulos, Papazoglou and Ross [59] and the induced gravity models of Dvali, Gabadadze and Porrati [60].

In the former case, known as bi-gravity (or multi-gravity), the set-up corresponds to two branes, each localizing gravity: for a finite distance between the branes, the corresponding zero modes mix, giving a massless graviton plus a very light one; the presence of a very light graviton modifies gravity at large distance.

In the latter case (induced gravity), there is an induced Einstein term on the brane and the full action reads:

$$S = \int d^5x \sqrt{-g} M_5^3 \frac{1}{2} R^{(5)} + \int_{\text{brane}} d^4x \sqrt{-h} M_P^2 \frac{1}{2} R^{(4)}. \qquad (44.37)$$

For distances r larger than a critical distance r_c given by

$$r_c = \frac{M_P^2}{2M_5^3} \qquad (44.38)$$

one recovers the five-dimensional $1/r^3$ behaviour: there is gravity 'leakage' into the extra dimension

For all these models, the critical distance must be cosmological [61, 62].

---

[3] In a dS background, a massive spin-2 theory is unitary only if $m^2 \geq 2\Lambda/3$ [54].

In the case of the induced gravity model, the late time evolution of the universe may be different from the standard scenario [63, 64]. Indeed, the Friedman equation takes here the form:

$$H^2 = \left(\sqrt{\frac{\rho}{3M_P^2} + \frac{1}{4r_c^2}} + \frac{1}{2r_c} \right)^2 - \frac{k}{a_0^2}. \tag{44.39}$$

This leads to an acceleration at late time, without a need for a cosmological constant!

44.8 Open problems

It would be very interesting to obtain experimental or observational signatures of braneworld cosmology.

The most obvious place to look is the cosmic microwave background [65–75]. There are however still no complete evaluation from the higher-dimensional point of view of the predicted C_l distribution for the cosmic microwave background. Difficulties already arise in the simplest case of the Randall–Sundrum model because the Kaluza–Klein modes do not decouple, even to linear order: this is a reflection of the fact that the brane is not a closed system. In the two-brane case, there is a need to define precisely which brane fluctuation modes are allowed (dynamical brane, orbifold fixed point, orientifold, etc.).

Another interesting aspect is the possibility of specific violations of Lorentz invariance [42, 76–79]. For example, above we have encountered models where the metric in the bulk has the form

$$ds^2 = - h(y) \, dt^2 + y^2 \, dx^2 + \frac{1}{h(y)} dy^2,$$

where $h(y)$ describes a black hole configuration (Schwarzschild or more elaborate). Since gravity waves are allowed to travel in the bulk, whereas electromagnetic waves are confined to the brane at $y = 0$, we deduce that the speed of light travelling between two points on the brane is different from the speed of gravitational waves (which have the possibility of travelling between the two points at non-zero y). This leads to violations of Lorentz invariance which might be detectable once gravitational waves are observed.

Most of the 'models' discussed above are mere scenarios or, at best, toy models. It may be wise indeed, in a subject which is still in its infancy, to explore all possible scenarios, and to disregard whether or not actual consistent models can be substantiated in such scenarios. This is why I have not done justice to a central issue in this game, which is supersymmetry. Supersymmetry, or more accurately supergravity, is presently an essential ingredient in constructing consistent brane models. Some of the scenarios that we have discussed are notoriously difficult to reconcile with supergravity. Once we obtain scenarios with decisively attractive features, it will still remain a major achievement to turn them into self-consistent models in the context of supergravity and string theory.

Acknowledgements

The title of this talk is borrowed from a recent article of Stephen Hawking [29]. On the occasion of his sixtieth birthday, it is but a small tribute to his profound influence on the field of cosmology and more generally on the evolution of ideas in physics over the last 30 years. He has led us, and will continue to lead us, to unexplored and exciting new worlds. Happy birthday!

References

[1] Kaluza, T. (1921), *Sitzungsberichte, Preussische Akademie der Wissenschaften* 966.

[2] Klein, O. (1926), *Z. Phys.* **37**, 895.

[3] Arkani-Hamed, N., Dimopoulos, S. and Dvali, G. (1998), *Phys. Lett.* **B429**, 263, [hep-th/9803315]; Antoniadis, A., Arkani-Hamed, N., Dimopoulos, S. and Dvali, G. (1998), *Phys. Lett.* **B436**, 257, [hep-th/980438]; Arkani-Hamed, N., Dimopoulos, S. and Dvali, G. (1999), *Phys. Rev.* **D59**, 086004, [hep-th/9807344].

[4] Hořava, P. and Witten, E. (1996), 'Heterotic and type I string dynamics', *Nucl. Phys.* **B460**, 506–524, [hep-th/9510209].

[5] Rubakov, V. A. and Shaposhnikov, M. E. (1983), *Phys. Lett.* **B125**, 139.

[6] Akama, K. (1983), 'Pregeometry, in *Gauge Theory and Gravitation, Lecture Notes in Physics', 176, Nara, 1982*, eds K. Kikkawa, N. Nakanishi and H. Nariai (Springer-Verlag) 267–271, [hep-th/0001113].

[7] Gogberashvili, M. (1999), *Mod. Phys. Lett.* **A 14**, 2025, [hep-ph/9904383].

[8] Randall, L. and Sundrum, R. (1999), 'An alternative to compactification', *Phys. Rev. Lett.* **83**, 4690, [hep-th/9906064].

[9] Binétruy, P., Deffayet, C. and Langlois, D. (2000), *Nucl. Phys.* **B 565**, 269, [hep-th/9905012].

[10] Binétruy, P., Deffayet, C., Ellwanger, U. and Langlois, D. (2000), *Phys. Lett.* **B477**, 285, [hep-th/9910219].

[11] Csáki, C., Graesser, M., Kolda, C. and Terning, J. (1999), 'Cosmology of one extra dimension with localized gravity', *Phys. Lett.* **B462**, 34–40, [hep-h/9906513].

[12] Cline, J. M., Grosjean, C. and Servant, G. (1999), *Phys. Rev. Lett.* **83**, 4245, [hep-ph/9906523].

[13] Bowcock, P., Charmousis, C. and Gregory, R. (2000), *Class. Quant. Grav.* **17**, 4745, [hep-th/0007177].

[14] Lukas, A., Ovrut, B. and Waldram, D. (1999), *Phys. Rev.* **D 60**, 086001, [hep-th/9806022].

[15] Randall, L. and Sundrum, R. (1999), *Phys. Rev. Lett.* **83**, 3370, [hep-ph/9905221].

[16] Mukohyama, S. and Kofman, L. (2002), *Phys. Rev.* **D65**,124025, [hep-th/0112115].

[17] Shiromizu, T., Maeda, K. and Sasaki, M. (2000), *Phys. Rev.* **D62**, 024012, [gr-qc/9910076].

[18] Maldacena, J. (1998), *Adv. Theor. Phys.* **2**, 231, [hep-th/9711200].

[19] Verlinde, H. (2000), *Nucl. Phys.* **B580**, 264, [hep-th/9906182].

[20] Gubser, S. S. (2001), *Phys. Rev.* **D 63**, 084017, [hep-th/9912001].

[21] Giddings, S. B., Katz, E. and Randall, L. (2000), *JHEP* **0003**, 023, [hep-th/0002091].

[22] Duff, M. J. and Liu, J. T. (2000), *Phys. Rev. Lett.* **85**, 2052, [hep-th/0003237].

[23] Arkani-Hamed, N., Porrati, M. and Randall, L. (2001), *JHEP* **0108**, 017, [hep-th/0012148].

[24] Rattazzi, R. and Zaffaroni, A. (2001), *JHEP* **0104**, 021, [hep-th/0012248].

[25] Hawking, S. W. and Page, D. N. (1983), *Comm. Math. Phys.* **87**, 577.

[26] Hebecker, A. and March-Russell, J. (2001), *Nucl. Phys.* **B608**, 375, [hep-th/0103214].

[27] Kanno, S. and Soda, J. [hep-th/0205188].

[28] Shiromizu, T., Torii, T. and Ida, D. (2002), *JHEP* **0203**, 007, [hep-th/005256]

[29] Hawking, S. W., Hertog, T. and Reall, H. S. (2000), 'Brane new world', *Phys. Rev.* **D62**, 043501, [hep-th/0003052].

[30] Hawking, S. W., Hertog, T. and Reall, H. S. (2001), 'Trace anomaly driven inflation', *Phys. Rev.* **D63**, 083504, [hep-th/0010232].

[31] Starobinsky, A. (1980), *Phys. Lett.* **91B**, 99.

[32] Hawking, S. W. and Hertog, T. (2002), 'Living with ghosts', *Phys. Rev.* **D65**, 103515, [hep-th/0107088].

[33] Kraus, P. (1999), *JHEP* **9912**, 011, [hep-th/9910149].

[34] Kehagias, A. and Kiritsis, E. (1999), *JHEP* **11**, 022, [hep-th/9910174].

[35] Gibbons, G. W. and Hawking, S. W. (1977), *Phys. Rev.* **D15**, 2752.

[36] Chamblin, H. A. and Reall, H. S. (1999), *Nucl. Phys.* **B562**, 133, [hep-ph/9903225].

[37] Khoury, J., Ovrut, B. A., Steinhardt, P. J. and Turok, N. (2001), *Phys. Rev.* **D64**, 123522, [hep-th/0103239].

[38] Arkani-Hamed, N., Dimopoulos, S., Kaloper, N. and Sundrum, R. (2000), *Phys. Lett.* **B480**, 193, [hep-th/0001197].

[39] Kachru, S., Schultz, M. and Silverstein, E. (2000), *Phys. Rev.* **D62**, 045021, [hep-th/0001206] *Phys. Rev.* **D62**, 085003, [hep-th/0002121].

[40] Förste, S., Lalak, Z., Lavignac, S. and Nilles, H. P. (2000), *Phys. Lett.* **B481**, 360, [hep-th/0002164] *JHEP* **0009**, 034, [hep-th/0006139].

[41] Binétruy, P., Charmousis, C., Davis, S. C. and Dufaux, J.-F., [hep-th/0206089].

[42] Csáki, C., Ehrlich, J. and Grojean C. (2001), *Nucl. Phys.* **B604**, 312, [hep-th/0012143].

[43] Golberger, W. D. and Wise, M. B. (1999), *Phys. Rev. Lett.* **83**, 4922, [hep-ph/9907447].

[44] DeWolfe, O., Freedman, D. Z., Gubser, S. S. and Karch, A. (2000), *Phys. Rev.* **D62**, 046008, [hep-th/9909134].

[45] Csáki, C., Graesser, M., Randall, L. and Terning, J. (2000), *Phys.Rev.* **D62**, 045015, [hep-ph/9911406].

[46] Mennim, A. and Battye, R. (2001), *Class. Quant. Grav.* **18**, 2171, [hep-th/0008192].

[47] Horowitz, G. T., Low, I. and Zee A. (2000), *Phys. Rev.* **D62**, 086005, [hep-th/0004206].

[48] Gregory, R., Rubakov, V. A. and Sibiryakov, S. M. (2000), *Phys. Rev. Lett.* **84**, 5928, [hep-th/0002072]; *Phys. Lett.* **B489**, 203, [hep-th/0003045].

[49] van Dam, H. and Veltman, M. (1970), *Nucl. Phys.* **B22**, 397.

[50] Zakharov, V. I. (1970), *JETP Lett.* **12**, 312.

[51] Kogan, I. I., Mouslopoulos, S. and Papazoglou, A. (2001), *Phys. Lett.* **B503**, 173, [hep-th/0011138].

[52] Porrati, M. (2001), *Phys. Lett.* **B498**, 92, [hep-th/0011152].

[53] Karch, A. and Randall, L. (2001), *JHEP* **0105**, 008, [hep-th/0011156]; *JHEP* **0106**, 063, [hep-th/0105132].

[54] Higuchi, A. (1987), *Nucl. Phys.* **B282** 397; Higuchi, A. (1989), *Nucl. Phys.* **B325** 745.

[55] Vainshtein, A. I. (1972), *Phys. Lett.* **39B**, 393.

[56] Deffayet, C., Dvali, G., Gabadadze, G. and Vainshtein, A. I. (2002), *Phys.Rev.* **D65**, 044026, [hep-th/0106001].

[57] Porrati, M. (2002), *Phys. Lett.* **B534**, 209, [hep-th/0203014].

[58] Fierz, M. (1939), *Helv. Phys. Acta* **12**, 3; Fierz, M. and Pauli, W. (1939), *Proc. Roy. Soc.* **173**, 211.

[59] Kogan, I. I., Mouslopoulos, S., Papazoglou, A. and Ross, G. G. (2000), *Nucl. Phys.* **B 595**, 225, [hep-th/0006030].

[60] Dvali, G. R., Gabadadze, G. and Porrati, M. (2000), *Phys. Lett.* **B485** 208, [hep-th/0005016].

[61] Binétruy, P. and Silk, J. (2001), *Phys. Rev. Lett.* **87**, 031102, [astro-ph/0007452].

[62] Bernardeau, F. and Uzan, J.-Ph. (2001), *Phys. Rev.* **D64**, 083004, [hep-ph/0012011].

[63] Deffayet, C. (2001), *Phys. Lett.* **B502**, 199, [hep-th/0010186].

[64] Deffayet, C., Dvali, G. and Gabadadze, G. (2002), *Phys. Rev.* **D65**, 044026, [astro-ph/0105068].

[65] Mukohyama, S. (2000), *Phys. Rev.* **D62**, 084015, [hep-th/0004067].

[66] Kodama, H., Ishibashi, A. and Seto, O. (2000), *Phys. Rev.* **D62**, 064022, [hep-th/0004160].

[67] Maartens, R. (2000), *Phys. Rev.* **D62**, 084023, [hep-th/0004166].

[68] Langlois, D. (2000), *Phys. Rev.* **D62**, 126012, [hep-th/0005025].

[69] van de Bruck, C., Dorca, M., Brandenberger, R. H. and Lukas, A. (2000), *Phys. Rev.* **D62**, 123515, [hep-th/0005032].

[70] Koyama, K. and Soda, J. (2000), *Phys. Rev.* **D62**, 123502, [hep-th/0005239].

[71] Langlois, D. (2001), *Phys. Rev. Lett.* **86**, 2212, [hep-th/0010063].

[72] Deruelle, N., Dolezel, T. and Katz, J. (2001), *Phys. Rev.* **D63**, 083513, [hep-th/0010215].

[73] Langlois, D., Maartens, R., Sasaki, M. and Wands, D. (2001), *Phys. Rev.* **D63**, 084009, [hep-th/0012044].

[74] Deffayet, C. [hep-th/0205084].

[75] Riazuelo, A., Vernizzi, F., Steer, D. and Durrer, R. [hep-th/0205220].

[76] Kalbermann, G. and Halevi, H. [gr-qc/9810083].

[77] Chung, D. J. and Freese, K. (2000), *Phys. Rev.* **D62**, 063513, [hep-ph/9910235].

[78] Chung, D. J., Kolb, E. W. and Riotto, A. (2002), *Phys. Rev.* **D65**, 083516, [hep-ph/0008126].

[79] Grojean, C., Quevedo, F., Tasinato, G. and Zavala C. I. (2001), *JHEP* **0108**, 005, [hep-th/0106120].

45

Publications of Stephen Hawking

[1] On the Hoyle–Narlikar Theory of Gravitation, *Proc. Roy. Soc.* **A286**, 313 (1965).

[2] Singularities in Homogeneous World Models. With G. F. R. Ellis, *Phys. Lett.* **17**, 246 (1965).

[3] Occurrence of Singularities in Open Universes, *Phys. Rev. Lett.* **15**, 689 (1965).

[4] Occurrence of Singularities in Cosmology, Part I, *Proc. Roy. Soc.* **A294**, 490 (1966).

[5] Occurrence of Singularities in Cosmology, Part II, *Proc. Roy. Soc.* **A295**, 490 (1966).

[6] Occurrence of Singularities in Cosmology, Part III, *Proc. Roy. Soc.* **A300**, 187 (1967).

[7] Singularities and the Geometry of Space-Time, Adams Prize Essay, Cambridge University (1966).

[8] Helium Production in Anisotropic Big Bang Universes. With J. R. Taylor, *Nature* **209**, 1278 (1966).

[9] Perturbations of an Expanding Universe, *Astrophys. J.* **145**, 544 (1966).

[10] Gravitational Radiation in an Expanding Universe, *J. Math. Phys.* **9**, 598 (1968).

[11] The Cosmic Black Body Radiation and the Existence of Singularities in Our Universe. With G. F. R. Ellis, *Astrophys. J.* **152**, 25 (1968).

[12] The Existence of Cosmic Time Functions, *Proc. Roy. Soc.* **A308**, 433 (1968).

[13] The Conservation of Matter in General Relativity, *Commun. Math. Phys.* **18**, 301 (1970).

[14] On the Rotation of the Universe, *Mon. Not. Roy. Astr. Soc.* **142**, 129 (1969).

[15] The Singularities of Gravitational Collapse and Cosmology. With R. Penrose, *Proc. Roy. Soc.* **A314**, 529 (1970).

[16] Stable and Generic Properties in General Relativity, *General Relativity and Gravitation* **1**, 121 (1970).

[17] Singularities in Collapsing Stars and Universes. With D. Sciama, *Comments on Astrophysics and Space Science* **1**, 1 (1969).

[18] Gravitationally Collapsing Objects of Very Low Mass, *Mon. Not. Roy. Astr. Soc.* **152**, 75 (1971).

[19] The Definition and Occurrence of Singularities in General Relativity, *Lecture Notes in Mathematics* **209**, Proceedings of Liverpool Singularities Symposium II, Springer-Verlag (1971).

[20] Black Holes, Gravity Research Foundation, First Award Essay (1971).

[21] Theory of the Detection of Short Burst of Gravitational Radiation. With G. W. Gibbons, *Phys. Rev.* **D4**, 2191 (1971).

[22] Gravitational Radiation from Colliding Black Holes, *Phys. Rev. Lett.* **26**, 1344 (1971).

[23] Black Holes in General Relativity, *Commun. Math. Phys.* **25**, 152 (1972).

[24] Black Holes in the Brans–Dicke Theory of Gravitation, *Commun. Math. Phys.* **25**, 167 (1972).

[25] Gravitational Radiation : The Theoretical Aspect, *Contemporary Physics* **13**, 273 (1972).

[26] Evidence for Black Holes in Binary Star Systems. With G. W. Gibbons, *Nature* **232**, 465 (1971).

[27] Solution of the Einstein–Maxwell Equations with Many Black Holes. With J. B. Hartle, *Commun. Math. Phys.* **26**, 87 (1972).

[28] Energy and Angular Momentum Flow into a Black Holes. With J. B. Hartle, *Commun. Math. Phys.* **27**, 283 (1972).

[29] Why is the Universe Isotropic? With C. B. Collins, *Astrophys. J.* **180**, 317 (1973).

[30] The Four Laws of Black Hole Mechanics. With J. M. Bardeen and B. Carter, *Commun. Math. Phys.* **31**, 161 (1973).

[31] *The Large Scale Structure of Space-Time.* With G. F. R. Ellis, Cambridge University Press (1973).

[32] The Event Horizon, *Black Holes*, eds DeWitt and DeWitt, Gordon and Breach (1973).

[33] The Rotation and Distortion of the Universe. With C. B. Collins, *Mon. Not. Roy. Astr. Soc.* **162**, 307 (1973).

[34] A Variational Principle for Black Holes, *Commun. Math. Phys.* 323 (1973).

[35] Causally Continuous Space-Times. With R. K. Sachs, *Commun. Math. Phys.* **35**, 287 (1974).

[36] Black Hole Explosions, *Nature* **248**, 30 (1974).

[37] The Analogy between Black-Hole Mechanics and Thermodynamics, *Annals of the New York Academy of Sciences* 4268 (1973).

[38] Particle Creation by Black Holes, *Commun. Math. Phys.* **43**, 199 (1975).

[39] Black Holes aren't Black, Gravity Research Foundation Award Essay (1974).

[40] Black Holes in the Early Universe. With B. J. Carr, *Mon. Not. Roy. Astr. Soc.* **168**, 399 (1974).

[41] The Anisotropy of the Universe at Large Times, *Proceedings of the I. A. U. Symposium on Cosmology (1973).*

[42] Black Holes are White Hot, *Annals of the New York Academy of Sciences* **262**, 289 (1975).

[43] Gravitational Collapse and After, address to the Pontifical Academy of Sciences on receipt of Pius XI Medal (1975). *Commentarii Pontificia Academia Scientiarvm* **3** (1976).

[44] A New Topology for Curved Space-Time which Incorporates the Causal, Differential and Conformal Structures. With A. R. King and P. J. McCarthy, *J. Math. Phys.* **17**, 174 (1976).

[45] Black Holes and Thermodynamics, *Phys. Rev.* **D31**, 191 (1976).

[46] Gamma Rays from Primordial Black Holes. With D. N. Page, *Astrophys. J.* **206**, 1 (1976).

[47] Breakdown of Predictability in Gravitational Collapse, *Phys. Rev. D* **14**, 2460 (1976).

[48] Path Integral Derivation of Black Hole Radiance. With J. B. Hartle, *Phys. Rev.* **D13**, 2188 (1976).

[49] Cosmological Event Horizons, Thermodynamics and Particle Creation. With G. W. Gibbons, *Phys. Rev.* **D15**, 2738 (1977).

[50] Quantum Mechanics of Black Holes, *Scientific American* **236**, 33 (1977).

[51] Action Integrals and Partition Functions in Quantum Gravity. With G. W. Gibbons, *Phys. Rev.* **D15**, 2752 (1977).

[52] Zeta Function Regularization of Path Integrals in Curved Spacetime, *Commun. Math. Phys.* **56**, 133 (1977).

[53] Gravitational Instantons, *Phys. Lett.* **A60**, 81 (1977).

[54] Black Holes and Unpredictability, *Annals of the New York Academy of Sciences* **302**, 158 (1977).

[55] Quantum Gravity and Path Integrals, *Phys. Rev.* **D18**, 1747 (1978).

[56] Generalized Spin Structures in Quantum Gravity. With C. N. Pope, *Phys. Lett.* **B73**, 42 (1978).

[57] Comments on Cosmics Censorship, *Phys. Rev.* **D6**, 1747 (1978).

[58] *General Relativity: An Einstein Centenary Survey*. Ed. with W. Israel, Cambridge University Press (1979).

[59] Introductory Survey, *General Relativity: An Einstein Centenary Survey. Ed. with W. Israel*, Cambridge University Press (1979).

[60] The Path Integral Approach to Quantum Gravity, *General Relativity: An Einstein Centenary Survey*. Ed. with W. Israel, Cambridge University Press (1979).

[61] Path Integrals and the Indefiniteness of the Gravitational Action. With G. W. Gibbons and M. J. Perry, *Nucl. Phys.* **B138**, 141 (1978).

[62] Spacetime Foam, *Nucl. Phys.* **B144**, 349 (1978).

[63] Euclidean Quantum Gravity, *Recent Developments in Gravitation*, Cargese Lectures, eds M. Levy and S. Deser (1978).

[64] Symmetry Breaking by Instantons. With C. N. Pope, *Nucl. Phys.* **B146**, 381 (1978).

[65] Gravitational Multi-Instanton Symmetries. With G. W. Gibbons, *Phys. Lett.* **B78**, 430 (1978).

[66] Classification of Gravitational Instanton Symmetries. With G. W. Gibbons, *Commun. Math. Phys.* 291 (1979).

[67] Yang–Mills Instantons and the S-matrix. With C. N. Pope, *Nucl. Phys.* **B161**, 93 (1979).

[68] Theoretical Advances in General Relativity, *Some Strangeness in the Proportion*, ed. H. Woolf, Addison-Wesley (1980).

[69] *The Limits of Space and Time*, Great Ideas Today (1979).

[70] Propagation of Particles through Spacetime Foam. With D. N. Page and C. N. Pope, *Phys. Lett.* **B86**, 175 (1979).

[71] Quantum Gravitational Bubbles. With D. N. Page and C. N. Pope, *Nucl. Phys.* **B170**, 283 (1980).

[72] Is the End in Sight for Theoretical Physics?, Inaugural Lecture, Cambridge University Press (1980).

[73] Acausal Propagation in Quantum Gravity, *Quantum Gravity: Second Oxford Symposium*, eds C. J. Isham, R. Penrose and D. Sciama, Oxford University Press (1981).

[74] *Superspace and Supergravity*. With Ed. with M. Rocek, Cambridge University Press, *1981* ().

[75] Interacting Quantum Fields around a Black Holes, *Commun. Math. Phys.* **80**, 421 (1981).

[76] Bubble Collisions in the Very Early Universe. With I. G. Moss and J. M. Stewart, *Phys. Rev.* **D10**, 2681 (1982).

[77] Why is the Apparent Cosmological Constant Zero, *Lecture Notes in Physics* **160**, 167, Unified Theories of Elementary Particles, Springer-Verlag (1981).

[78] The Boundary Conditions of the Universe, *Pontificiae Academiae Scientiarvm Scripta Varia* **48**, Astrophysical Cosmology (1982).

[79] Supercooled Phase Transitions in the Very Early Universe. With I. G. Moss, *Phys. Lett.* **B110**, 35 (1982).

[80] The Cosmological Constant and the Weak Anthropic Principle, *Quantum Structure of Spacetime*, eds M. Duff and C. J. Isham, Cambridge University Press (1982).

[81] The Unpredictability of Quantum Gravity, *Commun. Math. Phys.* **87**, 395 (1982).

[82] The Development of Irregularities in a Single Bubble Inflationary Universe, *Phys. Lett.* **B115**, 295 (1982).

[83] Positive Mass Theorem for Black Holes. With G. W. Gibbons, G. W. Horowitz and M. J. Perry, *Commun. Math. Phys.* **88**, 295 (1983).

[84] Thermodynamics of Black Holes in Anti-de Sitter Space. With D. N. Page, *Commun. Math. Phys.* **87**, 577 (1983).

[85] Fluctuations in the Inflationary Universe. With I. G. Moss, *Nucl. Phys.* **B224**, 180 (1983).

[86] Wave Function of the Universe. With J. B. Hartle, *Phys. Rev.* **D28**, 2960 (1983).

[87] Euclidean Approach to the Inflationary Universe, *The Very Early Universe*, eds G. W. Gibbons, S. W. Hawking and S. T. C. Siklos, Cambridge University Press (1983).

[88] The Boundary Conditions in Gauged Supergravity, *Phys. Lett.* **B126**, 175 (1983).

[89] The Cosmological Constant, *Phil. Trans. R. Soc. Lond.* **A310**, 303 (1983).

[90] The Cosmological Constant is Probably Zero, *Phys. Lett.* **B134**, 403 (1984).

[91] Quantum Cosmology, *Les Houches Lectures*, reprinted from "Relativity Groups and Topology", eds B. DeWitt and R. Stora, North-Holland (1984).

[92] The Quantum State of the Universe, *Nucl. Phys.* **B239**, 257 (1984).

[93] The Quantum Mechanics of the Universe, *Large-Scale Structure of the Universe, Cosmology and Fundamental Physics*, First E.S.O. CERN Symposium, 21-25 November, eds. G. Setti and L. van Hove. (1983).

[94] *The Unification of Physics*, Great Ideas Today (1984).

[95] The Isotropy of the Universe. With J. C. Luttrell, *Phys. Lett.* **B143**, 83 (1984).

[96] Higher Derivatives in Quantum Cosmology. With J. C. Luttrell, *Nucl. Phys.* **B247**, 250 (1984).

[97] Non-trivial Topologies in Quantum Gravity, *Nucl. Phys.* **B244**, 135 (1984).

[98] The Edge of Spacetime, American Scientific, July–August (1984). *New Scientist*, 16th August (1984).

[99] Limits on Inflationary Models of the Universe, *Phys. Lett.* **B150**, 339 (1984).

[100] Time and the Universe – Reply, *American Scientist* **73 (1)**, 12–12 (1985).

[101] Numerical Calculations of Minisuperspace Cosmological Models. With Z. C. Wu, *Phys. Lett.* **B151**, 15 (1985).

[102] The Origin of Structure in the Universe. With J. J. Halliwell, *Phys. Rev.* **D31**, 8 (1985).

[103] Operator Ordering and the Flatness of the Universe. With D. N. Page, *Nucl. Phys.* **B264**, 185 (1985).

[104] The Arrow of Time in Cosmology, *Phys. Rev.* **D32**, 2489 (1985).

[105] Quantum Fluctuations as the Cause of Inhomogeneity in the Universe. With J. J. Halliwell, *Proceedings of the Third Seminar on Quantum Gravity*, eds. M. A. Markov, V. A. Benezin and V. P. Frolov, Moscow (1984).

[106] Who's Afraid of (higher derivative) Ghosts?, paper written in honour of the 60th birthday of E. S. Fradkin (1985).

[107] Quantum Cosmology – Beyond Minisuperspace, with J. J. Halliwell, *Proceedings of the Fourth Marcel Grossman Meeting on General Relativity*, ed. R. Ruffini, Elsevier Science Publishing (1986).

[108] The Density Matrix of the Universe, *Physica Scripta* **T15**, 151 (1987).

[109] A Natural Measure on the Set of all Universes. With G. W. Gibbons and J. M. Stewart, *Nucl. Phys.* **B281**, 736 (1987).

[110] *Supersymmetry and its Applications: Superstrings, Anomalies and Supergravity. Ed. with G. W. Gibbons and P. K. Townsend*, Cambridge University Press (1986).

[111] Quantum Cosmology, *Three Hundred Years of Gravity*. Ed. with W. Israel, Cambridge University Press (1987).

[112] The Direction of Time, *New Scientist* **1568**, 46 (1987).

[113] The Ground State of the Universe, closing remarks given at Quantum Cosmology Workshop, Batavia, IL, May 1-3, 1987, Cambridge University Press (1987).

[114] The Schrödinger Equation in Quantum Cosmology and String Theory, Lecture given at the Schrödinger Conference, Imperial College (1987).

[115] Quantum Coherence Down the Wormhole, *Phys. Lett.* **B195**, 337 (1987).

[116] Wormholes in Spacetime, *Phys. Rev.* **D37**, 904 (1988).

[117] *A Brief History of Time*, Bantam Press (1988).

[118] How Probable is Inflation? With D. N. Page, *Nucl. Phys.* **B298**, 789 (1988).

[119] Baby Universes and the Non-renormalizability of Gravity. With R. Laflamme, *Phys. Lett.* **B209**, 39 (1988).

[120] Black Holes from Cosmic Strings, *Phys. Lett.* **B231**, 237 (1989).

[121] Do Wormholes Fix The Constants Of Nature, *Nucl. Phys.* **B335**, 155 (1990).

[122] The Spectrum of Wormholes. With D. N. Page, *Phys. Rev.* **D42**, 2655 (1990).

[123] Wormholes and Non Simply Connected Manifolds, Quantum Cosmology and Baby Universes, eds S. Coleman, J. B. Hartle, T. Piran and S. Weinberg, *Proceedings of 7th Jerusalem Winter School*, World Scientific Press , Singapore (1991).

[124] Wormholes in Dimensions One to Four, *Proceedings of PASCOS 90*, World Scientific Press, Singapore (1991).

[125] Alpha Parameters of Wormholes, *Physica Scripta* **T36**, 222 (1991).

[126] Gravitational Radiation from Collapsing Cosmic Strings, *Phys. Lett.* **B246**, 36 (1990).

[127] The Effective Action for Wormholes, *Nucl. Phys.* **363**, 117 (1991).

[128] Chronology Protection Conjecture, *Phys. Rev.* **D46**, 603 (1992).

[129] Wormholes in String Theory. With A. Lyons, *Phys. Rev.* **D44**, 3802 (1991).

[130] Selection Rules for Topology Change. With G. W. Gibbons, *Commun. Math. Physics* **148**, 345 (1992).

[131] Causality Violating Spacetimes, *Proceedings of PASCOS 91*, eds P. Nath and S. Reucross, World Scientific Press, Singapore (1992).

[132] The No-Boundary Condition and the Arrow of Time, *Physical Origins of Time Asymmetry*, eds J. J. Halliwell, J. Perez-Mercader and W. H. Zurek, Cambridge University Press (1992).

[133] Kinks and Topology Change. With G. W. Gibbons, *Phys. Rev. Lett.* **69**, 12 (1992).

[134] Evaporation of Two Dimensional Black Holes, *Phys. Rev. Lett.* **69**, 406 (1992).

[135] The Beginning of the Universe, *Annals of the New York Academy of Science* **647**, TEXAS/ESO-CERN Symposium on Relativistic Astrophysics, Cosmology and Fundamental Physics, eds. J. D. Barrow, L. Mestel and P. A. Thomas (1991).

[136] Naked and Thunderbolt Singularities in Black Hole Evaporation. With J. Stewart, *Nucl. Phys.* **B400**, 393 (1993).

[137] Origin of Time Asymmetry. With R. Laflamme and G. Lyons, *Phys. Rev.* **D47**, 12 (1993).

[138] Supersymmetric Bianchi Models and the Square Root of the Wheeler–DeWitt Equation. With P. D'Eath and O. Obregon, *Phys. Lett.* **B300**, 44 (1993).

[139] Quantum Coherence in Two Dimensions. With J.D. Hayward, *Phys. Rev.* **D49**, 5252–5256 (1994).

[140] *Black Holes and Baby Universes and Other Essays*, Bantam Books (1993).

[141] *Euclidean Quantum Gravity and other essays*, eds S. W. Hawking and G. W. Gibbons, World Scientific Press (1993).

[142] *Hawking on the Big Bang and Black Holes*, World Scientific Press (1993).

[143] The Superscattering Matrix for Two Dimensional Black Holes, *Phys. Rev.* **D50**, 3982 (1994).

[144] The Nature of Space and Time, [hep-th/9409195] (1994).

[145] The Gravitational Hamiltonian, Action, Entropy and Surface Terms.. With G.T.Horowitz, *Class. Quant. Grav* **13**, 1487–1498 (1996).

[146] Entropy, Area and Black Hole Pairs. With G.T.Horowitz and S. F. Ross, *Phys. Rev.* **D51**, 4302 (1995).

[147] Quantum Coherence and Closed Timelike Curves, *Phys. Rev.* **D52**, 5681 (1995).

[148] Duality of electric and magnetic black holes. With S. F. Ross, *Phys. Rev.* **D52**, 5865 (1995).

[149] Pair production of black holes on cosmic strings. With S. F. Ross, *Phys. Rev. Lett.* **75**, 3382 (1995).

[150] The Probability for Primordial Black Holes. With R. Bousso, *Phys. Rev.* **D52**, 5659–5664 (1995).

[151] Virtual Black Holes, *Phys. Rev.* **D53**, 3099–3107 (1996).

[152] The Gravitational Hamiltonian in the Presence of Non-Orthogonal Boundaries. With C. J. Hunter, *Class. Quant. Grav.* **13**, 2735–2752 (1996).

[153] Pair Creation and Evolution of Black Holes During Inflation. With R. Bousso, *Helv. Phys. Acta* **69**, 261–264 (1996).

[154] Pair Creation and Evolution of Black Holes During Inflation. With R. Bousso, *Phys. Rev.* **D54**, 6312–6322 (1996).

[155] Primordial Black Holes: Tunnelling vs. No Boundary Proposal. With R. Bousso, Contribution to the proceedings of COSMION 96, [gr-qc/9608009] (1996).

[156] Evolution of near extremal black holes. With M. M. Taylor-Robinson, *Phys. Rev.* **D55**, 7680–7692 (1997).

[157] Loss of quantum coherence through scattering off virtual black holes. With S. F. Ross, *Phys. Rev.* **D56**, 6403–6415 (1997).

[158] Trace Anomaly of Dilaton Coupled Scalars in Two Dimensions. With R. Bousso, *Phys. Rev.* **D56**, 7788–7791 (1997).

[159] Models for Chronology Selection. With M. J. Cassidy, *Phys. Rev.* **D57**, 2372–2380 (1998).

[160] (Anti-)Evaporation of Schwarzschild–de Sitter Black Holes. With R. Bousso, *Phys. Rev.* **D57**, 2436–2442 (1998).

[161] The Evaporation of Primordial Black Holes, Contribution to the proceedings of the 3rd RESCUE International Symposium, 185–197 (1998).

[162] Bulk charges in eleven dimensions. With M. M. Taylor-Robinson, *Phys. Rev.* **D58**, 025006 (1998).

[163] Open Inflation Without False Vacua. With Neil Turok, *Phys. Lett.* **B425**, 25–32 (1998).

[164] Is Information Lost in Black Holes, *Black Holes and Relativistic Stars*, ed. R. M. Wald, University of Chicago Press (1998) pp. 221–240.

[165] Open Inflation, the Four Form and the Cosmological Constant. With Neil Turok, *Phys. Lett.* **B432**, 271–278 (1998).

[166] Inflation, Singular Instantons and Eleven Dimensional Cosmology. With Harvey S. Reall, *Phys. Rev.* **D59**, 023502 (1999).

[167] Lorentzian Condition in Quantum Gravity. With R. Bousso, *Phys. Rev.* **D59**, 103501 (1999).

[168] Gravitational Entropy and Global Structure. With C. J. Hunter, *Phys. Rev.* **D59**, 044025 (1999).

[169] Nut Charge, Anti-de Sitter Space and Entropy. With C. J. Hunter and D. N. Page, *Phys. Rev.* **D59**, 044033 (1999).

[170] Rotation and the AdS/CFT correspondence. With C. J. Hunter and M. M. Taylor-Robinson, *Phys. Rev.* **D59**, 064005 (1999).

[171] A Debate on Open Inflation, pp.15–22, *Cosmo-98, Second International Workshop on Particle Physics and the Early Universe*, ed. David O. Caldwell, AIP Conference Proceedings 478 (1999).

[172] Charged and rotating AdS black holes and their CFT duals. With H. S. Reall, *Phys. Rev.* **D61**, 024014 (2000).

[173] Brane-World Black Holes. With H. A. Chamblin and H. S. Reall, *Phys. Rev.* **D61**, 065007 (2000).

[174] DeSitter Entropy, Quantum Entanglement and AdS/CFT. With J. Maldacena and A. Strominger, *JHEP* **0105**, 001 (2001).

[175] Stability of AdS and Phase Transitions, *Class. Quant. Grav* **17**,

1093–1498 (2000).

[176] Gravitational Waves in Open de Sitter Space. With Thomas Hertog and Neil Turok, *Phys. Rev.* **D62**, 063502 (2000).

[177] Brane New World. With T.Hertog and H. S. Reall, *Phys. Rev.* **D62**, 043501 (2000).

[178] Large N Cosmology, *Cosmo-2000: Proceedings of the Fourth International Workshop on Particle Physics and the Early Universe*, ed J. E. Kim, P. Ko and K. Lee, World Scientific Publishing (2000) pp. 113–125.

[179] Trace Anomaly Driven Inflation. With T. Hertog and H. S. Reall, *Phys. Rev.* **D63**, 083504 (2001).

[180] Chronology Protection, *The Future of Spacetime, Proceedings of Kipfest 2000*, W. W. Norton and Company Ltd. (2002) pp. 87–109.

[181] *The Universe in a Nutshell*, Bantam Press (2001).

[182] Living with Ghosts. With Thomas Hertog, *Phys. Rev.* **D65**, 103515 (2002).

[183] Why Does Inflation Start at the Top of the Hill? With Thomas Hertog, [hep-th/0204212] (2002).

Index